LET'S GO

■ PAGES PACKED WITH ESSENTIAL INFORMATION

"Value-packed, unbeatable, accurate, and comprehensive."

—The Los Angeles Times

"The guides are aimed not only at young budget travelers but at the independent traveler; a sort of streetwise cookbook for traveling alone."

—The New York Times

"Unbeatable; good sight-seeing advice; up-to-date info on restaurants, hotels, and inns; a commitment to money-saving travel; and a wry style that brightens nearly every page."

—The Washington Post

■ THE BEST TRAVEL BARGAINS IN YOUR BUDGET

"All the dirt, dirt cheap."

—People

"Let's Go follows the creed that you don't have to toss your life's savings to the wind to travel—unless you want to."

—The Salt Lake Tribune

■ REAL ADVICE FOR REAL EXPERIENCES

"The writers seem to have experienced every rooster-packed bus and lunar-surfaced mattress about which they write."

—The New York Times

"[Let's Go's] devoted updaters really walk the walk (and thumb the ride, and trek the trail). Learn how to fish, haggle, find work—anywhere."

—Food & Wine

"A world-wise traveling companion—always ready with friendly advice and helpful hints, all sprinkled with a bit of wit."

—The Philadelphia Inquirer

■ A GUIDE WITH A SPIRIT AND A SOCIAL CONSCIENCE

"Lighthearted and sophisticated, informative and fun to read. [Let's Go] helps the novice traveler navigate like a knowledgeable old hand."

—Atlanta Journal-Constitution

"The serious mission at the book's core reveals itself in exhortations to respect the culture and the environment—and, if possible, to visit as a volunteer, a student, or a teacher rather than a tourist."

—San Francisco Chronicle

LET'S GO PUBLICATIONS

TRAVEL GUIDES
Australia 8th edition
Austria & Switzerland 12th edition
Brazil 1st edition
Britain 2006
California 10th edition
Central America 9th edition
Chile 2nd edition
China 5th edition
Costa Rica 2nd edition
Eastern Europe 12th edition
Ecuador 1st edition
Egypt 2nd edition
Europe 2006
France 2006
Germany 12th edition
Greece 8th edition
Hawaii 3rd edition
India & Nepal 8th edition
Ireland 12th edition
Israel 4th edition
Italy 2006
Japan 1st edition
Mexico 21st edition
Middle East 4th edition
New Zealand 7th edition
Peru 1st edition
Puerto Rico 2nd edition
South Africa 5th edition
Southeast Asia 9th edition
Spain & Portugal 2006
Thailand 2nd edition
Turkey 5th edition
USA 23rd edition
Vietnam 1st edition
Western Europe 2006

ROADTRIP GUIDE
Roadtripping USA

ADVENTURE GUIDES
Alaska 1st edition
Pacific Northwest 1st edition
Southwest USA 3rd edition

CITY GUIDES
Amsterdam 4th edition
Barcelona 3rd edition
Boston 4th edition
London 15th edition
New York City 15th edition
Paris 13th edition
Rome 12th edition
San Francisco 4th edition
Washington, D.C. 13th edition

POCKET CITY GUIDES
Amsterdam
Berlin
Boston
Chicago
London
New York City
Paris
San Francisco
Venice
Washington, D.C.

LET'S GO GREECE

JULIA BONNHEIM EDITOR
SIMON WILLIAM VOZICK-LEVINSON ASSOCIATE EDITOR

RESEARCHER-WRITERS
B. BRITT CAPUTO
ALEX ECONOMOU
MISHY HARMAN
KEVIN PAIK
LAURIE SCHNIDMAN
JENNY WONG

KATHERINE J. THOMPSON MAP EDITOR
STUART J. ROBINSON MANAGING EDITOR

ST. MARTIN'S PRESS ❈ NEW YORK

Maps by David Lindroth copyright © 2006 by St. Martin's Press.

Distributed outside the USA and Canada by Macmillan.

ISBN:0-312-34885-1
EAN: 978-0-312-34885-4
Eighth edition
10 9 8 7 6 5 4 3 2 1

Let's Go: Greece is written by Let's Go Publications, 67 Mount Auburn St., Cambridge, MA 02138, USA.

Let's Go® and the LG logo are trademarks of Let's Go, Inc. Printed in the USA.

CONTENTS

HOW TO USE THIS BOOK

So you're probably pretty excited about your upcoming trip to Greece. We don't blame you—it's going to be incredible. Learning how to use this book, however, just might make it that much better.

COVERAGE LAYOUT. *Let's Go: Greece* begins in **Athens,** the heart of the country and a natural jumping off point. From there, coverage extends into the **Peloponnese,** up through mountainous **Central Greece,** and into the remote expanse of **Northern Greece.** Departing from the mainland, we embark on a tour of Greece's legendary islands, starting with the **Saronic Gulf Islands, Evia,** and the **Sporades,** then continuing into the Aegean sea to the **Cyclades, Dodecanese,** and **Northeast Aegean Islands.** The book winds up by darting west to the **Ionian Islands,** then south to **Crete.** Brand new **suggested itineraries** boxes at the beginning of each chapter point to the best spots in each region and can help structure either a long or short trip.

TRANSPORTATION INFO. For connecting between destinations, info is listed under the Transportation section of the departure city. Parentheticals usually provide the trip duration, frequency, and price, which is for one-way trips unless otherwise stated. For more general info on travel, consult the **Essentials** chapter (p. 8).

COVERING THE BASICS. Before hitting the road, check out the **Discover Greece** chapter (p. 1) for recommendations on when to go and country-wide suggested itineraries. The **Essentials** chapter (p. 8) has answers to a number of logistical and practical questions, and the **Life and Times** chapter (p. 54) gives a pocket overview of 5000 years of Greek history and culture. **Beyond Tourism** (p. 79) has suggestions about how to enrich your travel experience, from volunteer work to study abroad. The **Appendix** (p. 623) lists Greek phrases, pronunciations, and other quick reference info.

SCHOLARLY ARTICLES. At the end of Life and Times, **Gregory A. Maniatis** examines the presence of Greek culture outside of Greece, and then looks into its influence on the country itself (p. 78). After the Beyond Tourism chapter, Harvard Classics student and former *Let's Go* editor **Leanna Boychenko** shares her experiences on an archaeological dig in Athens (p. 89).

PRICE DIVERSITY. Our researchers list establishments in order of value from best to worst, denoting their absolute favorites with the *Let's Go* thumbs-up (🖐). Since the cheapest price does not always mean the best value, we have incorporated a system of price ranges for food and accommodations; see p. xvi.

PHONE CODES AND TELEPHONE NUMBERS. Area codes for each region appear opposite the name of the region and are denoted by the ☎ icon. Phone numbers in the text include the area codes and are also preceded by the ☎ icon.

LANGUAGE. The Greek name of each city and town is printed after its English name. Transliterations give syllabic pronunciation, with the stressed syllables capitalized. For a guide to the Greek alphabet, see the **Appendix** (p. 623).

A NOTE TO OUR READERS. The information for this book was gathered by *Let's Go* researchers from May through August of 2005. Each listing is based on one researcher's opinion, formed during his or her visit at a particular time. Those traveling at other times may have different experiences since prices, dates, hours, and conditions are always subject to change. You are urged to check the facts presented in this book beforehand to avoid inconvenience and surprises.

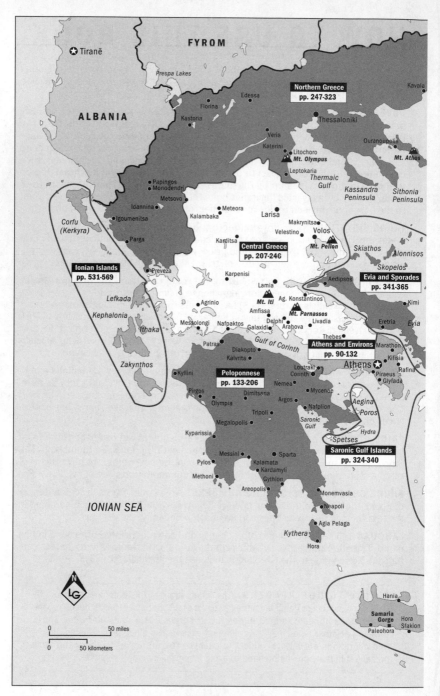

FYROM

★ Tiranë

Prespa Lakes

ALBANIA

Northern Greece
pp. 247-323

Kavala

Edessa

Florina

Kastoria

Veria

Katerini

Litochoro
▲ *Mt. Olympus*

Thessaloniki

Ouranoupolis

▲ *Mt. Athos*

Leptokaria

*Thermaic
Gulf*

*Kassandra
Peninsula*

*Sithonia
Peninsula*

Papingos
Monodendri

Metsovo

Idannina

Igoumenitsa

*Corfu
(Kerkyra)*

Meteora

Larisa

Kalambaka

Makrynitsa

Velestino

Volos

▲ *Mt. Pelion*

Skiathos

Alonnisos

Ionian Islands
pp. 531-569

Parga

Karditsa

Central Greece
pp. 207-246

Skopelos

Preveza

Karpenisi

Aedipsos

Evia and Sporades
pp. 341-365

Lefkada

Agrinio

Lamia

▲ *Mt. Iti*

Ag. Konstantinos

Kimi

Kephalonia

Amfissa

▲ *Mt. Parnassos*

Ithaka

Messolongi

Nafpaktos

Delphi

Galaxidi

Arahova

Livadia

Eretria

Evia

Patras

Gulf of Corinth

Thebes

Athens and Environs
pp. 90-132

Marathon

Zakynthos

Diakopto

Kalvrita

Loutraki

Corinth

Athens ★

Kifisia

Piraeus

Rafina

Glyfada

Kyllini

Peloponnese
pp. 133-206

Pirgos

Olympia

Dimitsena

Nemea

Mycenae

Aegina

Argos

Nafplion

Poros

Tripoli

*Saronic
Gulf*

Megalopolis

Hydra

Kyparissia

Messini

Sparta

Spetses

Saronic Gulf Islands
pp. 324-340

Pylos

Kalamata

Methoni

Kardamyli

Gythion

Areopolis

Monemvasia

Neapoli

IONIAN SEA

Agia Pelaga

Kythera

Hora

Hania

**Samaria
Gorge**

Hora
Sfakion

Paleohora

0   50 miles

0   50 kilometers

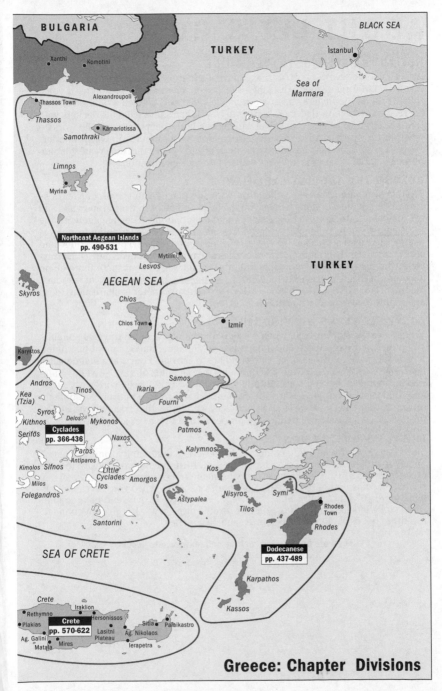

Greece: Chapter Divisions

BULGARIA

Xanthi
Komotini

TURKEY

BLACK SEA

İstanbul

Alexandroupoli

Sea of
Marmara

Thassos Town
Thassos

Kamariotissa
Samothraki

Limnos

Myrina

Northeast Aegean Islands
pp. 490-531

Mytilini
Lesvos

Skyros

AEGEAN SEA

Chios

TURKEY

Chios Town

İzmir

Karystos

Andros

Tinos

Ikaria

Samos

Kea
(Tzia)

Fourni

Syros

Delos

Patmos

Kithnos

Mykonos

Cyclades
pp. 366-436

Kalymnos

Serifos

Naxos

Paros

Kos

Antiparos

Kimolos

Sifnos

Little
Cyclades

Amorgos

Milos

Ios

Nisyros

Symi

Folegandros

Astypalea

Tilos

Rhodes
Town

Santorini

Dodecanese
pp. 437-489

Rhodes

SEA OF CRETE

Karpathos

Crete

Rethymno

Iraklion

Kassos

Plakias

Hersonissos

Crete
pp. 570-622

Sitia

Palaikastro

Ag. Galini

Lasitni
Plateau

Ag. Nikolaos

Matala

Mires

Ierapetra

ABOUT LET'S GO

NOT YOUR PARENTS' TRAVEL GUIDE

At Let's Go, we see every trip as the chance of a lifetime. If your dream is to grab a machete and forge through the jungles of Brazil, we can take you there. If you'd rather bask in the Riviera sun at a beachside cafe, we'll set you a table. We write for readers who know that there's more to travel than sharing double deckers with tourists and who believe that travel can change both themselves and the world— whether they plan to spend six days in London or six months in Latin America. We'll show you just how far your money can go, and prove that the greatest limitation on your adventures is not your wallet, but your imagination.

BEYOND THE TOURIST EXPERIENCE

To help you gain a deeper connection with the places you travel, our fearless researchers scour the globe to give you the heads-up on both world-renowned and off-the-beaten-track attractions, sights, and destinations. They engage with the local culture, only to emerge with the freshest insights on everything from local festivals to regional cuisine. We've also opened our pages to respected writers and scholars to hear their takes on the countries and regions we cover, and asked travelers who have worked, studied, or volunteered abroad to contribute first-person accounts of their experiences. In addition, we increased our coverage of responsible travel and expanded each guide's Beyond Tourism chapter to share more ideas about how to give back while on the road.

FORTY-SIX YEARS OF WISDOM

Let's Go got its start in 1960, when a group of creative and well-traveled students compiled their experience and advice into a 20-page mimeographed pamphlet, which they gave to travelers on charter flights to Europe. Four and a half decades later, we've expanded to cover six continents and all kinds of travel—while retaining our founders' adventurous attitude toward the world. Laced with witty prose and total candor, our guides are still researched and written entirely by students on shoestring budgets, experienced travelers who know that train strikes, stolen luggage, food poisoning, and marriage proposals are all part of a day's work.

THE LET'S GO COMMUNITY

More than just a travel guide company, Let's Go is a community. Our small staff comes together because of our shared passion for travel and our desire to help other travelers see the world the way it was meant to be seen. We love it when our readers become part of the Let's Go community as well—when you travel, drop us a postcard (67 Mt. Auburn St., Cambridge, MA 02138, USA), send us an e-mail (feedback@letsgo.com), or post on our forum (http://www.letsgo.com/connect/forum) to tell us about your adventures and discoveries.

For more information, visit us online: www.letsgo.com.

RESEARCHER-WRITERS

B. Britt Caputo
Athens and the Cyclades

Hailing from Manhattan, Britt knows her way around a big city. She took on Athens like a pro, never missing a beat whether she was strolling down its ritzy avenues or making fearless forays into its seedier districts. Along with covering what seemed like every inch of pavement in the sprawling capital, this accomplished squash player also got the scoop on the islands, from befriending hostel owners in Paros to finding her way to Naxos's citron distilleries.

Alex Economou
Crete and the Cyclades

Coming from a large Greek family and having lived in Athens for a year, Alex went to Crete ready for whatever Greece would throw at her. Though she ended up having more contact with German-tourist culture than that of her ancestral home, she nevertheless researched with spunky enthusiasm and an unrestrained love of gorgeous beaches. Her copy shone with the meticulous attention to detail that will serve her well in her job as a high-school teacher.

Mishy Harman
Northern and Central Greece

Mishy took budget traveling to a new level, hiking from destination to destination, sleeping on park benches, and getting chummy with train conductors in search of deals. Driven by a thirst to uncover the details of Greek history, Mishy infused his write-ups with fascinating background information and his offbeat sense of humor. In a near impossible feat, he managed to do thorough research and still finish early enough to get home for the Jerusalem Film Festival.

Kevin Paik
Evia and the Sporades, Central Greece,
the Peloponnese, and the Cyclades

Thrilled with the simple pleasures of his route, from a free glass of fresh-squeezed lemonade to a dancing grandmother on a ferry ride, Kevin approached both the mainland and the islands with genuine excitement. The self-described baklava and souvlaki connoisseur sampled the best of Greece's fast food while working arduously on thoughtful write-ups and prize-worthy maps.

Laurie Schnidman
The Dodecanese, Northeast Aegean,
and Saronic Gulf

Laurie managed to charm three entire island chains, befriending locals, securing a remarkable amount of free stuff, and even inspiring an impromptu marriage proposal. Visiting over half of Greece's islands, she climbed countless *kastros*, went to even more beaches, and learned that almost every island has a disappearing, reappearing icon. Though at the whim of unpredictable ferries, she kept a relaxed sense of cool and effortlessly crafted honest, witty copy.

Jenny Wong
The Peloponnese and the Ionian Islands

Unwaveringly cheery and fun-loving, Jenny sped breezily through her itinerary like wing-footed Hermes on a serious caffeine rush. She took southwestern Greece by storm, helping a domatia owner through an identity crisis and hanging out with former US president George H.W. Bush's coterie of Secret Service agents. Her countless phone calls, full of laughter and crazy stories, never failed to brighten her editors' weeks.

CONTRIBUTING WRITERS

Leanna Boychenko majored in Classics at the Harvard College. She was the Associate Editor of *Let's Go: Greece 2005* and the Editor of *Let's Go: New Zealand 2006*.

Gregory A. Maniatis is the founder of *Odyssey Magazine*, the leading international magazine about Greece and Greeks around the world. He has also contributed to *New York Magazine, The Independent, The Washington Monthly, Time-Life Books*, and other publications.

ACKNOWLEDGMENTS

TEAM GREECE THANKS: Our amazing, amusing, ridiculous, and always competent RWs. Stuart for keeping us in line, drawing us pictures, and always having our collective back. Katherine for making sure that our maps are stellar and that each of our sea monsters has a nice personal style. Ella for being the magical DA to our wizarding detectives in our synergistic pod. Greece for its unfailing tendency to be "vibrant and diverse."

JULIA THANKS: Simon for spelling skills and knowledge of the Greek alphabet. Stuart for being the best. Maya for being my number one source of fun this summer. Nahu for sharing in our ridiculous sublet experience. Meaghan 4 being 2 kewl 2 b 4gotten. Lisa and Jessica for being the *dulce de leche* in my *alfajore*. My family for love, support, and talking to me even when you thought I shouldn't walk and talk on the phone at the same time. And a final, loving shoutout to Sky "K9" Bonnheim.

SIMON THANKS: First and foremost, always and forever, ▓Sarah, καλή γλυκό μου, for being the best friend, companion, and love in the ancient or modern world, a better poet than Homer and a better teacher than Plato. Molly, you are my sibling, and that is crazy; I'll see you on the T. Thanks for fixing my pants yo. Alexander Graham Bell, for keeping it real. J.K., you got me through July, but what am I supposed to do for the next two years? Julia, thanks for hiring me. Big ups to my LowDiHa crew. D.Seltz, keep walking the road of truth. And, finally, June 2006: thank you, thank you, thank you for being on the way.

KATHERINE THANKS: Julia, Simon, and Stuart for being always on their game, and always game for sea creatures; David, Jess, and Kelly for working harder than belief; Ella (Law) and Laura (Order); Jeremy "Scissors" Todd; Mom, Dad, Jaxie, G&G, and Mimi for everything else.

Editor
Julia Bonnheim
Associate Editor
Simon William Vozick-Levinson
Managing Editor
Stuart J. Robinson
Map Editor
Katherine J. Thompson
Typesetter
Ansel S. Witthaus

LET'S GO

Publishing Director
Seth Robinson
Editor-in-Chief
Stuart J. Robinson
Production Manager
Alexandra Hoffer
Cartography Manager
Katherine J. Thompson
Editorial Managers
Rachel M. Burke, Ashley Eva Isaacson, Laura E. Martin
Financial Manager
Adrienne Taylor Gerken
Publicity Manager
Alexandra C. Stanek
Personnel Manager
Ella M. Steim
Production Associate
Ansel S. Witthaus
IT Director
Jeffrey Hoffman Yip
Director of E-Commerce
Michael Reckhow
Office Coordinator
Matthew Gibson

Director of Advertising Sales
Jillian N. London
Senior Advertising Associates
Jessica C.L. Chiu, Katya M. Golovchenko, Mohammed J. Herzallah
Advertising Graphic Designer
Emily E. Maston

President
Caleb J. Merkl
General Manager
Robert B. Rombauer
Assistant General Manager
Anne E. Chisholm

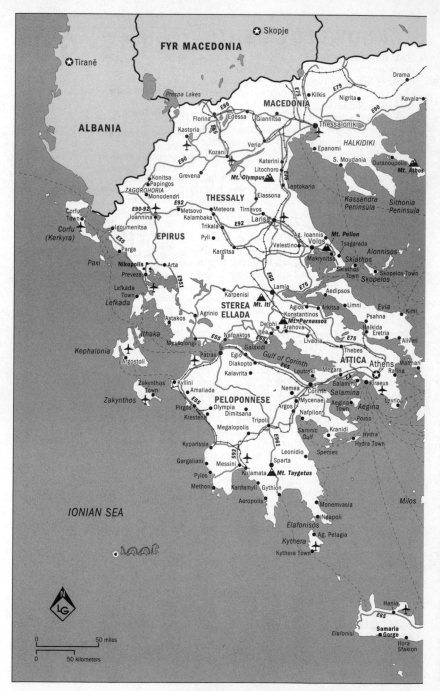

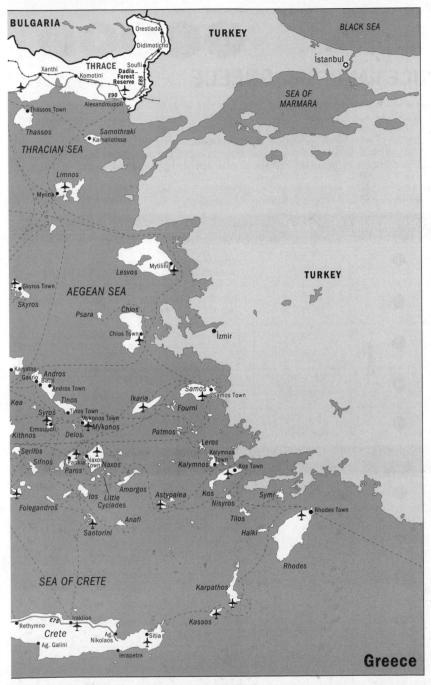

PRICE RANGES>>GREECE

Our researchers list establishments in order of value from best to worst; our favorites are denoted by the Let's Go thumbs-up (👍). Since the best value is not always the cheapest price, however, we have also incorporated a system of price ranges, based on a rough expectation of what you'll spend. For **accommodations,** we base our range on the cheapest price for which a single traveler can stay for one night. For **restaurants** and other dining establishments, we estimate the average amount a traveler will spend. The table tells you what you'll *typically* find in Greece at the corresponding price range; keep in mind that no system can allow for every individual establishment's quirks, and you'll typically get more for your money in larger cities. In other words: expect anything.

ACCOMMODATIONS	RANGE	WHAT YOU'RE *LIKELY* TO FIND
❶	under €15 / under US$19	Camping and most dorm rooms, such as hostels. Expect bunk beds and a communal bath; you may have to provide or rent towels.
❷	€15-25 / US$19-30	Domatia, high-end hostels, or small hotels. You may have a private bathroom.
❸	€26-35 / US$31-43	A small room with a private bath in a hotel or domatia. Decent amenities, such as phone and TV, and sometimes A/C. Breakfast may be included.
❹	€36-70 / US$44-85	Similar to 3, but may have more amenities, larger rooms, better views, or a better location.
❺	over €70 / over US$85	Large hotels or upscale chains. If it's a 5 and it doesn't have the perks you want, you've paid too much.

FOOD	RANGE	WHAT YOU'RE *LIKELY* TO FIND
❶	under €3 / under US$5	Mostly street-corner stands, gyro and souvlaki huts, bakeries, or fast-food joints. You may have the option of sitting down or getting take-out.
❷	€3-8 / US$5-10	Sandwiches, appetizers, or low-priced entrees. Generally a sit-down meal, sometimes with servers, but only slightly more upscale decor.
❸	€9-15 / US$11-18	Mid-priced entrees, seafood and exotic pasta dishes. More upscale ethnic eateries. You will have a waiter.
❹	€16-25 / US$19-30	A somewhat fancy restaurant or taverna. Few restaurants in this range have a dress code, but some may look down on t-shirts and jeans.
❺	over €25 / over US$30	Intricate, fancy entrees and a decent wine list. Slacks and dress shirts may be expected. Don't order PB&J.

DISCOVER GREECE

A land where sacred monasteries are mountainside fixtures, leisurely seaside siestas are standard issue, and circle-dancing and drinking until daybreak are summer rites, Greece's treasures are impossibly varied. Renaissance men long before their time, the ancient Greeks sprung to prominence with their philosophical, literary, artistic, and athletic mastery. Millennia later, schoolkids still dream of Hercules and Medusa; when those kids grow up, they hanker after Greece's island beaches, free-flowing booze, and gorgeous natural landscape. The all-encompassing Greek lifestyle is a deliciously frustrating mix of high speed chaos and sun-inspired lounging, as old men hold lively debates in town plateias, teenagers zoom on mopeds around the clock, and unpredictable schedules force a go-with-the-flow take on life.

FACTS AND FIGURES

OFFICIAL NAME Hellenic Republic

POPULATION 10,668,354

CAPITAL Athens

LENGTH OF COASTLINE PER GREEK CITIZEN 1.3m

AVERAGE BAR CLOSING TIME Sunrise or when the ouzo runs out

YEARS OF CIVILIZATION 5200

PERCENTAGE OF ISLANDS INHABITED 12%

RATIO OF FOREIGNERS TO LOCALS 9 tourists to every 10 Greeks

NUMBER OF GODS IN THE ANCIENT GREEK PANTHEON 12

NUMBER OF GODS IN THE GREEK ORTHODOX CHURCH 1

WHEN TO GO

June through August is **high season** in Greece. Bar-studded beaches set the scene for revelry and Dionysian indulgence, as the 100°F sun blazes over ancient cities and modern-day sun-worshippers alike. Hotels, domatia, and sights are, like the nightlife, in full swing. If the crowds or frantic pace of summer travel grate on you, consider visiting during May, early June, or September, when gorgeous weather smiles on thinner crowds. Avid hikers can take advantage of the mellower weather to traverse the unsullied expanses of Northern and Central Greece. In ski areas like Mt. Parnassos (p. 210), Kalavrita (p. 161), or Karpenisi (p. 223), winter brings another high season. Accommodations and food are cheaper in the **low seasons,** but many sights, restaurants, and nightlife options have shorter hours or close altogether. At this time of year, Greece takes a break from farming, fishing, and tourism; ferries, buses, and trains run less frequently; and life is quieter.

THINGS TO DO

Mountain chains, bougainvillea-speckled islands, silver-green olive groves, and the stark contrast of ochre land against the brilliantly blue Aegean comprise the refuge of mythological heroes and beasts. This varied land of isolated villages, jasmine-scented islands, and majestic ruins satisfies even the pickiest visitor with its infinite diversions. Don't be afraid to plot out your own route: the famous Greek hospitality

TOP TEN LIST

TOP TEN PLACES TO MEET A GREEK GOD

There once was a time when unicorns, centaurs, and gods roamed the earth. Now, finding the divine is hard, but if Hermes, the traveler god, doesn't befriend you, some other deity just might.

1. Visit the volcanoes of **Nisyros** (p. 469) and **Santorini** (p. 424) to see the forge of Hephaestus, god of fire.

2. Run through the **Dadia Forest Reserve** (p. 322) or the **Prespa Lakes** (p. 305) in search of Artemis, protectress of the woods.

3. **Mykonos** (p. 376) will put you in the alcoholic stupor needed to bond with wine god Dionysus, though **Ios** (p. 413) will do just as well.

4. Seek Athena's wisdom at none other than her patron city, **Athens** (p. 90), or try **Ithaka** (p. 550), home of one of her favorites, Odysseus.

5. Corfu's **Canal d'Amour** (p. 545) might help you find Aphrodite, or a mortal replacement.

6. A hike through Crete's **Valley of Death** (p. 621) might lead you to Hades.

7. You may run into Apollo at his oracle at **Delphi** (p. 216) or sanctuary at **Delos** (p. 383).

8. **Lesvos** (p. 503), home of the tenth Muse, Sappho, is a good place to seek the other nine.

9. Find Poseidon at his temple on **Cape Sounion** (p. 123), if you don't meet him first on a ferry.

10. **Mt. Olympus** (p. 295). Duh.

will make you feel welcome wherever you go. For more on regional bests, check out the **Suggested Itineraries boxes** that begin each chapter.

THE ROAD TO RUIN(S)

In Greece, it's harder to avoid ruins than find them. Since they survive in a broad spectrum of importance, quality of preservation, and overall impressiveness, you may find yourself bored unless you're a classicist or archaeologist. There are, of course, the not-to-be-missed biggies, which never disappoint. The perfectly proportioned columns of the **Parthenon** (p. 113), combined with the sun's beating rays and the brilliant gleam of marble, conjure up the same awe they inspired in centuries of worshippers. At Cape Sounion, the seaside **Temple of Poseidon** (p. 124) sits on a 60m promontory overlooking the Aegean. If you can catch the floating island of **Delos** (p. 383), birthplace of Apollo and Artemis, you will find an island-wide archaeological site. A voyage through the **Peloponnese** will take you back to the era of nymphs, satyrs, and gods in disguise. Sprint across the well-preserved stadium on the way to the original Olympic fields at **Ancient Olympia** (p. 169), wander through watery, fresco-covered tunnels at **Corinth** (p. 137), peer into Agamemnon's tomb at **Mycenae** (p. 149), or cry over an ancient tragedy in the theater at **Epidavros** (p. 151). Byzantine times stand still at the city-site of **Mystras** (p. 194), the former locus of Constantinople's rule in the Peloponnese. Back on the mainland, pilgrims can seek wisdom at the ancient **Oracle of Delphi** (p. 216), then wander up north to the dual ruins of **Pella** (p. 285) and **Vergina** (p. 284), once ruled by Philip II and his son Alexander the Great. **Samothraki** (p. 523), a pre-Hellenic cult-capital, will lead you out to the islands and farther back in time. The Minoan palaces of **Knossos** (p. 596) and **Phaistos** (p. 602) come straight out of mythology, and Santorini's **Akrotiri** (p. 424) shows you Minoan life, frozen in time by lava from a volcanic eruption.

ISLANDS IN THE SUN

The islands have long been a sun-worshipper's paradise, from those who follow Helios and Apollo to the disciples of Coppertone. Beachside days melt through spectacular sunsets into starry, disco-filled nights and back again, in a continuum of **hedonistic delight.** Besides the heavenly sands and turquoise waters, the islands offer ancient sites, intriguing museums, and peaceful small-town life.

▨ LET'S GO PICKS

BEST PLACE TO CONDUCT A CENSUS: The number of people in the village of **Agios Achillios** (p. 307) in Prespa can be counted on 1 person's fingers and toes. Counting the citizens of **Megalo Horio** (p. 226) in Evritania, however, would require 10 people's digits.

BEST PLACE TO THINK DEEP THOUGHTS: Take your most profound questions and ideas to Athens's **Agora** (p. 115), where master philosopher Socrates once taught. In **Vikos Gorge** (p. 266), any thought will be deeper than most on earth.

BEST EVIDENCE OF PLATE TECTONICS: The **Temple of Olympian Zeus** (p. 171), palace at **Knossos** (p. 596), and structures in **Akrotiri, Santorini** (p. 424), **Ancient Pella** (p. 285), **Ancient Dion** (p. 294), and **Sparta** (p. 190) were all destroyed by earthquakes.

BEST GIFTS: When Sir Frederic Adams, British High Commissioner to the Ionians, moved to Corfu, the British government gave him **2000 trees** (p. 538) as a house-warming gift. Franceso Gatelouzi received the entire island of **Lesvos** (p. 507), trees included, as a dowry.

BEST PLACES TO GET DIRTY: The mud from Messolongi's **lagoon** (p. 222) is said to have healing properties. The small town of Galaxidi marks the start of Lent each year with a **flour fight** (p. 217).

BEST OBJECTS M.I.A.: Greeks have been longing for their **Colossus of Rhodes** (p. 444) since it took its tumble into the Aegean in 226 BC. The celebrated **Winged Victory of Samothrace** (p. 526) resides in the Louvre in Paris. Ever since Lord Elgin decided to ship its marble reliefs to the British Museum in London, the **Acropolis** (p. 111) has been missing some key parts.

BEST EVIDENCE OF INBREEDING: The Prespa Lakes' **dwarf cows** (p. 307) were purposely bred small so that they wouldn't sink in the area's plentiful swamps. The **midget elephants** (p. 466) whose bones were found in Livadia on Tilos, however, did it all themselves.

MOST WELL-PRESERVED BODIES: **Mary Magdalene's hand** (p. 313) is kept in Simonos Petra monastery on Mt. Athos. The Osios Loukas monastery keeps its namesake **saint's body** (p. 212) in a Snow White-esque glass coffin. If you peek through the reliquary at Patras's Agio Andreas cathedral, you may see the top of **Saint Andrew's head** (p. 157).

BEST MULTI-PURPOSE BUILDINGS: The **San Marco Church** (p. 595) in Iraklion doubles as a venue for rotating art exhibits. Edessa's nighttime hotspot **Kanavourgeio** (p. 302) was once a hemp factory. **Anaplous** (p. 575), a restaurant in Hania, turned ruins into a dining room.

A favorite of international vacationers, **Skiathos** (p. 349), in the Sporades, harbors the piney Biotrope of Koukounaries beach and lovely Lalaria. In the Aegean Sea, **Santorini's** (p. 419) black-sand beaches soak up the sun's hot rays and stay warm long after the stunning sunsets over the Sea of Crete have faded. **Milos's** (p. 427) wide variety of beaches and multi-colored rocks seems like a rainbow-splashed paradise. Sea caves once ransacked by pirates on the coast of **Skyros** (p. 363) now welcome swimmers. Those basking on the **Lesvian shore** (p. 507) can multi-task as they stop to pay homage to **Sappho** or visit one of the only **Petrified Forests** in the world. Stumble out of all those pesky clothes at **Mykonos's** (p. 376) wild Paradise beach; if your eyes get tired of all the bare bodies, seek solace on a secluded strip of sand. Snorkeling, water-skiing, or just loafing in the sun fill the days on **Ios** (p. 413) and **Naxos** (p. 388). Signs of Odysseus are hidden on his home island, **Ithaka** (p. 550), and on **Corfu** (p. 531), where he was shipwrecked. Paleohora in **Crete** (p. 570) and castle-crowned Haraki beach on **Rhodes** (p. 437) beg travelers to drop their packs in the languid sun.

TAKE A HIKE

Take out your walking stick and rev up your engines. Hiking or motorbiking—or a combination of the two—lets you cruise between rural villages independent of sporadic bus schedules. On foot, you'll cross through graceful hills draped with olive groves, passing mountain goats and wildflowers along the way. To the delight of climbers, eighty percent of the Greek landscape is mountainous. Clamber to the abode of the gods at **Mount Olympus** (p. 295), ascending over 2900 steep, stunning meters to one of its eight peaks. During the summer, Dionysus's old watering hole, **Mount Parnassos** (p. 210), makes a great hiking and mountain-biking trip. The traditional villages of the **Zagorohoria** (p. 265) and their surrounding wilderness turn mere walking into an enticing adventure. On **Mount Athos** (p. 311), trails verge on sublime, as the paths from monastery to monastery scramble over grass-carpeted crags and yield divine views of the sea below. Neighboring **Vikos Gorge** (p. 266), the world's steepest canyon, challenges hikers with a 6hr. trek. The easier 11km hike between drowsy **Dimitsana** (p. 175) and cobblestoned **Stemnitsa** (p. 177) will remove you from the tourist bustle of the rest of the Peloponnese and treat you to beautiful Arcadian vistas. Odysseus's kingdom of **Ithaka** (p. 550) is an untapped hiker's paradise, where the Cave of the Nymphs—the hiding place for Odysseus's treasure—will seduce you. Northern **Thassos** (p. 526) is full of secluded ruins, superior hikes, and village-to-village strolls. **Alonnisos** (p. 359), a largely uninhabited Sporadic island, is criss-crossed by trails and moped-friendly roads, each hugged by beaches ideal for refueling after a tiring hike. In Crete, **Samaria Gorge** (p. 579), Europe's longest gorge, and the quieter **Valley of Death** (p. 621) plunge you below eagles' nests and trees that cling to the steep canyon sides. The trails around **Zaros** wind up to Zeus's childhood hiding place, **Kamares Cave** (p. 600).

SUGGESTED ITINERARIES

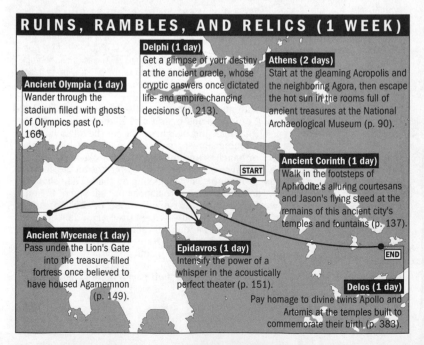

RUINS, RAMBLES, AND RELICS (1 WEEK)

Delphi (1 day)
Get a glimpse of your destiny at the ancient oracle, whose cryptic answers once dictated life- and empire-changing decisions (p. 213).

Athens (2 days)
Start at the gleaming Acropolis and the neighboring Agora, then escape the hot sun in the rooms full of ancient treasures at the National Archaeological Museum (p. 90).

Ancient Olympia (1 day)
Wander through the stadium filled with ghosts of Olympics past (p. 166).

Ancient Corinth (1 day)
Walk in the footsteps of Aphrodite's alluring courtesans and Jason's flying steed at the remains of this ancient city's temples and fountains (p. 137).

START

END

Ancient Mycenae (1 day)
Pass under the Lion's Gate into the treasure-filled fortress once believed to have housed Agamemnon (p. 149).

Epidavros (1 day)
Intensify the power of a whisper in the acoustically perfect theater (p. 151).

Delos (1 day)
Pay homage to divine twins Apollo and Artemis at the temples built to commemorate their birth (p. 383).

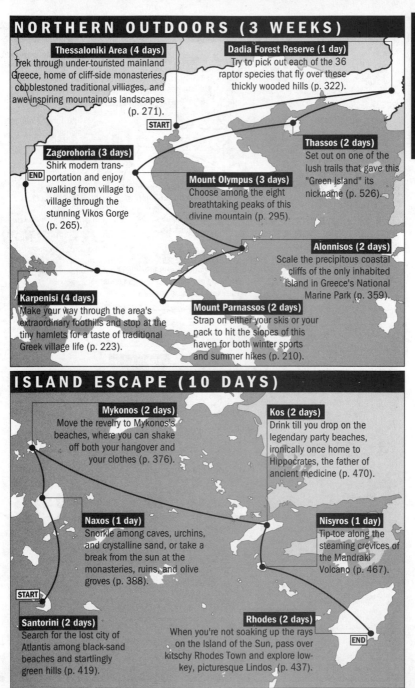

NORTHERN OUTDOORS (3 WEEKS)

DISCOVER

Thessaloniki Area (4 days)
Trek through under-touristed mainland Greece, home of cliff-side monasteries, cobblestoned traditional villiages, and awe-inspiring mountainous landscapes (p. 271).

START

Dadia Forest Reserve (1 day)
Try to pick out each of the 36 raptor species that fly over these thickly wooded hills (p. 322).

Thassos (2 days)
Set out on one of the lush trails that gave this "Green Island" its nickname (p. 526).

Zagorohoria (3 days)
END portation and enjoy
Shirk modern trans-
walking from village to village through the stunning Vikos Gorge (p. 265).

Mount Olympus (3 days)
Choose among the eight breathtaking peaks of this divine mountain (p. 295).

Alonnisos (2 days)
Scale the precipitous coastal cliffs of the only inhabited island in Greece's National Marine Park (p. 359).

Karpenisi (4 days)
Make your way through the area's extraordinary foothills and stop at the tiny hamlets for a taste of traditional Greek village life (p. 223).

Mount Parnassos (2 days)
Strap on either your skis or your pack to hit the slopes of this haven for both winter sports and summer hikes (p. 210).

ISLAND ESCAPE (10 DAYS)

Mykonos (2 days)
Move the revelry to Mykonos's beaches, where you can shake off both your hangover and your clothes (p. 376).

Kos (2 days)
Drink till you drop on the legendary party beaches, ironically once home to Hippocrates, the father of ancient medicine (p. 470).

Naxos (1 day)
Snorkle among caves, urchins, and crystalline sand, or take a break from the sun at the monasteries, ruins, and olive groves (p. 388).

Nisyros (1 day)
Tip-toe along the steaming crevices of the Mandraki Volcano (p. 467).

START

Santorini (2 days)
Search for the lost city of Atlantis among black-sand beaches and startlingly green hills (p. 419).

Rhodes (2 days)
When you're not soaking up the rays on the Island of the Sun, pass over kitschy Rhodes Town and explore low-key, picturesque Lindos (p. 437).

END

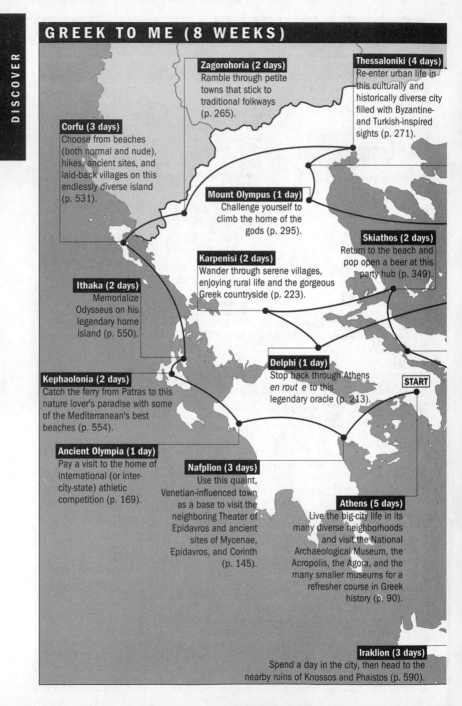

GREEK TO ME (8 WEEKS)

Zagorohoria (2 days)
Ramble through petite towns that stick to traditional folkways (p. 265).

Thessaloniki (4 days)
Re-enter urban life in this culturally and historically diverse city filled with Byzantine- and Turkish-inspired sights (p. 271).

Corfu (3 days)
Choose from beaches (both normal and nude), hikes, ancient sites, and laid-back villages on this endlessly diverse island (p. 531).

Mount Olympus (1 day)
Challenge yourself to climb the home of the gods (p. 295).

Skiathos (2 days)
Return to the beach and pop open a beer at this party hub (p. 349).

Karpenisi (2 days)
Wander through serene villages, enjoying rural life and the gorgeous Greek countryside (p. 223).

Ithaka (2 days)
Memorialize Odysseus on his legendary home island (p. 550).

Delphi (1 day)
Stop back through Athens en rout e to this legendary oracle (p. 213).

START

Kephaolonia (2 days)
Catch the ferry from Patras to this nature lover's paradise with some of the Mediterranean's best beaches (p. 554).

Ancient Olympia (1 day)
Pay a visit to the home of international (or inter-city-state) athletic competition (p. 169).

Nafplion (3 days)
Use this quaint, Venetian-influenced town as a base to visit the neighboring Theater of Epidavros and ancient sites of Mycenae, Epidavros, and Corinth (p. 145).

Athens (5 days)
Live the big-city life in its many diverse neighborhoods and visit the National Archaeological Museum, the Acropolis, the Agora, and the many smaller museums for a refresher course in Greek history (p. 90).

Iraklion (3 days)
Spend a day in the city, then head to the nearby ruins of Knossos and Phaistos (p. 590).

Vergina (1 day)
Stop by the tombs of Alexander the Great's illustrious, wealthy family (p. 284).

Limnos (2 days)
Loop down toward the Turkish coast to relax with packs of flamingoes on lovely beaches and sand dunes (p. 520).

Lesvos (3 days)
Pay a visit to Sappho's home and the petrified forest, one of only two in the world (p. 507).

Halkida (3 days)
Savor an urban metropolis that lacks the grit or chaos of Greece's biggest cities (p. 307).

Mykonos (3 days)
Join the pleasure-seekers and pelicans that gather at this hedonistic hotspot (p. 376).

Andros (2 days)
Relax in the rural paradise that practically begs hikers to explore its terrain (p. 366).

Delos (1 day)
Pay for the sins incurred on Mykonos with a daytrip to the sacred isle (p. 383).

Kos (2 days)
End your trip with one last 24hr. beach party. Because after all, who doesn't like hung-over plane rides home (p. 470)?

END

Naxos (2 days)
Visit olive groves, wineries, and ruins on Dionysus's home island (p. 388).

Santorini (3 days)
Marvel at the white cliff-side buildings, black volcanic beaches, and jewel-toned sea (p. 419).

Rhodes (2 days)
Stand in awe before Helios, god of the sun, and imagine the long-gone glory of the Colossus of Rhodes (p. 437).

Sitia (1 day)
Alternate between sun and shade at Vai's beach and palm-tree forest (p. 617).

ESSENTIALS

PLANNING YOUR TRIP

> ### ENTRANCE REQUIREMENTS
> **Passport** (p. 9). Required for citizens of Australia, Canada, Ireland, New Zealand, the UK, and the US.
> **Visa** (p. 10). Required only for stays over three months for citizens of Australia, Canada, Ireland, New Zealand, the UK, and the US.
> **Work Permit** (p. 11). Required for all EU citizens planning to work in Greece for over three months and all other foreigners planning to work in Greece for any length of time.
> **Inoculations**. Not required.

EMBASSIES AND CONSULATES

GREEK CONSULAR SERVICES ABROAD

Australia: 9 Turrana St., Yarralumla, Canberra, ACT 2600 (☎02 6273 3011; fax 02 6273 2620). **Consulates:** 300 Flinders St., Adelaide, SA 5000 (☎08 8232 2036; fax 08 8232 3184); 37-39 Albert Rd., Melbourne, VIC 3004 (☎03 9866 4524; fax 03 9866 4933); 16 St. George's Terr., Perth, WA 6000 (☎08 9325 6608; fax 08 9325 2940); 15 Castlereagh St., Sydney, NSW 2000 (☎02 9221 2388; fax 02 9221 1423).

Canada: 80 MacLaren St., Ottawa, ON K2P 0K6 (☎613 238 6271; www.greekembassy.ca). **Consulates:** 1170 Pl. du Frère André, Ste. 300, Montreal, QC H3B 3C6 (☎514 875 2119; www.grconsulatemtl.net); 365 Bloor St. E., Ste. 1800, Toronto, ON M4W 3L4 (☎416 515 0133; www.grconsulate.com); 500-688 West Hastings St., Vancouver, BC V6B 1P1 (☎604 681 1381; www.vancouver.grconsulate.ca).

Ireland: 1 Pembroke St. Upper, Dublin 2 (☎1 676 7254; fax 1 661 8892).

New Zealand: 5-7 Willeston St., Box 24066, Wellington (☎4 473 7775; fax 4 473 7441).

UK: 1a Holland Park, London W11 3TP (☎020 7229 3850; www.greekembassy.org.uk). **Consulate:** 1a Holland Park, London W11 3TP (☎020 7221 6467; fax 020 7243 3202).

US: 2221 Massachusetts Ave. NW, Washington, D.C. 20008 (☎202 939 1306; www.greekembassy.org). **Consulates:** Tower Place, Ste. 1670, 3340 Peachtree Rd. NE, Atlanta, GA 30326 (☎404 261 3313; www.greekembassy.org/atlanta); 86 Beacon St., Boston, MA 02108 (☎617 523 0100; www.greekembassy.org/boston); 650 N. St. Clair St., Chicago, IL 60611 (☎312 335 3915; www.greekembassy.org/chicago); 520 Post Oak Blvd., Ste. 450, Houston, TX 77027 (☎713 840 7522; www.greekembassy.org/houston); 12424 Wilshire Blvd., Ste. 800, Los Angeles, CA 90025 (☎310 826 5555; www.greekembassy.org/losangeles); 2 Canal St., Ste. 2318, New Orleans, LA 70130 (☎504 523 1167; www.greekembassy.org/neworleans); 69 E. 79th St., New York, NY 10021 (☎212 988 5500; www.greekembassy.org/newyork); 2441 Gough St., San Francisco, CA 94123 (☎415 775 2102; www.greekembassy.org/sanfrancisco).

CONSULAR SERVICES IN GREECE

Australia: Level 6, Thon Building, Kifisias and Alexandras, Ambelokipi, Athens 11523 (☎21087 04 000; www.ausemb.gr).

Canada: Ioannou Genadiou 4, Athens 11521 (☎21072 73 400; www.dfaitmaeci.gc.ca/canadaeuropa/greece). **Consulate:** Tsimiski 12, Thessaloniki 54624 (☎23102 56 350).

European Community: Vas. Sofias 2, Athens 10674 (☎21072 51 000; fax 21072 44 620).

Ireland: Vas. Konstantinou 7, Athens 10674 (☎21072 32 771; fax 21072 93 383).

New Zealand: Kifissias 268, Halandri, Athens 15232 (☎21068 74 700; fax 21068 74 444).

UK: Ploutarchou 1, Athens 10675 (☎21072 72 600; www.british-embassy.gr).

US: Vas. Sofias 91, Athens 10160 (☎21072 12 951; www.usembassy.gr). **Consulate:** Tsimiski 43, Thessaloniki 54623 (☎23102 42 905; www.usconsulate.gr).

TOURIST OFFICES

Start early when trying to contact tourist offices—like most things Greek, they run on their own relaxed schedule. Polite persistence coupled with genuine excitement and interest works wonders. Two national organizations oversee tourism: the **Greek National Tourist Organization (GNTO)**, known as the **"EOT"** in Greece, and the **tourist police.** The GNTO can supply general information about sights and accommodations throughout the country. The main office is in Athens at Tsoha 7 (☎21087 07 000; www.gnto.gr). Another information desk is located at El. Venizelos Airport (☎21035 45 101 or 21035 30 445). Tourist police deal with local travel issues like finding a room or bus schedules. Officers are often quite willing to help, though English may be limited. *Let's Go* lists locations and contact information for tourist offices and the tourist police in the **Practical Information** section of each city or town. There are also official Greek tourism boards in several countries:

Australia and New Zealand: 51-57 Pitt St., Sydney, NSW 2000 (☎02 9241 1663; fax 02 9235 2174).

Canada: 1300 Bay St., Toronto, ON M5R 3K8 (☎416 968 2220); 1170 Place du Frère André, Montreal, QC H3B C36 (☎514 871 1535; fax 514 871 1498).

UK and Ireland: 4 Conduit St., London W1S 2DJ (☎020 7495 9300; www.touristoffices.org.uk).

US: Olympic Tower, 645 Fifth Ave., Ste. 903, New York, NY 10022 (☎212 421 5777; www.greektourism.com).

DOCUMENTS AND FORMALITIES

PASSPORTS

REQUIREMENTS

Citizens of Australia, Canada, Ireland, New Zealand, the UK, and the US need valid passports to enter Greece and re-enter their home countries. Greece does not allow entrance if the holder's passport expires in under six months; returning home with an expired passport is illegal, and may result in a fine.

ESSENTIALS

ESSENTIALS

NEW PASSPORTS

Citizens of Australia, Canada, Ireland, New Zealand, the UK, and the US can apply for a passport at any passport office or at selected post offices and courts of law. They may also download applications from the official website of their country's government or passport office. Any new passport or renewal applications must be filed well in advance of departure, though many offices offer rush services for a steep fee. Note that "rushed" passports still take up to two weeks to arrive.

ONE EUROPE. European unity has come a long way since 1958, when the European Economic Community (EEC) was created to promote European solidarity and cooperation. Since then, the EEC has become the European Union (EU), a mighty political, legal, and economic institution. On May 1, 2004, 10 Southern, Central, and Eastern European countries—Cyprus, the Czech Republic, Estonia, Hungary, Latvia, Lithuania, Malta, Poland, Slovakia, and Slovenia—were admitted to the EU, joining 15 other member states: Austria, Belgium, Denmark, Finland, France, Germany, Greece, Ireland, Italy, Luxembourg, the Netherlands, Portugal, Spain, Sweden, and the UK.

What does this have to do with the average non-EU tourist? The EU's policy of **freedom of movement** means that border controls between the first 15 member states (minus Ireland and the UK, but plus Norway and Iceland) have been abolished, and visa policies harmonized. Under this treaty, formally known as the **"Schengen Agreement,"** you're still required to carry a passport (or government-issued ID card for EU citizens) when crossing an internal border, but once you've been admitted into one country, you're free to travel to other participating states. On June 5, 2005, Switzerland ratified the treaty, and will become fully participant by 2007. The 10 newest member states of the EU are anticipated to implement the policy after 2006. Britain and Ireland have also formed a **common travel area,** abolishing passport controls between the UK and the Republic of Ireland.

For more important consequences of the EU for travelers, see **The Euro** (p. 14) and **European Customs** and **EU customs regulations** (p. 13).

PASSPORT MAINTENANCE

Photocopy the page of your passport with your photo, as well as your visas, traveler's check serial numbers, and any other important documents. Carry one set of copies in a safe place, apart from the originals, and leave another set at home. Consulates also recommend that you carry an expired passport or an official copy of your birth certificate in a part of your baggage separate from other documents.

If you lose your passport, immediately notify the local police and the nearest embassy or consulate of your home government. To expedite its replacement, you will need to show ID and proof of citizenship; it also helps to know all information previously recorded in the passport. In some cases, a replacement may take weeks to process, and it may be valid only for a limited time. Any visas stamped in your old passport will be irretrievably lost. In an emergency, ask for immediate temporary traveling papers that will permit you to re-enter your home country.

VISAS, INVITATIONS, AND WORK PERMITS

VISAS

EU citizens do not need a visa. Citizens of Australia, Canada, Ireland, New Zealand, the UK, and the US do not need a visa to enter Greece for stays under 90 days, though this period begins upon entry into any of the countries in the EU's **freedom of movement** zone. For more information, see **One Europe** (above). Those staying longer than 90 days may purchase a visa from the Greek embassy or consulate in the area of your permanent residence. Visas allow the holder to spend six months in Greece. If you decide to stay in Greece longer than planned, make sure to apply for a visa extension well in advance—applications must be submitted at least 20 days before the three-month expiration date of normal non-visa travel.

Double-check entrance requirements at the nearest embassy or consulate of Greece (listed under **Greek Consular Services Abroad,** on p. 8) for up-to-date info before departure. US citizens can also consult http://travel.state.gov.

Entering Greece to study requires a student visa. For more information, see **Beyond Tourism** (p. 82).

WORK PERMITS

Admission as a visitor doesn't include the right to work, which is authorized only by a work permit. Permits are granted by the Ministry of Labor, and often require a letter from an employer. EU residents can work in Greece for up to 90 days with no permit, but need one for longer stays. For more info, see **Beyond Tourism** (p. 85).

IDENTIFICATION

When you travel, always carry at least two forms of identification on your person, including a photo ID; a passport and a driver's license or birth certificate is usually an adequate combination. Never carry all your IDs together; split them up in case of theft or loss, and keep photocopies of all of them in your luggage and at home.

STUDENT, TEACHER, AND YOUTH IDENTIFICATION

The **International Student Identity Card (ISIC),** the most widely accepted form of student ID, provides discounts on sights, accommodations, food, and transportation; access to a 24hr. emergency helpline; and insurance benefits for US cardholders. In Greece, ISIC offers discounts on entrance to archaeological sites, restaurants, equipment outfitters, and more. Applicants must be full-time secondary or post-secondary school students, at least 12 years old. Because fake ISICs are common, some services (particularly airlines) require additional proof of student identity.

The **International Teacher Identity Card (ITIC)** offers teachers the same insurance coverage as the ISIC and similar but limited discounts. For travelers who are under 26 years of age but are not students, the **International Youth Travel Card (IYTC)** also offers many of the same benefits as the ISIC.

Each of these identity cards costs US$22 or equivalent. ISICs and ITICs are valid until the new year unless purchased between September and December, in which case they are valid until the beginning of the following new year. Thus, a card purchased in March 2006 will be valid until December 31, 2006, while a card purchased in November 2006 will be valid until December 31, 2007. IYTCs are valid for one year from the date of issue. To learn more about ISICs, ITICs, and IYTCs, try www.myisic.com. Many student travel agencies (see p. 26) issue the cards; for a list of issuing agencies or more information, see the **International Student Travel Confederation (ISTC)** website (www.istc.org).

The **International Student Exchange Card (ISE Card)** is a similar ID available to students, faculty, and youths aged 12 to 26. The card gives discounts, medical benefits, and access to a 24hr. emergency helpline and student airfares. An ISE Card costs US$25; call ☎800 255 8000 for more info, or visit www.isecard.com.

CUSTOMS

Upon entering Greece, you must declare certain items from abroad and pay a duty on the value of those articles if they exceed the allowance established by Greece's customs service. Note that goods and gifts purchased at **duty-free** shops abroad are not exempt from duty or sales tax; "duty-free" merely means that you

need not pay a tax in the country of purchase. Duty-free allowances apply to those arriving from outside the EU. Upon returning home, you must likewise declare all articles acquired abroad and pay a duty on the value of articles in excess of your home country's allowance. In order to expedite your return, make a list of any valuables brought from home and register them with customs before traveling abroad, and be sure to keep receipts for all goods acquired abroad. Greek antiquities, including rocks from archaeological sites, may not be taken out of Greece. Doing so could result in large fines or even time in prison.

 CUSTOMS IN THE EU. As well as freedom of movement of people within the EU (see p. 10), travelers in the 15 original EU member countries (Austria, Belgium, Denmark, Finland, France, Germany, Greece, Ireland, Italy, Luxembourg, the Netherlands, Portugal, Spain, Sweden, and the UK) can also take advantage of the freedom of movement of goods. This means that there are no customs controls at internal EU borders (i.e., you can take the blue customs channel at the airport), and travelers are free to transport whatever legal substances they like as long as it is for their own personal (non-commercial) use—up to 800 cigarettes, 10L of spirits, 90L of wine (including up to 60L of sparkling wine), and 110L of beer. Duty-free allowances were abolished on June 30, 1999 for travel between the original 15 EU member states; this now also applies to Cyprus and Malta. However, travelers between the EU and the rest of the world still get a duty-free allowance when passing through customs.

MONEY

CURRENCY AND EXCHANGE

The currency chart below is based on August 2005 exchange rates between European Union euros (EUR€) and Australian dollars (AUS$), Canadian dollars (CDN$), New Zealand dollars (NZ$), British pounds (UK£), and US dollars (US$). Check the currency converter on websites like www.xe.com or www.bloomberg.com, or a large newspaper, for the latest exchange rates.

EUROS (€)		
AUS$1 = €0.62		€1 = AUS$1.60
CDN$1 = €0.67		€1 = CDN$1.50
NZ$1 = €0.56		€1= NZ$1.78
UK£1 = €1.44		€1 = UK£.069
US$1 = €0.81		€1 = US$1.23

As a general rule, it's cheaper to convert money in Greece than at home. While currency exchange will probably be available in your arrival airport, it's wise to bring enough foreign currency to last for the first 24 to 72 hours of your trip.

When changing money abroad, try to go only to a bank (τράπεζα, TRAH-peh-za) that has at most a 5% margin between its buy and sell prices. Since you lose money with every transaction, **convert large sums** (unless the currency is depreciating rapidly), but **no more than you'll need.**

If you use traveler's checks or bills, carry some in small denominations (the equivalent of US$50 or less) for times when you are forced to exchange money at disadvantageous rates, but bring a range of denominations since charges may be levied per check cashed. Store your money in a variety of forms; ideally, at any given time you will be carrying some cash, some traveler's checks, and an ATM and/or credit card. All travelers should also consider carrying some US dollars (about US$50 worth), which are often accepted, or even preferred, by local tellers.

THE EURO. The official currency of 12 members of the European Union— Austria, Belgium, Finland, France, Germany, Greece, Ireland, Italy, Luxembourg, the Netherlands, Portugal, and Spain—is now the euro.

The currency has some important—and positive—consequences for travelers hitting more than one euro-zone country. For one thing, money-changers across the euro-zone are obliged to exchange money at the official, fixed rate, and at no commission (though they may still charge a small service fee). Second, euro-denominated traveler's checks allow you to pay for goods and services across the euro-zone, again at the official rate and commission-free.

TRAVELER'S CHECKS

Traveler's checks are one of the safest means of carrying funds. American Express and Visa are the most-recognized brands. Many banks and agencies sell them for a small commission. Check issuers provide refunds if the checks are lost or stolen, and many provide additional services, such as toll-free refund hotlines abroad, emergency message services, and assistance with lost and stolen credit cards or passports. Traveler's checks are readily accepted all over Greece, and can be cashed in all Greek banks and exchange bureaus, though they are used less and less frequently. Ask about toll-free refund hotlines and the location of refund centers when purchasing checks, and always carry emergency cash.

American Express: Checks available with commission at select banks, at all AmEx offices, and online (www.americanexpress.com; US residents only). American Express cardholders can also purchase checks by phone (☎800 721 9768). Checks available in Australian, British, Canadian, European, and US currencies, among others. American Express also offers the Travelers Cheque Card, a prepaid reloadable card. Cheques for Two can be signed by either of two people traveling together. For purchase locations or more information, contact AmEx's service centers: in Greece ☎21032 62 626, in Australia 800 688 022, in New Zealand 423 74 409, in the UK 0800 587 6023, in the US and Canada 800 221 7282; elsewhere, call the US collect at 801 964 6665.

Travelex: Thomas Cook MasterCard and Interpayment Visa traveler's checks available. For information about Thomas Cook MasterCard in Canada and the US call ☎800 223 7373, in the UK 0800 622 101, in Greece 008 00441 31 409; elsewhere call the UK collect at 44 1733 318 950. For info about Interpayment Visa in the US and Canada call ☎800 732 1322, in the UK 0800 515 884, in Greece 008 00441 31 411; elsewhere call the UK collect at 1733 318 949. For more info, visit www.travelex.com.

Visa: Checks available (generally with commission). To find the nearest office, call the Visa Travelers Cheque Global Refund and Assistance Center: in the UK ☎0800 515 884, in the US 800 227 6811, elsewhere call the UK collect at 2079 378 091. Checks available in British, Canadian, European, Japanese, and US currencies, among others. Visa also offers TravelMoney, a prepaid debit card that can be reloaded online or by phone. For more info, see http://usa.visa.com/personal/using_visa/travel_with_visa.html.

CREDIT, DEBIT, AND ATM CARDS

Credit cards often have superior exchange rates—up to 5% better than the retail rate used by banks and other currency exchangers. They may also offer services like insurance or emergency help, and are sometimes required to reserve hotel rooms or rental cars. **MasterCard** and **Visa** are the most frequently accepted; **American Express** cards work at some ATMs, at AmEx offices, and at major airports.

The use of ATM cards is widespread in Greece. Depending on the system that your home bank uses, you can most likely access your personal bank account from abroad. ATMs get the same wholesale exchange rate as credit cards, but there is often a limit on the amount of money you can withdraw per day (usually around US$500). There is typically also a surcharge of US$1-5 per withdrawal.

Debit cards are as convenient as credit cards but have a more immediate impact on your funds. A debit card can be used wherever its associated credit card company (usually MasterCard or Visa) is accepted, yet the money is withdrawn directly from the holder's checking account. Debit cards often also function as ATM cards and can be used to withdraw cash from associated banks and ATMs throughout Greece. Ask your local bank about obtaining one.

The two major international money networks are **MasterCard/Maestro/Cirrus** (for ATM locations ☎ 800 424 7787 or www.mastercard.com) and **Visa/PLUS** (for ATM locations ☎ 800 843 7587 or www.visa.com). Most ATMs charge a transaction fee that is paid to the bank that owns the ATM.

> **ATMS AND PINS.** To use a cash or credit card to withdraw money from a cash machine (ATM) in Europe, you may need a four-digit **Personal Identification Number (PIN)**. If your PIN is longer than four digits, ask your bank whether you can just use the first or last four, or whether you'll need a new one. **Credit cards** don't usually come with PINs, so if you intend to hit up ATMs in Europe with a credit card, call your credit card company before leaving to request one.
>
> Travelers with alphabetic, rather than numerical, PINs may also be thrown off by the lack of letters on European cash machines. The following are the corresponding numbers to use: 1=QZ; 2=ABC; 3=DEF; 4=GHI; 5=JKL; 6=MNO; 7=PRS; 8=TUV; and 9=WXY. Note that if you mistakenly punch the wrong code into the machine three times, it will swallow your card for good.

GETTING MONEY FROM HOME

If you run out of money while traveling, the easiest and cheapest solution is to have someone back home make a deposit to your bank account. Failing that, consider one of the following options.

WIRING MONEY

It is possible to arrange a **bank money transfer,** which means asking a bank back home to wire money to a bank in Greece. This is the cheapest way to transfer cash, but it's also the slowest, usually taking several days or more. Note that some banks may only release your funds in local currency, potentially sticking you with a poor exchange rate; inquire about this in advance. Money transfer services like **Western Union** are faster and more convenient than bank transfers—but also much pricier. Western Union has many locations worldwide. To find one, visit www.westernunion.com, or call in Australia ☎ 800 173 833, in Canada and the US 800 325 6000, in the UK 0800 833 833, or in Greece 21090 05 000. To wire money using a credit card (Discover, MasterCard, Visa), call in Canada and the US ☎ 800 225 5227, in the UK 0800 833 833. Money transfer services are also available to **American Express** cardholders and at selected **Thomas Cook** offices.

US STATE DEPARTMENT (US CITIZENS ONLY)

In serious emergencies only, the US State Department will forward money within hours to the nearest consular office, which will then disburse it according to instructions for a US$30 fee. For this service, you must contact the Overseas Citizens Service division of the US State Department (☎ 202 647 5225 or 888 407 4747).

COSTS

The cost of your trip will vary considerably, depending on where you go, how you travel, and where you stay. The most significant expenses will probably be your round-trip (return) **airfare** to Greece (see **Getting to Greece: By Plane,** p. 26) and a **railpass** or **bus pass** (p. 31). Before you go, spend some time calculating a reasonable daily **budget.**

STAYING ON A BUDGET

In general, a bare-bones day in Greece (camping or sleeping in hostels, buying food at supermarkets) costs US$48-72 (€40-60); a slightly cushier day (sleeping in hostels, domatia, or a budget hotel, eating one meal at a restaurant, going out at night) costs US$65-90 (€55-75); and for a luxurious day, the sky's the limit. Remember emergency reserve funds (at least US$200) when planning how much money you'll need.

TIPS FOR SAVING MONEY

Some simple ways include finding free entertainment, splitting accommodation and food costs with trustworthy fellow travelers, and buying food in supermarkets rather than eating out. Bring a **sleepsack** (p. 18) to save on sheet charges in hostels, and do your **laundry** in the sink (unless you're explicitly prohibited from doing so). Museums often have certain days once a month or once a week when admission is free; plan accordingly. If you are eligible, consider getting an ISIC or an IYTC; many sights and museums offer reduced admission to students and youths. For getting around quickly, bikes are the most economical option. Renting a bike is cheaper than renting a moped. Don't forget about walking; you can learn a lot about a city by seeing it on foot. Drinking at bars and clubs quickly becomes expensive. It's cheaper to buy alcohol at a supermarket and imbibe before going out. That said, don't go overboard; though staying within your budget is important, don't do so at the expense of your health or a great travel experience.

TIPPING AND BARGAINING

Greek law stipulates that restaurant and cafe prices include a 13% gratuity surcharge. It is common to round up your check to the nearest euro. You do not need to leave a tip unless you want to show your appreciation for a particularly good server (around 5% over your total). Similar rules apply to taxi rides.

Bargaining skills probably won't get you as far as they would have even five years ago, but you can try your luck when appropriate. Paying the

TOP TEN WAYS TO SAVE IN GREECE

Though Greece has certainly become more expensive in the past few years, it's still accessible to the budget traveler—provided you know a few tips, that is.

1. Buy food at outdoor markets, grocery stores, or gyro stands instead of dining out at tavernas.

2. Try to stay in domatia where you can—they're often cheaper than hotels and will give you more of a local experience.

3. Plan your route around what you want to do, not where you want to go. For example, if you want to visit island beaches, the Dodecanese will be much cheaper than the Saronic Gulf.

4. Bargain (where appropriate).

5. Rent a moped, not a car. They can usually get you where you need to go for under €10 per day.

6. Watch for days when you can get into museums for free.

7. Build outdoors experiences into your itinerary. Hiking or laying on a beach won't cost a euro.

8. Instead of buying drinks at bars or clubs, get your buzz on before you go out at *ouzerias*, or with the free shots of ouzo or *tsipouro* you get after many taverna meals.

9. Visit the free (or very cheap) archaeological sites to get your ancient fix instead of going to the archaeological museums.

10. Bypass the waterfront establishments, and head inland. Everything—food, rooms, and sights—will be cheaper.

asked price for street wares might leave the seller marveling at your naïveté, while bargaining at the shop of a master craftsman would be disrespectful. The price tends to be more flexible in informal venues. If unclear whether bargaining is appropriate in a situation, hang back and watch someone else buy. Also, if you seem unsure, merchants might start the negotiations themselves. Merchants with any pride in their wares will refuse to sell to someone who has offended them in the negotiations. **Domatia** (p. 42) prices rise in summer and drop in winter (unless you're visiting a mountain town known for winter activities). You'll likely have success bargaining in domatia and other small hotels. If your **taxi** trip won't be metered or ticketed—though you should generally seek out metered rides—bargain before you get going.

TAXES

Greece imposes a value added tax (VAT) on sales, which is included in the retail price—16% on purchases made on the mainland, 11.5% on purchases made in the Aegean islands. Travelers from non-EU countries who spend more than €120 in one shop in one day are entitled to claim some of their VAT on these items when leaving Greece, as long as they take the items out of Greece within three months of their purchase. Claiming your VAT refund can involve complicated paperwork; try to ask about VAT at any shops where you make substantial purchases, or contact **Global Refund** (☎ 21032 30 730; www.globalrefund.org) for more information.

PACKING

Pack lightly: lay out only what you absolutely need, then take half the clothes and twice the money. The Travelite FAQ (www.travelite.org) is a good resource for tips on traveling light. The online **Universal Packing List** (http://upl.codeq.info) will generate a customized list of suggested items based on your trip length, the expected climate, your planned activities, and other factors. If you plan to do a lot of hiking, also consult **The Great Outdoors**, p. 46. Some frequent travelers keep a bag packed with all the essentials: passport, money belt, hat, socks, etc. Then, when they decide to leave, they know they haven't forgotten anything.

Luggage: If you plan to cover most of your itinerary by foot, a sturdy **frame backpack** is unbeatable. (For the basics on buying a pack, see p. 47.) Toting a **suitcase** or **trunk** is fine if you plan to stay in one or two cities and explore from there, but not a great idea if you want to move around frequently. In addition to your main piece of luggage, a **daypack** (a small backpack or messenger bag) is useful.

Clothing: If you are in Greece at the height of summer, you'll need little more than **comfortable shoes,** a few changes of **light clothes,** and a **jacket.** When Greece gets chilly in the winter months, rains come frequently, so bring a **rain jacket** (Gore-Tex® is both waterproof and breathable). **Flip-flops** or waterproof sandals are must-haves for grubby hostel showers. To visit monasteries or churches, men will need a lightweight pair of **pants** and women will need a **long skirt;** both will need clothes that cover the shoulders. If you plan on taking ferries you'll want a **windproof jacket,** and, if you want to hike, add sturdy shoes or **hiking boots,** and **thick socks.** You may also want one outfit for going out, and maybe a nicer pair of shoes.

Sleepsack: Some hostels require that you either provide your own linen or rent sheets from them. Save cash by making your own sleepsack: fold a full-size sheet in half the long way, then sew it closed along the long side and one of the short sides.

Converters and Adapters: In Greece, electricity is 220 volts AC, enough to fry any 120V North American appliance. 220/240V electrical appliances won't work with a 120V current, either. Americans and Canadians should buy an adapter (which changes the shape of the plug; US$5) and a converter (which changes the voltage; US$20-$30).

Don't make the mistake of using only an adapter (unless appliance instructions explicitly state otherwise). Australians and New Zealanders (who use 230V at home) won't need a converter, but will need a set of adapters to use anything electrical. For more on all things adaptable, check out http://kropla.com/electric.htm.

Toiletries: Toothbrushes, towels, cold-water soap, talcum powder (to keep feet dry), deodorant, razors, tampons, and condoms are often available, but may be difficult to find; bring extras. **Contact lenses** are likely to be expensive and difficult to find, so bring enough extra pairs and solution for your entire trip. Also bring your glasses and a copy of your prescription in case you need emergency replacements. If you use heat-disinfection, either switch temporarily to a chemical disinfection system (check first to make sure it's safe with your brand of lenses), or buy a converter to 220V.

First-Aid Kit: For a basic first-aid kit, pack bandages, a pain reliever, antibiotic cream, a thermometer, a multifunction pocketknife, tweezers, moleskin, decongestant, motion-sickness remedy, diarrhea or upset-stomach medication (Pepto Bismol® or Imodium®), an antihistamine, sunscreen, insect repellent, burn ointment, and a syringe for emergencies (get an explanatory letter from your doctor).

Film: Greeks tend to develop film very well (about €8 for a roll of 24 color exposures). However, film and processing can get expensive, so you might consider bringing along enough film for your whole trip and developing it at home. Less serious photographers may want to bring a disposable camera. Despite disclaimers, airport security X-rays can fog film, so buy a lead-lined pouch at a camera store or ask security to hand-inspect it. Keep film in your carry-on luggage, since higher-intensity X-rays are used on checked luggage. If you don't want to bother with film, consider using a digital camera. Just be sure to bring along a large enough memory card and extra (or rechargeable) batteries. For more info on digital cameras, visit www.short-courses.com/choosing/contents.htm.

Other Useful Items: For safety purposes, bring a **money belt** and a small **padlock.** Basic **outdoors equipment** (plastic water bottle, compass, waterproof matches, pocketknife, sunglasses, sunscreen, hat) may also prove useful. **Quick repairs** of torn garments can be done on the road with a needle and thread; also consider bringing electrical tape for patching tears. If you want to do laundry by hand, bring detergent, a small rubber ball to stop up the sink, and string for a makeshift clothes line. Other things you're liable to forget include: an umbrella, sealable plastic bags (for damp clothes, soap, food, shampoo, and other spillables), an alarm clock, safety pins, rubber bands, a flashlight, earplugs, garbage bags, and a small calculator. A **cell phone** can be a lifesaver (literally) on the road; see p. 40 for information on acquiring one that will work in Greece.

Important Documents: Don't forget your passport, traveler's checks, ATM and/or credit cards, adequate ID, and photocopies of all of the aforementioned in case these documents are lost or stolen (see p. 10). Also check that you have any of the following that might apply to you: a hosteling membership card; driver's license (see p. 38); travel insurance forms (see p. 22); ISIC (see p. 11); and/or rail or bus pass (see p. 31).

SAFETY AND HEALTH

GENERAL ADVICE

In any type of crisis situation, the most important thing to do is **stay calm.** Your home country's embassy abroad (p. 9) is usually your best resource when things go wrong; registering with that embassy upon arrival in the country is often a good idea. The government offices listed in the **Travel Advisories** box (p. 21) can provide information on the services they offer their citizens in case of emergencies abroad.

LOCAL LAWS AND POLICE

Greek police are used to having foreigners around, but that does not mean they allow them to break the law. Photographs and notes cannot be taken near military establishments (including docks). The purchase of pirated goods (including CDs) is illegal; keep your receipts for proof of purchase. Taking objects or rocks from ancient sites is forbidden and can incur fines or prison sentences. Drunk driving and indecent behavior (including mooning) also can result in arrest, fines, and imprisonment. A passport or photo ID should be carried with you at all times.

DRUGS AND ALCOHOL

Visitors of all ages generally have little difficulty obtaining alcohol in Greece. Drugs laws are very strict. Conviction for possession, use, or trafficking of drugs, including marijuana, will result in imprisonment and heavy fines. If you use **prescription drugs,** have a copy of the prescriptions themselves and a note from a doctor available, especially at border crossings. Keep all medication with you in your carry-on luggage. Authorities are particularly vigilant at the Turkish and Albanian borders.

SPECIFIC CONCERNS

EARTHQUAKES

Greece experiences frequent and occasionally large earthquakes. Earthquakes cannot be predicted and can occur at any time of day. If an earthquake does occur, it will last only a few minutes. Protect yourself by moving underneath a sturdy doorway, table, or desk. In mountainous regions landslides may follow quakes.

DEMONSTRATIONS AND POLITICAL GATHERINGS

Strikes and demonstrations occur often in Greece and can be inconvenient, but more serious civil disorder is not generally a problem. Still, it is wise to pay attention to where demonstrations are, and try to avoid them as there is always the possibility of violence. Common areas for protest include Exarhia (especially by the Polytechnical University), Omonia, Pl. Syndagma and Pl. Mavili (near the US embassy) in Athens, and the area near Aristotle University in Thessaloniki.

TERRORISM

As in any other part of the world, the threat of terrorism exists in Greece. The best thing you can do is be aware of your surroundings, especially in crowded areas or tourist sites. Domestic terrorism in Greece is mostly by anarchist groups, but it tends to be on a lower scale and directed at the government. The box below on **travel advisories** lists offices to contact and webpages to visit to get the most updated list of your home country's government's advisories about travel.

PERSONAL SAFETY

EXPLORING AND TRAVELING

To avoid unwanted attention, try to blend in as much as possible. Respecting local customs (in many cases, dressing more conservatively than you would at home) may placate would-be hecklers. Familiarize yourself with your surroundings before setting out, and carry yourself with confidence. Check maps in shops and restaurants rather than on the street. If you are traveling alone, be sure someone at home knows your itinerary, and never admit that you're by yourself. When walking at night, stick to busy, well-lit streets and avoid dark alleyways. If you ever feel uncomfortable, leave the area as quickly and directly as you can. Solo travelers

> **!** **TRAVEL ADVISORIES.** The following government offices provide travel
> information and advisories by telephone, by fax, or via the web:
> **Australian Department of Foreign Affairs and Trade:** ☎ 1300 555 135;
> www.dfat.gov.au.
> **Canadian Department of Foreign Affairs and International Trade (DFAIT):**
> ☎ 800 267 8376; www.dfait-maeci.gc.ca. Call for their free booklet, *Bon Voy-*
> *age...But.*
> **New Zealand Ministry of Foreign Affairs:** ☎ 044 398 000; www.mft.govt.nz/
> travel/index.html.
> **United Kingdom Foreign and Commonwealth Office:** ☎ 020 7008 1500;
> www.fco.gov.uk.
> **US Department of State:** ☎ 202 647 5225; http://travel.state.gov. Visit the
> website for the booklet *A Safe Trip Abroad.*

ESSENTIALS

may feel like they stand out among Greeks, who don't usually travel alone. West-
erners may also feel uncomfortable around anti-American and anti-Western graffiti. If you encounter anti-Western sentiment, just walk away.

There is no sure-fire way to avoid all the threatening situations you might
encounter, but a good **self-defense course** will give you concrete ways to react to
unwanted advances. **Impact, Prepare, and Model Mugging** can refer you to local
courses in the US. Visit the website at www.modelmugging.org for a list of nearby
chapters. Workshops (2-4hr.) start at US$50; full courses (20hr.) run US$350-500.

If you are using a **car,** learn local driving signals and wear a seatbelt. Children
under 40 lbs. should ride only in specially designed carseats, available for a small
fee from most car rental agencies. Study route maps before you hit the road, and if
you plan on spending a lot of time driving, consider bringing spare parts. If your
car breaks down, wait for the police to assist you. For long drives in desolate
areas, invest in a cellular phone and a roadside assistance program (see p. 36).
Park your vehicle in a garage or well-traveled area, and use a steering wheel lock-
ing device in larger cities. **Sleeping in your car** is one of the most dangerous (and
often illegal) ways to get your rest. For info on the perils of **hitchhiking,** see p. 39.

POSSESSIONS AND VALUABLES

Never leave your belongings unattended; crime occurs in even the most demure-
looking hostels and hotels. Bring your own padlock for hostel lockers, and don't
ever store valuables in a locker. Be particularly careful on **buses** and **trains;** horror
stories abound about determined thieves who wait for travelers to fall asleep.
Carry your pack in front of you where you can see it. When traveling with others,
sleep in alternate shifts. When alone, use good judgment in selecting a train compartment: never stay in an empty one, and use a lock to secure your pack to the
luggage rack. Try to sleep on top bunks with your luggage stored above you (if not
in bed with you), and keep important documents and valuables on your person.

There are a few steps you can take to minimize the financial risk associated with
traveling. First, **bring as little with you as possible.** Second, buy a few combination
padlocks to secure your belongings either in your pack or in a hostel or train station locker. Third, **carry as little cash as possible.** Keep your traveler's checks and
ATM/credit cards in a **money belt**—not a "fanny pack"—along with your passport
and ID cards. Fourth, **keep a small cash reserve separate from your primary stash.** This
should be about US$50 (US$ or euros are best) sewn into or stored in the depths of
your pack, along with your traveler's check numbers and important photocopies.

In large cities **con artists** often work in groups and may involve children. Beware
of certain classics: sob stories that require money, rolls of bills "found" on the

street, mustard spilled (or saliva spit) onto your shoulder to distract you while someone snatches your bag. **Never let your passport and your bags out of your sight.** Beware of **pickpockets** in city crowds, especially on public transportation. Though Greece has typically had very low petty crime rates, complaints of pickpockets, especially around Athens, have increased. Also, be alert in public telephone booths. If you must say your calling card number, do so very quietly; if you punch it in, make sure no one can look over your shoulder.

If you will be traveling with electronic devices, like a laptop computer or a PDA, check whether your homeowner's insurance covers loss, theft, or damage when you travel. If not, you might consider buying a separate insurance policy. **Safeware** (☎ 800 800 1492; www.safeware.com) covers computers and charges US$90 for 90-day comprehensive international travel coverage up to US$4000.

PRE-DEPARTURE HEALTH

In your **passport,** write the names of people you wish to be contacted in case of a medical emergency, and list any allergies or medical conditions. Matching a prescription to a foreign equivalent is not always easy, safe, or possible, so if you take prescription drugs, consider carrying up-to-date, legible prescriptions or a statement from your doctor with the medication's trade name, manufacturer, chemical name, and dosage. Be sure to keep all medication with you in your carry-on luggage. For tips on packing a **first-aid kit** and other health essentials, see p. 19. Names of drugs in Greek tend to mimic their English names (i.e., Greek doctors and pharmacists recognize the words "antibiotic", "penicillin", "acetaminophen", etc.).

IMMUNIZATIONS AND PRECAUTIONS

Though no immunizations are needed to travel in Greece, travelers over two years old should make sure that the following vaccines are up to date: MMR (for measles, mumps, and rubella); DTaP or Td (for diphtheria, tetanus, and pertussis); IPV (for polio); Hib (for *haemophilus influenzae* B); and HepB (for Hepatitis B). For recommendations on immunizations and prophylaxis, consult the CDC (see below) in the US or your home country's equivalent, and check with a doctor for guidance.

USEFUL ORGANIZATIONS AND PUBLICATIONS

The US **Centers for Disease Control and Prevention (CDC;** ☎ 877 394 8747; www.cdc.gov/travel) maintains an international travelers' hotline and an informative website. The CDC's comprehensive booklet *Health Information for International Travel* ("The Yellow Book"), a biannual rundown of disease, immunization, and general health advice, is free online or US$29-40 via the Public Health Foundation (☎ 877 252 1200; bookstore.phfg.org/cat24.htm). Consult your home government's appropriate agency for consular information sheets on health, entry requirements, and other issues for various countries (see the listings in the box on **Travel Advisories,** p. 21). For quick information on health and other travel warnings, call the **Overseas Citizens Services** (☎ 888 407 4747, from overseas 202 501 4444; M-F 8am-8pm), or contact a passport agency, embassy, or consulate abroad. For information on medical evacuation services and travel insurance firms, see the US government's website at travel.state.gov/travel/abroad_health.html or the **British Foreign and Commonwealth Office** (www.fco.gov.uk). For general health info, contact the **American Red Cross** (☎ 800 564 1234; www.redcross.org).

STAYING HEALTHY

Common sense is the simplest prescription for good health while you travel. Drink lots of fluids to prevent dehydration and constipation, and wear sturdy, broken-in shoes and clean socks. The Greek sun can be especially brutal in the summer, so also be sure to bring a hat and sunscreen.

ONCE IN GREECE

ENVIRONMENTAL HAZARDS

Heat exhaustion and dehydration: Greece will make you sweat if you travel in the summer; watch out for the nausea, excessive thirst, headaches, and dizziness that can be caused by heat exhaustion. Avoid these symptoms by drinking plenty of fluids, eating salty foods (e.g., crackers), and abstaining from dehydrating beverages (e.g., those containing alcohol or caffeine). Continuous heat stress can eventually lead to heatstroke, characterized by a rising temperature, severe headache, delirium, and cessation of sweating. Victims should be cooled off with wet towels and taken to a doctor.

Sunburn: Always wear sunscreen (SPF 30 is good) when spending excessive amounts of time outdoors, or you may end up toasted like Icarus. If you do fall victim to Helios's wrath, drink more fluids than usual and apply an aloe-based lotion. Severe sunburns can lead to sun poisoning, a condition that affects the entire body, causing fever, chills, nausea, and vomiting. Sun poisoning should always be treated by a doctor.

High Altitude: It's not easy for mortals to scale Mt. Olympus. If you're visiting Greece's mountainous regions, allow your body a couple of days to adjust to less oxygen before exertion. Note that alcohol is more potent and UV rays are stronger at higher elevations.

FOOD- AND WATER-BORNE DISEASES

Prevention is the best cure: be sure that your food is properly cooked and the water you drink is clean. Though Greece's tap water is very safe, it is generally a good idea to peel fruits and vegetables and drink bottled water in rural areas of the more remote islands. Watch out for food from markets or street vendors that may have been cooked in unhygienic conditions. Other culprits are raw shellfish, unpasteurized milk, and sauces containing raw eggs. Buy bottled water, or purify your own water by bringing it to a rolling boil or treating it with **iodine tablets;** note, however, that some parasites such as *giardia* have exteriors that resist iodine treatment, so boiling is more reliable. Always wash your hands before eating or bring a quick-drying purifying liquid hand cleaner.

 Due to the plumbing system in Greece, toilet paper should not be flushed. A trash can is generally provided for anything you might throw into the toilet.

Traveler's diarrhea: Results from drinking fecally-contaminated water or eating uncooked and contaminated foods. Symptoms include nausea, bloating, and urgency. Try quick-energy, non-sugary foods with protein and carbohydrates to keep your strength up. Over-the-counter anti-diarrheals (e.g., Imodium®) may counteract the problems. The most dangerous side effect is dehydration; drink 8 oz. of water with ½ tsp. of sugar or honey and a pinch of salt, try uncaffeinated soft drinks, or eat salted crackers. If you develop a fever or your symptoms don't go away after 4-5 days, consult a doctor. Consult a doctor immediately for treatment of diarrhea in children.

INSECT-BORNE DISEASES

Many diseases are transmitted by insects—mainly mosquitoes, fleas, ticks, and lice. Be aware of insects in wet or forested areas, especially while hiking and camping; wear long pants and long sleeves, tuck your pants into your socks, and use a mosquito net. Use insect repellents such as DEET and soak or spray your gear with permethrin (licensed in the US only for use on clothing). **Mosquitoes**—responsible for diseases including malaria, dengue fever, and yellow fever—can be particularly dangerous in wet, swampy, or wooded areas. **Ticks**—which can carry Lyme and other diseases—can be particularly dangerous in rural and forested regions, particularly in Northern and Central Greece.

Tick-borne encephalitis: A viral infection of the central nervous system transmitted during the summer by tick bites (primarily in wooded areas) or by consumption of unpasteurized dairy products. The risk of contracting the disease is relatively low, especially if precautions are taken against tick bites.

Lyme disease: A bacterial infection carried by ticks and marked by a circular bull's-eye rash of 2 in. or more. Later symptoms include fever, headache, fatigue, and aches and pains. Antibiotics are effective if administered early. Left untreated, Lyme can cause problems in joints, the heart, and the nervous system. If you find a tick attached to your skin, grasp the head with tweezers as close to your skin as possible and apply slow, steady traction. Removing a tick within 24 hours greatly reduces the risk of infection. Do not try to remove ticks with petroleum jelly, nail polish remover, or a hot match. Tick bites usually occur in moist, shaded environments and heavily wooded areas. If you are going to be hiking in these areas, wear long clothes and DEET.

Other insect-borne diseases: Lymphatic filariasis is a roundworm infestation transmitted by mosquitoes. Infection causes enlargement of extremities and has no vaccine. **Leishmaniasis,** a parasite transmitted by sand flies, can occur on both the islands and the mainland. Common symptoms are fever, weakness, and swelling of the spleen, as well as skin sores weeks to months after the bite. There is a treatment, but no vaccine.

OTHER INFECTIOUS DISEASES

Rabies: Transmitted through the saliva of infected animals; fatal if untreated. By the time symptoms (thirst and muscle spasms) appear, the disease is in its terminal stage. If you are bitten, wash the wound thoroughly, seek immediate medical care, and try to have the animal located. A rabies vaccine, which consists of 3 shots given over a 21-day period, is available, but is only semi-effective. Rabies is found all over the world, and is often transmitted through dogs.

STAYING HEALTHY ■ 25

Hepatitis B: A viral infection of the liver transmitted via blood or other bodily fluids. Symptoms, which may not surface until years after infection, include jaundice, loss of appetite, fever, and joint pain. It is transmitted through activities like unprotected sex, injections of illegal drugs, and unprotected health work. A 3-shot vaccination sequence is recommended for health-care workers, sexually-active travelers, and anyone planning to seek medical treatment abroad; it must begin 6 months before traveling.

Hepatitis C: Like Hepatitis B, but the mode of transmission differs. IV-drug users, those with occupational exposure to blood, hemodialysis patients, and recipients of blood transfusions are at the highest risk, but the disease can also be spread through sexual contact or sharing items like razors and toothbrushes that may have traces of blood on them. No symptoms are usually exhibited, but if there are any, they can include loss of appetite, abdominal pain, fatigue, nausea, and jaundice. If untreated, Hepatitis C can lead to liver failure.

AIDS and HIV: For detailed information on Acquired Immune Deficiency Syndrome (AIDS) in Greece, call the US Centers for Disease Control's 24hr. hotline at ☎800 342 2437, or contact the Joint United Nations Programme on HIV/AIDS (UNAIDS), 20 Ave. Appia, CH-1211 Geneva 27, Switzerland (☎22 791 3666; fax 22 791 4187).

Sexually transmitted diseases (STDs): Gonorrhea, chlamydia, genital warts, syphilis, herpes, and other STDs are easier to catch than HIV and can be just as deadly. **Hepatitis** B and C can also be transmitted sexually. Though condoms may protect you from some STDs, oral or even tactile contact can lead to transmission. If you think you may have contracted an STD, see a doctor immediately.

OTHER HEALTH CONCERNS

MEDICAL CARE ON THE ROAD

All travelers from the EU receive free health care in Greece with the presentation of an **E111 form.** A doctor can be found on every inhabited island and in every town; emergency treatment is available to travelers of all nationalities in public hospitals. While Greece offers outstanding medical training, the healthcare system is vastly underfunded. Public hospitals are overcrowded; in some locations, their hygiene may not be the best. Private hospitals generally provide better care and heavier bills; to use them you will need good **health insurance.** If your regular policy does not cover travel abroad, you may wish to buy additional coverage.

Pharmacies (φαρμακία, far-mah-KEE-ah), labeled by green or red crosses, are common. In most towns and cities, at least one pharmacy is open at all hours—most post listings of available 24hr. pharmacies in their windows.

If you are concerned about medical services while traveling, you may wish to employ special support services. The *MedPass* from **GlobalCare, Inc.,** 6875 Shiloh Rd. East, Alpharetta, GA 30005, USA (☎800 860 1111, fax 678 341 1800; www.globalcare.net), provides 24hr. international medical assistance, support, and medical evacuation resources. The **International Association for Medical Assistance to Travelers (IAMAT;** US ☎716 754 4883, Canada 519 836 0102; www.iamat.org) has free membership, lists English-speaking doctors worldwide, and offers detailed info on immunization requirements and sanitation. If your regular **insurance** policy does not cover travel abroad, you may wish to buy additional coverage.

Those with medical conditions (such as diabetes, allergies to antibiotics, epilepsy, or heart conditions) may want to obtain a **MedicAlert** membership (first year US$35, annually thereafter US$20), which includes a stainless steel ID tag, among other benefits, like a 24hr. collect-call number. Contact the MedicAlert Foundation, 2323 Colorado Ave., Turlock, CA 95382, USA (☎888 633 4298, outside US 209 668 3333; www.medicalert.org).

WOMEN'S HEALTH

Women traveling in unsanitary conditions are vulnerable to **urinary tract (including bladder and kidney) infections.** Over-the-counter medicines can sometimes alleviate symptoms, but if they persist, see a doctor. **Vaginal yeast infections** may flare up in hot and humid climates. Wearing loosely fitting pants or a skirt and cotton underwear will help, as will over-the-counter remedies like Monistat® or Gyne-Lotrimin™. Bring supplies from home if you are prone to infection, as they may be difficult to find on the road. And, since **tampons, pads,** and reliable **contraceptive devices** are sometimes hard to find when traveling, bring supplies with you. **Abortion** is legal in Greece. A useful resource for reproductive health is the **Family Planning Association of Greece** (☎21072 86 332), Alkaiou 10, Athens 11528.

GETTING TO GREECE

BY PLANE

When it comes to airfare, a little effort can save you a bundle. If your plans are flexible enough to deal with the restrictions, courier fares are the cheapest. Tickets bought from consolidators and standby seating are also good deals, but last-minute specials, airfare wars, and charter flights often beat these fares. The key is to hunt around, to be flexible, and to ask persistently about discounts. Students, seniors, and those under 26 should never pay full price for a ticket.

AIRFARES

Airfares to Greece peak between June and August; holidays are also expensive. The cheapest times to travel are October and late March. Midweek (M-Th morning) round-trip flights run US$40-50 cheaper than weekend flights, but they are generally more crowded and less likely to permit frequent-flier upgrades. Not fixing a return date ("open return") or arriving in and departing from different cities ("open-jaw") can be pricier than round-trip flights. Patching one-way flights together is the most expensive way to travel. Flights between Athens and regional hubs and islands will tend to be cheaper.

If Greece is only one stop on a more extensive globe-hop, consider a round-the-world (RTW) ticket. Tickets usually include at least five stops and are valid for about a year; prices range US$1200-5000. Try **Northwest Airlines/KLM** (☎800 225 2525; www.nwa.com) or **Star Alliance,** a consortium of 16 airlines including United Airlines (www.staralliance.com).

Fares for roundtrip flights to Athens from the US or Canadian east coast generally cost US$700-800 in low season (Oct.-Mar.) and US$1200-1600 in high season (June-Sept.); from the US or Canadian west coast US$900-1100 in low season and US$1200-1600 in high season; from the UK, UK£70-100 in low or high season; from Australia AUS$1500-1900 in low season and AUS$1800-2000 in high season; from New Zealand NZ$1900-2500 in low season and NZ$2100-2700 in high season.

BUDGET AND STUDENT TRAVEL AGENCIES

While knowledgeable agents specializing in flights to Greece can make your life easy and help you save, they may not find you the lowest possible fare—they get paid on commission. Travelers with **ISICs** and **IYTCs** (p. 11) qualify for big discounts from student travel agencies. Most flights from budget agencies are on major airlines, but in peak season some may sell seats on less reliable chartered aircraft.

STA Travel, 5900 Wilshire Blvd., Ste. 900, Los Angeles, CA 90036, USA (24hr. reservations and info ☎800 781 4040; www.sta-travel.com). A student and youth travel organization with over 150 offices worldwide (check their website for a listing of all their offices), including US offices in Boston, Chicago, Los Angeles, New York, Seattle, San Francisco, and Washington, D.C. Ticket booking, travel insurance, railpasses, and more. Walk-in offices are located throughout Australia (☎03 9349 4344), New Zealand (☎09 309 9723), and the UK (☎08701 600 599).

Travel CUTS (Canadian Universities Travel Services Limited), 187 College St., Toronto, ON M5T 1P7, Canada (☎800 592 2887; www.travelcuts.com). Offices across Canada and the US including Los Angeles, New York, Seattle, San Francisco.

USIT, 19-21 Aston Quay, Dublin 2, Ireland (☎01 602 1904; www.usit.ie). Ireland's leading student/budget travel agency has 20 offices throughout Northern Ireland and the Republic of Ireland. Offers programs to work, study, and volunteer worldwide.

Wasteels, Skoubogade 6, 1158 Copenhagen K., Denmark (☎3314 4633; www.wasteels.com). A huge chain with 180 locations across Europe. Sells Wasteels BIJ tickets discounted 30-45% off regular fare, 2nd-class international point-to-point train tickets with unlimited stopovers for those under 26 (sold only in Europe).

FLIGHT PLANNING ON THE INTERNET. The Internet may be the budget traveler's dream when it comes to finding and booking bargain fares, but the array of options can be overwhelming.

Many **airline sites** offer special last-minute deals on the Web. **Cheap-Flight-To** (www.cheap-flight-to.com/greece.htm) and **GreeceFlights** (www.greece-flights.com) specialize in booking discounted flights, and **easyJet** (www.easy-jet.com) finds cheap flights from major European cities to Athens.

STA (www.sta-travel.com) and **StudentUniverse** (www.studentuniverse.com) provide quotes on student tickets, while **Orbitz** (www.orbitz.com), **Expedia** (www.expedia.com), and **Travelocity** (www.travelocity.com) offer full travel services, as does **Opodo** (www.opodo.com) in Europe. **Priceline** (www.price-line.com) lets you specify a price, and obligates you to buy any ticket that meets or beats it; **Hotwire** (www.hotwire.com) offers bargain fares, but won't reveal the airline or flight times until you buy. Other sites that compile deals include www.bestfares.com, www.flights.com, www.lowestfare.com, www.one-travel.com, and www.travelzoo.com.

Increasingly, online tools can help sift through multiple offers; **SideStep** (www.sidestep.com; download required) and **Booking Buddy** (www.booking-buddy.com) let you enter your trip information once and search multiple sites. An indispensable resource on the Internet is the **Air Traveler's Handbook** (www.faqs.org/faqs/travel/air/handbook), a comprehensive listing of links to everything you need to know before you board a plane.

COMMERCIAL AIRLINES

The commercial airlines' lowest regular offer is the **APEX** (Advance Purchase Excursion) fare, which provides confirmed reservations and allows "open-jaw" tickets. Generally, reservations must be made seven to 21 days ahead of departure, with seven- to 14-day minimum-stay and up to 90-day maximum-stay restrictions. These fares carry hefty cancellation and change penalties (fees rise in summer). Book peak-season APEX fares early. Use **Expedia** (www.expedia.com) or **Travelocity** (www.travelocity.com) to get an idea of the lowest published fares, then use

the resources outlined here to try and beat those fares. Low-season fares should be appreciably cheaper than the **high-season** (June-Sept.) ones listed here.

TRAVELING FROM NORTH AMERICA

Most direct flights from North America to Greece leave from New York, and there are no direct flights from the West Coast. Standard commercial carriers like **American** (☎800 433 7300; www.aa.com), **United** (☎800 538 2929; www.ual.com), and **Northwest** (☎800 447 4747; www.nwa.com) will probably offer the most convenient flights, but they may not be the cheapest, unless you grab a special promotion or airfare war ticket. You will likely find flying one of the following "discount" airlines a better deal, if their limited departure points are convenient for you.

> **Finnair:** ☎800 950 5000; www.us.finnair.com. Cheap round-trips from New York, San Francisco, and Toronto to Helsinki; connections throughout Europe.

> **Icelandair:** ☎800 223 5500; www.icelandair.com. Free stopovers in Iceland on most transatlantic flights. For last-minute deals, subscribe to their email Lucky Fares.

> **SWISS:** ☎ 877 359 7947; www.swiss.com. Inexpensive flights to Athens from New York and Boston; usually connects through Zurich.

TRAVELING FROM THE UK AND IRELAND

Because of the many carriers flying from the UK to the continent, *Let's Go* only includes discount airlines or those with cheap specials. The **Air Travel Advisory Bureau** in London (☎0870 737 0021; www.atab.co.uk) provides referrals to travel agencies and consolidators that offer discounted airfares out of the UK. **Cheapflights** (www.cheapflights.co.uk) publishes airfare bargains.

> **British Airways:** UK ☎0870 850 9850; www.britishairways.com. London to Athens round-trip from UK£96.

easyJet: UK ☎0871 750 0100; www.easyjet.com. London to Athens (£72-141).

KLM: UK ☎0870 507 4074; www.klmuk.com. Cheap round-trip tickets from London and elsewhere to Athens and other European cities.

TRAVELING FROM AUSTRALIA AND NEW ZEALAND

Qantas Air: Australia ☎96 91 36 36, New Zealand 0800 808 767; www.qantas.com.au. Flights from Australia and New Zealand to London for around AUS$2500. Then catch connections on other airlines to Greece from London.

Singapore Air: Australia ☎13 10 11, New Zealand 0800 808 909; www.singaporeair.com. Flies from Auckland, Sydney, Melbourne, and Perth to Athens.

Thai Airways: Australia ☎1300 65 19 60, New Zealand 093 773 886; www.thaiair.com. Flies from Auckland, Melbourne, Perth, and Sydney to Athens.

AIR COURIER FLIGHTS

Those who travel light should consider courier flights. Couriers help transport cargo on international flights by using their checked luggage space for freight. Generally, couriers must travel with carry-ons only and deal with complex flight restrictions. Most flights are round-trip only, with short fixed-length stays (usually one week) and a limit of a one ticket per issue. Most of these flights also operate only out of major gateway cities, mostly in North America. Round-trip courier fares from the US to Greece run about US$600. Most flights leave from Los Angeles, Miami, New York, or San Francisco in the US; and from Montreal, Toronto, or Vancouver in Canada. Generally, you must be over 18 (in some cases 21). In summer, the most popular destinations usually require an advance reservation of about two weeks (you can usually book up to two months ahead). Super-discounted fares are common for "last-minute" flights (3-14 days ahead). The organizations below provide members with lists of opportunities and courier brokers for an annual fee.

International Association of Air Travel Couriers (IAATC; www.courier.org). From 7 North American cities to European cities, including Athens. Membership US$45.

Couriertravel, 1148 S. Valentine Way, Lakewood, CO 80228 (www.couriertravel.org). Flights from New York to Athens, US$628 in low season. Membership US$40, contact larry@couriertravel.org.

STANDBY FLIGHTS

Traveling standby requires considerable flexibility in arrival and departure dates and cities. Companies dealing in standby flights sell vouchers rather than tickets, along with the promise to get you to your destination (or nearby) within a certain window of time (typically 1-5 days). You call before your specific window to hear your flight options and the probability that you will be able to board each flight. You can then decide which flights you want to try to make, show up at the appropriate airport at the appropriate time, present your voucher, and board if space is available. Vouchers can usually be bought for both one-way and round-trip travel. You may receive a monetary refund only if every available flight within your date range is full; if you opt not to take an available (but perhaps less convenient) flight, you can only get credit toward future travel. Carefully read agreements with any company offering standby flights, as tricky fine print can leave you in the lurch. To check on a company's service record in the US, contact the Better Business Bureau (☎703 276 0100; www.bbb.org). It is difficult to get refunds, and clients' vouchers will not be honored when an airline fails to receive payment in time.

TICKET CONSOLIDATORS

Ticket consolidators, or **"bucket shops,"** buy unsold tickets in bulk from commercial airlines and sell them at discounted rates. The best place to look is in the Sunday travel section of any major newspaper (such as *The New York Times*), where many bucket shops place tiny ads. Call quickly, as availability is typically extremely limited. Not all bucket shops are reliable, so insist on a receipt that gives full details of restrictions, refunds, and tickets, and pay by credit card (in spite of the 2-5% fee) so you can stop payment if you never receive your tickets. For more info, see www.travel-library.com/air-travel/consolidators.html.

TRAVELING FROM THE US AND CANADA

NOW Voyager, 315 W. 49th St. Plaza Arcade, New York, NY 10019, USA (☎212 459 1616; www.nowvoyagertravel.com) arranges discounted flights to Europe, mostly from New York. Other consolidators worth trying are **Rebel** (☎800 732 3588; www.rebeltours.com) and **Cheap Tickets** (www.cheaptickets.com). More online consolidators include **Flights.com** (www.flights.com) and **TravelHUB** (www.travelhub.com). Keep in mind that these are just suggestions to get you started in your research; *Let's Go* does not endorse any of these agencies. As always, be cautious, and research companies before you hand over your credit card number.

CHARTER FLIGHTS

Charters are flights a tour operator contracts with an airline to fly extra loads of passengers during peak season. Charter flights fly less frequently than major airlines, make refunds particularly difficult, and are almost always fully booked. Schedules and itineraries may also change or be cancelled at the last moment (as late as 48hr. before the trip, and without a full refund), and check-in, boarding, and baggage claim are often much slower. However, they can also be cheaper.

Discount clubs and fare brokers offer members savings on last-minute charter and tour deals. Study contracts closely; you don't want to end up with an unwanted overnight layover. **Travelers Advantage** (☎877 259 2691; www.travelersadvantage.com; US$90 annual fee includes discounts and cheap flight directories) specializes in European travel and tour packages.

BY FERRY OR BUS

BY FERRY. Ferries are a popular way to get to and travel within Greece; ports can be reached from countless points and finding a boat agency to facilitate your trip should not be difficult. Be warned that **ferries run on irregular schedules.** A few websites, such as **www.ferries.gr,** have tried to keep updated schedules online but are often incomplete. Try to look at a schedule as close to your departure date as possible; you can usually find one at a tourist office or posted at the dock. That said, you should also make reservations and **check in at least 2hr. in advance;** late boarders may find their seats gone. If you sleep on the deck, bring warm clothes and a sleeping bag; reclining deck chairs rarely work. Bicycles travel free, but motorcycles cost extra. Bring food to avoid high prices onboard.

The major ports of departure from Italy to Greece are Ancona and Brindisi, in the southeast. Bari, Otranto, Trieste, and Venice also have a few connections. For Greece-Italy schedules, see Patras (p. 153), Kephalonia (p. 554), Corfu (p. 531), or Igoumenitsa (p. 249). Patras travel agency **Manolopoulos,** Othonos Amalias 35 (☎26102 23 621), offers deck passage to Brindisi (14½hr., 6am, €41) and can provide useful info. Ferries also run from Samos, Chios, and Kos to various Turkish ports. Though no ferries run directly from Albania, several have connections to Bari and Brindisi, where you can switch ferries to catch one to Greece.

BY BUS. There are very few buses running directly from any European city to Greece. **Eurolines,** Via Mercadante 2/b, Firenze 50144, Italy (☎055 35 71 10; www.eurolines.it) and **Busabout,** 258 Vauxhall Bridge Road, London SW1V 1BS, UK (☎020 7950 1661; www.busabout.com), transport travelers to Italian ports including Brindisi, Venice, and Ancona on their own buses, then arrange ferry transport to locations in Greece. From there, travelers can catch connections to locations throughout Greece. Both Eurolines and Busabout offer **international bus passes,** which are often cheaper than railpasses and allow unlimited travel on a hop-on, hop-off basis between major European cities.

BY TRAIN

A number of international train routes connect Greece via Thessaloniki to most European cities. **Eurail** (www.eurail.com) passes are valid in Greece, and may be a useful purchase if you plan to visit one of the 16 other European countries in which they are valid. Unfortunately, the Greek rail system is one of Europe's most antiquated and least efficient. A trip from Vienna to Athens takes about three days. For routes and info on special offers, see the **OSE** website (www.osenet.gr).

SHOULD YOU BUY A RAILPASS? You can either buy a **railpass,** which allows you unlimited travel within a particular region for a given period of time, or rely on buying individual **point-to-point** tickets as you go. Railpasses were conceived to allow you to jump on any train in Europe, go wherever you want whenever you want, and change your plans at will. In practice, it's not so simple. You still must stand in line to validate your pass, pay for supplements, and fork over cash for seat reservations. More importantly, passes don't always pay off. Because of Greece's limited railway system, you may not be able to use the train enough to pay off the cost of a pass. In most cases, buses will likely be preferable.

MULTINATIONAL RAILPASSES. Eurail is **valid** in most of Western Europe: Austria, Belgium, Denmark, Finland, France, Germany, Greece, Hungary, Ireland, Italy, Luxembourg, the Netherlands, Norway, Portugal, Romania, Spain, Sweden, and Switzerland. It is **not valid** in the UK. Several plans are available to fit a variety of itineraries. Passholders receive a timetable for major routes and a map with details on possible ferry, steamer, bus, car rental, and hotel discounts. Passholders often also receive reduced fares or free passage on many bus and boat lines. Eurailpasses are designed by the EU, and can be bought only by non-Europeans, almost exclusively from non-European distributors. The passes are sold at uniform prices determined by the EU. Some travel agents tack on a US$10 handling fee, and others offer bonuses with purchase, so shop around. Keep in mind that prices usually go up each year, so you can save by purchasing before January 1 (you have 3 months from the purchase to validate your pass in Europe).

It is best to buy your Eurail before leaving; only a few places in major European cities sell them, and at a marked-up price. You can get a replacement for a lost pass only if you have purchased insurance on it under the Pass Protection Plan (US$8.50-17). Eurailpasses are available through travel agents, student travel agencies like STA and Council, and **Rail Europe** (Canada ☎800 361 7245, UK 08 708 371 371, US 877 257 2887; www.raileurope.com) or **DER Travel Services,** whose services are available at several outfits across the US (☎800 782 2424; www.der.com).

If your travels will include the Balkan countries bordering Greece, a regional pass often provides a good value. The **Balkan Flexipass,** which is valid for travel in Bulgaria, Greece, the Former Yugoslav Republic of Macedonia, Romania, Serbia and Montenegro, and Turkey, allows the pass owner five days out of one month in 1st-class for only US$189 (2nd-class under 26 US$112).

ESSENTIALS

GETTING AROUND GREECE

BY BOAT

If you spend any time on Greece's many islands, you will get to know their wide-spread, unpredictable system of ferries and other aquatic transport very, very well. Arrive at the dock 1-2hr. before departure for a decent seat, though ferries could depart at any point, from 5min.-early to 3hr.-late. Bring a **windbreaker** if you want to wander the deck when at sea. For short distances, indoor seats fill up quickly.

FERRIES

MAKING SENSE OF FERRIES. Ferries are absolutely essential for reaching the Greek islands, but with schedules that sometimes change week-to-week (or day-to-day), they can leave travelers baffled. The key to making good use of ferries is understanding ferry routes and planning your trip accordingly. The ferry service in Greece is sparse during low-season months, but begins to pick up as summer approaches and brings waves of island-seeking tourists. Most ferries, rather than shuffling back and forth between two destinations, trace a four- or five-port route. Many ferry companies will allow you to buy your round-trip ticket **"split,"** meaning that you can ride the Piraeus-Syros-Tinos-Mykonos ferry from Piraeus to Syros, get off, get back on when the same ferry passes Syros several days later, proceed to Tinos, and so on. Remember that geographic proximity is no guarantee that you'll be able to get to one island from another. Also note that there is very little service from the Cyclades to the Dodecanese. Understanding the routes will also help you make sense of discrepancies in ticket prices and travel times.

MAJOR PORTS AND SCHEDULES. As the millennia-old port of Athens, **Piraeus** is the heart of the ferry routes through the Aegean Sea. Routes run to most major islands in the Cyclades, as well as Crete, the Saronic Gulf Islands, several major islands in the Dodecanese and Northeast Aegean Islands, and Turkey. **Rafina,** Athens's smaller, eastern port, sends ferries to Evia, some of the northernmost Cyclades, and many of the Northeast Aegean Islands. To reach the Ionian Islands, most ferries depart from **Patras** or **Kyllini** on the Peloponnese or **Igoumenitsa** in Epirus. **Agios Konstantinos** and **Volos** handle most ferries to the Sporades and Evia.

Available from ferry companies or posted at the port police, regional schedules are published weekly and give the departure times, routes, and names of each departing ferry. Make sure to look at the most updated version of the ferry schedules or call the agency on the island from which you want to leave. As particular ferries, even within companies, vary widely in quality, local travelers should pay close attention to the model of the ferry that they will be riding. Ask around or check on the web (www.ferries.gr) for tips, ferry schedules, and prices.

HYDROFOILS AND CATAMARANS

Hellas Flying Dolphins (☎21041 99 000; www.dolphins.gr or www.hellenicsea-ways.gr) runs most of the hydrofoils and catamarans.

DOLPHIN RIDES. Flying Dolphins, the standard name for hydrofoils in Greece, go twice as fast and look twice as cool, but cost twice as much. If you have cash to spare and want to minimize travel time, these crafts provide extensive, standard-ized, and sanitized transport between islands; offices and services are listed in the **Transportation** sections of all cities and towns.

Keep in mind that traveling by Dolphin is like traveling by seaborne airplane: passengers are assigned seats and required to stay in the climate-controlled cabin for the duration of the trip, which may be less than ideal for the easily seasick.

There's also something somewhat unfortunate about sailing the Aegean in a craft that won't let you get salt on your fingers and wind in your hair.

CATAMARANS. These high-speed double-hulled boats are similar to hydrofoils in speed and cost, but are generally more reliable. They are also very popular with tourists, so don't expect to be able to buy a same-day ticket.

BY PLANE

Olympic Airlines, Greece's national carrier, can be found at Syngrou 96-100, Athens 11741 (☎21092 69 111), and in many other cities. The Olympic Airways website (www.olympicairlines.com) lists information for every office around the globe. **Aegean Airlines** (☎80111 20 000 or 21062 61 000; www.aegeanair.com), a smaller Crete-based airline, also offers flights throughout the mainland and to many of the islands. For flight info within Greece, check regional **Practical Information** listings of airports, destinations, and prices, or get a brochure at any airline office. In recent years, Greece's domestic service has increased appreciably; from Athens a 1hr. flight (US$75-150) can get you to most islands. Even in low season, remote destinations are serviced several times weekly, while more developed areas can have several flights per day. Try to reserve tickets one week in advance.

No-frills airlines have made hopscotching around Europe by air increasingly affordable and convenient. Though these flights often feature inconvenient hours or serve less-popular regional airports, with one-way flights averaging about US$80, it's never been faster or easier to jet across the Continent. The airline with the most inexpensive flights from the UK to Greece is **easyJet** (UK ☎0871 244 2366; www.easyjet.com); it serves 62 destinations in Belgium, the Czech Republic, Denmark, Estonia, France, Germany, Greece, Hungary, Italy, Latvia, the Netherlands, Poland, Portugal, the Slovak Republic, Slovenia, Spain, Switzerland, and the UK.

The **Star Alliance European Airpass** (www.staralliance.com) offers economy-class fares as low as US$65 for travel within 41 European countries. The pass is available to transatlantic passengers on Star Alliance carriers, including Air Canada, Austrian Airlines, Lufthansa, Scandinavian Airlines System, Singapore Airlines, Thai Airways International, United Airlines, US Airways, and others. In addition, a number of European airlines offer discount coupon packets. Most are only available as tack-ons for transatlantic passengers, but some are stand-alone offers. Usually they must be purchased before departure. Finally, check out the *Flight-Pass* offered by **Europe by Air** (☎888 387 2479; www.europebyair.com), which allows you to country-hop to over 150 European cities (US$99 per one-way flight).

BY BUS

Buses are an essential part of travel in Greece. Service is more extensive, more efficient, and often more comfortable than on trains, and fares are cheap. Unless you're sticking close to train routes, **KTEL** bus service should be sufficient for longer bus trips. Always check with an official source about scheduled departures. Posted schedules are often outdated and all services are curtailed significantly on Saturday and Sunday; bus schedules on major holidays run according to Sunday schedules. Unless they are going longer distances, buses rarely run at night. The English-language weekly newspaper *Athens News* prints Athens bus schedules; they are also available online (www.ktel.org). Try to arrive at least 10min. ahead of time, as Greek buses have a habit of leaving early. In major cities KTEL bus lines may have different stations for different destinations, and schedules generally refer to **endpoints** (e.g. "the bus leaves Kalloni at 3pm and arrives in Mytilini at 4pm") with no mention of the numerous stops in between.

Ask the **conductor** before entering the bus whether it's going to your destination (the signs on the front can be misleading), and ask to be warned when you get there. If stowing bags underneath, make sure they're in the compartment for your destination (conductors take great pride in packing the bus for easy unloading, and may refuse to open the "final destination" compartment at the "halfway" stop). If the bus passes your stop, stand up and yell "**STAH-see**" ("στάση"). On the road, stand near a sign (reading "στάση") to pick up an intercity bus. KTEL buses are **green** or occasionally **orange** or **yellow**, while intercity buses are usually **blue**. For long-distance rides, **buy your ticket beforehand** in the office (otherwise, you may have to stand for the entire journey). For shorter trips, pay the conductor after you have boarded; reasonably close change is expected.

BY TRAIN

Although trains in Greece are cheap, they run less frequently than buses and don't cover as wide a geographic area. They are also generally slower than other European trains and can get pretty gritty. If you're lucky, you may come across a new, air-conditioned, intercity train, which is worth the slightly more expensive price.

The **Hellenic Railways Association,** or **OSE** (www.osenet.gr), connects Athens to major Greek cities (like Thessaloniki, Patras, and Volos). Lines do not yet go to the mainland's west coast (although plans are in progress to extend the railway to Ioannina), and they are rarely useful for remote areas or archaeological sites. Bring food and water, because the on-board cafe is pricey. Second-class compartments, which seat two to six, are great places to meet fellow travelers. However, it is wise to lock your compartment and keep valuables on your person; for safety tips, see p. 19. For long trips, make sure you are on the correct car, as trains sometimes split at crossroads. Towns listed in parentheses on European train schedules require a train switch at the town listed immediately before the parenthesis.

DOMESTIC RAILPASSES

If you are planning to spend much time within Greece, a national pass—valid on all rail lines in Greece—may be more cost-effective than a multinational pass.

NATIONAL RAILPASSES. The domestic analog of the Eurailpass, the **Greek Flexipass Rail 'n Fly** offers three days of unlimited 1st-class travel in one month on railways throughout Greece and two flight coupons for travel on Olympic Airways to selected locations in Greece. This pass must be purchased from a travel agent or **Rail Europe** (p. 34) before you leave for Europe, and costs US$251 for adults, US$244 for the under-26 youth pass, and US$136 for children 12 and under. It requires that all airline bookings go through **Ionian Travel.** You also need to get your pass validated before you use it on a plane or train; just bring the pass and your passport to an official in the train station prior to use so that he or she can record the first and last day of the eligibility of the pass. The pass must be validated within six months of issue in order to remain effective. For more information, check out http://www.raileurope.com/us/rail/passes/greek_flexipass_rail_fly.htm.

EURODOMINO. Like the Interrail Pass, the EuroDomino pass is available to anyone who has lived in Europe for at least six months; however, it is only valid in one country (which you designate when buying the pass). It is available for 27 European countries (including Greece) plus Morocco. Reservations must be paid for separately. The pass must be bought within your country of residence; each country has its own price. Inquire with your national rail company for more info.

BY CAR

Cars offer speed, freedom, access to the countryside, and an escape from the town-to-town mentality of trains. Although a single traveler won't save by renting a car, four usually will. Cars are a good choice in Greece, a country where public transportation is generally nonexistent in the night hours; they are especially useful in regions like Crete, where buses between nearby small towns often follow maddeningly indirect routes. Ferries will take you and your car island-hopping if you pay a transport fee for the car. Drivers in Greece must be comfortable with a **standard transmission,** winding mountain roads, and the Greek alphabet—signs in Greek appear roughly 100m before the transliterated versions. Driving is especially useful for exploring remote villages in northern Greece. **Petrol (gasoline)** prices vary but average about €0.90 per liter in Athens.

With a fatal accident rate that tops those of most countries in Europe, driving in Greece can be a dangerous enterprise. Drivers are notoriously reckless (especially in Athens), often driving on sidewalks and expecting pedestrians to move out of the way. Speed limits often go unposted and are utterly ignored. So it's important to always drive defensively in Greece. You must be 18 to drive, and both front-seat passengers are required by law to wear seatbelts; common sense says that all passengers should be strapped in. As in the US, cars drive on the right-hand side of the road. For an informal primer on European road signs and conventions, check out www.travlang.com/signs. The **Association for Safe International Road Travel (ASIRT),** 11769 Gainsborough Rd., Potomac, MD 20854, USA (US ☎301 983 5252; www.asirt.org), can provide more specific information about road conditions.

CAR ASSISTANCE. The **Automobile and Touring Club of Greece (ELPA),** Messogion 395, Athens 15343 (☎21060 68 800; www.elpa.gr), provides assistance and offers reciprocal membership to foreign auto club members. They also have 24hr. emergency road assistance (☎104) and a tourist information line (☎174 in Athens).

TAXIS. Taxis can be an invaluable means of transportation in areas where towns are close together but bus routes are sparse. Prices vary throughout Greece. When taking taxis, be aware that some drivers tinker with their meters, while others may not turn their meter on at all, taking you somewhere and then charging an exorbitant fee. Ask the cost of the fare in advance, and if you don't see the meter running yell "taxi-MEH-tro!" (meter). Also, if you ask for a hotel, the taxi driver may have another one in mind—one that has paid him a commission to bring you there. Be firm about where you're going; don't trust a driver who says your hotel is closed.

RENTING

Agencies may quote low daily rates that exclude the 18% VAT and **Collision Damage Waiver (CDW)** insurance. Some places quote low rates and then hit you with hidden charges, such as refueling bills if you come back with less than a full tank, or up to €300 drop-off or special charge. Most companies won't let you drive the car outside Greece. Foreign drivers are required to have an **International Driving Permit** and an **International Insurance Certificate** to drive in Greece (p. 38), but EU drivers only need their EU driver's license. Smaller rental cars may have difficulty getting up some of Greece's mountainous roads with four or five people onboard.

RENTAL AGENCIES

You can generally make reservations before you leave by calling major international offices in your home country. However, occasionally the price and availability information they give doesn't jive with what the local offices in your destination will tell you. Try checking with both numbers to make sure you get the best price and accurate information. Local desk numbers are included in town listings; for home-country numbers, call your toll-free directory.

To rent a car in Greece, you need to be at least 21 years old. Some agencies require renters to be 23 or 25. Policies and prices vary from agency to agency. Small local operations occasionally rent to people under 21, but be sure to ask about the insurance coverage and deductible and always check the fine print. For more specific information about car rental in Greece, contact the **Greek Car Rental Association** (☎21099 42 850) or the **Panhellenic Federation of Offices for Car & Motorbike Rentals** (☎28102 80 914). Rental agencies with operations in Greece include:

Auto Europe, 39 Commercial St., P.O. Box 7006, Portland, ME 04112, USA (US and Canada ☎888 223 5555 or 207 842 2000; www.autoeurope.com).

Avis (Greece ☎21032 24 951, Australia 1300 137 498, Canada 800 879 2847, New Zealand 09 526 2847, UK 08706 060 100, US 800 230 4898; www.avis.gr).

Europe by Car (US ☎800 223 1516 or 212 581 3040; www.europebycar.com).

Europcar (US and Canada ☎877 940 6900; www.europcar.com).

Hertz, Viltanioti 31, Kifisia 14564 (Greece ☎21062 64 000; www.hertz.gr).

COSTS AND INSURANCE

Rental cars start at around €35 per day. Expect to pay more for larger cars and for four-wheel-drive. **Standard transmission** is really your only option when renting cars in Greece. Most packages offer unlimited kilometers. Return the car with a full tank of petrol (gasoline) to avoid high fuel charges. Be sure to ask whether the price includes **insurance** against theft and collision. Remember that if you are driving a conventional rental vehicle on an **unpaved road,** you are almost never covered by insurance; ask before leaving the rental agency. Beware that cars rented on an **American Express** or **Visa/MasterCard Gold** or **Platinum** credit card in Greece might *not* carry the automatic insurance that they would in some other countries; check with your credit card company. Insurance plans almost always come with an **excess** (or deductible) of around €300. This means you pay for all damages up to that sum, unless they are the fault of another vehicle. The excess you will be quoted applies to collisions with other vehicles; collisions with non-vehicles such as trees (sometimes known as "single-vehicle collisions") will cost you even more. The excess can often be reduced or waived entirely if you pay an additional charge, around €15 per day. National car rental chains often allow **one-way rentals,** picking up in one city and dropping off in another. There is usually a minimum hire period and sometimes an extra drop-off charge of several hundred euros.

DRIVING PRECAUTIONS. When traveling in the summer, bring substantial amounts of **water** (a suggested 5L of water per person per day) for drinking and for the radiator. For long-distance drives, make sure tires are in good repair and have enough air, and that you have good maps. A **compass** and a **car manual** can also be very useful. You should always carry a **spare tire** and **jack, jumper cables, extra oil, flares, a flashlight (torch),** and **heavy blankets** (in case your car breaks down at night or in the winter). If you don't know how to **change a tire,** learn before heading out, especially if you will be in deserted areas. Blowouts on dirt roads are exceedingly common. If you do have a breakdown, **stay with your car;** if you wander off, there's less likelihood trackers will find you.

DRIVING PERMITS AND CAR INSURANCE

INTERNATIONAL DRIVING PERMIT (IDP)

If you plan to drive while in Greece, you must be over 18 and have an International Driving Permit (IDP). Although Greek proprietors may ignore the law, get one if you plan on driving. A valid driver's license from your home country must always accompany the IDP. Your IDP, valid for one year, must be issued in your own country before you leave. An IDP application usually requires one or two photos, a current local license, an additional form of identification, and a fee. To apply, contact your home country's automobile association. Be careful when purchasing an IDP online or anywhere other than your home automobile association. Many vendors sell permits of questionable legitimacy for higher prices.

CAR INSURANCE

Most credit cards cover standard insurance. If you rent, lease, or borrow a car, you will need a **Green Card,** or **International Insurance Certificate,** to certify that you have liability insurance and that it applies abroad. Green cards can be obtained at car rental agencies, car dealers (for those leasing cars), some travel agents, and some border crossings. Rental agencies may require you to purchase theft insurance in countries that they consider to have a high risk of auto theft.

BY MOPED

Motorbiking is a popular way of touring Greece's winding roads. Although renting mopeds is the most cost-efficient way to avoid unreliable public transportation, they can be uncomfortable for long distances, dangerous in the rain, and unpredictable on rough roads. On many islands, roads suddenly turn into tiny trails that must be walked. Moped (μηχανάκι, mee-hah-NAH-kee) rental shop owners often loosen the front brakes on the bikes to discourage riders from using them (relying on the front brakes makes accidents more likely), so use the back brakes. If you've never driven a moped before, a cliffside road is not the place to learn.

! UNSAFE AT ANY SPEED. A word of caution: most tourist-related accidents occur on mopeds, and the majority of deaths of US tourists in Greece involve mopeds. Regardless of your level of experience, winding, poorly maintained roads and reckless drivers make using a moped hazardous. Always wear a helmet and never ride with a backpack.

Shops renting mopeds are everywhere. Although a law was passed in 2000 mandating that mopeds could only be rented to those licensed to operate such a vehicle, this is rarely, if ever, enforced. Bike quality, speed of service in case of breakdown, and prices for longer periods vary drastically, but expect to pay at least €10 per day for a 50cc scooter, the cheapest bike that still has the power to tackle mountain roads. More high-tech bikes cost 20-30% more and usually require a Greek motorcycle license. Many agencies will request your passport as a deposit, but it's wiser just to settle up in advance. Ask before renting if the price quote includes tax, insurance, and a full tank of gas, or you may pay a few unexpected euros. Information on local moped rentals is in the **Practical Information** section for individual cities and towns.

BY THUMB

> ▼ *Let's Go* never recommends hitchhiking as a safe means of transportation, and none of the information presented here is intended to do so.

Let's Go strongly urges you to consider the risks before you choose to hitchhike. Hitching means entrusting your life to a stranger and risking assault, sexual harassment, theft, and unsafe driving. For women traveling alone (or even in pairs), hitching is just too dangerous to risk in Greece. A man and a woman are a safer combination; two men will have a harder time getting a lift, and three men will go nowhere. Greeks are not eager to pick up foreigners and foreign cars are often filled with other travelers. Safety-minded hitchers do not get in the back of a two-door car and never let go of their backpacks. If they feel threatened, they insist on being let off, regardless of where they are. They may also act as if they are going to open the car door or vomit on the upholstery to get a driver to stop.

KEEPING IN TOUCH

BY EMAIL AND INTERNET

The Internet becomes more accessible each year in Greece. In all big cities, in most small cities and large towns, and on most islands, you can find Internet access easily. **Internet cafes** are listed in the **Practical Information** sections of towns and cities. Expect to pay €3-6 per hour. Though in some places it's possible to forge a remote link with your home server, in most cases this is a much slower (and thus more expensive) option than taking advantage of free **web-based email accounts** (e.g., those offered at www.hotmail.com and www.yahoo.com).

Increasingly, travelers find that taking their **laptop computers** on the road can be a convenient option for staying connected. Laptop users can call an Internet service provider via a modem using long-distance phone cards specifically intended for such calls. They may also find Internet cafes that allow them to connect their laptops to the Internet. And most excitingly, travelers with wireless-enabled computers may be able to take advantage of an increasing number of Internet "hotspots," where they can get online for free or for a small fee. Wireless is most easily found in Athens. Newer computers can detect these hotspots automatically; otherwise, websites like www.jiwire.com and www.locfinder.net can help you find them. For information on insuring your laptop while traveling, see p. 22.

BY TELEPHONE

CALLING HOME FROM GREECE

Your best bet for international calls from Greece is to buy a prepaid phone card from a company like **@bcard** or **OTE.** The cheapest kind comes with a PIN and a toll-free access number which you dial to make international as well as domestic calls. These cards are sold by euro amount rather than time limit; rates vary, so shop around. Phone rates typically tend to be highest in the morning, lower in the evening, and lowest on Sunday and late at night. You can easily buy prepaid cards throughout Greece at Internet cafes, kiosks, and OTEs.

PLACING INTERNATIONAL CALLS. To call Greece from home or to call home from Greece, dial:
1. The **international dialing prefix.** To call from **Australia,** dial 0011; **Canada** or the **US,** 011; **Ireland, New Zealand,** the **UK,** or **Greece,** 00.
2. The **country code** of the place you're calling. To call **Australia,** dial 61; **Canada** or the **US,** 1; **Ireland,** 353; **New Zealand,** 64; the **UK,** 44; **Greece,** 30.
3. The **city/area code.** *Let's Go* lists the city/area codes in Greece opposite each city or town's name at the beginning of its listing, next to a ☎.
4. The **local number.** Note that in the text of this book, all phone numbers are listed with the full 10 digits, including both city/area code and local number.

CALLING WITHIN GREECE

The only way to call within the country is to use a **prepaid OTE phone card** available at kiosks and OTEs. There are local OTE offices in most towns and cardphones are often outside. Swipe your card in the payphone and the computerized phone will tell you how much time, in units, it has left.

CELLULAR PHONES

Greece has very good cell phone coverage, and as all incoming calls are free, a cell phone might be a good investment. Buying an international cell phone that can be used in Greece, however, can be extremely expensive. Stick to a Greek cell phone; a bare-bones model will probably cost around €50. The international standard for cell phones is **GSM,** a system that began in Europe and has spread to much of the rest of the world. To make and receive calls in Greece you will need a **GSM-compatible phone** and a **SIM (subscriber identity module) card,** a country-specific, thumbnail-sized chip that gives you a local phone number and plugs you into the local network. Many SIM cards are **prepaid,** meaning that they come with calling time included and you don't need to sign up for a monthly service plan. When you use up the prepaid time, you can buy additional cards to get more. For more information on GSM phones, check out www.telestial.com, www.roadpost.com, or www.planetomni.com. Companies like **Cellular Abroad** (www.cellularabroad.com) rent cell phones that work in destinations around the world.

TIP **GSM PHONES.** Just having a GSM phone doesn't mean you're necessarily good to go when you travel abroad. The majority of GSM phones sold in the United States operate on a different **frequency** (1900) than international phones (900/1800) and will not work abroad. Tri-band phones work on all three frequencies (900/1800/1900) and will operate through most of the world. Some GSM phones are also **SIM-locked** and will only accept SIM cards from a single carrier. You'll need a **SIM-unlocked** phone to use a SIM card from a local carrier when you travel.

TIME DIFFERENCES

Greece is two hours ahead of **Greenwich Mean Time (GMT),** seven hours ahead of New York, ten hours ahead of San Francisco and Vancouver, and eight hours behind Sydney. Greece observes **daylight saving time,** though it may be at a different time than your home country. More info is at www.worldtimeserver.com.

The following table applies from late October to early April.

4AM	5AM	6AM	7AM	8AM	NOON	2PM	10PM
Vancouver Seattle San Francisco Los Angeles	Denver	Chicago	New York Toronto	New Brunswick	London	Athens	Sydney Canberra Melbourne

This table is applicable from early April to late October.

4AM	5AM	6AM	7AM	8AM	NOON	2PM	9PM
Vancouver Seattle San Francisco Los Angeles	Denver	Chicago	New York Toronto	New Brunswick	London	Athens	Sydney Canberra Melbourne

BY MAIL

SENDING MAIL HOME FROM GREECE

Airmail is the best way to send mail home from Greece. **Aerogrammes,** printed sheets that fold into envelopes and travel via airmail, are available at post offices. Write "airmail," and "par avion" on the front. Most post offices will charge exorbitant fees or simply refuse to send aerogrammes with enclosures. **Surface mail** is by far the cheapest and slowest way to send mail. It takes one to two months to cross the Atlantic and one to three to cross the Pacific—good for heavy items you won't need for a while, such as souvenirs or other articles you've acquired along the way that are weighing down your pack. The Greek Post has a website in both Greek and English (www.elta-net.gr), which provides basic information. Postcards and letters to international locations (up to 20g and 16.5cm by 24.5cm) cost €0.65 for standard mailing. Within Europe, they should take 3-4 days to arrive. Outside of Europe, they should take 7-10 days.

SENDING MAIL TO GREECE

To ensure timely delivery, mark envelopes "airmail" and "par avion." In addition to the standard postage system whose rates are listed below, **Federal Express** (www.fedex.com; Australia ☎ 13 26 10, Canada and the US 800 463 3339, Ireland 1800 535 800, New Zealand 0800 733 339, the UK 0800 123 800) handles express mail services from most countries to Greece; for example, they can get a letter from New York to Greece in one to two days for US$40, and from London to Greece in three to four days for UK£30. Sending a postcard or letter within Greece (up to 20g and 16.5cm by 24.5cm) costs €0.49.

Australia: Allow 5-7 days for regular airmail to Greece. Postcards cost AUS$1.10; letters 20-500g AUS$2-11; packages up to 2kg AUS$9.50-53. Express courier service can get a letter to Greece in 2-3 days for AUS$38.50. www.auspost.com.au/pac.

Canada: Allow 2 weeks for regular airmail to Greece. Postcards and letters up to 30g cost CDN$1.45; packages up to 0.5kg CDN$12; 2kg package CDN$17 by surface, CDN$41 by air. Purolator International can get a letter to Greece in 2-4 days for CDN$45. www.canadapost.ca/personal/rates/default-e.asp.

Ireland: Allow 4-6 days for regular airmail to Greece. Postcards and letters up to 50g cost €0.55-1.20; packages up to 0.5kg €2-4, up to 2kg €6-13. Swiftpost International can get a letter to Greece quickly for €5.20. www.letterpost.ie.

New Zealand: Allow 1-2 weeks for regular airmail to Greece. Postcards and letters up to 200g cost NZ$1.50-5; packages up to 0.5kg NZ$6-15, up to 2kg NZ$15-47. International Express can get a letter under 0.5kg to Greece in 2-5 days for NZ$45. www.nzpost.co.nz/Cultures/en-NZ/OnlineTools/RateFinder.

UK: Allow 3 days for regular airmail to Greece. Letters up to 20g cost UK£0.42; packages up to 0.5kg UK£0.60-5, up to 2kg UK£5-18. UK Airsure delivers letters a day faster for UK£4 more. www.royalmail.co.uk.

US: Allow 4-10 days for regular airmail to Greece. Postcards cost US$0.70; letters up to 16oz. US$0.80-8.70; packages up to 5 lbs. US$22.75. Global Express Mail takes 2-3 days and costs from US$23. http://ircalc.usps.gov.

RECEIVING MAIL IN GREECE

There are several ways to arrange pick-up of letters sent to you by friends and relatives while you are abroad. Mail can be sent via **Poste Restante** (General Delivery) to almost any city or town in Greece with a post office, and it is generally reliable. Address *Poste Restante* letters like so:

Xena WARRIOR PRINCESS

Hania Post Office

Hania, Greece 73100

Poste Restante

The mail will go to a special desk in the central post office, unless you specify a post office by street address or postal code. It's best to use the largest post office, since mail may be sent there regardless. Bring your passport (or other photo ID) for pick-up; occasionally there is a small fee. If the clerks insist that there is nothing for you, have them check under your first name as well. *Let's Go* lists post offices in the **Practical Information** section for each city and most towns.

ACCOMMODATIONS

DOMATIA (ROOMS TO LET)

Private homes all over Greece put up signs offering domatia (rooms to let). Domatia are perhaps the ideal accommodations; they are cheap and let you absorb some local culture by staying in a Greek home. Always negotiate with owners before settling on a price. You may be greeted by domatia owners as you step out at a bus stop or port; though this is illegal in many areas, it is still common. Have a destination in mind when you arrive and look for people whose rooms are where you want. Many rooms offered at the port or bus stop are inexpensive; since proprietors are in direct competition with other owners, good deals abound. Make owners pinpoint the location of their house and don't pay until you've seen the room.

While domatia may be run like small hotels in tourist towns, in out-of-the-way places they can provide warm coffee at night and friendly conversation. Prices vary depending on region and season. You can expect to pay about €15-25 for a single in the more remote areas of Northern and Central Greece and €25-40 for a single (€25-45 for a double) on heavily traveled islands. Never pay more for domatia than you would for a hotel in town, and remember that domatia owners can often be bargained down, especially when the house is

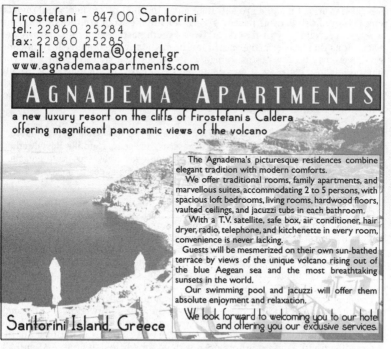
not full. If in doubt, ask the tourist police: they may be able to set you up with a room and conduct the negotiations. Most private rooms operate only in high season and are the best option for those arriving without reservations.

HOSTELS

Many hostels are laid out dorm-style, often with large single-sex rooms and bunk beds, although private rooms that sleep two to four are becoming more common. They sometimes have kitchens and utensils for your use, bike or moped rentals, storage areas, transportation to airports, breakfast and other meals, laundry facilities, and Internet access. There can be drawbacks: some hostels close during certain daytime "lockout" hours, have a curfew, don't accept reservations, impose a maximum stay, or, less frequently, require that you do chores. In Greece, hostel beds average around €15-25.

 A HOSTELER'S BILL OF RIGHTS. There are certain standard features that we do not include in our hostel listings. Unless we state otherwise, you can expect that every hostel has no lockout, no curfew, a kitchen, free hot showers, some system of secure luggage storage, and no key deposit.

Hostels are not as prevalent in Greece as they are throughout the rest of Europe. Those that exist (usually in the most popular tourist destinations) are almost never affiliated with an international hosteling organization. Thus a hosteling membership won't do you much good. Hostels are not regulated, so don't be surprised if some are less than clean or don't offer sheets and towels. Some Greek hostels offer private rooms for families and couples, and others have a maximum stay of five days. Greek **youth hostels** generally have fewer restrictions than those farther north in Europe. Many are open year-round and few have early curfews (some curfews, however, are strictly enforced—you may be left in the streets if you come back too late). In summer they usually stay open 6-10am and 1pm-midnight (shorter hours in winter). It's advisable to book in advance in the summer at some of the more popular hostels in Athens, Santorini, Crete, or Nafplion.

> **BOOKING HOSTELS ONLINE.** One of the easiest ways to ensure you've got a bed for the night is by reserving online. Click to the **Hostelworld** booking engine through **www.letsgo.com,** and you'll have access to bargain accommodations from Argentina to Zimbabwe with no added commission.

HOTELS AND PENSIONS

Hotel singles in Greece start at €20 per night, doubles €30. You'll typically share a hall bath; a private bath will cost extra. Smaller **guesthouses** and **pensions** are often cheaper than hotels. If you make **reservations** in writing, indicate your night of arrival and the number of nights you plan to stay. The hotel will send you a confirmation and may request payment for the first night. Often it is easiest to make reservations over the phone with a credit card.

The government oversees the construction and classification of most hotels, which are grouped into six classes: "L," "luxury," is followed by "A" through "E," in descending order of amenities. Greece is gradually transitioning to the star-based classification system used by many other European nations, but the process is slow. Assume hotels do not have amenities such as A/C and TV unless they are specified. More information is available from the **Hellenic Chamber of Hotels,** Stadiou 24, Athens 10564 (☎21033 10 022; www.grhotels.gr). If a hotel owner solicits you, offering to drive you, make sure you establish the location on a map; it may be miles away. Late at night, in low season, or in a large town, it's a buyer's market and bargaining is appropriate. As a security deposit, hotels often ask for your passport and return it when you leave. Don't give it to them—suggest that they take down your passport number or offer to pay up front. Sleazy hotel owners may offer you only their most expensive rooms, compel you to buy breakfast, squeeze three people into a hostel-size triple and charge each for a single, or quote a price for a room that includes breakfast and private shower and then charge extra for both. Don't pay until you've seen the room. If a room seems unreasonably expensive, stress that you don't want luxuries and they may give you a cheaper option. If you think you've been exploited, threaten to file a report with the tourist police. The threat alone often resolves "misunderstandings."

HOME EXCHANGES

Home exchange offers travelers various types of homes, plus the opportunity to live like a native and cut down on accommodation fees. Contact HomeExchange.com, P.O. Box 787, Hermosa Beach, CA 90254, USA (☎800 877 8723; fax 310 798 3865; www.homeexchange.com), or Intervac International Home Exchange, Perikleous 34, Maroussi, Athens 15122 (☎21080 61 943; www.intervac.com).

ESSENTIALS

LONG-TERM ACCOMMODATIONS

Travelers planning to stay in Greece for extended periods of time may find it most cost-effective to rent an **apartment**. A basic one-bedroom (or studio) apartment in Athens will range €600-1000 per month. Besides the rent itself, prospective tenants usually are also required to front a security deposit (frequently one month's rent) and the last month's rent. Newspapers like *Athens News* (www.athensnews.gr) and websites like www.expatriates.com and Craigslist (http://athens.craigslist.org/apa/) can be useful in finding an apartment or house.

CAMPING

Camping in Greece provides refuge from the regulations of hostels and the monotony of hotel rooms—and saves you a lot of money. The Greek National Tourist Organization (GNTO; p. 9) is primarily responsible for campgrounds; most GNTO campgrounds have drinking water, lavatories, and electricity. To find these, contact the Panhellenic Campings Association, Solonos 102, Athens 10673 (☎/fax 21036 21 560). Many campgrounds rent tents. Ask at local tourist offices for more info on the **Hellenic Touring Club,** which runs a number of campgrounds, especially in Northern Greece. Greece also has many private campgrounds, which may include pools, mini-marts, and tavernas. Prices depend on the facilities; you'll likely pay €4-8 per person and €2-3 per tent. See **The Great Outdoors,** (p. 46).

THE GREAT OUTDOORS

The **Great Outdoor Recreation Pages** (www.gorp.com) provides excellent general information for travelers planning on camping or spending time in the outdoors.

USEFUL RESOURCES

A variety of publishing companies offer hiking guidebooks to meet the educational needs of novices or experts. For information about camping, hiking, and biking, write or call the publishers listed below to receive a free catalog.

Automobile Association, Contact Centre, Carr Ellison House, William Armstrong Drive, Newcastle-upon-Tyne NE4 7YA, UK (☎08706 000 371; www.theAA.com).

The Caravan Club, East Grinstead House, East Grinstead, West Sussex, RH19 1UA, UK (☎01342 326 944; www.caravanclub.co.uk). For UK£32, members receive access to sites, insurance services, equipment discounts, maps, and a monthly magazine.

Sierra Club Books, 85 Second St., 2nd fl., San Francisco, CA 94105, USA (☎415 977 5500; www.sierraclub.org). Publishes general resource books on hiking and camping,

The Mountaineers Books, 1001 SW Klickitat Way, Ste. 201, Seattle, WA 98134, USA (☎206 223 6303; www.mountaineersbooks.org). Over 600 titles on hiking, biking, mountaineering, natural history, and conservation.

NATIONAL PARKS

Although the environment and wildlife in Greece were largely ignored in the past, the situation has been improving greatly. The EU required that Greece set up a managed wildlife preserve on Zakynthos in 2000, and set 274 areas—which total to cover 18% of Greece—as protected. There are also now several opportunities for people interested in volunteering to work for the environment (p. 80).

In addition to these protected sites, there are 10 National Parks in Greece, covering 169,709 acres. These are Mt. Aenos in Kephalonia, Vikos Gorge and the Aoos River canyon in Ioannina, Lefka Ori (Samaria Gorge) in Hania, Crete, Mt. Iti in Fthiotida, Mt. Olympos in Pieria, Mt. Parnassos in Fokida and Viotia, Mt. Parnitha in Attica, Cape Sounion in Attica, the Pindos Mountains in Ioannina, and the Prespa Lakes in northern Greece. There are two protected marine parks, around Alonissos and Zakynthos. Dolphins and monk seals make their home near Alonissos, while Zakynthos's Laganas Bay is the home of the loggerhead turtle, an endangered species (p. 80). Wetlands throughout Greece are also protected.

> **LEAVE NO TRACE.** *Let's Go* encourages travelers to embrace the "Leave No Trace" ethic, minimizing their impact on natural environments and protecting them for future generations. Trekkers and wilderness enthusiasts should set up camp on durable surfaces, use cookstoves instead of campfires, bury human waste away from water supplies, bag trash and carry it out with them, and respect wildlife and natural objects. For more detailed information, contact the **Leave No Trace Center for Outdoor Ethics,** P.O. Box 997, Boulder, CO 80306, USA (☎800 332 4100 or 303 442 8222; www.lnt.org).

WILDERNESS SAFETY

Staying **warm, dry,** and **well-hydrated** is key to a happy and safe wilderness experience. For any hike, prepare yourself for an emergency by packing a first-aid kit, a reflector, a whistle, high energy food, extra water, raingear, a hat, mittens, and extra socks. For warmth, wear wool or insulating synthetic materials designed for the outdoors. Cotton is a bad choice since it dries painfully slowly.

Check **weather forecasts** often and pay attention to the skies when hiking, as weather patterns can change suddenly. Always let someone—a friend, your hostel, a park ranger, or a local hiking organization—know when and where you are going. Know your physical limits and do not attempt a hike beyond your ability. See **Safety and Health**, p. 19, for information on outdoor medical concerns.

CAMPING AND HIKING EQUIPMENT

WHAT TO BUY

Good camping equipment is both sturdy and light. North American suppliers tend to offer the most competitive prices.

Sleeping Bags: Most sleeping bags are rated by season; "summer" means 30-40°F (around 0°C) at night; "four-season" or "winter" often means below 0°F (-17°C). Bags are made of **down** (warm and light, but expensive, and miserable when wet) or of **synthetic** material (heavy, durable, and warm when wet). Prices range US$50-250 for a summer synthetic to US$200-300 for a good down winter bag. **Sleeping bag pads** include foam pads (US$10-30), air mattresses (US$15-50), and self-inflating mats (US$30-120). Bring a **stuff sack** to store your bag and keep it dry.

Tents: The best tents are free-standing (with their own frames and suspension systems), set up quickly, and only require staking in high winds. Low-profile dome tents are the best all-around. Worthy 2-person tents start at US$100, 4-person at US$160. Make sure your tent has a rain fly and seal its seams with waterproofer. Other useful accessories include a **battery-operated lantern**, a plastic **groundcloth**, and a nylon **tarp**.

Backpacks: Internal-frame packs mold well to your back, keep a lower center of gravity, and flex adequately to allow you to hike difficult trails, while **external-frame packs** are more comfortable for long hikes over even terrain, as they carry weight higher and distribute it more evenly. Make sure your pack has a strong, padded hipbelt to transfer weight to your legs. There are models designed specifically for women. Any serious backpacking requires a pack of at least 4000 in^3 (16,000cc), plus 500 in^3 for sleeping bags in internal-frame packs. Sturdy backpacks cost anywhere from US$125 to US$420—your pack is an area where it doesn't pay to economize. On your hunt for the perfect pack, fill up prospective models with something heavy, strap it on correctly, and walk around the store to get a sense of how the model distributes weight. Either buy a **rain cover** (US$10-20) or store all of your belongings in plastic bags inside your pack.

Boots: Be sure to wear hiking boots with good **ankle support.** They should fit snugly and comfortably over 1-2 pairs of **wool socks** and a pair of thin **liner socks.** Break in boots over several weeks before you go to spare yourself blisters.

Other Necessities: Synthetic layers, like those made of polypropylene or polyester, and a pile jacket will keep you warm even when wet. A **space blanket** (US$5-15) will help you to retain body heat and doubles as a groundcloth. Plastic **water bottles** are vital; look for shatter- and leak-resistant models. Carry **water-purification tablets** for when you can't boil water. Although most campgrounds provide campfire sites, you may want to bring a small **metal grate** or grill. For those places that forbid fires or the gathering of firewood, you'll need a **camp stove** (the classic Coleman starts at US$50) and a propane-filled **fuel bottle** to operate it. Many campgrounds in Greece, however, have kitchens or kitchenettes. Also bring a **first-aid kit, pocketknife, insect repellent,** and **waterproof matches** or a **lighter.**

ESSENTIALS

WHERE TO BUY IT

The online/mail-order companies listed below offer lower prices than many retail stores. A visit to a local camping or outdoors store will give you a good sense of the look and weight of certain items before you buy.

Campmor, 28 Parkway, P.O. Box 700, Upper Saddle River, NJ 07458, USA (☎800 525 4784; www.campmor.com).

Cotswold Outdoor, Unit 11 Kemble Business Park, Crudwell, Malmesbury Wiltshire, SN16 9SH, UK (☎08704 427 755; www.cotswoldoutdoor.com).

Discount Camping, 880 Main North Rd., Pooraka, South Australia 5095, Australia (☎08 8262 3399; fax 8260 6240; www.discountcamping.com.au).

Eastern Mountain Sports (EMS), 1 Vose Farm Rd., Peterborough, NH 03458, USA (☎888 463 6367; www.ems.com).

Gear-Zone, 8 Burnet Rd., Sweetbriar Rd. Industrial Estate, Norwich, NR3 2BS, UK (☎1603 410 108; fax 1603 413 537; www.gear-zone.co.uk).

L.L. Bean, Freeport, ME 04033, USA (US and Canada ☎800 441 5713; UK 0800 891 297; www.llbean.com).

Mountain Designs, 443a Nudgee Rd., Hendra, Queensland 4011, Australia (☎07 3856 2344; www.mountaindesigns.com).

Recreational Equipment, Inc. (REI), Sumner, WA 98352, USA (US and Canada ☎800 426 4840, elsewhere 253 891 2500; www.rei.com).

ORGANIZED ADVENTURE TRIPS

Adventure tours are another way of exploring the wild. Activities include hiking, biking, skiing, canoeing, kayaking, rafting, climbing, photo safaris, and archaeological digs. **Specialty Travel Index,** P.O. Box 458, San Anselmo, CA 94979, USA (US ☎888 624 4030, elsewhere 415 455 1643; fax 415 455 1648; www.specialtytravel.com), lists over 20 trips in Greece. Tourism bureaus can often suggest parks, trails, and outfitters. Organizations that specialize in camping and outdoor equipment like REI and EMS are also good sources for info.

SPECIFIC CONCERNS

SUSTAINABLE TRAVEL

As the number of travelers on the road continues to rise, the detrimental effect they can have on natural environments becomes an increasing concern. With this in mind, *Let's Go* promotes the philosophy of **sustainable travel.** By remaining sensitive to issues of ecology and sustainability, today's travelers can be a powerful force in preserving and restoring the places they visit.

Ecotourism, a rising trend in sustainable travel, focuses on the conservation of natural habitats and using them to build up the economy without exploitation or overdevelopment. Travelers can make a difference by doing advance research and by supporting organizations and establishments that pay attention to their impact on their natural surroundings and strive to be environmentally friendly.

In Greece, travelers have ample opportunity to put the sustainable travel ethos into practice. Because so much of the country is undeveloped, backpackers play an important role in keeping the environment pristine. Small actions, like packing out excess waste when leaving a campground, using environmentally-friendly shampoo when bathing in the outdoors, and picking up trash on a beach go a long way. You can also promote ecotourism by supporting organizations that synthesize tourism with conservation. The **Ecotourist Centre of Dadia** (http://ecoclub.com/dadia/lodge.html), for example, supports conservation efforts in the Dadia Forest. See this book's **Beyond Tourism** chapter (p. 79) for opportunities to volunteer for environmental causes in Greece.

ECOTOURISM RESOURCES. For more information on environmentally responsible tourism, contact one of the organizations below:
Conservation International (www.conservation.org).
Green Globe 21 (☎+61 2 6257 9102; www.greenglobe21.com/Travellers.aspx)
International Ecotourism Society, 733 15th St. NW, Washington, D.C. 20005, USA (☎202 347 9203; www.ecotourism.org).
United Nations Environment Program (UNEP; ☎+33 1 44 37 14 41; www.uneptie.org/pc/tourism).

ESSENTIALS

TRAVELING ALONE

There are many benefits to traveling alone, including independence and greater interaction with locals. On the other hand, any solo traveler is a more vulnerable target of harassment and street theft. As a lone traveler, try not to stand out as a tourist, try to look confident, and be especially careful in deserted or very crowded areas. Stay away from areas that are not well-lit. If questioned, never admit that you are traveling alone. Maintain regular contact with someone at home who knows your itinerary, and always research your destination before traveling. For more tips, pick up *Traveling Solo* by Eleanor Berman (Globe Pequot Press, US$18), visit www.travelaloneandloveit.com, or subscribe to **Connecting: Solo Travel Network,** 689 Park Rd., Unit 6, Gibsons, BC V0N 1V7, Canada (☎800 557 1757; www.cstn.org; membership US$30-55).

WOMEN TRAVELERS

Women exploring on their own inevitably face some additional safety concerns, but it's easy to be adventurous without taking undue risks. If you are concerned, consider staying in hostels which offer single rooms that lock from the inside or in religious organizations with rooms for women only. Stick to centrally located accommodations and avoid solitary late-night treks or metro rides.

Always carry extra cash for a phone call, bus, or taxi. **Hitchhiking** is never safe for lone women or two women together. Look as if you know where you're going and ask older women or couples for directions if you're lost or uncomfortable.

Generally, the less you look like a tourist, the better off you'll be. Dress conservatively, especially in rural areas. Wearing a conspicuous **wedding band** sometimes helps to prevent unwanted overtures.

Your best answer to verbal harassment is none at all; feigning deafness, sitting motionless, and staring straight ahead at nothing in particular will do a world of good that reactions usually don't achieve. The extremely persistent can sometimes be dissuaded by a firm, loud, and very public "Go away!" (FEE-ghe!). Remember the word for police: αστυνομία (ah-stee-no-MEE-a). **Older Greek women** can help you in a bind; they're sharp, wise, fearless, and your best allies if you need information, advice, or a respite from persistent amorous attempts. If that fails, don't hesitate to seek a police officer or passerby if you're being harassed. Memorize the emergency numbers in places you visit, and consider carrying a whistle on your keychain. A **self-defense course** (p. 21) will prepare you for a potential attack and raise your awareness of your surroundings. Also be sure you are aware of the health concerns that women face when traveling (see p. 26).

GLBT TRAVELERS

Though legal in Greece since 1951, homosexuality is still socially frowned upon, especially in more conservative villages, and gay, lesbian, bisexual, and transgendered (GLBT) individuals are not legally protected from discrimination. That said, cosmopolitan regions like Athens and Thessaloniki offer some gay bars and clubs. The islands of **Hydra, Lesvos, Rhodes, Ios,** and **Mykonos** (arguably the most gay-friendly destination in Europe) offer gay and lesbian hotels, bars, and clubs.

To avoid hassles at airports and border crossings, **transgendered travelers** should make sure that all of their travel documents consistently report the same gender. Many countries (including Australia, Canada, Ireland, New Zealand, the UK, and the US) will amend the passports of post-operative transsexuals to reflect their gender, although governments are generally less willing to amend documents for pre-operative transsexuals and other transgendered individuals.

Listed below are organizations, mail-order bookstores, and publishers that offer materials addressing some specific concerns. **Out and About** (www.planetout.com) offers a weekly newsletter addressing travel concerns and a comprehensive site addressing gay travel concerns. The online newspaper **365gay.com** also has a travel section (www.365gay.com/travel/travelchannel.htm). The website **http:// greekgayguide.net** provides information on the GLBT scene throughout Greece.

Gay's the Word, 66 Marchmont St., London WC1N 1AB, UK (☎020 7278 7654; www.gaystheword.co.uk). The largest gay and lesbian bookshop in the UK, with both fiction and non-fiction titles. Mail-order service available.

Giovanni's Room, 1145 Pine St., Philadelphia, PA 19107, USA (☎215 923 2960; www.queerbooks.com). An international lesbian/feminist and gay bookstore with mail-order service (carries many of the publications listed below).

International Lesbian and Gay Association (ILGA; ☎+32 2 502 2471; www.ilga.org). Provides political information, such as homosexuality laws of individual countries.

▼ **FURTHER READING: GLBT.**
Spartacus: International Gay Guide. Bruno Gmunder Verlag (US$33).
Damron Men's Travel Guide, Damron Accommodations Guide, Damron City Guide, and *Damron Women's Traveller.* Damron Travel Guides (US$18-24). For info, call ☎800 462 6654 or visit www.damron.com.
Ferrari Guides' Gay Travel A to Z, Ferrari Guides' Men's Travel in Your Pocket, Ferrari Guides' Women's Travel in Your Pocket, and *Ferrari Guides' Inn Places.* Ferrari Publications (US$16-20).
The Gay Vacation Guide: The Best Trips and How to Plan Them, Mark Chesnut. Kensington Books (US$15).

TRAVELERS WITH DISABILITIES

The **Paralympic Games,** which took place in Athens in September 2004, inspired Greece to begin improving its facilities for disabled people. Now, the country is slowly beginning to respond to the needs of travelers with disabilities. Hotels, train stations, cruise ships, and airports are increasingly installing facilities for the disabled, and special air transportation is available aboard Olympic Airways to many of the larger islands. Still, Greece's mountainous terrain and uneven, windy streets can prove difficult for travelers with disabilities, and few of the archaeological sites or smaller towns are wheelchair-accessible. Those with disabilities should inform airlines and hotels when making reservations; time may be needed to prepare special accommodations. Call ahead to restaurants, museums, and other facilities to find out if they are handicapped-accessible. For **guide dog owners,** note that there is **no quarantine** for taking dogs in and out of Greece. While rail is probably the best form of travel for disabled travelers in Europe, the railway systems of Greece have limited wheelchair accessibility. For those who wish to rent cars, some major **car rental** agencies (e.g., Hertz) offer hand-controlled vehicles.

USEFUL ORGANIZATIONS

Access Abroad, www.umabroad.umn.edu/access. A website devoted to making study abroad available to students with disabilities. The site is maintained by Disability Services and the Learning Abroad Center, University of Minnesota, University Gateway, Ste. 180, 200 Oak St. SE, Minneapolis, MN 55455, USA (☎612 626 7379).

Accessible Journeys, 35 West Sellers Ave., Ridley Park, PA 19078, USA (☎800 846 4537; www.disabilitytravel.com). Designs tours for wheelchair users and slow walkers. The website has tips and forums for all travelers.

Flying Wheels, 143 W. Bridge St., P.O. Box 382, Owatonna, MN 55060, USA (☎507 451 5005; www.flyingwheelstravel.com). Specializes in escorted trips to Europe and the Middle East for people with physical disabilities; plans custom trips worldwide.

Mobility International USA (MIUSA), P.O. Box 10767, Eugene, OR 97440, USA (☎541 343 1284; www.miusa.org). Provides a variety of books and other publications containing information for travelers with disabilities.

Society for Accessible Travel and Hospitality (SATH), 347 Fifth Ave., Ste. 610, New York, NY 10016, USA (☎212 447 7284; www.sath.org). This advocacy group offers free online travel info and the travel magazine *OPEN WORLD* (annual subscription US$13, free for members). Annual membership US$45, students and seniors US$30.

MINORITY TRAVELERS

Greeks stare, point, whisper, and gossip as a daily pastime. The first thing to notice is that they're not just staring at *you*. While Greeks tend to hold stereotypes about every group of people imaginable, they place a great value on **individualism;** you may be asked (out of curiosity, not malice) all manner of questions or referred to continually as "the [insert your nationality here]," "the [insert religion here]," or simply "the foreigner." Greece presents two strong and entirely different views about foreigners, and travelers should expect to encounter both. On the one hand, the Greek tradition of **hospitality** is unmatched. Greeks consider it almost a sacred duty to help travelers, loading them with homemade food and advice. On the other hand, it's important to remember Greece's historical position as the crossroads of empire: most European nations have at one time or another invaded, burned, betrayed, or colonized part of Greece, forging an intense "us-versus-them" mentality. If you're not obviously Greek, everyone will want to know who you are. Greeks are very proud of their heritage and nationality, and often tend to view racial, religious, and cultural diversity as detrimental to society. That said, it is rare that **minority travelers** ever face any overt discrimination or violence; in fact, any negative comments are just as likely to come from tourists from other countries as they are from Greeks. Non-white travelers will admittedly have more trouble blending in and will be at the receiving end of more stares, questions, and comments. Once their curiosity is satisfied, however, you should be welcomed.

DIETARY CONCERNS

Vegetarians can make do in Greece if they don't mind making a meal of appetizers—green beans (φασολάκια, fah-so-LAH-kia), Greek salad (χοριατική, ho-ree-ah-tee-KEE), spinach pie (σπανοκόπιτα, spa-no-KO-pee-ta), and boiled greens (χορτά, hor-TAH). **Ask before you order;** many seemingly vegetarian entrees (like the myriad stuffed vegetables) can contain meat. **Vegans** should be aware that it is virtually impossible to avoid all animal products in Greek food. One exception occurs during **Lent,** when meat and meat stock disappear from many dishes. There are almost no Greek vegetarians, so if questioned your best bet is to argue weather ("It's so hot I only want vegetables") or allergies ("I'm allergic to pork and beef"), as opposed to some kind of ideology. This book has made an effort to list some of the few vegetarian restaurants in Greece; others are listed online at www.happy-cow.net. The travel section of the The Vegetarian Resource Group's website, at www.vrg.org/travel, has a comprehensive list of organizations and websites that are geared toward helping vegetarians and vegans traveling abroad. For more information, visit your local bookstore or health food store, and consult *The Vegetarian Traveler: Where to Stay if You're Vegetarian, Vegan, Environmentally Sensitive,* by Jed and Susan Civic (Larson Publications; US$16). For travelers with food-related **allergies,** the same rule applies: ask before you order, especially at local tavernas that simply serve whatever they have cooking. Travelers who keep **kosher** will likely run into difficulty in Greece. There are few kosher establishments. Observant travelers should contact synagogues in larger Greek cities where they still exist (Thessaloniki is one) for information on kosher restaurants. Your own synagogue should have access to lists of Jewish institutions across the nation. If you are strict in your observance, you may have to prepare your own food. A good resource is the *Jewish Travel Guide,* edited by Michael Zaidner (Vallentine Mitchell; US$17). Travelers looking for **halal** restaurants will likely find them in areas with large Muslim populations in Northern Greece; in other regions you may have to make your own meals.

ADDITIONAL RESOURCES

Let's Go tries to cover all aspects of budget travel, but we can't put *everything* in our guides. Listed below are books and websites that can serve as jumping-off points for your own research.

USEFUL PUBLICATIONS

Greece: An Oxford Archaeological Guide, Tony Spawforth, Christopher Mee, and Anthony Spawforth. Oxford Press, 2001. Thorough and wide-ranging guide to visiting Greece's ancient sites.

A Literary Companion to Travel in Greece, Richard Stoneman. J. Paul Getty Museum Publications, 1994 (US$20; US$14 on www.amazon.com). A collection of writings and artwork inspired by the natural beauty of Greece, arranged topographically.

Odyssey: The World of Greece, www.odyssey.gr. Intelligent bi-monthly magazine about Greece written for people of the diaspora.

Hunter Publishing, P.O. Box 476, Walpole, MA 02081, USA (☎800 255 0343; www.hunterpublishing.com), has an extensive catalogue of travel guides and diving and adventure travel books.

Rand McNally, P.O. Box 7600, Chicago, IL 60680, USA (☎847 329 8100; www.randmcnally.com), publishes road atlases.

WORLD WIDE WEB

Almost every aspect of budget travel is accessible via the web. In 10min. at the keyboard, you can make a hostel reservation, get advice on travel hotspots from other travelers, or find out how much a train from Athens to Thessaloniki costs.

DATE	NAME AND LOCATION	DESCRIPTION
September 8	The Virgin Mary's Birthday	Celebrates Mary's birthday; some villages finance a feast by auctioning off the honor of carrying the Virgin's icon.
October 26	Feast of St. Demetrius	Coincides with the opening of a new stock of wine. Celebrated enthusiastically in Thessaloniki.
October 28	Ohi Day	Commemorates Metaxas's cry of "Όχι!" ("NO!") to Mussolini's demand to occupy Greece.
December 25	Christmas	Remembers Jesus's birth. Greeks celebrate both Christmas Eve and Christmas day, when children make the rounds singing *kalanda* (carols).

ADDITIONAL RESOURCES

BOOKS

John Boardman. *Oxford History of Classical Art* (Oxford University Press). Details the history of Greek and Roman aesthetic innovation.

Paul Cartledge. *Cambridge Illustrated History of Ancient Greece* (Cambridge University Press). A well-written, comprehensive look at all aspects of ancient Greece.

Richard Clogg. *A Concise History of Greece* (Cambridge University Press). An overview of modern Greek history from the 18th century through today.

Edith Hamilton. *Mythology* (Back Bay Books). A standard introduction to Greek myths.

Henry Miller. *Colossus of Maroussi* (Norton). Zealous account of Miller's travels in Greece at the start of WWII.

Patricia Storace. *Dinner with Persephone* (Vintage Books). With dry humor and gorgeous detail, the American poet meditates on her travel in Greece in the early 1990s.

FILM

Troy (2004). Draining the depth out of Homer's epic story in exchange for choreographed action scenes and Brad Pitt in a battle costume, this high budget, low emotion film attempts to retell the events of the battle of Troy.

Hercules (1997). Disney's version of the heroic demigod learns the importance of having a strong heart inside a strong body, through physical challenges, singing, and dancing.

Mediterraneo (1991). Eight soldiers find themselves stranded on an anonymous Greek island during WWII in this Italian comedy.

Z (1969). Directed by Costa-Gavras, the thinly veiled depiction of a conspiracy to assassinate a liberal Greek politician won the Academy Award for Best Foreign Film.

Zorba The Greek (1964). An exuberant, sentimental film based on the novel by Nikos Kazantzakis. The most well-known movie about Greece.

The Greeks are everywhere: 1.5 million in America, over a half million in Germany, at least that many in the former USSR, and hundreds of thousands in Canada, South Africa, Asia, and Australia. All told, five million self-described Greeks live outside Greece. Melbourne, Toronto, New York, and Chicago all describe themselves as the "biggest Greek city outside Greece."

A disproportionate number of famed Greeks are from the diaspora. Aristotle Onassis (Turkey), Maria Callas (New York), and Spain's Queen Sophia come to mind, as do the poet Constantine Cavafy (Egypt), film director Costa Gavras (France), and actress Jennifer Aniston (California). George Stephanopoulos and Michael Dukakis (both Massachusetts) trail-blazed for the legions of Greek-Americans in politics. Pete Sampras and hockey star Chris Chelios are two of many sports world stars. Nicholas Negroponte (UK), founder of the Media Lab at MIT, is one of the diaspora pioneers in academia.

But in leaving their home, Greeks always looked back—nostalgia, after all, is a Greek word. Rather than fade into their adopted cultures, they maintained *arriktoi desmoi*—unbreakable bonds—with their heritage. The very idea of modern Greece was imported by diaspora Greeks. Before the 1821 Revolution, most Ottoman subjects in the Greek peninsula were uneducated peasants. The Western-educated diaspora taught these Greeks about their history, explaining that they were the inheritors of ancient Greece.

The independence movement began in Paris and Vienna, where the first Greek newspapers and books were published in the 18th century. It was in Paris, too, where Adamantios Korais revived the Classical Greek language; his synthetic version of it, *katharevousa*, remained Greece's official tongue until the 1970s. In London, Alexandros Mavrokordatos used his connections to finance the revolt against the Ottomans. In Odessa on the Black Sea in 1814, Greek merchants founded the society Filiki Etairia, which became the revolution's nexus.

During the following decades, diaspora Greeks built the country's most prestigious schools, the National Library, the Archaeological Museum, the University of Athens, the Ath-ens Observatory, and much of the infrastructure. This tradition of using hard-won earnings from abroad to finance good works at home continues: until the 1990s, diaspora remittances were Greece's largest source of foreign currency.

The diaspora elite's role in the Revolution was so profound that it sparked conflict with native Greeks—who, having suffered the Ottoman yoke, felt they had a greater claim to the new nation. But the historical vision of a Greece rooted in antiquity and Byzantium ultimately prevailed, expanding the notion of Greekness. Said one rousing orator in 1844 in the Greek parliament: "The Kingdom of Greece is not Greece. It constitutes only one part, the smallest and poorest. A Greek is not only a man who lives within the Kingdom, but also one who lives in Ioannina, Serrai, Adrianople, Constantinople, Smyrna, Trebizond, Crete and in any land associated with Greek history and the Greek race."

This notion of "cultural Greekness" was translated into the Great Idea, which guided Greek foreign policy for almost a century and sought to unite Greece with the capital of Byzantium, Constantinople (now İstanbul), and the Asia Minor coast. That dream ended in 1922, when Kemal Atatürk, the founder of Turkey, led an assault on Smyrna that killed tens of thousands of Greeks. The following year, the Treaty of Lausanne sent over one million Greeks from Asia Minor, their home for over 3000 years, to Greece, a homeland they had never known. A similar fate befell the 100,000 Greeks in Egypt, driven out by Nasser's 1952 revolution. The most recent flood of ethnic immigration came in the 1990s, when hundreds of thousands of Greeks liberated from communist rule in Albania and the former USSR made their way home.

Today's diaspora communities are largely the product of two great waves of economic emigration from Greece: the first at the turn of the 20th century, the second after World War II. The Greek-American community has grown vastly in size, influence, and economic might—they constitute the most prosperous ethnic group in the US. Similar success stories can be told of the communities in Australia, Canada, and in 70 other countries around the world.

Gregory A. Maniatis is the founder of Odyssey Magazine, *the leading international magazine about Greece and Greeks around the world. He has also contributed to* New York Magazine, The Independent, The Washington Monthly, Time-Life Books, *and other publications.*

BEYOND TOURISM

A PHILOSOPHY FOR TRAVELERS

BEYOND TOURISM HIGHLIGHTS IN GREECE

EXCAVATE the ruins of Apollo's most sacred site at Delphi (p. 85).

RESCUE endangered sea turtles on the beaches of Zakynthos (p. 80).

TEACH English to students of all ages in Crete (p. 81).

SCULPT like Phidias in the marble studio on Tinos (p. 84).

Let's Go believes that the connection between travelers and their destinations is an important one. We know that many travelers care passionately about the communities and environments they explore, but we also know that even conscientious tourists can inadvertently damage natural wonders and harm cultural environments. With this Beyond Tourism chapter, *Let's Go* hopes to promote a better understanding of Greece and enhance your experience there. You'll also find Beyond Tourism information throughout the book in the form of special "Giving Back" sidebar features that highlight regional Beyond Tourism opportunities.

RESPONSIBLE TOURISM. In this chapter, you'll find many opportunities for those who want to do more than just travel. Responsible tourism in general, however, starts with a few simple guidelines. Be respectful of local religious and social customs. Staying aware of cultural expectations on dress and behavior is essential if you want to appreciate Greece's many sacred sites. Minimize environmental impact—Greece's natural beauty has lasted for thousands of years, and we owe it to future generations not to litter or otherwise desecrate the land we visit. In general, try to be fair to the people you meet—don't be rude or inconsiderate, and don't take advantage of your hosts.

There are several options for those who seek to participate in Beyond Tourism activities in Greece. Opportunities for **volunteerism** abound, both with local and international organizations. As a volunteer in Greece, you can participate in projects from wildlife conservation to archaeological excavations, either on a short-term basis or as the main component of your trip. You can protect the beachside nests where baby sea turtles hatch, or dig up secrets of the past. Later in this chapter, we recommend organizations that can help you find the opportunities that best suit your interests.

Studying, whether through direct enrollment in a local university or on an independent research project, can be an excellent way to both visit and learn about Greece. Studying in Greece, however, doesn't mean you'll spend all day with dusty scrolls, as study programs are often coupled with travel opportunities and tours of the beautiful Greek countryside.

Working is a good way to both immerse yourself in the local culture and finance your travels. Many travelers also structure their trips by the work that they can do along the way—either odd jobs as they go, or full-time stints in cities where they plan to stay for some time. Athens and many of the Cyclades and Ionian Islands—popular tourist destinations—are great places to look for jobs. It is important to note that you must get a work permit to work legally in Greece (p. 10).

Start your search at ■ **www.beyondtourism.com,** Let's Go's new searchable database of alternatives to tourism, where you can find exciting feature articles and helpful program listings divided by country, continent, and program type.

VOLUNTEERING

Doing more than just sightseeing on a trip to Greece is as easy (and as challenging) as offering some of one's own time. Though Greece is considered wealthy by international standards, there is no shortage of aid organizations to benefit the very real issues the region faces. From preserving storied remnants of the past (see **Studying**, p. 82) to ensuring the survival of wildlife species for the future, Greece has plenty of opportunities to give back. Most people who volunteer in Greece do so on a short-term basis, at organizations that make use of drop-in or summer volunteers. These can be found in virtually every city and are referenced both in this section and in the town and city listings. Short-term social services in Greece range from geriatric assistance, medical care, and work with refugees to wildlife and environmental conservation. The best way to find opportunities that match your interests and schedule may be to search online at websites like www.idealist.org and www.timebank.org.uk; most programs have contact information, and many provide detailed descriptions and instructions on the Internet. Those looking for longer, more intensive volunteer opportunities usually go through an organization that handles logistical details and often provides a group environment and support system—for a fee. These costs can be surprisingly hefty (although they frequently cover airfare and most living expenses).

> **WHY PAY MONEY TO VOLUNTEER?** Many volunteers are surprised to learn that some organizations require large fees or "donations." While this may seem ridiculous at first, such fees often keep the organization afloat, and cover airfare, room, board, and administrative expenses for the volunteers. (Other organizations must rely on private donations and government subsidies.) If you're concerned about how a program spends its fees, request an annual report or finance account. A reputable organization won't refuse to inform you of how volunteer money is spent. Pay-to-volunteer programs might be a good idea for young travelers who are looking for more support and structure (such as pre-arranged transportation and housing), or anyone who would rather not deal with the uncertainty inherent in creating a volunteer experience from scratch.

WILDLIFE CONSERVATION

SEA TURTLES

Archelon Sea Turtle Protection Society, Solomou 57, Athens 10432 (☎/fax 21052 31 342; www.archelon.gr). Non-profit group devoted to studying and protecting sea turtles on the beaches of Zakynthos, Crete, and the Peloponnese. Opportunities for seasonal field work and year-round work at the rehabilitation center. €100 participation fee includes lodgings for those who work at the center. Field volunteers are put up at private campgrounds, but must provide their own camping equipment.

Earth, Sea, and Sky Ionian Nature Conservation, P.O. Box 6051, Weymouth, Dorset DT4 4AH, England (www.earthseasky.org). Promotes awareness of sustainable tourism and conservation. Although particularly concerned with sea turtles, they organize a variety of volunteer programs and preservation activities. Centered on Zakynthos.

The Katelios Group for the Research and Protection of Marine and Terrestrial Life, Kephalonia 28082 (☎26710 81 009; www.kateliosgroup.org). Organizes volunteer efforts to protect hatchling sea turtles and to promote sustainable development on Kephalonia. Volunteers pay €50 per month to participate in the summer.

The Mediterranean Association to Save the Sea Turtles (MEDASSET), Likavitou 1c, Athens 10672 (☎21036 13 572 or 21036 40 389; www.euroturtle.org/medasset). Assesses the condition of sea turtles throughout the Mediterranean, with sites at Zakynthos and Kephalonia. Volunteers can receive free lodging for at least 3 weeks of work at the Athens office.

OTHER FAUNA

Fiskardo's Nautical & Environmental Club (FNEC) and Ionian Sea Research Centre, Fiskardo, Kephalonia 28084 (☎26740 41 081; www.fnec.gr), conducts marine research, promotes environmental awareness, and engages volunteers in conservation efforts. Volunteers patrol the region on horseback to aid in forest fire protection, run an education museum and radio station, participate in local community service projects, catalog marine mammals, and help with other environmental research.

Hellenic Ornithological Society, Vas. Irakleiou 24, Athens 10682 (☎/fax 21082 27 937; www.ornithologiki.gr/en/enmain.htm) and Kastritsiou 8, Thessaloniki 54623 (☎/fax 23102 44 245), organizes volunteer field work to protect endangered species of birds. Also seeks volunteers to help with office work and educational presentations.

Hellenic Society for the Study and Protection of the Monk Seal (MOm), 18 Solomou, Athens 10682 (☎2105 22 2888; www.mom.gr), runs a rehabilitation center on Alonnisos for the highly endangered Mediterranean monk seal. Also conducts information sessions for local fishermen and the general public about how to further conservation efforts. Volunteers should have a basic knowledge of Greek.

Lesbian Wildlife Hospital, O. Christofa I Chatzigianni, Agia Paraskevi, Lesvos 81102 (☎22530 32 006; www.wildlifeonlesvos.org), provides medical aid for needy wildlife on the northeast Aegean island.

SOCIAL WELFARE

Global Volunteers, 375 E. Little Canada Rd., St. Paul, MN 55117 (☎800 487 1074; www.globalvolunteers.org/1main/greece/volunteer_in_greece.htm), sends volunteers to various locations in Crete to teach English to students or to provide care for and teach computer skills to physically and mentally handicapped individuals.

Medecins du Monde-Greece, Sapfous 12, Athens 10553 (☎21032 13 150; www.mdmgreece.gr/organization). A member of the international Medecins du Monde, the Greek branch brings together doctors, nurses, and non-medical personnel to provide medical care for refugees and victims of war, natural disasters, and other catastrophes in Greece and developing countries.

Multi-Functional Centre of Social Support and Integration of Refugees is an initiative of the **Hellenic Red Cross** (www.redcross.gr) that provides social support to refugees and asylum seekers and helps integrate them into Greek society.

OTHER OPPORTUNITIES

The American Farm School, Office of the Trustees and Greek Summer, 1133 Broadway, Ste. 1625, New York, NY 10010 (☎212 463 8434; www.afs.edu.gr) and P.O. Box 23, Thessaloniki 55102 (☎23104 92 700). Runs community service projects in rural villages. 6-week summer program for high school students in Thessaloniki, US$4300.

BEYOND TOURISM

Conservation Volunteers Greece, Veranzerou 15, Athens 10677 (☎21038 25 506; www.cvgpeep.gr). Volunteers aged 18-30 participate in 2- to 3-week community programs in various areas of Greece. Projects range from reforestation to preserving archaeological sites. Accommodations provided.

Service Civil International Voluntary Service (SCI-IVS), 5474 Walnut Level Rd., Crozet, VA 22932 (☎/fax 206 350 6585; www.sci-ivs.org), arranges placement in a wide variety of volunteer work camps in Greece for those over 18. Registration fee US$175.

Volunteers for Peace, 1034 Tiffany Rd., Belmont, VT 05730 (☎802 259 2759; www.vfp.org), arranges placement in work camps in many countries, including Greece. Membership (US$20) required for registration. Programs US$200 for 2-3 weeks.

Youth Action for Peace UK (YAP UK), P.O. Box 43670, London SE22 OXX, England (☎08701 927 657; www.yap-uk.org), offers volunteer opportunities in work camps in Greece. Membership £25, students £10; work camp placement fee £110.

STUDYING

Study abroad programs range from basic language and culture courses to college-level classes, often for credit. In order to choose a program that best fits your needs, research as much as you can before making your decision—determine costs and duration, as well as what kind of students participate in the program and what sort of accommodations are provided.

VISA INFORMATION

Passport-bearing citizens of Australia, Canada, the EU, New Zealand, and the US are all allowed a 3-month stay in Greece, though they are not eligible for employment during that time. Apply for visa extensions at least 20 days prior to the 3-month expiration date. If you plan to study in Greece for longer than 3 months, a student visa is necessary. You must first obtain admission into an academic or language program in Greece. Then, as long as you can prove financial support, apply to your embassy for a student visa for however long you want to study. Obtain a visa well before you leave.

In programs that have large groups of students who speak the same language, there is a trade-off. You may feel more comfortable in the community, but you will not have the same opportunity to practice a foreign language or to befriend other international students. Traditionally, Greek college students live in apartments as opposed to dorms, so you will be hard-pressed to experience dorm life studying abroad in Greece. A more likely scenario is that the study abroad program will place you, along with other students in the program, in an apartment. If you live with a Greek family, there is a potential to build friendships with natives and to experience day-to-day life in more depth, but conditions can vary greatly from family to family and from region to region.

UNIVERSITIES

Most university-level study abroad programs are conducted in Greek, although many programs offer classes in English and lower-level language courses. Those relatively fluent in Greek may find it cheaper to enroll directly in a university abroad, though getting college credit may be more difficult. You can search www.studyabroad.com for various semester-abroad programs that meet your criteria, including your desired location and focus of study. Most of the study programs based in Greece are located in highly-traveled areas, especially in Athens, on Crete, and in the Cyclades. Programs vary tremendously in expense, academic quality, living conditions, and exposure to local culture and languages. The following is a sampling of organizations that can help place students in university programs abroad, or have their own branch in Greece.

AHA International, 741 SW Lincoln St., Portland, OR 97201 (☎800 654 2051; www.aha-intl.org). 12-week terms in the fall and spring. Costs start at US$7510.

American College of Thessaloniki (ACT), P.O. Box 21021, Pylea, Thessaloniki 55510 (☎23103 98 238 or 23103 98 239; www.act.edu); study abroad admissions at Anatolia College Trustees Office, 130 Bowdoin, Ste. 1201-1202, Boston, MA 02108 (☎617 742 7992). ACT offers the opportunity to study in Greece in a predominately Greek student environment. Foreign students choose to enroll either for a term abroad or as an exchange student. Study abroad student fee starting at US$6836.

Arcadia University for Education Abroad, 450 S. Easton Rd., Glenside, PA 19038 (☎866 927 2234; www.arcadia.edu/cea), operates programs in Greece. Costs range from US$11,330 (fall or spring) to US$19,520 (full-year).

The Athens Centre, Archimidous 48, Athens 11636 (☎21070 12 268; www.athenscentre.gr), offers language, classics, poetry, and theater classes. Many universities also are affiliated with the Athens Center. Semester courses €320-590; summer €2000-2100.

College Year in Athens, P.O. Box 390890, Cambridge, MA 02139 (US ☎617 868 8200, Greece 21075 60 749; www.cyathens.org), runs semester-long, full-year, and summer programs that focus on ancient Greek civilization, East Mediterranean area studies, and modern Greek language for undergraduates. All courses taught in English. Scholarships available. Students housed in apartments in Athens's posh Kolonaki district. Summer programs include intensive modern Greek instruction on Paros and a 3-week archaeology program on Crete or Santorini.

Deree College, The American College of Greece, Gravias 6, Agia Paraskevi 15342 (☎21060 09 800; www.acg.gr/deree). Bachelor's degrees granted in a wide variety of subjects; classes taught in English. Open to students of all international backgrounds.

New York University in Athens, 19 University Pl., Room 510c, New York, NY 10003 (☎212 998 3990; www.nyu.edu/studyabroad/athens). Undergraduate- and graduate-level classes in the heart of Athens. Luxurious accommodations at the Park Hotel. Excluding housing, undergraduate US$3480; graduate US$574 per credit; program and activities fee US$300.

Odyssey in Athens, University of Indianapolis Athens Campus, Ipitou 4, Athens 10557 (☎21032 37 077; www.odysseyinathens.org), offers fall and spring semesters at the University of Indianapolis Athens branch. Provides students with residential hall housing in Plaka. Also organizes summer study programs. Semester US$7900; full-year US$17,500; summer program US$2500.

SUNY Brockport, Office of International Education, SUNY Brockport, 350 New Campus Dr., Brockport, NY 14420 (☎800 298 7869; www.brockportabroad.com/thirdlvl/greece_3rd.html), offers a 2- to 3-week summer Mythological Study Tour in Greece. Program visits ancient sites and relates ancient myths to Greek life.

LANGUAGE SCHOOLS

Language schools can be independently run by international or local organizations or divisions of foreign universities. Though they rarely offer college credit, they can be a good alternative to university study if you desire either a deeper focus on the language or a slightly less rigorous courseload. These programs are also good

BEYOND TOURISM

for younger high school students who may not feel comfortable with older students in a university program. Some programs include:

Greek Language Institute, National Registration Center for Study Abroad, P.O. Box 1393, Milwaukee, WI 53201 (☎414 278 0631; www.nrcsa.com/country/greece.html). Branches in Athens, Thessaloniki, and Hania, Crete offer immersion-based classes. 2-week courses begin at US$1441; 4-week US$2781.

Kentro Ellinikou Politsmou (Hellenic Culture Center), Tilemahou 14, Athens 11472 (☎21036 03 379; www.hcc.gr) and Arethoussa, Ikaria 85302 (☎22750 61 140). Seminars in modern Greek language in Athens and on Ikaria. Courses from €440.

Omilo, Tsaldari 13, Marousi 15122 (☎210 612 2896; www.omilo.com). Language courses for a range of proficiency levels offered in Athens, Nea Makri, Limni, and Nafplion. 2-week course €480; 3-week €690.

School of Modern Greek Language at the Aristotle University of Thessaloniki, Thessaloniki 54124 (☎23109 97 576; www.auth.gr/smg). Year-long and seasonal intensive programs offered. Limited scholarships available; consult website. Courses from €410; intensive courses from €350.

ART STUDY

Aegean Center for the Fine Arts, Paros 84400 (☎22840 23 287; www.aegeancenter.org), offers a spring session in Paros and a fall session in both Paros and Tuscany, Italy. Singing, painting, drawing, photography, sculpture, print making, literature, creative writing, and art history classes. Studio apartment housing in Greece; villa accommodations in Italy. University credit available. Financial aid available. Fall term €8000; spring term €7000.

Art School of the Aegean, P.O. Box 1375, Sarasota, FL 34230 (☎941 351 5597; www.greecetravel.com/schools/aegeanartschool), offers 1- to 3-week summer programs in painting, ceramics, and creative writing on Samos. Over 18. US$950-2050.

Cycladic School, Folegandros 84011 (☎/fax 22860 41 472; cycladicschool.cndo.dk). 6- to 12-day classes on the history and culture of Greece, particularly on Folegandros. Features drawing and painting instruction.

Dellatolas Marble Sculpture Studio, Spitalia, Tinos 84200 (☎/fax 22830 23 664; www.tinosmarble.com). Offers artists' workshops in a functioning marble studio; classes run May-Oct. 2-week course €980, each additional week €400.

The Glorious Greek Kitchen Art Classes (☎21437 31 161; www.cuisineinternational.com/greece). Art classes are held on Ikaria with artist Vassilis Stenos. 6-day class and housing US$1875-2250. (Cooking classes also available, p. 85.)

Island Center for the Arts, Skopelos 37003 (www.islandcenter.org), runs painting and photography classes from Skopelos. 2-week courses from US$2795.

ARCHAEOLOGICAL DIGS

Students interested in Classics and archaeology are often those who find their way to Greece to study abroad. **Archaeologic Institute of America,** 656 Beacon St., Boston, MA 02215 (☎617 353 9361; www.archaeological.org), puts out the annual *Archaeological Fieldwork Opportunities Bulletin*, which lists sites in Greece and is available online at www.archaeological.org. Print editions of the *Bulletin* cost US$20 and must be bought from the David Brown Book Co., P.O. Box 511, Oakville, CT 06779 (☎800 791 9354; www.oxbowbooks.com). The **Hellenic Ministry of Culture** (www.culture.gr) maintains a complete list of archaeological sites in Greece. Below is a limited list of organizations that can help you find an archaeological dig with participation opportunities.

The American School of Classical Studies at Athens, Souidias 54, Athens 10676 (☎21072 36 313; www.ascsa.edu.gr). Since 1881, American graduate students and professors have flocked here to participate in ongoing excavations of ancient sites, including Corinth and the ancient Athenian agora. A 6-week summer program (US$2950) allows undergraduates to work at its sites and others. Visit the website to find a list of publications and links to other archaeological programs.

Archaeology Abroad, 31-34 Gordon Sq., London WC1H OPY, UK (☎20 8537 0849; www.britarch.ac.uk/archabroad), is a magazine about archaeology that contains biannual bulletins with fieldwork opportunities. Individual subscriptions £20-24.

British School in Athens, O. Souidias 52, Athens 10676 (Athens office ☎21072 10 974 or 21072 92 146, UK office 20 7862 8732; www.bsa.gla.ac.uk), conducts fieldwork annually; courses for undergraduates, postgraduates, and teachers also available. Recent work has been conducted at Athens, Delphi, and Pylos.

Canadian Archaeological Institute in Athens, Dion. Aiginitou 7, Athens 11528 (☎21072 23 201; caia-icaa.gr), focuses archaeological fieldwork and research on various sites throughout Greece.

German Archaeological Institute, Fidiou 1, Athens 10678 (☎21033 07 400; www.dainst.org). Ever since Heinrich Schliemann found what he thought was mythic king Agamemnon's Mycenaean tomb in the late 19th century, Germans have maintained a strong presence in the Greek archaeological scene. The Institute currently runs digs at Aegina, Athens, Olympia, and Thebes.

OTHER INSTRUCTION

Athens Institute of Sailing, Alimos Marina, Athens (www.sailingcoursesingreece.com), runs basic and intermediate sailing and yachting classes run out of an Athens marina. Taught in English. Classes from €370.

Dora Stratou Dance, Scholiou 8, Plaka, Athens 10558 (☎21032 44 395; www.grdance.org), offers folk dance and culture classes. 1-week workshop €120.

The Glorious Greek Kitchen (☎21437 31 161; www.cuisineinternational.com). Cooking classes are held on Ikaria where instructor Diane Kochilas used to own a restaurant. 6-day class and housing US$1875-2250. (Art classes also available, p. 84.)

Ionian Village, 83 St. Basil Rd., Garrison, NY 10524 (☎646 519 6190; www.ionianvillage.org). The Greek Orthodox Archdiocese of America runs this religious and cultural summer camp for teens and young adults up to the age of 30, most of whom are Greek Orthodox or of Greek descent. Programs are based at a resort-like facility west of Patras. Full registration including travel US$3950.

Skyros, 92 Prince of Wales Rd., London NW5 3NE (☎020 7267 4424; www.skyros.com), has 1- to 2-week sessions in the Sporades on various topics ranging from writing to yoga. Courses from £385.

Tasting Places, Unit 108, Buspace Studios, Conlan St., London W10 5AP (☎20 7460 0077; www.tastingplaces.com), offers a 1-week cooking class on Santorini with trips and tastings.

WORKING

Work opportunities tend to fall into two categories. Some travelers want long-term jobs that allow them to get to know another part of the world as a member of the community, while others seek out short-term jobs to finance the next leg of their travels. Those who can teach English will find many job openings in Greece. Students can check with their universities' foreign language departments, which may

> **VISA INFORMATION**
> For **legal employment** in Greece, foreigners must apply for a work permit from the Ministry of Labor, Pireos 40, Athens 10182. Permits can be difficult to acquire, so apply well in advance. EU residents can work in Greece for up to 3 months without a work permit, but one is required for longer stays.

have connections to jobs abroad. Friends in Greece can expedite work permits or arrange work-for-accommodations deals.

Many popular youth hostels have bulletin boards with both long- and short-term employment opportunities. **City News** (http://athens.citynews.com/Employment.html) is a good resource listing updated opportunities for work in Athens. So are websites like **www.jobs-in-europe.net.** EU citizens will have a much easier time finding work and will generally make better pay than those from outside the EU.

LONG-TERM WORK

If you're planning on spending more than three months working in Greece, search for a job well in advance. Be aware that work permits can be hard to come by, and make sure that you will be employed by a company that will assist you in getting one. **International placement agencies** are often the easiest way to find employment abroad, especially for teaching English. **Internships,** usually for college students, are a good way to segue into working abroad; though they are often unpaid or poorly paid, many say the experience is well worth it. Be wary of advertisements for companies who ask for fees to get you a job abroad—often the same listings are available online or in newspapers. One reputable organization is **AIESEC International,** 127 W. 26th, 10th fl., New York, NY 10001, which coordinates business jobs that aim to promote "peace and fulfillment of humankind's potential" in over 80 countries, including Greece. (☎212 757 3774; www.us.aiesec.org.) Another interesting opportunity is **Trekking Hellas,** Filellinon 7, Athens 10557, which hires experienced travelers to guide others on various expeditions throughout Greece, including mountain treks and sea kayaking. Applicants, who are generally between 22 and 35 and are fluent in more than one language, must go through extensive training to demonstrate their abilities in the outdoors. (☎21033 10 323; www.trekking.gr. Salary €35-65 per day.)

TEACHING ENGLISH

Teaching jobs abroad are rarely well-paid, although some elite private American schools offer competitive salaries. Volunteering as a teacher in lieu of getting paid is a popular option; even then, teachers often receive some sort of a daily stipend to help with living expenses. In almost all cases, you must have at least a bachelor's degree to be a full-fledged teacher, although college undergraduates can often get summer positions teaching or tutoring. Those who wish to teach English in Greece should have a university degree (preferably in English literature or history) and a solid command of English. To obtain a teaching license, you must present your diploma and your passport translated into Greek, among other things; for current requirements contact the **Hellenic Ministry of Education,** Mitropoleos 15, Athens 10185. (www.ypepth.gr.) Greek schools rarely require teachers to have a **Teaching English as a Foreign Language (TEFL)** certificate, but certified teachers often find higher-paying jobs. Native English speakers working in private schools are most often hired for English-immersion classrooms where no Greek is spoken. Placement agencies or university fellowship programs are the best resources for finding teaching jobs in Greece. The alternative is to make contacts directly with schools or just to try your luck once you get there. If you are going with the latter, the best time to look is several weeks before the start of the school year in September. The following organizations are helpful in placing teachers in Greece.

GoAbroad.com, 8 E. First Ave., Ste. 102, Denver, Colorado 80203 (☎720 570 1702; www.goabroad.com or www.teachabroad.com). Its "Teach Abroad" section has useful listings for various teaching opportunities in a number of countries, including Greece.

International Schools Services (ISS), 15 Roszel Rd., Box 5910, Princeton, NJ 08543 (☎609 452 0990; www.iss.edu). Hires teachers for over 200 schools; applicants must have experience teaching or with international affairs. 2-year commitment expected.

Office of Overseas Schools, US Department of State, Room H328, SA-1, Washington, DC 20522 (☎202 261 8200; www.state.gov/m/a/os), keeps a comprehensive list of both schools abroad and agencies that arrange for Americans to teach abroad.

AU PAIR WORK

Au pairs are typically women (although sometimes men), aged 18-27, who work as live-in nannies, caring for children and doing light housework in foreign countries in exchange for room, board, and a small spending allowance or stipend. Most former au pairs speak favorably of their experience. One perk of the job is that it allows you to really get to know the country without the high expenses of traveling. Drawbacks, however, often include mediocre pay and long hours of constantly being on duty. Au pairs in Greece generally work 30-45 hours a week, including a few evenings, for €45-70 per week, depending on the number of children, duties, and qualifications. Much of the au pair experience depends on the family with whom you're placed. The agencies below are a good starting point for looking for employment as an au pair.

Au Pair in Europe, P.O. Box 68056, Blakely Postal Outlet, Hamilton, Ontario, Canada L8M 3M7 (☎905 545 6305; www.princeent.com).

Lucy Locketts & Vanessa Bancroft Nanny and Domestic Agency, 400 Beacon Rd., Wibsey, Bradford, West Yorkshire BD6 3DJ, England (☎/fax 012 74 402 822; www.lucylocketts.com), places au pairs and experienced nannies in Greece.

Nine Muses, El. Venizelou 4B, P.O. Box 76080, Nea Smirni, Athens 17110 (www.ninemuses.gr), is an agency with online applications that places au pairs who are EU nationals with families in Greece.

SHORT-TERM WORK

Since traveling can get expensive, many travelers try their hand at odd jobs for a few weeks at a time to help finance another month or two of touring around. For citizens of Greece and of EU countries, getting a job in Greece is relatively simple. For all others, finding work in Greece can be difficult, as job opportunities are scarce, and the government tries to restrict employment to citizens and visitors from the EU. If your parents were born in an EU country, you may be able to claim dual citizenship or at least the right to a work permit. Arrive in the spring and early summer to search for **hotel jobs** (bartending, cleaning, etc.). Most nightspots offer meager pay but don't require much paperwork. Check the bulletin boards of hostels and the classified ads of local newspapers, such as the *Athens News*.

Another popular option is to work at a hostel in exchange for free or discounted room and/or board. Most often, these short-term jobs are found by word of mouth, or simply by talking to the owner of a hostel or restaurant. Due to the high turnover in the tourism industry, many places are eager for help, even if it is only temporary. *Let's Go* tries to list temporary jobs like these whenever possible; look in the practical information sections of larger cities. Available short-term jobs in popular destinations include:

Milos Beach Bar and Cafe (May-Oct. ☎26710 83 188; Nov.-Apr. 26710 83 231) Skala, Kephalonia. Hires waitstaff, bartenders, and chefs for summer. Payment depends on qualifications like experience. Call in advance and ask for Joya Grouzi.

The Pink Palace (☎ 26610 53 103; www.thepinkpalace.com). Near Sinarades, Agios Gordios, Corfu 49084. Hires hotel staff, nightclub staff, and DJs. Send a letter of introduction, a résumé, and a photo to Dr. George (georgegrammenos@yahoo.gr). Min. 2-month commitment required (p. 543).

FURTHER READING ON BEYOND TOURISM

Alternatives to the Peace Corps: A Directory of Global Volunteer Opportunities, edited by Jennifer S. Willsea. Food First Books, 2003 (US$11).

Back Door Guide to Short-Term Job Adventures: Internships, Extraordinary Experiences, Seasonal Jobs, Volunteering, Working Abroad, by Michael Landes. Ten Speed Press, 2002 (US$22).

Green Volunteers: The World Guide to Voluntary Work in Nature, edited by Ausenda and McCloskey. Universe, 2003 (US$15).

How to Get a Job in Europe, edited by Sanborn and Matherly. Planning Communications, 2003 (US$23).

How to Live Your Dream of Volunteering Overseas, by Collins, DeZerega, and Heckscher. Penguin Books, 2002 (US$17).

International Directory of Voluntary Work, by Whetter and Pybus. Peterson's Guides and Vacation Work, 2000 (US$16).

International Job Finder: Where the Jobs Are Worldwide, by Lauber and Rice. Planning Communications, 2002 (US$20).

Invest Yourself: The Catalogue of Volunteer Opportunities, published by the Commission on Voluntary Service and Action (☎646 486 2446).

Live and Work Abroad: A Guide for Modern Nomads, by Francis and Callan. Vacation-Work Publications, 2001 (US$16).

Summer Jobs Abroad 2005, edited by Woodworth and Pybus. Vacation Work Publications, 2002 (US$18).

Volunteer Vacations: Short-term Adventures That Will Benefit You and Others, by Cutchins and Geissinger. Chicago Review Press, 2003 (US$18).

Work Abroad: The Complete Guide to Finding a Job Overseas, by Hubbs, Griffith, and Nolting. Transitions Abroad Publishing, 2002 (US$16).

Work Your Way Around the World, by Susan Griffith. Vacation Work Publications, 2005 (US$22).

EXCAVATING IN ATHENS

Arriving in a new country alone, late at night, with no knowledge of the native language is always a nerve-wracking experience. Things get even more complicated when the sites you're planning on visiting haven't seen daylight in a couple thousand years. So needless to say, I was a little anxious when my plane landed in Athens. I had arrived just in time to get a few hours of sleep before starting a summer of volunteer work on an archaeological dig—if I could make it to the apartment where I would be living, that is. Luckily, the world-famous Greek hospitality came through for me, as after knocking on the wrong door for 20 minutes and then wandering around asking strangers where to go, I found myself safely in my new home. For the next two months, I would live there while I helped dig at the ancient Athenian Agora with the American School of Classical Studies.

At first, I was in awe. At 7am the morning after my arrival, we met at the site and got a tour of the ancient marketplace. I wondered how people could go on vacation to destinations that didn't have amazing artifacts like the Acropolis looming over them. Why would anyone go to just a "normal" city? Although I got accustomed to walking by the waterclock of the Roman Agora every day on my way to work and eating lunch under the shadow of the Hephaestion, the ruins never ceased to impress me.

Still, my archaeological summer wasn't all gawking at towering monuments. It became immediately apparent, for instance, that the term "digging" would more accurately be described as "slowly scraping away." Excavating is far too delicate a process to just pull out a shovel and go; in fact, I never even saw a shovel the entire time I was there. A pick, however, can be a surprisingly delicate instrument. Although there were a few "big picks" used to take down strong walls, mostly we used the blunt end of miniature picks to steadily work away at the dirt. Our main instrument was a trowel, something I had once thought was only used for laying the mortar on bricks. I also came to realize that a tiny speck of green in the dust can be incredibly exciting—it could be a coin, you see—and that a toothbrush is very useful when cleaning shards of pottery.

There were disappointments, of course, like the time I watched as a potential tomb turned out to be maybe a latrine or just an ancient hole. The possibilities, however, were limitless. Working on a dig in which something fantastic could be discovered any second gave a constant adrenaline rush. One day, the entire site stopped work and watched as a large statue head was pulled out of the ground. Another time, I myself was lowered into the dark ground, sitting on a rope while two other workers cranked me down into a 2m deep well and then sent my tools in after me. It was there that I found a loom weight, one of my four personal discoveries of the summer (I also found three coins).

Since we did not work on the weekends, I had the time to take short trips to explore other areas of Greece. I went to see the oracle of Delphi, the monasteries of Meteora, the sacred island of Delos, and Milos's volcanic sands. On the weekends when I didn't go away I got to experience modern Athenian culture, sipping Nescafe, going to nightclubs where nobody was dancing, visiting the city's museums, and hanging out in the bars.

Living and working in Athens, I was able to see and do much more than the casual tourist. Instead of just breezing through and seeing the sights, I touched and helped uncover the sites. I did all of the typical tourist activities, but I also got to live in Athens, where I became used to the cries of "*malaka*" by angry residents upset that archaeologists took down modern buildings. I learned to order vegetarian in Greek, and I got accustomed to ignoring the locals' perplexed looks when I walked through their ritzy neighborhoods covered in dirt. Now, at least, I can always introduce myself as an amateur archaeologist—and as long as I don't get too specific, for all they know I spent my summer in Greece becoming a swashbuckling adventurer.

Leanna Boychenko majored in Classics at Harvard College. She was the Associate Editor of Let's Go: Greece 2005 *and the Editor of* Let's Go: New Zealand 2006.

ATHENS Αθήνα AND ENVIRONS

 During the construction of the Athenian metro 10 years ago, several unexpected obstacles obliged workers to pause abruptly. As they plunged their shovels into undisturbed earth, they stumbled upon dozens of ancient relics requiring immediate excavation. Today, these bits of sculpture and pottery rest behind a glass display case in the Pl. Syndagma station, which, like its sister stops, sparkles with efficiency. More than even the other Greek cities inhabited since ancient times, Athens is tied to its illustrious past. Thousands of years worth of ghosts gaze down from every hilltop and peek around each alleyway. Athens, however, is also a daring and modern place; its fiercely patriotic citizens pushed their capital into the 21st century with massive clean-up efforts and building projects before the 2004 Olympic Games. Contemporary art galleries flourish in the literal shadow of their older counterparts. Scores of outdoor theaters with views of the Acropolis play domestic and foreign films. Creatively international menus, hipster bars, and large warehouses converted into performance spaces crowd the streets among Byzantine churches, traditional tavernas, and toppled columns. Whether making your home here or passing through on your way to the islands, don't miss the chance to explore a city that, against all odds, is more energetic and exciting than ever.

SUGGESTED ITINERARIES: ATHENS AND ENVIRONS

THREE DAYS Thank Athens's ancient builders for putting everything so conveniently close together, as you can check out the **Parthenon** (p. 113) and the surrounding sites of the **Acropolis** (p. 111) and **Agora** (p. 115) in one afternoon. Spend the rest of your time finding your way through Athens's **Byzantine churches** (p. 117) and varied **museums** (p. 119). Reserve 1 night for the hip restaurants and bars of **Exarhia** (p. 108) and **Plaka** (p. 110).

ONE WEEK First, find your bearings at **Mount Lycavittos** (p. 118), whose stunning 360° view will give you an idea of how far Athens sprawls. Tackle the classics around the Acropolis (p. 111) first, then make your way through the nearby neighborhoods. After getting your fill of the city, enjoy the beachside pleasures of **Glyfada** (p. 125) and its many nightclubs, then sprint over for an afternoon at **Marathon** (p. 126).

HISTORY

If you reach back far enough, Athens's history blurs into myth. In the first of what would be many epic struggles over this capital, **Poseidon** and **Athena** were said to have fought for the right to be the city's patron god. Poseidon struck the Acropolis with his trident and water gushed forth, but it was Athena's wiser gift, an olive tree, that won the city's lasting admiration and worship. Moving forward to the age of humans, ancient Athenians believed that their *polis* had been united under the sword of **Theseus,** the Minotaur-slayer, as early as the 16th century BC. Capturing both the artistic and the political world by the 8th century BC, Athens's initial fame for Geometric pottery foreshadowed a bright future. Two hundred years later, law-giver **Solon** ended the servitude of native citizens, restored rights to some slaves, and established democratic law. Thus began Athens's long, often tortured relationship with popular government.

Victory over Persia in the 5th century BC brought a **Golden Age** of democracy and art to the new Athenian empire. Philosophers like **Socrates, Plato,** and **Aristotle,** joined by playwrights like **Aeschylus, Aristophanes, Euripides,** and **Sophocles** gave Athens its legendary status as the birthplace of Western thought. Athens, however, didn't remain the center of the world for long. Militaristic Sparta crushed it in the bloody, drawn-out **Peloponnesian War** (431-404 BC), and power shifted northward when **Philip II** and **Alexander the Great** of Macedonia conquered Athens and the rest of the known world. By the AD 2nd century, the **Roman Empire** ruled the city, and in AD 324 **Constantine** simply ignored it, establishing his grand imperial capital in Constantinople. **Justinian** delivered a further blow to Athens in 529, banning the teaching of Classical philosophy and allowing the once-great city to fall into ruin.

Five hundred years later, Byzantine emperor **Basil II** ordered Athens's glory restored; in the coming centuries, it passed (along with much of Greece) through the hands of the **Franks,** the **Catalans,** and of **Venetian** merchants. In 1456, the **Ottoman Turks** began their 400-year regime, leaving Athens a backwater. The success of the Greek independence effort in 1829 ushered in a new era of extensive restoration and passionate nationalism. Today, Athens's plateias, wide boulevards, and National Gardens follow the plan of architects hired by modern Greece's first king, the unpopular German prince **Otto** (p. 60).

The 1923 **Treaty of Lausanne** and **population exchange** (p. 60) with Turkey brought Athens an influx of ethnic Greeks who had been living in Asia Minor. Rural workers then flocked to Athens, further swelling its ranks. In the past 100 years, the city's population has exploded from a paltry 169 families to almost half of Greece's 11 million residents. Preparations for the 2004 Olympic Games fueled another age of urban renewal in Athens; the transit authority fought the sinister *nefos* (smog) by banning cars from historic Plaka and by further restricting drivers' access to downtown areas. With its magnificent new public transportation system, Athens no longer suffers from the confounding urban sprawl produced by years of turnover. The new Eleftherios Venizelos Airport, which lies to the city's southeast, has been consistently rated among the world's best airports since its 2001 opening.

■ INTERCITY TRANSPORTATION

Flights: Eleftherios Venizelos (☎21035 30 000; www.aia.gr), Greece's international airport, operates as 1 massive but easily navigable terminal. Arrivals are on the ground floor, departures on the 2nd. The **Suburban Rail** runs along the middle of the new Attiki Odos highway and serves the airport from the city center (30min.). Since it is connected with Neratziotissa on green line 1 and Doukissis Plakentias on blue line 3, the most central stations are, respectively, Omonia and Syndagma. 4 **bus** lines run to and from the airport from Athens, Piraeus, and Rafina. To get from **Plateia Syndagma** in the city center to the airport take the **E95** (40min., every 20min. 24hr., €3). Pick it up on Amalias, to the right of the top right corner of Pl. Syndagma. From the **Ethniki Amyna** metro station, take the **E94** (every 10min. 7:30am-11:30pm; €3; wait by the metro exit) or the E95. From **Piraeus,** take the **E96** (every 20-40min. 24hr., €3). Catch the bus in Pl. Karaiskaki on the waterfront, on Akti Tzelepi, across from Philippis Tours. From **Rafina,** the bus (€3) leaves every 30min. from the stop midway up the ramp from the waterfront. Buses drop off at 1 of the 4 departure

ATHENS

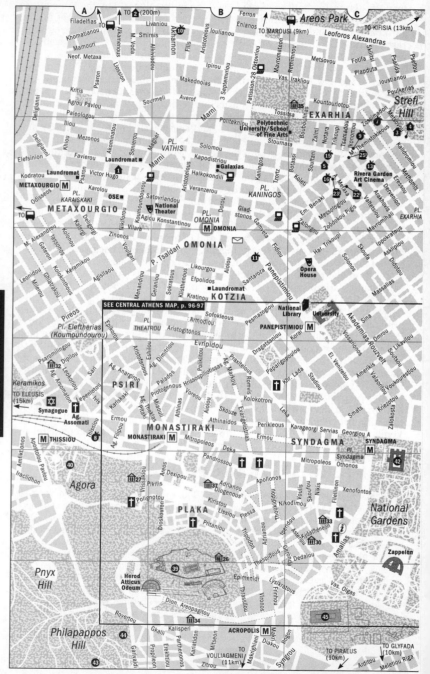

Athens

▲ ACCOMMODATIONS

Athens International Hostel, 1	A2
Hotel Aphrodite, 2	A1
Hotel Dryades, 3	C2
Hotel Orion, 4	C2
The Exarcheion, 5	C2
Youth Hostel #5, 6	E6

❤ FOOD

Ama Lahei, 7	C2
Attalos, 8	A4
CrepeXaria, 9	C2
Dafni Taverna, 10	B1
Healthy Food Vegetarian, 11	B3
Kallimarmaron, 12	D6
O Barba Giannis, 13	C2
Posto Cafe, 14	D6

Savvas,	15	C2
Souvlaki Kavouras,	16	C2

🍺 NIGHTLIFE

Briki,	17	F2
Cafe 48,	18	E4
Ellas Espresso,	19	D6
Flower,	20	F2
Haritos bars,	21	D4
Korso,	22	C2
Rock Underground,	23	C2
The Daily,	24	E3
Wunderbar,	25	C2

🏛 MUSEUMS

Acropolis Museum,	26	B5
Agora Museum,	27	A5
Benaki Museum,	28	D4
Byzantine Museum,	29	D4
Frissiras Musuem,	30	C5

Goulandris Museum,	31	D4
Islamic Museum,	32	A4
Jewish Museum,	33	C5
Lalaounis Jewelry Museum,	34	B6
National Archaeolgical Museum,	35	C1
National Gallery,	36	E4
Popular Musical Instruments Museum,	37	B5
War Museum,	38	E4

● SIGHTS

Acropolis,	39	B6
Hephaesteiou,	40	A5
Panathenaic Stadium,	41	D6
Parliament Building,	42	C5
Philopappos Monument,	43	A6
Socrates's Prison,	44	A6
Temple of Zeus,	45	C6

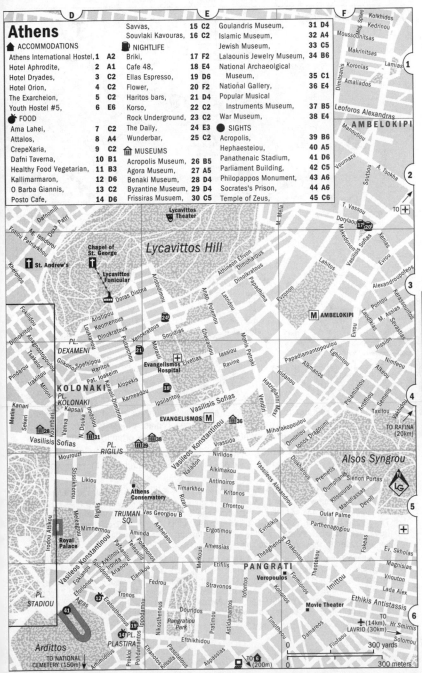

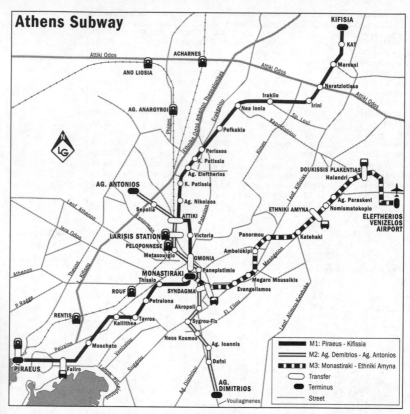

Athens Subway

KIFISIA
KAT
Attiki Odos · ACHARNES
ANO LIOSIA
Marousi
Attiki Odos
Neratziotissa
Iraklio · Attiki Odos
Irini
AG. ANARGYROI · Nea Ionia
Sp. Loui
Pefkakia
Perissos
A. Patissia
Ag. Eleftherios · DOUKISSIS PLAKENTIAS
Halandri
AG. ANTONIOS · K. Patissia
Ag. Nikolaos · Ag. Paraskevi
Sepolia · ETHNIKI AMYNA · Nomismatokopio
ATTIKI · ELEFTHERIOS VENIZELOS AIRPORT
LARISIS STATION · Victoria · Panormou · Katehaki
PELOPONNESE
Metaxourgio · Ambelokipi
OMONIA
MONASTIRAKI · Panepistimio
Thissio · Megaro Moussikis
ROUF · SYNDAGMA · Evangelismos
Petralona · Akropoli
RENTIS · Tavros
Kallithea · Sygrou-Fix
Neos Kosmos · Ag. Ioannis
Moschato · Dafni
PIRAEUS · Faliro
AG. DIMITRIOS
Vouliagmenes

■■■ M1: Piraeus - Kifissia
═══ M2: Ag. Demitrios - Ag. Antonios
▪▪▪ M3: Monastiraki - Ethniki Amyna
◯ Transfer
● Terminus
── Street

entrances, and wait outside the 5 arrival exits. **Taxis** from the airport to Pl. Syndagma run €18-25, including the extra €0.29 charge for each piece of luggage over 10kg and a €3 surcharge from the airport. Watch drivers carefully; they often rig the meters.

Trains: Hellenic Railways (OSE), Sina 6 (☎21036 24 402, reservations 21052 97 777, timetables in Greek 1440; www.ose.gr). Contact the railway offices to confirm schedules before your trip.

Larisis Station: ☎21052 98 829. Ticket office open daily 5am-midnight. Trains go to Northern Greece. Take **trolley #1** from El. Venizelou (Panepistimiou) in Pl. Syndagma (every 10min. 5am-midnight, €0.45) or take the metro to Sepolia. Trains depart for **Thessaloniki** (regular: 7hr., 5 per day, €14; express: 5½hr., 6 per day, €28). To get to **Bratislava, Bucharest, Budapest, İstanbul, Prague, Sofia,** and other international destinations, take a train from Larisis Station to Thessaloniki and change there.

Peloponnese Train Station: ☎21052 98 735 for buses to Albania, Bulgaria, and Turkey. Ticket office open daily 5:45am-9pm. Open 24hr. From Diligani, easiest entry is through Larisis Station; exit to your right and go over the footbridge. From El. Venizelou (Panepistimiou) in Syndagma, take blue bus **#057** (every 15min. 5am-11:30pm, €0.45). Serves **Kalamata** (6½hr., 3 per day, €7), **Nafplion** (3½hr., 2 per day, €5), and **Patras** (regular: 4¼hr., 3 per day, €5.30; express: 3½hr., 5 per day, €10). **Luggage storage** available (€2-3 per piece per day).

Buses: Athens has 4 bus terminals.

Terminal A: Kifissou 100 (☎21051 24 910 or 21051 32 601). Take blue bus **#051** (every 15min. 5am-11:30pm, €0.45) from the corner of Zinonos and Menandrou near Pl. Omonia. Don't mistake the private travel agency at Terminal A for an information booth. Buses depart for: **Corfu** (10hr., 4 per day 7am-8:30pm, €30); **Corinth** (1½hr., every 30min. 5:45am-10pm, €5); **Igoumenitsa** (8hr., 5 per day 6:30am-9pm, €30); **Patras** (regular: 3hr., every 30min. 6am-10pm, €13; express: 2½hr., 20 per day 6am-7pm); **Thessaloniki** (6hr., 11 per day 7am-11:45pm, €30) via **Larisa; Zakynthos** (6hr.; 4 per day 6am-7pm; €23, includes ferry).

Terminal B: Liossion 260 (☎21083 17 153). Take blue bus **#024** from Amalias near Pl. Syndagma outside the National Gardens or Panepistimiou (45min., every 20min. 5am-midnight, €0.45). Watch the numbers on street signs—Liossion 260 is near several car mechanic shops. Buses go to: **Delphi** (3hr., 6 per day 7:30am-8pm, €11), **Halkida, Evia** (1½hr.; every 30min. 5:30am-9pm, 9:45, 10:30pm; €5), and **Katerini** (5hr., 3 per day 9:45am-10pm, €25).

Mavromateon 29: ☎21082 10 872. In Exarhia. Walk farther up Patission from the National Archaeological Museum and turn right on Enianos. It's on the corner of Areos Park. Take **trolley #2, 5, 9, 11** or **18**. Buses to: **Agia Marina** (2½hr., M-Sa 5 per day 6am-4:30pm, €3.50) from which ferries depart for **Evia; Lavrio** (1¾hr., every 30min. 5:45am-9:30pm, €3.30); **Marathon** (2hr., every hr. 5:30am-10:30pm, €2.50); **Nea Makri** (1¼hr., every hr. 5:30am-10:30pm, €2); **Rafina** (1hr., every 30min. 5:40am-10:30pm, €2); **Sounion** (2hr., every hr. 6:30am 5:30pm, €4.30). Tickets are sold from 2 stands 50m apart.

Plateia Eleftherias: From Pl. Syndagma, go west on Ermou, turn right on Athinas, turn left on Evripidou, and walk to the end of the street. Buses **A16** or **B16** go to **Daphni monastery** and **Eleusis** (10-20min. 5am-11pm, €0.45).

Ferries: Check schedules at the tourist office, in the *Athens News*, with the Port Authority of Piraeus (☎21042 26 000), over the phone (☎1440), or at any travel agency. Ferry schedules change daily, so check close to your departure and be flexible. Most ferries dock at **Piraeus**, others at nearby **Rafina**. Those headed for the Sporades leave from **Agios Konstantinos** or **Volos**, and those going to the Ionian Islands leave from **Patras, Kyllini**, or **Igoumenitsa**.

Piraeus: Take M1 (green) south to its end or take **bus #040** from Filellinon and Mitropoleos right off **Plateia Syndagma** (every 15min.). To nearly all Greek islands other than the Sporades and Ionians: **Iraklion, Hania,** and **Rethymno, Crete; Aegina, Hydra, Poros,** and **Spetses; Astypalea, Kalymnos, Kastelorizo, Kos, Leros, Patmos,** and **Rhodes; Amorgos, Anafi, Donousa, Folegandros, Iraklia, Ios, Kimolos, Kithnos, Koufonisia, Milos, Mykonos, Naxos, Paros, Santorini, Schinousa, Serifos, Sifnos, Sikinos, Syros,** and **Tinos; Chios, Ikaria, Lesvos, Limnos,** and **Samos.** See **Piraeus** (p. 130) for prices, frequencies, and durations.

Rafina: From Athens, buses leave for Rafina from Mavromateon 29, 2 blocks up along Areos Park or a 15min. walk from Pl. Syndagma (1hr., every 30min. 5:40am-10:30pm, €2). Ferries to: **Andros, Evia, Marmari, Mykonos, Naxos, Paros,** and **Tinos.** High-speed **catamarans** (often known as **"Flying Dolphins"**) sail to: **Andros, Mykonos, Naxos, Paros, Syros,** and **Tinos.** See **Rafina** (p. 132) for prices, frequencies, and durations.

✈ ORIENTATION

Athenian geography can mystify newcomers. When you're trying to figure out the city, check out the detailed free **maps** available at the tourist office (p. 101); the city map includes bus, trolley, and metro routes. *Now in Athens* magazine has a more detailed street plan. If you lose your bearings, ask for directions back to well-lit **Syndagma**. The **Acropolis** is a good reference point, as is **Mount Lycavittos**. Athenian streets often have multiple spellings or names, so check the map again before you panic about being lost. Several English-language **publications** can help you navigate Athens. The weekly *Athens News* gives addresses, hours, and phone numbers for weekly happenings, as well as news and ferry information (€1).

ATHENS

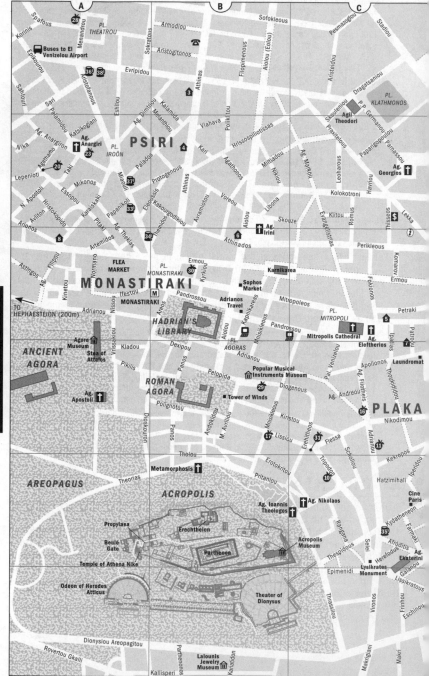

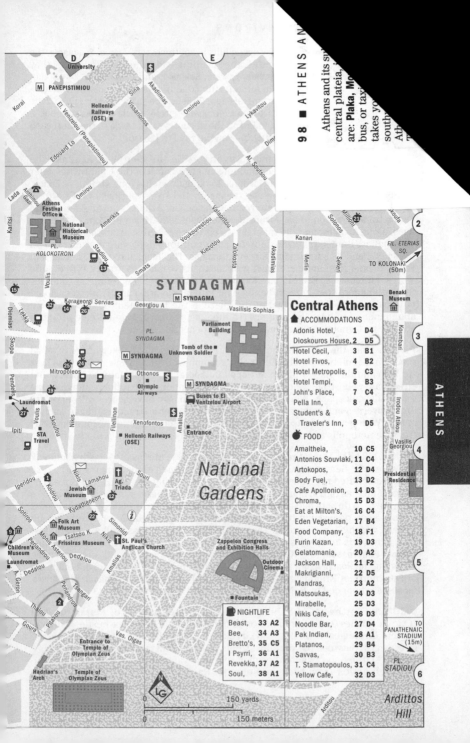

burbs occupy seven hills in southwestern Attica. **Syndagma,** the
s encircled by the other major neighborhoods. Clockwise, they
nastiraki, Psiri, Omonia, Exarhia, Kolonaki, and Pangrati. A 30min. car,
ride south—keep in mind traffic conditions vary greatly in Athens—
u to the seaside suburb of **Glyfada. Piraeus,** the primary port, lies to the
est of central Athens. In a wider clockwise circle, **Kifisia** and **Marousi** outlie
ens to the north; the port of **Rafina** to the northeast; and **Lavrio** to the southeast.
he new airport, **Eleftherios Venizelos,** is on the road to Lavrio.

SYNDAGMA. Plateia Syndagma (Συνδάγμα) is the center of Athens. The
stately, Neoclassical Parliament building and the Tomb of the Unknown Soldier
rest at the foot of the National Gardens, looking down the long stretch of **Ermou,**
populated with both trend-seeking teenagers and street performers. Fast food
spots and elegant restaurants alternate with some of Athens's best museums and
public transportation hubs. Airport-bound buses leave from in front of the Gardens, along **Amalias,** and the main metro entrance is across from the Parliament
on Amalias. Banks, luxurious hotels, and enormous department stores crowd
the square and its surrounding streets, **Georgiou, Filellinon,** and **Othonos. Nikis** and
Voulis, behind Filellinon, are lined with inexpensive eateries, tourist offices, and
stores. **Mitropoleos,** Ermou, and **Karageorgi Servias** (later becoming Perikleous,
then Athinados) start here and extend far into Monastiraki and Psiri. Occasional
public concerts, the changing of the guard at the Parliament building, and an
abundance of unlicensed vendors (to the dismay of frustrated police officers)
add to Syndagma's status as an eventful and energetic center.

PLAKA. Once the center of the Old City, Plaka (Πλάκα), the busy maze of small
roads on the hill beneath the Acropolis, is bounded by the **Temple of Olympian Zeus**
(p. 116) and the plateia of the **Mitropoli Cathedral** (p. 117). Many of its winding
streets are pedestrian (and moped) only, and vendors take full advantage of the
extra sidewalk space. While **Kydatheneon** and **Adrianou** have scores of tourist-oriented tavernas and souvenir shops, the smaller, quieter streets still have antique
charm. With reasonable accommodations and appealing eateries just meters away
from the Acropolis and other ancient sites, Plaka is an excellent place to stay.

MONASTIRAKI. Monastiraki (Μοναστηράκι; Little Monastery) hosts a fantastically frenetic flea market. Pedestrians wade through stalls heaping with fresh
fruit, handcrafted rugs, and stacks of jewelry of varying originality and price. The
pungent aromas of fish markets and souvlaki vendors permeate the vibrant square
from dawn to dusk, while crowded tavernas and the nearby colony of trendy bars
in Psiri keep pedestrian traffic flowing late into the night. Monastiraki's main
plateia, which shares its name, has a large metro station as well as several fast
food joints; it is located just off the main thoroughfare of **Ermou** and borders **Mitropoleos, Pandrossou,** and **Ifestou.** Many Byzantine churches and ancient ruins,
including the **Roman Agora** and **Hadrian's Library,** crowd this area. The old buildings
of **Psiri,** north of Ermou, and along the major thoroughfares of **Miaouli** and **Aristo-
fanous,** are bounded by **Evripidou** to the north and **Athinas** to the east.

OMONIA. Northwest of Syndagma, the busy melting pot of **Plateia Omonia**
(Ομονία) defies Greece's reputation of homogeneity. The square bustles with ethnic and ideological diversity, and Greek is far from the only script you'll see on
street signs. Between the parallel streets of **Agiou Konstantinou** and **Evripidou** is a
kind of "Little Asia," where the smell of curry wafts through the stalls and vendors sell goods from their homelands. Radical politics have traditionally

shared space with this vibrant mix of cultures, and a large red sign still hangs over the headquarters of the **Greek Communist Party (KKE).** Omonia is also a center of learning: **Polytechnic University** and the **National Library** are on **Panepistimiou** between the two plateias of Omonia and Syndagma. **Larisis Station,** serving Northern Greece, and **Peloponnese Station,** serving the south, are both located on **Konstantinoupoleos,** northeast of **Plateia Karaiskaki,** and are accessible from **Deligiani.** Omonia's old image as a shady haven for illegal activities hasn't deterred tourists, but despite great efforts in recent years to deal with both the district's crime problems and its reputation, visitors should be wary of pickpockets, particularly at night.

EXARHIA. In 1973, progressive Exarhia (Εξάρχια) was the site of a massive demonstration against the right-wing dictatorship. Today, students from the bordering university fill the same graffiti-covered streets as their former, more radical counterparts, though they gather now for a somewhat different cause. Their non-negotiable demand? Hip products, for sale at the at the thrift shops and record stores that pack this anarchist-enclave-turned-bohemian-mecca. The **Archaeological Museum** is here, among countless cafes pumping alternative music.

KOLONAKI. Athens may be the birthplace of Western democracy, but a modern-day plutocracy is alive and well in Kolonaki (Κολωνάκι). Euros flow like water in Athens's poshest district, nourishing the chic designer shops and upscale restaurants that crop up on its sidewalks almost as often as shady trees. Kolonaki's **Benaki** and **Byzantine Museums** are equally as valuable as the goods in the neighborhoods' stores (if not far more so), but, with their reasonable entrance prices, are far more palatable to the budget traveler. Kolonaki lies (very far) uphill from Syndagma, on the foot of **Mount Lycavittos;** most of its commerce centers on glitzy **Patriarchou Ioakeim,** while restaurants, bars, and cafes populate smaller **Plutarchou, Haritos,** and **Loukianou.** Every Friday, **Xenokratous** is overtaken by the humbler pleasures of fresh fruits and vegetables, sold in the crowded **laiki** (farmer's market).

PANGRATI. Youths and yuppies chat over Fanta or coffee, jabber into cell phones, and play backgammon in Pangrati (Παγκράτι), southeast of Kolonaki. Though close to the city center, Pangrati is remarkably intimate. The wide, tree-lined streets allow for quiet strolls, and the bevy of cafes provides for casual evenings sipping cocktails or coffee. Interesting shops less oriented toward tourists add a real-life city feel to Pangrati. The area's major monuments are its Byzantine churches, the **Olympic Stadium,** and the **National Cemetery. Pangratiou Park,** however, a reputed druggy hangout (particularly at night), is a reminder of the days before the area's gentrification. Take trolley #2, 4, or 11 from Syndagma.

☰ LOCAL TRANSPORTATION

Buses: KTEL buses (the **yellow** ones) leave from Terminals A and B, Mavromateon 29, and Pl. Eleftherias, and travel all over the Attic peninsula. Unlike much of Greek transportation, they are punctual, so be on time. Buy KTEL bus tickets on board. The other buses frequently visible around Athens and its suburbs are **blue,** designated by 3-digit numbers. Both are good for travel throughout the city and ideal for daytrips to **Daphni** and **Kesariani,** the northern suburbs, **Glyfada** and the coast, and other destinations in the greater Athens area. Buy blue bus/trolley tickets (good for both) at any street kiosk and validate them yourself at the orange machine on board. A standard 1-way ticket costs €0.45. Children under 6 ride free. There are several options for those who

ATHENS

plan to use buses and trolleys frequently. You can buy many tickets at once, or opt for an "Airport 24hr." ticket (€3), which grants unlimited travel on city bus, trolley, and metro within 24hr. of its validation and, despite its name, need not be used solely to get to the airport. A weekly card (€10), valid on all forms of public transport, is also available. **Hold on to your ticket.** If you drop or don't validate it—even when it seems like nobody is there to make you pay—you can be fined €18-30 on the spot by police. The metro stations' and tourist offices' maps of Athens label all of the most frequented routes. Buses run M-Sa 5am-11:30pm, Su and public holidays 5:30am-11:30pm. The **E95** from Syndagma to El. Venizelou airport, **E96** from Piraeus to El. Venizelou airport, and **#040** from Piraeus to Syndagma all run 24hr. Check KTEL bus schedules by calling Terminal A (☎21051 24 910) or B (☎21083 17 153).

> ▶**TIP**◀ **EASY RIDER.** Unlimited passes for travel on any mode of public transportation are available for €10 where bus, metro, and tram tickets are sold. If you're in Athens for a week or more, it's a bargain: 7 daily round-trip journeys plus 1 more ride, and you break even.

Trolleys: Yellow, crowded, and sporting 1- or 2-digit numbers, trolleys are distinguished from buses by their electrical antennae. Buy a bus/trolley **ticket** ahead of time at a **kiosk** (€0.45). Service is frequent and convenient for short hops within town. See the detailed metro and tourist office map for **routes** and stops. Trolleys operate M-Sa 5am-midnight, Su and public holidays 5:30am-midnight.

Metro: Most of the Athens metro was rebuilt for the 2004 Olympics. It is now fast, convenient, and gleaming. The underground network consists of 3 lines. **M1**, the green line, runs from northern Kifisia to the port of Piraeus. A new station, Neratziotissa, between the stations of Eirini and Marousi, close to the northern end of the line, intersects with the Suburban Rail. **M2**, the red line, currently runs from Ag. Antonios to Ag. Dimitrios. It will eventually continue from Ag. Antonios to Anthoupoli and from Ag. Dimitrios to Helliniko toward the Saronic Gulf. **M3**, the blue line, which goes from Monastiraki in central Athens to Doukissis Plakentias (where it intersects the Suburban Rail) and the airport, will continue northwest from Monastiraki to Haidari, and ultimately may be extended to Port Zea in Piraeus. A €0.70 ticket allows for travel along any of the lines (transfer is permitted) in 1 direction for up to 1½hr. after its validation. For shorter jaunts around the city center, tickets range €0.30-0.60. Buy tickets at metro stations; tell the cashier your destination or buy a ticket from one of the many automatic machines. Trains run 5am-midnight. Remember to **hold on to your ticket** to avoid a fine.

Trams: Noiseless and electrically-powered, 2 new tram lines opened in July 2004, right before the Olympic Games. Line 1 runs from Pl. Syndagma, in the city center, down to the coast and continues south to Helliniko. It connects with the M2 (red) in Neos Kosmos. Line 2 begins in Neo Faliro, where it connects with the M1 (green). From there it continues along the Apollo Coast until Glyfada.

Taxis: Meter **rates** start at €0.85, with an additional €0.30 per km within city limits and €0.56 outside city limits. Midnight-5am everything beyond the start price is €0.53 per km. There's a €3 surcharge for trips from the airport, and a €0.80 surcharge for trips from port, bus, and railway terminals; add €0.29 extra for each piece of luggage over 10kg. Pay what the meter shows, rounding it up to the next €0.20 as a **tip.** Hail your taxi by shouting your destination—not the street address, but the area (e.g., "Pangrati"). The driver will pick you up if he feels like heading that way. Get in the cab and tell the driver the exact address or site. Many drivers don't speak English, so write your destination down (in Greek if possible); include the area of the city, since streets in different parts of the city may share the same name. It's common to ride with other passengers going in the same direction. For an extra €1.50-2.50 for pick-up by appointment, call a radio taxi: **Ikaros** (☎21051 52 800); **Ermis** (☎21041 15 200); **Kosmos** (☎1300).

Car Rental: Try the places on **Syngrou**. €35-50 for a small car with 100km mileage (including tax and insurance); about €200-350 per week. Student discounts up to 50%. Prices rise in summer.

⊉ PRACTICAL INFORMATION

TOURIST AND FINANCIAL SERVICES

Tourist Office: Information Office, Amalias 26 (☎21033 10 392; www.gnto.gr). The staff is extremely friendly and offers brochures on travel throughout Greece and an indispensable Athens map (the same one is offered in larger metro stations). They can also give the most up-to-date bus, train, and ferry schedules and prices and lists of museums, embassies, and banks. Their website is also a good source of information. Going straight to a travel agency (see below), however, is generally a quicker and easier way to make specific plans. Open M-F 9am-7pm, Sa-Su 10am-3pm.

Budget Travel: STA Travel, Voulis 43 (☎21032 11 188). Open M-F 9am-5pm, Sa 10am-2pm. **Consolas Travel,** Aiolou 100 (☎21032 19 228), on the 9th fl. above the post office. Open M, Sa 9am-2pm, Tu-F 9am-5pm. **Adrianos Travel, Ltd.,** Pandrossou 28 (☎21032 31 015; www.adrianostravel.gr), near Mitropoli Cathedral in Plaka, on the 2nd fl. Open M-F 9am-6pm, Sa 9am-1pm.

Embassies and Consulates: See **Embassies and Consulates** (p. 8).

Banks: National Bank, Karageorgi Servias 2 (☎21033 40 500), in Pl. Syndagma. Open M-Th 8am-2:30pm, F 8am-2pm; open for **currency exchange** only M-F 3:30-5pm, Sa 9am-2pm, Su 9am-1pm. AmEx, the post office, some hotels, and other banks (list available at tourist office) offer currency exchange. Commission about 5%. 24hr. currency exchange at the airport, but commissions there may be exorbitant.

LOCAL SERVICES

Luggage Storage: Pacific Ltd. (☎21035 30 160; www.pacifictravel.gr), in El. Venizelos Airport's arrivals terminal across from the large cafe, stores baggage. Open 24hr. Main branch at Nikis 26 (☎21032 41 007) in **Syndagma.** €2 per day, €30 per month. Open M-Sa 8am-8pm, Su 9am-2pm. Many **hotels** have free or inexpensive luggage storage.

Bookstores: Around Syndagma, there are 2 ⬛**Eleftheroudakis Book Stores,** Panepistimiou 17 (☎21032 58 440) and Nikis 20 (☎21032 29 388). The air-conditioned, 8-floor Panepistimiou location, with a Food Company cafe, is a mecca for English, French, and German speakers nostalgic for fiction, reference, and travel books in their native tongue. Open M-F 9am-9pm, Sa 9am-6pm. AmEx/MC/V. **Compendium Bookshop,** Nikodimou 5, just off Nikis on the left (☎21032 21 248), has new and used books, large fiction and poetry sections, poetry readings in winter, and a children's book room. Open M, W 9am-5pm, Tu, Th-F 9am-8pm, Sa 9:30am-3:30pm. **Zoodochou Pigis,** off of Akademias in Omonia, is lined with bookstores frequented by students at the nearby university, selling old, new, and foreign books, magazines, and newspapers.

Libraries: The **British Council Library,** Pl. Kolonaki 17 (☎21036 71 300 or 21036 33 211), offers books on English literature and language. Open July-Aug. M-F 9am-2pm; Sept.-June M-Sa 10am-7pm. **Hellenic American Union Library,** Massalias 22 (☎21036 80 000), on the 4th fl. of the Hellenic American Union behind Panepistimiou, has a wide variety of English books on Greece. Open M, Th 10am-5pm, Tu 10am-8pm, W 10am-6pm, F 10am-4pm.

ATHENS

Laundromats: Most *plintirias* (launderers) have signs reading "Laundry." Be sure to specify if you don't mind mixing colors or you'll end up paying for several loads. **Angelou Geront 10** in Plaka will wash, dry, and fold your laundry for €9. Open M-Sa 8am-8pm, Su 8am-2pm. Syndagma has **National**, a laundromat and dry cleaners, at Apollonos 17 (☎21032 32 226). Wash, dry, and fold €4.50 per kg. Open M, W 8am-4pm, Tu, Th-F 8am-8pm. **Zenith,** Apollonos 12 and Pentelis 1 (☎21032 38 533), offers wash and dry (€4.50 per kg). Open M, W 8am-4pm, Tu, Th-F 8am-8pm. Launder 1 load for €9 near the train stations at **Psaron 9** (☎21052 22 856). Open M-F 8am-8pm, Sa 8am-5pm, Su 8am-noon.

EMERGENCY AND COMMUNICATIONS

Emergencies: Police ☎100 or 133. **Ambulance** ☎166. **Doctors** ☎105 or 21064 67 811; line available 2pm-7am. **Poison control** ☎21077 93 777. **AIDS Help Line** ☎21072 22 222. *Athens News* lists hospitals. Free emergency health care for tourists.

Tourist Police: Dimitrakopoulou 77 (☎171). Great for information, assistance, and emergencies. English spoken. Open 24hr.

Pharmacies: Marked by a **green cross** hanging over the street. They're everywhere. About 1 every 4 blocks is open 24hr.; they rotate. Once a pharmacy closes, it will list on its door the nearest ones that are open 24hr.; the "Useful Information" section of *Athens News* also lists the day's emergency pharmacies.

Hospitals: Emergency hospitals/clinics on duty can be reached at ☎106. **KAT**, Nikis 2 (☎21080 14 411), is located between Marousi and Kifisia. **Geniko Kratiko Nosokomio (Y. Gennimatas; Public State Hospital),** Mesogion 154 (☎21077 78 901). A state hospital, **Aeginitio,** Vas. Sofias 72 (☎21072 20 811) and Vas. Sofias 80 (☎21077 70 501), is closer to Athens's center. Near Kolonaki is the public hospital **Evangelismos,** Ypsilantou 45-47 (☎21072 01 000).

Telephones: OTE, Patission 85 (☎21082 14 449), Athinas 45 (☎21032 16 699), or Stadiou 15. Has phone books for most European and Anglophone countries. Overseas collect calls can only be made at Patission location. For information on **overseas calls,** dial ☎161 from any land-line phone; for **directory assistance** in and outside of Athens, dial ☎131. Most phone booths in the city operate by **phone cards** (€3, €6, €12, or €24), available at OTE offices, kiosks, and tourist shops. For rates and general OTE info, call ☎134 (English spoken); for a domestic English-speaking operator, call ☎151. Open M-F 8am-2pm.

Internet Access: Athens teems with Internet cafes. Expect to pay €3-6 per hr.

Arcade Internet Cafe, Stadiou 5 (☎21032 48 105), up Stadiou from Pl. Syndagma, in a shopping center about 15m from the main thoroughfare. Complimentary coffee. €3 per hr., €0.50 each additional 10min.; €2 min. Open M-Sa 9am-10pm, Su noon-8pm.

Rendez-Vous Cafe, Voulis 18 (☎21032 23 158), in Syndagma. Sip coffee or snack on freshly made white chocolate chip cookies (€0.40) while computing. €3 per hr., €1 min. Open M-F 7:30am-9pm, Sa 7:30am-6pm.

Bits'n Bytes Internet, Kapnikareas 19 (☎21038 22 545; www.bnb.gr), in Plaka. This mother of new-age Internet cafes has fast connections in a spacious, air-conditioned, black-light lit joint. 9am-midnight €5 per hr., midnight-9am €3 per hr. Vending machines sell coffee, juice (€1), and sandwiches (€1-2). Open 24hr. Second location in Exarhia, Akadamias 78 (☎21052 27 717).

Cafe 4U, 3 Septemvriou 24 (☎21052 01 564), in Omonia. A refuge off busy 3 Septemvriou, this cafe offers fast access for €2.50 per hr., €1.50 min.

Deligrece Internet Cafe, Akademias 87 (☎21033 01 895), in Exarhia. A relaxing place to hang out in central Athens independent of its Internet access (€2.35 per hr.), Deligrece has satellite TV and cheap espresso (€2). Open daily 8:30am-midnight.

Quicknet Cafe, Glathstonos 4 (☎21038 03 771), just off of Patission, in Exarhia. Extremely fancy with large new flat-screen PCs, fast connections, air-conditioning, and comfortable swivel chairs. €2.50 per hr., €1.50 min. Cappuccino €1.50. Open 24hr.

Lobby Internet Cafe, Imittou 113 (☎21070 14 607), by Pl. Pangratiou, in Pangrati. Mainly a cafe with a few computers and a printer (€0.25 per page). €4 per hr., €2 min. Open daily 9am-1am.

Post Offices: For customer service inquiries call the Greek National Post Office (ELTA; ΕΛΤΑ) at ☎80011 82 000.

Syndagma branch (☎21062 26 253), on the corner of Mitropoleos, sells stamps, **exchanges currency,** and will hold **Poste Restante** items. **Postal Code:** 10300.

Omonia branch, Aiolou 100 (☎21032 53 586). Machine distributes stamps 24hr. (bring credit card). Holds **Poste Restante** and accepts parcels up to 2kg sent abroad. Open M-F 7:30am-8pm, Sa 7:30am-2pm. **Postal Code:** 10200.

Exarhia branch, at the corner of Zaimi and K. Deligiani. **Exchanges currency** and accepts **Poste Restante.** Open M-F 7:30am-2pm. **Postal Code:** 10022.

Acropolis/Plaka branch (☎21092 18 076). **Exchanges currency** and accepts **Poste Restante;** sends packages up to 2kg abroad. Open M-F 7:30am-6pm. **Postal Code:** 11702.

Shipping: To send packages abroad, try parcel post at the Syndagma ELTA branch at **Mitropoleos 60** (☎21032 42 489; open M-F 7:30am-8pm). **Postal Code:** 10033.

⚑ ACCOMMODATIONS

The reception desk at **Youth Hostel #5,** Damareos 75, in **Pangrati,** also acts as the **Greek Youth Hostel Association** and lists 10 other affiliated hostels in Thessaloniki, Patras, and Olympia as well as on Santorini and Crete. (☎21075 19 530. Open M-F 9am-3pm.) The **Hellenic Chamber of Hotels,** Stadiou 24, provides info and reservations for hotels throughout Greece. Reservations require cash deposit, length of stay, and number of people; contact a month in advance. (☎21033 10 022; www.grhotels.gr. Open May-Nov. M-F 8:30am-1:30pm.)

ACCOMMODATIONS BY PRICE

UNDER €16 ❶			
Athens International Hostel (HI; p. 106)	OMN	🏨 Hotel Orion (p. 106)	EXR
🏨 Youth Hostel #5 (p. 107)	PAN	John's Place (p. 103)	SYN
€16-25 ❷		**€36-70 ❹**	
Hostel Aphrodite (HI; p. 106)	OMN	Dioskouros House (p. 105)	PLK
Hotel Fivos (p. 106)	MON	Hotel Cecil (p. 105)	MON
🏨 Pella Inn (p. 105)	MON	Hotel Dryades (p. 106)	EXR
Student's and Traveler's Inn (p. 105)	PLK	Hotel Metropolis (p. 105)	SYN
		Hotel Tempi (p. 105)	MON
€26-35 ❸		The Exarcheion (p. 106)	EXR
Adonis Hotel (p. 105)	PLK		

EXR Exarhia **MON** Monastiraki **OMN** Omonia **PAN** Pangrati **PLK** Plaka **SYN** Syndagma

ACCOMMODATIONS BY AREA

SYNDAGMA

Tourist services are easy to find in the heart of Athens, but cheap, quality accommodations are difficult to track down. Though it can be noisy, Syndagma is a good, central location; just be wary of overpriced, underwhelming tourist traps.

John's Place, Patroöu 5 (☎21032 29 719), near Mitropoleos. Off the major streets, John's quiet rooms are large and have A/C. Dim hallways and high ceilings enhance the Old World feel. Singles €35; doubles €50; triples €75. ❸

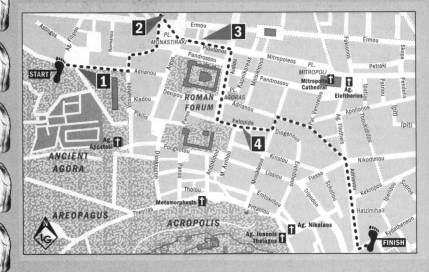

1. ANCIENT AGORA. As you emerge from the bustling streets of Plaka into this wide expanse of marble, crickets, and pines, you may be struck by the silence. For 1000 continuous years, however, this was the busiest place in Athens. The Hephaesteion, on the hill to your right, and the reconstructed Stoa of Attalos, on your left, are still real enough for you to imagine the generations of Greeks and foreigners who came here to haggle over mandarins. Picture Socrates lounging in the shops on the southwestern part of the square (p. 115).

START: Adrianou, entrance to Agora
FINISH: Kydathenenon 41
DISTANCE: 1.5km
DURATION: 2-3hr.
WHEN TO GO: Late morning

2. THE POET'S SANDAL SHOP. In the shadow of the Acropolis, Stavros Melissinos works the two crafts that have drawn Jacqueline Kennedy Onassis, John Lennon, ex-Prime Minister Kanellopoulos and Gary Cooper—sandalmaking, that is, and poetry. His wonderful raw-leather sandals line the shop's narrow walls, and samples of his poetry lie around for patrons of his shop to read. "A writer who does nothing but write," the poet once said, "is like the moon which gives off some light, but it's borrowed, taken from the sun. A writer needs first-hand experience which only working in another field can give him. Otherwise, he is rewriting what he's read in other books." *(Melissinos Art, 2 Agias Theklas.* ☎ *210 321 9247. Open M-F 10am-6pm, Su 10am-2:30pm. Sandals €13-27.)*

3. SAVVAS. Perhaps the most widely renowned among Athenians themselves, this is the best place to order souvlaki and run. Why? Well first, it's the best souvlaki out there. Second, it's a sixth of the price (literally) when you take it to go (p. 109).

4. BRETTO'S. Barrels of wine on the right side of this one-room, high-ceilinged, 112-year-old wooden distillery are filled with sweet red wine. At midday, you might prefer a chilled glass of *topio* (local) or a small ice-cubed ouzo cocktail, but whatever you do, you must have a taste, a sip, a drink, a whatever while you're here (p. 122).

Hotel Metropolis, Mitropoleos 46 (☎21032 17 469; www.hotelmetropolis.gr). Balconies with excellent views of the square or the Acropolis make this otherwise simple hotel distinct. Elevator, A/C, TV, phones. Free luggage storage. Laundry €10 per load. Singles €35-50; doubles €40-60; triples €60-75. AmEx/MC/V. ❹

PLAKA

Student's and Traveler's Inn, Kydatheneon 16 (☎21032 44 808; www.studenttravelersinn.com), has a lively atmosphere, A/C (in all rooms except dorms), and an around-the-clock cyber cafe (€3 per 30min.). The Inn courts backpackers with its balconies, large courtyard, and helpful management. Breakfast (6am-noon) €3-4.50. Storage €15 per month, €7 per week, free for 1 day. Reception 24hr. Call ahead for reservations; if you are going to be late, call and your room will be kept without charge. Co-ed dorms €16-20; doubles €50, with bath €60; triples €72/84; quads €88/100. For the cheapest digs, request the "dungeon" downstairs, a windowless co-ed dorm (€12). ❷

Adonis Hotel, Kodrou 3 (☎21032 49 737). From Filellinon on the way from Syndagma, turn right on Nikodimou and then left on Kodrou, which meets Voulis. This family hotel has private baths, satellite TV, and phones. Breakfast included and served on roof-top with Acropolis view. A/C €10 extra per person. Reserve in advance (1-2 months in high season). Singles €50, in low-season €30; doubles €70/45; triples €90/60. Up to 10% discount for stays longer than 2 days. ❸

Dioskouros House, Pitakou 6 (☎21032 48 165), at the southwestern corner of the National Gardens, by the Temple of Olympian Zeus. Simple, wood-floored rooms. Breakfast included. Luggage storage (€1) and book exchange. Singles €40; doubles €60; triples €90; quads €100. Discounts for calling ahead or staying multiple nights. ❹

MONASTIRAKI

With its nearby markets, Monastiraki will always be noisy, but the neighborhood's activity and central location make it an appealing place to set up camp. There is no shortage of cheap, high-quality accommodations, and ancient sights and buzzing nightlife are just a short walk away.

▧ **Pella Inn,** Karaiskaki 1 (☎21032 50 598). From the Monastiraki metro station, walk 2 blocks down Ermou, away from Pl. Syndagma. Tidy, well-equipped rooms overlook a street which, though bustling and often noisy, is particularly well-situated. On the dividing line between the old sights below the Acropolis and the newer, trendy nightlife of Psiri, Pella is minutes from many of Athens's best draws. From private balconies or a large roof-top seating area, guests enjoy beautiful, unobstructed views of the Acropolis. Shared baths. All rooms have fans, phones, and hot water. Breakfast included in room prices, €3 extra if you stay in dorms. Free luggage storage. Dorms €15; doubles €40-50; triples €60; quads €80. Prices drop in low season. ❷

Hotel Cecil, Athinas 39 (☎21032 17 079), on the border of Psiri, just a few blocks down from the Varvakia market and 4 blocks from the Monastiraki metro. Cecil has wood-floored, high-ceilinged rooms with spotless, private bathrooms, A/C, and TV. Roof bar with Acropolis view. Breakfast included. Free luggage storage. Singles €65; doubles €95; triples €120; quads €145. Ask about low-season discounts. AmEx/MC/V. ❹

Hotel Tempi, Aiolou 29 (☎21032 13 175; www.travelling.gr/tempihotel). Wedged between an assortment of street vendors and garment shops, Tempi rents simple rooms with A/C, TV, and private baths upon request. Make your own breakfast using the kitchen. Free luggage storage. Check-out 11am. Singles €38; doubles €58; triples €70. Prices can be up to 20% cheaper in low season. ❹

Hotel Fivos, Athinas 23 (☎21032 26 657; www.consolas.gr). Blocks away from the Monastiraki metro station, Hotel Fivos offers adequate accommodations in a convenient and lively location. Families and student travelers congregate here, where large windows add cheer to unadorned rooms. A/C and private baths available. Breakfast included. Internet access. Singles €45; doubles €55. ❷

OMONIA

Hurried travelers will appreciate Omonia's location by the bus and train stations, and their wallets will appreciate its accommodations' low prices. Though they lack glamour, the hostels here are some of the cheapest and friendliest in the city.

Hostel Aphrodite (HI), Einardou 12 (☎21088 10 589; www.hostelaphrodite.com). From the Victoria metro station, follow Heyden downhill for 2 blocks, then continue along Peioniou for 2 more. Turn right on Michail Voda and left on Einardou. From the train station, take Filadelfias to Michail Voda, then turn left and continue until you hit Einardou. Clean, simple rooms with A/C and phones. Bar in the basement. Breakfast €3-7. Laundry €11. Internet access €5 per hr. Safety deposit box. Free luggage storage. Reception 24hr. Dorms €17; doubles €45; triples €60; quads €72. Reduced prices in low season. HI discount. ❷

Athens International Hostel (HI), Victor Hugo 16 (☎21052 32 540; www.hostelbooking.com). Walk down 3 Septemvriou from Pl. Omonia and take a left on Veranzerou, which becomes Victor Hugo after crossing Marni (minutes from the Metaxourgio metro stop). Super-cheap lodgings in a gritty neighborhood. You'll need to be an HI member or buy a membership (€15) to stay here. Hot water 6am-midnight. Shared kitchen. Laundry €6. Reservations required. Email for reservations; priority given to those with previously purchased HI membership. Dorms €8; doubles €16. ❶

EXARHIA

Near the university bars and the Archaeological Museum, Exarhia is within walking distance of major public transportation. It's also quieter and brighter than nearby Omonia, making it a convenient and peaceful place to stay.

▨ Hotel Orion, Em. Benaki 105 (☎21038 27 362; fax 21038 05 193). From Pl. Omonia, walk up Em. Benaki, or take bus #230 from Pl. Syndagma. Filled with hip travelers intent on experiencing Athens away from the tourist machine, Orion rents small rooms with A/C, TV, and shared baths. Sunbathers relax on the exquisite roof-top with music, TV, and board games. Internet access €2 per hr. Breakfast €5. Kitchen open 24hr. Laundry €3. Singles €30; doubles €40; triples €48. Bargain for better prices. ❸

Hotel Dryades, Dryadon 4 (☎21038 27 116). Orion's luxurious sister is one of Athens's nicest mid-level accommodations, with large rooms and baths. Full kitchen and TV lounge. Breakfast €5. Internet access €2 per hr. Singles €40-45; doubles €50-60. ❹

The Exarcheion, Themistokleous 55 (☎21038 00 731), fuses Old World glamor with modern comforts. Up a marble spiral staircase, bright, spacious rooms have phones, TV, baths, A/C, and balconies overlooking Exarhia. Internet access (€3 per hr.), roof garden with a bar, and free exercise machine. Breakfast €5. Reservations recommended. Singles €35-40; doubles €45-50; triples €60-70. Prices drop 10% in low season. 10% discount for *Let's Go* readers; €10 discount for reserving online. ❹

KOLONAKI AND PANGRATI

Kolonaki's high prices may scare off budget travelers, while Pangrati has a few affordable accommodations.

Youth Hostel #5, Damareos 75 (☎21075 19 530). From Omonia or Pl. Syndagma take trolley #2 or 11 to Filolaou (past Imittou) or walk through the National Garden, down Eratosthenous Efthidiou, then 3 blocks to Frinis, and down Frinis until you come to Damareos; it's on your right. There's no sign for this cheery, family-owned hostel—just the number 75 and a green door. TV lounge and full kitchen. Hot showers €0.50 for 7min. Sheets €2 for the 1st night, free afterward. €4 to wash, then hang clothes to dry on the roof, or €7 for wash and dry combo. Quiet hours 2-5pm and 11pm-7am. Dorms €10-12. When the hostel fills up, the owner opens the roof (€6 per person) to travelers; bring a sleeping bag. ●

☐ FOOD

FOOD BY PRICE

UNDER €4 ●			€4-8 ❷, CONTD.	
Antonis Souvlaki (p. 108)	PLK		▨ Food Company (p. 111)	KOL
Artokopos (p. 108)	PLK		Gelatomania (p. 109)	MON
Cafe Apollonion (p. 107)	SYN		Healthy Food Vegetarian (p. 110)	OMN
CoffeeRight (p. 109)	MON		Nikis Cafe (p. 108)	SYN
CrepeXarhia (p. 111)	EXR		Noodle Bar (p. 108)	SYN
Everest (p. 109)	MON		▨ O Barba Giannis (p. 110)	EXR
Goody's (p. 109)	MON		Pasta Cafe (p. 110)	EXR
Makrigianni (p. 107)	SYN		Platanos (p. 108)	PLK
Matsoukas (p. 107)	SYN		T. Stamatopoulos (p. 109)	PLK
▨ Mirabelle (p. 107)	SYN		Yellow Cafe (p. 108)	SYN
Posto Cafe (p. 111)	PAN			
▨ Savvas (p. 109 and p. 110)	MON, EXR		€9-15 ❸	
Souvlaki Kavouras (p. 110)	EXR		Chroma (p. 108)	SYN
			▨ Cookou Cook (p. 110)	EXR
€4-8 ❷			Furin Kazan (p. 108)	SYN
Ama Lahei (p. 111)	EXR		Jackson Hall (p. 111)	KOL
Amaltheia (p. 109)	PLK		▨ Kallimarmaron (p. 111)	PAN
Attalos (p. 109)	MON		Mandras (p. 109)	MON
Beast (p. 110)	EXR		Pak Indian (p. 110)	OMN
Body Fuel (p. 108)	SYN			
Dafni Taverna (p. 110)	OMN		€16-25 ❹	
Eden Vegetarian Restaurant (p. 108)	PLK		Eat at Milton's (p. 109)	PLK

EXR Exarhia **MON** Monastiraki **OMN** Omonia **PAN** Pangrati **PLK** Plaka **SYN** Syndagma

FOOD BY AREA

SYNDAGMA

Just beyond the main square's local chains, several inexpensive eateries offer quick, delicious options. Like their franchise counterparts, **Makrigianni ●**, Nikis 54 (open daily 6am-7pm), and **Cafe Apollonion ●**, Nikis 10 (open daily 6am-9pm), sell sandwiches and pastries for €2-3. ▨ **Mirabelle ●**, Nikis 34, is a corner deli buzzing with locals. Make-your-own sandwich ingredients range from fried eggs to fresh zucchinis, and just €2-6 will buy you sausage and potato, a stuffed tomato, or baklava. (☎21033 12 612. Open daily 7am-11pm.) **Matsoukas ●**, Karageorgi Servias 3, lines its walls with chocolates, cookies, and other traditional sweets. (☎21032 52 054. Open daily 8am-10pm.)

ATHENS

Chroma, Lekka 8 (☎21033 17 793). Join trendy diners on the red and white leather couches at this upscale swankfest for grilled salmon with vegetables and rice (€13), or sip a mixed drink when the cafe becomes a bar in the evening. Open daily 8am-2am or later. Kitchen open 1pm-midnight. ❸

Body Fuel, Stadiou 3 (☎21032 57 772). This new-age food bar in a sleek metal and glass setting focuses on providing a healthy alternative to fast food. Young Athenians stop in on their lunch breaks to energize themselves with a shrimp and tuna sandwich (€4), sushi platter (€7), or fresh smoothie (€3-5) at the long shared table upstairs. Open M-F 10:30am-8pm. ❷

Furin Kazan, Apollonos 2 (☎21032 29 170). Follow Nikis to Apollonos, which is parallel to Mitropoleos and begins 1 block away from the square. Sushi, rice dishes, and noodles in an informal, cafe-like setting. Salmon roll €10.50. Yakisoba noodles with shrimp and vegetables €8. Open M-Sa 11:30am-11pm. ❸

Nikis Cafe, Nikis 3 (☎21032 34 971), near Ermou. Nestled in a lively corner, Nikis is both a light cafe (caesar salad; €7) and a bustling bar (strawberry or banana margaritas; €8). Savory crepes €5-7. Food available noon-midnight; bar open 7pm-2am. ❷

Yellow Cafe, Karageorgi Servias 9 (☎21033 19 029), on Voulis. Light streams through open windows cheerily highlighting the expected yellow walls. Enjoy smoothies like the Pink Monkey (strawberry, banana, and vanilla; €5), sandwiches (€4-5), espresso (€2.30), or mixed drinks (€4-7) to a jazz-pop soundtrack. Open daily 10am-9:30pm. ❷

Noodle Bar, Apollonos 11 (☎21033 18 585). This bright, spotless cafe offers Greek salads to please even the feta-phobic. Light options, including the wasabi salad (lettuce, tomato, cucumber, and mayo-wasabi dressing; €4) and Thai chicken coconut soup (chicken, chili, straw mushrooms, and coconut milk; €4.10), are served on glossy black tables. Take-out available. Open M-Sa 11am-midnight, Su 5:30pm-midnight. ❷

PLAKA

Plaka teems with lively dining options. During the day, ubiquitous **mini-marts** sell yogurt, spanakopita, and fresh fruit. **Vendors** roast souvlaki by the bushel, and **gelaterias** open their doors for icy treats. **Artokopos ❶**, Kydatheneon 1, across from Student and Travellers' Inn, has amazing warm bread. After nightfall, the old district's crowded streets fill with the glowing lights and live music that radiate from nearby tavernas. Wade through the small army of aggressive waiters vying for your attention, and pick from one of the many spots with uninterrupted views of the Roman Agora, Mt. Lycavittos, or the Acropolis.

Eden Vegetarian Restaurant, Lissiou 12 (☎21032 48 858; edenvegetarian.gr), corner of Mnissiklous. Pink walls, purple tablecloths, and stained-glass windows make this restaurant seem more like an eccentric Victorian teahouse than a Greek taverna, and the vegetarian menu makes it a rare paradise for those who shun meat. Souvlaki soya (€7) and vegetarian moussaka (€7) are good takes on dishes that the rest of Greece prepares with thoroughly animal-derived ingredients. The Mediterranean tart (eggplant, feta, olives, and sundried tomatoes; €6.50) is also a good option. Spicy olive paste served with the table bread is excellent. Open M, W-Su noon-midnight. ❷

Platanos, Diogenous 4 (☎21032 20 666). Just meters away from the touristy bustle of Adrianou and Kydatheneon, Platanos offers authentic, traditional fare in a secluded setting. Under a plant-draped trellis or inside the cozy taverna, diners choose from a wide-ranging menu. Tomato salad €3. Lamb with string beans €7. Open M-Sa noon-4:30pm and 7:30pm-midnight, Su noon-4:30pm. ❷

Antonis Souvlaki, Adrianou 118 (☎21032 46 838). The great deals at this tiny, unlabeled storefront would be easy to miss if not for the crowds of locals at its door. Pork kebab €1.50. Mythos beer €1.20. Open daily 10am-10pm. ❶

Amaltheia, Tripodon 16 (☎21032 24 635). The marble tables, antique mirrors, and delicate flower arrangements give a French feel to this welcoming spot, which serves sweet crepes (€3-6), yogurt desserts (€3-5), and frappés (€3). At night, warm, glowing lights illuminate the buzzing cafe. Open M-Th, Su 10am-1am, F-Sa 10am-2am. ❷

T. Stamatopoulos, Lissiou 26 (☎21032 28 722). Family-owned since 1882, this popular restaurant has a bright outdoor terrace and lively Greek music 9:30-11pm. Veal in wine sauce €7.30. Open M, W-Su 7pm-3am. ❷

Eat at Milton's, Adrianou 91 (☎21032 49 129; eatatmiltons.gr). An oasis of modern hipsterdom among ancient ruins and traditional tavernas, Eat at Milton's serves classy-cool dishes like poached salmon (€17). If that's too pricey for dinner, take a day-time dessert break (lemon cake with coconut ice cream; €7) or coffee (€2-3.50). ❹

MONASTIRAKI

A cluster of inexpensive tavernas and fresh takeaway options sits across from the metro, where Ermou meets Athinas. A kind of upscale McDonald's, **Goody's** ❶ serves inexpensive, uninspiring sandwiches, pastas, and gyros (€2-6) and attracts legions of Athenian teenagers who watch music videos in this popular chain. **Everest** ❶ (baguette sandwiches and pastries; €1-4) and **CoffeeRight** ❶, a ubiquitous espresso bar with excellent frappés (€1-3) and pastries (€2-4), are also nearby.

Savvas, Mitropoleos 86 (☎21032 45 048). Cab drivers and kiosk vendors recommend this famous souvlaki joint as the best in town. Save money by eating on the fly; restaurant prices for gyros (€6-9) shrink to €1.70 for take-out orders. Open daily 10am-3am. ❶

Mandras, Ag. Anargiron 8 (☎21032 13 765), at Taki. Live, modern Greek music plays for a young, buzzing crowd of locals in this attractive brick building in the heart of Psiri. *Pleurotous* (mushrooms grilled with oil and vinegar; €6.20) makes a great light meal. Spicy grilled chicken €9.20. Open daily 8am-4am. Music 2pm-4am. ❸

Attalos Restaurant, Adrianou 9 (☎21032 19 520), near the Thisseon area. On the edge of the Agora and the Temple of Hephaestus, outdoor tables have excellent views. Large white umbrellas and yellow tablecloths make the restaurant bright and inviting. The menu ranges from mussels *saganaki* (€5.50) to a vegetarian's dream plate of zucchini, eggplant, and tomato croquettes (serves 2-4; €8). Open daily 10am-1am. ❷

Gelatomania, Agatharho 21 (☎21032 30 001), at Taki. Ice cream has always been cool, but Gelatoma-

ESPRESS-YO' SELF

Good coffee can be hard to come by in Greece. Those who don't know how to order will find themselves sucking down cup after tedious €2 cup of instant Nescafé, the unofficial national beverage. In reality, traditional Greek coffee is on par with Italian brews and comes in a surprising variety of preparation styles. Long before the invention of *sanka*, Greek men gathered at *kafeneios* for backgammon, gossip, and good Greek java. Pull up a chair at a traditional cafe and savor the local flavor.

Steely-eyed, iron-jawed village men take their coffee *sketos*, straight from the pot and unadulterated by milk or sugar. Order just a *kafe* and it typically comes *metrios*, with one spoonful of sugar mixed in after boiling. Those with a sweet tooth should try *kafe glukus*, with a subtle honey flavor produced by boiling the sugar with grounds (*katakathi*). To get rid of the bitter surface foam, order sweet, double-boiled *kafe glukus vrastos*. Sip your coffee with some cold ice water, but don't swallow the sludge at the bottom. Hotels with kitchens almost always provide the small metal *briki* for boiling; the rule is one tablespoon per cup. Boil until a thick froth forms, then drink without stirring. Making your own *kafe* is cheaper, but you'll miss the socializing that goes with the laid-back buzz of the *kafenion*, always good to the last drop.

nia makes it trendy. The enormous glass walls of this hip parlor fold away in warm weather, so the corner spot becomes a sheltered outdoor space in the middle of buzzing bars and restaurants. Red-cushioned couches and small black tables fill the cafe, where heaping displays of homemade ice cream tempt with creative flavors like wafer and gum (one scoop; €2). A great place for day or night. Iced chocolate €3.50. Waffle with ice cream €5.50. Open daily 10am-3am. ❷

OMONIA

Fast food chains and kiosks fill the frenetic square with quick, inexpensive fare. More interesting ethnic and vegetarian options are a bit farther from the metro. Those with kitchen access should consider **Galaxias Discount Market,** 3 Septemvriou 26. At the marketplace on Athinas, between Monastiraki and Omonia, all-night restaurants satisfy stomach rumblings 3pm-7am.

Pak Indian Restaurant, Menandrou 13 (☎21032 19 412). From Omonia metro, head down P. Tsaldari (despite street sign identification, known to all as "Pireos"), turn left on Menandrou, and walk past Indian and Middle Eastern grocery import stores for 1½ blocks. Dark mirrors, earth-colored pillows, Indian lanterns, and pungent scents may make you wonder if you've stepped into a land where generic souvlaki joints are just an idle dream. Veggie *samosa* €1.50. Lamb *rogan josh* (with ginger, tomato, onions, and spices) €10. Open daily 2pm-midnight. MC/V. ❸

Healthy Food Vegetarian Restaurant, Panepistimiou 57 (☎21032 10 966). This meatless kitchen makes heaping portions of cooked vegetables and fresh fruit smoothies. Cheese pie €4.50. Open M-Sa 9am-10pm, Su 10am-4pm. ❷

Dafni Taverna, Ioulianou 65 (☎21082 13 914). From Pl. Victoria, walk down Aristotelous 2 blocks and turn right on Ioulianou. This walled-in outdoor taverna serves daily specials, on display at the counter. Simple food is authentic and satisfying. Moussaka €4.50. Lamb in lemon and olive oil €5. Open daily noon-1am. ❷

EXARHIA

Hungry 20-somethings demand cheap food around Exarhia. Many of the options are basic but tasty, with cheap, speedy souvlaki (€1-2) easily accessible at the second location of famous ▨**Savvas ❶,** on Pl. Exarhia at Spirou Trikouri 3 (☎21095 12 143), or at **Souvlaki Kavouras ❶,** Themistokleous 64.

▨ **O Barba Giannis,** Em. Benaki (☎21038 24 138). From Syndagma, walk up Stadiou and make a right on Em. Benaki; it's the yellow building on the corner with tall green doors. "Uncle John's" is informal, but that's how the locals like it—just ask the Athenian students, CEOs, and artists who count themselves among this taverna's regulars. Specials €5-10. Open M-Sa noon-1:30am. ❷

▨ **Cookou Cook,** Themistokleous 66 (☎21033 01 369). Yellow walls, mosaic tables, and eccentric decorations adorn this funky spot, which fuses creative gourmet with speed and informality. Greek salad €4.50. Stuffed tomatoes €4.50. Open M-Sa 1pm-1am. Closed 2 weeks in Aug. V. ❸

Pasta Cafe, Em. Benaki 58 (☎21038 38 186), 5min. from the Omonia metro. Glass walls and low brown booths make this small, square room feel spacious and welcoming. Feet away from his customers, the chef cooks up fresh vegetable dishes (€3-6) and flavorful pastas (€3-8). Open M-F 10am-10pm, Sa noon-8pm. ❷

Beast, Em. Benaki 45 (☎21033 00 010), near Pasta Cafe. Modern decor belies the menu's taverna flavor. Hanging lamps and small white lights illuminate this simple indoor-outdoor space where daily specials are listed on colorful photographic placemats. Pastas €5-6. Italian-influenced salads €4-5.50. Open M-Sa 1pm-midnight. ❷

CrepeXaria (☎21038 40 773), on the corner of Ikonomou and M. Themistokleous on Pl. Exarhia. Some take-out places throw your food in a styrofoam box before you dash off. Here, they wrap your concoction of choice in a warm, fresh crepe: just as fast and twice as tasty as the average doggie bag. Choose your own savory or sweet combinations—spinach, cheese, and onion (€2.80) and chocolate, strawberry, and hazelnut (€3) are particularly good. Open daily noon-5am. ●

Ama Lahei, Kalidromiou 69 (☎21038 45 978), at the foot of Strefi Hill. Big, weedy gates and a flight of stairs give this spot a sense of intrigue. Grilled salmon €10. Meatballs in tomato sauce €6.50. Open daily 8pm-2am. ●

KOLONAKI

The weekly *laiki* every Friday is your best bet if you're on a budget, but Kolonaki is more than ready to assist those who get their kicks from fine-dining splurges.

■ **Food Company,** Anagnostopoulou 47 (☎21036 16 619), on the corner of Dimokritou, 4 blocks up Lycavitto from Pl. Kolonaki. This gourmet deli displays a handful of delicious pre-prepared dishes under a glass counter. Cute and bright, the popular eatery has outdoor benches and cafe tables. Lentil salad with feta, parsley, and red peppers €4. Roast chicken with plums and olives over rice €6.50. Open daily noon-11:30pm. ●

Jackson Hall, Millioni 4 (☎21036 16 546). In Kolonaki, even the lowly hamburger can be elegant. This trendy steakhouse will charge you €13 for a New York Burger (lettuce, tomato, and onion), but the wood-paneled ambience comes free. Upstairs, the bar fills with locals at night. Chocolate mousse €6. Open daily 9:30am-2am. MC/V. ●

PANGRATI

Pl. Caravel has relaxing cafes and the large supermarket, **Veropoulos,** Formionos 23 (open M-F 8am-9pm, Sa 8am-6pm).

■ **Kallimarmaron,** Eforionos 13 (☎21070 19 727). With your back to the old Olympic Stadium, take the closest street on the right and walk 1.5 blocks. Eat like Justinian at this taverna that specializes in ancient and Byzantine recipes (typical fare is also available for those with incorrigibly modern taste). Spiced chicken on a spit €11. Filet of sardines in vine leaves €5. Open Tu-Sa noon-3pm and 8pm-1am, Su noon-3pm. DC/MC/V. ●

Posto Cafe, Pl. Plastira 2 (☎21075 10 210). In a small storefront tucked behind a large white awning, Posto's is a relaxed place for a fresh, quick bite to eat. Try the vegetable pizza (€1.50) or *spanakopita* (€1.50). ●

◉ SIGHTS

ACROPOLIS

Reach the entrance on the west side either by walking north from Areopagitou, by following the signs from Plaka, or by exiting the Agora to the south, by following the path uphill and turning right. The well-worn marble can be slippery, so wear shoes with good traction. ☎21032 10 219. Open daily 8am-7pm; in winter 8am-2:30pm. Admission includes entrance to Hadrian's Arch, the Olympian Temple of Zeus, and the Agora, within a 48hr. period. €12, students €6, under 19 free. Tickets can be purchased at any of the sites.

Some national sites become hopelessly trite over the centuries, as ceaseless reproduction of their images and exploitative tourism reduce monumentality to near meaninglessness. The Acropolis, however, has withstood such threats just as resiliently as it once repelled ancient invaders. Ever majestic, the 5th-century BC Parthenon continues to tower over the Aegean, and the Acropolis's looming structures do not fail to awe even the most jaded local eye. Visit as early in the day as possible to avoid massive crowds and the humbling midday sun.

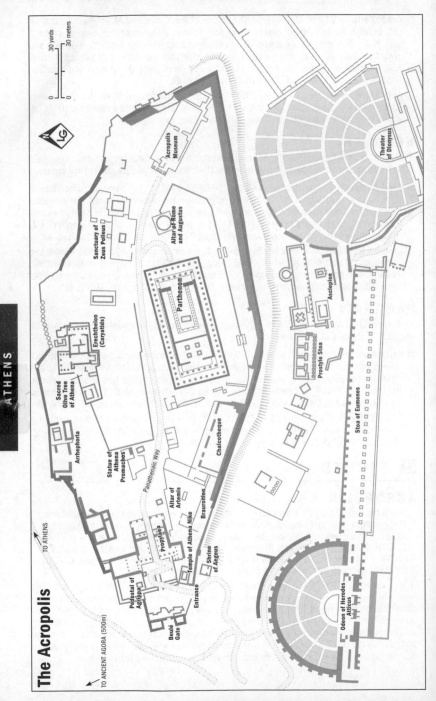

The Acropolis

TO ATHENS

TO ANCIENT AGORA (500m)

ATHENS

0   30 yards
0   30 meters

N

Beulé Gate

Pedestal of Agrippa

Propylaia

Temple of Athena Nike

Entrance

Shrine of Aegeus

Brauronion

Altar of Artemis

Panathenaic Way

Statue of Athena Promachos

Arrhephoria

Sacred Olive Tree of Athena

Erechtheion (Caryatids)

Sanctuary of Zeus Polieus

Acropolis Museum

Altar of Rome and Augustus

Parthenon

Chalcotheque

Theater of Dionysus

Asclepion

Prostyle Stoa

Stoa of Eumenes

Odeon of Herodes Atticus

HISTORY

BEGINNINGS. The area of the Acropolis was originally the tiny city of Athens, inhabited by **Mycenaeans** worshipping a nature goddess. As the fledgling *polis* grew into a sprawling military power, the strategic hilltop site was fortified into a refuge for Athenians in times of war. Wealthy **aristoi** took control of Athens in the 12th century BC, moving power downhill to the Agora and leaving the Acropolis as a purely religious site. A wooden shrine went up to Athena Polias, defender of crops and fertility, and her alter ego Pallas Athena, the city's virgin protectress.

PERICLEAN PROJECT. The Acropolis as it stands today owes much of its existence to the determination of **Pericles**. After Athens's victory against Persia left it in control of a growing empire, the Classical leader commissioned a series of grand architectural displays. Basking in post-Marathon glory, Pericles convinced members of the Delian League to donate great sums to the *polis's* beautification campaign. This imperial fundraising footed the bill to secure legendary artists including **Iktinos**, **Kallikrates**, and **Phidias**, for the site's new design. In 447 BC, a miraculous 10 years after construction commenced, they unveiled the completed **Parthenon**, dedicated to Athena. Work on the **Propylaea**, the **Temple of Athena Nike**, and the **Erechtheion** soon followed. Even in the Golden Age of Athens, however, citizens were quick to complain that Pericles's Acropolis project was excessively extravagant. Plutarch memorably blasted the leader for "gilding and bedizening" Athens like a "wanton woman adding precious stones to her wardrobe." Thankfully for modern viewers, Pericles persisted, commissioning more temples on the Acropolis, the **Hephaesteion** in the Agora, and the **Temple of Poseidon** at Sounion.

THE TEST OF TIME. Almost as soon as the Acropolis was completed, it fell to Sparta. Ever since, its function has changed whenever it changed hands, and the Parthenon's columns have welcomed the services of faiths that Athena couldn't recognize if her *aegis* depended on it. Byzantine Christians renamed it the "**Church of Agia Sophia**," worshipping there (and defacing the pagan sculptures) until **Frankish Crusaders** made the building a fortified palace for the Dukes de la Roche in 1205. Catholics came to use the space as a church again, dedicating it to **Notre Dame d'Athènes**, and by the 15th century **Ottoman** rulers had cast it as a mosque.

Throughout these identity crises, the Acropolis's buildings themselves remained remarkably intact—at least until a Venetian siege in 1687, when the attackers' shells accidentally blew up a Turkish supply of gunpowder stored under the Parthenon's roof. Its structure has deteriorated since then; by the dawn of the 19th century, British Lord Elgin was blithely chiseling the most stunning marble reliefs off of the Parthenon and carting them to London, where they remain, displayed in the British Museum and the subject of much controversy. Large-scale restoration efforts on the Acropolis have also caused concern, and much of the Parthenon statuary that Elgin didn't make off with has recently been relocated to the Acropolis Museum to shelter it from acid rain. Still, there's something awe-inspiring about the fact that almost all the damage dealt to Pericles's buildings over the millennia has been done by human hands, not gravity or the elements.

RUINS

The first structure within the site's gate is the reconstructed **Temple of Athena Nike**. Along the path where a Classical ramp once lay, visitors walk through the Roman **Beulé Gate**, named for the French archaeologist who unearthed it, past the **Propylaea**, the unfinished entrance attributed to Mnesikles. Famous for its ambitious multi-story design, the Propylaea combines Ionic columns with a Doric exterior.

⧆ PARTHENON. The ancient architect Iktinos, who designed the **Temple of Athena Parthenos**, more commonly known as the "Parthenon," was not the kind of person who glosses over details. Instead of the typical six, he placed eight columns at the front of the temple. Fearing that perspective would make them look spindly from a low vantage point, Iktinos made each column bulge ever so slightly to create an optical illusion of perfect symmetry. When it came time to plot the temple's dimensions, he followed a meticulous four to nine ratio, a variation on the aesthetically-ideal Golden Mean. Iktinos's obsession with proportion and order, traits that came to epitomize Classical architecture, pushed the Parthenon past traditional Doric boxiness into the sublime.

ATHENS FOR POCKET CHANGE. Budget travelers, rejoice: you're in Athens, where the wine is cheap, the food is cheaper, and the sights are (almost) free. Most of the ruins are outdoors, letting visitors ramble around the **Rock of Saint Paul** (p. 122), the **Philopappos Monument** (p. 117), and **Mount Lycavittos** (p. 118) without dropping a euro. After leaving your bags at the **Student's and Traveler's Inn** (p. 105), pick up local wine, beer, or juice (€1-3) from a corner kiosk and a gyro (€1-2) from **Savvas** (p. 109), and picnic at 1 of these ancient sights with great Acropolis views. Also note that the **Benaki Museum of Islamic Art** (p. 120) is free on Wednesday, the **Ilias Lalounis Jewelry Museum** (p. 121) is free on Wednesday after 3pm and on Saturday 9-11am, and the **War Museum** (p. 120) and **Popular Musical Instruments Museum** (p. 121) never have admission fees.

Ancient Athenians saw their city as the capital of civilization, and the **metopes** (scenes in the open spaces above the columns) which once bordered the sides of the Parthenon celebrated Athens's rise to such greatness. On the far right of the southern side, the Lapiths battled the Centaurs, while on the east the Olympian gods triumphed over the Titans. The north side faintly depicted the victory of the Greeks over the Trojans and the western facade reveled in Athens's triumph over the Amazons. A frieze around the interior walls showed a group of Athenians mingling with gods. The **pediments** at either end marked the zenith of Classical decorative sculpture. The **east pediment** once depicted Athena's birth, while the **west pediment** showed Athena and Poseidon's contest for the city's devotion. Many of these celebratory pieces, damaged over the centuries, are now in London's British Museum or in the Acropolis Museum.

Inside the temple, in front of a pool of water, stood Phidias's greatest sculptural feat: a 40 ft. tall gold and ivory statue of Athena. Although the statue has since been destroyed, the National Museum houses a 2nd-century Roman copy, which is fearsomely grand even at one-twelfth the original size.

TEMPLE OF ATHENA NIKE. This tiny temple was constructed in the middle of the Peloponnesian War, during a brief respite known as the "Peace of Nikias" (421-415 BC). Ringed by eight miniature Ionic columns, it housed a statue of winged Nike, the goddess of victory. When the Athenians were seized by a paranoid fear that Nike would flee and take any chance of victory in the renewed war, they clipped the statue's wings. The remains of the 5m thick **Cyclopean wall** which once surrounded the entire Acropolis lie below this temple.

ERECHTHEION. The Erechtheion, to the left of the Parthenon, was built in 406 BC, just before Sparta defeated Athens in the Peloponnesian War. It is named after a snake-bodied hero whom Poseidon speared in a dispute over the city's patronage. When Poseidon struck a truce with Athena, he was allowed to share her temple—the eastern half is devoted to the goddess of wisdom and the western part to the trident-bearing god of the sea. The eastern porch, with its six Ionic columns, contained an olive-wood statue of Athena; like the Temple of Athena Nike, it contrasts with the Parthenon's dignified Doric columns. The Erechtheion's southern side is supported by six women frozen in stone, the Caryatids. They're actually copies, as all the originals except one are safe in the Acropolis Museum.

■ **ACROPOLIS MUSEUM.** The Acropolis Museum is arguably the most striking part of the entire complex, with a collection composed exclusively of master-pieces. Visitors are welcome to peer at the treasures, inches from their surfaces and far from (most of) the tourist mob and the beating sun. Five of the original Erechtheion **Caryatids** appear monumentally huge in their small glass casement. From the stiff Archaic **calf-bearer** to the Classical **Kritios Boy,** Greek artists' develop-ment of anatomical detail and emotional expression is on fine display. Notice the empty space where room has been left for the British to return the missing Elgin marbles. *(Open M 11am-7pm, Tu-Su 8am-7pm; low season M 11am-2pm, Tu-Su 8am-2pm. No flash photography. English labels. Avoid going 10am-1pm, when it is most crowded.)*

ELSEWHERE ON THE ACROPOLIS. The southwestern corner of the Acropolis looks down over the reconstructed **Odeon of Herodes Atticus,** a functional theater dating from the Roman period (AD 160). Consult *Athens News* for schedules. You'll also see nearby ruins of the **Classical Theater of Dionysus, the Asclepion,** and the **Stoa of Eumenes II.** *(Entrance on Dionysiou Areopagitou. ☎ 21032 32 771. Open daily 9am-2pm and 6-9pm. Though the Odeon is closed to general admission, performances are held throughout the summer. Tickets around €30, but range €20-500. Students with ID, children 6-18, large groups or families, and tickets in the upper tier and D zone half price. Theater open M-Sa 8am-7pm. €2, students €1, visitors with an Acropolis ticket free. MC/V.)*

AGORA

Enter the Agora either off Pl. Thission, off Adrianou, or as you descend from the Acropolis. ☎ 21032 10 185. Guide pamphlets provided, but extra resources recommended. Open daily 8am-7:30pm. €4; students and seniors €2; EU students, under 18, and visitors with an Acropolis ticket free.

If the Acropolis was the showpiece of the ancient capital, the Agora was its heart and soul, serving as the city's marketplace, administrative center, and focus of daily life from the 6th century BC through the AD 6th century. Many of the great debates of Athenian democracy were held here; Socrates, Aristotle, Demos-thenes, Xenophon, and St. Paul all instructed in its stalls. After its original hey-day, the Agora, like the Acropolis, passed through the hands of innumerable conquerors. The ancient market emerged again in the 19th century, when a resi-dential area built above it was razed for excavations.

■ **HEPHAESTEION.** The Hephaesteion, on a hill in the northwestern corner of the Agora, is the best-preserved Classical temple in Greece. The 415 BC temple retains some of its original **friezes,** which depict Hercules's labors and the adven-tures of Athenian hero Theseus.

ODEON OF AGRIPPA. The Odeon of Agrippa, a concert hall built for Roman Emperor Augustus's son-in-law and right-hand man, now stands in ruins on the left of the Agora as you walk from the museum to the Hephaesteion. When the roof collapsed in AD 150, the Odeon was rebuilt at half its former size. From then on, it served as a lecture hall. The actors' dressing room was turned into a porch sup-ported by colossal statues, three of which still guard the site.

STOA OF ATTALOS. The elongated Stoa of Attalos, home to informal philoso-phers' gatherings, was a multi-purpose building filled with shops. Attalos II, King of Pergamon, built the Stoa in the 2nd century BC as a gift to Athens, where he had received his education. Reconstructed between 1953 and 1956, it now houses the

Agora Museum, which contains relics from the site. The stars of the collection are the **black figure paintings** by Exekias and a **calyx krater** depicting Trojans and Greeks quarreling over the body of Patroclus, Achilles's closest companion and possible lover. (☎ 21032 10 185. Open daily 8am-7:20pm.)

STOA BASILEIOS. Plato reports that Socrates's first trial was held at the recently excavated Stoa Basileios, or **Royal Stoa.** It served as the headquarters for the ancient Athenian political and religious figure known as the "King Archon." (As you cross the metro tracks at the Adrianou exit, it's on the left.)

OTHER ANCIENT SITES

ROMAN AGORA. The Roman Agora was a large rectangular structure built between 19 and 11 BC with donations from Julius and Octavian Caesar. The ruined columns of the two surviving **prophylae,** a nearly intact entrance gate, and the **gate of Athena Archgetis** stand as testaments to what was once a major meeting place for Athenians. Proving that people take interest in anything as long as it's old, the AD first-century **vespasianae,** or public toilets, are a popular site. A mosque dating from 1456 sits nearby. Yet by far the Agora's most intriguing structure is the well-preserved (and restored) **Tower of the Winds.** This octagonal stone tower, built in the first century BC by the astronomer Andronikos, was initially crowned with a weathervane. The top of each side of the tower has a carving of the personification of each of the eight winds. On the walls are markings that allowed the structure to be used as a sundial from the outside and a water-clock from the inside. Since its construction, the tower has also functioned as a church and a Dervish monastery. (☎ 21032 45 220. Open daily 8am-7:30pm. €2; students €1; EU students, under 19, and visitors with an Acropolis ticket free.)

TEMPLE OF ZEUS AND HADRIAN'S ARCH. Fifteen majestic Corinthian columns—the remnants of the largest temple ever built in Greece, dedicated to Zeus—stand on the edge of the National Gardens. Several shifts in power delayed the temple's completion until AD 131 under Hadrian's reign, six centuries after its first stones were set. To commemorate his monumental feat, Hadrian built an adjacent arch with two inscriptions. Facing the Acropolis, the arch reads "This is Athens, the ancient city of Theseus." On the other side, facing the emperor's addition, it proclaims, "This is the city of Hadrian and not of Theseus." Nearby, at Vas. Olgas and Amalias, is a memorial to a man whose ambitions were a bit less worldly, though no less grand: the English Romantic poet Lord Byron, who lost his life fighting for Greek independence. (Entrance on Vas. Olgas at Amalias, across from the entrance to the National Garden. ☎ 21092 26 330. Open daily 8am-5pm. Temple admission €2, students €1, under 19 free. Arch free. A €12 ticket gives access to the arch, the Acropolis, the theater of Dionysus, the Ancient Agora, the Roman Agora, and the Keramikos.)

KERAMIKOS. Most sites in the Agora are more dead than alive, but the Keramikos is especially so, as it includes a large cemetery built around a segment of the **Sacred Way,** the road to Eleusis. The Sacred Gate arched over this road, which was lined with **public tombs** for state leaders, famous authors, and battle victims. Worshippers began the annual Panathenaic procession along its path. Also within the site is a section of the 40m wide boulevard that ran through the Agora and Diplyon Gate and ended at the sanctuary of Akademes, where **Plato** founded his Academy in the 4th century BC. The **Oberlaender Museum** displays finds from the burial sites; its pottery and sculpture are highlights. (Northwest of the Agora; archaeological site begins at the acute angle where Ermou and Pireos intersect. From Syndagma, walk toward Monastiraki on Ermou for 1km. ☎ 21034 63 552. Open Tu-Su 8:30am-7pm. €2, non-EU students and EU seniors €1; EU students, under 19, and visitors with an Acropolis ticket free.)

PHILOPAPPOS HILL. Philopappos Hill, just southwest of the Acropolis and Agora, is a lush respite from park-deprived Athens. A marble road weaves past **Agios Dimitrious** and the serene cafe in back, where you're likely to stumble upon a wedding ceremony. According to legend, Dimitrious persuaded God to smite 17th-century Turkish invaders with lightning before they could harm the worshipers in this small, icon-filled church. Just before Ag. Dimitrious, a narrow dirt path veers off toward a stone cave with plain iron bars. This non-descript opening was once, as a small sign indicates, **Socrates's Prison;** check out the shadows cast on its wall and you might catch a glimpse of an ideal form or two. Farther upwards, toward the Acropolis, are the ruins of **Pnyx Hill,** where the Athenian Assembly once met, and the **Hill of the Nymphs,** which looks out on an ancient observatory.

The peak, where the marble **Monument of Philopappos** stands, has Athens's best view of the Acropolis. The angles and distance that render the view so breathtaking also made the Acropolis an unfortunate target in 1687. It was from this peak that the disastrous Venetian volley was shot, detonating the Parthenon's gunpowder stores. The small but elaborate monument was erected between AD 114-116 in memory of Julius Antiochus Philopappos, a Roman dignitary who settled on the hill after being exiled from his home in the Near Eastern kingdom of Commagene.

HADRIAN'S LIBRARY. Just north of the Roman Agora, by the Monastiraki metro station, are ruins that give new meaning to the phrase "rise and fall." Hadrian's Library, situated around a large central courtyard, was originally built in AD 132, damaged by a Herulian invasion in 267, then rebuilt from 407 to 412. The ruins of a 5th-century church, a 7th-century church, and a 12th-century cathedral sit on the same site. (☎ 21032 49 350. Open M-F 8am-2pm. €2, students €1, EU students free.)

BYZANTINE ATHENS

Hours depend on each church's priest; mornings are best. Modest dress required.

Athens teems with places to pray. Sanctuaries pepper tiny streets, squeeze between modern buildings, and hide under porticos, their modest facades almost overwhelmed by modern architecture. Inside their doors, ornate, icon-filled rooms unfold, dimly lit and smelling of incense. If no service is in session (services usually Su morning or 6pm every evening), a recording of chanting may be playing.

Many historians see Constantine's establishment of a Christian empire in 324 BC as a death-knell for Classical culture. But the 11th- and 12th-century golden age of Byzantine art has left behind its own share of masterpieces—devotional mosaics, delicate icons, and cross-shaped domed buildings—many of which can be found on the streets of Athens. **Kapnikaria Church,** sunk just below ground-level on Ermou and Kalamiotou, has typically Byzantine architecture; the frescoes inside are by a 20th-century painter, Photis Koruglou. Dedicated to the Virgin Mary, this church was built above the ruins of a temple to a female goddess, probably Athena or Demeter. Down Mitropoleos from Syndagma, where the street intersects with Evangelistras and Pandrossou, are **Agios Eleftherios** and the **Mitropoli Cathedral,** under construction after a recent earthquake. A frieze with the Attic calendar of feast days adorns the front facade. **Agia Apostoli,** which stands at the eastern edge of the Agora on Dioskouron and Polingnotou, dates from the early 11th century, making it one of Athens's oldest churches. White-walled **Metamorphosis,** on Theorias and Klepsidras, off Pritanou in Plaka, was also built in the 11th century, and was restored in 1956. Eleventh-century Russian Orthodox **Agia Triada,** a few blocks from Pl. Syndagma at Filellinon 21, is filled with silver angel icons. Farther on Filellinon is the **Sotira Lykodimou,** the largest medieval building in Athens, dating from 1031. Built as part of a Roman Catholic monastery, it is now a Russian Orthodox church. In **Ambelokipi,** north of Kolonaki next to Areos Park, Byzantine religiosity meets modern commercial development rather jarringly. Tiny **Panagitsa** (little Virgin) sits literally in the middle of Alexandros Hotel's driveway on T. Vassou, and 11th-century **Agioi Pantes** sleeps humbly at the back entrance of the Panathenaic stadium on A. Tsochas. The **Chapel of Saint George,** another small but elaborate structure, looms over Athens from the peak of Mt. Lycavittos, on top of a ruined temple to Zeus.

MODERN ATHENS

■**MOUNT LYCAVITTOS.** From the peak of Mt. Lycavittos, the tallest of Athens's seven hills, visitors can see every inch of the city. A **funicular** rail (2min.; every 15-30min. 9am-3pm; round-trip €4, under 5 free) travels to the top, and a trail from Ploutarchou in **Kolonaki** takes about 15-20min. Hikers should bring water, watch out for cacti and slippery rocks, and not climb alone, especially at night. The quaint **Chapel of Saint George** and a pricey restaurant sit at the peak. You'd be missing the point, though, if you didn't take a few minutes to appreciate the astounding 360° view, spanning from the mountains, over the Acropolis, to the water. Using the Acropolis as a point of reference, the neighborhoods of Monastiraki, Omonia, and Exarhia are on your right. Continuing clockwise, you will see Areos Park behind the small circular patch of green that is Strefi, another of the seven hills. The flashy lights and music of the Lycavittos Theater are 180° from the Acropolis. The eastern view gazes down onto more parks and Mt. Hymettus, and offers a glimpse of the Panathenaic Olympic Stadium, the National Garden, and the Temple of Olympian Zeus back toward the Acropolis.

PANATHENAIC STADIUM. Also known as the "Kallimarmaro" ("Pretty Marble"), the Panathenaic Stadium is wedged between the National Gardens and Pangrati, carved into a hill. The Byzantines destroyed the Classical stadium, but in 1895 it was restored in Panteli marble. The stadium was the site of the first modern Olympic Games in 1896 and lay under a cloud of disappointment in 1996 when the centennial games were held in Atlanta. Still, in 1997, it held the opening ceremonies of the World Track and Field Championships and is the perennial finish line of the **Athens Marathon,** which begins 42km (26.2 mi.) away in Marathon. Seventy thousand people can pack in the stands of this marble preserve for athletes and sunbathing students; military parades and gymnastic displays are held here as well. Marble steles near the front honor Greece's gold and silver medalists. The stadium was refurbished once again for 2004's Olympic Games, where it served as the finish line for marathon events that matched Phidippides's 490 BC route (p. 126). *(On Vas. Konstantinou. From Syndagma, walk up Amalias 15min. to Vas Olgas, and follow it to the left. Or take trolley #2, 4, or 11 from Syndagma. Open daily 8am-8:30pm. Free.)*

AROUND SYNDAGMA. Every hour on the hour, a small but eager crowd of attentive tourists assembles in front of the Parliament building to witness the **changing of the guard.** In precisely seven minutes, the *euzones* (guardsmen) on duty synchronize a series of jerky marionette moves that lead them away from their posts. Once new guards are in place, an attendant hurriedly adjusts ruffled collars and stray hairs. Longer, more elaborate ceremonies take place on Sundays at 11am.

The ■**National Gardens** sprawl serenely behind the Parliament building. Broad stripes of white gravel weave past patches of dense plant life, artificial ponds, and the occasional fallen column. A quiet refuge in the middle of Athens's busiest center, the gardens have shade and plenty of places to sit. Near the Zappeion, a building of exhibition and conference halls, are less natural diversions: an outdoor movie theater and a breezy patio restaurant. The park's dingy zoo is its least attractive (though perhaps most amusing) draw. A handful of ostriches wander as peacocks flash their long wings at the stray dogs barking nearby.

OUTDOOR MARKETS. Athens's markets attract bargain-hunters, browsers, award-winning chefs, and a lot of *yiayias* (grandmothers dressed in widows' black). The **Flea Market,** adjacent to Pl. Monastiraki, is like a festive garage sale where old forks and teapots are sold alongside family heirlooms. Try to go on a Sunday. *(Open M, W, Sa-Su 8am-8pm.)* **Varnakios,** the biggest outdoor food market in Athens, is on Athinas between Armodiou and Aristogeitonos. *(Open M-Th 6am-7pm, F-Sa 5am-8pm.)* Not for the faint of heart, the **meat market,** which closes at 3pm, overwhelms with the sights and smells of livers, kidneys, and skinned rabbits. Early risers can jostle with Athenian cooks for choice meats, fish, fruits, vegetables, breads, and cheeses. Moving farmers' markets, or *laikes,* pulsate throughout central Athens, stopping every morning to take over a specific *stenodthromos* (narrow street) in one particular neighborhood of the city. Other than following a trail of corn shucks and peanut shells, the best way to track them is to call the Athens office of **Laikes Agores,** Zoödochou Pigis 2-4 (☎21038 07 560).

NATIONAL CEMETERY. The National Cemetery in **Pangrati** provides a morbid thrill for anyone obsessed with obscure antiquity or the mildly famous. Within its gates are the graves of politicians, actors, poets, and foreigners who died in Athens, from archaeologist **Heinrich Schliemann,** excavator of Troy and Mycenae, to **Melina Mercury,** the Greek film icon who starred in *Never on Sunday* before becoming the nation's Minister of Culture. There is a chapel on the main path where ceremonies are held. *(From Pl. Syndagma walk down Amalias, turn left on Ath. Diakou, and then walk down Anapavseos. ☎21092 36 118. Open daily in summer 8am-8pm; in winter 8am-6pm. Free. For guided tours call the Cultural Center, Akademias 50, at ☎21036 12 705; if it is closed, call the cemetery office directly. Modest dress required.)*

🏛 MUSEUMS

🖼 NATIONAL ARCHAEOLOGICAL MUSEUM

Patission 44. A 20min. walk from Pl. Syndagma down Stadiou to Aiolou. Turn right onto Patission. Take trolley #2, 4, 5, 9, 11, 15, or 18 from the uphill side of Syndagma or trolley #3 or 13 from the north side of Vas. Sofias. Or take the metro to Victoria and after exiting, walk straight to the 1st street, 28 Oktovriou. Turn right and walk 5 blocks. ☎21082 17 717. Open Apr.-Oct. Tu-Su 8:30am-3pm; Nov.-Mar. M 10:30am-5pm, Tu-Su 8:30am-3pm. €6, students and EU seniors €3, EU students and under 19 free. No flash photography; no posing in front of exhibits.

The National Archaeological Museum's collection consists almost exclusively of masterpieces. Countless spectacular objects trace the rich development of Greek art through its many successive periods. Heinrich Schliemann's golden **Mask of Agamemnon** (p. 149) shines brilliantly despite having belonged to a king who lived at least 300 years before the mythic Mycenaean leader, and a female **Cycladic statue** stands as not only the most intact but the largest such sculpture to survive, topping 1.5m. Abundant **kouroi** (p. 69) from the 8th century BC onward lead toward the Classical bronze **spear thrower** who represents either Poseidon or Zeus. In the museum's lovely basement garden, mosaics and more sculptures line a cafe.

OTHER MUSEUMS

🖼 BENAKI MUSEUM. Over the course of his travels through Europe and Asia, philanthropist Antoine Benaki assembled a formidable collection of artwork and artifacts. They're now displayed (along with numerous additions) in his former home, a looming, white Neoclassical structure that is something of a masterpiece itself. Among the diverse media represented are Neolithic, Classical, and

Roman Period sculpture, Geometric pottery, traditional Greek costumes, and wonderfully recreated Byzantine period rooms. The museum also exhibits metalwork, jewelry, and paintings, which focus primarily on the Greek War of Independence. *(Vas. Sofias and Koumbari 1 in Kolonaki. ☎ 21036 71 000; www.benaki.gr. Open M, W, F-Sa 9am-5pm, Th 9am-midnight, Su 9am-3pm. €6; seniors and adults with children €3; students with ISIC or university ID, teachers, and journalists free.)*

■ BENAKI MUSEUM OF ISLAMIC ART. Large glass windows, spotless marble staircases, and sparkling white walls give a new-minted sheen to this fabulous museum, which opened in 2005. Organized chronologically, the collection of brilliantly colored, well-preserved tiles, metalwork, and tapestries documents the history of the Islamic world from the 12th to 18th centuries. The exhibit includes many examples of pottery and text with elegant Kufic inscriptions, as well as a marble reception room transported from a 17th-century Cairo mansion. The basement exhibits a ruin as exciting as it is out of place: during the construction of the museum, builders discovered parts of the famed Themistoclean Wall, which the Greeks built in 478 BC to defend against Persian invaders. *(Ag. Asomaton 22 on Dipylou, in Psiri near Thissiou metro. ☎ 21032 51 311; www.benaki.gr. Open Tu, Th-Su 9am-3pm, W 9am-9pm. €5, students and seniors €3; W free.)*

GOULANDRIS MUSEUM OF CYCLADIC AND ANCIENT GREEK ART. This 19-year-old museum houses a comprehensive collection of early Aegean art, ranging from 3000 BC to AD 300. Hundreds of clay pots, painted amphoras, and pieces of jewelry fill the compact space. The celebrated marble Cycladic figurines, one of them almost life-size, are prized possessions. A glass corridor leads visitors to the extension, a recently renovated Neoclassical house which holds further information and temporary exhibitions. *(Neophytou Douka 4. Walk 20min. toward Kolonaki from Syndagma on Vas. Sofias; turn left on Neophytou Douka. It's half a block up. Accessible by trolleys #3 and 13. ☎ 21072 28 321. Open M, W-F 10am-4pm, Su 10am-3pm. €5, seniors and students €2.50, archaeologists and archaeology students free with university pass.)*

■ BYZANTINE AND CHRISTIAN MUSEUM. Within its newly renovated glass and marble interior, this well-organized museum documents the political, religious, and mundane aspects of life during the Byzantine Empire. Its collection of metalware, mosaics, sculpture, and painted icons presents Christianity in its earliest stages, emphasizing how the fledgling religion sprung out of a largely polytheistic culture. One display describes the conversion of the Parthenon into the Church of Agia Sofia. Videos and photographs of the artifacts' original locations put them in context. A post-Byzantine collection is scheduled to open in 2006. *(Vas. Sofias 22. ☎ 21072 11 027. Open Tu-Su 8:30am-3pm. €4; students and seniors €2; EU students, under 18, disabled persons and an escort, families with 3 or more children, members of the Chamber of Fine Arts of Greece, persons serving in the armed forces, and classicists free.)*

NATIONAL GALLERY. The Gallery, also known as "the Alexander Soutzos Museum," traces Greek artists' experiments with Orientalism, Impressionism, Symbolism, Cubism, and more, from the 18th to the 21st centuries. Greece's War of Independence is memorialized in the ground floor's 19th-century portraits and other images. This floor also houses a handful of older paintings by masters from Italy, France, the Netherlands, and Spain, including several notable works by Domenikos Theotokopoulos, whose peers in late Renaissance Toledo found his Cretan origin notable enough to dub him "El Greco." The second floor shows more conceptual contemporary works and has space for temporary exhibits. *(Vas. Konstantinou 50, where Vas. Konstantinou meets Vas. Sofias by the Hilton. ☎ 21072 35 857 or 21072 35 937. Open M, W-Sa 9am-3pm, Su 10am-2pm; temporary exhibit also open M, W 6-9pm. €6.50, students and seniors €3.50, under 12 free.)*

WAR MUSEUM. The War Museum, in a fortress-like building itself, documents Greece's martial history with weapons and uniforms from ancient times until the present. Relevant newspaper clippings, letters from soldiers, flags, and photographs complement detailed curatorial descriptions of battles and their outcomes. A small room contains artifacts from the extended conflict in Cyprus. The outside of the museum is guarded by tanks, cannons, and fighter jets that visitors can explore. *(Rizari 2, next to the Byzantine Museum, slightly off Vas. Sofias. ☎21072 52 974. Open Tu-F 9am-2pm, Su 9:30am-2pm. Free.)*

POPULAR MUSICAL INSTRUMENTS MUSEUM. This interactive museum is no place for silent contemplation. Audio headsets reproduce the music of the *kementzes* (bottle-shaped lyres) and *tsambouras* (goatskin bagpipes) on display. Exhibits showcase antique instruments from the 18th, 19th, and 20th centuries. *(Diogenous 1-2 in Plaka. Going uphill on Pelopida, it's the green door on your left directly after you pass the Roman Agora. ☎21032 50 198. Open Tu, Th-Su 10am-2pm, W noon-6pm. Free.)*

ILIAS LALAOUNIS JEWELRY MUSEUM. At this unusual museum, you can see the more dazzling aspects of human history. Lalaounis, the 20th-century Greek jeweler and goldsmith who lived at the site of the museum, created masterpieces inspired by civilizations from the Byzantines to the Vikings, and by structures as basic as the web-like pattern formed by microscopic human cells. His designs are joined here by the gleaming adornments worn by people through the ages—"from prehistoric man to contemporary woman." *(Kallisperi 12, south of the Acropolis. ☎21092 21 044. Open M, Th-Sa 9am-4pm, W 9am-9pm, Su 11am-4pm. €3, students and seniors €2.30. Free W 3-9pm, Sa 9-11am.)*

FOLK ART MUSEUM. For a crash course in Greek cultural history, visit this well-organized collection of traditional costumes, metalwork, ceramics, embroidery, and other art created outside the academy. One room, covered in murals by the folk artist Theophilos Chatzimichael, has been transported intact from its original house. The informative, enchanting little museum also hosts temporary exhibitions. *(Kydatheneon 17, in Plaka. ☎21032 13 018. Open Tu-Su 10am-2pm. €2, students €1, EU students and children free.)*

JEWISH MUSEUM. This collection documents over two millennia of Jewish life in Greece with letters, costumes, photographs, religious items, and reconstructed spaces including the interior of Patras's old synagogue and a living room from the Ottoman period. The museum's fourth floor memorializes the tens of thousands of Greek Jews murdered by the Nazis and the resistance groups who fought to save them. The exhibit also highlights the tiny Jewish community of about 5000 remaining in Greece today. *(Nikis 39, in Plaka. ☎/fax 21032 25 582. Open M-F 9am-2:30pm, Su 10am-2pm. Library open Tu, Th 11am-1pm, by appointment. €5, students and seniors €3.)*

FRISSIRAS MUSEUM OF CONTEMPORARY EUROPEAN PAINTING. This marvelously modern museum's location in the center of the Old City makes its white galleries and asymmetrical architecture still more striking. The collection itself rotates, and is comprised of contemporary painting that focuses on the human figure. The second building, about 70m from the first, houses temporary exhibitions. *(Monis Asteriou 3 and 7, off Kydatheneon in Plaka. ☎21032 34 678; www.frissirasmuseum.com. Open W-F 10am-5pm, Sa-Su 11am-5pm. €6; AICA, groups of 4 or more, members of the Chamber of Arts, over 65, students of schools of Fine Arts, under 25 €3; guides, members of ICOM, students of schools of Fine Arts, and persons with special needs free.)*

▨ NIGHTLIFE

Many already-lively neighborhoods burst with life after dark. Quiet cafes become festive bars; restaurants vibrate with buzzing chatter and live music; outdoor theaters unlock their doors; people swarm around brilliantly-illuminated ruins; and late-night clubgoers get the parties started. Athens offers an abundant array of unique entertainment, ranging from **movie screenings** in the

National Gardens to live performances at the **Odeon of Herod Atticus** (☎21092 82 900; hellenicfestival.gr). The English-language monthly magazine *InsideOut* offers valuable information on events and festivals in Athens.

PLAKA

Locals avoid joining Acropolis-bound tourists during the day, but they flock to ancient sights at night. Enormous, bright outdoor lights make most of the city's famous ruins breathtakingly visible from any modest height. Before hitting the inviting bars below, join young Athenians wandering about the **Odeon** theater, hanging out in the **Acropolis**, or playing guitar and sharing beers on **Saint Paul's Rock.** You might also catch the views from one of Athens's several outdoor rooftop movie theaters. **Cine Paris**, Kydatheneon 22 (☎21032 25 482), plays Hollywood films with Greek subtitles and sells movie posters. (Shows 8:45 and 11:10pm. Tickets €7.30.) **Bretto's**, Kydatheneon 41 (☎21032 32 110), between Farmaki and Afroditis, serves almost exclusively local alcohol. Colorful bottles, giant barrels, and other ouzo paraphernalia line the walls of this one-room establishment, while mellow but upbeat crowds sample native drinks. €5 per bottle of sweet red wine; €2 per glass. Open daily 10am-midnight.

MONASTIRAKI AND PSIRI

The district's two neighborhoods follow opposite clocks. Just when the frenetic market roads of Monastiraki shut down for the day and silence finally reigns, the bar-heavy, club-speckled streets of Psiri awaken to prove their reputation as some of Athens's hippest and loudest.

☒ I Psyrri, Miaouli 19 (☎21032 44 046). Kitsch is cool at this spot, where the chintzy wallpaper and 1950s posters somehow don't clash with the contemporary music. Cafe by day, bar by night, I Psyrri's outdoor area is crowded with locals. Coffee €3. Mixed drinks €7. Open daily 10am-late.

Beast, Lepeniotou 1. Young Athenians sit in the cushioned enclaves of this dimly-lit, cavernous bar, drinking *sangria* (€6) and beers (€3-5). Open daily 8pm-late.

Bee, Miaouli 6 (☎21032 12 624), off Ermou at the corner of Miaouli and Themidos and a few blocks from the heart of Psiri. A hive of neon-colored plastic lights, Bee offers margaritas (€9) and other mixed drinks (€7) on a busy corner whose tables provide opportunity for endless people-watching. Open M-Th 7pm-3am, F-Sa 7pm-6am.

Soul, Evripidou 65 (☎21033 10 907), in Psiri, plays hip-hop, R&B, and dance music in a chic garden. Open May-Sept. M-Th, Su 9:30am-3:30am, F-Sa 9:30am-5am.

Revekka, Miaouli 22 (☎21032 11 174), on Pl. Iroön, in the center of Psiri. This 2-floored eclectic cafe-bar blossoms at night, when tables take over the sidewalk and darkness invites music and flowing drinks. Beer €2. Open daily 11am-5am.

EXARHIA

Exarhia is the student crowd's counter-culture heaven. Energetic bars fill the streets, blasting music from jazz to death metal. *Athens News* has lists of movies played at the outdoor **Riviera Garden Art Cinema,** Valtetsiou 46 (€7, students €5).

Rock Underground, Metaxa 21 (☎21038 22 019). Punky teenagers enjoy the immortal pairing of heavy-metal headbanging and backgammon in this smoky, brick-walled hangout. The sign hanging out front that mimics the logo of London's Tube system hints at the slightly British flavor of the hard rock reverberating through this cafe-bar. Beer €2-5. Mixed drinks €5. Open daily 10am-3am.

Wunderbar, Themistokleous 80 (☎21038 18 577), on Pl. Exarhia, plays pop and some electronic music. Local DJs often spin. Star-shaped paper lanterns decorate the interior, while late-night revelers lounge under large umbrellas outside. Beer €5-6. Mixed drinks €8-9. Open M-Th 9am-3am, F-Su 9am-sunrise.

Korso, Em. Benaki 72 (☎21038 42 077). High celings, bright walls, and Pollock-esque paintings characterize this breezy spot, where alternative music sets the background for board games or rounds of drinks. Frappé €3. Open daily 10am-2am.

KOLONAKI

Haritos, to the right of Plutarchou, and **Millioni** are the hottest spots for summertime action as long as you're prepared to shell out major euros for your buzz. At **City, Azul, Baila,** and **Mousa,** all at Haritos 43, sophisticated patrons sip beer (€5-6) and mixed drinks (€8-10) on tables that spill into the street. Summertime performances are staged in Lycavittos Theater as part of the **Athens Festival,** which has hosted acts from the Greek Orchestra to Pavarotti to the Talking Heads. The **Festival Office,** Stadiou 4, sells student tickets. An English-language schedule of events is available in mid-June. (☎21032 21 459. Tickets range €10-110. Open M-Sa 8am-4pm, Su 9am-2pm and 6-9pm.) In summer, open-air **Dexameni** cinema, in Pl. Dexameni on Lycavittos, plays movies. (☎21036 02 363. Shows daily 8:45, 11pm. €7, students €5, children under 5 free.) **Athinaia,** Haritos 50, is another outdoor movie theater. (☎21072 15 717. Shows 9, 11pm. €6.50.)

Flower, Dorylaou 2 (☎21064 32 111), in Pl. Mavili. An intimate little dive, Flower offers drinks in a casual, mellow setting. Shots €3. Mixed drinks €5. Open daily 6pm-late.

The Daily, Xenokratous 47 (☎21072 23 430), nestles under a covered trellis at the foot of Mt. Lycavittos. TVs show sports games and reggae rocks quietly at this cozy cafe-bar. Open-air seating in summer. Pints of Heineken €3.50, 0.5L €5.50. Mixed drinks €6. Open daily 9am-2am.

Briki, Dorylaou 6 (☎21064 52 380), in Pl. Mavili next door to Flower, is a retro bar with mod geometric-patterned lights and hanging decorations. Snack on free sliced cucumber and green olives splashed with vinegar. Martinis €7. Margaritas €7.50. Open daily 8am-3:30am, Sa-Su 8am-late.

Cafe 48, Karneadou 48 (☎21072 52 434), 3 blocks down Ploutarchou from Haritos; take a left and walk to the end of the block. This pink-walled, diner-like cafe-bar plays American music and serves a remarkable variety of beer. Board games and darts in the back room. Beer €3.50. Mixed drinks €6. Open daily 9am-2am.

PANGRATI

A colony of bungalow-like structures hovers above **Imittou,** where it meets **Efthikhidou.** Alike in their breezy settings, with white-curtain ceilings and mod geometric lights, the individual cafes blend into a massive congregation of coffee- and cocktail-drinking yuppies. Movies play twice nightly at Imittou 107 (€6.50). **Village Cinemas,** Imittou 10, on the second floor of the Millennium Centre, shows the latest blockbusters in state-of-the-art theaters. (☎21075 72 440. Call for listings and times.) **Ellas Espresso,** Pl. Plastira 8, plays pop and Greek music in a shaded terrace and indoor bar with four TVs. (☎21075 62 565. Frappés €4. Open daily 9am-3am.)

▓ DAYTRIPS FROM ATHENS

▓ CAPE SOUNION PENINSULA Ακρωτήριο Σούνιο ☎22920

Orange-striped KTEL buses go to Cape Sounion from Athens. 1 leaves from the Mavromateon 14 bus stop (near Areos Park, on Alexandras and 28 Oktovriou-Patission) and stops at all points on the Apollo Coast (2hr., every hr. 6:30am-6:30pm, €4.50); the other follows a less scenic inland route that also stops at the port of Lavrio (2¼hr., every hr. 6am-6pm, €4). The last coastal bus leaves Sounion at 9pm, the last inland at 9:30pm.

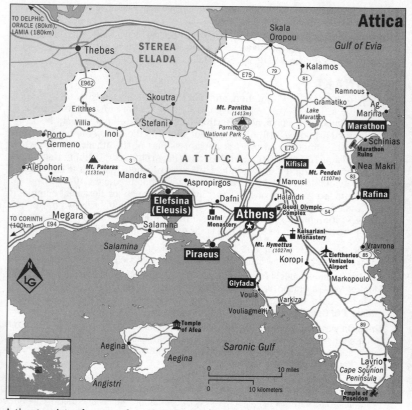

A tiny tourist colony perches atop the sharp cliff of Cape Sounion, where ancient Greeks built the enormous **Temple of Poseidon** in 600 BC. Today, visitors flock to the area to see the 16 Doric temples that remain from Pericles's reconstruction in 440 BC. Hundreds of names are scribbled into the monumental structure; look closely for Lord Byron's on the square column as you face away from the cafeteria. Across the street 500m below is the more deteriorated **Temple of Athena Sounias.** (☎ 22920 39 363. Open daily 10am-sunset except on Christmas, Easter, and May 1. €4, students and seniors over 65 €2, EU students and children under 18 free. Nov.-Mar. Su free.) The Cape has a handful of attractive beaches and hotels, down the inland side of the temple. Swarming with vacationing families, the beaches along the Apollo Coast between Piraeus and Cape Sounion have a carnival atmosphere on summer weekends. Towns often have free public beaches, and, despite the area's crowds, some seaside stretches along the bus route remain uncrowded. Drivers will let you off almost anywhere if you ask. If you stay here, **Camping Bacchus ❶**, 50m farther toward Lavrio from Saron, is a decent option. Ask to stay by the entrance to avoid loud family caravans. The site has a bar, restaurant, laundry, and mini-mart. (☎ 22920 39 572. €7.50 per person; €6.50 per tent, tent rental €10.) Next to the bus station, **Cafe Naos ❶** more than redeems its unspectacular food with one of the best views in Attica. While eating, diners can gaze at the temple and over the Aegean. (Salami sandwich €2.80. Open daily 9am-after sunset.)

MOUNT PARNITHA

Bus #714 (Sa-Su 6:30am, 2:30pm; €0.45) leaves from Acharnon off Stounari, in a parking lot near Vathis Square, opposite Aristoteles Hotel. It's best to buy a ticket at a metro station or kiosk in advance; few places in the vicinity sell them, especially in the morning.

When the bus lets you off at the majestic peak of Mt. Parnitha, about 1hr. outside Athens, you will see, of all things, the tastelessly glitzy **Mont Parnes casino** (☎21024 69 111; open daily at 8:30am) and the cable car (every 30min. 8:30am-3pm, every 10min. after 3pm; €1) that takes you there. Luckily, this decidedly unnatural wonder is a lone intrusion, and there is still a vast national park to explore. Its many trails feel a world away from the city, though few are far from public transportation and well-equipped rest stops. The 19th Parnitha station, a few meters from Hotel-Chalet Kyklaminia and the **Tradia Chapel,** is a good place for hikers to begin; several trails start behind the kiosk. At the fork in the road toward Athens, a map with Greek labels marks paths uphill away from Mont Parnes. Hikes of varying levels of difficulty will lead you along paved roads, gravel paths, and narrow trails to **Skipiza Spring,** the **Caves of Pan,** and **Bafi Refuge ❶** (Μπαφι), a hostel and cafeteria with a beautiful look-out point and detailed trail maps. (☎21021 69 050. Beds €10.) To reach Bafi, turn uphill away from Mont Parnes at the fork in the road 0.5km below the casino. Follow signs to the white gravel path until trails diverge at a quarry-like ravine. From there, follow red markings past a small patch of steep rock after about 15min. and continue for another 10min. It's a fairly easy hike of about 3km. The bugs are particularly audacious, so insect repellent is a good idea.

GLYFADA AND THE COAST   ☎210

Buses A2, A3, and B2, which travel from Vas. Amalias (at the upper right corner of Pl. Syndagma) along the coastline on Poseidonos, reach the town in 30-40min. (€0.75). The spotless, air-conditioned tram (€0.60) leaves from the same place every 8min. until midnight and is uninterrupted by traffic.

Stretching along the sea from Faliro to Sounion, Glyfada has become synonymous with swanky clubs and crowded beaches. Glyfada Town is a densely packed commercial center that teems with designer shops and a wide array of ethnic cuisine. Both **tram** and bus hug the sea as they head from Athens to Glyfada, so you can scope out the **beaches** just beyond stops named after them. The closest, **Edem, Batis,** and **Kalamaki,** are less than pristine, but charge no admission. Kalamaki in particular is known for its loud music and drunken, dancing masses. For a slightly quieter but still well-attended shore, head to Batis. Beyond Platas Glyfadas toward suburbs **Vouliagmeni** and **Varkiza,** beaches are cleaner and more secluded. Entrance fees of €5-10 often include use of pools and bungalows.

With beach views and hipster crowds, the clubs of Glyfada have earned their hot rep. They tend to be expensive, but cabs of trendy Athenians still flock here nightly. **Mao** (☎21089 44 048; pool open during the day €8), on Diadohou Paulou in Glyfada, **Island** (☎21096 53 563), on Limanakia Vouliagmeni in Vouliagmeni, and **Balux,** Vas. Georgiou B58 in Glyfada (☎21089 41 620), are three colorful, beachside options. Also look for **Prime, Envy,** and **Plus Soda.** Cover is usually €10-15, and clubwear (i.e., no shorts) is expected. Drinks typically range €4-10 but can go as high as €100 for a bottle of vodka and mixers for your table. Envy and Mao are accessible by tram, but the best bet for most clubs is to call a **taxi** (☎21096 05 600). A cab to Glyfada should cost about €8, but traffic and nighttime charges can make rates swell to €10-15. Ask the price in advance; if they pack the cab with more than just your party, don't let them swindle you into a set price per individual.

ATHENS

Most daytime activity in Glyfada Town spreads along **Lazaraki** and **Metaxa,** both U-shaped avenues inland from and parallel to the nighttime strip that runs down the coast. Restaurants line Konstantinopoleos, including **Sushi Bar ❸,** Konstantinopoleos 15, on a breezy veranda. (☎21089 42 200. Salmon, avocado, and cucumber rolls €6.50. Open daily 12:30pm-12:30am. MC/V.) Next door, **San Marzano ❷,** Konstantinopoleos 13, serves Italian classics. (☎21096 81 124. Margherita pizza €6.60. Open daily 1pm-1am. AmEx/MC/V.) **Garden of Eden ❸,** Zerva 12, is a block from Hotel Ilion away from the center. Lebanese dishes like *makdous* (baby eggplants stuffed with walnuts and spices; €3.50) and *kas-kas* (meatballs in spicy tomato sauce; €8) are accented by stained-glass windows and hookahs. (Open daily 8:30pm-midnight. DC/MC/V.) Four blocks inland in Ag. Gerasimon, **outdoor fruit markets** set up shop almost daily.

On the Third Marina (toward the beach from tram stop Paleo Demarhio, opposite the church) is a **Seaturtle Rescue Center,** where visitors can walk around pools that contain injured turtles rescued in Greece. Located inside old train cars, the center is Athens's only turtle hospital. The staff is eager to offer information and readily accepts volunteers. (☎21089 82 600. Open daily 9am-2pm and 5-8pm. Free.)

MARATHON Μαραθώνας ☎22940

The bus from the Mavromateon 29 station in Athens goes to Marathon (1½hr., every hr. 5:30am-10:30pm, €3). Look for the "Marathon" label, sit in front, and remind the driver of your destination. When returning to Athens, look for an orange-striped bus among scores of tourist-tour ones and flag it down. A car or taxi (☎22940 66 277) is the best way to see the sights; they are spread out and there is often no public transportation.

Toward the end of the Persian Wars in 490 BC, an overjoyed messenger ran 42km (26¼ mi.) from here to bring his fellow Athenians two words: "Νίκη ήμιν!" ("Victory to us!"). Though **Phidippides** collapsed and died of fatigue immediately afterward (this last 42km followed a grueling 450km the week before), his feat of endurance has made the town of Marathon's name a household word. In addition to the countless marathon races across the globe, runners today trace Phidippides's famous route twice annually here, where it all started. To tour Marathon and the surrounding area, most people find themselves taxis or cars, or just go straight to Marathon beach and stay there. At **Ramnous,** 15km northeast, lie the ruins of the **Temple of Nemesis,** goddess of divine retribution, and **Thetis,** goddess of justice. To reach the **Archaeological Museum of Marathonas,** it's best to call a taxi, but if you're up for a walk, ask the bus driver to drop you at the "Mouseion and Marathonas" sign, after Marathon Town and the beach. Follow the signs through 2km of farms, bearing right at the fork, to the end of the paved Plateion road at #114. As you might expect, the museum highlights the pivotal battle against Persia that occurred here. An atrium displays the **Athenian trophy,** as well as gifts and slabs from tombs of the 192 Athenians who died in battle. The exhibits also include a fairly unusual collection of **Egyptian-style statues,** which wear Pharaoh costumes and symbols of control over Lower and Upper Egypt. Some 4th-century Greeks re-appropriated artistic traditions originally used for worshipping the Egyptian goddess Isis to create images for their cult of Demeter. Also on the museum grounds is a **burial site** which archaeologist Spyros Marinatos uncovered in 1970. A wooden walkway surrounds the spooky mound of rocks, where visitors can peer into glass planks and see the remains of ancient skeletons buried there in 2000-1600 BC. The grassy **Tomb of the Fallen,** where the war victims from 490 BC are buried, is 15km from the town, behind the mountains and accessible only by private transport. (☎22940 55 155. Open Tu-Su 8:30am-3pm. €3; students €2; EU students, children under 18, classicists, and archaeologists free.)

Marathon beach, a slightly more hectic version of a sleepy seaside town, is a nicer place to dine or stay than central Marathon. Some tavernas are set along the decent, well-attended beach, and businesses center on the small plateia. **Marathon Hotel ❸,** Ag. Pantalimonos 25 (☎22940 55 222), 50m before the plateia on the road coming from Athens, has rooms with A/C, TV, fridges, balconies, and baths. (Breakfast included. Singles €35; doubles €45; triples €55; quads €60.) A **supermarket** is half a block inland from the plateia on Dimosthenous. (Open daily 8:30am-10pm.) Beachside taverna **O Vrahos ❸,** Chrisis Aktis 14, is a few buildings to the right of the plateia. (☎22940 55 297. Calamari €7. Fresh fish €20-60 per kg. Open daily noon-1am.) **Avlaia ❷,** Poseidonos 7, on the beach, is a few doors down to the left of the plateia. (☎22940 56 300. Spicy cheese dip €4. Fried fish €7.50.) Marathon beach also has an extensive, multi-building movie theater, **Village Cool Cinema** (☎22940 55 603), 1, 2, and 3 Tymbos, off Eleftherias, which plays mainstream English-language films with Greek subtitles nightly at 9 and 11:15pm.

ELEUSIS Ελευσίνα ☎21055

Take bus A16 or B16 from Pl. Eleftherias in Athens (also called "Pl. Koumoundourou"); purchase tickets at adjacent kiosks. Buses take about 45min.-1hr., and leave every 20min. ☎21055 43 470. €3, students and seniors €2, EU students free. Open Tu-Su 8:30am-3pm. To find the ruins from the bus stop in Elefsina, follow signs, look for Odos and Dimitros streets, or walk toward the Greek flag on top of the Eleusinian acropolis.

Though the gritty industrial town Elefsina doesn't seem to have much in the way of secrets, revealing the details of the cult worship that took place here was once punishable by death. When **Hades** abducted her daughter **Persephone,** harvest goddess **Demeter** was traumatized enough to begin inflicting the ravages of the four seasons on the earth. Here, myth held, she found solace in the kindness of Eleusinians. In honor of the saga, countless ancients took part in a secretive nine-day ritual here each year, from Mycenaean times to AD 400. Initiates were rumored to have seen the darkest truths of life and death, and modern historians have speculated that gory sacrifices and powerful hallucinogens were involved in the rites. Ever since Roman Emperor Theodosius put an end to the pagan celebration, though, the precise components of the Eleusinian rites have remained unknown—just as Demeter's priests would have wanted it.

Today, fallen columns and crumbled arches mark the hill where the rituals took place. Brochures available at the ticket office provide a detailed blueprint of the original layout, and the **museum** houses two miniature plaster models. Despite the curators' best intentions, however, the ancient structures are largely unrecognizable. Years of erosion and attack have reduced the once monumental acropolis to a sprawl of expansive, indistinguishable ruins; the intriguing history surrounding them can be amply appreciated without actually visiting the site itself.

KIFISIA Κηφισιά ☎210

Things haven't changed much since the shady pine trees of this quiet, posh suburb drew Athenian aristocrats during Roman times. A large, manicured park and pristine marble streets lie 12km north of the city—just a few stops on the metro, but a wealthy world away from urban Athens.

▆▋ TRANSPORTATION AND PRACTICAL INFORMATION. Kifisia is best reached by rail but is also accessible by bus. Take **M1,** the **green line,** all the way to the last, northernmost stop (30min., daily 5am-12:30am, €0.70). You can also take either the **A7** or **B7 buses** (30min., €0.45) from Akademias and Themistokleous in Omonia, which will drop you in front of the National Bank on Kifisias. **Taxis** (☎21062 33 100 or 21080 84 000) are available 24hr.

Kifisia has an astonishing concentration of large banks downtown, so you'll have no trouble finding one. **Eurobank,** Kifisias 271, **exchanges currency** and traveler's checks.

ATHENS

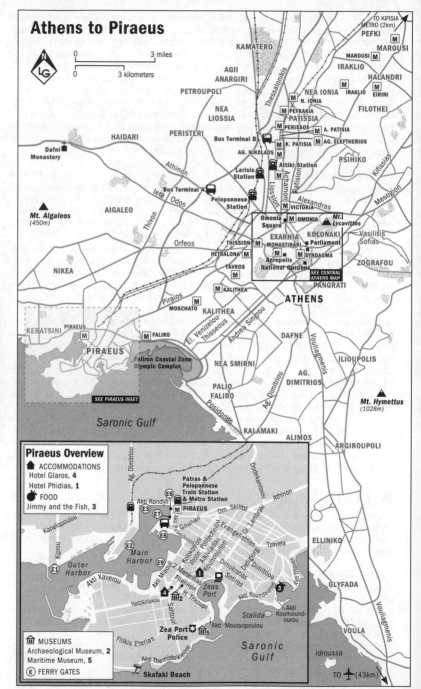

(Open M-Th 8am-2:30pm, F 8am-2pm.) **Citibank,** Levidou 16, also has a **24hr. ATM. Eleftheroudakis Bookstore** is at Kifisias 268. (Open M-F 9am-9pm, Sa 9am-5pm. AmEx/ DC/MC/V.) The **police,** Othonos 94 (☎21062 34 450; open 8am-1:30pm), near the Natural History Museum, can be reached 24hr. at ☎171. Dial ☎166 for an **ambulance.** The **OTE** is at Papadiamanti 8. (☎21062 32 899. Open M, W 7:30am-3pm, Tu, Th-F 7:30am-8pm, Sa 8am-3pm.) The **post office,** Levidou 3a, set in a mini-square off the sidewalk, accepts **Poste Restante.** (☎21080 17 665. Open M-F 7:30am-2pm.) **Postal Code:** 14503.

⊓⊓ ACCOMMODATIONS AND FOOD. If you're looking to slim down your bank account, Kifisia's hotels will be glad to help; otherwise, don't bother staying here. One comparatively modest (though still ridiculously expensive) option is **Hotel des Roses ❺**, Militiadou 4, just off of Kyriazi. Rooms have A/C, TV, fridges, baths, and views of the hills. (☎21080 19 952. Singles €90; doubles €115.)

Food in Kifisia is slightly more budget-friendly. **Dos Hermanos ❸**, Kyriazi 24, serves excellent Mexican fare. (☎21080 87 906. Mexican omelette €9.50. Chili con carne €14. Open Tu-Su 7pm-1am; in winter open Su 1pm. DC/MC/V.) **Pappa's Restaurant ❷**, Kifisias 222 and Drosini 3, makes spaghetti Neapolitana (€4), chicken with mustard sauce (€7.10), and a variety of pizzas (€5-8) in a huge, air-conditioned expanse. (☎21080 18 463. Open daily noon-1am. AmEx/MC/V.) At **Yo Sushi ❸**, Kifisias 238-240, salmon sashimi (€5.50), tuna maki (€6), and edamame (€3.50), among other sushi standbys, are served in the outdoor terrace. (☎21062 32 346; http://yosushi.gr. Open daily 1pm-1am.) Kifisia also has many affordable take-out options, including the several kiosks and cafes within or near the park, like **Crepes Kifisia ❶.** (☎21062 31 371. Most crepes under €3. Open M-Th, Su 11am-4am, F-Sa later.) ▨ **Varsos ❶**, Kassaveti 5, is a factory-like dessert complex. Famous apricot-custard tarts (€2.20) and brioche (€1) have made this patisserie a Kifisia classic. (☎21080 12 472. Open M-F 7am-1am, Sa 7am-2am, Su 7am-midnight.) **AB Supermarket,** on the corner of Levidou and Kassaveti, has an extensive selection for the picnic-bound. (☎21080 82 812. Open M-F 8am-9pm, Sa 8am-6pm. AmEx/MC/V.)

◙◙ SIGHTS AND ENTERTAINMENT. The **Goulandris Museum of Natural History,** Levidou 13, has taxidermied birds and mammals native to Greece, as well as displays of insect, reptile, mollusk, and plant biology. A room dedicated to geology features a collection of minerals from across the planet along with a few Jurassic bones and fossils. (☎21080 15 870. Open M-Th, Sa-Su 9am-2pm. Closed Aug. 1-18. €4, students and children 5-18 €1.50, children under 5 free.) The **Gaia Center,** Othonos 100, is around the corner and filled with multimedia exhibits to help the visitor understand the planet's ecological systems. Unfortunately, the lack of English labels reduces it to a soothing display of bells and whistles for a non-Greek speaker. (Open M-Th, Sa-Su 9am-2:30pm. €4.50, children €1.50.)

Cine Boubouniera, on the corner of Papadiamanti and Levidou, shows American and English movies in an outdoor garden during the summer. (Ticket office open daily 8:50-noon. €7.) The **Bowling Center,** Kolokotroni 1, is a popular nighttime destination. (☎21080 84 662. Open daily 10am-2am. Game of bowling or 30min. billiards M-Th, Su €2-4; F-Sa €4-5.30. Beer €2. Mixed drinks €4-6.) Kifisia is hard to handle as more than a daytrip, but if you stay late you'll find some popular suburban bars including **Windows Kefalari,** in Pl. Kefalari (open daily 9:30am-1:30am), and **Big Deals,** 50 H. Trikoupi (☎21062 30 860; mixed drinks €8-9; open daily 8pm-3:30am, F-Sa 8pm-later).

PIRAEUS Πειραιάς ☎210

The natural harbor of Piraeus has been Athens's port since 493 BC, when Themistocles concocted a plan to create a naval base for the growing Athenian fleet. A hilly peninsula studded with big apartment buildings, Piraeus is one of the busiest ports in the world. Though its charms may not be immediately obvious, Piraeus does have trendy shops, orange trees, and plenty of outdoor park space. Sprinkled among the fast food joints and traffic are hip bars, coffee shops, and Internet cafes, where young people congregate in festive, noisy throngs.

▐ TRANSPORTATION

Ferries: Most ferries circling Greece run from Piraeus. Unfortunately the ferry schedule changes on a daily basis; the following listings are only approximate. **Be flexible** with your plans, as ferries are notoriously fickle. Check *Athens News* and the back of the *Kathimerini* English edition or stop by a travel agency for updated schedules. Ferries sail directly to nearly all major Greek islands except for the Sporades and Ionians. To: **Aegina** (1¼hr., every hr., €6); **Amorgos** (10hr., 5 per week, €24); **Anafi** (11hr., 3-4 per week, €25); **Astypalea** (10hr., 3 per week, €32); **Chios** (9hr., 1-2 per day, €22.30); **Donousa** (7hr., 2 per week, €20); **Folegandros** (9hr., 4 per week, €20); **Hania, Crete** (11hr., 1-2 per day, €20); **Hydra** (3¼hr., 2 per day, €9); **Ikaria** (8hr., 1-2 per day, €20); **Ios** (7½hr., 3 per day, €22); **Iraklia** (7hr., 3-4 per week, €22); **Iraklion, Crete** (11hr., 1-3 per day, €24); **Kalymnos** (12hr., 5 per day, €34); **Kimolos** (6½hr., daily, €19); **Kithnos** (3hr., 1-2 per day, €13); **Kos** (13½hr., 1-2 per day, €36); **Koufonisia** (8hr., 1 per week, €21); **Leros** (10hr., daily, €31); **Lesvos** (12hr., daily, €26); **Limnos** (18hr., 3 per week, €26); **Milos** (7hr., 1-2 per day, €20); **Mykonos** (6hr., 2-4 per day, €20); **Naxos** (6hr., 5-7 per day, €24); **Paros** (5hr., 4-7 per day, €24); **Patmos** (8hr., daily, €30); **Poros** (2½hr., 5 per day, €9); **Rethymno, Crete** (11hr., 3 per week, €24); **Rhodes** (14hr., 2-5 per day, €43); **Samos** (10hr., daily, €27); **Santorini** (9hr., 3-5 per day, €28); **Schinousa** (8hr., 2 per week, €23.10); **Serifos** (5hr., 1-2 per day, €15.20); **Sifnos** (6hr., 1-2 per day, €18); **Sikinos** (8hr., 4 per week, €24); **Spetses** (4hr., daily, €12); **Syros** (4hr., 2-3 per day, €15); **Tinos** (5hr., 2 per day, €22.20). International ferries (2 per day, around €30) head to destinations in **Turkey.**

High Speed Ferries: To: **Aegina** (every hr.); **Amorgos** (1 per week); **Hydra** (6 per day); **Ikaria** (3 per week); **Ios** (6 per week); **Kithnos** (5 per day); **Milos** (1-2 per day); **Mykonos** (2-4 per day); **Naxos** (1-3 per day); **Paros** (1-4 per day); **Poros** (6 per day); **Samos** (2 per week); **Santorini** (daily); **Serifos** (6 per week); **Sifnos** (1-2 per day); **Spetses** (6 per day); **Syros** (2-4 per day); **Tinos** (2-4 per day).

Buses: The **#96** bus shuttles to and from the airport every 30min. (€3). Pick it up across from Philippis Tours on Akti Tzelepi. The **#40** goes between Syndagma and Piraeus (every 15min. 5am-12:45am, €0.45).

Metro: To get to Piraeus from Athens, take the **M1** (green) line **Kifisia/Piraeus** to the last stop, **Piraeus** (20min., €0.70). The metro station is the big building by a busy square on Akti Poseidonos (300m from Akti Tzelepi).

▟ ▐ ORIENTATION AND PRACTICAL INFORMATION

Piraeus can seem chaotic and confusing, but there is a method to the madness. The system of gates has changed; until recently, there were five gates, organized by letter. Now, gates are organized by number, all preceded by the prefix "E"; each gate is a dock for boats heading to specific destinations. Ferries for the Dodecanese leave from gate **E1**. For Chios and Lesvos, ferries depart from gate **E2**. For Crete, go to **E3**. Ferries for the Cyclades leave from **E7**, and ferries for the Saronic Gulf leave from **E8**. For Ikaria and Samos, ferries leave from **E9**. A free shuttle takes travelers from the metro to gate E1 every 15min. The large, busy street running alongside **Akti Miaouli** and **Akti Kondyli** is **Akti Poseidonos**. The remaining hydrofoils leave from the port of **Zea** on the other side of the peninsula, a 10min. walk up and then downhill along any of the streets running inland off Akti Miaouli.

Budget Travel: Most ticket agencies can be found on Akti Tzelepi and Akti Poseidonos. Bypass them for the extremely helpful █ **Philippis Tours**, Akti Tzelepi 3 (☎ 21041 17

787 or 21041 33 182). From the metro, go left and walk 200m until you come to Pl. Karaiskaki. Walk toward the water; it's on the left side of the cluster of offices. They sell ferry and plane tickets, help with accommodations, store baggage for free, and rent cars. Open daily 5:30am-11pm.

Banks: Most **banks** along the waterfront **exchange currency. Citibank,** Akti Miaouli 47-49, has **ATMs.** (☎21092 93 000. Open M-Th 8am-2:30pm, F 8am-2pm.)

Laundromat: Drop your clothes off at **Hionati Laundry,** Bouboulinas 50 (☎21042 97 356) in Zea, where a nice old man cleans them for €4 per kg. Open M-F 8am-2pm and 5-9pm, Sa 8am-3pm.

Emergency: Call the Athens **police** at ☎100 or an **ambulance** at ☎166. The **port police** (☎21042 26 000) are on Akti Tzelepi in the mirrored building. **Zea** has separate port police (☎21045 93 144) along the water and under the sidewalk. The **tourist police** can be reached at ☎171.

Telephones: OTE, Dimitriou 19. Open M, W, Sa 7:30am-3:30pm, Tu, Th-F 7:30am-7:30pm.

Internet Access: LaserNet (☎21041 29 905), in Kenari Square on Port Zea, is a large dim room with a bar filled with young people and narrow blue lights. €2 per hr.; afternoon €1.50 per hr. Open 24hr.

Post Office: The **main branch** (☎21041 71 5184) is on Tsamadou, a few blocks from Polytechniou. Open M-F 7:30am-8pm. **Postal Code:** 18501.

ACCOMMODATIONS AND FOOD

Inexpensive, quality accommodations are much easier to find in Athens, but the unglamorous **Hotel Glaros ❹,** H. Trikoupi 4, off Akti Miaouli toward the Expo Centre, is an adequate option. (☎21045 15 421; www.glaros-hotel.gr. A/C, TV, phone, fridge. Singles €36; doubles €56. MC/V.) Pleasant, quiet **Hotel Phidias ❹,** Koundouriotou 189, between Bouboulinas and 2 Merarhias, offers spacious rooms with large private baths, TV, and A/C. (☎21042 96 160. Breakfast €7.50. Singles €50; doubles €60; triples €70; quads €80. MC/V.) Bakeries and breadshops are a tasty, thrifty, and speedy dining alternative. **Aptos & Vyeia** (☎21058 22 883), just off Gounari, is one of several places that sell fresh breads and pastries for a few euros. Several **supermarkets** are also available, including one at 2 Merarhias and Karaiskou. Open M-F 8am-9pm, Sa 8am-6pm. Inviting but pricey restaurants line the waterfront around Microlimano, the small bay to the south of the main port. If you're looking to splurge, join the swanky diners of **Jimmy and the Fish ❹,** Akti Koumoundorou 46. (☎21041 24 417. Mussels with tomato sauce and parmesan €12.50. Saffron risotto with porcini mushrooms €19. Strawberry soup with ice cream €7. Open daily 12:30pm-1am. AmEx/DC/MC/V.)

SIGHTS

The prized possession of the **Piraeus Archaeological Museum,** H. Trikoupi 31, is the second floor's **Piraeus Apollo,** a hulking hollow bronze figure with outstretched arms. A huge grave monument which consists of three statues—the deceased, his father, and his slave—dated to about 330 BC is across the hall as you walk in. Found on the Black Sea coast, the monument was once painted in full color. Three other bronze statues of Athena and Artemis were found near the port in 1959, shelved in a storeroom for safekeeping when Sulla besieged Piraeus in 86 BC. The strange spots of color in their eyes are precious stones. (☎21045 21 598. Open Tu-Su 8:30am-3pm. €3, students €2, children under 16 free.) Farther south at Zea, the ramp to the dock at Akti Themistokleous and Botassi leads to the **Hellenic Maritime Museum,** which traces naval history using detailed ship models. Inside its main entrance, the building includes part of the 5th-century Themistoclean wall, which protected the three ancient ports of Kantharos, Munychia, and Zea. Of particular note in Room B is a model of an Athenian *trireme* used in the Persian Wars. The courtyard holds torpedo tubes, naval weapons, and part of a WWII submarine. (☎21045 16 264. Open Tu-Sa 9am-2pm. €2, children and students €1.50.)

RAFINA Ραφήνα ☎22940

Rafina is like a smaller, quieter version of Piraeus. It's Attica's second-most prominent port, though ferry service from Rafina has recently decreased. Compared to its larger counterpart there's less to do, but it's easier on the eyes, ears, and lungs.

Don't stay in Rafina unless you're stuck here: it's boring and expensive. Down from the plateia overlooking the water to the right (facing the water), **Avra Hotel** ❹ boasts decked-out rooms with A/C, TV, phones, and hair dryers. The hotel has both a restaurant and a bar. (☎22940 22 780. Breakfast included. Singles, doubles, and triples €60-130.) Smaller **Hotel Corali** ❸, Pl. Plastira 11, rents standard rooms with baths, fridges, TV, A/C, and phones. (☎22940 22 477, owner's home 22940 28 900. Singles €30-60; doubles €50-90; triples €60-110; quads €70-130.) Head right at the top of the ramp, right again at the end of the blue fence, and then follow the coast to find tiny inlets. If you keep walking, you'll get to a long beach with rough sand, and a waterfront lined with cafes, pizzerias, and tavernas. **O Vrahos** ❸, Vas. Pavlou 1, in front of the plateia, is toward the water on the left. The family which owns the taverna catches the fish they serve daily. (☎22940 25 912. Mussels with rice €13. Open daily 11am-midnight.) Early ferry-catchers can try **Fournos tis Plateias** ❶, a bakery on the right side of the plateia when you're facing the water. (☎22940 26 083. Fresh bread €0.60. Various croissants from €1.20. Open daily 6:30am-11pm.) A **mini-mart** (open daily 8am-2pm and 5-10pm) sells fruits, vegetables, and toiletries off Pl. Plastira, around the corner from the bakery.

Buses from Athens's station at Mavromateon 29 (1hr., every 30min. 5:40am-10pm, €2) or **shuttles** from the airport (every 40min. 6:15am-9:15pm) will take you to Rafina at the waterfront ramp. **Ferries** go to: Andros (2hr., 5-6 per day, €9); Marmari, Evia (50min., 5-8 per day, €7.50); Mykonos (5hr., 4-6 per day, €15); Paros (1-2 per day, €19); Syros (2 per week, €13); Tinos (4hr., 5-6 per day, €14). **Flying Dolphins** zip daily to: Mykonos (1½hr., €30); Paros (€30); Syros (€25); Tinos (€26). The **port authority** (☎22940 22 300) supplies info. Along the waterfront, **Blue Star Ferries** (☎22940 23 561), **Rafina Tours** (☎22940 22 700), and **Hellas Flying Dolphins** (☎22940 22 292) sell tickets for ferries and catamarans. (All open daily 6am-9pm.) **Taxis** (☎22940 23 101) line up in front of the plateia. Both the **Commercial Bank,** two blocks inland from the plateia (☎22940 25 184; open M-Th 8am-2:30pm, F 8am-2pm), and **Alpha Bank** (☎22940 24 159; open M-Th 8am-2:30pm, F 8am-2pm), one block beyond the far left corner of the plateia, **exchange currency** and have **24hr. ATMs.** The waterfront also has 24hr. ATMs. Reach the **police** at ☎22940 22 100. There is a **pharmacy** (☎22940 23 456; open M-F 8:30am-2pm, Tu, Th-F 8:30am-2pm and 5:30-9pm) one block to the right of the plateia's right inland corner. For a **doctor,** call ☎22940 22 633 or 22940 28 428. In a **medical emergency,** dial ☎166. The **OTE** is in the unmarked building inland from the plateia, beside the church. (☎22940 25 182. Open M-F 7:30am-3pm.) Facing inland at the dock, the **post office** is two streets to the right on El. Venizelou. **Postal Code:** 19009.

PELOPONNESE
Πελοπόννησος

 Stretching its fingers into the Mediterranean, the Peloponnese transports its visitors to another time through its rich history and folklore. The achievements of ancient civilizations dot the peninsula's landscape, as most of Greece's significant archaeological sites—including Olympia, Mycenae, Messini, Corinth, Mystras, and Epidavros—rest in this former home of King Pelops. Breathtaking scenery, from the barren crags of Mani to the forested peaks and flower-blanketed pastures of Arcadia, imbues the land with astonishingly timeless natural beauty. Away from large, urban transportation hubs, the serene, sparsely populated mountain and seaside villages welcome visitors to traditional Greek living at its best.

 SUGGESTED ITINERARIES: PELOPONNESE

THREE DAYS Stay in picturesque **Nafplion** (p. 145), and take daytrips from there to the pre-Classical palace at **Mycenae** (p. 149) and the acoustically perfect theater at **Epidavros** (p. 151). On your last day, relax in the sleepy mountainside villages of **Dimitsana** (p. 175) or **Stemnitsa** (p. 177).

ONE WEEK After a couple of days at the ancient sites around Nafplion (p. 145), swing westward through the idyllic towns of **Arcadia** (p. 172), then take a few laps around the stadium when you reach **Olympia** (p. 166). A final weekend in **Patras** (p. 153), a modern college town, will bring you back to the urban world.

CORINTHIA Κορινθία AND ARGOLIS Αργολίδα

Legend holds that Argos, a monster endowed with 100 unblinking eyes, once stalked the northern Peloponnese subduing unruly satyrs and burly bulls. While these creatures have left no tangible evidence behind, the region does provide some of the most impressive archaeological sites in the country near secluded mountainside villages and bustling seaside cities. Nafplion (p. 145) makes a good base for exploration, since this city, with its majestic Venetian architecture, allows easy access to Epidavros, Mycenae, Corinth, and other destinations.

NEW CORINTH Κόρινθος   ☎27410

For the last few millennia, life in Corinth has been about location, location, location. The ancient city was a bustling commercial crossways, doing brisk business from its position on the isthmus separating the Peloponnese from the Greek mainland. Today, that convenient placement has made New Corinth a busy transportation hub through which travelers must pass, and accordingly, its streets are supersaturated with fast food, designer shops, and 24hr. ATMs. Despite the urban sprawl, though, the pedestrian streets of downtown New Corinth and Kalamia Beach have a charming, small-town feel.

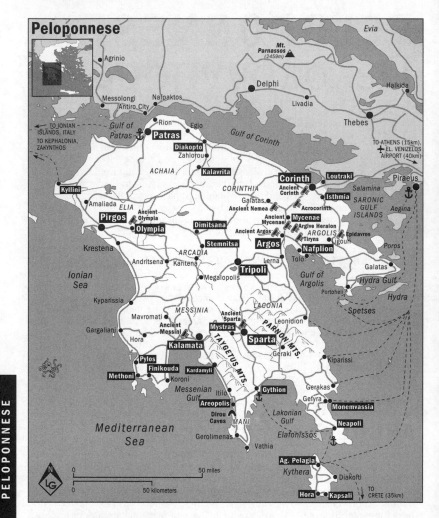

☐ TRANSPORTATION

Trains: The **station** (☎27410 22 522) is on Dimokratias, off Damaskinou. There are express trains to more popular locations, but they usually cost twice as much. To **Athens** (regular: 2hr., 7 per day, €3; express: 1½hr., 6 per day, €5.20). 2 major train lines serve the Peloponnese: 1 travels the northern coast from Corinth to Pirgos and south to Kyparissia; the other goes south from Corinth to Tripoli and Kalamata. To: **Argos** (1hr., 5 per day, €2); **Diakopto** (regular: 1½hr., 2 per day, €2.10; express: 1hr., 6 per day, €5); **Kalamata** (4½hr., 2 per day, €6); **Kyparissia** (5hr., 2 per day, €7); **Nafplion** (1½hr., 2 per day, €3); **Pirgos** (regular: 4½hr., daily, €6; express: 3½hr., 6 per day, €10); **Tripoli** (2hr., 3 per day, €3).

Buses: There are 3 bus terminals in town.

Terminal A: ☎27410 75 424, beyond the train station on Dimokratias. To: **Athens** (1½hr., every 30min. 5am-9:30pm, €7).

Terminal B: ☎27410 75 425. Walking inland on Eth. Antistasis, turn right on Koliatsou, halfway through the park; the terminal is outside a bakery, on the corner of Koliatsou and Kolokotroni. To: **Ancient Corinth** (20min., 15 per day 6:10am-9:10pm, €1).

Terminal C: The **Argolis Station** (Nafplion or Mycenae routes ☎27410 24 403; Isthmia, Nemea, Loutraki routes ☎27410 25 645) is also outside a bakery, at the intersection of Eth. Antistasis and Aratou, 1 block past the park. The station has 2 counters, each serving different destinations. The first counter on the right as you enter off Eth. Antistasis serves: **Ag. Vasileio** (40min., 2 per day, €2.10); **Athikia** (30min., 7 per day, €1.50); **Hiliomodi** (20min., 11 per day, €1.50); **Isthmia** (15min., 6 per day, €1) **Katakali** (30min., daily, €2); **Klenia** (40min., 7 per day, €1.50); **Korfos** (1hr., 2pm, €4); **Loutraki** (20min., every 30min. 7:30am-10pm, €1.40); **Nemea** (1hr., 7 per day 7:30am-5pm, €3.50); **Sofiko, Almiri, Loutra, Xilokeriza** (15min.; 9 per day; €3, €2, €1.50, €1 respectively); **Spathovouni** (30min., 1:45pm, €2.50). The counter on the left has buses to: **Argos** (1hr., 3 per day, €3.50); **Mycenae** (45min., 3 per day, €3) via **Fihtia; Nafplion** (1½hr., 4 at 7am and then every hr. 8:30am-9:30pm, €4.40). To get to **Sparta** or other points south, take the Loutraki bus to the Corinth Canal and take the Athens bus to Sparta, Kalamata, Koroni, or Tripoli. Or depart for these destinations from the bus station south of town; taxi €3.

Taxis: ☎27410 73 000. Along both sides of Eth. Antistasis (in front of the park and the Court of Justice).

■❋🏃 ORIENTATION AND PRACTICAL INFORMATION

New Corinth is a neat grid, so it's fairly simple to navigate. The palm-lined main street, **Eth. Antistasis,** runs perpendicular to the waterfront. **Ermou,** the central walkway, and **Kolokotroni** run parallel to Eth. Antistasis, on its left (northwest) and right (southeast) respectively as you look away from the waterfront. All three intersect **Damaskinou,** which runs along the harbor. Most of the town's shops, restaurants, and hotels are found on these four streets. Two blocks inland from the shore, between Eth. Antistasis and Ermou, is the city's central **park.** Opposite the park stands the **Court of Justice,** which makes a good reference point; taxis regularly line up here. Bus terminal A and the train station are a few blocks southeast. To find the waterfront from the train station, turn left out of the building onto Dimokratias, then take the first right onto Damaskinou. Much of New Corinth's nightlife centers on **Kalamia beach.** To reach it, walk to **Ap. Pavlou,** the third parallel to the right of Eth. Antistasis as you look inland. Take Ap. Pavlou inland, then make a right on **Notara** after the beautiful St. Paul Cathedral to reach the beach.

Tourist Office: Ermou 51 (☎27410 23 282; emergencies 27410 23 100). Doubles as the **tourist police.** Provides maps, brochures, and assistance. Some English spoken. Open daily 8am-2pm.

Banks: National Bank, Eth. Antistasis 7 (☎27410 23 934). 1 block up from the waterfront. Offers **currency exchange** and a **24hr. ATM.** Many banks with these services are also within a few blocks of Eth. Antistasis. Most open M-F 8am-2pm.

Public Toilets: Across from the park on Eth. Antistasis. €0.50. Open 7am-10pm.

Police: Ermou 51 (☎27410 81 100), across the park from the courthouse. Open 24hr.

Pharmacies: Many on Eth. Antistasis, Koliatsou, and Ermou. Typically open M-F 8am-2pm and 5-8pm.

Hospital: ☎27410 25 711. On Athinaion; cross the train tracks and turn left, about 5-6 blocks from the train station. Take a cab or call the hospital for an **ambulance** (☎100) in an emergency. Open 24hr.

Internet Access: Diadiktio (☎27410 73 707), 2 blocks from the corner of Damaskinou and Eth. Antistasis, near Vibes bar. Coffee €2. Drinks €1.50-4.50. Internet €2.40 per hr. Plasma TV and computer room upstairs. Open daily 8am-2am. **Stretto,** Pilarinou 70

(☎27410 25 570), just off the first block of Eth. Antistasis. Coffee €2.30. Internet €3 per hr., €1.50 min. The central location makes up for the cramped computer area. Open daily Sept.-June 8:30am-11pm; July-Aug. 8:30am-2:30pm and 5-11pm.

Post Office: ☎27410 80 050. Adimantou 35, facing the park, between Eth. Antistasis and Ermou. Open M-F 7:30am-2pm. **Postal Code:** 20100.

⌐ ACCOMMODATIONS

New Corinth's hotels, found mainly along Eth. Antistasis and Damaskinou, offer generic, clean rooms for generally affordable prices. Campgrounds can be quite a distance from the city, making it difficult for those who need to catch an early bus. The best option for those on a looser budget is **Hotel Ephira ❹**, Eth. Antistasis 52. Between downtown and Kalamia Beach, it has a comfortable garden as well a large second floor dining room. Recently redecorated, each room comes with TV, A/C, and phone. (☎27410 22 434. Singles €40; doubles €50; triples €60. MC/V.) **Hotel Apollon ❹**, Damaskinou 2, located one block away from the train station, has modern, recently renovated rooms with TV, A/C, and Internet access. Party-hoppers should keep in mind that though convenient to some transportation, Hotel Apollon is about a 25min. walk from Kalamia Beach. (☎27410 25 920. Breakfast €7. Reservations recommended. Singles €40; doubles €60; triples €70.) **Hotel Akti ❷**, Eth. Antistasis 1, offers the best choice for the budget traveler hoping to stay downtown. The lobby's leopard-print theme brings character to the otherwise plain and sparsely furnished hotel, but the lack of A/C may make summer nights feel like you're actually in the jungle. The great price and friendly owners (who are willing to bargain), though, make Hotel Akti a popular place for European backpackers. (☎27410 23 337. Singles €20; doubles €30. Cash only). The tourist-friendly campgrounds of **Blue Dolphin ❶**, on Lecheon beach (6km outside downtown Corinth), offer both rooms and camping facilities. At the on-site restaurant and bar, the owners invite guests to wake up with bread and milk (€2) or relax with ice cream (€1). Buses leave for Lecheon beach every 30min. on weekdays and every hour on weekends from the Terminal A bus stop. (☎27410 25 766; www.camping-blue-dolphin.gr. Kitchen and laundry facilities. Check-out 3pm. No curfew. Camping €4-6 per person; singles €15; doubles €22. Tents also available to rent; prices vary according to tent size. Parking and electricity extra.)

⌐ FOOD

After 9pm, the harbor perks up as residents flock to the waterfront to dine outdoors in the balmy evening air. Because fast, generic, and cheap food abounds in New Corinth, visitors often find themselves deciding where, not what, to eat. If you want to dine in the center of the city, stroll past the tavernas on Damaskinou by the waterfront plateia for meat and fish specialties. For the best tavernas, walk down to Kalamia beach. Original entrees, traditional decor, and speedy service make stopping at ⊠**Kioupia ❷** a must. The *mezes tes amartias* (food of sin) is indeed sinfully delicious (€8), as is the mushroom pie (€5.50). Energetic and friendly owner Lakis Giannidakis loves to share stories with his guests, adding to the cozy, personal atmosphere. (☎27410 81 818. Open M-F 5pm-midnight, Sa-Su 12:30pm-midnight.) Right as you hit the beach, on the corner of Meg. Alexandrou and Palama, family-run **Arodo ❸** (☎27410 71 500) serves lunch and dinner on a spacious, comfortable deck from 9am "until everyone is done eating" (usually around 2am). Try the *kolokithokeftedes* (cheese and zucchini croquettes; €2.64) or any of the day's fresh fish (€40-60 per kg). If you crave a specific type of fish or lobster not on the menu, call in the day before and Arodo will buy and prepare it fresh for you. Back downtown, one of the few tavernas open for breakfast, **Akhinos ❸**, Damaskinou 41, serves classic staples among kitschy murals. (☎27410 28 889. Souvlaki €7. Omelette €5. Rabbit *stifado* €9. Beer €2.50. Open daily 8am-1am.) **Neon Cafe ❷** delights locals with its slice of prime real estate—the outdoor seating overlooks the harbor. This modern cafeteria, at the corner of Damaskinou and Eth. Antistasis, serves coffee and mixed drinks, along with a selection of entrees (€3-5.50). The *gemisha* (peppers and tomatoes stuffed with rice; €5.50) is a good option for vegetarians. (☎27410 84 950. Open daily 8am-1am.)

☕ NIGHTLIFE

Corinth can't boast much crazy clubbing after sunset, but at least you can see and be seen at Kalamia Beach, which pulses to a techno sound track that comes free of charge. Cell-phone-crazed teenagers, 30-something bar-hoppers, and older couples all share a single walkway overlooking the sparkling lights of Loutraki. Visitors may find **Tango Bar,** at the far end of the beach, to be a fresh break from the trendier-than-thou people-watchers along the main stretch; the well-coiffed clientele keeps the hip establishment busy far into the evening, but the relaxed staff and delicious drinks (beer €4-5; mixed drinks €7) give the place a more manageable feel. (Open daily 10am-4am, Sa-Su 10am-6am). **Unique** (beer €3; mixed drinks €6), which ironically follows the latest trends, opens at 9pm and rocks until even the night owls retire. **Freedom Music Bar** (beer €4; mixed drinks €6) balances over the beach on an overhanging platform, tempting some partiers into taking a moonlight swim. (Open until 3am.) The blaring music quiets down near the cafes along Pilarinou, where people can enjoy an early evening drink in relative peace.

🔎 DAYTRIPS FROM CORINTH

ANCIENT CORINTH Αρχαία Κόρινθος   ☎27410

7km southwest of New Corinth. Buses leave from outside the bakery on Koliatsou and Kolokotroni (20min.; every hr. 6:10am-9:10pm, return buses leave at half past the hr.; €1). ☎27410 31 207. Open daily 8:30am-7:30pm. Guidebooks €4-7. Museum and site €6, students €3, EU students and under 18 free. Every Su from Nov. 1-March 31; last weekends of Apr., May, June, and Sept.; and major holidays free.

Ancient Corinth's opulent wealth and risque delights were anything but old-fashioned. Prosperous merchants swung by here to line their pockets and mingle with **hetairai,** famously clever courtesans in the service of Aphrodite. But don't go looking for their pleasure palaces: what remains of the Classical world's Sin City is buried under the ruins of the settlement the Romans built there after sacking Corinth. Remnants of both the Greek and Roman cities stand side by side.

◼ FORTRESS AND ACROCORINTH. The acrocorinth is located a steep 3.5km uphill from the museum. At the top of the hill stands a magnificent fortress built in the 10th century; its walls encircle the ruins of buildings from the 14th to 18th centuries. The easiest way up the acrocorinth is by taxi from the center of the village of Ancient Corinth (€7). Taxis are lined up by the hub of touristy restaurants and souvenir shops, and will even wait at the top of the acrocorinth to drive you back down (€15). The walk up the hill takes a little over an hour.

Those who want to experience the entire fortress should head past the first three gates and toward the summit. Here, where sacred *hetairai* once initiated disciples into the "mysteries of love" (read: engaged in crazy sex acts) at Aphrodite's altar, and where myth tells that Jason's flying horse, Pegasus, quenched its thirst, only a small chapel to St. Dimitrios remains. The dazzling view of Corinthia, however, is still wholeheartedly intact. Time permitting, venture around the rest of the relatively empty fortress, which contains acres of towers, mosques, gates, and walls. Don't forget sturdy shoes, sunscreen, and water; be careful on the rocks— they're slippery when wet. *(Open daily 8am-7pm.)*

ANCIENT SITE. The remains of the ancient Roman city stand with the older Greek ruins at the base of the Acrocorinth against a scenic mountain and ocean backdrop. Conspicuous and breathtaking, seven of the original 38 columns from the **Temple of Apollo** have defiantly endured the trials of time since the 6th century BC. As you walk toward the remains of the temple, climbing over the engraved friezes and pediments dispersed around the courtyard, a small edifice with hollowed entryways is on the left. Here, located behind the museum, is the **Fountain of Glauke,** named after Jason the Argonaut's second wife. After Medea, Jason's seriously bitter ex, gave her an enchanted robe which burst into flames, Glauke legendarily sought refuge in a fountain and drowned. In front of the Temple of Apollo, toward the mountainous Acrocorinth, lie the remains of the **forum,** the center of Roman civil life. Walk down the row of central shops to the **Julian Basilica,** which served as a courthouse and once held statues of the family of Julius Caesar.

To the left, near the exit at the edge of the site farthest from the museum, a broad stone stairway descends into the **Peirene Fountain,** which once stood over 20 ft. tall. Although smoothed by the water that still flows today, the columns and fresco-covered tunnels inside the fountain survived the centuries unharmed. Peirene was the daughter of the river god Asopus; when Cenchrias, one of her sons with Poseidon, was killed by Artemis, she shed endless tears and became the spring. Just past the fountain is the **Perivolos of Apollo,** an open-air court surrounded by still more columns. Although no guided tours are available through the museum, a careful walk and a handbook should be enough to appreciate all the treasures within this site.

ARCHAEOLOGICAL MUSEUM. Tracing Corinth's history through Greek, Roman, and Byzantine rule, the Archaeological Museum proudly showcases its restored collection of impressive statues, such as those from the Julian Basilica (27 BC-AD 4), statues of Augustus Caesar and his family, and tiny clay figurines dating back to the Neolithic period. The expansive array of ancient works in the permanent exhibit ranges from a marble statue of a sphinx to a series of restored mosaics from a nearby ancient Roman villa. The Roman frescoes and mosaics date from the same period as Pompeii, and changes in pottery technique trace Greece's evolution from Neolithic to Byzantine times. The museum's collections of sarcophagi and headless statues in the open-air courtyard are morbidly appealing. While the exhibits are noteworthy, it's worthwhile to purchase a guidebook (€4-7) because there is little accompanying explanation. *(Open daily 8am-7pm.)*

ANCIENT NEMEA Αρχαία Νεμέα   ☎ 27460

5km from modern Nemea; coming by bus from Corinth (45min.-1hr., 7 per day, €3), ask to be let off at the ancient site (☎ 27460 22 739). Museum open Tu-Su 8:30am-3pm, site and stadium open daily 8:30am-3pm, but call ahead to confirm. Site and stadium each €4, students and seniors €2, EU students and under 18 free.

Ancient Nemea might never have been excavated if a disastrous series of earthquakes in the 1880s hadn't led to construction and digging near the site. Today the ruins are a refreshing, albeit much smaller, silver lining for those feeling overwhelmed by more commercialized ancient sites in Corinthia. A spacious and well-maintained museum proudly displays the history of both the site and its excavation with a sizeable collection of coins, tools, and statuettes. Excellent explanatory notes and videos in English help convey the historical significance of an area that once held the **Temple of Nemean Zeus.** Outside, three massive columns still stand starkly against the mountainous backdrop. Visitors are greeted by an encased skeleton from an early Christian tomb, and can explore an ancient bathing chamber. Self-guided tours of the stadium, 200m up the road to the left, allow visitors to occupy the very track that once hosted Panhellenic contests linked with those at nearby Isthmia, Delphi, and Olympia.

ISTHMIA Ισθμία   ☎27410

At Terminal C, catch the bus from New Corinth to Isthmia (15min., 6 per day, €1). Ask to be let off at the museum (☎27410 37 244), or get off at the Isthmia stop. Go straight 1km, turn right for 300m, and then turn left on the uphill road; the museum is on the right. Alternatively, take a taxi from Corinth (€5-6). Open Tu-Su 8:30am-3pm. Guidebooks €4. €2, students and seniors €1, EU students free.

Held every other year during the springtime Festival of Poseidon, the Isthmian games attracted the best athletes from all of Hellas in a series of contests. According to legend the games grew out of funeral rites put on by Sisyphus for the child-hero Melikertes, in whose honor the champions donned pine and laurel crowns. Today little of the hillside site remains, save the foundation of the **Temple of Poseidon** and the **Later Stadium** used for the contests, both of which are open to the public. The adjacent museum holds a humble collection of artifacts like the glass opus sectile and 87 mosaic panels from the temple of Isis which miraculously survived an earthquake at Kenchreai in AD 375. The American School of Classical Studies in Athens is still excavating the site.

LOUTRAKI Λουτράκι   ☎27440

Since ancient times travelers have come to Loutraki—not for its pebbled beach tucked in the Gulf of Corinth's inner fold, but for its natural springs, said to have medicinal powers. The relaxed vacation atmosphere and long, beautiful waterfront lined with lively cafe-bars and restaurants make it a popular destination. Even after you leave Loutraki though, Loutraki never quite leaves you, as its brand-name mineral water is sold in distant lands' supermarkets.

▣ TRANSPORTATION. The KTEL bus station (☎27440 22 262) is located at a triangular road island where **Eleftheriou Venizelou,** the main street, meets **Periandrou** and **Iasonos.** Running parallel to the water, El. Venizelou curves away from Corinth at the northern end of the strip and becomes **Giorgiou Lekka.** The change from El. Venizelou to G. Lekka marks Loutraki's central square, but most of the tourist activity is located along the beach boardwalk and on El. Venizelou. **Buses** leave the station for Athens (1¼hr., 9 per day 6:05am-9pm, €7) and Corinth (25min.; M-F 2 per hr. 5:30am-9:30pm, service reduced Sa-Su; €1.40). To reach Isthmia and the Corinth Canal, take the Corinth bus and get off just over the canal near the train station. The Loutraki **Railway Station** (☎27440 61 277) provides alternative train service to Athens (12:37, 6:14pm; €4), at the corner of the El. Venizelou info kiosk. **Boat excursions** are also available at the dock past the park. Cruises sail north to beautiful Lake Vouliagmeni and south down the Corinth Canal. Times and prices vary; contact the tourist office for more information. **Taxis** (☎27440 61 000), available 24hr., stop by the stand next to the tourist info kiosk on El. Venizelou. To rent your own car, try the **Hertz** up the road at G. Lekka 10. (☎27440 62 950. Open M-Sa 9am-1pm and 6-9pm.) **Moto-Rent "Christos"** at Meleti-Spirogiannaki 14 rents **mopeds** and **bicycles** for €25 per day and €10 per day respectively. (☎27440 61 770. Open daily 8am-8pm.)

◪ PRACTICAL INFORMATION. Loutraki has two **tourist information kiosks**, both of which provide a helpful free **guidebook**. One (☎27440 67 770) is located on El. Venizelou, four blocks south of the bus station; the other (☎27440 62 791) is after the curve at the central plateia on G. Lekka, at the end of the town park. (Both open daily 9am-1pm and 5-9pm.) The **Municipal Enterprise for Tourism** office, in the central square, can tell you about water parks, scuba diving, horseback riding, bike tours, and cruises. (☎27440 26 001; www.loutraki.gr. Open M-F 8am-3pm.) To get to the **National Bank**, with a **24hr. ATM**, follow El. Venizelou, with the water on your left, to the central plateia. (☎27440 22 220. Open M-F 8am-2pm.) The fourth side street on the right coming from the bus inland (with the water on your left) is home to **SIC Laundry Service**, Lekka 3. (☎27440 63 854. Wash and dry €12. Open M, W, Sa 8:30am-2pm, Tu, Th-F 8:30am-1:30pm and 6-9pm.) The **police** and the **tourist police** are in the same building, about 3km south of downtown Loutraki on El. Venizelou and the first left after the athletic stadium. (☎27440 63 000. Open 24hr.) One of several **pharmacies** is at El. Venizelou 24. (☎27440 64 528. Open daily 8am-2pm and 5:30-8pm; in winter M, W 8am-2:30pm, Tu, Th-F 8am-2pm and 5-8pm.) The **hospital** is roughly a 30min. walk from the center of town; head five blocks up from El. Venizelou on Hatzopoulou, across from the information kiosk; follow the signs by turning right on Karaiskaki and continue straight for three blocks. (☎27440 26 666. Open 24hr.) The **OTE** is at El. Venizelou 10, on the left as you walk from the bus station with the water on your left. (☎27440 61 999. Open M-F 7am-2:40pm.) **Las Vegas Internet Cafe,** El. Venizelou 40, just past the information kiosk, offers **Internet access** as well as a pool table and bar. (☎27440 69 397. €5 per hr., 15min. min. Open daily 8am-11pm). **Zoom,** just north of the bus station at El. Venizelou 18, also has Internet access. (☎27440 23 117. Open daily 8am-12:30am. €2 per hr.) Walking down El. Venizelou with the water to your right, you'll find the **post office** about a block after the BP gas station on your right between El. Venizelou 46 and 48. (☎27440 22 328. Open M-F 7:30am-2pm.) **Postal Code:** 20300.

⌂ ☈ ACCOMMODATIONS AND CAMPING. Visitors to Loutraki are never far from a roof over their heads with nearly 60 different hotel options in the city itself. Those on a budget can try the hotels in the center of town, where El. Venizelou becomes G. Lekka; more expensive hotels sit closer to the waterfront, particularly in the quieter stretch past the park. For **domatia,** call ☎27440 22 456 or consult the tourist office in the central plateia. To reach ▨**Le Petit France ❷,** M. Botsari 3, take the third right on El. Venizelou, walking from the bus station with the water on your left. Dina, the friendly, multilingual owner of this quaint, blue-shuttered hotel, extends her hospitality. Visitors can eat breakfast in the garden or in the lobby, which has a TV for guest use. Rooms come with balconies, ceiling fans, and baths. (☎27440 22 401. Breakfast €3.50. A/C €5 extra. Singles €25-30; doubles €32-47. Family-style rooms available.) Nearly on the beach on the next street south of the bus station, **Hotel Marko ❷,** L. Katsoni 3, offers attractive rooms with fridges, A/C, private baths, TV, phones, and balconies. Breakfast is served in the eye-catching dining area downstairs which, later in the day, also serves as a bar. (☎27440 63 542. Breakfast €5. Singles €30; doubles €35; 5-person suite €50.) **Hotel Possidonion ❷** is on the right hand side of the central plateia, coming from El. Venizelou. Spacious rooms with high ceilings and hardwood floors have phones, A/C, TV, private baths, and balconies with a view of the square. (☎27440 22 273. Breakfast €3. Singles €25; doubles €35.) **Camping** is available 16km away at stunning **Lake Vouliagmeni ❶** (☎27410 91 230 or 27410 91 229). To get there, travel north out of town on G. Lekka and follow the signs. You can also camp at **Isthmia beach ❶** on the Corinth Canal, where coin laundry machines are provided. (☎27410 37 447; www.isthmiacamping.gr. 1-person tent €5, 2-person tent €13.)

❏ FOOD. The beachfront, Posidonos St., is lined with numerous cafes and restaurants. Many hotels on El. Venizelou and the streets between it and the water also have good dining options. Several **supermarkets** are scattered along El. Venizelou; the one at El. Venizelou 59, across the street from the gas station, is the largest. (☎27440 68 166. Open M-Sa 8am-9pm, Su 9am-2pm.) Locals flock to **Strougka ❸**, Posidonos 69, at the Corinth end of the waterfront, for their mouthwatering beef tenderloin (€10) and souvlaki (€6) served in plentiful portions. (☎27440 65 747. Entrees €10-15. Open daily noon-1:30am.) About an 8min. walk from the center of town, the chefs at **Grill House 71 ❶**, El. Venizelou 71, work furiously behind the searing grills to make inexpensive, scrumptious meals. Locals claim it serves the best pita souvlaki (€1.50) around. (☎27440 61 776. Take-out and delivery available. Open daily 5:30pm-1am or later.) **Caravella Beer House ❸**, El. Venizelou 8 and Posidonos 5, serves an arsenal of crepes, salads, and 110 different types of beer. The potatoes with sausage (€6.50) or an assortment of cheeses complement both the beer and the view of the bay of Corinth. (☎27440 65 204. Entrees €5-12.) Stylish **Pizza Ami ❷**, Posidonos 33, past the bars, offers reasonably priced Italian cuisine (€3.20-8.50) and a wide selection of appetizing pizzas. (☎27440 22 175. Takeout and delivery available. Open M-F 6pm-2am, Sa-Su 11am-3am. MC/V.)

❄❐ NIGHTLIFE AND ENTERTAINMENT. Nightlife in Loutraki means eating and dancing. Waterfront restaurants swell in summer, staying full well past midnight. Along the boardwalk, **Sax, Cafe Coral, Paul's, Jamaica, Cameo,** and **El Niño** pump music for steady crowds. (Mixed drinks €3-7.) After midnight, taxis transport the party-hungry to discos on the city's edges. **Hype,** on Athinon Rd. toward Corinth, fills with sweaty bodies pulsing past dawn. (☎27440 66 996. Cover €8; includes 1 drink. Open F-Sa 11pm-7am.) **CoCoon,** Posidonos 2, opens onto the boardwalk, filled for the day by day and alcohol by night. (☎27440 26 342. Beer €5. Mixed drinks €7. Open daily 10am-2am.) Loutraki is the birthplace of casinos in Greece, so if you're feeling lucky, stop by **Club Hotel Casino Loutraki,** Posidonos 48, down the beachfront. It features 600 slot machines and 70 gambling tables with roulette, cards, and dice, as well as a swimming pool and hot tubs for its guests. (Casino ☎27440 65 501, resort 27440 60 300; www.club-hotel-loutraki.gr. 23+. Cover M-F €10, Sa-Su €15; includes free drinks at games. Open 24hr.)

❖ WATER. If you seek solace in Loutraki's famous healing waters, make an appointment at **Therma: Hydrotherapy Thermal Spa,** G. Lekka 14, across from the park. (☎27440 22 215. Open M-Sa 8am-1pm and 4-6pm, Su 8am-1pm.) The well-maintained **waterfalls,** a 12min. walk from the central plateia on G. Lekka, offer a view of the fountains from the cliff's base that seems even cooler with ice cream from the adjacent cafe. (☎27440 66 700. Open daily 10am-1am.) **Lake Vouliagmeni,** 16km up the coast, is known for its beautiful blue water and tranquil atmosphere. A bus runs from the station in Loutraki to the lake from mid-June to late August (1 per day 9:30am); for visits at other times of year, taxis (€8) are available. A 15min. taxi south of Loutraki will take you to **Water Fun,** a waterpark with waterslides for all ages. (☎27410 81 400; www.water-fun.gr.)

ARGOS Άργος   ☎27510

According to Homer, Argos followed native hero Diomedes into war under the flag of Mycenae's mighty king, Agamemnon. Said to be the longest continuously inhabited city in the western hemisphere, Argos remained the most powerful state in the Peloponnese through the 7th century BC. In a famous 494 BC battle, even formidable Sparta was unable to get past the city walls, defended mightily by Argive women. Later Argos stood with Corinth and Sparta as the pillars of the Peloponnesian League. But these events that shaped the city's illustrious legacy are obviously far in the past, leaving the modern traveler questioning what there is to see in Argos today. Its archaeological museum and ancient theater have captured hints of the city's former glory and made them accessible to current visitors. You may, however, be tempted to devote more time to picturesque Nafplion nearby.

⌐ TRANSPORTATION

The train station (☎27510 67 212) is 1km from the plateia. Walk down Nikitara past the OTE and follow the signs to Nafplion. Then, signs for the police station will guide you to 25 Martiou; the train station is straight ahead. **Trains** go to Athens (3hr., 5 per day 2:40am-7:30pm, €3.50) via Fihtia (€0.60), Corinth (1hr., €1.80), and Nemea (20min., €1.20). The Argolida station (☎27510 67 324), on Kapodistriou, which runs parallel to and one block behind the side of the plateia with Hotel Morfeas, sends **buses** to: Athens (2½hr., 15 per day 5:30am-8:30pm, €8.70) via Corinth (€4); Mycenae (30min., 5 per day 7am-6:30pm, €1.10); Nafplion (30min., every 30min. 6:30am-9pm, €1); Nemea (1hr.; 6:30am, 1pm; €2.20); Tripoli (1hr., 4 per day 8:45am-4:45pm, €4). Service is reduced on weekends.

✈ 🛈 ORIENTATION AND PRACTICAL INFORMATION

Argos is a sprawling city with few landmarks, but most services are in or around the plateia, marked by the large **Church of Saint Peter.** If you arrive by bus, go right out of the station and turn left at the first intersection onto **Danaou.** The plateia will be on your left and a small, taverna-lined park will be on your right.

Bank: National Bank, Nikitara 2 (☎27510 65 029), off the plateia behind the small park to the left as you face Hotel Morfeas, has **currency exchange** and a **24hr. ATM.** Open M-Th 8am-2:30pm, F 8am-2pm.

Police: ☎27510 67 222, Ag. Artemiou 4. Head out from Vas. Sofias or follow the signs from the train station. Some English spoken. Open 24hr.

Hospital: ☎27510 24 455. 1km north of the plateia on Korinthou. Open 24hr.

Telephones: OTE, Nikitara 8 (☎27510 67 599). From the main plateia, walk 60m along the left side of the park past the ATM. Open M-F 7am-2pm.

Internet Access: Center for Youth Information (☎27510 25 314), 50m to the left of the bus station, facing the plateia, in the building in the playground. Free Internet access with the purchase of a snack or drink. Open 10am-2:30pm and 5:30-10pm.

Post Office: 32-34 Kapodistrou (☎27510 67 366). 3 blocks toward the plateia from the bus station. Follow the signs from the plateia. **Exchanges currency.** Open M-F 7:30am-2pm. **Postal Code:** 21200.

🛏 🍴 ACCOMMODATIONS AND FOOD

Argos's accommodations are fairly disappointing, with a few mid-range hotels around the main plateia. The luxurious ▨**Hotel Morfeas ❸,** Danaou 2, on the plateia, has unexpectedly reasonable prices. The modern rooms come with A/C, TV, phones, sleek private baths, and balconies; many have unobstructed views of St. Peter's. There is also a cafe in the lobby. (☎27510 68 317; www.hotel-morfeas.gr. Free Internet. Breakfast €5. Singles €25; doubles €35; triples €35. MC/V.) Don't be put off by the dark lobby at **Hotel Apollon ❷,** Papaflessa 13; the rooms themselves are spacious and light, with balconies, A/C, and TV. (☎27510 68 065.

Singles €20-25; doubles €29-35; triples €38-50. Discounts for shared baths.) The **Hotel Palladion ❷**, Vas. Sofias 5, just off the plateia, has colorful rooms with funky decorations; they include A/C, TV, phones, baths, and balconies. (☎27510 67 807. Singles €25-40; doubles €30-50; triples €40-65. MC/V.)

Argos has the Peloponnese's largest **open-air** **market** in the empty lot 20m from the museum when walking away from the plateia. (Open W, Sa 7am-3pm.) Fast food junkies can get their fix at the greasy gyro joints that clog the arteries of the plateia and the surrounding area. There are many supermarkets throughout the center of town, including gigantic **Atlantik Supermarket,** 50m to the right of the bus station facing the plateia. (Open M-F 8am-9pm, Sa 8am-6pm.) For a quick bite, locals consistently recommend **La Prima ❶**, Vas. Georgiou 8, in the park by Dia Discount Supermarket. This hip joint serves Italian and grilled Greek fare; cramped seating makes take-out and delivery options appealing. (☎27510 68 188. Salads €2.50-4. Pasta €3-5.) Those who prefer a more formal meal may be disappointed by the sit-down options, as there is only one taverna around the plateia.

👁 SIGHTS

ARCHAEOLOGICAL MUSEUM. Argos's superb archaeological museum has a large Mycenaean collection, Roman sculptures, several ancient weapons, and a garden courtyard with notable **Roman mosaics.** In the most striking of the mosaics, 12 figures personify the months of the year in their dress and expressions. Another mosaic similarly portrays the four seasons. Inside the museum, the Lerna Collection displays pottery from a prehistoric settlement, including pots imported from Troy. The statues on the second floor of the museum are mainly Roman copies of Classical designs, demonstrating Rome's admiration of its Greek territory. Though the explanations are in Greek and French, a small English pamphlet outlines the basic organization of the museum. *(Kallergi and Vas. Olgas 1. Follow Vas. Olgas from the plateia for 50m. ☎27510 68 819. Open Tu-Su 8:30am-3pm. €2, students and seniors €1, EU students and children free.)*

ANCIENT ARGOS. Though most of the ancient city of Argos remains buried beneath the modern version, major ongoing excavations have taken place on the city's western fringe at the site of the ancient agora. Unfortunately, many of the potentially fascinating sights aren't in the best shape. With a seating capac-

THE HIDDEN DEAL

A PERFECT FIT

The hectic open-air market in Argos has as many bargains as any in Greece. Villagers catch the early morning bus into town to score some cheap vegetables and teenage hipsters rummage through the clothing piled across the plateia, looking for something tight and low-cut enough. Strewn in this blissfully budget haze is the best deal of all: the shoes.

Fine-leather footwear is scattered throughout the market's clothing section. Sandals, loafers, and slippers come in all sizes and colors, everything from standard brown to white with purple swirls. Many stalls sell the same items, so shop around before making a purchase. You should be able to grab any pair for €10-15—a fraction of what you'd spend in a store. Most of the shoes on sale are factory rejects, but by and large their defects are undetectable. For some, the supposed problem may have been aesthetic (again, white with purple swirls), which means there are plenty of opportunities to find something that will assert your own unique style. Other shoes may have just been over-produced. Regardless of why they're there, though, the soft calfskin and super-low prices guarantee you'll leave the market with a new spring in your step.

Walk toward the Archaeological Museum from the plateia and continue for 30m. Open W, Sa 7am-3pm.

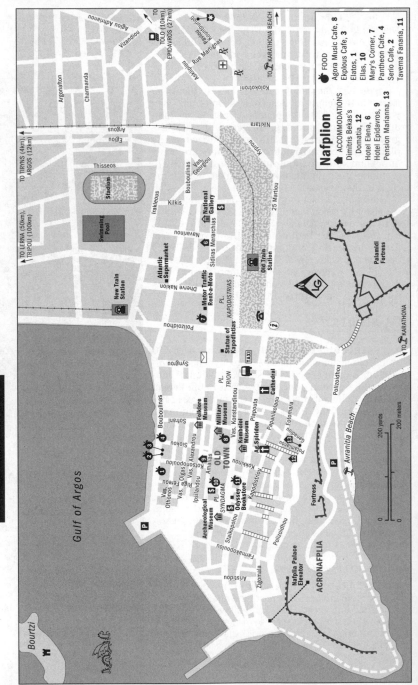

PELOPONNESE

Nafplion

ACCOMMODATIONS
Dimitris Bekas's
Domatia, **12**
Hotel Elena, **6**
Hotel Epidavros, **9**
Pension Marianna, **13**

FOOD
Agora Music Cafe, **8**
Ekplous Cafe, **3**
Elatos, **1**
Ellas, **10**
Mary's Corner, **7**
Pantheon Cafe, **4**
Serio Cafe, **2**
Taverna Fanaria, **11**

TO TOLO (10km),
EPIDAVROS (27km)

TO Aglou Adrianou

Vizandiou

Paflon Koutounin

TO KARATHONA BEACH

Rue Marignas

Rue Nezidou

Argonafton

Charmanda

Kolokotroni

Niklatra

Kipou

TO TIRYNS (4km),
ARGOS (12km)

Eflou

Argous

Thisseos

Stadium

Irakleous

Kilkis

Bouboulinas

Vas.
Georgiou

25 Martiou

TO LERNA (50km),
TRIPOLI (100km)

**Swimming
Pool**

Navarinou

**National
Gallery**

Sidiras Merarchias

**Atlantic
Supermarket**

Dherve Nakion

**Motor Traffic
Rent-a-Moto**

PL.
KAPODISTRIAS

**Old Train
Station**

**New Train
Station**

Polizoidhon

**Statue of
Kapodistrias**

Syngrou

TAXI

TO KARATHONA

Gulf of Argos

Bouboulinas

Sofrani

Siokou

**Folklore
Museum**

PL.
TRION

Vas. Konstandinou

**Military
Museum**

**Komboloi
Museum**

Ag. Spiridon

Papanikolaou

Cathedral

Papaniko

Plapouta

Fotomara

Genadiou

Vas. Alexandrou

Kotsonopoulou

Kokkinou

Vas. Olgas

Vas. Rini Ferou

Vas.
Othonos

Ipsilandou

**Archaeological
Museum**

Amalias

SYNDAGMA

**Odyssey
Bookstore**

**OLD
TOWN**

Kapodistriou

Staikopolou

Farmakopoulou

Zigomala

Arsidou

Polizoidhou

Avrantia Beach

P

Fortress

**Napfla Palace
Elevator**

ACRONAFPLIA

Polizoidhou

**Palamidi
Fortress**

0   200 yards
0   200 meters

Bourtzi

ity of 20,000, the 5th-century BC **☒theater** was the largest of its time in the Greek world. Although it's not as well-preserved as its famous counterpart in Epidavros, its sheer size is still impressive. What was once an extensive **Roman bath complex** nearby is now little more than two red brick walls, though many of the original floor mosaics are intricate, colorful, and intact. Similarly, the **Roman odeum**, 30m to the left of the baths (with your back to the entrance), survives mostly as an outline, since its rows dissolve into the hillside. Across the street are the scattered remains of the **agora,** built in the 5th century BC and destroyed by Alaric's Visigoths in AD 39. *(From the museum, turn left and walk toward the large space that holds the open-air market. Turn left onto Phidonos and walk 5min. until the road ends. Make a right on Theatrou and walk to the end. Open daily 8:30am-3pm. Free.)*

THE CASTLE OF LARISA. Franks, Venetians, and Ottomans all captured and ruled Argos in turn. As a result, the town's fortress is an architectural hodgepodge, combining disparate medieval and Turkish elements with Classical and Byzantine foundations. The Cyclopean walls are nearly 4000 years old. The ruins, about 4km above the city, also provide stunning sunset views. *(Walk along Foroneos for about 1hr. or take the path from the ruins of the ancient theater. The road to the castle is mostly unshaded, and it can get swelteringly hot in the summer, so bring water or take a taxi (€5). Open 24hr. Free.)*

OTHER SIGHTS. The **Argive Heraion,** 10km northeast of Argos, dedicated to Hera, goddess of the Argives, was built in the 5th century BC. It prospered well into the AD 2nd century, hosting the celebrations that followed the official ending of the Heraia Games (archery contests held at Argos in the second year after each Olympics) and other annual festivals. Fifteen kilometers from Argos is the ruined city of **Dendra,** where tombs yielded the preserved suit of bronze armor now in the Nafplion Archaeological Museum.

NAFPLION Ναύπλιο   ☎27520

Before 15th-century Venetians tried their hand at urban design, Nafplion consisted entirely of two hilltop fortresses above a swamp. It has since flourished into one of the most desirable getaways in Greece. Although the modern New Town is not so appealing, the Old Town is composed of charming tavernas and craftshops spread across a maze of trellised alleyways and plateias that extend to the waterfront promenade. With its pebbly beaches, Venetian architecture, ancient fortresses, and majestic harbor, Nafplion is one of the Argolid's most precious treasures.

▐ TRANSPORTATION

The **bus station,** Syngrou 8 (☎27520 27 423), across from the park, has service to: Argos (20min., 2 per hr. 5am-9:30pm, €1); Athens (3hr., 15 per day 5:10am-8pm, €10) via Corinth (2hr., €4); Epidavros (40min., 4 per day 10:15am-5:30pm, €2.20); Mycenae (45min., 3 per day, €2.20); Tolo (20min., every hr. 7am-8:30pm, €1); Tripoli (1½hr.; 4 per day 8:30am-4:20pm, service reduced Sa-Su; €4). **Taxis** (☎27520 24 120 or 27520 24 720) congregate on Syngrou near the bus station. One block past the post office, away from the Old Town, **Motortraffic Rent-A-Moto,** Sidiras 15, rents mopeds. (☎27520 22 702. €10-15 per day. Includes helmet and insurance. Open M-F, Su 7:30am-9:30pm, Sa 7:30am-11:30pm.)

▄✦ ▐ ORIENTATION AND PRACTICAL INFORMATION

Bouboulinas is the waterfront promenade. To get there, turn left out of the bus station and follow **Syngrou,** which runs to the harbor, perpendicular to Bouboulinas. Three principal streets stretch west off **Syngrou** into the **Old Town.** Moving inland

from Bouboulinas, the first is **Amalias**, the shopping street. **Vasileos Konstandinou**, the second, ends in **Plateia Syndagma**, the site of many tavernas, a bookstore, bank, and museum. The third is **Plapouta**, which becomes **Staikopoulou** in the vicinity of Pl. Syndagma. Across Syngrou, heading away from the Old Town, Plapouta becomes **25 Martiou**, Nafplion's largest avenue. Syngrou, behind the statue of Kapodistrias, marks the division between the Old Town and the modern **New Town**.

Tourist Office: 25 Martiou (☎27520 24 444), across from the OTE. Free **maps** and brochures on Nafplion and the surrounding area. Open daily 9am-1pm and 4-8pm.

Banks: Alpha Bank (☎27520 23 497), in Pl. Syndagma, has a **24hr. ATM** and **currency exchange.** Open M-Th 8am-2:30pm, F 8am-2pm. The **National Bank of Greece,** with a **24hr. ATM,** is on the corner across the street from the National Gallery on Sidiras Merarchias. Open M-Th 8am-2:30pm, F 8am-2pm.

Bookstore: Odyssey (☎27520 23 430), in Pl. Syndagma, sells stamps, newspapers, souvenirs, and books in English, French, and Greek. Open daily 8:30am-midnight.

Police: ☎27520 22 100. Take Sidiras Merarchias east, turn left when you get to Asklipiou, go right on Rue Martignas, then left up Pavlou Kountourioti; it's on the right. Open 24hr. **Tourist police** (☎27520 28 131) at the same address. Open daily 8am-2am.

Medical Services: Nafplion Hospital (☎27520 27 309), a 15min. walk east on Sidiras Merarchias and a left onto Asklipiou. Hospital is on the right, although the main entrance is on the opposite side of the block.

Telephones: OTE, Polizoidhou 2 (☎27520 22 139). On the left side of 25 Martiou as you walk toward the New Town. Open M, W, Sa 7:30am-3pm, Tu, Th-F 7:30am-8pm. **Pay phones** scattered throughout Pl. Syndagma.

Internet Access: Internet Cafe Dadis, Asklipiou 15 (☎27520 29 688). On the left side walking up Asklipiou in the New Town. Fast connection and comfortable atmosphere. Serves whiskey. €1 per 10min., €2 per 30min., €3 per hr. Open daily 9am-2am.

Post Office: (☎27520 24 855), on the corner of Syngrou and Sidiras Merarchias. **Western Union** available. Open M-F 7:30am-2pm. **Postal Code:** 21100.

▐ ACCOMMODATIONS

Rooms in the Old Town are charming and beautifully situated, which explains why they go quickly in summer. A number of unremarkable accommodations in the New Town can serve as a last resort. Pricier options lie on Bouboulinas and in the Old Town near the waterfront.

▧ **Pension Marianna,** Potamianou 9 (☎27520 24 256; www.pensionmarianna.gr). From the bus station, turn right and head south on Syngrou; turn right at Fotomara and follow the signs. Tucked quietly into the mountainside, this gem has jaw-dropping views of the city and handsomely adorned rooms with A/C, TV, phones, minibars, and baths. The cordial English-speaking owners serve lemonade worth writing home about. Breakfast €5. Singles €50-55; doubles €60-70; triples €75. MC/V. ❹

Hotel Epidavros, Kokkinou 2 (☎27520 27 541), just off Amalias, next to the Emporiki Bank. Centrally located in the Old Town, mere steps from the Nafplion nightlife, this hotel offers hardwood floors, A/C, TV, inviting beds, and private baths. The owner also runs the **Tirins Hotel,** Othonos 41 (☎27520 21 020), just a block from the port, with slightly larger rooms. Singles €30-45; doubles €45-65. ❸

Dimitris Bekas's Domatia, Efthimiopoulou 26 (☎27520 24 594). Follow Fotomara past Pension Marianna, turn left up the stairs at the Catholic church, right onto Zygomala, then left up the first stairs. This small pension exudes energy and offers a breathtaking view of Nafplion from the roof deck. Cozy rooms with shared bath and fridge; some have a bal-

cony and many have TV. Friendly manager Dimitris loves to chat, and shares lemons and oranges fresh from his trees. Reservations recommended. Singles €19; doubles from €25; triples €33. ❷

Hotel Elena, Sidiras Merarchias 31 (☎/fax 27520 23 888). 1 block behind Plaza Kapodistrias, away from the Old Town. Ample rooms come with A/C, TV, phones, baths, and huge balconies. Breakfast €7. Singles €50; doubles €60. ❹

🍴🍷 FOOD AND NIGHTLIFE

The Old Town's picturesque alleyways showcase countless romantic tavernas lit by soft lights amid flowers, balconies, and foot traffic. Fish restaurants that line the waterfront may charge as much as €70 per entree. Many of the best dining options are on Staikopoulou, the street inland from Pl. Syndagma, behind the bank. **Atlantic Market,** Bouboulinas 4, a block north from the far end of Pl. Kapodistrias, is an excellent modern supermarket with a great selection. (☎27520 26 626. Open M-F, Su 8am-9pm, Sa 8am-6pm.) **Ellas ❷,** in Pl. Syndagma, is refreshingly inexpensive, with a cheerful staff and outdoor seating that extends into the plateia. (☎27520 27 278. Veal with potatoes €6.50. Pasta dishes €3-4.50. Open daily 11:30am-4pm and 7:30-10:30pm.) **Taverna Fanaria ❷,** Staikopoulou 13, provides a peaceful, intimate atmosphere in which to enjoy traditional Greek entrees or simply to watch people walk by. (☎27520 27 141. Soup €3-6. Spaghetti bolognese €4.50. Fish dishes €4.60-7. Open daily noon-midnight.) **Mary's Corner ❶,** Sidiras Mirarchias 11, at the corner of Polizoidhou, is a fresh, cheap alternative to the standard sit-down restaurant, with delicious pitas (€1.20-2.30), salads (€2-6), and other entrees (€6-7) made in front of you. Many patrons elect to take their orders to the outdoor tables in the park. (☎27520 23 803. Open M-Th, Su 8am-4am, F 8am-6am, Sa 24hr.) Head along the waterfront to **Elatos ❷,** Bouboulinas 71, and savor their wide array of fresh local seafood. Enjoy typical taverna fare or treat yourself to the highly recommended scorpion fish, priced at €42 per kg. (☎27520 27 011. Appetizers €3-5. Entrees €4.50-7. Open daily noon-midnight.)

International and Greek pop music float out into the evening air at **Agora Music Cafe,** Vas. Konstandinou 17, where you can get excellent coffee (€3-6) or ice cream (€4-5) after dinner. (☎27520 26 016. Open daily 8am-2am.) At night, the trendy cafe-bars strung along the waterfront, such as **Pantheon, Ekplous,** and **Seirio,** surge with young heartthrobs and pounding

THE LOCAL STORY

DON'T WORRY, BEAD HAPPY

From the flashes of amber on the street to that whirring, clicking sound on the bus, you'll notice *komboloi* (come-boh-LOY), the fidget toy of the modern Greek, everywhere. Their name is rather self-explanatory, deriving from *kombos,* which means "knot," and *loi,* which refers to a group. Though almost always a loop of string filled with 16-20 beads, *komboloi* can range in shape and size, and the beads are made of materials ranging from amber and coral to bone and ivory. The *komboli,* the only secular beads of their type, are used primarily by men as a sort of stress reliever.

There are a number of theories as to *komboloi*'s origin. Some claim they are an adaptation of the rosary-like *komboskini* used by the monks of Mt. Athos to count prayers. Others suggest that the strung beads, like so much else in Greece, were born out of resistance to the Ottoman occupation, as a mockery of the Turks' 40-bead prayer strings. Still others say that *komboloi* are a relatively recent fashion, imported from Asia Minor in the population exchange of the 1920s.

*Learn more about the trend at Nafplion's **Komboloi Museum,** 25 Staikopoulou (☎27520 21 618). Open M-Sa 9:30am-9:30pm, Su 10:30am-9:30pm; in low season M, W-Sa 9:30am-9:30pm, Su 10:30am-9:30pm. €1.50, students and children free.*

beats. They offer beverages including beer (€3-5), mixed drinks (€5.50-6.50), and tasty "sippings" like almond-flavored white chocolate (€3). The search for alternative nightlife may land you in a taxi (€8) for the 15min. ride to **Tolo,** a tourist-packed beach resort. You can also take a **minicruise** of the harbor and get a close-up view of the *bourtzi*. Small boats leave from the end of the dock. Times and prices vary.

👁 🌊 SIGHTS AND BEACHES

Characterized by its architectural diversity, the Old Town is a display of history. Pl. Syndagma alone boasts a Venetian mansion, a Turkish mosque, and a Byzantine church, while Ottoman fountains, cannons, monuments, and statues sit in the alleyways. After passing from the Venetians to the Ottomans and back again, in 1821 Nafplion served as headquarters for the Greek revolutionary government and as Greece's first capital (1821-1834). President John Kapodistrias was assassinated here in Ag. Spiridon Church; the bullet hole is still visible in the church wall. The city's three fortresses stand as testaments to this politically checkered past.

▧**PALAMIDI FORTRESS.** The daunting 999 steps (though travelers attest that there are fewer—around 860) that once provided the only access to the 18th-century fort have since been supplemented by a 3km road (taxis €3.50-5). If you opt to brave the steps, they begin up from Polizoidhou past the park, and are marked by two cannonballs; bring water and try to go in the morning, when the steps are shaded. The spectacular views of the town, gulf, and much of the Argolid at the top of the fortress make the climb well worth it. For two weeks in June, coinciding with the full moon, there is a classical music festival with concerts every night. *(☎ 27520 28 036. Open daily 8:30am-6:30pm; low season 8:30am-5:45pm. €4, students and seniors €2, EU students and under 19 free.)*

ACRONAFPLIA. The fortress walls of the Acronafplia, the acropolis of Nafplion, were fortified by three successive generations of conquerors—Byzantines, Franks, and Venetians. To reach the fort, take the tunnel that runs into the hill, at the end of Zygomala, to the Nafplia Palace elevator, or follow the signs from the bus station. The views of the Palamidi Fortress, the Gulf, and the Old Town are fantastic. Ludwig I, King of Bavaria, had a huge Bavarian Lion carved out of a monstrous rock to guard the graves of the men who died in an epidemic in 1833-34.

MUSEUMS. Opened in 2004, the **National Gallery-Nafplion Annex,** Sidiras Merarchias 23, on the left heading toward the New Town, is a must-see stop for the art lover or history buff. The museum houses a wide array of 19th-century oil paintings that depict the 1821 Greek Revolution and has a section for temporary art exhibits. *(Open M, Th, Sa 10am-3pm, W, F 10am-3pm and 5-8pm, Su 10am-2pm. €3, students and seniors €1.50, children 12 and under free. M free.)* The fascinating **Komboloi Museum,** Staikopoulou 25, in the heart of the Old Town, allows visitors to explore all facets of the famous Greek *komboloi* (worry beads). *(☎/fax 27520 21 618. Open M-Sa 9:30am-9:30pm, Su 10:30am-9:30pm; closed Tu in low season. €1.50, students and children free.)* Nafplion's **Folklore Museum,** Vas. Alexandrou 1, in a lovely yellow building, is four blocks from the water at Sofrani. The award-winning collection includes an exhibit devoted to the progression of Greek fashion from antiquity to the 21st century. *(☎ 27520 28 379. Open M, W-Su 9am-3pm. €4, students and children €2.)* The **Military/War Museum,** Amalias 22, toward the New Town from Pl. Syndagma, displays a collection of historic firearms. *(☎ 27520 25 591. Open Tu-Sa 9am-2pm, Su 9:30am-2pm. Free.)*

BEACHES. Arvanitia, Nafplion's secluded, pebbly beach, is farther along Polizoidhou, past where the steps of Palamidi begin. On hot days, pop music blares over the noise of the sun-soaked crowd. For a cleaner, more serene alternative, take the footpath that runs along the water from the Arvanitia parking lot. The 45min. walk will reveal three quiet, rocky **coves**. If you're dying for a long, sandy beach, try the mostly undeveloped **Karathona** beach, a 3km hike along the coast from Arvanitia (taxi €3), or head to **Tolo**, where you can rent watersports equipment (€8-15). Buses head there from Nafplion every hour (€1).

DAYTRIPS FROM NAFPLION

MYCENAE Μυκήνες

Buses go to modern Mycenae from Nafplion (45min.; 10am, noon, 2pm; €2). To reach the ancient site, walk a shadeless 25min. uphill from town or take the bus to where it stops at the end of the asphalt road in the parking lot; the ruins are on the right. Open daily June-Oct. 8am-7:30pm; Nov.-May 8am-3pm. Museum open M noon-7pm, Tu-Su 8am-7pm. Site, museum, and Agamemnon's Tomb €8, students and seniors €4, EU students and children free. Guidebooks €3.50-6.50. Bags larger than book-size are not allowed in the acropolis.

The spectacular remains of ancient Mycenae, legendarily founded by Perseus, are on a rocky knoll between Mt. Ag. Elia to the north and Mt. Zara to the south. Gargantuan **Cyclopean walls**, 13m high and 10m thick, surround the site. Outside the central fortified city, down the road toward town, several *tholoi* tombs—most notably the so-called **"Treasury of Atreus"**—hint unsubtly at the magnificence that lies over the horizon. Today the bulk of the well-preserved ruins date from 1280 BC, when the city was the center of a vast Mycenaean Empire. The relics unearthed here number among the most celebrated archaeological discoveries in modern history, including countless jewels and the famous Mask of Agamemnon. As a result, many have been taken to the National Archaeological Museum in Athens (p. 119) instead of the new museum within the gate of the site itself.

HISTORY. Mycenae's origins, interactions with other Near Eastern civilizations, and subsequent decline have long puzzled historians. Thought to have been settled as early as 2700 BC by a tribe from the Cyclades, Mycenae, along with other nearby cities, remained under the shadow of the Minoans for centuries. It wasn't until the collapse of Minoan civilization in the mid-15th century BC that Mycenae surged to the head of the Greek world (p. 54). Mycenaean culture flourished for centuries until the 12th century BC, when the belligerent Dorians attacked from the north. Burning and looting anything in their path, the Dorians successfully conquered Greece, and Mycenae lost its grasp on the culture it had helped to create. The city continued to be inhabited through the Roman period, but by Byzantine times it had been swallowed by the earth and forgotten.

In 1874, the German businessman, classicist, and amateur archaeologist **Heinrich Schliemann** burst onto the Mycenaean scene. Fresh from his lucrative dig at Troy and eager to further establish the historical validity of Homeric epics, he began a quest to uncover Agamemnon's city. To his delight, he found massive walls which surrounded elaborate tombs laden with dazzling artifacts. It was impossible to overlook the possible connection between these finds and Homer's description of a "well-built citadel... rich in gold." Schliemann began his dig just inside the citadel walls at the spot where several ancient authors described royal graves. Discovering 15 skeletons "literally covered with gold and jewels," Schliemann decked his new 17-year-old Greek bride with the baubles and had her pose for photographs. Believing he had unearthed the skeletons of Agamemnon and his cohorts, he sent a telegram to the Greek king that read, "Have gazed on face of Agamemnon."

PELOPONNESE

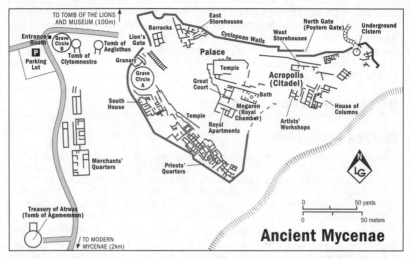

Ancient Mycenae

Moments after he removed its mask, however, the "face" underneath disintegrated. Modern archaeologists, who still cringe at the thought of such reckless excavation, now date the tombs and mask to four centuries before the Trojan War.

RUINS. Across from the entrance booth is **Grave Circle A,** where Schliemann found most of his artifacts. This hollow area contains six 16th-century BC **shaft graves** that have yielded 14kg worth of gold. Uphill from the entrance booth, you'll spot the imposing **Lion's Gate,** the portal into the ancient city, with two lions carved in relief above the lintel (estimated to weigh some 20 tons). Their heads—now missing—once bore eyes of precious gems. The sculpture, from 1240 BC, is one of the earliest known examples of statuary incorporated into a structure's support system. The barracks are up the stairs to the left after the gate. The gate and the walls of the upper citadel are from the 13th century BC.

The ruins on the hillside are the remnants of homes, businesses, and shrines from the formerly bustling complex. The **palace** and **royal apartments** are at the highest part of the citadel on the right. The open spaces include guard rooms, private areas, and a particularly impressive staircase; look for the **megaron,** or royal chamber, with its round hearth framed by the bases of four pillars. To the left of the citadel are the remaining stones of the ancient **temples,** thought to have been dedicated to Athena or Hera. At the far end of the city, between the palace and the **postern gate,** is the **underground cistern,** which guaranteed water during sieges. You can enter the silent and completely dark space at your own risk, but bring a flashlight and be careful—the steps are worn and slippery and drop off suddenly.

Follow the asphalt 400m back toward the town of Mycenae to the **Tomb of Agamemnon** (a.k.a. the "Treasury of Atreus"), the largest and most impressive *tholos,* named by Schliemann for the king he desperately wanted to discover here. On your way, stop at two often-overlooked *tholoi,* the **Tomb of Aegisthus** and the even more interesting **Tomb of Clytemnestra,** both outside the Lion's Gate near the town. Take the paths on your left and keep your flashlight handy. Once you get to the main structure, head down a 40m passage cut into the hillside that leads to the grave itself, and glance up to see the 120 ton lintel stones above you. The dim interior of the *tholos* conveys a ghostly majesty, but, to the dismay of both archaeologists and tourists, the tomb was found empty, having lost its valuables to robbers.

To reach the **museum,** with an impressive display of pottery and ancient script, follow the signs from the entrance booth, bearing left from the acropolis. The ceramics show evidence of trade with areas as far as Spain and Afghanistan. While the most important artifacts found at the site are in the National Archaeological Museum in Athens, the museum offers a detailed history of the ancient city, gorgeous views of the neighboring hills, and blessed air conditioning.

If you take longer than expected at the ruins and need to stay the night, try **Dassis Rent Rooms ❷,** in modern Mycenae, which has bright-blue rooms with A/C, TV, balconies, and wrought-iron beds. (☎27510 76 123. Singles €25-30; doubles €30-35; triples €35-40.) Food options are underwhelming, but funky and popular **Salt and Pepper ❷** (salads €2.50-3.50; entrees €2.50-7) has a 10% discount for students.

EPIDAVROS Επίδαυρος

Buses go there from Nafplion (40min.; 10:15am, 12:14, 2:30, 5:30pm; €2.20). A snack bar and restaurant-cafe serve the site but visitors may want to bring lunch. Museum ☎ 27530 22 009. Site open daily 8am-7pm; in low season 8am-5pm; festival season F-Sa 8am-9pm. Museum closed M 8am-noon. For a detailed explanation of the ruins, visitors may want to purchase a guidebook (€2-10). Ticket includes entrance to the museum and archaeological site and a small map of the ruins; €6, students and seniors €3, EU students and children free.

Like Olympia and Delphi, Epidavros was once both a town and a sanctuary sacred first to ancient deity Maleatas, then to Apollo, who assumed aspects of the former patron's identity. Eventually the energies of the sanctuary were directed toward Apollo's son, the medically gifted demigod Asclepius. When the good doctor got a little overzealous and began to raise people from the dead, Zeus legendarily felled him with a thunderbolt. Asclepius, however, continued to guard over Epidavros, which became famous across the ancient world as a center of medicine. The prestige of the ancient health center reached its peak in the early 4th century BC, when sick people traveled across the Mediterranean for medical and mystical cures to a disastrous onslaught of plagues. Asclepius (or one of his sacred creatures, the dog and the snake) made diagnoses in dream visitations; recent finds indicate that surgeries took place here as well. Over the centuries, the complex became increasingly lavish with former patients' assistance, growing to include temples dedicated to Aphrodite, Artemis, and Themis. Operating until AD 426, the sanctuary complex was closed along with all other non-Christian sanctuaries by Emperor Theodosius II.

With its world-renowned acoustics, the theater, built in the early 2nd century BC, is without a doubt the site's most splendid structure. Initially constructed to accommodate 6000 people, its capacity was expanded to 12,300 in the next century. Despite severe earthquakes in AD 522 and 551, the theater is still almost perfectly intact, and has recently come alive again after centuries of silence: during July and August it hosts the ▨**Epidavros Theater Festival.** The National Theater of Greece and visiting companies perform Classical Greek plays translated into modern Greek. Performances begin at 9pm, and tickets can be purchased at the site. (€17-40, students and children €8.50. Children under 6 prohibited from the front sections.) You can also buy tickets in advance at the Athens Festival Box Office (☎21032 21 459) or Nafplion's bus station. On performance nights, KTEL buses make a round-trip trek from Nafplion (7:30pm, €4), returning to Nafplion 20min. after the performance ends.

▨ **THEATER.** Built into a hillside in the 3rd century BC, the 55 tiers of the **Theater of Epidavros** face half-forested, half-flaxen mountains so awe-striking they almost distract from the tragedies played out on the stage. Though it is often said that the theater was designed by Polykleitos the Younger, architect of an even larger companion theater at Argos, it is not old enough to have been his work. The theater's acoustics defy belief, as yelling, singing, coin-dropping, whispering, and even match-lighting tourists from all nations enthusiastically demonstrate from the stage area—every sound made there can be heard, even in the last row of seats. The secret to the theater's acoustic perfection is its symmetrical architecture; the entire amphitheater was built in proportion to the **Fibonacci sequence.**

MUSEUM. The **Archaeological Museum** lies between the theater and the ruins. While most of the museum's exquisite pieces have been hidden from visitors because of restoration efforts, three open rooms still display a worthwhile collection. The room closest to the entrance holds a fascinating array of ancient medical instruments, as well as a series of engraved stone tablets, some of which describe the miraculous cures of Asclepius in lengthy detail. Make sure to check out the marble statue of bearded Asclepius, complete with thigh-high *caduceus*. The room farthest from the entrance is filled with intricate **entablatures** from the Temple of Asclepius and the *tholos*. Most impressive, however, is the perfectly preserved, authentic Corinthian capital, regarded as the architect's prototype for all of the capitals of the Temple of Asclepius.

SANCTUARY OF ASCLEPIUS AND THOLOS. The extensive ruins of the sanctuary, currently undergoing restoration, have somewhat limited access and can be confusing to decipher. Walking from the museum, you'll first pass the **Xenon,** an ancient hotel that now resembles little more than a maze of foundations. The **gymnasium** containing the remains of a **Roman odeon** is the first structure of the more concentrated complex of ruins. To the left is a **stadium,** of which only a few tiers of seats and the athletes' starting blocks survive. Two of the most important structures of the ancient sanctuary, the **Temple of Asclepius** and the famous **tholos,** are in front and to the left as you approach the ruins from the museum area. The *tholos,* thought to have been built by Polykleitos the Younger in the mid-4th century BC, is a richly carved architectural masterpiece. Beside the *tholos* are the remains of the **abaton,** where ailing patients would wait for Asclepius to reveal the proper treatment. Farther along the path on the eastern edge of the site lie the ruins of 2nd-century **Roman baths.**

TIRYNS Τίρυνθα

Take the Argos bus from Nafplion (10min., 2 per hr. 5am-9:30pm, €1). ☎ 27520 22 657. Guidebooks (€5) outline the history of the city. Open daily 8am-7pm; low season 8am-3pm. €3, students and seniors €2, EU students and under 18 free.

About 4km northwest of Nafplion on the road to Argos lie the Mycenaean ruins of Tiryns, or **Tiryntha,** birthplace of Hercules. Heinrich Schliemann's excavation of the site began in 1875 and has been continued by the German Archaeological Institute (p. 85) ever since. Perched atop a 25m hill that provides a 360° view of the Argolid, Tiryns was nearly impregnable during ancient times until its stunning capture and destruction by the Argives in 468 BC. Parts of the stronghold date as far back as 2600 BC, but most of what remains (including the walls) was not built until 1000 years later in the Mycenaean Era. At 8m tall, the massive walls surrounding the site reveal the immensity of the original fortifications; the walls on the eastern and southern slopes of the ancient acropolis reach a width of 20m. Vaulted galleries are concealed within these structures; however, many of the site's gems, like the palace's frescoes, have been taken to the National Archaeological Museum in Athens (p. 119), rendering the site significantly less interesting. Follow the signs leading to the left to a preserved *tholos* tomb from the Mycenaean era in a hillside.

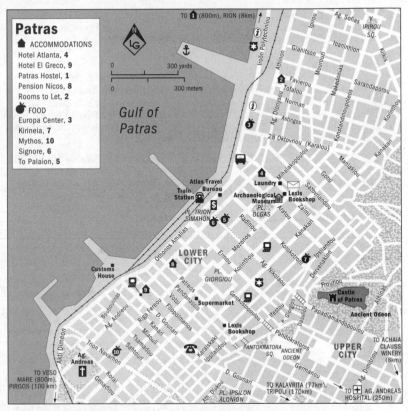

Patras

🏠 ACCOMMODATIONS
Hotel Atlanta, 4
Hotel El Greco, 9
Patras Hostel, 1
Pension Nicos, 8
Rooms to Let, 2

🍴 FOOD
Europa Center, 3
Kirineia, 7
Mythos, 10
Signore, 6
To Palaion, 5

Gulf of
Patras

ELIA Έλεια AND ACHAIA Αχαία

In rural Elia and Achaia, tomatoes (from three major factories in the area) and beachgoers (from all over the world) redden together beneath the blazing sun. Studded with cornfields and golden beaches, the mountainous region was first settled by Achaians from the Argolid, and later ruled by Romans. Afterward Franks, Ottomans, and Venetians all violently disputed this land, leaving a visible wake in the occasional ruins that crop up across the area's terrain.

PATRAS Πάτρας   ☎ 26106

Greece's third-largest city spreads from its harbor in a mixture of urban and Classical, Greek and international styles. Island-bound tourists often view the conveniently-located city as a stopover, and thus never look beyond the tourist agencies and cafes lining Pl. Trion Simahon. Yet Patras, a college town, is young, diverse, and vibrant throughout the year. Its noisy exuberance makes for a lively social atmosphere, as cafe-lined plateias and pedestrian-only streets, interspersed seamlessly with heavenly churches, overflow nightly. The prevalence of ancient theaters and modern festivals in Patras are just two of the many reasons it was named the European cultural capital for 2006. From mid-January to Ash Wednesday, Patras breaks out with pre-Lenten Carnival madness—music, food, and all-night revelry. The port becomes one vast dance floor and, for once, people stand a chance against speeding vehicles.

▙ TRANSPORTATION

If you're coming from Athens by car, choose between the **New National Road,** which runs inland along the Gulf of Corinth, and the slower, scenic **Old National Road,** which hugs the coast. From central Greece, take the brand-new **Rion-Antirio** bridge to Rion on the Peloponnese, then hop on bus #6 from Rion to the stop at **Kanakari** and **Aratou** (30min., €1), four blocks uphill from the main station.

Trains: Oth. Amalias 47 (☎26106 39 108, info 26106 39 109, tickets abroad 26106 39 110). To: **Athens** (regular: 4¼hr., 8 per day 2:40am-7:20pm, €5.30; express: €10); **Egio** (regular: 35min., 8 per day 6am-9pm, €1.20; express: €4); 1 bus runs to **Kalamata** (5½hr., 3 per day 6:15am-5:15pm, €6) through **Pirgos,** where you can catch a bus to Olympia (2hr.). The trains to Athens are packed, so reserve seats even if you have a railpass. **Ticket booth** open daily 6am-2am. MC/V.

Buses: KTEL (☎26106 23 886, 26106 23 887, or 26106 23 888), on Oth. Amalias between Aratou and Zaïmi. Buses go to: **Athens** (3hr., 33 per day roughly every 30min. 2:30am-9:45pm, €14); **Egio** (17 per day roughly on the hr., 7am-10:15pm, €3); **Ioannina** (4hr., 3 per day 12:30-5:30pm, €17); **Kalamata** (3hr.; 8am, 2:30pm; €16.40); **Kalavrita** (2hr., 4 per day 5:30am-4pm, €6); **Pirgos** (2hr., 10 per day 5:30am-8:30pm, €7.20); **Thessaloniki** (7hr.; noon, 3:15, 9pm; €33); **Tripoli** (2hr.; 7:15am, 2pm; €12); **Volos** (5hr., Su-F 2:30pm, €20). The **blue buses** around town are city buses. Buy tickets either on the bus or at 1 of the many white kiosks; there's 1 in Pl. Giorgiou and another next to the bus station. Tell the person at the kiosk your desired bus number and destination. Make sure to get a ticket for the return trip.

Ferries: From Patras, boats reach **Kephalonia, Ithaka,** and **Corfu** in Greece, and **Brindisi, Bari, Ancona,** and **Venice** in Italy. Most ferries to Italy leave at night. Daily ferries to **Vathy** on Ithaka (3½ hr.; 12:30, 8:30pm; €14) via **Sami** on Kephalonia (3hr., €13.50) and to **Corfu** (7hr., midnight, €29). Prices to Italy vary depending on type of passage and ferry line, so check the travel offices along Oth. Amalias and make sure to check prices for more than one line. **Railpasses** won't work for domestic ferries, but for international ferries, **Superfast Ferries,** Oth. Amalias 12 (☎26106 22 500; open 10am-9pm), which operates Blue Star lines, is the only company that accepts Eurail passes. For domestic and international departures, head to **Atlas Travel Bureau** (☎26102 24 439) opposite the train station (open M-F 9am-7pm, Sa-Su 9am-1:30pm and 3:30-6pm). For info on ferry departures, call the **Port Authority** (☎26103 41 002) or contact the Info Center or tourist police.

Car Rental: Many along Ag. Andreou. **Hertz Rent-A-Car,** Karalou 2 (☎26102 20 990). Turn right between the train station and the information center. Rates from €65 per day. Open M-Sa 8am-2pm and 4:40-8:30pm, Su 9:30am-1pm and 5:30-8pm. AmEx/MC/V.

Taxis: Line up in plateias and by the bus station. 24hr. **Radio Express** ☎26104 50 000.

▚ ▞ ORIENTATION AND PRACTICAL INFORMATION

Patras is divided into an upper and a lower city, both of which are arranged in a grid; most hotels, restaurants, and shops are in the heart of the lower city. **Othonas Amalias** (called **Iroön Polytechniou** past the new port) runs parallel to the waterfront. There are three main squares downtown. One block from the train station along Oth. Amalias is **Plateia Trion Simahon,** with palm trees, cafes, and kiosks. **Agios Nikolaou** runs inland from the plateia and intersects the city's major east-west streets. From the corner of Ag. Nikolaou and **Mezonos,** walk three blocks south on Mezonos to find **Plateia Giorgiou,** whose sculpted fountains make it seem like a little piece of Italy. The heart of New Patras, lined with designer clothing shops, is between Pl. Giorgiou and **Plateia Olgas,** three blocks to the left, with your back to the water. Access the upper city by walking away from the water on Ag. Nikolaou.

Tourist Office: The **Info Center,** Oth. Amalias 6 (☎26104 61 740 or 26104 61 741; www.infocenterpatras.gr), between 28 Oktovriou and Astingos, is the most comprehensive information center in Patras, providing festival schedules, transportation info, museum info, maps, brochures, and bicycles to explore the area (all free). It also offers information on all of Greece in English, French, Italian, German, and, of course, Greek. The center displays artwork, regional products, and a diverse selection of local wines, along with directions to local wineries. Open daily 8am-10pm. There is also a smaller information kiosk in Pl. Trion Simahon.

Banks: National Bank (☎26106 37 400), in Pl. Trion Simahon on the waterfront, has a **24hr. ATM** and **currency exchange,** as do other banks on the plateia and around Kolokotroni. Open M-F 8am-2:30pm.

Luggage Storage: Europa Center (p. 156) will store your bags for free. You can also store them at the port (€1.20; open 8am-10pm) and the train station (€3.20).

International Bookstore: Lexis Bookshop, Mezonos 38-40 (☎26102 20 919). By the Archaeology Museum. Has English and Greek books on Greek culture, history, and travel, as well as useful dictionaries. Open M-F 8:30am-2pm, Tu, Th-F also 5:30-9pm, Sa 9am-2pm. Their store at Patreos 90 (☎26102 74 831) carries only English books.

Laundromat: There are quite a few down Zaïmi, but try the one at 21 Zaïmi (☎26102 78 189) 3 blocks from the bus station. Wash and dry €7. Open M, W, Sa 9am-2pm, Tu and Th-F 9am-2pm and 5:30-9pm.

Police: ☎100. On the corner of Ermou and Karaiskaki, 6 blocks up from the waterfront.

Hospital: Ag. Andreas Hospital (☎26102 27 000), on Patron-Class past the church and on the left. For an **ambulance,** dial ☎100.

Telephones: OTE, at the corner of D. Gounari and Kanakari. Open M, W, Sa 8am-3pm, Tu and Th-F 8am-3pm and 5:30-8pm.

Internet Access: There's no lack of Internet cafes in Patras. **The Web,** Gerokostopoulou 34, 1 block above Pl. Giorgiou on your right, is a good, central option. Billing itself as "the ultimate Internet and gaming experience," The Web masquerades as a trendy nightclub with a dark bar and blue neon lights. €0.10 per min., €1.50 per hr. Open 24hr. **Ametron,** Korinthou 204 (☎26102 76 749), offers coffee (€2) and beer (€2) while you surf. €3 per hr. Open 8am-midnight. Another popular option is **Lanarena,** Ag. Andreou 149 (☎26102 73 063), whose low rates attract budget travelers and teenagers playing the latest computer games. €1.50 per hr. Open 24hr.

Post Office: ☎26102 74 642. On Mezonos at the corner of Zaïmi. Open M-F 7:30am-8pm, Sa 7:30am-2pm. **Postal Code:** 26001.

▐ ACCOMMODATIONS

Most hotels in Patras are on or near Ag. Andreou to the left of Pl. Trion Simahon facing inland, or on Ag. Nikolaou. Others are near the train and bus stations. While many are budget in appearance but not in price, some are diamonds in the rough.

▨ **Rooms to Let Spyros Vazouras,** Tofalou 2 (☎26104 52 152; www.patrasrooms.gr), 2 blocks up from the harbor, across from the new port entrance. This urban domatia has a personal feel, with large, bright rooms equipped with A/C, TV, and clean baths. Other perks include a communal fridge and a roof-top lounge with ocean views. Singles €30; doubles €40; additional bed €10. ❸

Pension Nicos, Patreos 3 (☎26106 23 757), 2 blocks off the waterfront. The best bet in Patras for price and convenient location, 3 blocks from Pl. Trion Simahon. This hotel features large wood-paneled and high-ceilinged rooms with balconies and clean, modern shared baths. Bar and roof terrace have excellent sunset views of the harbor. From the lobby, ring the bell and pick up the phone to connect to the 3rd-fl. office. Singles €20; doubles €30; triples €40-45. ❷

Hotel El Greco, Ag. Andreou 145 (☎26102 72 931; fax 26102 72 932). Walking along Andreou with the water on your right, it's 4 blocks past Pl. Trion Simahon on your left. It's nothing special, but clean rooms have baths, TV, fridges, and A/C. Breakfast €6. Check-out noon. Singles €38; doubles €50; triples €60. ❹

Patras Hostel, Iroön Polytechniou 62 (☎26104 27 278). From the port, walk away from town with the water on your left for about 1km. A cheaper option offered by the same owner as Rooms to Let, Patras Hostel occupies a creaky turn-of-the-century mansion that sat empty for 43 years after being used by occupying Germans in WWII. The gorgeous view and relative abundance of flora and fauna make up for the stark rooms, and the lack of constant moped noise is refreshing. Leave valuables at reception desk. Check-out 10:30am. Dorms €10. Sheets €.50 ❶

Hotel Atlanta, Zaïmi 10 (☎26102 78 627). 2 blocks away from the bus station in a residential area, Hotel Atlanta offers all the amenities found at downtown hotels at a cheaper price. The modern rooms have clean bathrooms, minibars, TV, A/C, and balconies. Breakfast €5. Singles €30; doubles €50. MC/V. ❸

◖ FOOD

Walk along the waterfront and through any of the main plateias for options ranging from gyro stands to fancy Italian restaurants to quiet creperies. Better quality and more traditional tavernas can be found by walking to the top of Kolokotroni from Pl. Olgas. **Supermarkets** are scattered throughout town.

Europa Center (☎26104 37 006), on Oth. Amalias between the information center and bus station. This friendly cafeteria-style eatery is run by Greek-Americans ready to assist weary backpackers. The food caters accordingly to tourists, but Europa Center provides very useful services such as free luggage storage, Internet access (€4 per hr.), a few old-school arcade games, and valuable local tips and resources. Appetizers €2.50. Salads €2.50-4. Entrees €3-7, including many vegetarian options. MC/V. ❷

Mythos (☎26103 29 984), on the corner of Riga Fereou and Trion Navarhon near Agios Andreas. This whimsical eatery calls itself a cafe, but it could be mistaken for a plant shop because of the flowers. Though the menu is modest, they have a fairly large selection of Greek salads (€4.70-5) and pastas (€6-8). The decor is a major draw in a city filled with generic cafes: bright potted plants are adorned with pinwheels, lanterns, and lights, while plates and serving dishes hang from the walls. Open daily 8pm-2am. ❷

Kirineia, Kolokotroni 63 (☎26102 74 340, delivery 26106 22 435), just above the corner of Karaiskaki and Kolokotroni. Adding much-needed diversity to Patras's food options, Kirineia offers a comfortable atmosphere and large portions. With a tasteful and romantic rustic kitchen theme, it serves Cypriot specialties such as grilled *haloumi* cheese and *seftalia* (Cyprus burger with spices and cheese; from €5). Entrees €4-8. ❷

Signore (☎26102 22 212), on Ag. Andreou across from Pl. Trion Simahon. Bustles with families grabbing pizza before a ferry ride to Italy and young hipsters looking for a bite to eat before a night of clubbing. This bright, airy quasi-Italian sit-down or take-out place serves everything from salads (€5-7) and pizza (€1.75 per slice) to large crepes (€2-4). Watch the young chefs theatrically toss your pizza dough up in the air. Try the veggie pizza (full pie; €8) for a meatless meal. Delivery available. Open 24hr. ❷

To Palaion, Ag. Nikolaou 13 (☎26102 66 435), between Mezenos and Mihalakopoulou. With Greek, French, and Italian food, this cafe attracts an older crowd. Salads €5-8. Entrees €7-15. Desserts €4-6. Coffee €1.50-3. Open daily 7:30am-1am. MC/V. ❸

Coffee Right, Pl. Giorgiou (☎26102 41 241). A beach bum's dream, this bright smoothie bar is in the middle of town where it helps locals bear the scorching summer heat with frozen drinks (€3-4). Other treats include ice cream with intriguing flavor names such as "Love Potion" and "Magic Soft," pastries, and desserts (all under €2), and some sandwiches (€2.50). Open 7am-11:30pm. ❶

🔎 SIGHTS

ACHAIA CLAUSS WINERY. A narrow road meanders uphill through grapevines and shaded countryside to the castle-like, internationally renowned 🏰 **Achaia Clauss winery,** 8km southeast of Patras. Founded in 1861 by German-born Baron Gustav von Clauss, its weathered stone buildings have aged as well as its wine. Try a complimentary sample of its famous Mavrodaphne, a superb and sweet dessert wine reputedly named for the black eyes of Clauss's lost love, Daphne. Not only is the wine renowned in the international community—numerous awards, diplomas, and letters from grateful ambassadors adorn the walls—but the staff is friendly and incredibly knowledgeable. Be sure to take a tour of the old wine cellars to see the Imperial Cellar, where images of Dionysus rowing wine to shore grace the beautifully-carved barrels. The oldest wine, a €1250 Mavrodaphne from 1873, is bottled for rare and special occasions, most recently the 2004 Olympics in Athens. Visitors can buy other wines (€2-30) on the spot. Before you leave, wander around the main house to catch a breathtaking view of the ocean and Patras. (☎26103 68 276. Take bus #7 from the intersection of Gerokostopoulou and Kanakari towards Seravali; it stops at the main gate to the winery (30min., €1.20). A 10min. walk up the winding road will get you to the winery. Open daily May-Sept. 11am-7pm, tours noon-3pm; Sept.-April 10am-5pm, tours 11am-3pm. Free. Free English tours every hr.)

AGIOS ANDREAS. The largest Orthodox cathedral in Greece, with a dome that soars to 46m and a capacity of 5500 people, is dedicated to St. Andrew. The saint was martyred here in the AD first century on an X-shaped crucifix (he felt unworthy of dying on a cross like Jesus's). A decade ago the Catholic Church returned St. Andrew's holy head to this place of martyrdom. The top of the head is visible through its reliquary, an ornate silver replica of the cathedral itself, in front of the remains of St. Andrew's crucifix on the right of the church. The cathedral's frescoes, gold mosaics, and delicately-latticed windows are both religiously significant and artistic masterpieces. One highlight is the large, intricately carved wooden chandelier in the center. Behind the cathedral on Eth. Korai is the equally beautiful **Church of Saint Andrew,** the original church built between 1836 and 1843. This building has bright frescoes, chandeliers, and a small well allegedly built by the saint himself, which can be found through a doorway to the right of the church. Legend holds that anyone who drinks from the well will return again to Patras. *(About 1.5km from the port. Walk along the waterfront or Ag. Andreou with the water to your right until you reach the cathedral; it will be on your left. Open daily 7am-dusk. Modest dress required.)*

THE CASTLE OF PATRAS. Built over the ruins of an ancient acropolis using many of the same materials, Patras's castle remains relatively intact considering its continuous, turbulent use from the AD 6th century to WWII. Controlled by the Byzantines, Franks, Turks, Venetians, and even the Vatican, the castle serves as a tribute to both the city below and to the various influences that have helped shape it. While the Slavs and Saracens have long departed, the castle maintains its aggressive spirit by hosting the occasional death-metal concert (among others) in the courtyard. The castle's high location makes it a perfect spot to get a bird's-eye view of the city. *(Walk to the upper city from Ag. Nikolaou. Then walk about 10min., following the fortress wall on Papadiamandopoulou, to the main entrance at the opposite side of the castle along Athinas.* ☎ *26106 23 390. Open Tu-Sa 8:30am-3pm. Free.)*

ANCIENT ODEION. Southwest of the castle in the upper city, this Roman theater, which was built before AD 160 and used until the 3rd century, once held an audience of 2500. Ancient travel writer Pausanias described it as the second most impressive theater in Greece after Athens's Theater of Herodes Atticus. Excavated in 1889, the theater was restored after WWII. Visitors can now make out the ancient *cavea*, orchestra, and *proskenion*, the wall at the back of the stage. *(*☎ *26102 76 207. Open Tu-Su 8am-6pm. Free.)* The theater hosts the **Patras International Festival,** where music groups play nightly. *(Every summer mid-June to Sept. Check at Info Center for performance times and prices.)*

ARCHAEOLOGICAL MUSEUM. This two-room museum's most striking pieces are its Roman artifacts. Highlights include the marble statue of Athena and the two cases containing amazingly intact gold jewelry, including a pair of earrings shaped like birds and a delicate gold-leaf necklace. *(Mezonos 42, next to Pl. Olgas at the corner of Mezonos and Aratou.* ☎ *26106 20 413. Open Tu-Su 8am-3pm. Guidebooks €3. Free.)*

🎵 📷 ENTERTAINMENT AND NIGHTLIFE

For a relaxed night out, head along the waterfront with the water on your right. Walk about 10min. past Ag. Andreas Cathedral and you'll come to the two-story **Veso Mare,** Akti Dymaion 17 (☎ 26103 65 500). Featuring a 16-lane bowling alley (€6 per game), eight movie theaters, and many restaurants and cafes, the complex pleases both Greek teens and families. Open daily 9am-2am.

At night, cafes and pubs downtown swell with patrons of all tastes: hard-core beer-swillers rub elbows with spiked-frappé sippers. Teenagers from the suburbs hop out of taxis dressed to the nines, and cigarette smoke pervades the air while the crowd jabbers into cell phones. Ag. Nikolaou and Radinou (a pedestrian-only alley one block south of Pl. Olgas) cater to the trendy club crowd, while Pl. Olgas and Pl. Giorgiou host older couples and families. Consistently the most popular bar on Ag. Nikolaou, **Cibo Cibo** serves Italian food all day (salads €6; entrees €5-12) and mixed drinks late into the night, when its deep red lights emit a fiery glow as the young come out to play. (☎ 26106 20 761. Open daily 7am-3am.) The party moves to the upper part of Gerokostopoulou (extending uphill from Pl. Giorgiou) for late-night cocktails at cafes underneath the romantic, dimly lit archways and along the steps to the Upper City.

Though Patras has much to offer in the way of bars and cafes, some of the wildest partiers head out of town. **Rion**, a beach satellite 9km to the northeast, accommodates Patras's club junkies. Some of the biggest clubs, like **H20** or **Oggi**, pass out flyers around town for their weekend pleasure-fests. Take bus #6 from Kanakari and Aratou (30min., €0.90) to the port, past the beach. Get off the bus just after the port before it turns left to head back to Patras; the strip is ahead as you walk with the water on your right. Buses to Rion only run until 11pm, so count on taking a cab home (€3-6). If none are immediately available, head over to the port near the beginning of the strip. Along the strip, beer runs €2-3. Mixed drinks are €5-7.

DIAKOPTO Διακοφτό   ☎ 26910

The village of Diakopto combines many of Greece's natural beauties: turquoise waters, picturesque houses, and mountains bursting with lush vegetation. Though famous among travelers for its 19th-century rack-railway trains which climb over 700m in 22.5km over the Vouraikos Gorge to Kalavrita, Diakopto remains largely isolated from the droves of tourists that have infested the more famous sights. It is only in July and August that the village comes alive, drawing visitors to its peaceful beaches, dramatic mountains, and nearby historical gems.

🖪 **TRANSPORTATION AND PRACTICAL INFORMATION.** Visitors may find Diakopto confusing at first; street names change often, and even the locals are often unfamiliar with their most current titles. Residents are eager to help, though, and the small downtown area is fairly easy to navigate. The well-lit area's many fountains pour much-desired water to drink in the summer heat. The train station (☎ 26910 43 206) intersects Diakopto's two main roads. The main commercial street—sometimes called "Mihalakopoulou," but usually left without a name—is perpendicular to the tracks on the side of the station, and is flanked by bakeries, pharmacies, and cafes. On the side of the tracks closest to the beach (opposite the station), **Filippopoulou**, which is also perpendicular to the tracks, runs straight to the beach and harbor. Tiny rack-railway trains from the station to Kalavrita (1hr., 4 per day, €4) make for a breathtaking ride through the forested mountains of Upper Diakopto and over the Vouraikos Gorge. The Kalavrita train also makes "halfway rides" to Zahlorou (45min., €3.30). **Trains** to Athens (regular: 3½hr., 8 per day 7am-3:30am, €4; express: 3hr., €8.50) via Corinth (regular: 90min., €2.10; express: 1hr., €5) leave from the opposite side of the tracks from the train to Patras (regular: 1hr., 8 per day 9:15am-1:45am, €2; express: 45min., €4.40). The station also offers **luggage storage.** (€3.20 per item per day, €2 if traveling by train. Open daily 6:30am-8:30pm.) There is no bus station in Diakopto (all buses come from nearby Egio), but the **bus stop** is outside the train station on the inland side. For more information about schedules, call ☎ 26910 22 424.

Most of the town's services are on the main street; turn right as you exit the train station on the inland side, and take a left after the kiosk between an electronics shop and a convenience store. Past the **police station** (☎ 26910 41 203; open daily 7am-2:30pm), which is on the second floor of a building on your right side, you will see a **pharmacy** on the right. (☎ 26910 42 885. Open daily 8am-2pm and 5-9:30pm; call ahead on Su to check hours.) The **National Bank,** which offers **currency exchange** and a **24hr. ATM,** is on the left. (☎ 26910 42 180. Open M-Th 8:45am-12:45pm, F 8:45am-12:15pm.) The nearest **hospital** (☎ 26910 22 222) is 20min. away in Egio, and is accessible only by bus or by **taxi** (☎ 26910 41 402). For **emergencies,** call for an ambulance (☎ 100) or call the doctor at the local **clinic.** (☎ 26910 41 260.

Open M-F in the morning, W open later.) The **post office** (☎26910 41 343; open M-F 7:30am-2pm) is on the first side street to the left off of the main road as you walk inland from the train station. **Postal Code:** 25003.

⌐ ACCOMMODATIONS. With a lack of domatia, the town has few accommodations that are worth their prices. ◼**Hotel Lemonies ❷**, closest to the nightlife (halfway between the train station and the beach on Filippopoulou), offers the best deal in town: clean rooms with private baths, comfortable beds, A/C, balconies, and TV for a low price. It also offers two floors of well-lit indoor and outdoor seating areas for late-night socializing. The hotel is surrounded on two sides by busy elementary schools, though, so don't expect to sleep in when school is in session. (☎26910 41 820; fax 26910 43 710. Singles €24-30; doubles €35-45.) **Chris Paul Hotel ❸**, one block inland from the train station and a left off the main road, sits conveniently in the quaint downtown. Although it has an impressive marble lobby, private pool, dining room and full bar, and A/C, its plain rooms are not necessarily worth the higher prices. (☎26910 41 715; www.chrispaul-hotel.gr. Breakfast €5. Wheelchair accessible. Singles €35; doubles €55; triples €70. MC/V.) Though formal campgrounds along the beach have shut down, travelers have been known to take their RVs to the shoreline and camp for the night. Eleon Beach, 5-8km from Diakopto (follow the signs from the train station), has campsites.

◖◗◗ FOOD AND NIGHTLIFE. Food options in Diakopto are limited to a few souvlaki joints and a couple of sit-down tavernas. The nicest place in town, **Kostas ❷**, on the main street a few stores past the pharmacy, is also one of the most affordable. On the edge of the commercial district, the well-lit canopy and patio provide an unobstructed view of the mountains. Try the *lamb giouvetsi* (pasta dish; €6.50), or *pastitsio* (€5). Fish lovers can walk down to the harbor, where **Kohili ❸** serves fresh seafood caught that morning by its own fishing boats. Dishes range €4.50-7. Try the taverna's specialty, *psarosoupa* (fish soup; €8), or grilled calamari (€7), highly recommended by locals. (☎26910 41 844. Open daily noon-5pm and 7:30pm-late.) **Thrifonayoanides ❶**, the local bakery across from the train station, offers filling spanakopita (€1.30) to match its mouthful of a name. Bustling with locals, the small room has shelves lined with all types of freshly baked bread. (Open daily 8am-2pm.) Travelers can find the town's modest supermarket, **El Var,** by the end of the railroad tracks. After exiting the train station, take a right and walk straight until the road ends. The market remains conveniently open while the town shuts down for a collective afternoon nap and offers mostly fruit and non-perishables. (Open daily 8am-8pm.)

After dinner, young people leave behind their espresso-sipping parents and head toward the beach. At the end of the main road on the right, **Fuego** offers patrons of all ages a pleasant evening of drinks (beer and ouzo €2; mixed drinks €5), Greek pop music, and large straw umbrellas by the sea. (☎26910 43 291. Open June-Aug. 10am-2am.) The same owners run **Hrisi Pili** (the bar/club next door) in the winter, with *boutzakya*, traditional Greek entertainment with live music and dancing all night. (Mixed drinks €6. Open Sept.-May 10pm-6am.) **Egkali beach,** about 2km outside of town, attracts the region's trendiest teenagers and 20-somethings to revel by the cheesy tiki huts. At the harbor, take a right down the road by Fuego and Hrisi Pili. When the road ends, either walk along the beach and take a right or follow a residential street and take a left immediately before the train tracks. The gorgeous views and general trendiness of this short stretch of pebble beach make up for the hike from Diakopto. The first club on the beach, **Pili,** offers live Greek music with dancing and general debauchery. (Mixed drinks €8. Open Th-Sa noon-7am.) Homesick partiers can check out the American electronic-music DJs of **Blue**

Beach Club, where, despite its name, everything has been painted white. (Open 10am-5am. Beer €4. Mixed drinks €6.) **Koursaros,** with a wooden patio right by the water, serves coffee (€3) and *pastitsio* (€4.50) from the best spot on the beach. (☎ 26910 43 100. Open daily June-Sept. 10am-7am.)

KALAVRITA Καλάβρυτα ☎ 26920

Although most famous for its ski resort, which comes alive in the winter, the town of Kalavrita has much to offer year-round. From dramatic hikes to religious and historical monuments, a journey through Achaia is incomplete without a visit to this close-knit mountain village.

⊏⊡ TRANSPORTATION AND PRACTICAL INFORMATION

To reach the bus station (☎ 26920 22 224), take the first right off Eth. Antistasios onto Kapota, walking away from the train station; it's on your left one block down at the intersection of three roads. **Buses** go to: Athens (3hr., 2-3 per day, €12.30); Egio (1¼hr.; M-F, Su 2 per day; €4) via Diakopto; Patras (2hr., 5 per day 6:15am-4:45pm, €6); Tripoli (2hr., daily 9:30am, €6.20). Call ahead as bus schedules can change unpredictably. **Taxis** (☎ 26920 22 127) line up along the side of the plateia, as well as by the train station.

Kalavrita is accessible by a renovated, rack-railway line from **Diakopto** (1hr., 8am-3:50pm, €4). The three roads perpendicular to the train station that lead to the plateia are **Konstantinou** (which becomes **Agios Alexiou**) to the left, **Syngrou** in the center (initially a pedestrian road, which later becomes **25 Martiou**), and **Ethnikis Antistasios** on the right (initially **Kallimanti**). The **central plateia** with the town's main church is within these three streets, 100m from the train station. The **National Bank,** 25 Martiou 4, 100m before the central plateia, offers **currency exchange** and a **24hr. ATM.** (☎ 26920 22 209. Open M-Th 8am-2:30pm, F 8am-2pm.) Across from the bank is a **laundromat,** 25 Martiou 5, that charges €10 per load. (☎ 26920 22 189. Open daily 8am-8pm.) Walking from the train station, the **police,** Fotina 7, are to the right off of Ag. Alexiou, four blocks beyond the central plateia. (☎ 26920 23 333 or 26920 22 213. Open 24hr.) The **hospital** is three blocks from the train station: take a right out of the station and go straight. (☎ 26920 22 222. Open 24hr.) Kalavrita has four **pharmacies.** While they try to be open during normal business hours (M-F 8am-2pm), their hours may vary; if one pharmacy is closed, it will post the phone number of an alternate place on its door. Find one across the street from the hospital (☎ 26920 22 097). **Phones** can be found in the central plateia and by the train station. The **post office** is down the road at Ag. Alexiou 17. (☎ 26920 22 225. Open M-F 8am-2pm.) **Postal Code:** 25001.

⌐ ACCOMMODATIONS

The few hotels in Kalavrita make good use of their dominance over local accommodations. Rooms are decent and clean, but prices sky-rocket during ski season. The best bet is to try any of the plentiful affordable, well-appointed **domatia;** numerous signs behind the train station will lead you to them.

Hotel Veelakalvika (☎ 26920 22 712 or 26920 22 845) is the best option for groups looking to spend more than a few nights in Kalavrita. Directly across from the train station, the apartment-style rooms have kitchens, baths, heating, and balconies for up to four people. The owner, Kostas, a former ship's captain who has traveled the world, also runs a restaurant downstairs and a lounge with TV and board games. Prices are negotiable depending on duration and time of stay. May-Nov. €40-70; Dec.-Apr. €100. ❹

Hotel Maria (☎26920 22 296; www.kalavrita.biz/maria.htm), 1 block up from the train station on the right side of Syngrou, offers bright, clean rooms, some with balconies, in a central location. Breakfast €5. In summer singles €35; doubles €50; triples €65. In winter doubles €70; triples €90. ❷

Hotel Filoxenia, Eth. Antistasios 10 (☎26920 22 422; www.hotelfiloxenia.gr). Though a bargain only in the summer, Filoxenia's 28 rooms delicately combine modern comforts with old-fashioned European beauty. A/C, private baths, TV, telephones, and minibars. Some rooms have balconies and jacuzzis. Breakfast included. English-speaking staff. Reservations recommended. In summer singles €40; doubles €55; triples €70. In winter €86/100/120. MC/V. ❹

Anesis Hotel (☎26920 23 070; www.anesishotel.gr), in the central plateia. A lovely stone hotel owned by friendly Greek-Australian brothers. Has 14 well-furnished, renovated rooms with phones, TV, baths, minibars, and temperature control during the winter. Breakfast included in winter. In summer singles €30; doubles €40; triples €48. In winter €70/75/90. V. ❹

🖪 🄬 FOOD AND NIGHTLIFE

Indistinguishable tavernas and fast food joints line Ag. Alexiou and Syngrou. Most serve classic Greek staples (entrees €5-7). For better food in a less touristed area, head to 🄫**Spitiko ❷,** right across from the bus station. Ignore the menu and ask owner Dimitrio to pick your meal for you, then savor the delicious concoction that he brings out. (☎26920 24 260. Entrees €5-7. Open daily 9am-1am.) The **Hotel Maria Cafe ❷,** right outside the hotel on Syngrou, serves scrumptious breakfast foods in large portions (omelettes €5). After breakfast, shirk social norms by getting desert—the traditional goat-milk yogurt with honey is too good to miss. Don't be put off by the kitschy neon sign; many locals also come sit in the outdoor space and delight in the self-proclaimed "best breakfast in town."

The most happening place in the winter is, unsurprisingly, the ski center, where the town gathers for evening drinks. A number of clubs have recently started entertaining Kalavrita's youth, though many are closed in the summer. On weekdays, nightlife centers around cafes on Syngrou and on the central plateia. The main dance club in town, the **Evdomi Techni** music club (take a right from Eth. Antistasios at the plateia), holds up to 1000 people and is almost always packed. (☎69459 35 662. Mixed drinks €5. Open F-Sa 11pm-morning.) **Portokali** dance club at the train station offers some variation with Greek pop and light traditional music all night long. Catering to a younger crowd, **Diadromes** music club (drinks €5) has a small bar and crowded dance space with rock tunes. Those in the mood for classic rock from Greece and the US might prefer the vinyl stylings of **Skiniko,** a few blocks up from the plateia at 25 Martiou 59. (Mixed drinks €5. Open Sept.-May.) Next door to the church in the central plateia, **Slalom** serves drinks and snacks into the night, and has some of the best outdoor seating in town under dim lamps strung through trees. (Coffee €2. Mixed drinks €5. Open 9am-2am.) **Bresler's Cafe,** Ag. Alexiou 1, plays mainly American club hits and pop for a hip, hair-gelled crowd, and serves coffee (€2), beer (€2), snacks (€1.20-1.50), and mixed drinks (€4) all day long. (☎26920 24 459. Open 6am-1am.)

👁 🄭 SIGHTS AND OUTDOOR ACTIVITIES

KALAVRITA SKI CENTER. Fourteen kilometers from downtown Kalavrita, the Kalavrita Ski Center operates eight lifts with 13 ski slopes of varying difficulty.

With ski schools, restaurants, and Saturday-night skiing, the center caters to the needs of experts, beginners, and non-skiers. (☎ *26920 24 241; www.kalavrita-ski.com. Taxis (☎ 26920 22 127; €20) and private buses run from the town to the mountain. Open Dec.-Apr. when there is snow 8:30am-4pm.)*

SITE OF SACRIFICE. The site held most dear to the townspeople of Kalavrita is the Site of Sacrifice monument, a tribute to the Kalavritans who were massacred on December 13, 1943. In retaliation for the murder of one of their troopers, the occupying Nazis gathered all of the town's men and boys over age 13 on a hill outside of town under the pretext of a stern reprimand for the death. Instead, at 2:34pm, lurking troopers opened fire on the men and their sons. Immediately after, they locked Kalavrita's women and children in the town's school (now called the **Museum of Kalavritan Holocaust**) and set fire to the school and town. Today, one of the clocks of the town's reconstructed church is set permanently to 2:34, and an extensive memorial stands at the site itself. Heart-wrenching gravestones detail the names and ages of the victims, eternally commemorating them beneath an overarching Greek flag and striking white cross. *(Walk up Ag. Alexiou from the train station and turn left at the signs near the square. The site is about 200m up the hill.)*

VOURAIKOS RIVER RAVINE. Perfect for summer hiking, the ravine is a celebration of Greece's mountainous beauty. Its wild cliffsides, natural waterfalls, caves, and untouched fauna and flora are so treasured by the town that, every May, Kalavrita's town hall organizes a communal hike through the ravine. Among the natural beauties is the River Styx, where the Olympian gods took their most sacred oaths. *(Explore the ravine by train or foot. A good starting point is Zachlorou, the halfway mark of the Diakopto-Kalavrita railroad. Information ☎ 26920 22 346 and 26920 23 043.)*

AGIA LAVRA MONASTERY. Greece's revolutionary fighters were placed under oath at this site—it was the monks of Ag. Lavra who officially initiated the Revolution on March 25, 1821. The monastery was burned by both the Ottomans and Nazis, but an icon of the Virgin Mary made in the 16th century along with other important religious relics survived the flames. *(☎ 26920 22 363. 7km outside of Kalavrita. Taxi €15. Open in summer 10am-1pm and 4-5pm, winter 10am-1pm and 3-4pm.)*

CAVE OF THE GREAT LAKES. Alluded to in Greek mythology but only "discovered" by locals in 1964, this cave's natural stalactites and stalagmites pose in uncanny rock formations. Unlike many of Greece's caves, however, this one, 17km outside of Kalavrita, has three levels of beautiful lakes that, when the snow melts, leave visitors gawking at the waterfalls that form inside the earth. *(☎ 26920 31 001 or 26920 31 633. English signs point the way from the road behind the Site of Sacrifice. Taxi from Kalavrita, €18, takes about 1.5hr. Open Sept.-May M-F 9:30am-4:30pm, Sa-Su 9am-6pm; June-Aug. 9am-6pm. €8-9.)*

▶ DAYTRIP FROM KALAVRITA

▦ GREAT CAVE MONASTERY Μόνη Μεγάλου Σπηλαιού

Sixteen centuries of religious history lie 950m above sea level, hidden in a monumental cave near Kalavrita. Built in AD 362, the Great Cave Monastery is the oldest monastery in Greece and is home to the wax icon of the Virgin Mary that was sculpted by St. Luke 2000 years ago. According to the friendly monks who will give you "tours" around the monastery, the icon was discovered by a local saint, St. Efrosini, in the cave itself and has performed wondrous miracles ever since. Check out the church with ancient mosaic floors, frescoes, and a bronze door. As you walk in, head toward the staircase that lies just right of the small gift shop—four cannons point the way to the museum (€2). Captions in both English and Greek help differ-entiate between all of the communion cups, clerical vestments, and religious manu-scripts from the 11th-13th centuries. Especially noteworthy is the group of 400-year-old handmade crosses on the left wall and famous frescos. Follow a footpath uphill from the monastery and reach the "hole in the rock," an aptly named rock formation with a hole in it, through which a mysterious whistle is sometimes heard. Unless you are driving, transportation is fairly difficult. Buses from Kalavrita to Egio run twice a day; a 15min. ride will take you to the landmark (ask to be let off at the monastery). Taxis are also available (☎26920 22 127; €20 roundtrip). For a particularly scenic route, take the rail to Diakopto, get off at Zachlorou, and climb an ancient and well-marked footpath for 45min. (Open daily 7am-7pm.)

KYLLINI Κυλλήνη ☎26230

For a port town that handles almost all the tourist traffic to Zakynthos, Kyllini is surprisingly undeveloped; the town has almost no bus service, few accommoda-tions, and a handful of cafes. This otherwise disappointing town's highlight is its sandy, isolated beach—since most travelers don't spend too much time here, the beach is splendidly undisturbed. If you're considering bypassing Kyllini entirely, keep in mind that some buses leave from Zakynthos Town, take a ferry to the mainland, and continue to places like Patras and Athens.

If you plan on spending the night, **Sea Garden Domatia ❷**, above the Sea Garden Res-taurant two blocks inland from the port, offers nothing spectacular but is your best bet for a relatively inexpensive night's rest. Rooms have TV, baths, balconies, and a com-munal kitchen; some have white Italian furniture, a nice improvement over the others' basic wooden beds. (☎26230 92 165. Singles €25; doubles €30.) **Hotel Ionion ❹**, across from the Sea Garden Restaurant, lies on a beachside street that has a few domatia. Ion-ion may not seem like much at first but rents surprisingly large rooms with A/C, TV, mini-fridges, and private baths. (☎26230 92 318. Singles €35; doubles €45.) At **Stivas ❷**, one block past Sea Garden Domatia on the right, diners eat on the blue and yellow side patio and have ample opportunity to ponder why the caged birds (hanging from the trellis overhead) sing. Dishes change daily, so ask before you look at a menu. (☎26230 92 045. Entrees €5-8. Seafood from €30 per kg.)

Ferries sail from Kyllini to Argostoli, Kephalonia (2hr., 8pm, €11), Poros, Kepha-lonia (1½hr., 6-9 per day, €7.40), and Zakynthos (1hr., 5 per day 8am-9:45pm, €6). Buy tickets from one of the three kiosks on the dock; the kiosk on the right, facing the port entrance, sells tickets to Zakynthos, and the two on the left sell tickets to Kephalonia. The prices to Kephalonia are standard, but one of the ferry lines doesn't sail to Argostoli, so be sure to ask both the kiosks for information. To leave Kyllini by land, take the **bus** from the stop next to the kiosk across from the port gate to Pirgos (1½hr., 4 per day 7am-9:30pm, €3.50). Once in Pirgos, you can catch a bus to Olympia (30min., 14 per day, €1.40) or a train to Athens, Ioannina, or Patras. For all other bus connections you will have to spend €12 on a **taxi** (☎26230 71 764) to Lehena, the nearest town on the main Patras-Pirgos highway. Taxis line up by the same kiosk where the buses depart. There is no police station in Kyllini; the closest one is in Lehana (☎26230 22 333). A **24hr. ATM** is on the dock next to the Killini Port Restaurant. To find the town's **pharmacy/shoe store,** walk straight from the dock past the Sea Garden Restaurant and turn left. The **post office** is a block past the pharmacy. (Open M-F 7:30am-2pm.) **Postal Code:** 27068.

PIRGOS Πύργος ☎26210

A small city that manages some first-rate urban sprawl, Pirgos is as disorienting as many of the biggest metropolises in the Peloponnese. Fast food joints and cafes for Greek youth are the rule, and the buildings here are not exactly beautiful. But, on the bright side, because Pirgos is a transportation mecca, its bus and train stations are disproportionately modern and efficient. If you have time to kill between buses, lively Pl. Kyprou will keep you occupied.

⬛ TRANSPORTATION. Pirgos has earned its reputation as an important Peloponnesian transport hub, with an efficient bus and train system that will get travelers around most of the Peloponnese and even up to Athens. The train station, Ypsilantou (Υψηλαντου) 12 (☎26210 22 576), 450m downhill from the statue of Kolokotronis along Patron, has **trains** to: Athens (regular: 7hr., 9:56am, €7; express: 4hr., 5 per day 4:28am-12:05am, €14) via Patras (1½hr., €5.40); Kyparissia (regular: 1hr., 4 per day 8:10am-7:20pm, €2; express: 4:21am, 8:40pm, €4.40); Olympia (45min., 5 per day 6:50am-2:05pm, €0.70). The brand-new, ultra-modern KTEL bus station is downhill from the train station. Walk down Patron and turn left after the BP gas station onto Erithrou Stavrou. **Buses** run to: Amaliada (25min.; M-F 15 per day 5:30am-9:15pm, Sa-Su 10 per day 5:30am-12:30am; €1.50); Kyllini (1½hr.; 10:30am, 2:35pm; €3.50); Olympia (35min.; M-F 16 per day 5:15am-9:45pm, Sa-Su 11 per day 6:30am-9:45pm; €1.60). **Taxis** (☎26210 25 000) line up in the center of town by the OTE.

⬛⬛ ORIENTATION AND PRACTICAL INFORMATION. The main road in Pirgos, **Mitropoliti Antoniou** (referred to by locals as **"Patron"**), runs up from the bus station to the main square, **Plateia Kyprou.** The plateia and its side streets are the center of the local youth's afternoons and nights, drowned in cafes and restaurants. The road that begins from the train station and continues upward to the plateia is **Themistokleous.** This road and Patron meet at the beginning of the plateia and intersect **Manolopoulou** perpendicularly. At the intersection of these three roads, you will see a large bronze statue of the Greek independence hero, Kolokotronis. From there, take any of the small pedestrian side streets on the right facing uphill to reach the plateia.

Banks can be found along Patron, next to the statue, and in the plateia. **Piraeus Bank,** next to the statue, has **24hr. ATMs** and **currency exchange.** (Open M-Th 8am-2pm, F 8am-1:30pm.) The **police station** (☎26210 22 100) is three blocks uphill from the train station. Walk up Patron and turn left on Karkarvitsa, next to Hotel Olympus. (Open daily 7:30am-10pm, for emergencies 24hr.) The local police also serve as the **tourist police** (☎26210 81 767). **Pharmacies** (most open M-F 8am-2:30pm) cluster around the intersection of Patron and Manolopoulou. To get to the **hospital** (☎26210 22 222), walk downhill on Patron toward the bus station. At the intersection of roads to Patras and to Olympia, turn right. The creatively-named **Internet Cafe** is in Pl. Kyprou on Letrinon, behind Goody's. (☎26210 24 033. €4 per hr.; €1 min. Open daily 9am-midnight.) The **post office** is at the corner of Manolopoulou and Grigoriou; facing uphill, take a right onto Manolopoulou at the statue. (☎26210 33 117. Open M-F 7:30am-2pm.) **Postal Code:** 27100.

⬛⬛ ACCOMMODATIONS AND FOOD. Backpackers who love the smell of pre-owned hostel sheets and high-rollers who live for complimentary bathrobes will be disappointed by the accommodations in Pirgos. Options are limited to the C-level hotels that cluster along Patron and on the parallel streets between the bus and train stations. Hotels don't pay attention to low or high season, and prices vary little depending on time of year. Rates and amenities tend to be consistent, so you may end up choosing based on arbitrary details like color scheme or headboard shape. **Hotel Ilida ❸,** Patron 50 and Deligianni, to the right of the train station, is the classiest of the mediocre choices. The lobby shines with cushy leather chairs and leads upstairs to bright rooms with shell-shaped headboards (definitely one of the

TOP TEN ARCHAEOLOGICAL BLUNDERS

Archaeological treasures inevitably get scuffed, but Greece's ancient sites have suffered a remarkable number of indignities.
1. The Byzantines built a church directly on the site of Phidias's workshop in **Olympia** (p. 169).
2. The ruins at **Dion** (p. 294) are treated with care—except when tides flood them in the winter.
3. The city of **Pella** (p. 285) was undone by both a Roman invader and a devastating earthquake.
4. Heinrich Schliemann ripped off what he thought was Agamemnon's face-mask at **Mycenae** (p. 149), pulverizing the features of his delicate discovery.
5. Arthur Evans reconstructed (painted over) the murals at Knossos (p. 596) based on pure fantasy.
6. At Crete's **Dikteon Cave** (p. 614), Evans was so impatient that he used destructive dynamite to open its entrance.
7. An even worse detonation demolished most of the **Parthenon** (p. 113) in 1687, when Turks stored gunpowder there.
8. Later, pilfering British Lord Elgin chiseled the best marble reliefs off of the Parthenon.
9. Finally, the few remaining sculptures there were deteriorated by decades of acid rain.
10. The Athenians, worried about losing the Peloponnesian War, cut off the wings of their own statue of **Nike** (p. 114) to make sure that she wouldn't fly away and take victory along with her.

more exciting shapes), large beds, A/C, TV, phones, and private baths. (☎26210 28 046. Breakfast €5. Singles €43; doubles €60; triples €75. MC/V.) **Hotel Pantheon ❹,** Themistokleous 7, two blocks uphill from the train station, caters to those who need a little color to perk up a bland stay in Pirgos. Lime-green doors and bright green carpeting introduce business travelers to rooms with A/C, fridges, hair dryers, spacious yellow beds, and blue-tiled baths. (☎26210 29 746. Singles €45; doubles €55; triples €80. MC/V.) One block uphill from the train station, **Hotel Marily ❸,** at the intersection of Themistokleous and Deligianni, looks older than some of its peers. Its 30 rooms have A/C, TV, phones, hair dryers, freezers, and baths. Hotel Marily's quiet location makes it a good place for a restful night if you don't mind the exposed pipes and dim lighting. (☎26210 28 133. Singles €35; doubles €45; triples €60. MC/V.)

It is difficult to find a good, full meal in Pirgos, since the scene is dominated by fast food joints, cafes, and souvlaki stands. For something less on-the-go, **Restaurant Milano ❷,** on Themistokleous, which is speedy, cheap, and very tasty, is a good choice for vegetarians and Italian cuisine enthusiasts. (☎26210 23 291. Salads €3-4. Pizza €4.50-6.50. Pasta €4. Open 6pm-1:30am.) **0 Vasilis ❷** (O Βασιλης) (☎26210 31 104), across from the Internet Cafe, is quick but satisfying, serving meal-sized souvlaki (€3-5) and salads (€5) next to the main plateia.

OLYMPIA Ολυμπία ☎26240

Set among quiet meadows of cypress and olive trees, modern Olympia bears little resemblance to its cosmopolitan past. Though it is most famous as the home of the ancient Olympic Games, travelers can also enjoy Olympia's pristine natural setting. The city teems with tourist shops and hotels, but retains a relaxed pace of living that makes visiting its ancient sites and stunning surroundings a pleasure.

▐▀ TRANSPORTATION

Trains go from Olympia to Athens (6hr.; 1:06, 3:28pm; €25) and Pirgos (25min., 5 per day 7:20am-3:30pm, €0.70). Contact the train station (☎26240 22 677) for updated information, as schedules and prices can change. The **bus stop** is about 100m down Kondili from the tourist office, toward the ruins. It is the bench across from the town hall. **Buses** go to Pirgos (35min., 11-16 per day, €2) and Tripoli (3½hr.; M-F 8:45am, 12:30, 5:30pm; Sa-Su 8:45am, 5:30pm; €8).

✈ 🔞 ORIENTATION AND PRACTICAL INFORMATION

Olympia consists primarily of **Kondili**, the 1km main street. Maps of the town are pinned up on billboards at the street's ends, so it's difficult to get lost. At the end of Kondili you will see signs pointing to the museums and ancient sites. As you walk toward them, the main tourist office will be on your right next to the National Bank. The train station, a convenience store, and pricey tavernas sit on the side road that intersects Kondili at a fork across from the youth hostel.

Tourist Office: ☎26240 23 173. On Kondili, toward the ruins. Helpful staff provides bus schedules, information, and free **maps**. Open daily 9am-8pm.

Bank: National Bank (☎26240 22 501), on Kondili next to the tourist office, has **currency exchange** and a **24hr. ATM.** Open M-Th 8am-2:30pm, F 8am-2pm.

Police: Em. Kountsa 1 (☎26240 22 100), 1 block up from Kondili, behind the tourist office. Open 24hr. Also serve as the **tourist police.**

Medical Services: ☎26240 22 222. Olympia uses **Pirgos's hospital** but has its own 24hr. **health center.** Walk from the ruins to the other end of Kondili and turn left before the church on your left. Continue straight as the road winds to the right, then turn right.

Telephones: Can be found along Kondili across from the youth hostel.

Internet Access: Epathlou Cafe, Stephanopoulou 2 (☎26240 23 894), rents nifty laptops so you can settle in its leather booths and listen to the latest pop songs, played so loudly you might mistake this place for the dance club next door. Turn off Kondili with the Youth Hostel on your right; it's on the left. €3 per hr. Open daily 9am-2am.

Post Office: ☎26240 22 578. On Pierre de Coubertain, the side street past the tourist office on the right. **Poste Restante.** Open M-F 7:30am-2pm. **Postal Code:** 27065.

🏠 ACCOMMODATIONS AND CAMPING

The prices of Olympia's hotels are set according to amenities and location. Since tourist traffic doesn't fluctuate much with the seasons, prices stay stable throughout the year. Call ahead for hotels, as they are often completely booked by tour groups. Singles range €20-30 and doubles range €22-85.

Youth Hostel, Kondili 18 (☎26240 22 580). A great place to get to know international backpackers, this hostel is in a good location and has the cheapest rooms in town. Helpful brochures introducing the ancient site and nature activities are posted up in the lobby. Sheets €1. Lockout 11pm. Dorms €9; doubles €22. ❶

New Olympia (☎26240 22 547), on the road that leads diagonally to the train station. The decor is a little behind the times—maybe retro chic, if you stretch your imagination— but the rooms are spacious with A/C, TV, phones, balconies, and large private baths. Be prepared to bargain. Breakfast included. Singles €30; doubles €50; triples €70. ❸

Hotel Ilis (☎26240 22 348), along Kondili next to the church, has not only the basic amenities (TV, A/C, private baths), but also a bright red lobby and orange doors, great views of the neighboring church, and use of the pool at Hotel Antonio just up the hill. Reservations recommended. Singles €30; doubles €50; triples €60. ❸

Hotel Hercules (☎26240 23 035) could be mistaken for a ski lodge from the inside: wood paneling leads upstairs to large, basic rooms with bright orange baths, A/C, TV, and balconies. Turn left on Kondili before the church, on the road to the health center, and it's 2 blocks on your right. Singles €25; doubles €30; triples €40. ❸

Hotel Kronio, Tsoureka 1, on the road perpendicular to the train station on the side closest to Kondili. At a nice balance of price and quality, Kronio has large, bright rooms with

A/C, TV, and private baths. The free Internet in the lobby makes up for the jarring fluo-rescent lighting. Breakfast included. Singles €30; doubles €44; triples €50. ❸

Pension Poseidon (☎26240 22 567). Turn off Kondili with the Youth Hostel on your right; it's at the top of the hill on the left. The simple, clean rooms don't come with much except for the relatively low prices. Singles €30; doubles €35; triples €40. ❷

Camping Diana (☎26240 22 314), uphill from the Sports Museum, has hot water, help-ful transportation info, a swimming pool, a mini-mart, and a restaurant that serves breakfast (€5), snacks, and ouzo. Shielded from the hot summer sun by trees and flow-ery fresh bushes, it's cooler than other accommodations down the hill. €6 per person; €4 per small tent, €7 per large tent; €4 per car. ❶

Olympia Palace, Kondili 2 (☎26240 23 101; www.olympia-palace.gr), is as close to Ancient Olympia as you can get (location-wise—don't expect naked athletes murmuring prayers to Apollo). Rooms are elegant and modern, with A/C, satellite TV, safety deposit boxes, room service, private baths with large bathtubs, Internet, and huge balconies. Breakfast included. Singles €60-70; doubles €75-85; triples €95-105. MC/V. ❹

🚻🍴 FOOD AND NIGHTLIFE

Along Kondili, **mini-marts, bakeries,** and **fast food** joints compete for your attention and cash. Most are overpriced, but a short walk up the hill leads to solid, less expensive tavernas. The constant influx of crowds keeps most open 8am-1am. For a filling meal that's as Greek as it gets, try **Vasilakis ❷**, at the corner of Karamanli and Spiliopoulou. (☎26240 22 104. Open noon-midnight.) Take a right off Kondili before the Youth Hostel, or follow your nose to the delicious meat dishes (€5-10) whose aroma wafts through the entire block. **Aigio ❷** is on the side street to the train station next to New Olympia Hotel. Pick from the ever-changing daily spe-cials, or get one of the meals, which come with salads and soft drinks or ouzo. (Moussaka meal €6. Souvlaki meal €6. Open 11am-late.) **Poseidon Restaurant ❷**, two blocks uphill from the Youth Hostel, is a romantic sanctuary away from busy Kondili. Patrons come for the *retsina* (€4 per L), distilled from the grapes that hang on the lattices overhead. (☎26240 22 567. Entrees €5-11. Souvlaki plate €11.)

At night, locals and tourists mingle in the tavernas and bars along Kohili; around 1am, the younger crowd moves to the dance clubs. Conveniently, the clubs pump the latest pop tunes right in the middle of town. **Gallery,** next to the Internet cafe, is one of the most popular ones, due more to its central location than stellar ambience. But it's a good place to meet well-coiffed locals. Open daily 10pm-4am. Mixed drinks €5.

🜨 SIGHTS

Olympia has several museums that examine the town's ancient legacy and sur-roundings and are definitely worth a visit. Beyond these, however, the natural beauty of the area is a sight in itself. Organized walks, river parties, rafting, and kayaking are just a few activities available through July and August. Participation is free, but early reservation is absolutely necessary. For more information visit the tourist office which can provide both info and schedules.

🏛ANCIENT OLYMPIA ARCHAEOLOGICAL MUSEUM

☎26240 22 742. Through the parking lot opposite the ancient site. Open M 12:30-7:30pm, Tu-Su 8:30am-7:30pm. Flash cameras prohibited. €6; with ancient site €9.

Many find ancient Olympia's gleaming new museum a greater attraction than the ancient site itself. A team of French archaeologists began unearthing the site from 1400 years of silt in 1829; the systematic excavations that continue today started in 1875, and most of what has been extracted in these 129 years resides in the museum. Since military victors from across the Greek world sent spoils and pieces of their own equipment to Olympia as offerings to the gods, the museum doubles as a display of Greek military history, with entire rooms filled with helmets, cuirasses, greaves, swords, spear points, and other military paraphernalia. The most spectacular military offering is a common **Corinthian helmet** (490 BC), partially destroyed by oxidation. While richer, better preserved headgear can be found elsewhere in the museum, this helmet has a faint inscription on the chin guard that reads "Miltiades dedicated this to Zeus." The victor of one of the most famous battles in all antiquity, **Miltiades** led the outnumbered Greeks to victory over the Persians at Marathon in 479 BC; he may have worn this helmet in the battle. Beside it is another headpiece, whose inscription reveals it to be from the Persian side of the same battle.

The museum's array of sculpture includes some of the greatest extant pieces in the world. One stunning centerpiece is the large western pediment from the Temple of Zeus, which depicts a myth about a group of centaurs who attended the wedding of the king of Lapiths. After having a few too many drinks, the horse-men made the mistake of trying to abduct the Lapith women, a move they surely regretted in the morning after the vicious battle which ensued. A 3m tall Apollo stands in the center of the scene, imposing peace and order on the group. The pediment's fragments have been dramatically reassembled along one wall of the main room. Even the overlooked objects here astound—every case holds pieces that would be highlights of a lesser collection. Don't miss the room dedicated to Phidias, including some of his tools and, best of all, shards of a plain drinking cup that, when they were cleaned and mended, bore the inscription "I belong to Phidias."

ANCIENT OLYMPIA (SITE)

Site: ☎ 26240 22 517. Open daily 8:30am-7:30pm. €6, seniors and students €5, EU students and children under 18 free; museum (p. 168) and site €9. The ruins are practically unmarked. Several guides are available at the site—try those by A. and N. Yalouris (€7.50), Monolis Andronicos (€5.50), or the Ministry of Culture (€9). Maps €2-4.

Before there were photo finishes, drug tests, and aerodymanic unisuits, there were the games of Olympia. A green tract between the rivers Kladeo and Alphios, the city was one of the ancient world's most important cultural centers for a millen-

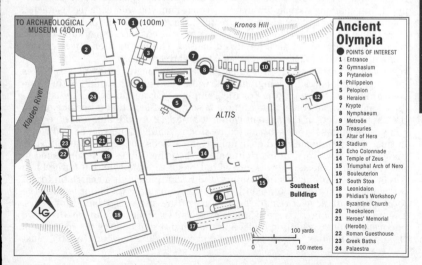

Ancient Olympia

● POINTS OF INTEREST
1 Entrance
2 Gymnasium
3 Prytaneion
4 Philippeion
5 Pelopion
6 Heraion
7 Krypte
8 Nymphaeum
9 Metroön
10 Treasuries
11 Altar of Hera
12 Stadium
13 Echo Colonnade
14 Temple of Zeus
15 Triumphal Arch of Nero
16 Bouleuterion
17 South Stoa
18 Leonidaion
19 Phidias's Workshop/
   Byzantine Church
20 Theokoleon
21 Heroes' Memorial
   (Heroön)
22 Roman Guesthouse
23 Greek Baths
24 Palaestra

TO ARCHAEOLOGICAL MUSEUM (400m)
TO ❶ (100m)
Kronos Hill
ALTIS
Kladeo River
Southeast Buildings
0   100 yards
0   100 meters

nium. Participants from Sicily, Asia Minor, North Africa, Macedonia, and Greece once convened here to worship, compete, and learn among masterpieces of art and architecture and the most cultured poets and musicians. Every four years for 1169 years, warring city-states would call a sacred truce and travel to Olympia for the most splendid Panhellenic assembly of the ancient world.

Olympia was first settled in the 3rd millennium BC, when it was dedicated to **Gaia**, the Earth Mother, who had an oracle at the site. The first athletic contests commenced in Zeus's honor, only to be forgotten again until 884 BC. Ancient history credits divine intervention for the first Olympic revival, which took place on the Oracle of Delphi's orders to Iphtos, King of Elia; prophecy told that the Games would save Greece from civil war and plague. The first recorded Olympiad was in 776 BC—which must have been a peaceful, disease-free year—and initially the most athletic men, naked as jaybirds, competed only in a simple *stadion*, or footrace, lasting 192m (the stadium's length). As the Games's popularity broadened, longer races, wrestling, boxing, the pentathlon (long jump, discus, javelin, running, and wrestling), the hoplite race (in full bronze armor), and equestrian events joined the slate of events. The Olympics were celebrated through the AD 4th century, until Emperor Theodosius concluded that the sanctuary (and thus the Games themselves) violated his anti-pagan laws. Soon thereafter earthquakes in AD 522 and 551, fulfilling their role as the thorn in the side of every archaeologist, destroyed much of the Olympic site.

The central sanctuary of the Olympic complex, eventually walled and dedicated to Zeus, was called the **Altis**. Over the centuries, it held temples, treasuries, and a number of monuments to the gods. The complex was surrounded by various facilities for participants and administrators, including the stadium on the far eastern side. **Pausanias**, a traveler-historian in the AD 2nd century, noted a whopping 69 monuments built by victors to thank the gods. Although the ruins are not especially well preserved, a few sections are roped off; you can climb up the steps of the Temple of Zeus and wander about as you please.

As you enter the site, facing south, follow the path which veers slightly to the left to reach the **training grounds**. Here you'll find the remains of the 2nd-century BC **gymnasium**. This open-air quadrangle surrounded by Doric columns was reserved for athletes like runners and javelin throwers who needed space to practice. If you continue straight through the gymnasium, you will reach the re-erected columns of the square **Palaestra**, or wrestling school, built in the 3rd century BC. More than a mere athletic facility, the Palaestra ensured that competitors wouldn't become one-dimensional, uncivilized brutes. The young men wrestled one moment and studied metaphysics the next in nearby rooms.

As you continue south and slightly west, the next group of structures includes a reddish, surprisingly intact, walled-in building, which is the **workshop of Phidias**, the sculptor. For the Temple of Olympian Zeus, Phidias produced an ivory and gold statue of the god so magnificent that it became one of the **Seven Wonders of the Ancient World**. It stood 12.4m tall and portrayed the god seated on his throne with an expression revealing benevolence and glory. In tune with the themes of the Olympic Games, Zeus cupped a statue of Nike, the goddess of victory, in his right palm. When the Games were abolished in the 4th century, the statue was moved to Constantinople, where it burned in a fire in AD 475. Adding insult to injury, the Byzantines built a **church** on top of the workshop in the AD 5th century, constructing new walls but leaving the foundation intact. As a result, the identity of the site was debated for years. The traditional sources were affirmed by recent excavations, though, that have uncovered molds, sculpting tools, and the famous cup bearing the inscription "I belong to Phidias." These finds are currently in the museum (p. 168). Just past the workshop and slightly to the left is the huge **Leonidaion,** built in 330 BC by a wealthy man from Naxos named Leonidas. Though the building was officially dedicated to Zeus some time after 350 BC, it served a primarily secular role, often hosting officials and other VIPs.

At the **Bouleuterion,** east of the Leonidaion, to the right as you face the entrance, lie the remains of the South Processional Gate to the Altis. The procession of athletes and trainers entered the sacred area on their way to the Bouleuterion (to the right of the gate), where the ancient Olympic council met. Each athlete was required to make a sacrifice to Zeus and take the sacred oath, swearing his eligibility and intent to abide by the rules of the Games.

North of the Bouleuterion (toward the entrance) are the ruins of the once-gigantic **Temple of Olympian Zeus,** the centerpiece of the Altis after its completion in 456 BC. Home to Phidias's awe-inspiring statue, the 27m long sanctuary was the largest temple completed on the Greek mainland before the Parthenon. The temple's elegant facade, impressive Doric columns, and accurately modeled pedimental sculpture exemplified the Classical design that evolved before the Persians invaded Greece. Today only a half-column stands, while the rest of these tremendous pillars, toppled in segments, lie as they fell after a 6th-century earthquake.

Past the temple, to the right as you face the entrance, you will reach the remains of the **Echo Colonnade,** which was used for competitions between trumpeters and heralds, whose musical prowess was no doubt enhanced by the colonnade's rumored sevenfold echo. At the northern edge of the colonnade, stone blocks that once supported statues of victorious athletes lead to the **Krypte,** the official entrance to the **stadium** used by athletes and judges. This domed passageway (of which only one arch survives) and the stadium as it stands today are products of the Hellenistic period, built over the remains of the earlier, similarly positioned stadium. Having survived the effects of powerful earthquakes, the stadium appears much as it did 2300 years ago. The judges' stand and the start and finish lines are still in place, and the stadium's grassy banks can still seat nearly 40,000 spectators; you may feel inspired to take a lap or two to bond with Olympians of millennia past. As you leave the passageway to the stadium, the remains of **treasuries** erected by distant states to house votive offerings sit in a row on the northern hillside to your right. Continuing left as you face the hill, you'll see the space that once held the small-scale temples donated by individual cities. Beyond the treasuries are the remains of the **Nymphaeum** and the **Metroön,** an elegant 4th century BC Doric temple dedicated to Zeus's mother, Rhea. Along the terrace of the treasuries stand the remains of the bases of 16 bronze statues of Zeus, built with money from fines collected from cheating athletes.

To the left facing the hill, past the Metroön and the Nymphaeum, are the dignified remains of the ■**Temple of Hera,** or **Heraion.** Erected around 600 BC, the temple is the oldest building at Olympia, the oldest Doric temple in Greece, and the best-preserved structure at the site. Originally built for both Zeus and Hera, it was devoted solely to the goddess when Zeus moved to his grander quarters (ironically now in far worse shape) in 457 BC. The *cella* of the temple is where the magnificent **Hermes of Praxiteles** was unearthed during excavations; the statue is now displayed in the site's museum. This temple figured prominently in the **Heraia,** a women's footrace as old, if not older, than the Olympic Games, which was also held every four years. Today's ■**Olympic flame** is lit every other year at the Altar of Hera, at the northeastern corner of the temple. From here, it is borne by a variety of means to the site of the modern Games. This trip can involve thousands of runners passing the torch hand-to-hand, and has also drawn on more current forms of transportation like boats, planes, and even laser beams (as in the unique case of the 1976 Montreal Games). The **Prytaneion** is

PELOPONNESE

northwest (toward the entrance) of the Temple of Hera, and contains a hearth, the Altar of Hestia. The spirit of the Games reached its culmination here with feasts, held on behalf of the victors and official guests, which expressed an appreciation for the virtues of discipline and honor embodied by the athletes.

MUSEUM OF THE HISTORY OF THE OLYMPIC GAMES IN ANTIQUITY

At the end of Kondili, before the incline toward the ancient site; look for the signs.
☎ 26240 29 119. Open Apr.-Oct. M 12:30-7:30pm, Tu-Su 8:30am-7:30pm; Nov.-March M
12:30-3pm, Tu-Su 8:30am-3pm. Free.

This museum is jam-packed with info about the ancient **Olympic Games,** with explanations in four languages of the different events and antiquity's various other athletic festivals. Beyond a historical outline, specific artifacts from the Games (dating back to the 9th century BC) are displayed, arranged by event, from bronze **tripod cauldrons,** to portions of the original wreaths given as **prizes,** to intact **shields** and even a **wheel** from an iron chariot used in races. One highlight is a remarkably well-preserved mosaic floor from a Roman house in Patras that depicts Olympic events. Although the explanations of the Games are very thorough, many specific objects have little or no explanation, so ask for assistance from one of the staff members who are more than willing to provide further explanation.

MUSEUM OF THE HISTORY OF EXCAVATIONS IN OLYMPIA

Next door to the Museum of the History of the Olympic Games in Antiquity. If it is locked,
ask a staff member at the Olympic Games museum to open it.

The one small room that houses this museum presents a brief, nostalgic glance at the long process of excavation in Olympia, dating back to 1829. Beyond newspaper clippings from the 1800s and the official documents that allowed for excavations, the smaller objects on display—like a box filled with tickets to the old museum, inventory lists from the daily excavations, and pages from excavation diaries and manuscripts from 1908—add depth to the story of discovery. The museum also has a large collection of instruments used in the original excavation. Though small, this museum is valuable for understanding the more practical side of the site's archaeology.

MUSEUM OF THE OLYMPIC GAMES

2 blocks from Kondili, on Avgerinou. Turn next to Hotel Ilis; it's the large white building at
the end of the street. ☎ 26240 22 544. Open daily 8am-3:30pm. €2. Guidebook €6.

Tracing the modern Games from 1896 to 2004, this museum shows pins, stamps, photographs, and posters from each Olympiad, as well as biographies of prominent athletes. Notice how the shape and style of the Olympic Torch has changed over the past century, and don't miss the silver medal from the 1996 Games in Atlanta, donated by Niki Bakoyianni, the women's high-jump medalist.

ARCADIA Αρκαδία

Beyond the noisy bustle of urban Tripoli, mountainous and heavily-forested Arcadia is lightly speckled with red-roofed villages and lonely monasteries. Introduced into mythology and literature for its serene landscape, "Arcadia" became synonymous with pastoral paradise. Well past ancient times, an archetypal image lingered of a green idyll inhabited by Pan, Dionysus, nymphs, satyrs, and the lucky mortals who cavorted with them. While few foreign tourists venture as far as Arcadia's outer reaches, those who do enjoy the rare company of mountain goats on the precipitous slopes. A visit to one of the small villages like Dimitsana or Stemnitsa brings complete immersion into traditional Greek culture.

TRIPOLI Τρίπολη   ☎2710

Tripoli, Arcadia's capital, will probably not be the high point of anyone's vacation to Greece. Its central location, however, means that many visitors pass through this urban hub daily. Exploring the museums or one of the large plateias, which come alive at night, is the best use of time at this unavoidable stop.

☞ TRANSPORTATION

Buses: Tripoli has 2 bus stations; both are outside of town, 5min. taxi rides or 15-20min. walks from Pl. Kolokotronis. You can also take a blue bus from stops around town. Ask at the nearest kiosk. The **KTEL Arcadias Station** (☎27102 22 560), Nafpliou 50, sends buses to: **Andritsena** (2hr.; 11:45am, 7:30pm; €6); **Athens** (2hr., 17 per day 5am-10pm, €12); **Dimitsana** (1½hr.; 1:30, 6:30pm; €3.75-5); **Megalopolis** (45min., 7 per day 10am-10:15pm, €3); **Nafplion** (1hr., 6 per day, 7am-6:30pm, €4) via **Argos; Pirgos** (3½hr.; 8:30am, noon; €10.50). Blue buses leave from Arcadias Station for **Mantinea** and **Tegea** (1hr., every 15min., €1). Walk along Nafpliou, the street across from Vas. Giorgiou in Pl. Kolokotronis, for about 15min. It's on the right. The **KTEL Messinia and Laconia** depot (☎27102 42 086) is housed in a convenience store across from the train station. From Pl. Kolokotronis, take the road to the left of Nafpliou facing the square and turn left at the first traffic light. Buses go to: **Kalamata** (1½hr., every hr. 8am-1am, €6); **Patras** (3hr.; 6am, 2:45pm; €12); **Pylos** (3hr.; 10:30am, 5:30pm; €9.50); **Sparta** (1hr., every hr. 9am-10pm, €4).

Trains: ☎27102 41 213. Facing the Messinia and Laconia bus depot. Trains go to: **Argos** (1hr., 6:30pm, €2); **Athens** (4½hr.; 9:30am, 6:25pm, 1:20am; €5) via **Corinth** (2hr., €3).

Taxis (☎27102 33 010) line up in Pl. Ag. Vasiliou.

⬛⁊ ORIENTATION AND PRACTICAL INFORMATION

Think of Tripoli as a cross. **Plateia Agiou Vasiliou,** marked by the Church of Ag. Vasiliou, sits at the central joint. Four other plateias form the ends of the cross, at the ends of the four roads that branch out from Ag. Vasiliou. From **Plateia Kolokotronis, Vasiliou Giorgiou,** to the left as you face the National Bank, takes you to Pl. Ag. Vasiliou. Facing the church in Pl. Ag. Vasiliou, turn left and head north onto **Ethnikis Antistasis** to reach **Plateia Petrinou,** recognizable by the large, Neoclassical Maliaropouli Theater. Continue on Eth. Antistasis past pedestrian-only **Deligianni,** which runs perpendicular to Eth. Antistasis. Farther up, the city **park** will be on your right. At the center of the park, to the left of Eth. Antistasis as you face Pl. Ag. Vasiliou, is **Plateia Areus,** with a 5m tall statue of war hero Kolokotronis.

Bank: National Bank, in Pl. Kolokotronis (☎27103 71 110). Another is on Eth. Antistasis (☎27102 34 878), 1 block from Pl. Ag. Vasiliou; take the first left as you head down Eth. Antistasis toward Pl. Petrinou. Both **exchange currency** and have a **24hr. ATM.** Both open M-Th 8am-2:30pm, F 8am-2pm.

Police: ☎27102 24 847 or 100 in an emergency. About 1km from Pl. Kolokotronis. Walk toward the train station and go right at the traffic light; it's another 150m. Open 24hr.

Hospital: ☎27102 38 542. On Panargadon. Walk straight ahead with your back to the church from Pl. Ag. Vasiliou; the road becomes E. Stavrou, which intersects with Panargadon after 500m. At the intersection, turn left. After 300m, look right, and you'll see the hospital. In an **emergency,** dial ☎166 or 100.

Telephones: OTE, 28 Oktovriou 29 (☎27102 26 399). From Pl. Ag. Vasiliou, take Eth. Antistasis and go left on 28 Oktovriou. Offices are upstairs. Open M-Sa 7am-5pm.

Internet Access: Cinema Billiards Club (☎27102 38 010), 45 Kennedy or 2 Deligianni, on the corner of Deligianni and Eth. Antistasis. €2 per hr.; €1 min. Open 10am-2am. **Memories Cafe** (☎27102 35 600), on Dareioutou off Eth. Antistasis, before Deligianni. €2 per hr.; €1 min. Open 7:45am-3:30am.

Post Office: ☎27102 22 565. Behind Galaxy Hotel in Pl. Ag. Vasiliou. Turn right 1 block past the war museum onto Nikitara. Open M-F 7:30am-8pm. **Postal Code:** 22100.

ACCOMMODATIONS

Most of Tripoli's hotels are in or near the plateias. As a transportation hub with some of the best nightlife in the region, the city draws village youth looking for weekend clubs, businessmen attending conventions, and a diverse mix of international travelers stuck for the night. **⬛Hotel Anaktorikon ❸,** Eth. Antistasis 48, between Deligiannis and the city park, offers Old World elegance and perks for half the price you might expect. The plush red carpeting leads to sitting areas with artwork, luxurious red brocade couches, and a piano. Rooms have large baths with tubs, A/C, TV, phones, and balconies. Shrewd bargaining can lower prices by €10-15. (☎27102 22 545. Singles €40-55; doubles €60-75; triples €90.) In Pl. Kolokotronis, travel into the past at **Arcadia Hotel ❸,** where the charmingly old-fashioned rooms come with leather-backed chairs and other classy furnishings. Each has a private bath, A/C, TV, and a unique wallpaper pattern. The five floors and roof-top garden provide much-needed peace and quiet from the constant traffic below. (☎27102 25 551. Singles €30; doubles €47; triples €55. V.) **Hotel Alex ❸,** Vas. Giorgiou 26, on the other hand, caters to those who prefer contemporary and super-trendy furnishings. Its leather and marble lobby and silver elevator give way to spotless white rooms with baths, A/C, TV, phones, and balconies. (☎27102 23 465. Singles €30-40; doubles €50-60; triples €65-70. Suites available.)

FOOD

The restaurants in Tripoli aren't generally anything to write home about. There are a few good options bordering the park, though, and sandwich shops on Eth. Antistasis and Vas. Giorgiou pile baguettes with meat and cheese (around €2-3). **Klimataria ❸,** Kalavriton 11a, four blocks past the park as you walk from Pl. Petriou down Eth. Antistasis, has romantic garden seating with fountains and grapevines that accent the traditional delicacies. Turkey with pepper (€6) and pork with celery (€7) are local favorites. (☎27102 22 058. AmEx/MC/V.) After a few hours exploring Tripoli's underwhelming eateries, you may answer the query posed by **Hungry? ❶,** on the corner of Deligianni and Eth. Antistasis, with an emphatic "Ναι!" The large portions of delicious pizza (€2.50 per slice) leave no doubt as to why Tripoli's youth regularly stop at this 24hr. eatery.

SIGHTS AND ENTERTAINMENT

The **Archaeological Museum** is on Evangelistrias, in a pink building surrounded by rose bushes and sculpture. Walking from Pl. Kolokotronis to Pl. Ag. Vasiliou, take the first left and then turn left again. The museum has a large collection, with rooms of pottery and weaponry from the Neolithic to Roman periods. (☎27102 42 148. Open Tu-Su 8:30am-2:45pm. €2, students and seniors €1, children free. Photography prohibited.) Walk to the left of the Galaxy Hotel in Pl. Ag. Vasiliou to find the **War Museum** on the left side of the street, marked by a large cannon in front. Look for the old photograph of Peristera Kraka, the female "Captain of West Macedonia." (Open Tu-Sa 9am-2pm, Su 9:30am-2pm. Free.)

Local high school students crowd the cafe-bars in the narrow, pedestrian-only hot spot around Deligianni and Eth. Antistasis. At **Vivace**, pop music plays as patrons lounge on trendy, alluring white and red leather couches. (Open daily 10am-3am. Beer €3. Mixed drinks €5.) Across the street from Hungry?, **Prince** combines Middle Eastern flair with whimsical wall ornaments and a very chill atmosphere. The only thing missing here is a hookah. (Open 9am-3am. Beer €3-4. Mixed drinks €6.) The side roads branching off of and parallel to Deligianni are home to some lackluster clubs (cover €10). In summer, posters advertise dance groups, choirs, and plays performed in the city's main plateias and nearby villages. Traveling companies and local performers stage Greek shows in the attractive **Maliaropouli Theater,** on Eth. Antistasis between Pl. Vasiliou and Pl. Petrinou. The **Lera Panigyris** is a 20-day theater and dance festival in the region, kicked off each year on August 15.

DIMITSANA Δημητσάνα ☎27950

The quintessential Arcadian village of Dimitsana clings to a steep, pine-covered mountainside about 65km from Tripoli. Built on the ruins of ancient Teuthis, Dimitsana has been a center of Greek learning and revolutionary activity since the 16th century. Trendy travelers may find little to keep them in this blatantly un-cosmopolitan town for long, but Greek city-dwellers have been working to resettle Dimitsana, bringing the money and energy to keep the town's historical buildings in good repair. With stunning views of endless mountains and the twinkling lights of Megalopolis, Dimitsana offers cozy hospitality in the winter and first-rate hikes along the Lousios River in the summer.

▐▀▐ TRANSPORTATION AND PRACTICAL INFORMATION. Getting around can be tricky in the mountains, where the villages are far apart and public transportation is almost non-existent. When planning trips, keep in mind that the town's two taxi drivers might siesta all afternoon. There is no Dimitsana bus station, only a **bus kiosk,** by the health center, and buses pick up passengers at several different locations. Talk to the locals to find out approximate times and places to catch a bus, but don't be surprised if these estimates turn out to be off by an hour. You may want to try taking a bus from the nearby village of Karkalou if Dimitsana's options are too limited. The bus station in Tripoli (☎27102 22 560) will have the latest updates, especially for weekends and national holidays. **Buses** should run at 7:30am to Tripoli (1hr.) via Stemnitsa and at 7:30-8pm to Tripoli via Karkalou. Both fares are €5. A bus to Pyrgos meets the 7:30-8pm bus from Dimitsana in Karkalou. When you leave the bus kiosk, make sure to tell the driver where you want to go. The bus deposits those arriving on **Labardopoulou,** the main street, near the **taxi** stand (☎27950 61 400), 30m downhill from the town center. Walking uphill into the town center, you'll pass a string of cafes and stores to the left and a small grocery store (open daily 7:30am-10:30pm) just before a turn in the road. There you will find a **National Bank** with a **24hr. ATM** and **currency exchange.** (☎27950 31 503. Open M-Th 8am-2:30pm, F 8am-2pm.) Opposite the grocery store is an alley leading to rooms and the Ecclesiastical Museum. The worn-down **police station**, which has a flag hanging from its balcony, is just before the bank. To get upstairs, take the alley by the station and go around to the side of the building. (☎27950 31 205. Open 24hr.) The **health center** (☎27950 31 401 or 27950 31 402; open 24hr.) is next to the bus kiosk, a 10min. walk down the road toward Karkalou; the closest **hospital** is in Tripoli. A small **pharmacy** is on your right, walking uphill from the bus stop. (☎27950 31 233.) The **post office** is next to the bank, after the road turns. (☎27950 31 234. Open M-F 7:30am-2pm.) **Postal Code:** 22100.

⚐⚐ ACCOMMODATIONS AND FOOD. For its small size, Dimitsana has an impressive number of rooming options. Though **domatia** can be just as expensive as the hotels, there's no doubt that you get what you pay for. Most are beautifully furnished and built along the cliffside, yielding fantastic mountain views. High and low seasons are reversed here—the rooms get cheaper as it gets warmer. Off the main road but still close to the town center, **Vasilis Tsiapa ❸**, among fields of bright, chaotic wildflowers, overlooks the mountains. Traditional stone rooms come with high wood ceilings, TV, private baths, and fully-stocked kitchenettes. As you walk up the main road from the bus stop, turn right into the alley opposite the National Bank, pass the Ecclesiastical Museum and a parking lot, and the rooms will be on your left. (☎27950 31 583. Breakfast included. Singles €25-35; doubles €35-80.) At the home of **Georgios Velissaropoulos ❸**, a short 3min. walk from the main road, the small gardens and magnificent valley views supplement rooms with kitchenettes and access to a comfortable living room. To find the house, follow the road across from the police station and turn right after 25m; signs point the way. (☎27950 31 617. Singles €35-55; doubles €40-60; 2- to 4- person apartments €50-90.)

Though Dimitsana's dining options are limited—the five restaurants in town all serve the same traditional dishes—your meal's mountain backdrop is worth every euro. In an elegant country house, **Drymonas ❸**, 200m past the post office on the road leading to Stemnitsa, has a rotating menu of classic Greek staples. Pork, lamb, and rabbit dishes (€7-9) come in large portions and are delicately seasoned. (☎27950 31 116. Salads €3-5. Rabbit with lemon sauce €8. Open daily noon-12:30am.) **To Baroytadiko ❷**, next to the pharmacy, heaps plates with giant portions in a pleasant outdoor dining area that gives way to disco space in the winter. (Beef pasta €7.50. Open daily noon-midnight.) Have a snack or drink at relaxed **Cafe-Bar Brahos**, at the turn onto the road to Stemnitsa after the bank. Forgotten American pop plays inside Dimitsana's only steady semblance of nightlife, and the mountain views make the already lovely outdoor seating magnificent. (Mixed drinks €5.)

◙ SIGHTS. Dimitsana has an impressive collection of museums that proudly commemorate its ecclesiastical, scholarly, and revolutionary heritage. The pride of the town, the **Historical Museum** was formerly the library of a ministry school that was established in 1764. Its collection of over 5000 books was almost completely decimated when the books were used as gunpowder during the War of Independence. The revamped and very much restocked library-museum now holds over 35,000 books. Some items from the original library are still on display, including a handful of Greek-Latin **incunabula,** 16th-century books from Venice and Basel that are among the first books ever printed. To find the library and museum, walk up the alley next to the police station and look for the courtyard with the statue and a large church; the entrance to the museum is on the wall farthest from the street. (☎27950 31 219. Open Tu-Sa 9am-2:30pm. Free.) Another smaller but still fascinating sight, the **Ecclesiastical Museum,** is in the alley opposite the National Bank. Located in the old mansion of Patriarch Gregory V, the museum also contains the saint's church in its basement. The collection includes local icons and religious artifacts from the 17th century, including exceptionally well-preserved Bibles and the saint's own robes. (☎27950 31 468. Open Apr.-Nov. M-Tu, Th, Sa-Su 10am-1:30pm and 5-7pm; Dec.-Mar. Sa-Su 10am-1:30pm and 4-6pm. Free.) Dimitsana is also home to an **Open-Air Water Power Museum,** 1.6km from the village; take the main road as it turns past the bank and follow signs at the first fork downhill to the right. The exhibit brings back to life the tanneries and mills that were operated in the 16th through 20th centuries using the waters of the Lousios River. (☎27950 31 630. Open Apr. 11-Oct. 10 M, W-Su 10am-2pm and 5-7pm; Oct. 11-Apr. 10 M, W-Su 10am-4pm. €2, EU students and seniors €1.)

If you have your own transportation, the old **Filosofou Monastery** is worth visiting for its role in the Greek independence movement, a great source of local pride. Built in the Lousios Gorge in AD 963, the monastery was the location of the famous *krifto scholio* (secret school) where priests covertly maintained Greek education and the revolutionary spirit under Ottoman rule. To reach the **Lousios River,** take the road to Stemnitsa and follow the signs at the fork. There is another entrance along the mountain road, 2km from Stemnitsa. Summertime visitors seek adventure on the rapids, swim in the river, and gaze at the multicolored butterflies that migrate to the area. A hike through the gorge takes about 3½hr., but the best part of the trek starts after the Filosofou Monastery. Rafting (including whitewater), horseback riding, and river tours are available. For more information, contact **Hellas Trekking** (☎27102 21 912).

STEMNITSA Στεμνίτσα ☎27950

From Dimitsana, you can walk an easy, scenic 10km (2hr.) along the winding road, catch the 7:30am bus, or pay for a taxi to Stemnitsa (€7). With its unspoiled mountain scenery and abundant flowers, greenery, and hidden courtyards, it is easy to see why this town has been called one of the most beautiful in Greece.

At the **Folk Art Museum,** 300m down the road leading away from Dimitsana, a series of rooms displays antiquated techniques once used by cobblers and candlemakers in an 18th-century mansion. Well-preserved, bound Bibles are as beautiful as the fake, life-sized cobbler is cheesy. (☎27950 81 252. Open July-Sept. M 11am-1pm, W-Th, Sa-Su 11am-1pm and 6-8pm, F 6-8pm; Oct.-Jan., Mar.-June M, W-F 11am-1pm, Sa-Su 11am-2pm. Free. No photography.) Between Dimitsana and Stemnitsa there are several monasteries, a few built right into the mountain face. Some of the roads and paths are unsuitable for cars and are best attempted on foot. A loop from Dimitsana to a monastery and then to Stemnitsa, however, could be up to 30km, so plan accordingly. The 12th-century monastery of **Agios Ioannis Prodromos,** 10km from Stemnitsa and 16km from Dimitsana, is currently inhabited by three or four monks. During the War of Independence, it was a hospital and sanctuary for revolutionaries. Its icons are painted on the bare stone walls and gravity-defying monastic cells that seem to hang off the mountain. Take the road toward Dimitsana for 4km, turn right at the sign, and follow the road for another 7km. Once you hit the dirt path, the monastery is another 30min. by foot. (☎27950 81 385. Open daily dawn-dusk. Modest dress required. Free.)

If you need to spend the night in the village, **Stemnitsa Domatia ❷**, a traditional stone building on the road from Dimitsana, has spacious rooms with private baths. With balcony space and a cozy living room with a fireplace, the elegant domatia offers characteristic Stemnitsan peace and quiet. (☎27950 81 349. Breakfast included. Doubles and triples €40-50.) Stemnitsa's mini-marts sell sweet honey,

PELOPONNESE

but once you've tasted that you may initially be disappointed with the town's food. Luckily, **Restaurant Stemnitsa ❸**, in the plateia, serves its tasty traditional dishes in very filling portions. There's no menu; make your choice based on which dishes in the kitchen look the best. A reliable staple is *aubergines* with cheese and tomatoes (€5). Stemnitsa's other restaurant is tiny, inexpensive **Taverna Klinitsa ❹**, outside the plateia on the way to Dimitsana. (Entrees €3.50-6. Open Sept.-June.)

Buses do come through Stemnitsa, but as with Dimitsana and other mountain villages, they are not necessarily regular or on time. On weekdays and some weekends, there are usually buses to Dimitsana at 2:15pm and to Tripoli at 7:30am. At the **town hall**, in the plateia, people are extremely friendly and helpful and speak English. (☎27950 81 280. Open M-F 8am-3pm.) **Postal Code:** 22024.

MESSINIA Μεσσηνία

Messinia is a lush and largely tourist-free oasis in the arid Peloponnese. Renowned olives, figs, and grapes spring from the rich soil, and its dense forests hide the ruins of Venetian castles and Turkish fortresses. Most Messinians live at the head of the gulf around the sprawling labyrinth of Kalamata, though visitors may prefer to stay in the sleepy coastal towns of Pylos, Methoni, Koroni, Kardamyli, or Finikouda, with their clean beaches, quiet streets, and breathtaking sunsets.

KALAMATA Καλαμάτα ☎27210

On March 23, 1821, two days before a Greek revolt was to begin, impatient Kalamatans massacred local Ottomans as they slept. Today, Kalamata has shed such brutality for a far more banal horror. The second-biggest city in the Peloponnese, it isn't quite cosmopolitan, but is still large enough to suffer from loud traffic and dizzying urban sprawl. Still, sandy beaches and a growing nightlife can help visitors passing through the city make good use of their time.

◧ TRANSPORTATION

Trains: ☎27210 95 006. Where Sid. Stathmou dead-ends at Frantzi. As you walk away from the Old Town and toward the waterfront in Pl. Giorgiou, turn right on Frantzi at the far end of the plateia and walk a few blocks. To: **Athens** (6½hr., 3 per day 7:11am-11pm, €7) via **Tripoli** (2½hr., €3), **Argos** (4hr., €4.40), and **Corinth** (5¼hr., €6); **Kyparissia** (2hr., 4 per day 4:53am-3:20pm, €2); **Patras** (5½hr., 3:20pm, €5); **Pirgos** (3¼hr.; 6:30am, 3:20pm; €3).

Buses: Leave from the station on Artemidos (☎27210 22 851; open 7am-10pm), inland from Pl. Giorgiou and across the river from Aristomenous. To get to the waterfront from the bus station, take a taxi (€3) or walk down Artemidos and eventually cross to parallel Aristomenous, which leads to Pl. Giorgiou. It's about a 40min. walk. Buses go to: **Athens** (4hr., 13 per day 4:45am-10:45pm, €16) via **Megalopolis** (1hr., €4); **Finikouda** (1½hr., 4 per day 5am-5:30pm, €5.40); **Koroni** (1½hr., 8 per day 5am-7pm, €3.50); **Mavromati** and **Ancient Messini** (1hr.; 5:40am, 2pm; €2); **Methoni** (1¾hr., 6 per day 5am-7:45pm, €4.30); **Patras** (3½hr.; 8:30am, 2:30pm; €16.40) via **Pirgos** (2½hr., €9.30); **Pylos** (1½hr., 9 per day 5am-7:45pm, €3.30); **Sparta** (2hr.; 9:15am, 2:30pm; €4) via **Artemisia** (1hr., €2); **Tripoli** (2hr., 8 per day 6am-10pm, €6). To get to **Areopolis,** go to **Itilo** (2hr., 3 per day 7:30am-5pm,

€5.20) on the 7:30am or 1:15pm bus and take the Areopolis bus (15min., €0.80) from there. The bus to Itilo also stops in **Kardamyli** (€3) and **Stoupa** (€3.10).

Public Transportation: Unfortunately for the traveler without a vehicle, the local city buses (€0.80 per ride) are very limited. City buses depart from near Pl. 25 Martiou in the Old Town; look for the large street off Aristomenous. **Bus #1** goes down Aristomenous to the water and then runs along the water. Stops can be found on all main streets. Buy your ticket onboard.

Taxis: ☎27210 26 565. Line up by the bus station and in Pl. Giorgiou.

Moped Rental: Alpha Rental (☎27210 93 423), on Vyronos 1 block from the waterfront. Map, helmet, and insurance included. From €16 per day. Open daily 8:30am-8pm.

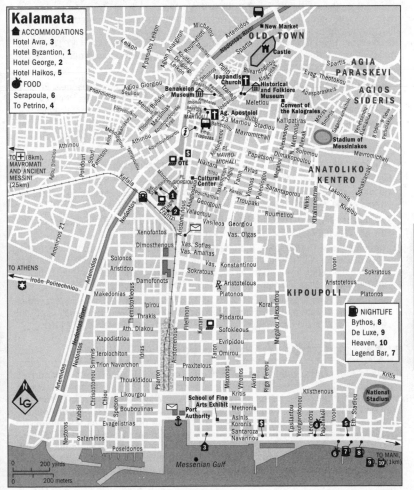

■✦ 🛈 ORIENTATION AND PRACTICAL INFORMATION

Kalamata, expanding inland from the beachfront, is frustratingly spread-out. Short-term visitors may want to spare themselves the trouble of navigating the interior and stay by the waterfront's convenient grid. The city is divided into three sections. Closest to the water is a **residential section**, distinguished by the municipal park; most of the hotels and restaurants are here, along **Navarinou**, the waterfront street. Heading inland, you will reach **Plateia Giorgiou**, home to the train station, the post office, stores, and banks. The **Old Town**, with the castle, market, and bus station, is farthest from the ocean. Navigating your way across the city can be confusing, so consider using a map. The bus station is on **Artemidos**. With your back to the station turn left, follow this street for about 500m, and cross the "river" on your left at the third crossing to **Aristomenous,** the main street. Eventually Aristomenous meets and runs along Pl. Giorgiou. Take the first crossing over the river and head directly away from the bus station to get to the Old Town and castle. To reach the waterfront from the Old Town, follow Aristomenous all the way along the left side of Pl. Giorgiou.

Tourist Office: A limited selection of pamphlets and free **maps** is available near Pl. Giorgiou at **DETAK,** Poliviou 6 (☎ 27210 21 700), just off Aristomenous. Walk up Aristomenous from Pl. Giorgiou and signs will point the way. Open M-F 8am-2:30pm.

Bank: National Bank (☎ 27210 28 047), on Aristomenous off the northern end of Pl. Giorgiou. Smaller branches are in the plateia and on Akrita on the waterfront. All have **24hr. ATMs** and **currency exchange.** Open M-Th 8am-2:30pm, F 8am-2pm.

Police: ☎ 27210 22 622. On I. Polytechniou. Take Artimidos to I. Poleytechniou, about halfway between the train station and the waterfront. Open 24hr.

Hospital: ☎ 27210 46 000 or 27210 45 500. Near the town of Sperchogia, accessible by car or taxi. Call ☎ 100 or 166 in a **medical emergency.**

Telephones: OTE ☎ 27210 92 999. In the northwestern corner of Pl. Giorgiou, opposite the National Bank. Open M-Th 8am-1:30pm, F 8am-1pm.

Internet Access: The Web, Sid. Stathmou 19 (☎ 27210 90 519), is next to Hotel Byzantio, 1 block from Pl. Giorgiou. At the southern end of the plateia, turn right; it's across from the train station. €2.50 per hr. Open 24hr. **Matrix,** Faron 154, is about 5 blocks up from the waterfront. €3 per hr.; €1.50 min. Open daily 9am-1am.

Post Office: On Vas. Olgas (☎ 27210 22 810). Turn left 1 block past the southern end of Pl. Giorgiou, toward the waterfront. Offers **Poste Restante.** Another branch is on the waterfront next to the tourist police. Open M-F 7:30am-2pm. **Postal Code:** 24100.

🏠 🍴 ACCOMMODATIONS AND FOOD

Hotels in Kalamata cluster around Pl. Giorgiou and the waterfront, but budget accommodations are few and far between. **Hotel George ❷,** on the corner of Dagre and Frantzi by the train station, is visible on Frantzi as you walk from the waterfront end of Pl. Giorgiou. With an intimate lobby that resembles a comfortable living room, this small hotel also provides A/C, TV, and private baths. As one of the cheapest places in town, it's often fully booked, so call ahead. (☎ 27210 27 225. Singles €20-25; doubles €25-30.) Another good bet is nearby **Hotel Byzantion ❸,** Sid. Strethmou 13, one block from the train station. Simple rooms come with A/C, TV, high ceilings, big baths, and balconies; those on the fifth floor are high enough to block out the city noise below. (☎ 27210 86 824. Singles €25-35; doubles €30-40.)

Beach bums and night owls who prefer to stay next to the lively waterfront may want to try **Hotel Avra ❷,** Santaroza 10, one block behind Navarinou between Kanari and Faron. The somewhat shabby exterior hides a bright, flower-strewn interior with a clean communal kitchen and shared bath. Large rooms have sinks, balconies, and a few magazines. **Hotel Haikos ❸,** Navarinou 115, rents colorful carpeted rooms with A/C, TV, balconies, and hair dryers. Adding depth to the decor, the rooms and hallways are lined with photos of 1930s Kalamata. (☎27210 88 902; www.haikos.gr. Singles €33-40; doubles €45-55; extra bed €5.)

The massive **New Market** is a must-see; with your back to the bus station, walk across the first bridge on your right. The market contains countless meat, cheese, and fruit shops, alongside stands selling every imaginable type of household good. You can sample famous Kalamata olives and figs at the daily farmers' market, which opens around 8am. For a sit-down meal, family-owned **Serapoula ❶,** Navarino 14, serves standard Greek dishes. In a central location on the waterfront, but quieter than its showy neighbors, it is perfect for those who want to have a relaxing meal and still be able to afford after-dinner drinks. (☎27210 20 985. Souvlaki pita €1.60. Salads €2.50-5. Open 8am-3am.) **To Petrino ❸,** Navarinou 93, has a drastic solution for those sick of traditional souvlaki. Adventure-seeking carnivores will be delighted by the ostrich (€15), crocodile (€27), and other "exotic hunting" the chef tosses on the grill. (☎27210 29 097. Open daily 11am-2am.)

🅖 SIGHTS

Having survived quite a turbulent history, the 13th-century **castle,** built by Wilhelm Villehardouin, crowns a hill above the Old City. From Pl. 25 Martiou, walk up Ipapandis past the large church on the right; turn right, walk around to the back of the church, and take your first left where you will see signs that point the way. Destroyed by Ottomans in 1685, the castle was rebuilt by Venetians a decade later. The restoration process that began after a devastating 1986 earthquake continues today, meaning access to the site may be limited on certain days. There are no written explanations, but feel free to ask any of the friendly staff for information. The castle also encircles an open-air theater, which hosts the **Cultural Summer of Kalamata** from mid-July to the end of August, with jazz, rock, and Greek drama. Ask at the tourist office for details. (Open M-F 8am-3pm, Sa-Su 9am-3pm. Free.) Near the castle in the Old Town is one of Kalamata's most famous gems, the **Convent of the Kalograies** (known locally as **"Moni Kalograion"**). Founded in 1796, the convent houses nuns who spend their days hand-weaving silks used for the priests' robes. To get there, walk down the hill from the castle toward Ipapandi church and take a left onto Patr. Poukoupaprio before the church, or follow the signs. (Modest dress required.) Closer to the New Town, in a corner by Pl. 25 Martiou, is the 14th-century **Church of the Aghioi Apostoloi** (Holy Apostles). The church first gained recognition when a doe-eyed icon of the Virgin Mary was found there. The name of the city reflects the icon's appearance—*kala mata* means "good eyes." (Open daily 6:30am-noon and 6-9pm. Modest dress required.)

After five years of restoration, the Old City's **Benakeion Archaeological Museum** proudly exhibits a small collection of statues, coins, and jewelry, with thorough captions in both English and Greek. The exceptionally preserved mosaic floor from Koroni, a ruined Roman villa nearby, is a particular highlight, along with the seals made from semi-precious stones on the second floor. (☎27210 26 209. Open Tu-Su 8:30am-3pm. €2, seniors €1, students and children free.) The **Historical and Folklore Museum,** in the same square as Ipapandi church, is currently closed for renovations, but in the past has exhibited everything from guns to icons to traditional costumes in its attempt to share Kalamata's rich historical traditions. Kalamata also proudly supports two professional **theaters.** Ask DETAK or the tourist police for info on events in the **Pantazopoulion Cultural Center** on Aristomenous. (☎27210 94 819, or call the municipality at 27210 28 000.) For information about and schedules of the widely known **Kalamata International Dance Festival,** contact the Kalamata International Dance Center (☎27210 90 886).

NIGHTLIFE

At night in Kalamata, the youth shimmy into skin-tight garb and head to either the cafes and bars on the waterfront or to the strip 1km east of the port. **De Luxe,** a 10min. walk with the water on your right, is a trendy urban oasis where Art Deco couches and multicolored canopies surround the circular bar and pool. (Mixed drinks €6. Beer €4. Open 10am-6pm and 10pm-4am. Pool open only in the daytime.) **Heaven,** Navarinou 302, two doors down from De Luxe, is a neon-colored, psychedelic paradise for the huge crowds that dance late into the night. (Open only in summer midnight-7am. Beer and mixed drinks €5.) Elsewhere on Navarinou, funky **Legend Bar's** large-screen TV broadcasts soccer matches for a rowdy clientele. (☎27210 97 690. Mixed drinks and beer €5. Open 9am-late.) Nearby, **Bythos Bar** sports blue and white decor in a large open-air space.

DAYTRIPS FROM KALAMATA

MAVROMATI
The town is 25km from Kalamata and within walking distance of Ancient Messini. Take the bus to Petralona and say that you want to get off here (1hr.; leaves M-Sa 5:40am, 2pm, returns 3:30pm; €2). Taxis €16-18.

The small town of Mavromati is charmingly impervious to the tour groups that file in and out of the nearby site. Visitors who stop into the tiny mountain village itself are treated to incredible views of the site below. The main square contains the **Klepseydra fountain,** where clean, clear water runs from a dark hole in the rocks that resembles a black eye, or *mavro mati* in Greek. The 17th-century **Voulkanou Monastery,** 2.5km outside town, was a staging point for rebels in the War of Independence. Its library holds priceless manuscripts.

ANCIENT MESSINI
Take the Petralona bus to Mavromati; it's 300m downhill from the main square. Or take the bus to Valira and get off at Lambena. From there, take a taxi (€5). Since there is only 1 taxi in town, however, you may wait all morning for it. ☎27240 51 046. Site open 8am-8pm. Free. Museum open Tu-Su 8am-2:30pm. €2, seniors €1, students free.

Pausanias wrote a detailed journal entry about his tour through thriving Messini in the AD 2nd century, and his account has been particularly useful for the excavations on **Mount Ithomi.** Over the last two decades, diggers have uncovered what is quickly becoming one of the most impressive ancient sites in Greece. Archaeologists believe the city dates back 2300 years, and there are signs of human settlement from thousands of years before. Fortunately, much of the city was buried by earth, preventing other cities from being built on top, and the artifacts have been protected from thieves and natural destruction. When the battle of Leuctra in 371 BC ended Spartan domination of the Peloponnese, Theban general and statesman **Epaminodas** built Messini, and named the new capital after the region's first queen. While the remains of a theater, stadium, gymnasium, public baths, and nine different temples have been uncovered, it is the city's **defensive walls** that receive the most attention. The 3m thick walls circle 9km and represent the massive heft of 4th- and 3rd-century BC military architecture. The partitions were constructed so well that the city lay unharmed for 700 years. Originally, huge gates with towers and battlements interrupted the circuit. Of the four that survive, the **Arcadian gate** is in the best shape. Also impressive is the **fountain of Arsinoe,** whose waters flow through ancient tunnels from the Klepsydra fountain in the village of Mavromati. The temples of Demeter, Dioscuri, and Artemis Orthia are some of the best-preserved sacred monuments discovered in Messini. The **Ekklesiasterion,** a small theater used for political and cultural gatherings, has also been admirably restored. The site is unmarked, so purchasing a guidebook (€13) is a good idea. A **museum,** outside of Mavromati, is the artistic highlight of the site. Numerous marble statues found intact in the temples below, such as the 2m tall statue of Hermes of Messini and the larger-than-life sandstone lion, still stand proudly.

KARDAMYLI Καρδαμύλη ☎27210

This sleepy one-road town has endless opportunities for long walks through lush forests and flower-scented streets. The rugged mountains and relaxing beaches have long attracted artists and writers; by the time they got to know the friendly locals, many refused to leave. Along with its own charms, Kardamyli offers easy access to the southern Peloponnese and the magnificent Mt. Taygetus region.

▐▌ TRANSPORTATION AND PRACTICAL INFORMATION. Six **buses** run daily from Kalamata, dropping off near the *periptero* by the main plateia. There is no posted schedule, but the locals will tell you when the buses stop in town. If you're headed to Athens, take a bus to Kalamata (1hr.; M-F 6 per day 7:15am-8pm, Sa-Su 3 per day 10:30am-8pm; €3). Buses also go to Itilo (1hr.; M-F 3 per day 8:30am-6pm, Sa-Su 8:30am; €2.40), where you can transfer to the Areopolis or Gytheio bus (20min.; M-Sa 7:10, 9:30am, 3:20pm; €1). A bus headed to Areopolis will sometimes wait for connecting passengers; inquire with the driver.

Most of the businesses in this small town are on the main road, and the others all have signs pointing the way from the main road. The **bank,** with a **24hr. ATM,** is one block from the main plateia, on the main road toward Itilo. (☎27210 73 697. Open W 9:30am-1pm.) The **bookstore,** two doors down from the post office, has a large selection of bestsellers in English, along with **maps,** tourbooks, phone cards, and hiking brochures. (Open 8:30am-12:30am.) To get to the **police station,** walk 5min. along the road to Kalamata and over the bridge; the station will be on a street to the left by the large school—look for signs. (☎27210 73 209. Open 24hr.) The **pharmacy** is in the main plateia, across from the post office. (☎27210 73 512. Open M-F 8:30am-2pm and 6-9pm, Sa-Su 10am-1pm and 7-9pm.) Walking toward Itilo, turn right across from the post office to **Cafe Internet Koursaros,** next to Olympia Domatia, for **Internet access.** (☎27210 73 148. €3 per 30min., €5 per hr. Open M-W 7:30pm-1am, Th-Su 6pm-1am.) The **post office** is also on the main road to Itilo; there are signs from the plateia. (Open M-F 7:30am-2pm.) **Postal Code:** 24022.

▐▌ ACCOMMODATIONS AND FOOD. Travelers to tiny Kardamyli will be glad to discover that there's no shortage of reasonably priced rooms. ▨**Olympia Domatia ❷,** on the side street across from the post office, rents breezy, immaculate rooms with personal fans, TV, and a shared kitchen. Olympia herself is the town's real prize, handing weary travelers a cold drink, a cup of coffee, and a map of hiking routes upon their arrival. (☎ 27210 73 623. Singles €20-25; doubles €25-35.) Across from Olympia Domatia, the amiable and energetic **Stratis Bravakos ❸** lets spacious rooms that have small kitchenettes, fans, private baths, big beds, wood-paneled furnishings, and balconies that overlook the lush, green courtyard. (☎ 27210 73 326. Singles €20; doubles €25-30; triples €35-45.) Closer to the ocean, you'll find **Pension Voula ❷** a few doors down from the police station. Run by a Norwegian company, it offers basic rooms with balconies, sea views, fridges, and a large communal kitchen with a stove. (☎ 27210 73 400. Doubles €35.) Travelers planning an extended stay in the area may want to consider **Hotel Anniska ❹**, one block before the bank coming from the plateia, which rents apartments for families (children must be under 16 years old) and studios. You can stay at either of its two buildings which both have lovely dining areas. All rooms include balconies, kitchens, TV, A/C, phones, and private baths. (☎ 27210 73 601 or 27210 73 600; www.anniska.gr. Studios €50-70; apartments €70-90. MC/V.)

Two large **supermarkets** can be found past the plateia on the road to Kalamata. **Spidarus,** with the yellow awning, has a larger selection. (Open daily 7am-10:30pm.) Tavernas in Kardamyli tend to cater to the small tourist population; nearly all the menus are multilingual and generally include traditional Greek dishes. ▨**Koumaristria ❷**, at the end of the downhill road by the bank, serves home-cooked specialties and uncommon dishes from across Greece. Jovial owner Gregory recommends the Adrakia salad (€5) with onion and tomatoes and the lamb *kleftiko* (€10) with cheese, potatoes, and green peppers. (☎ 27210 73 250. Entrees €6.50-12. Open daily in summer noon-late; in winter 5pm-late.) As you walk past Olympia's rooms to the waterfront, turn right at the junction; after about 50m you'll see cozy **Lela's Taverna ❷**. The tree-covered patio juts onto the rocks, granting a magnificent waterfront view. (Mixed vegetables €5.30. Roasted chicken with potatoes €6.30. Open daily 12:30-4pm and 5-11pm.)

▣▨ **SIGHTS AND BEACHES.** Beyond its large pebble beach, Kardamyli is an excellent starting point for hikes in the surrounding region. A short stroll up the road toward Kalamata will bring you to the small but worthwhile ruins of the **Old Town,** highlighted by the 17th-century Church of Ag. Spiridon and the Mourtzinos Tower. The site has detailed explanations in English and an information booth. (Open Tu-Su 9am-2pm. Free.) On an enormous natural bay encircled by lush mountains, the white-pebble shore of the magnificent **Ritsa beach** is ideal for a leisurely early-evening walk. From the main road to Kardamyli, take the small path to the beach after the bridge, and then walk along the beach for 1km to reach Ritsa.

▨ **HIKING.** The hiking terrain surrounding the village competes with the enticing beaches as Kardamyli's main draw. Southeast of Kalamata, the limestone **Taygetus Mountains** divide Messinia and Laconia, running from Megalopolis down through the Taenarian promontory. Sacred to Apollo and Artemis, the mountains were named after **Taygete,** daughter of Atlas, mother of Lacedaemon, and lover of Zeus. Since those mythological origins, ancient and modern poets alike have glorified the range for its sheer size. Lampito declares in Aristophanes's *Lysistrata,* "I would climb as high as the peak of Taygetus, if thus I could find peace," while Nikiforos Vrettakos describes Mt. Taygetus as "the masculine child of [the Peloponnese]." With such a prestigious reputation, it is not hard to see why many travelers make the mountain a necessary stop on their trips through southern Greece. Adventure-seekers are drawn to the challenging paths that lead to the mountain's peak at Profitis Ilia (elev. 2704m), and history buffs treasure the lower regions for their assortment of Byzantine churches, Venetian towers, Frankish forts, and Mycenaean tombs. Human hikers aside, 26 species of plants, 58 species of birds, and 35 species of reptiles (including the rare *Testudo marginata* turtle and a few varieties of snake) call the mountain home. The early morning reveals a hidden paradise of multicolored insects and a variety of reverberating animal sounds. The entrance from Kardamyli offers many day-hike trails with varying levels of difficulty. One popular 2hr. path begins at Kardamyli, goes through Old Kardamyli, up to Ag. Sophia (elev. 200m) and back to town via Petrovouni (elev. 180m). The trail is initially marked with yellow and black rectangles. Toward Petrovouni, follow the markers with red circles inside the white squares. More experienced hikers may be interested in the 4hr. path that leads from Ag. Sophia to Kato Chora (elev. 450m), past the Vyros Gorge to Moni Satiros (elev. 150m), and finally to Kardamyli via a walk through a river bed. All of the paths are narrow and rocky, and the area is filled with bugs, so it's a good idea to wear long pants.

PYLOS Πύλος   ☎ 27230

In Homer's *Odyssey*, Odysseus's son Telemachus came to Pylos to seek the counsel of wise old Nestor, who returned here after the Trojan War. Today the city is mystifyingly free of visitors, despite the presence of an Ottoman fortress, quaint waterfront tavernas, and splendid views of the Peloponnese's largest natural bay—surely more enticing than that wizened horse-tamer could have been. Stop by this site to see Pylos's red-roofed houses clinging spectacularly to the hills at sunset and the town plateia lighting up at night.

▐▘▐ TRANSPORTATION AND PRACTICAL INFORMATION. Most of the town's businesses line the plateia, the waterfront, and the roads leading uphill to Methoni and Hora. The tiny **beaches,** one sand and one pebble, lie to the right of the waterfront as you face inland, as does the 16th-century Ottoman **Neocastro** on a forested hill. **Buses** (☎ 27230 22 230) go to: Athens (6½hr.; 9am, 4:30pm; €20); Finikouda (20min., 4 per day 6am-7:15pm, €1.10); Kalamata (1½hr.; M-Sa 9 per day 6:30am-9:20pm, Su 5 per day 9am-9:20pm; €3.50); Kyparissia (1½hr.; M-Sa 5 per day 6:40am-4:30pm, Su 11am, 4:30pm; €4) via Nestor's Palace (30min., €1) and Hora (45min., €1.20); Methoni (15min.; M-Sa 6 per day 6am-9pm, Su 11am, 4:20pm; €1). No buses travel directly to Koroni, but you can go through Finikouda and take a bus to Horokorio, the stop nearest Koroni. Bus service is reduced on weekends. Tickets are sold and schedules posted at the tiny KTEL office in the far right corner of the plateia, facing inland; buses leave from the back of the plateia. **Taxis** (☎ 27230 22 555) line the left side of the plateia. A **National Bank** with a **24hr. ATM** is in the plateia. (Open M-Th 8am-2:30pm, F 8am-2pm.) The **police** are in a building on the left side of the waterfront. (☎ 27230 22 316. Open 24hr.) They double as the tourist police. To get to the **hospital,** take the road right from the plateia. (☎ 27230 22 315. Open 24hr.) For the **OTE,** pass the post office, take the first left, then the second right. (Open M-F 7:30am-3pm.) The **post office** is on the road toward Hora and Kyparissia, on the right uphill from the bus station, facing inland; it offers **currency exchange.** (☎ 27230 22 247. Open M-F 7:30am-2pm.) **Postal Code:** 24001.

▐▘▐ ACCOMMODATIONS AND FOOD. You'll spot "rooms to let" signs as the bus descends into town from Kalamata. They are farther away from the water and plateia, but are likely to offer slightly lower prices. Expect to pay €20-30 for singles, €25-50 for doubles, and €35-50 for triples. **◙Hotel Miremare ❸,** on the waterfront, provides welcome relief to those sick of bland wood furniture and white rooms. Open since 1945, this Pylos institution has bright and colorful rooms with

TV, fridges, private baths, balconies, and many posters and decorations. Don't be surprised if the friendly staff offers you a room for a fraction of the prices listed. (☎27230 22 751. Singles €30-55; doubles €58-68; triples €70-80; quads €80-92.) **Hotel Nilefs ❸,** Rene Pyot 4, behind the Archaeological Museum, has big rooms with colorful baths, A/C, TV, and some balconies. It's on the road uphill from the waterfront on the right side of the plateia, facing inland. (☎27230 22 518. Singles €25-40; doubles €35-60; triples €50-75.) **Navarino Beach Camping ❶,** 6km north of town at sandy, shallow Yialova beach, has a mini-mart, restaurant, communal kitchen, showers, public toilets, and laundry facilities. Internet access €3 per hr. Look for signs pointing off the road between Kalamata and Pylos. (☎27230 22 761. Electricity €3. €4 per person, €2.50 per child age 4-10, children under 4 free; €4 per small tent, €5 per large tent.)

Many waterfront restaurants prepare taverna staples served alongside fabulous sunset views. The road leading uphill from the left of the plateia is also packed with excellent options. The best of four eating establishments with the same name, the ▧**Navarino ❷,** around the corner from the port police on the waterfront, has good, cheap meals served in large portions away from the bustling cafes of the plateia. Don't be discouraged if there are too many locals around to get a table at first—service is speedy and friendly. (☎27230 22 564. Salads €2.40-3.40. Entrees €4-9. Stuffed peppers €5. Open daily noon-4:30pm and 6pm-midnight.) Behind the bus station in the petite Pl. Economidis, **La Piazza ❷** creates wonderful pastas and pizza. Try the "La Piazza" pizza (loaded with feta, bacon, peppers, and olives; whole pie €6.30-7.50), a house specialty. (☎27230 23 780. Open daily 6pm-midnight.) **Four Seasons ❷,** the last taverna on the water to the right of town (facing inland), serves some of the freshest fish in town, with tables on the water. Ask about the delicious, perpetually evolving dessert menu. (☎27230 22 739. Fish €45-50 per kg. Entrees €4-7. Open daily 11am-midnight.) **1930 Restaurant ❸,** on the road from Kalamata, is accented by wood paneling and antique fishing gear. Don't miss the creative decorations, depicting scenes from, you guessed it, 1930. (☎27230 22 032. Salads €4.50-8.50. Grilled octopus €8. Greek dishes €4.50-9. Open daily 12:30-3:30pm and 6pm-1am. V.)

◙◪ SIGHTS AND BEACHES. Fortresses guard both sides of Navarino Bay. **Neocastro,** to the south, is easily accessible from the town; walk up the road to Methoni and turn right at the sign reading "Φρουριο" (Frourio). Built by the Turks in the 16th century, the fortress was won by the Greeks during the War of Independence. The well-preserved walls enclose 19 acres of land. Boasting a magnificent view of the bay, inside are a citadel and graceful church, which was originally a mosque. Also on display are old cannonballs and weapons from the war. Little explanation is offered around the site, but skip the guidebooks (€20) and ask a friendly staff member. The **Museum of the Rene Puaux Collection,** to the left as you enter the site, contains artistic works celebrating Greek triumph in the War of Independence from the personal collection of French journalist Rene Puaux. Prior to the museum's creation, the building was a maximum security prison and occupied by Germans. (☎27230 22 010. Site and museum open Tu-Su 8:30am-3pm. €3, seniors and students €2, EU students and children free.) At the **Archaeological Museum,** an unassuming white building on the uphill road to the right of the plateia, facing inland, you'll find mostly pottery from Mycenaean palaces and jewelry from *tholos* tombs on display. The sophisticated Hellenistic glass vases in the back and the Mycenaean boar's tusk helmet catch the eye. (☎27230 22 448. Open Tu-Su 8:30am-3pm. €2, seniors €1, students and children free.)

NAP TIME. From about 2-5pm in Greek summers, the heat peaks—and the crowds virtually disappear. Those intrepid travelers who wander through these blistering hours will find little to do: throughout the country, cafes will be empty, streets will be barren, and nearly every shop closed up for a lunch break. This siesta leaves you with one option: make like a native and head for the beach!

Just offshore is the island of **Sfakteria,** famed as the site of a rare Spartan defeat during the Peloponnesian War (p. 56) and home to the remains of a defensive wall built during that period. Sfakteria also has a number of war memorials and a wooden church built by Russian soldiers without the use of a single nail. And aging aristocrats desperate for an heir may want to make use of the island's natural arch; legend has it that any pregnant woman who walks under it will bear a male child. To see the islands up close, you can take a **boat tour** from the port. Inquire at the small booth on the waterfront across from the port police. (☎27230 23 115. 1½hr., €7 per person.) The same booth also rents **motorboats** for you to tour the region yourself (€7-10 per hr.). If the tiny plots of sand that locals call "the beach" in Pylos don't do it for you, small but comparatively sizeable **beaches** surround the town. Although the sand is devoured by the ocean when the tide is in, families take to the waters on most summer afternoons. The sandy, shallow, and much wider **Yialova beach** is 6km north of town; sunken ships poke out from its waters. Buses to Athens and Kyparissia pass by. The **Navarino fortress** lies at the end of the beach. Most famous is the seemingly never-ending **Xrisi Ammos** (Golden Sand) beach, which runs all the way to Hora. Buses to Kyparissia can drop you off on a side road, and the beach is 3km away. Because of the infrequency of public transportation (especially on weekends), you may want to use private transportation.

🔁 DAYTRIP FROM PYLOS: NESTOR'S PALACE. Pylos was second only to Mycenae during Mycenaean times in wealth and artistic development. The centerpiece of the archaeological site is the **palace** where, according to Homer, Nestor met Telemachus, Odysseus's son. The palace is thought to have been built in the 13th century BC by Nestor's father Neleus, the founder of the Neleid Dynasty. It was destroyed by fire around 1200 BC. Under excavation since the early 20th century, the thigh-high remains of the site comprise three buildings. The main building, thought to be the king's residence, originally had a second floor with official and residential quarters and storerooms. The central throne room still contains a well-preserved hearth. Scholars believe an older, smaller palace stood to the southeast, while the ruins of a complex of isolated workshops and storerooms marked for oil and wine sit to the northeast of the main palace. Archaeologists have turned up pottery, jewelry, various bronze and ivory objects, and a cache of over 600 **Linear B tablets** (p. 54) explaining some of the palace's administrative operations. Most finds are displayed at the National Archaeological Museum in Athens, though some pottery and surviving fragments of wall paintings are at the **museum** in Hora, 3km away. (☎27630 31 358. Museum open Tu-Su 8:30am-3pm.) The chimney pipes that were once over the hearth and the gigantic *pithos* in the back room are particularly impressive. You can supplement your tour with the University of Cincinnati's *Guide to Nestor's Palace* (€5). **Buses** from Pylos run through **Kyparissia** (1½hr., 5 per day, €4) and stop at **Nestor's Palace** (30min., €1); service tends to run late and is reduced on weekends. Check for the return times before getting off the bus—the last, and sometimes only, bus returns at 7pm. (☎27230 31 437. Site open daily 8:30am-3pm. €3, seniors and students €2, EU students and children free.)

A **Mycenaean tholos tomb** from around 1550 BC, thought to have held 17 graves, is across from the lower parking lot. Its size signifies a large settlement up on the hill dating back to 1600 BC. Fortunately for archaeologists, hasty thieves left much of the tomb untouched during a gold-raiding escapade. Most of the artifacts are on display in Athens, but visitors can still explore underneath the dome of the *tholos*.

METHONI Μεθώνη ☎ 23530

Methoni's relaxed atmosphere is a restorative reprieve from the bustle of Kalamata and Tripoli. Some claim that Miguel de Cervantes found Methoni so comfortable that he managed to pen several romances while imprisoned by Ottomans in the town's spectacular castle. Cervantes wasn't alone in his awe for the area, as Agamemnon used the promise of Methoni's steep-cliffed beauty to lure sulking Achilles back to war in *The Iliad*. Today, a long stretch of quiet beach is all it takes to draw visitors to this enchanted village.

[⌐ꟷ] TRANSPORTATION AND PRACTICAL INFORMATION. The town's two main streets form a Y where the Pylos-Finikouda buses stop. Facing the fork, the lower road, **Mezonos,** is on the left and leads to the beach and castle. The upper road is lined with administrative offices and small businesses. There is no bus station in town, so your best bet is to ask locals for bus times. Since the buses arriving in town are coming from as far away as Athens, they can often run late. **Buses** go to Finikouda (30min.; at least 3 per day around 11am, 3, 8pm; €1) and Pylos (15min., at least 5 per day 7am-9pm, €1); service is reduced on weekends. Buses also head daily to Athens (6hr., €21) via Pylos and Kalamata (2hr., €4.20). The town's main **beach** is toward the end of Mezones; turn left at **Plateia Syngrou,** recognizable by its waterless fountain, to reach the beachfront square, **Plateia Paralias.** A stroll along the beach road, **Poseidonos,** leads to the campgrounds and several bars. The **National Bank** with a **24hr. ATM** is 40m down the right fork. (☎27230 31 295. Open M-Th 8am-2:30pm, F 8am-2pm.) There is no OTE in town, but public **phones** can be found at the bus stop and in the beachfront plateia. Methoni has a small **police** force, open 1-2hr. per day next to the National Bank on the upper road, although it relies primarily on the **Pylos police.** (☎27230 21 203. Open 24hr.) The **Trojan Horse,** on the left before the castle, offers **Internet access.** (€3 per hr.; €1 min. Open daily 8am-3am.) The **post office** is two blocks down the lower street on the left side. (☎27230 31 266. Open M-F 7:30am-2pm.) **Postal Code: 24006.**

[ꟷ] ACCOMMODATIONS AND CAMPING. Since Methoni receives a fair amount of tourism, accommodations can get pricey, especially in August. On the other hand, there is certainly no shortage of rooms in town. Several "rooms to let" signs hang along both forks of the main road. Although they usually lack luxurious amenities, domatia are a bit cheaper than many of the area's hotels. Near the end of the lower road, eight blocks from the bus stop, turn left at Pl. Syngrou to find **Hotel Alex ❸** in the beachfront plateia. Spacious, recently renovated rooms are superbly located and have A/C, private baths, and balconies. (☎27230 31 219. Singles €35-40; doubles €45-55; triples €55-65.) Next door at **Hotel Giota ❸,** Alex's owners rent somewhat smaller rooms for the same price. (☎27230 31 290. Singles €35-40; doubles €45-55; triples €55-65.) Walking down the lower road, the pink building before the first plateia is **Hotel Finikas ❸,** which has big rooms with colorful baths, TV, A/C, and fridges. (☎27230 31 390. Singles €30; doubles €40; triples €50.) **Seaside Camping Methoni ❶,** on Poseidonos, is a 5min. walk down the beach with the sea on your right. The public campground has a mini-mart, showers, hot water, toilets, and a nearby restaurant. (☎27230 31 228. €3.60-4.10 per person, €2-2.50 per child, €2.50-2.90 per small tent, €2.80-3.20 per large tent, €2-2.50 per car. Electricity €3.)

🖺🕯 **FOOD AND NIGHTLIFE.** Several excellent tavernas and restaurants pepper Methoni. No-frills **Nontas ❶** is simple and authentic with high-quality, low-priced food. Walking from the bus stop, turn left one block down the lower road. (☎27230 31 791. *Tzatziki* €2. Gyros €1.80. Souvlaki €1.50.) **Nikos ❷**, on Andromos Aftos, serves staples in a quiet, romantic atmosphere. It's the first left off of the road left of the plateia, facing inland. Chicken in lemon sauce (€4.50) is a favorite, and vegetarian entrees are also available. (☎27230 31 282. Salad €2.50-3.50. Entrees €4.50-6. Open daily noon-late.) In the waterfront plateia, the multilingual proprietor of **Meltemi ❷** makes creative versions of traditional dishes. (Fish and shrimp souvlaki €5.50. Vegetable plate €5. Open daily noon-4:30pm and 7pm-midnight.) While the clubbers head to nearby Pylos on the weekends, Methoni has a few late-night bars like **John's Rock Bar,** on the upper road.

🄶 **SIGHTS.** No visitor to the southwestern Peloponnese should miss Methoni's breathtaking █**Venetian fortress,** a 13th-century mini-city. To get there, follow the lower street to its end. Walk to the right on the path outside the castle for a great view of the open sea and fortified back wall, as well as an engraving of a griffin. Behind the fortress's fortified gate, paths ramble alongside towering arches, walls, and rainbow-colored wildflowers. Frankish foundations, Venetian battlements, and Turkish steam baths all testify to the castle's unstable, multinational history. Occasionally in the spring and summer, the moat hosts Greek rock concerts. (Open M-Sa 8am-9pm, Su 8:30am-9pm. Free.) The town's sandy **beach** is a few blocks to the left of the end of the lower street.

FINIKOUDA Φοινικούντα ☎27230

The tiny beach hamlet of Finikouda lies just 20km south of Methoni. Its popularity has grown as tourists have discovered the shallow, perfectly clear waters that lap at its never-ending stretch of sand. Though the land along the beach and main road is largely filled with bustling campgrounds or domatia, the small village itself is quiet and tame. It doesn't have a police station or post office, but there is a **24hr. ATM** on the main road as you walk toward the waterfront from the bus station. Some of the best **beaches** on the Peloponnesian coast are within easy walking distance of the town; locals will be able to provide directions. Should you opt to stay in Finikouda, find one of the many **domatia** along the waterfront or head to the closest campground, █**Camping Anemomilos ❶**, on the beach just north of town. Situated among flowering shrubs and with easy beach access, the site also has laundry, a mail drop, a restaurant, a mini-mart, a bar, showers, and Internet access (€3 per hr.). To reach the campsite, walk out of town on the road past Hotel Finikouda, then walk 300m toward Methoni and turn left toward the beach at the signs. (☎27230 71 360. €4.50-5 per person, €2.50-3 per child, €3.50-4.50 per tent.) At **Hotel Finikouda ❸,** next to the bus stop and a block from the water, large rooms with TV, A/C, and fridges are comfortable and squeaky-clean, and the reception has a book exchange. (☎27230 71 208. Breakfast €4. Singles €25-40; doubles €40-60.) Another good option is the **Hotel Finissia ❸,** at the far right of the waterfront as you face inland. The lobby with padded leather chairs is amazingly luxurious, and the clean rooms have A/C, TV, fridges, large baths, and balconies. (☎27230 71 457. Doubles €40-60; triples €48-72.) Restaurants are by no means hard to find, but if you want a view, walk to the left end of the waterfront (facing inland) to the enormous taverna **Elena ❷**, on the cliffside. The establishment is popular with families and tourists, as it offers half-portions for kids and has a helpful pronunciation guide in the menu. (☎27230 71 235. Salad €3-7.50. Vegetable dishes €5-5.50. Seafood €6-12.50. Open daily 11am-2am.) A step up from its fast food neighbors, **Aeomera ❶**, a little farther to the right (facing inland) from the ATM, serves cheap, delicious souvlaki and gyros in a pretty, mellow beachside setting. (☎27230 71 292. Souvlaki pita €1.60. Gyros €1.80.) **Vinnitiko ❸**, between the ATM and Aeomera, on a small, colorful platform above the sand, makes both standard and unusual Greek dishes. (Salads €2-4. Fish €5-11.) **Buses** head to Kalamata (1½hr., 3-4 per day 7am-8pm, €4.20) via Pylos (30min., €2), Methonia, and Harakopio (40min., €1.25). Service is reduced on weekends. The bus drops off and picks up at the plateia one block up from the waterfront, outside Hotel Finikouda.

LACONIA Λακώνια

Laconia, the territory of the ancient Spartans, has long prided itself on its minimalist image. The Spartans were ferocious in war, simple in lifestyle, and terse in speech. Such a regional disposition seems to have worn off on the landscape, with the stark, imposing Taygetus Mountains towering over ancient olive trees. Ornate Byzantine ruins and pockets of vivid green cypress trees crop up unexpectedly, oases in the harsh, barren setting.

SPARTA Σπάρτη ☎27310

Built directly on top of the ancient city, modern Sparta's gritty urban sprawl obscures the remains of the city that brought the world beautiful Helen and heroic Leonidas. Still, it's by far the best base for exploring the ruins of Byzantine Mystras, 6km away. Sparta's role in shaping the fate and legends of ancient Greece was monumental. The bellicose state dominated the Peloponnese with its legendary discipline and invincible armies, tracing its austere daily regimens back to 8th-century BC law-giver Lycurgus, who demanded plain dress, simple food, and strict training for all citizens from a young age. Men and women were educated differently, but both were held to severely rigid standards. The Spartans produced almost no literature, art, or architecture, as they preferred to expend all of their creative energy on the art of war. Finally capturing Athens in 404 BC to end the 28-year Peloponnesian War (p. 56), Sparta won its greatest victory and effectively ruled Greece. Though it had earned its historical place as the military giant of Greece, Sparta's hold on power declined following challenges from the Thebans and the Macedonians in the 4th century BC. Earthquakes and slave revolts didn't help, and further losses in 222 and 195 BC to the Macedonians and the Romans, respectively, sapped the city's strength. Sparta slipped into obscurity until the modern city, whose citizens make olive oil, not war, was founded in 1843.

▐ TRANSPORTATION

To get to the bus station (☎27310 26 441), walk downhill on Lykourgou toward the Archaeological Museum, continuing past a small forested area on your right; the station will be on your right, 10 blocks from the town center. The bus station is often crowded and not particularly tourist-friendly, as there are often confusing and unmentioned transfers on the bus routes. If you pay attention to the drivers and ask questions, though, you should end up where you want to be. **Buses** go to: Areopolis (1½hr., 4 per day 8am-6pm, €5); Athens (3½hr., 11 per day 5:45am-8pm, €14.30) via Tripoli (1hr., €4) and Corinth (2½hr., €9); Gerolimenas (2hr.; 6:45am, 2:30, 5:30pm; €7.30); Gythion (45min., 6 per day 7:30am-7pm, €3.10); Kalamata (1hr.; 9am, 2:30pm; €4); Monemvasia (2hr., 4 per day 5:45am-5:15pm, €6.30); Neapoli (3½hr., 4 per day 6am-5pm, €10.30) via Molai (€7); Pirgos Dirou (1½hr., 9am, €7). Buses to Mystras (20min., 10 per day 7:20am-8:20pm, €1) stop at the corner of Lykourgou and Leonidou, two blocks past the plateia away from the station.

ORIENTATION AND PRACTICAL INFORMATION

Sparta is a grid. The main streets, **Paleologou** and **Lykourgou**, have most essentials and intersect in the center of town. From that intersection, the plateia is one block uphill along Lykourgou away from the bus station. Walking right facing uphill toward the plateia along Paleologou, you will hit Ancient Sparta. To reach the center of town from the bus station, go about 10 blocks slightly uphill on Lykourgou.

Tourist Office: ☎27310 26 771. On the 3rd fl. of the town hall, the glass building in the corner of the plateia. English spoken. Not particularly helpful, they offer info about Sparta only (not Mystras), and can direct you to a nearby photo shop to pick up a free **map.** Some hotel information also available. Open M-F 8am-2pm.

Banks: National Bank, Paleologou 106 (☎27310 23 845), 3 blocks toward Ancient Sparta from Lykourgou and the town center. Has a **24hr. ATM, currency exchange,** and long lines. Open M-Th 8am-2:30pm, F 8am-2pm.

Police: ☎27310 26 229. On Ep. Vresthenis, off Lykourgou, 1 block past the bus station toward the plateia. Open 24hr. The **tourist police** (☎27310 20 492) are in the same building. Open daily 8am-9pm. In an emergency, dial ☎100 or 27310 29 106.

Pharmacy: Nikon Pharmacy, 1 block from the National Bank (☎27310 25 041). Many are on Lykourgou and Paleologou. Most open M-F 8am-2pm and 6-9pm.

Hospital: ☎27310 28 671 or 27310 28 675. On Nosokomeio, 1km north of Sparta. 7 buses per day (€1) go there. Open 24hr.

Internet Access: Ladas Cafe (☎27310 83 016) is visible from the plateia. 20m up on Lykourgou, on the right. The oldest cafe in town but with ultra-modern

THE IDIOT'S GUIDE TO DRINKING OUZO

When you go out for your first meal in Greece, don't be surprised, shocked, or flattered if your waiter rushes out before your entree arrives to present you with a shot glass full of opaque liquor and the simple command, "Drink!" He's just assuming that you, like almost every Greek, wants to cleanse your palate and ease your mind with some ouzo.

There's an art to enjoying the anise-flavored national drink, however, which is important to know if you don't want to reveal yourself as a neophyte. First, don't take that shot like a frat boy. Good ouzo is around 40% alcohol by volume and it just isn't made to be chugged. It's invariably served with a glass of water for the purpose of mixing; that's what turned your shot milky-white. The key is to keep adding water as you drink to avoid dehydration and other ill effects. Second, snack on some *mezedes* while you take your ouzo. Munching on a salad, some cheese or vegetables will temper the alcohol and prolong the experience. That's the point, after all: Greece's obsession with ouzo is not really focused on getting plastered on something that tastes like licorice. Instead, it's about drinking lazily, relaxing in a *kafeneion*, and chatting with friends for the entire afternoon until the sun sets and dinner begins.

computers. €3 per hr. Open daily 7am-midnight. **Cosmos Internet Cafe,** Paleologou 34 (☎27310 21 500), south of Lykourgou, away from Ancient Sparta. On the 2nd fl. of the video store. €3.50 per hr.; €1 min. Open daily M-Su 8am-11pm.

Post Office: ☎27310 26 565. Archidamou 84, off Lykourgou, about halfway between the bus station and the town center. Open M-F 7:30am-2pm. **Poste Restante** available. **Postal Code:** 23100.

▐▀ ACCOMMODATIONS AND CAMPING

It's hard to find a bargain among the numerous mid-range hotels grouped on Paleologou, but, as a small consolation, TV and private baths are widespread. **Hotel Cecil ❸,** Paleologou 125, is five blocks north of Lykourgou toward Ancient Sparta, on the corner of Paleologou and Thermopilon. It may look scruffy on the outside, but the small intimate lobby gives way to pleasant, simple rooms with TV, A/C, balconies, large baths, phones, and low beds. The small hotel's hallways contain a surprising amount of sitting room. (☎27310 24 980. Reservations recommended. Singles €30-35; doubles €40-45; triples €55-60.) **Hotel Lakonia ❷,** Paleologou 61, is the cheapest option in the center of town, though the dingy bathrooms and loud street noise indicate that you get what you pay for. The basic rooms come with A/C and TV, but the management turns the A/C off at night; if you ask repeatedly, they will very reluctantly turn it back on. (☎27310 28 951. Breakfast €5. Singles €20; doubles €35; triples €45.) **Hotel Apollon ❸,** Thermopilon 84, across Paleologou from Hotel Cecil, appeals to guests' playful side, with colorful rooms that have large, deep, blue baths and bright quilted bedspreads. (☎27310 22 491. TV, A/C, phones, and balconies. Breakfast €5. Singles €33; doubles €40-45; triples €53. V.) Offering some of the more luxurious rooms in Sparta, **Hotel Maniatis ❹,** at the intersection of Lykorgou and Palelogou 72-76, has big, carpeted rooms with A/C, TV, baths with tubs, and balconies. They're not, however, as flashy as the spaceship-like lobby suggests. (☎27310 22 655. Breakfast included. Singles €42-52; doubles €55-65; triples €66-76. MC/V.) To find **Camping Castle View ❶,** 2km from Mystras, take the Mystras bus and get off at the signs. The site has a pool, showers, bathrooms, laundry (€4), mini-mart, restaurant, cafe, and bar. (☎27310 83 303. €6.50-7 per person, €4 per tent, €3.50 per car.)

◖▐ FOOD AND NIGHTLIFE

Sparta's restaurants serve standard menus at pretty reasonable prices. **Supermarkets** and **bakeries** fill the side streets of Paleologou, while cheap fast food joints surround the main plateia. A large, fresh selection of local specialties and traditional Greek dishes keep **Elyssé Restaurant ❷,** Paleologou 113, across from the National Bank, busy at all times. The staff recommends one of their many vegetable entrees (€1.80-5.50) or the *bourdouniotiki* (€5.80), a regional dish of chicken in tomato sauce, onions, and feta. (☎27310 29 896. Open daily 11am-11pm.) **Parthenon ❶,** on Vrasida two blocks north of the intersection with Paleologou and one block east toward the bus station, boldly claims to make the "best food in Greece." Though this turns out to be glorified fast food in a cheesy faux-rustic kitchen, the low prices and young, energetic regulars will help you forgive the slight misrepresentation. (☎23767 20 444. Souvlaki €1.20-1.80. Gyros €1.40-1.60.) The elegant **Menelaion Hotel** may not be in the budget traveler's price range, but its popular **restaurant ❷** certainly is. Promising to please even the most epicurean, dishes from its huge menu are served either pool-side or in a beautiful dining room. The fabulous sourdough bread is an added plus. (Salads €2.50-4.50. Fish €5-12 or €38 per kg. Open daily noon-4pm and 7pm-midnight.) **Diethnes ❷**, on Paleologou, a few blocks to the right of the main intersection facing the plateia, offers tasty Greek food in an intimate garden with orange trees and the occasional turtle and stray cat. Though it has a few vegetarian options (€2.50-3.80), the restaurant specializes primarily in lamb entrees, which come paired with all types of sides (€6.50).

At night, the side streets off Paleologou swell with young people, while the plateia draws families and an older crowd which drinks away the hours at outdoor cafes. Due to the literally Spartan laws, nightlife ends earlier on the weekdays than in many other Greek cities (3:30am). Outside the plateia, **Ministry Music Hall**, on Paleologou one block north of the intersection with Lykourgou, is always packed. Brimming with energy and, of course, loud music, the Ministry is the place that Sparta's hipsters go to be seen. The interior is adorned with unicycles and mandolins, but despite this slightly odd decor, the atmosphere is comfortable and welcoming. (Beer €2.50-4.50. Mixed drinks €5. Open daily 8am-3am.) **Leghi Spartis**, a cafe in the beautiful Old Town Hall in the plateia, caters to those seeking a slightly calmer scene. Popular with families, it offers coffee (€3), mixed drinks (€6), and spectacular desserts. (Open 9am-3am.) **Caprice** is a small but popular club tucked behind neon green lights and small palm trees in the back of the plateia. White leather-backed chairs support Sparta's chicest as they stiffly sip their drinks of choice. (Beer €2.30-4.50. Mixed drinks €6. Open daily 11pm-3am.)

◎ SIGHTS

What little remains of **Ancient Sparta** lies in an olive grove 1km north of the town plateia down Paleologou. An enormous statue of **Leonidas**, the famous warrior king who fell at the Battle of Thermopylae in 480 BC, looms over the northern end of the street. The Spartans built a large tomb for their leader, but his body was never found. The tomb, therefore, still lays empty in a public park to the left of the road heading up to the ruins. Along with a few fragments of the acropolis, the otherwise unimpressive site is highlighted by the outline and lower rows of an **ancient theater.** To reach the theater, turn right after the statue and follow the signs; it's the first mound of ruins you pass.

Sparta's **Archaeological Museum**, on Lykourgou across from the OTE, is in a beautiful, well-kept park with a fountain and assorted ancient statuary. Headless statues usher visitors into the museum, which features a large collection of everything from beautiful mosaics to haunting votive masks used in ritual dances at the sanctuary of Artemis Orthia. The rooms to the right, facing inward, display various representations of the Dioscuri—the twins Castor and Pollux—locally revered as symbols of brotherly love and honor, as well as larger-than-life 3rd-century BC marble heads of Hercules and Hera. One room is devoted to prehistoric pottery, weaponry, and jewelry. English captions accompany all the artifacts. (☎27310 28 575. Open Tu-Sa 8:30am-3pm, Su 9:30am-2:30pm. €2, students and seniors €1, EU students and children free.) The **National Art Gallery**, Paleologou 123, next to Hotel Cecil, has a small permanent collection of 19th-century French and Dutch paintings, including one by Gustave Courbet. Upstairs, the gallery hosts temporary exhibits from the National Gallery in Athens. (☎27310 81 557. Open Tu-Sa 9am-3pm, Su 10am-2pm. Free.) For something refreshingly different, visit the **Museum of the Olive and Greek Olive Oil**, Othonos Amalias 129. If you walk three blocks to the left of Lykourgou as you face the plateia, and four blocks to the right, the museum will be on the left as the road ends. In this beautiful building that stands out among the ubiquitous concrete apartment complexes, three floors of exhibits explain the economic, technological, and cultural significance of the olive. (☎27310 89 315. Open M, W-Su 10am-5pm. €2, students and seniors €1.)

Many of the ruins surrounding Sparta are reachable by foot, though a few require a car; the tourist office and the tourist police have maps. From the northeastern corner of town, near Hotel Apollon, a 10min. walk east along Odos Ton 118 toward Tripoli leads to the **Sanctuary of Artemis Orthia**, where Spartan youths proved their courage by enduring repeated floggings. Three remaining platforms of the **Shrine to Menelaus and Helen** are 5km away in the same direction. The ruins of a **Shrine to Apollo** are south on the road to Gythion in the town of Amiklai.

🖺 DAYTRIP FROM SPARTA

🖺 MYSTRAS

Buses leaving Sparta's main station and the corner of Lykourgou and Leonidou (20min., 10 per day 7:20am-8:20pm, €1) stop at the restaurant Xenia near the main entrance at the bottom of the hill. It gets hot and requires some scrambling around, so go early, bring water, and wear comfortable hiking shoes. Consider getting another resource like Guidebook Mystras, by Manolis Chatzidakis (€6.50), to supplement your exploration. Free maps are also available. ☎27310 83 377. Open daily 8am-7pm; in low season 8:30am-3pm. €5, students and children €3, EU students free.

Once the religious center of all Byzantium and the locus of Constantinople's rule over the Peloponnese, Mystras lays dormant, a magnificent fortified city saturated with remains of Byzantine churches, chapels, and monasteries. Founded by French crusader **Guillaume de Villehardouin** in 1249 with the building of a central castle at the top of the hill, the city first experienced a change of ownership in 1262 when it was captured by the Greeks. Under Greek rule, the town flourished; in the following centuries it grew to a city, draining Sparta of its inhabitants as they sought protection in the city's fortress. By the early 15th century, Mystras was an intellectual and cultural center with a thriving silk industry. But even the booming economy couldn't keep the lower classes at bay. Unhappy under the thumb of oppressive feudal lords and clergy, restless country folk eventually surged into town, set up schools, and created an early bourgeoisie. The glory days ended, however, when Turks invaded in 1460 and, over the next few centuries, the city crumbled to ruin. When King Otto founded modern Sparta in 1834, Mystras's fate was sealed with a table-turning exodus to its revived neighbor.

An intricate network of paths traces through three tiers of ruins, descending from royalty to nobility to commoners. Although not as well preserved as many of the religious edifices that encircle it—they're almost completely intact, if a bit faded at the frescoes—the dramatic **castle** delivers a breathtaking view of the site and the surrounding countryside. Most people climb to the castle first and work their way down. The **palaces,** which date from the AD 13th-15th centuries, are downhill from the castle, and feature a large throne-room among their pointed arches and dressed stone walls. Next to them is **Agia Sophia,** built by Manuel Katakouzenos, the first despot of Morea. This is where the city's royalty was buried, among the still-visible striking frescoes. Farther downhill lies the magnificent **Pantanassa,** a convent with an elaborately ornamented facade, frescoes, and an icon of Mary said to work miracles. The ground floor also displays many paintings from the 17th and 18th centuries. On the lower tier you can find the **Metropolis of Agios Demetrios,** with its detailed frescoes, flowery courtyard, and small museum of architectural fragments, clothing, and jewelry. Its air-conditioned room holds everything from 14th-century manuscripts, to marble sculptures, to a reconstruction of a Byzantine woman's shoe. Also on the lower tier are the two churches that comprise the fortified monastery of **Brontochion**. The first, **Aphentiko** (a.k.a. **"Hodegetria"**), glows with magnificent two-story frescoes depicting saints; **Agios Theodoros** is its neighbor. Quietly tucked away in the far corner of the lower tier, every centimeter of the awe-inspiring **Church of Peribleptos** is bathed in colorful, exquisitely detailed religious paintings.

MANI Μάνη

The name of Mani comes from *manis*, which means "wrath" or "fury." Sparsely settled and encircling the intimidating Taygetus Mountains (p. 184), the region juts out vulnerably into the surrounding sea. During Roman times, Mani founded the league of Free Laconians and threw off Spartan domination. Ever since, Maniots have ferociously resisted foreign rule, boasting even today that not one Ottoman set foot on their soil. While historically fierce and proud of it, Maniots are still warm hosts to those who visit their well-preserved villages and unique gray stone tower houses. Home to Byzantine ruins, small fishing villages, world-class beaches, and even the famous *Caretta caretta* sea turtle, Mani continues to surprise visitors with its deeply contrasting diversity. The landscape follows suit, as the lush north gives way to stark southern mountains, which strike against the piercing-blue oceans and endless stretches of sand and pebbles.

GYTHION Γύθειο ☎ 27330

Gythion is much livelier than the desolate terrain to its south; colorful waterfront houses and friendly locals give this surprisingly modern city a small-town feel. Bright fishing boats bustle in and out of the port, where dockside tourist restaurants hang strings of octopi out to dry, and the ancient ruins and quaint Neoclassical buildings combine to create picture-perfect views. A short causeway connects Gythion to the tiny island of Marathonisi, where Paris and Helen consummated their ill-fated love.

▐ TRANSPORTATION. The bus station (☎27330 22 228), on the northern end of the waterfront, opposite a park, sends **buses** to: Areopolis (1hr., 4 per day 10:15am-6:45pm, €1.90) via the campgrounds (€1); Athens (4½hr., 6 per day 7:30am-7pm, €17.40) via Tripoli (2hr., €7.10) and Corinth (3½hr., €12.50); Gerolimenas (2hr.; 1, 6:45pm; €4.40); Kalamata (3hr.; 7:30am, noon; €6); Pirgos Dirou (45min., 10:15am, €3); Sparta (40min., 6 per day 7:30am-7pm, €3.10). Departure and return times are posted outside the station. **Ferries** go to Diakofti, Kythera (2½hr., 5 per week, €9.50) and Kasteli, Crete (7hr., 1 per week, €21). **Rozakis Travel**, on the waterfront by the police station, sells ferry tickets. (☎27330 22 207. Open M-F 8:30am-2pm and 5:30-8:30pm, Sa 9am-1pm and 5:30-7pm, Su 10am-1pm and 5-7:30pm.) **Taxis** (☎27330 23 400) line up outside the bus station and in the plateia and are available 24hr. **Moto Makis Rent-A-Moped** (☎27330 25 111), on the waterfront between the plateia and the causeway, rents mopeds from €15 per day, including tax, insurance, maps, and helmets. (Open daily 9am-1:30pm and 6-8pm.)

▇▐ ORIENTATION AND PRACTICAL INFORMATION. Going south from the bus station along the main harbor road, **Vasileos Pavlou**, with the water on the left, you will find most hotels on your right. Stores and offices crowd around the inland plateia by the bus station. The small **Plateia Mavromichali** appears as the road curves and continues to the dock. Vas. Pavlou turns into Proth. Genataki after the plateia, which ends at the causeway to Marathonissi.

To find the **tourist office**, facing the bus station, go around the left corner and bear left around the small plateia, following the road for 150m. (☎27330 24 484. Open M-F 8am-2:30pm.) The **National Bank,** next to the bus station, has **currency exchange** and a **24hr. ATM.** (☎27330 22 313. Open M-Th 8am-2pm, F 8am-1:30pm.) The **police station** (☎27330 22 100), on Vas. Pavlou, halfway between the bus station and Pl. Mavromichali, is open 24hr. A **pharmacy** is across from the bus station (☎27330 22 036; open M-F 8am-2pm and 5-9pm), and others are scattered throughout town. The nearest **hospital** is in Sparta, but a **health clinic** (☎27330 22 001, 27330 22 002, or 27330 22 003) is on Proth. Genataki en route to the causeway. For an **ambulance,** dial ☎166. **Mystery Cafe,** on Kapsali, around the corner from the National Bank, has **Internet access.** (☎27330 25 177. €3 per hr.; €1 min. Open daily 8am-3am.) Facing the bus station, go around the left corner and trace the plateia to Archaiou Theatrou. Follow it to the right for two blocks to the **post office,** Ermou 18. (☎27330 22 285. Open M-F 7:30am-2:30pm.) **Postal Code:** 23200.

🏠🍴 ACCOMMODATIONS AND FOOD. Gythion has an overabundance of seaside domatia and hotels, which keeps prices low and negotiable. With the same modern amenities and a cozy, at-home feel, the cheaper domatia are a better option than the impersonal hotels that line the waterfront. Gythion's campgrounds are located on Mavrovouni beach, an area popular with locals, 4km out of town toward Areopolis. They can be reached by bus (4 per day, €1) or taxi (€4). The charming Voulas family has been running 🏆**Xenia Karlaftis Rooms ❷,** to the very left of the waterfront, facing inland, for over 25 years. Now run by Xenia's charming daughter, who offers juice and homemade desserts to her guests upon arrival, the domatia's clean rooms have private baths and views of Marathonissi. Each floor has a kitchen with free coffee and a fridge. In the summer, they also rent apartments 3km from town, suitable for families with a car. (☎27330 22 719. Singles €20-25; doubles €25-30; triples €30; quads €40; apartments €30-60.) Another fantastic domatia along the waterfront, **Matina Rooms ❷,** Vas. Pavlou 19, rents spacious rooms with A/C, TV, wood furniture, private baths, and sea views in a central location near the police station. (☎27330 22 578. Fridge on every fl. Singles €20; doubles €20-40; triples €30-50.) **Meltemi Camping ❶,** 4km south on the road to Areopolis, has an overwhelming number of amenities including showers, cooking area, washing machines (€4), market, restaurant, cinema, water sports equipment, and pool. (☎27330 22 833. €5 per person, €3.50 per child; €4.50 per large tent, €4 per small tent; 2- to 5-person bungalows €20-55. Electricity €3.50.) **Gythion Bay Campgrounds ❶,** 5km south on the road toward Areopolis, has a large site shaded by orange, fig, and olive trees with laundry (€5), a mini-mart, restaurant, and showers. (☎27330 22 522. www.gythiocamping.gr. €6 per person, €3.35 per child; €4 per tent; wood tent rental €7.40. Electricity €3.)

Virtually identical waterfront tavernas with lovely views serve seafood at moderate prices. A **bakery** sits across the street from Masouleri Kokkalis, and many **supermarkets** and **fruit stores** cluster around the bus station. (Most open 7:30am-2pm and 6-9pm.) The food at **Masouleri Kokkalis ❶** is deliciously greasy and served on a pleasant patio in the back of the plateia. (Souvlaki €1. Pita gyros and pita souvlaki €1.40. Other meat dishes €5-6.) Outdoor **Taverna To Nisaki ❷,** on Marathonissi, provides an airy, calm setting for anyone looking to escape the waterfront tavernas' noisy crowds. (☎27330 23 830. *Tzatziki* €3.20. Grilled entrees €4-8.) **Saga ❷,** the classiest of the restaurants on Proth. Genataki between the causeway and the plateia, prides itself on its fresh fare and excellent service. (☎27330 23 220. Salads €3-7. Entrees €4-8. Fish from €7. Open daily 8am-1am. MC/V.)

🔲🔲 **SIGHTS AND BEACHES.** **Marathonissi,** Gythion's must-see site, is a small wooded island laden with mythology and history. While Paris and Helen are nowhere to be found these days, lovebirds flock to the island's small chapel for frequent weddings. Also on the island is the **Museum of Mani,** which features pictures and stories detailing the unique region. (Open Tu-Su 8am-2pm.) The masterfully built **ancient theater** of Gythion, spanning 240°, has endured the centuries remarkably well. Even its class distinctions remain—note the differences between the seats for dignitaries in front and the simpler seats farther back. Though the ruins themselves are very well-preserved, the current use of the surrounding field as a parking lot somewhat spoils the effect. The crumbling remains of ancient Roman walls that were destroyed by an earthquake lay scattered on the nearby hill. Heading away from the bus station, walk past the post office on Archaiou Theatrou until it dead-ends at the theater entrance. (Open daily 8am-8pm.) One of the last of its kind in the Peloponnese, the **Paliatzoures Antique Shop,** Vas. Pavlou 25, a few doors down from the police station, has furnished a number of museums in its day, as owner Costas will gladly tell you. The store's specialty is 18th- and 19th-century weapons, with amazing pieces such as the prized, intricately engraved silver sword from 1734. Beauty, status, and history don't come cheap, though; the sword is priced at €5800. Other items include everything from paintings to chandeliers to gongs. (☎27330 22 944. Open daily 11am-2pm and 6-9pm.) When traveling from Gythion to Areopolis, look for the Frankish **Castle of Pasava,** less than 5km from Gythion on the right (taxi €8). The road is dangerous, but domatia owners and the local consulate (☎27330 22 210) can keep you posted on whether it's been improved. Farther along, another Frankish castle, the **Castle of Kelefa,** looks out to sea. To get there, take the bus to Areopolis and ask to be dropped off as close as possible; it's a 5km walk from the road. A taxi there runs about €15.

There is a disappointing **public beach** north of the bus station; the better beaches are outside of town. **Mavrovouni,** home to the campgrounds, is a short 2km from Gythion toward Areopolis. Winds and deep waters make it a popular surfing spot, though plenty of beachgoers also hang out at one of the nearby bars along the 4.5km long beach, where beer runs €3-4, and mixed drinks €5. Home to **Caretta caretta,** an endangered sea turtle, Mavrovouni is also the site of a great deal of scientific research regarding the species. Visitors should ask the local tour agencies about precautions necessary to protect the turtles. From Areopolis, take one of the four daily buses, a €4 taxi, or walk 30-40min. Three kilometers north is rocky **Selinitsa,** known for its incredibly clear water and outstanding views of Gythion at night; to get there take a taxi (€3) or walk, following the signs that point the way. **Vathy,** a well-know and well-loved spot among locals, 10km along the road to Areopolis, has a mix of sun and shade that appeals to both the sun worshippers and the sun-burned.

AREOPOLIS Αρεόπολη ☎27330

Areopolis neighbors both the sea and the mountains, yet it is the incredible Old Town that dominates the scenery: stone tower houses and cobbled streets just wide enough for donkey carts are framed by the dramatic peaks of the Taygetus. Tourists on their way to nearby coastal towns often pass right through Areopolis, leaving plenty of accommodations available in the traditional tower houses that once defended the mighty insular clans of the Mani. The town takes its name from

Ares, god of war, making it rather appropriate that the modern War of Independence began here. A tamer village today, Areopolis is a town made for wandering, as its winding alleyways beg visitors to let themselves get delightfully lost.

▐▐ TRANSPORTATION AND PRACTICAL INFORMATION. All services can be found in the plateia or off **Kapetan Matapa**, the main road running into the Old Town from the plateia. The **bus station** (☎27330 51 229), a table with a single employee, is next to the Romeo Pub and Europa Grill, on the eastern edge of the plateia, between the church and Hotel Kouris. **Buses** from Areopolis go to Athens (5hr., 4 per day 8am-6pm, €20) via Gythion (35min., €1.90) and Sparta (1½hr., €5) and Itilo (20min.; M-Sa 6:30, 9am, 1:45pm; €1). From Itilo, you can catch a bus to Kalamata (4 per day). A bus running into Mani takes you to the **Dirou Caves** (leaves 10:50am, returns 12:45pm; €1), Gerolimenas (40min., 3 per day 11:30am-7:30pm, €2), and Vatheia (1½hr.; M, W, F 1:45pm; €2), with limited service on Sunday and holidays. To find the **National Bank,** with a **24hr. ATM,** walk down Kapetan Matapa, turn right at the first small church, and continue up the street or walk on the road away from Dirou Caves, making a left on the street closest to the gas station. (☎27330 51 293. Open M-F 9am-1pm.) The **police** are 500m out of town on the road toward Pirgos Dirou. (☎27330 51 209. Open 24hr.) As you walk facing the sea, a **pharmacy** is two doors down from the post office. (☎27330 29 510. Open M 8am-2pm, Tu-F 8am-2pm and 5-9pm.) A 24hr. **health center** (☎27330 51 242 or 27330 51 259) is 50m down a street that starts in the main plateia and runs away from the ocean, next to the first church; signs point the way. Opposite is the **OTE.** (☎27330 51 299. Open 8am-1pm.) The **post office** (☎27330 51 230; open M-F 7:30am-2pm) is on the street with the National Bank, across from Hotel Mani. It **exchanges currency** and traveler's checks, and offers **Poste Restante. Postal Code:** 23062.

▐▐ ACCOMMODATIONS AND FOOD. Though you won't find much variety in price, Areopolis's rooms range from century-old tower houses to modern hotels. Follow Kapetan Matapa and turn left at the end to get to ▓**Tsimova's Rooms ❷**, behind the church in the Old Town. A haven for history buffs, this 300-year-old house supposedly once hosted Kolokotronis. Unfortunately, the war hero wasn't timely enough to enjoy the now-installed A/C, TV, mini-fridges, and private baths. War memorabilia, religious pictures, and various knick-knacks give each room in the house and self-proclaimed war museum a distinctive character. (☎27330 51 301. Singles €25-60; doubles €35-60; triples €40-60.) On the same road as the National Bank, **Hotel Trapela ❹** combines the rustic beauty of its stone rooms and wood-paneled ceilings with elegant, modern furnishings. Each room comes with A/C, TV, and fridges, and some have a view of the intimate backyard courtyard. (☎27330 52 690; www.trapela.gr. Singles €40-50; doubles €55-70; triples €65-75; quads €60-80. Discounts for stays over 3 days.) Across from Hotel Trapela, the friendly Apelis family rents **rooms ❷** in a quiet location close to the plateia. The large doubles have marble floors, private baths, TV, A/C, pleasant wood furniture, and access to the family's garden. (☎27330 51 479. Doubles €25-40; apartments with kitchen €60-80.)

The dining options in Areopolis are basically indistinguishable from each other. All serving traditional Greek cuisine, the restaurants cluster in the plateia and around the Old Town. A few quality options, however, are hidden among the cookie-cutter masses. **Mparmpa Petros Taverna ❷** is along Kapetan Matapa between the plateia and the Old Town. The specialty dishes, like pork with wine sauce (€7), use pork raised on the owners' family farm. Before settling into the romantic garden seating area, you can take the friendly staff's tour of the kitchen. (☎27330 51 205. Entrees €5.50-7.

Open 1pm-late.) Across from the church in the Old Town, quiet **Lithostroto ❸** serves more upscale food. Quiet, with a spectacular view of the old church, the restaurant specializes in grilled meats (€4-9); the local pork dish, *moutzoupoula* (€7.30), should not be missed. (☎27330 54 240. Cover €1.20. Salads €2.50-4.50.) In the plateia, **Nikola's Place ❷** serves Greek dishes in plentiful portions. Feel free to disregard the menu, as the waiters are happy to bring you into the kitchen to let you choose whatever looks good. (☎27330 51 366. Entrees €5-8. Open daily noon-midnight.) You can also head to one of the area's **supermarkets**. There's one just off the plateia on the road from Dirou Caves and another on the road to the Old Town.

◪ DAYTRIP FROM AREOPOLIS: DIROU CAVES. Part of a subterranean river, the unusual **◪Dirou Caves (Spilia Dirou** or **Vlihada Cave**) are cool and quiet. The caverns are strung with tiny crystalline stalactites, while vermillion stalagmites slice the 30m deep water's surface. Discovered at the end of the 19th century and opened to the public in 1971, the caves have yet to be fully explored. Experts speculate that they are 70km long and may extend all the way to Sparta. The 1.3km boat ride through the freshwater cave lasts about 30min., followed by a 10min. walk out of the caves. The tiny boats, guided only by a small oar, rock their way through the narrow, incredibly low channels. Passengers often have to duck and lean to avoid the stalactites, which change from brilliant orange to green in the various small enclosures. Floating lights illuminate the tour, but unlit recesses branch off on each side. (☎27230 52 222. Open daily June-Sept. 8:30am-5:30pm; Oct.-May 8:30am-3pm. The caves are a 300m walk downhill from the ticket booth. €12; students, seniors, and children €7.) On your way out, you can also visit the small **Neolithic Museum,** which displays findings from Alepotrypa Cave at Dirou. The unique olive leaves have remained relatively intact from Neolithic times, and the complete skeleton of a young woman is morbid, but intriguing. (Open Tu-Su 8:30am-3pm. €2, students and seniors €1.) A small pebble beach, popular with local children, sits to the side of the caves' exit.

MONEMVASIA Μονεμβασία   ☎27320

Byzantine enthusiasts on their way to Monemvasia's sights may be puzzled when the bus drops them off in an unabashedly modern town. Still, the New Town of Monemvasia (a.k.a. "Gefyra") is a logical starting point for entry onto the island that contains the famed historical city. Below the monumental fortress built into precipitous cliffs, Old Town Monemvasia's winding cobblestone paths, low archways, and narrow flights of stairs highlight the town's origins in the Middle Ages. "The Rock" looks uninhabited from the mainland; only after crossing the causeway and walking along the main road do the Old Town's walls and gate appear, opening into an anachronistic fantasy world. Though it has capitalized on its own style by adding hotels, quaint shops, and restaurants, the Old Town's modern additions do not disrupt the overwhelming sense of having traveled back in time.

PELOPONNESE

▐▇ ▐▌ TRANSPORTATION AND PRACTICAL INFORMATION

The bus station is located in the helpful **Malvasia Travel Agency,** on Spartis. The travel agency also rents mopeds (€15 per day), **exchanges currency** (with the standard 3% commission, €3 min.), and sells tickets for ferries and Flying Dolphins. (☎27320 61 752. Open daily 7am-3:30pm and 5-8pm, hours reduced in low season.) All **buses** connect or stop in **Molai.** Daily buses at 7:15am, 2:15, 5:15pm leave for: Athens (5½hr., €22) via Molai (30min., €2); Ithsmos (4½hr., €17); Sparta (2hr.,

€7.30); Tripoli (3hr., €11.20). An express bus to Athens switches in Sparta (5:15am, daily, €22). Buses also run to Piraeus daily (M, F 8:30am, 5:15pm; Tu-Th, Sa-Su 5:15pm; €20). A local shuttle runs between Geyfra and the Old Town, picking up passengers at the kiosk before the bridge in the New Town, and outside the main gate of the Old Town (daily every 20min. 8am-midnight, €0.50). **Taxis** (☎27320 61 274) drive around town, and a few can be found at the beginning of the bridge near the bus stop. The most reliable way to find one is by phone. Facing the fortress from the village, the harbor is to the right, and a pebbled beach is to the left. The main street, **23 Iouliou,** runs inland from the causeway before becoming **Spartis.** Most offices are on this street; smaller offshoots contain hotels and restaurants. Across from the bus station, the **National Bank** has a **24hr. ATM** and **currency exchange.** (☎27320 61 201. Open M-Th 8am-1:30pm, F 8am-1pm.) The **police** are on Spartis, 50m to the right of Malvasia Travel. (☎27320 61 210. Open 24hr.) **Internet access** is available at the **Baywatch Cafe,** on the left 25m down the pebble beach. (€4 per hr.; €2 min. Open daily 10am-2am.) The **post office** is next to the National Bank. (☎27320 61 231. Open M-F 7:30am-2pm.) **Postal Code:** 23070.

ACCOMMODATIONS AND CAMPING

As accommodations tend to be expensive—expect to pay at least €30 for singles and €40 for doubles—**domatia** are your best bet (doubles €25-40). A room (doubles from €60) in one of the Old Town's traditional hotels will cost even more. One of the New Town's better hotels is ☒**Hotel Belessis ❸,** a picturesque stone building within walking distance of the bridge. The friendly management provides cozy, comfortable rooms with A/C, TV, baths, and lots of wood paneling that make you feel like you're staying in the Old Town at half the price. (☎27320 61 217. Singles and doubles €30-45; 4-person apartment with kitchenette €50-60.) **Petrino Domatia ❸,** another stone building along the harbor, rents clean rooms with A/C, TV, fridges, and strikingly clear views of the Rock. Take a right after the National Bank, and then another right; it will be 100m on your right. (☎27320 61 136. Singles €25-55; doubles €30-55; triples €40-60.) **Hotel Akrogiali ❷,** across from Malvasia Travel on Spartis, has simple, clean rooms with A/C, TV, fridges, and private baths. Though it can get noisy, the location is excellent. (☎27320 61 360. Singles €20-30; doubles €30-40.) **Camping Paradise ❶,** 4km along the water on the mainland, offers free hot water, a restaurant, a cafe, and a mini-mart. Follow the signs from the main road where the bus drops off. (☎27320 61 123; www.camping-monemvasia.gr. €5.50 per person, €3 per child; €3.50 per small tent, €4 per large tent. Electricity €1.80-3.60. Discounts for extended visits.)

FOOD

Dining in Old Monemvasia is a must, if only for the chance to gaze at the endless ocean. ☒**Pipinellis Taverna ❷** (☎27320 61 004), 2km from Monemvasia on the road to Camping Paradise, serves fresh, excellent homegrown produce (onions or beans €4.50). It may be out of the way, but unrivaled meals like veal in lemon sauce (€6.50) explain why it continues to be a favorite with locals. One of the first tavernas on the main road on the right is **Restaurant Matoula ❸,** whose outdoor garden gives diners a gorgeous view. The oldest taverna in town, it justifies its €7 moussaka with friendly service and quaint wooden menus. (Entrees €6-15. Open daily noon-midnight. V.) Bakeries and fast food are to the left off of Spartis as the road forks by the harbor. In a central waterfront location, **The Korali of Monemvasia ❶** makes cheap and delicious souvlaki pitas that threaten to run its more expensive neighbors out of business. (Open daily 11am-2am.) Take a left two blocks down off of Spartis, across from Malvasia Travel, to find **Lekakis Supermarket.** (☎27320 61 167. Open daily 7am-9pm.)

SIGHTS

⊠**Old Town Monemvasia** deserves the constant attention it receives. An undeniable other-worldliness shrouds the city, adding an aura of medieval mystery to every tunnel and turn. The town's name means "one way," which makes sense once you've passed through the single gate to Old Town Monemvasia, entering a city frozen in time. No cars or bikes are allowed through the gate, so packhorses bearing groceries and cases of beer are led back and forth to restaurants. Upon entering the gate, a cobbled street, lined with the surprisingly charming and whimsical decorations of tourist shops, winds through to the central plateia. There, the 1697 church of **Christos Elkomenos** (Christ in Chains) is on the left as you face the ocean next to the bell tower. The **Archaeological Museum,** on the right of the plateia, is a nicely air-conditioned former mosque where Monemvasia's 13th-century prominence and strong commercial ties to the Western world are chronicled. (☎27320 61 403. Open Tu-Su 8:30am-3pm. Free. Maps of the Old Town €2.) The Old Town's

> **⚡TIP** **HANDICAPPED INACCESSIBLE.** Old Town Monemvasia's shortage of sidewalks, ramps, and elevators makes it nearly impossible for disabled travelers to explore the small island. The tourist office may be able to help make arrangements for visiting Monemvasia and other nearby challenging areas.

greatest charm, unsurprisingly, lies in the winding, nameless side streets to the fortified sea wall. To get to the often-photographed 12th-century **Agia Sofia,** balanced on the edge of the rock cliffs that also hold the remains of the city's **castle,** take a right off the main road up the stairs marked for "Kate's Apartments" and continue uphill. Although invading Turks defaced Agia Sofia's frescoes, its beauty is still breathtaking, as is the dramatic drop to the sea behind the church. There are no signs that point the way, so you may want to purchase a map (€2) from a local store or the Archaeological Museum. Walking along the walls of the castle toward the New Town, you will reach a **cistern** that still provides the town's water. Rain was once Monemvasia's only source of water, and the complex network of cisterns have continued to collect and distribute water since their conception. The hike along it is full slippery stones and uneven ground, so wear suitable shoes.

NEAPOLI Νεάπολις   ☎27340

The most convenient gateway to Kythera from mainland Greece, Neapoli is a small seaside destination in itself. Its quiet pebble and dark sand beaches and long strip of waterfront restaurants make the town a lovely place to either pause en route to Kythera or to stay and enjoy for its own rich charms.

Besides a few luxury hotels, the smaller and more basic options are virtually indistinguishable from the waterfront domatia, as both offer spacious rooms with standard amenities for similar prices. Because travelers flow through Neapoli on their way to summer vacations in Kythera, hotel prices sky-rocket mid-July through August. A particularly colorful option is **Hotel Arsenakos ❸,** Akti Voion 198, whose bright yellow and red rooms have A/C, TV, baths, phones, balconies, and fridges. A 5min. walk from the pier with the water on the left, the hotel is across the street from the beach. (☎27340 22 991. Breakfast included in high season. Singles €25-55; doubles €30-60; triples €40-65; quads €45-80; 4-person suites €55-95. V.) Across the street, the rooms in bright white **Domatia Chrysoula** ❹ are spacious and clean, with TV, A/C, kitchenettes, and lots of closet space. Many of the pleasant rooms have balconies, and are across the street from the beach. (☎27340 23 951. No English spoken. Singles €25-65; doubles €25-65; triples €35-65; 4-person apartments with full kitchens €50-65.) A bargain in high season, **Aivali** ❸, at the corner of the street to the post office next to the bridge, rents large rooms with lots of natural light, A/C, TV, fridges, and balconies. (☎27430 22 561. Singles €25-40; doubles €30-45.) The local cuisine is one of the first things travelers to Neapoli encounter as they stumble off the ferry; most restaurant owners grill octopi outside all day long. As you walk past the pier, with the water on your right, many of the restaurants are similar in both food and price. **Tzivaeri** ❷ serves affordable seafood dishes (€3-12) and zesty dips (garlic dip; €2) to patrons seated in padded yellow chairs. **Moreas** ❷, two blocks past Aivali with the water on the left, makes delectable meat and fish dishes for a mostly local clientele. Its outside tables are pulled as close to the beach as they can get, so you can watch the waves crash while you choose from the rotating menu. Indoors, the elegantly appointed dining room is set with non-paper tablecloths, a rarity on the taverna scene. (☎27340 23 845. Entrees €5-12. Fish €40-48 per kg.)

Directly across from the pier, a few storefronts up an unnamed street, **Vatika Bay Travel** sells tickets for the Kythera ferries. (☎27340 24 004. Open daily 8am-8pm.) Though hawkers may try to sell tickets by the pier, it is illegal to sell anywhere but in a travel shop. **Ferries** leave for Diakofti, Kythera (M-W, Su 10am, 2pm; €7). On Tuesday, the only ferry is a 10am boat to Antikythera, Kythera's diminutive neighbor. The bus station (☎27340 23 222) is on an unmarked street off the right side of the waterfront as you face inland, two blocks from the pier. **Buses** leave at 8:15am, 1:45, and 5pm for: Athens (6hr., €25) via Ag. Nikolaos (20min., €1); Molai (1½hr., €5); Sparta (3hr., €10.30); Tripoli (4hr., €14.20). Buses also run to Pounta, the port for Elafonissos (M-F 4 per day 7am-1:45pm, €1). A **National Bank** and **24hr. ATM** are on the waterfront across from the pier. (Open M-Th 8am-2:30pm, F 8am-2pm.) The **port police** (☎27340 22 228) are one block from the National Bank in a small plateia behind the statue. The **post office** is one block inland on Dimokratias on the left of the waterfront as you face inland, past the bridge. (Open M-F 7:30am-2pm.) **Postal Code:** 23053.

KYTHERA Κύθηρα

According to myth, the island of Kythera rose from the waters where Zeus cast his father Cronus's severed head into the sea after castrating him. Springing from Cronus's foamy remains, Aphrodite washed up onto Kythera's shores and made it her homeland. In antiquity, the island held a large temple to the goddess, where she was worshipped as Aphrodite Urania, goddess of chaste love. Though one might not associate the island's barren, mountainous landscape with Aphrodite's famous worship-worthy fertility, its flowering shrubs, green valleys, and secluded villages hold a potent beauty. Today, the island remains blissfully untouched by mass tourism; its visitors are primarily Greek-Australians returning to visit family, not jet-setters looking for a year-round spring break. Kythera has a veritable laundry list of amazing things to see—whitewashed Cycladic houses, Byzantine churches, Venetian castles, widely varying beaches, deep canyons, and crystal-clear blue-green waters.

AGIA PELAGIA Άγα Πελαγία ☎ 27360

With the most hotels on the island and close proximity to six beautiful beaches, Agia Pelagia is a good place to set up camp. The town is less picturesque than southerly Hora or Kapsali, but accommodations and moped rentals are cheaper, and its waterfront tavernas offer some of the only nightlife on the tiny island.

⌐⏸ TRANSPORTATION AND PRACTICAL INFORMATION. All of Kythera's ferries go in and out of Diakofti. The bus runs twice a day between Ag. Pelagia and Diakofti, and taxis cost about €18-23. From Diakofti, **ferries** go to: Gythion (2½hr., 4 per week, €10); Kalamata (5hr., 1 per week, €15); Kasteli, Crete (4hr., 3 per week, €21.30); Neapoli (1hr.; daily noon, 4pm; €7). **Flying Dolphins** leave Diakofti for Piraeus (7hr., 2 per week, €21.30). Ferry tickets are sold in a kiosk by the mini-mart at Diakofti's pier. The island's only **bus** runs mid-July through August three times per day between Agia Pelagia and Kapsali in the south; it stops in small villages connected by subsidiary roads. The route travels down the island's main road, K. Dromos, and passes through Potamos (the largest town), Livadi, and Hora (Kythera). You can rent a **bicycle** (€10) or **car** (from €30 per day) from **Active Rent-A-Car** along the waterfront. (☎ 27360 33 207. Open daily 9:30am-9:30pm.) **Motorbike rentals** can be found in a field next to Taverna Faros, on the left side of the waterfront facing inland (from €15 per day, ask in the taverna). The cottage 20m from Hotel Kythereia heading away from town is the **information office.** Though not an official tourist office, its staff has information about accommodations, sights, and flight and ferry schedules, as well as an infinite amount of patience for travelers trying to get their bearings. In Agia Pelagia, a cottage to the left of the dock as you face inland is a **tourist office,** which also has information about the island. (☎ 27360 33 815. Open 10am-2pm and 4-8pm.) The nearest **bank** (☎ 27360 33 209; open M-Th 8am-2pm, F 8am-1:30pm), **pharmacy** (☎ 27360 34 220; open M-F 8:30am-2pm and 6-9pm), **hospital** (☎ 27360 33 203), and **post office** (☎ 27360 33 225; open M-F 7:30am-2pm) are all in Potamos. The **port police** (☎ 27360 33 280) are 50m to the right of the port, facing inland, above Stella Restaurant. **Postal Code:** 80200.

⌐⏸ ACCOMMODATIONS AND FOOD. You can find high-season bargains at the many domatia in town—doubles range €40-50, compared to hotels' €60-80. The tourist office has a list of domatia owners and can put you in contact with them. Blue and white **Hotel Kythereia ❷,** opposite the dock and the beach, is run by a spectacularly helpful and hospitable Greek-Australian family. The hotel's simple rooms have colorful baths, A/C, TV, and shared fridges. It fills up quickly, so calling ahead is recommended. (☎ 27360 33 321. Singles €18-30; doubles €30-50. MC/ V.) Another good option is an unnamed **domatia ❷,** farther left along the beach as you face inland, 150m after you bear left at the fork in the road. In a white-washed house with bright blue shutters on Neo Kosmos Beach (p. 204), the domatia's easy access to the beaches and distance from all non-ocean noise make its simple rooms with fridges, kitchenettes, baths, and huge balconies peaceful and relaxing. Some larger rooms have a shared shower and kitchen. (☎ 27360 33 895. Singles €20-30; doubles €25-35; 3- to 4-person suites €40-45.)

Stella ❷, two doors from the Hotel Kythereia, has a giant selection of traditional and creative fare with over 65 main dishes. Though it's hard to choose just one entree, the stuffed calamari with cheese (€7) and the "Special Veal" (€6) with cheese and eggplant are both delicious options. The bread never stops coming, and every meal ends with complimentary watermelon. To the right as you face inland on the waterfront, next to the town map, **Restaurant Kaleris ❷** serves mostly local cuisine to a mix of natives and visitors. The specials change daily, but the wild goat in oven (€8) is a popular standby. On summer nights, families gather there to eat and watch soccer games on TV. For a less authentic but still lively atmosphere, keep walking with the sea on the right to **Moustakias ❸**, which features live Greek music every Saturday. If you look past the picture-menu that screams "tourist," the food, such as the beef or rabbit *stifado* (€6.50), is actually quite good. (☎27360 33 519. Entrees €5-6.50.) The town's **supermarket** is next to Moustakias.

⚏ BEACHES. Agia Pelagia boasts six beaches, all within a short distance of the town center. Starting from the main beach, continue south toward Potamos with the water on your left to five more beaches; bear left when the road forks. The road is initially paved as you pass the second beach, **Neo Kosmos,** about 300m from town, and turns to dirt after the Aphrodite Pelagia Hotel. Next is stunning **Fyriamo Beach** (500m from town), with its long stretch of red sand and dramatic cliffs in the background. About 1km farther is **Kalamitzi Beach;** the path there is difficult to find off the main road, so ask for directions at the information office. The gorgeous landscape, however, justifies the circuitous route. From there, the last beaches are easy to find. Isolated **Lorenzo Beach** is in a small cove that provides shade from the hot midday sun. **Lagatha** lies at the base of a dramatic ⚏canyon at the end of the road, separating the ocean from the deep green waters of Lake Pekelagada.

AROUND KYTHERA

The island has a lion's share of sights, enough to keep any visitor occupied. From the peaceful beach town of **Kapsali,** 2km east and downhill from Hora, a beautiful view unfurls, spanning two nearby lighthouses, the tall surrounding mountains, and the castle at Hora. The beach, with clear waters and a long sandy shore, is packed with waterfront tavernas and pedal boat rental agencies. At Paleohora, in the east opposite the canyon, are the ruins of the former fortified capital of the island, **Agios Dimitrios,** built during Byzantine rule. Despite the walls, the town was destroyed in 1537 by pirates led by the notorious Barbarossa. The village of Milopotamos on the western side of the island is home to two of Kythera's most magnificent sites, including the **Milopotamos waterfall.** Its surrounding forest and sparkling waters provide a scenic, albeit cold, spot for a swim. Also near the village is the **Cave of Agia Sofia.** The most impressive of the island's several caves, Agia Sofia's walls are adorned with beautiful **frescoes** and are framed by eerie stalactites and stalagmites. The cave is an easy walk from Milopotamos; follow the signs until the dirt road ends, then take the footpath about 30m downhill. Though a short taxi ride from Milopotamos, many drivers are reluctant to drive on the dirt road, especially during low season. The modest but well-preserved remains of an over 1300-year-old **Venetian castle** sit steps from the center of town. Once in the castle, follow the signs to the church of Ag. Ioannis for a spectacular view of Kythera's mountains, valleys, and cliffs. The island's **beaches** are gorgeous as well, as the ocean's blue contrasts sharply with the bare, brown landscape. The best beaches are a bit difficult to reach, accessible only by dirt roads that can be perilous for mopeds or buses—a car is safer. On the eastern coast, a long staircase leads down to the often-empty ⚏**Kaladi beach,** with sparkling coves and striking rock formations. **Halkos,** near Kalamos on the southern coast, is an isolated beach that shimmers with a quiet beauty.

HORA Χώρα ☎ 27360

Hora (also called "Kythera"), the island's southern capital, is most famous for its large castle and whitewashed houses. Though usually a small, low-key community, it's often overwhelmed in high season with visitors from Kapsali and Diakofti. The few accommodations that cater to visitors offer similar views and amenities, but domatia may have kitchens and lower prices. Hotels and domatia are mostly clustered around and along the main road leading to the police. At **Castello Apartments ❷**, to the left of the main road as you approach the fork from the plateia, airy rooms come with A/C, TV, kitchens, baths, and large balconies behind a charming white facade. Follow the path leading to the back of the building to find the reception. (☎ 27360 31 069; www.castelloapts-kythera.gr. Singles €30-40; doubles €35-45; triples and studios €55. MC/V.) Though a little more removed from the center of town, the unnamed **rooms ❸** above Salonikios include A/C, TV, phones, kitchenettes, and balconies with beautiful views of the nearby mountains. Walk up the stairs to the right of the post office and turn right at the road; it's 20m down on the right. (☎ 27360 31 404. Singles and doubles €30-60.) Though people gather to sip frappés in the plateia, only one taverna in this small town actually serves meals. At family-run **Salonikios ❷**, diners are invited into the kitchen to choose their meals by sight. Head up the stairs to the right of the post office and turn right. (☎ 27360 31 705. Appetizers €2-4. Salads €2.50-5. Entrees €4-6.)

Flights depart Kythera for Athens (daily, €43). **Kithira Travel**, 50m uphill from the plateia, has ferry schedules and tickets for **Olympic Airways** flights and **Flying Dolphins**. (☎ 27360 31 390. Open daily 8:30am-2pm and 6:30-9:30pm.) The **bus** drops off outside town at the museum, and then continues to Kapsali before returning to Ag. Pelagia. From the bus stop, walk downhill on the main road to get to the center of town. **Taxis** (☎ 27360 31 720), which line up in the plateia, will take you to Diakofti (€23). Many taxi drivers take an all-afternoon siesta, though, so plan your ride in advance. There is a **National Bank** with a **24hr. ATM** in the plateia. (Open M-Th 8am-2:30pm, F 8am-2pm.) **Public toilets** are below the Agricultural Bank in the plateia; follow the steps outside the bank. Facing the water, Hora's main street begins in the plateia's lower left corner and runs downhill. Along it you'll find the **police**, 150m after you make a right at the fork in the road, on the street toward the castle. (☎ 27360 31 206. Open 24hr.) The nearest **hospital** is in Potamos. **Internet access** is available at the one computer at **Typographics**, on the main road toward the police station. (☎ 27360 39 016. €5 per hr.; €2 min. Open daily in high season 8:30am-1pm; in low season 8:30am-2pm and 5-10pm.) The **post office**, which has **Poste Restante**, is in the plateia. (☎ 27360 31 274. Open M-F 7:30am-3pm.) **Postal Code:** 80100.

ELAFONISSOS Ελαφόνησι ☎ 27340

Elafonissos (Deer Island) received its name at the end of the 19th century when its first inhabitants found it, peculiarly, filled with deer. Locals say that a boat carrying deer from Africa sunk near the island, allowing some animals to make it to shore. Unfortunately, no deer remain today, though Elafonissos has since become famous for the breathtaking waters of Simos beach, which are thought by some to be the best in Greece. The island's port that goes by the same name is a quiet fishing town that remains calm and unspoiled for the majority of the year. Its blue-shuttered buildings, winding roads, and easy access from the Peloponnese draw huge weekend crowds of Greek youth and a handful of artsy older visitors.

Just about everyone under the age of 40 camps on Elafonissos. Free camping is officially prohibited, though groups are known to stake out sites on the small beach of **Simos**, 5km from the port. To reach the beach's established campground, either hop on a ferry or take the road from the port and keep going straight when signs for the campground point to the right. **Simos Camping ❶**, though relatively expensive, is large and well-organized. Renowned for its cleanliness, it also has free hot water, bathrooms, laundry, communal kitchens, and restaurants. (☎ 27340 22 672; www.simoscamping.gr. €6.30, children €3.10, tents €7.80; tent rental €5.80.) In high season, waterfront rooms fill up quickly, and prices shoot up throughout town. Your best bet indoors is **Filoxenia ❸**, on the road toward the police station. The blue and white building covered in flowers and vines has pastel rooms with A/C, TV, fridges, kitchen supplies, large baths, and balconies. (☎ 27340 61 240. Singles and doubles €25-50; triples €30-60.) Run by sweet Katerina, **Pallas Hotel ❹**, on the waterfront, rents cozy rooms with A/C, TV, fridges, balconies, and walls adorned with Katerina's own art. One of the larger and more popular hotels on the island, Pallas fills up quickly, so reservations are highly recommended. (☎ 27340 61 142. Singles €30-40; doubles and triples €35-70.) The waterfront restaurants serve generic food for high prices, but bargains can be found farther inland. Numerous **supermarkets** and fast food sandwich shops line the street to the police station. Despite its cheesy theme ("the Lord of the Taste") and garish colors (jarringly bright orange), **El Gordo ❶** makes tasty pressed sandwiches (from €2). The popular nighttime spot, **Remezzo Cafe,** on the waterfront, is surprisingly hip and classy given its strange blend of a pirate-themed interior and Indian-influenced outdoor area. (Frappés €2.50. Mixed drinks €6.)

Large ferries arrive and depart from the very left side of the pier, facing inland, and small fishing boats dock at the center. **Ferries** run from Pounta, on the mainland, to Elafonissos (every hr. 7am-11pm, €1). The easiest way to reach Pounta is from Neapoli, where you can hop onto one of the few buses in the morning (20min., 4 per day 7am-1:45pm, €1) or take a taxi (€10). Buses return to Neapoli from Pounta just after the ferries arrive. On the island, ferries also go back and forth between the village and Simos Beach (25min., daily, €1-6.50). There is **no public transportation,** so a car or moped is necessary if you don't want to walk 4km every time you need something. There is also **no bank** on the island, so make sure you have enough cash. The **police station** is near the waterfront. As you walk with the water on your right, past Remezzo cafe, turn left onto the side street to the left of Spiros and Spiridoula tavern; the station is 30m farther on your left. (☎ 27340 61 111. Open mornings and afternoons in high season.)

CENTRAL GREECE

Situated at the crossroads of Greece, the expansive region of Central Greece is as diverse as its terrain is mountainous. Stretching from the foothills of Mt. Olympus in the north to the peaceful seaside villages that dot the shore of the Gulf of Corinth, Central Greece is charming, rugged, and authentic. Tiny villages cling to their cliff-side perches in the towering peaks surrounding Karpenisi, while the magnificent views from the lush terrain of the Mt. Pelion Peninsula let visitors gaze down at the twinkling lights of Volos. The region is home to the ruins of the ancient oracle at Delphi and the Byzantine monasteries atop immense stone pillars at Meteora, two must-see sights for any itinerary.

⏵ SUGGESTED ITINERARIES: CENTRAL GREECE

THREE DAYS Take advantage of summer discounts and gorgeous hikes in **Arahova** (p. 210), a ski town where low and high seasons are reversed. Seek Apollo's guidance on how to spend the money you've saved at the **Delphic oracle** (p. 216). From there, go to **Galaxidi** (p. 217), where you will get an introduction to Greece's small-town countryside culture.

ONE WEEK Traverse some of Greece's best hiking country, starting with **Mount Parnassos** (p. 210), which will be pleasantly empty when the weather's nice. Next, hike between the small towns in mountainous **Evritania** (p. 223), a region known as "the Switzerland of Greece." End your trip up north by climbing to the death-defying midair monasteries of **Meteora** (p. 244).

STEREA ELLADA

For millennia, advice-seeking pilgrims from across the ancient world gravitated to Sterea Ellada to inquire at the Oracle of Delphi. Many years later, 10th-century Orthodox saint Osios Loukas built a masterful Byzantine monastery nearby, which ailing believers continue to visit today in search of a sacred cure. Though perhaps in a less-spiritual way, Sterea Ellada continues to cater to both the mind and the body; its small mountain villages offer thrilling ski slopes and some of the world's finest honey, the western coast is covered in deep forest, and the monumental ruins shed light on tales of history.

THEBES (THIVA) Θήβα ☎ 22620

Buried beneath the low-rise apartment buildings and lazy tavernas of modern Thebes lies its claim to fame: an illustrious and notorious past. History has literally surfaced in spots throughout the city, as attempts at construction have revealed the edifices of ancient Thebes. Theban buildings grace the avenues of Cadmus (the city's legendary first king), Oedipus (exiled king and namesake of the Complex), and Epaminonda (the general who ended Spartan dominance). Rising to prominence in the heyday of the Greek city-state (600-400 BC), Thebes capitalized on its fertile plains and strategic location between Northern Greece and the Peloponnese to become a cultural center and the inspiration for great works by Sophocles, Euripides, and Aeschylus. Alexander the Great's army cut this prosperity short around 335 BC by maliciously setting fire to the city, reducing it to rubble; only temples and Pindar's ancestral home were spared. Modern Thebes, a tiny,

unremarkable city, has a vast reputation to live up to, and may never be able to revive its former splendor. Nevertheless, the unique combination of archaeological sites and inviting cafes makes it an excellent daytrip for any wayfarer.

☞ TRANSPORTATION. The main **bus station** (☎ 22620 27 512) is in the valley below Thebes at Estias 10. From there, buses depart for Athens (1½hr., every hr. 6am-8pm, €6). If you miss the direct bus between Thebes and Halkida (7:20, 10am; €3), take the Thebes-Athens bus and get off at the Skimatari stop (30min., €2); wait at the sheltered bus stop, then catch the Athens-Halkida bus (10min., every 30min., €1.30). Regular buses run to Livadia (45min., every hr. 7:40am-9:40pm, €3.20) from a stop about 2km out of town; walk all the way down Pindarou past the Archaeological Museum and go down the steps. Take the left fork then the right onto Laiou (Λαιου). Take a left onto St. Athanasiou and follow the blue signs to Livadia (Λειβαδια) to the small bus shelter before the gas station on your right. Buy your ticket onboard. For **taxis,** visit Pindarou 45, where they wait in front of the garden 24hr., or call ☎ 22620 27 077.

▦ 🛈 ORIENTATION AND PRACTICAL INFORMATION. If you ask nicely upon arrival, your bus driver might let you off in the center of town. Otherwise, with your back to the station and the dirt parking lot on your left, follow the road on your right and take the first right as it enters the rotary. Follow **Eteokleous** up the hill to a plateia where first **Pindarou** and then **Epaminonda** veer to the right. Turn right onto Epaminonda to find hotels, tavernas, and other points of interest. Thebes is built on a high hill. Two parallel main streets, Epaminonda and Pindarou, run from the top of the hill into the valley below. Epaminonda hosts a variety of cafes and shops; Pindarou is lined with small retail stores and businesses. The **National Bank,** Pindarou 94, has a **24hr. ATM.** (☎22620 23 331. Open M-F 8am-2:30pm.) The **hospital** (☎22620 24 444) has recently moved out of town and is best reached by taxi (€3-5). An **OTE,** Vourdouba 20, is between Epaminonda and Pindarou (☎22620 81 220. Open M-Th 7:30am-2pm, F 7:30am-1:30pm). To get to **Genesis Internet Cafe,** Oedipus 30, turn onto Oedipus from the pedestrian-only plaza on Epaminonda and walk one block away from Pindarou. (☎22620 89 500. €3.25 per hr. Open M-Sa 9am-2am, Su 2pm-2am.) The **post office,** Drakou 17, lies on a side street between Pindarou and Epaminonda in the opposite side of the square from the hotels. **Poste Restante** is available. (☎22620 27 810. Open M-F 7:30am-2pm.) **Postal Code:** 32200.

🛏🍴 ACCOMMODATIONS AND FOOD. If you decide to spend the night in Thebes, there are only two options in town. The rooms at **Hotel Meletiou ❸,** Epaminonda 58, have A/C, TV, fridges, and baths in graceful, carpeted surroundings. (☎22620 27 333. Breakfast €5. Singles €25-35; doubles €30-40; triples €36-46.) Across the street, the friendly English-speaking staff at **Hotel Niovi ❸,** Epaminonda 63, offers rooms with A/C, TV, and beautifully tiled private baths. (☎22620 29 888. Breakfast €3. Singles €35; doubles €40; triples €45. AmEx/MC/V.)

By evening, people fill the pedestrian-only sections of Thebes as cafes and tavernas move tables into the street. Most restaurants from Epaminonda to Pindarou offer similar fare at similar prices. The new, chic **Cafe Theatro ❷,** Epaminonda 79, is the square's most lively venue, with a DJ spinning bouncy pop for young hipsters who congregate outside on posh couches. (☎22620 26 370. Tea and coffee €1.50-2.50. Mixed drinks €4. Open daily 8:30am-4am.) Across the way, the **Athinaikou Cafe ❷,** Epaminonda 72, caters to a slightly older crowd and serves traditional dishes (souvlaki plate €3.50) to the tunes of mainstream music. **Dionysos ❷,** Epimanonda 88, just past the plateia, has been cooking traditional fare longer than the rest, first opening its doors in 1922. (☎22620 24 445. Entrees €4.50-6. Open daily 8am-5pm and 7pm-2am. V). Bakeries, fruit stands, and gyro and souvlaki restaurants scattered around the area provide cheaper options (€1-3).

◙ SIGHTS. Thebes's antiquities are its main attraction. The **Archaeological Museum,** Threpsiadou 1, at the end of Pindarou, has an extensive collection of art and artifacts from roughly 45 centuries of history (3000 BC-AD 1500). On display are Boeotian statues from the 5th and 4th centuries BC, including several well-preserved *kouroi,* and noteworthy red and black figure vases and Geometric vases dating from 900 to 700 BC. (☎22620 27 913. Open daily Tu-Su 8:30am-3pm. €2, students and seniors €1, children and EU students free.) You can peer into the open **excavation pits**—the source of the museum's collection—sprinkled between buildings throughout the city, but most holes are disappointingly empty of anything but rocks. Segments of a Mycenaean palace and acropolis (c. 1400 BC) are partially visible. The largest of these, the **House of Cadmus,** shows its ancient walls; it is on the left-hand side along the way to the museum, a block after the taxis, behind a green fence. Also nearby are the ancient **Mycenaean Chamber Tombs,** which have since closed to the public, but whose entrance is still visible. Take Vourdouba downhill from Pindarou, turn left on Avlidos, and then right up the stone stairs.

PARNASSOS Παρνασσός AND ARAHOVA Αράχωβα

☎ 22670

The crowds at Mt. Parnassos (2457m) hit their peak in the winter, when Apollo and the Muses share their peaceful sanctuary with the ski and snowboard enthusiasts who flock to the best slopes in all of Greece. By night the frostbitten masses thaw out in the cobblestone village of Arahova, the country's largest ski resort, located a convenient 24km away. In the summer months, crowds desert both mountain and village, allowing the opportunistic traveler to hike the broad slopes undisturbed. Peaceful Arahova offers local delights like delicious unresinated red wine, Boeotian honey, and *tsipouro*, a peculiar grape-seed brandy. Known for the pivotal role it played in Greece's War of Independence, Arahova attracts quite a crowd each spring as residents don traditional garb and host a festival in honor of St. George, the renowned dragon-slayer and the town's patron saint.

☎☒ TRANSPORTATION AND PRACTICAL INFORMATION. Buses to Arahova stop at the end of town closest to Delphi, next to the kiosk in front of the main plateia. There is no bus station—ask at the information office for bus schedules. From the stop, **buses** go to Amfissa via Delphi (10min., 6 per day 9:45am-10pm, €1), Athens (2hr.; 6 per day M-Sa 5:45am-6:15pm, Su 7:45am-9:15pm; €12), and Livadia (35min.; M-F 3 per day 7am-4:30pm, Sa 12:50, 4:30pm, Su 4:30, 6:30pm; €4). Getting from Arahova to Parnassos is slightly easier during ski season, when a bus runs from Pl. Xenia (M-Th 8am, F-Su 3 per day 8:30am-2:30pm; €5). During the summer, go by **car** or **taxi** (☎ 22670 31 566; round-trip €30) from Pl. Lakas. When negotiating the price, arrange for the driver to pick you up.

Arahova centers on **Delphon**, which points uphill toward Athens and has all the essentials. **Plateia Xenia**, the main square, is joined by **Plateia Lakas** and **Plateia Pappaioannou.** An **information office** is on the right before you enter town from Delphi, and can help with everything from trail info to discounted ski packages. (☎ 22670 31 630. Open M-F 8:30am-8:30pm, Sa-Su 8:30am-2:30pm and 5:30-8:30pm.) For the **police,** upstairs on the left side of Delphon past the town center, call ☎ 22670 31 333. The **OTE** is just before the town center on the right. (☎ 22670 31 099. Open M-Th 7:30am-1:30pm, F 7:30am-1pm.) One of many **pharmacies** is across from the OTE. (☎ 22670 31 252. Open daily 8am-5:30pm.) Just after Pl. Xenia on the left is the **National Bank,** with a **24hr. ATM.** (☎ 22670 31 496. Open M-Th 8am-2:30pm, F 8am-2pm.) **Alpha Bank,** in Pl. Lakas on the right, **exchanges currency.** (☎ 22670 32 561. Open M-Th 8am-2:30pm, F 8am-2pm.) To find the **post office,** turn right in Pl. Xenia; it's uphill and on the right. (☎ 22670 31 253. Open M-F 7:30am-2pm.) **Postal Code:** 32004.

☎☐ ACCOMMODATIONS AND FOOD. Hotels, pensions, and domatia cluster near Pl. Xenia and along Delphon toward Athens. High season here is winter and low season is summer; prices fluctuate accordingly. ◪**Pension Petrino ❸,** down the first alley on the right after Pl. Xenia, invites guests to unwind in cabin-style rooms with TV and private baths. A second-story loft accommodates larger groups. Some rooms have balconies. (☎ 22670 31 384. Breakfast included. Singles €75; doubles €95. Low season singles €25; doubles €35. 40% discount M-F in ski season; 10% off for stays longer than 3 days in summer. MC/V.) Spend a hard day's night at **Pension Nostos ❸,** past the information office off Pl. Xenia. Its cozy, well-appointed rooms with fridges, TV, private baths, and balconies hosted the Beatles in 1967. (☎ 22670 31 385. Breakfast included. Singles €35-65; doubles €50-95; triples €50-90. 8% discount for *Let's Go* readers. MC/V.) Down the road past the town center, **Hotel Parnassos ❷** has tidy rooms with the bare essentials and shared hall baths.

Some rooms have balconies with views of the surrounding mountains. (☎22670 31 307. Singles €20-35; doubles €30-45.) Several signs throughout the town marked "rooms to let" advertise **domatia.** Prices and availability vary by season.
The **bakeries** along the road to Delphi sell fresh bread and pastries (€0.50-2), and several small markets offer self-service options. **Pizzaria Kellaria ❶,** on the right past Pl. Lakas, serves pizzas (€5-10) and calzones (€5-8.50) from its brick oven, as well as savory and sweet crepes (€3-5). On soccer nights, patrons crowd to watch the game on the giant flat-screen TV. (☎22670 31 167. Open daily 8am-12:30am.) The roof-top dining area at **Taverna Karathanassi ❷** (☎22670 31 360), up from Pl. Lakas on the right, infuses the grilled meats (€3-6.50) with fresh mountain air.

⊞⊞ SKIING AND HIKING. Winter activities are accessible at the two main **ski centers: Kellaria** and **Parnassos** (☎22340 22 693 for both). Each center has tavernas, equipment rental, and childcare services. Ski season runs from December 15 to May 1. (M-F €12 per day, Sa-Su €25 per day; full week €80. Discounts available for students, children, and families.) Fourteen lifts service 20 slopes, which have a combined length of 14,000m.

> **TIP**
>
> **THE FAR SIDE OF THE MOUNTAIN.** Though skiing on Mt. Parnassos can be a sinkhole in your wallet, you can save some money by either skiing during the week or buying your weekend lift ticket for the Fterolaka side of the mountain (dally €12) instead of for Kelaria, the more heavily trafficked face (M-F €12, Sa-Su €25). Trails at the top of Fterolaka connect to Kelaria anyway, and, as an added plus, the lines to get on the lifts won't be as long.

Though more goats than tourists frequent Parnassos in the summer, it's a peaceful spot for hiking and rock climbing, with literally breathtaking views—the air becomes noticeably thinner higher up. The **E4** trail, one of the two main hiking routes in the area, begins in Delphi and runs north to south. The more popular **22** sprawls across the mountain to the east, around the ski centers. The conditions and difficulty of each trail can vary drastically depending on location and season, so be sure to inquire at the information office for details to plan your trek.
Rich foliage and wildlife surround the trail on a scenic walk near **Panagia.** Those searching for open air and the more expansive vistas of the rocky mountainside can start at any of the ski centers on the mountain, which provide free parking and a convenient base for most trips. **Kelaria** is the best starting point for a climb to **Liakoura,** the summit. Consult the **Greek Alpine Club** in Athens (☎21032 12 429) or the **Skiing and Mountain Climbing Association of Amfissa** (☎22650 28 577) about routes and refuges for climbers. If you don't speak Greek, ask the information office in Arahova to call for you. In most cases, the hike will take no more than 3hr. Trails are poorly marked and usually deserted (goats aside), so bring water, consider hiking with a partner, and be wary of the rock paths.

⊡ DAYTRIP FROM ARAHOVA: LIVADIA/KRYA SPRINGS. Renowned long ago as the site of the **Oracle of Zeus Trofonios,** the town of Livadia has now become an urban jumble of small boutiques and plazas that cater mostly to businesspeople. This makes for an enjoyable afternoon lunch stop on the way through Sterea Ellada, but Livadia can be an expensive place to spend the night.
Beyond its streets and shops, however, is the peaceful brook of Krya Springs, lined with arched stone bridges, luscious flora, and shaded cafes. A stone path leads upstream past the outdoor cafes to Livadia's historical sights. When you reach the tower marked as the **medieval castle,** turn right and follow the steep road uphill. Near the top, if you enter the castle and follow a footpath through over-

grown greenery, you will find another crumbling tower, a **Byzantine church,** and a beautiful view. An **outdoor theater,** built into the side of the hill below, is the site of the 20-day cultural festival of Trofonia held each September. Although it has been marred by graffiti, the theater still boasts spectacular acoustics and a seating capacity of 1500. Near the end of a stone path at the foot of the hill, a series of just over 500 rock steps winds up the mountain past the former site of the Oracle of Zeus Trofonios, now marked by two small churches. Make sure to bring water and be careful near the top where the steps become particularly steep as they lead to the upper church; a dazzling view of the city and theater below, however, are apt rewards. As you walk toward the spring, the city's **clock tower** looms overhead to your right. The tower was originally used as a lighthouse during the French occupation, but was converted in 1803 when Lord Elwin donated the clock to gain favor with locals so he would be permitted to begin archaeological excavations.

After your hike, **Krya Taverna ❷,** Trofonion 13, with the green awning at the base of the springs area, serves traditional Greek meals. (☎ 22610 26 764. Souvlaki €1.20. Steaks and fillets €6.50-12. Open daily 9am-midnight.) **Xenia Cocktail Bar ❶,** which sells cold drinks and ice cream near the base of the steps, is an excellent stop for an after-climb treat. (☎ 22610 29 479. Open daily 9am-midnight.)

Take the **bus** to Livadia (35min.; M-F 3 per day 7am-4:30pm, Sa 12:50, 4:30pm, Su 4:30, 6:30pm; €4) and ask to be let off in the center of town, near the outdoor garden in Pl. L. Katsonis. To reach Krya Springs, take Papaspirou until it branches into Boufidou. Continue past the plateia as Boufidou becomes El. Venizelou; at the end of the street, a right turn will bring you to the base of the springs.

OSIOS LOUKAS Όσιος Λουκάς   ☎ 22670

Stunning Byzantine architecture, gold-laden mosaics, vibrant frescoes, and intricate brick and stonework adorn ▨**Osios Loukas,** perhaps the most striking monastery in Greece. Built in the 10th and 11th centuries and still in use today, this exquisite complex on the green slopes of Mt. Elikon, over 500m above sea level, overlooks the orchards and vineyards of Boeotia and Phokis. Ironically, Christian saint Osios Loukas was born in AD 896 in Delphi (p. 213), a center formerly dedicated to the Olympian gods and polytheistic worship. Inclined to an ascetic life from early on, he became a monk at the age of 14. In 946, Osios Loukas settled at the lush and enchanting site of the monastery that now bears his name, building a cell, a small church, and a garden. Rumors that his church's relic worked miracles brought believers, which led to an expansion of the grounds and the establishment of a monastery. With aid from fellow hermits and money from admirers, Osios Loukas began construction of two larger churches. The first, the **Church of the Panagia** (Church of the Virgin Mary), was finished soon after his death in 953. The larger and more ornate **Katholikon of Osios Loukas,** built in 1011, became the site of his reliquary. Unfortunately, the monastery is still scarred from 13th-century Frankish occupation and German bombing during WWII.

The complex consists of the two churches, a crypt, a bell tower, and monks' cells. The **Archaeology Museum,** on the right after the arched stone gate, sells guidebooks (€2.50-4) and tickets for entrance into the monastery. The one-room museum, formerly a workplace and refectory, has remnants from Osios Loukas's architectural past and merits only a glance. The Katholikon of Osios Loukas, however, past the museum on the right, is the monastery's most impressive area. Built on the "Greek cross" basilica plan, the church is resplendent with mosaics made of stone, enamel, and gold, as well as frescoes depicting scenes from Christian lore.

A small passageway in the Katholikon's northwestern corner, at the front of the sanctuary on the left, links it to the Church of the Panagia. In this passageway is the monastery's most prized relic: the desiccated body of the saint himself, lying in a transparent glass coffin. Pilgrims come to pray at Osios Loukas's velvet-slippered feet, and thousands have said that his tomb cured them of various ailments. Some have been even bolder: Loukas's left hand, protruding from his habit to hold a rosary, has lost a few fingers to relic-seekers. The crypt is between the museum and the churches, accessible by an entrance in the exterior of the Katholikon. Protected from the elements, its stunning frescoes have retained their original splendor. Past the crypt entrance is a small courtyard; walk in and to the left to peek inside at the luxurious digs enjoyed by medieval monks. Climbing the tower at the far end of the courtyard yields a stunning view. (☎22670 22 797. Open daily May 3-Sept. 15 8am-2pm and 4-6pm; Sept. 16-May 2 8am-5pm. Modest dress required. €3, seniors and students €2, children and EU students free.)

The few buses from Arahova force you to take a car or **taxi** (☎22670 31 566). When negotiating the price, ask the taxi driver to bring you back from the monastery too; most taxis will wait an hour or two at a slightly higher cost (25min., €20).

DELPHI Δέλφοι ☎22650

The sign along the road that marks the entrance to Delphi proclaims, "Every intellectual human being of free will deserves to be regarded as a citizen of the town of Delphi." Locals take this mentality to heart as they host the countless travelers who come to marvel at Delphi's wonders. This town of 2500 was once so significant that Greeks felt it was the *omphalos* (belly button) of the earth. Myth tells that Zeus simultaneously released two eagles, one toward the east and one toward the west. They collided directly over Delphi—a sacred stone marks the spot. Nearby stood the impressive sanctuary of Apollo, home to the most important oracle of antiquity. Gaia (Mother Earth) was worshipped here until around 800 BC; according to later myth, Apollo defeated her snaky son Python at the site of the oracle, marking the advent of the Olympian gods. From then on, pilgrims from far and wide flocked to the oracle, seeking the cryptic guidance of Apollo's priestess. Delphi was also the site of the Pythian Games, held every four years in Apollo's honor. Athletes and poets would descend upon the theater and stadium to compete for the victor's laurel crown. Although the ancient oracle's temples and treasury have mostly crumbled to rubble, largely due to an earthquake in the AD 7th century, Delphi remains a place of pilgrimage—for tourists. Jewelry stores, expensive restaurants, "Greek art" trinket shops, and hotels now decorate the town that lies down the road from the ancient city. Beyond the tourist facade, however, are the magnificent ruins, hospitable residents, and beautiful views that make Delphi a must-see.

⬛ TRANSPORTATION. The bus station is at the western end of town, on Pavlou, and could easily be mistaken for a souvenir shop if not for the words "bus station" painted in red down the side of the building. (☎22650 82 317. Open daily 8am-10:10pm.) From Delphi, **buses** go to: Amphissa (30min., 4 per day 10:15am-8:15pm, €1.50); Athens (3hr., 6 per day 5:30am-6pm, €12) via Livadia (50min., €3); Lamia (2hr., 3 per day 6:30am-3pm, €6.50); Nafpaktos (2½hr., 3 per day 10:15am-3:45pm, €8) via Galaxidi (1hr., €3); Patras (3hr.; M-F 1:15pm, Sa 3:45pm; €10); Thessaloniki (5hr.; M-Th 10:15am, F-Su 3pm; €25) via Katerini (€21), Larisa (€16), and Velestino (€13). **Taxis** (☎22650 82 000) wait at the eastern end of Pavlou.

⬛⬛ ORIENTATION AND PRACTICAL INFORMATION. Delphi's main street, **Friderikis-Pavlou** (referred to here as "Pavlou"), goes east-west through town. **Apollonas** runs uphill from and parallel to Pavlou. Standing at the bus station facing the city, Apollonas snakes uphill to the left and Pavlou veers to the right, passing directly through the town. The oracle and museum are on Pavlou at the opposite end of town, toward Athens. The **tourist office,** Pavlou 12 or Apollonas 11, is in the town hall. From Pavlou, headed toward Athens, the office is up a flight of stairs on your left in a stucco courtyard, marked by an "Information" sign. ◖Efi Tsiropoulou can assist you with buses and accommodations. She also provides maps, information, and guidebooks. (☎22650 82 900. Open M-F 8am-2:30pm.) If the office is closed, the bus station can help you out. The **National Bank,** Pavlou 16, has a **24hr. ATM.** (☎22650 82 622. Open M-Th 8am-2:30pm, F 8am-2pm.) The **police** (☎22650 82 222), available 24hr., are located at Sygrou 3, directly behind the church that sits at the peak of Apollonas. The **OTE,** Pavlou 10, is just past the steps to the information office. (Open M-F 7:30am-3:10pm.) The cafe on the ground level of **Hotel Parnassos,** on Pavlou across from the Down Town Club, has four computers with **Internet access.** (☎22650 82 321. Open daily 7:30am-11:30pm. €4 per hr.; €2 min.) You can also get Internet at **Cafe Delfikon,** on the right side of Pavlou (facing Athens) past Hotel Sibylla. (☎22650 83 212. €4.20 per hr.; €2 min. Open daily 9am-midnight.) The **post office,** Pavlou 25, provides **Poste Restante.** (☎22650 82 376. Open M-F 7:30am-2pm.) **Postal Code:** 33054.

ⵕⵕ ACCOMMODATIONS AND CAMPING. Delphi is full of expensive hotels. Prices rise during ski season, holidays, and festivals. **Hotel Sibylla ❷,** Pavlou 9, has comfortable rooms with TV, fans, wonderful views, private baths, and the best prices in town. The reputable, friendly staff can help orient you in Delphi, provide free maps, and even exchange currency. (☎22650 82 335. Singles €20; doubles €26; triples €34. *Let's Go* readers €18/24/34. MC/V.) At **Pitho Rooms ❸,** Pavlou 40A, across from the Down Town Club, rooms are immaculate and have beautifully tiled private baths, A/C, and TV. Breakfast, included in room prices, is served in a lovely marble lounge. (☎22650 82 850; http://pithorooms.tripod.com. Singles €35; doubles €45; triples €60. *Let's Go* readers can call or email in advance to negotiate a discount. MC/V.) **Hotel Artemis ❸** and **Hotel Pan ❸,** across the street from each other at Pavlou 60 and 53, about 100m from the bus station, are under the same management. Both rent rooms with refreshing decor, A/C, TV, and private baths with tubs. Pan has better views and slightly cheaper prices. (☎22650 82 494. Breakfast €5. Singles €20-40; doubles €28-55; triples €35-65. 10% discount for *Let's Go* readers. MC/V.) Buses heading west out of Delphi can drop you off at one of the nearby campsites. **Camping Apollon ❶** is the closest, only 1.5km out of town. It has a swimming pool, laundry (€5), mini-mart, restaurant, and great views. (☎22650 82 762; www.apolloncamping.gr. €7 per person, €4 per tent. Tent rental €5 and 20% off total price.) You'll also find laundry (€5) and pools at **Delphi Camping ❶,** 4km out of town. (☎22650 82 745. €6 per person, €4 per tent.)

⬠ FOOD. Several **mini-marts** and a **bakery** line Pavlou and Apollonas and four **pizza** places beckon from the western end of Pavlou. While many tavernas are indistinguishable, with the same view and slightly pricey food, locals rave about **Vakchos ❷,** Apollonas 31, just below the church, on top of the stairs from Pavlou. (☎22650 83 186. Salad €3-6. Soup €3.50-5.50. Veal and rabbit €7.20. Open daily noon-4pm and 7-11pm.) You'll also find locals mixed in with tourists at **Gargantuas ❷,** Dimou Fragkou 10, a few doors toward town from the bus station. The grilled lamb (€8) is the most expensive item on a menu that also offers salad (€2.50), spanakopita (€4.50), and other Greek standbys. (☎22650 82 488. Open daily noon-3pm and 7pm-1am.) For the best cup of coffee in town, stop into **Melopoleio ❶,** Pavlou 14, near the town hall. Melopoleio's name means "honey shop" which appropriately alludes to the delicious pastries they serve along with their famous coffee. (☎22650 83 247. Coffee €1.50-3. Pastries €2-3. Open daily 7am-11pm.)

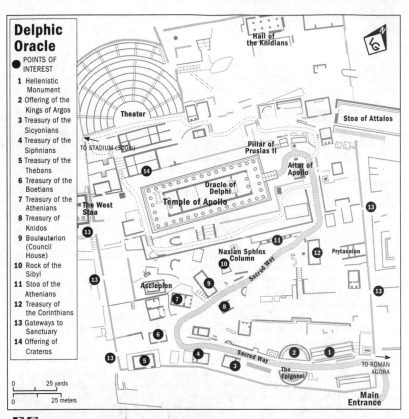

Delphic Oracle

● POINTS OF INTEREST
1 Hellenistic Monument
2 Offering of the Kings of Argos
3 Treasury of the Sicyonians
4 Treasury of the Siphnians
5 Treasury of the Thebans
6 Treasury of the Boetians
7 Treasury of the Athenians
8 Treasury of Knidos
9 Bouleuterion (Council House)
10 Rock of the Sibyl
11 Stoa of the Athenians
12 Treasury of the Corinthians
13 Gateways to Sanctuary
14 Offering of Crateros

🎭🎵 **ENTERTAINMENT AND NIGHTLIFE.** The **European Cultural Center of Delphi** (☎22650 82 731) puts on a **Festival of Greek Drama** with performances in the ancient theater in July. They also have temporary international art exhibitions. Contact their office in Athens (☎21033 12 781) for more information. Delphi is home to several other summer **festivals,** so ask around and keep an eye out for posters. Delphi's only two nightclubs are within stumbling distance of most hotels on Pavlou. Both open at 10pm and stay open until the customers leave (substantially later on weekends and during peak tourist periods). **Katoi Club** is about 75m up from the bus station on Pavlou. Moving lights suspended above the dance floor combined with a soft glow from the private tables create an electric atmosphere. The DJ plays a mix of American and international pop and is open to requests. (☎69325 26 578. Beer €3. Mixed drinks €5-8.) You'll hear **Down Town Club,** Pavlou 33, before you see it. Grab a drink at the bar or take advantage of the large dance floor. (☎69465 02 043. Beer €3. Mixed drinks €5. €3-10 cover; no cover for *Let's Go* readers.)

🥾 **HIKING.** Delphi offers several hiking trails with amazing views. The **E4** trail begins at the steps on the eastern end of Apollonos where it meets Pavlou. Here you will find a detailed map of the trails that you can follow up Mt. Parnassos and the surrounding peaks. Climb the steps up to Sygrou and follow the road to the

CENTRAL GREECE

right, past the Museum of the Delphic Festivals, until it turns to dirt. Look for the metal pole on the left that marks the continuation of E4, where you will find a spectacular view of the ancient stadium. The trail is relatively well marked but extremely rocky, so hikers should be careful and consider going in pairs. A 1hr. trek up the footpath will reach the top of the mountain. Hiking up for another few hours will lead to the **Corycian Cave,** an ancient sanctuary of Pan and the woodland nymphs. Consult the tourist information office to learn more about hiking trails.

THE DELPHIC ORACLE

A sacred site from 1500 BC or earlier, the Oracle of Delphi became the most important source of sacred wisdom in the ancient world from around the 7th century BC until the advent of Orthodox Christianity. When the oracle answered a pilgrim's pressing question, usually with just a few pithily ambiguous words, its authority was almost universally accepted. After all, it was the Delphic oracle that had foretold Cadmus's founding of Thebes and prophesied Oedipus's horrific fate. But the oracle held sway over more than religious matters and personal fortune-telling; Delphic approval sanctioned many political decisions, including the reforms that led to democracy in Athens. The oracle's pronouncements altered the courses of nations and set off (and sometimes extinguished) military conflicts. Hoping to make powerful friends and receive positive forecasts, city-states from all over the Greek world erected treasuries and donated immense sums to the oracle.

At the Pythian Games, athletes, musicians, and poets were judged by Apollo's golden rule of harmony and balance. Legend says that when the great Greek poet Homer participated in the Pythian Games, he lost because, although his poetic talent was unrivaled, his musicianship could not match it. From Delphi, head out of town on the road toward Athens and follow the highway to a paved path on the left, leading to the ruins and museum.

⬛ ARCHAEOLOGICAL SITE. The inscription "Know thyself" has long since crumbled from the portal of the ancient temple, but it still governs the meditative atmosphere of peaceful, windswept Delphi. Cut into the steep mountainside, the ancient sanctuary reigns over the brush-dotted valley below and overlooks eagles that fly under the lofty temple. Now, as in the past, the **Temple of Apollo** is the centerpiece of the oracle site. A largely wooden incarnation of the temple was burned in 548 BC, was demolished again by an earthquake in 373 BC, and still lies in ruin today. Ancient proclamations etched along the stone base are still visible. To reach the Temple of Apollo, follow the **Sacred Way,** which winds up the site in the footsteps of ancient pilgrims. To the left are the treasuries of supplicant cities, including the reconstructed **Treasury of the Athenians,** excavated in the early 20th century. Past the Temple of Apollo, the theater, a picture of geometric perfection and amazing acoustics, is no less impressive. After one glance at the view, you will understand why performances held here never used any backdrops. For a glimpse of ancient Delphi as an athletic arena, make your way up the slick steps to the **stadium** at the very top of the hill, and sit among the Greek and Roman ghosts in the stadium's seats. A sprint across the stadium while imagining the cheering crowd is a decidedly good use of time. (Open daily 7:30am-7:30pm. €6; site and the museum €9.) Guidebooks and maps (€3-15) are sold at the entrance, but the tourist office in town can provide similar materials for free. The site is staffed by knowledgeable guides who lead the groups from tour buses. They won't mind if you tag along and will be happy to answer your questions, especially if you give them a tip. Make sure you get a registered tour guide; unqualified imposters may charge ridiculous prices and fill your head with nonsense.

ARCHAEOLOGY MUSEUM. The museum, before the ruins on the left as you head out of town, houses artifacts exclusively from the ancient city. Among the notable collection are enormous 7th-century bronze **shields,** the frieze of the **Siphnian Treasury,** the two kouroi **Kleobis** and **Biton,** the altar from the **temple of Athena Pronaia,** a Naxian **sphinx,** the haunting bronze ▓**Charioteer of Delphi,** and many of the impressive gifts presented as offerings to the oracle. The excavations that yielded these treasures began in 1892 and were completed in 1935 by the **Ecole Française d'Athens.** (☎ 22650 82 312. Open daily 7:30am-7:30pm. €6; site and the museum €9.)

OTHER SITES. Before calling upon the oracle, pilgrims cleansed themselves both physically and spiritually in the **Kastalian Spring,** 200m past the main ruins along the road to Athens. ▓**Drinking** from the spring is said to confer the gift of eloquence, but the danger of falling rocks has indefinitely closed the spring to visitors, dooming them to a life of mumbling. Just past the spring, on the opposite side of the road, are the remains of an ancient **gymnasium** where athletes trained for the Pythian Games. All participants arrived one month before the competition to train in the gymnasium so that they would all be accustomed to the thin mountain air. Another 200m farther down the road (also accessible from the gymnasium), the Temple of Athena Pronaia was the ancient entrance to Delphi and served as a lounge and campground for pilgrims bound for the sanctuary. Three remaining Doric columns of the original 20 of the **tholos,** a round building used for an unknown purpose, are the sole evidence of its architectural mastery.

While in Delphi, consider visiting the small, fascinating **Museum of the Delphic Festivals,** which chronicles the celebrations held here in 1927 and 1930. At the peak of Apollonos, walk uphill to the church, turn right onto Sygrou, then go uphill to the museum on the left. The museum is in the former house of Eva Sikelianos (originally Eva Palmer of New York) and her husband Angelos, a Greek poet, who planned and staged recreations of the Pythian Games in the ancient theater and stadium. The productions were the first performances in an archaeological site, and paved the way for other venues like Epidavros. The museum displays a collection of the costumes that Eva designed from studying pictures on ancient vases and wove by hand on a loom, as well as the original sheet music and photographs from the two festivals. (Open daily 8:30am-3pm. €1, students and groups €0.35.)

GALAXIDI Γαλαξίδι   ☎ 22650

Peaceful little Galaxidi is situated around a relaxed harbor and pebble beaches that invite weary travelers to slow down and enjoy their charms. The town's dominant naval activity, which scholars date back to as early as 3000 BC, is evidenced by artifacts recovered from shipwrecks that are on display at the Nautical History Museum. Seafaring, in its modern incarnation, has evolved into pleasure boating, as locals lead tours for vacationing Europeans. Though quiet during most of the year, Galaxidi erupts into glorious mayhem on Kathari Deftera, ushering in the Orthodox Lent with a huge annual flour fight.

▐▓ **TRANSPORTATION AND PRACTICAL INFORMATION.** The two notable landmarks in town are the monument-centered main plateia and the waterfront. The bus stop is in the plateia, by the start of the main street, **Nikolou Mama,** which leads to the harbor. **Buses** run to Itea (20min.; M-F 6 per day 7:15am-8pm, Sa-Su 4 per day 10am-8pm; €1.20) and Nafpaktos (1½hr., 5 per day 6:20am-9:20pm, €5.30) where you can transfer to Delphi (1hr., €3). Buy tickets at **Kourdisto Portokali Cafe,** across Nik. Mama from the bus stop on the right. Call ☎ 22650 42 087 for schedules. **Taxis** (☎ 22650 41 243) are available

FLOUR POWER

While much of Greece is winding down from the pre-Lenten Carnival season on *Kathari Deftera* (Clean Monday), the real party is just getting underway for the citizens of Galaxidi—and it's definitely not very clean.

In accordance with an over 200-year-old annual tradition, the people of this otherwise serene seaside town bring in the first day of Orthodox Lent with a massive flour war. Residents and visitors of all ages throw on goggles, masks, and overalls, and scramble to chuck fistfuls of flour and ash at their closest neighbors, random townspeople, and the nearest hard surface. The flour is usually dyed a variety of bright colors, so both the people and the town end up blanketed in vivid, chaotic, Jackson Pollock-esque swirls and blobs.

After all of the flour has been thrown, the powdery people crowd into the center of their powdery town to continue the revelry with drinking, dancing, carousing, and eating. Some leap into the harbor to wash themselves off, while others take turns jumping over fire, a wild tradition that has somehow worked its way into the festivities' canon. In the end, everyone is happy and dirty, and the mess is left until morning to clean up.

24hr. The **National Bank** with a **24hr. ATM** is several blocks farther down Nik. Mama, past Hotel Poseidon on the left. (Open M-Th 8:30am-2:30pm, F 8:30am-2pm.) The **police** station (☎22650 41 222; open daily 8am-2pm) is in the main plateia across from the bus station. A **pharmacy**, Nik. Mama 17, is one block from the bus station. (☎22650 41 122. Open M-F 8:30am-1:30pm and 6-9:30pm, Sa 9am-1:30pm.) Galaxidi's **post office** is next to the bank on Nik. Mama and receives **Poste Restante**. (Open M-F 7:30am-2pm.) **Postal Code:** 33052.

ACCOMMODATIONS AND FOOD. Look for **domatia** on side streets off Nik. Mama mixed in with the expensive pensions and unremarkable hotels along the waterfront. Facing the bus stop from the main plateia, follow Nik. Mama to the right until you reach **Hotel Poseidon ❸** in the middle of the street. This home-turned-hotel is blessed with a vivacious manager, Costas, who personifies Greek hospitality, and may break open a bottle of ouzo on the evening of your arrival. The rooms' hardwood floors, high ceilings, A/C, and TV make them just as warm and inviting as the welcome. (☎22650 41 426. Breakfast included. Some rooms with bath. Singles €30; doubles €55; triples €71.) To reach **Hotel Galaxidi ❸**, Sigrou 11, turn right after the bank and continue down the street. Lovely rooms have A/C, TV, small balconies, and sailboat shower curtains. (☎22650 41 850. Breakfast €5. Singles €30-53; doubles €55-80.) **To Perasma ❶**, Nik. Mama 40, across from the National Bank, has a carefully cooked, deliciously seasoned selection of traditional mainstays. (☎22650 41 742. Gyros €1.70. Pita souvlaki €1.80. Open daily 5pm-midnight.) For an authentic Greek-kitchen experience, take your appetite to **Taverna Albatross ❷**. Turn left on Kon. Satha before Hotel Poseidon, and then take a right before the church. Meals here start with oven-roasted meats (€4-6) or stuffed grape leaves (€6), and finish with complimentary *pergamoto*, a sweet citrus fruit. (☎22650 42 233. Open daily 8am-3pm and 6pm-midnight.) If you're willing to splurge for seafood, head to one of the tavernas along the harbor for a great view and tasty catch. Turning left at the bottom of Nik. Mama, you'll find a steady crowd vying for the blue and yellow tables at **O Tasos ❷**, which offers its own name-brand wine and serves giant, mouthwatering portions. (☎22650 42 101. Grilled dishes €6-7. Fresh fish €44-60 per kg. Open daily 11am-midnight. MC/V.)

⚅⚄ **SIGHTS AND BEACHES.** On Kon. Satha, left off Nik. Mama, the **Church of Agios Nikolaos** houses fine mosaics and ornate wood carvings. (☎ 22650 41 682. Open daily 8am-8pm. Modest dress required.) The 13th-century **Monastery of the Metamorphosis,** high in the hills 6km from Galaxidi on the uphill road outside of town, has an amazing view of the town and harbor. Though the unshaded trip takes an hour by foot, the hike is enjoyable on a cool day and the spectacular views are certainly worth it; follow K. Papapetrou from the main plateia out of town past the school, beneath the highway, and follow the signs through the terraced orange orchards. The **Nautical History and Archaeological Museum,** on the first side-street to your right on Kon. Satha, displays impressive artifacts from the town's past, including *amphorae* (jugs) recovered from the bottom of the gulf that prove Galaxidi was an active trading port even in prehistoric times. Other rooms show guns used during the War of Independence and nautical instruments. (☎ 22650 41 558. Open daily July-Sept. 10:10am-1:30pm and 5:30-8:30pm; Oct.-May 10:10am-4:15pm. €5, seniors €2.50, students and groups €1, under 12 free.)

Look for small, pebbly **beaches** scattered over the rocky shoreline that stretches out past the docks on the forest side of the harbor. Walk along Nik. Mama to the waterfront, then follow the harbor toward the forest to your left until you find a resting place that suits you. Several tiny islands are within swimming distance.

NAFPAKTOS Ναύπακτος ☎ 26340

With its majestic hilltop fort and inviting beach-lined harbor, Nafpaktos is a popular destination, but shows no signs of becoming a generic family resort town. Vacationing urbanites and Greek children sunbathe side by side on the city's long, pebbly beaches, which grace both sides of the picturesque Old Port. The tree-lined waterfront avenues are blocked off for pedestrian use only, and are packed with cafes, tavernas, and playground equipment, which create the ideal atmosphere for bike-riding or enjoying an evening stroll.

☏ **TRANSPORTATION.** Nafpaktos has two bus stations, one near Pl. Farmaki, the main plateia, and the other east on Athinon by Pl. Kefalovrisou. The first station is located at Manassi 16 (☎ 26340 27 224), which is perpendicular to Athinon just before the main plateia. Facing west on Athinon, turn left onto Manassi to find the station on the left, across from the back of the church. From here, **buses** serve Athens (3½hr.; 10am, 5pm; €15), Messolongi (1¼hr.; 6:30, 9:30am, 1pm; €3.50), and Thessaloniki (8hr.; 10:45am, 3:15pm; €28) via Lamia (3hr., €11). You can also take a bus to Antirrio (15min., 2 per hr. 5:50am-9:30pm, €1) to catch the hourly bus to Athens and the ferry that serves the Peloponnese. The second station, Asklipiou 1 (☎ 26340 27 224), is about six blocks east from the main plateia on Athinon, across from Pl. Kefalovrisou. Walking east, you'll find the station at Asklipiou to the left. Buses from here go to Amfissa (2hr.; 5 per day 5:45am-6:45pm, service reduced Sa-Su; €7.50) via Galaxidi (1½hr., €5.50) and Itea (1¾hr., €6.50), Delphi (2½hr.; 4 per day 5:30am-1:30pm, service reduced Sa-Su; €8), and Larisa (5hr., 8:30am, €22). **Taxis** (☎ 26340 27 792) line up in front of the main plateia.

▇▐ **ORIENTATION AND PRACTICAL INFORMATION.** Coming from the east, **Athinon** leads into the town's central plateia, where it becomes **Ilarchou Tzavela** and then **G. Ath. Nova** as it continues past the **Old Port.** At the Old Port, one block toward the water from Athinon, **Noti Botsari** runs one way, away from the Old Port headed east. The **National Bank,** Il. Tzavela 86 (☎ 26340 27 304), and **Alpha Bank,** Il. Tzavela 81 (☎ 26340 29 291), both just off the main plateia, **exchange currency** and have **24hr. ATMs.** (Both open M-Th 8am-2:30pm, F 8am-2pm.) The **police** station (☎26340 27 258) is located off G. Ath. Nova, about six blocks west of the Old Port. **Pharmacies,** all with varying hours, sit around the plateia and down Athinon; if one is closed, there should be a sign indicating which others are open. Call the police or a taxi to arrange transportation to the nearest **hospital** (☎26340 23 690). **Hobby Club,** on Navmachias at the start of Psani beach, past the Old Port, has **Internet access.** (☎26340 22 288. €2 per hr.; €1 min. Open daily 8:30am-1am.) The **post office,** Il. Tzavela 33, is several blocks down from the banks, on the right. (☎26340 27 232. Open M-F 7:30am-2pm.) **Postal Code:** 30300.

▮▯ ACCOMMODATIONS AND FOOD. Accommodations in Nafpaktos range from rather mediocre hotels along G. Ath. Nova to more expensive options by Gribovo beach. In the heart of town, just past the Old Port plateia on G. Ath. Nova, dainty ▨**Hotel Diethnes ❷** (Διεθνες) rents bright, colorful rooms with hardwood floors, A/C, TV, balconies, and private baths. English-speaking owner Spiros is a native of Nafpaktos and can answer questions about the city. (☎26340 27 342. Singles €25-30; doubles €30-40.) **Hotel Akti ❸,** left on Gribovo from Pension Aphrodite and in front of the fountain, is a brand-new hotel whose vibrant, sizeable rooms have A/C, fridges, TV, phones, balconies, and swanky private baths. (☎26340 28 464. Breakfast €5. Singles €30-40; doubles €40-50. Prices may vary, so check in advance. MC/V.) At **Pension Aphrodite ❷,** just steps away from clubs Cinema and Empire on Apokafkou, you'll find white rooms with A/C, TV, balconies, and adjoining baths. Head one block east from the main plateia on Athinon, then turn right on Arvanti and walk to the beach; the pension is on the right; don't confuse it with the Hotel Aphrodite, which is also in town. (☎26340 27 370. Singles €25-30; doubles €30-40; triples €40-45.) To camp, follow G. Ath. Nova 4km out of town to **Platanitis Beach Camping ❶,** which has its own minimart, restaurant, and wooded campsites that extend to the pebbly beach. (☎26340 31 555. €4.50 per person, €3.50-4 per tent; tent rentals €6. Electricity €3.50.)

Bakeries, souvlaki stands, and fast-food restaurants clutter the central plateia area and Old Port. Head to the waterfront along Gribovo beach (just a few blocks down from the main plateia) for tavernas. The first of the bunch, **O Stavros ❷** (O Σταυρος), Gribovo 7, serves succulent entrees from rabbit with onions (€6.50) to pasta (€3-5) at tables on the beachfront. (☎26340 27 473. Open daily noon-1am.) On the other side of the Old Port near the middle of Psani beach and across from the playground, **Taverna Rotunda ❷,** Navmachias 2, has a wide selection of traditional Greek dishes. (☎26340 23 553. Moussaka €6. Stuffed tomatoes €4.50. Fresh seafood from €5. Open daily 10am-late.)

▣ SIGHTS. The ▨**Venetian Castle,** one of the most important examples of fortress architecture in Greece, dominates the picturesque town from its hilltop perch, 200m above sea level. Besides having the best vista around, the citadel also contains the tiny **Church of the Prophet Elias,** the remains of a **Byzantine bath** and **church,** and a large **cistern** to help the fortress weather sieges. Its walls, which reach down to the port, formed five zones of fortification, and are now woven into the construction of modern houses on the hill. Footpaths wind around the walls, past fountains, and through century-old gates; one begins off Il. Tzavela just past the post office. Look for the cobblestone steps and the sign that says "ΚΑΣΤΡΟ/Castle" on the right. A leisurely walk up to the fortress takes about 30min. When you hit the road just below the main fortifications, follow it uphill 1km to reach the castle. Alternatively, drive to the castle by following Athinon-Tzavela past the Old Port where it becomes G. Ath. Nova; veer right on Thermou and follow the signs.

The **Old Port,** enclosed by low walls and watchtowers, is a romantic backdrop for the town's hottest cafes. Plaques on the walls commemorate the October 7, 1571 **Battle of Lepanto** in which the united Christian fleet defeated the Ottomans, bringing an end to their naval superiority. A statue also honors the battle hero— **Miguel de Cervantes Saavedra**—who wrote of his experiences in *Don Quixote.* Both the castle and the Old Port are lit up spectacularly at night. Most leisure time around Nafpaktos is spent on the town's beaches, which form a large crescent with the Old Port at the center. Facing the water at the Old Port, **Gribovo beach** is to the left and **Psani beach,** the more popular choice for sunbathers and families with its playgrounds and **public showers,** is to the right.

⚑ 🎵 ENTERTAINMENT AND NIGHTLIFE. Follow Psani beach away from the Old Port to its end to reach **Na Blue,** a waterpark with a pool, waterslides, bar, and free lounge chairs and umbrellas that line the beach. (Pool and waterslides €5-8, children €3. Open daily 11am-8pm.) Nafpaktos's week-long **Carnival,** held annually during the week before Lent, features music, dancing, and free wine and souvlaki. Cafes and *ouzerias* along Psani beach and in the Old Port are filled with customers from 8:30 to 11:30pm, when those who don't hit the hay hit the clubs. Just off Gribovo, two doors down from Pension Aphrodite, is ultrahip **Empire,** Apokafkou 20, whose sophisticated hanging lantern lights illuminate the beachfront bar as party-hungry patrons grind to blasting pop tunes. (Beer €5. Mixed drinks €6. Cover €3. Open daily 11pm-late.) **Club Cinema,** farther down at Apokafkou 12, blasts syncopated mixes of international pop over a large dance floor. (☎ 26340 26 026. Cover €5. Open F-Sa 11pm-late.)

MESSOLONGI Μεσολόγγι ☎ 26310

Though the bleak, modern buildings may give it an initial big-city appearance, Messolongi, actually centered on a single plateia, has an intimate community and rich history. Children play soccer and ride bikes along the numerous pedestrian-only streets during the day, while the entire town retires to the central plateia at night to relax in the cafes and *ouzeria.* As evening sets in, wander to the port to soak in the shimmering colors of the sunset over the picturesque lagoon.

🖂 🚍 TRANSPORTATION AND PRACTICAL INFORMATION. Buses leave from the bus station, Mavrokordatou 5, just east of the central plateia, to: Agrinio (45min.; M-F 17 per day 6:15am-10pm, Sa-Su 12 per day 7:45am-10pm; €3); Athens (4½hr., 9 per day 6:30am-10:30pm, €17); Nafpaktos (1¼hr.; M-F 6 per day 8:40am-6:30pm, Sa-Su 3 per day 10am-2:30pm; €3.50); Patras (45min.; M-F 9 per day 5:45am-7:30pm, Sa-Su 7 per day 7:20am-7:30pm; €4.10); Thessaloniki (10hr.; 10:10am, 2:30pm; €31.50). **Taxis** (☎ 26310 22 623), available 24hr., wait in the central plateia. The entrance to Messolongi is marked by a **stone gate** once part of its fortifications. The road running south through the city splits into **Spyrou Moustakli** to the left, which leads to the water, and **Eleftheron Poliorkimenon** to the right, which goes to the central plateia, **Plateia Markou Botsari.** From there, **Charilaou Trikoupi** goes east-west. Its many off-shoots are filled with cafes, bakeries, and tavernas. **Lord Byron** is the first street perpendicular to Charilaou Trikoupi west of plateia, and connects it to **Pazekotsika,** which runs parallel to the south. Most necessities are in the central plateia. **Eurobank,** Deligiorgi 2 (☎ 26310 24 220), on the northern side of the plateia, has a **24hr. ATM.** Go past Hotel Avra on Charilaou Trikoupi and turn right onto Lord Byron to find **Alpha Bank** and **National Bank,** which **exchange currency.** (Both open M-Th 8am-2:30pm, F 8am-2pm.) To reach the 24hr. **police station,** A. Damaskinou 11 (☎ 26310 55 715) from the plateia, take the second right off Charilaou Trikoupi.

One of several **pharmacies** is by the bus station. (Open daily 8am-3pm.) To get to the 24hr. **hospital** (☎26310 57 110), turn right out of the stone gate and go 3km. The **OTE**, Spirou Trikoupi 5, is across from the bus station. (☎26310 59 303. Open M-F 8am-9pm, Sa 8am-2pm.) Find **Internet access** at **Challenger,** Petropoulou 7, the building between Alpha and National Banks on the opposite side of the street. (☎22310 24 220. 11am-10pm €2 per hr., 10pm-midnight €1 per hr. Open daily 11am-midnight.) The **post office** is on S. Moustakli, outside the central plateia. Take Spirou Trikoupi east and turn left on S. Moustakli; it's on your left. (☎26310 22 605. Open M-F 7:30am-2pm.) **Postal Code:** 30200.

⌐ ACCOMMODATIONS. Messolongi's accommodations are limited and expensive. The cheapest hotel in town is also the oldest and one of the best. **Hotel Avra ❸,** Charilaou Trikoupi 1, in the main plateia, treats its guests to hallways painted with beautiful watercolor seascapes and rooms with tiled private baths, A/C, TV, and phones. (☎26310 22 284. Singles €30; doubles €40; triples €50.) For a comfortable stay at the water's edge, **Hotel Theo Xenia ❹,** Tourlidos 2, 1km from the central plateia, rents carpeted rooms with A/C, TV, phones, private baths, hair dryers, minibars, and balconies. Follow S. Moustakli to the water and turn right, then continue along the water until you reach the hotel. (☎26310 23 303. Breakfast €5.50. Singles €40-50; doubles €55-75; triples €70-90. AmEx/MC/V.)

◫◲ FOOD AND NIGHTLIFE. Besides the cafes that line the main plateia, most of Messolongi's dining options lie in the lively pedestrian-only area behind Hotel Avra. **Pizza Remezzo ❷,** Pazikotzika 2, on the corner one block south of the square, makes hot, delicious pastas (€2.50-4.50) and pizzas (€4.50-6). The mouthwatering Ripieno pizza (€4.50), with gouda, feta, parmesan, and fresh butter, is a dairy-lover's dream (and a vegan's nightmare), at nearly half the price you would pay anywhere else. (☎26310 23 837. Open daily 5:30pm-1am.) **Mezedopoleio ❷,** past Pizza Remezzo at Pazikotzika 11, draws local regulars for its scrumptious appetizers (€2-5) like sliced potatoes with feta cheese. The Greek entrees (€3-9.50) and fresh fish are consistently good. (☎26310 23 237. Cover €0.50. Open daily noon-2am.) On D. Makri, the second left off of Charilaou Trikoupi, trendy **Anakapa Cafe ❶** brims with an energetic crowd all day long, with drinks served street-side as bubble gum pop tunes bounce out from indoors. (☎26310 51 532. Coffee and frappés €2-3. Beer €3-4. Mixed drinks €3-5.50. Open daily 8:30am-late.) For seasoned souvlaki, visit **O Lampros ❶,** Lord Byron 6, next to Alpha Bank, which makes it for only €0.90 per stick. (☎26310 22 707. Open daily 5pm-midnight.)

Nightfall brings the locals out into the main plateia, as cafes turn up the music for a more bar-like atmosphere. Several **clubs** open for the summer; look for posters and ask at cafes for locations. By day, **Plaza Club,** next to Hotel Theo Xenia 1km from town, serves fresh Messolongi fish (€7-8) and grilled entrees (€5-12). Enjoy a poolside drink (€2-4) or take a dip in the pool itself (€2 per person). At night, traffic picks up at the **outdoor bar,** as the music gets louder and the crowds arrive. (☎26310 25 122. Open in summer daily 9am-3am.)

◪ SIGHTS. Naturally gorgeous and teeming with wildlife, the **lagoons** at Messolongi also attract visitors for the acclaimed therapeutic value and skin-rejuvenating properties of their mud. Near the stone gate that marks the entrance to town sits the **Garden of Heroes,** a collection of monuments honoring the nearly 10,000 citizens of Messolongi who died in the War of Independence trying to flee to freedom, an event known as the "Exodus of 1826." The walls that enclose the garden, part of the city's original fortification, still have cannons mounted on them. (Open daily 9am-9pm. Free.) Outside the garden stands a statue honoring **Lord Byron,** who inspired the Messolongians to fight for independence. A memorial to his life and work is housed inside the town's **History Museum,** in the middle of the central plateia. The museum also has a large picture gallery which showcases Messolongi's struggle for freedom. (☎26310 22 134. Open daily 9am-1:30pm and 4-6pm. Free.) A short car or taxi ride will bring you to the field containing the ruins of **Ancient Pleuron,** 6km outside of town, where you can climb into the remains of Greek baths and admire the stonework in the walls of the former water reservoirs.

EVRITANIA Ευριτανια

With its towering alpine peaks, it is no surprise that Evritania is often referred to as the "Switzerland of Greece." This mountainous land was once a refuge for Greeks escaping Ottoman rule, but since then has evolved into a wildlife sanctuary. Hikers and adventurers can explore green forests of fir and walnut and trails that wander past tiny mountain villages to the highest peaks of the Louchi Mountains. Old churches and monasteries dot the mountains and overlook steep gorges where water enthusiasts hop in their rafts, canoes, and kayaks, and try to tame the rushing Karpenisiotis, Krikelopotamos, and Tavropos rivers. The best way to explore Evritania is by foot. Take a stroll up and down the sunny streets of a hillside town, or hike to the peak of the closest mountain for a breathtaking change of perspective. A car, however, is the most sensible (and frequently the only) option for reaching the more remote villages. Rent one elsewhere before you come; no car rentals exist and buses are sporadic.

> In winter, backpackers can contact the **Hellenic Alpine Club (EOS),** which runs several mountain refuge huts throughout Evritania. (Karpenisi office ☎22370 23 051, Lamia 22310 26 786.) Outfit yourself at **Trekking Hellas,** past the Karpenisi plateia down Karpenisioti on the right (☎22370 25 940), which offers kayak, rafting, and ski packages. Maps of the region are available at the information office in Karpenisi's main plateia.

KARPENISI Καρπενήσι   ☎22370

The alpine resort town of Karpenisi, at the tip of a long series of hairpin roads, is Evritania's relaxed capital and the perfect base for outdoor explorations in the surrounding countryside and villages. Founded when five agrarian settlements in the foothills of Mt. Timfristos merged early in the era of Ottoman rule, Karpenisi suffered for years as an economic backwater, weakened by emigration and unemployment. However, in recent years a thriving tourism industry has breathed new life into the city, bringing increased prosperity as outdoor enthusiasts discover the region's extraordinary beauty. Winter marks the peak tourist season, when Mt. Velouchi opens its six lifts to skiers and snowboarders. South of Karpenisi, the streets give way to rolling pastures and the Karpenisiotis river gorge.

☐ TRANSPORTATION. The bus station (☎22370 80 013) is on Char. Trikoupi, a 10min. walk southeast of the plateia. **Buses** run to: Agrinio (3½hr.; M-Th, Sa 9am, F 9am, 3:15pm, Su 1:15pm; €8); Athens (4½hr.; 9am, noon, 3:30pm; €18.20); Koryshades (10min.; Tu, Sa 6:30am, 1pm; €1); Lamia (1½hr., 5 per day 5am-3:30pm, €5.20); Megalo Horio and Mikro Horio (20min.; 7am, 1pm; €1); Proussos (1¼hr.; 6am, 1pm; €2.50). Ask at the station about service to smaller villages. In winter, buses to the Velouchi Ski Center (12km) can be arranged for large groups. **Taxis** (☎22370 22 666), available 24hr., wait at the stand at the high end of the plateia.

FROM THE ROAD

AN ASIAN AMERICAN IN GREECE

As a solo traveler, I've gotten used to receiving stares while dining alone. Especially in Greece, where so much emphasis is put on community and good company, I imagine that the people at the tables around me are speculating why I'm sitting by myself. Or perhaps they're all looking at me because I'm the only Asian within a 50km radius.

Greece is renowned for its supreme warmth and hospitality, but it's also marked by an overwhelming ethnic homogeneity. Understandably, then, the rare outsider attracts attention—not necessarily out of prejudice, but more out of unwavering curiosity. Sometimes it's as subtle as a shifting glance as I raise my head. Other times, people take the direct approach, asking me outright if I'm from "Cheena? Kor-eah? Jah-pan?" When I tell them that I was born in California, it seems to throw them for a loop, as if they can't imagine someone living outside of their place of ethnic origin. Once I heard a whistle while I walking down the street, and turned to see a teenage boy running toward me, waving the display of his camera-phone. He wanted to know if the Chinese tattoo his buddy just got actually said "harmony." "Sorry," I told him, "I can't read Chinese."

—Kevin Paik

◪ ⁊ ORIENTATION AND PRACTICAL INFORMATION. Karpenisi is at the foot of Mt. Velouchi, about 75km west of Lamia. To get to the main plateia from the bus station, follow **Charilaou Trikoupi** downhill as it forks right and gradually curves north, then make a right up steep **Karpenisioti,** which leads to the square. Arriving in the plateia, **Zinopoulou** is the parallel street to your right, bordering the plateia's eastern side, and from which Karpenisioti branches off as the two streets head downhill. The other main road, **Ethnikis Antistasis,** splits off from Zinopoulou at the top end of the plateia. As Eth. Antistasis passes the plateia, **Grigoriou Tsitsara** runs downhill to the left, between the church and the OTE, running roughly parallel to Zinopoulou and Karpenisioti. The largest **church** and the **town hall** are on the northern end of the plateia, near a **monument** to soldiers who died in 20th-century wars.

Directly across from the taxi stand, the **tourist office** is behind an inconspicuous door beneath a faded green sign labeled "Γραφειο Τουρισμο." The English-speaking staff downstairs offers maps and brochures and can help with outdoor excursions. (☎/fax 22370 21 016. Open M-F 9am-2pm and 5-8pm, Sa 10am-2pm and 5-8pm, Su 10am-2pm.) There are a number of **24hr. ATMs,** including one at the **Alpha Bank,** Zinopoulou 7, in the plateia, which also **exchanges currency.** (☎ 22370 25 612. Open M-Th 8am-2:30pm, F 8am-2pm.) For **laundry,** visit **To Ariston** at Karpenisioti 30. (☎ 22370 22 887. €5-10 per load. Open M-Sa 5am-9pm.) The 24hr. **police station,** Eth. Antistasis 9 (☎ 22370 89 160), is down the street from the **OTE,** Eth. Antistasis 3 (open M-F 7:30am-1:30pm). The **hospital** (☎ 22370 80 680), on P. Bakogianni, is a 10min. walk past the police station; signs point the way. Free, fast **Internet access** is available at the **library.** Take the first left after the police station and head straight through two intersections. After the second intersection, it is up the hill about 200m on the left. (☎ 22370 80 269. Open M, Th 4-9pm, Tu-W, F 10am-noon and 4-9pm.) The **post office,** Ag. Nikolaou 3 (☎ 22370 23 542; open M-F 7:30am-2pm), is off Karpenisioti to the left, and offers **Poste Restante. Postal Code:** 36100.

⌂ ACCOMMODATIONS. Though there is no shortage of hotels in Karpenisi, prices aren't budget-friendly, particularly on weekends and during the winter high season. The cheapest option is one of the local **domatia.** The tourist office lists rooms and prices. **Hotel Galini ❷** (Γαληινη), Riga Fereou 3, is set back on a nearby side street; to reach it, follow G. Tsitsara downhill and take the second right. True to its name, which means "serenity," the hotel offers quiet, comfortable rooms with balconies, fridges, TV, and private baths. (☎22370 22 914. Singles €20; doubles €30; triples €40. Longer stays may be discounted.) **Hotel Elvetia ❸**, Zinopoulou 17, has a comfy lounge and pleasant rooms with TV, large baths, phones, and balconies. (☎22370 22 465; www.elvetiahotel.gr. Breakfast €8. Singles €55; doubles €65; triples €80. In summer €35/45/60.) Conveniently located just off the plateia, **Hotel Apollonion ❹**, Karpenisioti 4, rents modern, carpeted rooms with TV, balconies, phones, fridges, and gleaming baths. (☎22370 25 001; www.hit360.com/apollonion/gr. Breakfast €5. Singles €60-70; doubles €65-75; triples €75-85. In summer €40-50/65-75/75-85.)

🛱 **FOOD.** In a small alley to the left of the first street off of Karpenisioti, **Folia ❷** (Φωλια) is a prime place to enjoy a Greek meal that won't break the bank. (☎22370 24 405. Salads €2-2.50. Entrees €6-8. Open M-Th 6:30pm-midnight, F-Su 10am-1am.) A short walk beyond Hotel Galini away from the plateia, **Taverna Panorama ❷**, Riga Fereou 18, serves meat dishes *tisoras* (charcoal grilled; €6-8.50) under a thick canopy of leafy vines. (☎22370 25 976. Veal with potatoes €7. Open daily 1-6pm and 7pm-midnight.) At **Pita Tso ❶**, Karpenisioti 7 (☎22370 21 241), you can indulge late-night food cravings with a souvlaki (€1) or a gyro (€1.50). Looking to upgrade your sweet tooth to saccharine? ▧**Kitsios ❶**, Zinopoulou 13, directly off the plateia, serves fresh Greek pastries, including sinfully decadent baklava (€1.30) drenched in honey. (☎22370 25 504. From €0.40. Open daily 9am-11pm.) To put together your own meal, visit the **Paneboriki Supermarket** (Πανεμπορικη Α.Σ), Karpenisioti 38, on the right (☎22370 21 102. Open M-F 8am-9pm, Sa 8am-6pm), or **Dia Discount Supermarket,** farther down on the left, at Karpenisioti 55. (☎22370 22 272. Open M-Sa 8am-9pm.)

🎦🎵 **ENTERTAINMENT AND NIGHTLIFE.** Throughout the summer, saints' days are celebrated with religious services in the morning and revelry at night. Beginning at the end of July and continuing for about 25 days, Karpenisi hosts **Yiortes Dassous** (Celebrations of the Forest), replete with theatrical performances, dances, food, and music. When the snowflakes start to fall, the **Karpenisi Ski Center,** located 11km up Mt. Velouchi from the town, comes alive. The mountain has six lifts and 12 slopes that weave down 2000m of powdery bliss. The slopes at the top of the mountain are best reached by car; follow the signs to the ski center (☎22370 21 111). Ask at the information office for any buses headed to the slopes. Ski season runs November through March.

The afternoon slides seamlessly into the evening as the small cafes where Karpenisians chat over iced coffee slowly evolve into crowded bars with hopping music. Three doors down from the plateia, mild-mannered **Peros,** Zinopoulou 4, sheds its cafe image around 10pm when it begins serving beer with astounding speed. (☎22370 22 382. Coffee and espresso €2-3.50. Milkshakes €4.50. Beer €4-5. Open daily 9am-1am.) Later, head down the street to **Byzantio,** Zinopoulou 12, the late-night bar of choice for most young Karpenisians. Pounding beats give way to more melodic Greek songs as the night wears on. (Beer €4-6. Mixed drinks €6. Cover €3; includes 1 drink. Open daily 10pm-3am.) A number of bars draw partiers out into the night just past the police station (be on your best behavior) on Eth. Antistasis. The most popular is breezy **Cinema Cafe,** which has an outdoor plateia and great mountain views. Take a left after the police station and it will be on the right. (Coffee €2-3. Beer €3-5.

Mixed drinks €3-6. Open daily 8:30am-late.) For live traditional Greek music, head to **Musikes Epafes,** Kosma Aitovou 17, down from the Klimataria Restaurant, above the billiard parlor. (☎22370 25 555. Open F-Sa.)

■ DAYTRIPS FROM KARPENISI. Outside Karpenisi, small villages and traditional settlements lure visitors to the sites of gorgeous rural views and hikes; old-fashioned stone houses rest on the shores of lakes while herds of goats snooze on hillsides. Getting to the small village of **Proussos** is an adventure in itself; enjoy the roadside scenery and admire your taxi driver's uncanny ability to maintain control of his vehicle as it swerves alongside steep ravines and past intermittent, flimsy guardrails. The **Monastery of the Virgin of Proussiotissa** is well worth the trip. Clinging spectacularly to the cliffside, the innermost sanctuary was blasted out of the stone itself. Inside is an icon of the Madonna said to have been painted by St. Luke the Evangelist and believed to work miracles, which may have something to do with the monastery's abundant stock of heavenly **■loukoumi** (Turkish jellied candy covered in powdered sugar), offered to visitors by the hospitable monks. In the evenings, the monks' chanting mingles with the sound of rushing water from the Karpenisiotis River and echoes through the ravine. (Modest dress required.) Proussos's **clock tower** belts out the hour from its precarious hilltop perch. The **Castle of Karaiskakis** is a small stone fortress, now more of a crumbling tower than a castle, near the monastery. The dark **Black Cave,** a rumored ancient oracle and a hideout for Greek women and children during the War of Independence, is along a trail that begins on the far side of the village near a bridge; bring a flashlight to explore. Proussos has no hotels, but as in most Evritanian villages, many homes offer fairly inexpensive **domatia;** most are in the main village. On the road above the monastery complex, the balcony tables at **Proussiotissa ❷** (☎22370 80 768) overlook the monastery, clock tower, and gorge below. The friendly, English-speaking owner serves local specialties like roast goat with tomato sauce (€5).

Proussos is 15km beyond Megalo Horio (32km beyond Karpenisi). Buses (6am, 1pm; €2.50) run from Karpenisi. You can also catch the bus as it heads by Megalo or Mikro Horio; walk back down to the main road or to the tiny hamlet of Gavros. Ask to be let off at the monastery, on the left side of the road before you enter the village. Verify the return time with your driver as you exit the bus.

MIKRO Μικρο AND MEGALO HORIO Μεγάλο χωριό ☎22370

Fifteen kilometers down the road from Karpenisi and accessible by bus (20min.; 7am, 1pm; €1) are the "Little Villages," divided into Neo (new) and Paleo (old). Paleo Mikro Horio was largely destroyed in WWII when bombs scarred the village and occupying Nazis executed the town's 13 leading dignitaries. The town's bad luck continued in a 1963 landslide which demolished the western section of the village. After the disaster, the population relocated down the hill to Neo Mikro Horio (pop. 250) on the slopes of **Mount Helidona.** The route to the top of the mountain (3hr.) starts near the bus stop; a view of the river valleys and Kremaston Lake is the reward for the uphill trek. Lodgings range from simple, cheap domatia to expensive ski-lodge-style hotels. **To Horiatiko ❷** (Το Χοριατικο), just on the left as you enter the village from the main road, is a restaurant that rents its upstairs rooms during low season. Colorful flowers pave the way to beautifully furnished, spacious rooms which have large balconies facing the mountains. (☎22370 41 103. Entrees €3-8. Doubles €30.) **Yonia ❸** (Γονια), a right-hand turn from the main road up past To Horiatiko, has white-walled, tiled rooms with baths and a small communal kitchen. (☎22370 41 393. Singles and doubles €35.) Down the road from Mikro Horio, headed toward Proussos, Megalo Horio (pop. 200) is not so much a village as a handful of stone houses tossed haphazardly down an Evritanian hillside. As you stroll from the top of the village down on roads that turn into staircases and back to roads again, tin-roofed, weather-torn huts gradually develop into sparkling mountain vacation homes. Perched midway up the hillside, the *kafeneion* tables on the plateia overlook the breathtaking gorge of the Karpenisiotis River. An enormous gnarled plane tree shades the plateia, and a semi-circle of lime trees fills the summer air with the delicate scent of their blossoms. A few meters above the plateia, the main road in Megalo Horio splits in two. The left branch houses the trailhead for the 3hr. climb up Mt. Kaliakouda, marked clearly to the top with red blazes. The right branch curves quickly downhill and meanders past gorgeous homes on its way to the **Folklore Museum,** where displays of costumes and household objects shed light onto life in this rural village. (☎22370 41 502. Open F-Su 10am-2pm. Free.) Like the rest of Evritania, Megalo Horio has a number of rooms to let scattered throughout the village. The captivating rooms at ⬛**To Petrino** ❸ (Το Πετρινο), down from the plateia and up the road by the church, are extremely well furnished, each with TV, fridges, and baths; some have balconies and fireplaces. (☎22370 41 187. Singles €30; doubles €30-45. Stays over 5 days discounted.) **Hotel Antigoni** ❷ (Αντιγονη), in the plateia, is a cozy and inviting place to stay with TV, baths, and balconies. Its staff serves sandwiches, omelettes, and coffee downstairs all day. (☎22370 41 395. Breakfast included. Singles €25; doubles €40; triples €55.) For a sit-down dinner, **Karveli** ❷ (Καρβελη), just past the plateia on the left, offers pizzas and other dishes. (☎22370 41 339. Beer €2-3. Entrees €4-7.) Reach Megalo Horio by the **bus** (25min.; 7am, 1pm; €1) that runs from **Karpenisi** and through **Mikro Horio.**

LAMIA Λαμία ☎22310

Sprawling Lamia is a jumping-off point for travelers bound for Northern or Central Greece. The city was important during the War of Independence and became the gateway for the newly independent Greece in 1884; currently, it serves as a decentralized and somewhat confusing transportation hub. Though most visitors only stay in Lamia long enough to see the inside of a bus station, the city has enough excitement to entertain those looking to take a break from traveling. With its shop-lined streets, engaging Archaeological Museum, swinging nightlife, and bustling plateias, Lamia is a rich, eclectic city.

⌐ TRANSPORTATION

Trains: There are 2 train stations in Lamia.

Local train station, Konstantinopoulos 1. Down the street from the local bus station, 2 trains per day head to **Athens** (3hr.; 5:40am, 6:30pm; €6.20).

Lionokladi train station (☎22310 61 061). Located about 10km west of Lamia, the Lionokladi station is the city's main rail stop and is along the Athens-Thessaloniki line. Intercity trains run to: **Athens** (3hr., 5 per day 9am-5am, €7) via **Livadia** (1hr., €5); **Thebes** (1½hr., €4.20); **Thessaloniki** (3¾hr., 5 per day 10:15am-10:50pm, €9.20). Express trains available at higher prices; call the station for information. To reach the station, catch the bus marked "Stavros" ("Σταυρος") either at the local bus station or the corner of Drosopolou and Hatzopolou at Pl. Parkou (10min., every hr. 6:05am-9:05pm, €0.70). You can also purchase train tickets at the **OSE office,** Averof 28 (☎22310 23 201), the 3rd

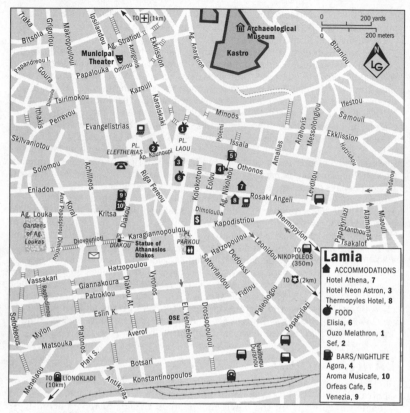

right down El. Venizelou from the southwestern corner of Pl. Parkou. There, a bus will bring you to the station (2 per hr.), but beware of extra charges (€2-5).

Buses: There are 4 intercity stations and 1 local station.

Papakiriazi 27 (☎22310 51 345). To **Athens** (3hr.; every hr. 5am-4pm, 5:30, 6:30, 9:15pm; €15). Take the Athens bus and ask to be let off at **Agios Kostantinos** (45min., €3.50) for ferries to the **Sporades.** Arriving from Athens turn left exiting the station and you will reach Satovriandou. Turn right and walk uphill to reach Pl. Parkou.

Botsari 5 (☎22310 28 955). Headed downhill from Pl. Parkou, walk down Satovriandou and turn right onto Botsari. The station, 1 block on the right, serves **Karpenisi** (1½hr., 5 per day 7am-9pm, €5.20) and the **Evritania** region.

Nikopoleos 1 (☎22310 22 802). Follow Thermopylon south away from the city. After the railroad tracks, Nikopoleos forks off to the left; the station is in a small shop on the left. Buses run to: **Agrinio** (4hr.; 2:30, 6:45pm; €17); **Delphi** (2hr.; M-Sa 3 per day 10:40am-7pm, Su 12:45, 7pm; €6.50) via **Amfissa** (1½hr., €5); **Halkida** (2½hr.; 1, 8pm; €11.30); **Karditsa** (M-Th, Sa 8 per day 10:45am-9:45pm, F, Su 7 per day 10:45am-9:45pm; €6.30); **Patras** (4hr.; M-F, Sa 4 per day 12:30pm-1am, Sa 3 per day 12:30-7:15pm; €14); **Thessaloniki** (4hr.; M-Sa 11am, 6pm, Su 11am; €19) via **Larisa** (2hr., €10); **Trikala** (2½hr.; M-Th, Sa 7 per day 10:45am-7:45pm, F, Su 6 per day 10:45am-7:45pm; €7.10).

Rosaki Angeli 69: (☎22310 22 627), near the meeting point of Rosaki Angeli and Kapodistriou. To: **Agia Marina** (20min., 4 per day 6:20-9am, €1), **Raches** (50min., 5 per day 5:45am-8pm; €2.40), and **Volos** (2hr.; M-F, Su 9:15am, Sa 9am; €9.30).

Local bus station, Konstantinopoulos 2 (☎22310 51 348), below the city, near the railroad tracks where Satovriandou intersects Konstantinopoulos. Several buses a day go to small towns and villages around Lamia. To the **Lionokladi train station** (15min., every hr. 6am-9pm, €1).

Taxis: (☎22310 34 555). At stands in each of the 4 main plateias. Available 24hr.

✦ 🛈 ORIENTATION AND PRACTICAL INFORMATION

Inland off the Maliakos Gulf and 160km north of Athens, Lamia climbs gently to a northwesterly ridge, crowned by the **kastro** in the north. The city sprawls out from the roughly rectangular arrangement of its four central plateias. Southeastern **Plateia Parkou** is broad, crowded, and lined with banks. Maps are posted at its northern edge. From Pl. Parkou's northeastern corner, past the National Bank, **Kolokotroni** leads north to leafy **Plateia Laou.** West from Plateia Parkou up **Karagiannopolou** is sleepy **Plateia Diakou.** Head up **Riga Fereou** in the northwestern corner of Pl. Parkou to reach **Plateia Eleftherias,** home of Lamia's trendiest nightlife. Pl. Eleftherias connects with Pl. Diakou via **Diakou** on its southern side and with Pl. Laou via **Apostoli Kounoupi** on the eastern side. A network of small streets including **Rosaki Angeli** and **Karaiskaki** interlaces the squares and bursts with small cafes.

Pl. Parkou teems with banks, including a **National Bank,** Kapodistriou 1, at the corner of Kolokotroni, which has a **24hr. ATM.** (☎22310 57 607. Open M-Th 8am-2:30pm, F 8am-2pm.) The **police** are about 2km out of town. To reach the station, take a taxi or follow Leonidou out of the city onto Athinon; it's on the right, about a block past Kavafi. (☎22310 56 845. Limited English spoken. Open 24hr.) The 24hr. **hospital** (☎22310 56 100 or 22310 56 200) is just over 1km north of the city on Karaiskaki. The **OTE,** Skilvaniotou 1, is on the western side of Pl. Eleftherias. (Open M, W, Sa 7:30am-2pm, Tu, Th-F 7:30am-2pm and 5:30-9pm.) **Internet access** is available at **Bet.Net,** Rosaki Angeli 40, across the street from Hotel Athena. The back room is lined with computers and comfortable chairs. (☎22310 67 424. Noon-midnight €2.50 per hr., midnight-6am €2 per hr., 6am-noon €1.50 per hr. Open 24hr.) You can also get connected at **INET Cafe,** Ipsilandou 6, just north of Pl. Eleftherias. (☎22310 46 388. €2 per hr. Open 9am-2am.) The **post office,** in Pl. Diakou, offers **Poste Restante.** (☎22310 22 237. Open M-F 7:30am-8pm.) **Postal Code:** 35100.

🛌 🍴 ACCOMMODATIONS AND FOOD

Those who choose to spend the night in Lamia can stay at any number of moderately priced hotels in the heart of the city, although the area is bustling and noisy all night long. **Hotel Neon Astron ❸,** Pl. Laou 5, offers comfortable rooms with TV, A/C, phones, and baths. (☎22310 26 245. Singles €28; doubles €34; triples €40.) **Hotel Athena ❸,** Rosaki Angeli 41, two blocks east of Pl. Laou, has new, sparkling rooms fully equipped with baths, hair dryers, TV, A/C, phones, and huge balconies. (☎22310 20 700. Singles €30; doubles €40; triples €50.) **Thermopyles Hotel ❸,** Rosaki Angeli 36, has 15 tidy rooms with TV, phones, A/C, small balconies, and baths. (☎22310 26 393. Singles €30; doubles €40.)

For fresh fruits and veggies, head to the markets along Rosaki Angeli and Othonos, both off Pl. Laou. **🗷Ouzo Melathron ❷,** Aristoteli 3, off Pl. Laou (the stairs on the northern side), has a 5 ft. long menu that brims with creativity as it combines exotic and reinvented traditional dishes. The food, beautifully presented in giant portions, is served in a lush courtyard under the glow of lanterns. Each meal comes with a complimentary crepe or scoop of ice cream served on a silver platter. (☎22310 31 502; www.ouzomelathron.gr. Entrees €4-8.50. Open daily 1pm-midnight.) For a traditional Greek meal, visit **Elisia ❷** (Ηλυσια), Kalyva Bakogianni 10, just off Pl. Laou, around the corner on the right from Hotel Neon Astron. Try the delicious moussaka (€3.60), or roasted veal, pork, or lamb.

(☎22310 27 006. Open daily 6am-midnight.) **Sef ❶** (Σεφ), Ap. Kounoupi 1, just off Pl. Laou, serves an arsenal of sweet and savory crepes (€1.50-3) to famished crowds well into the morning. (☎22310 42 001. Open daily 9am-late.)

👁 SIGHTS

The imposing remains of the **kastro** loom eerily over the city. Built in the Classical period, it has undergone many renovations under the Romans, Franks, Catalans, and Ottomans. Before Greece's 1884 annexation of Thessaly and Domokos, Lamia's *kastro* served as the core of the country's border defenses. The barracks building, built by King Otto in 1880, was used until WWII. It now serves as a spacious and well-organized **Archaeological Museum** that displays items found in tombs outside Lamia from the Neolithic to Roman periods. Aside from the numerous ceramic figurines and *amphorae*, highlights include the earliest preserved vase depicting a naval battle, a reconstructed floor mosaic, gold and bronze jewelry, and a fearsome collection of rusty weaponry. Head east out of Pl. Parkou on Kapodistriou and make the second left onto Amalias. Walk up the hill and cross Eklision when Amalias dead-ends to go up a stone stairway. Turn right and follow the road at the top of the stairs, with the *kastro* on your left. (☎22310 29 992. Museum and *kastro* open Tu-Su 8:30am-3pm. €2, students and under 18 free.) The way to the **Gardens of Agios Loukas,** a peaceful park on Ag. Loukas hill, begins at the top of Pl. Diakou behind a gloriously posed **Statue of Athanasios Diakos.** A War of Independence hero, Diakos was burned to death by the Turks in 1821. Take the steps up to the top, then go right to reach the gardens.

🎵 🎭 ENTERTAINMENT AND NIGHTLIFE

People congregate nightly in Pl. Eleftherias, filling the seats at the many cafes and nearby bars. From May through September, **Agora,** Othonos 8, two blocks east of Pl. Laou on the right and down the steps, entertains crowds in its outdoor courtyard where the DJ plays fast-paced dance music. (☎22310 51 350. Beer €4-6. Mixed drinks €6-7. Open daily 8pm-late.) Just past Agora and down the stairs at the **Orfeas Cafe,** Othonos 10, bright paintings and soft music set a mellower scene for the tables that fill its alleyway. (☎22310 50 645. Beer €2.50-5. Mixed drinks €5. Open daily 6pm-3am.) Several cafes on Diakou, the street that runs between Pl. Eleftherias and Pl. Diakou, shed their daytime roles to cater to the nighttime bar crowd. Those like **Venezia,** Diakou 6 (☎22310 46 525; open daily 8:30am-3am), and neighboring **Aroma Musicafe,** Diakou 8 (☎22310 36 808; open daily 8am-3am), compete with the other establishments on the street for Lamia's cosmopolitan youth.

AGIOS KONSTANTINOS Άγιος Κονσταντίνος ☎22350

Situated at the point where the mountainous mainland meets the Aegean Sea, Agios Konstantinos is the closest port to Athens that has ferries to the Sporades. It functions less as a destination in itself than as a gateway for those taking to the water. Still, its quaint personality makes waiting for a ferry or a bus easy to bear.

Accommodations in Agios Kostantinos are somewhat limited; hospitality, however, is not. Friendly **Hotel Olga ❷,** 11 Evoikou, is the first in the strip of hotels along the highway to the right of the plateia (facing inland). Spacious, white-tiled rooms have A/C, phones, fridges, TV, baths, and views of the harbor from private balconies. (☎/fax 22350 32 266. Singles €25-29; doubles €35-40; triples €35-50.) **Hotel Poulia ❷,** 4 Thermopylon, is in the center of town off the right side of the plateia. Small rooms come with varying levels of amenities, from stark singles with shared baths to doubles with TV, A/C, and private baths. Home-cooked breakfast is served at the bar downstairs. (☎22350 33 663. Singles €20-30; doubles €25-40; triples €30-40.) **Kaltsas Grill House ❷** on the right side of the plateia (facing inland) serves generous portions of meat. (☎22350 33 323. Pitas €1.30-2.20. Entrees €5-8. Open daily 9am-1am.) For something smaller to tide you over until the next meal, **Artopoeia ❶,** 3 Thermopylon, by Hotel Poulia, sells bread and pastries (€0.50-2) heaping with powdered sugar. (☎22350 31 684. Open daily 6am-10pm.)

Buses pick up and drop off those arriving or departing by ferry in front of the Galaxias Supermarket, 150m to the left (facing inland) on the waterfront. For times, call the bus station at ☎22350 32 223. **Buses** go to Athens (2½hr., 15 per day 5:45am-10pm, €11.50), Lamia (45min., every hr. 7:30am-7:30pm and 8:30-11:30pm, €3.50), and Thessaloniki (4hr.; 7am, 2pm; €24.50). The pier, immediately seaward of the plateia, serves both ferries and Flying Dolphins (☎22350 31 874). Buy your tickets at the right side of the plateia (facing inland). **Ferries** leave for Alonnisos (4½hr.: M-Th 11am; F 4pm; Sa 9am, 5:30pm; Su 1:30, 11:55pm: €31.20), via Skiathos (3hr., €23) and Skopelos (4hr., €31.20). Check departure times posted outside the ticket offices or call ☎22350 32 444. **Flying Dolphins** provide faster service for the same route, going to Alonnisos (2hr.: M-F, Su 10:30am, 7:15pm; Sa 10:30am, 1:15pm: €32), via Skiathos (1½hr., €23.30), and Skopelos (1¾hr., €32). **Taxis** (☎22350 31 850) line up behind the church. The **port police** (☎22350 31 920), above the ticket offices, can help with ferry schedules. Facing seaward in the plateia, turn right toward the bus station to find the **National Bank,** which has a **24hr. ATM.** (Open M-Th 8am-2:30pm, F 8am-2pm.) A left turn from the plateia takes you past the **OTE.** (Open M-F 8am-3pm.) A sign for the **post office,** 5 Riga Feraiou, 20m inland, is on the left (☎22350 31 855; open M-F 7:30am-2pm). **Postal Code:** 35006.

THESSALY Θεσσαλία

From the urban bustle of Volos and Larisa to the peaceful villages sprinkled across the Mt. Pelion Peninsula, Thessaly runs the gamut of lifestyles and attractions. The larger cities are home to some of the wildest nightlife on mainland Greece, while the otherworldly monasteries at Meteora define themselves by spiritual simplicity. Thessaly's plains tell the story of a more rural life, as they have long been home to farmers who tend sheep and goats in the summer before returning home to fish from the waters of the Pinios River. In this out-of-the-way region, you'll find a wealth of genuine hospitality but very little English.

VOLOS Βόλος ☎24210

Wayfaring Jason gave this city a permanent place in Greek mythology. It was from Volos that he and the Argonauts set sail on their quest for the Golden Fleece, a legend that the modern city has in no way forgotten: two main streets and half a dozen hotels are named in tribute to the ancient story. Much of contemporary Volos, however, has been shaped by historical rather than mythological events. In the 1923 population exchange (p. 60), many ethnic Greeks from Turkey came to the shores of the Pagasitic Gulf, significantly increasing the population of the city until it soon became one of Greece's largest. The Orthodox refugees brought their passion for carousing to Volos, establishing the countless *tsipouradika* that have brought the city national fame. Come nightfall, strolling couples fill Volos's harborside and dozens of cafes and seafood restaurants push tables up to the water.

▐ TRANSPORTATION

Trains: ☎24210 24 056. Take Lambraki out of town and turn right at the flags at the end of the park. Walk 2-3min. down the road parallel to the track. Trains go to **Larisa** (Intercity: 45min., 6:30am, €6; regular: 1hr., 15 per day 6am-11:20pm, €2.10). You must go to Larisa and change trains for **Athens** and **Thessaloniki.**

Buses: ☎24210 33 254. In the Old Town, about a 10min. walk up Lambraki. To: **Agios Ioannis** (2½hr., 3 per day 5am-1:30pm, €4.40); **Athens** (4½hr., 12 per day 5:30am-1am, €20); **Larisa** (1hr., 12 per day 5:45am-1am, €4.10); **Makrynitsa** (45min., 10 per day 6:15am-9:30pm, €1.10) via **Portaria** (40min., €1); **Milies** (1hr., 6 per day 6am-7:30pm, €2); **Thessaloniki** (3hr., 9 per day 4:30am-8:30pm, €13.40); **Trikala** (2½hr., 4 per day 6:30am-7pm, €10.10); **Tsagarada** (1½hr., 4 per day 5am-3:30pm, €3.30). Service reduced Sa-Su and in winter.

Ferries: To **Alonnisos** (4hr., 2 per week, €18), **Skiathos** (2¼hr., 2 per day, €13.10), and **Skopelos** (3½hr., 2 per day, €17). Waterfront agencies like English-speaking **Sporades Travel,** 33 Argonafton, sell tickets. (☎24210 23 400. Open daily 6am-9pm.)

Flying Dolphins: 3 per day go to **Alonnisos** (2hr.; 9:15am, 1, 7:30pm; €30) via **Skiathos** (1¼hr., €22), **Glossa** (1½hr., €24), and **Skopelos** (1¾hr., €28.20). The agencies near the pier all sell tickets. Try **Falcon Tours,** Argonafton 34. (☎24210 21 626; www.hellenicseaways.gr. Open daily 7am-10pm.)

Taxis: ☎24210 27 777. 24hr. taxis line up in front of Pl. Ag. Konstantinou.

Car Rental: Avis, Argonafton 41 (☎24210 20 849). Mopeds €25 per day. Cars from €59 per day. Open 8:30am-9:30pm. **European Car Rental,** Iasonos 83 (☎24210 36 238), has cars from €54 per day. Open M-Sa 9am-9pm, Su 9am-1pm, 6-9pm.)

◼✶▐ ORIENTATION AND PRACTICAL INFORMATION

Volos's bus station and tourist office are located on **Lambraki,** the city's main road, an easy 10min. walk west from the city and the waterfront. On its way into town, the road also runs past the train station and **Riga Fereou Park** before coming to an end at a fountain. **Argonafton,** the waterfront walkway, begins just farther down, and is home to lively tavernas and cafes, along with most of the city's foot traffic. Moving inland, **Iasonos** and **Dimitriados** are the next two parallel streets to the water; both are packed with banks, bakeries, and fast-food joints. After Dimitriados and also parallel to Argonafton, **Ermou,** a pedestrian-only street, contains boutiques that sell women's clothes and shoes. Near the center of the city, it leads into an open plateia with the **Church of Agios Nikolaos.** The point at which Ermou becomes **Polymeri** marks the start of the long seaside park. The **Church of Agios Konstantinos,** easily visible from the docks jutting out into the harbor, sits at the end of the park. Here, Argonafton and Dimitriados join to become **Nikolaou Plastira.** This quieter street heads past a local *ouzeria* to the hospital and the Archaeological Museum before ending at Volos's popular **Anavrou beach** in the residential section of town.

Tourist Office: ☎24210 20 273. Across the street from the bus station up Lambraki, in the large brick building with the fountain. Has **maps,** transportation timetables, and info about both Volos and the Pelion Peninsula. Open daily 8am-10pm.

Banks: There are several major banks on Iasonos, including 2 **National Banks** at Iasonos 50 and 91. (☎24210 90 800 and 24210 34 811. Open M-Th 8am-2:30pm, F 8am-2pm.) Most have **currency exchange** and **ATMs.** There's also a **Citibank,** Argonafton 27, on the corner of El. Venizelou, with a **24hr. ATM.** (☎24210 76 380. Open M-Th 8am-2:30pm, F 8am-2pm.)

Bookstore: Newsstand, Iasonos 78 (☎24210 23 200), 1 block inland from the meeting point of the port and Argonafton, sells a small collection of English novels, magazines, history books, and travel guides, including *Let's Go* titles. Open daily 8am-10pm.

Police: ☎24210 39 061. On the corner of Ath. Gazi and Ath. Diakou. Open 24hr. The **tourist police,** 28 Oktovriou 179 (☎24210 39 065), provide guides and free **maps** of the city. Open daily 8am-10pm.

Hospital: Polymeri 134 (☎24210 94 200), next to the museum. Open 24hr.

Telephones: OTE, El. Venizelou 22 (☎24210 95 936), on the corner of El. Venizelou and Sokratous. Open daily 7:30am-2pm.

Internet Access: ⊠The Network: Volos #1, Iasonos 141, is a gamer's paradise, lined with flat-screen computers. It also acts as the mother-ship to many smaller locations in the area, including **Volos #2** across the street. (☎24210 30 260. €2.50 per hr.; gaming €1.50 per hr. Open 24hr.) **Diavlos Youth Center,** Topali 14 (☎24210 25 363), off Dimitriados, has the best rates in town. €1.60 per hr. Open M-F 10am-10pm.

Post Office: Dimitriados 209 (☎24210 90 602). At the intersection of Dimitriados and Ag. Nikolaou. **Poste Restante** available. Open M-F 7:30am-8pm. **Postal Code:** 38001.

🏠 ACCOMMODATIONS

Volos's hotels vary little in location, appeal, and amenities and are almost never cheap. Most of the budget options are clustered along the waterfront or on the small streets leading away from the harbor. As usual, negotiating can slash prices.

Hotel Nefeli, Koumoundourou 10 (☎24210 30 211). Named for the queen who sent her children away from danger aboard Hermes's magic flying ram (before it provided the Golden Fleece, of course), Hotel Nefeli's friendly staff sees to its guests with comparable

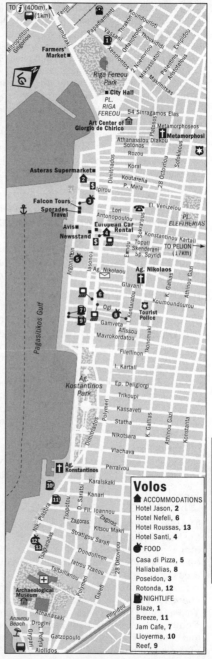

Volos

🏠 ACCOMMODATIONS
Hotel Jason, **2**
Hotel Nefeli, **6**
Hotel Roussas, **13**
Hotel Santi, **4**

🍴 FOOD
Casa di Pizza, **5**
Haliabalias, **8**
Poseidon, **3**
Rotonda, **12**

🌙 NIGHTLIFE
Blaze, **1**
Breeze, **11**
Jam Cafe, **7**
Lioyerma, **10**
Reef, **9**

care. Polished, yellow rooms come with TV, A/C, phones, balconies, and baths. Breakfast €6.50. Singles €35-48; doubles €50-58; triples €60-69. AmEx/MC/V. ❹

Hotel Roussas (Ρουσσας), Iatrou Tzanou 1 (☎24210 21 732), on the corner of Nik. Plastira and Iatrou Tzanou, in a peaceful section of town; look for the purple balconies. Though removed from the main waterfront, Roussas, whose attractive rooms have baths, fridges, phones, A/C, TV, and balconies, is ideal for those looking to spend time relaxing on the beach. Singles €30; doubles €38; triples €46. ❸

Hotel Jason, P. Mela 1 (☎24210 26 075), on the waterfront, across from the ferry dock, is a good deal considering its convenient location. Though only some of the gleaming, pink and white rooms have A/C, most have balconies overlooking the water, and all have phones, baths, fans, and TV. Singles €25-30; doubles €40-45; triples €60. ❸

Hotel Santi, Topali 13 (☎24210 33 341), off Argonafton. Basic rooms with miraculously soft pillows include private baths, TV, phones, A/C, and small balconies. Breakfast €5. Singles €25; doubles €40; triples €50. ❷

⬛ FOOD

Asteras Supermarket, Iasonos 34-38 (☎24210 31 524; open M-F 7:30am-9pm, Sa 7:30am-6pm), and a **farmers' market,** on Lambraki toward the bus station, can provide provisions for a seaside picnic. Splurging on ouzo and *tsipoura* at one of Volos's signature waterfront *ouzeria* will undoubtedly be memorable. Each has a wide selection of *mezedes*, including seafood plates with prawns and octopus.

▨ **Haliabalias,** hidden in a niche on I. Kontaratou; most locals will know where it is. There is no set menu, but patrons can walk inside and choose from the three or four deliciously filling home-style meals prepared for the day. Entrees €4-6. ❷

Poseidon, Argonafton 31 (☎24210 36 629), opposite the ferry dock. This governing seafood presence on the waterfront offers the day's fresh catches, staying impressively crowded well past midnight in the summer. Shrimp salad €9. Fish and seafood €35-60 per kg. Open daily 9am-3am. Neighboring **Iolkos,** Argonafton 32 (☎24210 35 227), offers similar dishes at identical prices and hours. ❸

Rotonda, Nik. Plastira 15 (☎24210 34 973), next to Hotel Roussas on the eastern edge of town. This popular lunch spot specializes in fresh whole fish and calamari and swordfish souvlaki. Fish and seafood €40-55 per kg. Open daily 8am-1am. AmEx/MC/V. ❸

Casa di Pizza, Argonafton 49 (☎24210 24 50), on the waterfront between Sp. Spyridi and Ag. Nikolaou, past Goody's heading east. As the name suggests, you can order pizza (large €6.20-7.80) and other Italian fare here. Open daily noon-2am. MC/V. ❷

◉ SIGHTS

The ▨**Archaeological Museum,** Athanasaki 1, a 20min. walk along the water from the ferry docks, occupies a Neoclassical mansion and displays fascinating reconstructed tombs and *stelae* from Demetrias. The panoply of miniature Neolithic objects includes figurines, seals, spindle whorls, bits of jewelry, carbonized seeds, and tools of bone and stone. (☎24210 25 285. Open Tu-Su 8:30am-3pm. €2, seniors €1, students free.) The museum can also provide English pamphlets about the nearby archaeological sites at **Dimini** and **Sesklo.** Both are close to Volos; Dimini is 4km west of the city center and Sesklo is another 5.5km farther along the connecting road. Taxis there range €4-7. Dimini dates from 4000 BC and contains two major sites; the main site was constructed sometime at the end of the 5th millennium BC, and the more recent of the two, southwest of the main site, was built during the Mycenaean period. Both sites have ruins of houses and evidence of early city planning. Sesklo is the oldest known settlement in Thessaly and has the oldest acropolis in all of Greece, dating from 6500 BC. (☎24210 85 960. Both open Tu-Su 8am-8pm. €2, seniors €1, students free. Tickets cover both sites.) The ⬛Art Center of Giorgio de Chirico, Metamorphoseos 3, next to the conservatory, showcases fascinating temporary exhibits of Greek modern art. The permanent collection upstairs is comprised of 19th- and 20th-century pieces. (☎24210 31 701. Open M-F 10am-1pm and 6-9pm, Sa 10am-1pm, Su 6-9pm. Free.)

🎵 NIGHTLIFE

The waterfront between the docks and Ag. Konstantinos becomes a hive of activity at night. Each of the cafes has its own character—you can "window-shop" while taking an evening stroll down the water's edge. Young Greeks congregate at **Jam Cafe,** Argonafton 62 (☎24210 76 156), and **Reef** (☎24210 24 168), next door with the blue phosphorescent glow, chatting over loud music and pings of the games from the arcade around the corner. (Beer €3.50-5. Drinks €6-7.50. Both open daily 9am-4am.) Cafe-bars toward the east, by the museum and beach, dominate with pounding beats. **Breeze,** Nik. Plastira 4B (☎24210 35 420; open daily 8am-3am), plays house and pop, and **Lioyerma,** nearby on the water, rocks an outdoor bar and a sprawling network of couches and tables (☎24210 36 178; beer €3.50-5; mixed drinks €6.50-7; open daily 9am-6am). After getting drunk enough to let loose on the dance floor, locals head to **Blaze,** by the train station. (☎24210 88 332. Mixed drinks €8. Cover €8; includes 1 drink. Open M-Th, Su until 3:30am, F-Sa until 6am.) For an even wilder time with a slightly heftier price tag, grab a cab (€4) to **Alykes.** This beach suburb hosts **Astra,** a popular traditional *bouzouki* haven. (☎24210 62 182. Cover €10; includes 1 drink. Open F-Sa midnight-4am.) For more *bouzouki* dancing and *rembetika* tunes, head to equally massive **Fengaria,** also in Alykes. (☎24210 88 733. Cover €8-9; includes 1 drink. Open W-Sa midnight-4am.) The disco of choice in Alykes is **Noa,** a restaurant and bar that switches gears around 1am, when it blasts music for countless young Thessalians who dance until dawn. (Mixed drinks €8-9. Open Su-Th until 3:30am, F-Sa until 6am.)

MOUNT PELION PENINSULA
Όρος Πήλιο

Way back before propriety, the Mt. Pelion Peninsula was home to a group of rowdy centaurs. These mythical half-men, half-horses—well known for their insatiable sex drives, which drove them to have their way with whatever hot young nymphets they could find—followed Chiron, their king, to the area. Also a healer and tutor to Achilles, Chiron was lured to Pelion by its abundant supply of over 1700 medicinal herbs. The cool, moist peninsula is a delicious anomaly in mostly sun-scorched Greece. Over the years, the mountains of Pelion have protected the area from invasion. While the rest of Greece groaned under Ottoman rule, the peninsula was a virtually autonomous center of Greek nationalism.

MAKRYNITSA Μακρυνίτσα   ☎24280

Perched in the Pelion mountain range, serene Makrynitsa soars over the Pagasitic Gulf. Its breathtaking views of the Volos metropolitan area have earned the town the apt nickname of the "balcony of Pelion." In contrast to the urban sprawl below, Makrynitsa, though touristed, is an escape from city life; the small town extends only a few hundred meters in three directions from the main plateia, and cars are

THE TOOTH FAIRY'S NIGHTMARE

The Italians have their gelato, and the French their fancy, creamy cheeses, but when it comes to decadent, caloric goodness, they've got nothing on the marvelously rich *glykismata* (desserts) of Greek cuisine.

Greek pastries are traditionally comprised of some combination of fresh honey, chopped nuts, and phyllo dough—a light, flaky-thin crust made from layers of butter. *Kadaife*, resembling an overgrown Kellogg's® mini-wheat, is a fine example of this blessed union: shredded wheat and phyllo crammed with nuts, honey, and cinnamon. *Galactobourico* is a slight variation on the rule, as the honey-draped pastry is filled with a dense egg custard rather a nut mixture. Coffee lovers should find a spot next to their *kafe* for *karidopeta*, a dark, moist nut cake similar in consistency to a coffee or carrot cake, and topped with a syrup coating. *Loukoumathes*, warm, deep-fried balls of dough, are the Greek equivalent of donuts, though they are usually eaten as an afternoon snack rather than a breakfast food. The celebrated granddaddy of all Greek *glykismata*, is, of course, baklava, comprised of layer upon layer phyllo filled with nuts, spices, and sticky honey syrup.

Most bakeries will offer to box your pastry to go, making it easy to enjoy it in a plateia whose public water fountains make cleaning up nice and convenient.

forbidden due to its designation as a protected traditional settlement. In the early evening, the setting sun illuminates the gulf with deep red and orange hues. Come nightfall, Makrynitsa looks down onto the indigo- and white-speckled valley like the best box seat in a giant opera house.

TRANSPORTATION AND PRACTICAL INFORMATION. Makrynitsa is accessible by daily **buses** from Volos (45min., 10 per day 6:15am-9:30pm; €1.10), which twist their way up the mountainside and through the neighboring village of **Portaria** (40min., €1). From the bus turnaround, a short walk up the hill takes you to the parking lot. Here, the left-most road, **17 Martiou,** leads to the plateia, and passes shops purveying tourist kitsch and medicinal and kitchen herbs. In Portaria, a 20min. walk from Makrynitsa's parking lot along the mountain road, you can catch buses to other Pelion destinations, including the beaches at Agios Yiannis and Milopotamos. A **police station** (☎24280 99 105; open 8am-2pm), **24hr. ATMs,** and a **post office** (☎24280 99 104; open M-F 8am-2pm) can be found in Portaria, and there are **pay phones** and a **mailbox** in Makrynitsa's plateia. **Postal Code:** 37011.

ACCOMMODATIONS AND FOOD. Because of its protected status, staying in Makrynitsa during the winter high season costs a fortune (singles around €65). Luckily, nearby Portaria has several exceptionally cheap **domatia** (singles around €20, doubles €30) and the upscale winter-tourist hotels offer summer visitors cheaper prices and posh rooms. On 17 Martiou headed into Makrynitsa's plateia, ⬛**Hotel Theodora** (Θεοδωρα) ❸ exudes luxury in its gorgeous, old-fashioned rooms, replete with wooden furniture, satin comforters, TV, phones, baths, and amazing views of the Pagasitic Gulf. (☎24280 99 179. Breakfast €5. Singles €30-40; doubles €50-60. MC/V.) Farther down 17 Martiou, just before the plateia, is **Hotel Kentavros** ❸, which has a garden and well-decorated rooms with TV, phones, and baths. (☎24280 99 075. Breakfast €4.50. Singles €30-50; doubles €30-70.) The rooms at **Hotel Pelia** ❸, one of two adjacent accommodations on the northern side of Portaria's plateia, have TV and baths and overlook a patio. (☎24280 99 290. Breakfast included. Singles €30; doubles €55; triples €60; quads €80.)

Several small restaurants have outdoor seating and spectacular views from elevated verandas. Most affordable is the local *ouzeria* **A-B** ❷, past the plateia on the small trail that skirts the church. From their porch at the end of town, patrons have a superb view of Makrynitsa, Volos, and the gulf far below. (☎24280 99 083. Entrees €4-6.) In the plateia, **Pantheon** ❷ monopolizes the spectacular vista of the Pagasitic Gulf, with tables that sit against the railing. The *moschari kokkonisto* (braised veal) and *kotopoulo fournou* (baked chicken) are both delicious. (☎24280 99 143. Entrees €4.50-8. Open daily 8am-midnight.) More touristed **Galini ❷** overlooks the plateia and is next to the large fountain. Sentimental tunes fill the air as diners feast on *spetsofai* (spicy sausage; €6) and rabbit stew. (☎24280 99 256. Entrees €6-7.50. Open daily 1pm-midnight.)

◙ **SIGHTS.** To reach the **Museum of Folk Art and the History of Pelion,** take the path that begins to the left of the church in the plateia and follow the signs. In a converted 1844 mansion, the museum highlights old stills used in making *tsipouro* and paintings by Christopoulos, all of which depict ships, gorgons, and sea-related subjects. (☎24280 99 505. Open Tu-Su 10am-2pm and 6-9pm. €2, students free.) In the plateia, the building across from the church contains a wall mural painted by famed folk artist **Theophilos Hadzimichali.** The town's remarkable churches include the **Church of Agios Yiannis the Baptist** in the main plateia and the peaceful church of **Kimisi Theotokou,** which once housed a *krifto scholio*, a secret school that taught the forbidden Greek language during Ottoman rule. (Churches open at the whim of their caretakers; early to mid-morning and evening are the best times to try visiting.) From the main parking lot, a road leads steeply uphill to the **Monastery of Agios Gerasimos** (20min. walking), which grants a beautiful view. (Open 7am-noon and 4-6pm.) Makrynitsa's old houses are a sight in themselves; stained-glass lanterns, false painted windows, and symbols to protect against evil spirits adorn the outer walls. You can answer that burning question of what it's like to be inside a tree just by the door of the main church in the plateia; the hollowed-out trunk of a tall, leafy tree has a handy opening that lets you slip in and out.

AGIOS IOANNIS Άγιος Ιωάννης ☎24210

Among the most distant Pelion villages from Volos, Agios Ioannis stretches along the Aegean Sea with light blue waters that lap onto lazy sand beaches. With its relaxing wonderland of forests and ferns, the small village is a favorite among travelers to the peninsula. Nearby coves and the *kalderimi* (laid stone trails) of Mouresi make for a wonderful morning or late-afternoon excursion.

▛▜ **TRANSPORTATION AND PRACTICAL INFORMATION. Buses** leave daily for Volos (2½hr.; M-F 3 per day 7:15am-5pm, Sa-Su 3 per day 8:15am-5am; €3.50) from the parking lot. **Taxis** (☎60946 08 968) are available by phone 24hr., but trips to nearby villages tend to be pricey. The entire town sits along a beachfront main street. Beginning at the town parking lot, the road heads past hotels, restaurants, and bakeries to the harbor at the far end. Near the parking lot, a bridge runs in the opposite direction over the often dry river and ends 100m farther at the beach of **Papa Nero.** The winding seaside lane will lead you to the town of **Damouhari,** 4km away. The **tourist office,** in the parking lot, dispenses **maps** and pamphlets. (☎24260 31 218. Open daily 9am-5pm.) Detailed info, boats (€55 per day), motorbikes (€20 per day), and rooms are available at the **Les Hirondelles** office, just past Plazza restaurant. (☎24260 31 181. Open daily 9:30am-10pm.) The **police** in Tsagarada can be reached at ☎24260 49 222. For **first aid,** call ☎24260 31 950. A **hospital** (☎24260 22 222) is 30km away in Zagora. **Internet access** is available at **Hotel Kentrikon** (€1.50 per 15min.), in the alley between Plazza and Kyma Taverna. An **ATM** and a **post office** (☎24260 49 215; open M-F 7:30am-2pm) are available in Tsagarada.

▛▜ **ACCOMMODATIONS AND FOOD.** Many of the hotels in Ag. Ioannis are controlled by Les Hirondelles, and are rather expensive for travelers who are not on one of their package tours. The best deal, hidden on a gravel path 300m past the river on the coastal road to Damouhari, is **Hostel Katerini ❸,** whose rooms have beach views, kitchens, and private baths. (☎24260 31 624. Doubles €45; triples €54.) Another option is **Eleni ❸**, across the river on the road to Papa Nero beach. Its comfortable rooms have baths, TV, and some kitchenettes. (☎24210 62 157. Singles €30; doubles €35; triples €40.) **Hotel Martha ❷**, toward the parking lot end of the strip, has clean rooms with private baths that practically bump up against the ocean. (☎24260 31 406. Singles €25; doubles €30; triples €35.) The **Papa Nero campground ❶**, near its namesake beach, is an ocean-front site with clean bathrooms. (☎24260 31 319. €5 per person, €4 per tent. Electricity €3.)

The strip is dominated by bakeries, cafes, supermarkets, and bars. Popular **Akrogiali ❷**, toward the far side of the walkway, serves a variety of cooked and grilled entrees (€6-10.50) to sunbathers just back from the beach. (☎24260 31 112. Pastas €3-5. Fish and seafood €40-49 per kg. Open daily 8am-midnight.) Near the middle of the strip, **Piazza ❷** serves pizza and pasta. (☎24260 32 110. Pizzas €7.50-9.50. Pasta €4.50-9. Open daily May-Oct. 11:30am-midnight.)

▓ **NIGHTLIFE.** During the summer, several waterfront bars keep the town buzzing late into the night. Ag. Ioannis's best club is **Kavos,** near the harbor, which blares house, pop, and Greek music into the steamy night. (☎24260 31 108. Beer €4. Mixed drinks €8. Open 11pm-late.) For a more intense clubbing experience, head to **Mamba,** 10km away in the Pelion beach village of Agia Saranta (taxi €7-9). A techno, house, and progressive haven for partiers looking to test their dancefloor stamina, Mamba shuts down for only 14 hours each week, officially "closing" at 8am and reopening at 10am for another day and night of hardcore partying. Enormous crowds fill the club on the weekends while international DJs spin the newest tracks. (Mixed drinks €8-9.)

DAMOUHARI Νταμούξαρη AND TSAGARADA Τσαγκαράδα

In contrast to Ag. Ioannis's packaged tourism, both Damouhari and Tsagarada are quiet, traditional villages. Tiny Damouhari consists of a handful of houses and a gorgeous cove. Next to the cove is a telephone, a convenience store, and the **Palia Damouhari ❷** taverna. (☎24260 49 175. Chicken €4.40. Octopus €7.50. Open daily 8am-midnight.) In stunning Tsagarada, immaculate gardens cascade downhill into violent bluffs as the peaceful Sporades sit far in the distance. Though reachable from Ag. Ioannis by climbing far up to the highway and then descending back down again, the village is most quickly and most spectacularly approached by walking the coastal lane to its end in Damouhari and then climbing the bluffs on a *kalderimi*. Tsagarada has succumbed to some tourism of the particularly expensive variety, but its sprawling layout preserves the village's charm. Spread across a wide area on the slope just below the highway, Tsagarada is comprised of four hamlets: Ag. Kyriaki, Ag. Paraskevi, Ag. Stefanou, and Ag. Taxiarhon. Visitors arriving by way of the Damouhari-Tsagarada *kalderimi* will enter at Ag. Paraskevi, and emerge onto the road by the charming **Villa Ton Rodon ❹**, whose rooms have private baths and TV. Shuttered doors opening onto porches perched above brilliant rose bushes and a panoramic view of the sea justify the higher prices. (☎24260 49 340. Breakfast included. Singles €40; doubles €65.) Turning left at the road, the hamlet's plateia is about 50m down and to the right. Here you will find the church of the hamlet's name and a massive 1000-year-old plane tree. From the plateia, a well-marked path leads 1hr. down to the blue-green waters and pearl-white stones of ▓**Milopotamos beach.** Up the road 20m in the other direction you'll pass the **tourist office** (☎24260 48 993; open daily 9am-3pm), and the **post office** (☎24260 49 215; open M-F 7:30am-2pm), before reaching the highway. The **ATM** is on your left when approaching the highway, and the stone-covered bus stop is just across the way. **Buses** go to Volos (1½hr., 4 per day 8am-5pm, €3.30).

WESTERN THESSALY

LARISA Λάρισα   ☎2410

As the fifth-largest city in Greece, the capital of Thessaly, and the location of a regional NATO office, Larisa is certainly of national importance. As most Greeks know, however, it's no tourism hotspot. Lacking notable sights and inherent charm, and often confusing to those unfamiliar with its numerous plateias and irregular streets, Larisa will likely be no more than a stop en route to more exciting destinations. Those who do end up staying the night, though, will find a large university community that supports some of the best nightlife in mainland Greece. During the day, tree-lined plateias, stork-crowned church domes, trendy boutiques, and chic cafes can keep you busy for a couple of hours.

▐▀ TRANSPORTATION

Trains: ☎24102 36 250. Head south on Panagouli and bear left (avoiding the sharp left) onto Paleologou at the 5-way intersection; the station is on the southern side of the small park. Intercity express trains run to **Athens** (4hr., 7 per day 3:35am-7:39pm, €10-30) and **Volos** (45min., 8:23pm, €6). Regular trains go to **Athens** (5hr., 5 per day 12:35am-9pm, €10), **Thessaloniki** (1¾hr., 8 per day 3:53am-9:19pm, €5), and **Volos** (1hr., 15 per day 5am-10:20pm, €2.10).

Buses: Buses from the main station (☎24105 37 777), 150m north of Pl. Laou at Olympou and Georgiadou, go to: **Athens** (4¼hr., 9 per day 7am-1am, €22); **Ioannina** (4hr.; 9am, 3pm; €13); **Kastoria** (4hr., 3 per day 12:30pm-12:30am, €15); **Thessaloniki** (2hr.; M-F 14 per day 9am-9pm, service reduced Sa-Su; €11); **Volos** (1hr., M-F 10 per day 7am-9:30pm, €4). The branch station, Iroön Polytechniou 14 (☎24106 10 124), sends buses to **Karditsa** (1hr., 9 per day 8am-8:30pm, €4.80) and **Trikala** (1hr., 13 per day 6:30am-8:30pm, €4.60). Head south on Olympou to Pl. Laou, where Panagouli begins; continue south on Panagouli, turn right at the 5-way intersection, and walk about 600m to the camouflaged gas station-bus stop on the left.

Taxis: ☎24106 61 414. Line up in Pl. Tahydromiou 24hr.

◪ ▮ ORIENTATION AND PRACTICAL INFORMATION

Surrounded by fertile corn and wheat fields, Larisa is just southeast of the **Pineios River**, in the middle of eastern Thessaly. The bus station in the north and the train station in the south mark the boundaries of the city's main commercial district, which forms a grid. From the bus station, **Olympou** heads south to **Plateia Laou**, one of Larisa's three main squares. Here you will meet **Panagouli**, a broad avenue that runs perpendicular to **Kyprou** and heads to the bottom of the city, where it crosses **Iroön Polytechniou** at a **five-way intersection**. Panagouli marks the eastern border of **Plateia Ethnarhou Makariou**, the town center, often called **"Plateia Tahydromiou"** ("Post Office Square"). The northern edge of this plateia is formed by **Papakyriazi**, which can be taken west three blocks to **Papanastasiou**. From here, Papanastasiou runs north to **Plateia Mikhali Sagika**, and south past the post office and tourist office. You will hit **Mandilara**, which runs east-west, two blocks south from the post office. A **map** is essential here, and you can grab one at most hotels for free.

Tourist Office: Ipirou 92 (☎24106 70 437). On Ipirou near the intersection with Botsari. Has **maps,** pamphlets, and advice. Some English spoken. Open M-F 7am-2:30pm.

Police: Papanastasiou 86 (☎24106 83 137 or 24106 83 146), 7 blocks south of Papakiriazi. Open 24hr.

Hospital: ☎24105 34 471. On Georgiadou, east of the main bus station. Open 24hr.

Telephones: OTE (☎ 24109 95 376) is across the street from the Folk Museum. Open M, W, F 8am-1:30pm and 5:30-8:30pm, Tu, Th 8am-1:30pm.

Internet Access: Chic cafe **Traffic,** Patroklou 14 (☎24102 50 210), at Rousvelt, has fast computers. €2 per hr., students €1 per hr. Frappés €2.50. Open 10am-3am.

Post Office: Papanastasiou 52 (☎24105 32 312). At Diakou. Open M-F 7:30am-8pm. **Poste Restante** and **currency exchange. Postal Code:** 41001.

🏠 🛏 ACCOMMODATIONS AND FOOD

Mid-range to upper-level hotels can be found along the side streets that connect the three main plateias. The cheapest options are near the train station and the smaller bus station, but they're a 1.5km hike south from the main bus station. In town, it's difficult to find a room for under €40. **Hotel Diethnes ❸,** Paleologou 8, on the left after exiting the train station, is a modern hotel with cool, nicely decorated rooms, a bar (drinks €5), and baths. (☎24102 82 749. Reception 24hr. Singles €27; doubles €33; triples €40.) One door down is **Hotel Pantheon ❸,** Paleologou 10. Its orange, yellow, and bright green rooms have TV, sinks, A/C, and phones; some have balconies and private baths. (☎24102 34 810. Singles €26, with bath €34; doubles €42.) **Hotel Doma ❸,** Skarlatou Soutsou 1, at the intersection with Kyprou, has spacious rooms with A/C, TV, phones, low-to-the-ground beds, and balconies in a central location. The shower in the tiny bathroom, however, is disturbingly close to the toilet. (☎24105 35 025. Breakfast €8. Singles €25; doubles €40; triples €50.)

Most of Larisa's cafes, bars, and tavernas are on Pl. Tahydromiou and its surrounding streets, where they blend into an uninterrupted river of chairs, tables, and TVs. Though crowded, the area manages to remain pleasantly lively rather than overwhelming. Tempting scents draw crowds into the *psistarias* (grills) on Panos, north of Kyprou, where lamb and whole chickens slowly turn on spits in the window of each establishment. On the southern side of Pl. Tahydromiou, **To Sidrivani ❷,** Protopapadaki 8, claims to be the oldest resturant in Larisa, though it was only established in 1974. The bubbling pots are full of delicious homemade Greek cuisine. (☎24105 35 933. Lamb with vegetables €6.50. Vegetarian entrees available. Open noon-midnight.) At **Frourio ❸,** located in the Byzantine fortress on the summit of Larisa's highest hill, straw tables covered in white tablecloths dot the grass, and are surrounded by ancient stone walls, flowering trees, and a stork-topped cathedral. (☎24109 37 173. Veal in red wine €9. Open 6pm-1am.)

🔆 SIGHTS

Larisa's disappointing archaeological sites are clustered on the city's northern hill. Two ancient theaters have been uncovered in the last century but neither is open to the public; they have been undergoing continuous restoration for over 10 years. The theaters, called **"Ancient Theater A"** and **"Ancient Theater B,"** both date from the late 3rd century BC to the beginning of the Roman period, and are located in Pl. Miteras, which begins at the corner of El. Venizelou and Papanastasiou and continues northward. In a field above Ancient Theater A are a couple of sections of columns from the ancient **acropolis,** which is no longer standing. The whole area is fenced off for construction, so all you can do is try for a quick peek. Beyond the remnants of the acropolis is the **Byzantine fortress,** where an equally tiny amount of the ruins is visible. (Open 24hr. Free.) Down the opposite side of the hill is the Peneios River. Crossing the river on Ag. Haralabous and turning right, you'll find shade-filled **Alkazar Park.** The park is without a doubt the most serene spot in the city—even the graffiti here seems decorative. At the intersection of El. Venizelou and 31 Augustou is a small yellow mosque with a single minaret that now serves as the **Archaeological Museum.** (☎24102 88 515. Open Tu-Su 8:30am-3pm. Free.) Also

showcasing Neolithic and Classical statues and ruins from the province, the collection's primary highlight is a **mosaic floor** that depicts Nike crowning Atton. The **Museum of Folk Art,** Mandilara 74, has rotating exhibits that illuminate different domestic and cultural aspects of Larisa's past. A permanent display features material elements of Thessalian culture, such as traditional costumes, weapons, coins, and embroidery. The museum also houses a large photo collection and the town's historical archives. (☎24102 87 516. Open M noon-7pm, Tu-Su 8am-5pm. Free.) The **Pinakothiki,** Mexali 28, on the corner of Patera and Mexali, about 5km from the center of town, has one of the best 20th-century art collections in Greece, with works by almost all of Greece's renowned modern artists. (☎24106 16 266. Open W-Su 10am-2:30pm and 6-8pm. €1. Students free.)

🔊 NIGHTLIFE

Larisa's lively bars rarely disappoint, as at night, the area around Pl. Tahydromiou becomes one large outdoor cafe. Dense with students, the bars and clubs generally have reasonably priced drinks (beer €3-4). Hip, young **Ermes,** Rousvelt 41, on Rousvelt and Mandilara in Pl. Trigoni, fills up before the other bars do. Though it's the least expensive of Larisa's bars, the red stools and cushy white couches make cheap feel swanky. (☎24106 21 022. Open 9am-3am.) Everything in **De-Tox,** Asclepiou 23, on the northern side of Pl. Tahydromiou, points to getting intoxicated— the menus, chairs, and bar are all a beer-colored translucent yellow, and pop music plays for drunken and still-drinking crowds. (☎24102 57 838. Beer €4.50.) Its next door neighbor, **Arco,** Papakiriazi 20, is another popular hangout, playing music late into the night. Tables spiral out into the plateia as English-speaking bartenders serve from the giant bar that dominates the middle of the cafe. (☎24105 36 798. Frappés €3. Beer €4. Mixed drinks €6. Open 9am-3:30am.) Larisa's impressive discos generally have a €5 cover (includes 1 drink). **Xilia Xeilia** (☎24102 88 845), which means "a thousand lips," is a €3 taxi ride from Pl. Tahydromiou. An enormous open-air nightclub boasting a row of towering fountains and 10 bars, it plays live Greek music every night, often featuring performances by the best *bouzouki* players in Greece. Open M-Th, Su 10pm-3:30am, F-Sa 10pm-later. **Red** is considered the hottest dance club in Larisa, about a €5-6 cab ride away. On especially wild nights, you may catch the bartenders diving into the indoor pool while the masses grind scandalously to Greek pop. (Open in summer 10pm-7am.)

KALAMBAKA Καλαμπάκα ☎24320

East of the North Pindhos mountain range is small, comfortable Kalambaka. The tourist-friendly town nicely complements nearby Meteora's spread-out, pious tone. Despite the volume of people passing through, Kalambaka remains fairly inexpensive, making it an able ambassador to the monastic community. The town's fabulously slow pace is evident in the relaxed attitude of its locals and the winding streets that make it nearly impossible to hurry without looking around.

📮 TRANSPORTATION. The distinctive yellow train station (☎24320 22 451), on the corner of Pindou and Kondyli, is clearly visible 50m to your left, one block down from the bus station. **Trains** go to Athens (4½hr., 4 per day 8:20am-8:47pm, €19.10) and Palaiofarsados (1hr., 11 per day 6:02am-10pm, €3), where you can change trains to reach Thessaloniki (3hr., 6 per day 11:18am-8:55pm, €6.20). The main bus station, Averof 2 (☎24320 22 432; open 6:15am-9pm), downhill from Pl. Dimarhiou on Rodou, past the taxi stand on the left, sends **buses** to: Athens (5hr., 7 per day 7am-6:30pm, €21) via Lamia (3hr., €9); Ioannina (3hr.; 8:50am, 3:20pm; €9) via Metsovo (2hr., €5.10); Patras (5hr.; Tu, Th 10am, F-Su 3pm; €22.30); Thessaloniki (3½hr.; 7:30am, 4:15pm; €15); Trikala (30min., every 30min. 6:15am-10:30pm, €2); Volos (3hr., 4 per day 7am-7pm, €12). Buses bound for Kastraki (5min., every hr. 7am-11pm, €0.80) and Meteora (15min.: M-F 9am, 1:20pm; Sa-Su 8:20am, 1:20pm: €1) leave from in front of Pl. Dimarhiou at the foot of the large fountain. The 9am bus to Meteora allows time to see the monasteries before taking the return bus back from Grand Meteoro at 1:30pm. Most visitors, however, walk back to Kalambaka (7km downhill), visiting monasteries along the way. **Taxis** congregate on Rodou, below the central plateia. (☎24320 22 310. Available 24hr.)

■**7** **ORIENTATION AND PRACTICAL INFORMATION.** Central **Plateia Dimarhiou** is uphill from the bus station. Standing at the plateia's roundabout with your back to the fountain and the Meteora cliffs, you will see **Vlachava** to the left, **Rodou** in front, and **Ioanninon**, the road to Ioannina, downhill to the right. **Patriarchou Dimitriou** goes uphill to the right, while **Trikalon** heads slightly left to sunny **Plateia Riga Fereou**, home to various trees, banks, and restaurants. A horde of cafes and bars, open at all hours, congregates on the pedestrian street **Dimoula**, two blocks down Trikalon from Pl. Riga Fereou. With the cliffs on your left, Kondyli branches off to the right at the end of Pl. Riga Fereou. Through a well-marked gate half a block down Kondyli on the right, the **tourist office**, Kondyli and Hatzipetrou 38, provides **maps**, hotel listings, and monastery hours. Helpful pamphlets are even available after hours in a box on the door. (☎24320 75 306. Open M-F 8am-3:30pm.) The **kiosk** by the taxi stand below Pl. Dimarhiou also has maps of both Kalambaka and Meteora. The **National Bank**, Sidirodromou 1, in Pl. Riga Fereou (☎24320 77 178), and the **Agricultural Bank**, Ioanninon 3, near the central plateia, have **24hr. ATMs**. (Both open M-Th 8am-2:30pm, F 8am-2pm.) The **police**, Ioanninon 17, are a 10min. walk from the center of town. (☎24320 76 100. Open 24hr.) They share a building with the **tourist police**. A 24hr. **health center** (☎24320 22 222) is 1km from town, on the road to Ioannina. The **OTE** is at Ioanninon 9; from the main plateia with your back to the cliffs, take a right. (☎24320 22 121. Open M-F 7:30am-2:30pm.) **Arena**, Dimola 21, a block down Dimoula off Trikalon, has the cheapest **Internet access** in town on fast terminals. (☎24320 77 999. €2 per hr. Open 10am-7am.) **Ouranio Toxo**, Trikalon 100, on the right at Trikalon's entrance to Pl. Riga Fereou, has five terminals and a bar. (☎24320 24 688. €3 per hr. Frappés €1.80. Beer €2. Open 10am-2am.) The **post office**, Trikalon 23, between the two plateias, has **Poste Restante**. (☎24320 22 467. Open M-F 7:30am-2pm.) **Postal Code:** 42200.

⌂ ACCOMMODATIONS AND CAMPING. Dock hawks offering **domatia** here are infamous for luring travelers with promises of good prices, then hitting them with exorbitant surcharges; make sure you know the details before agreeing to anything. The accommodations with the best views, comfort, and hospitality are in the quiet, high-rise-free Old Town near the foot trail to Meteora. A number of worthy campsites also line the roads around Kalambaka and Kastraki. In the Old Town at the base of Meteora, ◪**Alsos House ❷**, Kanari 5, has spacious rooms with breathtaking views of Meteora's pinnacles and the Ag. Triada Monastery; each includes a private bath, A/C, and a balcony. If you follow Vlachava from the central plateia until it ends, Alsos will be on your right. Amiable English-speaking proprietor Yiannis will pick guests up from the bus or train station and take them for walks on the hidden paths once used by monks. (☎24320 24 097; www.kalampaka.com/alsoshouse. Shared kitchen. Internet and laundry €5 each. Advance reservations recommended. Singles €25; doubles €35-40; triples €50; 2-room apartment with kitchen €60-65. Discounts for students. MC/V.) If Alsos is full, go one house down to **Elena Rooms ❸**, Kanari 3, which shares the same dazzling view. The owner, who greets you in a large room with farm-like wooden furniture, speaks four languages.

Rooms have baths, TV, A/C, and fridges. (☎24320 77 789; www.kalampaka.com/elena. Breakfast €5. Reception 24hr. Singles €30; doubles €40; triples €50; quads €60.) Farther up the road at the foot of the path that ascends the mountains, **Koka Roka ❷**, Kanari 21, rents large rooms. Always ready to chat, Aussie-accented Arthur serves his guests souvlaki every night. (☎24320 24 554. Breakfast €2. Laundry €10. Internet €3 per hr. Reception 24hr. Singles €20; doubles €30, with bath €32; triples €45.) **Vrachos Camping ❶**, 1km out of town toward Kastraki and the monasteries, is the most popular and best maintained of the area's campsites, with a pool, restaurant, and great views. (☎24320 22 293. Laundry €5. €6 per person, €1 per car; caravans with kitchen and bath €7. 10% discount for *Let's Go* readers.)

DOMATIA DILEMMA. It's true that prices can be flexible when bargaining for domatia. Keep in mind, however, that if you're too stingy in negotiations, you may be trading away your host's hospitality for a few measly euros.

🍴🍷 **FOOD AND NIGHTLIFE.** To save some cash or to slap together a picnic for a day at the monasteries, visit the 24hr. **supermarket** just off of Trikalon on Dimoula or the various **fruit stands** on Vlachava. On Friday, Vlachava and its main cross street, Kondyli, turn into a full-scale **marketplace** (open 7am-3pm) which sells fresh produce and household goods. Diners at 🍴**Arhondariki ❷**, Trikalon 9, at the left end of Pl. Riga Fereou when facing the cliffs, arc treated to magnificent views of Meteora. Though the restaurant's yellow theme is oddly banana-like, the food is fantastic and Sotiris, the owner, is a delight. The stuffed zucchini with rice and minced meat (€6) explodes with flavor. (☎24320 22 449. Entrees €4-8. Open noon-midnight.) **Restaurant Panellinio ❷**, Vlachava 3, on a cobblestone platform next to the fountain, is the life of Pl. Dimarhiou. Mrs. Soula cooks up a mean moussaka, along with over 30 different daily dishes, which are served either outside under hanging vines or in the costume-adorned interior. (☎24320 24 735. Entrees €3-9. Open daily 11am- midnight.) Conversation is lively and constant at **Koka Roka Taverna ❷**, Kanari 21, inside its namesake hotel at the top of town near the Byzantine church. The souvlaki has been described in the restaurant's guest book as a "religious experience." (☎24320 24 554. Open 8am-1am. Entrees €4-5.80.)

Nightlife centers on Trikalon, a street south of Pl. Riga Fereou, plastered with neon signs and fast-food joints. At traditional *ouzeria* **Plaka**, Sidirodromou 6, just below Pl. Riga Fereou, opposite the National Bank, the ouzo flows like water, and the sound of live *bouzouki* and laughter carries to the nearby Meteora cliffs. (Open 6pm-3am. Mixed drinks €4-6.) The fountain-lined pedestrian walkway of Dimoula hosts a trendier scene, with lively bars. From Pl. Riga Fereou, continue on Trikalon toward Trikala; Dimoula is the second right leading downhill.

🔲 **SIGHTS.** Kalambaka's foremost attraction is the Byzantine **Church of the Assumption of the Virgin,** which competes with the best of the area's many religious sites. Follow signs in the plateia; after several blocks that wind up to the foot of the slopes, you'll spy its stone bell tower. Built in the 7th century atop a Classical temple whose pagan mosaics are entombed beneath the floor, the main structure was remodeled in 1573. The baptism basin at the entrance remains from the original church. (Open 8am-1pm and 4-9pm. €1.50. Modest dress required.) Visitors wondering about all those gorgeous yet rigidly standardized gilded icons can visit the operating **Workshop of Dimitris Zervopoulos,** across from Camping Kalambaka 1km down the road to Trikala. While sipping complimentary ouzo or lemonade, you can watch monks as they paint the world's next generation of icons in this heavenly factory. During free tours, pleasant English-speaking guides explain production methods and even let you try applying 18-karat gold leaf to the unfinished icons. (☎24320 75 466. Open daily 9am-8pm.) In late July, the town honors its patron saint with a celebration complete with music, dance, and food. Nearby Kastraki holds a three-day **wine festival** with free samples in late August.

METEORA Μετέορα

Atop awe-inspiring peaks that ascend from the Thessalian plain to the sky is the monastic community of Meteora (meh-TEH-o-rah), whose name literally means "hanging in the air" or "in suspense." Believed to have been inhabited by hermits as early as the 11th century, the summits were chosen as the location of a series of 21 gravity-defying, frescoed Byzantine monasteries in the 14th century. Six of the monasteries are still in use and are open to the public, the largest and most popular of which are Grand Meteoro and Varlaam. The other four monasteries are less celebrated, which makes them refreshingly more quiet, charming, and intimate. Still, Meteora is hardly an undiscovered treasure, and gift shops and tourists are as common as the frescoes. Luckily, the most fantastic aspect of Meteora can be seen without having to wait in a crowded line—the construction of the buildings themselves, perching precariously on jagged boulders, is breathtaking.

📳 TRANSPORTATION AND PRACTICAL INFORMATION

Buses leave for Meteora from the Kalambaka fountain. (15min.: M-F 9am, 1:20pm; Sa-Su 8:20am, 1:20pm: €1.) Buy tickets onboard. You can also take a **taxi** (around €5) from Kalambaka. Each monastery closes one day per week. Opening hours vary from monastery to monastery and change often; consult the tourist office in Kalambaka for times. Even if a monastery is closed, it is still worth checking out, as the outside is often as spectacular as the interior. Photography is forbidden inside, and modest dress is required. Most of the monasteries close midday, so many people decide to pack picnics. (€2 per monastery, under 12 free.)

🚶 WALKING THE MONASTERIES

The origins of the settlements on the Meteora rocks are unknown: one story claims that the first recluse was **Barnabas,** a monk who founded the *skite* (a small, remote monastic cell) of the Holy Ghost in the mid-10th century. By the 11th century, hermits and ascetics followed his example, moving to the pinnacles and crevices of Meteora and worshipping in a church dedicated to the **Theotokos** (Mother of God), which can still be seen below the Ag. Nikolaos monastery. As persecution at the hands of Turkish and Frankish marauders increased in the 12th century, Orthodox Christians scurried to the summits of these impregnable columns of rock. In 1344, the region's first monastic community was founded when the monk **Athanasios,** his spiritual father **Gregorios,** and 14 fellow monks began to build Grand Meteoro. Athanasios was a well-educated monk whose journeys brought him to Constantinople, Crete, and finally Mt. Athos, from which he fled to avoid Turkish invasions. He occupied his time weaving baskets in a nearby cave, and referred to women as "the sling" (that vaults the stones of sin into men's hearts) or as "the affliction" (addicting men to the sinful pleasures of the flesh). He displayed this penchant for description slightly more constructively when he gave Meteora its name. Later, the Greek-Serbian king of Thessaly and Epirus, Ioannis Versis Angelos Komininos Palaeologos, traded regal comforts for Meteora's rugged rocks, and built many of its later monasteries. When the Ottomans ruled most of Greece, Meteora served as an outpost of Christianity. In the 16th century, it grew into a community of 21 monasteries which amassed large libraries of both religious and secular books and created dazzling icons and frescoes. When donations tapered off in the late 1700s and the popularity of monastic life waned, though, the Greeks sold many of these manuscripts and books for a fraction of their actual worth. Small brotherhoods still exist at **Grand Meteoro, Varlaam, Agia Triada,** and **Agios Nikolaos,** while **Agios Stephanos** and **Roussanou** are now convents.

The first ascetics scaled Meteora's cliffs by wedging timbers into the rock crevices to build small platforms; traces of these can still be seen in the walls. After the monasteries were completed, visitors arrived by means of extremely long rope ladders. Those who were too weak or too timid to climb were hoisted up in baskets. Once these devices were pulled up, though, the summits became inaccessible. Motorized winches have since replaced the rope-spool cranes (though the old pulleys are still visible at each monastery), and today only provisions are yanked up by rope. In 1922, in the ultimate facilitation of a quicker rise to heaven, bridges were built between the pillars, and steps were carved into the rocks.

It's easiest to begin your tour of Meteora in the morning at Grand Meteoro, the largest and most famous monastery, which also happens to be the location of the **bus stop.** You can then work your way down through its neighbors, Varlaam, Roussanou, and Ag. Nikolaos. After the big three, you can either head back to Kalambaka or grab a bite from a bagged lunch and start the hike to Ag. Triada and Stephanos. A sign on the highway between Varlaam and Roussanou marked "Ag. Triada" points into the bush to a short trail to Triada (20min.). The last monastery, Ag. Stephanos, is about 800m from Ag. Triada. Though it's probably a good idea to get a regional map before leaving Kalambaka, the monasteries are all within walking distance and are connected by a single road.

GRAND METEORO. The **Monastery of the Transfiguration,** known as "Grand Meteoro" (Μεγάλου Μετέορου), is the site at which St. Athanasios decided to begin his imitation of the community at Mt. Athos in the 14th century. Looming 475m above Thessaly's plain, the complex, known in its entirety as **Platys Lithos,** reached its peak in the 16th century, when it was visited by the reigning patriarch and accorded the same privileges as the autonomous Mt. Athos. Around this time, the **Church of the Transfiguration** was built and was capped by an exalted dome with a *pantokrator* (a central image of Christ). The *katholikon* (nave) stands 24m high, and is constructed in Byzantine style with a 12-sided dome. Murals created by the mid-16th century Cretan painter Theophanes Bathas-Strelitzas cover the walls. The sounds of chanting monks—emanating, disappointingly, from a stereo in the folk museum—fill the monastery; the monks themselves mostly keep to their private quarters. If you manage to get past all of the tourists you will find a former carpenter's workshop, the old kitchen (which still somehow smells delicious), and a museum. The museum's collection of early printed texts by Plato and Aristotle and old gospel parchments attest to the monastery's past preeminence as an intellectual center. (☎24320 22 278. Open M, W-Sa 9am-5pm. €2.)

VARLAAM. Varlaam, the second-largest monastery, is about 800m downhill from Grand Meteoro. The complex was founded in the 14th century by one of Athanasios's contemporaries who, in a display of true humility, named it after himself. The *katholikon's* 16th-century frescoes depict hermits, martyrs, an apocalyptic sea serpent swallowing doomed sinners, and St. Sisoes looking pitifully upon Alexander the Great's skeleton, symbolic of the vanity of worldly achievements. The monastery's **library** contains 290 manuscripts, including a miniature Bible from AD 959 that belonged to Emperor Constantine Porfyrogenitos. Varlaam also has a middle-school science teacher's dream toy—an extensive net and pulley system. It's now used for supplies, but also shows how earlier visitors were hoisted up to the building. (☎24320 22 277. *Open M-W, F-Su 9am-2pm and 3:20-5pm. €2.*)

ROUSSANOU. Bear right at the fork in the road to reach Roussanou. Visible from most of the valley, it is one of Meteora's most spectacularly situated monasteries. With steep sides, three of which overlook the drop to the valley below, Roussanou feels like a natural continuation of the boulders. Despite constant renovation, the interior, which includes a portrait of Constantine the Great, can't match the heavenly exterior, accessible even to those with no ticket. Still, the *katholikon*, illuminated by light that streams through stained glass, is beautiful. Roussanou proudly housed Greek refugees fleeing the Turks in 1757 and 1897; today it is home to an order of nuns. Though the crowds of tourists may make it difficult to see, the building contains fantastically strange frescoes of winged dragons, magical whales, and human-sized snakes. (☎24320 22 649. *Open daily 9am-6pm. €2.*)

AGIOS NIKOLAOS. Farther down the road is the 16th-century monastery of Agios Nikolaos Anapafsas, only 2.5km from Kastraki. Built on the ruins of an older monastery, it is situated on the summit of a very narrow boulder. Construction constraints meant that Agios Nikolaos had to be built vertically rather than horizontally, making it the second tallest monastery, next to Grand Meteoro. Standing at the top of the bell tower gives the impression that you're hanging in mid-air over mind-boggling depths. Allow 30min. for the walk past Roussanou to the next monastery, Agia Triada. (☎24320 22 375. *Open M-Th, Sa-Su 9am-3:30pm. €2.*)

AGIA TRIADA. On the metal bridge into Roussanou, face away from the monastery, and take the (mostly) paved path uphill on the right. When it hits the road, bear right and continue to find Agia Triada; movie buffs will recognize it from the James Bond flick *For Your Eyes Only*. Its peak yields a soul-searing view of red-roofed Kalambaka and the distant Pindos Mountains. Ambitious monk Dometius built the monastery in 1438, but many of the **wall paintings** weren't added until the 18th century. Unfortunately, most of the monastery's prized manuscripts and heirlooms were lost in WWII. (☎24320 22 220. *Open M-W, F-Su 9am-5pm. €2.*)

AGIOS STEPHANOS. At the end of the road, past Agia Triada, is Agios Stephanos. Originally a convent according to an 18th-century report, it became a monastery in the early 15th century. Today it is once again home to an active community of nuns. Of its two churches, the newer **Agios Haralambos,** built in 1798, is also the more impressive. The older church, **Protomartia Stephanou,** built in 1350, is beginning to show the wear of its age, with faded, disintegrating frescoes and cracked walls. The **museum** displays icons, manuscripts, liturgical vestments, and crosses. Its wooden iconostasis is intricately carved into figures of birds, animals, and people. (☎24320 22 279. *Open Tu-Su 9am-2pm and 3:30-6pm. €2.*)

NORTHERN GREECE

 Northern Greece does not experience the same mass tourism from which many other regions of the nation benefit. As you move inland, far from the cities and ever-popular beaches, the towns grow smaller, more self-contained, and more isolated from modern-day influences. Consisting of three provinces—Thrace, Macedonia, and Epirus—the region is starkly more Balkan than the remainder of Greece. With its proximity to and influence from the states of Albania, the Former Yugoslavian Republic Of Macedonia (FYROM), Bulgaria, and Turkey, tension from past disputes with both the Balkans and Turkey still hangs in the air. Thrace, the easternmost province, has a diverse population that includes a large number of Turkish Muslims and Eastern Orthodox immigrants whose influence is apparent in Thrace's architecture, markets, and cuisine. Macedonia is historically part of a much larger Greek province that extends into present-day Albania, FYROM, and Bulgaria, and has been a homeland of powerhouses ranging from antiquity's Alexander the Great to current urban giant Thessaloniki. Epirus, in the west, prospered under the imperial command of Ali Pasha in the early 19th century, but is currently best known as a hiker's haven with strikingly beautiful terrain. For travelers seeking distance from Athens and the islands, Northern Greece offers an idyllic escape, ripe with Byzantine heritage, countless traditional villages, and a landscape that soars from the depths of the Vikos Gorge, up to the heights of Mt. Olympus, and back over the serenity of the Prespa Lakes. A region largely connected, both ethnically and historically, to its Balkan neighbors, the north is where the modern, multicultural Greek state surfaces.

⊙ SUGGESTED ITINERARIES: NORTHERN GREECE

FIVE DAYS Base your trip in vibrant, cosmopolitan **Thessaloniki** (p. 271), whose prominent minarets and fortresses recall centuries of Turkish rule. See what remains of the region's ancient past as the center of Alexander the Great's Macedonian empire at the sites of **Vergina** (p. 284), **Pella** (p. 285), and **Dion** (p. 294).

TWO WEEKS After getting to know Thessaloniki (p. 271), leave the city life behind for the chilly shores and sparsely-populated villages of the **Prespa Lakes** (p. 305). As you travel southwest, take breaks to linger in the anachronistic hamlets of **Zagorohoria** (p. 265) before hiking the super-steep **Vikos Gorge** (p. 266).

EPIRUS Ηπειρος

If you came in search of serene isolation, consider roaming Greece's northwestern coast. The postcard-worthy towns and beaches of Parga see their share of tourism, but the Zagorohoria villages near the Vikos Gorge have retained a sense of timelessness, despite a recent influx of visitors. This mountainous region is world-famous for its beautiful trails, peaks, and reflecting lakes, and it draws international hikers for some of Greece's best outdoor treks. Those who enjoy exhilarat-

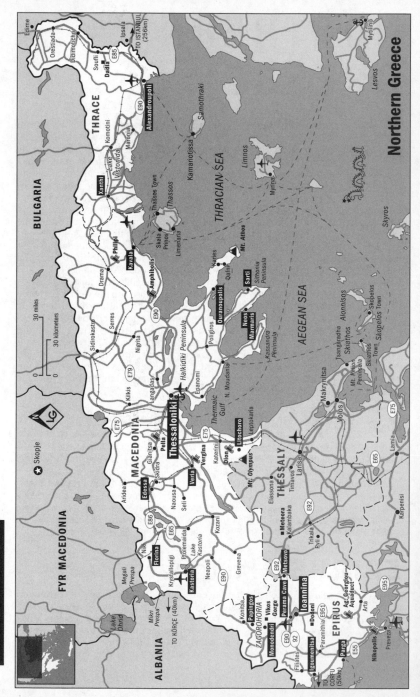

ing fresh air and quality trails will delight in the beauty of the Pindos Mountains region. Epirus links itself to a living past—the old dialect of Vlach, branched off from Latin, is still spoken in some of the towns, and the preserved mosques of the dynamic 19th-century ruler Ali Pasha still grace the city of Ioannina.

IGOUMENITSA Ηγουμενίτσα   ☎ 26650

A connection point between Italy and Greece, Igoumenitsa (ee-goo-men-IT-sa) is often a traveler's first or last glimpse of the Greek mainland. The town's enormous port, the third-largest in Greece, sends boats to four cities in Italy and to Corfu. Tourist agencies seem to outnumber people, harried backpackers scramble in search of their ships, and it appears as if life never stands still in this small town. Beneath the frenzy, however, are hints of a beach town's lazy lifestyle.

▐ TRANSPORTATION

Ferries: Igoumenitsa's endless **port** has 4 subdivisions; the 4th was recently completed to meet increased transportation demands. The **Old Port,** on the waterfront's northern edge (follow the signs), mostly sends boats to Italy. **Corfu Port** is south of the Old Port. Beyond Corfu Port is the **New Port,** whose boats go to both Italy and Corfu. The **Fourth Port** is at the southernmost point of the harbor and sends ships to Italy. Tickets to **Corfu** (1¼hr.; 5 per day 4am-10pm; €6, students €3, children €2.60) can be purchased at Corfu Port in 1 of several white kiosks. For tickets to **Italy,** shop around at the waterfront agencies, as some have student rates and some accept Eurail and InterRail passes; bargain before you buy. Destinations include: **Ancona** (14hr.; 11, 11:30pm; €54); **Bari** (9hr.; 9pm, midnight; €27-40); **Brindisi** (7hr.; 7:30am, 1:30am; €28-35); **Venice** (19hr., 10am, €57). Most boats depart before noon or late in the evening. Contact **Apeiros Travel,** Ethnikis Antistasis 20A, across from the entrance to the Old Port, for further information. (☎ 26650 26 944; www.aperios.gr. Open 8am-4pm and 6-11pm.)

Buses: To reach the bus station, Kyprou 29 (☎ 26650 22 309; open 5:30am-8:30pm), from the ports, walk north along the waterfront to 23 Fevruariou, turn right, then left 2 blocks later on Kyprou. The **ticket office** is behind a cafe on the left, marked with a blue and white KTEL sign. To: **Athens** (7hr., 4 per day 7:30am-8:30pm, €33); **Ioannina** (2hr., 8 per day 6:30am-8pm, €7); **Parga** (1hr., 4 per day 6am-5:15pm, €4.20); **Preveza** (2hr.; 11:45am, 3:30pm; €8); **Thessaloniki** (8hr., 10:30am, €30).

Taxis: ☎ 26650 25 000. Wait on Eth. Antistasis, especially by Corfu Port. Available 24hr.

Car Rental: Europcar, Pargas 5, just off the waterfront at the police station, 1 door down from Strad Marina restaurant. (☎ 26650 23 477. From €40 per day.)

◢◣ ▐ ORIENTATION AND PRACTICAL INFORMATION

Igoumenitsa is on the westernmost corner of mainland Greece, about 20km from the Albanian border. **Ethnikis Antistasis,** which becomes **Agion Apostolon** in front of the Corfu port, runs along the waterfront and overflows with travel agencies and banks. To the north, after it is separated by a lane divider, the tree-lined inland side of the street is bordered by the array of cafes and bars that mark it as the nightlife district. Igoumenitsa's main shopping area is on **Lamprari Grigariou,** the first pedestrian street parallel to the waterfront. To reach the central plateia, walk two blocks inland on **Eleftheriou Venizelou,** which begins across from the Old Port. The **tourist office** (☎ 26650 22 227; open daily 8am-2pm), at the entrance to the Old Port, helps with transportation and accommodations and supplies free **maps.** A **National Bank,** Eth. Antistasis 20 (☎ 26650 22 415; open M-Th 8am-2:30pm, F 8am-2pm), across the road from the Old Port, is in a string of

HOPE FLOATS. An inflatable pool raft (€4-6), popular among ferry-seasoned travelers, can be the beach-oriented backpacker's best friend. It provides endless hours of floating relaxation in the sun and can double as a comfy "bed" to help you get some shut-eye on a ferry ride.

banks that all **exchange currency** and have **ATMs**. The 24hr. **police station**, Ag. Apostolon 5 (☎26650 22 100), on the continuation of Eth. Antistasis, is across from Corfu Port. The **tourist police** are in the same building. (☎26650 29 647. Open 8:30am-1:30pm.) The **port police** are in a Corfu Port booth, near customs and passport control. The 24hr. **medical center**, Ag. Apostolon 7 (☎26650 24 420), next door to the police station, offers basic care. They can help you reach the **hospital** (☎26640 22 203), 15min. away in Filiates. The **OTE**, Grigariou Labraki 35, is at pedestrian Grigariou's end. (☎26650 23 499. Open M, W 7:30am-3pm, Tu, Th-F 7:30am-9pm, Sa 8am-2:30pm.) **All Time Cafe**, Dagli 18, off Eth. Antistasis, about 300m from Alekos, has **Internet access** (€2.50 per hr.) and serves drinks and coffee. (☎26650 21 080. Open 9am-1am.) The **post office**, Tzavelenas 2, 1km north along the waterfront on the corner of a playground, accepts **Poste Restante**. (☎26650 46 100. Open 7:30am-2pm.) **Postal Code:** 46100.

ACCOMMODATIONS

Accommodations in Igoumenitsa are surprisingly underdeveloped given the volume of travelers that pass through the city. Most hotels are run-down and generally unappealing. **Hotel Acropolis ❷**, Eth. Antistasis 58, has basic, slightly deteriorating rooms with a shared bath. Some rooms have sinks and views of the port. The leather couches in the dark common room are torn, but this is the cheapest option in town. (☎26650 22 342. Singles €20; doubles €30; triples €36.) Overlooking the Old Port, **Jolly Hotel ❹**, Eth. Antistasis 14, makes for a comfortable (albeit more expensive) alternative with its spacious, carpeted rooms and marble-tiled hallways. All of the mauve- and yellow-walled rooms have baths, A/C, TV, and phones; some of them have balconies and views of the harbor. (☎26650 23 971; www.jolly.50megs.com. Breakfast included. Reception 24hr. Singles €48; doubles €70; triples with fridge €85. MC/V.) Look for **Hotel Egnatia ❸**, Eleftherias 2, in the central plateia's far right corner. Simple, small rooms have tile floors, balconies, baths, TV, phones, and A/C. If you want to avoid being woken up by the morning traffic, ask for a room facing the quiet wooded area behind the hotel. (☎26650 23 455. Singles €31; doubles €44; triples €53; quads €61.)

FOOD AND NIGHTLIFE

The best of the city's restaurants are on the northern edge of the waterfront, past the ports. Dozens of **bakeries** and **markets** line the pedestrian street just inland from the harbor. **Alekos ❷**, Eth. Antistasis 84, at the beginning of the waterfront strip, north of the ports, specializes in fish caught in the harbor waters. Bright tablecloths and a cozy canopy augment the pleasant atmosphere. (☎26650 23 708. Entrees €4-6. Open 9am-12:30am.) **Mykonos ❷**, Eth. Antistasis 80, two doors before Alekos, toward the ports, has a vine-covered patio full of loquacious Greeks. Grilled octopus with calamari (€7.50) is the restaurant's specialty; the multilingual menu also includes pizza, pasta, Greek mainstays, and a few fish specialties. (☎26650 27 567. Entrees €4-8. Open noon-midnight.) **Strada Marina ❸**, Pargas 3, facing the police station between the Old Port and Corfu Port, has a multilingual menu of Greek favorites. You can watch your food being made from any vantage point in the restaurant or from inside the sidewalk seating area. (☎26650 23 549. Entrees €4-12. Open 9am-11pm.)

Igoumenitsa's bland nightlife centers on a strip of bars along the waterfront. An open-air **cinema** next to Taverna Alekos, which operates only in the summer, shows mostly American films (shows 9:30, 11:15pm; €5). At **Privilege** (☎26650 23 505) and **Envi**, a few doors down from Taverna Alekos, young tourists waiting for their ferries at cafe tables are entertained by American and Greek tunes on the weekends. (Beer €2.50. Mixed drinks €4. Cover €5; includes 1 drink. Open until 5am.) A short distance from the city, dance clubs **Clik** and **Ostria** attract a trendy local crowd peppered with stranded tourists. (Beer €2. Mixed drinks €5-6. Cover €8; includes 1 drink.) Buses (€0.80) run every hour from the center of town, but stop at midnight. Those returning later can catch a taxi (€5).

PARGA Πάργα ☎26840

Parga's marvelous port on the Ionian Sea, currently the seat of a major tourism industry, was historically the source of great hardship for Pargians. The port was almost continuously occupied from the Mycenaean period until its absorption into the modern Greek state in 1913. Its brief stints of independence were aided by protection from the Venetians and, later, the French. Parga's modern face has been built with the fruits of tourism, which pours northern Europeans through the town's waterfront and narrow, hilly streets. The otherwise dreary 2000-person village springs to life in the summer, and though the tourist-centered nature of the town can be somewhat overwhelming, the long stretches of light beaches are nice enough to attract a sun-seeking traveler to Parga.

⊏ TRANSPORTATION. The bus station (☎26840 31 218) is a small booth next to the Chinese (*Kineziko*) restaurant at the top of Sp. Livada. **Buses** run to: Athens (9hr., 3 per day 7am-5:30pm, €31); Igoumenitsa (1¼hr., 4 per day 7:15am-6:30pm, €4.40); Preveza (1½hr., 5 per day 7am-9:15pm, €5); Thessaloniki (9½hr., 7am, €34). **Ferries** head to Corfu Town (3hr., Th 8:30am, €35). **Taxis** (☎26840 32 855) wait in front of the OTE and can be called 24hr.

⊞ ⑦ ORIENTATION AND PRACTICAL INFORMATION. Parga is organized around its waterfront. The Norman Castle divides the town's two beaches, **Valtos** and **Krioneri**, and most of the city is located on southern Krioneri's side. The main waterfront road has three names: from west to east, they are **Gregoriou Labraki, Anexartisias,** and **Agiou Athanassiou.** Walking toward Krioneri beach, which runs alongside Athanassiou, the road forks just before the sand begins; the uphill branch is **Riga Fereou.** With your back to the dock, the street heading inland is **Alex Baga,** which goes uphill to most of Parga's municipal buildings. Al. Baga meets **Spyrou Livada** at the town's main intersection, by the OTE. Turning right on Sp. Livada takes you up to the highway and bus stop. Parallel to the waterfront, **Vasila** leads to **Abensberg,** which ascends to the **Venetian castle** at the far southwestern corner of town. From here, a stone path goes down the other side to **Valtos beach.**

There is no official tourist office in Parga, but private **tourist agencies** pack the streets around the waterfront, ready to help you find rooms, arrange daytrips, or rent a boat or car. The friendly, English-speaking staff at **ITS**, Sp. Livada 4, 20m down the hill from the bus stop on your right, has English newspapers, provides information about the area, arranges excursions, and **exchanges money.** (☎26840 31 833. Open 9am-10pm.) Waterfront souvenir shops sell **maps** of Parga (€4) at the end of Anexartisias. From the sea, walk two blocks left of the OTE on Sp. Livada to find the

National Bank, Livada 9, with a **24hr. ATM.** (26840 31 525. Open M-Th 8am-2:30pm, F 8am-2pm.) With the OTE on your left and the shore behind you, the **police station,** Baga 18, with a helpful tourist bureau, is straight ahead on your left. (☎26840 31 222. Open 24hr.) **Lenas Dimitrious Pharmacy,** Sp. Livada 6, is at the intersection of Sp. Livada and Baga, two doors down from ITS. (☎26840 31 195. Open M-F 8:30am-2pm and 6-9pm.) The 24hr. **health center,** Livada 71 (☎26840 31 233), is about 600m down Livada. In **emergencies,** you can also call the **port police,** Labraki 12, in the harbor. (☎26840 31 227. Open 24hr.) The **OTE,** Baga 7, is at the intersection of Sp. Livada and Baga. (☎26840 31 699. Open M-F 8am-1pm and 4-9pm.) **Internet access** is available at **Flamingo,** Baga 12, two doors down from the police station toward Sp. Livada (☎26840 32 207; €3 per hr.; open 8am-2am), and at **Net Zone,** R. Fereou 6, near the fork of Fereou and the waterfront walkway (☎26840 32 895; €3 per hr.; open 11pm-1am). The **post office** is on the first floor of the police station building. (☎26840 31 295. Open M-F 7:30am-2pm.) **Postal Code:** 48060.

⌂ ACCOMMODATIONS AND CAMPING. Parga's hotels can be expensive, and prices spike in July and August by about 30%. **Domatia** (€25-35) cluster near the highway, around the southern end of the town, and at the top of the hill in the small street leading up to the castle. Just below the entrance to the fortress, above a small bakery in a mustard-yellow building, **Kostas and Martha Christou ❷,** Patatokou 6, rent six clean, small, and simple rooms with heavy wood furniture, baths and balconies, just a 5min. walk from the shores of Valtos beach. The entire city and shoreline are visible from the balconies of the rooms that face the city. (☎26840 31 942. Breakfast included. Shared kitchen. Reservations recommended at least 1 month in advance. Rooms that can fit up to 3 people €25.) To find **Hotel Galini ❷,** walk down from the bus stop on Sp. Livada; after about 60m, you will see an orchard with a walkway to your right. Galini, whose signs are visible from Sp. Livada, is at the end of the walkway. The proprietor, Mr. Drakos, who speaks only German, rents quiet rooms with A/C, balconies, baths, and phones. (☎26840 31 581. Breakfast €4. Doubles €38-50; triples €46-60.) For spacious studios with full kitchens, A/C, TV, baths, and balconies, find Taso at **Thomas House ❷,** K. Tzavela 1. To get there, make the last right on Abensberg's stairs before Blue Star and walk past the mini-mart; you will see the hotel at the end of the hill, above a souvenir store that also belongs to Taso. Thomas House also offers regular rooms with baths and balconies. (☎26840 31 121. Doubles €30; triples €35; studios €40.) Some travelers on a tight budget choose to camp on nearby beaches, but those who want a shower stick to campsites. **Camping Valtos ❶** is clean and close to both town and Valtos beach; follow the signs to Valtos beach and you will see it right behind the Tango Club. Covered with mulberry trees, the site features a restaurant, mini-mart, bar, washing machines (€3 per load), and showers. (☎26840 31 287; www.campingvaltos.gr. Reception 24hr., but gates close to cars at midnight. €5 per person; €5 per large tent; €4.50 per small tent; €3 per car. Electricity €3.)

◖ FOOD. The price discrepancies between boardwalk corn-on-the-cob stands 50m apart should alert you to the often-arbitrary costs of a visit to this land of loose tourist cash. The waterfront restaurants aren't particularly authentic, and the farther you are from the water, the less you pay; venture into the heart of the city to find a tasty, well-priced meal. Perched on the hilltop just below the entrance to the fortress, **⬛Kastro Entasis ❸,** Abensberg 37, has it all, from sweeping views and soft Greek music to palm trees, a fountain, and absolutely superb food. Achilles, the owner, swears by his pork fillet (€14), which comes stuffed with two kinds of cheese, mushrooms, and peppers. (☎26840 31 119. Entrees €8.50-15.50.) Swanky peach colored **Rudis ❹,**

Anexartisias 8-12, across from the dock, serves creative Greek and Italian cuisine to tables on its balcony that overlooks the island. (☎26840 31 693. Entrees €8.50-18.) For a more affordable meal, try the delicious but noisy **Dokos Taverna ❷**, R. Fereou 13, 150m toward Preveza along the highway, whose excellent food and service make the journey worthwhile. Try the local special, *stifado* (lamb and beef with scallops; €5.50) or the €8 deal that includes an appetizer, entree, and dessert. (☎26840 31 574. Open 8am-1am.) A few doors beyond the ferry dock as you head toward Krioneri beach, **To Souli ❷**, Anexartisias 16, serves food that is as Greek as it gets. (☎26840 31 658. Lamb and feta *kleftiko* €5. Fish €35 per kg. Open noon-midnight.)

🎭🎵 **ENTERTAINMENT AND NIGHTLIFE. Tango Club,** at the far end of Valtos beach, is the most popular daytime party spot. Students crowd the bar and restaurant, while children fill the club's swimming pool. During the summer, owner Lefteris organizes beach soccer games starring the Greek national team. (☎26840 31 252. Drinks €6. Open 9am-2am.) At night, crowds of inebriated northern Europeans fill Parga's many waterfront bars and cafes. The population changes around midnight, when the older crowd heads to bed and the younger generation comes out to play. ◼**Blue Bar,** Abensberg 21, on the road leading to the castle, is, in one word, blue; the hue colors everything from the fans to the ash trays to the bartenders' hair. This hip hangout offers 120 cocktails, 42 of which were invented at the bar. The Happy Company (€24), serving four to six people, comes in a massive 5kg marble flower vase. (☎26840 32 067. Open 6pm-3am.) **Caravel,** Anexartisias 13, across the waterfront walkway from the ferry dock, is also popular, with blue nautical decorations and an upstairs balcony. Tourists fill the white-straw seats at all times of the day, sipping morning orange juice, afternoon iced coffee, and evening cocktails. (☎26840 31 359. Drinks €5. Open 7:30am-4am.)

In the summer, clubs stay open until 4am on weekdays and at least 6am on weekends; in the winter, they are only open on weekends. Cover is usually €5, which includes one drink. Though **Camares** is small, its blaring music and dazzling lights encourage its partiers to go all out, as freshly tanned northern Europeans blend together in one drunken, gyrating mass. (☎26840 32 000. Open M-Th, Su midnight-4am, F-Sa midnight-6am.) **Arena,** R. Fereou 1, sends its somewhat younger crowd into a dancing frenzy with its mirrored facade and loud hip-hop and Greek pop. (☎69442 22 709. Beer €3. Mixed drinks €5. Open M-Th, Su midnight-4am, F-Sa midnight-7am.) **Factory,** Themistokli 10, whose neon signs point up side streets near the dock, may not be as packed as the others, but it is a far funkier spot, with a live DJ who spins Greek pop, house, and rock over furniture that was originally factory machinery. (☎26840 32 625. Beer €4. Mixed drinks €5. Open M-Th, Su midnight-4am, F-Sa midnight-8am.) After July 10, the locally popular *bouzouki* club **Rendezvous,** at the top of Kanali above Valtos beach, opens its pounding doors. (☎26840 32 032. Coffee €2. Drinks €4. Open 6pm-2am.)

📷🏖 **SIGHTS AND BEACHES.** The **kastro** sits high on Parga's rocky headland. Built by the Normans, who later abandoned the city, the castle fell under the control of the Venetians from 1401 to 1797. In its glory days, the massive structure held 500 homes and 5000 Pargians. A surprising number of walls still stand, including the old barracks at the entrance, which are now the home of a small cafe. The cannons, however, which lined the top, have long since fallen and are strewn about the enclosure. Sitting high above the town, the castle is a perfect spot to escape the sun and tourists, and affords a stunning bird's eye view of Valtos beach.

The shady pine and olive trees seem to beg visitors to enjoy a picnic, take a stroll, or just imagine a Venetian-Ottoman battle. It's 5min. from the water; follow Abensberg up the hill to the castle spiked gates. (Open 7am-10pm.)

Krioneri, the closest beach to Parga's waterfront, just below Ag. Athanasiou, is also the most popular, attracting tons of daytime traffic. Paddleboats (€11 per hr.) or motorboats (€15 per hr.) are available for swimming-wary travelers who still want to make the 100m journey to the **Island of Panagia.** From the island's small beach, facing Krioneri beach, a hike past the **spring** and the small **Church of the Panagia** takes you to remains of Napoleonic fortifications. One building has the telltale inscription "De la Patrie 1808." On the other side of the island is a quiet pinnacle with views of Paxi and Antipaxi. The beach at **Paleo Krioneri,** a 5min. walk around the rocks at the end of Krioneri, is a bit more secluded. At **Valtos,** on the other side of the castle, a traditionally hipper group gathers as the crescent of sole-tickling pebbles turns to sand. From the end of Valtos beach, a trail leads past a **neromylos** (water mill) to **Ali Pasha's castle** on the top of the cliff, with views of the Ionians. Boats from the **Parga Mariners** that leave from the main dock in front of Caravel travel to smaller beaches, including cafe-lined **Lichnos** (2km), accessible by car or taxi boat (€4 round-trip). Though a boat no longer goes to secluded **Pogo,** ask the captain of the Lichnos boat to let you off there.

Tour companies along the waterfront and on the ferry dock book **excursions.** The 2hr. trips to uninhabited Antipaxi (daily 10am, €15) are most popular, though others that end up at Antipaxi also stop at its occupied neighbor Paxi and several inner island caves (daily 10am, €25). Summer-only voyages sail to the swampy **River Acheron,** the mythical gateway to the Underworld, and to **Necromanteion** (the Oracle of the Dead). It's a 1hr. trip (€9) past cliffs, caves, and coves, and then up the turtle- and snake-inhabited Acheron to the ancient swamp, now a corn field. A 30min. walk past fields and the occasional reed brings you to Necromanteion. The site is well-preserved with clay offerings, gigantic jugs, and a labyrinth meant to exclude sound from the windowless inner sanctum. A subterranean arched vault for communing with the dead, where Odysseus conversed with the shades of his fallen comrades and relatives, is also remarkably intact. (☎26840 41 206. Open 10am-4pm. €2, students €1, EU students with ID free.) Food is available in the nearby town **Mesopotamo.** The site can also be reached by taking the Preveza bus (20min.). Ask the driver to get off at Ammoydia and take a left on the dirt road; it's 2km away. To return, wait at the stop on the highway outside Mesopotamo for the Preveza-Parga bus. You can also call a taxi from Parga (€25) to come pick you up.

🖪 DAYTRIP FROM PARGA: NIKOPOLIS. Former allies **Octavian Caesar** (who later took the name "Augustus") and **Mark Antony** faced off in the waters off Preveza in the naval battle of **Actium,** which would ultimately secure Octavian's rise to power as a sole ruler. Though Antony, working with his lover, Egyptian queen **Cleopatra,** brought with him the powerful Egyptian fleet, many of his Roman friends ended up abandoning him and thus threw the battle to Octavian. This civil war effectively ended the Roman Republic and kicked off the Roman Empire. In celebration of his victory, Octavian built **◪Nikopolis** at the point where he had camped on the eve of the battle. Surrounding cities were emptied as both inhabitants and soldiers were resettled in this new capital. The well-preserved **odeon,** parts of fortification **walls, baths,** and the **nymphaion** (fountain pools at the end of the aqueduct) survive from this period and are within 10min. of the site's museum. The **stadium, gymnasium,** and **Actium victory monument,** perched above the city with a sweeping view of the waters, were later built outside the ancient city and are a

25min. walk away in modern Smyrntoula. When the Roman Empire declined, the city became an important early Christian center, and it is believed that St. Paul wrote his famous **Letter to Titus** here in the AD 1st century. Raids from northern barbarians and the fall of the western empire in the 5th century led to a contraction of the city. **Emperor Justinian** surrounded the now-smaller city with a new Byzantine fortification, which is the impressive tower-studded **wall** that is still visible. Look closely for pieces of friezes and reused Roman blocks in the wall, which reveal the fate of many of the city's lost monuments. The remains of three basilicas, whose amazingly ornate mosaics are now unfortunately covered with sand, date from this time. The site is extensive—as it was once a sprawling city, it requires a good deal of walking, some through high grass and thistles, so long pants and closed-toed shoes are recommended. Though the flocks of sheep, reed-filled basilicas, ocean views, and olive-grove-shrouded ruins make for a fascinating day of exploration, it's nearly impossible to imagine how Nikopolis looked in its heyday. Since the lack of signs (in Greek or English) makes the details of the site even more difficult to discern, you may want to get an outside resource. The small two-room **museum** houses sarcophagi, friezes, and a marble bust of **Agrippa**, Octavian's victorious admiral.

Take the bus to Preveza (1½hr., 5 per day 7am-9:15pm, €5) and ask the driver to let you off at Nikopolis. Specify that you are interested in the archaeological site, not the nearby club. To return, flag down the bus from Preveza to Parga (1½hr., 8 per day 7am-8pm, €5). The site is open 8am-7pm; museum 8am-3pm. €3, seniors €2, students and under 18 free.

IOANNINA Ιωάννινα ☎26510

The eighth-largest city in Greece, Ioannina reached its political peak after it was captured in 1788 by Ali Pasha, an Albanian-born leader and visionary. Although a subject of the Ottoman Sultan, Ali intended to make this city the capital of his own Greek-Albanian empire. His fiery nature earned him the title "Lion of Ioannina," and eventually caused the Sultan to view him as a threat, leading to his execution in 1822. Though in some ways still longing for the prominence of the Pasha days, present-day Ioannina is a charming, modern city worthy of a visit, though possibly not an imperial throne. With attractive avenues, a bustling waterfront, the monumental Frourio, vibrant nightlife, and easy access to Dodoni, the Perama caves, and the Vikos Gorge, Ioannina deserves its status as the hub and capital of Epirus.

☐ TRANSPORTATION

Flights: From **Ioannina National Airport** (☎26510 26 218). Flights go daily to **Athens** (1¼hr.: M-Th, Su 10:30am, 7:40pm; F-Sa 10:30am, 1:40, 7:40pm; €87) and **Thessaloniki** (55min.; M 1:35pm, Tu 3:35pm, F, Su noon; €73). To reach the airport, take bus #2 or 7 (€0.80) from the stop in front of the clock in the central plateia or get a taxi (€7-8). The **Olympic Airways office** (☎26510 23 120) is at Pl. King Pirus where G. Averof splits into Napoleonda Zerva and Leoforos Dodonis. Open M-F 9am-3:30pm.

Buses: There are 3 terminals in town.

Main terminal, Zosimadon 4 (☎26510 26 286). Buses go to: **Athens** (5½hr., 10 per day 7:15am-midnight, €29); **Igoumenitsa** (2hr., 8 per day 6am-7:45pm, €7); **Konitsa** (1hr., 7 per day 5am-8pm, €4.30); **Metsovo** (1¼hr., 4 per day 5am-2pm, €4.10); **Monodendri** (55min.; M, W, F 6:15am, 3:15pm); **Papingo** (1½hr.; F 5:15am, 2:30pm; €3.50); **Parga** (1½hr., daily Aug.-Sept. 9:30am, €9); **Thessaloniki** (4½hr., 3 per day 10:30am-10:30pm, €22.30) via **Trikala** (2½hr., €11), **Larisa** (3hr., €14), and **Volos** (5hr.; 3, 7pm; €17.50).

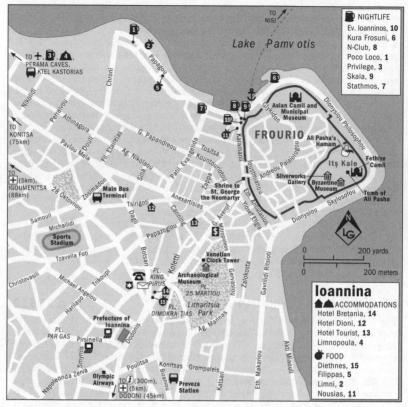

Preveza station, Bizaniou 28 (☎26510 25 014). To: **Agrinio** (3hr., 6 per day 6am-7pm, €11); **Arta** (1½hr., 10 per day 5:45am-8pm, €5); **Dodoni** (30min.; M, F 6:30am, 3:30pm; €2); **Patras** (4hr., 2 per day 9:30am-2:30pm, €15); **Preveza** (1¾hr., 8 per day 6am-8pm, €7).

KTEL Kastorias, G. Papandreou 58 (☎26510 30 006), goes to **Kastoria** (3hr.; 10am, 4pm; €15).

Ferries: Dock outside the Frourio on the waterfront and go to **Nisi** (every 30min. 7am-midnight; €1.30, students €1).

Taxis: ☎26510 46 777. Wait at the bus station and outside the Frourio before the gates that lead to the Municipal Museum.

■🛈 ORIENTATION AND PRACTICAL INFORMATION

Ioannina is at the center of Epirus, at the edge of Lake Pamvotis, and surrounded by the peaks of Pindos. Not far into the lake is a small, hilly island simply called **"Nisi"** or **"Nissaki"** ("the island" or "the islet"). **Plateia King Pirus,** the city center, contains the Venetian **clock tower** and is across from **Litharitsia Park. Georgios Averof** is a broad avenue that runs from the main gate of the Old City to the city center. After the plateia, G. Averof becomes **Dodonis,** the city's primary artery, full of shops, hotels, restaurants, and cafes. To reach the city center from the main bus station, turn left and walk uphill about 20m to an intersection where you'll see an Agricultural Bank. Facing the bank, walk uphill along the street on the left, which begins as **Dagli** and becomes **Markou Botsari** after a block—the Hotel Egnatia sign is a useful landmark. After three blocks, you'll emerge on G. Averof facing the park with the tall clock tower ahead of you. On your right, past the long building labeled "Prefecture of Ioannina" ("Νομαρχίον Ιωάννινων"), the road splits. The right branch (not the sharp right) is **Napoleonda Zerva,** and the left is Dodonis. To reach the **Frourio,** follow the signs from the city center to G. Averof's opposite end, and you will see its walls on your right. The street you will be on is **Karamanli,** which passes the main gate of the Frourio to the **waterfront.** All of Ioannina's nightlife and a long line of outdoor cafes are located down this same street, with the lake to your right.

🖾 **Tourist Office: EOT office,** Dodonis 39 (☎26510 46 662), about 500m down Dodonis on the left, just past the playground. Friendly, English-speaking Miltos provides free **maps,** info, and a list of domatia in the province. Open M-F 7:30am-2:30pm.

Banks: Dodonis and Averof are full of banks with **24hr. ATMs. National Bank,** G. Averof 4, is on your right just after Pl. King Pirus, walking toward the waterfront. (☎26510 264 34. Open M-Th 8am-2pm, F 8am-1:30pm.)

Police: 28 Oktovriou 11 (☎26510 38 600). Across Botsari from the post office. Open 24hr. The **tourist police** (☎26510 65 922; www.uoi.gr/tourist_police) are in the same building and have free **maps** and other info. Open daily 8am-10pm.

Hospital: 2 hospitals, each about 5km from the center of town. **Hatzikosta** (☎26510 80 111), on Makriani on the way to Igoumenitsa, handles emergencies on even dates; **University Hospital** (☎26510 99 111), on Universal, 5km from the end of Dodonis toward Dodoni, does so on odd dates.

Telephones: OTE, 28 Oktovriou 2-4 (☎26510 29 999). Open M, W 7am-2pm.

Internet Access: Online i-cafe, Pirsinella 4 (☎26510 72 512; www.onlinecafe.gr). On the 1st street on the right walking along Dodonis away from the waterfront. Has 75 terminals and even more overly enthusiastic gamers. Noon-midnight €2 per hr., midnight-6am €1.50 per hr., 6-7am and 9am-noon €1.20 per hr. Open 9am-7am.

Post Office: 28 Oktovriou 1 (☎26510 25 498), at the intersection of 28 Oktovriou and Botsari. Open M-F 7am-7pm. **Postal Code:** 45110.

🏠 ACCOMMODATIONS AND CAMPING

Hotels in Ioannina are either comfortable and expensive or uncomfortable, dirty, and cheap; this is a good place to consider **camping.** Otherwise head to one of the pricey but livable hotels on G. Averof. You can try one of Ioannina's cheaper options if you're not concerned with surroundings or amenities; located in noisy, sketchy back alleyways, they are worth what you pay (or less).

Limnopoula, Kanari 10 (☎26510 25 265). This unspectacular but well-priced campsite, near the town exit en route to Perama, has laundry (€5), a kitchen, a lake, public phones, and a mini-mart. Reception 7am-midnight. €6 per person, €4 per tent. ❶

Hotel Dioni, Tsirigoti 10 (☎26510 27 032; www.epirus.com/dioni). With your back to the bus station, follow Zosimadon for 1 block and turn left onto Tsirigoti. One of Ioannina's brightest, friendliest quasi-budget options, it has A/C, TV, phones, spacious blue-tiled baths, and balconies. Each floor also has a black marble lounge with couches and a TV. Breakfast €8. Laundry free. Singles €50; doubles €70. AmEx/MC/V.) ❸

Hotel Tourist, Kolleti 18 (☎26510 25 070). Walking from the *kastro* section on G. Averof toward the center of town, take a right onto El. Venizelou and then immediately another right; the hotel, with its huge neon sign, is on your right. Though it's in an unsettlingly dark area, the quiet, well-decorated rooms are far from G. Averof's incessant racket. Rooms have A/C, baths, phones, and TV. If you ask Costa, the manager, you may get a queen-sized bed. Reception 24hr. Singles €45; doubles €55; triples €66. ❸

Hotel Bretania, Pl. King Pirus 11a (☎26510 29 396), at G. Averof and Dodonis, opposite the clock tower in the city center. An excellent location, with easy access to the sweets shop downstairs. Clean rooms have bathtubs, A/C, TV, fridges, and lots of street noise. Breakfast €6. Singles €40; doubles €60; triples €72; quads €87. MC/V. ❸

🍴 FOOD

G. Averof is saturated with souvlaki, gyro, and hamburger joints. A line of more substantial restaurants on Papagou by the waterfront combines fresh air, sit-down meals, lake views, and live music. Follow G. Averof to the Frourio, and skirt the walls to the lake; as you walk away from the Frourio, cafes will soon give way to scenic tavernas. You can sample baklava and Ioannina's speciality, a tasty Turkish ice cream called *"kaimaki,"* at almost any of the ubiquitous sweet shops.

Limni, Papagou 26 (☎26510 78 988). This restaurant, whose name means "lake," is unsurprisingly located on the lakefront, with a charming patio and views of the mosque and mountains. The portions are huge, the prices are reasonable, and the vegetable pie (€3.50) is amazing. Entrees €4.50-7. Open 10am-3am. AmEx/MC/V. ❷

Filippas, Pamvotidos 5 (☎26510 31 170). Look for the yellow signs on the waterfront. The names of the delicious specials at this popular local spot all end with "Filippas," so there's no chance of forgetting where you're eating. The menu is an eclectic combination of different cultural cuisines, all prepared with a distinctly Greek spin. Pork parmesan (€7) breaks culinary rules with delicious flair. Entrees €6-11. ❷

Diethnes (☎26510 26 690), in Pl. King Pirus across from the clock tower. This shop has been keeping local dentists in business since 1950 by carrying every sugary food imaginable, including top-notch *kaimaki* (€1 per scoop). 4 other locations are spread around Ioannina, but this one is where it all began. Open 7am-2:30am. ❶

Nousias, Karamanli 1 (☎26510 33 233). Take the street that passes the main gate of the Frourio toward the dock and the waterfront; it will be on your left once you reach the lake. Confections and pastries are all baked fresh in the back, and include traditional and Turkish-influenced sweets. Ice cream €1 per scoop. Open 8:30am-1am. ❶

👁 SIGHTS

THE FROURIO. Ioannina's signature landmark, the **Frourio** (a.k.a. the **"kastro"** or the **"Old City"**), presides regally over the shore, with a slender minaret at each end. The fortress has witnessed 800 years of the city's history, from its stint as a humble Byzantine town to its mighty days under Ali Pasha. The Frourio is not a contained site, however, but a stretch of massive, overgrown stone walls that enclose a placid neighborhood of narrow streets, old Turkish-style homes, several museums, and all of Ioannina's major sights. Its several entrances are all open 24hr., as they are used by locals who live within the walls. Like that of any self-respecting fortress, the Frourio's main entrance on Karamanli has several sharp turns to make invasion slow and tricky. Just outside this entrance is an unmarked shrine to **Saint George the Neomartyr.** Ioannina's patron saint, he was tortured and hanged in 1838 by Turkish overlords for marrying a Christian. Most of the castle was built in the 13th century by **Thomas Preljubovic,** the Serbian ruler of Ioannina who was also known as **"Albanitoktonos"** ("Albanian-killer"). In order to secure a bloodless surrender in their conquest of 1430, the Turks assured Ioanninans that they could continue to remain in their houses within the fortress walls. After a failed 1611 Greek insurrection led by the fanatical Bishop of Trikala, however, the Turks cracked down. One Sunday, when all the Greeks were in church, the sneaky Turks seized their houses. Nicknaming the bishop **"Skilosofos"** ("he who has the wisdom of a dog"), they captured him and skinned him alive. When Ali Pasha came to power in 1795, he had his Greek subjects rebuild the walls on an even grander scale to fortify the capital of his dreamed-of empire. The area also saw the rise of a vibrant Jewish community that was tragically wiped out in the Holocaust.

THE ITŞ KALE. To reach the Itş Kale (the inner citadel), go into the Frourio's main entrance, take a right and then the first left; continue until you reach the long ramp that heads up to the site. This strategic high place was made the city's primary fortress in 1205 and later became Ali Pasha's headquarters, where he lived, built a mosque, and was buried. Though it was once enveloped in turmoil, the Itş Kale is now a peaceful area, surrounded by the Pindos Mountains and Pamvotis Lake. The small ruined buildings on both sides as you enter the walls were guard posts, and the cafe ahead of you on the left was originally a kitchen. To the immediate right along the wall are the remnants of Ali Pasha's **hamam** (baths), and around what is now the Silverworks Gallery of the Byzantine Museum is the *serai* (residence) that once housed Ali, his harem, and his ornately decorated audience chambers. Though hard to imagine in the serenity of today's site, Ali Pasha held most of his tortures and executions at the plane tree near the *serai*, running the gory gamut from skinning to impaling to suspending on hooks hung from the tree's branches. **Katsandonis,** a famed fighter in the War of Independence, is said to have sung patriotic hymns while being brutally hammered to death here, a scene re-enacted frequently in Greek folk shadow puppet theater. Though a **circular tower** is all that is left from the original Byzantine fortification, the **Byzantine Museum** has a small collection from the period that includes intricate wooden sanctuary doors, stone carvings, calligraphic manuscripts, and post-Byzantine icons. Plaques in English chronicle the history of Epirus and Ioannina. *(☎ 26510 27 761. Open M 12:30-7pm, Tu-Su 8am-7pm. €3, students free.)* The **Fethiye Camii** (Victory Mosque) to the right of the museum is the third mosque in its location, a space once occupied by a 13th-century church. The current mosque was rebuilt in 1795 by Ali Pasha himself. In front of the mosque, weeds and rubble obscure the **Tomb of Ali Pasha,** a sarcophagus that contains his headless body; his head and neck are buried in İstanbul. The gilded cage that originally decorated the tomb was looted by Nazis in 1943, but it was recently replaced by a green iron approximation. Ioannina is the silversmith capital of Greece, and at the **Silverworks Gallery,** to the left of the museum, you'll find snuffboxes, tea services, and belt buckles to prove it. An etching beside the desk depicts the Frourio as it looked in its glory days. *(☎ 26510 25 989. Site and museum open 8am-10pm. Show your Byzantine Museum ticket for admission.)*

MUNICIPAL MUSEUM. The smaller of the Frourio's walled inner areas is a little farther to the left of the Itş Kale—follow signs to the museum housed in the lovely **Aslan Pasha Camii,** whose rusting piles of cannon balls attest to the citadel's once-powerful status. On the left as you enter is the long, rectangular former *medrasa* (school for Qur'anic study). In front of it, the tombstones engraved in Arabic are the remains of an **Ottoman cemetary.** The small building behind the mosque is Aslan Pasha's mausoleum. In 1618, following the 1611 rebellion, the Turks destroyed the former church and replaced it with an elegant mosque. The Municipal Museum, in the former mosque, displays a beautiful *mimbar,* the pulpit from which the Imam recites readings from the Qur'an. The small but fascinating collection focuses on Ioannina's diverse ethnic past, and is divided into Jewish, Greek, and Muslim exhibits. The sword that belonged to War of Independence hero Karaiskaki and a golden dress worn by Lady Vasilikis, Ali Pasha's wife, are particularly impressive. (☎26510 26 356. *Open daily June-Sept. 7am-8:30pm; Oct.-May 8am-5pm. €3, students €12.*) Across from the Municipal Museum, down a set of stairs, is the private collection of **Fotis Rapakousis,** which houses Greek weapons from the 15th century through the Balkan Wars. *(Open M-F. Show your Municipal Museum ticket for admission.)*

NISI. Wandering chickens, cheap silver shops, a tiny whitewashed village, and five deteriorating monasteries cover this peaceful island, a 10min. ferry ride from the harbor and a world away from the noise and hectic rush of the city. It was here, surrounded by reeds and marsh, that Ali Pasha met his death after seriously falling out of the Sultan's favor. Attempting to hide from the certain punishment that awaited him, Ali fled to the second story of the island's **Saint Pantaleimon monastery.** He was soon found there, and subsequently killed by shots fired up through the floorboards—which are now, complete with bullet holes, displayed in the museum. The victors hung Ali's severed head for public viewing for several days before transporting it back to the Sultan in İstanbul. Though this event obviously marked the end of Ali's ruthless regime, Ioannina's claim to fame still rests on his now-detached shoulders. The monastery currently houses the two-room **Ali Pasha Museum,** which displays Ali Pasha's enormous bronze hookah, which he happily puffs in almost every portrait. A large painting of the Sultan ceremoniously receiving the head of his fearsome ex-governor adorns the opposite wall, a constant reminder of who was ultimately victorious. *(26510 81 791. Open daily 9am-9pm. €2.)* Signs point the way to St. Pantaleimon and the other four monasteries. A short walk from the museum, the **frescoes** of St. Nicholas Philanthropinos, painted by Katelanou in 1542, depict saints, the life of Jesus, and seven ancient sages, including Plato, Aristotle, and Plutarch, who were said to have foretold the coming of Christ. If the monastery is locked, ask politely at the house next door for a tour. The church is spectacular, with rays of light that beam through the windows and bathe the walls and frescoes in gold. At the nearby *krifto scholio* (secret school), the forbidden Greek language was kept alive during Ottoman reign. There is a crypt in the monastery of **Saint John Prodromos** that leads to a secret exit and path to the lake. *(☎26510 25 885. The 10min. ferries to Nisi from Ioannina's waterfront run every 30min. 7am-midnight; in winter every hr. 7am-9pm. €1.30, students €1.)*

◧ NIGHTLIFE

Most of Ioannina's late-night action takes place on the waterfront in two separate clusters, at different spots along the base of the Frourio walls: cafes and discos line the north, along the waterfront on Papagou, and bars sit in the south where Garivaldi meets Ethnikis. To reach a string of relaxed after-hours cafes, walk past the Diethnes sweet shop away from the Frourio walls to Soutsi and Mavili. The streets teem with locals sitting at music cafes, talking and enjoying the breezy waterfront area. More options are on the other side of the peninsula; you can either head back to Diethnes and walk along the perimeter of the walls for 400m or take Karamanli, which begins soon after the Ferris wheel, to Eth. Antistasios. You will then see a park, opposite which is a cluster of bars and clubs.

> **Kura Frosuni** (☎26510 73 984), right outside the fort, on the northwestern corner of the peninsula. Always crowded with young people, it has the tables closest to the water and a great view of Nisi. Open daily 9:30am-3am.

> **Stathmos,** G. Papagou 5 (☎26510 77 662; www.stathmos-ioa.gr), next to the Ferris wheel. Tables full of people relaxing with drinks sit on a giant dismantled train car. Open 9am-3:30am. Beer €3.50. Mixed drinks €6.

Poco Loco (☎26510 31 207), next to Limni, almost at the end of the waterfront. This open-air bar also serves Mexican food. Open 6pm-2am.

N-Club, Garivaldi 1 (☎26510 28 028), at the main gate to the Frourio. Light-emitting fiber-optic cables illuminate this super-modern club, which plays an unusual mix of ambient house, techno, Greek, and reggae music. Beer €3.

Skala (☎26510 37 676), behind N-Club. Locals come to this low-key hangout to hear pop and Greek tunes, and pre-game before hitting the clubs. Open 9pm-3am.

Ev. Ioanninos, Iourtorakis 18 (☎26510 21 669), around the corner from Skala. Its swanky, 3m tall bar is nearly impossible to miss. Mixed drinks €6. Open 10pm-4am.

Privilege (☎69324 25 258). Follow the signs after Poco Loco, walking away from the Frourio. Ioannina's biggest disco has gold-lit columns outside, and private booths and a pool-enclosed bar inside. You must be well-dressed (no shorts) and be over 20 with a photo ID. Beer €5. Cover €5. Open M-Th, Su midnight-3:30am, F-Sa midnight-6am.

⚡ DAYTRIPS FROM IOANNINA

▨ DODONI Δωδώνη

Buses to Dodoni run from Ioannina's smaller station (30min.; M, F 6:30am, 3:30pm; €2). Ask to be let off at the theater. You can also take a taxi there (at least €20) and take the bus (passes by daily around 4:45pm) back. If you're stranded, ask the famous oracle what to do. Otherwise, call a taxi (☎26510 46 777), but expect to pay a €2-3 surcharge. (☎26510 82 287. Open 8am-5pm. €2, students and seniors €1, EU students free.)

Ancient Dodoni, the site of mainland Greece's oldest oracle, lies at the base of a mountain 23km southwest of Ioannina. An oracle of Zeus and his consort Dione Naia, Dodoni's sacred oak tree was thought to be a portal of the divine wisdom of the king of the gods. Such worthy figures as Odysseus and Achilles sought advice under its leafy shade until the site was all but demolished by the Romans in 167 BC. At its height, Dodoni, consulted mostly on personal rather than political matters, was the second greatest oracle in the ancient world, surpassed only by Delphi. The **Naia festival,** an Olympic-like series of pan-Hellenic athletic and dramatic contests, was held here every four years in Zeus's honor.

The enormous **amphitheater** near the entrance to the site was built in the early 3rd century BC. The original design seated 17,000 before the Romans replaced the lowest rows with a retaining wall and improved the still-visible drainage system to accommodate their blood sports. The vast complex is staggering; every seat has an amazing view of the stage, and it is easy to picture the drama and violence that once occurred here. The acoustics are so good that whispers made on stage can be heard clearly even by those in the nose-bleed seats. Unfortunately the theater is currently undergoing restoration, and so much of it is off limits. Beyond the amphitheater are the ruins of the oracle itself, where the sacred oak (or a new sacred oak) has recently been replanted. Unlike the complicated hexameters which served as answers at Delphi, Dodoni's replies were either "yes" or "no," expressed through the doves nestling in the tree, the rustling of its branches, or the soft murmuring of the nearby spring. According to Herodotus, a dove was the original settler of the oracle. Myth tells that an Egyptian priestess who was kidnapped by Phoenician sea traders transformed into a dove to escape captivity. She settled at Dodoni and convinced Zeus that the serene spot was where he should establish his oracle. A clan of priests called the **Hellopes, Helloi,** or **Selloi** guarded the heavenly site, but were eventually replaced by three priestesses called **Doves.** Little remains today of the original building that housed the tree and its hordes of pilgrims. A 5th-century BC temple and the 350 BC **bouleuterion** and **prytaneion,** now almost totally vanished, once surrounded the oracle. Following the Aetolian sack in 219 BC, a larger Ionic temple to Zeus was built in 167 BC. Later, in the AD 5th century, the site was home to some of the largest early Christian basilicas.

AGIOS GEORGIOS AQUEDUCT

Take the bus to Preveza (1hr., 8 per day 6am-8pm, €6) and ask the driver to let you off at Agios Georgios. Once you get off, cross the highway and take the road leading downhill for about 1km. To return, go back up the road to take the bus back to Ioannina (1hr., 10 per day 6am-7:30pm, €6).

The location alone of the remains of Nikopolis's (p. 254) Roman **aqueduct,** high in the mountains, is gorgeous, but the well-preserved structure crossing the Louros rapids has a beauty of its own. Construction of the aqueduct at such an altitude was a major feat of contemporary engineering, which hints at the importance of Nikopolis to Roman interest in the region. Over 50 years later, the aqueduct was connected to the city's **nymphaion fountain.** Although the site has no signs or explanations, the area is serene and beautiful, and it's still fascinating to watch the stream flow under the ancient construction.

PERAMA CAVES

Take local bus #16 from the park behind the city center (15min., every 15min. 6:30am-10pm, €0.80). At Perama, follow the multiple "ΣΠΗΛΑΙΟ" signs to the cave. Turn right at the blue sign in the middle of Spileou. ☎ 26510 81 521. Open daily in summer 8:30am-6pm; in winter 9am-5pm. €6, students €2.50, children under 12 free. Tours every 15min.

A 500-step stairway leads through the spectrally lit, glimmering Perama Caves, among the largest in the Balkans. The path leads from narrow passageways to immense **caverns** filled with eerily hanging rock formations. The huge cavities were discovered accidently by two locals who were seeking shelter from Nazi bombs during WWII. Subsequent excavations have uncovered bears' teeth and bones in the nearly two-million-year-old stalagmites and stalactites. The 45min. Greek-only guided tour mainly introduces stalagmites that have been named after other objects they vaguely resemble: "Tower of Pisa," "Egyptian Sphinx," "The Statue of Liberty," and so on. Hovering around a comfortable 17°C/62°F inside, the cave offers natural relief during the scorching Greek afternoons. The exit puts you 600m away from the entrance, but luckily the walk back yields some beautiful vantage points from which to see Ioannina, the lake, and Nisi.

METSOVO Μέτσοβο ☎ 26560

On the steep western slope of the 1690m Katara Pass lies the quaint alpine town of Metsovo. Built into the side of a mountain, the town itself is a piece of art, maintained in near-perfect condition by the fortune left by Metsovite-turned-Swiss-banker Baron Tositsas. Though frequented during the day by tour buses that pause there during their journeys, the town has enough character and opportunities to be a fulfilling destination in itself. The self-proclaimed "Vlach capital" contains some of the last speakers of that Latin-based language, which is currently on the verge of extinction. Its position in the North Pindos mountains makes it a gold mine of exquisite hikes. The intricate local costumes and rugs, along with the festivals and traditional weddings that seem to be one continuous celebration in mid- and late July, display Metsovite culture in full form.

⌐ TRANSPORTATION. From the main plateia, **buses** depart for Ioannina (1½hr., 4 per day 6:30am-4:30pm, €4.20) and Trikala (2hr., 8:30am, €5) via Kalambaka

(1½hr., €4). The bus to Thessaloniki (5½hr., 5 per day 7am-10:30pm, €20) passes by on the main highway above town, but won't stop unless you flag it down. The *periptero* by the central plateia bus stop, across from the statue of a friendly bear, has schedules. **Taxis** (☎26560 41 393) wait in the plateia and can be called 24hr.

◼◪ ORIENTATION AND PRACTICAL INFORMATION. Though maps are not necessary to navigate Metsovo, if you feel lost, you can attempt to glean some information from the nearly illegible English-language town map on a stone wall. Metsovo extends through a few unnamed roads from the main plateia, which is the center of town life. The bus drops off in front of a sign for Hotel Egnatia information (not the hotel but a small souvenir shop bearing the same name). With your back to the sign and the park in front of you, there are two roads to your left. The road closest to you heads uphill toward Ioannina and Trikala after passing the Tositsas Museum and the **post office**, which has **Poste Restante**. (☎26560 41 245. Open M-F 7:30am-2pm.) There is a 24hr. **hospital** (☎26560 41 112) at the top of the town, along the same road. The **town hall**, on the second floor of the large white building that houses the Eurobank, is located where the road meets the plateia. If you walk around to the building's back, you will find a staff that can provide you with brochures about the area, info about hiking trails, and free **maps**. (☎26560 41 207. Open 7am-2:30pm.) The farther road to your left when standing at the bus stop leads to John Xaralabap-oulos's Rooms and Hotel Olympic. Past the parking lot and to your right are most of the town's restaurants and another section of the plateia, both blocked by the park. Walking 50m to your right will take you to Kria Folia, a restaurant at the northwestern corner of the square. From there, the street directly to your right goes slightly downhill to the municipal **police** (☎26560 41 233; open 24hr.) and the **OTE**, across the street (☎26560 42 199; open M-F 8am-2pm). The second road to the right runs downhill to the Agios Nikolaos monastery and to **Tsigas's Super Game Club**, which has **Internet access**. (☎26560 41 696. €2 per hr. Beer €1.50. Open 9am-2am.) In front of you to the right, another road wraps around the plateia and the public park, past the **National Bank** (☎26560 41 296; open M-F 8am-2pm) and **Agricultural Bank** (☎26560 41 160; open M-Th 8am-2:30pm, F 8am-2pm), which both have **24hr. ATMs. Postal Code: 44200.**

◪ ACCOMMODATIONS. Room prices spike outrageously during Metsovo's two high seasons (mid-July to Sept. and Dec.-March), making it near impossible to find accommodations that won't leave a gaping hole in your pocket. During these times, the town is best visited as a daytrip. In low season, however, the rooms are tranquil, charming, and far more reasonably priced. You can find **domatia** by veering left before the OTE and after the post office. Most offer simple rooms for about €25-30. Hands down the most welcoming option in town is ◪**Hotel Filoxenia ❷**, whose name (meaning "hospitality") says it all. British-educated proprietor Yiannis is a one-stop source for all things Mets-ovo. Full of wisdom, humor, and experience traversing the mountainous area, he has helpful information, arranges hikes in the nearby Valia Skalda National Park, and stores gear, even for hikers not staying at the hotel. The rooms have TV, mountainside balconies, and baths. (☎26560 41 021. Breakfast €4. Singles €25; doubles €35; triples 50.) **John Xaralabapoulos's Rooms ❷**, which all come with TV and phones, are large, comfortable, and have an understated charm. A handpainted sign labeled "Domatia-Rooms" marks the entrance, just past the basketball court. (☎26560 42 086. Singles €25; doubles €32; triples €36.) **Hotel**

Olympic ❸, behind John Xaralabapoulos's Rooms, has wood-paneled rooms with big soft double beds, baths, TV, and phones. (☎26560 41 337. Breakfast €7. Singles €30; doubles €35; triples €40. MC/V.)

◖◗◪ FOOD AND NIGHTLIFE. Many of the restaurants in Metsovo are similar, catering both to large groups of tourists as well as to locals. **Galaxias ❷,** in an ivy-covered mansion, serves a number of homemade local specialties such as veal with Metsovo village pasta (€7). With your back to the entrance of the town hall, take a left and walk past the small park; you'll see the huge sign reading "Galaxy." Though the mansion is appealing, the sunny, green-garden eating area has a more relaxed, summertime feel. (☎26560 41 202; www.metsovo.com/galaxyhotel. Entrees €5-9. Open 11am-11pm. MC/V.) Serving trout from Lake Metsovo, delectable soups (boiled goat meat soup with potatoes and carrots; €5) and the town's acclaimed vegetable pies, **To Koutouki Tou Nikola ❷** is found, as its name implies, in Nikola's basement, on the street toward the post office. With your back to the Hotel Egnatia bus stop, you will see the large sign if you look left. (☎26560 41 732. Open 11am-1am.) In the plateia itself, tourist favorite **Kryfi Folia ❷,** one shop down from the Agricultural Bank, is quite the grill master, with meat like *kokoretsi* (lamb intestines; 6.50) and *kontosoufli* (pork and lamb souvlaki; €6) cooked to perfection. (☎26560 41 628. Open 11am-midnight.) For a much cheaper meal, local fast-food stop **Mangare ❶,** just up the left branch of the road which forks at the post office, makes quick and satisfying souvlaki (€1.50) and sandwiches. (☎26560 41 101. Open 6pm-2am.) Metsovo does not offer much in the way of nightlife, but if you're itching to go out, drop by **Krini Club** (☎26560 41 184), one block up from the post office on the road to Ioannina. The club caters to older Metsovites looking for a good time, but is also a second home to Metsovo's youth—though they doesn't show up until after 12:30am, when the older crowd has dissipated. (Beer €3. Mixed drinks €6. Open M-Th, Su 6pm-3am, F-Sa 5pm-6am.)

◪ SIGHTS. Thanks to the Baron Tositsas and his nephew, Evangelos Averof-Tositsas, Metsovo has far more sights than you'd expect from a 4000-person town. Off the main plateia, the spacious **Evangelos Averof Gallery** exhibits 19th- and 20th-century Greek paintings, including Averof-Tositsas's private collection. Follow the road after the two banks; it's on your right after the bend around the park. (☎26560 41 210. Open M, W-Sa mid-July to mid-Sept. 10am-6:30pm; mid-Sept. to mid-July 10am-4:30pm. €3, students €2.) Just off the central plateia, between the National and Agricultural Banks, is the ◪**Workshop of George Boubas,** who handcrafts traditional costumes and silver jewelry. George guarantees that all of his goods are made with non-fading natural dyes, so souvenirs bought here promise to be of good quality. (☎26560 42 580. Open 8am-1:30pm and 3:30-9:30pm. AmEx/MC/V.) The **Tositsas Museum,** 50m up the hill in a mansion to the left of the main road opposite Krini Club, honors the generosity of the town's benefactors. Also known as the folk art museum, it displays traditional costumes, silverware, wooden carvings, along with a timeline of Metsovo's history. (☎26560 41 084. Open daily mid-July to mid-Sept. 8:30am-1pm and 4-6pm; mid-Sept. to mid-July 8:30am-1pm and 5-7pm. €3. Visitors are only admitted in small groups; wait at the door for the guide who appears every 30min.) The **Agios Nikolaos Monastery** is a 30min. walk from the plateia down the hillside; signs point the way. Built in the 14th century, the monastery was originally one of the most important in the area, though it soon fell into disuse. It was restored in 1700 before being abandoned once more. While it was officially empty, itinerant shepherds used its crumbling chapel as a refuge. The smoke from their fires completely covered frescoes that had been painted in 1702, perfectly preserving them until they were rediscovered in 1950 by Averof-Tositsas. Today, you can see the formerly covered icons and the famous moss-covered bell tower overlooking the picturesque valley below the town.

For info about **Valia Kalda National Park** (Vlach for "warm valley") and other outdoor activities in Metsovo, contact the town hall (☎ 26560 41 207) or the owners of Hotel Filoxenia (p. 263). One of the most important parks in Greece, Valia Kalda is home to 80 species of birds and a number of endangered animals such as the brown bear, the wild cat, and the wild goat. Its drastic landscape and gushing rivers are rich enough to occupy any outdoors enthusiast for days or even weeks. The town hall gives out an excellent free topographical map.

The village hosts a major *yiorti* (celebration) each year on July 26, which used to be the Vlach courting day; all women and most men dress in traditional bright costumes for the modern festivities, splashing the entire town with color. The residents then embark on an annual hike up to celebrate and carouse in honor of the Greek gods; the town elders decided that this was the only way to legitimately commemorate the generous Baron's belief in the Olympian pantheon. Reserve rooms at least two weeks in advance if you will be there for the festival.

> The ⚑Hellenic **Mountaineering Club (EOS)**, based in Ioannina, supplies information and leads weekend trips throughout the region. (☎ 26510 22 138. Open M-Sa 7-9pm.) The **Paddler Kayaking and Rafting School** (☎ 26550 23 777 or 26550 23 101), with offices in Konitsa and Megalo Papingo, gives lessons and oversees outings to local rivers. A major local outfitter is **Alpine Zone**, Josef Eligia 16 (☎ 26510 23 222; www.alpinesone.gr), located off Averof in Ioannina, which specializes in rafting equipment and outings. For more information, contact Marios at Pension Monodendri (☎ 26530 71 300) or Nikos at Koulis Restaurant (☎ 26530 41 115), in Monodendri and Papingo respectively. The best times for hiking are late May, early June, and September. April through June is the season to see alpine flowers. Colored foliage flares brilliantly in the dry autumns. The best season for rafting is April through May, when the full rivers start to warm up.

ZAGOROHORIA Ζαγοροχώρια

Between the Albanian border and the North Pindos mountain range, a string of 46 little hamlets (*horia*) quietly coexist, showing few signs of interference from modern-day society. A trip to these Zagorohoria immediately immerses visitors into the blissful relaxation of simple village life. The tiny, picturesque towns are a tapestry of narrow cobblestone roads and stone-tiled roof-tops, which give the area a magical "stone-age" atmosphere. While the villages themselves are well worth a day or two, most tourists come to the greater Zagorohoria region to hike around rough-riding rivers, stark peaks, and dark wet caves. The area's largest (or, shall we say, deepest) draw is Vikos Gorge, the world's steepest canyon. These natural treasures, in addition to the surrounding Vikos-Aoös National Park, which provides additional hiking and trekking opportunities, offer nature enthusiasts of every skill level an outlet for exploration.

MONODENDRI Μονοδένδρι   ☎ 26530

Many a traveler has passed dreamily through Monodendri's cobbled maze, illuminated only by twinkling stars and the summertime multitudes of fireflies. Though hikers bearing cameras and sunscreen are now as common as goats and sheep in the tiny village of 150, their presence has not changed Monodendri's character.

The area's natural and architectural beauty, location at the top of Vikos Gorge, and proximity to Ioannina make it an unrivaled base for hikers.

The bus stop, all of the hotels, and most of the restaurants cluster on Monodendri's one paved road. **Buses** go to Ioannina (1hr.; M, W, F 8am, 4pm; €3). **Taxis** can take you to Ioannina or Konitsa (€35). Monodendri's lower plateia is accessible by a footpath that descends to the right from the bus stop; follow the path downhill and turn left at the fork. The plateia is home to a cafe, a **phone**, a **post box**, and signposts for all the trailheads, and is also the starting point for all of the lookouts and hikes in Vikos Gorge. There is **no bank**; the closest are in Kalpaki and Konitsa. Some hotels accept traveler's checks and Pension Monodendri **exchanges currency** for guests of the establishment and *Let's Go* travelers. The nearest **hospital** is in Ioannina. Both the town kiosk, across from Arhondiko Zarkada Hotel, and Monodendri Hotel have good trail **maps** (around €7.50). **Postal Code:** 44007.

Opposite the bus stop, ◼**Monodendri Hotel ❷** has cozy rooms with colorful rugs. The owner's English-speaking son, Marios, is full of info about trekking in the area and picks up passengers from Vikos Village (€30) or Megalo Papingo (€40) after their hikes. (☎26530 71 300; www.monodendrihotel.com. Breakfast €5. Bag lunch for the trail €3.50. Laundry free. Reception 8am-11pm. Singles €20; doubles €25; triples €30. MC/V.) **Arhondiko Zarkada Hotel ❷**, on the left as you walk up from the bus station, has a pool as well as large, comfortable rooms with modern baths, TV, phones, and gorgeous stone balconies. (☎26530 71 305; www.epirus.com/zarkadas. Breakfast €6.50. Singles €25; doubles €30; triples €35. AmEx/MC/V.)

A few tavernas are scattered along the main road. The friendliest is ◼**Katerina's ❷**, on the porch of Monodendri Hotel, where Marios's mother, Mrs. Daskalopoulou, prepares the food. (Cheese pie €3.50. Lamb with potatoes €6.) **Restaurant Vikos Gorge ❷**, one door up in the upper plateia, has English-speaking waiters and a wide porch packed with locals. Stuffed tomatoes (€3.50) and *kotopita* (pizza-like pie; €4) are complemented by local wines. (☎26530 71 559. Open noon-2am.)

The must-see natural **overlook,** a very easy 1½hr. walk on the main road from the village, has breathtaking views of the entire **Vikos Gorge** (see below). A large section of the road can be bypassed by following a red-blazed trail that begins behind the Monodendri Hotel. As the harsh winters often leave the markers unclear, ask Marios at the hotel to show you the path. The road eventually gives way to a footpath which leads to the vantage point; the three main chasms' glow at sunset is spectacular. Another equally easy hike goes beyond the abandoned **Monastery of Agia Paraskevi** (20min.), which is 1km from Monodendri's lower plateia; many signs point the way. The monastery houses an operating icon-painter's workshop. A small terrace has stunning views of the beginning of the gorge trail, and an edgeless, meter-wide path is cut straight into the sheer rock wall. The treacherous path leads to a small cave once used by monks to hide from raiders. Signs from the plateia point along the slightly harder trail to **Megali Spilia** (30min.), another nearby cave where Zagorohorians used to hide from marauders.

VIKOS GORGE Φαράγγι Βίκου

Vikos Gorge, whose walls are 900m deep but only 110m apart, is the steepest on earth. In spring time, the river that has taken millions of years to form the gorge rushes along the 15km stretch of canyon floor. By summer, all that is left is the occasional puddle hidden among massive white boulders in the dry riverbed. Vikos Gorge seems to have been splashed with a beautifully faded mix of colors. Rusted iron deposits in the gorge's rock leave an orange-pink tint that drips over the gray walls, supplemented as the seasons pass by the brilliant hues of spring wildflowers, summer butterflies, autumn foliage, and views of the green waters running below Vikos Village. When night falls, listen for the shrill chirping of crickets and watch fireflies dance in trees, blending into the star-studded sky.

People have walked through the gorge's deep ravine since the 12th century BC, when early settlers took shelter in its craggy caves. Today, hikers follow its path, which stretches from the village of Kipi in the south to Megalo Papingo at its northernmost tip and winds its way through the center of the Zagorohoria. From the riverbed, nearly vertical canyon sides tower hundreds of meters overhead. The well-marked **trail** through the gorge is the **O3** domestic trail section of the Greek National E4 route, and it runs from the Aoös River near Konitsa all the way to Kipi. Before you go, be sure to get a **map** (€7.50), which are sold at the *periptero* on the main road through Monodendri, the Monodendri Hotel, and No Limits in Papingo. If you get confused, just look for the red diamonds on white square backgrounds with "O3" stenciled in them, which consistently mark the path. Most hikers enter the gorge from **Monodendri,** the highest of the villages, but it can also be accessed from **Kipi,** the **Papingo** villages, and from **Vikos Village.** It takes 5hr. to walk between Vikos Village and Monodendri and 6hr. between the Papingos and Monodendri.

To reach the gorge from Monodendri, take the marked path from the lower plateia. After about 10min. along the steep, winding descent, you'll reach a fork in the path (700m). Go left to enter the canyon's dry riverbed of smooth rocks, and head toward the far-off villages of the Papingos and Vikos. After about 1½hr. (4km), the right fork will bring you to the village of Kipi, with its trademark stone bridges. To descend down into the gorge, take the left fork as it climbs above the left bank of the riverbed. The path is fairly level and pleasant for some time, continuing through a shady woodland along the riverbank. On the way, you'll pass open groves mowed clean by grazing horses. About 4-5hr. (9km) from Monodendri, you'll reach the crossroads that lead up to Vikos Village. The trail suddenly becomes a meticulously cobbled stone path, which, after about 20m, makes a 90° turn up and to the left toward Vikos (300m; about 45min.). If you're Papingo-bound, you'll want to maintain a straight course that descends to your right, hugging the riverbanks into the grassy pasture. This area is a popular camping site among backpackers looking to avoid steep room rates. Keep your eyes on the stream's opposite bank because, about halfway through the grassy clearing, a frenzy of red arrows on the boulders marks the ford and continuation of O3 to Papingo. Another long hour out of the gorge brings you to the well-marked Megalo Papingo-Mikro Papingo split. From here, it's another 30min. to either village.

Hikers entering from the Papingo villages should follow signs from the plateias. Stone stairways lead you most of the way. The trailhead in **Vikos Village** is outside town across from Dinoulis Rooms. This intermediate trail slowly descends to **Voidhomatis springs,** the source of the Vikos river (1½hr.). The only other rooms in the tiny 30-person Vikos Village are at **Sotiris Karpouzis ❹.** (☎26530 41 176. Reception open until 1am. €45 for up to 3 people.) Both hotels have tavernas. At a third taverna in the plateia, the obliging owner provides rides (€30) to Monodendri.

THE PAPINGOS Τα Πάπινγκα ☎26530

Many travelers reach the two enchanting Papingo villages, Megalo (Μεγάλο; big) and Mikro (Μικρό; small), located north of the Vikos Gorge, after a long, tiring hike. As the most developed towns in all of the Zagorohoria, they boast 22 separate lodgings choices, which contrasts sharply with most of the other villages in the region, some of which have fewer than 25 residents. But even though Megalo is Zagorohoria's New York City, do not expect a huge metropolis—the village's total population is 117. Recently, the Papingos have become a vacation destination for

LOCAL LEGEND

MONSTER'S BRAWL

According to a widely known tale in the Zagorohoria villages, fire-spitting monsters used to traverse the Timfi mountain range. Though man and monster generally lived together in peace, the two fiercest monsters, Draco and Stella, occasionally grabbed a villager or two for a snack.

One day, both Draco and Stella had a craving for a delicious human, but got into a fight about who got first dibs. It started harmlessly enough, as they tossed archaic Greek obscenities back and forth. But then, as one would expect from a monster quarrel, things got out of control quickly. Draco began hurling boulders at Stella, while Stella retaliated by uprooting trees and throwing them at Draco.

No one knows who won the earth-shaking fight, but its aftermath is still visible today. Stella's former home, Storlyiki Lake is now littered with Draco's giant rocks. The trees Stella threw, however, didn't get quite high enough to reach Draco in his alpine abode at Dragomili Lake, so they landed on the nearby mountainside. Though the monsters are long gone (a monster's life span isn't infinite, you know), their descendants, the Alpine Newts, still roam around the area, and can be seen clinging to the grass around Dragomili Lake.

wealthy Greeks from Thessaloniki and Ioannina. Despite the boom in tourism, the villages still maintain the serenity that characterizes their neighboring hamlets.

◼◼ **TRANSPORTATION AND PRACTICAL INFORMATION.** The large, austere stone church and its attendant **bell tower** stand at the entrance to Megalo Papingo, to the left of the **bus stop.** From here, a cobblestone thoroughfare snakes around the town, first ascending to the top and then looping down again; it contains most of the villages' pensions and restaurants. The road to Mikro Papingo is clearly marked to the right of the church and the **trailhead** for Vikos Gorge is 20m down this road at the end of a well-marked dirt lane on the right. Don't follow the old, yellow sign 50m down the road—contrary to appearances, it does not actually lead to the Vikos trail. **Buses** go to Ioannina (1½hr.; M, W, F 5:15am, 3:30pm; €4.10). A more dependable alternative is to hike the 3hr. trail to **Klidonia,** where you can catch buses on the more frequent Konitsa-Ioannina route (1hr., 8 per day 5am-8pm, €4). Megalo Papingo has a **phone** by the church and a **mailbox** by Lakis Cafe. Mikro Papingo also has a **phone** at the town entrance, near the WWF center; a **mailbox** is by the trail signpost. Another entrance for Vikos Gorge is located here along with the trailheads for **Drakolimni, Mount Astrakas,** and the **EOS refuge.** For details about hiking, rafting, and paragliding, ask for Nikos at **No Limits,** an office that provides outdoor information, on your right about 10m up the cobblestone road. (☎26550 23 777. Open 10am-7pm.)

◼◻ **ACCOMMODATIONS AND FOOD.** The lodgings in the chic Papingos can be expensive as the recent increase in tourism has raised prices. If **pensions** and **domatia** are full or prices are at high-season levels, backpackers may want to huff it up to the EOS Refuge by Mt. Astrakas. Though it is illegal, many hikers have also been known to freelance camp. Popular locations include the Vikos Village crossroads in the gorge (p. 266), a small clearing halfway down the road from Megalo to Mikro Papingo on the left, and other areas surrounding the gorge. The beautifully furnished rooms at ◼**Pension Koulis ❷,** with fireplaces, wooden floors, TV, and baths, may remind you of an Alpine ski lodge. Facing the town from where the cobblestone road starts, take the first left after the church. The pension is on the corner of the next crossroads to the left. (☎26530 41 115. Breakfast included. Reception 24hr. Singles €25; doubles €50; triples €65. MC/V.) At **Vasiliki Nikolaus** ❸, simple, spacious farmhouse rooms come with access to a communal bath, fridge, and washing machine (free for guests). Go uphill from where the main road meets the cobblestone one facing the church, turn left after 50m up a small lane, and take the first left. Though the rooster might wake you at dawn, this domatia has an authentic small village atmosphere, complete with animals, the smell of manure, and fresh air. (Singles and doubles €35.) **Georgios Reppas's** ❹ homey rooms include quilted beds, TV, shared baths, and an amazing sense of tranquility. Look for his house immediately opposite the church. Though the prices are almost as steep as the nearby gorge, this little domatia will make you feel right at home. (☎26530 41 711. Breakfast €5 per room. Singles €40; doubles €47; triples €55.) Behind its vine entryway, the 120-year-old **Astraka** ❸, on the other end of the main road, feels familiar and well-loved, with comfortable rooms with baths, fireplaces, and TV, plus a cozy living room. (☎26530 41 693. Singles €35; doubles €45; triples €50; quads €60.)

Just outside town by the path to Vikos Gorge on the road to Mikro Papingo is ◪**Estiatorio** ❷. The owner, Costa, serves lamb from his father's flock, vegetables from his gardens, and his own feta. It is hard to decide whether to concentrate on the colorful plate in front of you or the gorge's surreal beauty, visible from your table. (☎26530 42 108. Entrees €5-8. Open 11am-1am.) **Restaurant Papingo** ❸, to the right of the bell tower in the Papingo Pension, near Pension Koulis, is a popular choice among visitors and serves a selection of meat dishes and salads. Though more tourist-oriented than Costa's place, the food is tasty and the portions are generous, making it a good place to satiate your hunger after a day of strenuous hiking. (☎26530 42 443. Entrees €7.50-13. Open noon-the last person leaves.)

◨◪ SIGHTS AND HIKING. Mikro Papingo hosts the Zagorohoria regional **World Wildlife Federation (WWF).** The office, located at the entrance to town in the former public elementary school, has a few nice exhibits about local wildlife, history, and culture. Follow the single road that goes through the village, and take the first right. (☎26530 41 071. Open M-Th 10am-5:30pm, F-Su 11am-6pm. Free.)

The most spectacular Zagorohoria hikes begin in Mikro Papingo. Besides Vikos Gorge, village visitors can climb **Mount Astraka** (2436m). The mountain's 407m deep cave, **Provatrina,** is filled with water; only geologists can descend into its dark mouth. Many footpaths go up to Mt. Astraka. Most of them take about 4hr. and are appropriate for intermediate-level hikers. Another option is to climb to the pristine ◪**Drakolimni** (Dragon Lake). This cloud-reflecting alpine pool (2000m) is filled with green and black and orange-spotted newts who hang motionless on the wind-whipped grasses. It is well worth the strenuous 4½hr. climb up—the pool's water mimics the sky like a perfect mirror and the air is crystal clear. Both hikes can be paired with a stay in the **EOS refuge** (1900m), on a ridge nearby (☎69732 23 100).

Those who can't get to the Papingos because of limited buses should consider hiking in from the Klidonia bus stop on the Ioannina-Konitsa line (1hr., 8 per day 5am-8pm, €4). From the bus stop, follow the Konitsa-bound bus along the highway to the town's main road on the right opposite a gas station. Ask at the gas station or one of the homes along the road to be pointed to the 5km **Klidonia-Papingo Trail** (Κλειδωνιά-Πάπιγκο). This easy walk, which takes around 1½hr., passes through green hills full of sheep and goats tended to by local shepherds. Before you get to the bridge of Aristi that goes over the river, you will see a stop at which there is a foot path for Klidonia. A more difficult but also more scenic option is to get to the Papingos via the trail up the mountain through the ghost town of **Ano Klidonia** (Upper Klidonia). From the trailhead, at a church visible above town, a well-marked path, highlighted by red blazes, leads up the mountainside. If you get off track, just follow the electric line, which goes along the trail, albeit without switchbacks. The first shoulder (1hr., 2km, intermediate) ascends 900m to yield awe-inspiring views of the Aoös River flood plain and a small abandoned church. This is Ano Klidonia, withered away from lack of a highway. Follow the sparsely marked dirt track to the church of Prositis Ilias, where the red blazed trail begins again. From here you have a sweeping view of Mt. Astrakas on the left and Vikos Gorge on the right. Perched in the distance on the ridges flanking this gaping crack are clustered houses. The right hamlet is Vikos; straight ahead is Papingo. After about one more hour on a fairly level path which traces a northern arch, you will take the dirt lane west of Papingo which marks the route's final kilometer.

To get to the **refuge** from Mikro Papingo, start walking on the trail leading to Drakolimni and Mt. Astrakas; signs saying "To the Refuge" ("Πρός Καταφύγιο") will guide you. This intermediate-level trail climbs past four **springs:** a chapel-topped faucet (Ag. Pandeleimon; 10min.), another faucet (Antalki; 1hr.), a frog-filled trough (Trafos; 2hr.), and a small, cold spring (Krouna; 2½hr.). The path is well marked with O3 triangles and red blazes throughout. Occasionally the trail spiderwebs, but usually all options are valid; keep a look-out for blazes. After the last spring, the trail is exposed and the ridge-resting refuge is visible. Another 30min. of views and knee-crunching brings you to the 60-bed **EOS refuge ❶**, 3km from Mikro Papingo. (☎26530 26 553 or 69732 23 100. €10 per person, members of any mountain club €8.) From here, a 2hr. trail scales Mt. Astraka (2km, difficult). A path (3km, 1¼hr.) from the same starting point descends into the blossom-dotted valley and then climbs a meadow on the opposite ridge, past Xeroloutsa, a shallow, life-alteringly beautiful Alpine lake, and onto Drakolimni. In the summer, the meadow's grasses are home to **sheep** and their shepherds, who are friendly and happy to gesture directions to the few visitors who make it up here. Give the flocks a wide berth as the sheep dogs are very protective and have been known to bite. From the refuge, multi-day treks deep into the Pindos are possible and hikers usually plan to end in the luxury of one of the valley villages.

MACEDONIA Μακεδονία

Macedonia earned itself a place in history when its native son Alexander conquered an empire stretching to Egypt and India by 323 BC. A few centuries later, the region served as the geographical entry point for St. Paul of Tarsus to bring Christianity to Europe for the first time. The historical boundaries of Greek Macedonia under the Byzantine Empire, meanwhile, were much greater than the modern province's current territory; pieces of the historical region of Macedonia lie within Albania, Bulgaria, and FYROM. In the last decades, Macedonia has become the focal point of a crisis between Northern Greece and the Balkan states; the slogan "Macedonia is Greece" has echoed as Greeks demand the return of formerly Hellenic lands or, at least, exclusive use of the name "Macedonia." Despite its identity struggle, Macedonia is one of Greece's most rewarding and multidimensional provinces. Offering a range of attractions— excellent archaeological sites, peaceful beaches, and beautiful and burgeoning urban areas—Macedonia keeps the visitor intrigued with endless surprises and historical flavor. For travelers looking to discover a new image of Greece, Macedonia waits with open arms.

THESSALONIKI Θεσσαλονίκη ☎ 2310

Thessaloniki (also called "Salonica") is one of the most historically diverse, cosmopolitan cities in Greece, second in size only to Athens. With its leafy avenues, charming squares, old churches and mosques, and ubiquitous ruins, Thessaloniki dazzles travelers as a large-scale monument to European history. The city was founded in 315 BC by Kassandros, King of Macedonia, who combined 26 smaller polities into a metropolis that defined ancient urban sprawl; he named this municipal collection after his wife, Thessalonice, whose half-brother was Alexander the Great. The city fell to the Romans in 164 BC, along with the rest of Macedonia, and soon became capital of the Roman Macedonian province. After the division of the Roman Empire, Thessaloniki flourished as the second city of the Byzantine Empire, leading to the construction of monumental churches throughout the city and sturdy protective walls surrounding it. Conquered by the Ottomans in 1430, it served as a place of refuge for many Sephardic Jews expelled from Spain during the Inquisition, who comprised half of Thessaloniki's population by 1873. The city became part of the modern Greek state in 1913 but was soon devastated by the Great Fire in August 1917, which destroyed much of the city's infrastructure. During WWII, the occupying Nazis exterminated 55,000 out of Thessaloniki's 59,000 Jews; today the city's Jewish community numbers just over 1000. Over the last half century, Thessaloniki has risen from these unstable conditions to develop into the major political center of the greater Balkan region. The cosmopolitan atmosphere and fashion-savvy population give this harbor city a booming young energy that shimmers through the strands of its rich and glorious past.

⊠ INTERCITY TRANSPORTATION

BY PLANE

Macedonia Airport (☎ 02319 85 000 or 02314 73 212), 16km east of town, can be reached by bus #78 (€0.50), which runs every 30min. from both the KTEL bus station and Pl. Aristotelous, or by **taxi** (€15). There's an **EOT** branch (☎ 23109 85 215) at the airport. **Flights** go to: Athens (55min., 24 per day 7am-10:30pm; €65); Chios (50min.; Tu 6:50am, W 4:40pm, Th 7:15am, Sa 3:15pm; €60); Corfu (55min.; Tu 5:40, W 2:05pm, Th 4:40pm, Su 4 and 5:30pm; €63); Hania, Crete (1½hr.; M 2:15pm, W-Th, Sa 10:40am; €115); Ioannina (35min.; M 10:45am, Tu 2:10pm, F, Su 11:05am; €60); Iraklion, Crete (1½hr., daily, €110); Larnaca, Cyprus (2hr., daily, €104); Limnos (50min.; M, W-Th 6:15am, F-Sa 7am, 7:15pm; €64); Mytilini, Lesvos (1½hr., daily 6:15pm, €87); Rhodes (2hr.; M-W 6:15am, F-Sa 7am, 5:30pm; €117); Samos (1½hr.; Tu 6:15am, F-Su 7am; €70). Times can change; check the most recent information before booking flights. For tickets, head to **Olympic Airways**, Kountouriotou 3, at the entrance to the port. (☎ 23103 68 311, reservations 23103 68 666. Open M-F 8am-4pm; reservations M-F 8am-5pm.) **Aegean Airlines**, 1 Nikis, is on the corner of Venizelou Ave., one block east from the port's passengers terminal. (☎ 23102 39 225.) Open M-F 8am-3pm, Sa 8am-2pm.

BY TRAIN

To reach the **main terminal** (☎ 23105 17 517) on Monastiriou in the western part of the city, take any bus down Egnatia (€0.50). **International trains** go to: İstanbul, Turkey (14hr., 7:17am, €14), Skopje, FYROM (4hr.; 9am, 6pm; €11), and Sofia, Bulgaria (7hr., midnight, €50). Tickets are sold at the **International Trains booth** at the train station. (☎23105 99 033. Open daily 7am-9pm.) Both regular **domestic trains** and high-speed **intercity trains (IC)** serve most destinations. Trains go to: Alexandroupoli (regular: 7hr., 3 per day 7:50am-10:25pm, €10; IC: 5hr., 4 per day 7:05am-1:45am, €25); Athens (regular: 7hr., 6 per day 8am-11:45pm, €14; IC: 5hr., 6 per day 7:05am-2:15am, €33); Drama (regular: 3hr., 3 per day 7:55am-10:30pm, €6; IC: 2hr., 3 per day 7:20am-1:50am, €16); Komotini (regular: 5hr., 3 per day 7:50am-10:30pm, €8.20; IC: 4hr., 3 per day 7:15am-1:45am, €20); Larisa (regular: 2hr., 8 per day 7:40am-11:45pm, €5; IC: 1hr., 6 per day 7:05am-2:15am, €12); Xanthi (regular: 4½hr., 3 per day 7:50am-10:35pm, €7; IC: 3½hr., 4 per day 6:43am-1:50am, €19). The Travel Office (☎23105 98 110) has updated schedules and prices in English.

BY BUS

KTEL buses connect Thessaloniki to most major Greek cities; except for the bus to the Halkidiki peninsula, all leave from the dome-shaped bus station west of the city center. **Bus #1** is a shuttle between the bus station and the train station (every 10min., €0.50). **Bus #78** connects the bus station to the airport, passing through the waterfront corridor (every 30min., €0.50). **International buses** (☎23105 99 100) leave from the main train station on Monastiriou in the city's western part; take any bus down Egnatia to get there (€0.50). **Buses** go to İstanbul, Turkey (12hr., Tu-Su 2:30am, €44) and Sofia, Bulgaria (6hr., 5 per day 7:30am-10pm, €19). **Domestic buses** leave from a dome 3km west of town. Take bus #1 from the train station. The dome also holds offices for each of the KTEL district booths. If you don't know in which district your destination lies, just pick a booth and ask.

Domestic buses to the Halkidiki prefecture leave from the **Halkidiki Station,** Kifisias 33 (☎23103 16 575), in the eastern outskirts of the city, near the end of Nea Egantia. Take bus #3 or 39 and ask the driver to tell you when to get off. Buses go to: Armenistis (2½hr., 4 per day 8:45am-6:30pm, €10); Ierissos (1½hr., 6 per day 6:15am-5:45pm, €8); Kalithea (1½hr., 13 per day 5:40am-9pm, €6.50); Nea Marmaras (2½hr., 3 per day 9:15am-5:15pm, €9.50); Ouranoupolis (2hr., 3 per day 6:15am-6:30pm, €9.10); Sarti (3hr., 6 per day 7:30am-7pm, €13.40).

DESTINATION	TIME	FREQUENCY	PRICE	TELEPHONE
Alexandroupoli	5hr.	8 per day 7:30am-11pm	€21.50	☎23105 95 439
Athens	6hr.	9 per day 7:30am-11:45pm	€30	☎23105 95 413
Corinth	7½hr.	11:30pm	€37	☎23105 95 405
Drama	2hr.	Every hr. 7am-7:30pm	€10	☎23105 95 420
Edessa	1½hr.	Every hr. 6am-9pm	€5.70	☎23105 95 435
Florina	3hr.	6 per day 7:30am-7pm	€11.30	☎23105 95 418
Grevena	2hr.	5 per day 8:30am-8pm	€12	☎23105 95 485
Igoumenitsa	8hr.	8pm	€30	☎23105 95 416
Ioannina	6½hr.	6 per day 7:30am-9:30pm	€23.30	☎23105 95 442
Karditsa	3hr.	5 per day 8am-8:30pm	€14.10	☎23105 95 440
Kastoria	3hr.	7 per day 7:30am-9pm	€14.30	☎23105 95 440
Katerini	50min.	Every 30min. 6:30am-10:30pm	€5	☎23105 95 428
Kavala	2½hr.	Every hr. 6am-10pm	€10.90	☎23105 95 422
Komotini	4hr.	7 per day 8:30am-11:30pm	€16.80	☎23105 95 419
Kozani	1½hr.	Every hr. 6am-10pm	€8.80	☎23105 95 484

DESTINATION	TIME	FREQUENCY	PRICE	TELEPHONE
Lamia	4hr.	9am, 3:15pm	€21.10	☎23105 95 416
Larisa	2hr.	Every hr. 7am-9:45pm	€10.90	☎23105 95 430
Metsovo	4½hr.	6 per day 7:30am-9:30pm	€19.20	☎23105 95 442
Parga	9hr.	10am, 9:30pm	€33	☎23105 95 406
Patras	7½hr.	4 per day 8:15am-9pm	€33	☎23105 95 425
Ancient Pella	1hr.	Every 40min. 6:30am-10:30pm	€2.50	☎23105 95 435
Pirgos	10½hr.	M-Th, Sa-Su 10:30am; F 3:30pm	€37.50	☎23105 95 409
Preveza	8hr.	10am	€30	☎23105 95 406
Serres	1½hr.	Every 30min. 6am-10pm	€6	☎23105 23 210
Trikala	3hr.	6 per day 8am-9pm	€13.70	☎23105 95 405
Veria	1hr.	Every hr. 8:12am-7:15pm	€5	☎23105 95 432
Xanthi	3hr.	9 per day 8am-11:30pm	€14	☎23105 95 423

BY BOAT

Buy tickets at **Karacharisis Travel and Shipping Agency,** Kountouriotou 8 (☎23105 13 005), one block to your left from the main entrance to the port. (Open M-F 8:30am-8:30pm, Sa 8:30am-2:30pm.) Three ferry lines run during high season. The **Chios line** to Chios (20hr., €34.20) via Limnos (8½hr., €22.10) and Mytilini (14hr., €34.40) leaves Sunday night at 1am. The **Iraklion, Crete line** to Iraklion, Crete (21-24hr., €34) via Skiathos (5½hr., €17), Paros (10-12hr., €37.50), Tynos (13hr., €37), and Santorini (17-18hr., €41) departs Tuesday at 2:30pm. The **Naxos line** to Naxos (14hr., €36) via Syros (12hr., €35) and Mykonos (13½hr., €37.50) leaves Thursday at 7pm. Buy **Flying Cat** tickets at Karacharisis. **Fast boats** go to Skiathos (3½hr., 1:45pm, €35.50) via Skopelo (2½hr., €35.30) and Alonnisos (3hr., €35.50)

◰ LOCAL TRANSPORTATION

Thessaloniki and its suburbs are connected by an extensive public transportation network. **Local buses** (€0.40 at newsstands, €0.50 on the bus) run throughout the city. An **office** opposite the train station provides schedules. **Maps** posted at many of the bus stops show the city routes. The **depot** most frequently visited by travelers is at the train station and is home to bus **#1,** which runs to the KTEL dome, bus **#8,** which goes to the White Tower stop, and bus **#73.** At the small depot at Pl. Eleftherias by the harbor you can catch **#5, 6,** and **33,** which navigate the waterfront on Tsimiski and Mitropoleos, and bus **#24,** which goes to the Old City. Buses **#10, 11,** and **31** run down Egnatia. **Taxis** (☎23105 51 525) run down Egnatia, Tsimiski, and Mitropoleos; stands are at Ag. Sophia and the intersection of Mitropoleos and Aristotelous. Rides within the city should not exceed €4, though ordering a taxi by phone adds €1.50 to the fare.

⊞ ORIENTATION

Thessaloniki stretches along the waterfront of the Thermaic Gulf's northern shore from the iconic **White Tower** in the east to the equally prominent **harbor** in the west. Its rough grid layout—established by French city planner Hebrard after the Great Fire of 1917—and the orienting presence of the sea make it nearly impossible to get lost. The most important arteries run parallel to the

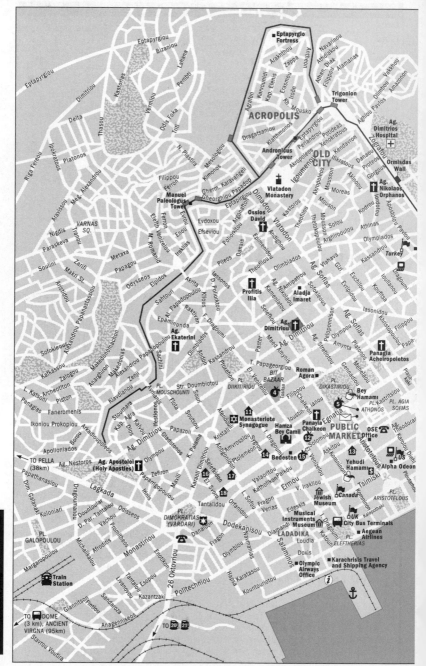

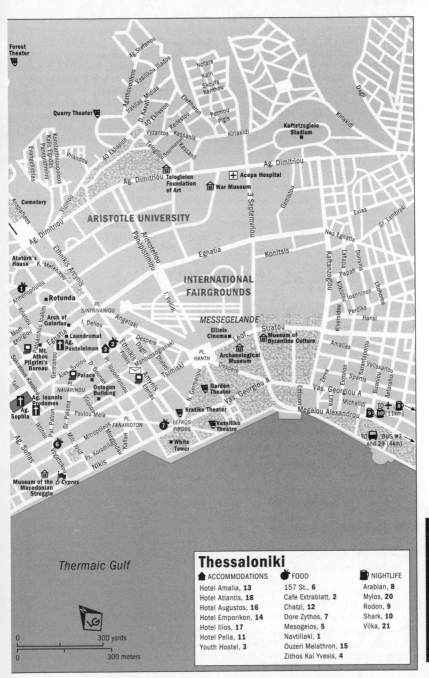

Forest
Theater

Ag. Stefanou

Notara
Kalri
Skoufa
Xanthou

Agathoupoleos
Vasilikou Iliados
IraKlias Midias
Eleftheron
Patmou
Pigis

D. Kavafi Midias

Quarry Theater

Kaftatzoglelo
Stadium

Kiriakidi

Dagri

40 Eklision

Vyzantos Kessanis Redestou
Teloglion Soumenanti Kessanli

Kiriakldi

Konstantinoupoleos
Kalis Elpidas
Panepistimiou
Evangelistrias

Vriandou

Vizinou

Ag. Dimitriou
Teloglelon
Foundation
of Art

Acepa Hospital

Ag. Dimitriou

Evias

Gr. Lambraki

Cemetery

Anapafseos

Ag. Dimitriou

Ethnikis Amynis

K. Melenikou

ARISTOTLE UNIVERSITY

Aristoteiou
Panepistimiou

Egnatia

3 Septemvriou

Gemistou

Nea Egnatia

Konitsis

Kaftanzoglou

Lahana
Papafi

Doiranis
Ioanninon
Klisdurs

Atatürk's
House

Armenopoulou

Rotunda

Arianou
Georgiou
Modi
Kavarchou

Patriarchou Ioakim

PL.
SINTRIVANIOU

I. Deliou

Angelaki

INTERNATIONAL
FAIRGROUNDS

I. Velidi

MESSEGELANDE

Ellinis
Cinema

Leof.

Stratou
Museum of
Byzantine Culture

Amallas

Kivernou
Perdika

Harisi

Litohorou

Lithaiou

Arch of
Galerius

Egnatia

Laundromat

Ag.
Panteleimon

Despere

Dagi

Ethnikis
Filkis

Manousogianaki
Dialeti Tsimiski

PL.
HANTH

Archaeological
Museum

Despere

Kaftanzoglou

Zervia
Evzonon
Spartis

Vas. Georgiou A

Michalidi

Sarantaporou
Velissarou
Bizaniou
Aetorahis

TO

(11km)

Mt.
Athos
Pilgrim's
Bureau

Sokratous Xandou

Germanou

Alex. Svolou
D. Gounari

Pl. Ippodromiou

Amynis

N. Germanou

Garden
Theater

Vas. Georgiou A

Megalou Alexandrou

Edisson

Tati

PL.
NAVARINOU

Palace

Octagon
Building

Eteras

TO

BUS #3
and 29 (4km)

Ag. Ioannis
Prodomos

Gr. Palama

Pavlou Mela

Vilaras

Kratiko Theater

Ag.
Sophia

Ikunou

Pal. Patron

Mitr. Iosf

Mitropoleos Morgenda

PL.
FANARIOTON

LEFKOS
PIRGOS

Vassiliko
Theatro

Ag. Sofias

Vogatsikou

Pr. Koromila

Kaftani

White
Tower

Museum of the
Macedonian
Struggle

Cyprus

Nikis

Thermaic Gulf

0   300 yards

0   300 meters

Thessaloniki

ACCOMMODATIONS
Hotel Amalia, **13**
Hotel Atlantis, **18**
Hotel Augustos, **16**
Hotel Emporikon, **14**
Hotel Ilios, **17**
Hotel Pella, **11**
Youth Hostel, **3**

FOOD
157 St., **6**
Cafe Extrablatt, **2**
Chatzi, **12**
Dore Zythos, **7**
Mesogeios, **5**
Navtiliaki, **1**
Ouzeri Melathron, **15**
Zithos Kai Yvesis, **4**

NIGHTLIFE
Arabian, **8**
Mylos, **20**
Rodon, **9**
Shark, **10**
Vilka, **21**

water. Farthest from shore is **Egnatia**, the city's busiest thoroughfare, a six-lane avenue. Next comes **Ermou**, named after the god of merchants (Hermes), which is, unsurprisingly, home to many stores; **Tsimiski, Mitropoleos,** and **Nikis** follow. Tsimiski's traffic and buses run from tower to harbor, while Mitropoleos has buses running the other direction. At the White Tower end, Tsimiski terminates in **Plateia Hanth** (XANΘ), Greek for YMCA. The plateia is a common reference point, bus stop, and base for museum exploration. **Nikis,** home to the city's main cafes, runs from the harbor to the White Tower. Further inland from Egnatia are **Agios Dimitriou** and the **Old City.** Intersecting all these streets and leading from the water into town are, in order from harbor to tower, **Ionos Dragoumi, Eleftherios Venizelou, Aristotelous, Agias Sophias,** and **Ethnikis Aminis.** Aristotelous, a wide pavilion where breezes sweep unobstructed from the ocean to the Acropolis, is the city's center, with a bevy of restaurants, businesses, and banks. The roads north of Ag. Dimitriou grow increasingly tiny and steep toward the Old City's ancient walls, panoramic views, and cheap tavernas. The area between Tsimiski and the Arch of Galerius, **Plateia Navarinou**, with the ruins of Galerius's palace, is a meeting ground for young locals, while the older crowd converses in the taverns of **Ladadika,** just behind the northern side (tower-side) of the port. Formerly the home of olive oil merchants, the back alleys have become a pocket of upscale cafes, bars, and tavernas.

ⓩ PRACTICAL INFORMATION

TOURIST AND FINANCIAL SERVICES

Tourist Offices: An **EOT** (☎23109 85 215) is at the **airport** (open 9am-9pm). **GNTO** (☎23105 00 310), in the port's passenger terminal. Provides free **maps** and info about sights, buses, and events in Thessaloniki. Open M-F 9am-9pm, Sa-Su 8am-2pm.

Permits for Mount Athos: Visit the **Holy Executive of the Holy Mount Athos Pilgrims' Bureau,** Egnatia 109, 1st fl. (☎23102 52 578; fax 23102 22 424); take bus #10 from the train station, or any point along Egnatia, and ask for number 109 or the Mt. Athos office (by the Kamara Galerius arch). No letter of recommendation needed; passport and personal appearance are required to pick up a permit. Only men are allowed to visit Mt. Athos (p. 311). English spoken. Open M-F 9am-2pm, Sa 10am-noon.

Consulates: see **Consular Services in Greece** (p. 9).

Banks: Banks with **currency exchange** and **24hr. ATMs** line Tsimiski, including **Citi Bank,** Tsimiski 21 (☎23103 73 300). Open M-Th 8am-2:30pm, F 8am-2pm. No bank accepts Bulgarian or Albanian currencies. Travelers coming from these countries must head to the **exchange booths** at El. Venizelou's intersection with Ermou.

LOCAL SERVICES

Bookstores: Molchos Books, Tsimiski 10 (☎23102 75 271), has an excellent selection of English, Classical, religious, political and art history books along with dictionaries and international newspapers. Open M, W, Sa 9am-3pm; Tu, Th-F 9am-2pm and 5-9pm. **Malliaris,** D. Gounari 39 (☎23102 77 113), has a large selection of English travel and leisure reading, computer equipment, magazines, and newspapers. Open M-F 9am-9pm, Sa 9am-4pm. **Newsstand,** Ag. Sophias 37 (☎23102 87 072), offers a wide selection of international newspapers and magazines. Open daily 7am-10pm.

Travel Books: For English travel guides, including ▨**Let's Go** titles, head to **Traveller Books,** Proxenou Koromila 41 (☎23102 75 215), 1 block inland from Nikis east of Aristotelous. Open M-Sa 9:30am-3pm, Tu, Th-F 9:30am-3pm and 5-9pm.

Backpacking Supplies: SurfoMania, Proxenou Koromila 48 (☎23102 31 351), has motorbikes and backpacking equipment. Open M, W, Sa 9am-3pm, Tu, Th-F 9am-9pm.

Laundromat: Bianca, Panagias Recsias 3 (☎23102 09 602), behind the church to the right. Wash and dry €6. Open M, W, Sa 8am-3pm, Tu, Th-F, Su 8am-8:30pm.

EMERGENCY AND COMMUNICATIONS

Tourist Police: Dodekanisou 4 on the 5th fl. (☎23105 54 871), carries free **maps** and brochures. Open 8am-10pm. For the **local police,** call ☎23105 53 800. There are also police booths at the train station.

Hospital: At both **Acepa Hospital,** Kiriakidi 1 (☎23109 93 111), and **Hippokratio Public Hospital,** Costantinos Polius 49 (☎23108 92 000), some doctors speak English. On weekends and at night call ☎1434 to find which hospital has emergency care.

Telephones: OTE, Karolou Diehl 33 (☎23102 41 999), at the corner of Ermou and Karolou Diehl, 1 block east of Aristotelous near the Ag. Sophia church between Ag. Sophia and Aristotelous. Open M, W 8:30am-2pm, Tu and Th-F 8:30am-2pm and 5:30-8:30pm. Another location (☎23105 51 599) by the intersection of 26 Oktovriou 1 and Pl. Dimokratias, at the west end of Egnatia near the city court. Open M-F 8:30am-2pm.

Internet Access: Behind the shopping complex housing the American Consulate, **E-Global,** Vas. Irakliou 40 (☎23102 52 780; www.e-global.gr), is 1 block to the right. Noon-4:30pm €1.80 per hr., 4:30-5pm free, 5-6pm €1.80 per hr., 6pm-midnight €2.40 per hr., midnight-noon €1.50 per hr. Open 24hr. Another location at Egnatia 17 (☎23109 68 404), 1 block east of the Arch of Galerius, has fast terminals. **Meganet,** Pl. Navarinou 5 (☎23102 50 331; www.meganet.gr), overlooks a charming fountain of a boy relieving himself and Galerius's Palace. Noon-midnight €1.80 per hr., midnight-noon €1 per hr. Open 24hr. **Bits and Bytes,** Vas. Irakliou 43 (☎23102 57 812). With 250 computers, this is a gamer's paradise. Noon-midnight €2 per hr., midnight-noon €1 per hr. Open 24hr.

Post Office: Aristotelous 26 (☎23102 68 954), just below Egnatia. Open M-F 7:30am-8pm, Sa 7:30am-2pm, Su 9am-1:30pm. A **branch** office (☎23102 27 604), on the corner of Eth. Aminis and Manosi near the White Tower, is in charge of parcels. Open M-F 7am-8pm. Both offer **Poste Restante;** to make certain your mail gets to the Aristotelous branch specify *Kentriko* (Center). **Postal Code:** 54101.

▛ ACCOMMODATIONS

Welcome to the big city—don't expect to find comfort and cleanliness at one low price. Thessaloniki's cheaper hotels (doubles around €35) are along the western end of **Egnatia,** between **Plateia Dimokratias** and **Aristotelous.** Most are a bit gritty, ranging from ramshackle sleaze to mere cheerlessness, but all are easy to locate, with neon signs that would make any Las Vegas resident feel at home. Egnatia is loud at all hours, but rooms on the street have balconies, while quieter back rooms have just a window. Some mid-level hotels (doubles €40) are farther away from the noise, set a few blocks behind Egnatia on **Dragoumi** around **Plateia Dikastiriou.** For more luxurious options, head toward the waterfront area two blocks west of Aristotelous. The closer you get to the water, the more you will pay.

Hotel Atlantis, Egnatia 14 (☎23105 40 131). Standard rooms have sinks, balconies, and decorative, gold-leafed ceilings; those on the 1st fl. are newly renovated. English-speaking management is warm and hospitable and keeps the rooms, shared baths, and fridges well-maintained. Breakfast €4. Reception 24hr. Singles €20, with bath €35; doubles €25/40; triples €30/45. ❷

NORTHERN GREECE

Hotel Ilios, Egnatia 27 (☎23105 12 620), on the western Egnatia budget strip, offers modern rooms with big windows, A/C, TV, phones, fridges, and baths. Rooms away from the street are quieter. Singles €35; doubles €49; triples €64. ❸

Hotel Pella, Dragoumi 63 (☎23105 24 221; www.pella-hotel.gr), 2 blocks north of Egnatia on Dragoumi. Pella has comfortably furnished rooms with desks, TV, phones, and baths, overlooking a quiet valley. Breakfast €6. Singles €46; doubles €61; triples €73. Rates reduced in low season. AmEx/MC/V. ❸

Hotel Augustos, El. Svoronou 4 (☎23105 22 955). Follow Egnatia down to Dimokratias Sq. and take a sharp right onto Karaoli. El. Svornou is your 1st right; turn and the hotel will be on your left. Cozy rooms have wooden floors, rugs, and high ceilings. Doubles and triples with baths also have A/C and TV. Reception 24hr. Singles €20, with bath €25; doubles €27/38; triples with bath €50. ❷

Hotel Amalia, Ermou 33 (☎23102 68 321). From Egnatia, turn right at Aristotelous and right again at Ermou; the hotel is just after the covered bazaar. Amalia's green-, red-, and blue-themed rooms have TV, A/C, phones, baths, radios, safes, and large balconies with double-paned windows. A bar on the 1st fl. serves drinks (€4.50). Breakfast €6. Reception 24hr. Reserve at least 2 days in advance. Singles €55; doubles €73; triples €86. 10-20% student discount. MC/V. ❹

Thessaloniki Youth Hostel, Alex. Svolou 44 (☎23102 25 946). Take bus #8, 10, 11, or 31 west down Egnatia, get off at the Arch of Galerius (Kamara stop), and walk down Gounari towards the water. Svolou is your 2nd left. The hostel's balconies are often filled with backpackers talking long into the hot nights, but you get what you pay for. 45 beds in 7 rooms. 5 day max stay. Reception open daily 9am-noon and 6-11pm. July 15-Sept. 15 €15 per person; Sept. 16-July 14 €13 per person. 10% discount with ISIC. ❶

Hotel Emporikon, Sygrou 14 (☎23105 14 431), on Sygrou and Egnatia, about halfway between Aristotelous and Dimokratias Sq. Rooms with bright balconies have a 1970s feel. A little quieter than the others that line Egnatia, the hotel has tiled shared bathrooms and hallway fridges. Singles €20; doubles €30, with bath €40; triples €40. ❷

◘ FOOD

Thessaloniki has eight main dining districts. Just behind the port is upscale **Ladadika,** whose restaurants wine and dine older patrons. Farther inland at the corner of **Dragoumi** and **Eleftherios Venizelou,** however, are more youthful restaurants. Between **Egnatia** and **Aristotelous,** a network of alleyways house vine-canopied *ouzeria* where roaming musicians strum tunes as they squeeze their way through tightly packed tables. A **public market,** with everything from fresh meat to Italian leather sandals, operates daily in the alleys between Egnatia and Aristotelous. Continuing eastward, **Plateia Athonos** is a student favorite, while **Plateia Navarinou** acts as a porch for the tables of well-priced *ouzeria* that overlook Galerius's Palace. Either behind the **Rotunda** or before the **White Tower,** find some ostentatiously positioned (and priced) but nevertheless tasty, avant-garde *ouzeria*. The **Old City** brims with tavernas and restaurants near the **fortress,** which have sweeping views of the gulf. Thessaloniki's restaurants have a delightful custom of giving patrons watermelon or sweets *gratis* after a meal. The local syrup-drenched cake, *revani,* a gift of the many refugees from Asia Minor, is especially good.

▨ **Dore Zythos,** Tsiroyianni 7 (☎23102 79 010; www.zithos.gr), is behind the grassy triangular plot across the White Tower. Sea breezes and superb views of the White Tower combine with the unusual menu to make this hot spot a local favorite. The Greek-Mediterranean food is served on wooden tables near a large bar that evokes images of 19th-century Paris. Try the Samothrakian fava bean salad (€4) or the Zythos lamb (meat ovals with garlic and cumin; €7.20), which can be washed down with any of their 47 beers (€3). Entrees €4.50-12. Open 10am-2am. V. ❷

🦊 **Chatzi,** El. Venizelou 50 (☎23102 79 058; www.chatzis.gr), has been acting as Thessaloniki's Willy Wonka since 1908. This bakery offers everything from the banal to the bizarre, including adaptations of traditional desserts like nuts *kataifi* (€3) and old-time favorites like *galakto-boureko*, a cream-filled delight (€2.20). The wall mountings, including various photographs of early-20th century Thessaloniki, are an even sweeter touch. Open daily 6:30am-3am. ❶

🦊 **Ouzeri Melathron,** Karypi 21-34 (☎23102 75 016). From Egnatia, walk past the Ottoman Bedesten on El. Venizelou and make a right into the cobblestone passageway; take the first left and follow the street. The witty, 4ft. long subtitled menus at this secluded gem feature chicken, lamb, snails, octopus, and a variety of cheese dishes. Entrees €4.30-13. Open daily 1pm-1am. Free round of drinks with ISIC. MC/V. ❷

Zithos Kai Yvesis (☎23102 68 746), by the intersection of El. Venizelou and Filipou. With your back to Egnatia, walk a half-block past the intersection and look for a sign reading "Venizelou 72" between a hair stylist and a gift shop; it's through the passageway on your left. The restaurant serves various appetizers and Greek food (€1.50-5.50) including *Vlachiko* (pig's intestine stuffed with meat and cheese; €3). Open daily 6pm-2am. ❷

Mesogeios, Balanou 38 (☎23102 88 460), east of Aristotelous, 1 block south of Egnatia, opposite the Bey Hamami baths on Egnatia, is the largest ouzeri in the area. The large portions of meat and seafood are popular among locals. Fried shrimp with lemon and sardines (€8) is too good to miss. Entrees €5-8.50. Open daily noon-1am. ❷

157 St., Kouskoura 6 (☎23102 54 444). Walking eastward on Egnatia, turn right onto Germanou, which becomes Kouskoura after the intersection with Tsimiski; 157 is on the left. This fast-food-like joint offers both pork and chicken gyros (€2.30), considered by locals to be the city's best, and delivers for no extra charge. Open daily 10am-1am. ❶

Navtiliaki, Pl. Ag. Georgiou 8 (☎23102 47 583), just behind the Rotunda. This ouzeri, known for its excellent seafood, also has some meat and vegetarian options in a relaxing, tree-covered setting. Octopus in vinegar €6.80. Eggplant with feta and tomato sauce €3.50. Entrees €8-10. Open daily 12:30pm-1am. Bar open until 2am. ❷

Cafe Extrablatt, Alex. Svolou 46 (☎23102 56 900), by the youth hostel. This cheerful, family-run restaurant blends German and Greek cuisine, with crepes, pasta, sausage and mushroom dishes, and over 50 beers. Entrees €7-17. Open daily 11am-1am. ❸

⊙ SIGHTS

🏛 **ARCH OF GALERIUS.** At D. Gounari and Egnatia stands the striking Arch of Galerius, known to locals simply as "*Kamara*" ("Arch"). Caesar Galerius erected the arch to commemorate his victory over the Persian Shah Narses in AD 297, covering it with relief sculptures detailing his triumphs and close rapport with his father-in-law, Diocletian. The masonry is still awe-inspiring almost two millennia later. According to legend, Christians, who suffered greatly under Galerius's persecutions, rubbed out his face in every panel. Many of the lower panels have faded, but one can still make out the Persians, with their distinctive headgear, and some elephants in the upper panels. From here, a colonnaded processional led north from the arch and nearby palace to the cylindrical rotunda. In AD 299, Galerius built a huge royal complex around the arch and made Thessaloniki his capital.

THE PALACE OF GALERIUS. A tiny piece of the once 150,000 sq. m royal complex is open for viewing in Pl. Navarino, two blocks seaward from the arch. The southeastern section of the mighty palace, which used to extend from the rotunda to the sea, was unearthed in excavations in the 1950s and 60s. The weathered geometric mosaic floors and partially preserved octagonal hall, believed to have housed Galerius's throne, are particularly notable. *(Open daily 8am-5:30pm. Free.)*

THE ROTUNDA. From the arch, turn up D. Gounari to see the most dramatic standing reminder of Thessaloniki's Roman heritage. The enormous rotunda, now **Agios Georgios,** was first built as a temple to Jupiter, the patron god of the eastern half of the tetrarchy, the Roman Empire's administrative system. Like the **arch** and the **palace,** the rotunda was erected by Galerius at the tail end of the AD 3rd century. In the 5th century, well after Christianity had become the Empire's official religion, the rotunda became a church filled with **mosaics** of saints martyred at the hands of Galerius and Diocletian, now considered heretics. Under the Ottomans, the rotunda sojourned as a mosque from 1590 to 1912. An estimated 36 million *tesserae* (small sea pebbles) were assembled to represent lavishly gilded facades, birds, and saints, though today they are barely visible. Only those highest in the dome have survived; bring binoculars. Despite the unfortunate lack of visibility, the interior is vast and very impressive. *(☎ 23109 68 860. Open Tu-Su 8am-5pm. Free.)*

ROMAN AGORA. The 2nd-century Odeon and covered market still stand at the top of Aristotelous. From Egnatia, go inland up Aristotelous; the site is at the end. The agora's lower square was once a Hellenistic colonnade which held eight **caryatids,** which have since been sent to the Louvre. Known in Ladino, the language of the Sephardic Jews, as "*las Incantadas*" ("the enchanted women"), they were thought to have been magically petrified. Though the site has been under construction, it is due to open in the summer of 2006. *(Open 8am-8pm. Free.)*

WHITE TOWER. Thessaloniki's most recognizable site, the White Tower, looms over the eastern part of the seafront like an oversized chess piece, acting as a symbol of the city and an easy rendezvous point. Originally part of the 15th-century Ottoman seawall, the tower became the Ottoman Death Row where **Janissaries,** members of an elite corps of Ottoman soldiers, carried out notoriously gruesome executions. Blood was so often seen seeping from the tower's stone walls that locals began calling it the "Bloody Tower." One prisoner, Nathan Gueledi, whitewashed the tower in 1890 in exchange for his release and thus inaugurated its current name. Though the walk up the winding stairway evokes a taste of the prisoners' fear as they marched to their death, the roof's view of the city and its shoreline is a marvelous trade-off. *(At the eastern end of Nikis. Take Bus #3, 5, 6, 33, or 39 to reach the tower. ☎ 23102 67 832. Open Tu-Su 8:30am-3pm. €2, students free.)*

OLD WALLS. Starting from the White Tower, walk inland along Filikis Eterias. Occasional strips of rubble mark the path of the old walls that surrounded the city under Ottoman rule. After Egnatia, head right for one block and continue up on Eth. Aminis. At Ag. Dimitriou, the walls rise to their ancient 10m glory. Here, just across from the hospital, a massive 5th-century **inscription** built into the brick arrogantly proclaims, "Ormisdas fortified the city with these indestructible walls." As the walls climb, a walking path leads toward the 15th-century **Trigonion Tower,** built as a guard post at the intersection of the city and acropolis walls. Enter the Old City, whose small, windy alleyways were all once part of a Byzantine city, through holes in the indestructible walls. Following the wall along Eptapyrigiou, you'll see multiple brick crosses and a large late Byzantine inscription built into the towers.

EPTAPYRGIO. Meaning "seven towers," this Byzantine and Ottoman fortress, once part of the Old City's outer wall, was a high-security prison until 1989. Today, it houses a small exhibit about the jail's history and is more a morbid monument to the penal system than a historical site. (☎ 23109 68 843. Open Tu-Su 8am-5pm. Free.)

OTTOMAN SIGHTS. The Ottomans ruled Thessaloniki for almost 500 years and left an indelible imprint on its landscape in the peppering of Turkish buildings and baths. **Bey Hamami,** built in 1444, was the first bathhouse of its kind in Thessaloniki. Its labyrinthine interior has a cool antechamber that leads to a tepid room and the immense domed sauna beyond. Today these decorated domes and colorful marble-tiled floors house art students' exhibitions. (On Egnatia, east of Aristotelous. Open M-F 8:30am-3pm. Free.) Built by a bey's daughter in 1467-68 as a *mesçid* (a hall of worship minus the minarets), **Hazma Bey Camii** gained both a minaret and official mosque status in the late 16th century. Although it was an active mosque for Thessaloniki's growing Muslim population for over three centuries, and was the largest mosque in Greece, today it is in danger of collapsing and is closed to the public. (On Egnatia, just past El. Venizelou.) A late 15th-century covered marketplace and craftsmen's workshop, the Ottoman **Bedesten** was said to emit delicious perfumes of musk and amber. Inscriptions carved into the domes in French, Greek, South Slavic, and Turkish evoke the variegated ethnicities of Thessaloniki in its cosmopolitan heyday. This still-busy marketplace houses merchants selling fabrics, fish, meat, and sewing supplies. (On El. Venizelou, 1 block south of Egnatia.)

🏛 MUSEUMS

📖 MUSEUM OF BYZANTINE CULTURE. This museum exhibits the largest collection of early Christian wall paintings in the world outside of the Vatican and illuminates bits of Byzantine life. The huge museum, keeping with Thessaloniki's former position as the second most important city in the Byzantine Empire, tells a far-ranging, secular tale. Through displays on daily life, economics, engineering, and imperial dynasties, visitors learn that the Byzantine Empire was neither the theocracy nor the monocultural Greek state that domestic museums often portray it to be. One of Thessaloniki's churches (Ag. Chalkeon) was actually rebuilt by a noble of Byzantine Lombardy, and the city's walls were repaired by the Emperor Leo, a Syrian. The painted funerary art with depictions of the Good Shepherd and AD 10th-century metal vessels that held holy myrrh from the graves of Thessaloniki's protector saints are particular highlights. (Stratou Ave. 2. Behind the Archaeological Museum, across 3 Septemvriou. ☎ 23108 68 570; www.mbp.gr. Open M 10:30am-5pm, Tu-Su 8:30am-3pm; in winter hours reduced. Wheelchair-accessible. €4, students and seniors €2, EU students and children free. Guided tours (around €15) can be requested.)

📖 ARCHAEOLOGICAL MUSEUM. This fantastic collection includes some of the area's most prized artifacts. The treasures from Vergina's royal Macedonian tombs, once the highlight of Thessaloniki's collection, were returned to Vergina (p. 284) in 1998, but the museum still displays enough jewels to thrill anyone attracted to sparkle. At a permanent exhibit on Macedonian gold with foil myrtle wreaths, the splendidly frail leaves vibrate with your footsteps. The **Derveni krater** from the late 4th century BC is probably the most important piece in the collection. This beautiful mixing vessel is made of an alloy of tin and bronze and depicts Ariadne and Dionysus's wedding. Particularly self-referential poems about the origin of the words used in the poems themselves grace Derveni papyrus fragments, also from the late 4th century. Sculptures of a famously erotic Aphrodite and parts of an enormous statue of Athena share space with a grand mosaic depicting Dionysus with Ariadne, Apollo stalking Daphne, and Ganymede in Zeus's eagle talons. The museum is a good place to visit before exploring the local Roman agora and the nearby sites of Vergina and Pella. *(At the eastern end of Tsimiski, across from the International Helexpo Fairgrounds. ☎ 23108 61 306. Open M 1-7:30pm, Tu-Su 8:30am-7:30pm; in winter hours reduced. Apr.-Oct. €4, students and seniors €2, EU students and under 18 free. Oct. 10, Nov.-March, April 18, May 1, May 18, June 5 free.)*

JEWISH MUSEUM OF THESSALONIKI. "A sign at the entrance to the museum proclaims, "Thessaloniki: The Metropolis of Sephardism." Inside, exhibits tell the tragic story of that metropolis's height and demise. Waves of Jewish refugees, fleeing 15th-century Reconquista Spain, were invited by the Ottoman sultan to settle in his lands. The museum's ground floor uses pictures, gravestones, and folk artifacts to show the subsequent 500-year history of Thessaloniki's Jewish community, once the largest in Europe. At its height, the Jewish population comprised more than half of the city, had over 30 synagogues, and led many of Thessaloniki's industries. The second floor features an extensive timeline of the city's Jewish history, telling the story of the Jews' migration to Palestine—founding ports like Tel Aviv and Haifa—in the 1920s and 30s after Thessaloniki's 1917 fire, and of pressure from Greek nationalism. The last room commemorates the Holocaust, when 96.5% of the city's Jewish members were murdered in concentration camps. *(Agiou Mina 13. ☎ 23102 50 406; www.jct.gr. Groups should call in advance. Open Tu, F 11am-2pm, W-Th 11am-2pm and 5-8pm, Su 11am-2pm. Free.)*

MUSEUM OF ANCIENT, BYZANTINE, AND POST-BYZANTINE MUSICAL INSTRUMENTS. Three floors of this upscale museum display replicas of contraptions used to please the ears, tracing their evolution from 2800 BC to the early 20th century. One particularly interesting exhibition demonstrates how ancient musical instruments were made. *(Katouni 12-14, at the western end of Tsimiski near the Ladadika district. ☎ 23105 55 265. Open M, W-Su 10am-2pm and 5-7pm. Free.)*

MUSEUM OF THE MACEDONIAN STRUGGLE. Once the Greek consulate to Turkish Thessaloniki (1892-1912), this house now contains memorabilia from the wars that made Macedonia officially Greek, focusing on the **Balkan Wars** (1912-1913). The exhibits include personal artifacts of rebel leader **Pavlou Melas**, along with captured war booty like Turkish and Bulgarian arms and treasure. The models and reproduced photographs shed light on the scope of this nationalistic struggle and its role as one of the triggers of WWII. The museum provides English pamphlets with facts about the collection and a historical overview of the Macedonian War. *(Koromila 23, 1 block from the water, halfway between the White Tower and Pl. Aristotelous. Take Bus #3, 5, 6, 12, or 39. ☎ 23102 29 778. Open Tu-F 9am-2pm, Sa 10am-2pm. Free.)*

ATATÜRK'S HOUSE. The three-story house that was the birthplace and childhood home of the man who brought Turkey into modernity now displays relics from his life. Pictures of the famed figure with various world leaders adorn the walls, and many items of clothing (including his bathrobe) are also in view. Aside from these artifacts, however, the house is surprisingly banal. Display signs are in Turkish and Greek only. *(Apostolou Pavlou 17. Ring the bell, then present your passport next door at the Turkish Consulate, Ag. Dimitriou 151. Open M-F 10am-5pm. Free.)*

TELOGLION FOUNDATION OF ART. The large museum of Teloglion is part of the Aristotle University complex. Here, some excellent rotating exhibits focus on topics from archaeology to modern art. *(Agiou Dimitriou 159A. ☎ 23109 91 610; www.auth.gr/teloglion. Open Tu-F 10am-2pm, Sa-Su 11am-6pm. Free.)*

WAR MUSEUM. Located behind the hospital in Aristotle University, this haven for gun lovers and war buffs features military paraphernalia used from the War of Independence through the Civil War. Also on display are some Ottoman military artifacts and weapons captured from Greece's many enemies. *(G. Labraki 4.* ☎23102 66 195. *Open Tu-F 9am-2pm, Sa-Su 10am-2pm. Free.)*

🎵 ENTERTAINMENT

Summer visitors looking for *rembetika* music should spend a weekend night at **Iyoklima**, a popular bar-cafe-club on tiny Axiou, south of Nikis near the port, or **Palios Stathmos** (Old Station), Voutira 2 (☎23105 21 892). **Alpha Odeon**, Tsimiski 43, in the same mall as the US Embassy, is an indoor **movie theater** (☎23102 90 100) that shows a variety of American films (€8). When skies are clear, head outside to catch a film under the stars. American movies with Greek subtitles play at the waterfront **Natali Cinema**, Vas. Olgas 3 (☎23108 29 457), 5min. past the White Tower, or at **Ellinis** (☎23102 92 304), at Pl. Hanth, across from the Archaeological Museum. (Films show shortly after 9pm and at 11:10pm. €6.) You can't miss the posters plastered all over town for the theater, music, and dance performances at venues like the **Dhasos "Forest" Theater** (☎23102 18 092), uptown in the forest near the acropolis, adjacent to the zoo. This green setting offers an opportunity to see city-quality theater away from a city-crazed lifestyle. **Kipos "Garden" Theater** (☎23102 56 775) in Pl. Hanth, **Damari "Quarry" Theater** (☎23102 06 930) in an old quarry in the Saranda Ekklesias district, **Moni Lazariston** (☎23106 52 020) in the old Catholic monastery, and **Kratiko** and **Vassiliko Theaters** (☎23102 23 785 for both) near the White Tower are also excellent venues. The **International Fairgrounds**, across from the Archaeological and Byzantine museums, holds festivals throughout the year. The **International Trade Fair and Song Festival** (Sept.), the **Dimitria Festival** (Oct.), which celebrates the city's patron saint with a number of theater productions, films, and dance performances, the internationally revered **Thessaloniki Film Festival** (Nov.; www.filmfestival.gr), and the new **Documentary Festival** (Mar.) all take place at the fairgrounds. Thessaloniki's **Wine Festival,** when different wineries offer tastings of their new wines, is celebrated at Nea Elvetia park.

🌙 NIGHTLIFE

There are four main hubs for late-night fun in Thessaloniki. The **Ladadika** district, which served as the city's red-light strip until the 80s, is now a sea of dance clubs. The bustling **waterfront** is filled with cafes and clubs. The dance-till-you-drop, tourist-saturated, open-air discos cluster around the **airport** (€8-9 taxi ride from the center). The **"Bit Bazaar"** area, encompassing 13 all-night wine bars, is popular with a low-key student crowd. Most clubs (cover €15; includes 1 drink) around the airport feature live modern or traditional Greek music. To get into many of the chicer establishments, you'll have to dress trendily and, if you're not one yourself, have an attractive woman on your arm. Though the clubs boom until dawn, the summer nightlife isn't much by Salonican standards—most head to the mega-beach clubs of **Kalithea** on Kassandra (p. 307). Every Monday during the summer, several boats transform themselves into floating clubs that play reggae, alternative, and disco music (beer €5). They depart from behind the White Tower.

   Shark, Themistokli Sofouli and Argonavton 2 (☎23104 16 855), in Kalamaria around the gulf. As the night progresses, this bar-restaurant clears out its tables, turns up the music, and becomes a full-fledged club. Waterfront views of the city's skyline from the balcony (only open in summer) thrill the dancing masses, comprised mostly of young professionals who haven't forgotten how to party. Mixed drinks €10. Open 9pm-4am.

Night Club Arabian (☎23104 71 135), along the highway toward the airport 13km from the city. Arabian supplies standard Greek fare in a pseudo-Middle Eastern venue, complete with belly dancers and Arabian music. Cover €10. Open 11:20pm-5am.

Mylos, Andreou Georgiou 56 (☎23105 16 945), in the far west of the city; take bus #31 or a taxi (€4). Once a mill, the building now features periodic art exhibits, a restaurant, and bars. The Turkish dessert *ek mek* (pastry made with milk, cake, and pudding and covered with syrup) is served nowhere else in the city. Open midnight-4am.

Vilka, Andreou Georgiou 21 (☎23105 15 006). Located in an old factory, this huge complex is an international-scale clubbing experience. Regularly playing modern Greek *bouzouki*, Vilka's stage also features local rock legends who perform alongside world-renowned DJs. Entrance can be difficult during popular events. Open midnight-8am.

Rodon (☎23104 76 720), east of the city along the main highway, on the right about 200m after the turn to the airport (follow the signs). The €10 cover charge (includes 1 drink) buys the opportunity to rub elbows with the city's hipsters in an amphitheater-like bowl or to join the crowd on stage with the live Greek pop band. Open 11pm-4:30am.

⚄ DAYTRIPS FROM THESSALONIKI

▨ ANCIENT VERGINA Βέργινα

Buses (☎23105 95 432) run from Thessaloniki (1hr., every hr. 8:12am-7:15pm, €5) to Veria. From Veria take the bus to Vergina (20min., 11 per day 6:50am-8pm, €1). Ask to be dropped off near the Vergina archaeological sites. Buses run out of Vergina back to Veria (20min., 10 per day 7:20am-8:20pm, €1) but are less reliable. Site open M noon-7pm, Tu-Su 8am-7pm; in winter Tu-Su 8am-7pm. Admission to all of Vergina's sights including tombs, theater, palace, and museum €8; students €4; EU students free.

Unearthing the ruins of Vergina, once the capital of ancient Macedonia, was an archaeological watershed. Among the finds were Greek inscriptions on Macedonian tombstones which bore Greek names, proving that the ancient Macedonians were in fact a Greek tribe. Scholars believe that the objects found in the tombs could have belonged only to the royal Macedonian family of Philip II, father of Alexander the Great (p. 56). This assumption was verified by the fact that the tombs date to 350-325 BC, the years of Philip's rule. The excavations began in 1856, when Macedonia was still under the Ottoman Empire. A French archaeologist uncovered a Macedonian tomb and other stones, but it was not until over 60 years later that the site underwent heavy excavation—in 1937 a professor from the University of Thessaloniki held classes at the site, and so the university was given excavation rights during WWII. The most impressive treasures, however, including the royal tombs and the acropolis, were not found until the late 1970s.

MUSEUM. At once morbid and dazzlingly beautiful, Vergina's museum is the highlight of the site. Visitors enter the ▨**Great Tumulus,** a massive burial mound traditional to the period, which is the largest in Greece (over 12m tall and 110m in diameter). It was built before the mid-4th century BC and housed the graves of Vergina's common citizens in addition to the massive royal tombs. The atmospherically dim-lit museum displays artifacts found in the Great Tumulus including Attic vases, clay and ivory figurines, gold jewelry, and carved funerary stelae (inscribed columns) of commoners' graves. Four of the **royal tombs** lie in their original locations, and each has an anterior Ionic or Doric colonnade decorated with mythological scenes. The large room behind the colonnade contains the deceased's remains and items to accompany him or her into the afterlife. Tombs I and IV belong to unknown royal family members. Tomb IV, looted in antiquity, stored well-preserved **frescoes**, possibly the work of master artist **Nikomachus**. The most intact of them depicts Persephone being abducted by Hades, while Demeter watches with cold sorrow. The other two tombs are among Vergina's most spectacular archaeological finds. The **Tomb of the Prince** probably belongs to Alexander IV, son of Alexander the Great. Born shortly after his father's death, the prince was murdered at the age of 13 by Cassander, one of his father's generals. The silver hydra containing his bones and his spectacular leaf-mimicking gold myrtle wreath are on display, along with other artifacts. The last tomb is that of Philip II, the conqueror who paved the way for his son Alexander's expansions. **Philip's tomb** held a number of the treasures, including a magnificent gold chest that held his remains, a gold wreath that sat on his head when he was placed on the funerary pyre, and fragments of his chryselephantine couch. Though the wood rotted away, the ivory faces, arms, and legs of the couch's diorama, depicting Philip hunting with a young Alexander, still remain. A glass case displays the charred remains of the offerings thrown on Philip's funeral pyre including animal offerings, figurines, and all of his most treasured possessions. When a king died, his consorts would be burnt alive alongside him; Philip's tomb thus also contained the remains of a woman, probably Meda, one of his seven consorts. Her gold couch, along with shreds of the gold-embroidered purple cloth that wrapped her bones, are still visible.

RUINS. To get to the **Palace of Palatitsa,** turn right as you exit the museum and make a left at the intersection. A short-cut through the bus parking lot followed by an uphill walk will get you to the ruins in about 20min. What remains of the 3rd-century BC palace is now little more than a collection of toppled columns and ancient rubble, which, after the riches of the museum, may come as somewhat of a disappointment. *(Open M noon-7pm, Tu-Su 8am-7pm. Included in museum ticket.)* On the walk up to Palatitsa, you'll encounter the **Macedonian Tomb,** believed to be that of Philip II's mother, **Queen Evridiki.** Walk down the steps to its doors to see a stately marble throne. Next to it is a second tomb with a fresco of Persephone and Hades in the underworld. On your left as you enter the palace, you will see a path leading downhill which you can take to get to the **ancient theater.** It was here, overlooking the plains of his kingdom, that Philip II was assassinated in 336 BC while celebrating the marriage of his daughter. Legend has it that he was punished for committing hubris by declaring himself a god.

▧ ANCIENT PELLA Πέλλα

Ancient Pella is on the main Thessaloniki-Edessa highway, 38km west of Thessaloniki. From the bus (1hr., every 40min. 6:30am-10:30pm, €2.50), make sure you're let off at "Ancient Pella," not "New Pella." The site is to the right of where the bus stops, and the museum is on the other side of the street. Buses to Thessaloniki (2 per hr.) pass the site; the bus stops across from the cafe by the archaeological site. Museum (☎23820 31 160) open Apr.-Oct. M noon-7:30pm, Tu-Su 8am-7:30pm; Nov.-Mar. Tu-Su 8:30am-3pm. Site and museum €6; students €3; seniors, EU students, and under 18 free.

Pella was the center of the world for over a century. When King Archelaus chose to move the capital of his Macedonian state here in 400 BC, the site, advantageously situated on what was then the shore of the Theramaic Gulf, fostered eastern trade and developed a rapport with southern Greece. Later, the capital prospered under Philip II. As Philip became a powerful leader in 4th-century Greece, Pella grew to be a major city. The splendid new palace was home to intellectual and artistic talents from throughout the Hellenic world; Aristotle was born in Pella in 356 BC. Alexander the Great, Philip's son, inherited the kingdom after his father's assassination in 336 BC. As he conquered and Hellenized eastward to present-day India, Pella remained the capital. But inheritance struggles and the subsequent division of Macedonian lands following Alexander's death in 323 BC weakened the empire, and recession of the sea soon made Pella an inconvenient port. The city's glory days ended in 168 BC when it was ransacked by Roman general Aemilius Paulus, who carried away most of the city's riches.

Pella only takes an hour to see, but the **museum** alone makes the trip worthwhile. Its treasures include gold-leaf jewelry, terra-cotta figurines, a magnificent white marble bust of Alexander the Great, and unusual molded pottery depicting some rather racy episodes. The collection's most important objects are the exquisite **mosaics** which show Dionysus riding a panther, a lion hunt, a female centaur preparing libations in the cave of the nymphs and Dionysus, and a winged griffin devouring a deer (highlighted by grisly splashes of blood). The mosaics are composed of *tesserae* outlined with thin lead strips; the characters' missing eyes were semi-precious stones. These are the earliest-known mosaics to mimic a three-dimensional look. The molds which once cast ceramic figures and bowls depict a series of Homeric and erotic scenes and mythological stories. Directly across the highway from the museum is Pella's vast **archaeological site**, still under excavation by young go-getters from the University of Thessaloniki. At the heart of the site are the remains of the **agora**, the commercial center of the ancient city, with the three wells from which much of the pottery in the museum was collected. To the left, the **House of Dionysus** and the **House of the Abduction of Helen** both have well-preserved mosaic floors with beautifully-executed scenes. The **House of Plaster** has a splendid rectangular Ionic colonnade. North of the houses and the agora are the **acropolis** and **palace**, which are off-limits to visitors and so can only be viewed from afar. Built in 10 stages, the palace is a blend of architectural styles. Expanded by Philip, it fell with the rest of Pella at the hands of Aemilius Paulus. A massive earthquake put the nail in Ancient Pella's coffin years later in the 1st century BC.

VERIA Βέροια ☎ 23310

For most, Veria is only a transit point en route to the archaeological allure of Vergina. But in their haste to see Macedonian ruins, travelers miss a city built around the remains of a completely different period of Greek history. With over 70 churches to accommodate a population of less than 40,000, Veria pays allegiance to the importance of Orthodoxy under the Ottoman Empire and provides an interesting view on the cultural remnants of the *Tourkokratia* (Turkish rule). Veria's enchanting Old City, small and relatively untouristed, also has a Jewish quarter which acts as a living testament to Macedonia's Jewish Golden Age.

⌐ TRANSPORTATION. The train station (☎ 23310 24 444), 3km from the town center, is best reached by taxi (€4). **Trains** go to Edessa (35min., every hr. 6:20am-11:15pm, €1.30) and Thessaloniki (1hr., every hr. 5:35am-11:10pm, €2.10). Veria's bus station, Iras 17, is near Pl. Antoniou. **Buses** head to Athens (7hr., 3 per day 8am-8pm, €30), Thessaloniki (1hr., every hr. 5:30am-9pm, €5), and Vergina (20min., 11 per day 6:50am-8pm, €1.10). **Taxis,** available 24hr., sit in Pl. Antoniou.

▓ ▨ ORIENTATION AND PRACTICAL INFORMATION. There are two main plateias, **Plateia Antoniou** and **Plateia Orologiou** (sometimes called "Raktivan"); both are on Veria's main avenue, **Eleftherios Venizelou,** which ends at the intersection with **Mitropoleos.** To reach Pl. Antoniou from the bus station, exit the station and turn left on **Iras.** At the intersection, turn right and **Therdrou** will be across from you; follow it until you reach El. Venizelou. Turn left there and continue to find Pl. Antoniou on your right. To find the second plateia, continue along El. Venizelou for three blocks after Pl. Antoniou and veer right on Mitropoleos. Follow Mitropoleos about 900m; you'll see the plateia at the end of the hill, by the huge sign for St. Paul's altar. Veria has **no tourist office** but maps of town are posted at the municipal bus stops along most of El. Venizelou and Mitropoleos. The **Bank of Attica**, El. Venizelou 21, one block down from Pl. Antoniou, has an **ATM**. Other ATMs line Mitropoleos. (☎23310 66 820. Open M-Th 8am-2:30pm.) The **OTE** is at Mitropoleos 53. (☎23310 36 110. Open M-Sa 7:30am-1:30pm, Tu, Th-F 5:30pm-9pm.) **Karagrapoulos Konstantinos Pharmacy**, El. Venizelou 28, is opposite the Bank of Attica and sells herbal medicines along with normal drugstore ware. (☎233102 23 34. Open M, W, Sa 8am-2:30pm, Tu, Th-F 8am-1:30pm and 5-8:30pm.) **Internet access** is available at **Para Pente Cafe**, Elias 6, one block from Pl. Antoniou off El. Venizelou. (☎23310 24 300. €2 per hr. Open 10am-2pm.) Veria's **post office** is at 72 Mitropoleos. (☎23310 22 333. Open M-F 8am-2pm.) **Postal Code:** 59100.

ⅠⅭ ACCOMMODATIONS AND FOOD. Accommodations are expensive in Veria and budget hotels are in short supply. **Hotel Veroi ❸**, Raktivan 10, just off Pl. Orologiou, has private baths, TV, and phones; some rooms have A/C and fridges. (☎23310 22 866. Singles €32, with A/C €35; doubles €48; triples €60.) More upscale **Hotel Villa Elia ❹**, 10 Elias, one block down from Para Pente Cafe, is a better choice if budget permits. Spacious rooms have A/C, baths, TV, and phones. (☎23310 26 800. Breakfast included. Reception 24hr. Singles €50; doubles €65; triples €75. MC/V.)

Veria's countless churches are rivaled by the town's multitude of bakeries. Luckily, almost every church has a public water faucet and basin to treat sticky hands. So find a church, check for a fountain, and drop by **Elit ❶**, one block from Pl. Antoniou on the corner of El. Venizelou and Vermiou, for fresh *tiropita* (€1.60), famous in the greater Veria region. (☎23310 67 301. Open daily 8am-10pm.) At **Byzantino Restaurant ❷**, 8 Pl. Orologiou, you can choose from traditional dishes lovingly prepared by the owner's mother and eat in a cozy, stone-covered interior. (☎23310 72 243. Veal €6. Open daily noon-midnight.) At **Restaurant Vergiotiko ❷**, Thomaidou 2, considered one of the best restaurants in Veria, bowls of *saganaki* (stew of cheese, tomatoes, and red chili; €3), are served in an old renovated building.

ⓖ SIGHTS. Despite Veria's astonishing number of churches, all but one is closed to the public. The **Resurrection of Christ**, Mitropoleos 3, is near the intersection with El. Venizelou. This 14th-century, one-room church is adorned with stunning frescoes by Verian iconographer George Kallierges. (Open Tu-Su 8:30am-3pm. Free.) At the beginning of Mavromihali, on Pl. Orologiou, is **Apostle Paul's altar**, a marble, mosaic-decorated monument on the site at which the saint is believed to have preached. Veria's **Byzantine Museum**, Thomaidou 26, is down the road that divides the plateia and the altar; after passing a small fountain, you will arrive at a kiosk where you should turn left onto Kaveskaki and go 200m. It's around a corner, in a remodeled stone building. The museum documents Veria's Byzantine past with icons and ruins. The small but beautiful collection of wooden iconographic art from the 9th to 15th centuries is all local—Veria used to be home to a prosperous icon-making industry. (☎23310 25 847. Open daily 8:30am-3pm. €2, students free.) The adjoining **southern fortifications** on Kyriotissis St. are also worth seeing.

KAVALA Καβάλα ☎2510

The gateway to eastern Macedonia and one of Greece's major port cities, Kavala exudes charm that far surpasses its commercial importance. Originally built by Thassian colonists in the 7th century BC, it was named "Neapoli" ("new city") to signify its centrality in the islanders' mainland expansion. The place where the apostle Paul first set foot in Europe, the city was renamed "Christopolis" ("city of

Christ") during the Byzantine period. Kavala was given its current name under the Ottoman empire, which conquered the city in the 14th century. Perched on the eastern hill of the city, the Byzantine district of Panagia shadows the modern city and the port with its meandering cobblestone streets, *kastro*, and Ottoman imaret. In the New City, the palm-lined port and Rapsani beach draw travelers seeking a relaxing but faster-paced experience than that on nearby islands.

TRANSPORTATION

Flights: The **M. Alexandrou airport** (☎25910 53 273) is 32km outside the city, accessible by buses to **Chrissoupolis**, which run every 30min. (6am-9pm, €2), followed by a short taxi ride (€3). You can also take a taxi (€22) directly from the city center. **Olympic Airways**, Eth. Antistassis 8 (☎25102 23 622), near the bus station west of the Thassos ferry dock on the waterfront corner with M. Chrisostomou, has daily flights to **Athens** (1hr.; 7am, 9:40pm; €65-98). Open M-F 8am-4pm.

Buses: ☎25108 37 176. At the corner of Filikis Eterias and M. Chrisostomou, between the waterfront and the post office. Buses go to: **Athens** (9½hr., 3 per day 9:15am-7:15pm, €42); **Drama** (1hr., every 30min. 6am-9:15pm, €3) via **Philippi** (20min., €1.40); **Thessaloniki** (2½hr., 15 per day 5:30am-8:40pm, €11); **Xanthi** (1½hr., 17 per day 4:45am-8:40pm, €4). To get to **Alexandroupoli** (2hr., 7 per day 9:30am-2am, €11), go to **Seven-Eleven**, M. Chrisostomou 4 (☎25108 37 176), a fast-food restaurant located directly opposite the main entrance of the bus station, where you'll find schedules, tickets, and the bus itself. Open 9am-midnight.

Ferries: Ferries leave from the east end of the port in front of several restaurants. **Nikos Milades**, Dimitriou 32 (☎25102 20 067), has info. In Karaoli Dimitriou Sq. in the port's northeastern corner, behind a large tree on the far right. Open daily 9am-1:30pm and 6-8pm. Every Su at 1pm a ferry goes to **Pireus** (32hr., €40) via **Limnos** (4½hr., €15.30), **Lesvos** (11hr., €26.30), **Chios** (15hr., €30.40), **Samos** (19hr., €37), and **Ikarike** (23hr., €36). Student tickets half price. **Saos**, K. Dimitriou (☎25108 35 671), 3 restaurants down from Milades toward the port, sells tickets to **Samothraki** (3½hr., 3 per week, €14.50). Buy tickets to **Thassos** (1hr.; 10 per day 8am-10pm; €3, students and children €1.50) at the white ticket kiosk on the Thassos dock.

Flying Dolphins: Leave for **Thassos** (40min., 4 per day, €8) from the eastern dock.

Taxis: ☎25102 32 001 Just behind the port in Pl. Eleftherias. 24hr.

ORIENTATION AND PRACTICAL INFORMATION

With its visible traces of the powers that once ruled Kavala, the city's most interesting area is the **Panagia District**. Located on a peninsula jutting into the Aegean northeast of the port, it is hemmed in by ancient walls under the turrets of the Byzantine fortress. The entrance is on **Poulidou** at the end of **Eleftherios Venizelou**, which runs parallel to the waterfront two blocks inland. The next parallel street seaward is hotel-lined **Erithrou Stavrou**, followed by **Ethnikis Antistasis**, which skirts the waves from the dock to beyond the Archaeological Museum and municipal park. A detailed **map** of Kavala can be found next to the small port police kiosk, at the Thassos ferry dock. For paper copies head to the **municipal information office.**

Tourist Office: The **Municipal Information Office** (☎25102 31 011), the large, windowed kiosk off El. Venizelou just behind the port at Pl. Eleftherias, is an English-language oasis of information. Free **maps**, brochures, and walking guides to Thassos's and Samothraki's ruins (€9) are available. Ferry schedules, bus schedules, and accommodations information are free. Purchase tickets to local performances at the ticket office window outside. **Internet access** is also available (€2 per hr.). Open M-Sa 8am-9pm.

Bank: Alpha Bank, El. Venizelou 28 (☎25102 29 084). On the corner of Mitropoleos and El. Venizelou, across from the public park. **Exchanges currency.** Open M-Th 8am-2:30pm. Pl. Eleftherias, on El. Venizelou by the tourist office, directly behind the port, is surrounded by banks with **ATMs.** Most open M-Th 8am-2:30pm, F 8am-2pm.

English-Language Bookstore: Papadogiannis, Omonias 46 (☎25102 25 885). At the northern side of Pl. Eleftherias. Has a good selection of European and American newspapers and magazines. The shop also has some books in English. Open 8am-9:30pm.

Police: Omonias 119 (☎25106 22 273), 4 blocks north of the port. Follow Averof to the OTE, then bear left. 24hr. **Tourist police** (☎25106 22 246) on the 3rd fl. of the police building. Open May-Nov. 8am-3pm.

Hospital: Stavrou 113 (☎25102 92 000), 4 blocks inland past Panagia. 24hr.

Telephones: OTE, ☎25105 61 160. In Pl. 28 Oktovriou, near El. Venizelou. Open M, W 7:30am-3pm, Tu, Th-F 7:30am-2:30pm and 6-8:30pm, Sa 8:30am-2:30pm.

Internet Access: Funtazia, El. Venizelou 43 (☎25108 36 660), has fast DSL connections and laptop access (€1 per hr.). Open 9am-3am. **Cyber Club,** El. Venizelou 56 (☎25108 31 295), has over 90 high-speed terminals and laptop access. €1 per hr. Frappés €1.50. Beer €2. Open 24hr.

Post Office: Main branch (☎25108 33 330) at Kavalas and Stavrou, 1 block north of the bus station, **exchanges currency.** Open M-F 7:30am-8pm. **Postal Code:** 65110.

⚑ ACCOMMODATIONS AND CAMPING

Domatia are scarce and hotels aren't cheap in Kavala, which can make it difficult to find a good place to crash. Camping, however, is a good option in Kavala's natural setting. A few indoor budget accommodations also exist.

▨ **George Alvanos Rented Rooms,** Anthemiou 35 (☎25102 21 781). Enter the Panagia District on Poulidou at the imaret. Turn left at the fork in the street and then take an immediate left up the stairs of Navarinou. Make a sharp left on Anathemiou; it's on your left. This centuries-old house has beautifully furnished, wooden-floored rooms far from the noise and fumes of the port. The owners, who treat guests as if they were long-lost grandchildren, offer modest-sized rooms that overlook the sea, a free laundry machine, and a full kitchen. Reserve at least one week in advance. Singles €20; doubles €25. ❸

▨ **Batis Beach campground** (☎25102 45 918) manages to have city conveniences far from city grime. The beach is 4km outside of Kavala. Blue bus #8 (€0.70) leaves from in front of the post office (near the bus station), at M. Chrisostomou and Erithrou Stavrou, and goes to Batis from Kavala every 20min. 6am-8pm. Mini-mart and outdoor cinema. €1 to swim in the pool. €5 per person, €7 per large tent, €4 per small tent. MC/V. ❶

Hotel Panorama, El. Venizelou 26c (☎25102 24 205), opposite Hotel Acropolis, has basic, run-down rooms with balconies, TV, phones, and colorful drapes; some have fridges. Breakfast €6. Singles €22, with bath €28; doubles €28/36; triples €42. ❷

Hotel Acropolis, El. Venizelou 29 (☎2510 223 543). From the bus station, walk 2 blocks away from the water and turn right on El. Venizelou; it's 1 block on your right. Large, bare but clean rooms have high ceilings, sinks, twin-sized beds, and TV. Singles €28, with bath €35; doubles €35/47; triples with bath €65. ❸

Oceanis Hotel, Erithrou Stavrou 32 (☎2510 221 981), at the intersection with Dagli. Colorful, carpeted, spacious rooms are fully equipped with TV, A/C, phones, large balconies, fridges, and sparkling baths. The bar and swimming pool on the roof provide exquisite views of the bay. Breakfast €9. Reception 24hr. Reserve 1 month in advance. Singles €68; doubles €88; triples €100. MC/V. ❹

🔆📷 FOOD AND NIGHTLIFE

Tavernas line Poulidou in Panagia and the area near the waterfront. A short distance from the imaret at Theodorou Poulidou 45, **Al Xalidi ❷**, a cozy, brick-lined taverna overlooking the cobblestone road, allows diners to sip wine from Limnos while enjoying the peaceful surroundings of the Old City. The tomato and cheese stew (€4.50) is a particular favorite. (☎25102 33 325. Appetizers €3-4. Entrees €5-7. Open noon-1am.) The easiest way to find **Mikros Mylos Bakery ❶**, Dagli 8, is to follow the delicious smells. If your nose's sense of direction is less than stellar, you can look for the corner of El. Venizelou and Dagli, one block inland from hotel Oceanis. The endless selection of freshly baked pastries and breads, chocolate truffles, and homemade jams (€7) will satiate any sweet tooth. (☎25102 28 132. Open 6:30am-10pm.) The staff at **Oraya Mytilini ❷**, across from the white bus station at the northeast end of port, is happy to give guided tours of the kitchen. Tastefully decorated with colorful tablecloths and a cozy atmosphere, the restaurant serves delicious seafood entrees (€4-8) like the "fruit of the sea" dish (rice with mussels, small shrimp, and octopus) and has a terrific view of the port. (☎25102 24 749. Entrees €5-9. Open 10am-midnight.) After hours, Kavala remains calm, though a few lively cafe-bars line the waterfront where the bulk of nightlife activity takes place. Winter clubbers inhabit the restored tobacco warehouses on Paleologou, but the real summer action moves to Kavala's suburban beaches. Take a taxi to nearby **Palio** (€6.50) or the beach at **Aspri Amos,** to the east of Kavala.

📷 SIGHTS

Once home to the Thassian colony of Neapolis, the **Old Town** is now the Panagia District. Perched above the town, this spiderweb of steep streets and Ottoman-style houses unfolds atop the promontory beside the port. Start your walk on Poulidou, which branches off Koundouriotou just as it intersects El. Venizelou.

BYZANTINE KASTRO (CASTLE). Follow the signs from Panagia's entrance on Poulidou to reach the *kastro*, which is visible from almost everywhere in Kavala. The current citadel was constructed in AD 1425 by the Venetians and was later renovated and enlarged by the Turks. Underneath are the remains of older Byzantine walls dating from the 5th century BC. Known by the locals as "Srourio," the *kastro* is divided into two open fields and separated by a tower and wall. A small **amphitheater** and three fortification towers are located in the outer field, while the inner one contains an early Byzantine cistern, an arsenal and food storehouse, and a guardhouse. In later periods the cistern was used as a prison. The amphitheater hosts occasional musical and cultural performances. In the **Eleftheria Festival** in late June, students celebrate Kavala's liberation from the Ottomans by performing dances at the castle. *(Open daily 8am-8pm. €1, students €0.50, EU students free.)*

OTTOMAN IMARET. A mind bogglingly expensive hotel (€1000 per night) is on the right as you enter Panagia at Poulidou 38, where the street forks and ascends to the *kastro*. This fantastically beautiful example of Islamic architecture was built in 1817 by native Kavalian Mehmet Ali, who later became pasha of Egypt. The imaret—a type of hospice often funded by wealthy Muslims to fulfill the Islamic principle of charity—was originally a seminary, poor house, and boarding school for less fortunate Kavalaians. While its current status as a protected hotel doesn't let tourists peek at the historical monument, if you win the lottery you may want to look into staying there (and probably buy a non-budget travel book).

MEHMET ALI'S HOUSE. Continue from Poulidou three blocks from the imaret, to where the cliff comes to an end. Ali's house survives at the very tip of the promontory. The founder of the last Egyptian dynasty, Ali was born in this house in 1769. He was recognized as the Pasha of Egypt in 1807 and given the island of Thassos as a gift. The Greeks of Egypt gave Ali yet another present: a bronze statue of himself mounted on a horse, which still stands there. From this point, there are splendid views of the sea and of Kavala. In front you can see green Thassos, an oil rig, and the uninhabited islet of Thassopoula to the left.

KAMARES AQUEDUCT. Kamares, erected in 1550 under Sultan Süleyman the Magnificent, connects the Old City with the New City and completes the circuit of Panagia. This colossal construction initially doubled as both a defensive wall and an aqueduct. The Ottoman city's guards would patrol on its top, while water from the nearby springs flowed through it to bring life to the city. To follow the aqueduct's path, retrace your steps to the imaret, following Poulidou, and make a right onto M. Ali. Take a left onto Navarinou and another left on Issidorou, which edges the western base of the *kastro*. Follow Issidorou and make a right at the end of the road, which will leave you right in front of the aqueduct.

OTHER SIGHTS. The **Archaeological Museum,** one of the region's largest, nicely complements any trip to Amphibolis or to the sights of Thassos. Many of its artifacts were plundered by the Bulgarians during WWII, but the museum was reorganized and restored in 1952. The gold jewelry and wreaths, elaborate Hellenistic funeral painting, and the reconstruction of a Macedonian burial chamber are worth checking out. *(In the park on the waterfront, between Ethnikis Antistasis and Erithrou Stavrou, by Farilou Park.* ☎ *25102 22 335. Open Tu-Su 8am-3:30pm.* €2, *students* €1, *EU students free.)* Kavala's **Municipal Folk Museum,** once home to tobacco trader Zachos Zachou, houses Kavala's municipal archives and a small but interesting collection. Of particular note are works by Thassian sculptor Polygnotos Vagis, an internationally acclaimed artist in the 1930s whose pieces blend archaic Greek styles with modern influences like Chagall and Matisse. The exhibit also includes local jewelry, games, and artifacts representing aspects of everyday life. *(Filippou 4. On the corner of Mitropoleos and Filippou near the public park.* ☎ *25102 22 706. Open M-F 8am-2pm, Sa 9am-1pm. Free.)*

There are a number of tobacco-related sights, including the **tobacco warehouse,** two blocks from El. Venizelou on the far side of Pl. Kapnergati; follow Averof, which runs inland from the port, up five blocks. Though it is currently undergoing renovations to accommodate the new municipal center which will share the building, the warehouse was once part of Kavala's booming tobacco industry. Built in the first decade of the 20th century, it has a beautiful pink facade and delicate stone masonry. In the same square, there is a monument to the tobacco workers.

There are 46km of **beaches** west of Kavala. Although it's not a particularly arduous walk from town, the easiest way to get to the water is by intercity bus. **Rapsani,** in the western part of Kavala, at the end of Eth. Antistasis, is currently under construction—you are more likely to encounter tractors than sunbathers. The sandy beach of **Kalamitsa,** however, 2km past Rapsani, has three bars, tavernas, and showers. **Batis** is next, 1km down the shoreline, followed by pebble-covered **Tosca,** which has received the EU's blue flag for clean water. The city's main resort beaches, with hot summer nightlife and long strips of sand, are **Palio,** 10km southwest, **Nea Iraklitsa,** another 2km, and **Nea Peramos,** 16km from Kavala. Buses leave from the post office near the bus station every 20-30min. Take blue bus #8 to all the beaches before Batis (20 per day 6am-8pm). To get to the farther beaches, take the green bus (30 per day 6am-10pm; Palio

€0.90, Nea Iraklitsa €1, Nea Peramos €1.40). Bus times are flexible. Ask at the bus station for hours. Alternatively, taxis to the beaches range from €2 to Kalamitsa to €9 to far-away Nea Peramos.

🔂 DAYTRIP FROM KAVALA

PHILIPPI Φίλιπποι

Take the bus from Kavala to Drama (every 30min. 6am-9:15pm, €1.40). Make sure to tell the driver you want the archaeological site of Philippi. The bus drops you off at the western section of the site, which holds the museum. ☎25105 16 470. Site open daily 8am-7pm; pavilion mosaics open Tu-Su 8am-3pm. €3, students and seniors €2, EU students free. The museum is undergoing renovations and is due to reopen in 2007.

About 15km north of Kavala, the once-proud city of **Philippi** lies in splendid ruin. Originally built on the site of a Neolithic settlement in 360 BC, Philippi was the final step in securing Thassian mainland expansion. With the establishment of Krenides, the islanders, who had previously expanded into mainland Greece by building Neapoli (present-day Kavala), achieved complete control of the Daton region. Rich in precious metals and agriculturally fertile, the area's Pangaion mountains attracted many to this Macedonian stronghold, and so the city was soon coveted by others in the region. Just four years later, **Philip II** of Macedon conquered the city and renamed it "Phillipi," after himself. The Macedonians controlled the city until the Roman conquest in 148 BC, and it was here that the Roman Republic met its demise. The **Battle of Philippi** between the combined armies of Brutus and Cassius and those of Octavian and Mark Antony was fought at the outskirts of the city in 42 BC. The defeat of the former, who had conspired in the death of Julius Caesar, opened the path to empire for Octavian, later called "Augustus Caesar," who would become Roman emperor in 28 BC.

A new phase in the city's history began in AD 49 with the visit of **Saint Paul.** In the Bible's Book of Acts, Philippi is referred to as "a leading city of the district of Macedonia and a Roman colony," and this is where Paul baptized Lydia, who became the first European Christian. In the mid-4th century, the first Christian church in Europe was built here, and in the 5th and 6th centuries, the city prospered as a religious center, inspiring people from across Europe to make pilgrimage. After Ottoman conquest, Philippi was not preserved.

The site contains the remains of 20 buildings of interest and a museum. The Kavala-Drama highway divides Philippi, leaving the central Roman ruins—the forum, the agora, the Via Egnatia (the street which passed though the city), and the baths—on your left as you exit the bus from Kavala. Across the street, in the western section, lie the Classical and Roman theater, the museum, and the prison in which St. Paul was kept. In the far northwestern corner is the city's acropolis, built between the 5th and 4th centuries BC and reconstructed under Byzantine control.

LITOCHORO Λιτόχωρο ☎23520

Though visitors rarely go to Litochoro for its own merits, as it is generally viewed as the gateway to Mt. Olympus, its charming small-town atmosphere, access to the party scene in nearby Plaka, and proximity to the archaeological site at Dion make it far more than a mere transportation hub. The town's twisting cobblestone paths lead down the mountainside to the plateia known as *"kentro"* ("center"), where locals relax in the shadows of Olympus. Litochoro is also, of course, a well of information about the mountain and its trails. Though it's possible to ascend the mountain from its western side, beginning in Kokkinopilos village, this treeless route can't match the lush canyon trails that originate in Litochoro.

⌐📱 TRANSPORTATION AND PRACTICAL INFORMATION. Buses (☎23520 81 271) depart from Litochoro's KTEL station, Ag. Nikolaou 20, under the wooden canopy, opposite the tourist office and next door to an Internet cafe. They go to: Athens (5hr., 3 per day 9:30am-midnight, €25); Larisa (2hr., 8 per day 6am-8pm, €5); Plaka (15min., every hr. 10:15am-7:15pm, €1.20); Thessaloniki (1½hr., 16 per day 6:15am-8:50pm, €6.50) via Katerini (30min., €1.70). Expect to wait 10-15min. for the Thessaloniki-bound bus at the Katerini bus station.

Agiou Nikolaou, Litochoro's main street, runs east-west leading up to a fountain at **Plateia Agiou Nikolaou,** the central plateia. The **tourist office,** down Ag. Nikolaou near the police station, by the park, provides excellent information in English, free **maps** of the town, and a €4.50 map of the mountain. (☎23520 83 100. Open daily July-Nov. 8am-2pm and 3-9pm.) There's a **National Bank** with a **24hr. ATM** in Pl. Ag. Nikolaou. (☎23520 81 025. Open M-F 8am-2pm.) The **police station,** Ag. Nikolaou 20, is just below the plateia, on the left as you walk downhill. (☎23520 81 100 or 23520 81 111. Open 24hr.) The **health center** (☎23520 22 222) is about 5km outside of town by the beach and has 24hr. **emergency** facilities. The **OTE,** Ag. Nikolaou 14, sits across from the tourist booth farther down the main street. (☎23520 84 099. Open 7:20am-2pm.) **Internet access** is available at many of the trendy cafe-bars toward the lower end of town. At **Cafe Artio,** Ag. Nikolaou 82, across from Hotel Park, patrons check email (€2.50 per hr.), sip frappés (€2), play pool (€4 per hr.), and listen to loud pop. (☎23520 21 051. Open 9am-2am.) The **post office** is at 28 Oktovriou 12. (☎23520 81 526. Open M-F 7:30am-2pm.) **Postal Code:** 60200.

🛏️🍴 ACCOMMODATIONS AND FOOD. Accommodations prices in Litochoro are fairly constant, and any price discrepancies can be eliminated with the usual negotiating. Though the cheapest options are the out-of-town campgrounds, there are some affordable indoor options. At **Hotel Park ❷,** Ag. Nikolaou 23, down Ag. Nikolaou from the plateia and past the long park, garish mosaic hallways lead into large rooms with A/C, baths, TV, fridges, phones, and large balconies. (☎23520 81 252. Breakfast €5. Reception 24hr. Singles €25; doubles €30; triples €35.) **Hotel Mirto ❸,** Ag. Nikolaou 5, on the left at the end of the first block coming from the plateia, has large, quiet rooms with private baths, TV, A/C, showers, and fridges. Beautiful pictures of the Greek landscape adorn each room, and the third-floor rooms overlook the mountain. (☎23520 81 398. Reception 24hr. Singles €30; doubles €38; triples €50.) **Papanikolau ❸,** Niko. Espik. Kitaus 1, behind the plateia on a road that veers off to the left, has tidy, well-maintained rooms. The sound of chirping birds and the smell of fresh bread that wafts from the breakfast room evoke Litochoro's small-town charm. Rooms have kitchenettes, TV, fridges, balconies, and fans. (☎23520 81 236. Breakfast €2.50. Reservations recommended 1 day in advance. Doubles €35; triples €45.) The beach, 5km from town, is chock full of campgrounds. **Olympus Zeus ❹** rents bungalows that resemble small houses, with fridges, private baths, and phones. Less crowded than the nearby Olympus Beach, this mix between a campsite and a resort also has two restaurants and a bar. (☎23520 22 115. Singles €40; doubles €50; triples €60; quads €70.) The complex has an actual **campground ❶** as well. (€6 per person, €3 per car, €3.60 per tent.) **Olympus Beach ❸** (☎23520 22 112; www.olympos-beach.gr.) has very simple bungalows for one to four people with small baths, beds, and fridges, all for a €40 flat rate. The area is like its own small town, with a supermarket, nightclub, 24hr. bar, beach, and plenty of weekend and high-season crowds. The owners also offer a nice **campsite ❶** adjacent to the bungalows. (Reception 24hr. €5.90 per person, €6 per tent, €2.90 per car. AmEx/MC/V.) Avoid camping on the northern side of the road between the town and the highway, as these areas are army training grounds.

For a final feast before heading for the hills, try ▧ **Gastrodromio En Olympo ❸**, just off the plateia by the church. Diners have a remarkable view of the mountain, and the plateia's sounds of pleasant chaos drift melodically up to the balcony. The menu features an array of meat dishes including rooster, rabbit, deer, and goat, along with excellent traditional meals. The wine menu is equally varied, with over 200 options. (☎ 23520 21 300; www.gastrodomio.gr. Entrees €8-13.50. Open 10am-midnight. MC/V.) The amazing lamb chops (€7.35) and chicken (€5) at **Fistaria Dias ❷**, Ag. Nikolaou 38, under a yellow awning on the left walking toward the plateia, have given the restaurant its reputation as the Grill King of Litochoro. (☎ 23520 82 225. Open 11am-1am.) **Ta Mezedakia ❷**, Vas. Ithakisiou 3, specializes in "little appetizers," as its name suggests. On the street that forks right at the police station, the restaurant grills tasty Greek classics, including *soustaki* (grilled beef; €5.50), and serves them in an outdoor seating area. (☎ 23520 84 574. Entrees €5.50-8.50. Open 5pm-midnight.) Those wisely seeking water and trail snacks for the arduous hike up Olympus should stay away from the expensive supermarkets just above the plateia, and instead try **Arvanitides**, Perikliko Torba 14, at the end of short, winding Odos Ermi, which branches off Ag. Nikolaou opposite the Demotic (Public) School just below the tourist office. (☎ 23520 21 195. Open 8am-9pm.)

▧ **NIGHTLIFE.** If you want to party before—or instead of—hiking, start your evening in the **bars** around the bottom of Ag. Nikolaou, about 6min. from the park. The action moves over to Plaka by midnight and continues toward the beach as the night goes on. **Abbia**, Ag. Nikolaou 100, 5min. past the tourist office, plays bass-heavy pop and Greek music for groups gathered around shockingly pink couches. (☎ 23520 23 520. Mixed drinks €7. Open 9am-5am.) **Bolero**, Ag. Nikolaou 98, just above Abbia, is a rock bar that serves some of the cheapest drinks (€5) in town. (☎ 23520 82 702. Open 8am-4am.) **Garage**, Ag. Nikolaou 102, just below Abbia, blasts pop music for a hip crowd. (Mixed drinks €5-6. Open 9am-5am.) On the road to Plaka, on the left side of Olympus Beach hugging the water, **Caprice** provides the full gamut of nightlife experiences. It has an eating area, dance floor, cafe, bar, and beach access. Special events include grill night and full-moon parties. (☎ 23520 22 506. Beer €4. Mixed drinks €6. Open 10am-5am). The sleekest and trendiest Litochorians get down at **White Shark**, a glass-walled disco perched on a cliff above the sea. (☎ 23520 22 930. Open 10am-5am.) Partying in Plaka can get expensive: a taxi costs around €6, cover is around €8, and the price of drinks can add up quickly. Fueling up on *retsina* and ouzo at one of the tiki-torch-lit *psistarias* (seafood grills) before hitting the clubs is a cheaper experience-enhancer.

▧ANCIENT DION Δίον ☎ 23510

Dion, at the foot of Mt. Olympus, is one of Greece's biggest and most fascinating archaeological sites. In Hellenistic times, Macedonian kings traveled great distances to the city to make sacrifices to Zeus. "Dion," in fact, is derived from a form of Zeus's name. The city was sacred to all Macedonians, not just royals, and it flourished during the Hellenistic and Imperial periods. At the **Greek theater,** Alexander the Great made sacrifices to seal the oaths of his assembled armies on the eve of the 334 BC campaign that led them to the far stretches of India. The city was also home to a number of cults worshipping various gods—temples to Artemis, Demeter, Zeus, and, later, Egyptian goddess Isis all cropped up here. In the spectacular ▧ **Villa of Dionysus,** a large, remarkably expressive mosaic of the god remains in excellent condition some 2300 years after it was created. Dion later fell to the Romans, who built elaborate **public baths.** The baths featured an underground steam system powered by open fires, which created heated air that traveled through dual-layered walls to create a sauna-like effect. Destroyed by a combination of earthquakes, fires, and the first German tourists—the Visigoths—in the AD 4th century, the city (or what remained of it) was preserved by subsequent mudslides. Underneath the wreckage, Christian basilicas lived in harmony with temples of the empire's old religions. Thessaloniki University has been excavating Dion since the 1930s, and has uncovered some spectacular artifacts. Almost every winter, however, the site, only 5m above sea level, fills with water, and excavations have to begin anew in the spring. The outstanding **museum,** in a two-story building just a 5min. walk into town, displays many of the treasures that have been recovered. Filled with pieces that would be the major highlight of a smaller collection, the museum also displays a 1st-century BC **hydravlis,** a forerunner to the pipe organ, the first ever of its kind found in Greece. The museum's lower level sheds light on everyday life in ancient Dion, with domestic objects including cosmetics, keys, and clothes. English explanations make the displays easily accessible. (Open M 12:30-7pm, Tu-Su 8am-7pm. €4, students and seniors €2.)

A taxi to Dion from Litochoro is about €10. The walk to Dion takes about 3hr., but it's pleasant, with a constant view of Mt. Olympus. (☎ 23510 53 206. Site open daily 8am-7pm. €4, students and seniors €2; combined ticket with museum €6.)

MOUNT OLYMPUS Ολύμπος Όρος ☎23520

Erupting out of the Thermaic Gulf, Mt. Olympus, the highest mountain in Greece, mesmerized the ancients so much that they believed it to be the dwelling place of their immortal pantheon. The sharp peaks saw no successful mortal ascent until 1913, when Christos Kakalos, a Litochorian shepherd, guided two Swiss photographers up to Mytikas's zenith. The group took the first photos of Mt. Olympus, and rumor tells that Kakalos became so famous that he never paid for a meal again. Since its initial conquest, Olympus has been harnessed by a network of well-maintained trails that makes the summit accessible to just about anyone with a head for heights, a taste for adventure, and about two days; the climb is strenuous but not technically difficult. As you ascend, you'll pass leafy, green woodlands and shadowy pine forests before emerging above the treeline to truly stunning views. Mt. Olympus has eight peaks: Ag. Andonios (2817m), Kalogeros (2701m), Mytikas ("The Needle"; 2918m), Profitis Ilias (2803m), Skala (2866m), Skolio (2911m), Stefani ("The Throne of Zeus"; 2907m), and Toumba (2801m). The mountain and its surrounding region became Greece's first national park in 1938, and are said to contain all the climates of Europe, from Litochoro's Mediterranean weather to the summit's snowy tundra. Twenty-three different types of flowers grow only on the mountain, and its tea leaves are well known throughout the country.

⁊ LOGISTICS OF THE CLIMB

You'll find the most reliable resources for all aspects of hiking—updates on weather and trail conditions, advice on itineraries and routes, and reservations for any of the **Greek Alpine Club** (EOS) refuges—at EOS refuge **Zolotas,** known as "Spilios Agapitos" (see **Accommodations,** below). The staff has years of experience and is happy to give information over the phone in English. As the refuge is 2100m up the mountain, it's best to call from Litochoro before embarking on the climb. (☎ 23520 81 800. Open for calls 6am-10pm.) The **EOS office,** the small stone building in the parking lot below Litochoro off Ithakisiou, has similar info and is in a far more accessible location. The parking lot is just below Gastrodromio En Olympo and the plateia. It's worth stopping by even if the office is closed—many of the members of the Mt. Olympus search-and-rescue team hang out there, and are glad to help hikers. (☎ 23520 82 444. Open M-F 9:30am-12:30pm and 6-8pm, Sa-Su 9am-noon.) The **SEO office** (Association of Greek Mountain Climbers; ☎ 23520 83 262),

NORHTERN GREECE

Mount Olympus

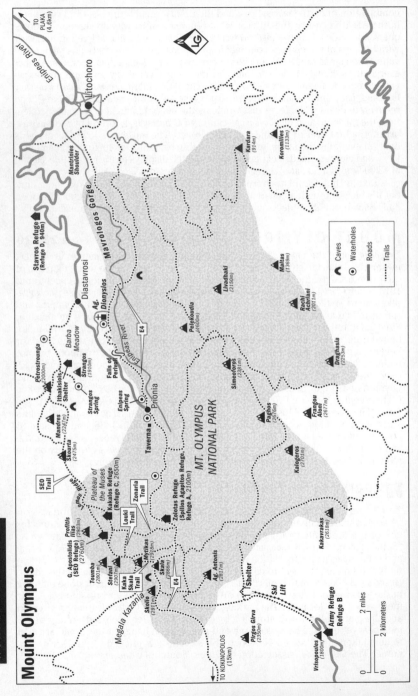

TO PLAKA
(4.6km)

Enipeas River

Litochoro

TO KOKINOPOLOS
(15km)

TO PLAKA

Mantrinies
Shoulder

Stavros Refuge
(Refuge D, 940m)

Diastavrosi

Ag.
Dionysios

Mavrologos Gorge

Barba
Meadow

Petrostrounga
(2000m)

Ithakisiolis
Shelter

Strangos
(1910m)

Falls of
Perivoli

Enipeas River

E4

Strangos
Spring

Priónia

Enipeas
Spring

Mandres

Skourta
(2475m)

SEO
Trail

Plateau of
the Muses

Kakalos Refuge
(Refuge C, 2650m)

Zonaria
Trail

Taverna

Louki
Trail

G. Apostolidis
(SEO Refuge)
(2760m)

Profitis
Ilias
(2803m)

Zolotas Refuge
(Spilios Agapitos Refuge,
Refuge A, 2100m)

Toumba
(2801m)

Stefani
(2907m)

Mýtikas
(2917m)

Kaka
Skala
Trail

Skala
(2866m)

Skolio
(2911m)

E4

Ag.
Antonis
(2817m)

Shelter

MT. OLYMPUS
NATIONAL PARK

Megala Kazania

Pagos Girva
(2350m)

Ski
Lift

Army Refuge
Refuge B

Vrisopoules
(1800m)

Kardara
(914m)

Koromilies
(1133m)

Maltas
(1365m)

Rachi
Asemani
(2011m)

Livadhaki
(2150m)

Draghasia
(2235m)

Simeoforos
(2381m)

Petelkoudia
(2400m)

Frangou
Aloni
(2677m)

Paghos
(2676m)

Kalogeros
(2701m)

Kakavrakas
(2618m)

Caves

Waterholes

Roads

Trails

0   2 miles

0   2 kilometers

behind Hotel Mirto, is more of a clubhouse than an official resource, but if you happen to catch someone there (which is rare), they have helpful information. You can buy a colorful bilingual fold-out map with contour lines and all the major trails at most local shops, kiosks, and bookstores for €4-5. A Road Editions map, produced with data from the Greek Army Geographical Service, is the best and most expensive map (€7.50) and comes with a handy plastic sleeve.

> **SAFETY ON THE MOUNTAIN.** Trails are well-marked and well-maintained and straying from them can be dangerous; most of the rescue team's calls are from lost climbers. Do not climb alone—even if you are traveling alone, try to find someone to hike with at a refuge. Also beware of **belladonna berries,** small, grape-like black fruit that grows on purple flowers. Though sweet, they are poisonous and just touching them, much less eating them, can cause unconsciousness. Though the climb is not recommended for those at risk of **altitude sickness,** the hike itself is accessible to people of any (or no) hiking experience.

Each winter, well over 7m of snow bury Mt. Olympus, and even in late July, snowfields linger in the ravines. Unless you're handy with an ice pick and crampons, you'll want to climb between May and October, when Persephone returns to Olympus from the underworld, and her mother, Demeter, warms the earth. Mytikas, the tallest peak, is not accessible without special equipment until June, and returns to the domain of professionals around September. **Weather** conditions can change rapidly near the summits; even in mid-summer, be prepared for anything from chilly clouds and rain to unrelenting sun. If you are climbing between June and September, you'll need typical **hiking equipment:** sturdy ankle-high shoes, sunscreen, a head covering, some snacks, at least 2L of water, light walking clothes, a warm wool or synthetic fleece sweater or jacket (the summit is 8-15°C/46-59°F in the summer), and, ideally, an extra shirt and waterproof windbreaker. Some hikers swear by trekking poles for maintaining balance and climbing steep terrain, but you will have to bring your own as there is no place to buy or rent them on the mountain. To avoid carrying necessary weight, take a small day-pack and leave your luggage in Litochoro; the EOS office stores bags for free.

ACCOMMODATIONS

Reaching Mytikas in one day is only recommended for experienced hikers up for an 8km, 6-8hr. ascent and a strenuous 4-6hr. hike back down. For those who want to savor the summit trails or are concerned about the possibility of altitude sickness from leaping from the Aegean to 3000m and back in one day, an overnight stay in one of the refuges is a good idea. They provide beds, blankets (no sheets or towels), meals, and water. Three refuges are near the summits, and all of them, particularly Zolotas, tend to fill up on weekends between June and October. Call at least one week in advance for reservations. At the refuges, breakfasts tend to run €3, soups and salads €2.50-3.50, and pasta and meat dishes €3-5. Bring a flashlight to navigate your way to the bathroom after the generator is shut down. The refuges' managers are also prepared to embark on emergency rescues if need be.

▨ **Zolotas Refuge,** (☎23520 81 800; elev. 2100m), also called "Spilos Agapitos" or "Refuge A"), is named after owner Constantine Zolotas. It's about 800m below Skala and Mytikas peaks, and can be reached by very easy walk on the E4 trail. The 110 beds, telephone, and very cold showers make this refuge the largest and cushiest, though also the most crowded—reservations are recommended. Curfew 10pm. Open mid-May to Oct. 6am-10pm. €10, with any Greek mountain club membership €8. You can also set up a tent nearby while using the refuge's facilities for €5. ❶

Kakalos (elev. 2650m), called "Refuge C," is much closer to the summit on the other side of the mountain in the Plateau of Muses. Accessible by a trail of intermediate difficulty, it has 18 beds and the same prices as Zolotas. Make reservations through Zolotas. Meals served 6am-9pm. Reception 24hr. Open mid-June to Sept. 15 F-Su only to groups (though stranded hikers are not turned away). ❶

G. Apostolidis (elev. 2760m), better known as **"SEO Refuge,"** is 15min. from Kakalos, beneath Stefani and Profitis Ilias, and has extraordinary sunrise views. Sleeps 100 and can accommodate extras and late-comers in its glass-walled porch or living room. Make reservations through the Thessaloniki SEO, which runs the refuge. (☎23102 44 710. Open M-F 8am-10pm; leave a message for reservations.) Meals served 9am-9:30pm. Reception 24hr. June-Sept. €10, with any Greek mountain club membership €8. ❶

✍ THE HIKE TO THE HEAVENS

There are three ways to tackle Olympus; all originate in **Litochoro** (elev. 500m). Two of the trails involve heading straight to the trailheads, while the third takes you to the trailhead along a more scenic route.

ASCENDING FROM PRIONIA. The most popular route begins at Prionia (elev. 1100m), about a 1hr. drive (taxi €20) or an easy 5hr. walk from Litochoro. At the trailhead, you'll find **drinking-water** taps, **toilets**, and a small **restaurant**. From here, a 3hr., 4km walk takes you to the Zolotas refuge. The well-marked trail is part of the European **E4** path from Spain to Greece. There's one last chance for water before the refuge, about 45min. from Prionia. After another 15min. you will be able to see the refuge, but it will still be another 2hr. before you reach it. As you approach the treeline, you'll be encouraged by bright clumps of wildflowers.

ASCENDING FROM DIASTAVROSI. The second trailhead is at **Diastavrosi** (also called **"Gortsia"**; elev. 1300m), 14km away, leading up to Kakalos and the SEO refuges. There are no buses to Diastavrosi so you must walk (4hr.), drive (40min.), or take a taxi (€11) from Litochoro. This longer (11km) but more picturesque route includes a stunning ridge-walk with views of the Aegean, the Macedonian plain, and Thessaloniki's smog. On cloudless days you may also be able to spy Mt. Athos and Thassos. As you climb higher, the difference in altitude is noticeable as the amount of vegetation dwindles. The well-marked trail reaches the **SEO** and **Kakalos refuges** in about 6-8hr. Begin at Diastavrosi's parking lot (turn right off the gravel road halfway between Litochoro and Prionia) by taking the uphill path on the left, and follow the red blazes, striped plastic strips on trees, and signs of the mule caravan that uses this route. In about 1hr., you'll pass through the **Barba Meadow,** which has a **water** tap. An hour later, you'll reach a cement water tank with an unhelpful painted map off to the left. Go straight here, not left, and the path leads up to **Petrostrounga** (elev. 1800m), about 3hr. from the trailhead. Four hours from the trailhead you'll begin approaching the treeline, reaching **Skourta Hill** in another 30min. or so. Here the trees will turn into small grassy fields. The beautiful **Lemos Ridge** leads you gently toward the peaks. About 5½hr. from the beginning of the hike you'll hit the **Plateau of the Muses** (Οροπέδιο Μουσόν; or-eh-PEH-thio moos-ON), a sweeping expanse of green under the Stefani, Toumba, and Profitis Ilias peaks. Take the clearly marked fork left for the Kakalos refuge (elev. 2650m) or right for the SEO refuge (elev. 2760m). A trail also goes up to the top of Profitis Ilias, where a tiny stone **church,** built in 1925, sits. You can usually find **water** in two places along the Diastavrosi trail: at the turn-off between Barba and Spilla (1½hr. from the trailhead, marked on the trail), and at Stragos spring. It's best not to depend on the springs, though, as they run dry in very warm weather.

ASCENDING FROM ENIPEAS GORGE. The third and most scenic route involves hiking to Prionia via a trail along the Enipeas Gorge; you begin in Litochoro and, after an easy 5hr. hike along a river, arrive at the Prionia trailhead. After spending the night at the Zolotas refuge, you'll ascend to the summit the next day and head to the SEO and Kakalos refuges. Hikers can stay another night there and walk down the next day to Diastavrosi (5-6hr., depending on how they fare going downhill), or pass the refuges and arrive at Diastavrosi in late afternoon. All of the trails to the refuges are simple to follow, and most are marked with red and yellow blazes. The low-key, beautiful trail from Litochoro to Prionia runs along an E4 trail by the Enipeas River through the Mavrologos Gorge—whose name means "black mountain," since the trees are so dense that you can't see the sun. The parts of the trail that go up through Enipeas Gorge are not difficult in themselves, but they add about 5hr. to the ascent from Prionia, which makes it a total climb of 8-9hr. Gorgeous stretches punctuate the 18km climb, but it's a long hike with many ups and downs on multiple bridges, so be sure to bring water. To find the trailhead, walk uphill from Litochoro's main plateia past the Hotel Aphrodite, and follow signs to **Mili** (Μύλοι), past the town cemetery, to the Restaurant Mili. There is **drinking water** at the trailhead. Continue past the restaurant to the left. When you reach the concrete walkway, make a right and walk along it for a short distance. At a fork in the trail, follow the yellow diamond markers reading "E4" up the left side of the Mavrologos Gorge. Keep following yellow diamonds, red blazes, spray-painted numbers, and orange and white plastic strips tied on trees, crossing over the river at the new bridges. Parts of the trail have views down into the gorge. When the trail descends to the river, you will see several lovely, clear green pools; though they couldn't be more tempting, swimming is forbidden. After 3hr. you'll reach the tiny **Chapel of Agios Spileo,** built at the source of a small spring inside a gaping cave. According to legend, drinking from it is extremely good for your health. About 20min. farther, after a bridge crossing, follow the dirt road for 60m before turning left up the hill to see the charred shell of the **Monastery of Agios Dionysios,** which was a refuge for Greek partisans during WWII until it was bombed by the Nazis. According to locals, when Ag. Dionysiou built the church in the 15th century, he was aided by a bear. After a short dispute that followed the church's completion, however, the saint petrified the bear, who can still be seen standing across the ridge from the church. You can fill your water bottle here and leave a small donation for the restoration of the large and beautifully situated monastery. Follow the outside wall of the monastery to a fork in the road and continue straight. You'll reach another fork after 15min. Take the left branch to go to for the **Falls of Perivoli** and the right to reach Prionia after another hour. Once you reach Prionia, follow the "Ascending from Prionia" section (p. 298).

ASCENDING MYTIKAS. From the refuges, the next step is conquering the top. Once you get there and meet the gods, make sure to write your name in the book underneath the Greek flag at the summit. There are only two trails, both classified as intermediate, to its top: **Louki,** "steep gorge," and **Kaka Skala,** "the evil staircase." Despite its ominous name, Skala is the easier of the two, though both have **sheer drops** and require some **scrambling.** Slightly longer, and a detour for hikers ascending from Kakalos or the SEO refuge, Kaka Skala climbs the ridge behind Zolotas on a broad but steep path to the Skala peak (2861m). From Zolotas, walk uphill. After about 45min. (1.2km), you'll find a **map** at a fork in the road. The left option takes you along the E4 trail to Skala and Skolio peaks; the right is the **Zonaria** trail, which leads to the Louki trail fork and the SEO and Kakalos refuge paths. If you're going via Skala, 50m beyond the signpost you'll find an unmarked fork. Take the right leg and continue ascending for about 1hr. (1km) along exposed terrain until you reach Skala peak. From here hikers can turn up to the Skolio peak (2904m) for a sweeping view of Mytikas and Profitis Ilias, or grab handholds on the mostly vertical "path" plummeting down to the sharp saddle point between Skala and Mytikas and then back up "The Needle." Those distracted by rocks loosed from climbers above should glance to their left—the 500m drop into **Kazania** ("The Cauldron"), named for the clouds of mist that steam up from it, will brush away all extraneous concerns. The climb, which is covered with snow most of the year, takes about 3hr.

The Louki trail should be used only for ascent; only serious climbers and those who have not yet decided whether their lives are worth living should attempt it for the descent. Louki branches off Zonaria about halfway (45min., 700m) between its endpoint on the Skala trail and SEO path respectively. After strolling the pleasant, precipitous Zonaria trail, hikers must turn straight up Louki's red-blazed gorge. During a pause in the shower of dust from climbers above, those with particularly good grips should peruse the plaques commemorating their unlucky predecessors, whose final handholds were not as secure as you hope your next one will be. Though 50 people have died trying to meet Zeus, most of the fatalities were caused by attempting ridiculous stunts like taking a picture while making a 50m jump (true story); the trail itself is quite safe. After 300m you will arrive at the top. A little closer to the SEO side of the Zonaria path, a slightly more dangerous trail goes up to Stefani peak, marked by a bent, rusted signpost. Past this is the SEO path, a 20min. walk to the SEO refuge and Plateau of the Muses. The bowl-shaped slopes are known as the **"Throne of Zeus,"** as the chief god is said to rest his enormous cranium on the Stefani (crown) peak above. Approaching the peaks from the Plateau of the Muses, it's about 1½hr. up to Mytikas via Louki, or 4hr. by the Skala route.

ASCENDING SKOLIO. If you decide to resist tempting the gods by climbing to Mytikas, you can take the 20min. hike from Skala to Skolio, the second-highest peak (2911m; 7m shorter than Mytikas). The best view of Olympus's sheer western face looks out from here. It takes about 2½hr. to reach the Skolio summit from the Zolotas refuge. From Skolio, a 1hr. walk south along the ridge takes you to the Agios Antonis summit and a path descending back to Zolotas.

EDESSA Έδεσσα ☎ 23810

An equidistant 50km from Kastoria and Thessaloniki, Edessa is drastically different from both Macedonian cities. The capital of the prefecture of the same name, the town spreads along the edge of a cliff, yielding sweeping views of Classical ruins and the plains, which stretch to Thessaloniki. This urban space, nicknamed the "Manchester of Macedonia" when its industrial factories boomed in the 1920s and 1930s, is nonetheless enveloped in a natural setting. Small rivers race along side streets and under bridges to leap off the cliffs, forming a notable series of waterfalls. Edessa's beautiful 19th-century cliffside water mills and stunning falls make it an ideal excursion for travelers through Macedonia.

⌐ TRANSPORTATION

From the train station (☎23810 23 510), at the end of 18 Oktovriou, **trains** run to: Athens (regular: 7hr., daily 10:06am, €15; intercity: 6hr., daily 1:04pm, €19) via Plati (50min., €2.10); Florina (2hr., 4 per day 8am-9:40pm, €3); Kozani (2hr., daily 8am, €3); Thessaloniki (regular: 1½hr., 9 per day 6:02am-10:42pm, €3; intercity: 1¼hr., 9 per day 4:59-9:36pm, €5) via Naoussa (35min., €1.20) and Veria (40min., €1.30). Edessa's main bus station, Pavlou Mela 13 (☎23810 23 511), is at the corner of Fillipou near the center of town. **Buses** go to Athens (8hr., 3 per day 8am-8pm, €34) via Litochoro (2½hr., €9.20) and Larisa (3hr., €13) Thessaloniki (1½hr., every hr. 6am-9pm, €6.20), and Veria (1hr., 6 per day 8am-4pm, €3.40). Buses leave for Florina (1½hr., 6 per day 8:45am-8:45pm, €7), Kastoria (2hr.; 11:20am, 1:45pm; €8.30), and Kozani (2½hr., 6 per day 10am-8:15pm, €8) from a stop outside the fast-food joint called Ta Souvrakia, 4 shops past the main bus station down Filippou in the direction of Pl. Timenidon. Look for schedules on the sign above the storefront or ask inside. Tickets are sold on the bus. **Taxis** (☎23810 23 392) congregate on Dimokratias, near the National Bank in Pl. Megalou Alexandrou.

▚ ⁊ ORIENTATION AND PRACTICAL INFORMATION

With your back to the ticket counter at the bus station, **Pavlou Mela** is in front of you. The street that intersects Pavlou Mela immediately to your right is **Filli-pou**; traveling two blocks to your left will lead you to the cliffside. If you turn to your right and then make a right onto Fillipou, **Plateia Timenidon** and the town center will be four blocks down the road. From the bus station, make a right onto Pavlou Mela and follow the street until it meets **Egnatia**. Here, in front of the Pella and Alfa Hotels, is the drop-off for buses stopping on the way from Kastoria or Florina to Thessaloniki. Egnatia forks right in front of the hotels; the branch closer to the hotels is the continuation of Egnatia, and the one closer to the park is **Dimokratias**. Facing the hotels, a left on Egnatia leads to the hospital and to Thessaloniki. On your right, Dimokratias goes past cafe-covered **Plateia Megalou Alexandrou** to an intersection by the stadium, marked by a park full of bars and cafes. The street on the right is **25 Martiou**, the left **18 Oktovriou**, and the sharp right **Filellinon**. Filellinon leads to the old district of **Varosi** and back to Pl. Timenidon, 25 Martiou goes to a series of right-branching side streets for the waterfalls, and 18 Oktovriou heads to the train station. The four rivers which run through the town can be very useful landmarks. Street maps are posted at many of the city's major intersections. The **tourist information office**, in the waterfall park behind the public waterfall center restaurant, provides free **maps** and brochures with information in English about sights, hotels, and transportation. The employees are happy to help with literally any question you could possibly dream up about Edessa or the surrounding area. (☎23810 20 300. Open daily 10am-8pm.) The **National Bank**, Arch. Panteleimonos 2 (☎23810 23 322), is located behind the taxi station in a old renovated house. Open M-F 7:30am-1pm. To find the 24hr. **police station**, Iroön Polytechniou 13 (☎23810 23 333), follow Dimokratias toward the waterfalls and turn left on Iroön Polytechniou; the station is at the intersection with Arhelaou. The large **hospital** is just outside town on Egnatia. The **OTE**, Nepma 11, is a blue and white building facing the clock tower on Ag. Dimitriou. (☎23810 27 441. Open M-F 7am-3pm.) For laundry, try **Kiknos**, Egnatia 37. From the Egnatia/Dimokratias fork in front of the hotels, follow Egnatia in the direction of the hospital. Kiknos will be 200m down on your left. (☎23810 22 872. €6.50 per load. Open M-F 8am-9pm, Sa 8am-3pm.) The local **pharmacy**, Egnatia 36, is across the street from Kiknos. (☎23810 22 232. Open M-F 8am-3pm and 5-9pm.) Net Station, Evripidou 6, next door to Emporiki Bank, has 30 terminals for **Internet access**. (☎23810 29 629; www.edessanet.com. €2 per hr. Coffee €1.50. Beer €2.) Edessa's **post office**, Pavlou Mela 10, one block up from the bus station on Mela, between the bus station and Egnatia, offers **Poste Restante** and **exchanges currency**. (Open M-F 7:30am-2:30pm.) **Postal Code: 58200.**

⌐ ⌐ ACCOMMODATIONS AND FOOD

There are a few good deals among Edessa's handful of hotels. ▨**Hotel Alfa ❸**, Egnatia 28, is located three blocks uphill along Pavlou Mela from the bus station and directly in front of the Kastoria-Thessaloniki stop. Comfortable blue rooms have baths, TV, A/C, fridges, and phones. (☎23810 22 221. English spoken. Breakfast €7.50. Reception 24hr. Singles €30; doubles €65; triples €78. MC/V.) A more luxurious option, **Hotel Xenia ❹**, Fillipou 35, offers well-furnished, carpeted rooms with A/C, baths, TV, fridges, a pool (open to the public for €2-3 per person), and spectacular cliffside views. A new western addition has sleek, modern rooms. (☎23810 29 706; www.xenia-edessas.gr. Breakfast included. Laptop Internet access in each room €1 per hr. Reception 24hr. Singles €60; doubles €85; triples €110; quads €150.) **Hotel Elena ❸**, Dimitriou Rizou 4, is near Varosi just off Pl. Timenidon; walk down Fillipou four blocks from the bus station. Simple white-tiled rooms have A/C, TV, and nice-sized balconies. (☎23810 23 218. Breakfast €5. Reception 24hr. Singles €30; doubles €40; triples €50.) **Hotel Olympia ❸**, 18 Oktovriou 51, is down the road to town five blocks from train station. This old-fashioned hotel rents standard rooms with no extra frills. (☎23810 23 544. Reception 8am-midnight; door locks at midnight. Singles and doubles €35.) Edessa suffers no shortage of **fast food**—cheese pies, rotisserie chickens, and gyros crop up on every street. Inexpensive restaurants are easy to find near the waterfall park and along Dimokratias. The most popular one in town is the ◪**Public Waterfall Center Restaurant ❷**, at the top of the falls. The sounds of rushing water and a stunning view of the plains accompany every meal at this giant tri-level complex. It serves local specialties like delicious *tsoblex* (potato, eggplant, and veal stew; €6) and has a large selection of domestic wines. (☎23810 27 810. Entrees €5-7. Open 8am-1am or until the last customer leaves. AmEx/MC/V.) From Hotel Alfa, **Taverna Arxontiko ❷**, Egnatia 60, is a short walk down Egnatia in the direction of the Thessaloniki highway. *Bouzouki* and guitar enhance the fresh, ambrosial dishes and authentic taverna experience. (☎23810 24 221. Soft pork kebab €5. Open 6pm-2am.)

🎵📷 ENTERTAINMENT AND NIGHTLIFE

The ◪**Cafe High Rock** has, hands down, the best view in town. Located on M. Alexandrou 2, in the southwestern corner of town on—surprise, surprise—a high rock perched on the cliff, the terrace seats seem like they're floating. Scrumptious desserts include the traditional *Revani* (€2.50), chocolate profiterol topped with cream (€3), and 18 different kinds of ice cream. (☎23810 26 793. Coffee €2. Beer €2.50. Entrees €5-7. Open 9am-2am.) You'll find dinner, drinks, and dancing at ◪**Kanavourgeio** and the adjacent club, **Aqua**, at the bottom of the glass elevators inside the huge old mill. The name derives from the Greek word *kanabis*, and refers to the building's past use as a hemp factory. The tableside machinery inside, now elegantly integrated into the wooden decor, once twisted fibers from the bountiful plant into thick ship's rope. Aqua's DJ blasts American music straight into space every Friday, Saturday, and Sunday night from mid-June to early September. (☎23810 20 070. Entrees €3.50-8. Cover €5; includes 1 drink. Open 8pm-6am.) Edessa's most popular club, **Paradise**, inside Hotel Xenia, sports both a pool and an amazing view from its spot at the tip of the cliff. The DJ spins Greek and American music every night of the week. (Beer €3. Mixed drinks €5-5.50. Open daily 24hr.) The other local club of choice, **Vanilla**, is beneath the cliff, 2km past the hospital on the left-hand side of the Thessaloniki-Pella highway. The already treacherous path down the cliff has the potential to be terrifying in the dark; a short taxi ride (€2.50) is probably a better transportation choice. Greek and American music plays in the well-decorated interior. (Beer €5. Open Th-Sa midnight-6am.) In the town center, nightlife centers on a tree-covered park off Dimokratias just before a Goody's restaurant. There, eight similar cafe-bars draw masses of people to sip coffee and chat late into the night. From July 1 to the end of August, open-air **movies** (€5) are shown just below the aquarium every night at 9pm. Most are American and European films with Greek subtitles.

◎ SIGHTS

WATERFALLS AND ENVIRONS. Edessa's best sights revolve around the *katarrakton* (waterfall), where the town's rivers spill over onto the plains below. Walk down Dimokratias past the stadium where it becomes 25 Martiou and watch for the signs—they'll tell you when to turn right. Alternatively, you can count the rivers you pass on the way, and turn left at the fourth. The edge of the park is the best vantage point from which to watch the powerful water flow over the falls which were formed in an 11th-century earthquake. The descending concrete terraces let you survey the waterfall and the agricultural plain below while catching a little spray on your face. A small cave with stalactites and stalagmites is beneath the rushing water. *(Open 10am-8pm. €0.50.)* The marble column ruins of an ancient city sit near a convent on the right-hand side of the valley. The cliffside was once also home to water mills, sesame mills, flour mills, and textile factories which all operated with water power. The companies, however, couldn't adjust to modern forms of production and closed in the late 1950s. They stood as deteriorating monuments to Edessa's industrial past until a recent European grant helped redesign and renovate the area, creating an open-air **Water Museum.** The museum now features preindustrial mills and tanneries, the wool mill, and the **cannabis factory.** Water still runs through the chutes alongside each mill, and plans are in the works to return the flour mill to working condition and reopen it as an educational museum. The tourist office has a free brochure showing the mill locations. The sesame mill has been converted into an **aquarium,** displaying indigenous amphibians, reptiles, and freshwater fish, all hand-caught by passionate town embryologist Mr. Tasos. This Greek-born, French biologist will be thrilled to recall his exciting snake stories for interested passersby. *(Open M, W-Su 10am-2pm and 5-9pm. €1.50, students €0.75.)* To reach the *kanavourgeio*, follow the steps down along the waterfalls. Those who don't particularly fancy the steps' wild thorns, puddles, and dirt might consider taking the two great **glass elevators.** Descending about 13 stories along the cliffs, they provide sweeping views and relief to ascending tourists.

VAROSI DISTRICT. The old town, built on the site of an ancient acropolis and containing several small churches dating back to the 14th century, still rests along the cliff's edge, beginning to the right of the waterfall park and continuing behind the walls of the stadium. Varosi retained an active Christian population even during Ottoman occupation, and was once surrounded by ancient city walls which held up for eight months of Turkish bombardment; when the Turks finally entered the city, they tore down the walls as a symbol of their victory. Though the fortifications are long gone, examples of traditional architecture abound: upper stories miraculously protrude out on creaky old wooden beams over stone bases. The quarter's location near the "safe escape" of the lowlands made it a popular spot for WWII resistance fighters who used the web of connected backyards to evade the Germans; much of the area, however, was later burned in the subsequent fighting. The new **Museum of Traditional and Folk Life,** which displays clothing, plates, and jewelry from the region, is located in one of the old buildings on the side of the drop. It's one block down from the intersection of Arch. Panteleimonos and M. Alexandriou and two blocks from High Rock. Ring the bell if the door is locked. *(☎ 23810 28 787. Open Tu-Su 10am-6pm, though hours vary. €1.50.)*

OTHER SIGHTS. Below the town, about 3km to the southwest, are the ruins of the **ancient city** of Edessa. Though little remains of the 4th-century BC city, a few columns still stand along the main avenue, including one from a temple devoted to the goddess of fertility. In the evening, the dying light makes the columns glow with celestial beauty. The guard is impressively informed about archaeology and will be happy to explain details about the site. Before the discoveries at Vergina, this ancient town was a leading candidate for the lost capital of the Macedonian Empire; proud Edessians still cling to the now-debunked theory. The fastest way to the ruins begins at the landing between the two glass elevators. Walk to the right on the sandy path over the little mound to find a winding path. Follow it downhill and go straight; you'll reach the city in 15min. Within Edessa, the **clock tower**, built in 1895, occupies a modern block at Pl. Megalou Alexandrou. The dilapidated remains of a 19th-century **Ottoman mosque**, which has been closed now for over 45 years, sink down on a side street. To find it, walk down Egnatia and take a right onto Miaouli; the mosque is three blocks uphill. The walls of this building, which now act as goals for local children's soccer games, once housed the artifacts unearthed in the archaeological excavations of the ancient city. To see Edessa's rivers united, follow any of the tributaries upstream until you hit the **Byzantine bridge**. The footbridge arches over the main stream that eventually splits off to form the countless rivers and channels that weave themselves through the city.

KASTORIA Καστοριά   ☎24670

Kastoria takes its name from the beaver (*kastori*) that was once the source of its prosperity in the fur industry. Though trade has declined, the city's shops and factories still claim a major share of the world's fur market. Kastoria also has 26 Byzantine chapels throughout the hilly landscape, offset by scenic Lake Kastoria below. The **Byzantine Museum** has a large exhibit of icons and manuscripts. (☎24670 26 7781. Open Tu-Su 8:30am-3pm. Free.) On the first weekend in August, the **Nestorio River Party** brings thousands of campers to the banks of the Aliakmonas River, 25km from Kastoria, for four days of live music and revelry. (☎24670 31 204; www.cultureguide.gr. Camping €10 per day, €25 for 4 days.)

Kastoria lacks budget accommodations. Luxurious ⬛**Hotel Kastoria ❹**, Nikis 122, rents spacious rooms with lake views, satellite TV, phones, A/C, and baths. (☎24670 29 453; www.hotelkastoria.com. Breakfast €6. Reception 24hr. Singles €40; doubles €55; triples €100. AmEx/MC/V.) The large rooms at **Hotel Europa ❸**, Ag. Athanasiou 12, have desks, TV, phones, and balconies. (☎24670 23 826. Reception 24hr. Singles €25; doubles €35; triples €45; quads €65. AmEx/MC/V.) There are many restaurants and cafes by the lake on Nikis and near the park on M. Alexandrou. **Mamm ❷**, Ptolemeon 6, serves juicy, tender meat dishes. From the taxi stand, follow 3 Septemvriou and make the first left. (☎24670 27 333. Sandwiches €2. Entrees €5-7. Open M-Sa 9am-2am.) **Nostalgia ❷**, Nikis 2, past the northern dock, offers grilled souvlaki, steak, veal, and lamb. (☎24670 22 630. Entrees €5-7.)

Aristotelis International Airport (☎24670 42 515), 13km from the city, has flights to Athens (1hr.; M, W-Th, Sa 1:45pm; €82). The bus station, Ath. Diakou 14 (☎24670 83 455), is two blocks ahead on the right. **Buses** go to: Amyntaio (1¼hr.; 2, 6:30pm; €5); Athens (9½hr., 3 per day 7:30am-7:30pm, €37.20) via Kozani (1¼hr., €7); Ioannina (3½hr.; 9am, 3:30pm; €14.10); Thessaloniki (3hr., 7 per day 6am-6:30pm, €14.30). **Taxis** (☎24670 82 100) line up 24hr. by the park at Ath. Diakou and M. Alexandrou. The **tourist office**, a kiosk in the public park, has excellent **maps** (€2.50) and info. (☎24670 22 292. Open M-F 8am-3pm, Sa-Su 8am-2pm.) There's an **Agricultural Bank** (☎24670 22 562; open M-F 7:30am-2pm) with an **ATM** in Pl. Davaki. **Eurobank** (☎24670 86 576), by the post office, **exchanges** currency. (Open M-Th 7:30am-2pm, F 8am-2pm.) Walk one block inland on Averof and turn right, and you will see the **police**, Grammou 25 (☎24670 21 517), on the left. The 24hr. **hospital** (☎24670 55 600) is 2km out of town on the road from Mavriozisa. The **post office**, M. Alexandrou 47, two blocks along the peninsula beyond the public park, accepts **Poste Restante**. (☎24670 80 779. Open daily 7:30am-2pm.) **Postal Code:** 32100.

FLORINA Φλώρινα ☎ 23850

Florina, almost entirely destroyed by fire and the Nazi occupation during WWII, now serves primarily as a connection point to the Prespas, offering few attractions of its own. If you're looking for a Northern Greek village completely untouched by tourism, however, this is as real as you'll get. The town's rough gem is the **Archaeological Museum,** by the train station at the end of Mela. (☎ 23850 28 206. Open Tu-Su 8:30am-3pm. €2, EU students free.) The lower floor focuses on sculptures from Roman Florina, while the upper contains Hellenistic finds from the area. A back room, with labels only in Greek, has beautiful mosaic fragments and icons from the Prespa churches. An **archaeological site,** where experts believe that Roman Florina once lay, is 2km up the hill outside town, but is currently closed to the public.

If transit schedules necessitate a bed in Florina, inviting **Hotel Hellinis ❷,** Pavlou Mela 31, has spacious rooms with phones, TV, balconies, and baths. (☎ 23850 22 671. Breakfast €4. Singles €26; doubles €37; triples €45. MC/V.) **Hotel Antigoni ❹,** Arrianou 1, at the intersection of Dragoumi and Makedonomachon, rents small, modest rooms with baths; some have A/C. (☎ 23850 23 180. Breakfast included. Singles €45; doubles €60; triples €5. MC/V.) Florina has many outdoor cafes, tavernas, and fast-food stops, most of which are clustered along Mela. Locals overwhelmingly recommend **Restaurant Afroditi ❷,** Megalou Alexandrou 6, a simple taverna that serves pizza along with baked pasta, pork, chicken, and veal dishes. (☎ 23850 28 188. Entrees €4-7. Open 8am-1am.) For dessert, try **Krinos bakery ❶,** Dragoumi 7, which specializes in every kind of cookie imaginable. Any assortment of cookies and/or pastries is €6. (☎ 23850 45 460. Open 8am-2pm and 5-10pm.)

With your back to the bus station, cross the stadium (the large park with a field of concrete), and continue walking until you hit Pavlo Mela; turn left and walk down three blocks. This brings you to the train station (☎ 23850 22 404) which serves Thessaloniki (4hr., 4 per day 5:30am-4:25pm, €5.20). Florina's main bus station (☎ 23850 22 430), Makedonomachon 2, opposite the stadium, sends **buses** to: Athens (9hr.; 8:30am, 8:30pm; €37); Kastoria (1hr.; M, Tu, Th 10:30am; €5); Kozani (1½hr., 8 per day 7am-8:30pm, €6.20); Prespa (30min.; M, W, F 6:45am, 2:30pm; €4); Thessaloniki (3hr., 6 per day 6:45am-6pm, €11.30) via Amyntaio (30min., €3). **Taxis** (☎ 23850 22 700) prowl the Dragoumi-Saradaporou-Makedonomachon intersection. With your back to the bus station, **Makedonomachon** is in front of you. If you take a right and start walking, this street turns into **Dragoumi** and takes you to the main square, **Plateia Modi.** Turning left from here will lead you through cafe-lined **Pavlou Mela.** Five blocks down Mela is **Ioanniou Arti,** which ends up at the train station. Turning left on I. Arti will put you at the **Plateia Megalou Alexandrou** rotary. **Alpha Bank,** Dragoumi 17, has **currency exchange** and a **24hr. ATM.** (☎ 23850 26 168. Open M-Th 8am-2:30pm, F 8am-2pm.) The **OTE,** Tyrnovou 7, is on the right one block down Tyrnovou. From the main plateia, walk on Mela and take the first right. (☎ 23850 22 299. Open M-Sa 7:30am-2:30pm.) A 24hr. **police station,** Iounnou Trypi 1 (☎ 23850 44 230), is off Mela. The **post office,** Kallergi 22, off Stephanou, accepts **Poste Restante.** (☎ 23850 22 236. Open daily 8am-2pm.) **Postal Code:** 53100.

PRESPA Πρέσπα ☎ 23850

In the far stretches of northwestern Greece, the cold waters of Lake Megali Prespa form the nexus of three countries. Territorially shared by Greece, Albania, and FYROM, the lake provides the most peaceful border imaginable. Once you enter this small region whose name literally means "a place surrounded by mountains," you are engulfed by a mixture of rolling green mountains, huge lakes, and small villages. Across a marshy isthmus lies a smaller lake, Mikri Prespa, which contains two islands that are home to 20 people. The remote shores are dotted with tiny, formerly Slavic neighboring villages that survive mainly on fishing and farming, forming a region that seems, in its serene lifestyle, set aside from the rest of Greece. A distinctly Greek history, however, still prevails throughout the region. The terrain is studded with beautiful ancient chapels, the earliest dating from AD 908, which act as reminders of the time when exiled Byzantine bureaucrats whiled away their days on the frigid shores of the Prespa Lakes.

◧ ☷ TRANSPORTATION AND PRACTICAL INFORMATION. Buses depart from the village square in Ag. Germanos to Florina (1hr.; M, W, F 8am, 4pm) via Laimos, Plati, and Lefkono. The stops at these other Prespa villages, however, are only made if they are requested in advance; call the bus station in Florina (☎23850 22 430). There are literally two **taxis** in the Prespa area. Both of the cars are owned by Yurgos (☎23850 51 207) who will take you around the villages for a hefty fee or to Kastoria or Florina (€30). Since the villages are far away and difficult to get to given the spotty public transportation, it is best to rent a car in Florina or Kastoria.

Visitors to Prespa will pass over a mountain and find Mikri Prespa pooled below them. The diminutive term "Mikri," however, may be misleading—this lake is huge. Farther along the road to the Prespas, **Laimos**, the regional center, is before **Agios Germanos**, which is at the eastern end of the road. Before the isthmus that divides the two lakes, the regional road forks; one direction continues south toward Trigono while the other crosses the isthmus to reach the town of Psarades, on the western side of Mikri Prespa. When crossing the isthmus from Laimos, Megalo Prespa is on the right and Mikri on the left. At the end of the isthmus is the small channel of **Koula**, a **beach** (on the Megalo side) of the same name, and the regional army post. Following the road left takes you to a floating causeway that passes through marshes, reeds, and the murky waters of the lake. On the other end is Ag. Achillios, an 11-house village on the island of Mikri Prespa. At Psarades, the regional road and Greece both end. The official **Prespa Information Center** (☎23850 51 452; open 9:30am-7pm), which is run by the Society for the Protection of Prespa and the World Wildlife Federation (WWF), is located on the road between Ag. Germanos and Laimos. You will see a sign and a small waterfall before the well-organized center that provides free information about the area's wildlife and history and sells a topographical **map** with marked hiking trails (€3). There are **no banks or ATMs** in the Prespas, but the grocer in Psarades is willing to **exchange currency**. Laimos houses both the **mayor's office** (☎23850 52 100; open M-F 8am-3pm), which has information on the area, and the **OTE** (☎23850 52 178; open M-F 8am-3pm). The **post office** (☎23850 51 249; open M-F 8am-2pm) is in Ag. Germanos's main square, next door to the 24hr. **police** station (☎23850 51 202). A small, one-doctor clinic is located in **Lefkona** (☎23850 46 372) and operates 24hr.

▛ ▟ ACCOMMODATIONS AND FOOD. Though inland Ag. Germanos offers the cheapest lodging, the best value is found in Psarades, where local **domatia** (€25-30) combine budget rates with serene lake views and an end-of-the-world sense of isolation. **Tasos's Domatia ❷**, on the right at the end of the lakefront road (ask anyone in this one-road village for directions), has four quiet, homey rooms with private baths and views of the inlet. Listen to a frog chorus at night and wake up to waterfowl, which, though pleasant in theory, may rouse even the heaviest sleeper around 5am. (☎69782 64 775. Singles €24; doubles and triples €28.) **Arhondiko ❸**, one block from Tasos on the continuation of the single road (ask at the lakeside taverna, Akrolimnia), has elegant, box-sized rooms with balconies, TV, and baths. The owner's daughter is a painter and made the wall paintings that adorn the inn. (☎23850 46 260. Singles €30; doubles €39; triples €47.)

Psarades has a handful of tavernas that serve tasty fresh fish from the lakes. ✉Syntrofia ❷, at the end of the waterfront, serves tasty food in a remote setting. The death of owners Lazarus and Georgia Christianopoulos threatened the continuation of this delicious dive, but their children have kept the taverna up, serving fresh fried and grilled fish. (☎ 23850 46 107. Grilled trout €5. Open 9am-11:30pm.)

◪ **SIGHTS.** Each village is separated by about 10km, so traveling requires a car or bike; still, the extra effort is well rewarded. Shallow Mikri Prespa, with a maximum depth of only 8m, lies almost entirely in Greece. Its islet hosts the 20-person village of **Agios Achillios.** This tiny town was once part of the mainland, but a slight raise of water levels disconnected them, leaving them attached to the shore only by an 800m floating causeway. Ag. Achillios contains the ruins of the **basilica** of the same name. Built in AD 980, it was sponsored by the Bulgarian Tsar Samuel to honor St. Achillios, the Bishop of Larisa, whose bones Samuel brought to the small islet. Difficult as it is to believe now, the Prespas were briefly the center of the Balkan world, when Samuel used the region as his capital. Its dominance ended, however, when Byzantine Emperor Basil II, nicknamed "Bulgarian-killer," crushed his defiant northern neighbor. The Prespas have 26 churches scattered throughout the region, a reminder of this remarkable history. Other sights of note are the 11th-century **Church of Saint Germanos** in **Agios Germanos,** featuring beautifully painted dark-hued **frescoes.** A rickety metal staircase will take you to the top of the adjacent ✉**bell tower.** The tower, with its gigantic steel bell, offers a stunning bird's eye view of Ag. Germanos and the isthmus between Mikri and Megalo Prespa. The 19th-century church of **Agia Paraskevi** sits north of Laimos, and is adorned with stained-glass windows that filter sun rays through the building. On the other side of Mikri Prespa, a unique breed of dwarf-cows wanders the cobblestones and pebble shores of ✉**Psarades.** These quadrupeds were bred to adapt to the swamps of the area, as legend tells that larger cows used to sink and drown in the swamps. As the Prespas have over 260 species of avian inhabitants, the isthmus between the lakes has observation areas for **bird watching;** bring binoculars and a camera. At both sunrise and sunset, you will see a remarkable number of birds crossing the isthmus between the Prespas. Another way to catch all of the bird action is to join one of the **boat trips** that leave from Megali Prespa. These excursions include stops at lakeside Byzantine rock paintings, ascetic caves, and monasteries, as well as a tour of the birds' nests hidden between the reeds. (☎ 69782 64 775. About €35 per hr. for 4-5 people.) Ask at the small dock in Psardes about the boat trip, or, if you are an early riser, you may be able to catch a 5:30am ride with one of the fishing boats that leave from the main dock.

HALKIDIKI Χαλκιδική

The three fingers of Halkidiki peninsula—Mt. Athos (Agion Oros), Sithonia, and Kassandra—point southeast into the Aegean, sporting spectacular scenery and amazing beaches. Central Europeans and urban Thessalonikans spread their oily bodies out on the two fingers of Sithonia and Kassandra to sunbathe in the shadow of Agion Oros, "The Holy Mountain," which continues its thousand-year tradition of Orthodox asceticism. Visits to Mt. Athos are strictly regulated and reservations for pilgrimages should be made a few months in advance to obtain the permits (p. 312). Visitors to Kassandra and Sithonia will find no barriers of entry, other than the Halkidiki public transportation system. Frequent buses run between the Kifisias 33 Halkidiki station in Thessaloniki (☎ 23103 16 575) and the three peninsulas, but bus service does not run from finger to finger; you have to return down the wrist to Thessaloniki. Kassandra is the most developed, as some of the largest nightclubs in Greece are located in Kalithea. While Sithonia is still heavily forested with a generally more rural atmosphere, souvenir merchandise has begun to infringe upon its natural setting. Private transportation allows for splendid cruises along Halkidiki's quiet, beautiful roads to your own personal beach.

SITHONIA PENINSULA Σιθωνιά

Tranquility persists on the isolated beaches of the southern and southwestern coasts of Sithonia, though like Kassandra, the peninsula has begun to sell its soul, plunging into the plastic world of souvenirs, tour buses, and charmless villages devoid of local character. Nevertheless, much of the land is, in an exhilaratingly refreshing combination, relatively untouched yet accessible to the budget traveler. Terrific camping sites dot the coves off the single road which loops around the coast, providing a very affordable window to the supreme nature of the peninsula. Internal transportation, however, can be a hassle.

NEOS MARMARAS Νέος Μαρμαράς   ☎23750

Many quaint Sithonian villages were founded on land taken from Mt. Athos's estates to provide for Greek refugees after the population exchange between Greece and Turkey. Neos Marmaras was one of these until tourism claimed the community. While sun-scorched vacationers are the most readily apparent sight, Neos Marmaras's beaches and sunsets are gorgeous, and the town is a good base for exploring the more rural areas of the peninsula. The town is a single strip, with restaurants and hotels on one side and water on the other.

Vacancies are scarce on summer weekends. Along the waterfront, signs with maps of the village list **domatia;** most singles run around €30, and anything below €20 will take haggling. **House Filippos ❷,** 20m down from Moto Rental on the main drag, is slightly removed from the waterfront's swarms of tourists. The large rooms have slate floors, TV, A/C, baths, and a huge balcony with hammocks. Each room comes with a full kitchen. (☎23750 71 963. Singles €20; doubles €30; triples €50.) For something cheaper and closer to Sithonia's breathtaking wilderness, try one of the numerous campsites. **◪Marmaras ❶,** in walking distance of the village, has pine trees, a private sand beach, and an amphitheater-like setting that gives every tent its own level and view of the beach and environs. Tents, which are provided by the campsite, come with tables, mosquito nets, and mattresses. (☎23750 71 901. Laundry €5. €5.70 per person, €6 for site and tent, €2 per car. Electricity €3.) Escape the afternoon heat for lunch under the namesake trees of **◪Tavern Ta Pefka ❷** ("pines"), which overlooks the water and Nea Marmaras's harbor. From the church, follow the waterfront for 7min. until you see the big sign. An intimate meal here of octopus (€6.50) or the less romantic stuffed beef burger (€6) is far from the noise and fumes of cars. (☎23650 71 763. Open 9am-2am.) For Greek classics, head to **Dionysios ❸,** in the first plateia, near the small kiosk where the second bus stop is located. Though some of the food caters to tourists seeking international standards, Dionysios spices many dishes up with local flavors or techniques. (☎23750 71 201. Entrees €5-9. Open 8:30am-3am. AmEx/MC/V.) Neos Marmaras's nightlife centers on the strip of bars between the two plateias and a pair of discos on the beach. At wave-side **Ploton,** 300m from Dionysios on the waterfront, heavy wooden doors open into a raging party of alcohol and smoke. (☎23750 71 704; www.sithonianet.gr/ploto. Beer €6. Mixed drinks €5-8. Open 10pm-4am.) Next door at **Molos,** Greeks and foreigners mingle, drink, and watch the surf. (☎23650 71 331. Beer €5. Mixed drinks €4.50-8. Open 10pm-4am.) The big disco, **Cassa Di Notte** (☎23650 72 900), 2km away, is on the single road that goes around the peninsula. Accessible by taxi (€3.50), this local lair blares Greek music. Opens in early July.

The **first bus stop** is where the road running along the shoreline begins. From here, the bus turns left and goes toward the sea. The **second stop** is at Dionysios restaurant. Immediately ahead is the **taxi stand,** followed by the docks, and the police station on the opposite side of the street; this is the **first plateia.** The road then angles right, following the shore. A seaside church follows on the high promontory. The road then descends until it arrives at the **second plateia,** which has a *periptero,* a **map** listing accommodations, and the **third bus stop.** The **fourth bus stop,** the last in Neo Marmaras, is 300m along the same road by the soccer stadium. **Buses** (☎23710 22 309 or 23710 22 909) run to Thessaloniki (2½hr., 3 per day 8:15am-6:30pm, €9.50) via nearby small towns, including Nea Moudania (1hr., €6). The bus coming from Thessaloniki continues to Sarti (1hr., 3 per day noon-8pm, €4). **Taxis** (☎23750 71 500) sit by the beach and by Dionysios. Because Sithonia's public transportation can be frustrating, renting a moped is probably the best way to see the peninsula. Try **Moto Rental,** two doors up from Filippos. (☎23750 72 224. €15 per day. Open 9am-10pm). The staff at **Marmaris Tours,** next to Dionysios and the second bus stop, recommends rooms and books excursions. (☎23750 72 010; www.marmaras.co.yu. Open daily 9am-2pm and 6-11pm.) The **National Bank,** with a **24hr. ATM** and **currency exchange,** is just after the police station on the main street in the middle of the first plateia. (☎23750 72 794. Open M-Th 8am-2:30pm, F 8am-2pm.) The **police station** is three doors up from the National Bank, opposite Dionysios. (☎23750 71 111. Open 7am-5pm.) **Internet access** is available at **Escape,** 100m down the road from Ariston. (☎23750 71 097. €2 per hr. Open 9am-1am.) The **post office,** in the second plateia across the street from the city map, accepts **Poste Restante.** (☎23750 71 334. Open M-F 7:30am-2pm.) **Postal Code:** 63081.

RURAL SITHONIA   ☎ 2 3 7 5 0

Explore more of Sithonia by renting a moped or taking the **bus** that goes around the peninsula and passes by deserted, unblemished turf. From Neos Marmaras you will cross shipping magnate Carras's extensive forests and olive orchards. The resort's white buildings—wonderful accommodations for those already missing the city—crash into the skyline of Neos Marmaras. The famous **Camping Armenistis ❶,** accessible from Thessaloniki by bus (2½hr.; 3 per day 11:15am, 2:45, 6:30pm; €9.40), is a king among campgrounds. It has every amenity imaginable (laundry, supermarket, cafe, bar, creperia, movie screenings, etc.) at an isolated site lined with golden sands, crystal water, and coves that come up to the forested eastern shore. This nomad village hosts numerous music festivals every summer featuring local rock legends. Check the website for events. (☎23750 91 487; www.armenistis.com.gr. Free movie screenings W, Sa 9pm. Reception 8am-midnight. €5.50 per tent, €6.50 per RV. Mobile homes available to rent €75. Electricity €3. MC/V.)

MOUNT ATHOS PENINSULA

OURANOUPOLIS Ουρανούπολις   ☎ 2 3 7 7 0

The last settlement in secular Athos, Ouranoupolis is at the very top of Halkidiki's easternmost finger. Strangely, it functions as both a gateway to monastic Athos and a hedonistic beach resort popular among German tourists. Halfway down the peninsula, 148km southeast of Thessaloniki, it lies just beyond a trans-peninsular depression dug by Xerxes as a canal for his invading fleet. There isn't much to see in Ouranoupolis beyond the beaches, and if you're not planning a visit to Athos's monasteries, Ouranoupolis is not worth the trip—even nicer beaches are plentiful on the other peninsulas, particularly Sithonia. Tickets for the **cruise around Athos,** whose name belies its route, which only traces the western side of the peninsula, can be purchased from the offices near the tower. (☎23770 71 370. 9am, 1:30,

NORTHERN GREECE

GIVING BACK

BEING A PILGRIM

Mt. Athos will likely induce complete culture shock. Understanding your surroundings, however, will enable you to get the most out of your experience while also remaining respectful of the monks and their lifestyle.

The monasteries use the **Julian calendar,** which lags by 13 days, and run on **Byzantine time,** marking sunset as midnight. Because of this schedule, then, it's normal for morning liturgy to stretch from 3am (regular time) until 8am. Only the most devout pilgrims attend the beginning of the service, but the ringing of bells and tapping of *talanto* (wooden planks) guarantees that almost everyone else will soon get up for church. Though being awake then may seem painful, the experience is worth the early rise.

In some monastaries, breakfast is served right after services in fresco-covered *trapezaries* to the sound of a **chanter,** who reads aloud about the life of the saint whose memory is commemorated on that particular day. Only the chanter talks during meals, and everyone stops eating when the chanter stops—eat quickly to make sure you get the food you want within the allotted time. Non-Orthodox pilgrims often sit at a separate table from both the monks and Orthodox visitors; at some monasteries they eat after everyone else. Breakfast and dinner both consist of vegetables, bread, water, and fruit. Fish and

4:30pm; €16.) If you wish to see the peninsula's eastern side, you must leave from Lerissos. Bear in mind, however, that cruises depend on weather conditions and are frequently changed or canceled. Also interesting are the **offshore isles.** You can explore the nearby coves in a rented boat or take the ferry from nearby Tripiti to **Amouliani,** a small village on an island known to the locals as the "donkey's island."

Those staying overnight in Ouranopolis have several reasonably affordable choices. Dozens of private houses offer **domatia** (around €25-20), and you will probably be greeted by offers as you disembark the bus. Make sure to see the room before committing to anything, however, as some can be run-down and even unpleasant. **Camping Ouranoupoli ❶** lies on a beach 1.5km outside of town along the highway (taxi €2.50) and has showers, a supermarket, laundry (€5 per load), and a restaurant. (☎ 23770 71 171. €5 per person, €7 per tent.) The rooms in **Hotel Athos ❷,** above a supermarket one street back from the waterfront, are small and snug but elegant, with a nice view of the beach. Finding the entrance is a bit tricky, so ask someone from the supermarket, which also functions as the hotel's reception during the day. (☎ 23770 71 368. Singles €25; doubles €32; triples €40.) Most places will also store luggage while you're on Athos. Those looking for a last supper before entering Mt. Athos—or a triumphant reward after the monks' spartan cuisine—should head to the row of tavernas on the waterfront. Most of them, however, are tourist-oriented and serve mediocre food at high prices.

The town of Ouranoupolis centers on the distinctive, medieval **Fosfori Tower,** by the sea. Though the tower is quite beautiful, it is permanently closed due to the constant danger of its collapse. The **bus stop** is in front of the tower in the parking lot. Ask the man in the kiosk next to the tower for schedules. Buses synchronized with the ferry from Athos go to Athens (7hr., 2pm, €30) and Thessaloniki (3hr., 6 per day 5:30am-5:30pm, €8.50). The sea makes a 90° angle at the tower. Facing town with your back to the tower, both the main taverna strip and the Athos **ferry office** are on your left. **Ferries** (€4.50) run only to Mt. Athos. (☎ 23770 21 041. Call to reserve tickets and receive information M-F 8:30am-7pm. Open 8:15am-11am.) The waterfront extends parallel to the road out of town. On a right side street two blocks down is an **Agricultural Bank** with a **24hr. ATM.** (Open M, Th 9am-2:30pm, F 9am-2pm.) Three blocks down is **Mamou-Nia Internet Cafe** (☎ 23770 71 577), which, despite its primary function as a bar, offers access on one computer. (€4 per hr. Open 10am-2am.) At the end of the waterfront road just before the parking lot, make a right and go up two blocks to reach the **Holy Executive of the Holy Mount Athos Pilgrims' Bureau,** which issues permits for Athos. Make sure you get to the office one day in advance to pick up your signed permit, and arrive well ahead of your ferry time since lines tend to be long. (☎ 23770 71 422. Open 8am-2:30pm.)

MOUNT ATHOS Άγιον Όρος

☎ 23770

The monasteries on Mt. Athos, Halkidiki's easternmost peninsula, have been the paradigm of Orthodox asceticism for over a millennium. Originally settled by five Hellenic cities, Athos, along with the rest of Greece, was conquered by the Macedonian Empire and then by the Romans. The settlements, then of a secular nature, thrived under Byzantine control until pirate attacks in the 7th century left the peninsula uninhabited. Athos's current status as a religious community began in AD 963 when Agios Athanasios Athonitis, a friend of the Byzantine emperor, created the first communal monastery on the peninsula; this monastery, known as **"Megistes Lavra,"** still stands today. For much of the Byzantine and Ottoman periods, Mount Athos formed the bedrock of Greek Orthodoxy, most notably speaking out against a unification with Western Christendom in the 15th century. Today, the Holy Community of Mount Athos is a semi-autonomous state comprised of 20 Orthodox monasteries, countless hamlets (*skites*), some 1800 monks, and at least as many full-time workers. The peninsula is covered with bushes and trees; only the jagged limestone peak of Mt. Athos itself, soaring 2027m above the waves, is exposed. Eagles and jackals roam the area, and natural springs deliver a wealth of water into the sea. The monks sequester themselves against the background of this lush sanctuary, shunning material pleasures to pursue a spiritual life. Emperor Constantine's edict of 1060 **forbids women and female domestic animals from setting foot on the peninsula,** with the exception of the female hens that provide the monks' eggs. Though this rule is officially considered to have come about out of respect for the Virgin Mary, it is more likely that it was enacted to end the scandalous frolicking between the monks and Vlach shepherdesses who had settled on the mountain. Long pants are mandatory on Mt. Athos and swimming is forbidden.

◪◪ TRANSPORTATION AND PRACTICAL INFORMATION. With **permit** in hand, arrive at the western port of **Ouranoupolis** or the less frequently used eastern port of **Ierrissos** the night before your entry date to Athos. Though it is possible to arrive in Ouranoupolis

other delicacies are served on feast days. Monks fast every Monday, Wednesday, and Friday, so meals are less formal then and there is no chanter.

Try to reach the monastery where you plan to stay by 4pm, making sure you're inside the walls before the gates close at sunset. When you arrive, look for the *archontariki* (guest house); a monk there will welcome you with a glass of cold water, *tsipouro,* ouzo, and a piece of candy as he explains the monastery's rules. The evening service varies within monasteries; some begin at 5 or 5:30pm while others start later. Though food and lodgings are free at every monastery, it's smart to make a reservation by calling between 11am and 1pm that same day. Phone numbers for every monastery are written on your Mt. Athos entrance pass.

Be as courteous and cooperative as possible, always addressing monks as *"Patera"* ("Father") and using the more formal "HAIR-eh-teh" instead of "hello" and "goodbye." Orthodox visitors may also say ev-lo-YEE-teh ("bless us, Father") to the monks. Take note of each monastery's restrictions for non-Orthodox visitors and avoid talking loudly, especially during siesta and at night. Sitting cross-legged or standing with your hands behind your back is considered disrespectful and arrogant, respectively. Though interaction with monks is limited, some monks, particularly the younger ones, are eager to engage visitors in conversation and discussion.

OBTAINING A PERMIT. Men who wish to see Mt. Athos must secure a permit in advance; call the **Holy Executive of the Holy Mount Athos Pilgrims' Bureau,** Egnatia 109 (☎23102 52 578; fax 23102 22 424), in Thessaloniki, 6 months in advance if you want to visit the community during Easter week or if you are not of the Orthodox faith. Sometimes there are still openings on days when the quota is not full, so even if you forgot to reserve a spot way in advance, it is worth calling to see if there is an opening. You are more likely to get a short-term permit if you are flexible as to the exact day you want to visit Mt. Athos. For Orthodox applicants, 100 daily permits are reserved, including a significant number set aside for Greeks living out of the country, but there are only 10 available for non-Orthodox men. Mail (don't fax) a copy of your passport to the office at Egnatia 109, Thessaloniki 54638; call 2 weeks ahead of your visit to confirm the reservation, and visit the office with your passport to pick up the permit. (Open M-F 9am-2pm, Sa 10am-noon; call ahead.) Though this process can be frustrating, the bureau will deny entry to anyone who fails to complete it. If departing for Mt. Athos from Ouranoupolis, **bring your permit and passport** to the Athos office (☎23770 71 422; open 8am-2:30pm) by 9am on the day your visit begins. At the end of the waterfront strip, take a right and walk 2 blocks uphill. At the office, you will receive your entrance pass, called the "*Diamonitirion,*" complete with the blue seal of the monastic community; you must present this before boarding the ferry to Mt. Athos. Visitors taking the 9:45am ferry must be in Ouranoupolis no later than 9am or at the dock of Ierissos no later than 8am; the boat leaves promptly at 9:45am from Ouranoupolis and, if you miss it, you will not be able to visit Athos. Arrive early as lines are long, especially when the 9am bus gets in. For the early morning ferry, and for the boat from Ierrissos, officials will be at the dock. This ferry leaves before the office opens, so it is smart to double check that you are on the list the day before by phone, or by stopping into the office. The regular permit is valid for a **4-day stay.** Passes cost €40 for foreigners and €20 for students under age 27 with ISIC. You must strictly observe the date of arrival on your permit—if you arrive a day late, you will be turned away. You will not be admitted without your **passport.** To extend your stay, you must ask at the peninsula's capital, Karyes. Unless you have an extremely compelling reason (e.g., you're becoming a monk), your request will almost certainly be denied. Unofficial extensions are easier to come by, when monks often allow considerate, interested visitors to stay longer.

that morning if you plan to take the 9:45am ferry, this can be dangerous given the unpredictable nature of Greece's public transportation. **Buses** run to Ouranopolis from Athens (7hr., 11pm, €30) and from Thessaloniki's Halkidiki station (2hr., 3 per day 6:15am-6:30pm, €9.10). Buses also depart from Thessaloniki for Ierrissos (1½hr., 6 per day 6:15am-5:45pm, €8). From Ouranoupolis, **boats** go to Dafni (2hr.; 6:30am, 9:45am; €4) and stop at each monastery on the way. The early-morning boat, called "Agia Anna," continues from Dafni at 8am to the *skiti* community of **Kafsokalivia** at the peninsula's tip. The boat stops at each monastery and *skiti* en route, both going and returning (€4). Arriving back at Dafni by 11:10am, Ag. Anna connects with the 11:30am arrival of the second boat from Ouranoupolis for a second trip down the peninsula at 12:45pm. Upon completing this trip, Ag. Anna stops at Dafni at 3:30pm, then returns to Ouranoupolis at 5:15pm. The second daily ship from Dafni to Ouranoupolis leaves at noon. To reach the peninsula's eastern monasteries, take the **bus,** synchronized with the ferry arrivals, from Dafni to Karyes. Get off the boat quickly, as the two buses fill up in a matter of seconds (30min.; €2.50), or sail with **Captain Spiro,** who travels to Vatopediou from Ierrissos (☎23770 21 041; call for schedule and prices as ferries are unreliable and canceled often). You can also hike (p. 315) or take the pricey monk-driven **taxis** (☎23770 23 267) between monasteries. But beware, a monk taxi trip to see all of the monasteries runs a wallet-defying €200.

Because Athos's hikes can be long, arduous, and often unmarked, grab a green **Mount Athos Tourist Map** (€7.50) or buy a **guidebook** with a map (€4-10) in Ouranoupolis or Karyes; a topographical map of the peninsula will be invaluable. Leave your pack in Ouranoupolis to avoid hiking with unnecessary weight. **Karyes**, the capital of Mt. Athos, has an **OTE** next to the Athonite Holy Council Building and a **hotel ❸** (€45 for up to 3 people). Under the hotel, a **restaurant ❷** serves spartan meals (€5-9), like those of the monasteries. To find the **post office**, continue straight ahead after disembarking from the bus and make a left after the large church. (☎23770 23 212; open M-F 8am-2:30pm.) Dafni also has a **convenience store**, a **police station**, and a **pastry shop**. **Postal Codes:** Dafni 63087, Karyes 63086.

THE HOLY MOUNTAIN. Named after a Thracian giant buried by Poseidon beneath the mountain, Athos predates Christianity. The Christian tradition began here when, according to legend, the **Virgin Mary** came to the mountain. After Jesus's death, the apostles divided up areas to visit to preach the "good news." Mary demanded to be allotted a region as well and was given Iberia in Asia Minor. On her way there, however, the archangel Gabriel directed her to the Athos. Even before Mary's time, many had tried to tame the rowdy peninsula, from Alexander the Great to Xerxes. But though the peninsula, then known as **"Akte,"** had been a notorious center of paganism, legend holds that the moment Mary's foot graced its soil, the false idols disintegrated in realization of their own worthlessness.

Although legend claims that the first monastic settlements were founded by Constantine the Great and his mother, Helen, record of monkish habitation does not come until the 10th century. Over the following centuries, Athos flourished periodically—at one point it contained 40 settlements and 40,000 monks—but its low points ached with natural disasters, pirate invasions, internal squabbling, and a lack of attraction to monastic ideals. Mt. Athos retained some degree of autonomy during the Turkish occupation by surrendering promptly to the Ottomans, accepting their rule, and sending heavy taxes to İstanbul. During the centuries preceding the Greek liberation of 1821, Mt. Athos was supported and populated by Serbs, Bulgarians, Romanians, and Russians, who still have affiliations with particular monasteries. At the height of imperial Russia's expansionist policies at the end of the 19th century, some 3000 Russian monks inhabited **Agios Panteleimonos**. After WWI, the Treaty of Lausanne made Mt. Athos an official part of Greece while still allowing it to retain much autonomy; a body of monks, elected from each of the 20 monasteries, was set up to legislate and govern the peninsula. Dwindling vocations through the 1950s threatened the stability of Mt. Athos, and it soon became a prime target for greedy real estate developers; the end of its 1000-year tradition of monastic asceticism seemed imminent. Athos has been rejuvenated in recent years, though, by hundreds of young men, many from Australia and Cyprus, inspired to take vows of Orthodox monasticism.

LIFE ON MOUNT ATHOS. Starting in the 14th century, financial difficulties brought on the practice of **idiorrythimico,** in which monks were allowed to keep their own money and eat and pray individually. Today, all the monasteries are run like communes, with shared money and duties. Athos retains an unsurpassed wealth of Paleologian and late Byzantine art, manuscripts, treasure, and architecture. Each monastery houses *lipsana*, remains of dead saints that only Orthodox men are allowed to see. Especially impressive are the **Hand of Mary Magdalene** (who bathed Jesus), which is said to remain (skin intact) in **Simonos Petra**, and the

belt of the Theotokos, also known as **"Agia Zoni"** ("the holy girdle"), the only extant relic of the Virgin Mary, in **Vatopediou.** Several monasteries possess fragments of the **True Cross.** The **Gifts of the Magi,** presented to Jesus at his birth, are said to be housed in **Agios Pavlou;** five of the 28 pieces are displayed for nightly veneration.

MONASTERIES. On the southeastern tip of the peninsula, **Megistis Lavras** (☎ 23770 23 754) is the oldest, largest, and wealthiest of the 20 monasteries on Mt. Athos. Its monks are known to be stern and conservative. Though it is one of the more frequently visited monasteries, you may find it somewhat impersonal. It's also the most isolated: to get there you will need to get a ride (€15-20 per person) from Karyes or embark on a long, tiring hike from either Iviron or Agia Anna. With thickly forested hills to the north and the ocean to the south, **Karakalou** (☎ 23770 23 225) is exceptionally picturesque and has the beautiful **brotherly kiss icon** depicting Peter and Paul. Karakalou's rules for non-Orthodox visitors are particularly strict, and its guest rooms are currently closed for renovation. **Philotheou** (☎ 23770 23 256), Greek for "God-loving," is one of Mt. Athos's most stunningly located monasteries, on a plateau over the northern coast. The abbey is surrounded by orchards, gardens, and lush chestnut forests. Philotheou, founded by monks from Megistis Lavra in 1015, is also one of the stricter monasteries: non-Orthodox guests must eat after the others and may not enter the church at all. Beautifully situated near a meadow overlooking the northeastern coast, **Iviron** (☎ 23770 23 643; reservations noon-2pm) was founded by Georgian monks in 980 and was the second monastery on Mt. Athos; it is currently among the most popular. Iviron is home to one of the most important icons in the Orthodox Christian world: the **Panagia Portaiatissa,** a depiction of Mary believed to have performed many miracles. **Pandokratoros** (☎ 23770 23 880) and nearby **Stavronikita** (☎ 23770 23 255; reservations noon-2pm) are on the northern coast, close to Karyes about 5km north of Iviron, accessible by bus. Home to a small community of friendly monks, Pandokratoros was the last monastery to leave the *idiorrythimico* and become communal in 1992, and is one of the few that imposes no special restrictions on its non-Orthodox visitors. Stavronikita is the smallest and "youngest" monastery, completed in 1536; it's also one of the friendliest and most peaceful. Don't miss the wonderful **mosaic of Saint Nicholas,** known as *Sterdas* ("the one with the oysters"), as it was supposedly found at sea with an oyster stuck to the saint's head. Moated and turreted like a medieval castle, **Vatopediou** (☎ 23770 23 219; reservations 9am-1pm) lies on the northern coast in a secluded bay and is now populated largely by Greek-Cypriot monks. Though tradition claims it was founded by Constantine the Great, the monastery was more likely erected by three brothers from Andrianoupolis in the late 10th century. Historically favored by emperors and princes, Vatopediou is the most visited monastery on Athos; call at least two weeks ahead for a reservation. Perched on the edge of a sheer cliff on southern coast, the breathtaking complex of **Simonos Petra** (☎ 23770 23 254; reservations 1-3pm) is spectacular, but only has room for 10 guests. The extremely kind and hospitable monks invite travelers to relax in the roomy guest quarters, which extend out on a balcony overlooking the cliff to the sea. Under constant renovation, this monastery is frequently booked; you'll need to call at least two weeks in advance to get a bed. In a secluded bay just southeast of Simonos Petra, **Grigoriou** (☎ 23770 23 668) is one of the more liberal monasteries. Guests are treated to their own private quarters just outside the monastery walls, with breeze-blown balconies that overlook the sea. Following Grigoriou southward, and accessible from the monastery Ag. Pavlou by a 30min. shore path, imposing **Dionysiou** (☎ 23770 23 687), resting on a rocky bluff over the Aegean, is one of Athos's biggest monasteries and its acting five-star hotel. The monks here are welcoming, English is prevalent, and guest quarters are luxurious. Most rooms are singles, and showers (rare on Athos) with hot water (still rarer) are available.

SLAVIC MONASTERIES. In addition to the Greek monasteries, Slavs, not to be outdone, inhabit several abbeys. The great migration of Slavs to the peninsula began in the 19th century with the emergence of the Pan-Slavic movement in the Balkans. Both political and religious ambitions converged to give the Slavs and Russians a piece of the monastic action. At one time, there were nearly equal numbers of Greek and Slavic monks on the mountain. However, political turmoil—notably the 1917 Russian Revolution—cut off the supply of funds and novices at the source, ending the Russian government's official role in the area. Today three Slavic monasteries remain: onion-domed Russian **Agios Panteleimonos** (☎ 23770 23 252; reservations 10am-noon), Bulgarian **Zografou** (☎ 23770 23 247), and Serbian **Hiliandariou** (☎ 23770 23 797). All Slavic monasteries welcome visitors.

SKITES AND HERMITAGES. Only a handful of Athos's monks still choose to live as ascetic hermits, eschewing material comforts and the "fast-paced" mainstream-monastic lifestyle in favor of caves and huts on the peak's harsh slopes. Though it seems as if the days of living in complete isolation are almost over, huts, cells, and tiny churches dot the southernmost end of the island, between Megistis Lavras and Ag. Pavlou. All are occupied by monks who have given their lives to meditation and the contemplation of God. These small communities are known as "*skites*," and each is affiliated with one of the larger monasteries. Many hermits will allow you to stay with them, but you must bring your own food and sleeping bag and be careful not to disturb their meditations. The barren southeastern slope of Athos, called **"Karoulia"** after the pulleys the monks use to bring food to their caves, is home to both some of the most extreme ascetics and some of the biggest *skites*. **Agia Anna** (☎ 23770 23 320), at the foot of Mt. Athos, is a *skiti* run by a brotherhood of nine warm, welcoming monks who offer pilgrims both rooms and meals.

HIKING. Hikes through Mt. Athos's winding mountain paths, high above emerald coves and speckled by fluorescent blue and yellow butterflies, rival any in Greece. All paths are marked with footprints and occasional signs in Greek. The trail from **Megistis Lavras** to **Agia Anna** is one of the wildest and most scenic among the Holy Mountain's family of trekking superlatives. The lack of auto accessibility in this area and the breathtaking bluffs plunging into the blue Aegean beside rocky peninsulas make this region a favorite among the most reclusive hermits. The path takes a good 8hr. but can be shortened to six by stopping at Kafsokalivia and taking the ferry to Agia Anna. Other popular hikes include the ascent of Athos's peak, a hot, dry 8hr. trek from **Agia Anna** (☎ 23770 23 320). A 6hr. climb will take you to the **Church of the Panagia**, which has mattresses for overnight stays and a small well to refill your water bottle, just 2hr. from the summit. An easier trail (2hr.) that traverses the Athos mountainside runs from Iviron monastery to Koutloumousiou, near Karyes. Catch a ride from Karyes back to Iviron or continue to another monastery in the vicinity. For any hike, it is advisable to take along a copy of the green **Mount Athos Road Editions Map** (Available in stores in Karyes; €7.50) or another Athos guide. **Paths** can be narrow and poorly marked, and those on the map might have been swallowed by brush. Stop frequently to verify directions. Bring lots of water and bear in mind the lay of the peninsula: western shore hikers will enjoy Athos's shadow until 11am, while the eastern shore is perfect for late afternoon rambles. Make sure to be back from your excursion by sunset, though, or you will be locked out of a meal and bed. The light monastic fare is insufficient for a long hike, so try to bring some nourishment from the outside world. If you tell the monks in your monastery that you are going to miss a meal, they may give you a modest amount of bread and vegetables. Alternatively, you can join most Greek pilgrims and hop into a monk-driven minibus for a bumpy ride back to Karyes. From there, ask around for another bus traveling in your direction.

THRACE Θράκη

The province that forms present-day Thrace, in the northeastern pocket of Greece, has historically been home to a people not considered ethnically Greek. In Roman times, Indo-European, non-Hellenic Thracians inhabited the mountainous region until they were subdued by Roman conquest in AD 46. The region then became an imperial trading card, passed from the Byzantine Empire to the Bulgarian Empire, back to the Byzantine Empire, and finally to the Ottoman Empire where it remained for 530 years. Only at the close of WWI in 1919, 90 years after Greece achieved independence, was the region completely returned to Greece. With a population of Greeks, Thracian Muslims, Bulgarians, and Albanians, Thrace bears the imprint of its historical path. Its villages, with their hectic jumble of people, food, architecture, and traditions, inspire visitors to discover the answers behind Thrace's complex mixture of cultures and religions.

XANTHI Ξάνθη   ☎ 25410

Xanthi, Thrace's gem, may be the most pleasant city in which to experience Thracian multiculturalism. The vivid landscape, framed by the Rhodopi Mountains to the northwest and the Nestos river to the west, provides a captivating backdrop, while a rich cultural mix colors the streets. Just a few steps away from the hustle, bustle, and fumes of the modern city, you can get lost among the cobbled streets of Xanthi's Old Town. These winding alleys thread through neighborhoods of Ottoman houses and elegant old mansions, the bounty of a tobacco industry that still buoys much of the town's economy. A student population from the University of Thrace gives the town a youthful spirit and sophisticated feel year-round.

⛶ TRANSPORTATION. Xanthi's train station (☎ 25410 22 581), at the end of Kondili, is about 2km southeast of the central plateia. Head down Karaoli, go right at the rotary of Pl. Baltadzi and, when the street forks, take a left onto Kapnergaton (a.k.a. Kondili); there are signs 100m past the stadium and the tennis courts. You can also take a taxi (€2) from the central plateia. **Trains** go to: Athens (regular:

12hr.; 2:40am, 2:15pm; €21.10. Regular intercity: 9hr., 10:30pm, €47. Express: 8hr.; 2:58, 8:10pm; €59); İstanbul, Turkey (9½hr., 10:40am, €26); Komotini (30min., 7 per day 3:05am-10pm, €2); Thessaloniki (regular: 4½hr., 3 per day 2:40am-5:50pm, €7; express: 3½hr., 4 per day 7:50am-10:30pm, €14). Tickets are sold at the train station and the **OSE Pilot Travel Office,** Thermopylon 2. (☎25410 74 018. Open M-F 8:30am-2pm and 5-9pm.) Though trains are the best way to get to and from Xanthi, the bus station, Dimokritou 6 (☎25410 22 684; open 5am-11pm), sends **buses** to: Athens (10hr.; 9:30am, 7pm; €46); Avdira and Myrodato beaches (30min., 6 per day 6am-8pm, €2.20); Drama (2hr., 4 per day 8am-6:30pm, €3.50); Kavala (1hr., every hr. 6am-10pm, €3.50); Komotini (45min., 14 per day 6:30am-8:30pm, €4); Lagos (30min., 9 per day 7am-7pm, €2); Mangana beach (30min., 7 per day 6am-10pm, €2); Thessaloniki (3½hr., 9 per day 6am-7pm, €14). **Taxis** (☎25410 72 801 or 25410 72 802) wait in Pl. Dimokratias and Pl. Baltadzi and run 24hr.

⚡🈯 ORIENTATION AND PRACTICAL INFORMATION. Thrace's western-most city, Xanthi is about 50km northeast of Kavala. Its central plateia, **Plateia Dimokratias,** has an impressive clock tower in the center. From the bus station, go out the door at the back of the seating area and **Dimokritou** will be in front of you. Head left past **Plateia Baltadzi,** a small traffic circle, as Dimokritou becomes **Karaoli** and leads into Pl. Eleftherias. Another main street, **28 Oktovriou,** whose name commemorates the day the Greeks beat the Nazis in WWII, runs parallel to Karaoli. **Vassilis Konstantinou** runs north to the Old Town across from the clock tower.

Xanthi has no tourist office, but the **town hall,** 6 Mavromihali, housed in a beautiful 19th-century mansion on the upper end of Vas. Konstantinou, provides free city **maps.** (☎25410 23 641. Open M-F 9am-7pm.) The **National Bank of Greece,** Konitsis 13, north of the main plateia, has a **24hr. ATM** and **currency exchange.** Take the first right off Konstantinou as you head toward the Old Town. (☎25410 45 844. Open M-Th 8am-2:30pm, F 8am-2pm.) The 24hr. **police,** Neston 2 (☎25410 22 654), is north of Karaoli near the bus station. **Laundry** can be done at **Alfa,** next to Hotel Orfeas. (☎25410 25 723. Open daily 8am-3pm.) Two blocks southeast of Pl. Baltadzi is the 24hr. **hospital** (☎25410 72 131). The **OTE** (☎25410 56 199), which is currently being renovated, is left of the central plateia as you face the large courthouse across from the prominent church; use the alternate entrance around the back as long as construction continues. (Open 7:30am-1pm.) **Internet access** can be found at **X-net,** Meletsidou 3, at the entrance to the Old Town, opposite a cluster of tavernas. (☎25410 84 463. €2.20 per hr. during the day, €1.70 per hr. at night. Coffee €2. Beer €2. Open 24hr.) The **post office,** Miltiadou 7, is just beyond the clock tower. (☎25410 21 166. Open M-F 7:30am-2pm.) **Postal Code:** 67100.

🖝🏠 ACCOMMODATIONS AND FOOD. Neither tourists nor budget hotels have discovered Xanthi; accommodations are scarce and expensive. The coastline resorts of **Mangana beach, Myrodato beach,** and **Lagos** have campsites and are served by daily buses to Xanthi. In town, your best bet is modern **Hotel Orfeas ❸,** Karaoli 40, whose carpeted rooms have A/C, TV, and balconies. Staff are very friendly and speak English. (☎25410 20 121 or 25410 20 122; www.ixanthi.gr/orfeas. Breakfast included. Singles €35; doubles €55; triples €65.) For a cheaper but less satisfying stay, try **Hotel Paris ❷,** Dimokritou 12, which offers clean but very small rooms with A/C. (☎25410 20 531. Breakfast €4. Singles €22; doubles €27; triples €32.) The **Hotel Democritus ❹,** 28 Oktovriou 41, just below the central plateia, is more luxurious, as reflected in its prices. The spacious rooms have TV, A/C, minibars, phones, and large balconies. (☎25410 25 111. English spoken. Internet access available. Breakfast included. Singles €45; doubles €62; triples €75.)

NORTHERN GREECE

A Turkish flavor pervades much of Xanthi's cuisine, with specialties like syrupy *kariokes* and *soutzouk-lokum*, known as "Turkish Delight." Restaurants, cafes, and bars concentrate on the central plateia. A **covered market**, off 40 Ekklision just south of the main plateia, has bustling stalls full of fruit, vegetables, and meat. (Open daily until 3pm.) Just north of the plateia, on a side street that leads to the National Bank, ⊠**Fanarakia Taverna** ❷, Stavrou 18, serves delicious local classics in a quiet courtyard. *Terlou terlou* (fried chicken and pork; €5.50) or minced meat rolls (€3.50) are among the restaurant's specials. (☎25410 84 540. Open daily 12pm-12am.) **O Metkos** ❷, Vasileos Konstantinou 26-32, is a student favorite known for its cheap, home-cooked dishes. (☎25410 25 410. Spaghetti and goulash €4. Open daily noon-9pm.) **Klimataria** ❷, under the shadow of the clock tower in the main plateia, features a number of local pork, veal, and fish dishes. Outdoor tables overlook the square. (☎25410 22 408. Appetizers €2-3. Entrees €4-7.)

◙ ▣ **SIGHTS AND ENTERTAINMENT.** Xanthi's museums, all in the Old Town, include the **Folklore Museum**, Antica 9, which houses traditional dresses and jewelry. (Open W-F 8:30am-2:30pm, Sa-Su 10:30am-3pm. Free.) **Christos Pavlides Painting Gallery**, Orfeos Pindarou Corner 24, has a bustling restoration workshop and paintings by local artists including (not shockingly) the 20th-century painter Christos Pavlides. (☎25410 76 363. Down the alley from the Folklore Museum. Open M-F 10:30am-1:30pm and 6:30-8:30pm. Free.) In the hills above Xanthi, frescoes adorn the walls of the **Panagia Archangeliotissa** convent, a 30min. cab ride from the center square (€11). The magnificent pictures depict Paul's missions to the area in the AD first century. (Open 7am-7pm.) The **Panagia Kalamou**, known for its archaeological collection, is farther down. (Open 8am-1pm and 4-8pm.)

Though Xanthi's nightlife may seem dull, its tavernas are actually full of students enjoying a drink between classes. Most of the action centers on the intersection of Sophias and Idras, at the edge of the University of Thrace's campus. Favorites include **Kyverneio**, Sophias 7a, the last cafe before the Old Town, which has a large bar, leather couches, and American music. (☎25410 77 577. Open M-Th, Su 9am-2am, F-Sa 9am-late.) **Baiser**, Vassilissis Sofias 5, is a sophisticated, modern bar that serves drinks and coffee. At night, it's packed with students showing off the latest Greek fashion fads. (☎25410 73 948. Open daily 9:30am-late.)

KOMOTINI Κομοτηνή ☎25310

The broad Thracian plain begins to rise into the Rodhopi Mountains at untouristed Komotini, 40km east of Xanthi. The city's population is about 20% Turkish ("Greek Muslim" according to the Greek authorities), and this influence is visible in the Old Town's architecture, where graceful minarets poke up from whitewashed apartments and church domes. A walk among the heavy weekday traffic along the bazaar gives a Greek-based taste of İstanbul's vibrant flavor.

▐ **TRANSPORTATION.** The **OSE office** is on Panayi Tzaldari 51 (☎25310 22 650. Open M-F 8am-3pm.) Komotini's train station (☎25310 22 650), in the southwestern corner of the city, is a 20min. walk from the city center. Standing on Orfeos facing the main plateia, go right and keep walking. At the railroad tracks, turn right on Kyprillou; it's seven blocks to the station. **Trains** go to: Athens (regular: 12hr.; 2:50pm, 11:55pm; €23; express: 8½hr.; 6:55am, 1:54, 8:37pm; €60); İstanbul, Turkey (10hr., 11:15am, €25); Thessaloniki (regular: 5hr., 3 per day 10:50am-2:10am, €9; express: 3½hr., 3 per day 7:45am-10pm, €15). The bus station, G. Mameli 1, is on the corner of Tsounta (☎25310 22 912). **Buses** go to: Alexandroupoli (1hr., 14 per day 6am-8:10pm, €5); Athens (10hr.; 8:30am, 6:30pm; €49); Kavala (1½hr., 8 per day 5:30am-8pm, €7); Thessaloniki (4hr., 8 per day 5:30am-8pm, €17); Xanthi (1hr., 11 per day 6:30am-8:30pm, €4). **Taxis** (☎25310 37 777) are available 24hr. by the OTE south of Pl. Eirinis, or in front of Hotel Olympus on Orfeos St.

▪▮ ORIENTATION AND PRACTICAL INFORMATION. To get to the city center from the bus station, turn right from the door and left at the first intersection; follow Ainou to the central **Plateia Eirinis. Orfeos** runs east-west directly above it; **Zoidou** is a few blocks south. Across Orfeos, a maze of streets, markets, and mosques marks the Turkish area. The open-air ▨**Turkish bazaar** centers on **Ermou.** Going east on Orfeos away from Pl. Eirinis, you will find **Plateia Vizinou** with a large white obelisk and wooded urban park. **Maps** and tourist pamphlets are available at the **information office** in the municipal Nomarhio office, Dimokratias 1, at the other side of the park. (☎25310 34 124. Open M-F 7am-2:30pm.) The **National Bank,** Thisauis 1, north of Pl. Eirinis at the east end of Orfeos, has a **24hr. ATM** and **currency exchange.** (☎25310 54 901. Open M-Th 8am-2:30pm, F 8am-2pm.) There is a **Bank of Greece,** Ag. Georgiou 1, at the eastern end (closest to Pl. Vizinou) of Pl. Eirinis. (☎25310 34 045. Open M-Th 7:45am-3:15pm, F 7:45am-2:45pm.) **Laundry** can be done at **Laundry Express,** Zoidou 35. (☎25310 21 511. Open daily 8am-2:30pm and 6-9:30pm. €7.30 per load.) Facing the white obelisk, go 500m north on Aghiadou to the **police station,** Aghiadou 8 (☎25310 83 205). The **hospital,** Sismanoglou 45 (☎25310 22 222 or 25310 24 601), is in the southeastern part of town; follow Georgiou east out of Pl. Eirinis. The **OTE** is at Parasiou 2, on a side street south of Pl. Eirinis across from Hotel Orpheus. (☎25310 56 171. Open M-Sa 7am-2:30pm, Tu-W 7am-2:30pm and 5:30pm-8:30pm). Find **Internet access** at **The Web,** A. Souzou 8. (☎25310 70 111. €2-2.40 per hr. Open 24hr.) Past the OTE is the **post office,** Parasiou 4. (☎25310 22 344. Open M-F 7:30am-2pm.) **Postal Code:** 69100.

▮ ACCOMMODATIONS. Like Xanthi, Komotini has few budget accommodations. ▨**Olympos Hotel ❹,** Orfeos 35, in a converted mansion, offers bright, carpeted rooms with TV, phones, fridges, hairdryers, and A/C. (☎25310 37 690; www.hotel-olympos.gr. Breakfast €4. Singles €40; doubles €50; triples €62. MC/V.) **Hotel Hellas ❷,** Dimokritou 31, is just north of the Archaeological Museum. With Pl. Eirinis on your left, follow Orfeos as it becomes Makedonias and pass its first intersection with Dimokritou, which bends back and re-intersects Makedonias three blocks down; it's on your right. Simple rooms with shared baths sit off hallways adorned with artwork created by the manager's wife. The hotel is in the couple's apartment, giving the entire establishment a home-like feeling. Language, however, might be a problem, as the staff does not speak English. (☎25310 22 055. Singles €20; doubles €28.) **Hotel Orpheus ❹,** Parasiou 1, south of Pl. Eirinis opposite the OTE, has cheerful rooms with TV, fridges, A/C, and balconies. (☎25310 37 180; fax 25310 28 271. Breakfast €4. Singles €37; doubles €47; triples €55. AmEx/MC/V.) **EOT's campsite ❶,** about a 30min. taxi ride out of town near Fanari, is a great option for anyone looking to save money. (☎25350 31 217. Electricity, drinking water, bath, and shower available. €4.50 per person; €7.50 per car.)

◨ FOOD. Dining centers on Pl. Eirinis. Excellent local fare abounds among the winding streets of the bazaar. Sweet shops display the colorful cubes and long sausages of Turkish Delights and back alleys host both Greek and Turkish eateries. One favorite, ▨**Taverna Petrino ❸,** Kiklis 8, is just two blocks from Orfeos. A delightful escape from both the summer sun and the traffic of Ermou, Petrino offers a variety of chicken, fish, and pork dishes served by a courteous English-speaking waitstaff. Don't miss the house specialty, octopus with ouzo (€5). (☎25310 73 650. Entrees €4.50-7. Open daily in summer 11:30am-3am; winter location is around the corner at Serron 25.) **Restaurant Ydroxos ❷,** Papaflessa 2, on a side street connecting Orfeos to Pl. Eirinis, has tasty local dishes and a

GIVING BACK

RESCUING RAPTORS

The Dadia forest was once home to hundreds of animal species. With the advent of logging in the 1970s, however, large portions of the animal population began to die out at a shocking speed. By 1980, many of the animals were at such risk of extinction that the government declared the area a protected region. Ever since then, a number of projects have been launched in order to save and document the endangered species. One such initiative, a joint collaboration between the World Wildlife Federation (WWF) and the European Volunteer Service (EVS), concentrates on Dadia's community of black vultures. The action group is comprised of 10-12 young Europeans who participate in an EU-run program that lasts six to nine months. The group members live in small apartments in the village of Dadia and spend their days feeding and caring for the raptors, monitoring their numbers—only 23 recorded pairs are known to remain in the reserve—and conducting DNA research.

Though only EU residents can apply for the full conservation program, the group is always more than happy to have visitors help for a few days. If you're interested, contact Lamprini Anastopoulou well in advance by email (ecodadia@otenet.gr) or phone (☎25540 32 210).

wide selection of homemade salads. Seating is available either under the vine-covered canopy looking over the bustling square, or in the air-conditioned interior. Ydroxos has an English menu and serves a delicious pudding desert on the house. (☎25310 33 786. Thracian pork dish with green and red peppers €5.) In the square, the balcony tables at **Oinopion ❸**, Pl. Eirinis 67, let you survey the plateia while enjoying the breeze. The tasty menu includes meat dishes like the famous Oinopion chicken (€5.50). (☎25310 36 082; www.oinopion.gr. Entrees €4-12.) For more of a Turkish taste, try out **Restauran ❶**, Bakkalbasi 4; its homemade authentic *kofte* (minced meat patties and rice; €2) and Turkish salad (€1.50) are locally popular. (☎25310 36 088. Open daily 6:30am-4:30pm.)

🄶 **SIGHTS.** To reach Komotini's **Archaeological Museum,** Simeonidi 4, follow Zoidou westward and bear right at the park onto the cement footpath. Arranged with helpful English explanations from the Neolithic to the Byzantine periods, the museum's exhibits focus on artifacts found in Thrace. The museum also features Early Neolithic Thracian wall-paintings from the 11th century BC, and artifacts from a barren Roman fortress at Nestos whose oft-raided walls protected the Via Egnatia and port of Neapolis. Highlights include the spectacular **golden bust** of Roman Emperor Septimius Severus from Plotinopolis, the 5th-century BC **Panathenaic amphora** depicting Athena holding a shield, and the 4th-century BC **Mask of Dionysus** from Maroneia. (☎25310 215 17. Open daily 8am-3pm. Free.) A 30min. taxi ride from Komotini brings you to the beach of **Maroneia,** which has a few archaeological sites including a well-preserved amphitheater.

ALEXANDROUPOLI
Αλεξανδρούπολη ☎25510

Travelers often rush through Alexandroupoli on their way to Turkey, the Northeast Aegean Islands, and the hinterlands of Thrace, and thus often overlook the charms of one of Thrace's most bustling port cities. Though Alexandroupoli does not have the ethnic diversity of Xanthi or Komotini, cobblestone streets, rows of fashionable stores, and a wooded waterfront make Alexandroupoli a pleasant pit-stop or a delightful place to get stranded. Music and chitter-chatter infuse the waterfront, making it a lovely place for an evening stroll, and the town is an excellent base for exploring the green hills of the Evros region.

TRANSPORTATION. Dimokritos Airport (☎25510 45 198), 6km east of town and only reachable by taxi (€3.80), sends planes to: **Athens** (1hr., 2-3 per day, €75-85); **Sitia, Crete** (2hr., 3 per week, €92); **Thessaloniki** (1hr., 3 per week, €65). Buy tickets at **Sever Travel** (☎25510 22 555) on Dikastarion and Karaiskaki. Walking inland from the lighthouse it is the first intersection on your left. The train station is at M. Alexandrou 1, 400m east of the lighthouse, in front of Pl. Eleftherias. (☎25510 26 395. Open 24hr.) **Trains** to: Athens (regular: 14hr., 5 per day 1am- 9:05pm, €23. Intercity: 9hr., 5 per day 1am-9:05pm, €49); İstanbul, Turkey (9hr, noon, €21); Komotini (regular: 1hr., 4 per day 1am-4:17pm, €2. Intercity: 50min., 4 per day 6:45am-9:05pm, €4.50); Thessaloniki (regular: 6hr., 4 per day 1am-4:17pm, €10. Intercity: 4½hr., 4 per day 6:45am-9:05pm, €17); Xanthi (regular: 1½hr., 4 per day 1am-4:17pm, €3. Intercity: 1½hr., 4 per day 6:45am-9:05pm, €7). The bus station, Maiou 14 (☎25510 26 479), is at the corner of El. Venizelou and Maiou, 500m inland from the docks, sends **buses** to: Athens (11hr., 6:30pm, €50); Didimotiho (1½hr., 17 per day 4:15am-8:45pm, €7) via Feres (30min., €2) and Soufli (1hr., €4.20); Kipi (45min., 5 per day 6:50am-7:30pm, €3); Komotini (1hr., 14 per day 6:10am-8:10pm, €5); Thessaloniki (regular: 5hr., 8 per day 5:15am-10pm; express: 4½hr.; 9:30am, 5pm; €22) via Xanthi (1½hr., 8 per day, €8) and Kavala (2hr., 8 per day, €11).

There are two main ferry lines. **Saos** lies a few doors up from the waterfront at Kyprou 15. (☎25510 26 721. Open M, W 8:30am-9pm, Tu, Th-F 7:30am-3pm and 5-9pm, Sa 8am-9:30pm, Su 8am-5:30pm.) **Ferries** run to Samothraki (2½hr.; 1-2 per day; €9, students €6). The Monday ferry continues to Limnos (5hr., 4pm, €18) and the Saturday ferry continues to Lesvos (12hr., 3pm, €25). **Flying Dolphins,** which run June 20 through September 20, zip to Samaothraki (1hr., 2-3 ferries per day, €18). **Kikon Tours,** El. Venizelou 68 (☎25510 25 455; open M-F 9am-2:30pm and 6:30-9:30pm, Sa 8:30am-2:30pm), sends one weekly ferry that leaves on Monday at 8:30am and stops at: Chios (12hr., €28); Kalimnos (22hr., €39); Kos (20hr., €39); Lesvos (10hr., €21); Limnos (4hr., €15); Rhodes (24hr., €44); Samos (16hr., €34). **Taxis** (☎25510 33 500) are available 24hr. Fares inside the city cost up to €3.30.

■♂ ORIENTATION AND PRACTICAL INFORMATION. Everything a traveler could need or want is within 10min. of the waterfront center, marked by a lighthouse. Standing at the lighthouse facing inland, the waterfront road, **Megalou Alexandrou,** stretches left to the row of cafes and right toward the train station. Halfway between the lighthouse and the train station, **Kyprou** leads inland to small **Plateia Kyprou.** The three main streets running parallel to Alexandrou (**Dimokratias, Eleftheriou Venizelou,** and **Paleologou**) are about three blocks inland, linked by narrow cobblestone streets. The **tourist police,** Karaiskaki 6 (☎25510 37 411; open M-Th 8am-2pm), supply info and share a building, two blocks inland from the water, just before the lighthouse, with the 24hr. **police** (☎25510 37 424). Dimokratias is one long string of banks with **24hr. ATMs,** including the **National Bank of Greece,** Dimokratias 240. (☎25510 64 612. Open M-Th 8am-2pm, F 8am-1:30pm.) There is a 24hr. **hospital** (☎25510 74 000) in the suburb of Hilli. **Net Gaming Network,** Xarilaou Trikoupi 2, has **Internet access.** Head west along Dimokratias until the road splits; take the left fork onto Trikoupi. (☎25510 29 751; www.gnet.gr. €2-3 per hr. Open 24hr.) The **post office,** M. Alexandrou 42, is on the water 20m west of the lighthouse. (☎25510 23 122. Open M-F 7:30am-2pm.) **Postal Code:** 68100.

⌐⌐ ACCOMMODATIONS AND FOOD. Like most of its neighbors, Alexandroupoli's lodgings are pricey. Most choices cluster near the bus and train stations. Call ahead, especially in the summer, for weekend stays. ◪**Hotel Alex ❸,** Dimokratias 292, one block south of the bus station by the town hall, has friendly management and comfortable rooms with baths, balconies, TV, phones, and ceiling fans. The decor is a throwback to the 80s. (☎25510 26 302. Singles €30; doubles €40; triples €52.) **Hotel Lido ❸,** Paleologou 15, behind the bus station, has a variety of simple rooms. Some rooms face the sea, others have a pleasant city view. Rooms with bathrooms are more expensive; the others share a common bathroom with a squat-style toilet (i.e., a hole in the floor). (☎25510 28 808. Singles €30, with bath €35; doubles €32/42; triples €45.) **Hotel Vergina ❸,** Karaoli 74, directly across the street from the train station at the point where M. Alexandrou becomes Karaoli, has 10 clean, well-furnished rooms with showers, TV, A/C and phones, three of which have a beautiful sea view. (☎25510 23 025. Singles €35; doubles €50; triples €70.) **Camping Alexandroupolis ❶** is 1km west of the town center on the water. (☎25510 28 735. €4.40 per person, €3.20 per tent, €1.80 per car.)

Fast food and cheap cafes line the waterfront and the area around Dimokratias and M. Alexandrou, while a number of good seafood restaurants put tables out along the shore. **Taverna Mylos ❷,** M. Alexandrou 2 (across from the post office—look for the windmill), serves delicious fresh seafood brought in every morning by Samothrakian fisherman on tables overlooking the Aegean. Ask for the celebrated crab salad served in a giant shell (€4), or plunge into the impressive ouzo and tsipouro selection. (☎25510 35 519. Entrees €2-8. Open until midnight.) Locals flock to **Kokoras ❷,** M. Alexandrou 4, 5min. east of the lighthouse on the waterfront, for freshly grilled meats at affordable prices. (☎25510 82 647. Entrees €1-6. Open 10am-1am.) **Neraida ❷,** Kyprou 5, a local favorite, is one block away from the waterfront in Politehneiov Sq. Facing the lighthouse, walk four blocks east and one block inland on Kyprou. The eclectic menu features Turkish, Greek, and Bulgarian food; try the Kokoretz stuffed lamb liver (€6), or any other of the 32 daily entrees which range €3-8. (☎25510 22 867. Open 9am-1am.) Down the street from Neraida, toward the water, you will find **Theofilos ❶** on the corner of Kyprou and M. Alexandrou. This popular cafe has an amazing variety of cheese and meat pastries (€0.60-2.70) and 12 homemade ice-cream flavors (€1.50). Sit on the second-floor balcony and watch the fishermen coming up from the harbor. (☎25510 33 882. Open 5am-1am.) The modest nightlife in Alexandroupoli centers almost exclusively on the waterfront where cafes, which put tables and chairs out on the sidewalk, play Mediterranean music and stay open very late.

◙ SIGHTS. Alexandroupoli's ◪**Ecclesiastic Art Museum** is inside of the Cathedral of Ag. Nikolaos, one block inland and one block east from the bus station. The little museum features a 19th-century gilded Bulgarian Gospel and wooden icons alongside a fascinating workshop that demonstrates the process of painting an icon. If you can, get Nectarius, the English-speaking priest, to give you a tour. (☎25510 81 281. Open Tu-Sa 11am-1:30pm. Optional donation €1.) The beautiful 19th-century church of **Agios Nikolaos** is in the same compound. The walls house unique artifacts like the Byzantine Virgin **"Trifotissa,"** a 13th-century icon of Mary and the baby Jesus from Aenos. Mary's almond shaped eyes are prominent and so the icon was worshipped as protection against bad eyesight. The altar is adorned with magnificent stained glass windows. (Prayers are held 7-9am and 6:40-7pm.)

DADIA Δαδιά   ☎25540

The **Dadia Forest Reserve** lies 40km northeast of Alexandroupoli. It covers over 18,000 acres of thickly-wooded hills near the Turkish border and extends into the Evros prefecture at the southeastern edge of the Rodophi mountain range. The forest serves as the home and breeding ground for hundreds of endangered raptors. Of the 38 European species of these huge hunters, 36 have been spotted in Dadia, and it is the only place in Europe where the four European vulture species (black, bearded, Griffon, and Egyptian) coexist. A well-maintained network of hiking trails runs throughout the reserve. Blazes light the way along the rugged ridges that break up the golden, untouristed Thracian plain. From the Ecotourist Center, a main trail leads up a hill to a bird hide, where you can watch raptors and vultures swoop down onto their prey. Follow the orange blazes uphill from the center for about 1hr. From the hide, trails extend in all directions, with most leading back to the Center. To head back down, take the trail marked with yellow blazes (45min.). The red trail takes you to the ruins of a Byzantine castle, built by Emperor Justinian on the peak of the Giberna mountain (2hr.), while the blue trail traverses the mountain side and returns to the Ecotourist Center (1½hr.). The center houses a modest museum which offers interesting information about the flora and fauna found in the Dadia forest. The village of **Dadia** is small, charming, and definitely worth a short visit if you are exploring the surrounding area. Official documents from the Ottoman empire call the town Cimkebir—"village of the great pine"—and the modern name, Dadia, comes from the same thematic root, meaning "pine wood torch." The local **monastery,** which lies 4km outside of the village, was first built in 1727 and rebuilt in 1950 after being destroyed in the Balkan wars; in addition, fourteen other churches serve the 600 villagers. The town hosts a number of local festivals and celebrations like the **Courbani Fair** on January 18, which celebrates an old custom meant to bring about good fortune for the crops and animals. On this day, the men of the village slaughter male goats and cook the meat all night in huge cauldrons by the chapel; in the morning, the food is distributed between houses in the village. To scare off the Christmas spirit known as "Kalikantzari" on **Epiphany** (Jan. 6), villagers carry icons out of the church and cling to them as they run through the village chanting "Lord have mercy."

A **small hotel ❸** shares the same building as the Ecotourist Center. The simple wooden-floored rooms with A/C, TV, and individual bathrooms are connected by a veranda that overlooks a picturesque courtyard. (☎ 25540 32 209. Reserve in advance. Singles €30; doubles €40; triples €50.)

To get to Dadia, take the **bus** from Alexandroupoli to Didimotiho and get off at Soufli (1hr., 18 per day, 4:15am-8:45pm, €4). From Soufli, catch the bus to the village of Dadia (20min., 3 per day 8am-2pm). The reserve is approximately 1km from the center of Dadia; follow the signs to the **Ecotourist Center.** If you miss the last bus back, taxis to Soufli cost about €10 (☎ 25540 22 888).

SARONIC GULF ISLANDS
Τα Νησιά του Σαρωνικού

The Saronic Gulf holds mixed blessings for the budget traveler. The intrepid will find a gold mine of history and natural beauty located just over an hour from Athens. They will, however, have to wade through a stream of five million party-crazed Athenians who invade on summer weekends—rendering prices and room availability just plain ugly—to find it. Mid-week and low-season travelers with time to explore will encounter a surprising diversity here; despite their geographic proximity, each island retains a distinct character. Aegina's throngs of beer-swilling beach-goers live in a different world than Poros's urbane upper crust, and Spetses's motorbiking hipsters are much farther from Hydra's mule-mounted artists than the 1hr. ferry between them would suggest.

SUGGESTED ITINERARIES: SARONIC GULF ISLANDS

FOUR DAYS Set off on a salty excursion to **Aegina Town, Aegina** (p. 326), where you can snack on more varieties of pistachio nuts than you ever dreamed of. The ferry you catch to **Hydra** (p. 332) the next day will very likely be the last motorized transport you use for a while—anything more advanced than a donkey is strictly forbidden at the popular honeymoon destination. Wind up with 2 days on arguably the best of the Saronic Gulf islands, **Spetses** (p. 336), with its amazing beaches.

AEGINA Αίγινα

White-washed Aegina is an easy daytrip for Athenians, and the bustle of Greece's capital is indeed transported to the island on summer weekends. In ancient times, though, relations between Athens and Aegina were not so chummy. The little island made up for its size with a self-determined spunk that irritated the haughty Athenians to no end. Aegina independently produced the first Greek coins (silver "tortoises"), and its sprinters, who practiced with jugs of water on their shoulders, zoomed past the competition at Panhellenic games. When Xerxes's army laid siege to Athens in 491 BC, kicking off the Persian Wars, Aegina made the foreign policy mistake of the century by siding against their Hellenic brethren. In 480 BC they humbly returned to the Greek side and won the praise of the Delphic Oracle for having the swiftest navy on the seas. The Aeginians apparently didn't learn from their own history, however, as in the next warring period, they were quick to join Sparta's insurgence against Athens. After getting trounced in 459 BC, the islanders soon found themselves displaced by Athenian colonists. Aegina soon sank into geopolitical obscurity, only to emerge over two millennia later, in 1827, as the temporary capital of then-partially liberated Greece.

Travelers to Aegina will find that its attractions are as rich as its legacy, though significantly less rebellious. Agia Marina, on the far side of the island from Aegina Town, boasts gorgeous beaches and wild nightlife, while the clean beaches of Marathonas, a quiet hamlet outside of Aegina Town, are ideal for a late-afternoon swim. A pleasant drive through olive-terraced mountains leads to the massive Church of

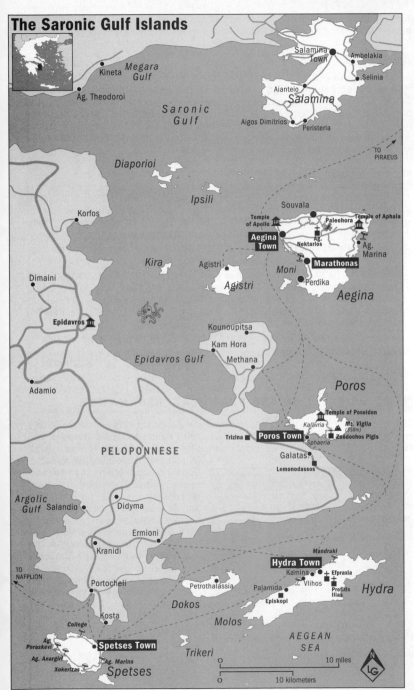

The Saronic Gulf Islands

Salamina Town
Ambelakia
Kineta
Megara Gulf
Ag. Theodoroi
Selinia
Aianteio
Salamina

Saronic Gulf

Aigos Dimitrios
Peristeria

TO PIRAEUS

Diaporioi

Ipsili

Souvala

Korfos

Temple of Apollo
Paleohora
Temple of Aphaia
Aegina Town
Ag. Nektarios
Ag. Marina

Kira
Agistri

Moni
Marathonas

Agistri
Perdika

Aegina

Dimaini

Kounoupitsa

Epidavros
Kam Hora
Methana

Epidavros Gulf

Poros

Adamio

Temple of Poseidon
Kalavria
Mt. Vigila (350m)
Trizina
Poros Town
Zoodochos Pigis
Sphaeria

PELOPONNESE
Galatas
Lemonodassos

Argolic Gulf
Salandio
Didyma

Ermioni

TO NAFPLION
Kranidi

Mandraki
Hydra Town
Portocheli
Kamina
Efpraxia
Petrothalassia
Palamida
Vlihos
Profitis Ilias
Episkopi
Hydra

Kosta
Dokos

College
Molos

Ag. Paraskevi
AEGEAN SEA
Ag. Anargiri
Spetses Town
Ag. Marina
Trikeri
Xokerizas
Spetses

0   10 miles
0   10 kilometers

SARONIC GULF

Agios Nektarios, and the well-preserved remains of the Temple of Aphaia, a fascinating reminder of the island's ancient glory, stand high on the western coast.

AEGINA TOWN   ☎22970

As soon as your ferry docks in Aegina Town, you'll know that you've entered "the pistachio capital of the world." With preserved, jellied, flavored, red, flaked, shelled, and regular varieties, there are as many ways to eat pistachios here as there are package tour boats from the mainland; fortunately, the tasty nuts are the stronger influence. Those looking for a carefree beachside romp will do well to stay in town. For a more substantive experience, rent a moped and delve deeper into the forested, temple-crowned terrain.

▐ TRANSPORTATION

Ferries: Saronikos Lines (☎22970 25 951). To: **Agistri** (20min., 1-2 per day, €1.70); **Hydra** (2hr., 1-2 per day, €7.50); **Piraeus** (1½hr., 11 per day, €5.50); **Poros** (1hr., 5-6 per day, €4.50) via **Methana** (45min., 3-4 per day, €3.40); **Spetses** (3hr., 9am, €10). Find schedules and tickets at the kiosks on the inland end of the ferry dock.

Hydrofoils: Hellas Flying Dolphins (☎22970 27 462) has a ticket stand on the quay and goes to **Piraeus** (35min., 12 per day, €9.50).

Buses: ☎22970 22 787. In Ethnegarcias Park, at the corner of the waterfront left of the ferry quay. Departure times change daily, so check with the station before making plans. Buses run to **Agia Marina** and the **Temple of Aphaia** (30min., 11 per day 6:30am-8pm, €1.70), **Perdika** (15min., 9 per day 6:30am-7:30pm, €1) via **Marathonas,** and **Souvalda** (25min., 8 per day 6:30am-8pm, €1.30).

Taxis: ☎22970 22 635. The station is just to the left of the quay along the waterfront.

Mopeds: Mopeds from Aegina's many rental agencies are €7-20 per day depending on bells, whistles, and paint jobs. The free **maps** at **Trust,** Leonardou Lada 1 (☎22970 27 010), 1 block inland from the waterfront, on the 2nd fl., boost it over its competitors.

⚞ ❼ ORIENTATION AND PRACTICAL INFORMATION

The central quay is expensive, but tavernas and hotels get cheaper toward either end of the waterfront street, which is, when facing inland, **Kazatzaki** to the left and **Toti Chatzi** to the far right. At a central point, it goes by **Dimokratias.** Running parallel and one block inland, **Pan Irioti** is lined with small shops, markets, tavernas, and the occasional moped rental shop. Sp. Rodi, farther inland and on a tangent curve to P. Irioti, becomes **Aphaias** at the intersection with **Aiakou.** Aiakou, perpendicular to Aphais, takes you back to the waterfront between the National Bank and the port authority. It's home to upscale shops, bars, and an Internet cafe. **Maps** of the town are posted on the waterfront across the street from the National Bank.

Budget Travel: Karagiannis Travel, Kanari 2 (☎22970 25 664), 1 block inland opposite the ticket kiosks. Ask the congenial staff for info about the island, free **maps,** and help with accommodations. Bike rentals €4.50 per day; mopeds from €10; cars from €35.

Bank: National Bank (☎22970 26 930), to the right of the waterfront quay, past the port police. **Currency exchange** and **24hr. ATM.** Open M-Th 8am-2:30pm, F 8am-2pm.

Police: ☎22970 22 100. Available 24hr. The **tourist police,** Leonardou Lada 11 (☎22970 27 777), are in the same courtyard as the police. Open daily 8am-8pm.

Pharmacy: 3 are along Aiakou. All open at 7:30am. 1 is always open until midnight.

Medical Center: ☎22970 22 222. 2km along the waterfront to the left of the ferries. The tourist police will arrange transport or refer you to doctors in town.

Telephones: OTE, Paleas Choras 6 (☎22970 22 399, assistance 161), up Aiakou to the right. Open M-Th 7:30am-1:30pm, F 7:30am-1pm.

Internet Access: Prestige Internet Cafe, at Sp. Rodi and Aiakou. €6 per hr. Open daily 10am-3am. Less-hip **Nesant Internet Cafe,** Aphaias 13 (☎22970 24 053), has computers with temperamental connections. €6 per hr. Open daily 9am-11pm.

Post Office: Kanari 6 (☎22970 22 398), in Pl. Ethnegersias, behind the bus station. **Poste Restante** available. Open M-F 7:30am-2pm. **Postal Code:** 18010.

▐ ACCOMMODATIONS

Though still pricey, rooms here are cheaper than those on any of the other Saronic Gulf islands, with high season doubles going for around €30-45. **Domatia** owners often meet the ferries; bargain and learn the location before committing. Surprisingly, the cheapest rooms are near the town center, so it pays to stick close to the port. Arriving midweek and avoiding the weekend Athenian flood may give you some bargaining power, but be prepared to dole out plenty of euros anyway.

Hotel Plaza, Kazatzaki 4 (☎/fax 22970 25 600), at the far left end of the waterfront when facing inland. Small, modestly furnished, shell-pink rooms. Prices vary according to amenities (A/C, TV, balconies). Book exchange available. Transportation schedules in the lobby. Singles €25-45; doubles €28-50. ❸

Hotel Avra (☎22970 22 303), at the far left end of the waterfront. Rooms have A/C, TV, phones, and baths; half have sea views from balconies. Note that a "triple" actually means "a double plus a cot." Singles €30; doubles €40; triples €50. ❸

Hotel Pavlou, Aeginitou 21 (☎22970 22 795), behind the church on the far right of the quay, facing inland, has comfortable rooms with A/C, fans, TV, phones, sinks, and balconies with a view of the domed church. Most rooms have baths. Payment required in advance. Singles €35; doubles €50; triples €60. ❸

Athina, on Telemonos, is run by the owners of Pavlou. Charming rooms with baths and fridges. Singles €35; doubles €40-47; triples €50. Discounts for longer stays. ❸

▐ ▐ FOOD AND NIGHTLIFE

Tavernas line P. Irioti along the right side of the harbor, though it can be hard to distinguish between the authentic and the tourist-centric. For a combination of the two, head to the strip of *ouzeria* at the far left of the harbor, past the bus stop. In general, the farther you stray from the ferry dock, the better the food will be. Tavernas around the fish market on Dimokratious (to the right when facing inland) are a good bet. Several **supermarkets** sit on P. Irioti. In an alley to the left, up Aikaou, **To Patitiri** ❷ welcomes guests into its courtyard for flavorful taverna fare served with unflagging courtesy. (☎22970 51 520. Entrees €4.50-8.50. Open 6pm-midnight.) If you can't eat another souvlaki, return to the staples—toast, baguettes, and ice cream—at **Yacht Club Panagakis** ❷, Dimokratious 20. Tire-sized crepes (€4.70-9) are made with fillings that range from chocolate and walnuts to turkey and mayo. (☎22970 26 654. Mixed drinks €7. Open daily 7am-late.) **Leo Confections ❶,** Aphaias 48, will delight your sweet tooth and challenge your pancreas with its gelato (€1) and pans of sugary pastries. (Open daily 8am-11pm.)

Past the church on the waterfront, the ◩**Inn on the Beach** bar sparkles with harbor lights. A chic crowd circulates between private tables, couches, and two well-stocked bars. Creamy frozen drinks (€10) and loud dance tracks let the good times roll. (☎22970 25 116. Occasional happy hour 3-4am. Cover €8; includes 1 beer. Open 10am-late.) Aegina's main dance club, **Ellinikon,** Toti Chatzi 10, down the street from Inn on the Beach, is a Gordian Knot of writhing limbs and swiveling hips that threatens to spill onto the street. (☎69361 11 213; www.ellinikon.net. Beer €4-5. Mixed drinks €6-7. Cover €8; includes 1 drink. Open daily 11pm-6am.)

◉ SIGHTS

Aegina Town's archaeological fame teeters on the last half-column of the **Temple of Apollo.** The 8m Doric column dates to 460 BC and stands on Kolonna Hill, ancient Aegina's acropolis. Excavation of the site, home to 10 consecutive early-Bronze Age (3000 BC) communities, is ongoing, and visitors can often watch the archaeologists in action. Today Byzantine-era cisterns and the foundations of prehistoric homes sit in stony silence alongside the monolithic column. Fortunately, the on-site **archaeological museum** speaks for them. Highlights include a magnificent early-Classical sphinx (460 BC), artifacts from the Temple of Aphaia, a statue of Hercules from the Temple of Apollo, and a small collection of Neolithic pottery. (☎22970 22 248. Museum and site open Tu-Su 8:30am-3pm. €3.) The underground church of **Faneromeni,** a 15min. walk inland just south of the town, contains a rare icon of the Virgin Mary. Locals say that the night before construction was to begin on a site above Faneromeni, the architect in charge had a vision instructing him to dig instead of build. Doing just that, he unearthed the icon. (Free. Dress modestly.)

▣ DAYTRIPS FROM AEGINA TOWN

MARATHONAS

7km south of Aegina Town. Buses run from Aegina Town to Marathonas (15min., 5 per day, €1). The schedule is irregular, though, so ask at the bus station.)

Nicer than Aegina Town and less peopled than Ag. Marina, the tranquil beach of **Marathonas** arcs gracefully along the island's western coast. Warm waters quietly lap the sandy shore, forming a shallow crescent with views of the Peloponnese. Approaching the town on the main road, veer right onto the unpaved road after the first stand of umbrellas to reach the beachfront. The seaside tables at family-owned **O Tassos ❷,** just before the church on the main road, let you wriggle your toes in the sand (or dip them in the water) as you eat. Homemade pastries, epic portions, and fresh vegetables from the family farm have earned this taverna well-deserved renown. (☎22970 24 040. Entrees €3-6.)

AGIOS NEKTARIOS

A 15min. bus ride from Aegina Town; ask to be let off here. Modest dress required.

Connected to a monastery and its patron saint's personal residence, this bronze and white church is massive. Built in honor of Agios Nektarios, the Orthodoxy's most recent saint, the compound is one of the largest places of worship in the Balkans. Several English-language publications (€5-25) available in the **bookshop** explain the details of Nektarios's life and work. The turn-off just after Agios Nektarios leads up to **Paleohora** (about 1km), the "town of 300 churches" and a former refuge from pirate invasions. It's worth making the short climb to explore the remaining 15 churches and take in the panorama from the top of the hill.

EASTERN AEGINA

Buses run from Aegina Town to Agia Marina (30min., 11 per day 6:30am-8pm, €1.50); for nearby sites, tell the driver your destination. You can buy bus tickets in Agia Marina at the kiosk in the plateia where the bus lets you off or in the adjacent tourist shop.

If interior Aegina's outdoor beauty starts to seem a little too, well, natural, head to **Agia Marina,** which will quell those cravings for kitschy beach bars and masses of sunburned bodies. The town has a beautiful but overcrowded beach and intense nightlife. If you don't want your partying hindered by bus schedules, consider staying at **Hotel Myrmidon ❷,** off Aphaias a few blocks before the bus stop. Rooms with A/C, baths, and fridges are supplemented by the hotel's courtyard with a swimming pool and lovely footbridge. (☎22970 32 691. www.hotel-myrmidon.gr. Singles €25; doubles €38; triples €44. 20% discount for *Let's Go* readers.) Pricey waterfront restaurants crammed with tourists crowd between the gyro and fast-food shops along Aphaias. For gourmet taverna fare, head back out of town and follow the signs uphill 1.5km to **O Kostas ❸.** Staple *mezedes*, *dolmades*, and *tzatziki* unite with their fancier cousins, caviar and escargot, on a barrel-lined terrace adorned with folk art. (☎22970 32 424. Entrees €6-12. Open Apr.-Nov. 9 daily; Nov. 10-Mar. F-Su.) **Restaurant Paradise ❷,** on the beach, gives diners a gorgeous view of the water from the tables under a cool canopy of trees. (☎22970 32 008. Open daily 10am-late.) **Crystal,** 200m out of town, with the water on your left, is a "snack bar" with a swimming pool, pool tables, and two outdoor patios. (☎22970 32 170. Mixed drinks €3-6. Open 10am-5am.) Trendy **Zorba's Castle** is a popular disco by the waterfront; turn right on Praxitelous two blocks past the bus stop, then follow the signs. (Open daily 11pm-late.) Summer dance club **Manos** is across from Crystal.

The ruins of the Doric **Temple of Aphaia** are 2km uphill from Agia Marina. Legend tells that this is where Aphaia, daughter of Zeus and Karme, was rendered invisible in a narrow escape from King Minos's unwelcome advances. Built in the 5th century BC, her temple still boasts a spectacular set of double-tiered columns that provided inspiration for the Parthenon. Evening visitors may be joined by peacocks from the surrounding hills. To get there, take the Agia Marina bus from Aegina Town and ask the driver to stop at the temple. (Open M-F 8:15am-7pm.)

POROS Πόρος

Poros is actually two islands separated by a shallow channel: larger Kalavria, which has preserved thick patches of woods and dark-watered beaches, and smaller Sferia, almost entirely geared toward tourists. The name "Poros" ("Passage") refers to the less-than-1km-wide strait, formed in 273 BC by a volcanic eruption, that separates the islands from the Peloponnese. In the 6th century BC, the Kalavrian League met in Poros to ward off hostile navies. They then ordered the construction of the Temple of Poseidon, by whose columns the great orator Demosthenes chose to commit suicide rather than face capture by the Macedonians.

Poros was sparsely populated until Greek refugees arrived from Turkey in the 1920s. Today, the island is hardly lacking for people—tourists have descended on its beaches, enjoying the many opportunities to soak up the sun.

POROS TOWN Πόρος   ☎ 22980

Beach shops and tavernas sprawl outward from the ferry dock in Poros Town like one long, tourist-snagging tentacle. While the waterfront offers an almost endless variety of places to spend money, actual sights and entertainment options are limited, even if you proceed inland. Up the hill, however, are a few quiet spots that provide lovely panoramas of Kalavrita's remaining wilderness. Look across the thin strait toward the mainland and you'll spy Galatas (Γαλατας), a working village with a grittier, more realistic feel than tourist-oriented Poros Town. Surrounded by beautiful farmland, Galatas gives the outdoors enthusiast a chance to uncover natural and ancient sights.

⌐ TRANSPORTATION. Ferries go to: Aegina (1hr., 3-5 per day, €5.50); Hydra (1hr., F-Su, €4.50); Piraeus (2½hr., 3-5 per day, €9.30) via Methana (30min., €3); Spetses (2½hr., F-Su, €7.20). You can buy tickets at **Family Tours Travel and Tourism Agency** (☎ 22980 23 743), across from the ferry dock, which also posts schedules and provides free **maps. Marinos Tours** (☎ 22980 23 423), 50m to the right of Family Tours facing inland, sells tickets for **Flying Dolphins,** which dock at the main landing in the center of town and go to: Ermioni (1hr., 3-5 per day, €11.30); Hydra (30min., 6-7 per day, €8.40); Piraeus (1¼hr., 8 per day, €16.50); Portoheli (1½hr., 1-2 per day, €14.40); Spetses (1hr., 2-3 per day, €13.50). The bus station (☎ 22980 22 480) is across from the car ferry dock, to the right of the water taxis. Buses leave from the main plateia (every 30min. 7am-11pm). The **green bus** goes to the Zoödochos Pigis Monastery (€1) via Askeli beach; the **white bus** goes to Russian Bay (€0.70) via Neorion. Buses leave Galatas for: Epidavros (3 per day); Methana (45min., 5 per day); Nafplion (3 per day); Trizina (20min., 3 per day, €1). **Water taxis** run 1km. from the main docks to Galatas (2min.; €0.50, after midnight €0.80). **Taxis** (☎ 22980 23 003) wait to the right of the ferry landing, facing inland, before the bus station. To rent mopeds (€7-12 per day) and bikes (€2.50), check out **Kosta's Bike Rental,** to the left of the waterfront past Diana Cinema. (☎ 22980 23 565. Open daily 9am-9pm.)

◼ 🛈 ORIENTATION AND PRACTICAL INFORMATION. Ferries and hydrofoils dock in the center of the waterfront, which traces the edge of the small island; the main plateia is to the right facing inland. **Galatas,** across the strait, also has food and lodgings. The **National Bank** is on the waterfront to the left of the docks, and has a **24hr. ATM.** (Open M-Th 8am-2:30pm, F 8am-2pm.) **Alpha Bank,** in the plateia to the right before the port police, also has a **24hr. ATM.** (Open M-Th 8am-2:30pm, F 8am-2pm.) **Suzi's Launderette Service** is left of the dock in an alley just past International Press. (Wash and dry €10. 2hr. service. Drop-off only. Open M-Sa 9am-2pm and 5-9pm.) To reach the **police** (☎ 22980 22 256) from the main plateia, turn right and head up the stairs to the left of Igloo Ice Cream. Then turn right at the church and continue downhill past Platanos Taverna. The **tourist police** (☎ 22980 22 462) are in the same \building. There is a **pharmacy** across from the ferry dock. (☎ 22980 25 523. Open daily 8:30am-2pm and 5-10pm.) **Galatas clinic** (☎ 22980 22 222) is open 24hr. **Emergencies,** including minor surgery, can be handled at the **Naval School;** contact the tourist police. The **OTF,** on the waterfront to the left of the National Bank, sells phone cards. (☎ 22980 22 199. Open M-F 7:30am-3pm.) It's easy to find **Internet access** along the waterfront. **Webworld Internet Cafe,** above Coconuts Bar, is in the plateia to the right of the ferry dock. (€6 per hr.; €1.50 min. Open daily 10:30am-3pm and 6:30-11pm.) **International Press,** left of ferry dock, also has Internet access. (€6 per hr.; €1.50 min. Open 8:30am-11pm.) The **post office** is in the first plateia to the right along the water. Specify Poros Trinzinias for **Poste Restante**. (☎22980 22 275. Open M-F 7:30am-2pm.) **Postal Code:** 18020.

⚑ᄃ ACCOMMODATIONS AND FOOD. The best deals in Poros Town are the **domatia**, advertised in almost every window; expect to pay €25-40 for a bare-bones single or double without A/C. Galatas's rooms are similar in both content and price. The knowledgeable staff at **Family Tours** can help you find a room in your price range and preferred location, and might even conduct negotiations with domatia owners. Those aching for luxury will find it at the superb, though pricey, **Hotel Seven Brothers ❹**, to the right of the ferry dock and inland past Alpha Bank. In a beautiful salmon-toned building, rooms are equipped with balconies, baths, TV, and A/C, encouraging guests to just lay back and relax. (☎22980 23 412; www.7brothers.gr. Singles €45-50; doubles €60-65. 20% discount for stays over 2 nights.) **Nikos Douros ❸** rents clean, simple rooms with fans, baths, fridges, coffeemakers, and TV; some have A/C. Facing inland, head left from the ferry dock, turn right after the supermarket, and then right on to Dimosthenous. (☎22980 22 633. Doubles €30-50; prices negotiable.) Across from the water-taxi landing in Galatas, **Saronis Hotel ❸** has basic rooms with A/C, TV, and baths. (☎22980 42 356. Doubles €35.) To find **Manos Pension ❸** in Galatas, walk left when you disembark the boat from Poros Town and go just past the playing field. Friendly owners Manos and Beatrix can tell you about the region, and the cozy rooms with private baths will make you feel at home. (☎/fax 22980 42 000. Doubles €30-35; triples €35-45.)

Restaurants with identical menus line the harbor and "charming" waiters try to coax tourists into €6 souvlakis. Prices and food don't vary much, so make your choice based on the view. Several **grocery stores** and **produce markets** cluster along the waterfront on either side of the dock; the best prices are found at the large supermarket up to the left, past the book market. Follow the alleyway to the right of the cinema and continue uphill about 50m to find **Taverna Karavolos ❷**, a family-run restaurant that rises above those lining the waterfront. The snails in tomato sauce (€4.50) are the house specialty. (☎22980 26 158. Entrees €4-8. Open daily 7:30pm-1am.) The traditional Greek dishes and seafood (from €5) at **Babi's Taverna ❷** (Ο Μπαμπης), in Galatas to the right of the water taxis, facing inland, are reasonably priced. (☎22980 23 629. Grilled entrees €4-7.) **Igloo Ice Cream ❶**, around the corner to the right of the post office, offers the uncommon single-scoop cone. (☎22980 25 515. €1.40 per scoop. Crepes from €2.20.) **Colona ❶**, just down the waterfront to the right of the dock, meets your fast-food needs in a nicer-than-average atmosphere. (☎22980 22 366. Pork gyro €1.50.)

◪ ⅃ SIGHTS AND ENTERTAINMENT. The two-room **Archaeological Museum,** in the middle of the waterfront, has tombstone shards and miniature ceramic works, though very few pieces actually come from Poros. (☎22980 23 276. Open Tu-Su 8:30am-3pm. Free.) For a view of the harbor, climb the stairs next to the library, one block inland, and follow the signs to the **clock tower.** Join the hordes of camera-toting tourists in time for sunset. The 18th-century **Monastery of Zoödochos Pigis** (Virgin of the Life-Giving Spring) is sequestered in an overgrown glade 6km from Poros Town. Greek naval leaders Miaoulis, Jobazis, and Apostolis met here to plan for the uprising of 1821. A tiny church features colorful frescoes and icons. Between the cafe and the small church is a fountain supplied by the ◪**life-giving spring.** Monks have been drinking these blessed curative waters since 200 BC, so fill up your water bottle and let the invigoration begin. To get to the monastery, take the green bus (20min., every hr. 7am-11pm, €0.90) from the stop by the main port. (Open daily in summer dawn-1pm and 4:30pm-dusk. Modest dress required.) To reach the 6th-century BC **Temple of Poseidon,** bear left at the fork in the road before the monastery—take a car or moped, as it's about 15km down the road. The ruins may be best appreciated by history buffs, but the view will inspire all.

Poros is not much of a party town, though there are a few options for a night out. Check billings by the bus station for the **Diana open-air cinema,** to the left of the ferry docks past Lela Tours, where you can catch American movies. (Shows 9 and 11pm. €6, children €4.) Young locals stop for an early frappé at **Centro Cafe Bar** before heading farther down the strip. (☎22980 26 745. Draft beer €2.50. Mixed drinks €7. Bar open 9pm-3am.) European tourists pack into tropical-themed **Malibu,** farther along the waterfront, which dominates the scene. (☎22980 25 267. Mixed drinks €5-7. Open daily Apr.-Oct. 9:30pm-3am.) Trendsters clad in the ubiquitous tight t-shirts meet at **Maskes Music Club,** about 100m past the church at the far right of the waterfront. Crowds sip drinks at either the ship-themed bar or the kindergarten-sized tables. Mirrored wall panels and medieval armor gleam under flashes of technicolor lights. (☎69723 98 513. Open daily 10pm-3am.)

■ ☀ **BEACHES AND OUTDOOR ACTIVITIES.** The white bus runs hourly to **Russian Bay,** where the Czar's ships docked in the early 19th century to aid the Greek rebels. Along the way it passes **Neorion,** with a sand beach, tavernas, and a watersports center, and **Love beach,** a secluded local favorite with blue-green waters and rocky sands. When Greeks were denied education during the Turkish occupation, the tiny island by the beach was a secret school. Ironically, it's now a popular spot for students to sunbathe while cutting class. On the way to the monastery, the green bus passes **Askeli,** which has tavernas, shops, and watersports.

In Galatas, if you follow the road heading left, facing inland from the ferry dock, about 3km out of town, you'll reach the enormous lemon grove of **Lemonodassos** (Lemon Forest). Follow the signs through the trees for about 1km to **Kardassi Taverna ❷** (☎22980 23 100) for a glass of fresh, tangy lemonade (€1.50) and a view of 38,000 lemon trees; take the first turn-off if you're in a car or moped, and the second if you're walking. In **Artemis,** 12km farther down the road, the ruins of a temple to the goddess are visible from underwater. **Trizina,** the mythical birthplace of the hero **Theseus,** is 15km from Galatas, in the other direction. Take a bus (20min., 3 per day, €1) or a taxi (about €7) from Galatas and follow the signs up the hill out of town. The lovely ◧**Devil's Bridge,** so named for the cloven-hoof footprint found in one of the rocks at the gorge's base, is just outside of town. The shady, lush area is a pleasant change of scenery from the rest of the island's scrubby growth, and the rushing water and cool mountain pools take the edge off the heat. Head uphill from the bus stop in the center of town and go right, following the paved road past olive trees and fragrant citrus groves. At the fork in the road, follow the dirt path heading left and uphill (right and downhill will take you to some meager ruins), passing the ancient **Tower of Diateichisma.** At the next fork, go right. Stay on the worn path and climb down to the bottom; ropes guide the way at the steepest points. Many sections of the path are closer to climbing than hiking, so be prepared to use both hands to clamber up and down the steep trail. Wear comfortable clothing and sturdy shoes with excellent traction; much of the path oozes with ankle-deep mud, so go closed-toed or get grimy.

HYDRA Ýδρα

Even bicycles are illegal on Hydra (EE-dthrah)—the steep streets only accommodate pedestrians, donkeys, and three garbage trucks, leaving the island blessedly free of mopeds but difficult to explore. Chosen in honor of the plentiful drinking water that once poured forth from the island's rocks, Hydra's name has long become ironic. An ancient fire rendered the soil fallow, the island barren, and the inhabitants completely dependent on the sea. Foreign exports flourished, and the impressive Venetian-built mansions of the merchants of Hydra's past dot the hills behind the harbor. During Ottoman rule, the Hydriots made a deal in return for the island's freedom, providing the Turkish navy with 30 young men every year. Hydriot youth thus learned the art of naval battle, a perk when, in 1821, Admiral Miaoulis and the Hydriot elite dedicated their fleet to the Greek revolution. Pride in this military courage persists today; the main thoroughfare is named for Miaoulis. In the 1920s, Pavlos Koundouriotis, grandson of one of the many Hydriot leaders in the War of Independence, took the national helm as president of Greece.

HYDRA TOWN Ύδρα ☎ 22980

Hydra Town's slippery, cobbled streets stretch like tendrils from the deep blues of the sea into the island's dusty hills. Art students and honeymooning couples mill around the crowded jumble of jewelry shops and cafes down by the port; away from this frenzy of foot traffic, donkeys and wheelbarrow-pushing fruit vendors share quiet, narrow alleys. As gorgeous as the summers are, the pink-blossomed spring and salt-winded fall give the town a low season like no other.

▐ TRANSPORTATION

Ferries: Hydreoniki Travel (☎ 22980 54 007) sells ferry and hydrofoil tickets; it's in the building with the gray door opposite the ferry dock. Open daily 9:30am-6:30pm. To: **Aegina** (2¼hr., 3 per week, €7); **Methana** (1½hr., 4 per week, €6.50); **Piraeus** (3¼hr., 4 per week, €10.40) via **Poros** (1hr., €4.50); **Spetses** (1hr., 4 per week, €5.10).

Flying Dolphins: To: **Ermioni** (30min., 3 per day, €7.10); **Piraeus** (1½hr., 8 per day, €19.40); **Poros** (30min., 5 per day, €8.40); **Portoheli** (45min., 4 per day, €11.30); **Spetses** (30min., 6 per day, €10).

Water Taxis: ☎ 22980 53 690. By the mule stand in the southeastern corner of the harbor, to the right of the docks. Each boat's price is divided among its passengers, so try to find a full one. Service to: **Agios Georgios** (€40); **Agios Nikolaos** (€50); **daytrip** around the island with beach stops (€120); **Hydra beach** (€50); **Kamina** (€8); **Mandraki beach** (€10); **Metohi** (€25); **Palamidas** (€15); **Vlihos** (€10).

▐▐ ORIENTATION AND PRACTICAL INFORMATION

Hydra Town's buildings form an amphitheater around the famously picturesque harbor, with the opening facing north. Yachts and fishing boats bob in the center, accompanied by water taxis in the southeastern corner. Ferries and Flying Dolphins dock on the eastern edge of the harbor. **Tombazi,** in the southeastern corner, runs inland from Alpha Bank past the Internet cafe and several restaurants. **Miaouli** heads into town from the center of the harbor. **Votsi,** in the southwestern corner just past the clock tower, goes inland past the OTE, police, and medical center. Although street names exist, don't be surprised if locals have never heard of them.

Banks: National Bank (☎ 22980 53 233), on the waterfront, has a **24hr. ATM.** Open M-Th 8am-2:30pm, F 8am-2pm. **Alpha Bank,** on the corner where Tombazi meets the waterfront, offers **currency exchange.** Open M-Th 8am-2:30pm, F 8am-2pm.

Laundromat: Yachting Center, in the southwestern corner of the harbor. Wash, dry, and fold (up to 4kg €12). Showers also available (€4). Open daily 8am-noon and 5-9pm.

Tourist Police: ☎ 22980 52 205. Follow Votsi inland and bear left at the fork. Look for the coat of arms, opposite the OTE. Open 24hr.

Pharmacy: On Tombazi, by the Amarillis Hotel. Open daily 9am-1:30pm and 5-8:30pm.

Hospital: ☎22980 53 150. Inland on Votsi, just past the tourist police. Look for a brown door with grates set in a stone wall. Open M-F 9am-1pm and by appointment. In an **emergency,** call the 24hr. nurse (☎22980 53 150) or the tourist police.

Telephones: OTE (☎22980 52 199), facing the tourist police. Open M-F 8am-1:30pm.

Internet Access: Flamingo Cafe (☎22980 53 485), 20m up Tombazi. €3 per 15min., €8 per hr. Open daily noon-3pm and 6-9:30pm. Also offered at the **Yachting Center** (see above). €3 per 15min., €7 per hr. Open daily 8am-noon and 5-9pm.

Post Office: ☎22980 52 262. 1 block inland in the alley just before Vicky's Shop. Open M-F 7:30am-2pm. **Postal Code:** 18040.

🛏 ACCOMMODATIONS

Hydra has the most expensive accommodations in the Saronic Gulf, and among the most expensive in Greece. Singles are almost nonexistent and doubles are at least €40 in high season. Without reservations, weekend accommodations are almost impossible to get; call ahead or arrive on a Thursday. Offers of **domatia** may be the cheapest option (rooms €40-60, in low season €30-40).

Pension Glaros (☎22980 53 679). Walk inland by Alpha Bank and turn left at the 1st small alley; look for the sign above the mini-mart. Spacious doubles with A/C, TV, fridges, and baths overlook a courtyard and a jungle of potted plants. Flower-shaped lights and tiled floors add a decorative touch. Singles €30-40; doubles €45-55. ❹

Pension Antonios (☎/fax 22980 53 227), on Spilios Charamis across from Christina's, a 5min. walk inland on Tombazi; follow the signs past Barba Dima's taverna. Small, orderly rooms furnished in dark oak have baths, fridges, and A/C. The cafe-style patio brims with flowers and stacks of magazines. Singles €30-40; doubles €50. ❹

Hotel Amarillis (☎22980 53 611; www.amarillishydra.gr). Walk inland on Tombazi and bear right at the fork. This welcoming, family-run hotel has brilliant blue rooms with fridges, TV, A/C, and baths. Singles €45-50; doubles €55-60; triples €60-65. MC/V. ❹

Hotel Mira Mare (☎22980 52 300; www.miramare.gr), at Mandraki beach. Low-lying, bunker-style rooms commandeer the tiny, sandy cove. The on-site restaurant and beach bar, packed all day long, mean many guests never leave the compound. Rooms 10m from the surf include TV, A/C, baths, and fridges. Complimentary water taxis shuttle guests from the ferry and into town. Doubles €60-125. Discounts for longer stays. ❺

🍴 FOOD

Most waterfront establishments have average food, burger-scarfing tourists, and prices that reflect the rent. A few restaurants, however, compensate for their more distant locations with superior fare at somewhat lower cost.

Barba Dima's (☎22980 52 967), a short walk up Tombazi, bearing right at Hotel Amarillis. Locals and Greek tourists crowd into this tiny orange taverna to savor Greek specialties. Entrees €3.50-6. Open daily 10:30am-1am. ❷

Christina's Taverna (☎22980 53 615), on Spilios Charamis to the right of Douskos, across from Pension Antonios. Most diners don't bother with the menu, ordering whatever Christina has in the kitchen. Entrees €4-10. Open daily 11am-11:30pm. ❷

Douskos (Taverna Xeri Elia; ☎22980 52 886), in a courtyard 5min. inland on Tombazi. The wide range of Greek dishes and nightly *bouzouki* music performances ensure you'll rub elbows with the local crowd. Entrees €4-9. Open daily 11am-1am. ❷

Artopoieion (☎22980 52 886), in the 1st alleyway to the left off Tombazi and next to Pension Glaros, has a small market and freshly baked goods (€1-2). The flaky *tiropita* is good for a breakfast on the go. Open daily 7am-10pm. ❶

Anemoni (☎22980 53 136), makes unusually large Greek pastries (€1.50-2). Bear left uphill from the OTE. Also serves fresh ice cream (€2 for 2 hefty scoops) and chocolatey little mouse-shaped cakes. Open daily 8am-11pm. ❶

⬤ SIGHTS

The **Tombazis Mansion,** on the southwestern side of the harbor, now houses a famous **Fine Arts School.** Climb the steep white stairs and look for paint-smeared artists on the balcony. The works of Hydriot painter Periklis Byzantios, who taught at the school, and those of his son, Constantinos, are displayed in the basement of the **Lazaros Koundouriotis Historical Mansion,** the yellow building high on the southwestern side of town. Head inland on Votsi to the fork in the road; bear right and follow the small blue signs. On the first and second floors, the museum showcases an extensive array of traditional Hydriot costumes and has a brilliant view of the town. (Open Tu-Su 10am-4pm. €4, students €2, children under 11 free.)

The white courtyard of the **Church of the Assumption of the Virgin Mary,** beneath the clock tower that dominates the port, offers sanctuary from the busy harbor just meters away. The small church is certainly worth a trip, if only for a peek at its gilded ceiling and a few blessed moments of peace and quiet. Built as a convent in 1648, it housed 18 nuns before becoming a monastery in 1770. It is now dedicated to the *kemesis*, the Ascension of Mary. The courtyard surrounds the tomb of Koundouriotis, his statue, and another of Miaoulis. Upstairs is the **Ecclesiastical Museum,** with brightly colored and beautifully preserved 18th- and 19th-century scenes from the life of Christ. (☎22980 54 071. Open Tu-Su 10am-5pm. €2. Modest dress required.) The **Historical Archives Museum,** to the left of the ferry building, houses old Hydriot costumes, census records, naval treasures, relics of the revolution, and a library. The heart of Admiral Andreas Miaoulis is preserved here in a silver and gold urn. (☎22980 52 355. Open daily 9am-4:30pm. €3, students €1.50.) An arduous 1½hr. hike will take you to the **Monastery of Profitis Ilias** and the **Convent of Efpraxia,** on the lower peak overlooking the harbor. To get there, take Miaouli up from the waterfront; signs point the way as you get higher. Wear sturdy shoes and don't forget to bring water. If they are available, monks may show you around the monastery, the prettier of the two structures. A donkey ride up the rocks costs about €30 and seems to wear out the donkey—inquire at the harbor. (Both open daily 9am-5pm. Modest dress required.) Hydra's celebration of Orthodox **Easter** is reputedly one of the best in the land—throngs of visitors crowd Kamini beach on Good Friday, where men of the church, in traditional attire like that in the museum, carry the Epitaph into the sea. If you're in Hydra Town during the **Miaoulia** (the last weekend in June), join the rest of the island in celebrating the feats of Admiral Andreas Miaoulis at an explosive mock battle held in the harbor.

▌ NIGHTLIFE

Hydra is more an island for lovers than swingers. Known internationally as a honeymoon destination, it doesn't have much crazy nightlife. You will, however, find a number of bars that play an eclectic sampling of music. The Hydriot pub crawl starts around 1am at **Amalour,** a short walk up Tombazi, and stumbles westward through the harbor. Just about everyone old enough to order a beer (€3) kicks off their night here to the ethnic rhythms that shake the shadowed orange walls. (☎09774 61 357. Mixed drinks €5-7. Open daily 8pm-late.) The younger set then heads to the **Pirate Bar,** in the southwestern corner of the harbor, where its members congregate around the lounge seats, listening to techno and American pop. (☎22980 52 711. Beer €4. Mixed drinks €6-8. Cafe open daily 10am; bar open 9pm-6am or later.) A small and trendy handful ducks into **Nautilus** on the western side of the harbor (beer €3; open daily 9pm-late), but most aim directly for **Saronicos**, farther down the western end, where live singers and guest DJs occasionally spice up the scene. (☎22980 52 589. Beer €4. Mixed drinks €7.50. Open daily 9pm-6am.)

◪ BEACHES

Many of the "beaches" by Hydra Town are actually industrial-looking cement slabs with a few aluminum ladders descending into the sea. Landings and stairs are cut into the rocks across the harbor from the ferry dock, providing access to a popular swimming area with cool, crystalline, and instantly deep waters. The first landing on the right is open to the public, but the next few are lined with cliffside cafes; daiquiris (€7) at **Hydronetta** are a delicious treat. (Open daily 11am-late.) A 15min. walk west along the coast takes you past the high-walled artists' colony of **Kamini**. Just beyond it is a tiny, pebbly beach where the drop to the sea is less severe and the water reasonably shallow. Walking another 20min. brings you to slightly more populous **Vlihos**, guarded by a regiment of Hawaiian-style beach umbrellas. Lively, overcrowded **Mandraki**, a coarse sand beach surrounded by the fortress-like Hotel Mira Mare, is east of town (30min. hike or 10min. water-taxi ride). This isn't the secluded beach of your dreams, but there are plenty of water toys to keep you busy. (Paddle boats €8 per hr., canoes €5 per hr., windsurfing €16 per hr., sailboats €6-16 per hr.) If you have the time and money, hire a water taxi to take you to the far side of the island, where there's room for you to find a quiet beach of your own; be sure to agree on a pickup time before getting out of the cab.

> **𝕽** **THE REAL DEAL.** In low season, the Saronic Gulf Islands can be a pleasant escape from the big city, and a quick, reasonable getaway for the budget traveler. But during high season, which lasts here from June until September, both crowds and prices skyrocket, making the islands painfully packed and devastatingly expensive. Although long ferry rides to farther islands may seem daunting, the cheaper prices and local ambience will often be worth the extra hours on the boat. If your schedule does not allow for such luxuries, then go to Spetses. Prices there are more negotiable in high season, and its beaches are cleaner, quieter, and far less crowded than those on neighboring Saronic Islands. —Laurie Schnidman

SPETSES Σπέτσες

A green cloak of pine trees and a gentle landscape distinguish Spetses from its rockier neighbors. Years ago, visitors were welcomed to the island by a cloying scent: the vegetation combined with an abundance of honey to produce a sweet, magical odor—hence the name "Spetses," derived from the Venetian term *spezzie* (aromatic or spiced). Perhaps the fact that there was something in the air explains Spetsiots' passionate devotion to their homeland. They played a crucial role in the War of Independence, fighting courageously and offering their fleet to the cause. Today Spetses is a summer-vacation haven, as the streets crowd in July and August with motorbikes and swimsuit-clad Athenians and Brits.

SPETSES TOWN   ☎22980

In the 1830s, 20,000 Greeks crowded into Spetses's tiny houses, sending the town sprawling up the hillsides. Due to pirate raids and Turkish invasions throughout the tumultuous 19th century, however, residents gradually moved onto the main-

land, contributing to Athens's population boom. Today, the 3500 islanders stick around Spetses Town, as close to the water as possible. Its 14km of thin, winding coast injects little pebble beaches into the procession of cafes and bars, turning the town into a round-the-clock beach club. Jet-setters dock in Spetses's Old Harbor, where the bars are somewhat closer together. Although topless sunbathing is technically illegal, Spetsiots know how to bend the rules.

TRANSPORTATION. Ferries depart 4 times per week to Aegina (3hr., €11), Methana (2½hr., €9), Piraeus (4hr., €14.30) via Hydra (1hr., €5.10), and Poros (2hr., €7.20). **Alasia Travel,** on the waterfront, sells tickets and posts schedules. (☎22980 74 098. Open daily 8am-9pm.) **Flying Dolphins** can be found inland from the dock, with service twice per day to Hydra (30min., €10), Piraeus (2hr., €25.50), and Poros (1hr., €13.50). From Ag. Mamas beach 500m down from the dock, **buses** go to Ag. Anargiri beach, and stop at Ag. Marina, Xokerizas on request, and Ag. Paraskevi (30min., 7 per day, €2). Buses leaving from the plateia by the Hotel Poseidono go to Anargirios College and Lioneri beach (30min.-1½hr., 18 per day, €1). **Taxis** wait in front of the travel agencies to the left of the ferry dock. Several rental agencies cluster past the Ag. Anargiri bus stop; veer right at the kiosk. Expect to pay €15-20 per day for a moped. Be aware, though, that from May-Oct. mopeds are prohibited on front roads after 2pm and from all roads 2am-7am. **Water taxis** (☎22980 72 072) dock inland off the ferry dock, and go to: Ag. Marina (€18); Anargiri or Paraskevi beach (€38); Costa (€13); Costoula (€15); daytrip around the island (€55); Emilianos (€25); Hinitsa (€22); Old Harbor (€12); Porto Heli (€30); Zogeria (€25). Prices are per boat. **Rent-a-Bike** (☎22980 74 143), on the street parallel to the harbor, unsurprisingly rents **bikes** (€4 per day).

⊞ ⁊ ORIENTATION AND PRACTICAL INFORMATION. The waterfront road runs from the left (facing inland) of the ferry dock to the **Old Harbor,** past **Agios Mamas** beach. To the right of the ferry dock restaurants and cafes line the way up the hill to **Plateia Bouboulina,** with a large playground. The first street inland parallel to the water, running to the left, has shops, pharmacies, and tavernas. The Old Harbor, home to bars and tavernas, is a 20min. walk, €12 water taxi, or €7 carriage ride from the town center; carriages wait by the bus stop.

Several **travel agencies** lie around the corner on the left side of the boat landing. The Kentros brothers at **Mimoza Travel** (☎22980 75 135) can help find accommodations and book Euroseas catamarans, and are a great source of info about the island. The **National Bank,** by the OTE, on the waterfront to the right of the ferry docks, has a **24hr. ATM.** (☎22980 72 286. Open M-Th 8am-2:30pm, F 8am-2pm.) The **police** are 150m before the Spetses Museum; follow signs to the museum. (☎22980 73 100. Open 24hr.) The **tourist police** (☎22980 73 744) are to the right of the ferry dock, by the National Bank, and share a building with the **OTE** (☎22980 72 199; open M-Th 7:30am-1:30pm, F 7:30am-1pm). The plateia has a **pharmacy** off the street running parallel to the waterfront. (☎22980 72 256. Open M-Sa 8:30am-1:30pm and 5-9pm, Su 10am-1:30pm and 5:30-9:30pm.) For the **first aid station,** dial ☎22980 72 472. (Open 24hr. for **emergencies.** Call the police to reach a doctor.) **1800 Cafe,** to the right of Hotel Poseidon, has **Internet access.** (☎22980 29 498. €6 per hr. Open daily 9am-2am.) The **post office** is left of the dock on the road parallel to the waterfront. (☎22980 72 228. Open M-F 7:30am-2pm.) **Postal Code:** 18050.

⌐⌐ ◖ ACCOMMODATIONS AND FOOD. Accommodations are expensive, with rooms scarcer and prices higher on weekends. A cornucopia of **domatia** opens up at both ends of town. For cheap rooms, head left toward the Spetses Museum; nicer accommodations cluster behind the House of Bouboulina. Dock hawks will pounce before you're halfway out of the ferry; bargain and pinpoint

LET'S HEAR IT FOR THE GIRL

In Greece's famously male-dominated society, the actions of women have long gone overlooked or under-rated. A rare exception to this rule is Laskarina Bouboulina, a woman who has earned a place, albeit an unofficial one, in the historical account of Greece's struggles against the Turks.

Intelligent, wealthy, and nationalistic, Bouboulina personally funded a defensive army, tricked the Turks into permitting the construction of her heavily armed battleship, and bravely commanded legions during the rebellion. She was the first to raise a Greek flag on Spetses in 1821, beginning the official rebellion against the Turkish occupiers, and she led an entire fleet of ships in the blockade and eventual victory at Nafplion.

Despite her invaluable contributions to the Greek struggle for independence, however, the Greek government did not initially honor her; rather, in 1825 it stripped her of any rewards given earlier in gratitude for her efforts. Although she has come to hold a cherished place in Greek history, to this day her official title remains the slightly derogatory "Lady Captain."

In an interesting twist of 19th-century international intrigue, it was actually the Russian monarchy that accorded this heroine her due respect. In 1816, before Bouboulina's involvement with the Greek struggle for

the location before committing. To find **Pension Theano** ❸, follow the signs for the Spetses Museum; it's parallel to the museum, to the right when facing inland. Spacious rooms have A/C, baths, and fridges. Angela and her husband wait at the docks when they have vacancies; if you call ahead, Angela will come to lead you through the unnamed streets. (☎ 22980 73 064. Singles €20-30; doubles €30-50.) The owners also run the gorgeous but pricier **Villa Christina Hotel** ❹, around the corner from the movie theater, inland from the ferry dock. Large rooms include A/C, baths, and fridges; some have kitchenettes, and all center on a courtyard covered in magenta bougainvillea. (☎ 22980 72 218. Singles €40; doubles €60-70; prices negotiable in low season.) **Hotel Klimis** ❹, on the waterfront, left of the ferry docks, is a short walk from the beach. Its rooms have baths, TV, balconies, and A/C. (☎ 22980 73 725. Breakfast €4.20-6.80. Singles €40-50; doubles €50-55; triples €70-80.)

Tavernas abound in this tiny town, but they tend to be expensive. You can economize by buying groceries at one of the many supermarkets. For the best seafood and the lowdown on town gossip, locals head to ▨**Bouboulina's** ❸, past Alasia Travel on the waterfront. Across from the fish market, it has first crack at the catch of the day. Char grilled octopus (€6) comes fresh out of the morning sea. (☎ 22980 73 033. Open daily 11am-1am.) **O Roussos** ❸, on the waterfront just before Ag. Mamas beach, has a similar menu but with a more touristy feel. In the afternoon, hawkers and musicians show off their wares between the tables. The *dolmades* (€3) are packed with flavor and rendered divine with a drizzle of lemon juice. (☎ 22980 72 212. Entrees €4-11. Open daily 11am-midnight.) **Politis** ❷, on the waterfront to the right of the ferry docks, serves decadent baklava (€3.50) and waffle breakfasts with bottomless cups of coffee (€6-7.50), a godsend for the under-caffeinated traveler. Butter-soaked croissant sandwiches (€3.50) and devilishly delicious dessert waffles (€6.50-8) make decadent snacks. (Open daily 8am-late.) **Quarter Pizza** ❷, in the plateia off the road running parallel to the water, is crowded with trendy teens smoking and eating gourmet pies. The pizzas (€6-10), cooked on a wood-fire stove, are available for take-out, delivery, or immediate consumption. (☎ 22980 72 027. Beer €2. Pasta €4-7. Open daily 11am-midnight.)

◪ **SIGHTS.** The creaking, crumbling **Spetses Museum** lurks off to the left, in the residential area of town. Follow the signs near the OTE and the National Bank; where the directions are unclear, stick to the larger road running left and inland. Enshrined in a 19th-century mansion once owned by Spetses's first governor, the collection includes traditional costumes, ancient maps, religious artifacts, and the remains of Laskarina Bouboulina. (☎22980 72 994. Open Tu-Su 8:30am-2:30pm. €3, students €2.) The **Monastery of Agios Nikolaos** stands above the old harbor, opposite a square of traditional mosaics. A plaque to the left of the entrance commemorates Napoleon's nephew, Paul Marie Bonaparte, who was preserved in a barrel of rum after he died in the War of Independence. The barrel was stored in a monastic cell here from 1827 to 1832. (Inconsistent hours. Modest dress required.)

📷📷 **ENTERTAINMENT AND NIGHTLIFE.** Spetses hosts many lively festivals, the best of which is the **Armada,** a mid-September celebration that reenacts Spetses's victory over the Turkish fleet early in the War of Independence. Islanders set off dramatic fireworks from a flimsy reconstructed Ottoman-style ship. The ship sinks soon after. Greeks, particularly Athenians, flood Spetses for this rowdy, memorable event; book accommodations early if you plan to join in.

Spetses's appeal lies mainly in its boisterous bar scene. A favorite vacation spot for restless youth, the island offers plenty of ways to pickle your liver. The bar crawl typically moves left, starting near the ferry docks and ending up in the Old Harbor. As much of the nightlife centers in the Old Harbor, save enough cash to hitch a carriage ride home in case you're too tipsy to tackle the 20min. stroll. On the road parallel to the water, the draw of 📷**Socrates's** €3.50 happy hour drinks (9:30pm-close) is a force to be reckoned with; you might not even make it to the Old Harbor after a few Malibu Beaches. The raunchy yet amusing truisms hanging above the bar get funnier with every drink. (☎22980 74 043. Open 7pm-3am.) Moving to the left, **Delfina Cafe,** at Ag. Mamas beach, intercepts those in transit between the harbors with its pulsing dance tunes. Grab a drink at a table (€4-6) or join the throngs of trendy teens jabbering on their cell phones on the sidewalk. (☎22980 75 051. Open M-Th, Su 9am-4am; F-Sa 9am-morning.) Continuing around the Old Harbor, **Diadromes** quickly reaches capacity after 12:30am, with live traditional music and an older crowd; not a spare seat remains in this oddly cafeteria-like bar. (☎22980 74 039. Mixed drinks €7. Open daily 12:30-4:30am.) You'll have to fight your way through the undulating crowds to the bar at **Brachera** and pray there won't be a fire—it gets so crowded after 1am that dancing is reduced to a rhythmic wiggle. (☎22980 73 581. Open M-Th, Su 10:30pm-5am; F-Sa 10:30pm-8am.) **Club Stavento,**

independence, the Turkish government tried to arrest her and claim her family fortune. Instead of despairing, the clever Bouboulina went to the Russian government for help, reminding them that her late husband had contributed his fleet to Russia during the earlier Turkish-Russian wars. Tsar Alexander agreed to protect her and her inheritance, arranging a successful meeting with the Sultan's mother to plead for her security.

The Russian government's respect for Bouboulina's actions grew during the course of the Greek's War of Independence. After her unceremonious murder due to an inter-family feud, the Russian government posthumously deemed Bouboulina "Admiral." The title stuck, and now even in Greece, Bouboulina is popularly known as "the only female admiral in Greek history." The Greek government, however, still never officially elevated her to this military status.

To learn more about Bouboulina, head to the 📷**House of Laskarina Bouboulina** by the park behind the National Bank and the OTE. Tours of her house provide a fascinating torrent of information about her life and belongings. Ticket proceeds go toward the house's restoration. ☎ *22980 72 416. Open for guided tours only; tours in English run every 1½hr. 10:30am-6pm. €5, students €3, children €1.*

blasting rhythmic dance music, is a few doors to the left. Up to 2000 people can pack inside the mod white room; fortunately, many choose to enjoy the excellent harbor view from the patio entrance. (☎22980 75 245. Cover €5; includes 1 drink.) At the farthest end of the Old Harbor waterfront, chic **Baltiza** plays the latest hits and classic mixes, and trendy Athenian guest DJs spin on weekends. (☎22980 29 456. Cover €7; includes 1 drink. Open daily midnight-6am.)

⌐ BEACHES. Spetses's warm waters are invitingly shallow. If you rent a moped, you can see all of the beaches on a 24km jaunt around the island, though the bus runs to many of them as well. Big sandy **Agii Anargiri,** across the island from Spetses Town, is the most popular beach, with a taverna and a host of watersports. (Waterskiing €15 per hr., canoes €10 per hr., windsurfing €12 per hr.) In the rear of the beach's sole restaurant are showers, changing rooms, and impeccable bathrooms. **Agia Paraskevi,** about 1km to the right when facing the sea, has the same blanket of pine trees and a sand and pebble surface without the accompanying hubbub. Midway along the bus route between Anargiri and Spetses Town is amazingly peaceful ▨**Xokerizas.** Pure white, smooth stones contrast with the bay's still, brightly colored waters. Hunks of watermelon from the nearby snack bar are big enough for two and make a perfect after-swim snack. Although it's easiest to take a moped there, the bus to Ag. Anargiri passes by the dusty road to the beach (10-15min. walk uphill); check with the driver about return times before you hop off.

EVIA AND THE SPORADES

 Stretching out into the azure depths of the Aegean, Evia and the Sporades are a mixture of natural, cultural, and archaeological treasures, topped off with a healthy dose of hedonism. Prominent Evia nudges the coast of Central Greece, stretching from Karystos in the south, through bustling Halkida, to the therapeutic springs of the northern villages. Beyond Evia, the Sporades arc across the sea to the north. Vibrant Skiathos has the liveliest reputation, flaunting her beach-ringed shores for summer travelers. Skopelos is widely known as one of the greenest islands in all of Greece, with Byzantine monuments and narrow streets sprinkled among the lush vegetation. Little Alonnisos harbors pristine wilderness crossed by hiking trails, while Skyros has successfully remained true to its old ways despite the demands of modern-day tourism. These islands have beckoned visitors to come bask on their sun-lit shores and trod their shaded forests since the earliest days of ancient Greece.

🕐 SUGGESTED ITINERARIES: EVIA AND THE SPORADES

THREE DAYS Use busy **Halkida** (p. 341) as a hub for exploring Evia, Greece's second-largest island. Soothe any burns incurred by a lazy afternoon on the famous beaches of **Eretria** (p. 346) by immersing yourself in **Aedipsos's** (p. 344) legendarily therapeutic hot springs.

ONE WEEK After a few days in Evia's (p. 341) towns, head for **Skopelos** (p. 355) and hike the green hills, where some say a fiery dragon met a brutal end. Finish by trekking through the gorgeous wilderness of **Alonnisos** (p. 359), a partially-inhabited island in the National Marine Park.

EVIA Εὔβοια

The second-largest island in Greece, with warm waters, forested highlands, archaeological treasures, charming villages, and therapeutic baths, Evia is synonymous with paradise to any pleasure-seeker. Its capital, Halkida, serves as a portal from the mainland into Evia, as a new suspension bridge allows visitors to traverse the Channel of Evripos with ease, though ferries also connect the island to Aedipsos, Marmari, and Karystos. Because of its proximity to Athens, floods of Greek vacationers arrive during the summer, but Evia effortlessly absorbs and delights the masses.

HALKIDA Χαλκίδα   ☎ 22210

Sprawling, Halkida, also known as "Chalkis," is the capital of Evia as well as its key transportation hub, connecting the island to the mainland. Bustling streets, lively plazas, and packs of young people keep the city at a continuous hum. The archaeological artifacts, nearby beaches, and urban vibe make Halkida the natural starting point to explore the more remote parts of the island.

📋 **TRANSPORTATION. Trains** go to Athens (1¼hr., 19 per day, €5). To get to the main part of Halkida from the train station (☎22210 22 386), cross the Old Bridge

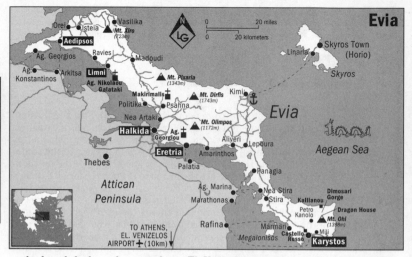

and take a left along the waterfront; El. Venizelou intersects it five blocks down. Halkida's hangar-like **bus terminal**, Favierou 28 (☎ 22210 22 640), is just off **Papanastasiou**, which intersects El. Venizelou. Heading out the front of the station, take a left, then a right, and then another left onto El. Venizelou, which leads to the waterfront. **Buses** travel to: Aedipsos (2½hr.; 12:30, 2:30pm; €9); Athens (1½hr.; 2 per hr. 5am-9pm; service reduced Sa-Su; €5.10); Karystos (3½hr.; 6am, 1, 5:40pm; €9); Kimi (1½hr., 9 per day 6am-8:15pm, €6.20); Limni (2hr.; 8:15am, 12:30, 5:15pm; €6). **Taxis** (☎ 22210 25 220) are located at the Old Bridge, Pl. Agios Nikolaos, El. Venizelou, and just outside the bus station. They run 24 hr.

■ ▐ **ORIENTATION AND PRACTICAL INFORMATION.** Halkida's main thoroughfare is **Eleftheriou Venizelou,** which runs perpendicular to the water and ends just before **Voudouri** (the waterfront promenade). Here, **Agios Goviou** runs off El. Venizelou to the left, behind and parallel to Voudouri and toward the Old Bridge; **Farmakidou** does the same, but to the right. **Avanton** goes behind Pl. Agios Nikolaos parallel to the water. The **Erippon Bridge,** or **Old Bridge,** connects Halkida to the mainland at the end of the waterfront and points west with Halkida at your back. Halkida also joins the mainland via the new **suspension bridge,** the connection for most ground transportation, on the city's southern edge.

The **port authority,** across the Old Bridge on Kostantinos Karamanlis, in the white building with blue shutters, dispenses info about the city. (☎ 22210 28 888. Open daily 24hr.) The **National Bank,** El. Venizelou 9, two blocks from the water, has a **24hr. ATM** and **currency exchange.** (Open M-Th 8am-2:30pm, F 8am-2pm.) Pl. Agios Nikolaos borders the waterfront and is home to the **public library** at the corner of Ant. Antoniou and M. Kakara. (Open M-F 7:30am-2:30pm, Sa 8:30am-2pm.) The **tourist police,** Arethousis 153 (☎ 22210 77 777), are available M-F 8am-2pm; their office is 25min. from the bottom of El. Venizelou, in the same building as the 24hr. **police** (☎ 22210 83 333). A **pharmacy** can be found at El. Venizelou 24. (Open M, W 8am-2pm, Tu, Th-F 8am-1:30pm and 6-9pm.) To get to the **hospital,** 48 Gazepi (☎ 22210 21 901), head up El. Venizelou away from the water and turn left onto Papanastasiou. Take the first right onto Kriezotou, then a left at the butcher shop; the hospital is 400m up the hill on the right. There is also a smaller emergency building by the museum. The **OTE** (☎ 22210 22 599) is at the intersection of El. Venizelou and Papanastasiou. For cheap, fast **Internet access,** go to **Surf on Net** between Hotel Kentrikon and John's Hotel on Ag. Goviou. (☎ 22210 24 867;

www.surfonnet.gr. €2.50 per hr., €1 9pm-6am. Open daily 24hr.) The **post office,** Karamourtzouniis 11, is the second left from the waterfront. **Poste Restante** and **Western Union** are available. (☎22210 22 211. Open M-F 7:30am-8pm.) **Postal Code:** 34100.

◪ ACCOMMODATIONS. Most hotels are of the €75-per-night variety, catering to business travelers or Athenian families. At the Old Bridge end of Ag. Goviou, **John's Hotel ❹,** Ag. Goviou 9, has rooms with plush carpeting, baths, A/C, phones, and balconies. Enjoy breakfast (€5) in the attractive dining area. (☎22210 24 996. Singles €45; doubles €60. AmEx/MC/V.) **Hotel Kentrikon ❸,** Ag. Goviou 5, by John's Hotel, has inviting rooms with TV, phones, and a shared fridge; some have A/C and private baths. The Canadian-Greek proprietor, George Grontis, can help you make sense of the city, and offers plenty of amenities—from a sewing kit to a bigger towel—to make your stay more comfortable. (☎22210 22 375; www.geocities.com/hotel_kentrikon. Breakfast included. Singles €30-40; doubles €35-49. Cash only.) To find **Hotel Hara ❸,** Karoni 21, bear right after crossing the Old Bridge, then take the stairs across from the fun-park. Simple, unadorned rooms come with A/C, TV, tiled baths, and balconies with a view of Halkida. (☎22210 76 305. Breakfast included. Singles €35-40; doubles €50-55; triples €60-65.)

◪◪ FOOD AND NIGHTLIFE. Many restaurants in Halkida can bust your budget, though the fresh, quality seafood available along the waterfront may justify the cost. Several bakeries hide on streets near Ag. Nikolaos and fast-food joints are bunched at the base of El. Venizelou and by the Old Bridge on the waterfront. Small supermarkets, like **Dia Discount,** Favierou 14, cluster around Papanastasiou off of El. Venizelou. (☎22210 78 960. Open M-F 8:30am-9pm, Su 8:30am-6pm.) Deliciously named pizzas like the Inferno and the Erotica (tomato, cheese, salami, pepper; €8) emerge from the oven at **Il Posto Ristorante ❷,** a smart Italian eatery on the waterfront offering an impressive selection of pastas (€6-10) and intriguing entrees including ostrich. (☎22210 73 841. Open daily noon-2am. MC/V.) For reasonably priced seafood, go around the corner from the OTE to **Tsaf ❷,** Papanastasiou 3, near the bus station. Dine on a wide variety of fresh fish (€26-55 per kg) at their outdoor tables as soft Greek music plays inside. (☎22210 80 070. Entrees €3-12. Open Tu-Su 1pm-1am. Cash only.) The shelves of fresh-baked cookies, cakes, and confections (€8 per kg) at **Cookie Land ❶,** Avanton 59, across from the shopping plaza, will satiate the sweetest tooth.

Halkida's thriving nightlife is not to be missed. Follow the party-hungry hordes to one of the bars on the waterfront for laughs and drinks. (Beer €4-5.50. Mixed drinks €6-8. Laughs free.) **Yacht Cafe** (☎22210 27 881), one block north of the Hotel Paliria, and **Jam,** Voudouri 10 (☎22210 22 157), near the Old Bridge, are two popular venues that blast pop music to their outdoor patios and are still both packed around 1am. (Both open 8:30am-late.) If you feel like burning off those beer calories, hop a cab (€4) to the suspension bridge and shake what your mama gave ya on the dance floor of **Gaz** or **Mist** (mixed drinks €3-6; cover €10).

◪◪ SIGHTS AND BEACHES. Palm-lined **Voudouri,** Halkida's waterfront promenade, makes for a splendid evening stroll. The hike up to the **Fortress of Carababa,** on the other side of the Old Bridge, has a great view of the city, ocean, and surrounding hills. From Halkida, cross the Old Bridge and head right. Once you reach the fun-park, take the stairs on the left, which lead all the way up the hill to the fortress. Built by Turks in 1688 to protect Halkida from Greek and Venetian marauders, the fortress is extremely well preserved. You can picnic, climb on the walls, and check out the lookout posts where Turks once guarded the city. (Open daily 8am-10pm. Free.) The **Archaeological Museum,** El. Venizelou 13, is full of finds from the Neolithic, Classical, and Roman eras. It has an impressive display of statues, pottery, and shimmering gold laurels—some pieces date as far back as 11,000 BC. (☎22210 76 131. Open Tu-Su 8:30am-3pm. €2, under 18 free.) The white **Church of**

Agios Nikolaos, at the far end of Pl. Nikolaos from the waterfront, has a vast collection of iconography and vaulted arches. (☎ 22210 24 815. Open daily 7am-1pm and 4:30-8pm. Modest dress required.) For a picnic or afternoon stroll, visit **Park Farou,** near the lighthouse, at the northern tip of the city by the beaches.

When you're in the mood to take a dip or soak in the rays, one of the best options is to catch the bus to **Eretria,** known for its beautiful beaches. Otherwise, Halkida has several beaches that attract bronzed sunbathers. The locals flock to the clean **Kourenti** and **Papathanasiou** beaches, both a 15min. walk from the Old Bridge. Follow Avanton four blocks after it becomes G. Chaina, then turn left onto Delagrammatika, which will take you to Kourenti. Walk across the parking lot and along Ethnikis Symfiliosis to reach Papathanasiou. For a beach closer to the center of town, head to **Souvana,** tucked away in a cove off of Farmakidou.

AEDIPSOS Λουτρά Αιδηψού ☎ 22260

For thousands of years, the health-afflicted and pleasure-seeking alike have come to be submerged in Aedipsos's hot springs. Greek mythology attributes the existence of the springs to a gift of health and strength from Athena to Hercules; affirmation of the waters' healing power can be found in texts by Plutarch and Aristotle. Today, the springs still flow, luring travelers from around the globe to this quaint, seaside town. Let your troubles melt away as you experience Aedipsos's laid-back atmosphere, palm-lined promenade, and serene sunsets.

▐▀▌ TRANSPORTATION AND PRACTICAL INFORMATION. Buses leave from the bus station (☎ 22260 22 250) at Thermopotamou 7 for Athens (3hr., 3 per day 7:45am-5:30pm, €10.10) and Halkida (3hr., 5:45am, €10). Alternatively, get to the mainland by catching a **ferry** to Arkitsa (45min.; M-Th 16 per day 5:30am-10pm, F-Sa 20 per day 5:30am-10pm, Su 22 per day 5:30am-10:30pm, service reduced in low season; €2.10) from the ferry terminal on 28 Oktovriou (☎ 22260 23 330; www.edipsouferries.gr). **Taxis** wait just outside the ferry terminal or call ☎ 22260 23 280. The main street, **28 Oktovriou,** runs along the waterfront. **Thermopotamou,** an extra-wide street, intersects 28 Oktovriou three blocks past the small boat dock when exiting the ferry terminal and heading right. Tourists can find helpful information at **City Hall,** 25 Martiou (☎ 22260 23 270). The **National Bank** can be reached by walking right onto 28 Oktovriou when exiting the ferry landing, then turning left onto Omirou, one street after Thermopotamou; it **exchanges currency** and has a **24hr. ATM.** (Open M-Th 8am-2:30pm, F 8am-2pm.) Find the **police** station (☎ 22260 23 333) on 28 Oktovriou, just across from the boat dock; follow the side alley next to the ice cream shop, then go up the stairs. A **pharmacy,** Omirou 12, can be found near the National Bank. (☎ 22260 24 000. Open M, W 8am-1:30pm, Tu, Th-F 8am-1:30pm and 5:30-9pm.) Follow 28 Oktovriou to the turn in the road where it becomes Posidonos, and turn left onto 25 Martiou to reach the **post office** on the left. (☎ 22260 22 252. Open M-F 7:30am-2pm.) **Postal Code:** 34300.

▐▐▐ ACCOMMODATIONS AND FOOD. There are a few reasonable accommodations in Aedipsos; many can be found on Ermou and its sidestreets. **Hotel Istiaia ❸,** 28 Oktovriou 2, the yellow, red, and brick building at the corner of 25 Martiou, is an excellent choice. Hospitable management offers attractive rooms with A/C, TV, fridges, baths, and balconies, many with views of the water. (☎ 22260 22 049. Breakfast included. Singles €25-35; doubles €35-60. MC/V.) To get to **Hotel Alex ❸,** Ermou 39, exit the ferry landing from the left end of the parking lot with the water at your back, then walk straight for one block and make a left onto Ermou. The immaculate rooms have baths, A/C, TV, fridges, balconies, and phones. A striking bar is downstairs. (☎ 22260 22 127. Singles €25-35; doubles €30-50.) Just past the National Bank, **Hotel Areti ❸,** Omirou 11, will greet you with a lovely lobby and the same amenities as Hotel Alex. (Singles €30-40; doubles €40-50. Cash only.)

Eateries and cafes border the waterfront, but most only serve drinks before 8pm. **To Steki ❸**, 28 Oktovriou 14, by the Omirou intersection, is recognizable by its blue canopy. It serves fresh seafood and traditional Greek fare to a steady crowd (☎22260 60 069. Souvlaki plate €6. Fish dishes €8-12. Open daily 9am-6pm and 8pm-1am. Cash only.) The mouthwatering pizzas at **La Luna ❷**, 28 Oktovriou 36, near the boat dock, have a buttery crust sublime enough to thrill even the most jaded pizza fans. (☎22260 69 446. Medium pizzas €8-9.50. Crepes €4-6. Open daily 9am-1am.) After a dip in the hot springs, cool off with an ice-cream cone (€1.20) at **Dodoni ❶**, next to La Luna (☎22260 60 226. Open daily 8am-2am.)

🅖 **SIGHTS.** Since antiquity, Aedipsos's main appeal has been and continues to be its **hot springs.** While the springs are often recommended by doctors to those suffering from arthritis, respiratory difficulties, and other ailments, even the perfectly healthy can come to relax and rejuvenate. If you'd rather not empty out your checkbook for a day of hydrotherapy treatments (€17-83) at the Thermae Sylla Spa in the Wellness Hotel, you can easily experience the springs for next to nothing. Heading right on 28 Oktovriou from the ferry terminal, follow the road along the waterfront as it turns into Posidonos. After you pass the Wellness Hotel, look for the stairs heading to the beaches on your right. The largest concentration of hot springs emptying into the sea is here at **Thermatiki beach**, where there are changing stations and a €1.60 entrance fee. (Open 8am-6pm.) You can also feel the warmth from the springs for free on the beaches on either side of Thermatiki.

LIMNI Λίμνη ☎22270

A 2hr. bus ride north from Halkida brings you to the wooded cove of Limni, where friendly villagers are curious about the rare outsider who stumbles upon their home. Fortunately for those looking to experience the unadulterated essence of Greece, this tranquil fishing village has remained a secret from most travelers. The splendid scenery and gorgeous surroundings, with dazzling sunsets and serene, star-filled nights, will stun you. Limni's **Folklore Museum**, Anagnosti Goviou 7, to the right of the plateia facing inland, houses an extensive collection of historic items from Limni households, including a mosaic floor and formal dining room. Ring the bell and ask the curator for a map of Limni that provides a history of the town. (☎22270 31 335. €2. Open M-Sa 9am-1pm, Su 10:30am-1pm.)

There are two hotels to choose from. **Plaza Hotel ❹**, to the left of the main plateia, has comfortable rooms with beautifully tiled floors, TV, A/C, phones, private baths, and wooden furniture. (☎22270 31 235. Singles and doubles €40-50.) For lower rates with fewer amenities, visit **Hotel Limni ❷**, to the far right facing inland, past the small boat dock. It has unadorned rooms with baths. (☎22270 31 316. Singles €16; doubles €30; triples €35. Rates reduced in low season.) For **domatia**, call ☎22210 31 640. (Singles €35; doubles €40.) After a morning museum trip, stop by **To Neon ❶** (☎22270 31 262), next to the National Bank, for a scoop of vanilla with honey swirls (€1) or your choice of sweet Greek confections. Before dinner, walk out on the pier to watch the sunset bend across the distant mountains. From 10pm to midnight, the waterfront restaurants serving nightly specials pick up steam. Try **Avra ❷**, just past the plateia, for a traditional Greek meal and friendly service. (☎22270 31 479. Entrees €5-8. Open daily mid-Feb. to mid-Dec. 8:30am-11pm. MC/V.) **Remetzo ❶**, to the left of the plateia, serves cold drinks (€1.30-5) all day and into the night (☎22270 32 510. Open daily 6am-3am or later.)

Buses in Limni stop at the main intersection; ask before you get off when the next one comes or inquire inside To Neon. Though Limni is on the Halkida-Aedipsos Springs bus line (2½hr., 2 per day, €9), the road to Aedipsos Springs has been closed to buses indefinitely due to treacherous conditions from yearly rain seasons. A **taxi** (€20) will help you make the 30km trip to northern Evia, and can be found up the road to Aedipsos and Athens, or by calling ☎ 22270 32 000. (Available 8am-1pm and 5-8:30pm.) Facing inland, turn right on the waterfront for **Plateia Eleftherios Antistasis,** the main plateia.

ERETRIA Ερέτρια ☎ 22290

Formerly one of ancient Evia's most important cities, modern Eretria is a popular destination for both beach-bound tourists and vacationing Athenians. A short bus ride from Halkida, the town provides an enticing escape from the big city and an ideal location to work on your tan. Beyond the happening waterfront, it is impossible not to be reminded of Eretria's past; exposed and magnificently preserved archaeological excavations are scattered throughout the streets.

▐▀ ▞ TRANSPORTATION AND PRACTICAL INFORMATION. Buses stop in Eretria (30min., 1-2 per hr. 6am-9pm, €1.50) on their way from Halkida to Amarinthos, Karystos, and Kimi. Tickets are sold out of the cafe that doubles as the bus station; consult the bus schedule posted outside for details about trips out of Eretria. Buses stop three blocks inland from and parallel to the waterfront on Filosofou Menedimou. The booth directly opposite the dock in the main port (☎ 22290 62 492) sells tickets for **ferries** to Skala Oropos (20min., 2 per hr. 5:45am-10:45pm, €1.40), where you can catch a bus to Athens (35min., every hr. 5:40am-8:45pm, €3.30). **Taxis** (☎ 22290 62 500) wait across from the ferry port and respond to calls 24hr. Archaiou Theatrou, the main street, is home to nearly everything you'll need in Eretria. Facing the street from the bus station, turn left; the main port and the waterfront are to the right, and the museum and House of the Mosaics to the left. The **National Bank** on the first corner toward Archaiou Theatrou from the bus station has a **24hr. ATM** and **exchanges currency.** (☎ 22290 62 203. Open M-Th 8:45am-1:45pm, F 8:45am-1:30pm.) The **pharmacy** is across the street from the bank on the right. (☎ 22290 62 775. Open daily 8:30am-2pm and 5-10pm.) The **OTE,** Archaiou Theatrou 17, is in the beige building just before the traffic circle on the right. (☎ 22290 60 399. Open M-F 7:30am-2pm.) To reach the **post office,** start toward Archaiou Theatrou from the bus station and take the first right, then turn left after one block. (☎ 22290 62 333. Open M-F 7:30am-2pm.) **Postal Code:** 34008.

▐▛▐▌ ACCOMMODATIONS AND FOOD. If you want to spend the night in Eretria, try **Pension Diamanto ❸,** on Archaiou Theatrou, past the traffic circle and on the left. If no one is at reception, visit the small store next door. The lightly colored rooms have TV, A/C, fridges, and baths; most have balconies with waterfront views. (☎ 22290 62 214. Singles €30; doubles €35; triples €40. Discounts for extended stays.) There are plenty of cheap fast-food options around the traffic circle, and several waterfront tavernas prepare delectable dishes at reasonable prices. **Remetzo ❷,** just before Pension Diamanto on the left, serves traditional favorites (moussaka €5.50), fresh seafood (calamari €6), and heaping salads (€3-5). Their delicious bread (included in the €1 per person cover charge) is more of a *bruschetta,* toasted and topped with fresh tomatoes, olives, and olive oil. (☎ 22290 61 446. Open daily 11am-1am. MC/V.) Those interested in stocking up on cheap snacks can head to **Atlantik Supermarket,** on the corner across the street from and to the right of the bus station. (☎ 22290 60 010. Open M-Sa 8am-9pm, Su 8am-2pm.)

▐▛▐▙ SIGHTS AND BEACHES. The courtyard of the **Archaeological Museum,** at the inland end of Archaiou Theatrou, is packed with marble statues, friezes, and pillars. Inside, several large black figure *amphorae* stand in the middle of the room, surrounded by display cases that contain ancient tools, statues, and figurines found throughout the city. The exhibits are in Greek and French, but you can buy an English guidebook (€6). Museum admission also lets you into the **House of the Mosaics,** a 10min. walk from the museum; trade your passport for the keys at the front desk. Coming out of the museum, head left to the main road and bear right for three blocks, turning left at the intersection of Antioxou Theodikou. The 4th-century BC mosaics are incredibly well-preserved, and are among the oldest in existence. Flicking the square switches will light up the floors behind the glass, making the exhibit significantly more illuminating. (☎22210 62 206. Open Tu-Su 8:30am-3pm. €2, students and children free.) On the other side of the main road from the museum is a large excavated portion of **ancient Eretria**, where visitors can peer at the ancient **theater** and the ruined foundations of the city's residential section. Unfortunately, the site is often locked behind a fence to protect the remains.

The best and most heavily populated **beaches** are along Archaiou Theatrou, past the tavernas and cafes. To escape the crowds, continue along as the waterfront bends to the left—the sandy beach stretches out for another 1.5km.

KARYSTOS Κάρυστος ☎22240

A sanctuary between the mountains and the sea, Karystos blooms in the summer. The nature-lovers and party fiends drawn here owe thanks to Otto (p. 60), Greece's first king, who ordered German architect Bierbach to lay out the modern city's streets in a grid. As a result, it's incredibly easy to find your way from one attraction to the next, though your eyes may be distracted by the sparkling panorama. The view of Marmari's bay more than compensates for the uneventful bus ride from Halkida; wind-generators stand guard over the sea's glittering waves.

◪◪ TRANSPORTATION AND PRACTICAL INFORMATION. The bus station (☎22240 26 303) is on I. Kotsika, which runs along the right side of the city hall. Take the **bus** to Marmari, where you can catch the **ferry** to Rafina (1hr.; M-Th 5-6 per day, F 7 per day, Sa 8 per day, Su 9 per day; €5.10). Buses from Karystos also go to Athens (4hr.; M-Sa 8am, Su 1:45pm; €7); Halkida (3hr.; M-F 5:30am, 1:45pm, Sa 6am, Su 1:45pm; €9); Marmari (20min.; M-Th 4-5 per day, F 5 per day, Sa 5 per day; €1.20); Nea Stira port (1hr.: M-F 5:30, 8am, 1:45pm; Sa 6, 8am; Su 1:45pm: €2.50) via Stira (45min., €2.20). **Taxis** (☎22240 26 500) are in the plateia 6am-2am. If you need after-hours service, get a driver's cell phone number. For comprehensive travel advice, head to ◪**South Evia Tours,** on the left side of the central plateia with your back to the sea, through Kosmos, where Nikos and his sister Popi can help with everything from **renting a car** (€30-45 per day), to planning local excursions, to booking accommodations. They'll also provide you with a free regional **map.** (☎22240 26 200. Open daily 9am-midnight.) The **Alpha Bank,** on Sachtouri, off the main plateia, **exchanges currency** and has a **24hr. ATM.** (☎22240 22 989. Open M-Th 8am-2:30pm, F 8am-2pm.) To find the 24hr. **police** (☎22240 22 262), turn into the small alley just past the bank and climb the stairs at the end of the block on the left. A **pharmacy** is at the head of the central plateia. (☎22240 23 505. Open M, Th, Sa 8am-1:30pm, Tu-W, F, Su 8am-1:30pm and 5-8:30pm.) The **OTE,** El. Amerikis 73, is to the right off I. Kotsika one block above the central plateia. (☎22240 22 399. Open M-Th 7:30am-2pm, F 7:30am-1:30pm.) **Internet access** is available for €3.50 per hr. at the sole computer in **Cafe Kalypso,** on the left side of Kriezotou, 200m past the *bourtzi.* (☎22240 25 960. Open daily 10am-midnight.) The **post office** is on Th. Kotsika, one street over from I. Kotsika, to the left facing inland, just above El. Amerikis. (☎22240 22 229. Open M-F 7:30am-2pm.) **Postal Code:** 34001.

◪◪ ACCOMMODATIONS AND FOOD. Hotels in Karystos start at €35 for singles and €45 for doubles during the summer, but South Evia Tours can help you find a cheaper **domatia** (€25-35). Follow the waterfront toward the *bourtzi,* turn left one block past the Archaeological Museum, and make the first right to find ◪**Rooms to Let ❹,** Sachtouri 42. Converted from a charming yellow home, the bright, well-decorated rooms burst with character and surround a courtyard garden. They come with TV, A/C, fridges, baths, and small kitchens. (☎22240 22 071. Laundry available. Singles, doubles, and triples €30-40.) **Hotel Als ❸,** in a convenient location on the corner of Th. Kotsika and the waterfront, rents spacious, tiled rooms that include TV, A/C, private baths, and balconies with a sea view. (☎ 22240 22 202. Singles €35; doubles €45; triples €60.) Opposite the beginning of Kremala beach at the corner of Kriezotou and Odysseos, **Hotel Galaxy ❸** is run by a hospitable English-speaking couple and has rooms with smooth earth-colored tiling, TV, A/C, baths, and balconies. Breakfast (€5) is served in the large downstairs lobby. (☎ 22240 22 600. Singles €35; doubles €45; triples €55. MC/V.)

The restaurants that line the waterfront have everything from fresh seafood to burgers and fries. ▨**Cavo Doro ❷**, in the alleyway left of the central plateia facing inland, just past the back entrance to South Evia Tours, serves deliciously light moussaka (€5) and vegetarian options (stuffed tomatoes; €4) to a small, loyal crowd of locals. The gregarious English-speaking staff will happily translate the menu and show you the dishes as they cook in the kitchen. (☎ 22240 22 326. Entrees €4-6. Open daily 11am-1am.) Popular **Marinos ❷** (Μαρινος), Kriezotou 98, on the waterfront to the right as you face the water, has a variety of seafood entrees like octopus with vinegar (€9) and traditional Greek-village dishes. (☎ 22240 24 126. Entrees €5-9. Open daily noon-5pm and 8pm-midnight. MC/V.)

◪ **SIGHTS.** Peek into one of the holes in the back of the **bourtzi**, on the left side of the waterfront. In the 11th century, the peep-hole was used to pour boiling oil on attackers. Today theatergoers invade the fort in August, as they crowd in to watch student productions; inquire at South Evia Tours about schedules. The **Archaeological Museum,** Kriezotou 58, is housed in the same building as the public library, just past the *bourtzi*. The exhibit includes a small collection of marble statues and inscribed tablets, along with artifacts from the *drakospita* of Stira and Mt. Ohi. (☎ 22240 25 661. Open Tu-Su 8:30am-3pm. €2, seniors €1, students free. Su free.) Located north of Karystos in the Old Town (accessible by taxi) are the **Montofoli Estate's** wine cellar and rolling vineyards. Built over the ancient site of the church of St. Marcus, the grounds also occasionally hold concerts. Guided tours of the estate occur every Wednesday and Saturday at 7pm from July to September. Inquire at South Evia Tours or call ☎ 22240 25 951 for more info.

◪ **NIGHTLIFE.** Start your evening at one of the bars that line Karystos's moonlit beaches. **Kohili Beach Bar** (Κοχυλι), on Psili beach, past Hotel Karystion, serves beer (€3.50-5) and mixed drinks (€5) throughout the day and night. (☎ 22240 24 350. Open daily 10am-late.) **Archipelagos** (Αρχιπελαγος), on Kremala beach at the right edge of the waterfront facing the sea, taps into the island atmosphere with wooden bars, ferns, hanging lanterns, and seating by the sand. A DJ spins nightly, and there is live music once a week. (☎ 22240 25 040. Beer €3. Mixed drinks €4.50-5.50. Open daily 8am-4am.) For a more active scene, try **Ostria Bar** (Οστρια), farther inland from Archipelagos, about a block past the fork and Hotel Galaxy coming from the plateia, on the right. Funky instrumental, house, and pop music fills the blue black-lit interior. (☎ 22240 25 678. Beer €4. Mixed drinks €5-7. Open May-Oct. 24hr.) Mostly locals party at **Chroma** (Χρομα), on the right side of the central plateia facing inland, where the drinks flow and the music thumps until the early morning. Colorful outdoor couches turn its section of the plateia into an upbeat lounge. (☎ 22240 23 085. Beer €4. Mixed drinks €6. Open 6pm-3am.)

◪ **DAYTRIPS FROM KARYSTOS.** The widely varied terrain of the Karystos region offers an abundance of spectacular daytrips and hikes for outdoor enthusiasts. The 4hr. hike up **Mount Ohi** (elev. 1398m) is awe-inspiring, with arresting vistas of southern Evia and the sea. Though May or early June have optimal climate and conditions for hiking, the mountain path is well marked and safe year-round. Be cautious, however, around rocky parts of the trails and in windy weather, and hike with a partner if you can. To get to the trailhead, take a car or taxi (€5) to the village of **Mili,** or walk the 3km distance yourself by following Aiolou, one block east of the plateia, out of town. A set of mysterious monolithic **columns** appears on the side of the trail about 45min. into the hike, where they were abandoned at the site of an ancient Roman marble quarry. The haunting ruins of the ◙**Dragon House** (*drakospita*) sit on the summit, which you will reach after another 3¼hr. of walking. Believed to date back to Neolithic times, the ruins represent a major ancient achievement—each stone, weighing several tons, was transported up the mountainside. The building may have served as a temple dedicated to Zeus and Hera, and local legend holds that it was inhabited by a dragon who terrorized the region. You can spend the night at the **Mount Ohi Lodge ❶** (elev. 1050m), about 3hr. from the bottom and 1hr. from Profitis Ilias Peak at the top, and catch the heavenly sunrise from the summit the next morning. (Lodge also accessible by four-wheel-drive. Contact Mr. N. Gkika ☎22240 26 417. €7 per person.)

Running from the back of Mt. Ohi to **Kallianou** (41km north of Karystos) and the sea, the **Dimosari Gorge** is a stunning example of natural architecture. Clear, cold water cascades down its length, shaded by the lush forest. The 3½-4hr. trail that takes you through the gorge is best accessed by car or taxi. A taxi to Petro Kanolo (a good starting point), an arranged pick-up at Kallianou, and a return trip to Karystos costs around €70. For true mountaineers, a combined ◙**Mount Ohi-Dimosari Gorge hike,** from Mili to Profitis Ilias Peak and down the northern side of Mt. Ohi through the gorge to Kallianou, can be completed in 8½-10hr. It makes more sense, though, to break the trek up into two days, staying the night at the Mt. Ohi Lodge. South Evia Tours organizes 6-7 group hikes along this trail per summer (€20); ask at Karystos's central plateia for schedules and info. **Klimataria Taverna ❷,** at the Mt. Ohi end of the gorge, is a convenient place to stop for a bite. Its owners also rent **rooms ❶** (€13) above the taverna. (☎22240 71 300. Open daily noon-midnight.) On the slopes above Karystos is the majestic **Castello Rosso** (a.k.a. "Kokkino Kastro" or "Red Castle"), named for the blood spilled there in the many battles for its control. From Mili, it's a 20min. hike up the hill on the left and across the stone bridge. Other interesting sites in the region include the **Roman aqueduct,** past the Red Castle, and the **stone church** and **cave** at **Agia Triada,** accessible by a 2hr. hike from **Nikasi,** where the bus (€1.30) can drop you off.

For a taste of the open sea, **day cruises** are available throughout the Evoikos Gulf, to the Petali Islands, and to the other Cyclades. The trip to the Petali Islands stops at private islands with villas built by Picasso and former Greek King Constantinos. The tour (€30-35), which can be booked through South Evia Tours, leaves from the waterfront at 10am and returns at 5pm.

SPORADES Σποράδες

SKIATHOS Σκιάθος

The most popular tourist destination in the Sporades, Skiathos offers everything from gorgeous beaches and majestic forests to serene boat cruises and vibrant nightlife. The waterfront is a busy mix of tavernas, tourist agencies, and rental shops, while side streets reveal an abundance of trinket stores and creperies that entice passersby into making a quick stop. Beyond Skiathos Town, the island's raw beauty is evident in the forests and beaches.

SKIATHOS TOWN Σκιάθος   ☎24270

Arriving in Skiathos Town can be overwhelming; crowds of shouting hawkers greet ferries at the landing, advertising domatia and waving flyers. Cafes and tavernas line every street, intermingling with tacky beach shops and expensive boutiques. But it isn't long before Skiathos draws you in (and it's not because of the

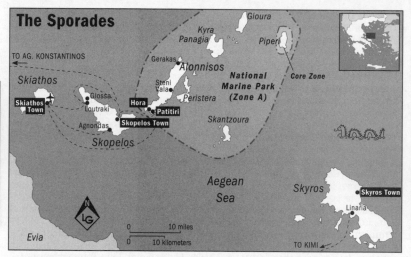

The Sporades

TO AG. KONSTANTINOS

Skiathos

Skiathos Town

Glossa
Loutraki
Agnondas
Skopelos
Skopelos Town
Hora
Patitiri
Steni Vala
Peristera
Gerakas
Alonnisos

Gioura
Kyra Panagia
Piperi

National Marine Park (Zone A)

Core Zone

Skantzoura

Aegean Sea

Skyros
Skyros Town
Linaria

Evia

0   10 miles
0   10 kilometers

TO KIMI

much-hyped 2-for-1 specials). Welcoming bars full of talkative travelers, warm taverna owners who invite you to dine with them, and an almost palpable spunky spirit quickly make you a part of the lively and constant buzz.

⌷ TRANSPORTATION

Flights: Olympic Airways (☎24270 22 229), at the airport. Open M-F 8am-4pm. Taxis (€3) get you from the harbor to the airport. 1 flight per day goes to **Athens** (50min.).

Ferries: Buy tickets at the office on the corner of Papadiamantis opposite the ferry landing (☎24270 22 209). Go to: **Alonnisos** (1¾hr., 2 per week, €9); **Glossa** (30min., 10:45am, €4); **Skopelos** (1hr.; M-Tu, Th-Su 6:40pm, W 10:45am; €6.20); **Volos** (2½hr.: M 12:15, 10:15pm; Tu, Th-Su 12:15am, 9:15pm; W 4:05pm: €13.10). Tickets to **Agios Konstantinos** (3hr.: M-Th 5:40pm; F 10:30pm; Sa 2:10pm; Su 10am, 6:50pm: €23.20) must be bought at the travel agency **Papathimas Alekos** (☎24270 22 204), by Alpha Bank.

Flying Dolphins: ☎24270 22 018. Buy tickets in the same office as the ferry tickets. To: **Agios Konstantinos** (1¼hr.: M-F, Su 8:20am, 5:20pm; Sa 8:20, 11:35am: €23.20); **Alonnisos** (40min., 5 per day 10:45am-9pm, €15); **Glossa** (15min., 4 per day 10:45am-9pm, €6.30); **Skopelos** (25min., 5 per day 10:45am-9pm, €10.30); **Thessaloniki** (3¼hr.; M-F, Su 8:30pm, Sa 2:35pm; €35.30); **Volos** (1¼hr., 3 per day 7:30am-5:45pm, €22).

Buses: Facing inland, turn right and follow the waterfront until the road continues left to the airport and branches right to the club strip. Continue left and walk 1 block to the **bus stop** on the corner. The bus to **Koukounaries beach** (30min.; every 15-20min. 7:15am-1am; €1.40, after midnight €1.75) makes stops at southern beaches. Heading outbound, sit on the driver's side for the best view. When returning, stop #4, on the **acropolis** hill, will likely be closest to your hotel or domatia. Follow the street downhill to where it intersects with the end of Papadiamantis and leads to the waterfront. A schedule is available at the information kiosk and is posted at most stops along the route.

Taxis: ☎24270 24 461. Line up along the waterfront 24hr.

Car and Moped Rental: Companies like **Avis** (☎24270 21 458) and **Heliotropio** (☎24270 22 430) are located along the waterfront and include insurance in the rental price. Mopeds €15-20 per day. Cars from €35 per day.

Charter Boats: From the Old Port. Circuits go around the island (€15) and stop at **Lalaria** and **Castro beaches.** Boats also run to **Tsougria** (€8) and **Skopelos** and **Alonnisos** (€20), among others. The boatmen along the Old Port have more info.

✈ 🛈 ORIENTATION AND PRACTICAL INFORMATION

Skiathos's waterfront is more or less an L shape; the **bourtzi**, the small tree-covered peninsula at its corner, divides the Old Port from the New Port. Facing inland in front of the Bourtzi, the **New Port** runs to the right and is the location of the ferry dock, rental agencies, tavernas, cafes, and tourist shops. The **Old Port** is perpendicular to the New Port and to the left of the Bourtzi. **Papadiamantis,** Skiathos Town's mostly pedestrian thoroughfare, overflows with cafe-bars, souvenir shops, and clothing stores; it intersects the main waterfront across from the ferry dock. Farther inland, **Evangelistra** (just before the post office) intersects Papadiamantis and connects it to **Polytechniou,** or "Bar Street," running parallel to Papadiamantis on the left. On the far right of the waterfront facing inland, the road splits. The branch that continues left passes the bus stop on its way to the airport and then follows the island's southern coast to **Koukounaries beach.** The **club strip** is before the bus stop on the right fork of the split road. Most of the shops and hotels along the waterfront and Papadiamantis give out a free **map** called "Skymap." Less-detailed maps (€1.50) of Skiathos are available at the info kiosk near the ferry landing.

Bank: National Bank (☎ 24270 22 400), midway up Papadiamantis on the left side, **exchanges currency** and has an **ATM.** Open M-Th 8am-2:30pm, F 8am-2pm.

Laundromat: Miele Laundry. From Papadiamantis, turn right onto the side street opposite the National Bank. Wash €7. Dry €3. Open daily 8am-10pm.

Police: ☎ 24270 21 111. Upstairs, on the left of Papadiamantis, just past where the road forks around a public water spout. Open 24hr. The **tourist police** (☎ 24270 23 172) are in small white building on the right side of Papadiamantis, by the school and opposite the police. Open daily May-Oct. 8am-9pm; in winter 7am-2:30pm.

Pharmacies: Several pharmacies line Papadiamantis. The one across from the National Bank (☎ 24270 24 515) is open daily 9am-2pm and 5pm-midnight.

Hospital: ☎ 24270 22 040. On the acropolis hill behind Skiathos Town. Open 24hr.

Telephones: OTE, ☎ 24270 22 399. On Papadiamantis, past the post office on the right. Open M-Th 7:30am-1:30pm, F 7:30am-1pm.

Internet Access: Internet Zone Cafe, Evangelistra 28 (☎ 24270 22 767), to the right off Papadiamantis. €3 per hr. Open daily 10:30am-1am. **Sixth Element,** G. Panora 15 (☎ 24270 24 032), next to the laundromat. €4.50 per hr. Open daily 9am-12:30am.

Post Office: ☎ 24270 22 011. On the right at the intersection of Papadiamantis and Evangelistra. Offers **Poste Restante.** Open M-F 7:30am-2pm. **Postal Code:** 37002.

🏠 ACCOMMODATIONS AND CAMPING

It's smart to make reservations for July and August, as tour groups book rooms a year in advance. Dock hawks meet the ferry, promoting **domatia,** which are generally the best deal in town; let them compete for you and be sure to bargain. Doubles run €20-30 in spring and fall; €25-50 in summer. The **Rooms to Let office** in the port's wooden kiosk has lists of available rooms. (☎ 24270 22 990. Open daily 9am-10:30pm.) In August, if you haven't already made reservations, forget about finding a room, much less a cheap one, and forgo sleep and party the night away.

Australia Hotel (☎ 24270 22 488). Turn right onto Evangelistra off Papadiamantis; it's in the 1st building alley to the left. Away from the bustle of town, Australia has rooms with A/C, TV, baths, fridges, and balconies. Ring the bell outside for service. Singles €20-40; doubles €25-50; triples €30-60. Discounts for extended stays. ❷

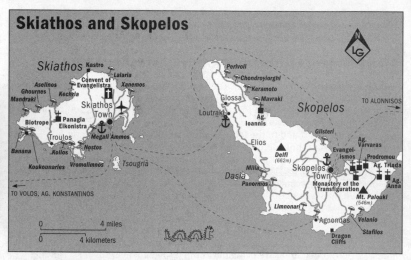

Skiathos and Skopelos

Pension Nikolas (May-Sept. ☎24270 23 062, Oct.-Apr. 23940 32 756.) Follow the left fork on Papadiamantis past McDonald's; it's on the right, just before Polytechniou and Kirki bar. Within stumbling distance of the bar strip, Nikolas's rooms have TV, fridges, baths, and balconies. A/C €5. Singles €30-50; doubles €35-60; triples €42-70. ❸

Pension Lazou (☎24270 22 324), on the hill overlooking the Old Port. Walk along the Old Port as it bends to the left, and climb the stairs at the very end. Has 12 uniquely furnished rooms with A/C, fridges, and baths. Some overlook the waterfront, but the best view is from the roof-top deck. Quiet hours 3-6pm and 11pm-9am. Call before arrival. Doubles €30-55; triples €45-65. Singles may be offered in low season. ❸

Camping Koukounaries (☎24270 49 250), on the bus route to Koukounaries, just before stop #23. Close to Koukounaries and Mandraki beach. Mini-mart on site. €7 per person, €3 per tent, tent rental €5.50, €3 per car. ❶

🍴 FOOD

Skiathan restaurants accommodate a wide range of tastes and budgets. Greek tavernas abound, but Italian restaurants and other ethnic cuisines are also available. Not surprisingly, though, more exotic food tends to be pricey; back-alley souvlaki stands and tiny tavernas off the main strip feed locals and broke backpackers.

Hellinikon (☎24270 23 225), left around the corner from Piccolo. Fish (€10) and lamb *kleftiko* (€7.50) are meticulously prepared and receive rave reviews. Nightly live music in the outdoor seating area. Open daily 11am-3pm and 6pm-late. AmEx/MC/V. ❸

Crepes Krepali (☎24270 23 840), up Papadiamantis on the right, at the next corner past the post office. Sweet crepes (€3-4.50) ooze with your preferred indulgence, from Nutella and white chocolate to piping hot caramel and bananas. Also has waffles, ice cream, and savory crepes. Save €0.50 by ordering take-out. Open 24hr. ❷

Piccolo (☎24270 22 780). From the Old Port waterfront, take the stairs on the right across from the cannon and flag, walk past the church, and turn right. Set in a romantic plateia, Piccolo serves ambrosial meals in a charming atmosphere. The cooks are committed to using only fresh ingredients and put a Greek spin on many Italian classics. Salads €5.50-6. Pizzas €7.50-9. Open daily May-Oct. 6:30pm-12:30am. ❷

To Bourtzi (☎24270 21 832), the only cafe on the Bourtzi peninsula, offers an unparalleled view of the sea and surrounding islands from a spot quietly removed from the glitz of Papadiamantis. Drinks and snacks only. Frappés €4.50. Open daily 8am-1:30am. ❷

👁 SIGHTS

Author Alexandros Papadiamantis's tiny 140-year-old house, set back off Papadiamantis about 1½ blocks inland, now serves as the **Papadiamantis Museum,** housing his few possessions. The exhibit honors the 19th-century realist, who was one of Greece's best-loved prose writers. Information and short stories are available in English. (Open Tu-Su 9:30am-1:30pm and 5-8:30pm. €1.) Ten kilometers from Skiathos Town on the northern coast of the island, accessible by private vehicle or by boat, are the unimpressive ruins of the island's **kastro.** In its heyday, the 16th-century walled castle was a refuge from marauding pirates. You can reach the **Skiathos Dog Shelter** (see **Dog's Best Friend**) and the neighboring **Monastery of the Panagia Eikonistra** or **Kounistra** by either hiking or driving. From bus stop #18, they are located near the top of the large hill, about 4km along the road. Follow the signs to the monastery. Panagia Eikonistra marks the spot where an old monk discovered a **miracle-working icon** of the Virgin Mary hanging from a tree, emitting light. Today the icon is in the **Cathedral of the Three Hierarchs,** up the steps from the Old Port, and is escorted back to the monastery every November 20 during the **Presentation of the Virgin.** People visit the monastery in search of oil from the church's lamp, which is said to have healing power. The **Convent of Evangelistra,** 4km north of Skiathos Town on the slopes of Karaflitzanaka, is where the first Greek national flag (a white cross on a blue background) was raised in 1807.

🏖 BEACHES

The most notable sights on the island are its many gorgeous **beaches.** The best of them, along the southern coast, are accessible by bus. Those looking for a more varied experience can consider taking a **charter boat** from the Old Port for a day-long excursion around the island (€15) or to the other Sporades (€20). The cruise around Skiathos stops at the island's *kastro* and at the small but picturesque **Lalaria** beach, reachable only by boat. A single paved road runs along the southern coast of Skiathos, between Skiathos Town and the most famous beach, **Koukounaries.** The bus makes many stops along the road, mostly at

GIVING BACK

DOG'S BEST FRIEND

Traveling in Greece, you've probably noticed the stray-dog population that roams almost every city's streets; you may have even been followed. The people of Skiathos, though, decided to take action about this pervasive problem, founding the Skiathos Dog Shelter to benefit both the island and the dogs.

Accepting canines of all breeds and in all sorts of conditions, the committed staff at the shelter works year-round to provide medical treatment and housing for the strays. They search both in Greece and abroad for permanent owners, and with the help of Danish, British, and German programs, the shelter has been vastly successful. According to Helen Bozas, the manager, in 2003 they were able to find homes for 320 pups. Still, the influx is constant, and, in its busiest months, the shelter can receive up to 14 dogs per day.

Volunteers—both locals and travelers—are eagerly welcomed to come in and play with the dogs or take them on walks. If you show up with treats from the supermarket, you'll be greeted with affectionate, slobbery kisses (from the pups, of course).

The Skiathos Dog Shelter is located about 4km up the hill on the road that intersects the main drag at bus stop #18. ☎24270 49 214; www.skiathosdogshelter.com. Arrive between 9am and 2pm to walk the dogs.

other beaches; a list of the stops is available at the bus station in Skiathos and at Koukounaries (stop #26). Soft sand curves between blue waters and the deep pines of the **Biotrope,** a protected forest area. Koukounaries is the island's most popular and activity-centric beach—expect crowds in July and August. The full slate of water sports includes kayaking (€6 per hr.), water skiing (€20 per 10min.), parasailing (€35 for 1 person, €50 for 2), banana boating (€8 per 10min.), and wind surfing (€15 per hr.). Showers, bathrooms, chairs with umbrellas (€8 per set per day), and bars also pepper the beach. For the best sunset views on the island, head to **Banana** and **Little Banana** (stop #26) at the end of the road up the hill across from the bus stop; signs lead the way. To get to curvy Little Banana from Banana, walk around the rocks on the right as you face the sea. Amusing in a middle-school sort of way, Little Banana is a predominantly **nude beach.** Down the street from stop #13 headed toward #14, follow the road on the left to **Vromolimnos,** where the staff at **Porto Paradiso** serves mixed drinks (€4-6.50) and milkshakes (€5-6) to cool off the crowds. (☎24270 49 257. Sandwiches €3.50-4.50. Open daily 10am-10pm.)

The bus also stops at other beaches, including **Megali Ammos** (stop #5), **Nostos** (stop #12), and **Kolios** (stop #14), though they tend to be crowded because of their proximity to the bus route. From the later stops, a 30min. walk through a pine forest brings you to the northern beaches, where winds are stronger and beach umbrellas less prominent. **Mandraki,** one of the better options, is up a sandy road from stop #23. To steer clear of the bus route altogether, a 45min. walk north of town past the airport will get you to **Xanemos,** frequented primarily by locals.

■ NIGHTLIFE

There is no shortage of nightlife on Skiathos, which designates the entire strip on the far right of the waterfront for nightclubs, and has great bars just above the Old Port and at the beginning of Polytechniou. At the bars, expect to pay €3-5 for beer, €5-7 for mixed drinks, and sometimes a €3-5 cover on very popular Saturday nights. Pillows serve as chairs on the hill outside lively **Rock and Roll Bar,** in the Old Port up the stairs across from the cannon and flag pole, which serves mixed and frozen drinks (€6-9) to hits from the 70s, 80s, and 90s. (☎24270 22 944. Half-priced drinks 7-9pm. Beer €4-5. Open daily May 1-Oct. 16 7pm-3am.) **Kentavros,** off Papadiamantis to the right beyond the Papadiamantis Museum, has been playing everything from British pop to world soul since 1978. (☎24270 22 980. Beer €2.50-4. Mixed drinks €5-6.50. Open daily 9:30pm-3:30am.) Turn left on Evangelistra from Papadiamantis to reach the Polytechniou bars. **Spartacus,** bursting with personality, is one of the oldest bars on the island and attracts a crazy young Scandinavian and British crowd. There are frequent themed evenings like "14 Beers Around the World Night" and contests where you can drink to win a free t-shirt. (2-for-1 9pm-midnight. Beer €2-4. Mixed drinks €5-7. Open daily 9pm-late.) The nearby wild English pub **Kazbar,** with darts and foosball, plays live music beginning at 11pm. (☎24270 21 781. Beer €3-4.50. Mixed drinks €4-5. Open daily 8pm-late.)

From October to May, Skiathos Town is a ghost town; by July it's hard to imagine anything being closed. Partiers stay out until dawn at the disco-bars that line the **club strip** on the right edge of the harbor, facing inland; things kick into gear around 11pm. While there is no cover, beer costs about €5-6, mixed drinks €8, and soft drinks €4, so you might want to pre-game elsewhere. Popular **Kahlua** is the big fish in the club strip's large, diverse pond, flaunting multiple red-lit bars playing an eclectic mix of international pop music. (☎69456 61 199. Open daily 10pm-late.) In the land of ubiquitous techno syncopation, the hip-hop and R&B classics at popular **Remezzo,** near the start of the strip, are a rare treat—though even these tunes can't escape being remixed. (☎24270 24 024. Happy hour 11:30pm-1:30am. Open 9:30pm-late.) Farther on, **Lobby** is elegant and sophisticated, with clean white decor that highlights the colorfully lit indoor dance floor. (☎69722 68 858. Open daily 9pm-late.) Following the illuminated steps behind Lobby will bring you to **Rodon** (Ροδον), an upscale, live-Greek-music club and the only non-disco on the strip. (Beer €8. Mixed drinks €10. Open daily 12:30am-late.) The **Harley Davidson** bar that rounds out the end of the strip caters to motorcycle enthusiasts and anyone who likes bikers. (☎24270 24 556. Open daily 10am-3am.) For more subdued entertainment, open-air **Cinema Attikon**, on Papadiamantis just before the bank and on the right, plays Hollywood's latest releases in English with Greek subtitles. (☎24270 22 352. Admission €7. Shows 9, 11:30pm.) During the summer, there are concerts at the bourtzi. Ask at the information kiosk in the harbor for schedules.

SKOPELOS Σκόπελος

Skopelos sits between the whirlwind of Skiathos and the largely untouched wilderness of Alonnisos, incorporating the best elements of both. Hikes and moped rides through shady forests lead to numerous monasteries, bright beaches, and white cliffs that drop into a sparkling-blue sea. By night, the town's waterfront strip closes to traffic, crowds swarm the streets, and a number of low-key bars and a few quality clubs keep partiers drunk and happy.

SKOPELOS TOWN Σκόπελος   ☎24240

Skopelos Town winds up the steep hills above the harbor. Close to the waterfront, the plethora of moped rental shops, cafes, and tavernas contrasts with the narrow streets farther up the hill, which twist among whitewashed buildings, beautiful churches, and precariously perched cafes.

▛ TRANSPORTATION

In good weather, ferries and Flying Dolphins dock at the landing on the left side of the harbor, facing inland, or at the ferry dock in the center of the waterfront. When it's windy, they go to **Agnondas,** 8km south of town. If you find that you have landed in Agnondas, wait for the bus at the end of the dock, which will take you to Skopelos Town (€1). In Skopelos Town, you can buy tickets for ferries and Flying Dolphins at the **ticket office** (☎24240 22 767), across from the central ferry landing. Ask where your ferry departs, as the walk between the central dock and the left side of the harbor is long enough that you can miss your boat if you pick the wrong location. **Ferries** run to Alonnisos (30min., 2 per week, €5), Skiathos (1hr., 8pm, €6.20), and Volos (3½hr., 8pm, €17). **Lemonis Travel** (☎24270 22 363; open daily 9am-10:30pm), to the right along the waterfront, facing inland, organizes ferry service to Agios Konstantinos (4hr.: M 4:30pm; Tu-Th 4:20pm; F 9:20pm; Sa 1pm; Su 9am, 4:45, 6:25pm: €32) and Thessaloniki (5½hr., Sa 12:45am, €19.40). **Flying Dolphins** head to: Agios Konstantinos (2hr.: M-F, Su 7:25am, 4:20pm; Sa 7:25, 10:35am: €32); Alonnisos (20min.; 5 per day M-F, Su 11:45am-10:05pm, Sa 10:35am-10:05pm; €8); Glossa (30min., 4 per day 6:30am-4:45pm, €8.40); Skiathos (45min., 6 per day 6:30am-6:45pm, €10.30); Thessaloniki (2½hr.; M-F, Su 9:30am, Sa 3:35pm; €35.30); Volos (2hr.; M 4 per day 6:30am-4:45pm, Tu-Su 3 per day 6:30am-4:45pm; €28.20). The bus stop is left of the ferry dock facing inland, on the left side of the road. From here, 13 **buses** per day go between Skopelos Town and Agnondas (€1), Milia (2.30), Panormos (€1.70), and Stafilos (€1). Eight per day head to Glossa (€3.20) and Loutraki (€3.20). Check the schedules at the Skopelos Town stop and be sure to note return times. **Taxis** (☎69448 43 738) are available 7am-2am at the waterfront next to the bus stop and can be called 24hr. **Motor Tours,** along the waterfront to the left (facing inland), past the port, rents **mopeds** (€10-14 per day) and **cars** (from

€30 per day), and has the largest fleet and the best prices. (☎24240 22 986. Open Apr.-Oct. 8:30am-10pm; return vehicle during store hours.)

⚡❓ ORIENTATION AND PRACTICAL INFORMATION

Tourist agencies, tavernas, and cafes line the waterfront. **Platanos**, a small plateia packed with souvlaki and gyro restaurants, is up the street, opposite the dock, with the small monument on your right and playground on your left. **Galatsaniou** darts upward about 200m to the right of the dock facing inland between Nostos and Aktaion restaurants. The staff at **Thalpos Travel Agency**, 5m to the right of Galatsaniou on the waterfront, provides **maps** and can help with everything from transportation to catching octopi. (☎24240 22 947. Open May-Oct. M-Sa 9am-2pm; Nov.-Apr. available by phone.) **National Bank**, on the right side of the waterfront, facing inland, has a **24hr. ATM** and **exchanges currency**. (☎24240 22 691. Open M-F 8am-2pm.) **Self Service Laundry** is just off the back right corner of Pl. Platanos coming from the water. (☎24240 23 123. Cold wash €9, warm wash €12, dry €6. Open daily 9am-1:30pm and 5:30-8pm.) The **police** (☎24240 22 295), above the National Bank, are available 24hr. The **pharmacy** in Pl. Platanos is across from the laundromat. (☎24240 22 252. Open daily 9am-2pm and 5:30-11pm.) Follow the left-hand road inland from Pl. Platanos past Ag. Ioannis to the dead end, then go right at the signs to find the **medical center**. (☎24240 22 222. Open M-F 9am-2pm, M-F 24hr. for emergencies.) The **OTE** is 100m from the water on Galatsaniou. (☎24240 22 139. Open M-F 7:30am-2pm.) An **Internet cafe** is on the road running through the back of Platanos. Coming from the waterfront, turn left at the back left corner of the plateia; it's across from Metro nightclub. (€4 per hr. Beer €2. Open daily 9am-midnight.) Look for the yellow postbox, 50m past the Internet Cafe on the same road, to find the **post office**. (☎24240 22 203. Open M-F 7:30am-2pm.) **Postal Code:** 37003.

🏠🍴 ACCOMMODATIONS AND FOOD

The **Rooms and Apartments Association of Skopelos,** in the stone building next to the town hall, around the waterfront to the right, facing inland, can provide a list of **domatia**. (☎24240 24 567. Open daily 10am-10pm.) Dock hawks greeting ferries may also offer reasonable rooms; bargaining is expected. Prices vary but run around €15-30 for singles and €20-40 for doubles. ▨**Pension Sotos ❷,** inside the inconspicuous door on the corner of Galatsaniou on the waterfront, has a fantastic location at a diamond-in-the-rough price. The renovated, 150-year-old house has 12 exposed-beam rooms with fans, coffeemakers, and private baths; some have A/C, TV, fridges, and balconies. A common kitchen, quiet courtyard, roof terrace, and book exchange are also available. (☎24240 22 549. Singles €18-28; doubles €21-35; triples €30-50; quads €32-55. Discount for extended stays.) At **Hotel Regina ❸,** off the back right corner of Pl. Platanos, and then off the second alley on the left, kind owner Viki will be happy to help make your stay comfortable. Simple yet cozy rooms include A/C, TV, some water views, overhead fans, baths, and fridges. (☎24240 22 138. English speakers should call Viki's son Iannis at ☎69788 64 092. Breakfast included. Singles €25-40; doubles €35-50; triples €40-60.) Follow the waterfront to the left (facing inland) past the park to reach **Hotel Akti ❷,** on the corner, where pretty tiled rooms have TV, fridges, baths, and balconies with waterfront views. (☎24240 23 229. Singles €25-30; doubles €30-40; triples €35-45.)

Also known as "Souvlaki Square," Pl. Platanos abounds with quick bites. For slower-paced dining, head to one of the tavernas along the waterfront. **Taverna O Molos ❷,** down the waterfront to the far right, facing inland, is beloved by locals (it's Hotel Regina's Iannis's favorite place to eat), serving delicious Greek food and overlooking the harbor. (☎24240 22 551. Entrees €5-12. Lamb *kleftiko*

€7.50. Open daily 11am-1am.) Follow the waterfront to the left, just past the park, to reach **Limni ❷**, whose traditional Greek cuisine, including fried zucchini (€2.50), is particularly good. (☎24240 24 781. Salads and appetizers €2.50-5. Entrees €5-8. Open daily 6pm-2am.) **Cafe Barramares ❶**, fewer than 100m to the right of the boat dock (facing inland), dishes out delicious, filling *tiropita* (€3), crepes to go (from €2), ice-cream sundaes (€3.50-7), and an array of enticing desserts. (☎24240 22 960; www.skopelosweb.gr/barramares. Open daily 8am-2am.) **Alpha-Pi Supermarket,** left from the back-left corner of the plateia and on the right, has groceries. (☎24240 23 533. Open daily 8am-midnight.)

◎ SIGHTS

While the island's main attractions are its beaches and hikes, Skopelos Town also has an abundance of **churches.** Thalpos Travel can provide a map that pinpoints many of them, but you may not be able to enter some as they do not have regular visiting hours. As you make your way from church to church, a good place to start is around the harbor to the far right, where beautiful whitewashed **Panagia ston Pirgo** perches on the rocks. From there, the stairs below the church climb up along the sea-edge of the city. The ascent passes tiny, simple **Evangelismos** and 11th-century **Athanasios,** the town's oldest church, just below the *kastro*. Just off to the left is **Genesis tou Christou,** a larger cruciform church with a round cupola and clock tower. Continuing up the side of the city, you will see the **kastro,** originally built by King Philip of Macedon in the 4th century BC. Today it is the site of a traditional taverna that features live Greek music. On the uphill side of the *kastro*, if you wind your way into town and head for the top of the hill, you will hit **Spiridon.** Slightly farther into the city lies **Papameletiou,** a cruciform basilica built in 1662 with a red-tile roof and small clock tower. **Agios Nikolaos,** just up Galatsaniou on the left, exhibits brightly colored icons and a marble statue of the Virgin. In **Mikhail-Sinnadon,** a stone basilica contains a remarkable iconostasis. The island draws international students and recognition for its **Photographic Center of Skopelos** (☎24240 24 121); call for more info. The **Folklore Museum,** 100m left past the OTE, has a small collection of island artifacts. The meticulously researched exhibit on popular religion is worth a longer look. (☎24240 23 494. Open daily 10am-10pm. €2.)

◨ NIGHTLIFE

A 10min. walk up the stairs by Platanos Jazz Club on the far right of the waterfront, keeping close to the coast on the way up, leads to ◨**Anatoli,** the haunt of Giorgos Xintaris, one of the world's last great *rembetika* singers. If you stop by the taverna for a drink after dinner (usually just before midnight), you may be lucky enough to catch him singing the old songs with a group of friends. (☎24240 22 851. Appetizers €2-5. Beer €3. Mixed drinks €3-7. Open daily 8pm-2:30am.) **Platanos Jazz Club,** on the far right of the harbor facing inland, near Taverna O Molos and the jetty, lets you relax with jazz, blues, and a drink under a hulking tree. (☎24240 23 661. Beer €3. Mixed drinks €6.50. Open 8am-3am.) **The Blue Bar,** two blocks up Galatsaniou in an alley on the right (past the church of Ag. Nikolaos), plays folk, rock, and blues music to accompany the €3 beers and impressive collection of malt whiskey. (☎24240 23 731. Mixed drinks €6. Open daily 9:30pm-2:30am.) Skopelos's **dance clubs** cluster midway up the street off the back left corner of Pl. Platanos. **Metro,** with a DJ, two bars, and flashing lights, is where local youth head to party the night away. (Beer €5. Mixed drinks €6. Cover €5; includes 1 drink. Open May-Oct. daily 11pm-3:30am; Nov.-Apr. F-Sa 11pm-3:30am.) Closer to the plateia on the same side of the street, **Club 54's** black and white checkered dance floor and neon photo-art work well as a mix of retro and modern. (☎24240 24 300. Beer €5. Mixed drinks €6. Cover €5; includes 1 drink. Open daily June-Aug. 1am-late.)

📷 BEACHES

Traveling Skopelos's road by bus or car gives you your pick of lovely southern beaches. Headed out from Skopelos Town, the first beach is crowded but dazzlingly beautiful **Stafilos;** it's by the hillside where archaeologists discovered the tomb of the ancient Cretan general of the same name. Nearby **Velanio**, over the hill to the left as you face the sea, is less packed. Named for the trickling spring that was a gushing fountain in Roman times, today Velanio is advertised as the only nude beach on Skopelos, though actually most swimmers are clothed. Past the small town of **Agnondas,** a paved road leads about 1km downhill to the secluded beach of **Limnonari**, which more than justifies the walk; ask the bus driver to let you off at the top of the road. Silvery **Milia**, accessible by bus, is the island's longest beach, with water sports and a rough surf on windy days. Closer to Loutraki, dirt paths lead to the northern beaches of **Spilia, Mavraki, Keramoto,** and **Chondroyiorgi.**

🥾 HIKING

Due to Skopelos's predominantly dirt roads, it is best explored on moped or foot. The island's 35km asphalt road runs from the Skopelos bus station through **Stafilos** (4km), **Agnondas** (8km), **Panormos** (18km), **Elios** (24km), **Loutraki** (30km), and **Glossa** (32km). Thalpos Travel and various souvenir shops carry *Skopelos Trails* (€11), a great guide to the island's hikes. According to local lore, a fierce 🐲**dragon** once went on a fiery rampage, eating almost everyone on Skopelos until Ag. Rigine killed it and became the island's protector. The **Dragon Cliffs** (*Drakondoschisma*), where the creature was hurled to its death, are now a quiet overlook with a sea view and an altar portraying the dragon's grisly demise. The beginning of the short 10min. walk is best reached by moped or bus, as it's just off the highway between Stafilos and Agnondas; look for the rusty "For Sale" sign about 2km after Stafilos next to a small dirt road that disappears into the woods on the left.

> 📙 **THE REAL DEAL.** The Dragon Cliffs of Skopelos aren't so exciting now that the resident fire-breather is gone, especially since abandoned sheds and machinery spoil the otherwise mediocre woodsy trail. Unless it's along the way on your beach-hopping trip around the island, consider spending your time lounging at Stafilos or Velanio beach instead. —Kevin Paik

Two paved roads leave the town from the bus depot on the left end of the waterfront (facing inland). To reach a set of monasteries, follow the road out of the harbor to the left (facing inland)—signs mark the way to those that ascend **Mount Palouki.** Small **Evangelismos** was built in the 17th century as part of the Monastery of Xiropotamos of Athos, but today is only inhabited by three nuns. Take the left-hand fork up the hot, winding mountain road for the 1hr., 2km hike; if you start early in the morning, you can avoid both the heat and the bugs and make it to the monasteries before the afternoon siesta. (Open 8am-1pm and 5-8pm. Ring the bell to be let in.) Up the right fork, a 45min. walk leads you to the **Monastery of the Transfiguration** (*Metamorphosis*). Its chapel, set in a flowered courtyard, dates from the 16th century. Another hour up the hill along the road takes you to two monasteries perched on ridges overlooking the sea. The first, the **Monastery of Agias Varvaras,** was built as a fortress in 1648. Nearby **Prodromou** contains several wall paintings along with icons dating back to the 14th and 15th centuries. Prodromou, whose astounding setting surveys the entire coast, is now a cloister dedicated to St. John the Baptist. The dirt path that begins behind the building leads to the smaller monasteries of **Agia Triada** and **Agia Taxiarches.** Farther up the road, a trail leads to beautiful **Agia Anna.** For a 4hr. round-trip hike from **Glossa,** take the dirt track across the island to the **Monastery of Agios Ioannis,** which clings spectacularly to a boulder above the ocean. From the main road east of Glossa, turn left on the first dirt road to Steki Taverna. At the road's end, a path drops to the sea, and stone steps that have been cut in the escarpment lead to the monastery.

ALONNISOS Αλόννησος

The only inhabited island within Greece's National Marine Park, Alonnisos is a pleasant starting point for those exploring the marine sanctuary. Carpeted with well-marked trails that stretch through the forested hills to the coastal cliffs, it's a veritable paradise for hikers. To its northeast, the small island of Gioura claims to have been the home of Polyphemus, the Cyclops whose eye was gouged out by Odysseus's sizzling lance. Though many islands claim this distinction, Gioura's rocky landscape best fits Homer's description of Polyphemus's cavern, complete with herds of the now-endangered brown goats with black crosses on their backs.

PATITIRI Πατητήρι   ☎ 24240

All boats dock at Patitiri, the island's main town. Tourist agencies clutter the waterfront between the cafes and tavernas that have recently undergone visible expansion to provide better outdoor seating. Though modest and somewhat congested, the town serves as an easily accessible base for exploring the rest of Alonnisos and the surrounding Marine Park.

▐ TRANSPORTATION

Ferries: To: **Agios Konstantinos** (4½hr.: M-Th 3:30pm; F 8:30pm; Su 5:35, 5:45pm: €31.20); **Kimi** (5hr., W 8:25pm, €10); **Skiathos** (2hr.: M 3:30, 8:30pm; Tu, Th 3:30pm; W 5:45am, 1:35, 3:30pm; F 8:30pm; Sa 1:35pm; Su 5:35, 5:45pm: €7.40) via **Skopelos** (30min.,€4); **Thessaloniki** (7½hr., Su 1:30pm, €23.20); **Volos** (5¼hr.: M 8:30pm; W 5:45am, 1:35pm; Sa 1:35pm: €15).

Buses: Run from where Ikion Dolophon hits the waterfront to **Hora,** also called **"Old Town"** (10min.; every hr. 9am-3:20pm, 2 per hr. 7pm-midnight; €1), and to **Steni Vala** (30min.; 9:20am, 2:35, 5:50pm; €1.10).

Flying Dolphins: To: **Agios Konstantinos** (2hr.: M-F, Su 7am, 4:45pm; Sa 7, 11am: €31.30); **Glossa** (25min., 4 per day 6am-4:15pm, €12.30); **Skiathos** (40min.; 5 per day M-F, Su 6am-4:45pm, Sa 6am-4:15pm; €15); **Skopelos** (15min.; M 6 per day 6am-9:05pm, Tu-F, Su 5 per day 6am-9:05pm, Sa 5 per day 6am-4:15pm;

Alonnisos

0   2 miles
0   2 kilometers

— Major Road
— Dirt Road
····· Hiking Trail

Gerakas Bay
Gerakas

Ag. Kostantinos
Ag. Dimitrios
Lechousa
Glyfa
Manolas
Steni Vala
Megali Ammos
Peristera
Ag. Anargiri
Leftos Galas
Kokkinocastro
TO SKOPELOS
Vrisitsa
Milia
Chrisi
Milia
Votsi
Hora
Patitiri
Mikros Mourtias
Megalos Mourtias

€8); **Thessaloniki** (3hr., 9pm, €35.30); **Volos** (2hr.; M 4 per day 6am-4:15pm, Tu-Su 3 per day 6am-4:15pm; €30). Boats going to **Agios Konstantinos** and **Thessaloniki** dock to the far left of the harbor, and not at the main dock.

Taxis: ☎ 24240 65 751. Along the waterfront. Run until 2am, but respond to calls 24hr.

Water taxis: Go to beaches on the eastern coast. Leave the dock between 10 and 11am and return from the northernmost beach, **Ag. Dimitrios**, at 5:30pm (round-trip €10).

Rentals: Motorbikes can be rented on Pelasgon and Ikion Dolophon. €10-15 per day.

➕🛈 ORIENTATION AND PRACTICAL INFORMATION

From the docks, **Pelasgon** on the left and **Ikion Dolophon** on the right, run inland.

Budget Travel: Alonnisos Travel (☎ 24240 65 188), on the waterfront. Sells **ferry tickets, exchanges currency,** and books excursions. Open daily 8am-11pm. **Flying Dolphin tickets** can be bought just to the left of Ikion Dolophon on the waterfront.

Bank: National Bank (☎ 24240 65 777), on Ikion Dolophon on the left from the water, has a **24hr. ATM.** Open M-Th 8am-2:30pm, F 8am-2pm.

Police: ☎ 24240 65 205. Past the fire station, up Ikion Dolophon. Open 6am-10pm.

Pharmacy: ☎ 24240 65 540. Before the Internet cafe. Open 8:30am-2pm and 5-10pm.

Hospital: ☎ 24240 65 208. Opposite the police. Open 9am-1pm, 24hr. in emergencies.

Internet Access: Play Cafe (☎ 24240 66 119), on Ikion Dolophon, has slow connections and an inflexible pay-before-use system. €4 per hr. Open 10am-2pm and 5-11pm.

Post office: ☎ 24240 65 560. A short walk up Ikion Dolophon on the right. Open M-F 7:30am-2pm. **Postal Code:** 37005.

⌂ ACCOMMODATIONS AND CAMPING

The **Rooms to Let Office,** to the right of Ikos Travel, can help find rooms. (☎ 24240 66 188. Open daily 10am-2:30pm and 6:30-10:30pm.) To reach **Panorama ❷,** head down the first alley on the left up Ikion Dolophon, walk up the stairs to the top of the hill, and turn into the blue-fenced courtyard. The bright rooms come with TV, A/C, fridges, baths, and a bougainvillea-covered common balcony with a port view. (☎ 24240 65 240. Singles €25; doubles €30; triples €35; 2-bedroom suite with kitchen €40-60.) Find lovely **Rooms and Studios ❸** with TV, A/C, baths, balconies, and kitchens about 200m down Pelasgon on the left, opposite I'm Motorbikes. (☎ 24240 65 451. Singles €20-40; doubles €25-45; studios €30-50.) Inquire at Boutique Mary, 100m from the waterfront on Pelasgon, about the simple, comfortable rooms with baths at **Dimakis Pension ❷,** next door. (☎ 24240 65 294. Singles €20; doubles €30.) One kilometer uphill on the first alley on the left of Pelasgon (look for signs) is the eminently punny **Camping Rocks ❶.** The sites, 50m from swimming rocks, have showers. (☎ 24240 65 410. €5 per person, €2.50 per tent.)

🍴🍷 FOOD AND NIGHTLIFE

Away from the chaos of the harbor, little *ouzeri* **To Kamaki ❷,** on Ikion Dolophon past the National Bank, serves delicious home-cooked seafood dishes like mussels *saganaki* (€6.50) at reasonable prices. (☎ 24240 65 245. Open daily noon-1:30am. MC/V.) **Tzitziphia ❷,** at the corner of Pelasgon on the waterfront, busily caters to a mixed crowd of locals and tourists looking for quality Greek fare. (☎ 24240 65 255. Moussaka €5.50. Entrees €6-8. €0.50 cover. Open daily 9am-midnight.) For cheap souvlaki and gyros (€1.80), stop by **To Steki ❶**, near the corner of Pelasgon on the left. (☎24240 66 292. Open daily 6pm-midnight.) Alternatively, you can buy **fresh fruits** and **vegetables** at the store past the first alley on the left of Ikion Dolophon. (☎24240 65 020. Open daily 8am-2pm and 5-9:30pm.) In the evening, people gather to sip cold drinks (€5) just above the beach at **Kactos Bar**, on the far left of the waterfront. (☎24240 66 054. Beer €2.50. Open daily 7pm-3am.) **Club Enigma**, a short walk on Pelasgon, and **B&B Club**, on Ikion Dolophon, entertain crowds with international pop. (Beer €3-5. Mixed drinks €6-8. Both open F-Sa 10pm-late.)

🞈 🞑 SIGHTS AND BEACHES

The **History and Folklore Museum** of Alonnisos, up the stairs to the far left of the waterfront facing inland, displays a wide variety of cultural artifacts. Exhibits include weapons used in the Balkan Wars and WWII, historical maps, and, downstairs, an excellent series of trade exhibits on everything from wine-making to pack-saddle construction. (Open daily 11am-7pm. €3, includes 1 soft drink.) Many **beaches** are accessible from the island's main road, which runs along the spine of the island from Patitiri to the port of Gherakas in the far north. A 50min. walk on this road from Patitiri takes you to **Votsi**, the island's other major settlement. Local children dive off the 15-20m cliffs near Votsi beach, just outside the village. The road then passes separate turn-offs for the pine-enclosed beaches of **Milia** and the shallower, sandier **Chrisi Milia**. Alonnisos's residents will tell you that **Agiou Dimitriou**, at the end of the coastal road, is the island's most beautiful beach. Along the coast from Chrisi Milia is the beach and archaeological site of **Kokkinocastro**, where swimmers occasionally find ancient coins. Nearby **Leftos Galas** has a sandy beach with two tavernas. The tiny fishing village of **Steni Vala**, 12km north of Patitiri, is the only other bus stop (30min., 3 per day, €1.10)—the **fish tavernas** here are fantastic. **Glyfa beach** is along the shore, a 5min. walk north of the village.

🞖 HIKING

Only the southern end of the island is inhabited, leaving large swaths of mountain wilderness to the north. Trails are marked at regular intervals and range from paved roads to steep, rocky paths. Blue maps, scattered throughout the island, mark trailheads and show routes, indicated by numerical yellow signs. Still, the purchase of a trail map (€3-5) or *Alonnisos on Foot* (€9), a walking and swimming guide, is recommended. Numbers below refer to those of the marked trails. The **Megalo Nero-Agii Anargiri-Megali Ammos-Raches-Votsi trail** (#5, 2½hr.) takes you along the southeastern side of Alonnisos to the secluded monastery of Ag. Anargiri and beach of Megali Ammos. The trailhead is along the main road near Votsi. Head out Ikion Dolophon from Patitiri to get to the main road, then follow the signs to Votsi and Steni Vala. From Megali Ammos, two trails (#7, 1½hr.; #8, 1½hr.) lead north to **Megalo Chorafi**, east of the main road, the hub for hikes to **Agalou Laka beach** (#14, 45min.) and the church of **Agios Kostantinos** (#6, 2hr.). From Ag. Kostantinos, the trails lead north to the church of **Agios Georgios** (#12, 1hr.) and **Melegakia** (#13, 1½hr.) in the more rugged part of the island. Hikes #12 and 13 both bring you back to the main road. From **Steni Vala**, hike #10 (1hr.) takes you past **Agios Petros beach** to **Isomata** and then to the main road. From Isomata, hike #9 winds its way down to **Leftos beach** (45min.). Far north, past Ag. Georgios, in Kastanorema, a dirt road leads to the #11 trailhead, to **Agios Dimitrios beach** (1hr.).

▶ DAYTRIPS FROM PATITIRI

HORA Χώρα

Buses run from Patitiri (10min.; every hr. 9am-3:20pm, 2 per hr. 7pm-midnight; €1); schedules are posted at each bus stop. Round-trip taxi €10.

Set high on a hill to ward off pirates, **Hora,** also called "Old Town" or "Paleo Alonnisos," welcomes visitors looking for the charm that Patitiri lacks. Its quiet, crooked alleys, which open suddenly onto incredible vistas of the island and wind their way into the dusty hills, have a bizarre origin. When settlers first came to Alonnisos, they performed a goat sacrifice, cutting the animal into pieces, and placed the pieces of meat at potential building locations. Over subsequent days, if the meat had kept, they concluded that the spot was prime for building, sheltered from the sun, pests, and other elements. Tiny 12th-century **Christ Church,** on the left fork from the bus stop, is run by Father Gregorias, the village priest and a legend in the area. If you choose to stay in Hora, bright and spacious **Hiliadromia ❹,** above the gift shop behind the church, has beautiful wood-accented rooms with stone floors, tiled baths, A/C, TV, fridges, and fantastic balcony views. (☎24240 65 814. Singles €30-50; doubles €45-50; studios with kitchen €60-70.) Hora is home to a variety of quaint cafes and tavernas, some perched on beautiful overlooks. **To Aloni ❺,** at the base of an old windmill (sans blades), to the right of the bus stop, serves Greek food to tables with views of the island. (☎24240 65 550. Veal steak €6. Moussaka €5.50. Open daily 8:30am-1am.) Four easy, enjoyable hiking trails lead from the center of Hora. A short walk along the main road headed back toward Patitiri will bring you to the trail to **Vrisitsa** (#3, 1km, 30min.), on the left. This miniature beach lies in a secluded cove that seems to smile up at you as you descend to its sandy shore. The trail to **Mikros Mourtias** (#1, 1.5km, 45min.) winds down the hill through the surrounding green trees, offering a fantastic view as it heads to the water. Beginning at the bus stop, walk through town, past the church, and up the stairs to a street lined with cafes. Turn left just before the street ends and walk down the steps of a narrow side street to the trailhead. Mikros Mourtias is a small, quiet beach with perfectly shaped skipping stones. A steeper climb to **Kalovoulos** (#2, 1.5km, 45min.) will bring you to one of the highest points on the island. To reach the path, continue on the main road past the bus stop and it will be on the left. As you start back on the main road to Patitiri, the trail **Patitiri** (#4, 1.5km, 35min.) is a pleasant stroll that connects Old and New Towns.

NATIONAL MARINE PARK

The park islands are accessible by specially licensed boats. Most trips, advertised and sold along the Patitiri harborfront, are all-inclusive single-day trips; a typical trip departs from the Patitiri dock around 10am, makes stops on 2 or more islands, visits the monastery on Kyra Panagia, and returns around 6pm. Ikos Travel, across from the dock, can assist with arrangements and info. (☎24240 65 620. Open daily 9am-2pm and 4-11pm.) Special hiking and stargazing trips are also available in May, June, and Sept. (€35-40. Most companies require you to sign up 1 day in advance.)

Surrounding Alonnisos are the 25 ecologically protected islets of the National Marine Park. The largest and most important are Peristera, Skantzoura, Piperi, Kyra Panagia, Jura, and Psatnoura. Psatnoura, Kyra Panagia, and Skantzoura are owned by nearby Mt. Athos (p. 311) and are used in part for grazing goats. Visiting Jura and Piperi is forbidden in an effort to protect their rare species, including the Mediterranean monk seal. Unless you're an MOm official (p. 81), forget about seeing the seals, but feel free to grab a "Save the Seals" poster from the gallery in MOm's headquarters across the dock in Patitiri. (☎24240 66 350, Athens headquarters ☎21052 22 888; www.mom.gr. Open daily June-Oct. 10am-midnight.)

SKYROS Σκύρος

Skyros is dominated by two forces—modern tourism and local tradition—that are as diametrically opposed as the terrain found on each side of the island. But while the barren landscape of the south and the green hills of the north will always remain separate, the two influences on Skyrian life are beginning to coexist. Preserving the island's folkways has been recognized as an important priority, and is a draw for travelers weary of tourist-infested islands. The trend promises to continue, as there is no longer a ferry link to Skyros from the other Sporades. Most visitors here are in the market for more than just a beach-and-bar tour.

SKYROS TOWN Σκύρος ☎ 22220

Like a gleaming pocket of snow, Skyros Town ("Horio"—"the village"—to locals) stands out in bright white contrast to the greens, yellows, and browns of the hills that surround it. Beyond the tavernas, cafes, and bars are the features that give the island its distinctive charm. The characteristically small Skyrian houses were all built between the 11th and 12th centuries. They owe their compact size to an effort to build the village so that all the homes would be out of view of marauding pirates. Among this maze of whitewashed houses, old men sew sandals by porchlight late into the evening and women embroider patterns they learned from those pesky pirates. During Carnival, the town erupts into a truly wild festival.

TRANSPORTATION. The airport (☎22220 91 625), 20km from Skyros Town, has **flights** to Athens (35min., 2 per week, €33) and Thessaloniki (45min., 3 per week, €57). Take a cab (€11) to get there. The best way to get to Skyros is to take the bus from Terminal B in Athens to Kimi, Evia (3½hr., 2 per day, €10), then the **ferry** (☎22220 22 020) from Kimi (1¾hr.: M-Th 6:30pm; F 2:30, 8pm; Sa noon, 6:30pm; Su 4, 9pm: €8.30). Ask for the bus that goes to the ferry dock, as the bus going to the town of Kimi will bring you to a station that is 5km from the dock. If you land in Kimi proper, take a **taxi** or walk down the long, winding road, following the signs for the port. No ferries or hydrofoils run to the other Sporades, making Skyros a difficult destination to reach on an island-hopping tour. The ferry to Skyros arrives in Linaria, the tiny western port; a **bus** to Skyros Town picks up when ferries arrive (15min., 5 per day, €1) and leaves Skyros Town about 1hr. before ferry departures. Another bus runs to Molos (10min., 6 per day, €1); if you ask, the driver can give you an exact schedule. Buses stop in Skyros Town at the base of Agoras, the town's backbone road. **Taxis** (☎22220 91 666) wait by the central plateia or the bus stop (unavailable late or in the afternoon). **Pegasus Rent A Car** runs out of Skyros Travel, and rents cars (€40-65 per day) with 24hr. pick-up and delivery to the airport, ferry dock, or anywhere else. For **moped rentals** (€10-15 per day), look for the sign that points right off Agoras, just after Skyros Travel.

ORIENTATION AND PRACTICAL INFORMATION. Agoras runs uphill from the bus stop, passing shops, pharmacies, bars, and restaurants along its way through Skyros Town. Maze-like streets scatter outward along the hillsides, and buildings are numbered counterintuitively. Few streets are named, so when venturing off Agoras, pick out landmarks. At the far end of town, looking out across the sea, is **Plateia Rupert Brooke,** dedicated to British poet Brooke and to "immortal poetry." You can reach Pl. Rupert Brooke by walking up Agoras through town until it forks left at Kalypso Bar, then heading left along the wall and walking up until you reach a sign pointing to "ΜΟΥΣΕΙΟ/MUSEUM." If you veer right, you can follow the stairs built into the narrow street to the plateia. At Pl. Rupert Brooke, the

Skyros

0   4 mi

0   4 km

stairs to the right pass the **Archaeological Museum** on a 15min. descent to the beach; another set straight ahead leads to the **Faltaits Museum.**

Skyros Travel, past the central plateia on the left of Agoras walking away from the bus station, sells **Olympic Airways** tickets, rents cars, organizes bus and boat excursions, and helps find rooms. Their port office in Linaria opens when ferries arrive. (☎22220 91 600; www.skyrostravel.com. Open daily 9am-2pm and 7-10pm.) The **National Bank,** past the central plateia on the left, has a **24hr. ATM.** (☎22220 91 802. Open M-Th 8am-2:30pm.) The **police** station is beyond Nefeli opposite the gas station. (☎22220 91 274. Open 24hr., but the small staff may be away on another call.) You can ask the police for info about **doctors.** A **pharmacy** is across from the bank (☎22220 91 617; open 8:30am-1pm and 6:30-10pm) and on the right past Skyros Travel (☎22220 91 111; open daily 9am-2pm and 6pm-1am). The **hospital** (☎22220 92 222) is just out of town behind Hotel Nefeli. **Mano.com,** past the plateia up Agoras on the left, has **Internet access.** (☎22220 92 473. €3 per hr.; €1.50 min. Open daily 8am-1pm and 6:30-11:30pm.) To get to the **OTE,** turn right at Skyros Travel, walk to the end of the road, and take another right. (☎22220 91 399. Open M-F 7:30am-1:30pm.) The **post office** is on the far side of the plateia from Agoras and offers **Poste Restante.** (☎22220 91 208. Open M-F 7:30am-2pm.) **Postal Code:** 34007.

⊓▢ ACCOMMODATIONS AND FOOD. Coming to Skyros and staying in a hotel is like coming to Greece to swim in a pool. For the real experience you've got to stay in a **domatia,** such as one of those offered by the old women at the bus stop. Thick-walled Skyrian houses are treasure troves, brimming with ceramics, Italian linens, icons, embroidery, metalwork, and fine china bought from long-dead pirates who looted the Mediterranean. Expect to pay €15-35 for a room; always bargain, and look carefully for landmarks and house numbers, as it's easy to lose your way in the maze of streets. If you arrive during siesta, your calls for domatia may be answered only with snores from within. If you don't feel like searching for a room, try **Hotel Elena ❸,** on the first right off of Agoras heading uphill from the bus stop. The clean and comfortable rooms have tiled private baths, A/C, TV, and fridges; some have balconies. (☎22220 91 738. Singles €30; doubles €35; triples €55.)

Skyros's amazing food perfectly satiates after-swim hunger. Look for the light-green chairs outside incredible ◼❍ **Pappou Kai Ego ❷** (Grandpa and Me), immediately after the sharp bend in Agoras, on the right. Known in town as "Pappou's," this restaurant serves a delicious Chicken O Pappous floating in cream sauce over rice (€7), a tender nanny goat au lemon (€6.80), and flaming meatballs with ouzo that are just really cool to see brought to the table. (☎22220 93 200. Entrees €4-8. Open daily 7pm-1am. AmEx/MC/V.) **To Metopo ❷,** on the left heading into town from the bus stop, is a hangout for Skyrian men looking for a good meal (octopus barbecue; €9) and good conversation. (☎22220 93 515. Entrees €5-8. Open M-Sa 1-5pm and 7pm-1am, Su 7pm-1am.) Past the central plateia on the right, **O Pantelis ❶** (Ο Παντελης) prepares tasty souvlaki with potatoes (€1) and gyros (€1.50) which are slow-cooked to perfection. (☎22220 92 225. Open daily 6pm-2am.)

◙▧ SIGHTS AND NIGHTLIFE. The ▧**Faltaits Museum,** just past Pl. Rupert Brooke, is the wonderful private collection of a Skyrian ethnologist. Inside are paintings by local artist, poet, and writer Manos Faltaits, who, well into his sixties, still produces masterful works of art. Tours (available in English) take you through the frozen-in-time ancestral home of the Faltaits family, one of the first larger homes to be built after fears of pirate raids had subsided. Conferences and cultural activities are held here throughout the year, including a **theater and dance festival** in late July and August; ask the staff for dates and times. (☎ 22220 91 232. Open daily 10am-2pm and 6-9pm. Admission and basic tour €2, comprehensive historical tour €5.) Down the stairs to the right of Pl. Rupert Brooke is the **Archaeological Museum,** with a modest collection of pottery, tools, clay figurines, and jewelry. (☎ 22220 91 327. Open Tu-Su 8:30am-3pm. €2, seniors €1, students free.) Both museums have rooms decorated like traditional Skyrian homes, but if you decide to venture out onto the village's labyrinthine streets, it's perfectly acceptable to knock on a door or two and ask to see the real thing. At the top of the hill on the way to Pl. Rupert Brooke before descending to the plateia, a sign points the way up marble-edged steps to the **Monastery of Agios Georgios** and the **castle.** Both are closed, but the climb yields an amazing view of the entire village. Closer to the beaten path, on Agoras after going left at Kalypso, is the "upper village," a stronghold of island tradition. Jewelry, sandals, and other Skyrian items are crafted and sold in its several shops. The museum shop, **Argo,** can also be found here, near Kalypso on the left. (Open daily 9:30am-1:30pm and 6:30-10:30pm.) The shop's proprietor, Niko Sikkes, also leads walking tours of the island (☎ 22220 92 707).

The central plateia is the heart of nighttime action, surrounded by crowded bars that keep the music loud and the drinks strong. **Kata Lathos** (☎ 22220 91 671; open daily 9am-3pm and 6pm-3am), across from the central plateia on Agoras to the right of equally popular **Iroön** (☎ 22220 92 648; open daily 8am-late), has a young, fun atmosphere, with a friendly English-speaking staff and a roof-top patio. (Beer €2.50-3. Mixed drinks €4.50-5.50.) **Kalypso Bar,** at the top of Agoras past Pappou's, has a calmer scene, as people gather to chat and sip a nightcap after a tasty Skyrian meal. (☎ 22220 92 160. Beer €2.50. Mixed drinks €5-6. Open May-Oct.)

◪ BEACHES. Standing in Skyros's pirate-proof streets, it's easy to forget how close you are to the water. A pleasant, sandy beach, however, stretches below the town, through the villages of **Magazia** and **Molos,** and continues around the point. Head down the stairs after the Archaeological Museum and follow the road leading to the left. The local nude beach, ironically named **"Tou Papa to Homa"** ("The Sands of the Priest"), remains clean and uncrowded, just south of the local beach. Walking 10-12min. to the right along the seaside road at the bottom of the steps, you'll reach a narrow, slippery dirt path lined with spiky plants that leads downhill along a wire fence—be careful as the last 4m is especially steep. From here, you'll have a beautiful view of the **Southern Mountain,** famous in local literature for its hourly color changes in the slanting island light. Locals recommend **Pefkos,** tucked into a cove up the coast from Linaria and accessible by taxi. Barren beaches and **Rupert Brooke's grave,** on the southern portion of the island, are accessible only by dusty paths or boat. Buses from Linaria to Skyros Town will stop at the beaches of **Aherounis,** on the western coast, and small **Mialos,** on the east, if you ask the driver in advance. Boats explore the former pirate grottoes at **Spillies,** on the southeastern coast, and **Sarakino Island,** one of the largest pirate centers in the Aegean. If you keep your eyes peeled, you may see one of the rare, wild ▧**Skyrian ponies.**

CYCLADES
Κυκλάδες

Sun-drenched white houses, winding stone streets, and trellis-covered tavernas define the Cycladic islands as a whole, but subtle quirks make each island distinct. Orange and black sands coat the shoreline of Santorini, rocky cliffs shape arid Sifnos, and celebrated archaeological sites testify to the mythical and historical legends surrounding Delos. Naxos and Paros offer travelers peaceful mountains and villages, Milos's coast is spectacularly unusual with its caverns and deeply colored sand, and notorious party spots Ios and Mykonos uncork some of wildest nightlife on earth. The Little Cyclades and islands like Serifos, closest to Athens, are blissfully under-touristed, populated only by locals and a smattering of Greek vacationers. Visitors to any island, however, can be sure to encounter large quantities of unadulterated local flavor, surrounded by the ever-present cerulean sea.

 SUGGESTED ITINERARIES: CYCLADES

FIVE DAYS Start your trip with a healthy dose of hedonism on **Mykonos** (p. 376), where the drinks are strong and the beaches are nude. Afterwards, a couple of days trekking through the delightful churches and villages hidden in **Naxos's** (p. 388) vast olive groves will clear your head. As you stretch out on **Santorini** (p. 419), thank an ancient volcanic blast for covering the island's beaches with distinctive black sand.

TWO WEEKS From **Tinos's** (p. 372) busy harbor, set sail for Mykonos (p. 376), whose delights are literally intoxicating. Take a daytrip to sacred **Delos** (p. 383) before exploring Naxos's (p. 388) caves and ruins. When you're ready to get back to the party, go to **Ios** (p. 413), where you'll be surrounded by as much alcohol as water. Soak up the sun on Santorini's beaches (p. 419), then head to ancient **Akrotiri's** (p. 424) lava-preserved streets.

ANDROS Άνδρος

The second-largest Cycladic island, Andros is a weekend destination for Greece's wealthy ship captains, many of whose families originated here. In their zeal to keep their hideaway unspoiled, the residents have restricted hydrofoil access to the island. Once you make it onto Andros, you'll understand why: the drive from the ferry landing at Gavrio to Andros Town yields magnificent panoramas of the island's beloved beaches. Towns are spread through Andros's mountain ranges, and narrow roads criss-cross their peaks and valleys, weaving down to the coast below. Stone walls outline green and purple fields, and the island's sandy beaches glow in solitude beneath the sun, each more breathtaking than the last. Though Athenians crowd in on the weekends, Andros generally remains a serene escape for international tourists who delight in untrammeled ground and quiet nights.

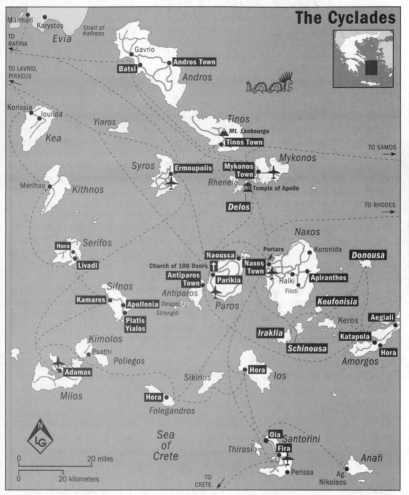

The Cyclades

Marmari
Karystos
Strait of Kafireos
TO RAFINA
Evia
Gavrio
Andros Town
Batsi
Andros
TO LAVRIO, PIRAEUS
Korissia
Ioulida
Kea
Yiaros
Tinos
Mt. Exobourgo
Tinos Town
TO SAMOS
Syros
Ermoupolis
Mykonos Town
Mykonos
Merihas
Kithnos
Rheneia
Temple of Apollo
TO RHODES
Delos
Hora
Serifos
Naxos
Koronida
Donousa
Livadi
Church of 100 Doors
Naoussa
Portara
Naxos Town
Antiparos Town
Parikia
Halki
Filoti
Apiranthos
Sifnos
Antiparos
Paros
Koufonisia
Kamares
Apollonia
Despotiko
Strongili
Keros
Aegiali
Platis Yialos
Kimolos
Iraklia
Katapola
Psathi
Poliegos
Schinousa
Hora
Adamas
Sikinos
Hora
Ios
Amorgos
Milos
Hora
Folegandros
Sea of Crete
Oia
Santorini
Thirasia
Fira
Anafi
Perissa
Ag. Nikolaos
TO CRETE
0 — 20 miles
0 — 20 kilometers

CYCLADES

BATSI Μπατσί   ☎ 22820

Climbing its way up the mountainside above a stretch of golden sand, Batsi is the tourist capital of Andros, with the liveliest nightlife and a wide variety of food and accommodations options. Visitors stroll the waterfront by night, pausing for a drink at a *kafeneion* or dancing away the hours in a club.

⊏ ⁊ TRANSPORTATION AND PRACTICAL INFORMATION. The bus stops by the town's long sandy beach in front of Andros Travel and in the small central plateia, where the bus schedules are posted. **Buses** pass through Batsi on their way to Andros Town (45min.; M-F 8 per day 7:30am-9:45pm, Sa-Su 6 per day 10am-9:45pm; €2.50) and Gavrio (15min., 5-7 per day 9am-8:15pm, €1.50) All ferries to the island arrive in Gavrio, where a bus immediately picks up passengers going to Batsi and Andros Town. If you miss the bus, a taxi will take you to Batsi for €6. From Gavrio, **ferries** sail to Mykonos (2½hr.: M-Sa 9:40am, 7:05pm; Su 9:40, 10:05am, 8:35pm: €9.50), Rafina (2hr.: M-Th 11am, 4:10, 9pm; F-Sa 1:30, 4:10, 9pm, Su 3:30, 4:10, 9pm: €9.10), and Tinos (2hr.: M-Th 9:40am, 7:05pm; F-Sa 9:40, 10:05am, 7:05pm, Su 9:40, 10:05am, 8:35pm: €7.20). **Taxis** (☎22820 41 081), available 24hr., line up just before the main plateia. Check schedules and prices in Batsi at **Andros Travel,** on the waterfront road just left of Dino's Rent a Bike, when facing inland. The agency provides a free tourist info booklet and **map,** books ferry tickets, **rents cars** (€35-60 per day), and gives helpful advice about hiking on Andros. (☎22820 41 252. Open daily 9am-1:30pm and 6-10:30pm.) If you want to book tickets and accommodations or search for tours while in Gavrio, **Hellas Ferries,** across from the ferry dock, can meet your needs. (Open daily 8am-11pm.) **Taxi boats** dock at the end of Batsi's wharf and go to Golden beach (round-trip €13). Head to **Dino's Rent a Bike,** on the waterfront road with the huge sign, where the friendly staff will help you learn to drive a **moped** before you rent one. (☎22820 41 003. Mopeds from €16, helmet and insurance included. Open daily 9am-1:30pm and 5:30-10pm.)

Heading up the hill past the plateia, the **National Bank** has a **24hr. ATM** and offers **currency exchange.** (☎22820 41 400. Open M-F 8:30am-1pm.) In an **emergency,** call the **police** (☎22820 41 204) or the **medical center** in Andros Town (☎22820 22 222 or 22820 23 333). To the left of the beach, behind a playground, is a small **medical office;** signs point the way. (☎22820 41 326. Doctor available 9am-1pm.) A **pharmacy** is all the way up the hill as it curves left, past the National Bank. (☎22820 41 541. Open M-Sa 9am-1:30pm and 6:30-8:30pm.) **Apomero Cafe,** which has **Internet access,** is a 5min. walk from the Gavrio port, before the BP gas station on the way to Batsi, on an uphill road to the right. (☎22820 71 681. €3.50 per hr. Open daily 10am-3pm and 5pm-3am.) The **post office** is between Andros Travel and Dino's Rent a Bike. (☎22820 41 443. Open M-F 7:30am-2:30pm.) **Postal Code:** 84503.

⌐⌐ ACCOMMODATIONS AND FOOD. Accommodations are generally easier to find in Batsi than elsewhere on the island, as the plentiful **domatia** here tend to be nicer than hotels for a comparable or lesser price. They can be found all along the waterfront and outside town off the main road as it doubles back past the National Bank; just look for signs. Expect to pay €20-30 per person per night (lower if you bargain well). Walk to the end of the waterfront, with the water on your right, to find Panayiotis Barous, the friendly owner of **Villa Lyra ❷.** Barous will most likely be at the souvenir shop he also runs, next to the National Bank. The pleasant, inexpensive rooms include TV, A/C, fridges, kitchens, baths, and balconies. (☎22820 41 322. Singles €19-25; doubles €22-38. MC/V.) **Villa Aegeo ❹** is up four flights of stairs to the right of Batsi Gold; past the tree, look for the small sign on the side of the building. The airy rooms have TV, A/C, private baths, fridges, kitchenettes, and balconies. Singles may not be available during high season. (☎22820 41 327. Call ahead for someone to meet you at the bus stop. Singles €40; doubles €55; triples €65.) **Hotel Chryssi Akti ❹** is easy to spot, directly across from the beach. Guests relax by the pool or laze around in plush, spotless rooms complete with TV, fridges, A/C, private baths, and waterfront views. (☎22820 41 236; www.hotel-chryssiakti.gr. Breakfast €4.50. Apr.-Oct. singles €48-53; doubles €58-66; triples €70-79; quads €87-110. MC/V.) For rooms near the beach with fans, fridges, baths, and balconies, see Mike Marinakis, the artist who owns the Glari Art Bar next to his **Glari Rooms for Rent ❸** (Γλαροι), just past Andros Travel as you walk with the water on the left. (☎22820 41 354. Doubles €45.) If you're not attached to staying in Batsi itself, you can camp at **Andros Camping ❶,** 300m from Gavrio (follow the directional arrows). This remote campground has a pool, clean bathrooms with showers, common kitchen, mini-mart, and laundry. (☎22820 71 444. Open Apr.-Oct. €5 per person, €3.50 per tent; tent rental €10-15.)

To find ▩**Restaurant Sirocco** ❸, climb to the top of the stairs between Hotel Chryssi Akti and the Chinese restaurant; two palm trees mark the bottom. Congenial owner Louie prepares unbelievably delicious meals out of his grandparents' former home. The Chef's Special (€11) is a divine steak filet covered with edam cheese, onions, and a burnt crust of mayonnaise, with a side of tangy tabasco sauce. (☎22820 41 023. Open daily 6:30pm-midnight.) On top of the steps just before the National Bank, **Stamatis** ❸ (Σταματης) serves traditional Greek entrees. The restaurant is particularly known for its lamb *kleftiko* (€8), which it only offers on Wednesday nights after slowly roasting the lamb all afternoon; call ahead to reserve a portion. (☎22820 41 283. Entrees €5-8. Open daily 6:30pm-midnight.) **Villy's Place** ❶, in the plateia across from the bus stop, is a perfect spot to grab a sandwich (€2.50) to bring to the beach. (☎22820 41 025. Open 24hr.) A **fruit market** (☎22820 42 333; open daily 8am-10:30pm) is under Capriccio Music Bar on the right side of the waterfront facing inland, and one of several **minimarts** is to the left of Andros Travel. (☎22820 41 315. Open daily 8am-11pm.)

◙◪ **SIGHTS AND BEACHES.** With its many ruins and first-rate beaches, Andros is best explored by moped or car. Near the back corner of the wharf's plateia, a gradual outdoor stairway leads upward through two stone walls and along the flowing waters of the town's **natural spring.** The trees, vines, and flowers lining the walls, along with the dim lighting, make this a lovely, romantic area for an evening stroll. The bus from Batsi can drop you off at the ancient capital of **Paleopolis,** where you can explore the remains of an ancient theater, stadium, and small stone houses. A 1hr. hike or faster taxi ride (€6) north of Gavrio will bring you to the stone **Tower of Agios Petros,** which provides superb views of the harbor below. If you crawl inside the bottom of the tower, built in the 4th century BC, you can gaze up at its interior where the floors have long since collapsed. The tower's original purpose remains unclear, but most believe that it once served as a *friktoria*—a building used to send torch signals. A bus from Gavrio (€3) runs twice per day to the **Bay of Korthi,** the site of a charming village and Andros's finest swimming. Korthi is also home to the 30 watermills that run alongside the **Dipotamata** (Twin River) as well as the remnants of the impressive **Castle of the Old Woman,** which once protected its inhabitants from attacking forces.

The bar at **Golden beach** (beer €2.50-4), accessible by water taxi (round-trip €13), taxi (round-trip €8, arrange a pick-up time), or foot (45min.), is a popular spot for daytime partying. The beach also offers a number of watersports. **Kipri,** 400m back on the road toward Batsi, is more low-key. Following the road toward Gavrio, you'll find **Agios Petros,** another secluded stretch of sand. You can also access the peaceful beach of **Vitali,** which sits in a small protected cove 26km north of Gavrio, by private vehicle. If you continue along the river bank in the back left corner of the beach for 200m, you'll find a cave with beautiful stalagmites.

▨ **NIGHTLIFE.** In the evening, the plateia along Batsi's wharf becomes the center of activity. **Porto Batsi,** across the parking lot by the National Bank, beckons with its blue-neon mermaid and breezy seaside seating. Live Latin music plays over the cozy dance floor on Thursday through Sunday nights. (☎22820 42 026. Happy hour noon-5pm. Beer €4. Mixed drinks €5-8. Open daily April-Oct. 10am-late.) Up the stairs just past the plateia and before the Thothoni, **Capriccio Music Bar's** classy outdoor patio is a great spot to people-watch while having a drink. The party moves to the indoor dance floor around midnight. (☎22820 41 770. Happy hour 7-9pm. Beer €4. Mixed drinks €9. Open daily 9am-late.) Around 1am, follow the locals to the clubs in the back of the plateia, behind the red glow of Cafe Avra, to see how Andros really parties. **Nameless** creates an upbeat atmosphere with a large dance floor, friendly bartenders, and loud mix of mainstream beats. (☎22820 41 698. Beer €6. Mixed drinks €7. Open daily midnight-late.)

CYCLADES

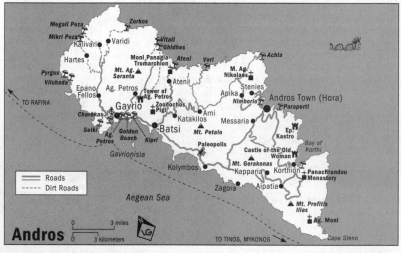

CYCLADES

ANDROS TOWN ☎22820

Andros Town (commonly known as Hora) is built on a peninsula capped by a medieval castle. It quietly charms its visitors with calm, cobbled streets that pass by shops, bakeries, and homes on their way to blue waves and black rocks. Though prices tend to be a bit high relative to the rest of the island, Andros Town makes a great place to spend a day or two soaking in local culture and visiting the exhibitions at its fantastic museums.

▐▌ TRANSPORTATION AND PRACTICAL INFORMATION. The **bus** leaving Andros Town for Gavrio (1hr., 5-7 per day 8:15am-7:30pm, €3) via Batsi (45min., €2.50) runs out of a depot by the main plateia where **taxis** (☎22820 22 171) wait. A schedule is posted in the outdoor waiting area. To get your own wheels, **Riva,** on the left by Faros Studios, all the way down the street, **rents mopeds** from €15 per day and **boats** from €80. (☎22820 24 412. Open daily 8am-10pm.) **Andros Island Travel,** across from the bank, can book tickets, find rooms, and plan excursions. (☎22820 29 220. Open M-Sa 8:30am-9pm, Su 9:30am-9pm.) **Alpha Bank,** G. Ebirikos 49, with a **24hr. ATM** and **currency exchange,** is down the street on the right as you turn right and walk toward the water. (☎22820 23 900. Open M-Th 8am-2:30pm, F 8am-2pm.) The **police station,** G. Ebirikos 2, is on the inland end of the main street to the left. (☎22820 22 300. Open 24hr.) One of several **pharmacies** along the main street sits right across from the main plateia at G. Ebirikos 29. (☎22820 23 203. Open daily 8am-3pm and 6-11pm.) In **medical emergencies,** dial ☎22820 22 222, or visit the **health center** in the back-right corner of the main plateia facing away from G. Ebirikos. The **OTE** is across from the plateia. (☎22820 22 099. Open M-F 7:30am-2:30pm.) **E-waves Internet Cafe,** along the main street before Pl. Kairis, has **Internet access** upstairs from its cafe-bar. (☎22820 29 129. €4.50 per hr.; €1.50 min. Open daily 9am-2am.) The **post office,** G. Ebirikos 14, is inland from the plateia on the main street. (☎22820 22 260. Open M-F 7:30am-2pm.) **Postal Code:** 84500.

▐▌ ACCOMMODATIONS AND FOOD. If you visit in high season be prepared to spend big, though accommodations still aren't cheap the rest of the year; **domatia** are the best options (rooms €35-50, in low season €25-35). The **tourist informa-**

tion kiosk in the main plateia has a list of names and numbers. (☎22820 25 162. Open 8am-11pm.) **Karaoulanis Rooms ❹**, down the street opposite Alpha Bank, on the left corner of Nimborio beach facing inland, rents rooms and studios with kitchens, baths, A/C, and TV. Ask at Riva for more info. (☎22820 24 412; www.androsrooms.gr. Doubles €30-60; studios €60-120.) **Hotel Niki ❹** (Νικη), before Pl. Kairis on the left side of G. Ebirikos, has rooms with TV, A/C, fridges, baths, and balconies. (☎/fax 22820 29 155. Singles €67; doubles €70; triples 86.)

In Pl. Kairis, tons of stands serve *mezedes*, milkshakes, and pizza. Family-owned cafes, restaurants, and markets line the main street and Nimborio beach. For a delicious traditional meal, try **Parea ❷** (Παρεα), in the corner of Pl. Kairis, overlooking Paraporti beach. The roasted red peppers stuffed with feta cheese (€3), seasoned Greek meatballs (€5.40), and roast veal (€6.10) are particularly good. (☎22820 23 721. Cover €1. Open daily noon-midnight. MC/V.) **Kokkini Piperia ❷** (Κοκκινη Πιπερια), in the bus depot parking lot, serves excellent *cacciatore* pasta (€7.20) and salads (€3.50-6.50), and has sweeping views of the valley below. (☎22820 22 778. Open daily noon-4pm and 8pm-1am.) For savory and sweet crepes (€2.50-4.70), head to **Sofrano Kreperi ❶** (Σοφρανο) on the left, across from Alpha Bank. (☎22820 24 152. Open daily 7am-3pm and 6pm-2am.)

◻◪ SIGHTS AND BEACHES. The **Archaeological Museum**, a large white building with a brown tile patio on the left as you enter Pl. Kairis, displays huge *pithoi* (storage jars) from the Geometric-era village of Zagora. The collection, comprised of artifacts from Andros's ancient past, includes a marvelous marble **statue of Hermes**. (☎22820 23 664. Open Tu-Su 8:30am-3pm. €3, students and seniors €2, EU students free.) Turn down the lane to the left upon exiting, and travel down four small sets of stairs (following the arrows on the left wall) to find the permanent wing of the ◪**Museum of Contemporary Art.** Its exhibit displays a wide selection of modern art by both Greek and foreign artists, including works by 20th-century Greek sculptor Michael Tombros. The weird noises are not a mechanical failure, but rather the acoustic stylings of the wonderful kinetic, **electromagnetic art,** which uses electromagnets to strike metal rods against plastic string, creating a fun-to-watch musical masterpiece. The museum's new wing is located two sets of steps farther down on the right, and houses three levels of contemporary art that circulates every summer. (☎22820 22 444. Open June-Sept. M, W-Sa 10am-2pm and 6-8pm, Tu, Su 10am-2pm; Oct.-May M, Sa-Su 10am-2pm. €6, students €3, seniors and children under 12 free.) Follow the main road past Pl. Kairis, turn left at the dead end, and continue down Michael S. Polemi to the end to reach the **Maritime Museum of Andros**, which houses models, paintings, and photographs of 19th- and 20th-century sailing vessels. (Open daily 8am-10pm. €1.50, seniors and children under 12 free.) Past the museum is a plateia where the larger-than-life **Alfanis Nautis Statue,** honoring lost soldiers, gazes out at the humble ruins of a **Venetian castle.**

Facing Hora from the sea, **Paraporti beach** is to the left and **Nimborio beach** is to the right. To reach Paraporti's isolated sands, take the steps down from Pl. Kairis past Heaven Rock Cafe. Nimborio, the more popular and more developed beach, is most easily accessed via the street that leads down to the water across from Alpha Bank. **Achla,** north of town, is considered one of Europe's most beautiful beaches, but is inaccessible to everything but mopeds and fishing boats. Just north of Achla lies **Vori,** where you can swim among shipwrecks; locals warn, however, to be careful of sharp metal in the wreckage. Those yearning to see more secluded spots— the many rivers, waterfalls, and monasteries of the island's interior—should inquire at Andros Travel. A beautiful hiking trail originates in **Apika,** 6km north of Andros Town, and leads past **Sariza Springs** to the village of **Stenies.** This small town is home to the largest **waterwheel** in the Balkans, and is the site of an old spaghetti factory that was accidentally burned down in 1916 by a Greek priest.

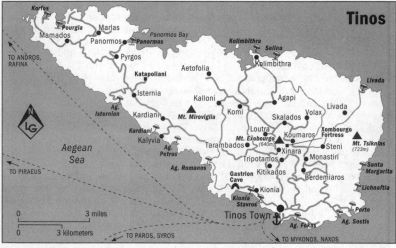

CYCLADES

TINOS Τήνος

Beneath the towering peak of Mt. Exobourgo and its impressive Venetian fortress, the island of Tinos consists of little more than a tourist-oriented harbor town and a number of remote villages that seem untouched by 20th-century commercialism. Tinos's main attraction is the Panagia Evangelistria Church, the largest contemporary shrine of the Greek Orthodox religion, where thousands of pilgrims have flocked every year since its miracle working-icon was unearthed in 1823.

TINOS TOWN   ☎ 22830

Tinos Town made history when, on August 15, 1940, an Italian submarine torpedoed the Greek cruiser *Elli* as it docked at the town's harbor for the observance of the Feast of the Assumption of the Virgin Mary. Mussolini declared war two months later. Tinos has since faded off of the international political map, now playing a dual role as a mecca for both pilgrims and tourists: peddlers sell standard souvenirs alongside the jugs pilgrims use to carry Panagia's sacred waters home. The cool, often unruly breezes that envelop the island explain why the ancient Greeks believed Tinos to be the home of Aeolus, the god of wind.

⬛ TRANSPORTATION. Ferry schedules vary, so check at the **port authority booth** (☎22830 22 220) in the central port or at one of the many **Blue Star ticket offices** (☎22830 24 241) along the waterfront. The largest one is directly across from the buses. **Ferries** run to: Andros (2hr., 2:25pm, €7.20); Mykonos (30min.; 11:20am, noon; €4.50); Paros (1hr.; W 4am, Su 12:15pm; €10); Piraeus (5½hr., 3pm, €23.20); Rafina (4hr.; 2:15, 2:25pm; €15); Syros (20min., 3pm, €5). The **Hellas Ferries office** next door has schedules and tickets for **Flying Dolphins** to Mykonos (15min.; M, W-Su 10:40am; €8), Piraeus (3hr.: M-W 10:40am, 9:15pm; Th 9:15pm: €38.20), and Syros (20min.; M, W-Su 10:40am; €8). There are three ferry ports in Tinos (see below), so ask where you're leaving from when buying tickets. From the central port, **buses** run to: Agios Fokas (5min., 4 per day 11am-5:30pm, €1); Kalloni (45min.; 6:45am, 12:15, 3:45pm; €2.20); Kionia (7min., 11 per day 8am-7:30pm, €1) Skalados (20min.; 6:45am, 12:30pm; €1.60); Steni (30min., 7 per day 6:45am-6pm, €1.30); Porto (6 per day 8am-7pm, €1); Pyrgos (45min., 4 per day 6:30am-5:30pm, €2.70). A schedule is posted at the KTEL ticket agency across from the central port, next to a Blue Star ticket office. (☎ 22830 22 440. Open daily 8am-9:30pm.) **Taxis** are one block past the waterfront base of Evangelistrias, with the water on your right. (☎ 22830 22 470. Available 6am-1:30am.) For **car and moped rental**, try **Vidalis**, which also has free **maps**, at one of its several waterfront locations. (☎ 22830 23 400. Mopeds €16-20. Cars €30-45. Open daily 9am-9pm.)

■ ▐ **ORIENTATION AND PRACTICAL INFORMATION.** The town's central port, across from the bus depot, is the docking point for many ferries. Catamarans and hydrofoils dock at the port to the left, facing inland. The newest port, farther to the left around the waterfront, past a playground, is equally trafficked. Activity centers on wide **Megalochares** and parallel, pedestrian **Evangelistrias** (known as "Bazaar") to the right, facing inland. Among the restaurants near the base of Megalochares, an alley leads away from the central port, through a small plateia with a dolphin statue, to a handful of restaurants and Tinos's cafes and clubs. Many domatia are off Evangelistrias and **Zanaki Alavanou**, on the right of the waterfront. A labeled map of Tinos sits to the left of the central port.

The English-speaking staff at **Windmills Travel**, Kionion 2, behind the playground by the far left port, can arrange accommodations and rental cars (from €40). They also offer bus tours of the island (€12), excursions to Delos and Mykonos (10am-7pm, €20), and day-long tours (€45) around the island. (☎ 22830 23 398. Open 9am-3pm and 6-9pm.) Banks with **currency exchange** and **24hr. ATMs** line the waterfront, including a **National Bank**, opposite the bus depot (☎ 22830 22 328; open M-Th 8am-2pm, F 8am-1:30pm), and an **Alpha Bank** (☎ 22830 23 608; open M-Th 8am-2:30pm, F 8am-2pm), by the post office. The **police** (☎ 22830 22 100) share a building with the **tourist police** (☎ 22830 23 670; open daily 8am-10pm), 5min. out of town on the road to Kionia, and can be reached by phone 24hr. There is a **pharmacy** just to the right of the base of Evangelistrias, next to a Hellas Ferries ticket office. (☎ 22830 22 272. Open M-F 8am-2pm and 6-9:30pm.) There is a **medical center** (☎ 22830 22 210) up Megalochares on the right. The **OTE** is up Megalochares on the right. (☎ 22830 22 499. Open M-F 7:45am-1:30pm.) The **Symposion Cafe**, Evangelistrias 13, on the left up the stairs above a photo shop, has **Internet access** on two high-speed computers. (☎ 22830 24 368. €5 per hr.; €3 min. Open daily 8am-1:30am.) The **post office**, on the right end of the waterfront, also sells phone cards. (☎ 22830 22 247. Open M-F 7:30am-2pm.) **Postal Code:** 84200.

▐ **ACCOMMODATIONS AND CAMPING.** Tinos has plenty of accommodations, but rooms fill up around Easter and on weekends in July and August. Most hotels are expensive, so try bargaining with the crowd holding "rooms to let" signs as you disembark the ferry. Family-run ▧**Nikoleta Rooms to Let ❷**, Kapodistriou 11, is on the second right off the traffic circle uphill from the post office; look for the sign on the left near the end as you walk down the street. Bright rooms just 100m from Agios Fokas beach include TV, A/C, fridges, and balconies. Though only some rooms have baths and kitchenettes, the common kitchen, beautiful garden courtyard, and laundry facilities are available to everyone. (☎ 22830 24 719. Singles €20-25; doubles €25-35; triples and quads €35-45.) **Dimitris-Maria Thodosis Rooms ❷**, Evangelistrias 33, midway up the road to the left with blue balconies and shutters, rents cozy rooms with a central kitchen and common baths. They also have apartments on Marcos Psaros which have more amenities. (☎ 22830 24 809. Open Mar. 25-Oct. Singles €20; doubles €30; triples €35; 2-person apartments €40.) If you want high-class service, call ahead to reserve one of the stylish rooms at **Hotel Tinion ❹**, K. Alvanou 1, which come with TV, A/C, fridges, phones, and baths; some have balconies. Facing inland, follow the main port road to the right; it's on the left by the post office. (☎ 22830 22 261; www.tinionhotel.gr. Breakfast €9. Singles €50-60; doubles €60-70; triples €75-85; quads €80-90. MC/V.) To the left of Windmills Travel, turn left at the top of the stairs and then right at the street to find **Faros ❸**, Foskolou 2, on the right, whose common balconies have harbor views.

The rooms include baths and TV, and some have A/C. (☎22830 22 712. Singles €35; doubles €50; triples €70.) Off the traffic circle past the post office, signs point the way to **Tinos Camping ❶,** whose grounds have a kitchen, laundry, showers, restaurant, and bar. Watch out for the chickens and ducks; you probably won't step on one, but you may step on their droppings. (☎22830 22 344. July-Aug. €6.50 per person; May-June and Sept.-Oct. €5.50 per person, €3.50-4 per tent. Tent rental €7-7.50. 2- to 5-person bungalows €35-47. Discounts for stays over 6 days.)

⬛⬛ FOOD AND NIGHTLIFE. In the middle of the line of tavernas that starts at the base of Megalochares, **Mesklies ❷** is known all over town for its delicious pizza (€10-16; take-out €7.50-13) and Greek salads. (☎22830 22 373. Open daily 10am-2am. MC/V.) Turning into the alleyway just before Mesklies and following it past the plateia with the dolphin statue, you will find **Palaia Pallada** (Παλαια Παλ–λαδα) ❸, on the right. The taverna, with an attractive seating area, has earned its reputation for serving authentic favorites like grilled lamb (€7), carefully prepared vegetable dishes (€3-6), and pasta. (☎22830 23 516. Open daily noon-3:30pm and 7:30pm-midnight. MC/V.) For a cheaper bite to eat, head up the alley around the corner, past Palaia Pallada to **Sikoutris ❶** (Συκουτρης). This diamond-in-the-rough souvlaki stand has cheap beer (€1.50-3) that undercuts the neighboring clubs and hot pitas (€1.70) served with a tasty mayonnaise-mustard sauce. (☎22830 25 680. Open daily 5pm-3am.) **Palamares supermarket** (Παλαμαρες) is on the corner before the post office. (Open M-Sa 8am-9:30pm, Su 9am-2pm.)

For a religious center, Tinos has a surprisingly healthy nightlife scene; at night the cafes lining the street between the plateia with the dolphin statue and the children's playground become happening bars. **Remetzo Cafe,** with its trendy white decor, attracts a chic crowd. (☎22830 25 727. Beer €3-5. Mixed drinks €5. Open daily 9am-2am.) Colorful hanging bobbles and stashes of pirate booty adorn the popular **Koursaros Music Bar** (a.k.a. **"Corsaire"**), 10m seaward from Mesklies, on the corner. (☎22830 23 963. Beer €2.50. Mixed drinks €5-6. Open daily 8am-4am.) To reach Tinos's festive nightclubs, head past Sikoutris up the alleyway and turn right onto Taxiarchon. **Sibylla,** Taxiarchon 17, has a marble dance floor and a DJ who mixes Greek and Euro dance music. (Beer €4. Mixed drinks €6. Open daily 10pm-3am.) Next door, at **Volto** (Βολτο), Taxiarchon 24, clubbers dance under flashing laser lights. (Beer €4. Mixed drinks €7. Open daily 10:30pm-late.) For an unbeatable view and American and international pop music, take a taxi (€2) to **Kactus Bar,** at the base of a windmill above Tinos Town. (Beer €5-6. Mixed drinks €8. Open 10pm-7am.) Those still raring to go when the bars shut down can grab a taxi (€2) to **Paradise,** a thatched-roof "after-club." (Open 3am-9am.)

⬛ SIGHTS. In 1822 a Tiniot nun, Sister Pelagia, had a vision in which the Virgin Mary told her about an icon buried in a field, once the site of a church destroyed by 10th-century pirates. A year later, the prophesied icon was unearthed, and **Panagia Evangelistria** was built to house it. The church draws daily visits from those who consider it evidence of the Virgin's divine power. The relic is said to have healing powers and is credited with ridding Tinos of cholera, saving a sinking ship, and giving a blind man sight. Gifts of gold, diamonds, jewels, and countless *tamata*—plaques praising Mary's healing powers—cover the chapel. The famous **icon** sits up the red-carpeted flight of steps. More devout pilgrims will approach on hands and knees, some beginning at the red carpet at the base of the church, others as soon as they get off the boat at the port, continuing all the way up the hill. The **Well of Sanctification** is a natural spring that appeared when the icon was found. Today it flows from one of many faucets in the church between two sets of marble entrance stairs to the chapel; visitors scoop up a bottle of it to drink or to carry as a talisman. To the right is the **mausoleum** of the Greek warship *Elli*, sunk by an Italian torpedo in 1940. (Open daily 6:30am-8:30pm. Modest dress required. Free.) Tinos's small **Archaeological Museum**, Megalochares 35, halfway up on the left and uphill from the OTE, displays an ancient sundial, sculptures from the sanctuary of Poseidon and Amphitrite at Kionia, a 5th-century BC relief from a cemetery at Xombourgo, and a 7th-century BC relief showing Athena bursting from Zeus's head. (☎22830 29 063. Tu-Su 8:30am-3pm. €2, seniors and students €1, EU students and children free.) Tinos is strewn with over 1000 large medieval birdhouses called **"dovecotes."** The island's symbol, they are made of intricate white lattices and are full of nesting birds. The largest and most impressive collection of dovecotes can be found in the village of **Tarambados**, 6km from Tinos Town, accessible by bus. To explore the poorly preserved ruins of the 4th-century BC **Temple of Poseidon and Amphitrite**, near the beach, drive left along the waterfront road. The picturesque town of **Pyrgos**, 27km northwest of Tinos Town, is home to Tinos's renowned marble sculptors as well as to a School for Fine Arts. Several museums and exhibitions are dedicated to past residents such as Giannouli Chalepas, whose *Sleeping Daughter* graces Athens's central graveyard.

◪ **BEACHES.** Sun-worshippers take a page out of the religious pilgrims' book and prostrate themselves before Tinos's beautiful beaches. Facing inland at the center of town, **Agios Fokas** is on the other side of the peninsula to the right. Midway down the beach, a cafe plays music, rents chairs (€8 for 2), and has volleyball and paddleball. Picturesque **Kolimbithra** is in a small cove 12km north of Tinos Town. To get there, catch the Kalloni bus at the central port and ask to be let off at Kolimbithra beach. The stretch of sand on the island's northern coast lies seductively below a few small tavernas. In the unlikely event that the beach gets crowded, facing the sea, walk uphill to the right and around the peninsula to remote **Selina**. If you find yourself in the Pyrgos or Panormos bay region, continue past the harborside village of **Panormos** and down to the small but lovely beach. The beach of **Kionia**, 3.5km from the center of town, is narrow and pebbly but still attracts a healthy crowd thanks to the frequent buses and multitude of nearby tavernas.

◪ **HIKING.** If you have a car or moped, the villages that ring **Mount Exobourgo** (Εξόβουργο Όρος; 14km north of Tinos Town) and the site of the Venetian Fortress **Xombourgo**, on the northeastern side of the mountain, are fascinating places to explore. After withstanding 11 assaults, the 13th-century capital fell to the Ottomans in 1715, becoming their last territorial gain. For a panoramic view of the entire island, drive up to the foot of the fortress itself. If you're feeling energetic, climb the mountain from the eastern foothill on a trail lined with wildflowers and brilliant orange moss. On a clear day, the peak offers a magnificent view extending as far as Santorini. At the gated entrance to Xombourgo, head left into the plateia to the little gate where the trail to the top starts. At a fork, the road detours to a church. Go straight to get to the fort. Strong winds buffet Exobourgo, causing the fort to close occasionally; stay low to avoid getting blown off balance.

The hike from Tinos Town to Mt. Exobourgo takes 3-4hr. Alternatively, the trip from Tinos Town to Loutra and back takes 3-4hr. and traverses much of the island's interior. Other routes, marked by wooden signposts, up Mt. Exobourgo don't cut through all the villages. For all of them, bring food, water, comfortable shoes, and a hiking partner. Stick to the trail and be prepared for extremely high winds. Travel agents in Tinos Town have more info the particular trails.

To ascend to the villages of **Kitikados** and **Xinara**, begin by heading left behind the Panagia Evangelistria Church to unmarked **Agios Nikolaos**. Follow this road straight up and to the left, where the asphalt gives way to a broad cobblestone path that takes you past two white chapels within 45min. Past the second white chapel is a small stone bridge with an arch. Cross the bridge if you want to stop in Kitikados; if not, stay on the main trail until you reach the asphalt road where you will turn left. Continue across the road and follow the path to the right of the windmill when you see a small trail marked with a wooden sign. Once you pass the windmill, there is another trail marker on your right. Written in Greek, it points to the climb up to Mt. Exobourgo. Xinara is ahead and **Tripotamos** is behind you. You can ascend Exobourgo from here or continue 1½hr. through quiet Xinara.

To get to the village of **Loutra** (2hr.), follow the road through town to the church plateia and then head left to the narrow trail. This path begins your descent to the village; turn right when you hit asphalt. Continue on the paved road past Loutra to Skalados; turn right to find a nice hillside taverna. From the taverna, head up and right on a street with steps to another asphalt road. Walk to the right about 15min. until you see the blue sign pointing toward **Volax**. It's worth stopping here to meander through the narrow, low-arched streets and peek into the many basket-weaving workshops in town. Retrace your steps to the blue Volax sign and turn left onto the road. At **Koumaros,** look for the **Association Lounge ❶,** which sells dirt-cheap drinks and snacks. Once it's passed through Koumaros, the road turns into a stone stair trail that will take you up the northeastern side of Mt. Exobourgo. At the foot of **Sacred Heart,** an impressive Catholic monastery, go diagonally through the plateia to the little gate on the left. The **Xombourgo fortress** is only 20min. up.

MYKONOS Μύκονος

Mykonos is known around the world as the party center of the Greek isles. Having come a long way since ancient times, when it was a mere stopping point on the way to sacred Delos, Mykonos is now one of the most heavily trafficked and lusted-after tourist destinations in Greece. The island's beautiful sand beckons to hedonists of every age, and whitewashed, narrow streets are lined with shops, restaurants, and every travel service imaginable. At sunset, the unparalleled island-wide party revs into high gear. Mykonos's gay scene, which reached its prime in the 1970s, remains alive and kicking as the island continues to be accepting in a way that most of Greece is not. In the end, everyone is drunk and happy.

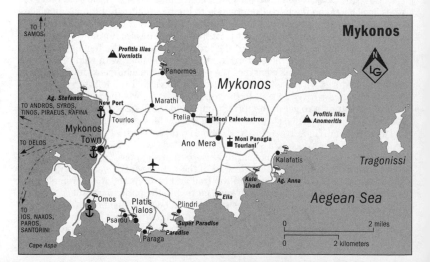

CYCLADES

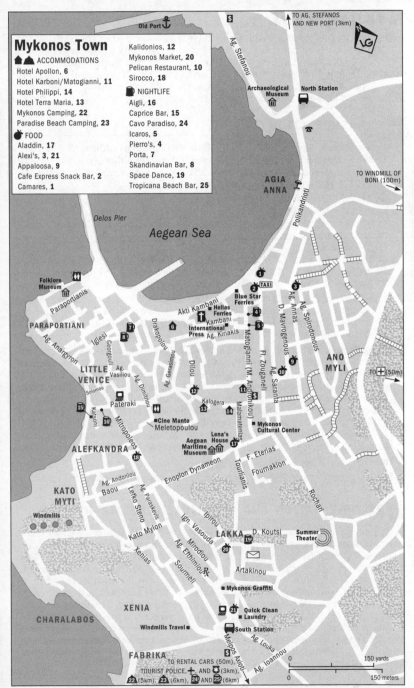

CYCLADES

Mykonos Town

🏠🏠 ACCOMMODATIONS
Hotel Apollon, **6**
Hotel Karboni/Matogianni, **11**
Hotel Philippi, **14**
Hotel Terra Maria, **13**
Mykonos Camping, **22**
Paradise Beach Camping, **23**

🍴 FOOD
Aladdin, **17**
Alexi's, **3, 21**
Appaloosa, **9**
Cafe Express Snack Bar, **2**
Camares, **1**

Kalidonios, **12**
Mykonos Market, **20**
Pelican Restaurant, **10**
Sirocco, **18**

📷 NIGHTLIFE
Aigli, **16**
Caprice Bar, **15**
Cavo Paradiso, **24**
Icaros, **5**
Pierro's, **4**
Porta, **7**
Skandinavian Bar, **8**
Space Dance, **19**
Tropicana Beach Bar, **25**

Old Port

TO AG. STEFANOS
AND NEW PORT (3km)

Archaeological Museum
North Station

Delos Pier

Aegean Sea

AGIA ANNA

TO WINDMILL OF
BONI (100m)

Folklore Museum

Paraportianis
PARAPORTIANI

Ag. Anargyron
Iglesi
Georgouli
Ag. Vasiliou
Solomou

LITTLE VENICE

Drakopoulou
Ag. Gerasimou
Diliou

Akti Kambani
Hellas Ferries
Kambani International Press
Ag. Kiriakis

Blue Star Ferries
TAXI

D. Mavrogenous
Ag. Annas
Ag. Spiridonous

Matogianni (M. Andronikou)
Fl. Zouganeli

ANO MYLI

TO ✚ (50m)

Pateraki
Karsoti

Mitropoleos

Kalogera

Ag. Saranta
Malamatenias

Mykonos Cultural Center

Cine Manto
Meletopoulou

ALEFKANDRA

Aegean Maritime Museum
Lena's House

F. Eterias
Fournakion

Enoplon Dynameon
Touriianis

Rochari

KATO MYTI

Ag. Andoniou
Baou
Lefko Steno
Kato Mylon
Ag. Paraskelis

Ipitou
Ign. Vasouda
Mirodiou
Ag. Efthimiou
Sourmeli
Xenias

LAKKA
D. Koutsi
Summer Theater

Windmills

Artakinou

Mykonos Graffiti

XENIA

Quick Clean Laundry

Windmills Travel
South Station

CHARALABOS

FABRIKA
TO RENTAL CARS (50m),
TOURIST POLICE, ✚, AND ✚ (3km)
22 (5km), **23** (6km), **24** AND **25** (6km)

Ag. Ioannou
Melpos Axioti
Ag. Louka

0   150 yards
0   150 meters

MYKONOS TOWN   ☎22890

Mykonos Town owes its labyrinthine streets, now closed to motor traffic in the afternoon and evening, to Mediterranean pirates. The city's maze was planned expressly to disconcert and disorient marauders, and now has a similar effect on tourists. Despite the massive influx of visitors, the town has resisted large hotel complexes, allowing historical churches, traditional fishing boats, basket-laden donkeys, and king-like pelicans to take center stage.

▐▀ TRANSPORTATION

Flights: Olympic Airways (☎22890 22 490) flies to **Athens** (30min., 4-5 per day, €88) and **Thessaloniki** (1¼hr., 2 per week, €99). **Aegean Airlines** (☎21099 88 300) also goes to **Athens** (30min., 4 per day, €51-100) and **Thessaloniki** (1¼hr., 3 per day, €140-227). Take a taxi (€5.20) to the airport.

Ferries: Most boats dock at the **Old Port** to the left of the waterfront, facing inland, but occasionally they arrive at or depart from the **New Port** near Ag. Stefanos beach, 3km away. Buy tickets at the Blue Star Ferries ticket office (☎22890 28 240) on the waterfront. To: **Andros** (2¼hr., M-F 2-3 per day, €9.50-11.40); **Naxos** (3hr., F 9:20pm, €9.50); **Piraeus** (6hr., 2:15pm, €25.50); **Paros** (3hr., M-F daily, €8.40); **Rafina** (4½hr.: M-W, Su 3 per day; F 4 per day: €17-20.40); **Syros** (2½hr., 2:15pm, €7.50); **Tinos** (35min.: M-W, Su 4 per day 1:15-4pm; Th, Sa 3 per day; F 4 per day 10:30am-2:15pm: €4-5). To get to **Santorini**, you must connect through Paros.

Flying Dolphins: Buy tickets at Delia Travel (☎22890 22 322) on the waterfront. To: **Ios** (2½hr., 2:30pm, €26); **Naxos** (1hr., 1-2 per day, €16); **Paros** (1hr.: M-Tu, Th-Su 11:15am, 2:30pm: W 2:30pm: €14); **Piraeus** (4hr., 2 per day, €42); **Santorini** (3hr., 2:30pm, €28); **Syros** (1hr., 2 per day, €12.30); **Tinos** (30min., 1-2 per day, €8).

Buses: KTEL (☎22890 23 360) has 2 stations. Unless noted, buses are €1 during the day and €1.30 after midnight. **North Station,** on the paved road from the ferry dock to the center of town, sends buses to **Agios Stefanos beach** (every 30min.), **Elia** (8 per day 11am-7:30pm) via **Ano Mera,** and **Kalafatis** (7 per day 7am-10pm) via **Ano Mera. South Station,** at the opposite edge of town, serves: **Agios Ioannis** (7:30am, every hr. 9:30am-5:30pm, 2 per hr. 6pm-1:30am); **Ornos beach** (7:30am, every hr. 9:30am-5:30pm, 2 per hr. 6pm-1:30am); **Paradise beach** (7:45, 9am, 2 per hr. 10am-7:30pm, every hr. 8pm-6am); **Paraga** (every hr. 9am-3am); **Plati Yialos beach** (7:50, 9am, 2 per hr. 10am-12:30am, 1, 2am). Schedules are posted at the stations.

Taxis: ☎22890 22 400. Wait at Taxi Sq., along the water.

Rentals: Agencies around the bus stops. Bargaining expected. **Mopeds** €15-25 per day.

◪ ▐ ORIENTATION AND PRACTICAL INFORMATION

Facing inland from the **Old Port,** the road leading to the right along the water takes you past **North Station** and the beach to **Taxi Square** and the waterfront. This same road heading away from Mykonos Town leads to **Agios Stefanos beach** and the **New Port** 3km away. On the right side of the waterfront is a pier from where excursion boats head to Delos dock. Past the pier is a series of white-washed churches, a lovely part of town called **"Little Venice,"** and a windmill-lined hill. Although plenty of action centers on the waterfront, most of the real shopping, fine dining, and partying occurs among the narrow, winding back streets. Some of the important streets to be familiar with are **Matogianni,** which leads inland from the water, **Enoplon Dynameon,** which catches the bottom of Matogianni, and **Mitropoleos,** which intersects E. Dynameon on its way from Little Venice to **Lakka** and **South Station.** Pick out landmarks for yourself along the way as navigating Mykonos's maze of streets is not an easy task. The road heading uphill from South Station goes to the **airport**, campsites, and **Paradise beach**. The town's essentials—post office, Internet, markets, and so forth—mostly lie near Lakka and South Station.

Tourist Information: Windmills Travel (☎22890 26 555; www.windmillstravel.com), on Xenias, around the corner from South Station, has maps and helps with everything from last-minute accommodations to scuba diving (2 dives €99) and snorkeling (€25) excursions. The staff also has tips and resources for gay travelers. Open daily 8am-10pm.

Banks: National Bank, Melpos Axioti 6 (☎22890 23 163), up the hill from South Station, and **Alpha Bank**, Matogianni 41 (☎22890 23 909), at the corner of Kalogera, **exchange currency** and have **24hr. ATMs**. Both open M-Th 8am-2:30pm, F 8am-2pm.

Bookstore: International Press, Kambani 5 (☎22890 23 316), in a small plateia opposite Pierro's; follow signs from the waterfront. Sells eclectic books, magazines, and newspapers in several languages including English. Open daily noon-1am.

Laundromat: Quick Clean (☎22890 27 323), just below South Station on the right, up 1 flight of stairs. Wash and dry €10. Open daily 8am-midnight.

Police: ☎22890 22 716. By the airport. Open 24hr. The **tourist police** (☎22890 22 482), with helpful English-speaking staff, are also by the airport. Open daily 8am-9pm.

Pharmacies: Ag. Efthimiou 57 (☎22890 24 188). Downhill from South Station. Open M-Sa 9am-2pm and 5-11pm.

Medical Center: ☎22890 23 994. On the higher road leading from the port to South Station. Open for **emergencies** 24hr.

Telephones: OTE ☎22890 22 699. At the left end of the waterfront in a big white building, uphill and to the right of the dock. Open M-F 7am-2:40pm.

Internet Access: Mykonos Internet World, Ag. Louka 8 (☎22890 79 194). Follow the signs up the stairs just past South Station. Also has international phone calls and laptop connections. €3.50 per hr. Open daily 9am-1am. Turning right from E. Dynameon onto Mitropoleos, green arrows point to **E@rthInternet Cafe**, Pateraki 4 (☎22890 22 791). €4 per hr. Open daily 9am-1am.

Post Office: ☎22890 22 238. Down the street to the right after South Station, by the police. **Exchanges currency**. Open M-F 7:30am-2pm. **Postal Code:** 84600.

ACCOMMODATIONS AND CAMPING

Mykonos is one of the most expensive of the Greek islands, and rooms are predictably pricey. Budget accommodations do exist, however, if you're willing to stay outside town. Most budget travelers find their niche at the island's campsites, whose options far surpass the standard plot of grass. The information offices by the dock are numbered according to accommodation type: "1" for **hotels** (☎22890 24 540; 9am-4pm), "2" for **rooms to let** (☎22890 24 860; 9am-11pm), and "3" for **camping** (☎22890 23 567; 9am-midnight). Signs on the streets advertise **domatia**, but the rooms farther from town, available through the information office, tend to have better amenities for lower prices. In high season, domatia doubles range €40-50.

■ **Paradise Beach Camping** (☎22890 22 852; www.paradisemykonos.com). Take the bus from South Station (15min., 2 per hr., €1). Free pickup at the port or airport (call when you arrive). This campsite on Paradise beach features clean showers and bathrooms, bars, a restaurant, and a dance club. Internet €4.50 per hr. Breakfast included. Luggage storage €1 per day. Camping €5-8 per person; €2.50-4 per small tent, €4.50-7 per large tent; 3-person tent rental with beds €8-18. 1- to 2-person cabin €15-40, 4-person cabin €40-100. Hotel doubles with A/C €40-90. Apartments also available. ❶

Mykonos Camping (☎22890 25 915; www.mycamp.gr), just above Paraga beach on the bus route to Paradise beach, provides a slightly more subdued camping experience. Free pickup and drop-off at the port and airport. Clean showers and bathrooms, a mini-mart, beachside cafe-bar, and restaurant are all on site. Internet €5 per hr. €5-8 per person, €4 per tent; tent rental €9. Dorms €15. 2-person bungalow €20-30. ❶

Hotel Philippi, Kalogera 25 (☎22890 22 294), across from Zorzis. The rooms in this light-blue shuttered hotel, which feels like your own private sanctuary, have baths, fridges, TV, phones, hair dryers, A/C, and balconies. The garden courtyard is gorgeous. Open Apr.-Oct. Singles €45-70; doubles €60-90; triples €72-108. AmEx/MC/V. ❹

Hotel Terra Maria, Kalogera 37 (☎22890 24 212, low season 22890 22 957), on a side street to the left of Kalogera off Matogianni, by the public gardens. Lovely rooms have A/C, baths, fridges, TV, and balconies. Breakfast (€5) is served in the cafe-bar or on the veranda. Singles €15-80; doubles €30-100; triples €36-120. AmEx/MC/V. ❹

Hotel Karboni/Matogianni (☎22890 22 217; www.webtourists.com/karbonimatogianni/index.html), located among Matogianni's shops. Owned by the same family, these 2 hotels have a private garden, comfortable lounge, and rooms with varying amenities. All have A/C and TV; some have fridges, balconies, and private baths. Signs point to the reception off Matogianni. Breakfast €4.40. Hotel Karboni singles €37-42; doubles €60-90; triples €69-99. Rooms at Matogianni are about 10% more. ❹

Hotel Apollon (☎22890 22 223), on the waterfront, is an antique-laden house with burgundy trim and a cheerful owner. Rooms are simple and cheaper than other rooms in town during the summer. Singles and doubles €50, with bath €70. ❹

◢ FOOD

Food is, not surprisingly, also expensive on Mykonos, but the produce stands around South Station and **Mykonos Market,** between the post office and South Station, are good for cheap meals. (☎22890 24 897. Open daily 8am-12:30am.) Creperies and souvlaki joints crowd almost every street. For the cheapest, most delicious crepes in town (from €3.50), head to Taxi Sq., where small **Cafe Express Snack Bar** ❶ (☎22890 27 998), is to the right with the water at your back. At the other waterfront corner of the square, **Camares** ❶, which also serves crepes, opens at 6pm.

Appaloosa, D. Mavrogenous 11 (☎22890 27 086), 3 blocks from Taxi Sq. Known as 1 of the classier restaurants in town, it serves large, creative salads (€8-12), pastas (€7-14), and a few Mexican entrees. The €2 cover includes bread with a delicious home-made olive pâté. Open daily 8pm-1am. MC/V. ❸

Pelican Restaurant (☎22890 26 226), past Appaloosa coming from Taxi Square, under a canopy of vines and flowers. The Greek entrees, such as seafood (€11-25) and lamb with yogurt (€11.50), are worth savoring. Open daily noon-1:30am. AmEx/MC/V. ❸

Sirocco, Mitropoleos 8 (☎22890 27 669), brings a taste of California to the Aegean, preparing fruit smoothies with sorbet, frozen yogurt, or ice cream (€5-6), along with crepes (€3.50-7) and bagel sandwiches (€3.50-5). Open daily 10am-1am. ❷

Kalidonios, Dilou 1 (☎22890 27 606), tucked away at the end of Dilou, a small street off of Kalogera. Serves a broad range of Greek and Mediterranean dishes made from scratch in a cozy, colorful interior. The staff recommends the *exohiko* (€15), a hearty pastry filled with lamb, vegetables, and feta. Open daily 1pm-1am. MC/V. ❸

Aladdin (☎22890 24 783), on E. Dynameon by the Dodoni ice-cream parlor, makes unique pastry masterpieces such as green pistachio baklava (€1.50), and has an assortment of fresh-brewed coffees (€3). Open daily 10am-4am. ❶

Alexi's, 1 at the back of Taxi Sq. (☎22890 26 904), and 1 near South Station (☎22890 26 393), is a good place to grab a cheap meal. Pitas €2. Souvlaki platters €6.50. Delivery available. Open daily 10am-late. ❶

SIGHTS

Losing yourself in its colorful alleyways is one of Mykonos Town's cheapest and most exhilarating experiences. A stroll to the **kastro** area—behind the Delos ferry pier, at the far left of the port when facing the water—will take you to the **Paraportiani,** a cluster of white churches. This is also a prime spot to encounter one of the island's famed local **pelicans,** who wait outside the tavernas in the square hoping for a tasty treat. From there, walk through **Little Venice,** where the Aegean's sapphire waters lap at the legs of cafe tables and chairs. The line of stalwart **windmills** along the waterfront is a fabulous sunset vantage point.

The **Folklore Museum** is divided among three of the island's most historically significant buildings. The main museum in the **House of Kastro** is just above the Delos pier, and has displays on traditional Mykonian household items. (☎22890 22 591. Open Apr.-Oct. M-Sa 5:30-8:30pm, Su 6:30-8:30pm. Free.) The **Windmill of Boni,** on the road that leads uphill from North Station, hosts a wine festival each September to celebrate the town's agricultural history. (Open daily Apr.-Oct. 4-8pm.) **Lena's House,** the third building, next to the Aegean Maritime Museum, is an 18th-century upper-middle class home preserved exactly as its owner left it. (☎22890 28 764. Open Apr.-Oct. M-Sa 6:30-9:30pm, Su 7-9pm. Free.) The beautifully manicured garden of the **Aegean Maritime Museum,** around the corner from the inland end of Matogianni on E. Dynameon, contains gigantic nautical instruments, including the largest lighthouse in the Aegean. (☎22890 22 700. Open daily Apr.-Oct. 10:30am-1pm and 6:30-9pm. €3, students and seniors €1.50, children free.) The **Archaeological Museum** is on the paved road between the dock and the center of town. It displays a large collection of pottery found throughout the island, including a renowned 7th-century BC *amphora* with scenes depicting the fall of Troy. (☎22890 22 325. Open Tu-Su 8:30am-3pm. €2, students and seniors €1, EU students and under 18 free.) The **Cultural Center of Mykonos,** on Matogianni, hosts fascinating rotating exhibits that feature the work of up-and-coming Greek artists. (☎22890 27 791. Open daily 11am-2pm and 7pm-1am. Free.)

NIGHTLIFE

At night, the young and beautiful descend upon Mykonos Town to mingle with mere mortals at cafes, nightclubs, and a handful of pubs. The most popular bars, packed from 11pm until morning, are in Little Venice and Taxi Sq. Mykonos's club scene is one of the most vibrant in Greece, with new establishments opening each summer. If you get tired of crazy par-

THE LOCAL STORY

PETROS: PELICAN OF MYSTERY

Every summer, tourist-paparazzi swarm around Mykonos Town, attempting to get a photo of the area's biggest celebrity in action— taking a stroll by the windmills, perhaps, or enjoying a seafood dinner in Little Venice, compliments of a taverna-keeper.

The town superstar isn't what you would call typical, though. In fact, he's a pelican named "Petros." In his standard pose, the white-and-pink bird can be hard to pick out against the town's white buildings—at least until he blinks his beady black eyes and extends his heavy wings and long, slender neck. Though he is constantly surrounded by his admirers, Petros's main concern is scoring free fish; if you feed him, be prepared to be followed and "asked" for more.

But Petros's obsessive fish habit, typical of most pelicans, may be hiding the fact that he's not really Petros after all. The first pelican known as "Petros" lived here for over 30 years after being stranded by a storm in the 1950s and adopted by locals. Since his death, though, any pelican in Mykonos gets the royal treatment; there are currently 2-3 regulars.

Petros (or possibly Petroses) has been sighted all over the northwestern city. To catch a glimpse, wander around the whitewashed churches of the Paraportiani and the surrounding tavernas. Just look for a crowd of tourists wielding cameras.

ties, head to **Cine Manto,** in Pl. Lymni, which shows English-language films. (☎22890 27 190. Shows 9, 11:30pm. €7.)

▓ **Caprice Bar,** in Little Venice, is a popular post-beach hangout. Crowds cluster around the candlelit bar, and jump and sing exuberantly with the loud, funky music. Gathering steam earlier than most other establishments on the island, it's a great place to watch the sun set and kick off the night. Beer €7. Mixed drinks €12. Open daily 6:30pm-4am.

▓ **Skandinavian Bar** (☎22890 22 669), near the waterfront. This 2-building complex includes a disco, 2 bars, and a cafe-like seating area. Though large enough for its massive crowds, it still has a casual, intimate atmosphere. Beer and shots €4-6. Mixed drinks from €7. Open M-Th, Su 9pm-5am, F-Sa 9pm-morning.

Cavo Paradiso (☎22890 27 205; www.cavoparadiso.gr) on the cliff over Paradise beach. As the club is considered 1 of the world's premier dance clubs, rumor says that even internationally renowned DJs will settle for a lower salary to spin at the open-aired venue. The debauchery centers on a glowing pool and continues well past sunrise. Cover €15-50. Open daily 3am-11am.

Pierro's, in Pl. Kiriaki on Matogianni, is the oldest gay bar in Mykonos and still the place to go for a good time. Spontaneous glitter parties and an annual summer theme event (e.g., jungle) keep the crowd on their toes. The owner also runs the calmer **Manto Cafe,** for those who need a breather from the party. Drag shows nightly at 1:30am. Beer €5. Mixed drinks €9-10. Open daily 10pm-5am.

Space Dance (☎22890 24 100; www.spacedance.gr), by the post office, is the nightclub your mother feared when you first told her you were going to Mykonos. Scantily clad dancers strut on elevated platforms, while spectacular light shows and pounding beats saturate the 2-story, notoriously crazy complex. When things get too hot, sweaty partiers cool off in the posh outdoor bar and lounge. Beer €6. Mixed drinks €8. Cover €10 women, €20 men, €25 couples; includes 1 drink. Open daily midnight-morning.

Icaros (☎22890 22 718), next door and upstairs from Pierro's, shares customers, atmosphere, and the drag show with its neighbor. Beer €4. Open daily 11pm-4:30am.

Porta (☎22890 27 087), tucked behind Niko's Taverna, is a popular, lively gay bar. Mellow tunes melt into upbeat disco as the night wears on. The lounge, however, with colorful pillow seating in the corner, stays quieter. Open daily 9pm-3:30am.

Aigli (☎22890 27 265), E. Dynameon, sheds its cafe image and becomes a lively, social bar after dark. The indoor and outdoor seating areas are perfect for a pre-gaming session or a night off from the ruckus. Mixed drinks €12. Open daily 11am-4am.

⚲ BEACHES

Mykonos has a beach to please everyone. Although all the island's beaches are **nude,** the degree of nudity depends on where you go. The small beach in Mykonos Town is nice for a quick swim, but the best beaches are out of town, accessible by bus or water taxi from **Ornos** or **Platis Yialos** (€1-3). Chairs and umbrellas (€4) line **Paradise** in front of the beachside bars and clubs. Widely known as the party beach, it blasts music and serves drinks all day; the revelry kicks into full gear between 5pm and sundown, when bars give away free drinks and t-shirts to get the beachgoers onto the dance floor. **Tropicana Beach Bar,** on Paradise beach, is where international youth go to make spring break last all summer. The most popular place to party your liver away by day, the crowd reaches its peak around late afternoon or early evening, and chugs on into the night. (☎22890 26 990. Open daily 8:30am-late.) Watersports (tubing €15, jet-skiing €30-50, water-skiing €30, wakeboarding €30) are available in the afternoon. Nearby **Paraga** beach is accessible by the same bus. Farther away from Mykonos Town, **Elia** is quieter, but still has a slew of watersports (jet-skiing €35, wakeboarding €13, paddle boats €15). Nearby **Kalo Livadi,** with similar activities, is more family-oriented, but is only accessible by a few buses per day from South Station. Otherwise, ask the bus to Elia to drop you at the top of the road to Kalo Livadi and walk the 2km down to the beach. **Agios Stefanos** has a magnificent view of the harbor and a small sandy beach perfect for relaxing and working on your tan. Fashionable, trendy **Psarou** stays crowded with vacationing Athenians, as waitresses in bikinis serve drinks from the pricey beachside cafes and restaurants. **Platis Yialos** offers a variety of watersports, and **Ornos** has a lifeguard on duty; both are geared toward families. (Chairs and umbrellas are both €8 for 2 of each.) **Panormos,** on the northern coast, 15km from town and accessible only by private vehicle, is remote and private, a relief for those trying to escape the crowds. Windsurfing and sailing are also available (€15-40). **Super Paradise,** accessible by water taxi or private vehicle, 8km from town, is a pebbly beach in a gorgeous setting, lined with bars and covered with umbrellas (€8 for 2). The beachgoers' tendency to display much more nudity than the other beaches attracts pleasure-seekers of all ages and sexual orientations.

⭐ DAYTRIP FROM MYKONOS

DELOS Δήλος

Excursion boats leave from the dock (20min., Tu-Su 4 per day 9am-12:50pm, round-trip €6.50-7). Buy tickets at either Hellas or Blue Star Ferries on the waterfront. An additional boat heads out from Mykonos's southern beaches 10-10:45am (€10). Most trips let you explore for only 3hr., but each boat line has several return trips, allowing for flexibility. Each company also offers guided tours (€30, including admission). A cheaper option is to buy a guidebook (€5-15) in town or at the entrance to the site with a map. Tinos, Naxos, Paros, and other islands run joint trips to Mykonos and Delos but allow less time to explore. Open Tu-Su 8:30am-3pm. €5, students and EU seniors €3, EU students free.

With its impressive ruins, continuing excavations, and fascinating museum, Delos—the sacred center of the Cyclades—is a must-see. The tiny island is home to the most important **Temple of Apollo,** built to commemorate the birthplace of the god and his twin sister, Artemis. A site of religious pilgrimage in the ancient world, today Delos is essentially a giant, island-wide museum.

HISTORY. According to mythology, after **Zeus,** the philandering king of the gods, impregnated the mortal **Leto** with Artemis and Apollo, he sent her away from Olympus in an attempt to shield her from the wrath of his jealous wife, **Hera.** Leto, desperately seeking a place to give birth, wandered the Aegean, but was refused by island after island, each afraid of Hera's fury. At last exhausted Leto came upon a floating island shrouded in mist but it too cowered under Hera's threats. Leto swore by the river Styx—the most sacred of all oaths—that if she were allowed to give birth on the island, it would no longer have to float and that her future son Apollo would bring fame and riches to its shores. Upon hearing this vow, the reassured island stopped drifting and welcomed her. Unhappy and vengeful, Hera made the goddess of childbirth, **Eilythia,** prolong Leto's labor for nine days in revenge. When the infants finally arrived, the mist disappeared and the island basked in light. The island's name was thus changed from "Adelos" ("invisible") to "Delos" ("visible"). True to Leto's vow, Delos soon became the seat of her son's worship. Attracting a multitude of pilgrims, Apollo's sanctuary grew to be one of the most important religious and cultural centers in ancient Greece.

Although Delos was colonized by the Ionians in the 10th century BC, its status as a center of worship arose only in the 8th century BC. After it emerged untouched from the **Persian Wars** (p. 55), Delos became the focal point of the **Delian League** (p. 56). During these years, the Athenians ordered at least two "purifications" of the island in Apollo's honor. The second, in 426 BC, decreed that no one should give birth or die on its grounds—an order worshippers took retroactively, exhuming graves and moving bodies to a "purification pit" on nearby **Rheneia.** After Sparta defeated Athens in the **Peloponnesian War** (p. 56), Delos enjoyed independence and wealth. This prosperity soured, however, during the Roman occupation in the 2nd century BC, when Delos became the slave-trading center of Greece. By the end of the AD 2nd century, after successive sackings, the island was left nearly deserted. Today its only residents are legions of lizards and members of the French School of Archaeology, which has been excavating here since 1873.

SIGHTS. Occupying almost 2.5 sq. km, the **archaeological site** includes the Temple of Apollo, the agora, Mt. Kythnos, and the theater quarter. While it would take days to explore the ruins completely, you can see the highlights in about 3hr. Most visitors follow a similar route when they disembark the ferry; reverse it for more privacy. Bring a hat, good shoes, and a water bottle. The cafeteria beside the museum is exorbitantly priced (orange juice; €4), so it's wise to pack some snacks as well.

The path beyond the admission booth points toward the **Agora of the Competaliasts,** where Roman guilds built their shop-shrines. Continue in the same direction and turn left onto the Sacred Road. Two parallel **stoas,** the more impressive of which (on the left) was built by Phillip of Macedon in 210 BC and dedicated to Apollo, adorn the walk. Bear right and follow this road to the **Sanctuary of Apollo,** a collection of temples built in the god's honor. The sanctuary complex begins when you reach the **Propylaea.** The biggest and most important of the temples is on the right. The famous **Temple of Apollo,** or Temple of the Delians, was completed at the end of the 4th century BC. Its immense, partially hollow hexagonal pedestal once supported an 8m marble statue of the god. Following the direction of the Sacred Road north, 50m past its end, will lead to the **Terrace of the Lions,** where replicas of the ancient marble felines overlook the Sacred Lake. Five of the original lions are still whole and are protected from the elements inside the museum, along with the partial remains of three others. The body of the ninth, pirated by Venetians, guards the entrance to the Arsenal in Venice.

Proceed up the small crest left of the terrace to the **House of the Hill.** Because the building was planted deep into the earth, this archetypal Roman house is still intact. The **House of the Lake,** with a well-preserved mosaic decorating its atrium, and the desecrated **Sacred Lake,** drained in 1925 to protect against malaria, are both downhill. Today, the round shape of the former lake appears as a leafy oasis with a lone palm tree at its center. On the lake's south side is the **Roman agora.**

From the **Archaeological Museum** (free with admission to the site), you can hike to the summit of **Mount Kythnos** (elev. 112m). Its peak provides such a good view of the island that Zeus used it to secretly watch his twins' birth. Wear sturdy, comfortable shoes; though the trail is not too difficult, it can be steep and some of the rocks dislodge easily. Ascending the mountain coming from the direction of the Temple of Apollo, you will pass temples dedicated to Egyptian gods. The elegant bust in the ▨**Temple of Isis** depicts the sun. The immense building blocks of the nearby **Grotto of Heracles** reflect Mycenaean architecture (though some experts suggest they're knock-offs). Coming down the mountain, bear left away from the museum to reach the **House of the Dolphins** and **House of the Masks,** which contain intricate mosaics of dolphins, as well as the most famous mosaic on Delos, *Dionysus Riding a Panther.* Continue on to the **ancient theater,** which has a sophisticated cistern (as cisterns go) called **"Dexamene,"** with nine arched compartments. As you weave down the rough path back toward the entrance, you'll see the **House of the Trident,** graced by a mosaic of a dolphin twisted around a trident; the **House of Dionysus,** containing another mosaic of Dionysus and a panther; and the **House of Cleopatra.** The famous statue of Cleopatra and Dioscourides is sheltered in the site's museum.

SYROS Σύρος

Syros first rose to commercial power as a Phoenician seaport, and later the 13th-century Venetians turned it into a trading capital. Steamships and the rise of Piraeus as the modern national port, however, ended Syros's glory days, until the last 20 years, when the shipbuilding industry has helped Syros regain its economic footing. Now, Syros is home to almost half of the Cyclades's permanent residents. Tons of Greek families have made their home in the seaside villages, and visitors are treated to an uncommonly bustling island lifestyle and the medieval settlement of Ano Syros, high on one of Syros's two peaks.

ERMOUPOLIS Ερμούπολις ☎22810

Busy Ermoupolis, the Cyclades's largest city and capital, is named in honor of winged messenger Hermes, god of commerce, communication, and travel. True to its name, the port hosts both shipping magnates and tourists; Neoclassical mansions, most of which now house government agencies, line quieter streets farther inland. Greek, Italian, and Bavarian design combine in the pastel colors and wrought-iron balconies that make the island feel dignified and cosmopolitan, and hint at its opulent past. In the background two church-topped hills vie for supremacy: Catholic church Agios Giorgos caps Venetian settlement Ano Syros to the left, while Greek Orthodox church Anastasis tops the mountain to the right.

🗐 TRANSPORTATION

Flights: 5 flights per week go to **Athens** (25min., €70). You must take a bus or a taxi to the **airport,** southeast of Ermoupolis (☎22810 87 025).

Ferries: To: **Crete** (10hr., 2 per week, €23); **Ios** (5hr., 5 per week, €15); **Mykonos** (1hr., 3-4 per day, €8); **Naxos** (1½hr., 1-3 per day, €10); **Paros** (1hr., 1-3 per day, €7.50); **Piraeus** (4½hr., 4-6 per day, €18.50); **Santorini** (6hr., 7 per week, €20); **Tinos** (45min., 4 per day, €4). Most boats depart from the right side of the harbor. **Flying Dolphins** go twice daily to **Mykonos** (1hr., €33), **Piraeus** (2hr., €36), and **Tinos** (30min., €8.30). Schedules vary by season; check with a travel agency.

Buses: ☎22810 82 575. Green **KTEL** buses leave from the depot near the ferry dock. Most buses follow a single loop around the island, departing counterclockwise on the hour (8am-midnight) and clockwise on the half-hour (7:30am-10:30pm). To: **Azolimnos** (45min., €1.10); **Finikas** (25min., €1.30); **Galissas** (15min., €1.10); **Komito** (30min., €1.30); **Megas Yialos** (35min., €1.30); **Posidonia** (€1.30). Another bus leaves 5

Syros

Trimeson Cape
Grammata
Marmari Kastri
Glyssoura
TO PIRAEUS
Lia
Sirigas Chalandriani
Varvarousa
Mytikas
Aegean Sea
Delfini Mt. Pyrgos (440m)
Kini
Kini Ano Syros
Ermoupolis Ag. Nikolaos
Ag. Varvara
TO TINOS, MYKONOS
Danakos Episkopio
Galissas Galissas Talanda TO PAROS, NAXOS
Armeos Pagos Agros Manna
Ag. Stefanos Faneromeni
Parakopi Azolimnos
Finikas Finikas Vissas
Chroussa
Kokkina Vari
Posidonia Megas Yialos
Agathopes Vari
Megas Yialos
Komito Abela
0 15 miles
0 15 kilometers
Ak. Viglostasi

times per day for **Episkopio** (€1), **Manna** (€1.10), and **Parakopi** (€1.10). 3-5 shuttle buses per day go to **Ano Syros** (€1), **Dili** (€0.70), and **Vrontado** (€0.70).

Taxis: ☎22810 86 222. Line up 24hr. in Pl. Miaouli.

Rentals: Rental agencies line the waterfront. Try **Enjoy Your Holidays Rent a Car,** Akti Paeidou 8 (☎22810 87 070), by the central port. Cars €30. Open daily 8am-11pm. **Sigalas Rentals** (☎22810 81 805) is farther down the waterfront in front of the Diogenis Hotel. Motorbikes €10; helmet included. Cars from €30. Open daily 9am-9pm.

⚡ 🛈 ORIENTATION AND PRACTICAL INFORMATION

Facing inland from the dock, head right and walk down the waterfront for 3min. to **Eleftheriou Venizelou,** the main street, beginning at the winged **statue of Hermes.** El. Venizelou runs inland to **Plateia Miaouli,** a large marble plaza marked by the Neoclassical town hall. Hotels and domatia can be found all along the waterfront and the surrounding streets. Generally, the farther you walk from the port, the nicer your surroundings. A labeled map of Ermoupolis and a listing of domatia are posted on two large signs at the bus depot.

Tourist Office: ☎22810 85 385. In 2 booths on the waterfront, 1 across from the ferry terminal; the other 100m toward El. Venizelou. Provide info on Syros's myriad hotels and domatia, as well as free **maps.** Open daily 11am-12:30pm and 3:30-10pm.

Budget Travel: Team Work (☎22810 83 400), past the ferry terminal on the waterfront toward the shipyard. Open daily 9am-10pm. **Vassilikos Tours** (☎22810 84 444), on the port across from the bus depot. Open daily 8am-midnight. Both provide ferry, hydrofoil, and flight schedules, prices, and tickets.

Bank: National Bank (☎22810 85 350), at the end of the 1st large street on the right off El. Venizelou from the waterfront, **exchanges currency** and has a **24hr. ATM.** Open M-Th 8am-2:30pm, F 8am-2pm.

Police: ☎22810 82 620. Behind the theater off the upper-right corner of Pl. Miaouli. Take the right inland street from the far-right corner of Pl. Miaouli, go right at the fork, and continue 200m to the station. Open 24hr.

Pharmacies: Akti Ethnikis Antistasis 42 (☎22810 82 220), on the waterfront behind the statue of Hermes. Others are scattered throughout the city. Most open M, W 8am-2pm, Tu, Th-Su 8am-2pm and 6-9pm. A few are open 24hr.

Hospital: ☎22810 86 666. At the left end of the waterfront (facing inland) at Pl. Iroön past the roundabout, a 20min. walk from Pl. Miaouli. Open 24hr.

Telephones: OTE (☎22810 86 099). At the right of Pl. Miaouli. Open M, W, Sa 7:20am-3pm, Tu, Th-F 7:20am-8pm.

Internet Access: Net Cafe (☎22810 85 330), in Pl. Miaouli, to the left of the town hall's staircase. €6 per hr.; €2 min. Open daily 9am-1am.

Post Office: ☎22810 82 590. Down the street from the National Bank. Offers **currency exchange.** Open M-F 7:30am-2pm. **Postal Code:** 84100.

🏠 ACCOMMODATIONS

Domatia abound, but you have to find them—look for signs. Prices are reduced 20-40% in low season. Cheaper accommodations are farther from the waterfront, or outside the city. A large map with info about hotels is at the ferry dock.

▨ **Hotel Aktaion** (☎22810 88 201). From the ferry landing, head to the far end of the waterfront past El. Venizelou and turn left along a narrow side street. The old, harborside building's refurbished rooms sport classy mahogany and stone trim along with TV, A/C, phones, and goodies like candy and soap. Singles €30-35; doubles €45-50. ❸

Hotel Almi (☎22810 82 812), on the left side of Kithnou across from the bus depot. Look for the dark wooden doors. Pink rooms with wrought-iron beds have a Neoclassical feel, but with far more modern conveniences. TV, baths, and fridges in each room and a common roof-top patio overlooking the sea. Doubles €20-45. ❸

Villa Votsalo, Parou 21 (☎22810 87 334; www.votsalo-syros.com). Walk inland on Hiou (before El. Venizelou from the port); Parou is the 1st left. In a cozy, traditional house, rooms are equipped with TV, phones, A/C, and baths. You can see the entire harbor from the roof-top veranda. Doubles €30-50; triples €65-80. ❸

Ariadni Rooms to Let, Nikolaou Filini 9 (☎22810 81 307), above Ag. Proiou and near the ferry dock. Turn left at the kiosk before the Hermes statue and head up the stairs (look for signs). Rooms include kitchenettes, baths, TV, phones, and A/C. The 3rd bed in some triples is on a loft above the bathroom. Doubles €30-60; triples €45-65. ❸

❐ FOOD

The plateia on Hiou has bakeries and fruit and seafood stalls. Halfway up from here is a **mini-mart.** (☎22810 81 008. Open M-F 8am-9pm, Sa 8am-4pm.) Sophisticated crowds flock to ⬛**To Archontariki** ❸, Em. Roidi 8, between the OTE on Pl. Miaouli and the waterfront, for its legendary cuisine. (☎22810 86 771. Mussels baked with feta and tomato €9. Open daily 10am-late. AmEx/MC/V.) **La Dolce Vita** ❹, Nikolaou Filini 3, serves classy Italian fare on a steep street above the harbor. (☎22810 86 199. Pasta €6-20. Meat dishes €12-25. Open daily 6pm-2am. MC/V.) **Kechayia Sweet Shop** ❶, on the waterfront corner of El. Venizelou, makes *chalvathopita* (almond paste, nuts, and chocolate; €1.50), *loukoumi* (fried dough; €2), and other fabulous local specialties. (☎22810 88 076. Open daily 8am-2am.)

❻ SIGHTS

The **Church of the Assumption** (Kimisis Theotokou), on Ag. Proiou at the end of the alley opposite the bus station, displays a painting finished in 1562 by a 20-year-old Domenikos Theotokopoulos, before he was known as **"El Greco."** The church's interior literally sparkles with its gleaming marble columns, crystal chandeliers, and mirrors. (Open daily 7am-2pm and 4:30-9pm. Free.) For a cultural interlude, visit **Theater Apollon** in Pl. Vardaka. With plush red-velvet balconies and a captivating ceiling mural depicting Mozart, Rossini, and Dante, this playhouse is a museum by day and stage by night. Greek shows, from ancient tragedy to Italian opera to modern comedy, are performed every evening at 9pm. (☎22810 85 192. Tickets €10-20. Discounts for students and seniors.) The town hall's **Archaeological Museum** has a small collection of Cycladic and early-Roman art. (☎22810 88 487. Open Tu-Su 8:30am-3pm. Free. No cameras.) Ascend the steps (30min.) at the far left of Pl. Miaouli or take the bus (€1) from the waterfront to **Ano Syros,** a medieval Venetian settlement which many of Syros's Catholics still call home. Facing inland, two house-covered hills topped by churches loom over the city; the higher one to the left is Ano Syros. Continue uphill past chalky, crowded houses to the lofty Church of Ag. Giorgios for a panorama of Ermoupolis and the coast below.

❽ NIGHTLIFE

The waterfront and Pl. Miaouli buzz with cafes, restaurants, dance clubs, and bars. Most of the popular waterfront locales open as cafes in the morning, turn into bars by night, and host DJs and dancing after midnight. Unpretentiously hip **Plaza,** past El. Venizelou on the waterfront when coming from the dock, lures young Syriots with port-side seating and a steady stream of international rock. (☎22810 85 337; www.plazacafe.gr. Beer €2.50. Mixed drinks €3-6. Open daily 9am-late.) Cavernous **Arxaion,** toward the port on the waterfront from El. Venizelou, is trendily futuristic, with modern Greek music, disco balls, and a dimly lit dance floor. (Beer €3-5. Mixed drinks €6-7. Open daily 9am-4am.) **Kimbara's** stylish bar crowd is accompanied by the butterflies on the walls. (☎22810 80 878. Beer €3. Mixed drinks €6. Cover €5 after midnight; includes 1 drink. Open daily 8am-5am.)

⚡ BEACHES

The closest access to the ocean is at sedate **Agios Nikolaos,** although it's more a seaside platform with ladders than a beach. To get there, walk up El. Venizelou through Pl. Miaouli to the right of the library. Head right and pass through Pl. Vardakas up to the right of the Church of Agios Nikolaos. Continue on the street until you see an archway and a stone stairway leading down to the beach. At **Galissas,** family vacationers crowd onto the main beach. You can fight for your eight inches of sand or climb past the chapel of Agia Pakou on the left side (facing the water) to discover a nudist's paradise in tiny, sheltered **Armeos.** From Ermoupolis buses go to Galissas (13-18 per day, €1.10), alternating between a direct 15min. route and a 45min. route that stops in other villages first. Taking the scenic route to Galissas allows you to see the rest of Syros's southern beaches. **Finikas** and **Komito** are popular for watersports like windsurfing. **Megas Yialos's** many small coves provide for a semblance of solitude, and **Azolimnos** is known for its large metal waterslide. The shallow waters and relaxed atmosphere at the beach resort of **Vari** attract families and package-tour groups. North of Galissas is the quiet fishing village of **Kini,** ideal for a romantic sunset. If you happen to be there on June 29, the **Church of Agios Petros** invites you and every other living thing within earshot to an all-night festival with revelry, *bouzouki,* and plenty of *kakavia* (fish soup).

NAXOS Νάξος

The gleaming marble Portara, the lone remaining arch of a once-grand temple to Apollo, beckons visitors to Naxos from its own unguarded peninsula. Naxos was once revered as the home of hedonistic Dionysus; centuries later, Venetians safeguarded their profits by making Naxos the capital of their mercantile empire. Modern visitors can take buses or rented cars from the cluttered eateries and shops of Naxos Town to small, placid villages like Halki and Apiranthos, dotted with old Venetian towers and early Christian churches. Mopeds are invaluable for winding through Naxos's terrain, where marble quarries and pristine beaches are secluded alongside vast vineyards and quiet olive groves. Hiking is another option; maps of trails and walking paths are available at the information center in town.

NAXOS TOWN   ☎22850

A dense collection of labyrinthine streets, bustling tavernas, and tiny museums radiates to the sea in Naxos Town. Despite its claim as the urban center of Naxos, the town retains an old island charm with its twisting historic quarter and the tightly packed buildings of Old Naxos, where stone archways curve over streets and trellises of flowers drape the whitewashed buildings and Venetian ruins.

▐ TRANSPORTATION

Flights: Olympic Airways (☎22850 23 292) has a desk in **Naxos Tours** (☎22850 22 095; www.naxostours.gr) on the left end of the waterfront. Flights go to **Athens** (€56).

Naxos

Aegean Sea

Main Roads
Dirt Roads
Hiking Trails

Kalantos Bay

0   4 miles
0   4 kilometers

CYCLADES

Ferries: All **ferries** to Naxos go to Naxos Town. 2 docks are at the left end of town: the bigger for large ferries, the other for smaller ferries and daily cruises. For updated schedules and prices, consult www.greekferries.gr. To: **Amorgos** (4½hr., daily, €9.30); **Crete** (7hr., 1 per week, €20); **Donousa** (4hr., daily, €6.30) via **Iraklia** (1hr., €5.50); **Ios** (1hr., daily, €8.20); **Kos** (7hr., 1 per week, €16); **Koufonisia** (3hr., €6.50); **Mykonos** (3hr., daily, €9); **Paros** (1hr., 4 per day, €5.50); **Piraeus** (6hr., 4 per day, €20); **Rhodes** (13hr., 1 per week, €20); **Santorini** (3hr., 3 per day, €13); **Schinousa** (2hr., €5.50); **Syros** (2½hr., daily, €9.30); **Thessaloniki** (14hr., €30); **Tinos** (4hr., daily, €9.50).

Buses: ☎22850 22 291. Tickets for all buses €1-3. Current schedules are available at the station (across from the largest dock) and at tourist offices. Buses to **Apollonas** (2hr., 3 per day 9:30am-1:30pm) and **Filoti** (30min., 5 per day 9:30am-3pm) are often packed. Buses also run to: **Apiranthos** (1hr., 5 per day 9:30am-3pm); **Engares** (2 per day); **Halki** (30min., 5 per day 9:30am-3pm); **Koronos** (4 per day); **Melanes** (3 per day 9am-3pm); **Plaka beach** (15min., every hr. 9am-9pm) via **Agios Prokopios beach** and **Agia Anna beach**; **Pyrgaki beach** (1hr., 2 per day) via **Tripodes**.

Hydrofoils: Flying Dolphins and Flying Cats to: **Astypalea, Crete, Ios, Mykonos, Paros, Piraeus**, and **Santorini**.

Taxis: ☎22850 22 444. On the waterfront, next to the bus depot.

Rentals: Rental Center (☎22850 23 396; www.rentalcenter.gr), in Pl. Protodikiou, is open 24hr. Also has **Internet access** (€3 per hr.) 8:30am-11pm.

ORIENTATION AND PRACTICAL INFORMATION

The waterfront along **Protopapadakis** to the right of the harbor is lined with cafes, tavernas, and clubs. After 500m the road forks inland; after another 70m, turn right to find the roundabout of **Plateia Protodikiou,** the central square, known for its lack of authentic food or establishments. The **Old Town** is to the left as you walk toward Protodikiou, accessible via any of the alleyways running inland.

Tourist Office (☎22850 25 201 or 22850 26 123), 300m from the dock, by the bus depot. Accommodations assistance, bus and ferry schedules, car rental, **currency exchange,** international telephone, **luggage storage** (€1.50 for the day until bus/ferry departure), safety deposit (€1.50), and **laundry** (€8). English-speaking Despina and Stavros have useful information and advice. Open daily 8am-11pm.

Budget Travel: Zas Travel (☎22850 23 330) has 1 location 2 doors down from the tourist center, and another 50m away from the port; both are on the waterfront. Sells ferry and plane tickets; offers information about day-trip cruises and tours of the island. **Internet access** available at the port location (€4 per hr.). Open daily 8:30am-11pm.

Bank: National Bank (☎22850 23 053) is one of many banks on the waterfront offering **currency exchange** and an **ATM.** Open M-Th 8am-2:30pm, F 8am-2pm.

Bookstore: Vrakas (☎22850 22 226), in an alley to the left of the first inland street before Vrakas jewelry, with blue signs reading "gold-silver, used books." Charming owner buys at half the original price, sells for €2-10. Open M-Sa 10am-2pm and 6-11pm, Su 6-11pm. **Zoom** (☎22850 23 675), right of the National Bank, has international magazines and photocopying (€0.15 per page). Open daily 8:30am-11pm.

Police: ☎22850 22 100 or 22850 23 280. On Amortou, the main road heading toward Ag. Giorgios beach from Pl. Protodikiou, 1km out of town. Open 24hr.

Port Police: ☎22850 22 300. On Protopapadakis, across from the small port dock.

Pharmacy: ☎22850 23 183. On the waterfront, right before the OTE. Open M, W-F 8:30am-2pm and 6-9pm.

Medical Services: ☎22850 23 333 or 22850 23 550. Turn inland at the fork in the road past the OTE, at the right end of the waterfront. Follow that road for about 500m; it is on your left. Helicopter to Athens available for **emergencies.** Open 24hr.

Telephones: OTE (☎22850 25 899), left of the fork in the road to the right of the waterfront. Open M-F 8am-2pm.

Internet Access: Readily available at many locations. **Matrix Cyber Cafe** (☎22850 25 627), just before the police station on the road leading toward Ag. Giorgios Beach away from Pl. Protodikiou, also offers laminating, printing, and digital photo service. €3.60 per hr. **Net Cafe,** on the eastern side of Pl. Protodikiou. €1.50 per 15min., €3 per hr. Also has **currency exchange.** Open 9am-10pm.

Post Office: Walk down the waterfront with the water on your right, and continue just beyond the main street that turns left. Pass a long playground on the right and the post office will be on your left, up 1 floor. Open M-F 7:30am-2pm. **Postal Code:** 84300.

ACCOMMODATIONS AND CAMPING

Avoid the dock hawks that will accost you as you disembark your ferry; the waterfront tourist information center (look for the "i") can help find suitable accommodations. Hotels in Naxos Town fill to capacity in the late summer, so if you're planning an extended stay, you might consider investigating renting options.

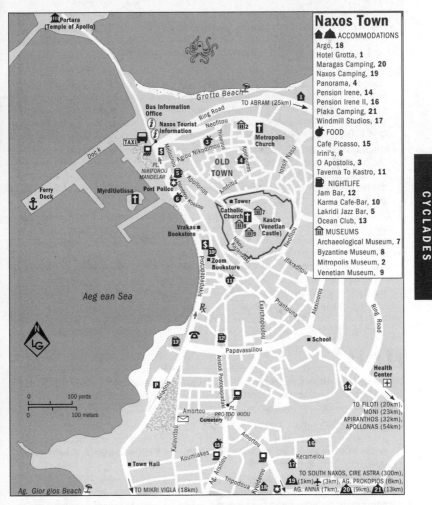

Naxos Town

▲ ■ ▲ **ACCOMMODATIONS**

Argo, **18**
Hotel Grotta, **1**
Maragas Camping, **20**
Naxos Camping, **19**
Panorama, **4**
Pension Irene, **14**
Pension Irene II, **16**
Plaka Camping, **21**
Windmill Studios, **17**

🍴 **FOOD**

Cafe Picasso, **15**
Irini's, **6**
O Apostolis, **3**
Taverna To Kastro, **11**

🍺 **NIGHTLIFE**

Jam Bar, **12**
Karma Cafe-Bar, **10**
Lakridi Jazz Bar, **5**
Ocean Club, **13**

🏛 **MUSEUMS**

Archaeological Museum, **7**
Byzantine Museum, **8**
Mitropolis Museum, **2**
Venetian Museum, **9**

CYCLADES

Naxos has three beach camping options, whose representatives wait eagerly at the dock. All of the sites have mini-marts, restaurants, Internet access, moped rentals, and laundry facilities. Prices similar at each campsite (€4-8 per person; tent rental €2). **Plaka Camping ❶** (☎22850 42 700), next to Plaka beach, is 12min. by car; it also offers cabins and rooms. By far the closest to town, **Naxos Camping ❶** (☎22850 23 500) is 150m from Ag. Giorgios beach and has a swimming pool. Bamboo walls divide camping areas. 10% discount for *Let's Go* readers. **Maragas Camping ❶**, on Ag. Anna, a 15min. drive from Naxos Town, also has studios and apartments. (☎22850 42 552 or 22850 42 599. Doubles €16-29.)

▨ **Windmill Studios** (☎22850 24 594; www.windmillnaxos.com). Take the first left after the police station heading away from Pl. Protodikiou toward Ag. Giorgios, then the first right. Mother and son proprietors are friendly and accommodating at this secluded but convenient hotel. Tidy, spacious rooms have A/C, TV, private baths, and kitchen facilities, with either a balcony or access to outdoor seating area. Free port shuttle available. Singles €18-25; doubles €20-55; triples €25-60. 20% discounts until June 10. Discounts at New Car Rentals, 100m away on the main street. ❷

▨ **Pension Irene** (☎22850 23 169) is 100m from Ag. Giorgios, 2 streets east of the main road. The owners, who volunteer information about directions and activities, offer rooms with A/C, TV, kitchen facilities, and private baths. Windows and balconies make suites pleasant and bright. A second location, Irene II, is 10min. away and includes a pool, which guests of either pension can use. Free port shuttle. Laundry €6. Singles €20; doubles €20-30; triples €25-35; 5-person apartments with kitchenettes €40-50. ❶

Panorama (☎22850 22 330). By both the waterfront and the most interesting sights in the Old Town. Make a left on the street labeled "Old Market," and then another left, following signs inland to "Panorama" and "Chateau Zevgoli." Kiki, the gregarious, grandmotherly owner, provides spacious rooms with fans and fridge. A serene roof-top garden overlooks the bay. Singles €25-35; doubles €30-50; triples €35-60. ❸

Argo (☎22850 25 330 or 22850 23 059; www.argo-hotel.com), 150m from Ag. Giorgios and 400m from the square; call for a port shuttle. Multilingual owners offer well-kept rooms with private baths, phones, and A/C. Breakfast €5. Doubles €25-60; 2-room apartments with kitchenettes €30-80. ❸

Hotel Grotta (☎22850 22 215; www.hotelgrotta.gr), is in a colony of hotels and mini-marts perched just above the Portara. Call for the free shuttle or follow Ring Rd. along the water and take the dirt path at the sign on the left. The welcoming dining area and spotless rooms have mountain and sea views. Indoor pool and jacuzzi. Rooms have fridges, A/C, balconies, hair dryers, satellite TV, safety deposit boxes, and telephones. Breakfast included. Laundry €8. Doubles €45-85; triples €55-104. MC/V. ❹

⬦ FOOD

Naxos brims with airy cafes and outdoor ouzeries, where chefs cook up fresh seafood and traditional dishes. Dozens of mini-marts offer tasty options for eating on the fly with ubiquitous vendors selling fruit, homemade bread, and local honey.

▨ **O Apostolis** (☎22850 26 777), on the old market street, at the foot of the Old Town among whitewashed walls and overhanging flowers. This traditional Greek restaurant serves excellent food in an informal outdoor setting. A fresh, whole fish is grilled for €11. Open noon-2am. AmEx/MC/V. ❷

Irini's (☎22850 26 780), the second taverna along the waterfront after Zas Travel. A cluster of blue and white checked tablecloths under a leaf-covered terrace, nestled in between the waterfront park area and the pedestrian path. The friendly waitstaff serves flavorful local fare. Fresh green peppers stuffed with sour cream and feta €5. Grilled chicken with mushrooms €6.50. Open daily noon-late. MC/V. ❷

Taverna To Kastro (☎22850 22 005) is just before the entrance to the *kastro*; turn left away from the waterfront after Rendez-Vous Cafe and follow signs for the castle and museums. For 27 years, the Naxian chef, Sulis, has been serving local specialties such as baked feta (€3.50), grilled calamari (€7), and his recommendation, rabbit cooked with onion and red wine (€8.50). High on the hill of Old Town, the taverna has unparalleled, spectacular views of the bay below. Open 6:30pm-late. ❷

Cafe Picasso Mexican Bistro (☎22850 25 408; www.picassoismexican.com), 1 block toward Ag. Giorgios beach from Pl. Protodikiou, serves Tex-Mex food in a lively, colorful setting. Quesadillas €5-6. Margaritas €4.50. Open 7pm-2am; kitchen closes at midnight. A second location at Plaka Beach (☎22850 41 188) opens at 1pm. MC/V. ❷

SIGHTS

Naxos Town is crowned by the **kastro**, whose gems are the small museums and churches within. Descendents of the Della Rocca Barozzi family, former Italian aristocrats, still inhabit a section of the castle, and have designated part of it as a **Venetian museum,** which showcases five period rooms and beautiful views. In his enchanting stone basement, the dignified and hospitable owner hosts frequent **Sunset Concerts** (tickets available at reception; €14-20) of classical music and traditional Greek dancing. (☎22850 22 387. Open daily 10am-3pm and 7-10pm. 30min. tours in English, French, and German throughout the day. €3, students and seniors €2; with tour €5.) Steps away is the **Byzantine Museum,** a two-room collection of artifacts from the 8th to the 10th centuries found on Naxos and other Cycladic islands. (Open M-Sa 8am-2pm. Free.) The **Archaeological Museum,** located in the former Collège Français where Nikos Kazantzakis (p. 73) studied, is also nearby. (Open Tu-Su 8:30am-3pm. €3, students €2.) The impressive **Catholic Church** is just around the corner. (Open 10am. Tours start at 5pm. Free. Modest dress required.) The **Mitropolis Museum,** next to the Orthodox Church, has elevated glass walkways that lead you over the reconstructed buildings of a 13th-century BC settlement. (☎22850 24 151. Open Tu-Su 8:30am-3pm. Free.)

From the waterfront, you can gaze at the chapel of **Myrditiotissa,** floating in the harbor on its manmade islet, and the marble **Portara** archway, on its own peninsula. Climb up to it and view the unfinished beginnings of an ambitious **temple** dedicated to Apollo, begun on the orders of the tyrant Lydamis in the 6th century BC.

NIGHTLIFE

Starting around 11pm, beat-heavy music leads partiers to waterfront clubs, and generously extended happy hours lure them into lively bars. The island's outdoor theater, **Cine Astra,** is another evening option, showing English movies with Greek subtitles at 9 and 11pm. The theater is a 15min. walk from the waterfront, on the road to Agia Anna from Pl. Protodikiou. (☎22850 25 381. Open daily May-Oct. €7.)

Karma Cafe-Bar (☎22850 24 885), in the center of the waterfront. Pointed arches and orange-pink walls beckon toward a metallic, vault-like interior. Daily happy hour 7pm-midnight offers 2-for-1 beers. Open 7pm-late.

Jam Bar (☎69420 19 426). First left after Klik Cafe, behind the OTE. Drink creative concoctions such as the

ON THE MENU

A DRINK TO REMEMBER

The island of Naxos is one of only three places in the world where fragrant citron trees grow. Two families in Halki, making maybe the best possible use of the rare plant, have been using its juices for over 100 years to produce a unique alcohol called "Citron." Today, fifth-generation members of the Vallindras family use the same recipe their relatives developed in 1896. Workers collect the thick leaves from October through February, when they have the best aroma. The plants are then put into the original family press, which, within hours, extracts a clear liquid. Manufacturers then mix in natural coloring to distinguish flavors and strength: the green is sweetest, the yellow is strongest, and the clear is in between.

The after-dinner drink is widely available throughout Naxos, but impossible to find anywhere else. The Vallindras distillery used to export all over the world, but since a shortage of trees has arisen, the distilleries have had to limit production until replacement trees have grown to maturity. Until then, Citron is only available in Naxos.

The Vallindras distillery in Halki offers free tours, brochures, and samples. ☎22850 31 220. Open daily. Representatives of the Promponas distillery also provide info and samples at their store in Naxos Town, across from Myroditissa. ☎22850 22 258.

Naxos Butterfly (€4) in either the cool, dim interior or the outdoor area, a small island of seats sectioned off by low pink walls and large, spherical lights. Shots €2-2.50. Open M-Th, Su 7pm-3:30am, F-Sa 7pm-late.

Ocean Club (☎22850 26 766). Facing the water at the right end of the harbor. Late-night revelers dance under swirling disco balls in this mod, white-surfaced hipster haven. Frozen strawberry daiquiri €4. Open M-Th, Su 11pm-late, F-Sa 11pm-morning.

Lakridi Jazz Bar (☎22850 25 013). In Old Naxos, on the old market street; take the first right. The sounds of Ella Fitzgerald and Billie Holiday seep out of this narrow nook, where people share small wooden tables. Frozen cocktails €6. Open 8pm-3:30am.

⚲ BEACHES

Beachgoers seeking solitude head away from Naxos Town, but the closest waters are equally beautiful. Buses (€1.20) run regularly from the bus stop to **Agios Proko-pios**, **Agia Anna**, and **Plaka** (a beach popular with nude bathers), while **Agios Giorgios** is a short walk from anywhere in town. Clear sparkling water laps up on the curvy shores of all of these pristine spots, where a wide variety of sporting activities are available. **Naxos Surf** (☎22850 29 170), **Flisvos Sport Club** (☎22850 24 308) on Ag. Giorgios, and **Plaka Watersports** (☎22850 41 264) at Plaka and Ag. Anna offer windsurf-ing, kayaking, and mountain biking equipment and lessons. Desert meets sea at the more secluded beaches of **Mikri Vigla**, **Abram**, **Aliko**, **Moutsouna**, and **Pyrgaki**, where scrub pines, prickly pear, and century plants grow on the dunes. All are accessible by bus from Naxos Town. Nude bathers gather on a small portion of the southern protuberance of **Kastraki beach**. **Walking tours** of the island (€22850 22 481) are avail-able, as is a 3hr. **horseback tour**. (Contact Iris Neubauer at ☎69488 09 142. €40.)

⚑ DAYTRIPS FROM NAXOS TOWN

▨ APIRANTHOS
Buses run the 32km from Naxos Town (1hr., 5 per day 9:30am-3pm).

Venturing into Apiranthos may feel like a trip back in time. Old men lead bucket-laden donkeys through crowded streets, and the townspeople speak a unique dia-lect—a gift of the political refugees who fled here from Crete in the late 18th cen-tury. A blue marble road leads into the modest plateia that is Apiranthos's center; beyond the row of tavernas overlooking the valley lie Venetian ruins and 400-year-old homes. The one-room **archaeology museum** exhibits early 3rd-century statues and pottery. (Open 8am-3pm. Free.) A €1 ticket grants admission to the **folk art museum** (in the main square; open 10am-1:30pm), the **natural history museum** (to the right of the bus stop; open 10:30am-2:30pm), and the **geological museum** (just beyond the natural history museum; open 10am-1:30pm). Apiranthos is also a good base for exploring Central Naxos's **olive groves**. At the start of the main road, steps veer downward and to the right toward marked walking paths. The small size and proximity to Naxos Town make the quiet village an ideal destination for a leisurely half-day trip. For lunch, try **Taverna O Platanos ❸**, a simple terrace restaurant with generous helpings of traditionally prepared local produce. (☎22850 61 460. Cap-puccino €2.50. Pork souvlaki €7. Open daily 10am-midnight.)

CENTRAL NAXOS AND THE TRAGEA
A bus runs the 17km from Naxos Town to Halki (30min., 5 per day 9:30am-2:30pm), from which hikers can access Mino, Filoti, and Pangia Drosiani. Passengers can ask to be let off between official stops; the path to Mt. Zeus is en route.

Ancient ruins, medieval churches, and quaint, untouched towns are scattered within the **Tragea**, central Naxos's enormous, picturesque olive grove. By far the best way to see the inner island is by private transport; the sights are primarily along one main road but are often several kilometers from the closest bus stop. Inexpensive cars, mopeds, and four-wheel go-cart-type vehicles (for those wary of motorcycling) are available in Naxos Town at **New Car Rental** (☎22850 23 595). An ambitious but feasible bike ride can also take you to the major sights.

Colorful buildings and Venetian towers make up **Halki,** the quiet village east of Naxos Town. The surrounding area is sometimes known as "Little Mystras" because of its enormous number of 6th- to 14th-century churches. In town, store owners hawk homemade linen, jam, and olive oil, while market vendors and the main taverna offer local produce. Halki boasts the Vallindras family's **citron** distillery, one of only two in the world (see **A Drink to Remember,** p. 393). Recently-uncovered frescoes from the 11th and 13th centuries are displayed at Halki's Medieval **Panagia Prottheroni.** The church, immediately adjacent to the bus stop, is often closed, but if you can find the priest, he'll open the doors.

Just north of Halki, on the road to **Moni,** is **Panagia Drosiani,** a well-preserved early Christian edifice with a beautiful miniature dome and 7th-century frescoes. The road south brings travelers to **Filoti,** another sleepy cluster of houses, tavernas, and small churches on a lush, steep hill. A 1hr. hike extends from Filoti to the mouth of the **Cave of Zeus,** a damp, dark grotto where an eagle gave the king of the gods his thunderbolts. Forty-five minutes from the cave is **Mount Zeus** (1008m), the tallest peak in Naxos, which usually takes visitors about 1½hr. to climb.

The stretch of road northeast of Naxos Town toward **Melanes, Kinidaros,** and **Keramoti** is also dotted with intriguing old sights. A half-finished but distinguishable 6th-century BC **kouros** lies on its back in a wild garden in **Flerio** (7km east of Melanes), where narrow dirt paths lead to a modest statue garden and small cafe. On the road back to Naxos Town, through Moni, Halki, and Filoti, you will pass the Timios Stavros (Holy Cross), a 17th-century nunnery, and the Temple of Demeter, which experts are currently restoring.

APOLLONAS AND NORTHERN NAXOS

Buses run from Naxos Town to Apollonas (2hr., 3 per day 9:30am-1:30pm).

Countryside views make the trip to and from Apollonas a peaceful, pleasant way to spend an afternoon. You'll pass the secluded beach at **Amiti,** down the road from Galini. Farther on is the monastery of **Faneromenis.** One of the more famous **kouroi** of Naxos is just a short walk from the harbor. This kouros (p. 69) is nearly 11m tall. From the Apollonas bus stop, walk back along the main road uphill to the fork in the road. Take a sharp right and walk up until you see the stairs at the sign reading "Προς Κούρο" ("toward the kouros").

LITTLE CYCLADES

Good things can come in small packages, and nothing proves it better than the Little Cyclades. These tiny isles bridging Naxos and Amorgos are a tranquil and rustic interlude between their larger, increasingly crowded neighbors. In their towns, goats often outnumber people, beaches outnumber goats, and star-studded nights center on a single town cafe.

KOUFONISIA Κουφονήσια   ☎22850

The smallest and most popular of the inhabited Little Cyclades, Koufonisia surrounds itself with dazzling beaches on the southeastern side of the island, called "Ano Koufonisia." The name, meaning "hollow," refers to the caves perforating the island's surface. Unlike on the other Little Cyclades, small clothing boutiques, cafes, and a lone ATM line Koufonisia's main street, which springs to life in the early evening. The simplicity of the setting lends itself to complete relaxation.

TRANSPORTATION AND PRACTICAL INFORMATION. The ferry ticket office, up the second road parallel to the beach, a few buildings past the blue-domed church, posts a schedule on its door. (☎22850 71 438. Open daily 8am-2:30pm and 5-11:30pm.) **Ferries** go to: Aegiali (2¼hr., 1-2 per day, €6.50); Iraklia (45min., 1-2 per day, €4.50); Katapola (3hr., 1-2 per day, €6.50) via Donousa (1½hr., €5); Naxos (2¼hr., 1-2 per day, €7) via Schinousa (30min., €4); Paros (3½hr., 4 per week, €13.50); Piraeus (7hr., 3 per week, €24). One **Flying Dolphin** stops at Koufonisia each week and goes to Amorgos (25min., €12), Naxos (30min., €12), and Piraeus (6hr., €42). Head straight off the ferry dock and hug the beach to find accommodations. You can also try following the road toward the town of Hora, the heart of which can be reached by turning left at the second road parallel to the beach, just past the card phone. Koufonisia's commercial center consists of two main streets. The shorter one runs inland from just past the port to the left of the mini-mart; the longer one springs from its left side, about 100m inland and parallel to the beach. The 24hr. **police** (☎22850 71 375) are on the right side on the road leading inland from the port, past Kalamia Music Cafe. Next door is the **medical center** (☎22850 71 370, doctor 69782 22 446. Open M, W, F 9am-2pm and 6-8pm, Tu, Th 9am-2pm. 24hr. emergency service.) The **OTE** is on the main road inland, across from Pension Melissa. (☎22850 22 392. Open 8am-2pm and 5-10pm.) **Internet access** is available at **Kohili** and **Kalamia Music Cafe** (see below). The **post office**, in a boutique next to the Keros Hotel, has **currency exchange** and a **24hr. ATM.** (☎22850 74 214. Open 11am-1:30pm and 5:30-11:30pm.) **Postal Code:** 84300.

ACCOMMODATIONS AND CAMPING. The pensions around town fill up fast, so call ahead. Many homes with rooms to let sit on the main road (doubles €40-55; in low season €20-30). **Maria Prasinou ❷,** the first hotel on the road past the beach, has a quaint cafe and rooms with private baths and beautiful harbor views. (☎22850 71 436. Doubles €25-60; triples €35-65. V.) **Sofia Soultania ❷,** next to Maria Prasinou, rents large, echoing rooms with TV, baths, and semi-private balconies. (☎22850 71 437. Doubles €35-55; triples €35-65.) **Keros Hotel ❸,** just before the post office, grants a view of the harbor from its large rooms with private balconies, baths, phones, fridges, and A/C. (☎22850 71 601. Doubles €40-84; triples €45-95.) **Harakorou Camping ❶,** with few amenities, is in a beautiful location 15min. from the wharf. (☎22850 71 683. €5 per person.)

FOOD AND NIGHTLIFE. The town has tons of traditional seafood and standard Greek fare (entrees €5.50-10). For tasty, cheap gyros (€1.80) or souvlaki (€1.80), swing by the enormously popular ▒**Strofi ❶,** a green window just around the corner from the church on the main road. (☎22850 11 818. Open 6:30pm-midnight.) **Kohili ❶,** on the main road past Strofi, has croissants (€1.20), coffee (€1.20-3.50), and great views of the harbor. (☎22850 74 279. Internet access €5 per hr. Open daily 9am-1am.) **Kalamia Music Cafe ❶,** 150m along the inland road, by the public phones, provides drinks (frappés €2.50), sweets (€2-4.50), breakfast (yogurt with honey; €4.50), and an eclectic blend of world music for a crowd of chic customers. (☎22850 71 741. Internet €8 per hr. Mixed drinks €6-7. Open daily 8am-3am.) People crowd into **Emplo's** purple-draped interior for late-night dancing. Walk uphill to the left of the port and listen for Greek music. (Beer €3. Mixed drinks €5. Open daily 10pm-late.)

BEACHES. You will find more stunning ▒**beaches** on little Koufonisia than on most of the Cyclades combined. The crystal-blue stretches spool out in a continuous ribbon along the southern coast. **Ammos** is closest to Hora, just to the right of the ferry dock, facing inland; you can spot nearby fishing boats here while spirited locals play soccer. Continuing 10min. down the road behind the sand leads you to pristine, popular **Finikas,** next to a convenient taverna. Much-quieter **Fanos** waits on the other side of the ridge. The farther you walk, the fewer people (and clothes) you'll see. A 30min. walk from Hora uphill along the road past the helicopter pad and across cow fields brings you to **Pori,** the best beach on the island, with brilliant blue, glassy water and fine, white sand, magnificent even by Greek-island standards. If the sand begins to burn, head for the shaded rocks behind the beach where cave-lined coves provide perfect snorkeling spots. Regular boats (10min., 4 per day, round-trip €3) also make trips to Pori from the dock at Hora. For those who hate sharing the sand, the daily ferry takes you to **Kato Koufonisia** (30min., 4 per day, round-trip €3), an oasis of quiet relaxation.

DONOUSA Δονούσα   ☎22850

Donousa, the most rural of the Cyclades, gives visitors a potent dose of local culture. Lacking banks and public transportation, the island beckons those eager to abandon modernity. Isolated, golden-sand beaches abound beyond the town's smattering of tavernas and pensions. The small **town beach,** with volleyball courts and shallow splashing amid fishing boats, also serves as a thoroughfare between the village and the pensions across the cove. **Kedros beach,** a nicer piece of shore, stretches out just over the ridge. Follow the road perpendicular to the town beach up the hill and around the bend to get to the tent-lined sand. The even more pristine **Livadi beach** is a 1hr. walk down this road.

The few **domatia** in town lie at the other end of the beach and across the cove from the main port; doubles are usually €20-50. Rooms fill up quickly in July and August, but owners are happy to direct visitors to a neighbor with vacant rooms. Keep inquiring until you find an available room. **Camping** is permitted only on **Kedros beach,** up the concrete road that begins at the beach and around the bend. Several tavernas are visible from the dock, all serving similar Greek food (entrees €3.50-7). **Meltemi ❷,** just to the right of the tourist office when facing inland, serves simple dishes and has spectacular sunset views. (☎22850 52 241. Moussaka €6. Open daily June-Oct. noon-4pm and 6pm-late.) Join the daily raid on the delicious goods at the **bakery ❶,** above the tourist office. (☎22850 51 567. Bread €1.50 per kg. Pastries €1.20-1.80. Open daily 8am-2pm and 5-10pm.) Bear right from the dock to find the small **mini-mart.** (☎22850 57 582. Open daily 8:30am-1pm and 4:30-9pm.) ▓**Skatzohoros,** just to the left of the dock facing inland, is the only nightlife option in town. Almost every evening, patrons sit and talk in the low light under tropical umbrellas, gazing contentedly out to sea. (☎22850 51 783. Beer €2.50-4. Mixed drinks €5-6. Open daily June-Sept. 9am-4am.)

> **CASH ONLY.** On the Little Cyclades, escaping the hassles of modern life also means forgoing some of its conveniences. The mini-islands have no banks and no establishments that accept credit cards, making those little plastic rectangles in your pocket seem awfully flimsy; the region's lone ATM, on Koufonisia, won't accept PINs with over 4 digits. So either bring a well-lined wallet, or get ready to wash some dishes for your dinner.

The ferry ticket office, across from the dock, **exchanges currency** and sells tickets for all lines except Blue Star. If it is closed during your visit, you can buy your ticket onboard. (☎22850 51 648. Open 8am-2pm and 5-10pm.) The ticket office for Blue Star Ferries is in the Iliovasilema restaurant, across the cove from the town, marked by a large sign. (☎22850 51 570. Open M, Su 8:30am-1am, Tu-Sa 10am-1pm and 5-7pm.) **Ferries** go to: Amorgos (1½hr., 1-2 per day, €6); Iraklia

(1½hr., 1-2 per day, €7); Koufonisia (1¾hr., 1-2 per day, €5); Naxos (1½hr., 1-2 per day, €7); Paros (2hr., 6 per week, €10); Piraeus (8hr., 4 per week, €22); Syros (4hr., 6 per week, €11.30). You can reach the **doctor** 24hr. (☎22850 51 506). To reach the island's **public phone**, walk 200m up the hill behind To Kima.

SCHINOUSA Σχοινούσα ☎22850

Isolated yet accessible beaches line the coast of untouched Schinousa, all but guaranteeing a peaceful communion with nature. The island is best enjoyed on foot, as you can explore its rustic, dusty, and donkey-patrolled interior and get to know the affable population—250 at last count.

⊡🛈 TRANSPORTATION AND PRACTICAL INFORMATION. All boats dock at the tiny **Mersini**, with the village, **Hora**, a 10-15min. walk uphill. **Ferries** go to: Aegiali, Amorgos (3hr., 1-2 per day, €7.50); Donousa (1½hr., 1-2 per day, €7); Iraklia (15min., 1-2 per day, €4); Katapola, Amorgos (3hr., 1-2 per day, €6) via Koufonisia (30min., €4); Naxos (1½hr., 1-2 per day, €6.20); Paros (2hr., 2-3 per week, €8.10); Piraeus (7hr., 3 per week, €24). Nearly everything you'll need in can be found on the main road, a 5min. walk from end to end. On the right coming from the port is **Panorama**, a hotel and restaurant which doubles as the **ferry ticket agent** for Blue Star lines and the **post office**. (☎22850 71 160. Open daily 8am-late.) Past Panorama on the main road, you'll see **Giorgos Grispos Travel Agency**, where you can **exchange currency** and buy **ferry tickets** for Small Cycladic Lines, which connects the Little Cyclades to each other. (☎22850 29 329. Open daily 9am-2pm and 6-9pm.) Note that there is **no bank or ATM** in town. **Maps** and **phone cards** are available at the minimarts lining the main road; the bakery sells a useful map (€4) of the Little Cyclades. The **doctor** (☎22850 71 385) is on the same road as Agnantema bakery in a clearly marked white building; 24hr. emergency care is available. Two public **card phones** are down at the port and in Hora's plateia. **Postal Code:** 84300.

🛏🍴 ACCOMMODATIONS AND FOOD. Nearly every restaurant or general store in town offers several rooms to rent and free port transfer in addition to moussaka and Fanta. Centrally located **Anesis ❸**, on the right past the turn-off to the bakery, has large, clean rooms with fridges, private baths, funky orange lamps, and panoramic balcony views. (☎22850 71 180. Doubles €30-50; triples €45-60.) The hospitable namesake of **Anna Rooms ❷**, on the left on the way to the bakery, rents rooms with common balconies, private baths, and kitchens. (☎22850 71 161. Doubles €30-50; triples €35-55.) **Iliovasilema Hotel ❸**, down the road on the left and run by Anna's daughter, has modern rooms with phones and balconies, and a cafe-terrace overlooking the harbor, hills, and ocean. (☎22850 71 948. Doubles €30-45; triples €35-50.) To find **Giorgios Grispos's domatia ❹**, follow the signs in Hora to Tsigouri beach on the main road and proceed 500m downhill. Grispos's rooms, in a pleasant beachside location, include A/C, TV, and fridges. (Doubles €40-75. AmEx/MC/V.) **Agnantema ❸** has a prime location above the bakery and taverna. The rooms, with baths, fridges, kitchenettes, phones, and TV, overlook a rocky terrace with a gazebo. (☎22850 71 987. Reserve in advance during high season. Doubles €30-40; 4-person studios €70 in high season. Taverna open 3pm-midnight.)

Off the main road, heading left, you'll find a street marked with signs for **Agnantema bakery and mini-mart ❶**, 250m downhill. (☎22850 71 987. Open daily 6:30-11pm.) **Loza Pizzeria ❷**, filled with traditional music, tasty food, and chatty locals, is in the main plateia. (☎22850 74 005. *Peiridi* (long pizza) €6-8. Baklava €1.30. Open daily 10am-12:30am.) At **Panorama ❷**, balcony seating provides an appropriately sweeping view of the sea beyond. (☎22850 71 160. Spaghetti €4. Moussaka €6. Octopus €8. Open daily June-Sept. 8am-midnight. V.)

NIGHTLIFE AND BEACHES. Tsigouri beach is Schinousa's only nightlife locale; **Ostria Cafe,** an outdoor bar and restaurant there, is pleasant and low-key. (☎22850 71 174. Beer €2.50-3. Mixed drinks €4-5. Open daily June-Sept. 15 10am-late.) The island's rocky, pothole-ridden dirt roads are virtually car-free, making it easy to explore the island on foot. Grab a bottle of water, glance at a map, and wander until a particularly alluring cove catches your eye. Tsigouri, 450m down the first road on the right heading into town from the port, is easily accessible and more developed than the other beaches, with a view of Iraklia. **Livadi,** a thin stretch of sand cradled by a small bay, lies at the end of a 15min. walk down the right fork of the road through Hora. Follow the dusty road 2km past the bakery, across the fields, and through the tiny village of Messaria to **Psili Ammos.** The secluded, rocky beach, on the far side of the island, is sheltered from the heavy surf.

IRAKLIA Ιράκλια ☎22850

Iraklia is another tiny island where a handful of people comes to escape the bustle of modern life. You won't have too much company on its peaceful beaches, and a cave with circuitous underground passages contributes to the hideaway feel.

TRANSPORTATION AND PRACTICAL INFORMATION. Ferries head to: Amorgos (2½hr., 1-2 per day, €8); Donousa (1½hr., 1-2 per day, €7); Koufonisia (45min., 1-2 per day, €4); Naxos (1½hr., 1-2 per day, €6); Paros (3-4 per week, €8); Piraeus (6hr., 3-4 times per week, €24); Schinousa (15min., 1-2 per day, €4); Syros (3hr., 1 per week, €12). Schedules are posted around the harbor. **Iraklia Rent a Scooter** in Panagia rents **mopeds.** (☎22850 71 991. €12 per day.) The largest settlement on the island, **Agios Giorgios** is the island's port; turn right off the dock past the beach to reach the center of town. This main road splits at multi-story, air-conditioned **Perigali** (☎22850 74 234; open daily 8am-11pm), the local mini-mart where you can buy a **map** (€1). A small ravine runs through the center of town; two roads run alongside it and merge at the top. The **medical center** is just above Perigali on the right branch. (☎22850 71 388 or 69730 62 550. 24hr. emergency service. Open Tu, Th-F 9am-1pm.) All-purpose **Melissa,** 50m farther along the right-hand road, is a general store, ferry ticketer, telephone operator, domatia (see below), and **post office.** (☎22850 71 539. Open daily 6am-11pm.) One of the island's two **card phones** is just outside; the second is in Panagia. **Postal Code:** 84300.

ACCOMMODATIONS AND FOOD. If you call ahead, your hosts will most likely pick you up at the port. ✹**Anna's Place ❷,** up the hill on the first left from the left fork of the main road, looks out over the port from its spacious balconies. Friendly Anna greets her guests with orange juice, while her comfortable rooms have fridges and private baths; the studios are palatial. (☎22850 71 145. Doubles €30-60; 3-person studios €40-65.) Turn right on the road after Anna's and then left on the second gravel road to find **Prasinos Nikolas ❷,** whose luxurious rooms have built-in beds, fridges, TV, private baths, and balconies. (☎22850 71 991. Doubles €20-40.) **Alexandra ❷,** at the top of Agios Giorgios just beyond Anna's, has four small, breezy rooms with baths and fridges, a shared kitchen, and a spacious common veranda with a hammock. (☎22850 71 482. Doubles and triples €20-40.) **Maria's ❷,** across the road, rents tiny, homey rooms with kitchenettes, private baths, and a shared balcony. (☎22850 71 485. Doubles €20-40.)

Ten minutes down the road to Livadi, you'll find a delicious variety of grilled fish and Greek specialties (€5-7) at ✹**Giorgios Gavalas's Place ❷.** Giorgios welcomes diners to his veranda, which has a top-notch view at standard taverna prices. He also offers free **camping ❶.** (☎22850 29 034. Open May-Sept. 24hr.) Across the road, **O Pevkos ❷,** up the left fork of the road past Perigali, makes fresh fish caught by the owner and tasty Greek salads with local feta. You can also buy raw fish (€10-20 per kg) to prepare at home. (☎22850 71 568. Prepared fish €20-40 per kg. Open daily 10am-10pm.) **Maistrali ❷,** up the hill just before O Pevkos, serves meals all day and sells postcards, foreign papers, and books, has an international telephone, Internet access (€3 per hr.), and exchanges currency. (☎22850 71 807. Omelettes €2-3. Grilled meat €4-7. Open daily 8am-late. AmEx/MC/V.)

◙ ⊡ SIGHTS AND ENTERTAINMENT. The shallow, clear waters of **Livadi beach** epitomize Iraklia's appeal: they draw only small crowds, even on hot summer days. If you wade out, you can look at the ruins of the **Venetian Castle** overhead. The water taxi "Anemos" (Tu, Th, Su departs 11am, returns 4pm; round-trip €8) will take you to **Karvounlakos** or **Alimia;** buy tickets at Perigali. To get a feeling for Greece as it was 40 years ago, continue past Livadi to the town of **Panagia** (45min. from Ag. Giorgios), where you'll find a church, some cows, and not much else. The taverna **To Steki ❷,** with roof-top seating overlooking hills and the sea, also serves as a general store, bakery, and the island's only gas station—fill up from a canister. (☎22850 71 579. Open daily 7am-2am.) For a more raucous hangout try **Bar Aki Music-Dance,** the island's only club, down the dirt road from Maistrali. (☎22850 71 487. Beer €3. Mixed drinks €6. Open daily 10pm-late.)

⚑ OUTDOOR ACTIVITIES. The ⊠**Agios Ioannis Cave,** with tiny waterways, dramatic depths, and a seemingly endless series of chambers, will fascinate more adventurous travelers. There is a rough but helpful map of the path on the back of the Iraklia map available in Perigali. Bring a flashlight, candles, matches, and a walking stick if possible, and get ready to get filthy. The steep, 1½hr. **hike** begins past the church in Panagia, where the first of a number of blue signs points away from the village. After 20min. along the stone-walled dirt path, you'll reach a fence at the bottom of a dip in the land and another sign pointing uphill. Follow the stone wall on your right until it meets another one. The path becomes difficult to follow; just stay near this wall. After you've climbed up, you will see the sea on the other side of the island and signs pointing to Agios Athanassis, Agios Giorgios, and the cave. From here, a more clearly defined trail marks the beginning of a 30min. descent down **Mount Pappas** toward the tiny, bright-white cave entrance; blue signs will direct you. Crawling through the small entrance brings you into the caves. You'll need your flashlight right away, leaving lighted candles along the way à la Hansel and Gretel to mark your path back. An icon of St. John, who is celebrated in an August **festival** at the cave, is to the left as you enter. There are said to be 15 rooms inside the cave; the final chamber is so deep that there is no oxygen inside. Be careful—the rocks are slippery and daylight vanishes quickly.

PAROS Πάρος

Pieces of Paros are sprinkled throughout the Western world in the form of its famed translucent marble. Many of antiquity's most celebrated statues and buildings—the Venus de Milo, the Nike of Samothrace, and parts of Napoleon's mausoleum in Paris—took their materials from this locale. Seemingly bottomless Parian quarries still export regularly, but today most ships entering the island bear tourists instead of merchants. The local population inflates to 10 times its low-season size in the summer, when the golden beaches and lonely mountains swell with travelers. The main port of Parikia is spread out along the water, making it less concentrated and congested than other Cycladic cities (though hardly less festive). Parties at the beach clubs in Parikia and Naoussa last late into the night.

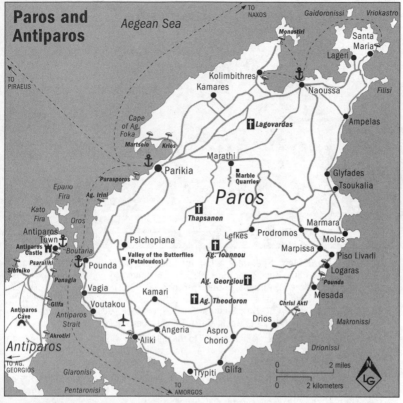

Paros and Antiparos

Aegean Sea

TO NAXOS

Gaidoronissi   Vriokastro

Monastiri

Santa Maria

Lageri

TO PIRAEUS

Kolimbithres
Kamares

Naoussa

Filisi

Ampelas

Lagovardas

Cape of Ag. Foka
Martselo   Krios

Marathi

Parikia

Marble Quarries

Parasporos

Glyfades
Tsoukalia

Epano Fira
Ag. Irini

Paros

Kato Fira   Oros

Thapsanon

Antiparos Town
Antiparos Castle
Boutaria
Psaraliki
Sitnelko
Panagia
Pounda

Psichopiana

Valley of the Butterflies (Petaloudes)

Lefkes   Prodromos

Marmara

Molos

Marpissa

Piso Livadi

Ag. Ioannou

Logaras
Pounda

Ag. Georgiou

Mesada

Vagia
Voutakou

Kamari

Ag. Theodoron

Chrisi Akti

Antiparos Cave
Antiparos Strait
Akrotiri

Glifa

Angeria

Aspro Chorio

Drios

Makronissi

Antiparos

TO AG. GEORGIOS

Aliki

Drionissi

Glaronisi

Trypiti   Glifa

Pentaronisi

TO AMORGOS

0   2 miles
0   2 kilometers

CYCLADES

PARIKIA Παροικία   ☎ 22840

Behind Parikia's commercial facade, flower-filled streets wind through arch-ways, past whitewashed houses, and by dozens of ancient, intimate churches. Wander through the agora to find trendy clothing, colorful jewelry, homemade goods, and many outdoor cafes. While the town's small, pebbly beaches are overpowered by souvenir shops and touristy tavernas, this transportation hub is a lively and convenient base for reaching more remote island locations.

▐ TRANSPORTATION

Flights: Olympic Airways (☎22840 21 900), in the plateia by the National Bank. Open M-F 9am-3pm. To **Athens** (M-Tu, Th, Su 3 per day, W and F 2 per day; €56).

Buses: ☎22840 21 395 or 22840 21 133. The **bus stop,** a booth surrounded by buses, is to the left of the windmill, on the water. Prices range from €1-2; consult timetable posted at bus stop. Buses run every hour to **Naoussa** (15min.) via **Kolimbithres.** 11 per day to: **Agia Irini** (10min.); **Parasporas** (5min.); **Pounda** (15min.). 8 per day to: **Mar-mara** (35min.); **Piso Livadi** via **Lefkes** (20min.); **Prodromos** (30min.). 7 per day to: **Age-ria** (25min.); **Aliki** (20min.); **Aspro Chorio** (1hr.) via **Naoussa** (20min.); **Chrisi Akti** (1hr.); **Piso Livadi** (45min.); **Pounda beach** (50min.); **Valley of the Butterflies** (12min.).

Ferries go to: **Amorgos** (3hr., 4 per week, €12); **Andros** (5 per week, €14.10); **Astyp-alea** (14 per week, €22.10); **Crete** (8hr., 5 per day, €27); **Folegandros** (4 per

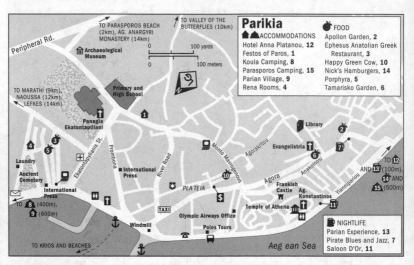

TO PARASPOROS BEACH (2km), AG. ANARGYRI MONASTERY (14km)

TO VALLEY OF THE BUTTERFLIES (10km)

Peripheral Rd.

🏛 Archaeological Museum

0   100 yards

0   100 meters

TO MARATHI (9km), NAOUSSA (12km), LEFKES (14km)

Primary and High School

Panagia Ekatontapiliani

Ekatontapyliani St.

Prombona

Laundry

Ancient Cemetery

International Press

International Press

TO 🔒 8 (400m), 9 (600m)

TO KRIOS AND BEACHES

Windmill

River Road

PLATEIA

TAXI

Olympic Airways Office

Polos Tours

Monte Mavrogenous

Agorakritou

Agora

Anakolnosi

Evangelistria

Frankish Castle Ag. Konstantinos

Temple of Athena

Library

Yianniparou

TO 12 AND 13 (100m), 14 AND 15 (500m)

Aeg ean Sea

Parikia

♠▲ACCOMMODATIONS
Hotel Anna Platanou, 12
Festos of Paros, 1
Koula Camping, 8
Parasporos Camping, 15
Parian Village, 9
Rena Rooms, 4

🍴 FOOD
Apollon Garden, 2
Ephesus Anatolian Greek Restaurant, 3
Happy Green Cow, 10
Nick's Hamburgers, 14
Porphyra, 5
Tamarisko Garden, 6

🍸 NIGHTLIFE
Parian Experience, 13
Pirate Blues and Jazz, 7
Saloon D'Or, 11

week, €9); **Ikaria** (4hr., 4 per week, €15); **Ios** (2hr., 2-3 per day, €9.50); **Kalymnos** (5 per week, €23.50); **Kos** (3 per week, €18.50); **Mykonos** (4 per week, €9); **Naxos** (1hr., 4-5 per day, €7); **Piraeus** (5-6hr., 5-6 per day, €22); **Rafina** (5-6hr., 4 per week, €22); **Rhodes** (16hr., 2 per week, €29); **Samos** (6hr., 4 per week, €18.50); **Santorini** (3hr., daily, €13.50); **Sikinos** (3hr., 2 per week, €8); **Syros** (1hr., 4 per week, €7); **Thessaloniki** (2 per week, €40); Tinos (4 per week, €11.50).

Taxis: ☎ 22840 21 500. Facing inland, walk to the right of the windmill and take the first left; taxis line up at the corner of the plateia. Prices range from €8 (to Naoussa) to €18 (to Agnat). Available 8am-3am.

Cars and Motorcycles: Rentals, which are readily available all over the waterfront, are a convenient traveling alternative for people 21 or older exploring the island. **Iria Rent-a-Car** (☎ 22840 22 132) rents cars for €20-50 per day.

◤▪ 🔁 ORIENTATION AND PRACTICAL INFORMATION

Cheap hotels, tourist offices, and the town beach lie to the left of the ferry dock. The plateia is straight ahead, past the windmill. To the right, a whitewashed labyrinth brims with shops, restaurants, and cafes. The island's party district awaits to the far right of the ferry dock and around the bend.

Budget Travel: Polos Tours (☎ 22840 22 092; www.polostours.gr), by the OTE, has transportation schedules and **car rental** (€25-79). Open 8am- 11:30 pm.

Banks: National Bank (☎ 22840 22 012 or 22840 21 663). From the windmill, head inland to the plateia and to the right. In the fortress-like building at the far corner. **24hr. ATM** and **currency exchange.** Open M-Th 8am-2:30pm, F 8am-2pm.

Luggage Storage: Several travel agencies by the waterfront offer luggage storage. **Paros Travel Agency,** directly opposite the windmill, charges €2 for each bag stored up to 12 hr. The "luggage deposit" behind the bus station holds bags for up to one day; €3.

Laundromat: Top (☎ 22840 23 424). Head right on the waterfront facing the water, and turn right after the ancient cemetery. Drop laundry off with attendant at the convenience shop down the street by the water. Wash and dry €9.

Police: ☎ 22840 23 333. Across the plateia behind the OTE, on the 2nd fl. Open 24hr.

Tourist Police: ☎22840 21 673. Shares the town police's building; tourist police are behind the door opposite the entrance stairs. Staff members are most useful for specific questions. Open daily 7am-2:30pm.

Hospital: ☎22840 22 500. "Health Center" is the first large white building on the waterfront, to the left of the windmill (facing inland), behind a small church. Open M-F 9am-2am. **Emergency** care available 24hr.

Telephones: OTE (☎22840 21 399). 1 block to the right of the windmill (facing inland). Open M-F 7am-2:40pm.

Internet Access: Internet cafes abound in Parikia. Many restaurants offer access for free; look for the "@" symbol. **Cybercookies** (☎22840 21 610), on Agora, charges €5 per 90min. Free 15min. with a food order, 35min. with 2 orders. Excellent smoothies. Open daily 8am-1am. **Memphis Cafe** is to the left of the windmills on the waterfront, past the church. €1 per 15min., €6 per 2hr. Open daily 9am-11pm. **Marina Internet Cafe** is on the waterfront, by the ancient cemetery. €1 per 15min., €3.50 per hr.

Post Office: ☎22840 21 236. On the left side of the waterfront facing inland. Open M-F 7:30am-2pm. **Postal Code:** 84400.

♠♦ ACCOMMODATIONS AND CAMPING

Hotels and **domatia** abound along the waterfront and in the Old Town. A slew of inexpensive pensions like **Pension Antoine** (☎22840 24 435) and **Pension Arian Hotel** (☎22840 21 490; cycladesnet.gr/arian) have recently opened throughout the city. Dock hawks are known to offer good deals in Naoussa, Piso Livadi, and Antiparos; remember to insist on seeing rooms before you pay.

▨ **Rena Rooms** (☎22840 22 220; www.cycladesnet.gr). Turn left from the dock and take a right after the cemetery or call ahead for a port shuttle. Owners George and Rena provide detailed information about the island, a welcoming atmosphere, and bright, clean rooms with fridges, ceiling fans, baths, and balconies. White walls and blue shutters are comfortable cottage-like. Free luggage storage. A/C and TV €5 extra. Doubles €20-40; triples €30-55. 20% discount for *Let's Go* readers. ❷

▨ **Festos of Paros** (☎ 22840 21 635 or 22840 24 192). About 150m from the port. Turn left at the yellow school building, and the blue fence entrance is on the left. A twentysomething English-speaking couple runs this simple, starkly decorated hostel. The doubles and triples, which surround a small courtyard, have few windows and thin walls, but the sheets, rugs, and private bathroom facilities are sparkling clean for dirt cheap. Breakfast included. Pets welcome. Prices are flexible; expect to pay €8 per person. ❶

Parian Village (☎22840 23 187), about 1km from the port. On top of a hill overlooking the bay opposite Parikia, accessible by the main waterfront road to the left of the windmill. Small rooms with A/C, phones, and fridges have spectacular bay views and beach access. Nestled in the hills, the sprawling stone terrace complex houses a gleaming pool, deck furniture, and a simple cafe. Doubles €60, low season €35. MC/V. ❹

Hotel Anna Platanou (☎22840 21 751). About a 10min. walk from the port and 5min. from Parikia's clubs. Turn right from the windmill and take a left onto the road adjacent to a light blue church and kiosk; the hotel is directly behind a square parking lot. Clean and attractive rooms have TV, fridges, balconies, and A/C. Some balconies are sheltered by hanging apricot trees. Doubles €50-60, low season €20-35. ❸

Parasporos Camping (☎22840 22 268 or 22840 21 100), 1.5km south of the port, away from the bustle of town, by Delphini beach. Shuttle service available. Showers, swimming pool, laundry, and kitchen. €6 per person, €2 per tent. Tent rental €4. ❶

Koula Camping (☎22840 22 081; www.campingkoula.gr), 400m from the dock, across the street from the town beach. A market, kitchen, and easy access to the town from a beachside location keep the backpackers flowing. €6 per person; €3 tent rental; tiny, tent-shaped cabin for 1 person €7, for 2 €12. MC. ❶

☐ FOOD

■ **Ephessus Anatolian Greek Restaurant** (☎22840 21 491), behind the hospital. Menus are available, but the waitress is likely to ask diners to choose from pre-made dishes on display, including flavorful moussaka and stuffed tomatoes. A popular option is the plate with samples of each daily special and a Greek salad (€9.50). The simple ambience is as home-style as the ordering process; the restaurant feels like an extension of the chef's dining room. Open daily 12:30-11:30pm. ❷

■ **Happy Green Cow** (☎22840 24 691), 1 block inland off the plateia in the narrow walkway behind the National Bank. Offers vegetarian and chicken dishes in an atmosphere that fuses traditional Greek ornamentation with the psychedelic 60s. Colorful walls, hanging lamps, crystal chandeliers, and mellow music make this restaurant a popular venue. The creative dishes which mix cheese, curry, and vegetables are matched by equally creative names, including the Cow's Orgasms (pastries with cheese and peppers; €12). Open daily Apr.-Nov. 7pm-midnight. ❸

Porphyra (☎22840 23 410), by the ancient cemetery on the right side of the waterfront. Under a plant-draped trellis with an ocean view, diners order from a seafood-only menu, that includes the namesake *porphyra* (the inhabitant of a conch shell; €4) and sea urchin (€4) harvested by the owner. Open daily Mar.-Oct. 7pm-1am. AmEx/MC/V. ❷

Tamarisko Garden Restaurant (☎22840 24 689), up Agora away from the main plateia, about 100m before Apollon Restaurant. A stone wall and plant-filled roof enclose several long tables lined with gregarious native customers and heaping plates. Greek salad €4.50. Mushroom pasta €7. Open Tu-Su 7pm-late. ❷

Apollon Garden Restaurant (☎22840 21 875). Take Agora away from Market and keep an eye out for the signs. Overflowing with opera music and lush plant life, Apollon's rotating menu caters to a sophisticated crowd. Chicken with mango and plum sauce €13. Salmon fillet €13. Open daily May-Oct. 6pm-1am. AmEx/MC/V. ❸

Nick's Hamburgers (☎22840 21 434). Walk right from the port; it's tucked away in Ventouris Square along the water. Large signs boasting "Pure 100% Beef" and "Fish n' Chips" lure carnivores to this American-diner-style burger joint. Cheeseburger €1.90. Hot dog €1.70. Fish and chips €4.20. Nickfeast (2 burgers, chips, and salad) €3.80. Open daily Apr.-Oct. 11am-2am. ❶

☉ SIGHTS

PANAGIA EKATONTAPILIANI. According to the local legend, St. Helen commissioned the construction of Parikia's largest church, the **Church of Our Lady of 100 Doors,** in the AD 4th century. On a mission in AD 326, the mother of Emperor Constantine the Great stopped to pray at the site, vowing to build a church on the spot if her quest for the Holy Cross was successful—which, as the lore goes, it was. The main structure of the complex is the mammoth **Church of the Assumption,** where Orthodox Christians make pilgrimage every August 15th in honor of The Feast of Panagia, or Ekatontapiliani. The **Church of Agios Nikolaos** (the oldest of the three) and the **baptistry** flank this centerpiece to the north and south, respectively. The white cloister at the entrance of the complex was built in the 17th century as a monastery, but now hosts church offices, an **Ecclesiastic Museum,** and housing for the Paros/Naxos High Priest's infrequent visits. In the museum's small, uncelebrated galleries are Byzantine religious icons and texts, including several gems. *(Church open daily 7am-10pm. Free. Mass M-Sa 7-7:30pm, Su 7:30-10am. Museum open daily 9am-10pm. €1.50. Modest dress required.)*

OTHER SIGHTS. The **Archaeological Museum** places masterpieces alongside curiosities, haphazardly displayed in a courtyard and three small rooms. Labels are few but informative; the museum claims fame for its glorious *amphorae*, its 5th-century wingless Nike, and its archaic statue of Gorgon, which was discovered a only few meters away from its display case. A slab of the marble Parian Chronicle, a history of Greece up to 264 BC, is also housed here. *(Heading away from the water, take a left after Panagia Ekatontapiliani; the museum is at the end of the road. ☎22840 21 231. Open Tu-Su 8:30am-2:45pm. €2, students €1, EU students free.)* A ramble through the Old Town will inevitably lead you past the lone remaining wall of the Venetian **Frankish Castle,** where you can see sections of marble and columns removed from the ancient Ionic Temple of Athena, built in the 5th century BC.

📷 NIGHTLIFE

The waterfront comes alive after dark. Throngs assemble on the sidewalk and the beach, and pedestrians stroll the beach road at all hours of the night. At midnight, the tourist traffic forms a stream flowing toward the clubs at the edge of town. **Pirate Blues and Jazz,** in V. Gravari square on Agora, is a tiny bubble of New Orleans jazz culture in the sprawl of Old Town Paros. Black and white photographs of John Coltrane, Ella Fitzgerald, and the Cotton Club dot the walls of this intimate, low-ceilinged establishment, and a DJ plays continuous jazz. (☎22840 21 114. Beer and wine €3. Mixed drinks €7. Open daily 7pm-3am.) Follow the spotlight and crowds to the far end of the harbor where **The Dubliner, Salsa Club, Scandi Bar,** and the **Paros Rock Cafe** all share one roof, connected by a spacious central courtyard. This sweaty, pulsating party complex, which calls itself **The Parian Experience,** attempts to cater to every type of tourist with its different themes—Irish bar, Scandinavian decor, and Latin dancing. (☎22840 21 113. Beer €3-5. Mixed drinks €5-6. Cover €3; includes 1 drink.) **Saloon D'Or,** a popular cafe right on the water, about 100m before the blue church, is Parian Experience's milder, more intimate cousin. Upbeat music plays over funky checkered floors and brightly colored couches. (☎22840 22 176. Beer €2-3. Mixed drinks €5-7. Open daily Apr.-Oct. 7pm-4am.)

📷 BEACHES

Almost every beach on Paros can be reached in under an hour's drive. In just the immediate vicinity of Parikia, though, there are some outstanding and easily accessible beaches. **Parasporos** is 2km to the south and is in a beautiful cove next to a beach club and restaurant (take the bus to Pounda or Ageria; about every hr., €0.90). **Krios** lies across the harbor from Parikia. The sand is less pebbly and more welcoming than the beaches in town, but it can be just as crowded. Krios is accessible by **water taxi** (every 30min. 10am-6pm, round-trip €2.30). To explore Paros on horseback, call **Horse Riding Koukou** (☎22840 51 818). For watery adventures, try the scuba lessons and tours offered by **Eurodivers Club** (☎22840 33 6464) or kiteboard with **Paros Kite** (☎22840 42 757; www.paroskite-procenter.com).

📷 DAYTRIPS FROM PARIKIA

Just 10km south of town is the shady **Valley of the Butterflies,** or Petaloudes, where the rare (and tongue-twisting) *Panaxiaquadripunctaria* moths return to the place of their birth to breed, lured back by their strong sense of smell. Petaloudes is one of the rare surviving sanctuaries for the moths. June provides only a smattering of the bright black and yellow moths, while the height of mating season (late July to late Aug.) sometimes draws millions in a miraculous display. Since the moths do not eat for their entire mating season, they can ill afford to expend energy by entertaining photo-hungry guests. Be considerate by not clapping, talking loudly, or shaking the bushes. Take the bus from Parikia to Aliki (12min., 7 per day, €0.90) and ask to be dropped off at Petaloudes. Follow the signs up the steep road for 2km. (☎22840 91 211. Open daily June-Sept. 9am-8pm. €1.50.)

Five kilometers from Parikia in the center of the island, **Marathi** is home to Paros's idle marble quarries. Still considered to be among the finest in the world, Parian marble is translucent up to 3mm thick, with one-third the opacity of most other marble. A visit to the quarries is a serious undertaking: bring a flashlight, strong shoes, and don't go alone. Buses run to Marathi approximately eight times a day. From the bus stop, signs will direct you to the quarries. Blink and you might miss **Lefkes,** a tiny town 5km from Marathi, which, as Parians moved inland to escape plundering coastal pirates, was the largest village on the island through the 19th century. Beautiful architecture and quaint, untouristed streets make Lefkes an attractive daytrip location.

NAOUSSA Νάουσσα ☎22840

Naoussa is Paros's second port, a natural harbor cradled by long, sandy beaches in the shape of crab claws. Persian, Greek, Roman, Venetian, Ottoman, and Russian fleets have anchored here over the years, leaving subtle marks on the sophisticated town, which overflows with unique shops, inviting coffeehouses, and trendy nightclubs. Naoussa is colorful and festive, but budget travelers should be wary: the upscale environment is pricey.

⌂⊿ TRANSPORTATION AND PRACTICAL INFORMATION. Naoussa is on two of Paros's bus lines, and **buses** leave for Naoussa once or twice an hour. Others run to nearby beaches. Check the schedule at the bus stop booth. **Water taxis** also go to the beaches. The blue booth on the waterfront sells round-trip tickets to: Kolimbithres (12min., 12 per day, €3); Lageri (20min., 5 per day, €4); Monastiri (15min., 5 per day, €3.50). **Taxis** (☎22840 53 490) are available 24hr. by the bus stop.

Naoussa can be hard to navigate, but the central bridge is a useful landmark. From the bus stop facing the water, the main road out of town is to the left and leads to the beaches of **Kolimbithres** and **Monastiri.** Buses also go to the nude beach at **Lageri.** From the bus station, facing away from the water, two roads head inland, one on the right with a stream down the middle and one on the left without a stream. Naoussa's **tourist office,** opposite the bus stop by the bridge, has info about the town and accommodations. (☎22840 52 158. Open daily June-Sept. 10am-3pm and 6-10:30pm.) An **Alpha Bank** is up the inland road on the left. (☎22840 28 233. Open M-Th 8am-2:30pm, F 8am-2pm.) For the **police,** call ☎22840 51 202. The **pharmacy** is on the left on the main street inland without the stream. (☎22840 51 550. Open daily 8:30am-2pm and 5-11pm.) A **medical center** (☎22840 51 216) is in the park just before the church when heading inland on the same road; the doctor is available 8:30am-2:30pm. In **medical emergencies,** call the clinic in Parikia at ☎22480 22 500. To find the **OTE,** walk along the main road out of town and turn left up a large set of stairs across from the beach; it's on the road at the top of the stairs. The **post office** is on the road out of town along the water, just beyond the Santa Maria turn-off. (☎22840 51 495. Open M-F 7:30am-2pm.) **Postal Code:** 84401.

⌂ ACCOMMODATIONS AND CAMPING. Though Naoussa has many places to sleep, prices skyrocket in summer when package-tour groups book hotels months in advance. Rooms to let cost about €30-45 for doubles and €35-50 for triples. Ask at the tourist office for help finding accommodations. **Pension Anna ❷** sits around the corner from the bus station, the first left on the road out of town. It has spacious rooms with A/C, TV, fridge, and shared balcony. (☎22840 51 328. Doubles €25-55.) A number of upscale pensions with spectacular views of the harbor lie to the right of the waterfront as you face away from the water. Around the corner to the right and up the hill is **Coral Rooms ❸**. The hostel advertises its slightly cheaper accommodations with a "backpacking" sign on its exterior. Small rooms with few windows come with refrigerators and breakfast. Internet and safe boxes available at the front desk. (☎22840 53 456. Singles €25-50; doubles €40-70 depending on the season. AmEx/MC/V.) 20m up the same hill is **Sakis Rooms ❸**, which provides weary travelers with luxurious lodgings in a welcoming atmosphere. Amenities include private baths, TV, A/C, fridges, and balconies overlooking the sea. (☎22840 52 171; www.parosonline.com. Doubles €35-60; 5-person apartments €50-130. MC/V.) At upscale **Atlantis Hotel ❹**, down the road from Pension Anna, bare but well-equipped rooms with A/C, phones, baths, and fridges are complemented by a pool and jacuzzi. (☎22840 51 340. Breakfast €7. Doubles €50-75; triples €65-90. AmEx/MC/V.) **Camping Naoussa ❶** is on the road to Kolimbithres. Call for the free port shuttle. (☎22840 51 595. €5 per person. €6 tent rental.)

◖◗ FOOD AND ENTERTAINMENT. Naoussan kitchens cook famously delicious seafood; their local specialty is the fish plate *gouna*. One of the many colorful, savory-smelling eateries clustering the waterfront is **Mouragio ❷**, a simple taverna with a limited seafood menu. (☎22840 51 405. Fried cod €5.50. Open daily Apr.-Nov. 9am-midnight.) **Diamantis ❷**, behind the church on the commerce road about 300m from the bus station, is a family-run restaurant featuring meat-heavy Greek fare. Sit on a tree-studded terrace just below the sidewalk and feast on lamb *diamantis* (€7), stuffed with feta, tomatoes, peppers, and onions. (☎22840 52 129. Open daily 7pm-1am. AmEx/MC/V.) A few meters above Diamantis, quaint blue and red doors open to reveal **Pervolaria ❸**, a multi-level terrace restaurant in a secluded, garden setting. Pervolaria has a second, almost identical location about 200m inland on the road along the stream, past the clubs. (☎22840 51 721. Seafood platter €12. Moussaka €8.50. Open daily 7pm-late. AmEx/MC/V.)

Posh **clubs** with cavernous dance floors and mod decor dominate Naoussa's high-season nightlife. Up the road with the stream 100m from the bus stop, several dance clubs grind away late into the night. **Privilege, Envy, and Nostros** lures chic customers with a spacious dance floor playing American music and gauze-draped couches in a palm-lined, pool-spotted courtyard. (☎22840 53 450. Mixed drinks €8-10.

PIRATES OF THE AEGEAN

In Naoussa, dreams do come true—at least if you're one of the many children who entertain fantasies of abandoning boring rules for the rough-and-tumble life of a pirate. Hopefully, though, the fun of jumping off ships and taking prisoners won't be spoiled by the fact that it's actually allowed.

Each year, August 23 marks the demurely named Nine Days of the Virgin Mary, commemorating the ninth day after the Assumption of the Virgin. Other islands observe the holiday with extended Orthodox services and the occasional mild feast. In Naoussa, however, the day is devoted to roaring merrymaking and wild play. Dressed in traditional pirate costumes, boys re-enact the naval battles of Barbarossa, a 16th-century Ottoman conqueror. They dive into the bay off fishing boats and run through throngs of revelers, picking up little girls and carrying them away from the crowds. When the costumes are shed and the captives returned, the entire island gathers to dance, feast, and celebrate. Fireworks explode overhead, adding color and chaos to the already festive shoreline. The Naoussan spirit is contagious and inclusive; boat captains will take visitors to the feasts for free.

Though things return to normal the next day, at least one pirate-themed day is better than none.

Cover €8-10; includes 1 drink. Open daily midnight-late.) If you're in Naoussa in low season before many of the clubs have opened, check out **Insomnia,** a two-level cafe and bar on the waterfront to the left of the bridge. A party atmosphere draws revelers to the balcony. (☎22840 53 388. Beer €5. Mixed drinks €7-8. Also opens at 8am as a cafe.) The **Aqua Paros water park** (☎22840 53 271), at Kolimbithres, is a pricey option for waterslide aficionados. On the first Sunday in July, eat, drink, and be merry as you cruise Naoussa's harbor and watch traditional dancing at the **Wine and Fish Festival;** call the tourist office for details.

EASTERN COAST OF PAROS

The quiet town of **Piso Livadi,** 11km from Lefkes, includes a handful of cafes and hotels clustered together on a pristine bay. While it feels isolated and remote, Piso Livadi is close to Paros's nicest beaches (e.g. **Logaras** and **Chrisi Akti**) and is easily accessible by public transportation. **Perantinos Travel & Tourism,** to the left of the bus stop facing the water, provides information about accommodations and ferries. (☎/fax 22840 41 135. Open daily June and Sept. 9am-2pm and 6-8pm, July and Aug. 9am-10pm.) The family owners of Perantinos also run the **Londos Hotel ❸,** on the first right 50m up the road towards Parikia. Its clean rooms come with fridge, private bath, and balcony. (☎22840 41 218. A/C and breakfast each €5 extra per day. Doubles Aug. €40; July €35; June and Sept. €20-25.) **Anna's Studios ❹,** toward the end of the wharf, offers spacious balconies directly overlooking the water. Fresh, clean doubles and triples include housekeeping and minifridges; studio apartments with full kitchens also available. (☎22840 41 320; www.annasinn.com. Doubles €45, low season €25.)

ANTIPAROS Αντίπαρος

Literally meaning "opposite Paros," Antiparos is so close to its neighbor that, according to local lore, travelers once signaled the ferryman on Paros by opening the door of a chapel on Antiparos. The small island is mostly undeveloped, with a modest population to match Antiparos's size. Most travelers visit Antiparos as a daytrip to see the caves, but it's easy to find a place to stay on the tiny island, which is sleepy and attractive.

ANTIPAROS TOWN   ☎22840

Virtually all of the island's 1000 inhabitants live in town, where the ferry docks and most accommodations are found.

◪⊟ TRANSPORTATION AND PRACTICAL INFORMATION. Take a direct **ferry** from Parikia (30min., 3 per day, €2) or a **bus** to Pounda (15min., 11 per day, €0.90), followed by a boat to Antiparos (10min., 30 per day, €0.60). The island has two bus routes. One leaves for the caves (6 per day 7:30am-2pm, round-trip €2); another travels to Soros via St. George (3 per day 7:30am-2pm).

Waterfront **Oliaros Tours** helps with accommodations, sells maps (€0.50), and has boat and bus schedules, **Internet** access (€6 per hr.), **currency exchange,** and information about cruises and vehicle rentals. (☎22840 61 231, low season 22840 61 189. Open daily 9am-10:30pm.) It may be better to get cash in Parikia; the **National Bank,** on the left up the road to the plateia, is only open April to October. (☎22840 61 294. Open M-F 9am-1pm.) The **laundromat** is behind the windmill, to the left of the port facing inland. (Wash, dry, and soap €8. Open 8am-9:30pm.) Reach the **police** 24hr. at ☎22840 61 202. To find the **medical clinic,** walk 200m inland on the main street and take a left before the post office. The number of the doctor on duty is posted. The **post office** is on the left side of the street leading from the water to the plateia. (☎22840 61 223. Open M-F 7:30am-1pm.) **Postal Code:** 84007.

⌂ ACCOMMODATIONS AND CAMPING. The **Mantalena Hotel ❸,** to the right of the dock when facing inland, has large rooms with baths, fridges, A/C, TV, and balconies. A family-owned establishment for 37 years, the pristine hotel has two large communal verandas. (☎22840 61 206. Doubles €35-60; triples €42-72. AmEx/MC/V.) At **Hotel Antiparos ❷,** the small, basic rooms include A/C, kitchen facilities, balconies, and phones. (☎22840 61 358; www.otenet.gr/antiparoshotel. Doubles €20-35; triples €30-45, with kitchen €35-60.) **Camping Antiparos ❶** is 800m northwest of town, on the well-marked way to Ag. Yiannis Theologos beach. Camping areas are separated by bamboo walls. The beachside has its own mini-mart and restaurant. (☎22840 61 221. Open May-Sept. May 1-July 14 €4 per person, €2 per tent; €4 tent rental. July 15-Sept. 30 €5.50 per person, €2.50 per tent; €4 tent rental.)

▣▣ FOOD AND ENTERTAINMENT. At the end of a small break in the buildings 100m up the main road on the left, **Taverna Klimataria ❷** is sheltered by hanging trees and low yellow walls and serves traditional dishes. (☎22840 61 298. Most entrees under €6. July 20 to late Aug. open 24hr., otherwise open 4pm-late.) The last building before the church on the right of the waterfront dock, **O Statheros ❷** dishes out fresh, hefty-portioned plates of seafood under a canopy of hanging octopi. (☎22840 61 172. Fried squid with mint €5.50. Open daily noon-midnight.) **Amargyros ❷** provides a similarly seafood-oriented menu in a more formal environment. (☎22840 61 204. Octopus stew €7. Goat with tomato sauce €6. Open daily Apr.-Oct. 7am-midnight. MC/V.) For a post-meal or pre-pub stop, **The Shipwreck ❶,** the first establishment past the post office on the left, plays jazz and mellow music in an airy, subtly schooner-themed interior. (☎22840 61 012. Frappés €2.50. Crepes €2-4. Mixed drinks €4-5. Open daily Apr.-Oct. 9am-3am.)

Bars, clubs, and late-night eateries cluster around the main plateia. Follow the music past the first sign for Taverna Klimataria on the left of the main road to **Cafe Yam,** an outdoor restaurant and cocktail bar, where live Brazilian music and colorful plants fill the large, trendy terrace. (☎22840 61 055. Most entrees around €8. Mixed drinks €6.50. Open daily July 11-Sept. 15, 8pm-4am). Tables, chairs, and drinkers spill out from **The Doors,** an intimate bar whose tiny space is covered with Jim Morrison memorabilia. (Beer €2-4. Mixed drinks €4-5. Open daily 9pm-late.) **The Stones** is a spacious bar with a dance floor and patio for people-watching. (Beer €2-4. Mixed drinks €4-5. Open daily 7pm-late.)

◧◪ SIGHTS AND BEACHES. The dank, wet stalactite **caves** at the southern end of the island are Antiparos's main attraction. **Buses** (20min., round-trip €2) run from Antiparos Town's port every hour from morning through early afternoon. Names of ancient visitors are written on the walls with their years of entry. Unfortunately, some of the stalactites were broken off by Russian naval officers in the 18th century and "borrowed" on behalf of a St. Petersburg museum, while still more were destroyed by Italians during WWII. Despite all this defilement, the caves, which plunge 100m into the earth, are dramatic; the stalactites stretch to over 7m in length, and the cavernous interior feels like a surreal, otherworldly landscape. (Open daily 11am-2:30pm. €3.50.) Go through the unpainted stone archway to the immediate right of the plateia to reach the meager ruins of the **Castle of Antiparos,** a village built by a 15th-century Italian to defend his holdings from rampant piracy. Though new buildings exist in place of the first ones, which were made with 3m thick walls, they retain Loredano's original layout. **Psaraliki,** a 5min. walk just to the south of town, is a pleasant place to bathe, as is **Glifa,** a 15min. ride to the east on the bus (every hour, €1) toward the caves. **Blue Island Divers** (☎22840 61 493; www.blueisland-divers.gr) runs scuba diving lessons and tours.

AMORGOS Αμοργός

King Minos of Crete was said to rule a kingdom on Amorgos in ancient times, a legend supported by the 1985 discovery of artifacts atop Mt. Moudoulia. Today, much of Amorgos resembles its most enduring sight, the Hozoviotissa Monastery, which burrows into the cliffs below Hora. The steep cliffs and clear waters were captured 20 years ago in the film *The Big Blue* (*Le Grand Bleu*); they remain just as startlingly big and blue now. Though tourism has boomed recently, Amorgos's small size and tight-knit local community have preserved an enduring tranquility. Infrequent ferry connections generally stop at Amorgos's two ports in succession—Aegiali in the northeast and larger Katapola in the southwest.

KATAPOLA Κατάπολα ☎ 22850

Whitewashed houses with blue trim, narrow streets, and an overhanging Venetian castle make up Katapola, Amorgos's central port. Free from the bustle of many other Cycladic port towns, the town retains a serene, communal atmosphere even as more visitors have come to the island. The small streets hardly extend beyond the water; a short walk will bring you to deserted beaches and Minoan ruins.

⌐⊠ TRANSPORTATION AND PRACTICAL INFORMATION. Ferries from both ports of Amorgos go to: Astypalea (3hr., 2 per week, €16); Donousa (1½hr., 4 per week, €6.50); Iraklia (2hr., 1-2 per day, €7.70); Koufonisia (1½hr., 1-2 per day, €6.40); Naxos (3-6hr., 1-2 per day, €12.40); Paros (4hr., 7 per week, €14); Piraeus (8½hr., 7 per week, €24.50); Schinousa (1¾hr., 1-2 per day, €6.20); Syros (5hr., 5 per week, €14.50). **Speedboats** go to Koufonisia (1hr., 3 per week, €18), Mykonos (1hr., 3 per week, €22), and Naxos (1½hr., 3 per week, €23). The bus station sits to the left of the dock facing inland, 200m past the ferry landings. **Buses** connect villages in the summer, running from Katapola to: Aegiali (45min., 4-6 per day, €1.70); Agia Anna (25min., 6-8 per day 10am-6pm, €1) via Hozoviotissa Monastery (20min., €1); Hora (15min., 11-15 per day 7:45am-midnight, €1); various beaches (9 per day 10am-6pm, €1). Call a 24hr. **taxi** at ☎ 69378 83 838.

The town surrounds the ferry dock in a horseshoe, with restaurants, bars, and accommodations on either side. The port is at the center; most tourist services are between the ferry dock and the road to Hora. Across from the large ferry dock is **Synodinos Tours,** which **exchanges currency** and sells ferry tickets. (☎ 22850 71 201. Open daily May-Oct. 8:30am-10pm and 1hr. before all boat departures; Nov.-Apr. 10am-1:30pm and 5-8:30pm and 1hr. before all boat departures.) **Agricultural Bank,** opposite the ferries, has a **24hr. ATM.** (☎ 22850 71 872. Open M-Th 8am-2:30pm, F 8am-2pm.) The **laundromat** is inland, past the docks on the way to the beach; take the first right after Pension Amorgos. (☎ 22850 71 723. Wash and dry €10. Open M-Sa 8:30am-4:30pm and 6:30-9:30pm, Su 10am-2:30pm.) The **police** (☎ 22850 71 210) are in Hora while the **port police** (☎ 22850 71 259; open 24hr.) are across from the ferry dock. The nearest **pharmacy** is in Hora. The **medical center** is at the far left end of the waterfront, in the white building behind the two statues. (☎ 22850 71 805. Open M-F 9am-2:30pm.) For **medical emergencies,** dial ☎ 22850 71 805 or 69776 63 558. **Minoa Cafe,** in the central plateia, has **Internet access.** (☎ 22850 71 480. €5 per hr.; €2.50 min. Open daily 11am-1:30pm and 5:30-10pm.) The small **post office** is located at the back left of the main plateia facing inland. (☎ 22850 71 884. Open M-Tu, Th 10am-1pm and 7-8:30pm, W, F 10am-1pm.) **Postal Code:** 84008.

⌐⊡ ACCOMMODATIONS AND FOOD. Katapola is a small town with few hotels and many **domatia.** At the far end of the beach from the port, **Titika Rooms ❷** surrounds a flowery, stone-lined garden; look for the green shutters. A free port shuttle takes you to the pleasant, if cluttered, rooms with private baths, fridges, TV, A/C, balconies, mosquito netting, and hair dryers. (☎22850 71 660. Breakfast €2.50. Doubles €25-45; triples €30-55.) To reach **Big Blue Pension ❷** from the ferry dock, turn right after the plateia and follow signs uphill. The pension is indeed big, with blue windows and doors. A free port shuttle, flower-studded walkways, and spectacular multi-level veranda views complement private baths, fridges, and TV. (☎22850 71 094. Doubles €25-55; triples €35-65.) **Pension Amorgos ❸,** across from the small ferry dock, rents small rooms directly on the water and has a roof-top veranda. (☎22850 71 013. Doubles €25-65.)

Katapola's outdoor restaurants and cafes have pleasant harbor views. If your taste buds need a change of pace, savor authentic Italian dishes like a delicious baked spaghetti (€6) at **Erato ❷,** the second-to-last cafe at the end of the wharf. (☎22850 74 102. Pizzas €5.50-8.10. Open noon-midnight.) **Aigaion Cafe ❶,** in the center of the main plateia, serves fruit juice (€3), crepes (€3-5), omelettes (€2.50-5), and mixed drinks (€5.50-6) to locals who lounge in the waterfront seats. Inside the funky interior, people play board games and listen to pop music. (☎22850 71 549. Open daily Apr.-Oct. 8am-3:30am; Nov.-Mar. 9am-midnight.) **Mouraylo ❷,** across from the dock, has authentic meals in a simple outdoor seating area. Inside, you can get a sneak preview of your meal in coolers full of fresh fish. (☎22850 71 011. Boiled octopus €6. Fried cod €5. Moussaka €5. Open 1pm-late.)

■ **SIGHTS AND BEACHES.** Follow the signs uphill and out of town past the church to begin the 2km hike to the ancient town of **Minoa,** inhabited between the 10th and 4th centuries BC. Look for the base of the temple among the otherwise-unimpressive ruins and the bust of a statue rising from within—the now barely distinguishable acropolis once stood on the plateau above the temple. Thorough signs explain the site's history and the former location of the city's main buildings. **Agios Pavlos's** shallow turquoise lagoon is exquisite and is only a short walk downhill from the bus stop. Take a bus toward Aigeiali and ask to be let off at Agios Pavlos (6 per day, €1.50). Various **nude beaches** provide sand and sun outside of town, opposite the dock. Smooth-stoned **Plakes** and the sandier **Agios Panteleimonas** are quiet, yet easily accessible by foot or boat—taxi boats leave from the left of the dock facing inland (5 per day, round-trip €2).

■ **DAYTRIP FROM KATAPOLA: HOZOVIOTISSA MONASTERY.** A trip to Amorgos is incomplete without a visit to otherworldly Hozoviotissa Monastery, an 11th-century Byzantine edifice built into a cliff face—one of the most exhilarating spectacles in all of Greece and an inspiration to the great 20th-century Swiss architect Le Corbusier, among others. Legend tells that attempts to build the monastery on the shore were inexplicably thwarted; when the workers discovered their tools hanging from the cliff, they figured it was an omen and started construction there. If you complete the hike (up 350 stairs), the monks may treat you to cold water, sweet ginger-flavored liquor, and *loukoumi.* Inside, visitors must lean to the left when climbing the narrow staircase to avoid the cliff face, which protrudes into the building's cave-like interior. At the top, a multilingual monk will greet you to provide a short history and answer questions. To see more of the building, come in November when the entire island celebrates the **Feast of Panagia Hozoviotissa** at the monastery. If you miss the bus back, take the stone stairway (10m uphill from the fork in the road leading away from the monastery). A 20min. climb up the stairs will lead you to Hora. The road from the monastery also takes you to the crystal waters of **Agia Anna** and its two beaches; from the bus stop, one is at the end of the path through the clearing, the other at the bottom of the central steps. Catch a **bus** (20min., 6 per day 10am-6pm, €1) from Katapola to the monastery. (☎22850 71 274. Open daily 8am-1pm and 5-7pm. Modest dress required. Free.)

CYCLADES

HORA Χώρα   ☎22850

Also known as Amorgos Town, the island's small, relatively untouristed capital lies 6km uphill from the harbor at the top of the mountains. A typical example of Byzantine village planning, Hora's winding streets were constructed to deter and confuse raiding pirates; they now allow visitors to meander aimlessly along the cafe-lined walk to **Plateia Loza,** at the far end of town. Sights include a 14th-century Venetian **fortress,** a row of 10 defunct windmills perched on the mountain ledge above town, numerous Byzantine churches, and the first secondary school in Greece, built in 1821. The remnants of Amorgos's Minoan civilization are visible in the statues and relief carvings at the **Archaeological Museum,** across from Zygos Cafe and downhill from the large church at Pl. Loza. (☎22850 71 831. Open Tu-Su 9am-1pm and 5-7pm. Free.) Rugged mountains and a placid coast run alongside the road from Hora to Aegiali. The clearly marked, sunny 4hr. hike begins behind Hora and stretches up the mountains to Potamos. You'll find the crumbling Byzantine church of **Christososmas** (The Body of Christ) hewn out of a small cave that was once a hermit dwelling, 40min. into the hike. The trail ascends past a series of monasteries before descending to views of miniature **Nikouria Island,** which experienced swimmers can reach from the beach by the main road. Lonely and deserted **Agios Mammas** church is the last significant marker before Potamos appears.

If you decide to spend the night in Hora, you can strike a deal with the **domatia** owners who meet your boat, or look for "rooms to let" signs along side streets. The reception for **Pension Ilias ❷** is along the road from Hora to the monastery, while the rooms are one street uphill. Rooms have baths, common balconies with views of the valley below, and fridges; the multi-room apartments include full kitchens. (☎22850 71 277. Doubles €25-50; apartments €55-70.) **Maria Economidou ❸** has modern, classy rooms. They all come with balconies, kitchenettes, and impeccable baths. (☎22850 71 111. Doubles €40; 2-person apartments €45-60.) Both establishments will pick you up at the port if you call ahead. ▨**Zygos ❶**, on the cafe-lined alley below Pl. Loza, serves peerless apple pie (€2.80), coffee (€1.50-3), and mixed drinks (€5) in a comfortable interior or on a vine-roofed patio across the street. Leisurely patrons play board games to the tunes of international music. (☎22850 71 350. Open daily 8am-3:30am.) **Liotrivi ❷**, near the bakery on the road to the monastery, prepares delicious twists on Greek standards—*kalogiros* (eggplant with veal, feta, gouda, and tomato) and *exohiko* (lamb and vegetables in pastry shell) are the house specialities. (☎22850 71 700. Entrees €5-7. Open daily May-Oct. noon-midnight.) The relaxed cafe downstairs at **Bayoko,** by the bus station, caters to coffee-sipping people-watchers. Upstairs, at one of Hora's only clubs, nightly DJs spin Greek dance hits over the small dance floor from 9pm until dawn. (Beer €2.50-4. Mixed drinks €6. Ouzo €1.50.)

You can find the **police** in the main plateia with the big church, by Cafe Loza. (☎22850 71 210. Open daily 8am-2pm.) The **pharmacy** is opposite the bus stop. (☎22850 74 166. Open M-F 9:30am-2pm and 6:30-9pm.) The **medical center** sits below the bus stop on the main road into Hora from Katapola. (☎22850 71 207. Open M-F 9am-2:30pm.) Hora is home to the island's **OTE** (☎22850 71 399; open M-F 8am-2pm), on the right 250m past Pl. Loza's major church, and the main **post office** (☎22850 71 250; open M-F 7:30am-2pm), in a corner beyond Pl. Loza.

AEGIALI Αιγιάλη   ☎22850

Aegiali, the island's other port, is as close as Amorgos comes to feeling touristy. As a result, the locals seem a little wearier of travelers here than on other parts of the island. With a beach and many accommodations, leisurely Aegiali serves best as a base for exploring the beaches clustered along the island's northern edge.

A number of pensions occupy the hillside inland of the waterfront. **Capetan Nikos ❷,** uphill and to the right before the medical center, has rooms with kitchenettes, baths, TV, and A/C. Colorful paintings adorn the walls and the common balcony offers a grand view of the harbor. (☎22850 73 026. Doubles €35-50.) **Poseidon Pension ❸,** past the pharmacy on the road inland, rents neat, trim rooms with kitchenettes, baths, and outdoor seating. (☎22850 73 453. Doubles €30-55; 3- to 4-person studios from €50.) **Camping Aegiali ❶** is just outside town, on the road to Tholaria. You can walk 10min. from the port to the campsite or take advantage of the free port transfer. The site has laundry and cooking facilities, free safety deposit boxes, a restaurant, bar, and impeccable showers. (☎22850 73 500. Quiet hours 3-6pm and 1am-9am. Check-out 3pm. €3.70-5 per person, €3 per tent; €5.70 tent rental.) On the opposite end of the beach, mellow out at cafe-club-restaurant **▨Disco The Que ❶.** They're too chill to have menus, but dreadlocked waiters can tell you which snacks (€3) and meals (€5-7) to munch on during the day and which beers (€2.50) and mixed drinks (€5) to down at night. Music ranges from reggae and psychedelic rock to trance and jazz. (☎22850 73 212. Open daily 10am-late.) **To Steki ❷,** at the edge of the beach past the bus stop, serves standard Greek fare in a simple, inviting outdoor setting. (☎22850 73 003. Amorgos cheeses €3. Fish €4-6. Pasta €3-5. Open daily 6pm-midnight. MC/V.)

For **ferry** and **high-speed boat** schedules, see the listings for Katapola (p. 410). **Bus** routes stop in several villages. They go to: Aegiali-Hora-Katapola (45min., 4 per day, €2); Meria-Hora-Katapola (2 per day, €1); Ormos-Lagada (6 per day, €1); Tholaria (4 per day, €1). **Taxis** (☎69321 03 077) can be reached 24hr. Aegiali is built along slope of the mountain foothills. Most tourist facilities are along the waterfront or just uphill. Facing inland, clubs are to the left along the beach, cafes are to the right. **Aegialis Tours** (☎22850 73 394) has **Internet access** (€5.70 per hr.), stores **luggage** (€1.50 per piece per day), and handles accommodations, **car rental** (€40-60), and bus or boat excursions. (Open daily Apr.-Oct. 9am-2pm and 6-10pm.) Across the street, **Nautilus Travel** helps with ferries and accommodations. (☎22850 73 032. Open daily 10am-10pm.) Both agencies are just inland from the waterfront. There is **no bank** in Aegiali. The **police** (☎22850 73 320) are located in Langada; the 24hr. **port police** (☎22850 73 620) are on the road inland to the bakery. A **pharmacy** is up the road by the Island Market, on the right. (☎22850 73 173. Open M-F 9:30am-3pm and 6-10pm.) The **medical center** is 100m uphill past the pharmacy near the road to Potamos. (☎22850 73 222. Open M, W, F 9:30am-2pm.) **Phones** are next door to the pharmacy. The **post office** is across from the pharmacy in the mini-mart. (☎22850 73 001. Open daily 8am-11pm.) **Postal Code:** 84008.

IOS Ίος

This drink-till-you-drop party island is rivaled only by Mykonos when it comes to nocturnal Dionysian rites. Daytime activity generally centers on the coast, as beachgoers soak up the sun's energy to prepare for the long night ahead. Ios has actually settled down a bit in the past few years, making a successful effort to bring families and older crowds to enjoy its more peaceful side. And despite the island's knack for revelry, only three of its 36 beaches have been fully developed for tourism, so there are plenty of places to stretch out and soothe that hangover.

HORA (IOS TOWN) Χώρα   ☎22860

If you're not drunk when you arrive, you will be when you leave. In Hora, beers go down and clothes come off faster than you can say "Opa!" You'll see everything your mother warned you about—wine swilled from the bottle at 3pm, all-day drinking games, partiers dancing in the streets, people swimming less than 30min. after they've eaten, and so much more. Those in search of quieter pleasures stay in Gialos (the port), while the party animals crowd into Hora.

⌐ TRANSPORTATION

Ferries: To: **Anafi** (3hr., 3-4 per week, €9); **Folegandros** (1½hr., 5 per week, €6); **Naxos** (1¾hr., 3 per day, €9); **Paros** (3hr., 3 per day, €9); **Piraeus** (8hr., 3 per day, €22); **Santorini** (1½hr., 2-3 per day, €7); **Sifnos** (3hr., 2 per week, €12); **Sikinos** (30min., 3-4 per week, €4); **Syros** (4hr., 3-4 per week, €15.20).

Flying Dolphins: To: **Iraklion, Crete** (2½hr., 3 per week, €36); **Milos** (3½hr., 3-4 per week, €32); **Mykonos** (2hr., daily, €27); **Naxos** (45min., daily, €18); **Paros** (1½hr., daily, €20); **Santorini** (45min., daily, €13).

Rentals: Jacob's Moto Rent (☎22860 91 700), by the bus stop at the port. Motorbikes €15-25; cars €35-80. **Ios Rent-A-Car** (☎22860 92 300), located in Acteon Travel in the port, has cars for €25-53. MC/V.

▰ ⁊ ORIENTATION AND PRACTICAL INFORMATION

Ios Town's action is based in three locations, each 20min. apart along the island's paved road. **Gialos**, the port, is at one end; **Hora**, the village, sits above on a hill; frenzied **Mylopotas beach** is 3km farther. During the day, the winding streets behind the church are filled with shops and postcard pushers. As the sun sets, they become the hub of nighttime activity. Buses shuttle between port, village, and beach (every 10-20min. 7:20am-midnight, €1). While people generally walk between Hora and Mylopotas after midnight, you may want to get one of the three island **taxis** (☎69326 80 896) to take you to and from Gialos.

Budget Travel: Acteon Travel (☎22860 91 343; www.acteon.gr), adjacent to the bus stop in the port, has 2 branches in Hora and 1 at Mylopotas beach. Sells **ferry tickets**, offers assistance with accommodations, **exchanges currency**, has **Internet access** (€0.10 per min.), and rents vehicles. Open daily 8am-11pm.

Banks: National Bank (☎22860 91 565), by the main church in Hora, has a **24hr. ATM.** Open M-Th 8am-2:30pm, F 8am-2pm.

Laundromat: Sweet Irish Dream Laundry (☎22860 91 584), by the club with the same name, on the main road from the port. Wash and dry load €8. Open 9:30am-9pm.

Police: ☎22860 91 222. On the road to Kolitsani beach, past the OTE. Open 24hr.

Pharmacy: ☎22860 91 562. In Hora, next to Acteon Travel. Open daily 8am-midnight.

Medical Center: ☎22860 28 611. At the port, 100m from the dock. Specializes in drunken mishaps. Open M-F 8:30am-2:30pm and 6-8pm for emergencies only. In Hora, you can reach a **doctor** (Yiannis) 24hr. at ☎22860 91 137 or 69324 20 200. His office is on the main road next to Fun Pub; open for emergencies 24hr.

Internet Access: All over the port and village. At the port, **Acteon Travel** charges €0.10 per min., €5 per hr. Open daily 8am-11pm. Try **Francesco's** (€6 per hr.) in the village, and **Far Out Beach Club** (€4 per hr.) on Mylopotas beach.

Post Office: On the main road coming from the port in Hora, take your 1st right after Sweet Irish Dream. Receives **Poste Restante.** Open M-F 7:20am-2pm. **Postal Code:** 84001.

⌂ ⁊ ACCOMMODATIONS AND CAMPING

Affordable accommodations can be found in both the frenetic village or in the quiet port. Each area has its own personality, so weigh your interests before making your choice. A tent, bungalow, or room on Mylopotas beach lets you roll hazily from blanket to beach, cutting out the bus ride in between.

Francesco's (☎22860 91 223; www.francescos.net), in the village. With your back to the bank, take the steps up from the left corner of the plateia, then take the 1st left. Owned by friendly Francesco, this hostel is right out of a hip backpacker's dream, with new people to meet, chill hangout space, and cheap dorms to crash in. Reception 9am-2pm and 6-10:30pm. Check-out 11am. A/C extra in low season. Dorms €8-13; 2-4-person rooms €10-22 per person. ●

Far Out Beach Club and Camping (☎22860 92 302; www.faroutclub.com), at the end of Mylopotas beach. A friend of Francesco's runs a hopping beachside version of his pal's top-notch hostel. Far Out has rooms for every budget, from tents to hotel studios, at rock-bottom prices. Restaurant, bar, mini-mart, volleyball court, swimming pools, bungee jumping, free new movies (shown every evening), showers, laundry, Internet access, live music, and nightly happy hour (5-8pm, 2-for-1 mixed drinks €5). Check-out noon. Open Apr.-Oct. €4-9 per tent, tent rental €1; cabins €5-12; bungalows €8-18; hotel rooms €10-35 per person. ●

Markos Village (☎22860 91 059), 1 block up from the village's main road. From the bus stop coming from Gialos, go uphill and to the left. Guests are treated to a poolside bar with frozen daiquiris and a great view. Dorms €10-15; doubles €20-45. MC/V. ●

Hotel George and Irene (☎22860 91 074), 2 blocks up the hill from Markos Village, away from the noise, but still near the action. Rooms have balconies, TV, A/C, private baths, and safety boxes. Internet access €0.10 per min. Laundry €3 per kg. Free transport to and from the port. Doubles €40-75. AmEx/DC/MC/V. ❸

The Corali (☎22860 91 272), on the peaceful port beach where umbrellas and beach volleyball courts spill onto the sand. At this family-oriented hotel, you can escape the heat in the flowered garden or the A/C-equipped rooms. High-season doubles €58; triples €65; quads €80. MC/V. ❹

Camping Ios (☎22860 92 035), all the way to the right side of the harbor from the port in Gialos, has immaculate grounds and a large pool. Amenities are similar to those at Far Out Camping minus the high volume and potentially wearying excitement. Check-out noon. Open May-Sept. €7 per person, tent and sleeping bag included. ●

FOOD

Most eating on Ios coincides with heavy drinking, peaking in the middle of the night at gyro joints. There are a few better restaurants, though, among the ubiquitous bars and disco, at the port, and on the beach. **Ios Market** (☎22860 91 035) is opposite the bus stop in Hora and a **supermarket** is in the main plateia.

Ali Baba's (☎22860 91 558), by the Ios gym. Coming down from the main plateia, take a right after you reach the fast-food restaurants. Continue down to the bottom of the road and take a left. Live hip-hop groups perform in the enclosed garden, and the menu has globe-trotting options from Asian dishes to burgers. Chicken *satay* €9. BLT €5.50. Open daily 6:30pm-midnight. ❷

Waves Indian Restaurant and International Cuisine (☎22860 92 145), to the left of the waterfront road as you disembark from the ferries. Run by a Welsh windsurfer couple who serve fabulous curry and tasty Chinese stir-fry. Entrees €6-14. Take-out available. Open daily 11am-midnight. ❷

Lord Byron's (☎22860 92 125). Look for the sign by the pharmacy directing you up 3 blocks. a classy bistro that puts a creative (and perhaps Romantic) twist on Greek staples, ending up with dishes like curry chicken with bacon and *tzatziki*. Entrees €9-15. Reservations recommended. Open daily 7:30-11:30pm. MC/V. ❸

Polydoros (☎22860 91 132), on Koumbara beach. Walk (1.75km) or take the bus (5min., 1 per hr.) on the road along the harbor's beach. The beloved hangout of many of Ios's residents, who will stand for nothing less than the freshest ingredients. Shrimp *saganaki* with feta €7.50. Open 1pm-midnight. ❷

🔍🔆 SIGHTS AND BEACHES

CYCLADES

Pay a visit to the Ios **Archaeological Museum,** in the town hall across from the bus stop, to view artifacts from Ios's long and rich history of habitation. Watch for a tablet that mentions Homerium, an ancient month named in honor of the ancient poet. (Open Tu-Su 8:30am-3pm. Free.) According to legend, Homer died and was buried on Ios; the supposed site of **Homer's tomb** has been worn to rubble, but the spot in Plakatos, on the island's northern tip, still draws a few dedicated tourists. To repent for the previous night's excess, walk toward the windmills to the path at the top of the hill, which leads to the solitary **monastery.** An **Open Theater Festival Program** is held every summer above the windmills on the island—inquire at a travel agency for more info. During the day, crowds lounge on the **beaches,** making sure they will look tan in the tight t-shirts that the night will surely require. **Mylopotas,** a 20min. walk downhill from Hora, has music blasting at every turn, and all parties flock to the debaucherous Far Out Beach Club (p. 415). The long, wide stretch of sand also has beach soccer and volleyball areas. **Koumbara,** 1.75km down the road that follows Gialos beach, draws a much smaller crowd to its large cove, which is a popular place for windsurfing. For those who just want quiet and beauty (of the natural variety), buses (25min., 2 per day, €5) go to the more secluded 🏖**Manganari,** the island's nicest stretch of sand. Gialos (the port beach), Mylopotas, and Manganari all offer watersports, from tubing (€12-22) to windsurfing (€14-40). Continuing uphill from the OTE, look for the path on the left that leads to the secluded beach and crystal pool of water at the little bay of **Kolitsani** (a 15min. walk from Hora). Nude **Psathi,** on the eastern coast, is accessible by moped and bus (2 per day 11am, 4pm).

🎵 NIGHTLIFE

Most of Ios's extraordinary number of bars are packed densely into the old village, making it easy to hit all the hot spots in one night. The central focus of the party can't really be determined until the night is underway, so people tend to walk around deciding where to go. The largest and loudest discos line the main road. Many start their night at roof-top bars, like those at **Francesco's** and **Markos,** swilling liquor from the bottle in the main plateia at sunset, hitting the village before 1am, then migrating to the discos and private liaisons before sunrise.

The Slammer Bar (☎22860 91 019), in the left inland corner of the main plateia. The bartender here will gladly whack your helmeted head with a blunt object before you down a tequila slammer (tequila, Tía María, and Sprite; €3), which gets you equally hammered. Open daily 10pm-4:30am.

Sweet Irish Dream, in a large building on the main road leading from the port. Most save this nighttime reverie for their last stop, pausing to dance on the tables before nodding off in the early morning sun. Beer €3. Cover 2:30am-4:30am. Open midnight-4:30am.

Blue Note (☎22860 92 488), off the main plateia, past the fast-food joints, and around the corner to the left. If you've had enough Mediterranean hedonism to last a lifetime, cool out with some Swedish pop at this Scandinavian bar. Open 10:30pm-4:30am.

Disco 69 (☎22860 91 064; www.disco69club.com), on the main bar street on the right, blares mainstream dance music; when the dance floor gets crowded, people hop onto the bar. Free shot with all drinks. Beer €5. Cover €6 midnight-4am. Open 10pm-4am.

Red Bull (☎22860 91 019), in the main plateia in the village. If flashing lights aren't your thing, this small, wood-trimmed bar, which plays loud 90s music, will give you wings. Beer €3. Open 9pm-4:30am.

Q Club, on the right side of the road to Mylopotas. Visiting international DJs spin hip-hop and R&B. Open daily midnight-4:30am.

Scorpion Disco, on the main road in town, strategically located *en route* to the beach, after Q Club. This super-sized techno emporium has a capacity of 2000, which it manages to reach night after night. Cover 2am-4:30am. Open daily midnight-4:30am.

FOLEGANDROS Φολέγανδρος

According to legend, King Minos's son made the first footprints on this island and gave it his name. For many years, few followed in the mythic leader's footsteps; Folegandros's high, rocky cliffs and inaccessible port secluded it from the outside. Unlike Mykonos and Santorini, Folegandros still remains off the beaten island-hopping path, and those who do come to visit tend to be Greek. Its dry, steep hills are terraced with low, snaking stone walls worn by centuries of fierce wind—the only tumultuous presence on this serene island.

HORA Χώρα   ☎22860

The capital of Folegandros, cliffside Hora sparkles with white-washed churches, blue shutters, and fuchsia bougainvillea vines. Hospitable villagers and easy accessibility from the port by bus make it the ideal base on the island.

🖂🔃 TRANSPORTATION AND PRACTICAL INFORMATION. After disembarking the ferry, you can board the bus from the port, Kararostassi, to Hora. **Buses** (10min.) head to the port before each ferry and then return with new arrivals (13 per day 7:20am-11pm, €1). Irregular **ferries** run to: Ios (1½hr., €5.50); Kithnos (5hr., €14.50); Milos (2hr., €7.10); Naxos (3hr., €10); Paros (4hr., €8); Piraeus (10hr., 5 per week, €20.50) via Kimolos (1½hr.); Santorini (1½hr., 4-5 per week, €7); Serifos (4hr., €10); Sifnos (3hr., €8); Sikinos (40min., €4.20). A **taxi** is available at ☎22860 41 048. **Moped rental** is cheaper at the port than in town. Try **Jimmy's** (☎22860 41 448. €15 per day. Open daily June-Oct. 15 9am-2pm and 5-8pm).

The **tourist information office exchanges currency,** runs boat tours around the island, **stores luggage,** sells **maps** (€3), and provides info on accommodations. (☎22860 41 158. Open 9am-9pm.) If you continue straight down the main road past the post office and turn left after Pl. Pounta, **Maraki Travel,** which rents cars (€30 per day), provides **Internet access** (€6 per hr.; €1.50 min.), and sells ferry tickets, will be 50m down to your left. (☎22860 41 273. Open daily 9:30am-midnight.) The only **ATM** on the island is in Pl. Kontarini, the main square. Make a right after Folegandros Snack Bar; it's tucked into the far corner of the plateia. The town's **laundromat** is on the road past Maraki Travel; keep walking for 300m. (☎22860 41 575. Wash €5, dry €2. Open daily 9am-2:30pm and 6-8:30pm.) Past Maraki Travel, head straight past the next two tree-filled plateias, cut across to the right, then head left. A sharp right before the market leads to the **police** (☎22860 41 249). The **pharmacy** (☎22860 41 540) is on the road to the port, after the post office. The **medical center** (☎ 22860 41 222) is on Pl. Pounta as you enter town from the main road. (Open M-F 9am-2pm; 24hr. in emergencies.) The **post office** (☎ 22860 41 299) is on the left as you enter town (open M-F 7:30am-2:30pm). **Postal Code:** 84011.

⊓ ACCOMMODATIONS AND CAMPING. A recent spike in Folegandros's popularity has created a shortage of space, so reserve ahead of time in high season. Most accommodations are pricey, and camping is the only real budget option. **Rent Rooms Evyenia ❸**, by the tourist office, near the center of town, has comfortable rooms with fridges and baths. (☎ 22860 41 006. Doubles €30-60; 4- to 5-person rooms €40-65.) Its owners also run **Hotel Aegeo ❷**, on the other side of the plateia, a slightly cheaper alternative with the same amenities and free port shuttle service. Inquire about either at Rent Rooms Evyenia. (☎ 22860 41 468. Doubles €25-50.) **Rent Rooms Lambrini ❷**, across from the police station, also offers reasonably priced accommodations. The tastefully decorated apartments have private balconies, TV, fans, fridges and coffeemakers. Inquire at Asyngrito Taverna in Plateia Maraki. (☎ 22860 41 266. Doubles €25-45.) Across the street from Rent Rooms Evyenia, **Hotel Polikandia ❸** has rooms with fridges, baths, fans, phones, and breezy balconies surrounding a lovely flagstone garden. (☎ 22860 41 322. Breakfast €5. Singles €17-50; doubles €30-60; triples €35-65.) To find **Livadi Camping ❶**, set back from the beach on the road from the port to Hora, take a left at the sign or call for a port shuttle. (☎ 22860 41 204. €5 per person, €2 per tent.)

◨◪ FOOD AND NIGHTLIFE. Fresh fruit and bread **markets** line the road from Kararostassi through Hora. At **◪Folegandros Snack Bar ❶**, across from Maraki Travel, owner Michailidia makes what could be the best cappuccino outside of Italy. He provides a wide array of fresh meals and snacks, including crepes (€4.50) and fruit juices (€3-3.50), along with music, games, books, maps, and info about the island. (☎ 22860 41 226. Open daily May-Oct. 7am-2am.) **Pounta ❷**, on your left just as you enter Pl. Pounta, the first square from the port road, is in a beautiful stone garden. (☎ 22860 41 063. Crepe with tomato, cheese, and *tzatziki* €3.50. Open daily 8:30am-3pm and 6pm-midnight.) **Kritikos ❷**, to the left after Pl. Pounta then straight through two more plateias, serves the freshest meat on the island, straight from the owner's herd. (☎ 22860 41 219. Grilled lamb €6.50. Open daily noon-1am.) **Piatsa ❶**, in the center of Pl. Kontarini, makes delicious traditional Greek meals. The *matzata* (pasta with pork or chicken; €7.50) is an island speciality. (☎ 22860 41 274. Open daily 10am-midnight. MC/V.)

In the summer, when the island's permanent population of 650 triples with the influx of tourists, weddings fill the town's plateias with roasting goats and local music. **Greco**, at the bus stop for Ano Meria, is a bohemian cafe-bar adorned with artistic lighting and Botticelli-esque murals. (☎ 22860 41 456. Mixed drinks €6-8. Open daily Apr.-Oct. 11:30am-2:30pm and 7pm-late.)

◙ SIGHTS. The **Church of Panagia**, above the town on Paleokastro Hill, is an unbeatable place to watch the sunset or photograph whitewashed domes against mountains and sea. When you get to Pl. Pounta, take two sharp rights and hike up the zigzagging path past a tranquil three-level cemetery. The torso of a marble Roman statue sits in the masonry of the bell tower. (Open in summer daily 7-9pm; in winter for religious festivals only.) Walking into town from Pl. Pounta, take your first right up the stairs through the narrow archway labeled "Kastro," into the triangular fortification of houses built under Venetian rule in the years following the Fourth Crusade of 1204. On your left after the church of **Agia Anargyron**, walk through the tiny corridor that centuries of townspeople used as a hideout to evade Romans, Franks, Venetians, and Turks. When plundering conquerors and raiding pirates invaded the town, 150 to 200 large families dwelled in this small cliff-top enclosure, each in its own *monospito* (one-roomed house). Continuing straight through the rows of these houses, you will come to the church of **Our Lady Panta-**

■ **Camping Milos** (☎22870 31 410), located at Hivadolimni beach, 7km from port; buses go to and from the port after the public buses stop running. A pristine, turquoise pool and open-air cafeteria, both overlooking Hivadolimni beach from the heights of a steep cliff, lend this newly renovated campsite a rare air of elegance and luxury. At dusk, a poolside bar and dance floor opens. Communal kitchen, laundry, and mini-mart on site; tent, bike, and car rentals available. €5 per person, €4 per tent; bungalow for 2 with fridge and bath €45-69. ❶

Anezina and Iliopetra (☎22870 24 009; www.anezinahotel.com), set back from the waterfront about 50m. These sister hotels offer colorful rooms with A/C and fridges, though they also come with a hefty high-season price. Doubles €30-80; triples €35-100; studio apartments with kitchens €50-120. MC/V. ❹

Kanaris Rooms to Let (☎22870 22 184 or 69467 52 275), 200m from the town center—look for the "Anezina" minibus when you disembark the ferry. If you're walking, take the first left after the laundromat's street; it's down on your right. Private baths, fridges, A/C, balconies, and ceiling fans. Doubles €20-42. ❷

╏ FOOD

At dusk, the dozens of waterfront tavernas on Adamas's shoreline fill up with lively diners and the glow of hanging lanterns. Most offer traditional Greek menus.

Navayio (☎22870 23 392), 100m down the road from the Agricultural Bank along the sea. This outdoor taverna serves excellent swordfish fillet (€10.30). Open 1-11pm. ❸

O Kinigos (☎22870 22 349), 50m from the main dock. Clear pots with floating rose petals and teal-colored chairs distinguish this traditional eatery from its plainer neighbors. Moussaka €4.50. Open daily. ❸

Artemis Bakery, on the corner at the fork in the road across from the bus station. Artemis is ideal for picnics or breakfast, with an unusually wide selection of freshly baked goods that includes bagels, foccaccia, and brownies. ❶

Pitsounakia (☎22870 21 739), opposite the Agricultural Bank. The souvlaki (€3) here is a tasty, fast option; those who want to linger can eat in the garden seating area. ❶

◎ ╏ SIGHTS AND BEACHES

A few meters beyond Adamas's narrow strip of activity is the icon-filled **Ecclesiastical Museum** (open daily 9:15am-1:15pm and 6:15-10:15pm; free). While visitors peruse the exhibit, they can often overhear music from the adjacent **Church of the Holy Trinity.**

Years of volcanic eruptions, mineral deposits, and aquatic erosion have carved each beach on Milos into a small natural wonder. The island's unique, impressive coast is comprised of dark, multicolored sand, cavernous rock formations, and steep, jutting cliffs. Swimmers wade between the rocks at the canyon of ⊠**Papafragas,** just off the Filokipi bus station, and look at years of graffitied engravings. Beachgoers can lie near the enormous orange- and red-striped sedimentary rocks at **Provotas,** tiptoe across a smooth, glacier-like stretch at **Paleohori,** stake out a spot at crowded **Hivadolimni,** and peek around the deep, secluded cave hideouts at a local favorite, **Kleftiko,** known to locals as "pirates' hideaway." If you're having trouble choosing which beaches to visit, you can check out pictures of each on postcards that are at literally every kiosk and tourist office. Boat and kayak excursions will take you to hard-to-reach spots like **Tsigrados,** a glittering beach only accessible by private transport on tricky roads. Buses, however, travel to the major shores every one to two hours for about €1. The tourist office or any tourist agency can help arrange all-day **boat tours,** which are usually about €20 per person and include a lunch stop in Kimolos. **Sea Kayak Milos** (☎22870 21 365) plans kayak trips (€30-50) and **Milos Diving** (☎22870 41 296; www.milosdiving.gr) provides a range of diving excursions.

▨ NIGHTLIFE

Nightlife in Adamas is less than wild, but the town's few bars are chic and popular. **La Costa's** sea of white chairs and cafe tables surround an enormous blue historic ship, complete with sails and rigging. With your back to the sea, make your way left past the tourist agency and around the curve of the beach cove adjacent to Adamas. You really can't miss the giant boat. (☎22870 24 008. Open 9pm-3am.) The white chairs, white balcony, and seaside view make **Aragosta Cafe**, both above and beside Milos Travel, exude a laid-back sense of cool. Late-night dancing takes place at the upstairs cafe. (Pina colada €10. Cafe open 8am-3am; club open 8pm-3am or 4am. MC/V.) Next door, the DJs at **Vipera Lebetina**, a dance club draped with sheer, blue curtains and metal decorations, spin mainstream foreign music until they switch to Greek tracks late into the night.

▨ DAYTRIPS FROM ADAMAS

PLAKA Πλάκα AND TRYPITI Τρυπητή

Buses from Adamas run to Plaka and Trypiti (15min., every hr., €1).

The cobblestone path adjacent to the bus stop leads to the large, yellow **Archaeological Museum**, which houses artifacts unearthed at Fylakopi, including the 14th-century BC painted statuette known as the "Lady of Fylakopi." (☎22870 21 620. Open Tu-Su 8:30am-3pm. €3, seniors €2.) For a 360° view of the island, climb upward for 15min. from the bus station to the **Panagia Thalassitra Monastery** at the top of the old castle, in the town of **Plaka**, 6km from Adamas. Opposite Plaka's police station, follow the signs downhill through twisting streets to the terrace of the **Church of Panagia Korfiatissa**, which opens directly onto the lush countryside and the bordering sea. Next door is the **Folk Museum**. (☎22870 21 292. Open Tu-Sa 10am-2pm and 6-9pm, Su 10am-2pm. €2, students and children €1.)

A 3min. walk from the Archaeological Museum (follow signs that begin across the street from it to the left) leads to the tiny town of **Trypiti.** From there, a paved road winds down past several sights, including the spot where the **Venus de Milo**, since moved to the Louvre in Paris, once stood, and a well-preserved Roman **theater** with a riveting ocean view; ask at the tourist office about performances there. At the end of the road and down a set of stairs, you will see signs for the **catacombs** (☎22870 21 625), an early-Christian burial site hewn into the cliff face. Virtually no painting or artifacts remain, but the well-lit cavern is eerily fascinating. Of the five chambers, only one is open to the public. (☎22870 21 625. Open Tu-Su 8am-7pm. €2, students €1. Su free.) You can also still see part of a Dorian stone wall built between 1100 and 800 BC. At the ruins of **Fylakopi**, 3km from the fishing village of **Pollonia** toward Adamas, British excavations unearthed 3500-year-old **frescoes**, now displayed in the National Museum in Athens; other treasures from the site are exhibited in Plaka's archaeological museum (see above).

KIMOLOS Κίμωλος

Ferries go from Adamas to Kimolos 1-2 times per week; smaller boats, which also transport mopeds and cars, make the journey from Pollonia (accessible by bus) 3 times per day at 7:15, 11am, and 2:15pm, weather permitting (€2).

Kimolos, with its secluded beaches and rarely explored roads, is a lovely distraction. Boats drop visitors off in the sleepy port of **Psathi,** where a few cafes serve frappés on the beach and the family-run taverna, ▨**To Kima ❷,** makes tasty traditional dishes. (☎22870 51 001. Zucchini pie €3.50. Fava beans €2.70. Chicken souvlaki €7. Open M-Sa noon-midnight.) An uphill, paved road directly across from the dock leads to stony **Aliki beach,** where pleasant and quiet **Sardis Domatia ❸** sits, a bit set back from the water. Recently renovated rooms are fully equipped with fridges, A/C, private baths, and coffeemakers. (☎22870 51 458. Taverna attached. Doubles and quads €30-70.) Farther along is the town of **Hora**, where travelers head to the *kastro* or embark on hikes through the mountains, toward the eastern shore. If you haven't rented a moped, traveling around the island is difficult, but the island's single **taxi** (☎22870 51 552) is available to take you wherever you please. A watertaxi, like **Delphini Sea Taxi** (☎22870 51 437), is also available to take you back and forth from hard-to-reach beaches.

SIFNOS Σίφνος

Ships to Sifnos drop visitors at Kamares, a charming, tiny collection of eateries and pottery shops that overflow with celebrated Sifniot *keramiko* (ceramics). Though the port has an abundance of appealing accommodations and a pleasant strip of beach, most travelers head straight to Apollonia or to the small villages on cove-like shores. While days in Sifnos are quiet and sleepy, nights often bring lively local festivals; each of the island's 365 churches hosts an annual celebration for the entire community on its patron saint's name day.

KAMARES Καμάρες   ☎22840

Kamares is a modest, attractive port. Hovering yachts, sailboats, and ferries almost overwhelm the thin strip of beach, which teems with tavernas and information offices. Peaceful and mellow, the town is filled with vacationing families who sun themselves on the shallow shore.

☐ TRANSPORTATION. Four **buses** leave daily from the main stop in Kamares, in front of the tourist office near the ferry landing, to Apollonia (10min., about every hr. 7:30am-8:30pm, €1), where you can change buses to get to Artemonas, Faros, Herronisos, Kastro, Platis Vathy, and Yialos; consult the schedule in the tourist office for more details. Most **ferries** from Sifnos travel in short routes with multiple stops. To: Folegandros (2 per week, €8); Ios (2 per week, €11.10); Kimolos (7 per week, €6); Kithnos (6 per week, €8); Milos (7 per week, €6.30); Piraeus (7 per week, €18); Santorini (2 per week, €12.50); Serifos (7 per week, €6); Sikinos (2 per week, €9.50). High-speed **catamarans** go to: Kithnos (1 per week); Milos (2 per week); Piraeus (2 per week); Serifos (2 per week). A number of **taxis** are available 24hr. on the island. You can also call the drivers' cell phones directly (☎69446 96 409, 69446 42 680, and 69444 44 904; complete list available in the tourist office). **Niki Rent a Car,** 200m down the main road from the dock, has some of the best rates. (☎22840 33 993 or 69456 56 147. Bikes €10-20. Cars €20-60. Prices vary with season, increasing from mid-June to Aug. AmEx/MC/V.)

⚡☑ ORIENTATION AND PRACTICAL INFORMATION. Just opposite the ferry dock, the extremely helpful Anglophones in the **information office** help visitors find rooms, store luggage (€0.50 per piece), and decipher boat and bus schedules. (☎22840 31 977. Maps €1.30-3. Open in high season daily 9am-midnight; in low season before and after ferry arrivals.) Along the waterfront as you walk from the dock to town, the English-speaking staff at **Aegean Thesaurus Travel Agency** happily provides the same services as the tourist office; they also sell tickets for ferries and Flying Dolphins. (☎22840 33 151. Open in high season daily 9:30am-10pm; in low season before and after ferries arrive.) **The Bookshop,** an international press a few stores down on the main strip, sells maps with hiking trails (€1.50), international newspapers, magazines, and fiction, and also offers a used book exchange. (☎22840 33 521. Open daily 8am-1am.) In an **emergency,** call the **police** (☎22840 31 210) in Apollonia. The **pharmacy** can be reached at ☎22840 33 541, and a **doctor** is on call 24hr. at the **medical clinic.** (☎22840 31 315. Open M-F 10am-1pm, Tu, Th also 5-7pm.) **Postal Code:** 84003.

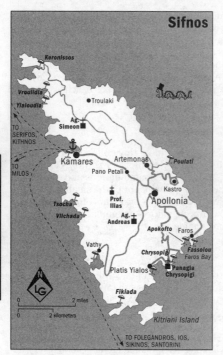

Sifnos

ACCOMMODATIONS AND CAMPING. During high season, it may be difficult to find a budget hotel room. **Domatia** are good options in terms of availability, price, and quality, and Kamares is full of them; the tourist office has an exhaustive list. To re-experience sleep-away camp, pitch a tent at ▧**Maki's Camping ❶**, where a friendly, conscientious staff creates a family atmosphere and volunteers information about the island. From the port, turn left toward Niki Rent a Car where a road descends to the left and leads to the site, 200m opposite the beach. The campgrounds include a taverna, mini-mart, laundry (€5 per load), common kitchen, and showers. Private rooms are also available. (☎22840 32 366; www.makiscamping.gr. €6 per person, €14 per tent; doubles €20-30.) A more secluded campsite, **Platis Gialos Camping ❶** is a 30min. bus ride from Kamares, then a 10min. walk down a rocky road away from the beach; follow the signs. (☎22840 71 286. €4 per person; tent rental €2.40.) If you turn right 10m uphill from Niki's Car Rental on the main road, the second building of its kind on your left is **Hotel Kiki ❹**. The spotless rooms with baths, TV, A/C, fridges, and balconies overlook Kamares and the harbor. (☎22840 32 329. Doubles €45-59; triples €49-62.) **Meltemi Rooms ❸**, behind Hotel Kiki, has clean rooms with A/C and private baths. (☎22840 31 653. Doubles €20-50; triples €30-60; quads with kitchen €50-90.)

FOOD AND NIGHTLIFE. Sifniot specialty *revithada* (chickpea soup; €2.50-5.50) can be found most everywhere that serves Greek cuisine. Most of the tavernas serve food of roughly the same quality and price, but some have the added bonus of seaside seating. **Ristorante Italiano de Claudio ❷**, up the main street toward Apollonia, serves memorable pizza (€6.50-10) and *rigatoni delicati* (€8.50), a pasta with chicken, asparagus, and cream sauce. (Open 6pm-1am. AmEx/MC/V.) Across the street, **O Kapetan Andreas ❷**, a lantern-lit terrace restaurant on the beach, specializes in seafood, with €2.50 fish soup. (☎22840 32 356. Open daily noon-midnight.)

Young locals spend late nights at trendy **Cafe Folie**, a cafe-bar about 150m along the beach, past Camping Maki. Turquoise cushions and orange lanterns decorate a wide outdoor terrace that extends out onto the ocean. (☎22840 31 183. Mixed drinks €6-7.50. Open daily 9am-3am.) The **Old Captain Bar**, midway along the waterfront strip, serves milkshakes (€4.50) and a variety of rum punches (€7) under thatched umbrellas on the sand. The unofficial pirate theme keeps the bar festive and amusing. (☎22840 31 990. Open daily 10am-3am.)

APOLLONIA Απολλώνια   ☎22840

The streets of Apollonia, the island's capital and heart, meander haphazardly about the hilltop, but each leads back to the main, paved road, from which buses carry beachgoers to nearby shore-side villages. Good restaurants and quaint houses carpet the small village, and the narrow lanes contain almost all of the island's nightlife.

⬛🚺 ORIENTATION AND PRACTICAL INFORMATION. All the essentials a traveler needs can be found in the main plateia, where the bus from Kamares makes its first stop. **Buses** to Artemonas and Kamares (10min., €1) wait in front of the post office; those to villages and beaches like Kastro (€1) and Platis Yialos (€1.50) stop around the corner on the mountain road next to the Hotel Anthousa. Buses run to these destinations at least once every hour. The schedules by the plateia stop outside the travel agency have exact times. **Aegean Thesaurus,** near the post office, offers **currency exchange,** accommodations assistance, bus and ferry schedules, a **24hr. ATM,** and useful €2 island information packs. (☎22840 33 151. Open daily 10am-10pm.) **Alpha Bank** is up the main road from the bus stop, on your left before Hotel Anthousa. It has a **24hr. ATM.** (☎22840 31 317. Open M-Th 8am-2:30pm, F 8am-2pm.) To get to the **police station,** walk up the main road from the plateia. Turn left at the fork in the road with the signposts. Walk up a ways, and it will be the building on your right with the large Greek flag in front. (☎22840 31 210. Open daily 9am-1pm.) There is a **pharmacy** next to the post office. (☎22840 33 541. Open daily 9am-2:30pm, 5pm-10pm.) The **medical center** (☎22840 31 315) is across from the police station, and an **OTE** is 50m down the road back to Kamares on the right (☎22840 31 215; open daily 7:30am-2:30pm). The **Billiard Cafe,** on the road out of Apollonia to the right, has the only **Internet access** on the island. (€6 per hr. Open daily 10:30am-midnight.) The **post office** is in the main plateia. (☎22840 31 329. Open M-F 7:30am-2pm.) **Postal Code:** 84003.

🏠 ACCOMMODATIONS. Summer vacancies are rare in Apollonia, and it's best to make reservations far in advance if you're traveling in July and August. **Hotel Anthousa ❸,** on the mountain road to Artemonas is above the pastry shop around the corner from the main plateia. From its clean rooms with A/C, TV, fridges, baths, and phones, you can see both the sea and the deep ravine over which it sits. The video arcade is an added perk for those who need their fix of push-button animation. (☎22840 31 431. Laundry €12. Singles €30-40; doubles €40-50. MC/V.) To find the **Sifnos Hotel ❸,** head up the paved road from the plateia. At the fork in the road, the hotel is on the corner on your right, above a bakery and a cafe. The hotel's spacious, inviting rooms include A/C, TV, fridges, private baths, and phones. (☎22840 31 624. Singles €25-40; doubles €30-60. MC/V.) **Hotel Sofia ❸** is just off the plateia, right by anything you could possibly want or need in town; head up the wide paved road from the plateia until you see it on your left, above the supermarket. (☎22840 31 238. TV, A/C, fridges, and private baths. Doubles €36-45.) **Nikoleta Rooms ❹,** across from the Eko gas station, rents quiet and clean doubles with TV, A/C, kitchenettes, phones, private baths, and balconies, some with a peaceful view of the sea. (☎22840 31 538. Doubles €35-53.)

📋 FOOD AND NIGHTLIFE. Along the road past Vegera, **Apostolos ❷** ladles out tasty stews and years of island wisdom. Fricassee of goat and rice in a ceramic pot (€6.50) and *arnaki mastelo* (lamb with red wine and dill; €8.50) are delicious options. (Open daily 4pm-1:30am. MC/V.) The restaurant at the **Sifnos Hotel ❷** serves *revithada* (€4.50) only on Sunday, but you can get *imam baldi* (eggplant with onions and tomato; €4.50), another favorite, any day of the week. (☎22840 31 624. Open 8am-1am. MC/V.) The strong coffee brewed at **Vegera ❶,** on your left just before the police station and clinic, makes their crepes (€3.50-5) and richly gooey caramel cake taste even sweeter by comparison. The expansive balcony which looks over Sifnos's gentle mountains provides a lovely setting in which to savor your dessert. (☎22840 33 385. Open daily 9am-3am.)

If you stroll up the hill toward Kastro on the road away from Hotel Anthousa, you will find the cafes and clubs that define Sifniot nightlife. Live Greek music plays every night until sunrise at the multi-tiered local hangout **Aloni,** on the road to the police station before Vegera, about 75m toward Artemonas on the left. The **Camel Club,** up the road toward Platis Yialos past the Eko gas station, blares international tunes and hints vaguely at a Middle Eastern theme with its arched entrance. (Open daily 9pm-4am or later.) **Veranda,** a mod-looking cafe-bar across from Anthousa, serves everything from breakfast and coffee (€2.50-4) to sweet crepes (€3) and mixed drinks (€3.50-9) on its colorful terrace. **Okiyialos,** next to Apostolos, serves over 40 kinds of ale and lager on brown furniture that implies that this is a serious beer drinker's joint which will have none of that fruity drink nonsense. (Open daily 7pm-2am.)

⚡ DAYTRIPS FROM APOLLONIA. Buses travel to enchantingly remote villages throughout the island—maps are available at bookstores and tourist agencies for €1.30-3. To see fascinating architecture and a slice of history, catch the bus to **Artemonas,** 1.5km from Apollonia (about a 10min. walk), where Greek aristocrats from Alexandria built mansions, or to **Kastro,** 2km east of Apollonia, a cluster of whitewashed houses perched dramatically on a mountain with a sweeping panorama of the steep drop to the sea below. You can also walk to Kastro along the road from Apollonia; it's mostly downhill with a stone path shortcut 300m from the bus stop. The quiet village has little activity, but the architectural remains, including remnants of homes from the Geometric period, a wall from the Classical period, and Venetian ruins give a broad overview of the island's past. The tiny **Archaeological Museum,** at the center of the town, houses a handful of clay figurines of goddesses from the Mycenaean period and the head of an archaic *kouros*. (Open Tu-Su 8am-3pm. Free.) There are no hotels in Kastro, but if you ask around, you will be able to find **domatia.** Visible from the path around the town's periphery and accessible by marked footpath, a stone cliff juts into the ocean. On it is the tiny **Epta Martires** (Seven Martyrs) church, as well as a popular spot for **cliff diving.** Another footpath leads to the sparkling cove at **Poulati,** which is a popular place for snorkeling.

Buses run hourly to **Platis Yialos,** 12km from Apollonia, a busy but still beautiful beach town. For a meal while you're there, **Kalimera ❸** serves French and Greek dishes and sugary desserts. (☎22840 71 365. Entrees €6-12. Open 9am-midnight.) **Faros,** the bus stop before Yialos, is a series of round shores connected by footpaths. Since there is plenty to do in the area and the public transportation is frustratingly infrequent, you may want to plan for this stop to be a full daytrip. Numerous little tavernas blend together at busy **Fasolou** and **Apokofto** beaches nearby. A mountainous footpath leads to the striking **Panagia Chrysopigi Monastery,** which sunbathers can see from Faros. To reach it, as well as the adjacent Chrysopigi beach, take the 20min. hike from Faros or walk 10min. from Platis Yialos. A bridge connects the 17th-century monastery's rocky islet to the mainland. Forty days after Easter, locals celebrate the island's largest name day, the two-day **Festival of Analipsos.**

SERIFOS Σέριφος

Stony Serifos's rocky terrain comes straight out of mythology. After Perseus decapitated the petrifying, snake-haired Medusa, he took her head back to King Polydectes of Serifos, who had sent him on the mission. When he found out the monarch was just trying to get him out of the way so he could put the moves on Perseus's mother, Danae, irate Perseus flashed Medusa's head at Polydectes, turning his royal court (and the island) to stone. Whether or not you believe in Gorgons, it's hard not to appreciate the rock cliffs that rise high above the water. Sitting by the chapel and crumbling *kastro* in Hora, hikers can see almost all of the small island's rugged, Alp-worthy landscape.

LIVADI Λιβάδι   ☎ 22810

Livadi is a pleasant spot to make a base. Uncrowded, traditional restaurants and busy bars keep visitors happily entertained. Hora, a small town nestled high above the port, is accessible by a steep hike or bus.

⌐ ⁊ TRANSPORTATION AND PRACTICAL INFORMATION

Almost all of the island's services are located on the waterfront. From Serifos, **ferries** travel at least once a day to: Kimolos (€8); Kithnos (€7.20); Milos (€7); Piraeus (€16); Sifnos (€6). Your ferry may stop at another island before getting to the one you want. **Catamarans** go daily to Milos, Piraeus, and Sifnos. **Buses** run from Livadi to Hora (14 per day 8am-10:30pm, €1); a return bus follows the same schedule with a 15min. delay. Another bus (Tu, Th, Sa-Su) heads to Koutalas and Megalo Livadi. Buses also go to the **monastery** daily, waiting 30min. before rumbling back to Livadi. For exact departure times, consult the schedule at the bus stop (on the left, directly across from the second newsstand on the way from the ferry landing to town; another is across from Condilis Supermarket). **Krinas Travel,** the first left as you walk from the dock, rents **cars** (€44-68 per day) and **mopeds** (€16-22) at the best prices on the island. (☎ 22810 51 500. Open M-Sa 9:30am-10pm, Su 9:30am-8pm). To contact one of the island's four **taxi** drivers, call one of their cell phones: ☎ 69738 01 051, 69444 73 044, 69449 08 637, or 69324 31 114.

    Apiliotis Travel, on the waterfront, on the left just before the butcher shop-fruit market, sells hydrofoil and ferry tickets and has English schedules. (☎ 22810 51 155. Open before and after ferry arrivals.) **Alpha Bank,** on the waterfront up the second flight of stairs on your left, has a **24hr. ATM.** (☎ 22810 51 780. Open M-F 8am-2:30pm.) For 24hr. **police,** dial ☎ 22810 51 300. To get to the **pharmacy,** take a left after the first supermarket from the dock, walk past the bakery, take a right, and go about 30m. (☎ 22810 51 205. Open daily 9am-2pm and 6-8pm.) The **medical center** can be reached at ☎ 22810 51 202. **Vitamin C** has **Internet access.** (☎ 22810 79 352. €3 per hr. Open 9am-2am.) On the way to Hora, behind Apilotis Travel, is an **OTE.** (☎ 22810 51 399.) The **post office** is across the street. (☎ 22810 51 239. Open M-F 7:30am-noon.) **Postal Code:** 84005.

⌐ ⌂ ACCOMMODATIONS AND FOOD

Though small, Livadi has a wide range of rooming options. The ▨**Coralli Campgrounds ❶,** popular with backpackers, is 20m from Livadakia beach and 700m left of the port. Call for the free minibus or continue along the beach from Alexandros-Vassilias. The stone-floored bungalows have TV, A/C, fridges, and private baths, and the grounds have a mini-mart, laundry, pool, cafeteria, common refrigerators, and kitchen sinks. (☎ 22810 51 500; www.coralli.gr. Camping €6, children under 11 €3; doubles €65; triples €72; quads €85; 6-person room €95.) **Hotel Areti ❸,** up the hill, has lovely rooms with harbor views, backyard terraces, private balconies, A/C, and fridges. Take the first left from the dock, then continue 60m to the end of a one-way road. (☎ 22810 51 479. Breakfast €5. Open Apr.-Oct. Singles €30-50; doubles €46-64; triples €48-77.) To reach **Alexandros-Vassilias ❹,** on Livadakia beach, take an immediate left when you get off the boat. Bear left and walk uphill for about 500m. When you come to a fork, take the left branch, and you will find this bustling, friendly establishment with an attached taverna. Its four-person studios (€100) with kitchens are perfect for families. (☎ 22810 91 119. Doubles €55-66; triples €84-95.) Sand and thatched beach umbrellas bump up against the charming facade of **Hotel Albatross ❸,** a few doors down from Maistrali. (☎ 22810 51 148. Singles €25-45; 4-bed suites €45-65; without A/C prices reduced.)

    Frutopoleio O Petros ❶, next to Apiliotis Travel, sells delicious fresh fruit, including apricots (€7 per kg) and oranges (€1 per kg). Restaurants and cafes spring from hotels and line the waterfront. For an inexpensive but amazingly filling meal, head to **Stamadis ❶** at the right end of the waterfront. (☎ 22810 51 729.

Stuffed zucchini €4. Fresh fish €5.10-9. Open daily noon-1am.) The restaurant at **Hotel Anna ❷**, where daily fish specials "depend on our local fisherman," serves Greek and Italian dishes. (☎22810 51 666. Traditional Greek noodles with prawns €13.50. Open daily 1pm-1am.) **Vitamin C ❷**, near the Hotel Serifos Beach, offers pizza (€8.50-10) and mixed drinks (€3.50-4.50).

🔊 🏊 NIGHTLIFE AND BEACHES

Karnayia, on the waterfront, a few doors past Hotel Anna and before Vitamin C, blasts classic tunes from the 70s and 80s. (Mixed drinks €6.50. Open daily 9am-3am.) **Hook,** a roof-top dance club next to Vitamin C, plays a mix of American Top 40 and Greek hits. (Drinks €3-7. Open daily 11pm-late.) The terrace of the **Yacht Club,** a beachside cafe-bar 50m down the waterfront, past Hotel Serifos Beach, is a popular evening destination despite its exclusive name. (☎22810 51 888; www.yachtclubserifos.gr. Drinks €3.50-7. Shots €3. Open 9am-late.)

Serifos's secluded **beaches** stretch along the island, with sand unblemished even by footprints. To reach **Psili Amos,** walk all the way along the beach to the right of Linadi, then follow the road over the headland. Stay on the road after it becomes paved. The walk is steep in places and takes at least 45min. To reach unnamed beaches, head north along Serifos's paved and dirt roads. For those without a vehicle or swift-footed mule, a bus travels once daily to **Mega Livadi** and **Koutalas.**

🔁 DAYTRIPS FROM LIVADI

HORA Χώρα
If you're feeling ambitious and energetic, you can take the steep 5km hike up to Hora. Otherwise, catch the bus (€1), which runs roughly every 45min.

Whitewashed Hora offers bits of history and culture, a likely relief for the beach-weary traveler. The bus from Livadi stops in a small square in front of a well-stocked **supermarket** and a few **tavernas.** If you climb up the first series of steps on the right, past the second plateia, to the small **chapel** that crowns the town, you will be rewarded with an absolutely amazing view. The crumbling remains of the **kastro** invite you to poke around; follow the signs painted along the numerous steps up. The **Archaeological Museum,** open only during high season, exhibits artifacts from Hora's Roman years. (Open Tu-Su 8:30am-3pm.) If you can't tear yourself away at night, **Apanemia Domatia ❷** is 200m down the stone path to the left of the green supermarket. There is no sign, but maroon shutters distinguish it from the neighboring buildings. (Doubles €24-30; 4-person apartments €50.) Look for the EOT sign next to a doorway, and ask for directions at the supermarket if you get lost. Other domatia in town go for similar prices.

NORTHERN SERIFOS

Serifos's interior is not easily accessible without a car or moped. Taxis will leave and pick up at a set destination; buses run once or twice per day to the monastery and to Galani.

Traditional villages and scattered churches, monasteries, and traces of ruins blanket the northern part of the island. The **Monastery of the Taxiarchs** (☎22810 51 027), 10km beyond Hora toward Galani, was built in 1400. Legend says a Cypriot icon mysteriously appeared in the monastery and returns whenever removed. The monastery also houses an Egyptian lantern, several Russian relics, and a 17th-century stone plate in the floor depicting the Byzantine Double Eagle, which appeared on the empire's flag. Between 1600 and the 1940s, 12 to 40 Orthodox monks lived together in this castle-like edifice. Today, if you arrive by bus, you may meet the lone monk who has lived here on his own for 30 years. Call ahead to arrange a visit. By foot, the trip takes 2hr.; the monastery and town by the port have no facilities, so bring provisions for the hike.

DODECANESE
Δωδεκάνησα

The Dodecanese are the farthest Greek islands from the mainland, closer to Asia Minor than to Athens—no small matter in Greece's centuries-long territorial battle with Turkey. Home to Hippocrates, the father of medicine, and the exile asylum of St. John, author of the *Book of Revelations*, the Dodecanese are marked by a history of persistent life in the face of seemingly constant conquests and invasions. Although the islands flourished culturally during the Hellenistic period, the Roman Empire soon took over. A favorite target of religious luminaries including St. Paul and St. John, the inhabitants of these islands were among the first to convert to Christianity. During the 14th century, Christian crusaders repaid the favor, building heavily fortified castles over many ancient temple grounds as bases for their religious wars. Ottoman rule began in 1523 and persisted largely until 1912. Due to their proximity to Turkey, the lucky Dodecanese received special concessions from the sultan and continued to prosper. Under the direction of Mussolini, Italian Fascists took over in 1912 and developed the islands primarily for use as naval bases. The Dodecanese ultimately joined the Greek nation in 1948. Eclectic architecture is the most visible legacy of all these comings and goings: Greek and Roman ruins, fortresses built by crusaders, Ottoman mosques, and stark Italian architecture coexist, mixed with locals' bright blue and white homes. The islands themselves are just as diverse in landscape and character. From Rhodes's fertile hills to Nisyros's volcanic terrain, and Kos's buzzing nightlife to Karpathos's secluded beaches, the Dodecanese will entice even the pickiest traveler.

SUGGESTED ITINERARIES: DODECANESE

FOUR DAYS On Rhodes (p. 437), bypass the main port and head for Lindos (p. 450), with its undisturbed, traditional charm. After wandering through its streets, lie before Helios on this island of the Sun. Then move on to **Kos** (p. 470) for more beaches and endless parties.

TEN DAYS After worshipping the sun on Rhodes (p. 437), spend 1 or 2 days on **Karpathos's** (p. 452) magnificent beaches, among the area's best. Stop back through Rhodes again on your way to the other islands, taking the chance to explore the winding streets of **Rhodes Town** (p. 439) or less touristed Lindos (p. 450). Peer into **Nisyros's** (p. 467) simmering volcano, then prolong the excitement at Kos's (p. 470) high-octane parties. Wrap up your trip on **Astypalea** (p. 477), whose small town friendliness and gorgeous surroundings will make you never want to leave.

RHODES Ρόδος

The ancients chalked up Rhodes's bright climate to a case of love at first sight. When the sun god Helios saw the nymph Rhodos swimming in the sea, it is said

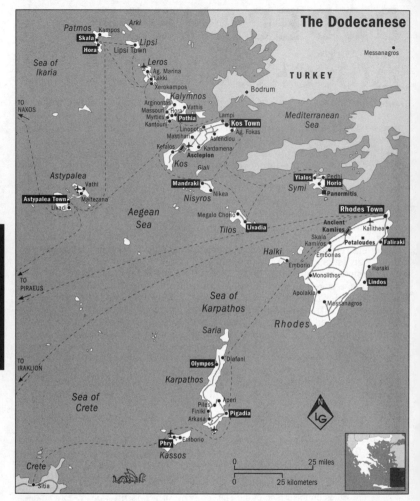

The Dodecanese

that he was instantly smitten. Her father Poseidon complied with Helios's request for marriage and called up a mountain from the sea beneath where the girl swam. As Helios descended to this island, the warmth of his affection dried its lakes and rivers, turning Rhodes into the Island of Sun. Today, sun worshippers still flock to Rhodes's welcoming shores, making the island the undisputed capital of the Dodecanese. Though touristy resort towns cluster in the north, Rhodes's natural wonders dominate other sections of the island, with sandy beaches stretching along the east coast, jagged cliffs skirting the west, and green mountains dotted with villages filling the interior. Beautiful ancient artifacts lingering from a storied past also carpet the island. Kamiros, Ialyssos, and Lindos show the clearest evidence of Rhodes's bygone days as a Hellenic power, while the slumbering medieval fortresses in Rhodes Town and Monolithos recall a history full of conquests.

RHODES TOWN   ☎ 22410

As locals like to say, Rhodes Town has always been a conquered city: first by the Turks, then by the Italians, and now by the tourists. Wandering the town is like being in a time machine. A hike to the ancient acropolis at sunset rewards trekkers with a view of a fire-streaked sky over the stadium, hinting at Rhodes Town's ancient vigor. Medieval times spring to life in the Old Town's walls and winding cobblestone paths. The New Town catapults visitors into modernity, offering raucous, tourist-packed bars and nightclubs amid seemingly ubiquitous shopping (souvenir) options. The beaches, however, are timeless; join the masses in soaking up Helios's joyous rays.

▐▀ TRANSPORTATION

Flights: Diagoras International Airport (☎ 22410 88 911), 16km out of town, near Paradisi; accessible by bus (25 per day 4:45am-11pm, €2) from the west bus station. **Olympic Airways,** Ierou Lohou 91 (☎ 22410 24 555), 2 blocks inland from the post office. Open M-F 8am-4pm. Flights to: **Athens** (5 per day 7am-10:55pm, €75); **Iraklion, Crete** (2 per day, €87); **Karpathos** (17 per week, €28); **Kassos** (9 per week, €28); **Kastellorizo** (5 per week, €25); **Thessaloniki** (3 per week, €117). **Aegean Airways** flies to **Athens** (5 per day, €67) and **Thessaloniki** (daily, €100).

Ferries: Ferries leave from the eastern docks in Commercial Harbor, across from the Milon Gate into the Old Town. Ferry schedules should be confirmed at a travel agency or the Port Authority upon arrival; try **Inspiration Travel,** Akti Sahtouri 4 (☎ 22410 24 294). Some services do not begin until late June. To: **Agios Nikolaos, Crete** (13hr., 3 per week, €25); **Halki** (2½hr., daily, €8); **Kalymnos** (1 per week, €22); **Karpathos** (5hr., 3 per week, €18); **Kassos** (7hr., 3 per week, €20); **Kos** (2½hr., 1-2 per day, €17); **Leros** (4hr., 6 per week, €23.20); **Patmos** (5½hr., 1-2 per day, €27); **Piraeus** (13hr., daily, €44.40); **Samos** (8hr., 1 per week, €27); **Sitia, Crete** (10hr., daily, €24.30); **Symi** (1½hr., 3 per week, €7); **Tilos** (1½hr., 3 per week, €18.50).

Flying Dolphins: Hydrofoils may sometimes run to Halki, Kalymnos, Kos, Leros, Marmaris, Nisyros, Symi, and Tilos; contact Inspiration Travel (p. 439) for more info. The **Dodecanisos Express** (☎ 22410 70 590), a high-speed catamaran, leaves from the western docks of Commercial Harbor. To: **Symi** (1hr., €21); **Kos** (2hr., €28); **Kalymnos** (3hr., €35); **Leros** (4½hr., €38); **Lipsi** (4½hr., €42); **Patmos** (5hr., €43.10). All trips leave Rhodes at 8:30am and return at 6:30pm. Daily catamaran excursions from Mandraki Port to **Kos** (round-trip €45), **Symi** and **Panormitis Monastery** (round-trip €22); prices may be negotiable if the boat isn't full.

Buses: Stations lie on opposite ends of Papagou at Pl. Rimini. The EOT has schedules. **East** station is served by **KTEL** (☎ 22410 27 706). Schedules listed are for M-Sa. Contact EOT or ask the station clerk for Su schedules. Service to: **Afantou** (12 per day 6:50am-7pm, €2); **Arkhangelos** (12 per day 6:50am-6pm, €2); **Faliraki** (17 per day 6:45am-9:15pm, €2); **Genadi** (8 per day 6:45am-7:30pm, €5); **Haraki** (10am, 4:30pm; €3); **Kiotari** (8 per day 6:45am-7:30pm, €5); **Kolymbia beach** (7 per day 9am-7:30pm, €3); **Laerma** (M-F 2pm, €5); **Lindos** (17 per day 6:45am-7:30pm, €4); **Malona** and **Masari** (4 per day 9am-2:30pm, €3).

West station is served by **RODA** (☎ 22410 26 300). To: **Damatria** (4 per day 6am-9:45pm, €2); **Embonas** (3 per day 4:45am-2:45pm, €4.10); **Fanes** (11 per day 4:45am-9:35pm, €2.10); **Kalavarda** (9 per day 4:45am-9:35pm, €4.10); **Kalithea, Calypso, Kastri, Faliraki** (26 per day 6:45am-11pm, €2); **Kamiros** (10:30am, 1:30pm; €4.10); **Koskinou** (8 per day 6am-9:10pm, €2); **Kritinia** (M-F, Su 1:30pm, Sa 8am, 2:05pm; €4.10); **Monolithos** (M-F 1:30pm, €6); **Paradisi Airport** (25 per day 4:45am-11pm, €2); **Pastida** and **Maritsa** (9 per day 5:40am-9:45pm, €2); **Salakos** (4 per day 4:45am-3:40pm, €3.20); **Soroni** (13 per day 4:45am-9:35pm, €2); **Theologos** (14 per day 4:45am-9:35pm, €2).

Taxis: ☎ 22410 27 666. In Pl. Rimini. Radio taxis (☎ 22410 64 712) also run 24hr.

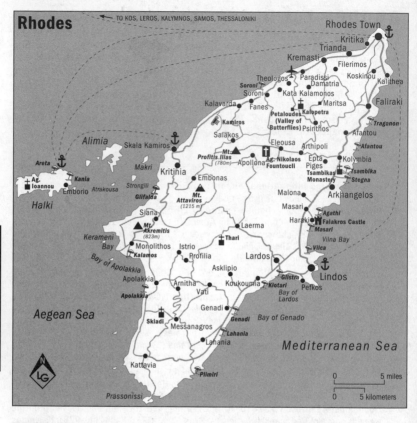

Rhodes

TO KOS, LEROS, KALYMNOS, SAMOS, THESSALONIKI

Rhodes Town
Kritika
Trianda
Kremasti
Filerimos
Theologos Paradissi Koskinou Kalithea
Soroni Damatria
Soroni Kata Kalamonos Maritsa Faliraki
Kalavarda Fanes
Petaloudes Kalopetra
(Valley of Psinthos
Butterflies) Traganon
Kamiros Afantou
Salakos Eleousa Arthipoli Afantou
Skala Kamiros Ag. Nikolaos Kolymbia
Mt. Apollona Fountoucli Epta
Profitis Ilias Piges Tsambika
Areta (780m) Tsambikas Stegna
Makri Monastery
Kritinia Malona Arkhangelos
Ag. Embonas Masari
Ioannou Kania Masari Agathi
Emborio Atrakousa Strongili Haraki Falakros Castle
Glifalda Mt. Masari
Halki Attaviros Vilna Bay
(1215 m) Laerma Vilca
Siana Thari
Kerameni Mt. Lardos
Bay Akremitis Istrio Lardos Lindos
(823m) Monolithos Profilia
Kalamos Asklipio Glistra
Bay of Apolakkia Koukoumia Kiotari Pefkos
Apolakkia Arnitha Bay of
Apolakkia Vati Genadi Lardos

Aegean Sea Skladi Genadi Bay of Genado
Messanagros Lahania
Lahania Mediterranean Sea

Kattavia
Plimiri

Prassonissi

0   5 miles
0   5 kilometers

⚡ 🛈 ORIENTATION AND PRACTICAL INFORMATION

The city is composed of two districts. The modern **New Town** spans the north and west with ritzy hotels, trendy boutiques, and a happening nightclub scene. The **Old Town** centers on touristy **Sokratous,** a bustling, cobbled street descending from the castle to the commercial harbor. The Old Town streets form a labyrinth of medieval structures still in use as houses, taverns, and souvenir shops. Keep your eyes open for Byzantine influences, and be prepared to get lost in the maze of narrow streets despite your best efforts to follow a map. Unless you're in the market for an "I love Rhodes" magnet, skip the central plazas and wander the outer streets, many of which still evoke an Old World charm.

Ferries depart from the **Commercial Harbor** outside the Old Town. **Mandraki,** the New Town's waterfront, is where private yachts, hydrofoils, and excursion boats dock. Town beaches lie to the north, beyond Mandraki, and along the city's west coast. The tourist office, both bus stations, and a taxi stand are in **Plateia Rimini,** beneath the fortress's turrets, at the junction of the Old and New Towns. From Mandraki, head a block inland with the park on the left. From the Old Town, walk out the D'Amboise Gate in front of the Palace and follow the road as it curves around the park. Or, follow Aristotelous to Ermou until it joins Mandraki. Tourist nightlife in the New Town swarms around **Orfanidou,** dubbed **"bar street,"** while the Greek scene converges mainly at **Militadou** in the Old Town.

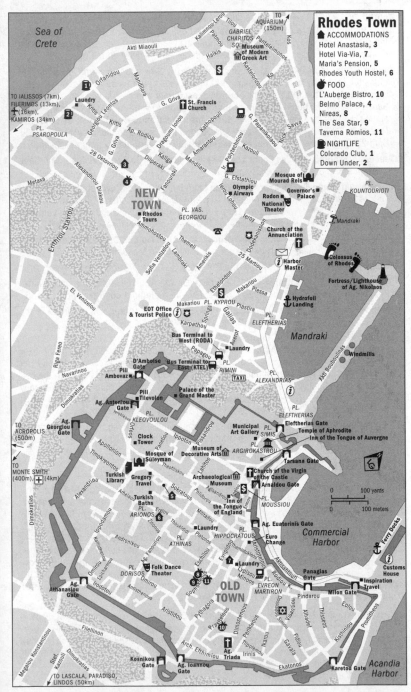

Sea of
Crete

TO IALISSOS (7km),
FILERIMOS (13km),
✝(16km),
KAMIROS (34km)

PL.
PSAROPOULA

NEW
TOWN

Metaxa

Rhodes
Tours

TO
ACROPOLIS
(500m)

TO
MONTE SMITH
(400m), ✝(4km)

OLD
TOWN

TO LASCALA, PARADISO,
LINDOS (50km)

TO
AQUARIUM
(150m)

GABRIEL
CHARITOS
SQ.
Museum of
Modern
Greek Art

St. Francis
Church

Mosque of
Mourad Reis

Governor's
Palace

Rodon
National
Theater

PL.
KOUNTOURIOTI

Mandraki

Church of the
Annunciation

Colossus
of Rhodes

Harbor
Master

Fortress/Lighthouse
of Ag. Nikolaos

Hydrofoil
Landing

Mandraki

Windmills

Olympic
Airways

PL. VAS.
GEORGIOU

EOT Office
& Tourist Police

Bus Terminal to
West (RODA)

Laundry

Bus Terminal to
East (KTEL)

D'Amboise
Gate

Pili
Ambovaz

Pili
Tilevolon

Palace of the
Grand Master

Ag. Antoniou
Gate

Ag.
Georgiou
Gate

PL.
KLEOVOULOU

Clock
Tower

Mosque of
Süleyman

Municipal
Art Gallery

PL.
SIMIS

Eleftherias Gate
Temple of Aphrodite
Inn of the Tongue of Auvergne

PL.
ELEFTHERIAS

PL.
ALEXANDRIAS

PL.
ARGIROKASTROU

Museum of
Decorative Arts

Turkish
Library

Gregory
Travel

Turkish
Baths

PL.
ARIONOS

Tarsana Gate

Archaeological
Museum

Church of the Virgin
of the Castle

Arnaldou Gate

Inn of
the Tongue
of England

PL.
MOUSSIOU

Commercial
Harbor

Euro
Change

Laundry

PL.
HIPPOCRATOUS

Ag. Euaterinis Gate

Folk Dance
Theater

PL.
DORISOS

PL.
ATHINAS

Laundry

PL.
EVREON
MARTIRON

Panagias
Gate

Inspiration
Travel

Milon Gate

Customs
House

Ag.
Athanasiou
Gate

Kosnikou
Gate

Ag. Ioannou
Gate

Ag.
Triada

Karetou Gate

Acandia
Harbor

Ferry Docks

100 yards

100 meters

Rhodes Town

ACCOMMODATIONS
Hotel Anastasia, 3
Hotel Via-Via, 7
Maria's Pension, 5
Rhodes Youth Hostel, 6

FOOD
L'Auberge Bistro, 10
Belmo Palace, 4
Nireas, 8
The Sea Star, 9
Taverna Romios, 11

NIGHTLIFE
Colorado Club, 1
Down Under, 2

DODECANESE

Tourist Office: EOT (☎22410 23 255; www.ando.gr/eot), a few blocks up Papagou from Pl. Rimini, at the corner of Makariou and Papagou. Provides helpful advice for day-trip planning, as well as free **maps**, brochures in several languages, and complete M-Sa bus schedules. English and Greek information desks. Open M-F 8am-3pm.

Banks: Banks and ATMs abound throughout both the New and Old Towns, ensuring that tourists have ready access to cash. The **Eurochange** booth (☎22410 31 847), at Pl. Hippocratous in the Old Town, has **currency exchange** and cash advances. Open daily 9am-10:30pm. **National Bank** has an office with an ATM in the Old Town at Pl. Moussiou. Open M-Th 8am-2:30pm, F 8am-2pm. The **Commercial Bank of Emboriki** (☎22410 22 123) is just across the way, on Ippoton, and also has an ATM. Open M-F 8am-2:30pm. In the New Town, **National Bank** in Pl. Kyprou has currency exchange.

American Express: Rhodos Tours Ltd., Amohostou 23, P.O. Box 252. Open M-F 9am-1:30pm and 5-8:30pm, Sa 7:30am-3pm.

Laundromat: Happy Wash Express Service Laundry, in the New Town at Alex. Diakou 38 (☎22410 35 693) and at Dilperaki 97 (☎22410 21 546), just off Orfanidou. Wash and dry €4. Open M-Sa 8:30am-11pm, Su 10:30am-11pm. In the Old Town, **Laundromat** (☎22410 76 047), 33 Platonos, by Pl. Athina, also offers wash and dry (€4.50).

Police: ☎22410 23 849. In an **emergency** dial ☎100. On Eth. Dodekanission, 1 block behind the post office. Open 24hr. **Lost and found** open M-F 9am-noon.

Tourist Police: ☎22410 27 423. In the EOT building. Open 7:30am-9pm.

Medical Services: Hospital ☎22410 80 000. On Ag. Apostoli. Open for emergencies 24hr. **Walk-in clinic** open noon-2pm and 5-7pm. In a **medical emergency** dial ☎166.

Telephones: OTE, Amerikis 91 (☎22410 24 599), at the corner of 25 Martiou in the New Town. Open M-Sa 7:30am-1:30pm.

Internet Access: Cosmonet Internet Cafe has 2 locations: in the Old Town at 45B Pl. Evreon Martiron (open daily 9am-9pm), and in a brand new 2-level cafe in the New Town, Papanikolaou 17e (☎22410 35 533; open M-Sa 3-9pm). Both locations €4 per hr. **Galileo Cafe,** Ir. Polytechniou 13 (☎22410 20 610; www.galileocafe.gr), at the corner of G. Efstathiou in the New Town. €1.20 per 30min. Mixed drinks €5. Open daily 9am-3am. In the Old Town, **Mango Bar,** Pl. Dorisos 3 (☎27210 86 565; www.karelas.gr). €4 per hr. Open M-Sa 10am-1am, Su 10am-midnight.

Post Office: Main branch (☎22410 30 290) on Mandraki, next to the Bank of Greece, has **Poste Restante.** Open M-F 7:30am-2pm. **Postal Code:** 85100.

▗ ACCOMMODATIONS

Most **pensions** in the **Old Town** are scattered about the narrow pebbled paths between Sokratous and Omirou. Bargaining with pension owners might be worth your while; just allow wild shock to register on your face upon hearing the original price and go from there. Many pensions are clean and decent, so don't settle for one that looks borderline, and always look for bedbugs (before they start looking for you). Flashing the cash will get you everywhere in the New Town, where charmless, expensive hotels seem to merge into one sprawling corporate Colossus. Some affordable and even delightful pensions, however, can be found a block or two inland from the waterfront and on the narrow streets of Rodiou, Dilperaki, Kathopouli, and Amarandou.

Hotel Anastasia, 28 Oktovriou 46 (☎22410 28 007; www.anastasia-hotel.com). Escape the hordes of rowdy tourists in the peaceful, vine-enclosed garden-bar of this family-run pension. Mihalis Aggelou, the friendly owner, readily shares the lowdown on Rhodes and her multilingual, free-to-borrow book collection. Bright, airy rooms include 2 twin beds (some with more), private baths, and large wardrobes. Be careful not to trip on the pet turtles roaming the garden. A/C €3 per day. Breakfast €3. Singles €25-28; doubles €30-37. V. ❷

Maria's Pension, Lisia 147 (☎22410 22 169), off Sokratous, right off the main touristy drag. This charming, family-run pension has freshly renovated, breezy rooms that over-look a lovely courtyard filled with colorful flowers. Doubles €25, with bath €30. ❷

Hotel Via-Via, Pythagora 45 and Lisipou 2 (☎22410 77 027; www.hotel-via-via.com). Lives up to its advertisement as a "Hotel de Charme." Owner Beatrice carefully designs each room with a subtle, artistic eye and a tendency toward the avant-garde. Rooms share bathrooms between them, and all have TV, A/C, and fridges. The nicest rooms open onto a roof-top veranda. Breakfast €5-7. Doubles €45; roof-top double €55. ❹

Mama's Pension, Menekleous 28 (☎22410 25 359), off Sokratous. Generous, gregari-ous owner Mike, an Old Town institution, says he runs his little pension on the code of music, peace, and love. Comfortable whitewashed rooms, clean shared baths, and a TV lounge foster a community feel. The view from the roof-top terrace spans both the har-bor and the Old Town. Kitchen access, book exchange, and work-for-board arrange-ments available. Laundry €5. Dorms €10, large groups €8; doubles €25. ❶

Rhodes Youth Hostel, Ergiou 12 (☎22410 36 746). Turn onto Fanouriou from Sokra-tous and follow the sign for the hostel. Lively travelers crowd into the smallish dorms with flaccid pillows and the enchanting musk of budget travel. The charge for toilet paper (€0.50), space-saving communal bathroom with shower heads in each toilet stall, and cheapest beer on the island (€1.50) make this hostel ideal if creature com-forts aren't a priority. Quiet hours after 11pm. Laundry €3. Check out 10am. Dorms €8; doubles and triples from €18. ❶

🍴 FOOD

Three types of restaurants dominate the Rhodes dining scene: overpriced, schnit-zel-touting tourist traps (mainly along Sokratous); small, classy bistros run by expat chefs; and tavernas where Rhodians might stop for lunch but stay for the afternoon. For those eating on the cheap, generic greasy fare abounds on Orfani-dou, and crepe stands (€2-5) line the streets of the Old Town. Some of the best dining options in the Old Town are clustered on Pl. Sophokleous; from Pl. Hippo-cratous, turn onto Pithagora, hang a right on Platanos, then veer left after the mosque to find this hidden street of excellent cuisine.

🏮 **Taverna Romios** Sophokleous 15, (☎22410 25 549), across from Nireas, offers a truly gourmet experience. The cushioned, canopy-covered sofa in the garden and romanti-cally lit alcove indoors are excellent places to relax and sip a glass of house wine (€6 for 0.5L). Toasted bread covered with garlic and tomato, accompanied by a flavorful tapenade, arrives in place of the generic bread basket. The rich caesura roll (cheese, pastrami, and tomato wrapped in phyllo dough and lightly fried; €4.50) is utterly divine, and the grilled octopus with orange sauce (€9) bursts with tangy-sweet flavor. Also has a large vegetarian menu (€3.50-8). Open 10am-1am. MC/V. ❷

The Sea Star (☎22410 22 117), in Pl. Sophokleous, right next to Nireas. One of the few establishments in the Old Town where the other patrons actually speak Greek. Fresh local fish (€30-40 per kg), flavored only with lemon and olive oil, arrives at your table straight off the charcoal. Indulge your sweet tooth with one of the candied fruit desserts, served with a scoop of dense homemade yogurt to soak up the sugary syrup. ❷

Belmo Palace (☎22410 25 251), 28 Oktovriou and Ionos Dragouni, has more of a neighborhood feel than some of its Old Town or harbor-side counterparts. Patrons often find themselves chatting with hospitable owner Yiannis and his son Antonio. The Greek platter (€8) comes piled with *tzatziki*, stuffed tomatoes, *dolmades*, and fava beans cov-ered with a tasty red sauce. Items such as pizza (€4) and spaghetti (€4) satisfy even the most basic craving. Open 10am-11:30pm. AmEx/MC/V. ❷

Nireas, Sophokleous 22 (☎22410 21 703). Midway on the gourmet scale between neigh-bors Sea Star and Taverna Romios, Nireas also serves high quality seafood, prepared according to local recipes. Try the *fouskes* (sea snails; €7.50), a local treat, or the lightly fried calamari (€6). Ordering a large fresh fish to share (most run €45 per kg) can be a good way to go for larger groups. MC/V. ❷

L'Auberge Bistro, Praxitelous 21 (☎22410 34 292; www.bistrotrhodes.com). From Pl. Hippocratous, turn onto Pithagora. Go left on Klevoulinis, continue until you reach Praxitelous, then turn right. Deliciously low-priced house wine (€4.50 per 0.5L) mingles with soft music in a breezy courtyard to create the mood for *l'amour.* Excellently executed French dishes (€7-11) burst with flavor. Open Tu-Su 7:30pm-midnight. MC/V. ❷

🗗 SIGHTS

Few places are known for a sight that no longer exists, but Rhodes, with its now-defunct **Colossus,** is one of them. The towering 33m bronze statue, one of the **Seven Wonders of the Ancient World,** once stood guard over Mandraki harbor. Rhodians, giddy over their defeat of Demetrius Poliorcetes, sold off the enemy's abandoned battle equipment and used the funds to build an enormous monument in the shape of Helios. Sadly, sunset came quickly for the Colossus—it only stood for about 54 years before breaking in an earthquake around 226 BC. Fearing a curse, Rhodians left the giant hunks of bronze undisturbed until AD 654, when they were carried off by Arab pirates raiding the town. Although it was once thought that the Colossus stood straddling the harbor, calculations now show this to be impossible. More likely, its "lovely light of unfettered freedom" shone in the courtyard of the temple of Helios. Today, the Colossus has left no earthly trace. Two bronze deer stand in commemoration on either side of the harbor entrance, marking the spots where the statue's gigantic feet are wistfully imagined to have been planted.

OLD TOWN

Plaques scattered throughout the medieval Old Town mark historical sites and museums constructed by the **Knights of Saint John.** At the height of their power in 1309, the Knights conquered the Dodecanese (with the exception of Astypalea, Karpathos, and Kassos), replaced their Hellenistic ruins with towering Gothic edifices, and revived trade with Europe. Strewn among the ruins of these two bygone ages, the influence of the **Ottomans,** who ousted the Knights in AD 1523, also permeates the town. Though the Turkish bazaar of old has long since transformed into Sokratous's kitschy shopping strip, a historic mosque, library, school, and even Turkish baths pay tribute to the city's Islamic ancestry.

▨ PALACE OF THE GRAND MASTER. At the top of the hill, a tall, square tower marks the entrance to the Palace of the Grand Master, erected by the Knights as a symbol of Rhodes's recovered military power. With moats, drawbridges, huge watchtowers, and enormous battlements, the 300-room palace stands in the center of the walls that enclose the Old Town; just outside of the old moat, it is bordered by a blossoming city park that stretches for blocks. The palace survived the long Ottoman siege of 1523, though it was converted into a prison by the Turks after their victory. In 1851 an earthquake damaged the building; the natural disaster was followed a short five years later by the devastating explosion of 300-year-old ammunition in a depot across the street. The citadel was restored to its former glory at the beginning of the 20th century during the Italian occupation under the watchful eye of Mussolini, who planned to use the palace as a summer home. Just after the Italians finished importing a collection of 16th- and 17th-century **mosaic floorwork** from Kos, however, WWII broke out, leaving little time for the dictator to take vacations. The mosaics, in addition to intricate wrought-iron light fixtures and exhibits on Ancient Rhodes, can be viewed Tuesday through Sunday 8:30am-7pm. (☎22410 25 500. €6, students €3, EU students free.) For an unparalleled bird's eye view of the entire fortified city, wait for a Tuesday or Saturday and take the

1.5km walk along the **city walls.** But come at 2:15pm sharp—there's only a 30min. window for admittance. *(Open Tu, Sa 2:30-3pm. €6, students €3.)*

PLATEIA ARGIOKASTROU. Dominating one side of the plateia with its halls and courtyards, the former **Hospital of the Knights** has been reborn as an **Archaeological Museum.** Its treasures include the exquisite marble statue from the late 4th century BC, *Aphrodite Bathing,* also called the "Marine Venus." After falling into the sea during an earthquake, centuries of erosion polished the statue's fluid contours. *(☎ 22410 27 657. Open Tu-Su 8:30am-2:30pm. €3, students €2.)* The cobbled **Avenue of the Knights,** or Ippoton, sloping uphill near the museum, was the city's main boulevard 500 years ago and is one of the few major streets free of souvenir shops. Perhaps because of the lack of kitsch, the street appears to the tourist-saturated eye as a bland slope of stone walls. During the Knights' reign, however, the **inns** of each of their different divisions lined the street. Each division, called a "tongue," maintained its own inn where members would gather to eat, socialize, and converse without pesky language barriers. The **Inn of the Tongue of England** is a 1919 copy of its 1483 predecessor, destroyed in one of the Knights' many defensive battles. At the foot of Ippoton, you'll find the **Church of the Virgin of the Castle,** an 11th-century Byzantine church, gradually reworked with Gothic elements up through the 14th century. *(Open Tu-Su 8:30am-2:40pm. €2, €1 student.)*

PLATEIA SIMIS. Inside Eleftherias Gate to the right, at the base of the Mandraki, the **Municipal Art Gallery** boasts 13 rooms of lithographs, sculptures, and oil paintings by contemporary local and national artists. You can gaze over the entire plateia from its cool, sunny rooms. *(Open Tu-Sa 8am-2pm and 6-9pm. €3, students €1.)* Behind the sandstone and stucco ruins of the **Temple of Aphrodite** (3rd century BC) in the middle of the plateia stands the 16th-century **Inn of the Tongue of Auvergne,** with an Aegean-style staircase and a photo-friendly fountain in the middle.

ORFEOS STREET. Evidence of the city's Ottoman past lines this street, especially toward the top of the hill. A walk down Orfeos will take you by a large **clock tower,** which was part of the Byzantine walls in the early 800s, and later marked the wall separating the Knights' quarters from the rest of the city. The highest point in the Old Town, the tower offers views of the city walls, the Old and New Towns, and the ancient stadium and acropolis just outside the city. *(€5; includes 1 drink in adjacent cafe.)* The **Mosque of Süleyman,** below the clock tower, was originally built after Sultan Süleyman the Magnificent captured Rhodes in 1522. Restored in the early 19th century, the mosque is still undergoing renovations and is closed to visitors.

TURKISH HORA. The **Hafiz Ahmed Aga Library** (Turkish Library), built in 1793 opposite the mosque, houses 830 volumes of handwritten 15th- and 16th-century Persian and Arabic manuscripts of classic literature. *(Open M-Sa 9:30am-4pm. Voluntary donation.)* Other Old Town Ottoman-era buildings and monuments are in various states of decay, though the still-operating 250-year-old **Turkish baths** in Pl. Arionos off Menikleous merit some exploration. *(Open M-F 10am-5pm, Sa 8am-5pm. €1.50.)*

JEWISH QUARTER. Plateia Evreon Martiron (Jewish Martyrs' Square) lies in the heart of the old Jewish Quarter. Sephardic Jews arrived on the island after fleeing the Spanish Inquisition in 1492 and added a distinctive flair to some of the Old Town's medieval architecture. In 1943, almost 2000 Jews were taken from this square to concentration camps. Pl. Evreon Martiron has since been overrun by tourist cafes and shops, though a small, touching memorial in the center pays tribute to the victims of the Holocaust. Although the streets in this area show some wear and tear, they provide a pleasant reprieve from the crazed main plaza. Down Dossiadou (off Pl. Evreon Martiron and Simiou) is the **Kahal Shalom Synagogue,** originally constructed in 1577 and restored by five Greek-Jewish families after WWII. Inside, intricate stone mosaics cover the floor and several "eternal lamps" hang overhead. Holocaust survivor Samuel Modiano, one of two Jews who lived through the concentration camps and returned to Rhodes, welcomes visitors to the synagogue and shares his touching personal story of survival. (☎ 22410 22 364. *Open 10am-4pm M-F; services F 5pm. Modest dress required.*)

NEW TOWN AND MANDRAKI

Stately Italian architecture permeates the modern business district. The bank, town hall, post office, and National Theater number among the weighty stone buildings inspired by the fascist aesthetic that dominates Eleftherias. Opposite them sits the majestic **Governor's Palace**, with its unique mix of Byzantine, medieval, and Spanish styles, and the **Church of the Annunciation**, built by the Italians in 1925 to replicate a much older cathedral destroyed in an 1856 explosion. Gorgeous Byzantine-style decor lines the church's interior, and chandeliers hang over the center nave. Three inoperable **windmills** stand halfway along the harbor's pier marking the path to the **Fortress of Agios Nikolaos**, which guarded the harbor from 1464 to the end of WWII. The **Mosque of Mourad Reis** is named after the Turkish admiral who died in the 1523 siege of Rhodes. His mausoleum, the domed building inside, served as the Turkish cemetery. Turbans indicate male graves; flowers, female ones. Rhodes Town's small **aquarium**, also a marine research center, exhibits its aquatic life from the Aegean. (*At the tip of Cos.* ☎ 22410 78 320. *Open daily 9am-8:30pm. €3.50, students €1.50.*) A few blocks inland in Gabriel Charitos Sq., you'll find the stately ■ **Museum of Modern Greek Art,** home to a well-rounded collection of 20th-century Greek oil paintings and sculptures; this museum is far more impressive than its counterpart in Pl. Simis. Follow signs from the EOT to reach the **Acropolis of Rhodes,** famous for its dazzling sunset vista. The ancient stadium, a popular place for locals to go running, stands below the temple.

OUTSIDE THE CITY

Excursion boats trace the coast from Rhodes Town to Lindos. Most leave the city around 9am and return at 6pm, making for a great escape to an ancient town less tinged by commercial materialism. The boats stop at the beaches at Kalithea, Faliraki, and Tsambika, among others. Schedules and prices are posted at the dock along the lower end of Mandraki (from €11). Excursion boats also go to nearby islands like Symi and Halki (round-trip €22). **Rodos Diving Center** (☎ 22410 20 207; www.rodosdiving.com) offers **scuba diving** lessons and fish-feeding dive trips to Kalithea (lessons €45; non-diving passengers €25).

♫ ♫ ENTERTAINMENT AND NIGHTLIFE

In the early evening, check out one of several cultural events before hitting the rowdy bars. **Saint Francis Church** (☎ 22410 23 605), at Dimokratias and Filellinon, echoes with sublime organ recitals. (Every W 9pm; check at the EOT to verify schedule.) In winter, the **National Theater** (☎ 22410 29 678), on Efstathiou Georgiou off Mandraki across from the Governor's Palace, stages productions. Nearby **Rodon,** behind the National Theater, shows new flicks and subtitled classics in an outdoor, vine-covered amphitheater (€4). In June, it hosts an annual Ecocinema week, showing environmentally and anthropologically themed documentaries. **Folk Dance Theater,** on Andronikou, has Greek song and dance performances during the summer. (☎ 22410 29 085. M, W, F 9:20pm; check with EOT to confirm.)

After indulging your intellect, let your animal instincts take the helm with a good old-fashioned pub crawl in either section of town. Nightlife in the Old Town focuses around **Militadou,** off Apelou. Bars line the street and music pours out of every door, creating a carnival atmosphere. By midnight, the boundaries between bars have completely disappeared, and there's not a bare spot to be found on the cushioned stone benches scattered along the street. There's almost never a cover charge, and drink prices are comparable everywhere: wine and mixed drinks €5-6, beer €4. If the bartender is in the mood, he might sit down with your table for shots of ouzo and more than a few cigarettes. Quieter bars more suitable for conversation can be found in the plateias between Ag. Fanouriou and Eschilou, where tourists and locals alike linger over mixed drinks and *mezedes*. Nightlife in the New Town has the youthful electricity of any large city. Popular bars and clubs are scattered throughout, but crowds of travelers converge on the "bar street" of **Orfanidou.** Popular places have expensive drinks; empty bars cut deals.

Colorado Club, Orfanidou 57, is the king of New Town nightlife, packing partyers into three floors of perpetually crowded rooms. One floor has a live rock band blasting 80s hits, the second plays smooth Euro techno, and the third provides a bump-and-grind venue. (☎22410 75 120; www.coloradoclub.gr. Mixed drinks €5-7. Cover €8; includes 1 drink.) **Down Under,** Orfanidou 37, features Aussie waitresses who dance on tables to loud pop and hip-hop. Two-for-one mixed drinks might just help you find a mate. (☎22410 32 982. Drinks from €4.50.)

▶ DAYTRIPS FROM RHODES TOWN

A few kilometers inland from the coast, the Rhodesian geography changes drastically. Beaches seamlessly rise into mountains, offering any wilderness aficionado opportunities for scenic hikes or quiet contemplation. These quieter spots are often left out of the party package tours, and so you are more likely to encounter families and older couples than young revelers. Sturdy shoes and bug repellent are a must for attempting these often steep and wooded trails.

VALLEY OF BUTTERFLIES. During the summer, Jersey tiger moths invade **Petaloudes,** or the Valley of Butterflies, 5km inland from Theologos, to live out their final days in the shade of the valley's fragrant Styrax trees. During this time, the moths fast, living only on water and body fat to conserve energy for rigorous mating sessions; afterward, in a sad state of post-coital affairs, they die of starvation. Although the butterflies can be elusive (particularly in early summer), the hike alongside a bubbling stream and cascading waterfalls still makes the valley a worthwhile destination. The bus drops off at the main entrance, located in the middle of the ascending path; visitors can also enter near the monastery on top of the mountain, or at the valley below. A **cafe** near the main entrance overlooks one of the larger waterfalls, and provides a break between the upper and lower parts of the steep trail. Tread softly and avoid clapping or stomping. (☎22410 81 801. Open daily 7:30am-7pm. June 15-Aug. €5; Sept.-June 14 €3. Buses run daily 9:30am and 1:30pm from Rhodes Town's west station to Petaloudes; 40min., €3.40.) If you still have energy left upon reaching the top of the 1km trail, continue 300m up to the **Monastery of Kalopetra** to see the restored mosaic and a panoramic view of the island.

EPTA PIGES. Eleven kilometers south of Faliraki, just before Kolymbia, a road to the right leads 3km down a less than scenic, unshaded highway and up a steep incline to Epta Piges. The aqueduct, built by Italians to bring water to Kolymbia, now quenches its visitors' thirst for excitement. Hurtling down the 150m pitch-black natural waterslide is the fastest way to reach the picturesque freshwater pool below. If the destination sounds nicer than the journey, take the path next to the tunnel that is used to return from the pool. Exploring the tunnel can also be fun; a flashlight is helpful to light the way. A streamside **taverna,** home to a family of peacocks, sits at the mouth of the aqueduct. Get off the Rhodes-Lindos bus at Kolymbia, and follow the sign to Epta Piges which you'll reach after a 50min. walk. Renting a car or moped is generally a much better way to get there, especially in the midday sun. Continue inland past Epta Piges to visit the 13th- and 15th-century frescoes of the Byzantine **Church of Agios Nikolaos Fountoucli,** 3km past Eleousa.

DODECANESE

TSAMBIKAS MONASTERY. From the coastal road, Tsambikas Monastery is marked by the restaurant that sits below it. A 1km road leads to the restaurant; the Byzantine cloister and its panoramic views are 1km farther up a steep, rocky trail. The monastery takes its name from the sparks (*tsambas*) that were reportedly seen atop the hill. Upon climbing up to investigate, locals discovered a Cypriot icon of the Virgin Mary that had mysteriously appeared there, miles from its home. Angry Cypriots ordered that the icon be returned and the locals obliged—but the icon kept coming back. By the third time, everyone agreed the icon belonged in Rhodes. To this day, some women ascend the mountain to pray to the Virgin Mary for fertility. If the prayer works, the baby should be named "Tsambikos" if it's a boy or "Tsambika" if it's a girl. Visitors can enter the monastery to escape the sun's beating rays and view the famed icon. (Modest dress required.) One bus runs to long, sandy **Tsambika beach,** 1km south of the turn-off for the monastery. Ask at the east bus station in Rhodes Town for times (€3). Buses to Arkhangelos, Faliraki, and other destinations that pass the turn-off will let you off for some rays.

KAMIROS. The smallest of Rhodes's three ancient cities, Kamiros surpasses Rhodes Town in intricacy and preservation. This Hellenistic city was built into a hollow and constructed in an impressive chessboard design. Three levels of settlement developed, and you can see how the lowest "public" level, slopes up like an amphitheater to the highest level which contains the acropolis. A visit to the precinct of Athena Kamiras on the acropolis gives a clear sense of the city's well-planned layout. The giant cistern on the north side of the temple (5th or 6th century BC) and the stone colonnade (2nd century BC) are other noteworthy archaeological finds. *(Buses run daily from Rhodes Town's west station to Kamiros 10:30am and 1:30pm, €4. ☎ 22410 40 037. Open Tu-Sa 8:30am-7pm. €4, students €2.)*

 ALL BEACHES ARE NOT CREATED EQUAL. Due to wind patterns in the Aegean Sea, Rhodes's beaches differ significantly depending on their location. Beaches on the western coast tend to have choppier, rougher water suitable for active swimming and water sports, while the eastern beaches, shielded from the wind by the interior mountains, are more tranquil and lagoon-like. The southern tip of the island is said to be the windiest; southernmost point Prassonissi is hailed by locals as the best windsurfing spot on the island.

FALIRAKI Φαλιράκι ☎22410

There's little to Faliraki besides bars and beach. A few years ago, the town was perennially packed with raucous European partiers, but due to recent bad press about its frat-boy image, the tour packages and party-hardy crowds have waned. Wandering down the main drag now feels like you're walking through more of a ghost town than a holiday playground. As a result, prices have nose-dived as locals hope simply to keep their establishments alive, and new, family-themed attractions like a waterpark provide safe preteen amusements.

⌐⎚ TRANSPORTATION AND PRACTICAL INFORMATION. Faliraki is 15km south of Rhodes Town. There are two main bus stops: one on the Rhodes-Lindos highway and one on the waterfront. **Buses** run to Lindos (15min., 16 per day, €3) from the former stop and to Rhodes Town (15min., 16 per day 6:15am-8:40pm, €2) from the latter. Ask the driver to stop. Faliraki is also a base for excursion boats to Lindos (round-trip €19) and Symi (round-trip €23). Grab a **taxi** (☎22410 85 444) at the stand next to the waterfront bus stop (€10 to Rhodes Town).

Hermou is the main road, connecting the beach to highway. If you get off at the Rhodes-Lindos highway stop, look for the Hawaii House BBQ on the corner and follow that road to the beach. The **Lydia Travel Agency,** at the corner of Hermou and the Rhodes-Lindos highway, next to Hotel Faliro, has **currency exchange,** an international phone, fax, excursion boat tickets, and **car rental.** (☎22410 85 483; www.falirakibay.com. Open daily 9:30am-1pm and 5-10pm.) The **Agricultural Bank** on Hermou (open M-Th 8am-2pm, F 8am-1:30pm) has a **24hr. ATM;** other ATMs sit at the intersection of Hermou and the highway. The **pharmacy** is on Hermou; look for the green cross. (☎22410 85 998. Open daily 9am-11pm.) Directly opposite the waterfront bus stop, to the right of Hermou, is the **first-aid station.** (☎22410 80 000. Open 8am-6pm.) The 24hr. **medical center** (☎22410 85 852) on the Rhodes-Lindos highway and the Faliraki 24hr. **emergency medical service** (☎22410 60 260 or 22410 43 302) are also options in a crisis. For **emergency care,** call ☎80011 60 260 to reach English-speaking doctors. Find **Internet access** at **Yasoo! Cyber Cafe** on a side street to your left as you walk up Hermou. (€1.50 per 30min. Open 10am-late.)

🛏️🍴 ACCOMMODATIONS AND FOOD. Since the European tour packages have abandoned the town, finding accommodations in Faliraki is fairly easy. Hotel owners, hoping desperately for bodies to fill their beds, will often negotiate. **Studio Zeus ❷,** across from the beach and behind the taxi stand, offers clean, spacious rooms with kitchenettes and private baths. Inquire at Jimmy's Pub; Jimmy's wife runs the hotel. (☎22410 85 643. Doubles €20.) **Hotel Faliro ❸** is inland on Hermou directly before it joins the Rhodes-Lindos highway. Rooms that open over lemon trees have private baths, balconies, safety deposit boxes (€8 per week), A/C (€5 per day), and pool access. But beware, there is a €20 charge if you vomit on the sheets. (☎22410 85 483. Doubles €28.) **Hotel Dimitra ❸** is another pleasant option on Hermou, with A/C (€4) and a fridge in every room. The lounge downstairs has a pool table, small bar, and a couple of TVs. (☎22410 85 309. Doubles €30.)

Fast-food joints that catered to the former university-age party crowd line Hermou. A number of sports bars advertise full English breakfasts. (€4.50 at most places.) The Rhodes-Lindos highway is filled with slightly pricier variations on a similar theme, plus several arch-stereotypical Chinese restaurants. An average meal runs €6-9. For a reprieve from the typical fast food, walk toward the highway on Hermou and go several blocks left on Apollonos. There you will find **Manolis ❷,** which has earned a reputation for the most authentic *mezedes* (€1.80-8) in Faliraki. (☎22410 86 561. Greek dishes €4-7.50. Open M-Sa 4pm-midnight, Su 1pm-midnight. MC/V.) Beachside **Dimitra ❷,** next to Chaplin's Bar, serves fresh local dishes (€4-15), including some vegetarian versions of traditional

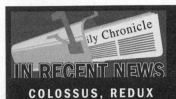

IN-RECENT NEWS

COLOSSUS, REDUX

Although no trace of the ancient Colossus, which toppled in 226 BC, remains, some creative Rhodesians plan to resurrect the former Seventh Wonder of the Ancient World in the near future. Though the 100 ft. tall statue of the sun god Helios originally towered over the entrance to Mandraki harbor in Rhodes Town, neighboring Faliraki, has agreed to provide a site for a replica of the famed statue. Attempting to shed their island's notorious reputation as a mecca of debauchery and to restore a now painfully slow tourist economy, Faliraki's local authorities hope to create a substantive site of cultural heritage.

Greek-Cypriot sculptor Nikos Kotziamanis, who has spearheaded the project in collaboration with other European artists and politicians, plans to recreate the Colossus with as much historical accuracy as possible. Falirakians working on the project have likened their vision to the Statue of Liberty in New York City, and hope that the reconstructed Colossus and a planned adjacent cultural center will generate the same kind of tourist appeal as its American counterpart. And like Lady Liberty, the new Colossus will be hollow, giving visitors dramatic views of the Aegean Sea from inside the statue's head. Although a far cry from the statue's ancient religious purpose, the reconstructed version might draw more much-needed tourists to Faliraki.

fare. (☎22410 85 756. Open 9am-midnight MC/V.) **Cookies Bakery ❶** (☎22410 86 276), on Hermou next to Breeze Bar, sells fluffy loaves of bread (€0.70) and savory pies (€1-1.60).

❻❼ ENTERTAINMENT AND NIGHTLIFE. Beach crowds need not wait for dark to pound one back—most bars are open all day. **Jimmy's Pub** (☎22410 85 643), inland on Hermou, is a British bar with Guinness on tap and soccer and car races on TV. For the steady of hand, Jimmy's hosts pool competitions every Saturday night at 9:30pm. Head up to the second floor to dance to a mix of oldies, techno, and R&B (open midnight-6am), or test your pipes, and perhaps your patience, at nightly karaoke. A number of bars on Hermou play American movies on their TVs during the afternoons. Catch up on your cinema over a burger (€4) and beer (€3) at the **Tropical Bar** (☎22410 85 143; www.tropicalbar.gr) or **Breeze Bar** (☎22410 85 145). When the music stops at midnight, crowds head toward a handful of popular dance clubs. **Chaplin's** (☎22410 60 222; www.chaplins.net), on Hermou by the beach, is one of the most popular 24hr. party spots, hosting a handful of dawn-to-dawn beach parties during the summer. Another option for Hermou indulgers is **Sinners** (☎22410 85 442; http://sinners-club.com), where transgressors try to save themselves in the Soul Room. A Funk Room and a Pop Room also exist for those less interested in salvation—or Aretha Franklin. (Cover €2.)

LINDOS Λίνδος ☎22410, 22440

To escape into the undisturbed past, pass over Rhodes's Old Town and head 50km south to Lindos. With whitewashed houses clustered at the foot of a castle-capped acropolis, Lindos is perhaps the most picturesque town on Rhodes. Vines and flowers line the narrow streets and black and white pebble mosaics tile courtyards and footpaths. Although touristy shops line the entrance to the town, most of the winding streets are still untouched by kitsch, and locals are proud of Lindos's balance between ancient ambience and modern Greek life. In July and August, room prices rise dramatically as accommodations become scarce. The natural beauty of Lindos, however, endures despite the summer's heavy traffic. From the ruins of the 4th-century BC Temple of Athena Lindia within the acropolis, Lindos's panoramic views of the aquamarine sea are hard to rival.

▐ TRANSPORTATION. Lindos is a pedestrian-only city—all traffic stops at the main road to Rhodes Town and Pefkos, where you'll find the **bus** and **taxi** stations. Buses in and out of Lindos fill quickly, so it's best to arrive early. Buses connect Lindos to: Afantou (12 per day 6:50am-7pm, €2.30); Arkhangelos (12 per day 6:50am-6pm, €1.50); Faliraki (12 per day 6:50am-6pm, €3); Kiotari-Genadi (8 per day 7:45am-8:30pm, €2); Kolymbia beach (3 per day, €3); Rhodes Town (15 per day 6:50am-7pm, €4). Check with the tourist office for recent changes to the bus schedules. **Free shuttles** run between the bus station and Kalithea (3 per day), the Lindos town plaza down the hill (every 10min. 9am-5pm), and the Lindos beach (every hr. 9am-5pm). **Excursion boats** from Rhodes depart at 9am and return at 5pm, hitting Rhodes Town (2½hr., €10) and other pit stops as they travel along the coast. Renting a **donkey** (€5), the only non-walking option in town, is a traditional way for visitors to ascend the mountain to the acropolis or head down the steep paths to the beach. Pick up a ride at the donkey stand just past the plateia.

▐▐ ORIENTATION AND PRACTICAL INFORMATION. It's best to find your way around Lindos by using landmarks; street signs are few and far between, and many simply don't have names at all. When asked, locals often won't recognize official street names, but will point you in the right direction. From the bus station, **Acropolis** leads down into town and up to the acropolis; signs point to the beach after

50m or so. **Apostolou Pavlou** crosses Acropolis just past the **Church of the Assumption of Madonna.** The **tourist information booth,** located in the plateia next to the bus stop, can equip you with a rudimentary free **map.** It also provides bus and excursion schedules, general info on Lindos and the acropolis, and help with accommodations. (☎22440 31 900. Open daily 8:30am-8:30pm.) A **24hr. ATM** is next to the tourist info booth. **Pallas Travel,** on Acropolis, **exchanges currency,** helps with accommodations, and arranges excursions. It also has free-to-borrow books and alarm clocks. (☎22440 31 494. Open 8am-10pm. Closed in winter.) Other services cluster around the intersection of Apostolou Pavlou and Acropolis. Sheila Markiou, an American expat, runs the superb ☒**Lindos Lending Library** with her daughter, offering more than 7000 English, French, German, Greek, and Italian books. You can buy a book second-hand or bring an old book to trade. When you are standing at the base of the westernmost pa.h leading up to the acropolis (by Il Forno), the library is just up the road on your right. (☎22410 31 443. Open M-Sa 9am-8pm.) Sheila also runs a **laundry** service out of the store, with the same hours. (Wash and dry €7.50.) **Public toilets** can be found in the plateia. The **police** are at Apostolou Pavlou 521. (☎22410 31 223. Open M-F 8am-2pm; 24hr. for emergencies.) The **pharmacy** is just past Yannis Bar, down the right side of Acropolis. (☎22410 31 294. Open daily 9am-9pm.) The **medical clinic** is to the left of the library before the church. (☎22410 31 840. Open M-Th 9am-1pm, F 9am-noon.) **Lindos Internet Cafe** (☎22440 32 100), up a small path off Acropolis just past the plateia, is a comfortable place to check email over a €4.50 full English breakfast. (Open daily 8am-1am.) The **post office** is uphill from the donkey stand right before the Internet cafe. (☎22440 31 314. Open M-F 8am-2pm.) **Postal Code:** 85107.

🛏 ACCOMMODATIONS. Package tours elbow into even the tiniest pensions, making Lindos a difficult place to spend the night in late July and August. If you get in a jam, try asking store owners or a local about domatia. A handful of small advertised pensions, whose prices are quite negotiable, sometimes have room for solo travelers. However, until the package tours leave the island, many tourists only stay for the day. Facing the acropolis when standing just a few paces before Il Forno, follow the signs pointing left to the beach instead of up the hill to find **Pension Katholiki ❸,** #65 on the unnamed street. The four spacious, whitewashed rooms include private baths, A/C, and kitchenettes. The decorated stone facade in the courtyard that dates from 1640 and roof-top view are added bonuses. (☎22410 31 445. Doubles €35-45.) **Pension Electra ❸,** next to Katholiki, has exceptionally clean, bright rooms, which open onto courtyards with gardens and dining areas. Each of the two floors share a full kitchen. Some rooms have A/C and private fridges, though rooms with private baths are about €5 extra. (☎22440 31 266. Singles €25; doubles €35-45. Prices are negotiable.) **Pension Lindos ❷,** #70 on the same stretch of winding road, offers clean rooms with sinks, fridges, and A/C. (☎22440 31 369. Shared baths. Singles €20; doubles €40.)

🍴 FOOD AND NIGHTLIFE. Creperies and snack bars on Acropolis near the plateia have the cheapest options; crepes start at €3, gyros at €1.80. Grocery stores can also be found along the two main streets. Many of the tavernas in town serve similar fare at reasonable prices; head up to one where you can enjoy the incredible views. Flaky croissants (€1) and truly spectacular olive loaves are lovingly handmade at **Il Forno Bakery ❶,** on Acropolis, heading up toward the top. Ingredients are imported from Italy, evident in the gigantic, distinctly Sicilian square pizza slices (€2.50). Look for the green bread basket as you head toward the ruins. (Open daily 8am-3pm and 5-8pm.) **I Love Billy's Bar ❶** because it's cheap (hamburgers €2.50; beer €2), because it's greasy (eggs with meat €2.50), and because large projectors show the latest soccer game on the first floor, and the roof-top terrace offers a great view of the town below. (☎22440 31 655. Look for the blue sign off Acropolis. Open daily 8am-1am.)

Lindos municipal law requires music to stop at midnight, but revelers carry on well past this stodgy deadline. The action begins at **Yannis Bar** (☎22440 31 245; open 8am-3am) on Acropolis (drinks €4-6), and continues across the street at **Arches** dance club, teeming with rowdy hedonists. (Open daily 11:30pm-3:30am, F-Sa 11:30pm-6am.) In the summer, catch a free late-night cab to the **amphitheater** and dance as you overlook Lindos's natural splendor. (Open June-Aug. daily midnight-4am. The opening times are fairly fluid—ask locals for details.)

◙ **SIGHTS.** Lindos's ancient **acropolis** stands on sheer cliffs 125m above town, caged by scaffolding and the walls of a crusader fortress. The site was excavated by the Danish Archaeological School between 1902 and 1912. The dig yielded everything from Neolithic tools to a plaque inscribed by a priest of Athena in 99 BC that lists the dignitaries who supposedly visited Athena's temple—Hercules, Helen of Troy, Menelaus, Alexander the Great, and the King of Persia. Just before the final incline, a carving of an ancient trireme, supposedly by Pythokreitos (famous for his Nike of Samothrace), is worth seeing. This rectangular relief of a ship remains a symbol of Lindos's ties to the sea. Lined with staircases, the daunting 13th-century **crusader castle** marks the site's entrance. The arcade, built around 200 BC at the height of Rhodes's glory, originally consisted of 42 Doric columns laid out in the shape of the Greek letter Π. The large stone blocks arranged against the back wall were bases for bronze statues that have long since been removed and melted down. The remains of the **Temple of Athena Lindia** comes into view at the top of the steps. The tomb of 6th-century BC tyrant Kleoboulos, who also built Athena's temple, is ironically inscribed with Aristotle's timeless maxim, "Nothing in excess," and sits across the way from the temple. At the foot of the acropolis lie the remains of the **ancient amphitheater.**

A cave called the **"Boukopion,"** on the north side of the rock face, may have been used for special sacrifices that could not be performed in the acropolis. Use of the cave probably dates back to the 9th century BC. The Dorians later transformed it into a sanctuary for Athena. Ask for the helpful pamphlet at the acropolis ticket window. The trek up the mountain is long, slippery, steep, and has no railings; if you're not in tip-top hiking shape, consider taking the €5 donkey express. (☎22410 31 258. Acropolis open daily 8am-6:40pm. €6, students €3.)

KARPATHOS Κάρπαθος

Ancient mythology claimed the island of Karpathos as the home of the Titans, a clan of giants who spawned the Olympian gods. Though one look at its austere mountain landscape makes the legend believable, today, the island is populated less by deities and more by portly European couples. Tourism has been a major boon to the Karpathian economy over the last 50 years, drawing travelers to its stunning pale-green coastline with the tantalizing offer of a slower pace of life. While the industry has changed the island, Karpathians' tie to their homeland remains strong. Though many fled to the United States after the Italian occupation during WWII destroyed their jobs, tons of Greek-Americans now return during July and August to run family-owned restaurants and shops. Pigadia was built exclusively to please its wealthy clientele, but the rest of Karpathos has plenty to offer the variety-seeking backpacker. The cultural traditions that have been preserved in the north and the hypnotically beautiful coves and beaches that stretch along the southeast make Karpathos an ideal stop for beach bunnies, mountain men, and anyone looking to kick back and relax with Mother Nature.

PIGADIA Πηγάδια ☎22450

This small but wealthy town has a double identity. In the winter it lies dormant, with only a few thousand residents wandering its unnamed streets. In the summer, however, the town surges with energy as thousands of Greek-Americans descend to reopen the shops, tavernas, and services, and prepare for the onslaught of mostly European tourists. Despite the large resort hotels and fast-food gyro stands, Pigadia retains a refreshing authenticity; the rampant touristy kitsch that has infected other islands is less pervasive here, perhaps due to the Greek-Americans' nostalgia for the utopian Karpathos of generations past.

⌐ TRANSPORTATION

Flights leave from **Pigadia Airport** and go to **Athens** (45min., 5 per week, €44), **Kassos** (15min., 2 per week, €33), and **Rhodes** (35min., 1-3 per day, €28).

Ferries: To **Kassos** (1½hr., 3 per week, €8), **Piraeus** (21hr., 3 per week, €32), and **Rhodes** (5hr., 3 per week, €18). You must connect through Rhodes to get to the other Dodecanese islands. **Chrisovalandou Lines** runs daily excursions to **Olympos** (leaves

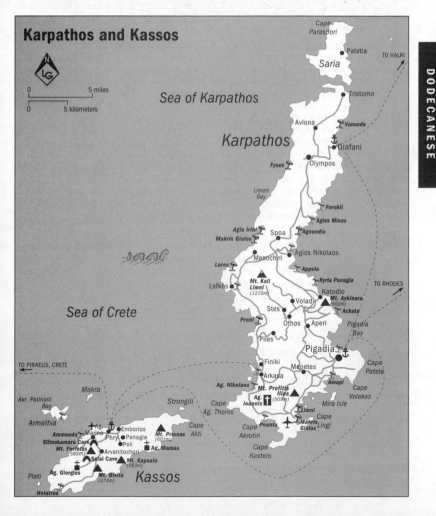

Karpathos and Kassos

8:30am, returns 6pm; €20 round-trip, €28 with guided tour). Schedules can change drastically, so check ahead and book reservations at **Possi Travel** (☎22450 22 235), or ask around near the docks.

Buses: All buses leave from the main station, on the 3rd street parallel to the water, west of the post office, next to the supermarket and the mini-golf course. Although there is another bus stop across from the taxi stand on Dimokratias, getting on at the origin is a better bet unless you are sure of the schedule. Buses don't run on a regular timetable until the end of June; check at the main station. Serves most villages on the southern part of the island (€1-3). Tickets sold onboard. No service Su or local holidays. Buses to: **airport** (15min.; 8am, 2pm); **Ammopi** (20min., 6 per day 8am-5:30pm); **Aperi** and **Apelia** (1¼hr.; M-Sa 9:30am, 3:40pm); **Kyra Panagia** (1hr.; M, W, F 9:30am, 3:40pm); **Aperi, Volada, Othos,** and **Piles** (40min., 4 per day 7am-5pm); **Arkasa, Finiki,** and **Lefkos** (1hr.; 9:30am, 6:30pm); **Mesohou, Spoa,** and **Lefkos** (3 per day 11am-6:30pm) via **Menetes, Arkasa,** and **Finiki** (45min.).

Taxis: ☎22450 22 705. Run 24hr., but are scarce 2-7am. Government-regulated taxi prices are posted at the station on Dimokratias across from the supermarket; the drivers, however, may not follow these guidelines. €5-15 to nearby villages; €12 to airport.

Rentals: Moto Carpathos (☎22450 22 382; www.motocarpathos.com). Facing inland from the taxi stand, walk right for 2 blocks. Motorbikes average €20 per day, including insurance. Min. age 21. Open 8am-1pm and 5-9pm. Continue walking to the right down the same street to find **Circle Rent A Car** (☎22450 22 690). Cars €35-45 per day. 10% discount for a 3-day rental. Open 8am-noon and 5-8:30pm.

➡ ⁊ ORIENTATION AND PRACTICAL INFORMATION

In Pigadia many of the streets are unnamed. Locals give precise directions, but pay no attention to the names of streets and restaurants. Three main roads run parallel to one another and to the waterfront. The first runs along the water and is lined with tavernas. The second extends one block up and inland from the dock, and has many shops, cafes, and rental locations. The police, post office, main bus station, and some domatia lie along the third. The taxi stand and a bus stop are on **Dimokratias,** one of the main streets perpendicular to the others.

Budget Travel: ◪**Possi Travel and Holidays** (☎22450 22 235; fax 22450 22 252), on the waterfront, sells ferry and plane tickets, books excursions, **exchanges currency,** and has bus and ferry schedules. **Western Union** available. Friendly, English-speaking staff is ready and willing to help with any logistical problem. Open M-Sa 8am-1pm and 5:30-8:30pm, Su 8-10am, and occasionally when late-night ferries arrive.

Banks: National Bank (☎22450 22 409), opposite Possi Travel, has **currency exchange** and an **ATM.** Open M-Th 8am-2:30pm, F 8am-2pm. **Agrodiki Bank,** by the police station, also has an ATM. Open M-Th 8am-2pm, F 8am-1:30pm.

Police: ☎22450 22 222. Just past Internet Cafe Potpourri. Open 24hr.

Hospital: ☎22450 22 228. Take the 2nd road parallel to the waterfront for 500m. The hospital will be on your left. English spoken. Open 24hr.

Telephones: OTE, ☎22450 22 609. Past the post office. Open M-F 7:30am-2:30pm.

Internet Access: Internet Cafe Potpourri (☎22450 29 073) is a short walk up the 2nd road from the seafront, at a 3-way intersection opposite Olympic Airways. Connect on newly-installed DSL lines over some crepes (€3.50) and Greek coffee (€1.50). €3 per hr. Open daily 7am-1am. **Caffe Galileo** (☎22450 23 606), a block east of Potpourri on the same street, has DSL connections, camera card readers, a full bar (drinks €2-6), and sandwiches (€3-4). €1 per 20min. Open 9am-2pm and 6pm-late.

Post Office: ☎22450 22 219. Take the 3rd street from the coast uphill, away from the docks; it's on your left. Open M-F 7:30am-2pm. **Postal Code:** 85700.

PIGADIA ■ 455

ACCOMMODATIONS AND FOOD

Christina's Rooms ❹ are palatial, with amenities fit for a king. From the water, walk up Dimokratias, take a left on the next major street, and look for the sign on a pink house. Rooms include private baths, balconies, TV, fridges, and an almost obscene amount of closet space; several rooms have kitchens. (☎22450 22 045. Singles €15; doubles €30; triples €40.) To find **Hotel Blue Sky ❷,** head right from Dimokratias on the second major street; it's on the first corner. Gigantic suites with sitting rooms, full kitchens, baths, TV, fridges, coffee-makers, large closets, and wrap-around balconies make this spot an excellent bang for your buck. The 1970s furniture and the silk flowers in the room give off a grandmotherly vibe, and Maria, the owner, may not let you leave the building without a juicebox and a pastry. Larger multi-room apartments could easily fit a family or group. (☎22450 22 356. Singles €15-20; doubles €30-40.) Facing inland on Dimokratias, you will see the sign for **Elias Rooms for Rent ❸** up the hill ahead; turn right at the taxi stand and take the first left. English-speaking Elias is friendly and can provide plenty of helpful information about the island. Ask about the traditional rooms with lofted beds. (☎22450 22 446. Singles €20-25; doubles €25-30.) **Harry's Rooms to Rent ❷,** right behind Blue Sky, have balconies, fridges, and shared baths with psychedelic flower tiling. (☎22450 22 188. Singles €12-16; doubles €15-20.) The rooms at **Chrissa Studios ❸,** arranged in three-room private suites, are equipped with baths, fridges, TV, and full kitchens. From the main bus station, walk up the hill and take the first right; the building is about 250m ahead. Balconies with ocean vistas and A/C in the bedrooms bring relief from the summer heat. (☎22450 22 548, ask for Chrissa; www.greek-tourism.gr/karpathos/chrissastudios. Doubles €30.)

A number of dinner options lie along the waterfront, and though some are tourist traps, the majority serves authentic, quality local fare. Sample an unending selection of traditional Karpathian and Greek *mezedes* at **Taverna Orea Karpathos ❷,** located right across from the ferry docks. Small plates designed for sharing range €3-7 and feature everything from local cheese-sprinkled *makarounes* to flavorful grilled squid. (☎22450 23 681. Open daily noon-late.) Seated under the stars at **Anemoussa ❸,** way up the staircase next to Liquid, you can satisfy your craving for Italian food while still sampling the local fruits of the sea. Sauces are as delicate as the classical music that floats in the air. (☎22450 22 164. Open daily 6pm-midnight. Entrees €5-10.) **The Life of Angels ❷** is a couple blocks past the National Bank and next to the church, on the second road from the water. Owner Zoe (Greek for "life") and her daughter, Angel, serve a mean Karpathian goat in wine sauce (€10), plus traditional foods like *spanakopita* (€3). Stop by after 8:30pm on Wednesday or Saturday to enjoy live Karpathian music over a glass of house wine. (☎22450 22 984. Open daily 10am-2pm and 5pm-midnight.)

NIGHTLIFE

Karpathians take their nightlife seriously. Lounges and bars fill up around 11pm as friends gather for drinks, and by 1:30am the tipsy crowds, complete with waiters from the tavernas, head out to the clubs. **Liquid,** a mod lounge past Possi Travel on the waterfront road, gets going around 10pm, and is a usual first stop in the summer barcrawl for both locals and tourists. Bounce your head to house and international music while sipping drinks (€4-6) with the tight-t-shirt crowd on the upstairs terrace. (☎69721 92 339. Open 7:30pm-late). Chill lounge **Anoi,** a few doors down from Liquid, provides a quieter, more relaxed atmosphere for the conversation-minded reveler. People lounge on the cushions on each step of the wide ascending staircase wrapping around the front of the bar. (Drinks €4-6. Open 10am-2:30pm and 6pm-1am.) Tropical-themed **Edem Music Cafe-Bar,** on the third parallel street, two blocks past Eth. Antistasis, starts drawing crowds around 11:30pm. Spinning rock, reggae, and the latest Greek hits, the tiki huts are packed with European tour groups, locals, and summer folk of all ages.

 TAKE A NICE, LONG DRINK. The "long drinks" ever-present on English-language bar menus in Greece are in no way related to the Long Island iced teas served in American bars. A long drink, which actually refers to the composition of a given beverage rather than to a specific drink, is made of a single alcohol mixed with juice or soda. This is not to be confused with a cocktail, which (in the Greek drinking world) includes two or more varieties of the nectar of the gods, and comes with a notched-up price tag to boot.

Uncommonly healthful bar food—cauliflower and marinated cucumbers—is tasty and goes strangely well with beer. (☎22450 23 681. Open nightly 8pm-1am.) By 1am, **Oxygen Club**, on the waterfront road, has attracted throngs of younger locals and tourists dancing to house and hip-hop. (Mixed drinks €2.50-6. Cover €6; includes 1 drink. Open M-Th, Su until 3:30am, F-Sa until 6am or later.) Next door, **Amnesia** packs them in so tight it's hard to move, which suits the crowd just fine—they're too busy drinking and flirting to actually dance to the R&B and house that echoes through the single room. (☎6930 34 403 to reach the owner, Yannie. Drinks €2-6. Cover €6; includes 1 drink. Open 1am-6am or later.)

OLYMPOS Όλυμπος ☎22450

Isolation defines Olympos's legacy. The inhabitants of two nearby villages founded the city after an earthquake destroyed their homes; they intentionally chose an inaccessible location, high in the mountains, to avoid pirate raids. Today, Olympos is a city of centuries-old customs that continue to fascinate ethnographers and linguists. Visitors weave their way through tightly packed white and blue houses and sit in tavernas between women in traditional garments and men speaking the archaic Dorian dialect. Yet Olympos is not a city entirely apart from time; though outside interest has led Olympians to preserve and, in some cases, rekindle craft traditions, the younger generation is growing further from its roots. Like their fellow Karpathians, many Olympians move to America during the winter, living most of the year as modern citizens and returning every summer to don traditional gear for busloads of history-minded tourists. The village, once famed for its insularity, now hangs in a precarious balance between past, present, and future, still unclear if it is a true relic of history or simply a reconstruction.

TRANSPORTATION AND PRACTICAL INFORMATION. From **Diafani**, take a **taxi** or the small **bus** that leaves shortly after the boat from Pigadia arrives (bus fare is included in the €20 excursion ticket). A dusty **hike** along the valley floor is another alternative if you have the time, energy, and drinking water—it's a long, hot, uphill trip. Chatting with Ana Protopapa, the English-speaking daughter of the family who runs the excursion boat, during the ride to Diafani will fill travelers in on what the village has to offer and how it has changed with time. From where the bus drops you off, navigation is fairly simple; one main road snakes uphill and connects to small side streets filled with tiny houses. The town's major attractions, tavernas, and markets are all primarily on the main road.

ACCOMMODATIONS AND FOOD. Most of the hotels and pensions in Olympos feature traditional *soufas* (lofted beds) in rooms which dazzle the senses. Luminous, colorful embroidery lines the windows, tables, and intricately carved, split-level beds; it is customary for children to sleep in the play-pen-like area on the top, and for parents to get the lower level. Some of the best accommodations in Olympos are at **Hotel Aphrodite ❸,** located just below the church and to the right, where big rooms, outfitted with their own baths and balconies, offer breathtaking views of the ocean below. Find the Baltimore-based proprietor Nikos Filipades at his nearby restaurant, the **Parthenon Cafe ❶,** where the homemade lentil soup (€3.50) and the Olympian version of *makarounes* (€3) are definite winners. (☎22450 51 307; hotel 22450 51 454. Call ahead for reservations. Doubles €35; triples €40.) **Pension Olympos ❷,** to the left of the bus stop near the start of the village, rents rooms with beautiful hand-carved *soufas*, private baths, and peaceful balconies with mountain views. (☎22450 51 252. Doubles €25.) The attached family-run **restaurant ❶** of the same name serves *makarounes* (€3.50) and *papoutsaki* (stuffed eggplant dish; €4), all handmade before your very eyes. To find **Milos Tavern ❶** (☎22450 51 333), follow the signs past Hotel Aphrodite; it's right next to the windmills. This scenic eatery dishes out *makarounes, tiropita,* and goat dishes. (Open daily 7am-10pm.) **Sinandes ❶,** across from Parthenos Taverna, offers honey-drenched, fried *loukoumades* (€3.50), a deliciously sticky dessert. If you're lucky, the local regulars will take a break from arguing Olympian politics to pull out their *zambuna* (bagpipe-like traditional instruments) and serenade you.

◪ **SIGHTS.** Olympos's traditional culture and crafts are the region's main draw; tourists marvel at the local women's black and white embroidered garb, and shops selling handmade scarves line the street. Also noteworthy are the locally grown spices, honey, and olive oil. At the two working **windmills** overlooking the western cliffs, Olympian women grind the flour that they later bake in huge, stone ovens. If you brave the tiny ladder inside one of the windmills, you can watch it whirl from behind the scenes. Just past Parthenos Taverna, near the windmills, is the lavishly decorated chapel **Kimisi tis Theotokou.** Gold foil blankets its wooden altar and centuries-old frescoes of biblical scenes adorn the walls. If the priest isn't around, you can ask at the restaurant for a key. (Modest dress required.) From the church, follow the road to the right and ask a local (or tour group leader) to point you in the direction of **Papa Yannis's house.** Inside, visitors can see an authentic Olympian *soufa* at its finest, with an overwhelming display of colorful embroidery and ceramic plates covering every inch of wall. (Free, though chatting with Yannis is appreciated.)

SOUTHERN KARPATHOS

West of Pigadia, winding roads climb toward enchanting villages and cloud-covered mountains before snaking down to the beach-laden west coast. A number of the island's mountain villages and coastal towns are accessible by bus from Pigadia. Check return trip times with your driver, but if you find yourself stranded, call a cab (☎22450 22 705) to pick you up; rides will run anywhere from €15 to 35, depending on the distance and the driver's mood. Hairpin turns in the road create a number of stupefyingly beautiful, postcard-worthy photo ops that can't be captured from a bus window. Renting a car or motorbike in Pigadia (p. 452) will give you maximum beach-going, photo-snapping, engine-revving freedom, but keep in mind that the steep, winding roads lack guardrails.

The southern city of **Aperi** was the island's capital in medieval times, when Arab raids and menacing pirates forced Karpathians to abandon their coastal homes and retreat inland. It is home to a *Panagia* (Virgin Mary) icon revered throughout Karpathos. According to local legend, a monk discovered the icon while chopping wood and blood began spurting from one of the logs. Each time the icon was moved, it would disappear—only to reappear in an old church in Aperi. A bishop's church, **Koimisis Theotokou,** was built on the spot in 1886. (Open daily 8-11am.)

West of Aperi lies **Piles,** where the winding skinny paths retain an old-world charm and quixotic appeal. A walk through the rows of traditional Karpathian houses (picturesque white boxes with decorative railings on the balconies) leads to olive groves and charming tavernas that serve the town's famous honey. Two kilometers west of Piles, the road hits Karpathos's stunning west coast.

The wind-swept remains of five parallel Cyclopean walls mark the town of **Arkasa,** home also to the ruins of an ancient acropolis that stands stoically atop the nearby cape of Paleokastro. Rounding out the town's archaeological riches are the mosaic floors of a 5th-century Christian basilica, preserved at the church of **Agia Sophia** on the shore. Although few hotels in Arkasa have single rooms, and high prices are the norm, some pensions do exist, and most places will discount for longer stays and multiple guests. ⊠**Pension Philoxenia ❷,** on the northern end of the main road, rents sparkling rooms with artful wooden decor, private baths, fridges, and in-room safes, all supplemented by the spectacular views of the water from the large balcony out back. (☎22410 61 341. Doubles €15-20.) South of Arkasa, campers can crash in a beach cove near sandy **Agios Nikolaos.**

North of Arkasa, the tiny fishing port of **Finiki** now consists mostly of tourist establishments. If you decide to stay, though, **Hotel Finiki View ❸,** on the cliffs overlooking the port, is an excellent option, with large, luxurious rooms that have island-wide views, private baths, kitchenettes, pool access, and terraces. (☎22450 61 400; www.finikiview.gr. Singles €20; doubles from €40.) ⊠**Taverna Under the Trees ❸,** 1km up the road from Finiki, serves Greek salads made from fresh veggies grown in its own garden (€3) under a canopy of lanterns. This romantic spot overlooking the beach also has charcoal-grilled fish (€7-10) and lounge chairs in the sun. (Open daily.) Farther north, the small beach town of **Lefkos** offers a gorgeous stretch of coast to naturalists who shy away from crowded beaches in favor of a quiet, rocky cove. Inland there is forested hiking terrain.

Karpathos is home to a number of blissful **beaches,** many of which can be found off the Pigadia Airport road. ⊠**Amopi,** voted one of the best in the Mediterranean, lives up to its record with golden sands that slide into stone-covered inlets and crystal-green waves. For the brave and beautiful, several of the pebbly coves are officially nude beaches. In a winning combination, beachside **Taverna Avra ❷** (☎22450 81 172) provides respite from the beating sun, but still has a breathtaking view of the water. The shrimp *saganaki* (Symi shrimp, feta, and tomatoes; €4.80) is heavenly. At least three walking routes run from Pigadia to Amopi; each takes about 1½hr. Head away from the ferry docks to the outskirts of Pigadia and take a left at the **7-11 Snack Bar ❶** (☎22450 22 885). A hike along the dusty but beautiful riverbed takes you to the main road. Take a right and walk on the paved road the rest of the way to Amopi or stick to the dirt road to find one of the less crowded but equally beautiful beaches. If you have transportation, the deep green-blue waves across from Mira Isle and the long coves between Cape Kastelo and Cape Akrotiri are also well worth a visit.

KASSOS Κάσος

Few landscapes evoke Homeric times better than the bare, rocky sprawl of Kassos. To short-term travelers, the island has little in the way of entertainment. For those willing to spend several days investigating, however, Kassos offers the vibrant and welcoming bustle of small-town life. The island's five small villages retain distinctive personalities, each with a monastery maintained by local volunteers and unique festival feast days for each village's patron saint. Spectacular beaches and a couple of intriguing caves give visitors to this sleepy, welcoming island even more options.

PHRY Φρύ ☎22450

The small port town of Phry may seem generic to passersby, but engaging with the locals reveals a unique, inclusive community that is an experience all its own. Phry's main attractions are the open arms, big hearts, and running mouths of its lifelong residents, who warm up quickly to those travelers who make the effort. Proud of their tiny island, locals will readily volunteer to serve as tour guides around the rocky, church-filled mountains, or take you down to the best beaches. Stay a week, and you'll experience tourism like it was 30 years ago—focused on personal touches and local color, rather than generic revelry.

E TRANSPORTATION. The **Olympic Airways** office is next door to the tourist agency. (☎22450 41 555. Open M-F 8am-3pm.) **Flights** go to Karpathos (7 per week, €22) and Rhodes (9 per week, €34). **Ferries** run to: Agios Nikolaos, Crete (4½hr., 3 per week, €17); Karpathos (1½hr., 3 per week, €7.50); Piraeus (17hr., 3 per week, €32); Rhodes (7hr., 3 per week, €22); Sitia, Crete (2½hr., 3 per week, €10). **Buses** make a loop from Phry through the surrounding villages (most locations less than €1). Check schedules at the tourist agency. **Taxis** are the most common way to get around. (☎69779 04 632. €3-5 between villages.) **Rent A Moto** rents mopeds (€15) and all-terrain vehicles (€20), and is located on the main street behind the tourist agency. (☎22450 41 746. Open daily 9am-1pm and 3-8pm.) Cars can be rented by request; inquire at the tourist agency.

■🛈 ORIENTATION AND PRACTICAL INFORMATION. Kassos's tourist services are in Phry. Emmanuel Manousos at **Kassos Maritime and Tourist Agency** (☎22450 41 323; www.kassos-island.gr), to the right of the port, by O Milos, provides maps, friendly advice, and timetables. Ask around to find **Elias Galanakis,** an expat from Zimbabwe who writes the local newspaper. A valuable source of information about accommodations, restaurants, and beaches, Elias is a good ally. (☎22450 41 145.) The **Cooperative Bank of Dodecanese,** just behind O Milos taverna, offers **currency exchange** and cash withdrawal. (☎22450 42 730. Open M-F 8:30am-1:45pm.) A conspicuous blue **24hr. ATM** sits in Pl. Iroön Kasou, by the ferry docks. The **police station** is just a block inland, on a narrow street to the left of Olympic Airways. (☎22450 41 222. Open 24hr.) The small **hospital** on Kriti, past the bus stop, provides emergency first aid only; serious cases are flown to adjacent islands. (☎22450 41 333. Open M-F 8am-3pm.) The **OTE** is a few blocks inland. (☎22450 41 300. Open M-F 7:30am-2:30pm.) A brand-new Internet cafe, **ACS,** is located just past the post office. (☎22450 43 751. €4 per hr. Open 10am-3pm and 6pm-midnight.) The **post office** is off Pl. Iroön Kasou. (☎22450 41 255. Open M-F 7:30am-2:30pm.) **Postal Code:** 85800.

🛏🍴 ACCOMMODATIONS AND FOOD. Except for the month of August and festival days, Kassos's hotels usually have plenty of vacancies. ❚**Elias Mariakis ❸** runs a new hotel just past the port on the left, above the taverna. Palatial rooms have private baths, fridges, TV, A/C, and balconies overlooking the sea. (☎22450 41 661. Doubles €30.) The English-speaking management at **Anagenesis ❸,** in Pl. Iroön Kasou next to the tourist agency, just to the left of the port, offers recently renovated rooms, most with TV, private baths, and balconies. Inquire at the travel agency. (☎22450 41 323; www.kassos-island.gr. A/C €7. Singles €25-32; doubles €32-42.) **Anesis ❸,** one street behind the tourist agency, has seven simple rooms with balconies and private baths; check in at the supermarket below. (☎22450 41 234. Singles €25; doubles €30.) Rooms to let, advertised by signs along the main road toward Emborio and the villages, charge €10-20 for basic singles or doubles. **Dimitrios Staurianos ❷** runs a small, unpretentious domatia near the port with clean rooms and private baths. (☎22450 41 393. Singles €20, for longer stays €15.)

Kassian cuisine has received some attention for its traditional macaroni dishes, locally churned butter, and flavorful dandelion leaves (*roikio*). Several restaurants are clustered near the church; if the owner of one is tired of cooking for the moment, he may just send you to his buddy next door. **Kafe Matheos ❷**, nicknamed "the Plateia," is the undisputed gossip hub and social center of Phry, and Matheos counts the mayor and visiting members of Parliament as patrons. (☎22450 041 320. Full meal €7-10. Fresh fish market 8-10am daily. Open daily 4:30am-2am.) Fishermen, large Kassian families, and the occasional daytripping tourist gather at **O Milos ❷** (☎22450 41 825), an open-air spot overlooking the sea next to the port, to smoke, argue Kassian politics, and chomp down tasty moussaka (€4.80) or rich macaroni with sitaka cheese (€5). Don't ask for the menu at beachside **Taverna Emborios ❷**, a 5-10min. walk on the road leading left from the port—the food changes daily depending on the fresh local catch and the chef's mood. (☎22450 41 310. Entrees €7-10. Open 6am-about 1am.) Classier **Apaggio ❷**, across from Matheos, provides a bit more privacy than you'll find at neighboring cafes. The food, like the mixed seafood grill (€10-15) is less traditional Kassiot and more gourmet. (☎22450 41 908. Open 8am-2pm and 6pm-2am.) Although the nightlife on Kassos isn't a bump-and-grind affair, Kassians do stay out late, often parking themselves in the tavernas and continuing their dinnertime discussions until the wee hours of the morning.

◪ ⚑ SIGHTS AND THE OUTDOORS. Though many of these daytrips are walkable from Phry, seeking an alternate form of transportation may be wise if you decide to go during the unforgiving heat of the afternoon sun. Most of the paths have no trees to provide shady spots of relief on the way, and routes are often uphill. Just a 10min. boat trip away, on a neighboring island, waits glistening ▨Armathia beach. This calm, well-sheltered stretch of soft sand remains untarnished by tourism and pollution. Locals hail Armathia as the finest beach in Greece—a true oasis, with turquoise waters as clear as the Caribbean and as warm as the south of Crete. George Manousos begins running the small boat in mid-July. (☎22450 41 047. €15-20 round-trip; set your own departure and pickup times.) Leisurely excursions by foot or private transportation to the residential villages above Phry give insight into the island's agriculturally centered life. For an interesting outing, try searching for the elusive cave of **Selai**, about 1.5km west, down the footpath beyond the cave **Ellinokamara**. Once there, wriggle on your belly to get inside and marvel at the stalactites and stalagmites of the cave's interior. To get to Ellinokamara, start by following the road past the airport through the village of Agia Marina. Stay to your right whenever the road forks, until you eventually reach a small dirt road (stop and ask for directions along the way). After a 15min. walk you should see a small wooden gate on your left leading up the mountain; hike up between the double stone walls until you see the entrance to the cave appear over the wall on your right. Foregoing the walk and taking a taxi will run €25-30.

The interior of the unpeopled monastery of **Agios Giorgios** at Hadies is filled with impressive, gold-painted icons and commands magnificent views of the gorgeous **Helatros beach** below. The older families of Phry still have cells at the monastery which they inhabit for the festival of St. George.

From **Poli**, a 40min. hike along an uphill asphalt road to **Agios Mamas Monastery** (4km from Phry) brings you to scenic views of the southeastern coast from atop a dangerously sharp cliff face. The boulders visible from the monastery are reputed to be the hulls of three ships, turned to stone by vengeful monks.

The tiny village of **Panagia** is notable for the showy homes left behind by Kassian sea captains of yore. Athenians and former Kassians who summer here are gradually refurbishing these wind-eroded but ever-proud houses.

SYMI Σύμη

Pastel houses bloom like wildflowers on the cliffs overlooking Symi's main port, which has welcomed the incoming boats of sailors, fishermen, and sponge divers for thousands of years. Each of the beautiful, warm-toned colonial homes can be singled out for its unique artistic flourishes and individual charms. The continued presence of a small, tight-knit community of artists and writers on Symi reminds visitors of the island's golden years in the 18th century, when the *belles artes* thrived under the special protection of the ruling Ottoman Empire. Symi's steep, barren shores belie the healthful, buoyant quality in the air, beckoning mostly families and older travelers looking to escape the decadence of the other islands. Most visitors who stop here *en route* from Rhodes to Kos understand why the expat population is growing—Symi's gorgeous coves and vibrant village life are undeniably alluring. Panormitis Monastery, on the southern side of the island, remains one of the holiest places in Greek Orthodoxy and an important point of pilgrimage.

SYMI TOWN   ☎ 22460

Symi Town, the heart of the island's activity and where all public boats arrive, is divided into two sections: Yialos, the harbor area, and Horio, the residential village perched on the hillside up a daunting flight of 500 steps. Another small village, Pedhi, sits in the valley below Horio, south of Yialos. The town was constructed in the Middle Ages as a fortification against pirate raids; trekking your way up to Horio under the hot Symian sun may give you an appreciation of the strengths of this particular urban planning tactic. Luckily, there is an hourly bus.

▐ TRANSPORTATION

Ferries: Ferry ticket offices sit at the dock, just after the footbridge, and on the next block; tickets are also available at travel agencies. 3-4 per week to: **Kos** (€9), **Piraeus** (€34), and **Rhodes** (€10). 2 per week to **Astypalea** (€26), **Kalymnos** (€14), and **Tilos** (€6.50). Prices and times can both vary significantly.

Hydrofoils: Hydrofoil to **Rhodes** (1hr., 2-3 per day, €13). The **Catamaran Dodecanisos Express** departs W, Su 9:30am to **Kalymnos** (€30), **Kos** (€19), and **Leros** (€36); Su 9:30am to **Patmos.**

Excursion Boats: The boats **Poseidon** and **Triton** offer day-long round-trip tours (€28; lunch included) around the island that stop at Panormitis Monastery and a number of coves and beaches. Find them at the docks just beyond the footbridge.

Buses: The green **Symi Bus,** stops at Pl. Ikonomou, across the harbor from the ferry dock. Every hr. 8:10am-11:10pm to **Horio** (5min., €0.70) and **Pedhi** (10min., €0.70).

Taxis: Congregate next to the bus stop on the eastern waterfront. The island's taxis must be reached individually (☎ 69452 26 348, 69746 23 492, or 69452 73 842). Those that serve small beaches and coves can be found at the docks at Yialos or Pedhi.

▐ ▐ ORIENTATION AND PRACTICAL INFORMATION

The main steps leading up to Horio are behind Vapori Bar and Kaledoukias Travel, but can be difficult to find. From the ferry port, head into town over the wooden footbridge and take the last street inland before the waterfront road curves. To reach Pedhi, a 30-40min. walk from Yialos, climb up to Horio and take the main road going down the other side.

Budget Travel: Symi Tours (☎ 22460 71 307), 1 block inland from the gold shop on the waterfront. Sells tickets for G.A. Ferries, DANE Lines, and the Dodecanisos Express. Also **exchanges currency,** and helps find accommodations. Open daily 9am-1pm and 5-

9pm. **Kalodoukas Holiday** (☎22460 71 077), behind Vapori Bar, to the left of the steps to Horio, sells hydrofoil tickets, **exchanges currency,** and arranges mountain walks. In emergencies, they may be able to arrange **cash advances** on credit cards. Open daily 9am-1pm and 5-9pm. **Sunny Land L.T.D.** (☎22460 71 320), to the left of the entrance steps to the church in Yialos, sells ferry tickets and provides helpful advice about the island. Open M-Sa 9am-2:30pm and 5:30-9pm, Su 10am-1pm and 6-8pm.

Banks: Alpha Bank, on the waterfront directly across from the footbridge, has a **24hr. ATM. National Bank,** farther into town, also has an **ATM.** Both open M-F 8am-2pm.

Police: ☎22460 71 111. Next to the Yialos clock tower in a big white building by the port. Some English spoken. Open 24hr.

Medical Services: ☎22460 71 290. To the back left of the church in Yialos, opposite Hotel Kokona. Open M-F 8am-1pm; call 24hr. for emergencies. The doctor in Horio can be reached at ☎22460 71 316. Serious medical concerns often taken to Rhodes.

Telephones: OTE (☎22460 71 212), inland along the back left side of the town square in Yialos; follow signs from Neraida restaurant. Open M-F 8am-1:30pm.

Internet Access: Roloi (☎22460 71 597), over the footbridge, set back about 50m from the corner of the harbor. Electronica and hand-painted murals set an unhurried mood that match the dial-up speeds. Open daily 9am-2am. €3.50 per hr. **Vapori Bar** also has a computer with similarly slow Internet access. €4 per hr.

Post Office: ☎22460 71 315. In the same building as the police, up the flight of stairs on the left. Open M-F 7:30am-2pm. **Postal Code:** 85600.

ACCOMMODATIONS

Accommodations get classier and pricier as you ascend toward Horio, but there are a couple more economical pensions closer to the harbor. If a pension owner approaches you at the docks, be persistent with your haggling and marvel as prices drop as much as 50%. **Pension Agli ❷,** just past the steps to Horio, behind Symi's Burger, has large suites, some with private baths, kitchenettes, and fridges. Affordable for one, the rooms are a steal for three, particularly as larger rooms include laundry. If no one's around, look for the owner, Chrissa, at the pharmacy. (☎22460 71 392. Singles €24; doubles €28-30; triples €35-45.) Manolis, the owner of **Pension Titika ❷,** will likely meet you at the docks. Otherwise find him in his tourist shop across from the footbridge; look for the hand-painted "rooms to let" sign. Rooms are centrally located and have baths, A/C, and fridges. (☎22460 71 501. Singles €25-30; doubles €30-35. Prices negotiable.) **Hotel Kokona ❸** is over the footbridge to the left of the church tower. Light breezes blow the scent of lemons through billowing curtains. Classy rooms overlooking a garden terrace all have baths, balconies, fridges, and A/C. (☎22460 71 549. Breakfast €5. Singles €35-40; doubles €40-50; triples €50-60.) **Hotel Maria ❸,** next to Hotel Kokona, has six spacious doubles with private baths. Wood furniture and paintings create an intimate feel at this family-run pension. (☎22460 71 311. Doubles €30.)

FOOD AND NIGHTLIFE

Like many island waterfronts, Symi's is lined with indistinguishable restaurants catering more to tourists than to local palates. More authentic options at reasonable prices are squirreled away in winding alleys, at the far end of the waterfront, and up in Horio's heights. Symian cuisine is renowned throughout the Dodecanese for its seafood preparation, particularly that of its delightful small shrimp. Inviting smells fill the air at **Georgios's Taverna ❸,** at the top of the stairs to Horio, one of the oldest and most respected tavernas in Symi. Traditional dishes, archways, and a hanging roof garden add rich local flavor. (☎22460 71 984. Prawns

€10. Entrees €7-11. Open daily 9am-4pm and 7pm-midnight.) **Meraklis Taverna ❷**, at the end of the road when walking inland from Symi Tours, has been an institution for over 20 years. The charming outdoor patio is packed every night with diners hankering for another mouthwatering seafood masterpiece. (☎22460 71 003. Entrees €4-7. Seafood €7-38. Open daily 11am-midnight.) To find **Milonos Restaurant ❸**, take a left at Georgios's; it's on the road with the many parked cars. Inside an 18th-century windmill with terrace seating, Milonos has Mediterranean-inspired dishes and a unique ambience. (☎22460 71 871. Entrees €7-12.) Try the small Symi shrimp (€8) or the stuffed vegetables (€6) at **Tholos ❷**, at the far end of the small harbor to the right of the dock. (Open daily 7-11:30pm.)

Nightlife in Symi tends to be bar-oriented, but two clubs—local favorite **Club Harani** and newer **The Club**—open in Yialos for July and August. ▓**Jean and Tonic Pub**, in Horio, up the hill from Georgios's on your right, is a particularly popular spot. Cheery owner Jean artfully converted this 500-year-old building into a snug, friendly late-night hangout, where the expat community and the artistic set mingle under a pomegranate tree. (☎22460 71 819. Happy hour 9-10pm. Open daily 9pm-6am.) Cosmopolitan **Vapori Bar** stacks recent foreign-language newspapers on its blue wicker chairs. By night, it attracts European leisure-class patrons. (☎22460 72 082. Frappés and ouzo €2.50. Happy hour 6:30-8:30pm. Open daily 8am-late.)

◎ ⌒ SIGHTS AND BEACHES

At the top of the road to Horio, signs point toward the quaint **Archaeological and Folkloric Museum**, which displays labeled sculptures, relics, costumes, and icons. The museum is housed in the **Chatziagapitos Mansion**, the former home of an old naval family, which also displays everyday objects owned by 19th- and early 20th-century Symiots. (☎22460 71 114. Open Tu-Su 8:30am-3pm. €2.) The **Naval Museum**, in a yellow Neoclassical building beyond the waterfront strip in Yialos, provides an interesting look at the island's maritime history and development. (☎22460 72 363. Open daily 10am-2:30pm. €2.) Signs lead through a maze of streets to a handful of ruins. After being used for ammunition storage during WWII, little remains within the walls of the dismantled 15th-century **Castle of the Knights of Saint John** aside from what is left of the **Church of the Virgin of the Castle**. If this isn't enough to fill your old ruins quota, follow the signs to **Pontikokastro**, a partially excavated prehistoric mound near the windmills.

A number of small excursion boats function as water taxis connecting Yialos, Pedhi, and several excellent coves and beaches. Look for signs by the small boats in the center of the Yialos harbor. **Agia Marina** is a small, charming island within swimming distance of the shore. **Agios Georgios,** reached only by excursion or taxiboat, has deep, glassy waters set against a stunning 300m vertical cliff. **Agios Nikolaos,** a 30min. walk or €5 round-trip boat ride from Pedhi, is a beautiful half-sand, half-pebble beach. Tiny **Nos** is a 10min. walk along the waterfront from Yialos, past the shipyard. In the southeast, **Nanou's** expansive bay and the narrow, pebbly strip of **Marathounda** also deserve mention.

▌⌂ DAYTRIP FROM SYMI

PANORMITIS MONASTERY

Weekly tour boats running from Yialos include Panormitis on day-long trips around the island; daily tour boats from Rhodes stop here as well for at least 1hr. A taxi ride is over €20 (almost as much as the round-trip tour boat) and is only advisable for those short on time. The steep, winding road has recently been resurfaced, but still makes for a treacherous moped ride. By foot, it's a rigorous full-day hike. Open daily 10am-3pm. Modest dress required; no bare shoulders or shorts. Entry to museums €2, under 12 free.

Panormitis Monastery, on the southern part of the island, is the second most important monastery in the Dodecanese (after the Monastery of St. John in Patmos), and is by far the most worthy sight on Symi. Dedicated to the Archangel Michael, the patron saint of sailors and travelers, Panormitis attracts hundreds of sailors the islands for the feast day on November 8. Throughout the year, visitors come to the monastery to pay homage to the saint, and couples, hoping for child-bearing luck, come offering votives. Though the monastery's founding date remains a mystery even to the monks, its most recent renovation was in the 1700s, when the affluent area entertained a flourishing art school. Other recently restored frescoes may be much older. The magnificent wooden altar screen, carved from a walnut tree, depicts a powerful St. Michael stepping on a dead man who represents evil and holding a small child who represents purity. The museums contain ecclesiastical relics, folk exhibits, and displays of silver tokens hammered into icons symbolizing different prayers, which were left by supplicants. If the doors are locked, head up the stairs and ask a monk if you can take a peek. The monastery will also supposedly let visitors spend the night in one of the many empty cells if they find themselves stranded without a return trip in sight. Arranging for round-trip transportation, however, is still a good idea.

TILOS Τήλος

Pure, peaceful, and famous for its alternative vibe, Tilos slips under the radar of most pleasure-seekers. With an earthier, more laid-back atmosphere than other islands, Tilos is a place where one is more likely to encounter dreadlocks and acoustic guitar jam sessions than slick trendsters. The 3000 goats and 300 permanent residents that call this island home have managed to fend off the stock-and-trade tourism of larger islands, leaving the serene, natural beauty that was praised by poet Irinna in 350 BC. Today, free thinkers of all ages are drawn to Tilos's hippie beach camps, red-sand beach, partridge-filled walking paths, and boundless wilderness to explore. With its independent mindset and secluded beaches, Tilos makes a perfect stop for travelers seeking a holiday that's off the beaten path.

LIVADIA Λιβάδια   ☎22460

Tilos's small port village nestles between mountains and sea; its handful of unnamed streets stretches along the length of a smooth-pebbled beach and wind up into the surrounding hills. Though crowded in August, Livadia slumbers for most of the year, with many of its shops and restaurants closed during the winter. Visitors in early summer or September and October will enjoy a quiet, friendly welcome and glorious solitude amid the warm waves. Currently, Livadia is in the midst of a town-wide face-lift; a waterfront sidewalk was recently installed, and a newly rebuilt fountain graces the central square.

⌐ TRANSPORTATION

Getting to Tilos can be difficult, as ferry schedules change weekly; those considering extending their stay may find the matter decided for them.

Ferries: To: **Kos** (3hr., 2 per week, €8); **Leros** (4hr., 2 per week, €12); **Nisyros** (2hr., 2 per week, €6); **Patmos** (2 per week, €16); **Piraeus** (2 per week, €29); **Rhodes** (3½hr., 2 per week, €11); **Symi** (2 per week, €7). Confirm times at Stefanakis Travel Service.

Hydrofoils: High-speed **catamaran** tickets can be purchased at the **Sea Star** office on the waterfront near the church, at the corner where the road takes a 90° turn into town. (☎22460 44 000. Open 8:30am-2:30pm.) To **Kamiros** (every Sa), **Nisyros** (30min., 2 per week, €10), and **Rhodes** (1½hr., 1-2 per day, €19).

Excursion Boats: Stelios runs an excursion cruise every Sa from mid-Apr. to Oct. to the island's many beaches for a cookout and swimming. (€29 including lunch and wine.) He also takes groups to swim on various beaches (M-F only, €15-17). Look for his waterfront "office," a table near the tavernas. **Tilos Travel** organizes a speedboat excursion cruise around the island (€25); inquire at the office for schedules.

Buses: Walk past the police station on the waterfront and turn right at the white mini-mart; the **bus stop** is 1 block inland, by a cafe. Buses leave 5 times a day to **Agios Antonio, Eristos beach,** and **Megalo Horio** (€0.60-1.20). An **excursion bus** runs to the **Monastery of Saint Pandeleimon.** (Every Su 11am, stays for 1hr.; €4 round-trip).

Taxis: The island's 2 individual taxis can be reached 24hr.; call **Nikos Logothetis Taxi** (☎22460 44 059) or **Taxi Anna** (☎22460 44 169). €2 surcharge after midnight.

Rentals: At the port, **Tilos Travel** rents **cars** (€35-50 per day) and **motorbikes** (€15-20 per day) with insurance. **Bicycles** (€8 per day) are also available. Open 9am-2pm and 6-8pm. Facing inland, go left from the square to find **Drive Rent A Car,** which has motorbikes (€15-22) and cars (€35-45 per day) with insurance. Open M-Sa 10am-10pm. The family that runs Calypso restaurant rents out **paddle boats** (€10 per hr.), **canoes** (€5 per hr.), and **windsurfs** (€12 per hr., additional €8 for a lesson). Discounts available for multiple hours. Look for stacks of canoes and paddle boats on the beach.

◀ ❼ ORIENTATION AND PRACTICAL INFORMATION

The main road begins at the port, curves through town and heads back to the waterfront; the far end is lined with tavernas and small beachfront hotels. Continuing up the mountain, you'll pass **Mikro Chorio** on the way to **Megalo Chorio.**

Budget Travel: Tilos Travel (☎22460 44 294; www.tilostravel.co.uk), at the ferry dock, sells **maps** when available (€2.50), **exchanges currency,** rents rooms and vehicles, and keeps scrapbooks about Tilos. Open daily 9am-2pm and 6-8pm. At the corner, **Stefanakis Travel Service** (☎22460 44 310) sells ferry tickets, provides accommodations advice, and rents cars (€35 per day). Open daily 10am-2pm and 7-9pm.

Bank: The **Cooperative Bank of the Dodecanese** (☎22460 70 703; www.bankdodecanese.gr), located just past the mini-mart, handles **currency exchange** and operates a **24hr ATM.** Open Apr.-Oct. M-F 9am-2pm; Nov.-Mar. M-F 10am-2pm.

Police: ☎22460 44 222. The white and blue building opposite Stefanakis. Open 24hr.

Medical Services: ☎09448 87 869. Behind the church. Doubles as the **pharmacy.** Open M-F 11am-1pm; emergency phone answered 24hr.

Internet Access: Kosmos (☎22460 44 074; www.tilos-kosmos.com), opposite the bakery near the center of town, has Internet in the back of their clothing shop. €6 per hr.; €3 min. Open daily 9:30am-1pm and 7-11:30pm.

Post Office: Turn right at the waterfront mini-mart and right again at the fountain. Open M-F 9am-1:30pm. **Postal Code:** 85002.

▮ ACCOMMODATIONS

Because Livadia is so small, hotel competition is fierce, and prices are uniformly high. Expect to pay around €30 for a single in low season and €45 in the summer. Very basic rooms at slightly lower rates cluster toward the outskirts of town or up the mountain road; by the sea, sprawling hotels cater to those looking to shell out for a luxury resort. Attached to Tilos Travel, ▧**Blue Sky Apartments ❸** features spacious two-level rooms with fantastic harbor views. Chic decor, A/C, and private kitchens, baths, and balconies are standard in rooms that approach budget travel's upper limits of comfort. Hair dryers, desks, and patio umbrellas make the rooms feel like actual apartments. (☎22460 44 294, or ask at Tilos Travel. Singles €35-60.) **Georgia's Rooms to Let ❸,** up the road from the church, offers doubles with private baths, fridges, kitchens, and balconies that overlook a perfectly manicured garden. (☎22460 44 261. Doubles €30.) Those on a tight budget can scrap the ocean view and hike up the hill to **Sevas Studios ❷**, where comfortable doubles with TV, A/C, baths, balconies, and kitchens run lower than more centrally located counterparts. Ask for Antonio at the supermarket next to Yannis's, left of the square, before you make the climb. (☎22460 44 237. Doubles €15-25.) Tilos Travel also manages the more economical **Golden Beach Studios ❷**, which is a 10min. walk along the beach away from the center of town, behind another hotel (about 20m from the water). Simple but large rooms have fridges, baths, and extra trundle beds under the sofas. (☎22460 44 294 or ask at Tilos Travel. Doubles €20-35.)

🎮🍴 FOOD AND NIGHTLIFE

Although traditional Greek tavernas dominate the Tilian dining scene, **⧉Calypso Cafe ❷**, up the perilous staircase behind Stefanakis Travel Service, epitomizes fusion at its finest. Caribbean, Vietnamese, and Greek culinary influences come together in an ever-changing menu of inventive dishes like the French-Caribbean *mezedes* plate, which includes lightly fried cod-cake bites, spicy prawns lit aflame at your table, and a minty rum cocktail (€6). On many summer nights, Matteo, affectionately nicknamed the "Bob Dylan of the Dodecanese," strums 1960s protest rock on his acoustic guitar, inspiring restaurant-wide, campfire-esque sing-alongs. (☎69472 13 279. Entrees €6-8. Open daily 7pm-late.) A variety of tavernas, cafes, and pizzerias are linked along the pebble beach. The first of these, **Sophia's ❷**, is a mother-and-son establishment that dishes up a delightfully bubbly clay pot of *moussaka* (€5.60) and daily vegetarian entrees. (☎22460 44 340. Entrees €4-7. Open daily 8am-3pm and 5:30pm-late.) Just up the hill from the police station, **Nick's Time Pita Time ❶** puts a Greek spin on supersized fast food, with volcanic, calzone-like covered pitas (€5) and pork or chicken gyros (€1.80) the size of rolled newspapers. Delivery is free 5pm-midnight to Livadia, Megalo Chorio, and even Eristos beach. (☎22460 44 148. Min. order €6.)

Livadia residents like their peace and quiet, and the town offers little in the way of nightlife. In July, the party is exported over the mountain to **Mikro Chorio**, the ancient capital city (5min. by taxi, €3-5), where colored lights and thumping Greek pop tunes flood deserted houses. Dancing in the streets lasts from midnight to 5am. While Mikro Chorio draws an older, touristy crowd, **Cafe Ino**, on the waterfront, caters to young locals looking for cocktails and conversation. On the waterfront just in front of the police station, Ino's yellow-toned, outdoor terrace is a relaxing place to sip a drink. (Open nightly 8:30pm-midnight.) **Cafe Akti**, next to Nick's Pita, also draws low-key crowds of locals to its roof-top terrace, and fills a similar niche as neighboring Cafe Ino. Blue-toned decor and soft techno beats make this chill spot ideal for grabbing a drink (€5-6) and gazing out at the sea. (Open nightly 8pm-midnight.)

👁 SIGHTS

The 15th-century village of **Mikro Chorio** sits 3km up the road from Livadia. Abandoned in 1960 as residents moved to open businesses in Livadia, the town today hosts a bizarre summer dance club for the middle-aged set between the castle ruins and Agia Zoni chapel. Six kilometers farther, in **Megalo Chorio**, lie the remains of the much larger **fortress** built by the ever-present Knights of St. John. Neolithic tools and midget elephant fossils dated roughly to 5000-2300 BC were unearthed in the **Cave of Harkadio** in 1971. Although the cave itself is closed to the public, paleontology buffs and circus fans curious to see the findings can check out the recovered bones which have been laid to rest in the nearby **museum**. (Open daily 9am-1pm. Free.) **Agios Antonios**, just outside Megalo Chorio, is an idyllic seaside village dotted with closet-sized chapels. Taking the road west leads to **Plaka beach;** continuing to the south will take you to the 15th-century **Monastery of Agios Pandeleimon** atop a rock, towering over cyprus trees and trickling streams. Inside the pebble yard stands a 200-year-old cyprus tree and an impressive icon of Jonas, the 15-century founder of the monastery.

Perhaps the best way to experience Tilos is to explore its wild sage patches and goat-filled grottoes on foot. **Walking maps** can be found at Tilos Travel or at the supermarket, along with advice on how to find the beaches accessible only from hiking routes. Several routes, varying in difficulty, steepness, and the rockiness of the terrain, all take about 1hr. from Livadia. Easily disoriented explorers can hire **licensed guides** Iain and Lyn from **Tilos Trails.** (☎ 22460 44 128. About €20.)

NISYROS Νίσυρος

Most visitors to Nisyros come to walk among the sulfur crystals and escaping steam of the five separate craters that make up its active volcano. Because day-tripping tourists to Nisyros move in predictable cycles from the dock of Mandraki to the volcano to the waterfront tavernas and back to the dock again, the rest of the island remains a quiet, peaceful place to unwind. Quiet villages are made up of winding streets and the whitewashed, boxy architecture typical of the Dodecanese that provides scenic views of the mountains and sea. Relics dating back to the Classical and Byzantine eras are sprinkled throughout the island, interspersed between the unusual sand and stone beaches tinted black with volcanic rock.

MANDRAKI Μανδράκι ☎ 22420

Mandraki's calm, leisurely rhythm of life seems immune to the volcano-minded tourists who arrive *en masse* on daytrips from Kos. Beyond the harbor, the winding, stone streets and handsome views make the city a pleasant stopover, though the steaming sulfur pit comprises the town's most exciting entertainment.

⌐ TRANSPORTATION

Ferries: GA Ferries provides the main ferry service connecting Nisyros to the rest of the world. **Kentris Travel** (☎ 22420 31 227), located on the main road past the town hall, sells tickets and has schedules. Open daily 9am-1pm and 5-9pm. To: **Kos** (1¼hr., 4 per week, €7.40); **Piraeus** (16hr., 2 per week, €31); **Rhodes** (5hr., 4 per week, €12); **Symi** (3hr., 3 per week, €10.10); **Tilos** (1½hr., 3 per week, €6.40).

Highspeed boats: Hydrofoil tickets are available at **Diakomichalis Travel** (☎ 22420 31 459); follow the main road 250m to the right, past the bank. The high-powered **Sea Star** departs on M for **Tilos** (30min., €10) and **Rhodes** (2hr., €20). On F afternoons, hydrofoils run to **Rhodes** (1½hr., €17) and **Kos** (45min., €13).

Excursion Boats: Enetikon Travel sends a daily commercial boat to the town of **Kardamena,** Kos (1hr., 7am, €7). Diakomichalis Travel also has boats that go to **Kardamena** (1hr., daily 3:30pm, €7.50) and **Kos Town** (M-W, Sa; €12.30).

Buses: A municipal bus makes rounds through the villages, leaving from the Mandraki harbor 6 times a day. To: **Emporio** (20min.); **Loutra** (4min.); **Nikea** (25min.); **Pali** (10min.); **White beach** (10min.). The municipal bus runs to the **volcano** (30min.) twice a day. Daily excursion buses also head to the volcano when the boats from Kos arrive, usually 10am-noon. €7 round-trip, includes volcano entry. Enetikon and Nisyrian Travel both have "volcano bus" stands at the docks where you can purchase tickets.

Taxis: Babis's (☎ 22420 31 460) is based in Mandraki. To Loutra and the White beach (€2-3), Lies beach (€10), and the volcano (€20).

Rentals: Yiannis (☎22420 31 750), located just to the right at the fork in the road, rents **motorbikes** from €12 per day. **Car** rental is available at **Diakomichalis Travel.** (€25-30 per day, minimal insurance included. Min. age 21.)

✦ 🔃 ORIENTATION AND PRACTICAL INFORMATION

The main road in Mandraki starts at the ferry docks and follows the waterfront (to the right as you face inland) until it forks at the bank. To the right, the road continues along the waterfront, leading to stairs that ascend to the monastery and, beyond them, to a small stony beach. To the left, the road takes you inland to **Plateia Ilikiomeni** (Old Woman Square), a cobbled plateia nearly overwhelmed by the ficus tree in its center and filled with cafes and tavernas.

Budget Travel: Nisyrian Travel (☎22420 31 411), to the left of the ferry dock. Provides historical info and arranges excursions, walks, accommodations, "Greek Evenings" with food and dancing (€15), and boat trips around the island (€10). Open daily 9am-9pm.
Enetikon Travel (☎22420 31 180), on the right side of the road leading into town from the docks, helps with tickets, hotel reservations, book exchange, and bus and boat tours. Friendly, multilingual staff. Open daily 9:30am-12:30pm and 6:30-9pm.

Banks: The **Cooperative Bank of the Dodecanese** (☎22420 48 900), the only bank on the island, is on the waterfront road; turn right from the dock. **Currency exchange** and cash advance available M-F 9am-2pm. A **24hr. ATM** is located right off the ferry docks.

Emergency: ☎22420 31 217 for an ambulance. The surgeon is located right before Pl. Ilikiomeni. Major medical emergencies are taken to nearby Kos for treatment.

Internet Access: Proveza (☎22420 31 386). Located far down the waterfront next to Kleanthis, this cafe has 1 computer with dial-up connection, but plans to install wireless in the near future. €2 per 30min. Open daily 10am-3pm and 6pm-late.

Police: ☎22420 31 201. In a white building near the dock. Phone answered 24hr.

Post Office: ☎22420 31 249. In the same white building as the police. Open M-F 7:30am-3pm. **Postal Code:** 85303.

🏠 🌙 ACCOMMODATIONS AND FOOD

Rooms can be scarce in Mandraki, especially during the August 15 Festival of the Panagia, so calling ahead is advisable. The 📱**Three Brothers Hotel ❸**, next to the ferry dock, is one of Mandraki's best. Its breezy lounge overlooks the harbor and is a great place to meet other guests or hang with the charismatic brothers themselves. Whitewashed rooms come with clean private baths and balconies. Studios with full kitchens, A/C, and TV also available. (☎22420 31 344. Singles €20-30; doubles €23-36; quads with kitchen €30-60; studios €35-55.) **Hotel Romantzo ❷**, a longstanding rival of the Three Brothers, is just across the street with an upstairs terrace that affords amazing views of the sea. Quiet, nice-sized rooms have private baths and fridges. (☎/fax 22420 31 340. A/C €4. Singles €15-20; doubles €20-30; triples €35-45.) **Volcano Studios ❷**, on the main road along the waterfront above the Volcano Cafe, rents simple rooms with fridges and private baths; some have balconies overlooking the water. (☎22420 31 680. Singles €15-20; doubles €20-30.)
Dining in Mandraki will inevitably mean enjoying standard Greek comfort food in a taverna or cafe, as few other options exist. Restaurants with similar menus and prices line the waterfront, and smaller cafes cluster in the plateia. Mandraki's best seafood may be at **Restaurant Kleanthis ❷**, far down along the waterfront, which prepares appetizing *mezedes*, shellfish entrees, and a variety of Nisyrian dishes. The *pithia* (chickpea fritters; €3) are a local specialty. (☎22420 31 484. Octopus in vinegar €4.50. Open 10am-midnight.) Head to **I Fabrika ❷**, on the main street past the Kentris Travel, in a basement between two tourist shops; keep your

eyes open, as it's easy to miss. Greek folk tunes play in the background as hungry patrons gobble down delectable *mezedes* (€3-6) or vegetarian specials. (☎22420 31 552. Open 8pm-4am.) At **Ilikomeni Irini ❶** in the plateia, a hotspot for local gossip, you can wander through the kitchen and pick what looks good or let Irini make you a mixed plate of her favorite dishes. The traditional Greek favorites range €4-6, and a variety of vegetarian dishes (€3-5) are usually available. (☎22420 31 365. Open daily 9am-late.) Patrons at **Cafe Fikos ❶,** next door, can lounge on a dark blue sofa while enjoying a cold *soumada* (€1.20), a sweet Nisyrian almond drink. (☎22420 31 215. Open daily 6am-1am.)

⚑ DAYTRIPS FROM MANDRAKI

▨MANDRAKI VOLCANO. Plug your nose and head down the steep, sandy trail into the bowels of Mandraki's enormous **Stefanos Crater,** where steam hisses from small crevices that still bubble with smoldering, viscous fluid. Yellow traces of sulfur crystals, responsible for the pervasive rotten-egg aroma, can be seen throughout the cracked, chalk-white earth. Aspiring geologists (or pyromaniacs) will want as close a look as possible, though visitors should tread lightly near the open pits—the earth here is delicate and has opened underfoot before. Although no special safety precautions are necessary, digging a hole in the spongy, steaming terrain would probably be a bad move. The volcano last erupted in 1872; now, geologists have determined that, though inactive, the volcano still causes earthquakes. A 10min. walk along the trail behind the snack bar leads to nearby **Polyvotis and Alexandros craters,** virtually unvisited but no less spectacular. Shoes with some traction are advisable for those wanting to venture into the craters, as the paths are sandy and steep. Bringing a bottle of water is also a good idea, as the crater provides no shade and the snack bar is a long way back up the trail. Two different routes lead from the volcano back to Mandraki; ask for a walking map at Nisyrian Travel. Both walks afford impressive views of the mountains and sea; neither is difficult, and each takes about 2½hr. to complete. *(Entrance €1. Municipal bus from Mandraki stays 45min. at the sight before returning; 30min., 2 per day, €3 round-trip. Excursion buses also leave regularly from the harbor; €7 includes admission.)*

MONASTERY OF OUR LADY SPILLANI. At the far end of Mandraki from the docks, a twisted stone staircase leads up a cliff past tiny cells carved into the rock face, once used to house anti-Turkish artillery. Perched at the top is a quaint, whitewashed church dating from the 17th century, which grants sweeping views of the sea below. An altar boy recently discovered the original iconographer's hidden portrait of St. Nikolaos on the rear face of an icon that had been covered with an old cloth for over two centuries. The **museum** at the bottom of the staircase houses a collection of precious votives, elaborately embroidered gowns, and other relics related to the church. *(Monastery open daily 9am-3pm. Donations welcome. Modest dress required. Museum open daily 10am-3pm. €2.)*

BEACHES. Because Mandraki's stony beach is small, jumping from the sidewalk near where the yachts dock into the sea is a more convenient option for swimming. The black pebble beach of **Hohlaki** is a short walk from the monastery stairs along a coastal footpath. **White,** on the road to Pali just past Loutra, is also almost entirely black despite its name. Dust from nearby pumice quarries once gave the pebbly beach a pale top layer, but now that the quarries are inactive, the beach's natural dark color has returned. Sandy, picturesque **Lies,** 3km east of Pali, is the island's optimal tanning spot. If there is sufficient demand, Enetikon and Nisyrian Travel run boats (€8 round-trip) to the beaches of **Yali,** a small island nearby that houses pumice stone quarries.

KOS Κως

Antiquity best knew Kos as the sacred land of Asclepius, god of healing, and the birthplace of Hippocrates, the father of ancient medicine, who wrested the science of human health away from magicians. Today Kos attracts a young, loud, intoxicated crowd more interested in sexual healing than anything else. If you've been meaning to reduce the blood in your alcohol stream or need a primer on the anatomy of the torso or backside, the rowdy beaches of Kos Town may be just what the doctor ordered. Though the more sedate traveler can escape to the mountains of central Kos or the relatively isolated beaches of the western coast, those allergic to the party may find Kos a tough pill to swallow.

KOS TOWN   ☎22420

Young foreigners eagerly overdose on Kos Town's cocktail of liquor, lights, and lovin'. The tourist industry has grown exponentially in Kos Town, and the army of five-star hotels based at its outskirts threatens to invade untouched beaches farther southwest; luckily, though, there are still beautiful swaths of terrain to explore if your liver needs a day off.

DODECANESE

⌐ TRANSPORTATION

Flights: Olympic Airways, Vas. Pavlou 22 (☎22420 51 567, reservations 22420 28 331), has flights to **Athens** (from €68). Open M-F 8am-2:30pm. Olympic runs a bus (€3) to the airport from Kos Town 2hr. before departure. Taxis to the airport €25.

Ferries: Schedules differ between companies; check schedules and prices at a travel agency. To: **Astypalea** (4hr., 2 per week, €13); **Kalymnos** (1hr., daily, €5); **Katapota** (7hr., 2 per week on Sa, €21); **Leros** (3hr., 1-2 per day, €7); **Mykonos** (7hr., W 3:30am, €31); **Nisyros** (1½hr., 4 per week, €5); **Patmos** (4hr., 1-2 per day, €10); **Piraeus** (11-15hr., 1-3 per day, €23); **Rhodes** (4hr., 2-3 per day, €15); **Symi** (3hr., 1 per week W, €1); **Syros** (5hr., 3 per week Sa-Su, €28). Boats also run to **Bodrum, Turkey** every morning (20min.; round-trip €15-40, port tax included).

Flying Dolphins: To: **Agathonisi** (3¼hr., 1 per week, €20.50); **Fourni** (4hr., 2 per week, €25); **Ikaria** (3½hr., 2 per week, €31); **Kalymnos** (45min., daily, €10); **Leros** (30min., daily, €14); **Lipsi** (2hr., daily, €14); **Patmos** (2½hr., daily, €20); **Pythagorio, Samos** (5hr., daily, €25); **Symi** (1½hr., 1 per week, €18). The **Dodecanisos Express** runs to: **Kalymnos** (40min., daily, €11.50); **Leros** (1¾hr., daily, €16.40); **Lipsi** (2hr., 4 per week, €16.40); **Patmos** (2½hr., 4 per week, €22.40); **Rhodes** (2hr., Tu-Su, €27.50); **Symi** (1½hr., 2 per week, €21).

Intercity Buses: ☎22420 22 292. Leave from the intersection of Kleopatras, Metsovou, and Pissandrou and from the junction of Vas. Pavlou and A. Koundourioti at the waterfront. Run M-Sa with reduced service Su to: **Antimachia** (40min., 6 per day 9:10am-9pm, €2); **Asfendiou-Zia** (40min., 3 per day, €1.30); **Kardamena** (45min., 6 per day 9:10am-9pm, €2.20); **Kefalos-Paradise** (1hr., 6 per day 9:10am-9pm, €3); **Marmari** (35min., 12 per day 9am-11pm, €1.30); **Mastihari** (45min., 5 per day, €2); **Pyli** (30min., 5 per day, €1.30); **Tigaki** (30min., 12 per day 9am-11pm, €1.30). Schedule posted by the bus stop and at the EOT; buy tickets onboard.

City Buses: A. Koundourioti 7 (☎22420 26 276), on the water. Fares run €0.50-1.20. To: **Agios Fokas** (#1, 20min., 46 per day 6:45am-11pm); **Lampi** (#2, 10min., 25 per day 6:30am-11pm); **Messaria** (#3, 10min., 10 per day 8am-8:45pm); **Platani** (#3, 5min., 5 per day 8am-10:45pm); **Thermae** (#5, 20min., 9 per day 9:45am-5:45pm).

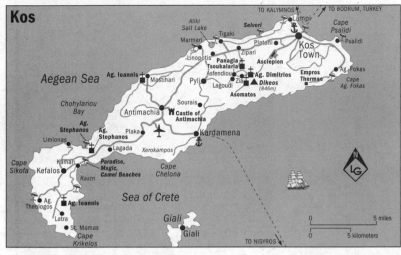

Blue mini-trains go from the EOT to **Asclepion** (15min., Tu-Su every hr. 8:15am-2:15pm, €3.50). **Citywide tours** on a green mini-train leave every 30min. 10am-6pm from the Municipality Building (€3).

Taxis: ☎22420 22 777. All taxis convene near the inland end of the Avenue of Palms, just after A. Koundourioti splits where the harbor curves. €0.50 surcharge with calls and midnight-5am. To the airport €20-25.

Rentals: Laws restricting rentals to those with proper motorbike licenses are more strictly enforced here than on other islands. Driving behavior does not reflect this stringency, however, so drivers should exercise caution. **Mike's** (☎22420 21 729), 20 Amerikis, at the corner of Amerikis and Psaron. Mopeds €9-15 per day. Bikes €2-4 per day. Open 9am-8pm. **George**, P. Tsaldari 3 (☎22420 28 480), near the port authority, rents mopeds from €10-12 per day. ATVs €20. Bikes €3. Open daily 8:30am-8pm.

✦🛈 ORIENTATION AND PRACTICAL INFORMATION

Street lamps, neon signs, and floodlit hotels shine like beacons on the coast, guiding ferries to dry land and young people to the watering holes. The coastal road (**Zouroudi** in the northwest; **Akti Koundourioti** curving around the harbor; and both **Akti Miaouli** and **Vasileos Georgiou B'** to the southeast, past the castle) are lined with standard theme bars and souvenir stands. On **Vasileos Pavlou**, just off A. Koundourioti, is a practical group of **travel agencies, banks,** and **24hr. ATMs**. The town centers on **Plateia Eleftherias**, just a bit farther inland, where you'll find the pint-sized **Archaeological Museum**, a large market, and some nondescript cafes. A plethora of pubs pack together on the cobblestone streets branching off **Nafklirou (Bar Street)** in the **Old City**, where the rollicking night kicks off in Kos Town. Nafklirou borders the ancient **agora**, and culminates at the gigantic **plane tree of Hippocrates** and the well-preserved **Castle of the Knights of Saint John**. South on Nafklirou takes you to **Grigoriou E'** with the **Odeon, Altar of Dionysus,** and **Casa Romana**. The club scene circles the **Dolphin Roundabout** and clusters on nearby **Kanari** and **Zouroudi**.

Tourist Office: ⬛EOT, Vas. Georgiou B' 1 (☎22420 24 460; www.hippocrates.gr). Free **maps**, bus and ferry schedules (and explanations of their quirks), event guides, and hotel review booklets. Open M-F 8am-2pm and 5-8pm, Sa 8am-2pm.

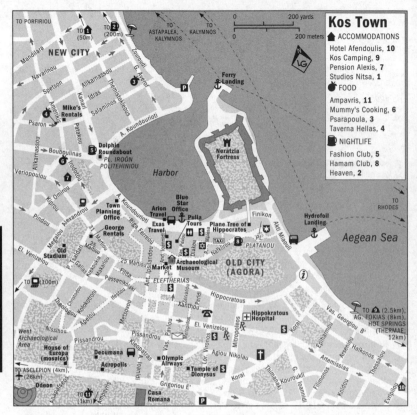

Kos Town

🔺 ACCOMMODATIONS

Hotel Afendoulis, **10**
Kos Camping, **9**
Pension Alexis, **7**
Studios Nitsa, **1**

🍴 FOOD

Ampavris, **11**
Mummy's Cooking, **6**
Psarapoula, **3**
Taverna Hellas, **4**

🌃 NIGHTLIFE

Fashion Club, **5**
Hamam Club, **8**
Heaven, **2**

Budget Travel: Though there are tons of travel agencies in Kos Town, most do not have complete boat information. **Pulia Tours** (☎/fax 22420 26 388; open daily 7am-11pm), Vas. Pavlou 3, is an exception, and can book tickets on any major ferry line or excursions to Turkey. Also offers rental assistance and **exchanges currency.** The patient, friendly staff at ▓**Exas Travel Service,** 4 Ioannidi (☎22420 29 900; www.exas.gr) provides oodles of transportation advice and books tickets for **GA Ferries, Catamaran Dodecanisos Express,** and various other air and sea lines. **Arion Travel,** Vas. Pavlou 1B (☎22420 49 930), next to Pulia Travel, has flying dolphin schedules.

Banks: You should have no trouble locating a bank on A. Koundourioti, between And. Ioannidi and Al. Diakou. Many have **24hr. ATMs.** Typical hours are M-Th 8am-2pm, reduced hours on F. **Alpha Bank,** Koundourioti 5 (☎22420 28 144), is between Vas. Pavlou and Al. Diakou. After banking hours, you can **exchange currency** at virtually any travel agency along the waterfront.

Emergency: ☎22420 22 100. For an **ambulance,** call ☎22420 22 300.

Police: ☎22420 22 100 or 22420 22 222. At A. Miaouli 2, in the big, white building next to the castle. Some English spoken. Open 24hr. **Tourist police,** ☎22420 22 444, are in the same building. Open daily 7am-2pm.

Pharmacy: On almost every major street. 1 is around the corner from the hospital at El. Venizelou 2 (☎22420 26 426). Prescriptions filled 24hr. Open 8am-midnight.

Medical Services: Mitropoleos 13 (☎22420 22 300), between El. Venizelou and Hippo-cratous. English spoken. Open 24hr.

Telephones: OTE, ☎22420 23 499. At Lor. Vironos and Xanthou, around the corner from the post office. Open M-F 7:15am-1:30pm.

Internet Access: A number of cafes and bars in Kos Town provide Internet with similar prices; expect to pay at least €4-6 per hr. **Del Mare Internet Cafe,** Meg. Alexandrou 4A (☎22420 24 244; www.cybercafe.gr), has admirably fast connections in a food-friendly environment. €4.50 per hr.; €2 min. Open daily 9am-1am.

Post Office: ☎22420 22 250. On Vas. Pavlou. From El. Venizelou, walk 1 block inland. Open M-F 7:30am-2pm. **Postal Code:** 85300.

ACCOMMODATIONS AND CAMPING

Vacancies are rare in August, so start searching for rooms early. Most budget options are on the right side of town when facing inland or back toward the ancient sites. It's best to avoid Kos's dock hawks, but if you do choose to haggle, ask for a business card, telling them you'll check out your options and come by later; if they can't produce a card, they may not be legit.

Pension Alexis (☎22420 28 798). From the port, head inland on Meg. Alexandrou; take the first right onto Irodotou and walk up 1 block. Kind, hospitable Sonia and her son Yannis preside over this beloved travel institution, offering transportation advice, maps, and insiders' tips on Kos. Spacious doubles with in-room sinks share recently-remodeled common baths with hot water and deliciously massage-like water pressure. Upper-story rooms have breezy private balconies, while rooms on lower floors share an attractive veranda. Breakfast (€5) is served on the 2nd-fl. terrace where guests gather to chat. If all rooms are full, Sophia will help arrange other accommo-dations or finagle a price break at her brother Alexis's elegant Hotel Afendoulis. A/C €3. Laundry €5. Doubles €20-22; triples €28-38. ❷

Hotel Afendoulis, Evripilou 1 (☎22420 25 321). From Vas. Georgiou B', take a right on Evripilou and walk 1 block; it's on the left. Always-cheerful Alexis's mantra is "everybody must be happy," and it is rare that guests leave his hotel any other way. Alexis will gladly pick you up from the port, recommend the best sites on Kos, and per-haps join you for breakfast. Quiet doubles have A/C (though the surprisingly cool basement rooms don't even need it), private baths, and balconies. The elevator is a welcome addition, making the hotel both wheelchair- and drunk-accessible. Breakfast €5. Laundry €5. Doubles €30-38; basement €24-30. ❸

Studios Nitsa, Averof 47 (☎22420 25 810). Take Averof inland from A. Koundourioti and it's on your left. Pleasantly large studios each include a fridge, bath, A/C, and bal-cony. Only 10m from the beach and close to the nightlife, this is a good choice for those planning to paint the town. Doubles €20-25. ❷

Kos Camping (☎22420 29 886), 2.5km southeast of the town center, is accessible by the buses that run to and from the site every 30min. (€0.65, get off at the 11th stop). This family-operated campground is a welcome break for those looking to escape the frenzy of Kos Town. The site is equipped with a mini-mart, bar, laundry, kitchen, postal service, pool, restrooms, showers, and security boxes. €7 per tent; tent rental free. ❶

FOOD

The major fruit and vegetable **market** in Pl. Eleftherias, inside the large yellow building, caters to tourists and is more expensive than it looks; the many **mini-marts** sell fruit at cheaper prices. Heaping portions of Greek food and sociable company characterize **Taverna Hellas ❷,** Psaron 7, down the street from Pension

DODECANESE

ROLLING WITHOUT THE HOMIES

Exploring Greece, land of the shameless stare, as a solo female traveler can be daunting; it's not unusual to be stared at, cat-called, invited to dinner, or propositioned, all before breakfast.

The overt staring will likely be most apparent as you walk down the street in the late afternoon and early evening. If it feels like all the eyes of the men seated at the sidewalk cafes are on you, you're not imagining it. They are. As the night progresses and cocktails replace coffee on the cafe tables, the stares are often accompanied by catcalls. Although slightly creepy, the leers and comments are usually harmless. If you continue walking and avoid meeting the onlooker's gaze, you will be left undisturbed. If the man is particularly persistent, continue playing the I-can't-hear-you game or politely refuse and move on. As it is uncommon for women, either alone or in groups, to eat out before sunset, if you buy yourself lunch or coffee, you will likely be the only woman in the taverna save for the occasional waitress; the stares will intensify.

The bar scene is actually less openly intimidating than the side-walk situation, but potentially more dangerous given the addition of alcohol. On the touristy islands that draw European partiers, a single female out at night is not unusual—just join in the

Alexis at Amerikis. Eager-to-please owner Dimitris has been known to invite solo diners to meet other patrons, creating a fun night for one and all. (☎22420 22 609. Entrees €4-8. Vegetarian options available. Open noon-late.) A pleasant mix of locals and tourists make up the constant stream of patrons at **Mummy's Cooking ②,** where the homemade food comes piled ridiculously high. From the Dolphin Roundabout, walk two blocks down Bouboulinas. Mummy's hospitable son Ilias will happily decode Greek menu items and provide suggestions. (☎22420 28 525. Entrees €6-8. Open M-Sa 7am-11pm.) **Psarapoula ③,** G. Averof 17, inland from the far end of the port, is another local favorite that serves a wide range of seafood and the usual Greek specialties. (☎22420 21 909. Seafood entrees €6-12. Open 1pm-late.) At **Ampavris ❶,** on Ampavris, a father-son team cooks and waits tables. Just outside of town, home-made Greek dishes are both authentic and cheap. Take Grigoriou E' and turn onto Ampavris, the road next to the Casa Romana; it's a 1km walk up the road on your left. (☎22420 25 696. Entrees €3-5.50.)

🜚 SIGHTS

Never satisfied without building a bevy of defensive island fortifications, the Knights of St. John erected yet another massive **castle,** the **⧏Neratzia Fortress,** in the early 14th century. To find it, take the bridge from Pl. Platanou over Finikon. The bridge once stretched across an outer moat filled with seawater and could draw back to cut the castle off entirely from the mainland. A second construction phase in the late 15th century added the now-distinctive stout towers and elaborate double walls. Unlike the ruins to the city's south, the fortress remains incredibly well preserved and is one of the best examples of medieval architecture in all of Greece. Those who make like the knights and patrol the tops of the exterior walls will be rewarded with unbeatable views from the former lookout and weaponry holes. (☎22420 27 927. Open Tu-Su 8:30am-3pm; last entrance at 2:30pm. €3, students €2, EU students free.)

In Pl. Platanou, the **plane tree of Hippocrates,** allegedly planted by the great physician 2400 years ago, has grown to an enormous 12m in diameter; it's so big that metal bars now support its branches. While it is alluring to envision Hippocrates teaching and writing beneath its noble foliage, the tree is actually only 500 years old, suggesting that the legend is honorary rather than historically accurate.

Among Kos's **Roman ruins** stands a desolate pair of Corinthian columns and the scattered remains of what was once a lively **agora** in the 4th century BC. The uninspiring field of broken masonry, in the heart of the Old City, has little more than unruly weeds, empty beer cans, and unremarkable stones. Other poorly tended ruins include the **Temple of Dionysus** and the **West Archaeological Area**, on Grigoriou E', where only the occasional plaque or broken obelisk separates the otherwise indistinguishable rocks. The West Archaeological Area does, however, contain an excellent floor **mosaic** of Europa's abduction by Zeus in the guise of a bull. As you walk down Grigoriou E', look on the other side of the road to see the noteworthy 3rd-century **Odeon** (Roman theater) and the **Casa Romana** villa which is currently being restored, but is scheduled to open soon. English labels guide you around the modest collection of Hellenistic through late-Roman sculptures in the **Archaeological Museum**. The 4th-century sculpture (presumably of Hippocrates) that graces the northwestern room and the central courtyard's Roman mosaic depicting Asclepius's arrival on Kos definitely merit a visit. (In Pl. Eleftherias. ☎22420 28 326. Open Tu-Su 8am-2:30pm. €3, students €2, EU students free.)

▣ NIGHTLIFE

Exuberance permeates the very air of Kos Town, where the party never stops. By 11pm, the masses converge around **Nafklirou** in the Old City and along **Porfirou** in the New City, between Averof and Zouroudi. In both areas, beers go for €3-6 and mixed drinks for €6-8. The sly greeters standing outside the bars are armed with clever ploys to reel in passing Anglophones. Unfortunately, the ubiquitous 2-for-1 drink specials often mean one standard-sized drink with a free miniature sidekick.

The cavernous, red and chrome **Fashion Club,** Kanari 2, by the Dolphin Roundabout, hosts Kos's wildest nights, attracting both trendy locals and tourists looking for a posh scene. Huge television screens broadcast the detached cool of runway models and funky wax-drip candelabras create an intimate atmosphere. Three bars, two dance floors, and a 1700-person capacity make Fashion Club Kos's biggest and most ostentatious nightclub. Wednesday night beauty contests and Sunday night dance marathons offer cash prizes of up to €300. (☎22420 22 592. Happy hour until midnight. Outdoor cafe no cover. Club cover F-Sa €10; includes 1 drink. Open daily 11pm-4am; cafe opens 7pm.) **Hamam Club,** Nafklirou 1, is inland from the Pl. Diagoras taxi station in the Old City. Outside, a 30-something touristy crowd gathers to hear live covers of popular songs and sip drinks

drunken crowds and keep your wits about you. In general, however, it's very strange for a woman to go out drinking alone, and this is particularly noticeable in bars frequented by locals. In such establishments, talk with the bartender or with other women (if there are any) to avoid unwanted overtures.

Greeks are not booty-shakers by nature, but enough alcohol will get them dancing. Avoid suggestive bumping and grinding unless you want the added attention, and refuse a potential dance partner unless you want to be dancing with him all night. Although some advise that a wedding band might prevent pick-ups, even the biggest bling won't put off a determined Greek suitor.

If a lusty guy won't stop bothering you, say "AH-se-meh!" meaning "leave me alone." If that fails, get the attention of a local woman, who, used to this game of sexual politics, will likely tell the guy off in not-so-nice terms and send him away, tail between his legs. This is especially effective on smaller islands, where the bar's clientele probably already know each another well.

If you there is someone who sparks your interest, returning the stare will signal to him that it's okay to proceed. If he is still interested, he'll send over a drink. If you're female, he'll be interested. Choose carefully, though—once you start talking, he'll expect to be with you the rest of the night.

—*Laurie Schnidman*

until around midnight. Afterward, the stone walls of this former Turkish bath echo with Greek, house, and American hits as young locals take to the dance floor. (☎22420 24 938. Mixed drinks €6. July and Aug. cover €5; includes 1 drink.) **Heaven,** on Zouroudi opposite the beach, often hosts guest DJs and, once the season gets going, has foam parties every Wednesday inside its sleek, metal-colored club room. Take Averof away from the harbor to K. Porfyriou, turn right, and follow the road as it bends left; continue walking for about 5min., past the sign for Petros Beach. (☎22420 23 874. Beer €4. Mixed drinks €7. Cover €10 for special events and guest DJs; includes 1 drink. Open M-Th, Su 10am-4am, F-Sa 10am-dawn.)

📌 DAYTRIPS FROM KOS TOWN

🏛 THE ASCLEPION

About 4km southwest of Kos Town. Take a 15min. ride on the blue mini-train to get there in summer. By bike or moped follow the sign west off the main road and go straight; taxis €6-7. ☎22420 28 763. Open Tu-Su 8am-2:30pm. €4, students €2.

The Asclepion was an ancient sanctuary devoted to Asclepius, the god of healing. In the 5th century BC, **Hippocrates** founded the world's first medical school and hospital here and forever changed the course of science and man's understanding of the body. Combining early priests' techniques with his own, Hippocrates made Kos ancient Greece's leading medical center. Present-day doctors still travel here to take their Hippocratic oaths and to pay homage to the original mastermind.

Most of the ruins date from the 2nd and 3rd centuries BC. The complex was built on three levels, called *"andirons,"* which were carved into a hill overlooking Kos Town, the Aegean, and the coast of Turkey. Although the intimidating staircases sit directly under the beating sun, trees surround the site and dot each level, providing much-needed shade and creating pleasant areas to gaze at the view while sitting on a historically important stone. The lowest *andiron* holds a complex of 3rd-century Roman baths, complete with a *natatio* (swimming pool), *tepidarium* (lukewarm pool), and *caldarium* (sauna); it was once home to the medical school and the anatomy and pathology museums. Elegant 2nd-century columns remain standing on the second level, which once contained a temple to Asclepius and a temple to Apollo. The 60-step climb to the third *andiron* leads to the forested remnants of the main **Temple of Asclepius** and a paramount view of the site, the town below, and Asia Minor across the sea. Although the temple is remarkably preserved, much of its structure is gone, recycled by the Knights of St. John in the building of the Kos Castle. The spectacular view and what remains of the once-grand layout, however, are still very impressive.

NORTHERN KOS

The Empros Thermae (hot springs) are east of Kos Town, along the coastal road; catch 1 of the regular buses at the town center (€1.20). The bus drops you off at the top of a steep cliff path which you have to descend to get to the springs. Open 24hr. Free.

The **Empros Thermae** are northern Kos's main attraction, drawing those with dermatological ailments or simply too much stress to its piping-hot, healing waters. Breathing in its sulfuric vapors while sitting elbow to elbow with shingles patients, however, may not exactly make your muscles melt in relaxation. Going in the evening when the medical and tourist crowds have somewhat dissipated allows for a more peaceful soak. Along the western coast, a small road suitable for biking extends parallel to the main road, giving ample opportunity to take a bike tour of the gorgeous island's less-visited areas. Sandy **Lampi beach** lies just a few kilometers northwest of Kos Town. About 8km from town, the beautiful **Selveri beach** has clear sand, shallow waters, and a panorama of the Turkish coast. Along the beach, the rusted husks of anti-Turkish artillery posts jut out like strange cattails, though as the tide at Selveri has been steadily encroaching on the land, some of these outposts are now half-submerged in the water. It is difficult to reach the beach without private transportation or a bike; as a result, it remains blissfully deserted.

CENTRAL KOS
Continue southwest along the minor coastal road.

The tourist resort beaches of **Tigaki**—"Sea sports and amusement on the waves!" promises the Kos travel brochure—and **Marmari**, both under 20km from Kos Town, are disappointingly developed. The savvy (and free-spirited) head for the middle section of the coast, overlooked by corporate conglomerates, where casinos have been replaced by a secluded nude beach. Close by, at **Aliki Salt Lake,** you may be able to spot a handful of loggerhead sea turtles coming to the northern coastline to lay eggs in the summer. Much farther south, along the main road, lies the village of **Antimachia,** worth visiting only for its annual **Honey Festival** in August. To the south of Antimachia lie the serene forests of **Plaka,** just past the airport, where full-feathered peacocks idly parade around in a truly stunning sight. Travelers should avoid **Kardamena** to the east, a slightly smaller version of Kos Town with all of the tourist industry but none of the charm.

SOUTHERN KOS
A moped allows unobstructed exploration; a taxi (€6-7) also does the trick. Heading south lands you at Camel; Paradise and Magic beaches are just beyond, with bright-white sand and breathtaking views of the southern peninsula. The bus (1hr., 6 per day 9:10am-9pm, €2.80) will let you off at any of the beaches.

Hills, ravines, and the occasional pasture roll across Southern Kos, surrounded by the island's most worthy **beaches.** A few ancient columns mark **Kefalos,** Kos's ancient capital, whose modern, crowded, and colorless town can be easily passed over for its surrounding beaches. North of Kefalos, the beach of **Agios Stephanos** lies next to well-preserved ruins of a basilica. Visitors can lie in the shade of olive trees among crumbling walls or swim to a nearby rocky islet, crowned with a small blue and white church. On the opposite side of the peninsula is the deserted, pebbly beach of **Agios Theologos,** whose foamy green waves batter the shore.

ASTYPALEA Αστυπάλια

Nicknamed "Banquet of the Gods" by the ancient Greeks due to its high-quality fish, bountiful flowers, and overflowing honey, Astypalea draws summer crowds of city-weary Greeks ready for astounding mountain-top views and a taste of a quieter life. Although local tourism spikes in July and August, few foreign travelers venture to this butterfly-shaped island, making Astypalea refreshingly off the beaten-to-the-ground path. Those who brave the ferry schedules and find their way here will discover pristine beaches, peaceful mountain hikes, relics of a rich history, and warm locals proud of their island's past and present.

ASTYPALEA TOWN ☎22430

Although development has begun to crawl into the neighboring villages of Livadi and Maltezana, Astypalea Town is still the heart of the island, with many of its services and residents. The town is composed of two main areas: Pera Gialos, the lower area by the port, and Chora, the section atop the steep hill. Picturesque white and blue houses cluster around the main road that connects the two areas as it snakes steeply uphill. Daunting staircases line the small side streets, providing a rather strenuous shortcut from the winding main road.

☐ TRANSPORTATION. Flights leave from **Astypalea Airport** and go to Athens (45min., 4 per week, €53) and Rhodes (1½hr., 3 per week, €46) via Kos (1hr., €46) and Leros (20min., €41). All flights are on Olympic Airlines; contact **Astypalea Tours** (☎22430 61 571) for schedules and tickets. **Ferries** head to: Amorgos (3hr., 3 per week, €12); Donousa (5hr., 2 per week, €13.30); Kalymnos (2½hr., 2 per week, €13); Kos (4hr., 1 per week, €13); Naxos (6hr., 4 per week, €27); Nisyros (5hr., 1 per week, €9.40); Paros (8hr., 4 per week, €28); Piraeus (12hr., 5 per week, €33.45); Rhodes (9-11hr., 2 per week, €21); Syros (9hr., 3 per week, €16); Tilos (6hr., 1 per week, €12). Confirm all ferry schedules at the **tourist office**, as they change regularly. **No hydrofoils or Flying Dolphins** serve the island. **Kostas Taxi** (☎69732 57 350) is available 24hr. **Vergouli Rent a Car** (☎22430 61 351), right behind the museum on the main road, rents **cars** (from €20; insurance included) to those over 21 and **motorbikes** (from €12). Open daily 9am-2pm and 4-9pm. **Buses** run to Livadi (30min., 3 per day, €1) and Maltezana (30min., 3 per day, €1). They leave from the bus station near the police and taxi stand, at the center of Pera Gialos, and stop several times before reaching their end destinations. During high season, the frequency often increases; check with the tourist office for schedules. The chalkboard near the bus stop lists specific times.

⚡🔊 ORIENTATION AND PRACTICAL INFORMATION. As Astypalea's settled areas are relatively small, getting around its unnamed streets is surprisingly easy. The main road starts at the port and continues to the right through the center of **Pera Gialos,** then turns left to head uphill to **Chora.** Once in Chora's main plaza, follow the road uphill to the left to reach the **castle,** or take the road right to the giant **windmills** and toward **Livadi.** A small **tourist office** is located on the docks. The amazingly friendly, English-speaking staff offers **maps,** ferry and bus schedules, and information and tips about the island. (☎22430 61 778; www.astypalaia.com. Open daily 10am-2pm and 6-10pm.) **Astypalea Tours,** up the hill on the main road just past the museum, sells airline and ferry tickets, can help decode schedules, and provides suggestions for accommodations. (☎22430 61 571. Open daily 9am-2pm and 5-9pm.) The **National Bank** is located under Hotel Paradissos on the main road near the port. (☎22430 61 224. Open daily 9am-2pm.) **Commercial Bank,** next to the police station, has a **24hr. ATM.** (☎22430 61 402. Open M-Sa 9am-2pm.) You can find the **police** (☎22430 61 207) in a white building with a Greek flag on the main road in Pera Gialos. The **port police** are in the same office. The **health center** (☎22430 61 222) is in the main plaza in Chora. In an **emergency,** call ☎69793 76 783 to reach the doctor. Midway up the main road between Pera Gialos and Chora is the **pharmacy.** (☎22430 61 544. Open M-Sa 9am-1:30pm and 6-10:30pm.) The **post office** sits on the main road, just before the central plaza in Chora. **Western Union** is available. (Open M-Sa 7:30am-noon.) **Postal Code:** 85900.

📷🍴 ACCOMMODATIONS AND FOOD. Although numerous accommodations exist, most are pricey studios and apartments aimed at summering Athenians. Less-expensive options cluster in Pera Gialos, and until the season picks up in mid-July, finding a room is fairly easy, and hotel owners may be willing to negotiate. When getting off at the port, follow the main road to find 🏨**Hotel Astynea ❷.** Palatial rooms with soaring ceilings include A/C, baths, fridges, TV, and more closet space than any backpacker would know what to do with. Private balconies overlooking the water are an added bonus. (☎22430 61 040. Singles €15-20; doubles €20-30; triples €30-40. MC/V.) For those wanting to stay closer to Chora, **Hotel**

Aegean ❷, about 50m uphill on the main road across from the gas station, rents spotless rooms with baths, fridges, TV, and balconies. Look for the owner in his china shop on the first floor. (☎22430 61 236. Doubles €25-35; triples €35-45.) **Camping Astypalea ❶**, 2.5km east of town, has clean bathrooms, a mini-mart, and a taverna that offers €5 barbecue dinners. Take the bus toward Maltezana (15min., €1) or follow the signs from the port. (☎22430 61 900. €5 per person, €2 per tent.) Camping anywhere else is **illegal**, and this rule is strictly enforced.

Restaurants cluster near the waterfront and on Chora's square. For a break from purely traditional fare, take the road behind the windmills in Chora to find ▨**Aiolos ❶**, a pizzeria that puts a distinctly Greek spin on the crispy-crusted Italian classic. The Aegean (€4.10) comes topped with shrimp, mussels, and gouda, and the Greek pizza (€3.50) is piled with tomatoes, olives, onions, and feta. (☎22430 61 359. Pizzas €3-5. Open daily 6pm-1am.) **To Akrogiali ❷** serves only the freshest of fish along with a variety of standard Greek dishes. From the main road in Pera Gialos, walk down onto the beach. The gigantic shrimp with feta and tomatoes (€8) and the flavorful grilled octopus (€5) taste even better when you eat them with your toes wriggling in the sand. (☎22430 61 863. Open daily 8am-2am.) At **Meltemi ❶**, in Chora's central plaza, locals gather day and night for coffee, drinks, and snacks. (☎22430 61 479. Greek salad €3. Beer €2. Open daily 8am-2am.)

🔲 ◪ **SIGHTS AND BEACHES.** The teeny **Archaeological Museum,** in Pera Gialos on the main road to Chora, just inland from the waterfront, houses a well-presented collection of artifacts unearthed from around the island. Amazingly preserved jars, tools, and other daily objects from the 2nd and 3rd centuries BC are displayed alongside fragments from Hellenistic sculptures and early-Christian pieces. Helpful English-language plaques by each item make the museum particularly accessible. (Open Tu-Sa 9:30am-1:30pm and 7-10pm. Free.) The Knights of St. John strike again in Chora, with the hilltop **kastro** that they built as a line of defense. Inside the stone walls of this medieval fortress are two quaint whitewashed churches, **Panagia of Kastro** and **Agios Giorgios.** Although the site is remarkably intact, it is currently undergoing restorations, so visitors are cautioned to tread lightly and beware of loose and falling stones. Despite the potentially perilous rocks and the long hike to the top, the views from the *kastro*'s peepholes are breathtaking. A striking row of **windmills** lines the main road near Chora's central plaza, and leads the way up to two more notable religious sites—the **Megali Panagia** on the road to the right and the **Portiaitissa Monastery** on the road to the left.

The beach at **Livadi** is only a few minutes' walk down the hill from Chora, but it becomes quite crowded over the summer. A 20min. hike southwest along the coast takes you to **Tzanaki beach,** a beautiful, uncrowded stretch that welcomes nude bathers. Four kilometers farther along a dirt path, the pebbly beach at **Agios Konstantinos** is one of Astypalea's best. Tranquil, secluded beaches like **Kaminakia** and **Vatses** lie in the southwestern part of the island, past Tzanaki, but are difficult to find without private transportation and good directions. From there, the hidden cave of **Vatses** is accessible by boat. A right turn after the sixth windmill in Chora begins the perilous 1hr. drive along a circuitous route that leads past a military base to the monastery of **Agios Ioannis.** The monastery overlooks a small waterfall which is perhaps the most charming sight on the island. Northeast of Astypalea Town, the main road leads toward the other "wing" of the butterfly-shaped island, passing the campsite and several sandy beaches. Another cave, **Spilia Negrou,** is in the northwestern section of this part of the island. Both of Astypalea's famous caves are dark and potentially dangerous to those unfamiliar with their geography. Knowledgable guides, however, are happy to lead even the most inexperienced visitor through them; the tourist office can help put you in contact with a guide. Wear sturdy shoes, and bring a flashlight.

Astypalea's locals have recently begun a concerted effort to facilitate exploration of the island's lesser developed areas. A **rock-climbing** area recently opened near Livadi, featuring planned climbs geared toward every level of difficulty. The site is free, but climbers should plan on bringing their own gear; an equipment rental system is in the works for the near future. If scaling a mountain seems a bit much, you can follow one of the newly marked **hiking trails** that start from the climbing area. Four different routes, between 90min. and 4hr. and of varying difficulty, wind down the mountain. Friendly, helpful **George Giannoulis** (☎22430 61 750; giannoulis@KLM.forthnet.gr), one of the organizers of this endeavor, is the ultimate source for information about Astypalea's outdoor opportunities.

KALYMNOS Κάλυμνος

Once famous for the "Kalymnian gold" its sponge divers fished up from the depths of the sea, Kalymnos's economy—and its golden reputation—has plunged. In the past, sponges were so valuable that Kalymniot men would spend five or six months of the year diving in the Libyan Sea. Today, however, sponges are of commercial value only to the extent that they can be hawked to tourists. The island's government has thus focused extensively on building its tourism industry, though these efforts have not had tremendous success. This is in part because locals are unwilling to pander to foreigners, but difficult ferry schedules are the biggest reason intense tourism has not flourished here. Kalymnos, however, does have many hidden treasures and natural sights to offer to those who make it there. The interior's rugged mountains cascade into wide beaches and blue-green water, delighting both divers and rock-climbers, and travelers can take advantage of Kalymnos's tourist facilities without the typically corresponding mob.

POTHIA Πόθια   ☎22430

Talk to a local, and he will proudly tell you that Kalymniots are the only "real" Greek islanders; they retain a vibrant culture, live there year-round, and shun the tourist-luring behavior so prevalent on other islands. A large, bustling port town, Pothia maintains the goods and services of a happening metropolis without spoiling its thriving local culture. Fast, fashionable youth nonchalantly speed by on motorbikes, but for the most part, life in Pothia is slow; in the port, people go to bed early and, except for July and August, most local bars are closed by 1am.

▐ TRANSPORTATION

Ferries: To: **Agathonisi** (6hr., 4 per week, €9.50); **Alexandroupoli** (20hr., 1 per week, €38.50); **Arki** (5hr., 4 per week, €8.50); **Astypalea** (3hr., 3 per week, €10.50); **Chios** (7½hr., 1 per week, €20); **Kos Town** (1hr., 6 per week, €6); **Leros** (1½hr., 6 per week, €9); **Limnos** (16hr., 1 per week, €34.50); **Lipsi** (2¾hr., 4 per week 7am, €9); **Mytilini** (10hr., 1 per week, €29.50); **Patmos** (4hr., 6 per week, €10); **Piraeus** (12hr., 4 per week, €35); **Rhodes** (5hr., 8 per week, €18); **Samos** (4hr., 1 per week, €18).

High-speed boats: Flying Dolphins go to: **Kos** (30min., 7 per week, €12); **Leros** (40min., 7 per week, €15); **Lipsi** (1hr., 7 per week, €15); **Patmos** (1¾hr., 7 per week, €20); **Samos** (2hr., 7 per week, €25.50). The **Catamaran Dodecanisos Express** runs to: **Kos** (40min., Tu-Su 3:30pm, €10.20); **Leros** (1hr., 6 per week, €15.40); **Lipsi** (2hr., 4 per week, €15.10); **Patmos** (1½hr., 4 per week, €20.10); **Rhodes** (3hr., daily 3:30pm, €35); **Symi** (2½hr.; W, F, Su 3:30pm, €28.50).

Buses: Leave from just past town hall in the harbor center. 16 times per day 6:50am-10pm to: **Hora** (10min., €0.30); **Kastelli** (50min., €0.90); **Massouri** (25min., €0.75); **Myrties** (20min., €0.75); **Panormos** (15min., €0.60). Buses also go to: **Argos** (8am, 1pm; €0.60); **Emporios** (9am, 4pm; €0.90); **Platy Gialos** (3 per day 9am-6:10pm, €0.75); **Vlihadia** (6 per day 7am-7:10pm, €0.60). The bus to **Vathis** (4 per day 6:30am-6pm, €0.90) departs from the far end of the waterfront, past the town hall when walking from the dock. Buy tickets at Themis mini-mart, next to the town hall; on the bus, insert them into the automated validating box or hand them to the driver.

Excursion Boats: Round-trip boats to the beaches on **Pserimos** (€3-6) and **Vlichadi** (€8) leave 9-10am from the harbor and return 5-6pm. Also go to **Bodrum, Turkey** (€30; bus tour in Bodrum included), **Leros** (€27), **Lipsi** (€27), and **Patmos** (€36). Inquire at **Magos Tours** (☎22430 28777) for more information.

Taxis: ☎22430 50 300. In Pl. Kyprou. €1 extra for port-side pickup. Available 24hr.

Rentals: Renting a vehicle is easy in Pothia, as similarly priced options line the waterfront and the sidestreets. If something seems too expensive, it probably is; head a few doors down to do some comparison shopping. **Kostas Moto Rentals** (☎22430 50 110), to the left of the port police when walking inland, rents **mopeds** with normal insurance for €10-12 per day. International driving license required. Open daily 9am-1pm and 2-9pm. **AVIS Rent A Car** (☎22430 51 630) is directly behind the church in the square by the town hall. Car rentals with full insurance from €35.

✈🔢 ORIENTATION AND PRACTICAL INFORMATION

Ferries arrive at the far left end of the port (facing inland). The road from the dock bends around the waterfront, and after a while becomes the road to **Vathi**. About halfway down the waterfront, this road meets a square that contains the large, cream-colored municipal building, a church, the Nautical Museum, and the town hall. Narrow, shop-lined **Eleftherias** heads in one direction inland at this point, leading to **Plateia Kyprou**, home to the taxi stand and pay phones, and, just beyond, the post office. Continue on Eleftherias to reach **Horio, Myrties,** and **Massouri.**

Tourist Office: A small tourist **kiosk** (☎22430 50 879; www.kalymnos-isl.gr) on the ferry dock is sometimes open when boats arrive. If you happen to catch someone in the office, he or she can provide free **maps** and help you bargain with hostels.

Budget Travel: Magos Tours (☎22430 28 777), on the main road next to Ciao Cafe, before the road curves to the right; look for the Blue Star Ferries sign. Sells ferry, hydrofoil, catamaran, and excursion tickets, as well as airline tickets from nearby Kos. Open daily 8:30am-4pm and 5:30-10pm.

Banks: A few banks along the waterfront have full services. **National Bank** (☎22430 51 501; open M-Th 8am-2:30pm, F 8am-2pm), on the waterfront, has a **24hr. ATM** and **currency exchange.** A few blocks farther inland, the **Agricultural Bank** (☎22430 28 305; open M-F 8am-2:30pm) also has an **ATM** and will **exchange currency.**

Police: ☎22430 22 100. Go up Eleftherias and take the left road inland from the taxi stand. In a blue and yellow building on the right. Open 24hr.

Hospital: ☎22430 23 025. On the main road to Hora, 3km from Pothia. Open 24hr.

Internet: Neon Internet C@fe (☎22430 28 343), on the waterfront in front of the ferry deck. 2 aging computers, full bar, and ice cream. €5 per hr. Open daily 7am-late. Its 2nd location, on a back street a few blocks behind the bus stop, has 1 slow computer, but charges only €3 per hr. Pool tables, video games, and a full bar make this location a teenage hangout. Open daily 9am-late.

Post Office: ☎22430 28 340. Up Eleftherias, just past the police station on the right. Has **currency exchange.** Open M-F 7:30am-2pm. **Postal Code:** 85200.

⚄ ⚄ ACCOMMODATIONS AND FOOD

Many of Pothia's accommodations are mediocre. Much nicer rooms are available in Myrties and Platy Gialos, though you can find decent lodgings by the port. The tourist information kiosk at the harbor maintains an exhaustive list of area accommodations and tracks customer satisfaction for each. Immediately out of the port, along the waterfront, is ▓Greek House ❷, above Ta Adelvia Flaskov Cafe. Though the rickety, treehouse-like stairs may be daunting, the rooms at the top are worth the climb. Most of the breezy, simply decorated suites have separate rooms for the living area and kitchen, along with French-doored balconies with panoramic harbor views. All rooms have TV, A/C, and private baths. If the Greek House is full, lovely owner Papadi will help you find another room. (☎22430 29 559. Singles €20-25; doubles €35. Rooms for 3 or more also available. Some haggling permitted.) **Pension Niki ❷** offers small but comfortable peach-colored rooms with TV, fridges, A/C, and baths. Niki's daughter Maria will be waiting at the docks if there are any vacancies. If you don't see her, head inland at the National Bank and follow the road as it curves to the right. Just past the wedding store, follow the sign for the pension, which points down the side street. (☎22430 48 135. Singles €20-25; doubles €25-30.) **Hotel Therme ❷** is on the waterfront before the town hall, above Cafe Kaike (look for the tiled sign hanging from a balcony). Therme keeps it hot with a 70s motel vibe that features retro turquoise halls, rotary phones, and olive-green bathroom fixtures. If you need to chill out, step onto the patio or switch on the A/C. (☎22430 29 425. Singles €20-25; doubles €25-35.) **Camping**, though uncommon, is legal on all the island's beaches.

A couple of good dining options are hidden among the standard array of waterfront tavernas and pizzerias, which are themselves better than those on most islands. ▓Thraka ❶, on the waterfront near Hotel Therme, prides itself on having souvlaki-shack prices with the quality and atmosphere of a good taverna. The astoundingly huge grill platters (€6-8) feature every kind of meat known to Greeks, fries, pita, and *tzatziki*. (☎22430 28 888. Gyros €1.50. Souvlaki €2.50. Open daily 9am-3pm and 5:30pm-late.) The octopus balls (€4) and the cheapest Greek salad in town (€2.50) hit the spot at **Orea Kalymnos ❷**, on the waterfront just past the town hall. (☎69488 30 028. Open daily noon-1am.)

⚄ ⚄ SIGHTS AND BEACHES

The **Nautical Museum,** on the second floor of a building a few doors down from the town hall, explains the life and work of the island's sponge divers. Though there are only a few signs (and fewer in English), a plethora of pictures tiles the walls, and a few of the old scuba suits are on display. For first-hand information, ask the English-speaking curator, a former diver. (☎22430 51 361. Open M-F 8am-1:30pm. €1.50.) The grossly misnamed **Archaeological Museum of Kalymnos** contains few artifacts. Its three paltry rooms are housed in the reconstructed former mansion of sponge barons Catherine and Nikolaos Vouvalis, with whom the museum is much more concerned. (☎22430 23 113. Open Tu-F 8am-2pm. Free.)

The sandy **beach** just to the left of the port police has clear water but a rather industrial backdrop. From the port police, take the road to the left to reach the beach at **Therma,** only 1km out of town. Arthritic patients once came to the sanitarium to wade in its soothing **sulfur mineral baths,** but now that its therapeutic reputation has declined, a pleasant, crowded beach has become Therma's main draw. A short walk around the bend leads to a quiet swimming spot. **Vlihadia beach,** 5km from Pothia and west of Therma, is perhaps the best beach on the island, with crystal-clear waters, fewer patrons than neighboring locales, and the **scuba diving** center, the only state-run facility of its kind. The center provides equipment and instruction for both beginners and seasoned divers. With over 12km of continuous approved diving area, this is the largest site in Greece. (☎22430 51 818. 1st group lesson €45, equipment included; discounts for subsequent sessions.) The **Sea World Museum** at the port in Vlihadia contains more sponge diving memorabilia and various underwater finds. (☎22430 50 662. Open daily 10am-10pm. €2, free with scuba session.) Each year at the end of August, divers from around the world descend upon the island for the **Annual International Kalymnos Diving Festival** to try out new gear, visit the trade show, and enjoy nightly parties. (☎22430 59 056 for specific info.)

Grass, wildflowers, mandarins, limes, and grapes cover the **Vathis Valley** (5.5km northeast of Pothia), which begins at **Rina** village. There's no beach here, but you can safely swim from the pier. Within swimming range on the northern side of the inlet is **Daskalio,** a stalagmite cave that you can explore on foot.

🎵 🎭 ENTERTAINMENT AND NIGHTLIFE

For a calm evening, **Cine Oasis,** at the end of a short alleyway off the waterfront, before the town hall, plays movies in English with Greek subtitles. The glass displays list current features and times. The building's open-air courtyard doubles as a community auditorium when it's not showing movies. (Tickets €5, children €4.)

In the words of one cab driver, people in Pothia have a "program": they eat from 8 to 10pm, drink coffee at the harbor until midnight, and then head up to the clubs in Massouri until sunrise. While this is undeniably true for the younger set, older and more low-key crowds fill Pothia's own lively cafes and bars until the wee hours. The ◪**Victor Hugo Galerie Bistro** is more high-class than high school. From the waterfront, go inland by the National Bank. Make the first left and follow the winding road until it turns right; the bistro is 50m farther. French owner and art scholar Charles Coulouriotis displays local art and reproductions of famous museum exhibits in an upscale, intimate environment. Patrons gather to sip after-dinner brandies, listen to hushed jazzy infusions, and discuss the finer points of art history. Although a variety of beverages are available, patrons are under no obligation to buy a drink; as Charles insists, the emphasis is on "galerie," and the cafe is simply a forum to discuss the works exhibited. A quiet evening here might replenish some of the brain cells wiped out by Massouri's alcoholic haze. **Blue Note** (☎22430 50 888), by the waterfront statue of Poseidon, mixes a wide variety of drinks (€3-6) for locals who mingle beneath palm trees bathed in aquamarine light. The wood and steel outdoor tables are just removed enough to allow for conversation over the techno and rock beats; the socially awkward can avoid that whole talking thing inside, where the music is so loud you just have to smile and nod. (Open 8am-late.) **Neon Internet C@fe,** favored by young, loud, motorbiking males, satisfies late-night solitaire cravings. (Beer €2. Open daily 9:30am-late.)

WESTERN COAST OF KALYMNOS ☎22430

The road north from Pothia is lined with intermingling villages. The first of these, **Hora,** was Kalymnos's capital until the threat of piracy made seaside living too dangerous. Scattered churches line Hora's streets, including the **Church of Christ Jerusalem,** built by Byzantine emperor Arcadius after he survived a storm at sea. The half-domed stone blocks with carved inscriptions are from a 4th-century BC temple to Apollo that stood on the same site. The beachside footpath leads to a quiet **cove** with strange and wonderful rock formations—though they often hide sea urchins ready to injure those not wearing waterproof shoes. Kalymnos also boasts some incredible cliffs for **rock climbing.** There are about 20 climbing areas located between Pothia and Emborios with 550 routes of varying levels of difficulty, ranging from level 4c to 9a. The **Municipal Athletic Organization** (☎22430 51 056; www.kalymnos-isl.gr/climb) has incredibly useful, specific info. Numerous mapped-out **hiking routes** cover the island and its surrounding islets, providing the opportunity to walk through the mountains, along the coast, through gorges and orchards, or all of the above. The **Municipal Tourist Organization** can provide detailed maps. (☎22430 59 056; www.kalymnos-isl.gr.)

> **PEACE AND QUIET FOR POCKET CHANGE.** Tired of loud, crazy Massouri? For €1.50, hop on a boat to vehicle-free, tranquil Telendo, an islet less than 1km away. Pristine pebble and sand beaches with nary a motorbike within earshot will revive even the most party-weary. A few pensions and tavernas line the waterfront. Boats leave from Myrties every 15-20min. 6am-midnight, and return at the same frequency.

The village of **Kantouni,** home to a popular if slightly unremarkable **beach** south of Panormos, is accessible by the Kasteli bus from Pothia. If you have both energy and waterproof shoes, clamber over the rocks past Domus Restaurant for about 10min. to reach the black-sand beach of **Plati Yialos. Pension Plati Yialos ❷** has rooms that overlook the coast from the cliffside. (☎22430 47 029. Doubles €25-30.) **Domus Restaurant and Bar ❷,** on the far end of the beach in Kantouni, is a nice place to sip a martini and watch the sunset. (☎22430 25 058. Mixed drinks €5.50. Restaurant open daily 7pm-1am; bar open daily 11am-4am.) **Cafe Del Mar ❷,** where the bus stops, transforms daily from a relaxing beachside cafe to a chill bar popular with Pothia's young clubbing crowd. On the weekends, patrons dance until dawn to American and Greek beats. (☎22430 48 018. Cafe open daily 8am-late.)

The mere mention of **Massouri** lights up the faces of young Kalymniots. With only one paved road, all the bars and clubs in this beloved nighttime destination are within a 10min. walk of one another. The last bus to Massouri departs at 10:20pm, but you'll find little to do in town before 1am; grabbing a taxi (€6-8.50; €15 after midnight) is recommended. The ever-lively Massouri **beach,** filled with local hipsters playing volleyball, stretches below the main street and down a steep cliff. **Stavedo Beach Cafe ❷** (☎22430 47 696; www.stavedo.com) provides snacks in the daytime and drinks at night. (Greek salad €4. Drinks €3-7. Open daily 10am-late. 2-for-1 happy hour 7-9pm.) Past the curve in the road from the bus stop, **Nadir Rock Cafe** plays classic rock under a Jim Morrison poster's watchful eye. (☎69746 06 471. Happy hour for draft beer 4-6pm, for mixed drinks 7-9pm. Open daily 4pm-late.) A few doors down is sizzlin' club **La Loca,** which spins house and R&B in its red and orange modern art interior. (☎22430 47 047. Karaoke every F. Cover €6 on Sa only; includes 1 drink. Open daily 10pm-late; in low season F-Sa only.) If the bus brings you into town early, **Neon Internet C@fe** (☎22430 48 318) can serve both your emailing (€3 per 30min.) and pre-gaming needs.

PATMOS Πάτμος

Lush mountainsides and acres of blooming wildflowers sprawl over Patmos, famed for its devotional and culinary masterworks. Ancient Patmians worshiped the huntress goddess Artemis, said to have raised the island from the sea. However, with the arrival of St. John, exiled from Ephesus in AD 95, Patmos became a center of fledgling Christianity. John purportedly wrote the Book of Revelations here, in a grotto overlooking the main town. In the 4th century, a basilica replaced the razed Temple of Artemis; in 1088 the fortified Monastery of St. John was built on a hill overlooking the entire island. This former "Jerusalem of the Aegean" now draws a less pious and more vacation-minded crowd to its holy hills. The narrow, well-balanced island offers a mix of tourist amenities and tranquil escapes, its local culture gloriously unaffected by the hordes of cruise ships that dock for the day. Whether meditating at the monastery or pursuing more temporal activities, almost everyone will find something praiseworthy about Patmos.

SKALA Σκάλα ☎22470

Built along a graceful arc of coastline, the colorful port town of Skala is mirrored by a virtual city of yachts docked in the water. Squeezed between its cafes and tourist shops, you'll find bakeries, traditional *ouzeria*, and the thriving undercurrent of a local artist community. The town's sense of creativity is immediately apparent; stores, cafes, and offices are all filled with handmade pottery and funky crafts. Skala is the most convenient place to stay on Patmos, as all administrative and practical offices converge around the port. A 10min. bus or moped ride connects you with most major villages and sights, and a 15min. walk gets you to the beach on the other side of the island.

⌐ TRANSPORTATION

Ferries: Tickets can be purchased at offices near the plateia; Blue Star tickets available at Apollon Travel. Ferries go to: **Kalymnos** (3hr., 2-3 per day, €9); **Kos** (4hr., 2-3 per day, €14); **Leros** (1hr., 2-3 per day, €8); **Lipsi** (1½hr., 5 per week, €4); **Piraeus** (10-12hr., 2 per week, €30.40); **Rhodes** (8hr., 2 per week, €27); **Samos** (3hr., 6 per week, €6); **Syros** (7hr., 2 per week, €24.50).

Flying Dolphins: 6 per week to **Rhodes** (5hr., €27.50) via **Kos.** 2 per day to: **Kalymnos** (1½hr., €20); **Kos** (2hr., €22.10); **Leros** (50min., €12); **Lipsi** (20min., €9); **Samos** (2½hr., €14). 2 per week to **Agathonissi** (1hr., €13).

Excursion boats: To **Lipsi, Fourni,** and **Ikaria;** prices are posted by the waterfront.

Buses: Next to the Welcome Cafe at the ferry docks. To **Grikos** (20min., 7 per day 9:30am-7:30pm, €1), **Hora** (10min., 10 per day 7:40am-8:40pm, €1), and **Kampos** (20min., 4 per day 8:15am-6:30pm, €1). Purchase tickets onboard.

Taxis: ☎22470 31 225. Congregate in main plateia 24hr. in summer, but can be difficult to catch elsewhere, especially during the post-disco flurry from 3-6:30am.

Rentals: Rent A Car Patmos (☎/fax 22470 32 923). Just behind the building with the post office and police, next to the Art Cafe. Cars from €35 per day. 10% discount when renting for 1 week or more. Open daily 8:30am-10pm. Walk down the main street toward the OTE to find **Aris Rent a Car and Moto** (☎22470 32 542), on the left side of the street. Cars from €30 per day. Small mopeds €8.50 per day. Large mopeds €9.50 per day. Call for delivery to your door. Open daily 8:30am-10pm. Moped rentals are widely available throughout Skala, mainly along the harbor.

◄★🔊 ORIENTATION AND PRACTICAL INFORMATION

Skala's amenities are mostly huddled around the port; a few are down the waterfront and around the main road. Excursion boats dock opposite the line of cafes and restaurants, while larger vessels park near the main plateia. The police, tourist office, and post office share the large Italian building by the port, making tourist orientation a one-stop shopping experience. Moving inland from this building, a street lined with shops and souvlaki stands leads to the OTE and continues until it dead-ends at peaceful **Holhaka Beach.** Across from the Welcome Cafe by the main docks, a parallel road is lined with pensions and rental shops. Facing the water, go right to get to **Hora** (4km) or left to go to **Meloi beach** (15min. on foot).

Tourist Office: ☎22470 31 666. Provides **maps**, brochures, bus schedules, help with accommodations, and the free *Patmos Summertime Guide*, which includes maps of Skala and the island. Open daily 9am-9pm, but it's often closed 2-6pm.

Budget Travel: All over the waterfront, though each may only offer info for the ferry lines it works with. Consult the tourist office for schedules, and then ask where to buy your ticket. **Apollon Travel** (☎22470 31 324) sells Flying Dolphin and Blue Star tickets, helps with accommodations and rentals, **exchanges currency**, and is the local agent for **Olympic Airways**. Open daily 8am-9pm.

Bank: National Bank (☎22470 34 050), in the far end of the plateia. Has MC/V cash advances, **currency exchange**, and **24hr. ATM.** Open M-Th 8am-2:30pm, F 8am-2pm.

Luggage Storage: Welcome Cafe, next to the dock. Open 24hr.

Police: ☎22470 31 303 or 22470 31 571. Above the tourist office. Open 24hr.

Hospital: ☎22470 31 211. On the main road to Hora, across from the monastery Apokalipsi (2km out of Skala). Open daily 8am-2pm. In an **emergency**, call the police—they know doctors' schedules and will contact them.

Telephones: OTE, ☎22470 34 137. Follow the signs in the main plateia. Open M-F 7:30am-3:10pm. The Welcome Cafe at the ferry dock has an international phone.

Internet Access: Interesting paintings and sculptures line the stone walls of **Millennium Internet** (☎22470 33 240), next to Rent A Car Patmos. €5 per hr. Open daily 10am-2pm and 5-10pm. **Internet Place** (☎22470 09 324), past the OTE on the road to Hohlaka Beach, has a more office-like environment, complete with a water cooler. €4 per hr. Open daily 9:30am-2pm and 3-10pm.

Post Office: ☎22470 31 316. Open M-F 8am-2pm. **Postal Code:** 85500.

🞑 ACCOMMODATIONS AND CAMPING

Domatia will run €15-20 for singles and €20-30 for doubles. To the right of the docks, facing the water, Vas. Giorgiou is lined with pensions. Nicer hotels can be found by walking about 10min. the other way.

▨ **Pension Augerinos** (☎/fax 22470 32 118), past the electrical company toward Meloi; look for the sign pointing uphill. Artfully decorated, jasmine-scented rooms are furnished with dark oak, and the cool blue-tiled private baths, balconies, and fridges make them hard to refuse. Breakfast €2. Singles €18-33; doubles €20-44. ❸

Katina's Rooms for Rent (☎22470 31 327), farther toward Meloi. Turn left at Celine's Music Club, then take the first right after the rocky wall on your right doubles in height; it's at the dead-end. If she has vacancies, Katina is usually at the docks with her car, ready to save you the 10min. trek in the sun. Large, whitewashed rooms come with kitchenettes, A/C, TV, and private baths. Doubles €25-30. ❸

Stefanos Flower Camping at Meloi (☎22470 31 821), 1.5km northeast of Skala, 20m behind Meloi beach. Follow the waterfront road along the port and all the way over the hill. Jungle-like rows of tall grass and flowers between tent sites provide ample privacy, while the mini-mart, restaurant, cooking and laundry facilities, clean showers, shared fridges, and hospitable managers foster a sense of community. For those in need of creature comforts, Stefanos also has spacious studios nearby with A/C, private baths, and kitchens. Scooter rental €10-15 per day. Parking €3, mopeds €1.50. Sites €6.50 per person, tent included; studios €25-35. ❶

Pension Sydney's (☎22470 31 689), just across the street from Pension Avgerinos. Comfortable rooms have private baths and balconies that overlook the mountains. The gracious owner gives her guests drinking water, Greek coffee, house wine, and the occasional information pamphlet at no extra charge. Singles €15-25; doubles €25-45. ❷

◘ FOOD

Patmos is not shy about its culinary reputation, and in Skala, the standard blasé tourist cafes give way to excellent fish tavernas and *patisseries*. Restaurants without set menus or with prices listed in pencil almost always have the freshest seafood. Don't settle if a plateia taverna looks suspiciously expensive; finding your way to a side street will more than likely reveal a similar menu with lower prices.

▧ **Koukoumavla** (☎22470 32 325; www.patmos-island.com/koukoumavla). Walking past the Welcome Cafe, Koukoumavla is up a small street where the harbor curves. The free-spirited owner sells handmade books and purses in this funky, fish-themed cafe, while her Italian husband brews freshly ground espresso (€2-3.50) to perfection. Various pressed sandwiches are big enough to share, heaped with tasty fillings like prosciutto, *manchego* (Spanish cheese), or *chorizo* (€3.50). Patrons can grab a seat at the lime-green bar or join the family-friendly crowd in adjacent "Elfland," a shady garden of colorfully painted furniture and toys. Open daily 8am-3pm and 6pm-12:30am. ❷

▧ **Chiliomodi** (☎22470 34 080), past Koukoumavla on the same side street. This small *ouzeri* has earned a stellar reputation among locals for its fresh, well-prepared seafood. The daily assorted grilled-fish platter (€5) will please discerning palates and satisfy ravenous appetites. The tasty eggplant pancakes (€4) are a good option if you need a break from marine life. Entrees €3-6. Open daily 6pm-late. ❷

To Kyma (☎22470 31 192), past Meloi beach, near Aspiris Bay. The 2km walk from town makes for a pleasant evening stroll. Follow the waterfront road around the port and up the hill; when you start descending, look for the sign and turn right, then continue for 200m. Your reward for the walk is fresh fish (€20-40 per kg) hot off the charcoals. From the campground, the walk only takes 5min. Open daily 6:30pm-2am. ❸

Loukas Taverna (☎22470 32 515), across from the OTE, is a traditional taverna that serves a variety of homemade Greek dishes, like pork marinated in mustard and wine sauce (€5). The friendly, familial staff, outdoor seating, and light Greek music create an inviting atmosphere. Open 10am-2pm and 7pm-late. ❷

Remezzo (☎22470 31 553), along the port-side road to Meloi, before the hill. The chef artistically prepares the house specialty, chicken with prunes and orange sauce (€9). Complimentary Patmian almond cake from a generations-old recipe sends you off with a sweet taste in your mouth. Open daily noon-2am; in low season 6pm-2am. ❷

◪ NIGHTLIFE

While Patmos's monastic pilgrims tend to be a high-minded set, the local youth know how to get their earthly pleasures. Entertainment options are rather spread out but can all be reached by foot.

▧ **Isalos Bar** (☎69761 25 881; www.12net.gr/isalos), behind the police station, down a side street near the bus stop. Blacklights and tealight candelabras cast mysterious shadows on the stone walls, arches, and urn-shaped tables at Skala's most popular club. Owner Yiannis's special coconut "summer shots" complement the veggie bar-food and come free at random intervals. Live folk music and other special events every 1-2 weeks. Beer €4. Mixed drinks €5-6. Open daily midnight-late; low season F-Sa only.

Koncolato (☎22470 32 060), on the waterfront across from the lighthouse. Popular with both locals and tourists, this club is packed late at night, but is almost empty before 2am. During the frequent *sfinakia* (shot) tradition, people line up at the bar and go bottoms up in unison. Open daily July-Sept. 11:30pm-late.

Lampsi Club (☎22470 33 334), near Remezzo. Blue dots of light undulate rhythmically on the walls, causing the gin and tonics (€4) to glow an eerie turquoise. A gymnasium-sized dance floor and an endless marble-topped bar easily accommodate the endless crowds. American music plays before 1am when the music switches to Greek hits. Beer €3. Open in summer M-Th, Su 11pm-4am, F-Sa 11pm-dawn.

▶ DAYTRIPS FROM SKALA

RURAL PATMOS

Though Skala has its own stretch of beach by the port, it is extremely crowded and not particularly scenic; far better beaches lie just a few minutes away. From Skala, the next closest beach is **Meloi,** an easy walk over the hill. Large trees envelop the sandy beach, creating a prime barbecue spot. At **Hohlaka,** at the end of the road with the Skala OTE, beachgoers can catch epic sunsets melting into the water. Follow the signs on the port-side road to Meloi to get to **Aspiris Bay,** which commands fantastic views of Hora and Skala. A bit farther north, **Agriolivadi** is yet another sandy beach, a nice alternative to more congested **Kampos.** Though its numerous hotels help pump in the tourists, the town of Kampos has an inviting plateia and a few waterfront restaurants and is still a pleasant option for those traveling by bus.

Over the hill from Kampos, **Vagia beach**—rocky, secluded, and serene—seems a world apart. Go east along the road to Livadia and follow the path down to find an appealing, **unmarked beach** set against a small bluff. A bit farther east, cliff-lined **Livadia beach** has spectacular views of the islets just offshore. While bus service extends only to Kambos, you can reach more secluded beaches by hiking or biking. **Lambi beach** is famed for its multicolored pebbles, which are now rare due to years of locals pillaging the beach for stones to use in their homes' floor mosaics. The strong winds that buffet the Lambi shore, though, make swimming difficult.

HORA Χώρα   ☎ 22470

The reverent solace of the monastery atop the hill diffuses through the sloped and crooked streets of Hora, while the intricate maze of divine white houses defies even the most adept cartographers. The town's cobbled paths reveal sprawling gardens behind grand doors and rusty-hinged gates. The turreted, 15m walls and imposing gateway built into the **Monastery of Saint John the Theologian** to combat piracy make it look more like a fortress than a place of worship. Founded in 1088 by Ag. Christodoulos as a memorial to St. John, the monastery once laid claim to all of Patmos and several neighboring islands. As the title deed still hangs in the treasury, some monks claim tongue-in-cheek that residents of nearby Samos are squatting on their land. Around the main courtyard's holy well, the walls are covered with 17th-century **frescoes,** including one portraying St. John's duel of faith with Kinopas, a local priest of Apollo. Legend tells that after the saint rebuffed Kinopas's "demons" and weathered a beating from his thugs, St. John called to Christ and made the sign of the cross. Kinopas turned to stone and sank to the bottom of the Skala harbor, and the townspeople turned to Christianity. During WWII, the Italians tried to remove the stone believed to have once been Kinopas, but their underwater bombs didn't leave a dent. A small buoy in Skala's harbor marks the spot. The excellent ◪**treasury museum** preserves 33 original pages from the Gospel of St. Mark, making it the second-largest collection in the world—though only one page is displayed at a time. Glass cases with helpful English placards guard numerous 12th-century icons, ornate ceremonial jewels, renowned works of 11th-century Cretan art, and a 7th-century Book of Job. Look for Helkomenos, an icon painted by **El Greco,** near the end of the exhibit. (☎ 22470 31 223. Monastery and treasury open M, W, F-Sa 8am-1:30pm, Tu, Th, Su 8am-1:30pm and 4-6pm. Monastery free; treasury €6, students €3. Modest dress required.) Within its walls, the monastery holds 10 chapels. The **Chapel of the Virgin Mary,** near the holy water well, is covered with gold-laden 12th-century frescoes, hidden behind the wall until they were exposed by 1956 tremors. The small door on the left before the exit allows visitors to view several famous skulls and the casket containing Ag. Christodoulos's entire corpse. The **Apocalypsis Monastery** is built on the site where St. John stayed while on Patmos. Today, that spot is 2km from both Skala and Hora, on the winding road that connects them. Most people come to this large, white complex of interconnected buildings to see the **Sacred Grotto of the Revelation,** adjacent to the **Church of Saint Anne.** This cave is said to be where St. John dictated the Book of Revelations after hearing the voice of God, whose power supposedly caused the crack still visible in the wall. Friendly, English-speaking priests stand guard over the site and retell the legend to fascinated visitors. (☎ 22470 31 234. Open M, W, F-Sa 8am-1:30pm; Tu, Th, Su 8am-1:30pm and 4-6pm. Modest dress required.)

If the monasteries have filled your religious quota but left your stomach empty, try popular **Vangelis Restaurant ❷,** in the central plateia, one of the only restaurants in town; follow the signs from the monastery. (☎ 22470 31 967. Moussaka €4. Entrees €4-6. Open daily 11am-2pm and 6-11pm.) Hora is 4km from Skala, a trip you can tackle by bus (10min., 10 per day, €1), taxi (€3), or foot. If you hike down, it's easy to find your way on the foot and donkey paths, and walking allows for frequent breaks to take in the unparalleled views of the entire island. The bus stops at the top of the hill outside the town, which is also the point of departure for buses from Hora to Grikos (15min., 5 per day, €1).

DODECANESE

NORTHEAST AEGEAN ISLANDS

Flung toward the outskirts of Greece, closer to İstanbul than to Athens, the islands of the Northeast Aegean remain sheltered from the cultural creep of globalization. With limited contact and transportation to even their Dodecanese neighbors, the islands go about life in the Aegean at their own pace with their own rules. Deck chairs and mass hotels are rarities in this part of Greece, where vast wilderness, local hospitality, and undisturbed beaches are commonplace. The strength of the cultural authenticity here is palpable, a traveler's welcome and reward.

SUGGESTED ITINERARIES: NORTHEAST AEGEAN ISLANDS

THREE DAYS Enjoy the enlightened atmosphere of Sappho's home, **Lesvos** (p. 507), and visit **Chios** (p. 500), whose time-honored gum resin will give you something to chew on.

TEN DAYS After embarking on the lush hikes on **Thassos** (p. 526), nicknamed the "Green Island", discover the dazzling

beauty hidden in **Limnos's** (p. 520) barren wilderness. Explore the many diverse towns in Lesvos (p. 507), with an extended stay in storybook village **Molyvos** (p. 514). Take a daytrip to the **Petrified Forest** (p. 519), 1 of only 2 in the world, before moving to the less-traveled villages and beaches on Chios (p. 500).

SAMOS Σάμος

Over the years, lush and lovely Samos has accommodated a more scholarly crowd than some of its wilder siblings in the Cyclades and Dodecanese. A procession of architects, sculptors, poets, philosophers, and scientists—among them Pythagoras, Epicurus, Aesop, and Aristarchus (who discovered that the Earth revolved around the sun 1800 years before Copernicus)—have all spent thoughtful hours on Samos's shores. Yet getting acquainted with Samos reveals its incredible diversity and depth; hiking paths through mountain forests lead to hidden caves and waterfalls, and luminous beaches lie just minutes from the port town's modern metropolis. By day, a wealth of historical sights beg to be explored. By night, the island takes off her glasses, shakes down her hair, and turns up the music in her city bars. Approaching Samos as a destination rather than a stepping stone to Turkey may prove its bookish reputation ancient history.

SAMOS TOWN (VATHY) Βαθύ   ☎22730

Though larger than Samos's second port, Pythagorio, Vathy receives far fewer tourists and remains a city for its residents. Waterfront tavernas unfurl along a

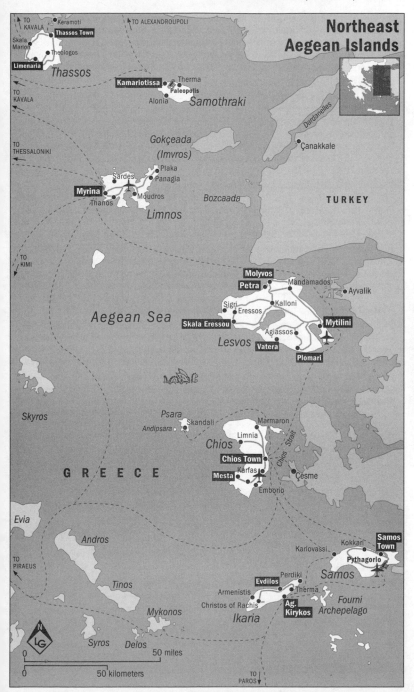

Northeast Aegean Islands

TO KAVALA

Keramoti

Thassos Town

Skala Marion

Theologos

Limenaria

Thassos

TO KAVALA

TO THESSALONIKI

TO KIMI

TO ALEXANDROUPOLI

Therma

Kamariotissa

Paleopolis

Alonia

Samothraki

Gokçeada

(Imvros)

Çanakkale

Dardanelles

Plaka

Sardes

Panagia

Myrina

Thanos

Moudros

Bozcaada

TURKEY

Limnos

Aegean Sea

Molyvos

Petra

Mandamados

Ayvalik

Sigri

Eressos

Kalloni

Skala Eressou

Agiassos

Mytilini

Lesvos

Vatera

Plomari

Skyros

Psara

Skandali

Andipsara

Marmaron

Chios

Limnia

Chios Town

Karfas

Mesta

Chios Strait

Cesme

Emborio

GREECE

Evia

Andros

Karlovassi

Kokkari

Samos Town

Pythagorio

TO PIRAEUS

Tinos

Perdiki

Evdilos

Therma

Samos

Armenistis

Christos of Rachis

Ag. Kirykos

Ikaria

Fourni Archepelago

Mykonos

Syros

Delos

N

LG

0   50 miles

0   50 kilometers

TO PAROS

NORTHEAST AEGEAN

graceful parabola of coastline. Behind them, narrow streets and stairways stretch up the neighboring hillside toward the residential area. Well-kept public gardens, a children's playground, hole-in-the-wall restaurants, and several excellent bars give Vathy a lived-in quality so often absent from large port towns. The entire town is referred to as either "Vathy" or "Samos Town;" both options are equally correct.

⌐ TRANSPORTATION

Flights: Olympic Airways (☎22730 27 237). Walk a few blocks up Kanari from the Archaeological Museum; it's on your left. To: **Athens** (1hr., 5 per day, €73); **Chios** (20min., 1 per week, €26); **Limnos** (25min., 1 per week, €36); **Rhodes** (40min., 2 per week, €36); **Thessaloniki** (1hr., 4 per week, €71). Open M-F 8:10am-3:30pm. The **airport** (☎22730 61 219), past Pythagorio, is only accessible by taxi (€15).

Ferries: To: **Agios Kirykos, Ikaria** (3hr., 1-3 per day, €9); **Chios** (3½hr., 2 per week, €13); **Evdilos, Ikaria** (3hr., Tu-Su 1 per day, €9); **Fourni** (2hr., Tu-Su 1-2 per day, €8); **Kos** (1 per week, €15); **Mykonos** (6hr., 4 per week, €19); **Naxos** (7hr., 2 per week, €22); **Paros** (8hr., 2 per week, €18); **Piraeus** (16hr., 1-2 per day, €27.50); **Rhodes** (10hr., 1 per week, €28); **Syros** (8½hr., 4 per week, €21).

High-speed boats: Catamarans run to: **Agios Kirykos** (3 per week, €16); **Evdilos** (1-2 per day, €15); **Karlovassi** (1-2 per day, €10); **Naxos** (daily, €38); **Paros** (daily, €31); **Piraeus** (1-2 per day, €49). **Flying Dolphins** leave from the port at Pythagorio heading to: **Agios Kirykos** (1½hr., 2 per week, €15); **Fourni** (1½hr., 2 per week, €14); **Kalymnos** (2hr., 2 per day, €25.50); **Kos** (5hr., daily, €25.50); **Leros** (1½hr., 2 per day, €18); **Lipsi** (1¼hr., 5 per week, €13); **Patmos** (1hr., daily, €13).

Excursion boats: Daily excursion boats go to **Kuşadası, Turkey** (1¼hr.; 8:30am; €40 round-trip, €9.13 Greek port tax); you can add a bus ride and tour of nearby **Ephesus** for €20 more. Turkish entrance **visas** (US$65) must be purchased at the border by citizens of Australia, Canada, Ireland, the UK, and the US planning to stay for over 1 day.

Buses: Follow the waterfront past Pl. Pythagoras, turn left onto Lekati, and continue 1 block to the station. To: **Heraion** (30min., 3 per day); **Hora** (30min., 3 per day); **Karlovassi** (50min., 2 per day); **Kokkari** (20min., 8 per day); **Potokaki** (25min., 3 per day); **Psili Ammos** (25min., 2 per day); **Pythagorio** (30min., 4 per day). Reduced ser-

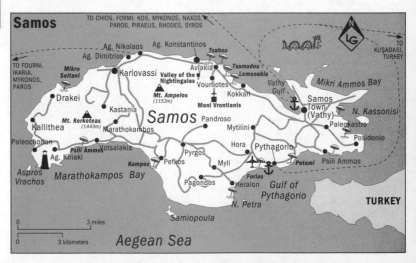

Samos

vice Sa-Su. Most fares €1-2. Bus tour around the island stopping at major sights including the **Valley of Nightingales** (Su 8:30am).

Taxis: ☎22730 28 404. Available 24hr. in Pl. Pythagoras.

■❄ ⁊ ORIENTATION AND PRACTICAL INFORMATION

The waterfront is home to most services. **Plateia Pythagoras,** identifiable by its four large palm trees, consists of cafes, a taxi stand, and a giant lion statue. It is located 250m to the right of the port when facing inland; head past Pl. Pythagoras until you see signs pointing to the **Archaeological Museum,** about a block inland and adjacent to the **Municipal Gardens.** Many of the town's public amenities, including the city hall, OTE, and post office, are nearby. To find the most densely packed pension neighborhood, head about 100m along the waterfront away from the port and walk a couple blocks inland when you see the sign for Hotel Aeolis. Many good accommodations are also located on the three step-lined streets that lead up the hillside. For nightlife, start up the hill to the left of the port (facing inland); the best bars and clubs are 400m up, though several can be found along the waterfront strip.

Tourist Office: ☎22730 28 530. On a side street 1 block before Pl. Pythagoras. Open mid-July to Aug. M-F 10am-1pm.

Budget Travel: ▧**ITSA Travel** (☎22730 23 605; www.itsatravel.com), on the waterfront opposite the port. Warm, English-speaking staff helps locate budget accommodations, has ferry and Flying Dolphin tickets and schedules, recommends sights and restaurants, plans excursions to Turkey, and offers free luggage storage. Open daily 7am-10pm and when boats arrive. **By Ship Travel** (☎22730 25 065), next to ITSA, has schedules of most ferry and Flying Dolphin connections. Both offices **exchange currency.**

Bank: National Bank, on the waterfront just beyond Pl. Pythagoras, has a **24hr. ATM.** Open M-Th 8am-2:30pm, F 8am-2pm.

Laundromat: Laundromatique (☎22730 28 833), the town's only self-service laundromat, is 1 block inland from Hotel Medusa. Purchase tokens at Mezefe Cafe next door. Wash €3.50, dry €3; detergent €0.60. Open daily 8am-11pm.

Police: ☎22730 22 100. After Pl. Pythagoras on the far right of the waterfront when facing inland. Doubles as the **tourist police.** Some English spoken.

Hospital: ☎22730 83 100. 10min. to the left of the ferry dock. Open 24hr.

Telephones: OTE, ☎22730 27 799. Facing inland from the Archaeological Museum, head right on Kanari; it's on your right, behind the big church. Open M-F 7:30am-3pm.

Internet Access: Pythagoras Hotel (☎22730 28 601), 600m up the hill from the port, by the hospital, has 3 fast computers. €3 per hr.; €1 min. **Diavos Net Cafe** (☎22730 22 469), on the waterfront 200m past Pl. Pythagoras, has reasonably quick connections. €4 per hr.; €1 min. Open daily 8:30am-midnight.

Post Office: ☎22730 28 820. On the waterfront, just before the military post and police. Open M-F 7:30am-2pm. **Postal Code:** 83100.

⌐ ACCOMMODATIONS

The limited availability of rooms during high season makes it advisable to call ahead or get help from a travel agent.

▧ **Pythagoras Hotel** (☎22730 28 601), across from the hospital. Rooms are clean and the cheapest in town. The location by the beach and several nightlife spots, combined with the snack bar, Internet access (€3 per hr.), and private baths makes this hotel a backpacker's heaven. The staff will pick up guests with reservations at the airport, port, and bus station for no extra charge. Singles €18-25; doubles €20-35. ❷

Pension Trova, Kalomiris 26 (☎22730 27 759). Head along the waterfront and go left when you see the sign for Hotel Aeolis; curve up the hill on Kalomiris and the pension will be on the right. Clean, open rooms have shared baths. The top-floor triple has a kitchen, fridge, and balcony. If you're planning a longer stay, you may want to ask about renting rooms in a nearby, fully equipped house for the same price. Singles €15-20; doubles €20-35; triples €30-40. ❷

Medousa Hotel, Sofouli 25 (☎22730 23 501), on the waterfront halfway between the port and Pl. Pythagoras. The most convenient accommodations in town, with no hill-climbing involved. An elevator goes up to well-appointed rooms that have private baths, TV, A/C, and hair dryers. Singles €20-25; doubles €25-30. ❷

Pension Avli, Areos 2 (☎22730 22 939). Walk along the waterfront away from the docks until you reach Hotel Aeolis. From there, take the next left onto Areos, and go 2 blocks and up the stairs. This former convent has 12 rooms, converted from the nuns' quarters, with vivid red bathrooms. Owner Spiros offers company and helpful advice about the island. Open May-Oct. Doubles €25-30. ❸

🍴🍷 FOOD AND NIGHTLIFE

In addition to the waterfront's standard assortment of beer-and-ice cream cafes and touristy establishments, excellent family-run tavernas on side streets serve homemade Greek dishes and freshly grilled fish. Samian cuisine leaves something to be desired—it's notable only for a sweet regional wine, which, depending on your taste, is either sickeningly saccharine or the nectar of the gods. Despite the lack of specialties, though, tavernas still make some mean renditions of national favorites. Locals rave about **Taverna Aprovado ❷**, located one block inland from Hotel Aeolis, for its authentic Greek dishes, huge portions, and unbelievably low prices—not to mention the free shot of ouzo that comes with every meal. (☎22730 80552. Entrees €2-6. Open noon-1am.) Just past the post office, **Grigori's ❷** serves a small selection of knockout home cooking. You'll probably have to point out what you want in the kitchen—a sign that you're getting the good stuff. (☎22730 22 718. Entrees under €6. Open daily 8:30am-3pm and 5pm-late.) **Christo's ❷,** in Pl. Nikolaos behind Pl. Pythagoras, adds its own touch to standard taverna fare. Inventive entrees, like stuffed chicken with dill and lemon sauce (€5), are a nice break from the *mezedes* routine, and vegetarians will be pleased to know that the feta-stuffed eggplants (€3) are excellent. (☎22730 24 792. Entrees €4-6. Open daily 10am-11pm.) A large **supermarket** sits behind the Archaeological Museum, and fruit and vegetable vendors line up in front of the OTE in the morning.

Vathy's most unusual nightspot is ▨**Sayang,** 400m toward the hospital. At this Turkish-themed bar (a rarity in the Greek isles), people lounge on divans as Turkish pop and house beats float through the incense-scented air. Fruity mixed drinks (€4-6) come garnished with a condom "just in case." (Open 11pm-late.) Even on a Monday night it's tough to find a seat at **Escape Music Bar,** across from Sayang, which looks out at a necklace of harbor lights. An upstairs dance club, Friday 80s nights, and live music in the summer make sure the venue stays fresh. (Happy hour 7:30-10pm with half-price drinks. Beer €3.50. Mixed drinks €7. Bar open May-Oct. 7:30pm-3am; club open July-Aug. nightly at midnight, Sept.-June F-Sa only.) On the waterfront, **Samos Music Cafe** at Hotel Samos has a relaxed atmosphere. Eye-popping art adorns the bar area, and dance music keeps the energy flowing for the mostly late-20s tourist crowd. (☎22730 28 377; www.samoshotel.gr. Beer €2. Mixed drinks €4. Open 10am-2:30pm and 10pm-3am.)

🔵 SIGHTS

The excellent, informative **Archaeological Museum** sits behind the municipal gardens, and contains more proof of the Heraion's bygone splendor than the crumbled remains of the site itself. The museum's two buildings house treasures from the ancient Heraion (the temple of Hera) and other local digs, explained in painstaking detail by near-encyclopedic English labels. The first building holds Laconian ivory carvings and some statues, most notably the colossal 5m **kouros** from 560 BC. Pieces of this magnificent figure were found built into existing walls and cisterns; its grey-white banded marble was a distinctive regional signature of ancient Samian sculptors. The same building houses the well-preserved Genelos group, which was a rather ostentatious offering to Hera that depicted the aristocratic donors, the Genelos family, themselves. The group once graced the Heraion's Sacred Way, and of the original series of six life-sized sculptures, four have survived. In the second building, an exhibit on Hera worship displays a rich collection of expensive and well-crafted votives to the goddess. Objects from ancient Egypt, Cyprus, and the Near East testify to the island's importance as a trade center. The last room, upstairs on the right, includes a case of fascinatingly nightmarish, gryphon-engraved **protomes** (cauldron handles) that should not be missed. (☎22730 27 469. Open Nov.-May Tu-Su 8:30am-3pm; June-Oct. 8am-7:30pm. €3, seniors and students €2, EU students free.)

🟥 DAYTRIPS FROM SAMOS TOWN

ANCIENT PYTHAGORIO Πυθαγόρειο

A bus from Vathy arrives at Pythagorio (20min., 4 per day, €1.20), now a modern beach town built on much of the ancient ruins, 14km south of Vathy.

The ancient city of Pythagorio, once the island's capital, thrived as a commercial and political center during the late 6th century BC under **Polykrates the Tyrant.** The writings of historian Herodotus recount how Polykrates undertook the three most daring engineering projects in the Hellenic world. Two are located in Pythagorio; the first, the **Tunnel of Eupalinus,** lies 1500m up the hill to the north of town. This 1.3km underground aqueduct diverted water from a natural spring on the hill to the city below. Climbing down a steep and high-walled staircase into the ground leads to a cool, slippery 200m passage hewn from the rock. Though the tunnel is an impressive feat of ancient engineering, there is not much on the walls to see, and its abrupt end forces a bottleneck of tourists to double back through the cave. Claustrophobes should also note that ceilings are low and the tunnel is narrow. To reach the passageway, walk back along the road to Vathy and follow the signs. The 20min. walk to the tunnel's entrance leads past minor ancient ruins, including a Hellenistic villa and some wells, along with picturesque rolling hills and grazing goats. (Open daily June-Oct. 8:15am-7:30pm, last entrance 6:45pm; Nov.-May Tu-Su 8:45am-2:45pm, last entrance 2:15pm. €4, seniors and students €2, EU students free.) Polykrates's second feat, the 40m deep **harbor mole,** is still in use today as a breakwater which supports the modern pier. Blocks, columns, wall fragments, and entablatures are strewn throughout the town of Pythagorio in random fenced-off plots of weeds. The ruins of the stubby **Castle of Lykurgus,** constructed during the War of Independence, are on the southern side of town. The **Church of the Transfiguration,** a pale-blue variant of classic Orthodox architecture, and the remains of a rather underwhelming **basilica** are also nearby.

HERAION Ἱραίον

A bus from Vathy (30min., 4 times per day, €1.70) drops off in Heraion Town. The temple is 1km back on the road from Vathy. ☎22730 95 277. Open daily June-Oct. 8am-7:30pm, Nov.-May Tu-Su 8:30am-3pm. €3, students €2. As transportation back is infrequent, be ready for some quality time with the rubble, or bring cash for a taxi (€8-10).

Polykrates's third engineering feat is the Heraion, or **Temple of Hera.** Fire damage in 525 BC left only one of the original 134 columns standing; the most interesting finds from the remains are stored in the Archaeological Museum in Samos Town. Samian devotees had worshipped Hera for seven centuries by the time that Polykrates began enlarging the temple in the 6th century BC. Although not much more than rocky rubble marks the site today, Hera's faithful once brought their offerings to the temple down the *kouros*-lined **Iera Odos** (Sacred Way) leading from Pythagorio to the temple steps. Though only minimally reconstructed after the fire, the 118-by-58m temple retained its historic prestige even after Samos's decline as a commercial power. In 80 BC Cicero convinced Roman authorities to turn the building into a kind of museum for earlier votive offerings, though it also became a place of unlimited asylum under the Romans, attracting vagabonds and miscreants. The temple fell into decay after the collapse of the Roman empire, but the later Byzantines erected a church on the site. Today the temple still merits a short visit, if only to wax poetic about its glory days. From the Sacred Way, a walk along the beach brings you back to the temple. If you can't enter through the beachside back gate, look for the path leading inland to the main road and the entrance, farther along the beach past two houses. Come prepared with a jug of libations, lest you suffer Hera's wrath in the form of heat stroke.

NORTHERN AND WESTERN SAMOS

The northern coast of Samos has many crowded, sandy **beaches** and a few less-frequented pebble beaches tucked into coves. Most of the coast is easily accessible from the road to **Karlovassi.** On a peninsula 10km west of Samos Town, you'll find the village of **Kokkari,** skirted by white pebble shores and clear waters. **Lemonakia beach,** 1km west of Kokkari next to Tsamadou, and the wide white beach west of **Avlakia** are both alluring. Kokkari, Lemonakia, and Avlakia are accessible from Samos Town via the irregular KTEL **bus** service; check with the bus station for the day's schedule. Infrequent buses (1-2 per day) shouldn't keep you from the splendid beaches of southwestern Samos—being stranded at one of them is more of a delight than a nuisance. From the red-roofed hamlet of **Marathokambos,** go a few kilometers west to find the spacious beaches at **Votsalakia** and **Psili Ammos.**

A small **waterfall** near Karlovassi is a nice location for a picnic lunch. Drive from the port up to Potami, the river road, and follow it for 1.5km. When you see a sign for the falls, park and hike 15min. to reach the lake where the small waterfall collects in three beautiful but freezing-cold pools. From the village of **Agios Konstantinos,** on the northern coast of Samos, you can hike into the mountains through the **Valley of the Nightingales,** where the songbirds' sweet melodies fill the wooded valley just after midnight. The village of **Vourliotes,** 5km south of Avlakia, was a favorite of renowned Greek actress Melina Mercury, who raved about the village for years after her visit there. Several kilometers above the town, the 16th-century monastery **Moni Vrontianis** watched over the populace below, though it is currently closed for renovation; consult the tourist office in Vathy for info. You can hike to three more waterfalls, 2km west of **Paleo,** in the island's northwestern corner.

IKARIA Ικαρία

Ikaria is named after the reckless young Icarus, whose wings melted away after he flew too close to the sun. A legendary rock marks the spot where he plunged to his watery demise. Ikaria's history matches the rebellious attitude of its namesake: during the Balkan Wars a revolutionary movement led to the formation of a short-lived Ikarian republic. With a predominantly agricultural economy and no major tourist industry, the island remains one of the poorest in the region. Perhaps consequently, the Communist Party (KKE) enjoys huge popularity with the island's residents; anti-EU banners make a jarring addition to the otherwise peaceful, relaxed landscape. Ikaria's lush coastline is speckled by serene, largely untouristed beaches, some with natural hot springs. Looming above the sea is an enormous chain of alpine green mountains that separates the north from the south. Besides providing dramatic vistas, the mountainous terrain makes transportation around the island difficult; visitors patient with the island's often inexplicable schedule, though, are rewarded with an unspoiled slice of Greece.

THE REAL DEAL. Ikaria has an unquestionable sense of authenticity that many travelers find refreshing. Precisely because the island doesn't cater to tourists, however, getting around can be frustrating and difficult on a budget. Be prepared either to rent a vehicle and tackle the long, winding mountain roads on your own or to spend a wad of cash on taxis if you can find a driver willing to take you where you want to go. —Laurie Schnidman

AGIOS KIRYKOS Άγιος Κήρυκος ☎22750

Ikaria's port town is little more than a shaded plateia stretching along giant steps that lead to the sea. The town is nearly deserted from 2 to 6pm, after which locals begin to hang out by the pier or circulate and sip frappés. Headquarters for both the KKE and a macho youth culture, the town plays by its own rules and keeps a baffling schedule; even at 1am you'll see small children playing energetically in front of the cafes as their parents chat and gossip.

TRANSPORTATION AND PRACTICAL INFORMATION. The town's pier is marked by a sculpture of Icarus plummeting to the ground. Coming off the ferry, walk up the pier onto the main waterfront road, then turn right to reach the town plateia, which is center for all tourist services and most of the town's daily life. The **airport** is on the island's northeastern tip, near Faros beach, and has flights to Athens (50min., 1 per day, €47); contact **Icariada Travel,** in the plateia. The English-speaking staff also provides ferry schedules and gladly helps with accommodations, excursions, and vehicle rental. (☎22750 23 322. Open daily 9am-2pm and 6-9:30pm.) **Dolichi Tours,** at the far end of the waterfront by the hydrofoil docks, helps with ferry tickets and moped rentals (€12 per day). Catching ferries to and from Ikaria can be tricky, as boats alternate departures and landings between southern **Agios Kirykos** and northern **Evdilos.** Be sure to plan ahead for this obstacle since public transportation between the port towns ranges from erratic to nonexistent; if you can manage to tear a taxi driver away from his afternoon coffee, the 45min. one-way taxi ride on the nauseatingly curvy mountain road will be about €25. **Ferries** run to: Fourni (1hr., 3 per week, €5.50); Paros (4hr., 2 per week, €14.30); Piraeus (10hr., daily, €22.50); Samos Town (3hr., daily, €9.10). **Flying Dolphins** go to Fourni (30min., 4 per week, €10), Kos (5hr., 1 per week, €31) via Patmos, Lipsi, Leros, and Kalymnos, and Pythagorio, Samos (2hr., 3 per week, €15). **Caïques** depart for Fourni (M, W, F 1pm; €5). As transportation in Ikaria tends to be private enterprise rather than public service, **buses** can be fickle, if they exist at all. Buses should go from Agios Kirykos to Evdilos (1hr.) and continue to Armenistis (2hr., 1-2 per day, €5). A fairly regular **green bus** runs to Therma every hour from 5 to 10pm (5min., €1).

Facing inland, the **National Bank** can be found toward the right side of the plateia. (☎22750 22 553. Open M-Th 8am-2:30pm, F 8am-2pm.) An **Alpha Bank** is next door to Dolichi Tours. (☎22750 22 264. Open M-Th 8am-2:30pm, F 8am-2pm.) Both banks have **24hr. ATMs.** The **police** (☎22750 22 222) are open 24hr. Climbing the steps left of Dolichi Tours and continuing up the road, you'll find the **pharmacy,** next to the G.A. Ferry ticket office in the plateia. (☎22750 22 220. Open daily 8:30am-2pm.) The local **hospital** (☎22750 22 330) is two streets inland from the pier. About 100m up the street are the **OTE** (☎22750 22 499; open M-F 7:30am-3pm) and the **post office** (☎22750 22 413; open M-F 7:30am-2pm). **Postal Code:** 83300.

⌂⌂ ACCOMMODATIONS AND FOOD. Finding lodgings can be tough, so check your port of arrival beforehand and call ahead for reservations. To reach **⌂Akti Hotel ❷,** climb the stairs on the right side of Dolichi Tours and take your first right. Guests often sit around the flower-filled seaside patio until 6am smoking, talking, and gazing at the rolling sea. The Greek-American owner Marsha knows the island inside-out and can direct you to the hot springs in the sea, nearby sandy beaches, and the best places to stop for a drink. Rooms are small, clean, and sunny, with private baths; larger rooms upstairs have newly remodeled baths, TV, A/C, and fridges. (☎22750 22 694. Singles €15-20; doubles €25-45.) On the road from the plateia, **Hotel Kastro's ❸** many amenities should placate the pamper-needy. Its spacious, modern rooms come fully loaded with TV, baths, balconies, phones, A/C, and fridges. (☎22750 23 480. Singles €35; doubles €40.) **Pension Ikaria ❸,** one block inland from the plateia, has simple, functional rooms perched above the main row of cafes, providing the perfect venue to play Peeping Tom—in a less creepy way, of course. (☎22750 22 108. Doubles €30-40. Discount for singles.) Next to Akti Pension is **Hotel O'Karras ❷,** which offers small, immaculately white rooms with A/C, fridges, and private baths that rival the rooms in terms of square footage. (☎22750 22 494. Singles €20-25; doubles €30-35.)

Agios Kirykos does not have a particularly noteworthy dining scene, mostly because there aren't many tavernas that serve full meals. Those that do tend to cook a couple of dishes in large batches and serve them to everyone, rather than making individual entrees to order. **Ston Tsouri ❷** (Στον Τσουρη), in the plateia, has an *Odyssey*-length menu but rotates what's available daily. Local cheeses and Ikarian wines make watching the stunning sunsets from the tables a multi-sensory experience. (☎22750 22 473. Omelettes €3. Greek entrees €3.50-6.) Taverna **Klimataria ❷,** a block inland from the plateia, serves standard Greek dishes. (☎22750 22 686. Entrees under €8. Open daily 11am-midnight.)

◧◪ NIGHTLIFE AND BEACHES. All of the town's nightlife is within a 20min. walk along the road heading left from the ferry dock, facing inland. Ikaria's low pollution leaves the stars strikingly visible, setting the scene for a lovely nighttime stroll above the sea. If you're headed to the bars, however, it's unlikely you'll be home before the sun comes up; nightlife gets started around 2am and peaks at 5 or 6am. As you walk from the dock, the bars are arranged in temporal sequence, perfect for one long pub crawl. Before 3am, **5 Minutes Til** (Παρα Πεντε) will be the only bar with patrons, as young locals stop here for some liquid courage and pulsating dance hits to get them revved up for the night ahead. (Mixed drinks €3-6. Open daily 11am-late.) The next stop is **Flic Flac,** about 10min. farther down the same road, catering to the town's clubbing needs with an outdoor dance floor, fog machine, and the occasional guest DJ. The indoor dance club below the bar is only open in the winter. (☎69732 07 115. Cover €6; includes 1 drink. Open F-Sa 11pm-late.) Pressing on up the road, **Wha Wha's** cool classic rock tunes spill over the three open-air terraces leading down to the beach. (Drinks €4-6. Open 11am-late.)

Incredible beaches sprinkled with boulders and pearl-white pebbles unfold between the coastal road and the glass-green sea. There are two natural ⌂**hot springs** in the ocean. The first is about 10min. farther down the same road as Flic

Flac and Wha Wha, just past the hotel under renovation. It can only be approached via a steep, rocky dirt path, as the staircase has long since collapsed. Look for steam rising from the water and for fire-red rocks, which are covered in a therapeutic mud that many bathers like to spread over their bodies. Lie back and relax; chances are you'll be the only person in sight. You can also bathe in the spring water at **Therma** (Θέρμα), 2km north of Agios Kirykos on the way to the airport. The green bus runs between the two beaches approximately every hour from 5 to 10pm (€1). You can also walk by taking the path by the police station. People with ailments ranging from rheumatism to neurological difficulties venture to Therma's three springs, which also attract a geriatric crowd. Unlike the ocean springs, the water from Therma is piped into a bathhouse containing 20 individual bathtubs in private little rooms. Each of the complex's springs is naturally radioactive, and the various springs' waters are used for different treatments. Twenty minutes in a warm bath costs merely €1.35, so you can take your time. Unlike the ocean springs, however, Therma's bathtubs have little space to explore and no view. For those without health problems, the ocean springs beat Therma hands down.

Farther north, by the airport, the small town of **Faros** offers a number of unremarkable but pleasant pebbled beaches. Buses to Faros exist in theory, but they hardly ever run; instead, take a taxi (€10-15) from Agios Kirykos.

🔼 DAYTRIP FROM AGIOS KIRYKOS. The **Fourni Archipelago** (Φούρνοι) makes a nice afternoon trip. Most of the island's 2700 residents are involved in some sort of maritime activity, meaning that the waterfront tavernas in Fourni, the sleepy port town, serve outstanding seafood. The coastal road south of the port leads to Kambi, whose lovely beach is set against windmill-laced hills. Weather permitting, Fourni is accessible by caïque from Ag. Kirykos (M, W, F 1pm; €4.50). There is limited ferry service three times per week between Fourni and Ag. Kirykos (€5) and once weekly from Fourni to Patmos (€6). Hydrofoils run twice per week to Fourni from Patmos (€13). Excursion boats also leave from Pythagorio, Samos, departing at 8:15am and returning by 7pm; contact ITSA Travel (p. 493) for more info.

EVDILOS Εύδηλος ☎22750

The dangerously narrow road from Agios Kirykos to Evdilos snakes up through sheer, craggy rock faces that peer over the golden coast and clean blue waters below. Only a few tiny villages and beaches lie between the ports, and the transportation hazards have limited the exchange of people and ideas among them. In serene, red-roofed Evdilos, things happen slower and earlier than in other island towns; you're not very likely to find a local who speaks much English. Because the town receives hydrofoils and has a central location convenient for visiting the many beaches and scenic villages of the northern coast, it serves as the main base for some visitors to Ikaria.

📭 TRANSPORTATION AND PRACTICAL INFORMATION. Buses are difficult to catch and service is spotty, but regular transport to Armenistis is supposed to exist. Check the bulletin board on the waterfront by the taxi stand for a schedule; if nothing is posted inquire at the kiosk in the plateia. **Taxis** are a pricier but far more reliable option; get a price quote before you get in the cab. (☎22750 31 275. Agios Kirykos to Evdilos €25; Agios Kirykos to Armenistis €27; Armenistis to Evdilos €9.) The staff members at **Blue Nice Holidays,** who speak only Greek, handle ferry and Flying Dolphin ticket sales, excursions, flights, and car rentals; they also **exchange currency** and post a weekly schedule for **ferries** serving Agios Kirykos and Evdilos, as well as for **Flying Dolphins** serving Agios Kirykos. (☎22750 31 990. Open daily 8am-2pm and 5-11pm.) There is a **24hr. ATM** next door to Blue Nice and at the opposite end of the harbor outside **Alpha Bank.** (Open M-Th 8am-2:30pm, F 8am-2pm.) Facing inland, stone steps at the right end of the harbor, past the pizza parlor, lead uphill; take a left for the **port police** (☎22750 31 007) and a **pharmacy** (☎22750 41 352) just beyond. In an emergency, call for **first aid** (☎22750 31 228). The **post office** is at the top of the stairs leading up the hill. (☎22750 31 225. Open M-F 7:30am-2pm.) **Postal Code:** 83302.

⌐⌐ ACCOMMODATIONS AND FOOD. Satisfactory accommodations are difficult to come by here; overpriced, ramshackle domatia and a luxury hotel are all you'll find at the harbor. Up the hill, the situation is a bit more promising, but the town has only one better-than-average option. The owners of **Apostolos Stenos's Rooms to Rent ❷** speak little English but still manage to have lengthy conversations with almost all of their guests. From the port, take the winding uphill road to the top and continue straight at the small square. Go right where the road splits at the bottom, then veer right at the church. When you see a bookstore, go past it to the right, then make an immediate left onto the adjoining coastal road; the pension is on your right—look for the red-roofed building with pink-arched windows. Rooms have private baths and incredible balconies that jut out over the crashing waves. (☎22750 31 365. Doubles €25; prices flexible.)

The usual assortment of small tavernas and *kafeneios* fills the plateia. **Cuckoo's Nest ❸,** whose tables surround the square's central monument, is a cheese-lover's paradise, with fondue and several dessert cheeses. The chicken in wine sauce (€5) is so tender that teeth are not required. (☎22750 31 540. Entrees €5-8. Open M-Sa 7pm-1am.) The Greek-speaking-only staff at an unnamed **taverna ❷,** in the old stone building near the pizza shop, serves standard fare for reasonable prices. (Greek salad €3.50. Open 6am-midnight.) Catering to late-night ferry arrivals with an array of sweets, coffees, and baked goods (€1.50), **Ta Kimata ❶** (☎22750 31 952), next to Blue Nice, is open 24hr.

⚡ DAYTRIPS FROM EVDILOS. One of the most popular resorts in Ikaria, **Armenistis** (Αρμενιστής), 15km west of Evdilos, boasts the beaches of **Livadi** and **Mesachti,** along with a few restaurants and bars. Though a challenge to get to, Armenistis has more tourist facilities than Evdilos and is close to some of the best beaches and hiking routes on the island. Idle stone fountains hidden under the canopy of shady green leaves mark the entry to the town of **Christos of Rachis** (Χριστός της Ράχης), a classic traditional Ikarian village (10km south of Armenistis). The best time to visit is after 11pm, when the locals have finished their daily farming and are ready to run their errands—though they continue shopping until 3 or 4am. Ikaria's best-organized hiking trails originate from here and are marked by little orange footprints. Pick up the very handy *Guide Map and Information* or *Round of Rahes on Foot* (€4).

The asphalt ends 5km west of Armenistis, leaving a dirt road that runs to **Nas,** one of the Aegean's undiscovered treasures. The sandy beach, flanked by huge rock walls, mediates between an aggressive sea and a serene river, ending in a freshwater pool. A 25min. hike south takes you to the small waterfall that forms its beginning. To reach the falls, head inland past the pool. The hike is best accomplished by hugging the river, so you may get your feet wet. Toward the end of the walk, you will see a cavernous rock enclosure on top of the eastern ledge, a favorite haunt for local goats. The waterfall is just a few minutes past this point.

CHIOS Χίος

Dusty, pine-speckled hills lend a wild feel to the interior of Chios. The port town is loud and glitzy, but the real charms lie deep in the heart of the island. Traditional villages and sandy shores in the north give way to fragrant orange, lemon, and mastic plantations that encircle Genoese mansions in the south. Southern Chios is the only place in the world that produces mastic, a gummy evergreen resin used since antiquity in medicines, chewing gum, and cosmetics. The local economy hinges on the toothsome substance, and though visitors descend *en masse*, the island refuses to succumb to the tourist trap mentality. Chios is an island worth savoring—allowing its wonders, including natural caves, thriving traditional artistry, and fields of native tulips, to resonate in all of their splendor.

CHIOS TOWN ☎22710

Chios's bustling port town has an electric pulse that doesn't pause for the wayward tourist. The waterfront showcases its slew of hip cafes where trendy young locals lounge, talking and drinking frappés all afternoon. The interior of the town is home to bustling fish and fruit markets, fancy shops, old tavernas, and a smattering of museums. The quieter residential section slumbers under the shadow of the castle walls, disturbed only by the occasional blare of a speeding moped.

▐ TRANSPORTATION

Flights: Olympic Airways, 50 Aigeou (☎22710 23 998), at the center of the waterfront, 2 doors past Villa Clio. Flights to: **Athens** (1hr., 2-5 per day, €65-83); **Limnos** (1¾hr., 2 per week, €36); **Mytilini, Lesvos** (30min., 2 per week, €40); **Rhodes** (1¾hr., 2 per week, €41); **Samos** (35min., €28); **Thessaloniki** (1-2hr., 4 per week, €60). Open M-F 8am-4pm. **Aegean Air** also flies to Athens (1hr., 2 per day, €50-84); contact Sunrise Tours for schedules (☎22710 93 586).

Ferries: Go to: **Agios Kirykos, Ikaria** (6hr., 3 per week, €13); **Alexandroupoli** (12½hr., 2 per week, €28); **Çesme, Turkey** (45min., 1-2 per day, round-trip €50); **Fourni** (7½hr., 1 per week, €13.50); **Kavala** (14½hr., 2 per week, €35); **Kos** (8½hr., 1 per week, €18); **Lesvos** (3hr., 1-3 per day, €14); **Limnos** (9½hr., 1 per week, €22); **Mykonos** (4½hr., 1 per week, €16); **Piraeus** (9hr., 1-2 per day, €24); **Rhodes** (12hr., 1 per week, €32); **Samos** (3½hr., 4 per week, €13); **Sitia, Crete** (22hr., 1 per week, €60); **Thessaloniki** (19hr., 2 per week, €31). Citizens of Australia, Canada, Ireland, the UK, and the US (among others) will have to purchase a visa (US$20) if staying more than 1 day in Turkey.

High Speed Ferries: Go to: **Kavala** (8hr., 1 per week, €70); **Lesvos** (1½hr., 5 per week, €20); **Limnos** (4¾hr., 2 per week, €35); **Piraeus** (5hr., 5 per week, €37); **Thessaloniki** (8¾hr., 1 per week, €70).

Excursion Boats: Travel around Chios and to **Çesme, İzmir, Ephesus,** and

Chios

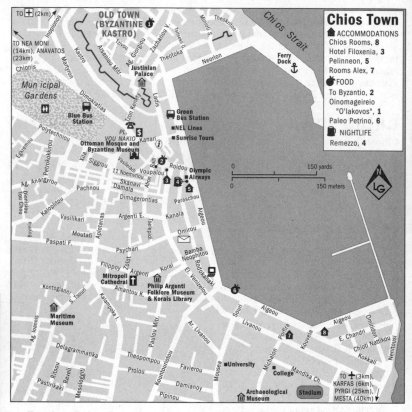

Chios Town

♠ ACCOMMODATIONS
Chios Rooms, 8
Hotel Filoxenia, 3
Pelinneon, 5
Rooms Alex, 7
🍴 FOOD
To Byzantio, 2
Oinomageireio
"O'lakovos", 1
Paleo Petrino, 6
🎵 NIGHTLIFE
Remezzo, 4

Kuşadası, Turkey. To book a trip, inquire at **Serafirm Travel** (☎22710 23 558) or at the EOT. **Kanaris Tours** (☎22710 42 490) gives a 50% discount after 3 excursions.

Buses: KTEL buses (☎22710 27 507) leave from both sides of Pl. Vounakio, right off the municipal gardens coming from the waterfront. Intercity bus service is split between 2 lines. **Blue buses** (office ☎22710 23 08, station 22710 22 079), just up from the plateia on Dimokratias, travel short distances from Chios Town. 1 regular route (15 per day 6:35am-9:10pm) travels south to **Karfas, Kontari, Megas Limionas, Thimania**, and smaller towns along the way; another heads west to **Dafnonas** (6 per day). Trips from €1; tickets available at the station, at kiosks, or onboard. **Green buses** (☎22710 27 507; open 6am-4:30pm), on the left side of the municipal gardens, go farther away to: **Agia Fotia Beach** (4 per day); **Armolia** (5 per day); **Emporios** (4 per day); **Kalamoti** (5 per day); **Kardamila** (6 per day); **Kataraktis** (6 per day); **Komi** (4 per day); **Lagada** (6 per day); **Lithi** (3 per day); **Mesta** (5 per day); **Nagos** (2 per day M, W, F); **Nenita** (6 per day); **Pyrgi** (7 per day); **Volissos** (2 per day M, Th). Tickets from €2.50; last buses leave at 4pm.

✴ 🛈 ORIENTATION AND PRACTICAL INFORMATION

Walking left from the ferry dock along the waterfront, you'll pass many cafes and restaurants. A right on **Kanari** takes you inland to **Plateia Vounakio**, the social center of town. Most services, buses, and taxis can be found there, on either side of the **Municipal Gardens**. In the gardens themselves you'll find a children's playground and **public bathrooms.** Left of Vounakio lies **Aplotarias,** the market street, with several groceries and bakeries. Between the ferry dock and the Municipal Gardens, fortress walls hug the predominantly residential **Old Town.**

Tourist Office: Kanari 18 (☎22710 44 344). Turn off the waterfront onto Kanari, walk toward the plateia, and look for the "i" sign on your left. English-speaking staff has **maps;** brochures; and bus, ferry, and airplane schedules. Open May-Oct. M-F 7am-2:30pm and 6-10pm, Sa-Su 9am-2pm and 6-10pm; Nov.-Mar. M-F 7am-2:30pm.

Tourist Agencies: Sunrise Tours, Kanari 28 (☎22710 41 390), a few doors down from the tourist office on Kanari, is 1 of the rare places open in the afternoons. Open M-Sa 9am-10pm. **NEL Lines,** Aigeou 16 (☎22710 23 971), has an agency where Kanari meets the waterfront road. Open daily 8:30am-2pm and 5:30-10pm.

Bank: National Bank, Kanari 3 (☎22710 22 820), next to the OTE in the plateia, **exchanges currency** and has a **24hr. ATM.** Open M-Th 8am-2:30pm, F 8am-2pm.

Hospital: El. Venizelou 2 (☎22710 44 306, first aid station 22710 44 302). 2km north of Chios on the coastal road before Vrondados.

Telephones: OTE, Tzon Kenety 1 (☎22710 40 167), up the block from the tourist office. Pay phones can be found on the waterfront. Open M, Th 7:30am-8pm, Tu-W, F 7:30am-2:30pm, Sa 8:30am-3pm.

Internet access: A number of cafes with fast connections can be found on the waterfront road. **Fantasy,** Aigeou 60 (☎22710 23 896), has tons of computers. (€3 per hr.)

Post Office: 2 Kanaki (☎22710 45 350). On the corner of Omirou and Kanaki, 1 block inland. Open M-F 7:30am-2pm. **Postal Code:** 82100.

ACCOMMODATIONS

Most accommodations are on the far end of the waterfront from the ferry dock. In high season, a tourist agency can help you find a room. Head to nearby Karfas if Chios Town gets too crowded. Soaring ceilings, hardwood floors, artful decor, and excellent harbor views make ▧**Chios Rooms ❷,** Aigeou 110, a great place to stay. The large, breezy rooms in a converted mansion share sparkling-clean bathrooms and a common kitchen. The New Zealand-born owner dispenses advice about the island and the occasional free cup of Greek coffee. (☎22710 20 198. Singles €18-22; doubles €23-25, with bath €35; triples with bath €40.) At **Hotel Filoxenia ❸,** Voupalou 8, just off the waterfront on Voupalou, guests can roll out of bed and be just steps away from both bus stations, the main shopping streets, the municipal gardens, and the waterfront. Its well-appointed rooms have A/C, TV, private baths, and fridges. (☎22710 22 813. Breakfast included. Doubles €40-45; triples €50-55.) Turn by Goody's, go one block inland, and walk left to find **Rooms Alex ❸,** Livanou 29. The six narrow rooms with fridges, A/C, TV, private baths, hair dryers, and coffeemakers connect to a roof-top garden filled with flags, canaries, and woodcuts. Alex, chairman of a local hosteler's union, can give you the low down on transportation and accommodations anywhere on the island. (☎22710 26 054. Singles 30-35; doubles €40-45.) **Pelinneon ❸,** Aigeou 54, is on the water near the Olympic Airways office; look for the sign outside Antena Rent-a-Car. Rooms come with A/C, TV, and private baths; slightly larger rooms also have balconies. The location couldn't be better, but it means that the rooms can get noisy. (Inquire at the Antena Rent-a-Car office. ☎22710 41 361; www.vilaclio.com. Doubles €30-40.)

FOOD

Vendors set up shop near Pl. Vounakio. For lunch on the cheap, grab a fresh *spanakopita* or *tiropita* (€1) available in one of the many **bakeries** and **cafes.** Quality tavernas can be found around Pl. Vounakio, just off the waterfront. For traditional Greek specialties prepared with an artistic eye and a more delicate hand than most tavernas, try ⊠**Oinomageireio "O'Iakovos" ❷**, Ag. Giorgiou 20. Garden tables inside the Old Town's stone walls are painted an inviting blue, making the eating experience as romantically relaxing as it is decadent. The superb staff will happily translate the entire menu and create mixed plates to relieve those struggling to choose between endlessly appealing options. (☎22710 23 858. Lightly fried shrimp and onions €5.50. Grilled local cheeses €3. Open daily 7pm-late.) **Taverna of Tassos ❸**, Livanou 8, is another excellent option. Facing the water, head right along the waterfront for about 10min., staying with the road as it curves and the scenery shifts from bustling port to quieter beachfront. Well-spaced tables in a tree-covered garden are a welcome break from the sidewalk traffic. The freshly prepared Greek fare is top notch, and the clay-pot broad beans in tomato (€3.80) will trounce any competition. (☎22710 27 542. Open daily 10am-late.) Ouzeri **Paleo Petrino ❷**, Leoforo Egeou 80, on the waterfront near Goody's and Il Fungo, serves delicious traditional dishes and has a nice selection of local ouzos. The stone facade adds a high-class touch to the outdoor tables. (☎22710 29 797. Most entrees €4-8. Open daily 11am-late.) Escape the waterfront's fashion parade at **To Byzantio ❷**, 9 Afron Ralli, around the corner from the mosque, near Hotel Filoxenia. Diners choose their meals from behind the counter at this friendly cafe. Homemade, tear-jerkingly spicy vinegar sits on each table, ready to add a potent kick to your meal. (☎22710 41 035. Most entrees under €5. Open M-Sa 7am-11pm.)

👁🎵 SIGHTS AND ENTERTAINMENT

Chios Town has many museums, some more compelling than others. The best in town is the 1200 sq. m **Archaeological Museum,** Michalon 5. The exhibits dissect ancient Chios's role in the Aegean, with an extensive collection of Neolithic, Archaic, and Classical artifacts and detailed explanatory placards in English. (☎22710 44 239. Open Tu-Su 8:30am-3pm. €2, students €1, EU students free.) To the right of Pl. Vounakio, follow Tzon Kenety toward the waterfront to enter the **Byzantine kastro,** reconstructed by the Genoese. Enclosing the narrow streets of the Old Town, the walls make the neighborhood seem like a museum itself. The castle also houses a handful of well-restored 14th-century Byzantine wall paintings in the small, overpriced **Justinian Palace.** (☎22710 22 819. Open Tu-Su 9am-3pm. €3, students €2, EU students free.) The mid-19th-century **Ottoman Mosque,** in Pl. Vounakio across from the gardens, currently houses the paltry collection of the **Byzantine Museum of Chios,** in which Jewish and Christian gravestones, column capitals, and Venetian cannons are littered throughout the small space in garage-sale fashion. The two large slabs depicting St. George slaying the dragon and the Genoese sculptures merit a lingering glance. Due to the renovations, however, both the Mosque and the Byzantine Museum are closed indefinitely. The slightly musty **Philip Argenti Folklore Museum,** Korai 3, above the **Korais Library,** next to the Mitropoli cathedral, examines traditional Chian embroidery and clothing through illustrations and figurines. More prominently featured, though, are numerous European-style portraits of various members of the Argenti family from the 18th century onward. (☎22710 44 246. Open M-Th 8am-2pm, F 8am-2pm and 5-7:30pm, Sa 8am-12:30pm. €1.50) Folklore fiends looking for a more focused (but also more cheesy) fix can try the **Folklore Museum of Kallimasia,** in a junior high school in the neighboring town of Kallimasia. The exhibit features a reconstructed early 20th-century Chian village filled with items donated by locals. (Accessible via Green bus; ask at the bus station for times. ☎22710 51 373. Open June-Aug. 9:30am-12:30pm and 6-8:30pm; Sept.-May during school hours. Free.) The **Chios Maritime Museum,** S. Tsouri 20, contains intricate wooden models and paintings of ships from a number of nations. Those without a specific interest in ships may find that the technical explanations inspire a deckside snooze. (☎22710 44 140. Open M-Sa 10am-2pm. Free.) In July and August, the Prefecture of Chios finances **free guided tours** of the island's monuments. Visitors must provide their own transportation to the various sites, where a guide will wait at set times each day. For more information, contact the **Ena Chios Development Corp.** (☎22710 44 830; www.chios.gr.)

Tired travelers or those weary of the Greek practice of having your first drink at 1am and your last at 8am are in luck in Chios, where the nightlife gets going surprisingly early. Waterfront bars overflow with chic clientele by 10pm, and packs of wandering trendsters take over the sidewalks not much later. Chios's scene revolves around the numerous hip bars and handful of clubs on the waterfront. **Remezzo,** 51 Aigeou, draws twice the crowd of its neighbors. The young and beautiful don their tightest clothing and coolest attitude and mingle in packs inside this bustling, bow-shaped bar. (☎22710 42 848. Mixed drinks €5. Open 10am-3:30am.) For a game of billiards (€6 per hr.) and a beer (€3), head to **Fantasy,** which also has Internet access (see above). An **open-air cinema** in the public gardens shows films nightly (€6.50), many of which are in English.

◘ DAYTRIPS FROM CHIOS TOWN

▨ MESTA Μεστά

Green buses run from Chios Town to Mesta M-F 5 times per day (€3.10-3.50).

One of the most fascinating villages in southern Chios, Mesta's name comes from the Greek word *"mesto,"* meaning "a very well thought-out idea." The town was founded in 1038, when representatives from four neighboring towns put their heads together to solve the perennial pirate problem. Their solution was to build a town where the houses were all connected to one another, forming a fortification wall like that of a castle. Today Mesta looks almost exactly as it might have during the Byzantine era; due to archaeological decree, all new houses must be built in the same original style with delightful stonework, rounded arches, and painted wooden doors. It's easy to get lost in the narrow, cobbled streets, but most wind up back at the central plateia, the nucleus of village life and home to the town's two tavernas. **Meseonas Cafe ❶** offers intriguing Chian drinks, like mandarin and sour cherry juices, mastic liquors (most €2.50), and a local, ouzo-like fig liquor called *"souma,"* which goes down surprisingly smoothly considering its 70% alcohol content. (☎22710 76 050. Open daily 6am-late.)

> **⚡TIP** **BUS-TING A MOVE.** When visiting walled cities, make sure to ask your bus driver where the return bus stops to pick people up. Although it may be just where the bus left you, sometimes the stop is at another entrance to the city, and running through a maze of winding streets at the last minute to find the bus may leave you stranded in medieval times.

While its quaint Byzantine design is an attraction in itself, Mesta houses two beautiful **churches** that are well worth a look. The newer one, the **Great Taxiarchi,** in the main plateia, was constructed 300 years ago and is the third largest in Greece. The impressive pale-blue interior is filled with silver votives and chandeliers. From there, ask the church keeper to take you to the town's original church, the **Older Taxiarchi.** Dating from 1412, this church contains an enormous walnut iconostasis, carved over the course of 40 years in the early 18th century.

The church keeper can narrate every Biblical scene depicted in the intricate carvings. Make sure to see the **Iron Door**, also known as the Door to the Captain, which served as the original gate to the city, before the church keeper returns to the bigger church. (Great Taxiarchi open M-F 10am-3pm and 4-6pm. Older Taxiarchi open by request. Modest dress required. No flash photography.)

◾ PYRGI Πυργί

Take the Pyrgi bus from Chios (7 per day, €2.40). Pyrgi and Mesta are on the same bus route, making for a convenient daytrip combination; ask at the Chios bus station for information on how to time your visits to catch the bus en route.

The villages in the southern half of the island, called "Mastichohoria," cultivate the lentisk trees that produce Chios's famous resin. High in the hills, 25km from Chios Town, the village of Pyrgi greets visitors with its buildings' intricate black and white geometric facades. In the afternoon, old men congregate in the central plateia by the church to gossip over ouzo; their wives pass the time chatting in the rustic narrow alleyways that separate their tiny, tattooed homes. Pyrgi is also home to the 12th-century **Agioi Apostoloi** church, a replica of the Nea Moni, in a small alley off the plateia. Thirteenth-century frescoes cover the interior of the church. (Open M-F 10am-1pm. Free. Modest dress required.)

NEA MONI Νέα Μόνι AND ANAVATOS Ανάβατος

Blue buses run to Nea Moni Tu, Th at 9:50am and return at 11:30am. ENA guides lead free tours from the entrance of the monastery on Th at 10am and noon.

On the eastern half of the island, several sites, among them Nea Moni and Anavatos, recall the Ottoman Turks' invasion of the island in 1822. Pine-covered mountains 16km west of Chios Town cradle **Nea Moni** (New Monastery). Built in the 11th century, the monastery was inspired by the miraculous appearance of an icon of the Virgin Mary to three hermits—the skull of one, covered in gold and silver adornments, is in the back corner of the church. The complex is one of the world's most important Byzantine monuments. Though an 1881 earthquake destroyed much of it, most structures have been carefully restored. Before entering the main chapel, you'll see five 11th-century **floor mosaics**, which are stunning despite their age. The artists who created them were also responsible for those of Hagia Sophia in İstanbul. A few meters before the entrance to the complex, up a small dirt path, lies Nea Moni, where an arched crypt contains the grisly skulls and bones of monks and villagers massacred by the Turks during the 1822 invasion. The skeletons are the remains of the 600 priests and 3500 women and children who sought refuge from the attacks in the chapel. An adjoining chapel just inside the entrance houses a **memorial** to the tragic event. (Open daily 9am-1pm and 4pm-sunset. Free. Modest dress required.) An on-site **museum** displays church garments and religious items. (Open daily 9am-1pm. €2. Nov.-March Su free.) Unfortunately, the famed church is undergoing massive renovations and will be closed to visitors at least through the end of 2007. Though the skeletons and memorial are interesting in a disturbing sort of way, the current inability to enter the church makes the 45min. bus ride to the site far less appealing.

For a memorable if somewhat haunting experience, head to **Anavatos**, an abandoned village built into the hillside, 15km west of Nea Moni. The village's women and children threw themselves from these cliffs in resistance to the Turkish invasion; today the red ruins, the pines below, and a statuette of an angel near the village's entrance pay tribute to their sacrifice. A walk through the fortifications provides amazing views of the surrounding hills. The church near the right of the site's entrance has a folk-art rendition of the tragic event. (Open daily 10am-2pm.)

SOUTHERN CHIOS

Karfas, 6km south of Chios Town, is home to the sandiest, most tourist-covered beach on the island. Many take up temporary residence here, close to both the beach and to Chios Town's amenities. Karfas is also a refuge for vacationers unable to find lodgings in the capital. Karfas's main beach offers watersports and scuba diving (☎/fax 22710 32 434). ■ **Emporios Beach,** by the island's southern tip, however, is the better bet. Spectacularly beautiful, the beige cliffs collide against the black stones and tranquil blue water. One part of the beach is up the only road to the right (when facing the water). A smaller, less crowded shore is up the stairs to the right from the first beach. When you've had enough of the sunshine, descend into the **Cave of Olympi** and spelunk to your heart's content. Though known for centuries, the cave was only opened in 1985. Its Jurassic-era stalag-mites and stalactites are still growing, thanks to the mineral-rich waters that con-tinue to drip in the interior. The cave is inaccessible by public bus. If you have private transportation, take the main road from Olympi southwest toward the coast. On Fridays, Kanaris Tours runs a bus tour (€17) that visits Armolia, Pyrgi, Olympi, the Cave of Olympi, and Mesta; this is the best option for those without their own wheels. (☎22710 44 830. Open Tu-Su 10am-8pm. Free.) Though domi-nated by pricey beachfront resorts, a few moderately more economical options do exist. **Karfas Bay View Studios ❸,** in a charming blue and white townhouse just off the cafe-lined street on Karfas beach, rents cavernous apartments with kitchens, baths, balconies, A/C, and TV. Though expensive for one, the studios, which sit above and behind a small cafe, are a good deal for three, as the price stays the same. (☎22710 92 053. Studios €30-50.) **Markos's Place ❸,** up the hill about 500m at the far end of the beach (look for a blue gate), has small rooms in tiny buildings spread out within a relaxed, 8000 sq. m compound. The area, adjacent to a monas-tery, also includes a yoga room and breakfast nook. (☎22710 31 990. Shared baths. Minimum 4- to 5-day stay. Doubles €30.) The helpful, English-speaking staff at the **tourist office,** across the street from the bus stop, keeps a list of accommodations in town and can help you find a room. (☎22710 31 222. Open daily 10am-10pm.) Blue **buses** run from Pl. Vournakio in Chios Town (every 30-45min., €1.20).

NORTHERN CHIOS

The pleasant, pebbly shores of **Vrondados** and **Daskalopetra** are 9km north of Chios Town. Blue **buses** from Pl. Vournakio in Chios Town run to both. A 2min. walk inland from the shore of Daskalopetra takes you to the **Sanctuary of Cybele.** Stat-ues dating from the site's glory days as a center of worship are now in the Archae-ological Museum in Chios Town (p. 504), but you can still find the **Stone of Homer,** where the poet is rumored to have held lectures. A circle of stone seats surrounds the prestigious rock, which affords a magnificent view of the sea from behind a thicket of trees. After Daskalopetra, the main roads wind northwest along the coast past Marmaron to **Nagos,** a rocky beach and perhaps once a popular spot to go to when cutting Homer's class. High in the hills near the center of the island, the village of **Volissos** is crowned by a Byzantine fort.

LESVOS Λέσβος

Ouzo, olive groves, monasteries, parched hillsides, lush green expanses, sandy beaches, and a petrified forest all harmonize on Lesvos in an irresistible siren song. Unlike the tiny islands in the southern Aegean, Lesvos defies categorization, often feeling like its own country; the distinctiveness of its towns, not to mention the inconvenient bus system separating them, makes them feel like their own islands. Lesvos's cultural riches match those of its terrain: 7th-century BC poet Sappho, fabulist Aesop, philosopher Aristotle, empiricist Epicurus, Nobel Prize-winning poet Odysseas Elytis, artist Theophilos Hadzimichali, and art critic Tériade have all called the island home. Despite the diversity of its famous citizens, legend has it that Lesvos's population was once entirely female; the tale may date back to the Athenian assembly's 428 BC decision to punish the unruly residents of Mytilini by executing all adult males on Lesvos. Though the assembly repealed the sentence, the idea of an Amazonian island appeals to girl-power pilgrims who come to pay homage to Sappho and the etymological roots of the word "lesbian." Whether or not you number among them, arriving with an open mind and a healthy wanderlust ensures that the island will enchant you. For the traveler wanting to see the many sides of the Greek islands without ferrying around, Lesvos is the perfect destination, as each of the towns is completely unlike the ones next door.

MYTILINI Μυτιλήνη   ☎ 22510

Each morning, the capital's wide harbor yawns into a modern, working city marked by glitzy shops, bustling local markets, and hordes of chic Greeks spilling out of waterfront *kafeneios*. Most visitors to Mytilini come on business or *en route* to the rest of Lesvos, leaving the city as a playground for trendy college students. The commercial beat only goes so far, though—exploring some of the many winding side streets farther inland will reveal a much calmer Mytilini.

⌐ TRANSPORTATION

Flights: The **airport** (☎22510 61 590) is 6km south of Mytilini; take a **green bus** from the intercity bus station. **Olympic Airways,** Kavetsou 44 (☎22510 28 659; open 8am-3:30pm), has another office at the airport, as does **Aegean Airlines** (☎22510 61 801). Tickets for both Olympic and Aegean flights can be purchased at almost any travel agency in town. To: **Athens** (1hr., 4 per day 8am-6:10pm, €65); **Chios** (25min., 2 per week, €25); **Limnos** (35min., 5 per week, €36); **Rhodes** (1hr., 5 per week, €53); **Samos** (45min., 2 per week, €35); **Thessaloniki** (2 per day, €87).

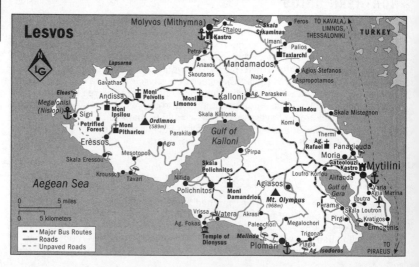

Ferries: NEL Lines, Pavlou Koundourioti 67 (☎22510 46 595), on the far right side of the waterfront facing inland, before the string of cafes. Open daily 7am-10pm. Service to: **Ayvalik, Turkey** (1½hr.; 4 per week; €49, includes Greek port tax); **Chios** (3hr., 11 per week, €14); **Kavala** (11hr., 3 per week, €29); **Limnos** (5hr.; 2-3 per day M-Tu, F-Su; €20); **Mykonos** (15hr., 1 per week, €26); **Piraeus** (12hr., 10 per week, €31); **Thessaloniki** (13hr., 2 per week, €35).

High-speed ferries: To: **Chios** (1½hr., 5 per week, €27); **Kavala** (5hr., 3 per week, €53); **Limnos** (2½hr., daily, €36); **Piraeus** (7hr., daily, €58); **Thessaloniki** (6½hr., 2 per week, €69).

Intercity Buses: Intercity bus station, Pl. Andrea G. Papandreou (☎22570 28 873). Buses crisscross the island with Mytilini as the home base. From outlying cities, you will have to head back to Mytilini in order to get somewhere else on the island. It is possible

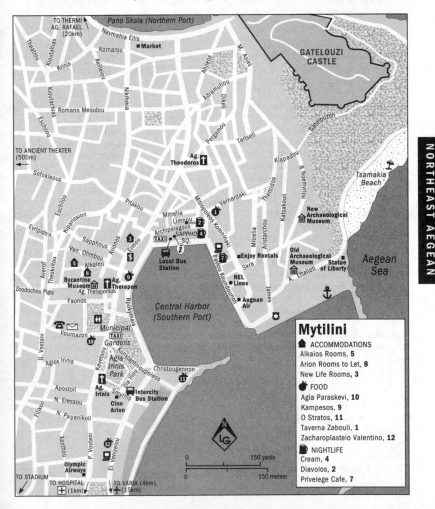

Mytilini

🏠 ACCOMMODATIONS
Alkaios Rooms, **5**
Arion Rooms to Let, **8**
New Life Rooms, **3**

🍴 FOOD
Agia Paraskevi, **10**
Kampesos, **9**
O Stratos, **11**
Taverna Zabouli, **1**
Zacharoplasteio Valentino, **12**

🌙 NIGHTLIFE
Cream, **4**
Diavolos, **2**
Privilege Cafe, **7**

NORTHEAST AEGEAN

to transfer buses at Kalloni and at the fork for Eressos and Sigri, but this takes careful planning and some assistance from a local who's incredibly familiar with all things bus-related. Schedules for the island's buses are available at the intercity bus station in Mytilini and at most information or tourist agencies throughout Lesvos. Buses go to: **Agiassos** (25min., 5 per day); **Mandamados** (1hr., 3-4 per day); **Mistegna** (20min., 3-4 per day); **Molyvos** (2hr., 4 per day, €5) via **Kalloni** and **Petra; Plomari** (30min., 3-5 per day, €3.10) via **Gera; Polichnitos** (1½hr., 3-4 per day) via **Vatera; Sigri** (3½hr., 1-2 per day) via **Eressos** and **Kalloni**. Buses run July-Aug. 9am-6pm; Sept.-June 9am-3:15pm. Reduced service Sa-Su. €2-7, depending on distance.

Local Buses: ☎ 22570 28 873. At the northern end of the waterfront on Koundourioti, in Sappho Sq. Schedules change daily; check with the bus station to get the day's routes. To **Agia Marina** (45min., every hr. 6:50am-8:40pm, €0.90) via **Varia** (€1), **Agios Rafael** (every 30min. 6am-9:40pm, €1.05) via **Thermi** (€0.90), and **Loutra** (every hr. 6:15am-8:30pm, €0.90) via **Koundourtias** (€0.55).

Taxis: ☎ 22510 23 500. Line up on the corner of Ermou and Vournazon by the municipal gardens and where Pavlou Koundourioti meets Archipelagous in the main plateia.

Moped Rentals: Enjoy Rentals (☎ 22510 42 242), on Tenedou, a small street off Koundourioti next to the NEL office. From €20, includes helmet and insurance. Open daily 8am-1:30pm and 5:30-10pm. Discounts for longer rentals.

■ 🛈 ORIENTATION AND PRACTICAL INFORMATION

Mytilini's harbor opens to the south, and cafes, bars, and hotels line the waterfront street **Pavlou Koundourioti**. The **old market** stretches along **Ermou,** home to pharmacies, boutiques, and bakeries. Ermou becomes **Kavetsou** at its southern end, where it intersects **Vournazon** one block inland on the harbor's western side. The **tourist office** is in Sappho Sq. by the local bus station. It has free **maps** and info about the island, and showcases an amusing collection of mannequins dressed in traditional Lesvian gear. (☎ 22510 44 165. Open in summer Tu, Th 9am-2pm, M, W, F 9am-2pm and 6-9pm.) A **National Bank,** 28 Kounodourioti, in the inner harbor two doors south of Hotel Lesvion, has a **24hr. ATM.** (Open M-Th 8am-2:30pm, F 8am-2pm.) A number of ATMs are also on Ermou, between Archipelagous and the municipal gardens. There are **public toilets** in the park. The **tourist police,** on Aristarchou by the ferry docks, provide brochures. (☎ 22510 22 776. Open 7am-2:30pm.) The 24hr. **hospital** (☎ 22510 40 401), is southwest of town on P. Vostani and Navmachias Elis. For an **ambulance,** dial ☎ 166. The **OTE** is at Vournazon 8. (☎ 22510 29 999. Open M-F 7:20am-1:30pm.) Find blissfully cheap **Internet access** in the northeast harbor, at both **Sponda** and **Internet Club,** along Mitropoleos Komninaki, by turning inland by the NEL ferries office. (€1.50 per hr.; €1 min.) In the southwest gardens region, **Cafe Play Field,** on El. Venizelou 1½ blocks south of the intercity bus station, also has Internet access. (☎ 22510 24 751. €4 per hr.; €1 min. Open daily 10am-2pm and 5pm-late.) The **post office,** next to the OTE, at 2 Vournazon, **exchanges currency.** (☎ 22510 28 836. Open M-F 7:30am-2pm.) **Postal Code:** 81100.

🛏 ACCOMMODATIONS

The hotels on the waterfront are elegant but pricey; head to Ermou to find plentiful **domatia.** If you are met at the ferry, be sure to negotiate, and keep in mind that longer stays often result in lower rates. Doubles run €20-23 before July 15, and anywhere from about €35 to €55 in late summer. **Alkaios Rooms to Let ❸,** Alkaiou 16, rents soothing peach-colored rooms with lovely wood furniture, high celings, TV, A/C (€3), hair dryers, and private baths with showerheads fit for a king. The elegantly furnished hallways have common fridges and a handy free map marked with important sites. (☎22510 47 737. Doubles €30-35; triples €40-50.) **Arion Rooms to Let ❸**, at Alkaiou and Arionos 4, is beautifully decorated, with light gold-toned walls that frame hand-painted murals. From the waterfront, go inland on Alkaiou for two blocks and turn left on Arionos. Small rooms with lustrous hardwood floors have A/C, private baths, and TV. (☎22510 42 650. Singles €30; doubles €40.) **New Life Rooms ❸**, at Ermou and Olympou, in a beautiful Art Nouveau building, has a handful of simple rooms with fridges and baths. The lone triple has a private kitchen. (☎22510 46 100. Singles €30; doubles €35; triples €50.)

🎵🍴 FOOD AND NIGHTLIFE

Walking seaward on the southwestern quay brings you to Mytilini's best tavernas. Fresh octopi hang to dry in front of tables right by the water at **O Stratos ❷**, which offers an ocean's worth of freshly prepared fish in a large, shaded seating area. Ask the eager-to-please staff for a sampling of local specialties if choosing just one item from the huge menu seems impossible. (☎22510 21 739. Entrees €4.50-6.50. Open daily 11am-late.) From Ermou, head right on Mitropoleos Komninaki and then left on Vernardaki to find **Taverna Zoubouli ❷**, Vernardaki 2, one of the oldest in Mytilini. The gigantic greengrocer's salad (small €3, large €4.50) adds beans, capers, lettuce, and cabbage to the usual Greek salad in a tasty break from the routine. The list of house specials (€5), like the *tabakas* (veal stewed with tomato, feta, and yogurt) makes navigating the large menu a bit easier. (☎22510 21 251. Open daily 11am-late.) **Agia Paraskevi ❶**, on Vournazon past the intersection with Kavetsou, is home to the best souvlaki in town, with meat that's fresh, slow-roasted, and well-seasoned. (☎22510 46 666. Entrees €1.50-4. Open daily 6am-2:30am.) For a sugar high that will last all day, head to **Zacharoplasteio Valentino ❶**, El. Venizelou 6, which sells tantalizing almond confections and €0.10 cookies. (☎22510 23 989. Open daily 9am-8:30pm.)

Mytilini's nightlife centers on the waterfront. Early on, head to the posh, pastel **Privelege Cafe,** Koundourioti 47, on the northeastern side of the waterfront, for a live DJ and fashionable drinks. To take full advantage of the experience, down a few shots (from €2.30) and head upstairs to the trippy ⬛**neon bowling alley,** where blacklights, music videos, and glow-in-the-dark pins and balls put a new spin on the old game. (☎22510 46 884. Mixed drinks from €4.50. Bowling €2.50-3 per person per game. Cafe open daily 7:30am-1am; bowling alley open 5:30pm-late.) The bartenders make a concerted effort to ensure

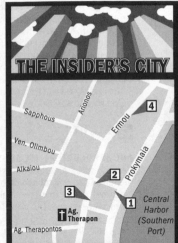

THE INSIDER'S CITY

Sapphous · Arionos · Ermou · Ven. Olimbou · Alkaiou · Prokymaia

[4] [2] [3] [1]

Ag. Therapon
Ag. Therapontos

Central Harbor (Southern Port)

PASTRY PILGRIMAGE

Although Mytilini has impressive sights, it is the tantalizing aroma wafting from its many bakeries that is most noticeable (and most delicious) about the city.

[1] **Kampesos,** (☎22510 81 122) Koundourioti and Alkaiou, has no-frills, divine doughnut-like pastries smothered in honey, nuts, and cinnamon.

[2] The treats at **Maskotitsa,** Alkaiou 2 (☎22510 26 181), are a step up on the intricacy scale. Their speciality is *tsoureki,* a sweet bread flavored with *mahlepi,* a cinnamon-like Turkish spice.

[3] **Fantastico,** Ermou 23 (☎22510 28 257), has the best variety of local treats, including *platseda,* a syrupy, walnut-filled pastry.

[4] **Flokaki,** on Ermou (☎22510 28 588), specializes in *kombehai,* an almond cake saturated with sweet syrup. They also have airtight packages ready for shipping that will keep pastries fresh for a month.

that each person who comes to **Cream,** behind the local bus station, has a good time. Cubist plastic lanterns, candy-colored couches, and bubble-gum wallpaper draw a hip, vibrant crowd. (☎22510 47 995. Open daily 8pm-2:30am.) You can exchange bump and grind for drinks and conversation at **Diavolos,** Ladadika 30. Vaulted wooden ceilings, stonework walls, and a gregarious 30-something crowd welcome newcomers for a quieter evening. (☎22510 22 020. Open daily 8am-late.) **Cine Arion,** on Smyrnis across from the intercity bus station, plays mostly American films nightly on the theater's two screens. (☎22510 44 456. Weekly schedules at the ticket window. €6-7.)

🅖 SIGHTS

ARCHAEOLOGICAL MUSEUMS. Two museums share Mytilini's extensive collection of archaeological relics. Tickets are good for both on the same day. The well-designed 🔳**new Archaeological Museum,** on 8 Noemvriou, contains the permanent exhibit "Lesvos from the Hellenistic to Roman Times." Displayed are finds ranging from 2nd-century BC cooking utensils to AD 3rd-century Roman sculptures and busts. The undisputed highlights, though, are the fully restored mosaic floors from ancient villas at Ag. Kyriaki, which are displayed in their original layout; they are placed under glass tiles, allowing you to walk on top. Most exhibits have English signs and the museum is handicapped-accessible. (☎22510 40 223. Open Tu-Su 8am-7:30pm. €3, students €2, EU students and under 18 free.) The **old Archaeological Museum,** Argiri Eftalioti 7, up the hill behind the main port, has a less-inspiring roundup of Lesvian artifacts from prehistoric to Roman times. Each exhibit, however, is accompanied by fascinating signs that use both mythological and historical elements to explain the significance of these fragments of ages past. The collection focuses on earthenware jars and small figurines found during the excavations at Thermi. The smaller building hiding behind the museum contains administrative and legal tablets written in the rare Aeolian dialect, now known to scholars primarily through the writings of Sappho. (☎22510 28 032. Open Tu-Su 8:30am-3pm.)

VARIA. Only 4km south of Mytilini along El. Venizelou, the tiny, unassuming village of Varia (Βαριά) surprises wayfarers with the 🔳**Theophilos Museum,** which exhibits 86 paintings by self-taught Greek artist Theophilos Hadzimichali. His vivid natural and patriotic works are internationally recognized. (☎22510 41 644. Open Tu-F 9am-2pm and 5-8pm, Sa-Su 9am-2pm. €2, students and children under 18 free.) Next door the **Musée Tériade** has an excellent—if somewhat crowded—collection of Picasso, Miró, Léger, Chagall, and Matisse lithographs with captions in Greek, English, and French. Tériade, a native of Lesvos (born Stratis Eleftheriadis), was a leading 20th-century publisher of graphic art in Paris. (☎22510 23 372. Open daily 9am-2pm and 5-8pm. €2, students and children free.) Local **buses** to Varia leave Mytilini every hour (20min., €1). Tell the driver you're going to the museums.

AGIOS RAFAEL. Twenty kilometers into the hills above Mytilini is the **Monastery of Agios Rafael.** The saint was particularly active in working modern-day miracles, making his chapel and grave a major place of pilgrimage. The door on the bottom level of the church marked "Αγιασμα" leads to a source of holy water. (Bus from Mytilini runs every hr., €1.)

OTHER SIGHTS. The sprawling **Gatelouzi Castle** extends over a pine-covered hill near the museums, above the port. Though the original building was erected in AD 483-565 by Emperor Justinian, the castle bears the name of Franceso Gatelouzi, who received the entire island of Lesvos as a dowry in 1354. Centuries of Genoese, Ottomans, and Greeks have maintained the castle walls and underground tunnels that once hid women and children in times of war. Because locals took stones from the castle to rebuild fallen structures throughout Mytilini after WWII, little more than rubble remains of its interior. Wear a sturdy, comfortable pair of shoes for wandering around and climbing to the top of the rocky walls. (☎ 22510 27 970. *Open Tu-Su 8am-2:30pm. €2, EU students and children under 18 free.*) The highest point on the northern side of Mytilini is the 3rd-century BC **ancient theater**, from the Hellenistic period, where 15,000 spectators attended performances and enjoyed near-perfect acoustics. The effect was so impressive that it inspired Pompeii to build Rome's first stone theater. *(Open Tu-Su 8:30am-7pm.)* The late 19th-century **Church of Agios Therapon,** on the western side of the harbor and one block inland on Ermou, is impressive for both its enormous size and its cherished icons. *(Open 9am-7pm. Free. Modest dress required.)* Across the square, the **Byzantine Museum,** on Pl. Ag. Therapon, contains Christian iconography from the 13th through 19th centuries along with other ecumenical treasures. (☎ 22510 28 916. *Open M-Sa 9am-1pm. €2.*) Inland and north of the harbor (one block off Ermou) is the **Church of Agios Theodoros,** the oldest in Mytilini, which houses the bones and skull of its patron saint.

⚡ DAYTRIPS FROM MYTILINI

VATERA

To get to Vatera (58km from Mytilini), you can take the bus (1½hr.; M-F 4 per day, Sa-Su 3 per day; €4.20). It enters on the main road, runs the length of the beachside road, and drops off and picks up anywhere along the beach. A 1-way taxi ride is about €40. If you have private transportation, you can also visit Vatera as a daytrip from Plomari or Polichnitos.

With calm waters and 8km of wide, unbroken sands, Vatera is Lesvos's premier **beach.** The ruins of the **Temple of Dionysus** sit to the right of the beach (when facing the water) at the cape of **Agios Fokas.** Some of the column remnants are from 300 BC, while others date to AD 100, when early Christian temples were built over the site. The ruins aren't hugely impressive, but the sunsets from the beach on the other side of the point are truly awesome. The journey is long by foot but makes for a pleasant bike ride. Follow the road along the beach to the right facing the water and veer left across the bridge at the sign for Villa Pouloudia. Bring water and avoid the midday heat; the latter half of the ride is quite hilly. **Hotel Aphrodite** ❹, 800m down from the main intersection, on your left, has rooms with A/C, TV, fridges, kitchenettes, private baths, and hair dryers. (☎ 22520 61 588. Breakfast included. Singles €70; doubles €45. In low season singles €45; doubles €55.) Two **supermarkets** are 50m to the left of the intersection and the beachside road is lined with tavernas. Candlelit **Mylos Cafe,** 100m left of the intersection on the beach, is a chill nightspot. (☎ 22520 61 161. Beer €2.30-4. Mixed drinks €5. Open late.)

PLOMARI

Plomari is a 40km bus ride from Mytilini (1½hr., €3.30). The bus stops in Plomari's main plateia, next to the taxi stand.

The vibrant, traditional flavor of this tiny fishing village is unlike any other on Lesvos. Home to several of Greece's most vital ouzo distilleries and surrounded by olive groves, Plomari's faded, crumbling buildings glow with the luster of small-town life. Originally a Turkish region, Plomari was first home to Greeks in 1841 after a fire in nearby Megalochorio drove residents southward. The village's warmth now attracts an influx of tourists, some who breeze through on their way west to Vatera, and others who stay to explore Plomari's cultural heritage. Lesvos is renowned for its ouzo production, and Plomari in particular is known for its local brews. The **Barbayanni Ouzo Factory,** about 2km east on the road to Agios Isodoros, is the production site for one of Greece's oldest and most beloved privately owned ouzo companies, still controlled by the founding family. You can take a peek at 19th-century distillation devices in the adjacent **Ouzo Museum** in addition to observing the fascinating production process in the current factory. (☎22520 32 741; www.barbayanni-ouzo.com. Ask at the factory for a free tour of the museum. Open M-F 10am-2pm.) Beaches appear intermittently around the town. To reach small, rocky **Ammoudeli beach,** follow the waterfront road out of town to the right from the bus stop, facing the water. Continuing straight past the beach brings you to **Agios Nikolaos,** a church that sparkles with icons spanning 400 years. About 3km east of town past the ouzo factory, the sandy, golden expanse of **Agios Isodoros beach** draws a large, bronzed following. An annual, week-long **Ouzo Festival** takes place in late August and features song, dance, and—of course—free ouzo. Plomari also holds several summertime religious celebrations and cultural events. The one-week **Festival of Benjamin,** in late June, commemorates War of Independence leader Benjamin of Lesvos with dancing and theatrical presentations. On August 15, the town celebrates the **Panagia** in time-honored style.

While Plomari is best as a daytrip, it does have accommodations for those who have had too much ouzo to make the last bus back. **Pension Lida ❷** is housed in two adjacent buildings; look for signs from the main plateia. The rooms in Lida 1 come with private baths and either a balcony, stone terrace, or arched window. Smaller and less snazzy Lida 2 has serviceable rooms with private baths. (☎/fax 22520 32 507. Book exchange available. Breakfast from €3. Singles €23; doubles €30-32; triples €36-38.) Tavernas line Platanos and the road leading to the main plateia. For fresh-grilled entrees, friendly owners Nikos and Nikos at **Bacchus ❷,** on the waterfront side of Hotel Oceanis, serve celebrated meatballs with bacon (€6) and *souvlaki bacchus* (€6.50) to tables overlooking the harbor. (☎22520 31 059. Entrees €5-8. Open daily 6pm-late.)

MOLYVOS Μόλυβος ☎22530

Hilly and cobbled, the town of Molyvos (a.k.a. "Mithymna") is a quintessential storybook village, winding up from the sea toward a towering castle. Home to an illustrious school of fine arts, a number of galleries, and a gaggle of artsy trinket shops, Molyvos breathes with the sensibility of an artists' colony. Though frequented by tourists, its atmosphere remains serene and its prices reasonable.

⊡⊠ TRANSPORTATION AND PRACTICAL INFORMATION. The most posh local bus imaginable, equipped with a TV, bathroom, and luxuriously soft seats for the 10min. (at most) rides, stops at the base of town on the main road. **Buses** run to Anaxos (7 per day) via Petra, Eftalou, and Skoytaros. All fares €1. Ask at the tourist office for schedules. The intercity bus runs to Mytilini (1½hr., 5 per day, €5). To the immediate left of the National Bank, **Kosmos Rentals** rents **mopeds** (€14-24 per day) and **cars** (from €35). Prices include full insurance, tax, and unlimited mileage. (☎22530 71 710. Open daily 8am-1pm and 5-9pm.) **Taxis** (☎22530 71 480) stop at the intersection on the main road heading into town from the bus stop.

Molyvos has three primary roads that run along different levels of the hill. The **main road** leads from the bus station past the tourist information office and bank and runs to the port on the far side of town. Down on your left as you enter town, another road borders the beach past hotels and restaurants. The third road veers right and uphill as you enter town and goes through the agora past shops and restaurants. At the edge of the left side of town, on the main road, is the **tourist information office,** where the friendly, informative staff provides updated bus schedules, info about Molyvos and Lesvos, and accommodations advice. They can also help decode the mysterious intercity bus schedule, providing much-needed insight on how to get around without returning to Mytilini. (☎22530 71 06. Open

Apr.-Oct. M-F 8am-5pm, Sa-Su 10am-5pm.) The **National Bank** is next door and has a **24hr. ATM.** (☎22530 71 210. Open M-Th 8am-2:30pm, F 8am-2pm.) The road forks just beyond the bank; head right, uphill, and left at the second fork, and you'll find the local **laundromat,** where €8 will get you one load of clean clothes. (☎22530 71 622. Open 9am-2:30pm and 5:30-9pm.) Signs will direct you to the **police station** (☎22510 71 222). Along the main uphill road, just after the National Bank, a **pharmacy** is before the road to Nassos Guest House. (☎22530 71 903. Open daily 9am-3pm and 6-10pm.) Continue along the road to the top of the hill and go right at the fork to reach a **medical office** (☎22530 71 702). **Internet access** isn't hard to find in Molyvos. Take a left at the fork in the uphill road for **Centraal.** (☎22530 72 556. €4.50 per hr.; €1.50 min.) Several other places with comparable prices are close to the harbor. The open-air **Cinema Arion** is just up from the bus stop. (☎22530 71 078. €4.40 per hr.; €1.50 min. Open in summer daily 9am-11pm.) Take a right at the fork at the top of the hill to reach the **post office.** (☎22530 71 246. Open M-F 7:30am-2pm.) **Postal Code:** 81108.

⌐⌐ ACCOMMODATIONS AND FOOD. Signs for **domatia** dot the town; the tourist office can help you find a bed. Expect to pay €25-40 for a double in high season and €15-25 in low season. In general, the farther uphill you go, the cheaper the rooms will be. Petra and Anaxos have better and often significantly cheaper options. ⚐**Nassos Guest House ❸** is on the road up the hill into town; head right at the first steep switchback and look for the Nassos sign. Homey, inviting, and thoughtfully decorated rooms have a youth hostel's atmosphere with the common kitchen, balcony, and bath. The staff moonlights as bus tour guides, able to answer any Lesvos-related question in English, Greek, or Dutch. Book exchange and private balconies with breathtaking views of the town and water below add to the appeal. (☎22510 71 432; www.nassosguesthouse.com. Open Apr.-Oct. Reservations recommended in Aug. Doubles €30-35; triples €35-45. Discounts for longer stays.) **Evaggelia Teke ❷,** on the uphill road at the corner of the port, has large rooms with fridges, clean private bathrooms, and lovely views. (☎22530 71 158. Inquire at one of the art galleries next door if no one's around. Singles €25; doubles €40-45.) **Camping Mithimna ❶,** a spacious campground 1km out of town on the road to Eftalou, has 24hr. hot showers, laundry, a common picnic area, and barbecue equipment for the budding chef. Bring your own food from town, as there is no place to buy it at the site. (☎22510 71 169. €5.60 per person, ages 4-10 €3, under 4 free; €3 per small tent, €3.50 per large tent.)

There are several **mini-marts** on the main road. Molyvos's harbor, at the far end of the main road, is crammed with restaurants, each offering fresh seafood and tables by the water. The fisherman who supplies **The Captain's Table ❸** is reputedly one of the island's best. The captain's platter for one (€12) or two (€23) lets you taste the full range of his talents along with the complimentary olives and sweet cinnamony bites. (☎22530 71 241. V.) **Octapus ❷,** one of the town's oldest tavernas, provides a similarly worthy seafood menu. Most fish run €45 per kg. (☎22530 71 317; www.octapus-restaurant.com. Open daily 10am-late.) Harbor restaurants may stretch the pocketbook, but many tavernas farther inland serve excellent food for more reasonable prices. **Taverna O Gatos ❷,** midway up the hill before the post office, has served fresh, traditional fare for over 20 years, including artfully prepared lamb with feta and tomatoes (€7.50). The sea breeze and sunset from the roof-top tables garnish the down-home dishes. (☎22510 71 661. Entrees €4-8. Open 9am-late.) Herbivores can finally taste a genuine gyro at **Friends Gyros Stand ❶,** on the main road, where several meatless pitas are stuffed with cucumbers, french fries, green peppers, feta, tomatoes, and other tasty ingredients. Luckily for demanding carnivores, the standard options are available as well. (☎22510 71 567. Pitas €1.40-1.60. Open daily noon-late.)

NORTHEAST AEGEAN

◙ ◪ **SIGHTS AND ENTERTAINMENT.** The dominant feature of Molyvos's skyline is the **kastro**, the medieval castle whose view alone is worth the climb. (Open Tu-Su 8am-2:30pm. €2, students and children free.) The superbly preserved castle, repaired by Gatelouzi in 1373 and later buttressed by the Turks, was once an important transfer point for trade in olives and oil. The former theater of war now hosts theatrical events; ask at the tourist information office, call the town hall (☎ 22510 71 313), or keep an eye out for signs. On summer nights, head to **Bazaar**, on the right side of the hill heading down to the harbor. House, techno, and blue floor-lights bounce off cave-like walls. (Open daily 11pm-late.) **Conga's Beach Club**, accessible from both the waterfront and main roads, helps you while away entire days in a haze of beach, bongos, and booze. Pool tables and tropical decor, complete with hammocks and tiki lamps, entertain a tourist crowd. (☎ 22530 72 181. Beer €3-5. Mixed drinks €7. Cover €5; includes 1 beer. Open daily 10am-3:30am.) **Nuevo**, on the beachside road, to the right of the Olive Press Hotel facing the water, is decorated with funky orange cubes and occasionally has live Greek music and theme parties. (Open daily 11pm-6am. Cover for theme nights €6; includes 1 drink. Mixed drinks €7. Beer €3.)

◪ **BEACHES.** A narrow, pebbly beach stretches to the south toward Petra and is accessible from the first road to the left as you enter Molyvos. Beach umbrellas abound, and showers and changing rooms are both free. More inviting shores can be found at **Eftalou**, whose beautiful black-pebble beaches make a pleasant daytrip from Molyvos. The bus from Molyvos drops off in the middle of the main beach. Walk about 300m to the end of road and around the rocks to find Eftalou's spa-like **thermal baths**, whose 44-46.5°C waters are amazingly relaxing and said to be medicinally potent. The knowledgeable, multilingual staff is happy to give advice on proper soaking procedures and can answer all questions concerning the baths' health benefits. (☎ 22530 71 245. €3.50 for 45min. in the pool, €5 for 15min. in a private bathtub; includes free locker storage. Towel rental €1. Children under 7 free. Pool open daily 10am-2pm and 4-8pm. Baths open daily 9am-4pm.) The beach continues well beyond the baths. The farthest cove is populated by **nude** bathers.

PETRA Πέτρα ☎ 22530

Named for the monolithic rock in the town center, quiet Petra extends along a sunny plain 5km south of Molyvos. Though it is basically an outgrowth of Molyvos, the village ambience and long beach make it a popular daytrip or an alternative place to stay in the area. If you can peel yourself off the sand, you can watch ouzo being bottled at **Ouzo Petras**, Ermou 31, an ouzo store with its own equipment. (Open daily 10:30am-1:30pm and 6:30-10:30pm.) Before downing your bottle of anise-flavored goodness, head up Theodokou past the post office to find the town's namesake, a 27m rock. The 114 steps nearby lead to the endearing **Church of the Holy Mary with the Sweet Smile**, which grants stunning views of the village and the sea. (Open daily 8:30am-9pm. Modest dress required.) The **Vareltzidaina House Museum** (open in summer Tu-Su 8:30am-7pm), an opulent mansion, is also in town.

Rooms in Petra are slightly cheaper than in Molyvos but are still more than in neighboring Anaxos. Walk past Nirvana Travel about 75m and turn left at the sign to find **Marina Rooms ❷**, at the end of the cul-de-sac. Pretty pink rooms with private baths offer peaceful, house-like repose. (☎ 22530 41 571. Singles €20; doubles €30.) The town's many delectable products are brought together at the **Agricultural Cooperative of Petra**, at the fork before town off the main road—a cornucopia of local wines, olive oils, and cheeses. They also sell fresh produce in the morning. (☎ 22530 41 208. Open 8am-1pm and 7-9pm.) The beachfront hosts the usual slate of indistinguishable tavernas. If you're looking for a less run-of-the-mill dinner, follow Theodokou past the steps leading to the church, and continue to your left at the fork in the road. The long walk along cobbled streets leads to **Rigas ❷**, the oldest taverna in town, which serves home-cooked Greek fare. (☎22530 41 405. Entrees €4-8. Open daily 7pm-late.)

Local **buses** go to Molyvos in the summer (7 per day 10:10am-7:05pm, €1) and stop 200m down the beach. **Taxis** are just a phone call away (☎22530 42 022). Parallel to the water one block inland, **Ermou** is lined with bakeries and shops. To the right on the water is **Nirvana Travel**, which has info, **currency exchange,** book exchange, and excursion bookings; it can also help with accommodations or car rentals. Additionally, Nirvana Travel organizes yoga, painting, and Greek dancing classes. (☎22530 41 991; www.nirvanatravel.gr. Open daily in summer 9am-2pm and 6-9:30pm.) A **24hr. ATM** is by the OTE on the main road. Next to Nirvana Travel is a **pharmacy.** (☎22530 41 319. Open 9am-2pm and 6-9pm.) A few paces farther down the same road is a **medical office** (☎22530 42 205; open 7:30am-1:30pm) and a private **hospital** (☎69449 75 219; open 24hr.). The **OTE** (☎22530 41 399; open M-F 7:30am-1:30pm) is to the left of the plateia on the road to Molyvos. **Internet access** is available at **Cafe Reef,** on the road to Molyvos, which is a full-on English pub complete with live soccer, Guinness (€4), and Indian food (chicken curry €5.50) on Tuesday. (☎22530 42 146; www.cafereef.com. €4 per hr.) The **post office,** which **exchanges currency,** is straight inland from the central plateia, on Theodokou. (☎22530 41 230. Open M-F 7:30am-2pm.) **Postal Code:** 81109.

SKALA ERESSOU Σκάλα Ερεσού ☎22530

Laid-back and open-minded, Skala Eressou, Sappho's birthplace, welcomes families, archaeologists, and lesbian couples alike to share in its golden, sandy embrace. Though the town isn't much, the beach, stretching for kilometers between two mountainous heights, has won awards as one of the world's best. In the spirit of free love, nude bathers frolic on part of the endless shore.

📭🔁 TRANSPORTATION AND PRACTICAL INFORMATION. An early-morning **bus** runs between Skala Eressou and Mytilini via the fork for Sigri and Kalloni (3hr., daily, €7.40). From July 5 to September 10, extra buses run at 11am and 6pm. The bus stops in a large parking lot on the main road two blocks from the waterfront. There is only one **taxi** driver (☎22530 54 327) in the area, based out of Sigri, 26km to the northwest; a one-way taxi to Sigri will run about €20.

The main road hits the waterfront just a few meters to the right of a short footbridge, which divides the town. Though the restaurants and cafes to the left of the bridge have a bit more soul than those to the right, the entire beach strip radiates fun and relaxation. Joanna and the incredibly helpful, English-speaking team at 🏠**Sappho Travel,** one block from the bus stop before the waterfront, provide info about the town, help with accommodations, and **exchange currency.** (☎22530 52 140; www.sapphotravel.com. Open daily 9am-3pm and 6-10pm.) Though there is **no bank** in Skala Eressou, a **bank-on-a-bus** rolls through town every Tuesday and Thursday from 11am to 1pm. Though infinitely less amusing, the **24hr. ATM** outside Sappho Travel is more convenient. The nearest **police** are in Eressos (☎22530 53 222). The town's sole **doctor** commutes between the **clinic** in Skala Eressou (☎22530 53 221; open June-Sept. M, W, F 9am-1pm), behind Hotel Sappho, and his office in Eressos (☎22530 52 132; open Tu, Th). In case of **emergency,** call the **health center** (☎22530 56 440, 22530 56 442, or 22530 56 444), in Antissa, 11km from Skala Eressou. A few card **phones** sit along the main road running from the bus stop to the beach; there is also one by Hotel Sappho. **Internet access** is available at the **Internet Cafe,** just past the bridge on Kanari. (€2 per 20min., €5 per hr.; additional time €0.05 per min. Unlimited coffee €1.50. Open 11am-10pm.) The **post office** is in Eressos. (☎22530 53 227. Open M-F 8am-2pm.) **Postal Code:** 81105.

⌂ ACCOMMODATIONS. Skala Eressou first draws visitors for weeks of stunning sunsets; many vacationers end up staying for good. Consequently, studios and long-term lodgings are plentiful, though there are reasonably priced rooms for brief stays as well. To find a room, call Sappho Travel's special line for help with accommodations (☎22530 52 202). Call ahead for reservations in high season, as the rooms fill up quickly. **Hotel Sappho ❷**, on the waterfront to the right (facing the water), is a lesbian-friendly, women-only hotel with an open feel and original artwork decorating the walls. Simple, spacious rooms have private baths. The lobby contains a book exchange and several lesbian-oriented magazines. (☎22530 53 495. Singles €15-35; doubles €40-56.) The good-humored couple who runs **Pension Krinelos ❷**, just behind the bus stop, offers affordable, homestyle lodgings. Clean rooms have baths, A/C (€5), and common fridges. (☎22530 53 246. Book exchange available. Quiet hours 2-5pm and midnight-8am. Singles €20-25; doubles €25-35.) As you enter town, turn right past the bus stop and walk 50m to find the new, women-only **Hotel Mascot ❸**. Its 10 rooms have the amenities found in larger hotels—A/C, fridges, baths, balconies, phones, and Internet jacks—at a fraction of the cost. Breakfast (included) in the common dining nook and teas at the small, tree-sheltered patio encourage guests to mingle. Ask about the women's writers group and ecotourism hikes. Reservations are booked through Sappho Travel. (☎22530 52 140. Doubles €35.) Across the street, **Katerina Rooms ❷** has bright, sun-warmed rooms with fridges and baths and overlooks a well-tended fruit garden. (☎22530 53 640. Doubles €25-35.) **Camping** on the beach is **illegal** and the town's police have been increasingly strict about this policy.

◧⌕ FOOD AND ENTERTAINMENT. Food in Skala Eressou is generally very good and the town is a vegetarian paradise—at least by Greek standards. **Sappho Restaurant ❷**, at Hotel Sappho, has a spunky, alternative vibe. Excellent, meatless dishes like the tasty falafel platter (€6.50) are served to a soundtrack of female singer-songwriters. (☎22530 53 233. Entrees €6-8. Open daily 9am-11pm.) To the right along the waterfront, **Ouzeri Soulatso ❸** is the most traditional Greek taverna in town, treating diners to a deep-sea harvest of fresh fish along with their ouzo. (☎22530 52 078. Grilled entrees €5; seafood prices fluctuate around the catch and season. Open daily noon-midnight.) Farther down to the right is **Eressos Palace ❷**, a family-run taverna whose huge portions of fresh food come at deliciously low prices. The fisherman's souvlaki (€5.50) is made with a variety of skewered and grilled fish, and a number of vegetarian dishes are available as well. (☎22530 53 858. Entrees €4-8. Open daily 8am-1am.)

The nightlife scene, dominated by chill beachfront cafes and bars that spill onto the sand, is (unsurprisingly) lesbian-friendly. On hot summer evenings, join the crowd for a late-night plunge in the Aegean to clear your head. **The Tenth Muse** is a popular bar in the main plateia. (☎22530 53 287. Beer €2-4.50. Mixed drinks €5. Open 9:30am-4am.) **Friends,** along the waterfront to the left, draws an international crowd with a plethora of creative non-alcoholic drinks (€6) plus all the intoxicating standbys. Stop by during the day to take advantage of its all-day breakfasts. (☎22530 53 178; www.friends-bar.net. Open 10am-late.) **Naos Music Club,** at the far end of the parking lot on the main road to Eressos, has a massive bar and mostly local clientele. The wide variety of music is so dance-able that it's a challenge to stay seated. (☎22530 53 787. Open 11pm-late.)

🗿 **SIGHTS.** Sappho fans beware: though useless trinkets and statues of the poet are easy to find in town, actual collections of her work are not. A few photographs of the landscape that inspired her might make better souvenirs. The 5th-century mosaics once housed in the early-Christian basilica of **Agios Andreas,** three blocks north of the beach, are now in Mytilini's new Archaeological Museum (p. 512). Though the church was named after the apostle Ag. Andreas, a Cretan archbishop of the same name happened to die nearby just a couple centuries later. His grave, the **Tomb of Agios Andreas** (open 9am-9pm), was incorporated into the site, though it only contains half of his remains; the other portion was claimed by Crete. The **river,** just west of Skala's center, is home to many rare and exotic birds. Peak **bird watching** season is from April to May. About 11km north of Sigri on the main road is the spectacular **Ipsilou Monastery,** which dates back to AD 800. Sitting on the peak of the Ordymnos volcanic dome, the Byzantine monastery commands an amazing view of northwestern Lesvos's rugged, yellow hills. (☎22530 56 219. Open daily 9am-9pm. Free. Modest dress required.)

🚌 **DAYTRIPS FROM SKALA ERESSOU.** A **petrified forest,** 4km from **Sigri,** is one of only two such forests in the world (the other is in the southwestern United States). The remains of the fossilized trunks scattered throughout the parched hillside are around 20 million years old, and the more massive remnants are over 20m in length. The trees were preserved in exquisite detail during an ancient volcanic meltdown that almost instantaneously blanketed the original forest. Molecule-by-molecule, silicon carried by the volcanic goo replaced the plants' organic matter. A 2.5km long walking trail brings visitors to the site, and the forest itself takes at least 1hr. to appreciate fully; make sure to bring water and a hat. (Open daily July-Aug. 8am-7pm; Sept.-June 8am-3pm. €2, children under 15 free. For more info, call the museum or the parks office in Mytilini at ☎22510 40 132.) In Sigri, the 🏛**Natural History Museum of the Lesvos Petrified Forest** has fascinating exhibits on plant fossils, both from Lesvos itself and from around the world, dating back to the Paleozoic Era. The museum, well-designed enough to turn even the biggest rockhead into an aspiring geologist for an hour, also contains exhibits on general geology and the geological history of the Aegean. (☎22530 54 434; www.aegean.gr/petrified_forest. Open M-Sa 8:30am-6pm, Su 9am-6pm; later in Aug. €2, children free.) The site and museum are only accessible by private vehicle, but the road that runs directly from Eressos to Sigri is not passable. Head back toward Andissa on the main road for 10km and turn left at the fork for Sigri; on the way you'll pass the road up to Ipsilou Monastery. No buses currently run to Sigri or to the forest. A one-way taxi from Skala Eressou to the village of Sigri will run about €20. Bus service does exist between Mytilini and Sigri (3hr., 3 per day 6:15am-1:15pm, €7.40), however, making the forest accessible as an extra-long daytrip. A network of hiking **trails** connects Eressos to the petrified forest and Sigri; get a detailed map of the trails from a travel agency or the museum before a hike.

The small fishing village of Sigri is worth a look if you make the trip to the museum. Several small tavernas cluster near the plateia on your left as you approach the harbor on the main road. **Una Fazzia, Una Razza ❷,** an Italian restaurant with welcoming owners, serves the cheapest lobster in the area (€35 per kg) along with excellent pasta dishes. (☎22530 54 565. Entrees €5.50-8. Open daily Apr.-Oct. 9am-4pm and 6:30pm-late. MC/V.) Sandy and calm, Sigri's **beach** is protected from the northern winds by the town's 18th-century **Turkish castle.** Less-frequented beaches lie farther down the road. If you decide to stay longer in Sigri, Sappho Travel in Skala Eressou (p. 517) can organize accommodations. Sappho

Travel also has an office in Sigri that doubles as a shipping agency for the newly opened commercial port; although no major ferry routes use the port yet, contact Sappho for information about cruises and docking private boats.

LIMNOS Λήμνος

Remote and arid, Limnos can intimidate travelers with its uninviting austerity. But just as the dry, apparently unmanageable soil yields a surprising wealth of products to wise Limnian farmers, the lively island reveals its treasures—well-preserved wetlands and archaeological sites, majestic sunsets, sparkling beaches, silent sand dunes, bustling local communities, and a pack of migrating flamingoes—to travelers with the patience to meet the land on its own terms.

MYRINA Μύρινα   ☎ 22540

Myrina has a small-town feel to it, largely because of the cobbled main road, where residents and visitors stroll after sunset to window-shop and gossip. Two waterfronts split the town's duties admirably: one greets ferries and brings in the fishermen's daily catch, while the other buzzes with trim waiters and idle beachgoers as the sun sinks behind distant Mt. Athos. The impressive, illuminated Venetian Castle dominates the evening skyline.

▐ TRANSPORTATION. The **Olympic Airways** office, next to the post office, sells plane tickets. (☎ 22540 22 214. Open M-F 8am-3:30pm) **Flights** go to: Athens (50min., 2 per day, €68); Chios (2hr., 2 per week, €36); Lesvos (35min., daily M-Sa, €36); Thessaloniki (6 per week, €71). **SAOS** and **G.A. Ferries** are the two lines that serve Limnos. **Ferries** run to: Alexandroupoli (6hr., 1 per week, €18); Kavala (5hr., 5 per week, €16); Lavrio, near Athens (10hr., 5 per week, €33.20); Mytilini, Lesvos (5½hr., 3 per week, €20); Piraeus (25hr., 1 per week, €30); Samos (13hr., 1 per week, €29); Samothraki (2½hr., 4 per week, €13); Volos (10hr., 2 per week, €28). The **SAOS office,** at the far end of Pl. 8 Oktovriou, where the port-side road meets Kyda, sells tickets. (☎ 22540 29 571. Open daily 8am-1:30pm and 6-10pm.) The bus station is in Pl. El. Venizelou, the second plateia along Kyda in the far-left corner between a tourist agency and a coffee shop. In theory the **buses** should serve all island villages. They are inconvenient and unreliable, though, and you run the risk of getting stranded; check with locals to find out if they are running at all. Many visitors choose to rent a **bicycle** (€6), **moped** (€12-20), or **car** (€30) at one of the countless harbor-front agencies. Limnos is not the place to pinch pennies on vehicles—many of the roads to ecological sites are broken dirt paths that require good traction to navigate safely. **Taxis** (☎ 22540 23 033) are available in the main plateia.

▐▌ ORIENTATION AND PRACTICAL INFORMATION. The city has two main waterfronts on opposite sides of the castle. **Turkikos,** facing Turkey, is the active port, with Myrina's best fish tavernas and a sandy, shallow beach at its far end. **Romeikos,** on the northern side of the castle, is a family-friendly waterfront lined with parks, playgrounds, and hip cafes. To find it, head inland up **Kyda,** past most of the town and take a left when you can spot the sea in between the buildings. The **tourist office,** just off the ferry docks, provides a variety of elementary-school-style multilingual handouts that give an incredibly useful overview of the island, including ferry and flight schedules, accommodations information, and summaries of historical sights. (☎ 22540 22 935. Open daily 7am-3pm and 6-9pm.) Kyda is the town's commercial artery; it leads inland from Pl. 8 Oktovriou to the town's central plateia and contains the **National Bank,** which has a **24hr. ATM** (☎22540 23 541; open M-Th 8am-2:30pm, F 8am-2pm), **taxis** (☎22540 23 820), and **card phones.** One block farther on Kyda, **Garofallidi** runs to the right; following it will take you to a self-service **laundromat** in the Hotel Astron. (☎22540 24 392. €6.50 per 1-2kg load, €8 per 5-6kg. Open daily 8am-2pm and 5-9pm.) Down Garofallidi is a large intersection with the **police station** on the corner. (☎22540 22 200 or 22540 25 555. Open 24hr.) There are several **pharmacies** on Kyda. From the post office, turn left and take the first right, following the signs to the **hospital.** (☎22540 82000. Open 24hr.) Farther up Garofallidi on your right is **Joy Games,** which has **Internet access.** (☎22540 25 453. €3 per hr.; €1 min. Open daily 9am-2pm and 5:30-10pm.) The **post office** is two doors up. (☎22540 22 462. Open M-F 7:30am-2pm.) **Postal Code:** 81400.

⊓⊓ ACCOMMODATIONS AND FOOD. Most hotels in town are expensive. If you have a phone card and a little patience, try calling some of the **domatia** advertised around town to compare prices. In high season, however, you may end up paying top dollar regardless of your efforts. **Hotel Aktaion ❷,** on the waterfront in the first plateia on the left from the ferry dock, has simple rooms with small balconies and fridges. The rooms with shared baths are an amazing deal, as prices remain constant throughout the summer. (☎22540 22 258. Singles €15, with bath €20-25; doubles €20/25-30.) In Romeikos, the **Blue Waters Hotel ❹,** housed in a mid-19th-century mansion, has beautifully decorated rooms with A/C, fridges, TV, and modern baths; larger rooms come with kitchens. (☎22540 24 403. Doubles €45-50; quads €55-65.) **Hotel Lemnos ❸,** near the ferry dock in Turkikos, rents clean, standard rooms with A/C, TV, fridges, phones, balconies, and harbor views. (☎22540 22 153. Singles €30-35; doubles €40-45; triples €50-55.)

High-quality, reasonably priced food is easy to find in Myrina; both Turkikos and Romeikos are lined with quality tavernas and cafes. For some of the best fish in town, head past the port-side cafes to the *limanaki* (little port), on the marina near Pl. 8 Oktovriou. **To Limanaki ❷,** on the far end, lets patrons choose whatever fish their hearts desire from the icy vats near the kitchen. A heaping plate of grilled sardines (€4) may be enough for a satisfying seafood fix. (☎22540 23 744. Fish €27-47 per kg. Open daily 7am-late.) The sea literally crashes up to the tables at **Taverna Kosmos ❷,** along Romeikos to the left when facing the water. A slew of Greek

THE LOCAL STORY

SPINNING A CURE

In 1916, the small village of Varos, in the center of Limnos by the present-day airport was struck by a horrible plague. As the disease quickly decimated the population, one woman in the village had a vision it, Agios Charalambos, one of the Greek Orthodox Church's saints, directed her to spin thread from locally produced cotton, and wrap it around the village's borders to ward off the plague. The next morning, the woman shared her vision with her weakening townspeople. Eager to try anything that might eradicate the epidemic, a large group congregated to join her in immediately setting upon the task of spinning large amounts of thread. They surrounded Varos with the seemingly never-ending strand and sure enough, the plague disappeared from the village.

Today, Varos's residents commemorate this story during Lent. The village women re-enact the frenetic spinning session, making 13 balls of thread from local cotton. The thread is then taken to the small Church of Saint Charalambos, where the villagers pray to the saint, thanking him profusely for saving their village. After the service, the townspeople, continuing the re-enactment of the original wrapping, symbolically bind the village with the thread, draping it around the village's borders for an entire day.

comfort foods, including moussaka (€4.50) and beef in tomato with fries (€6), dominate the well-rounded menu. (☎22540 22 050. Open daily.) The many shops along Kyda make fresh souvlaki, gyros (€1.50), and spanikopita (€1.50), all perfect for a quick bite. **Taverna Oi Tzitzifies ❷** (Οι Τζιτζιφιες), about 50m to the right of the archaeological site when facing the water, is a popular lunch spot due to its location on the sand. Throw a towel over your suit and follow the crowds into the kitchen to see what's cooking. (☎22540 23 756. Greek salad €3.50. Eggplant with bechamel €4. Open daily 11am-1am.)

⑥ SIGHTS. The **kastro**, piercing the skyline and dividing the waterfronts, is home to several dozen deer. If you don't catch sight of them, you can at least enjoy the stunning view and the ruins of the 7th-century BC fortress, reworked by Venetians in the 13th century. It takes about 1hr. to clamber through the buildings, so wear good shoes and watch for deer droppings and prickly weeds. Follow signs from Myrina harbor for the easiest ascent. At the far end of Romeikos, to the right when facing the water, the well-curated **archaeological museum** has a collection of artifacts with informative English, German, Greek, and Italian explanations. Finds from the ancient settlements of Hephaestus, Poliochni, and the Kabeiron include a series of terracotta siren sculptures and an impressive skeleton of a sacrificed bull calf. (☎22540 22 990. Open Tu-Su 8:30am-3pm. €2, seniors and students €1, EU students and children free.) About 100m past the museum along the waterfront is the fascinating **archaeological area,** where catwalk-like paths lead visitors through the well-preserved remains of a 4th-millennium BC proto-urban settlement. The stone building, which sits at the site's entrance, continuously plays an amusing and informative video with English subtitles that uses computer simulations to show what the village looked like in its heyday. Detailed cyber tours of each building's interior pan by several animated Neolithic people, adding a touch of human interest. (☎22540 22 257. Open Tu-Su 9am-8pm. Free.)

Though most of the island's attractions are best reached by car or moped, a couple of travel agencies arrange bus excursions around Limnos. **Petrides Travel** (☎22540 22 039; www.petridestravel.gr), on Kyda, runs six different trips (all €15 per person) a few times per week. Full-day trips leave at 9am and include lunch, while others are only in the evenings. Taxis go from Myrina to all sites for €10-20 each way but will expect to be paid for waiting time while you explore; negotiate a total price with the driver before departing. Limnos has a number of notable **archaeological sites,** all on the opposite side of the island from Myrina. **Poliochni,** on the eastern coast, is the oldest proto-urban settlement discovered in all of Europe, dating from the late-Neolithic period (5000-4000 BC). One of the most complex fortified cities of its time, it is credited with being the site of Europe's first parliament. **Ancient Hephaestia,** on the northeastern coast of the island, was the location of a sanctuary to Hephaestus, god of fire and metallurgy, whose divine forge was supposedly on the island; the idea may have arisen because of Limnos's volcanic soil and the metalworking skills of its ancient inhabitants. Farther up the coast is the **Kaveiron,** an 8th-century BC sanctuary once used by a secret cult to worship the Kaveiroi, Hephaestus's children. Ceremonies were held to honor the birth of humanity and the rebirth of nature. Near the sanctuary is the cave, which can now be explored by foot, where Philoctetes, a Greek archer in the Trojan Wars, lived after he was bitten by a snake and abandoned by his companions. During full moons, islanders and visitors still gather on the nearby beach to celebrate with food, drink, guitars, and good spirits.

Limnos also has to a number of ecological sights, including the longest **sand dunes** in Europe (near Gomati beach, on the northern coast), the **waterfalls** near Kaspakas, and the **hot springs** at Therma. Ask around regarding the latter two, as the island's water supply has a great deal to do with their magnificence (and even existence). During winter and spring, the western salt plain of Lake Aliki hosts thousands of migrating flamingoes who descend on the island in a blur of pink. If all of the sightseeing has worked up an appetite, head to one of the best—and also one of the only—restaurants in the central western part of the island, **Taverna Mandela ❷** (☎22540 61 899), in Sares. A friendly South African expat serves village rooster with fresh *flomari* pasta (€6.55) and other tasty specialties.

Most of Limnos's sandy **beaches** are near Myrina. The most popular beach on the island is shallow **Riha Nera,** just north of Romeikos. **Avlonas,** on the way to Kaspakas, is large and uncrowded, with two islets of its own; go along the steep mountain road to find **Agios Yiannis** nearby. On the road to Kontias is **Nevgatis,** an easily accessible beach with 2km of unbroken sands.

SAMOTHRAKI Σαμοθράκη

Samothraki (also called "Samothrace") was once a place of pilgrimage for Thracian settlers who belonged to a cult that worshipped the great Anatolian gods. When those first colonists arrived in the 10th century BC, they saw an incredible vista that is still visible from the ferry port: dry grassy fields surrounding the base of the Aegean's tallest peak, the pine-blanketed Fengari (meaning "moon"). Remote and dominated by wilderness, Samothraki attracts visitors who prefer swatting mosquitoes in a tent to clubbing until dawn—there are more hiking boots than high heels, and guitars outnumber cell phones as hand-held accessories. This laid-back crowd lends the place a grungy *joie de vivre* which can be a refreshing change from the run-of-the-mill summer glitz of other islands.

KAMARIOTISSA Καμαριώτισσα ☎25510

This transportation hub is an excellent settling place for exploring and surveying Samothraki's charms. Kamariotissa has a serene attitude which is apparent even amid tourist agencies along the waterfront and the occasional traffic from the arrival and departure of buses and boats; compared to the surrounding wilderness, however, Kamariotissa feels like a major urban center.

⌐ TRANSPORTATION. Ferries dock on the southern edge of town and run to: Alexandroupoli (2½hr., 1-2 per day, €9); Kavala (3½hr., 2 per week, €16); Lesvos (7hr., Sa 5:15pm, €28); Limnos (3½hr.; M-Tu 6:15pm, Sa 5:15pm; €15). **Flying Dolphins** run to Alexandroupoli from mid-June to mid-September (1hr., 1-2 per day, €16). For tickets and schedules, ask the port police or **Saos Tours** (☎22510 23 512; open daily 10am-1pm and 6-9pm). **Niki Tours** doesn't sell ferry tickets, but the friendly Hatzigiannakaidis brothers there can help with accommodations, flight tickets, group excursions, and general information about the island. (☎25510 41 230 or 25510 41 465. Open daily 9am-2pm and 6-10pm.) **Buses** stop on the waterfront across from Saos Tours and go to **Hora** (7 per day, 8am-7:40pm, €1), **Profitis Ilias** (5 per day, 6:30am-8pm, €1.50) via **Alonia** and **Lakoma,** and **Therma** (4 per day, 7:10am- 5:15pm, €2). Schedules and prices fluctuate often; consult the bus drivers for more information. **Taxis** wait on the waterfront (☎25510 41 733. 24hr.). The best way to get around the island is by car or moped, which you can rent from **Kyrkos Rentals,** located on the waterfront where you disembark from the ferry. (☎25510 41 620. Mopeds and bikes €10 per day; cars €20-50 per day. Open daily 24hr.)

◼ ⁊ ORIENTATION AND PRACTICAL INFORMATION. Everything in Kamariotissa is located on one street along the waterfront. The waterfront road runs out of town to the northeast, and the road to Hora runs east out of town just past the bus stop (at the stop sign). The **National Bank** with a **24hr. ATM** and **currency exchange** is two stores down from Niki Tours. (☎22510 41 750. Open M-Th 8am-2:30pm, F 8am-2pm.) A Greek flag marks the 24hr. **port police** whose station is five shops down from the bank (☎22510 41 305). The **pharmacy** is 10m east of the only stop sign in the village on the road to Hora. (☎25510 41 698. Open daily 9am-2pm, M-F also 6-9pm.) The town's pharmacies rotate 24hr. duty; check the schedule posted on the door of any one for more information. **Cafe Aktaion**, on the waterfront across from the ferry docks, entertains the video game generation with 10 computer stations, three pool tables (€5 per hr.), and **Internet access** on eight computers. (☎25510 41 056. €3 per hr. Open daily 8am-2am.) The **police station** (☎22510 41 203; open 24hr.), **medical clinic** (☎22510 41 217; open 24hr.), and **OTE** (☎22510 41 299) are in Hora. The **post office** (☎22510 41 244) is at the end of the main port road; facing the ferries, go left for about 100m. **Postal Code:** 68002.

⚞⚟ ACCOMMODATIONS AND CAMPING. Samothraki's main draw is its pristine wilderness, high peaks, and crystal clear beaches; consequently, many travelers breeze through Kamariotissa on their way to **Therma** and the campsites. Some camp illegally in the surrounding area, but there's no reason to avoid the established campsites. Kamariotissa is the island's transportation hub and the only place to stay before early-morning ferries. **Domatia** signs abound along the waterfront road and prices for a single range €20-30. ▓**Camping Platia ❶**, 15km from Kamariotissa and 2km beyond Therma on the coast, has showers, baths, a minimart, and phones. This excellent choice is bounded by the wilderness on one side and a spectacular view of the Aegean on the other. (☎25510 98 244. €3 per person, 12 and under €2; €2.50 per tent.) **Brisko Rooms ❸** has quiet accommodations off its flower-lined terrace. To get there, turn left out of Cafe Aktaion and take the next left inland. Only some of the rooms have an ocean view, but all rooms come with A/C, TV, fridges, baths, and balconies. (☎25510 41 328. Singles €27; doubles €35; triples €47.) **Hotel Kyma ❸**, on the waterfront at the outskirts of Kamariotissa on the beginning of the road to Therma, has clean, simple rooms close to the stone beach. Rooms have small private baths, fridges, and A/C. (☎25510 41 263. Doubles €50; triples €65. Low season prices reduced.) **Camping Varades ❶**, 5km from Therma on the coastal road, has similar amenities to Camping Platia as well as a cafe, but this added luxury means there is more concrete than greenery. (☎25510 98 291. €3 per person, €2 per child under 15; €2.50-3 per tent.)

⚞⚟ FOOD AND NIGHTLIFE. Waterfront tavernas specialize in fresh seafood. At **Klimataria ❷**, adjacent to hotel Kyma, enticing home-cooked dishes await your selection behind a glass counter in the kitchen. Chicken fillet stuffed with tomato and feta (€8), pork roasted with potatoes, yogurt, eggs, and cheese (€8), and "goat in oven" (€7) are just some of the specialties. (☎25510 41 535. Open daily noon-5pm and 7pm-1am.) **Sinatisi ❷**, a few doors down from Niki Tours, is a favorite for fresh fish. The menu is only in Greek, so stroll in and simply point at the fish of your culinary dreams. (☎25510 41 308 or 25510 41 214. Entrees €5-7. Open daily 8am-5pm and 8pm-late.) **Cafe Moka ❶**, on the waterfront, will satiate any sweet tooth with its 26 flavors of homemade ice cream, and an overwhelming variety of pastries and cakes. (☎25510 41 093. Greek coffee €1.80. Strawberry milkshake €3.50. Ice cream €1 per scoop. Open daily 6am-midnight.)

Kamariotissa's tavernas often stay open late into the night for nightlife; the younger set flocks to the bars that have dance floors. **Cafe-Bar Diva**, on the waterfront, plays up-to-date MTV-style hits during the day and popular Greek music at night. (☎22510 41 060. Mixed drinks €2-6. Open 8am-late.) **Rebel**, a dance club to the right of the docks on the waterfront, appropriately shirks Cafe-Bar Diva's music strategy, playing mostly Greek music until mid-summer, when it changes to

American hits to fit the more touristy audience. (☎25510 41 554. Open June-Sept. midnight-8am.) **Cafe Therma** at the entrance to the nearby village of Therma, is another nightlife favorite. Tables overlook the sea while guests sit in the shade of old sycamore trees. Flanked by two creeks gushing down from the peak of Fanagri, this understated cafe offers both drinks and *mezedes* (€4) in addition to a general air of tranquility. Live music is played at night. (☎25510 938 325. Open 24hr.)

◪◪ **BEACHES AND THE OUTDOORS.** This verdant gem of an island holds a wealth of trails leading to cascading waterfalls, mountain vistas, and the summit of Fengari. Trails are generally unmarked; the best way to explore is to rent a vehicle in Kamariotissa and head to the coast or interior. Hiring a local tour guide, available for a negotiable fee at some of the trailheads, is also a good idea, as trekkers who attempt to ascend unaided can get lost or injured in the wild terrain. Ask locals from the villages that dot the mountain's flanks for directions to trailheads.

The most convenient hub for outdoor activities is the small town of **Therma,** about 13km from Kamariotissa. Its houses, spread out on the mountainside, are framed by two streams. Tavernas and domatia dominate the village, making it a quiet, down-to-earth, and attractive alternative to Kamariotissa, especially for stays of multiple days. A multitude of local mini-marts and equipment stores can outfit your camping trip. **Buses** from Kamariotissa stop at the base of town, next to the refreshing **thermal springs** that give the town its name. Thermal water bursts from the springs at a scorching 92°C and is cooled down to 42°C for public use. (Entrance to both private and public baths €2.)

The trail to the **summit of Fengari** (4hr.) is accessible from Therma. Ask around at the base of town for the best way up. Be sure to fill up your water bottles at the fountain at the base of town and don't hike alone. Enchanting ◪**Fonias waterfall,** also accessible from Therma, will revive any tired soul slowed by the scorching Aegean sun. From the bus stop, take the left fork through town. Take the first right after a mini-mart and follow this road past tavernas and a bakery. When the road dead-ends, turn left and follow the unpaved road; when it meets an asphalt-paved road, turn right. The road dead-ends again at Taverna Filarakia, where you should turn right and head up the shaded road. The dirt trail follows the stream on the right side of the road; head right 20m before the Marina Hotel. The easy 2km hike meanders alongside a gurgling stream and beneath gnarled trees. The trail ends at a sheer cliff face at a cascading waterfall. The trail can be slippery, so watch your step. Some hikers shed their clothes and jump into the pool at the waterfall's base carved out of the rock below, or carefully climb up the rock face to the right of the stream for a magnificent view of the falls and the mountains.

The island's only sand beach is the soft arc of **Pahia Ammo** on the southern coast, whose radiant blue water could have splashed off of a postcard. The best way to get to Pahia Ammo is to rent a car or moped, as buses are infrequent. Stony black beaches ring the rest of the island. Ask a bus driver to drop you anywhere, then hunt down an isolated stretch of shore. At the end of the line along the northern coast is popular **Kypos,** whose main attraction is a cave which looks out at the rocky beach. Three white **buses** per day go to Kypos. Schedules change frequently; ask bus drivers in Kamariotissa for schedules.

◪ **DAYTRIP FROM KAMARIOTISSA.** ◪**Paleopolis** and its **Sanctuary of the Great Gods** lie 6km east of Kamariotissa and are Samothraki's premier attractions. Take the bus to Therma and ask to be let off there. Before the island's 4th-century BC Aeolian colonization, pre-Olympian gods ruled over Samothraki: the Great Mother goddess **Axieros** and her cronies **Axiokersa, Axiokersos,** and **Kasmilos.** Members of the secret cult that worshipped these gods were among the island's earliest inhabitants, possibly dating back to 7th century BC. Since disclosing initiation secrets was punishable by death, today very little is known about their rituals. Purification rites took place in the **Anaktoron,** at the lowest part of the temple complex, and the **Hieron,** a courtyard whose re-erected columns now form the site's central attraction. In the **palace** at the southern end of the site, aspiring initiates donned special vestments, and were inducted at the adjoining Anaktoron.

It is reported that Philip II of Macedon, Alexander the Great's father, first met Olympias, a princess from Epirus and Alexander's mother, at their initiation into this cult. Thereafter the site was of special importance to the new Macedonian empire. The enormous cylindrical **Arsinoëin Rotunda,** given to Samothraki by Queen Arsinoë II of Egypt (288-270 BC), demonstrates the continued patronage of the site by Alexander's successors, the Ptolemys. The sacrificial site's walls (now in the museum) are decorated with rosettes and oxen heads. In the center, the **Doric Hieron**—containing pits for sacrifices, an altar for libations, and seats for the audience—saw the final stage of initiation in which the candidates were purified after confessing their worst deeds.

The **Winged Victory** (or **Nike**) **of Samothrace,** the pride of the island, stood upon a marble base here before it took a mid-nineteenth-century trip to Paris, where it currently perches in the Louvre. The remains of an **ancient theater** sit on the overlooking hillside. Above the sanctuary are the remains of the **ancient town** of Samothraki where the apostle Paul stopped in AD 49-50 on his way from Ephesus in Asia Minor to Phillipi. It is believed that the AD first-century **Christian Basilica,** whose ruins lie at the eastern edge of the ancient harbor, was built in commemoration of Paul's visit. (Site open Tu-Sa 8:30am-8:30pm. €3 including museum admission, students €2, EU students free.)

Sitting beside the ruins, the ◪**Paleopolis Museum** houses many of the site's artifacts such as libation vessels and figurines. Of particular note are the giant entablatures from the Arsinoëin rotunda and the Hieron, a bust of the blind Samothrakian prophet Tiresias, and a galling cast of the missing-in-action Nike. Other highlights of the exhibition include the beautiful winged and draped Akroterial statue of victory from the Hieron, an inscription from the Anaktoron in Greek and Latin forbidding the uninitiated from entering the inner sanctum (AD 200), and the erotic scenes depicted on a first-century BC pot. (☎25510 41 474. Open Tu-Su 8:30am-3pm.)

THASSOS Θάσος

Just 20km off the coast of Kavala (p. 287) lies Thassos, a green jewel which has run into an inordinate amount of trouble over the centuries. According to legend, Thassos's origins are wrapped in misfortune: After Europa's devoted brother finally gave up chasing his sister—who had met the all-too-common fate of being abducted by a lusty Zeus—he built the first settlements on this remote island. Despite Europa's brother's scorn for Zeus's actions, Thassos soon fell victim to a less mythic type of lust. As an ancient exporter of gold, silver, and its famous wine, Thassos attracted the unwelcome attention of Phoenician, Athenian, and Roman conquerors. Those Thassians who were not killed or sold into slavery during the conquests were forced to hide, fleeing to mountain villages or caves. This "Green Island" sweetened its lot with a thriving beekeeping culture, producing jam and honey that was renowned through the ancient world. Since then, the island's greenery has been threatened by a new foe: massive forest fires. The forests are slowly coming back, though, and the northeastern regions around Thassos Town which escaped the fires are especially beautiful. In recent years, Thassos has escaped its historic woes to become a tourist-oriented island, attracting throngs of Northern Europeans who seek a quiet place in the sun. Its cool, shaded mountains and isolated southern coast are a hiker's paradise.

THASSOS TOWN
☎ 25930

The island's capital and tourist center is built atop the foundations of the ancient city, and ruins crowd the Old Port area. Also known as Limenas (from *limani*, meaning "harbor"; not to be confused with nearby Limenaria), Thassos Town sees the highest concentration of tourists on the island. The surprisingly quiet town, however, lacks the fast pace that characterizes many islands' main cities—the friendly, inviting locals say it is common for people to leave doors open at night.

TRANSPORTATION

Ferries: The arrival and departure point for ferries from Kavala is not in Thassos Town, but in the village of **Skala Prinos** (18km west). From **Skala Prinos** ferries go to **Kavala** (1½hr.; 10 per day 6am-8:30pm; €3.30, cars €15). Bus schedules between Skala Prinos and Thassos Town are synchronized with the ferries, so it is easy to then get to Thassos Town by hopping on a nearby bus. In Thassos Town both the **Port Police** and the **ticket booth** (located at opposite sides of the new harbor) post schedules. Ferries go to **Keramoti** (30min., 20 per day 5:45am-9pm, €2).

Flying Dolphins: Hydrofoils zip to **Kavala** from Thassos Town (45min.; 4 per day 8:10am-3:45pm; €9, children €4.40), and from Limenaria, on Thassos's southern coast (45min.; 8:20am, 3pm; €11). Schedules are posted at the port police and ticket booth, and docked boats indicate departure times with signs above their doors. You can buy tickets either prior to boarding or onboard.

Buses: When you arrive in **Skala Prinos** from Kavala, walk left to find buses for Thassos Town and Limenaria, whose departure times correspond with the arrival of the ferries from Kavala. The **Thassos Town** bus station (☎ 25930 22 162) is located across from the hydrofoil landing on the waterfront. Open daily 7:30am-8:15pm. To: **Aliki beach** (1hr., 3 per day 10:45am-4:15pm, €3); **Limenaria** (1hr., 9 per day 6:20am-6:20pm, €3.30) via **Skala Prinos** (25min., €2); **Panagia** (15min., 12 per day 6:45am-6pm, €1); **Skala Potamia** (30min., 12 per day 8:10am-6pm, €1.30); **Theologos** (1½hr., 6 per day 9am-4:15pm, €4.30); **around the island** and back to Thassos Town (3hr., 5 per day 6:20am-4:15pm, €8). Ask at the **Thassos tourist services** or bus office for paper schedules in English.

Taxis: ☎ 25930 23 391. Near the ports.

Water Taxis: ☎ 25930 22 734. Run once daily from Thassos Town to **Golden beach** (€3 one-way) and **Makryamos** (€3 one-way). Schedules change frequently—call the tourist office for departure times.

Rentals: Cars and mopeds can be rented all over Thassos Town. **Budget,** on Theagenus (☎ 25930 23 150; fax 25930 22 421), rents cars (€30-50 per day including 100km and damage waiver). Open 9am-1:30pm and 5-9pm.

ORIENTATION AND PRACTICAL INFORMATION

A small crossroads near the bus station and the National Bank connects the waterfront road leading to **Agousti Theologiti Cafe** and **18 Oktovriou**, a jungle of souvenir shops that runs parallel to the water one block inland. With your back to the water, the **Old Port**, the ancient **agora**, and the nearest beach are on the left. The small central plateia is about two blocks farther inland.

Budget Travel: Thassos Tours (☎ 25930 22 546), under the yellow sign on the waterfront. Helps with accommodations and island tours, and rents motorbikes (€15-22) and cars (€25-50). International license required. Open daily 8:30am-midnight.

Thassos Tourist Services (☎ 25930 22 041), on 18 Oktovriou behind the row of tavernas. **Exchanges currency** and has **maps.** Karin, who speaks English, is helpful and informative. Open M-Sa 9am-1:30pm and 6-9pm.

Bank: The Commercial Bank (☎25930 22 703), next to Thassos Tourist Services, **exchanges currency. Agricultural Bank** (☎25930 22 970) is across the road. Both have **ATMs** and are open M-Th 8am-2:30pm, F 8am-1:30pm.

Pharmacy: ☎25930 23 210. In the central plateia, 3 blocks inland from the waterfront. Open 8am-10pm.

Police: ☎25930 22 500. On the waterfront by the port police. Open 24hr.

Medical Services: Health Center (☎25930 71 100). In Prinos. Open 24hr. Although there are 6-7 doctors, there is no hospital on Thassos; the nearest is in Kavala.

Telephones: OTE, On 18 Oktovriou, 1 block inland from Thassos Tourist Services. Open M-F 7:30am-3:10pm.

Internet Access: Millennium Net (☎25930 58 089). From the tourist office, turn left and continue walking past Hotel Xenia. 6 computers. Internet €3 per hr. Beer €2. Coffee €1.50. Also try **Corner Net Cafe** (☎25930 58 086), 2 blocks in from the police station down the street from Lena Hotel. €4 per hr. €6 per 2hr. Open 10am-2am.

Post Office: ☎25930 22 114. Across the street from Corner Net Cafe. Open M-F 7:30am-2pm. **Postal Code:** 64004.

⚐ ☕ ACCOMMODATIONS AND FOOD

There's no need to stay in a hotel on Thassos if you're traveling on a budget—the plentiful **domatia** are a much better deal. The streets behind 18 Oktovriou are crammed with "rooms to let" signs; most cost €20-25 per single. They usually offer a clean room, and a Greek breakfast of salad, feta cheese, and pastries. Ask to see the room before settling in—many are not worth the money. The best value in Thassos Town is ▧**Hotel Lena ❷**, located next to the post office on M. Alexandrou, four blocks inland from the beach. The management is personable and courteous and the recently renovated building has 22 large rooms with A/C, TV, private baths, balconies, and a shared refrigerator. Reserve rooms a week in advance during high season. (☎25930 22 933. Breakfast included. English spoken. Open May-Oct. 10% discount for *Let's Go* readers. Rooms €25.) **Hotel Athanassia ❷** seems more like domatia than an actual hotel. Walk down the waterfront with your back to the Old Port, and make a left immediately after the Hotel Xenia. The hotel is on the right at the end of a narrow lane, swallowed by grapevines and plane trees. Away from the touristy area, this is one of the quieter and more serene options in town. There are spacious rooms, some with bath. (☎25930 22 545. Singles and doubles €25; triples €30.) With kitchen facilities in each of the eight rooms and a shared barbecue, fridge, and garden, **Studio Amy ❷** caters to the self-sufficient traveler. This studio complex, which belongs to the same owner as Hotel Lena, is on the main road going to Prinos across the street from the Elin gas station. Send a fax 10 days in advance to reserve during the summer. (☎25930 22 933; fax 25930 23 873. English spoken. Doubles €25.)

The waterfront is packed with restaurants designed to cater to a wide range of European tastes. The promenade is extremely tourist-oriented; multilingual menus offer "full English breakfasts" along with plates of schnitzel, pizza, and pasta. To hunt down more genuine Greek flavor, head toward the tavernas along the Old Port, where fresh fish and octopus appetizers dominate. Established in 1952, **Simi Restaurant ❷**, in the Old Port, was the first restaurant in town and is currently considered the most popular. Though you might be forgotten by waiters in this laid-back atmosphere, the fish and shellfish are irresistible. Don't miss the €7 tender El Greco pork fillet with mustard sauce. (☎25930 22 517. Reservations required for parties of more than 5. Entrees €6-10. Open 10am-12:30am. MC/V.) **Restaurant Syrtaki ❸,** 150m past Simi and the Old Port at the end of the waterfront

To Do:
Buy Let's Go Europe
Buy Eurail Pass
~~Check euro conversion rate~~
Ask about Roman hostels
Visit letsgo.com

Photo credits, clockwise from top left: Jeremy Todd, Samuel Perwin, Kristin Lee, Yaa Bruce, Nick Elprin, Dham Choi

LETSGO.COM
Here today, wherever you're headed tomorrow.

Whether you're planning your next adventure or are already far afield, LETSGO.COM will help you satisfy your wanderlust. Peruse our feature articles and destination write-ups as you select the spots you're off to next. Consult fellow travelers on our discussion and photo forums, or search for anecdotal advice in our researchers' blogs. From embassy locations to passport laws, we keep track of all the facts, so discover what you need to know, book that high-season hostel bed, and hit the road. *READY. SET. LETSGO.COM.*

road, is especially famous for their *mezedes* (€10 per person). With an ocean view, tables on the beach under a shaded canopy, and live Greek folk music Wednesday, Saturday and Sunday nights, however, food is just one of the many draws. (☎25930 23 353. Entrees €4-11. Open noon-midnight. AmEx/MC/V.)

🔎 🎵 SIGHTS AND ENTERTAINMENT

For a small town, Thassos has a huge number of ancient sites. Maps of the **Old Town** are available at Thassos Tourist Services. Just behind the Old Port are the ruins of the ancient **agora.** (Open 8am-7pm.) From here, or from the promontory beyond the Old Port, trails lead to the 4th-century BC **theater** (closed). Climbing past the theater, a lighted trail leads to the **acropolis,** home to a **Genoese fortress.** Lights continue to the **Temple of Athena** and the rock-carved **Altar to Pan,** above which is the scenic peak and a **secret stairway** down. Marble **Cyclopean walls** that once circled the city are well preserved here. Continuing down the walls is the **Gate of Parmenon,** with a lintel, and an eerie **Evil Eye** rock facing downhill. Even the archaeologically drained will enjoy a trip to the **⬛Gate of Silenos,** which is an ancient main gate graced with a full-length, excited centaur. Follow Scolis several blocks out of the town center, or turn left after a block onto Scolis after re-entering town from the Gate of Parmenon on Akropoleos. Beyond Silenos the walls continue past the **Gate of Hercules** and **Gate of Zeus and Hera,** which both have reliefs.

Beach lovers may have a hard time choosing among Thassos's beautiful sands. Between Panagia and Potamia, the popular **Chrisi Ammoudia,** better known as the "**golden beach,**" stretches endlessly. Take the bus or a water taxi to this favorite, known for its long sandy beaches packed with young German and British tourists. To the south, **Aliki's** twin coves shelter slabs of bleached white rock and crevices ideal for snorkeling. More isolated spots can be found along the clear turquoise water in both directions from Limenaria—just rent a bike or head out on foot, and pick a cove. Ask at the bus station to find out which bus heads past a particular beach. You can find superb **hiking** in the relatively untouched interior, as many unmarked trails snake into the mountainous inland.

For a night out, try **⬛Zorbas,** two blocks inland from the police station on Polignotou Vagi St. Down a few ouzos and join the welcoming Greek regulars and musicians for songs and dance accompanied by *bouzouki* and guitar players. (☎25930 22 704. Ouzo with lemonade €2. Mixed drinks €6. Stuffed Zorbas burger with cheese and mushroom €8. Open 6pm-1am.) **⬛Cafe Karnagio** is perched on a cliff at the end of the waterfront walkway, past the old harbor far from the racket made by motorbikes. Thoughtful night owls can sip ouzo and watch the stars and dark waters from a seat on the wooden roof. (☎25930 23 170. Beer €2. Open 9am-2am.) Locals and tourists flock to a number of music bars and dance clubs, blending in a haze of alcohol and loud bass. **The Grand Cafe,** on K. Dmitriadi one block inland from 18 Oktovriou, doubles as a quiet coffee shop during the day and a club blaring house, Greek, techno, and pop music at night. (Mixed drinks €8. Open 11am-6am.) The younger locals gravitate to the **Just in Time Club,** across the road from the Grand Cafe. This pick-up scene is American-owned and plays progressive and hip-hop music. (Mixed drinks €6. Open 9:30am-4am.)

LIMENARIA Λιμενάρια   ☎25930

Thriving auxiliary town Limenaria is across the island from Thassos Town on a curve of stony beach at the island's southern tip. Smaller and more relaxed than its bustling counterpart, Limenaria is a haven of unhurried calm, breeze-blown waves, and lazy sunsets. Unfortunately, Limenaria is no longer a secret—a resort feel prevails as the island is invaded by sun-craving Europeans every summer.

Subsequently, the village is turning into one big tourist attraction which closes down from October to April; hotels are high in both quality and price. Still, the area itself is spectacular, and a 1902 German steel factory perched on the cliff outside of the village offers a magnificent look at the beaches and mountains.

Hotels and rented rooms abound throughout Limenaria, with many hotels stationed on the waterfront and **domatia** scattered throughout town. ▨**Hotel Molos ❷** has bright, pleasant rooms with TV, baths, and balconies overlooking the water. Walk down Eth. Antistasis and turn right at the waterfront; Molos is 50m down, on your right. (☎25930 51 389. Breakfast €3, lunch €6, dinner €8, all meals €10. Singles €20-30; doubles €30-40; triples €35-45. MC/V. Discount for *Let's Go* readers.) **Hotel Asterias ❸,** on the waterfront about 60m down from Molos, has sunny air-conditioned rooms with kitchen, fridge, and pale-blue walls. (☎25930 52 497. Breakfast included. Reception open 8am-1am. English spoken. Singles €35; doubles €45; triples €50. AmEx/MC/V.) **Avgoustos Rented Rooms ❷** offers standard domatia amenities, but rooms also have private bath, Spanish-style balconies, and A/C. Walk down Eth. Antistasis, turn right, and follow the waterfront road until it bends inland; go another block and look right. (☎25930 52 310. Open late June to early Sept. Doubles €33.)

The entire waterfront fuses into one tacky mega-restaurant, comprised of the town's numberless tavernas and snack bars. To get to **Il Mare ❷,** walk down to the waterfront on Eth. Antistasis. Homemade delicacies like the lamb *kleftiko* (broiled in oven with feta cheese; €7) are cooked by the owner and served on romantic tables along the water. (☎25930 53 170. Entrees €4-8. Open 11am-1am. AmEx/MC/V. 10% discount for *Let's Go* readers.) Down the waterfront 200m past the intersection with Eth. Antistasis, on the left, is **Restaurant Maranos Flisvos ❷,** with a large wine cask teetering precariously over the entrance. It offers a calm, easygoing environment with the sounds of classic *rembetika*, and a variety of fish choices. (☎25930 51 239. Entrees €4-8. Open 8am-2am. AmEx/MC/V). Come nightfall, the wall of waterfront restaurants becomes a single long bar. **Istos Cafe-Bar, Nile Bar,** and **Larry's Bar** are all in a row, blaring a jumbled audio mess of Greek and American favorites. (Beer €3. Mixed drinks €5-6.)

Limenaria, like most resort towns, spreads along the waterfront. The road leading out of town, Eth. Antistasis, runs perpendicularly away from the shore to an intersection with Polytechniou, one block inland. From the main intersection of Eth. Antistasis and Polytechniou, **buses** go to: Thassos Town (45min., 8 per day 6:30am-6:30pm, €3.30) via Skala Prinos (20min., €2); Theologos (15min., 8 per day 7:20am-7:20pm, €1.30); around the island (stops in Limenaria twice a day 7:30am, 3:50pm; 1 day of unlimited rides €8). For car rental, go behind the Agricultural Bank ATM to **Speedy Rent-a-Car.** (☎25930 52 700. Cars €15-25. Open 9am-1:30pm and 5-10pm.) On the waterfront 150m right of Hotel Molos is **Blue City Tours,** which arranges excursions and has information on buses, ferries, and flights to Kavala. (☎25930 51 695. English spoken. Open 8:30am-1:30pm and 6-8:30pm.) A few meters past the OTE, **Agricultural Bank** has an **ATM.** (☎25930 52 683. Open M-Th 8am-2:30pm, F 8am-2pm.) The **police** are at the inland waterfront, before the National Bank. (☎25930 51 111. Open 24hr.) The **OTE** is on Antistasis. (☎25930 51 399. Open M-F 7:30am-3:10pm.) There is no readily available Internet access in Limenaria; you must travel 2.6km southeast to Potos. The **post office** is on the inland waterfront, close to the police station. (☎25930 51 296. Open M-F 7:30am-2pm.) **Postal Code:** 64002.

IONIAN ISLANDS
Νησιά Του Ιόνιου

Just west of mainland Greece, the Ionian Islands entice travelers with their lush, green vegetation that rolls gently to the edge of the shimmering turquoise waters. The unusual architecture and colors in the villages hint at a different history than much of the rest of Greece—these islands were never conquered by Ottomans, but instead bear the marks of Venetian, British, French, and Russian occupants. Each of these civilizations has left its own cultural fingerprint. Today, the islands are a favorite among Western Europeans and adventurous travelers seeking the unconventional. Multicultural for millennia, each of the Ionian Islands maintains a unique identity while sharing an unparalleled beauty.

SUGGESTED ITINERARIES: IONIAN ISLANDS

FOUR DAYS Lounge by **Kephalonia's** (p. 554) sky-blue water, then push past the crowds on **Zakynthos** (p. 562) to appreciate the Venetian arches, isolated beaches, and brilliantly green foliage.

ONE WEEK Start in **Corfu** (p. 531), checking out beaches and cultural sights during the day, then heading to the Pink Palace Hotel in **Agios Gordios** (p. 543) at night for some general carousing. Help protect sea turtles on Zakynthos (p. 562) and swim through Kephalonia's (p. 554) underground lakes. After seeing why Odysseus was so determined to get back to **Ithaka** (p. 550), test your windsurfing skills in **Vasiliki, Lefkada** (p. 548).

CORFU Κέρκυρα

Homer first sang Corfu's praise by writing of its "honeyed fig," "unctuous olive," "boisterous waves," and friendly inhabitants, who helped Odysseus in a desperate time of need. Corfu itself, however, had powerful helpers of its own. In 743 BC, it was colonized by Corinth, a close ally of Sparta; when the island broke into conflict with its mother city a few centuries later, it was joined by Athens, sparking the Peloponnesian War. Handed down from the Franks to the Venetians to the British to today's tourist masses, Corfu (Κέρκυρα, KEHR-kee-rah) has captivated them all. The island is large enough to have both lively nightlife and quiet traditional villages, and as in most of Greece's beautiful places, those who stray from the beaten path discover uncrowded, unspoiled beaches. Budding archaeologists will find ruins galore, sun seekers can sprawl out on stunning beaches, those tired of clothes can strip down at any number of nude beaches, and people seeking a laid-back village experience will stumble on it without even having to look. Corfu's natural and man-made treasures make the Homeric fuss fully justifiable.

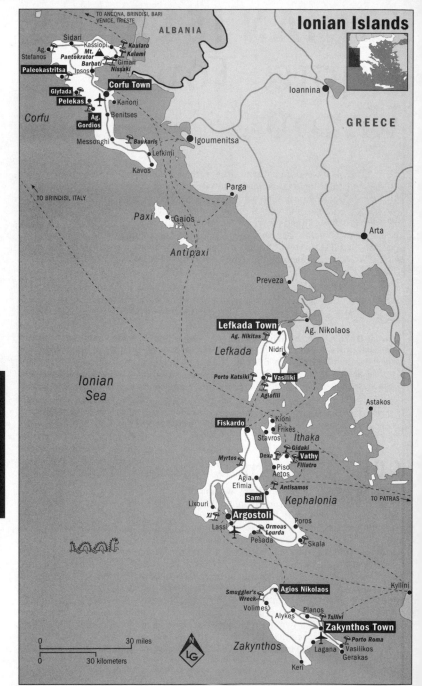

Ionian Islands

TO ANCONA, BRINDISI, BARI
VENICE, TRIESTE

ALBANIA

Sidari
Kassiopi • **Kaulara**
Ag. • **Mt.** • **Kalami**
Stefanos • **Pantokrator**
Barbati • Gimari
Paleokastritsa • Ipsos • **Nissaki**
Corfu Town
Glyfada
Pelekas • Kanoni
Ag. • Benitses
Gordios
Corfu
Messonghi • **Baukaris**
• Lefkimi
Kavos

Ioannina

GREECE

TO BRINDISI, ITALY

Paxi • Gaios

Igoumenitsa

Parga

Antipaxi

Arta

Preveza

Lefkada Town
Ag. Nikitas
Lefkada • Nidri

Ag. Nikolaos

Ionian
Sea

Porto Katsiki • **Vasiliki**
• **Agiofili**

Astakos

Fiskardo
• Kioni
• Frikès
Stavros • **Gidaki**
Ithaka
Myrtos • *Dexa* • **Vathy**
Piso • **Filiatro**
Agia • Aetos
Efimia
Antisamos
Lixouri
Xi • **Sami**
Lassi • **Argostoli** • Poros
Ormous
Lourda
Pesada
Skala

TO PATRAS

Kephalonia

Smuggler's • **Agios Nikolaos**
Wreck • Planos
Volimes • **Tsilivi**
Alykes
Zakynthos Town
Lagana • **Porto Roma**
Zakynthos • Vasilikos
Keri • Gerakas

Kyllini

0 ____ 30 miles
0 ____ 30 kilometers

N

CORFU TOWN ☎ 26610

Corfu Town hums with activity day and night. Encouraging you to get lost in the most positive sense of the word, the town teems with delicious distractions. Laundry lines stretching from ornate iron balconies, fragrant yellow roses, Venetian buildings, and green-shuttered alleyways exhibit the genuine flavors that have made this a lively center of Mediterranean culture.

TRANSPORTATION

Flights: Olympic Airways, Iak. Polila 11 (☎ 26610 38 694, reservations 26610 38 695). From the post office, walk 1 block on Rizopaston Voulefton toward the Old City and turn right. Open M-F 7:30am-7:30pm. Flights go to **Athens** (1hr., 2-3 per day, €102-120) and **Thessaloniki** (1hr.; Tu, F, Su 11:40pm; €63-84). In summer, almost 50 charter flights per day fly through Corfu's airport; book 2-3 days in advance. A 5min. taxi ride (agree on about €10 beforehand) is the quickest way to the **airport** (☎ 26610 33 811), but you can get off nearby if you take **blue bus #11** to Pelekas (tell the driver), or ask at the info kiosk at the blue bus station which bus can take you by the airport next.

Ferries: Get your tickets at least a day in advance during high season; when traveling to **Italy,** find out if the port tax (€6-7) is included in the cost of your ticket. Prices vary according to season, ferry line, and class. Try **Fragline** or **HML** for **Brindisi** and **Strindzis Lines** for **Venice. International Tours,** El. Venizelou 32 (☎ 26610 39 007),

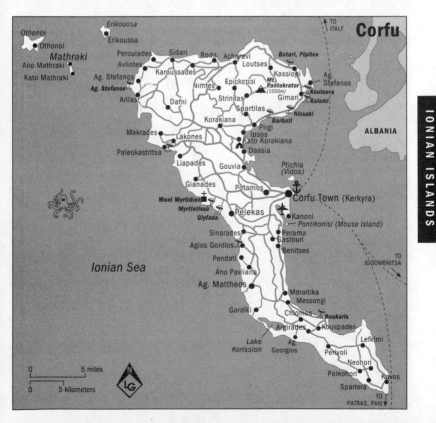

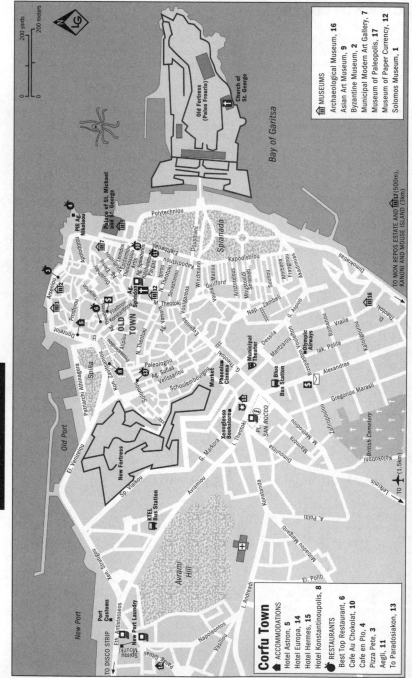

IONIAN ISLANDS

Corfu Town

▲ **ACCOMMODATIONS**
Hotel Astron, 5
Hotel Europa, 14
Hotel Hermes, 15
Hotel Konstantinoupolis, 8

● **RESTAURANTS**
Best Top Restaurant, 6
Cafe Au Chokolat, 10
Cafe en Plo, 4
Pizza Pete, 3
Aegli, 11
To Paradosiakon, 13

🏛 **MUSEUMS**
Archaeological Museum, 16
Asian Art Museum, 9
Byzantine Museum, 2
Municipal Modern Art Gallery, 7
Museum of Paleopolis, 17
Museum of Paper Currency, 12
Solomos Museum, 1

Bay of Garitsa

Old Fortress
(Paleo Frourio)

Church of
St. George

Palace of St. Michael
and St. George

New Fortress

New Port

Port
Customs

New Port Laundry

TO DISCO STRIP

Avrami
Hill

British Cemetery

KTEL
Bus Station

Blue
Bus Station

Municipal
Theater

Phoenix
Cinema

Market

Xenoglosso
Bookstores

SAN ROCCO

Olympic
Airways

OLD
TOWN

Spianada

TO MON REPOS ESTATE AND 🏛17 (500m),
KANONI AND MOUSE ISLAND (3km)

TO (1.5km)

TO LEFKIMIS

and **Ionian Cruises**, El. Venizelou 38 (☎26610 31 649), both located across the street from the Old Port on El. Venizelou, can help you with your scheduling woes. Ferries to: **Bari, Italy** (10hr., M-F 8:30-10:45pm, €49); **Brindisi, Italy** (8hr., 1-2 per day, €32); **Igoumenitsa** (1½hr., every hr. 5:45am-10:45pm, €5.10); **Patras** (8hr., 1-2 per day, €27); **Paxi** (2:30, 3:30pm; €14); **Venice, Italy** (24hr., daily, €64).

Buses: Green KTEL buses (☎26610 30 627) go between I. Theotoki and the New Fortress (accessible from I. Theotoki or Xen. Stratigou), and **blue municipal buses** (☎26610 31 595) leave from Saroco. For a schedule with return times and prices for both types, ask at the white info kiosk at the station (open 8am-10pm). The tourist info office in the green kiosk in Saroco has English timetables for all buses.

Green buses: Agios Gordios (45min.; M-Sa 4per day 8:15am-5:30pm, Su 2 per day 9:30am-5:30pm; €2); **Agios Stefanos** (1½hr.; M-F 4 per day 5:15am-4pm, Sa 3 per day 5:30am-2pm; €3); **Barbati** (45min.; M-Sa 5 per day 9am-4pm, Su 9:30am; €2); **Glyfada** (45min.; M-Sa 4 per day 9am-4pm, Su 3 per day 9am-4pm; €2); **Ipsos** and **Pirgi** (30-45min.; M-F 9 per day 7am-8pm, Sa 5 per day 9am-4pm, Su 9:30am; €1.20); **Kassiopi** (1hr.; M-Sa 5 per day 5:45am-4pm, Su 9:30am; €2.50); **Cavos** (1½hr.; M-Sa 10 per day 5am-8pm, Su 3 per day 5am-3:30pm; €3.30); **Messonghi** (45min.; M-F 6 per day 9am-3:30pm, Sa 4 per day 9am-3:30am, Su 4 per day 5am-3:30pm; €2); **Paleokastritsa** (45min.; M-Sa 6 per day 9am-6pm, Su 3 per day 10:30am-4pm; €2); **Sidari** (1hr.; M-Sa 8 per day 5:15am-8pm, Su 9:30am; €2.50). Buy tickets onboard. **KTEL** also runs to **Athens** (8hr.; 8:45am, 1:45, 7:15pm; €33) and **Thessaloniki** (8hr., 7am, €31); prices include ferry. Buy tickets at the green bus station.

Blue buses: Achilleon (30min.; M-Sa 6 per day 7am-8pm, Su 4 per day 9am-8pm; €1); **Agios Ioannis** and **Aqualand** (30min.; M-F 13 per day 6:15am-10pm, Sa 12 per day 7:10am-10pm, Su 6 per day 8am-9pm; €1); **Benitses** (30min., 13 per day 6:45am-10pm, €1); **Kanoni** and **Mouse Island** (30min.; M-F 2 per hr. 6:30am-10pm, Sa every hr. 6:30am-9:30pm, Su every hr. 9:30pm-9:30pm; €1); **Pelekas** (30min.; M-F 7 per day 7am-8:30pm, Sa 6 per day 2:15-8:30pm, Su 8 per day 10am-8:30pm; €1). Buy tickets at the kiosk.

Taxis: ☎26610 33 811. At the New and Old Ports, the Spianada, Pl. San Rocco, and Pl. G. Theotoki. Ask for the price before you get in—they may vary a great deal, especially for short distances. Taxis respond to calls 24hr.

Car Rental: Both **Europcar**, Venizelou 30 (☎26610 46 931; www.europcar.com.gr) and **InterCorfu Rent a Car**, Venizelou 46 (☎26610 41 709), on the water at the New Port, offer reasonable rates. A small car starts at €45-60 per day, but price varies by season. Ask if 20% tax, 3rd-party insurance, and mileage over 200km are included.

Moped Rental: Travelers should note that many roads, especially those far from Corfu Town, are not well-paved and can present serious risk to moped drivers; stick to the main roads, which have fewer potholes. If you do decide to rent, there are various places along the waterfront, especially near the New Port. **Easy Rider**, 3rd Parodos El. Venizelou (☎26610 43 026), across from the customs house on the corner of Xen. Stratigou, has mopeds from €25 per day (helmet included). Rental fee should include 3rd-party liability and property damage insurance. Open daily 9am-9pm.

■✦ 🛈 ORIENTATION AND PRACTICAL INFORMATION

Befuddling alleys and ubiquitous waters may add to Corfu Town's charm, but they can also cause stress for anyone with a plane or ferry to catch. Most visitors arrive in the **New Port,** which sits next to the **Old Port** in front of a large square on the town's northern coast. The **New Fortress** is the conspicuous edifice by the ports and is a good reference point. From the customs house at the New Port, it's about 1km to the center of town, **Plateia San Rocco;** locals will say and understand "Saroco" for short. To get there from the New Port, cross the intersection at the light, turn right, and walk uphill on **Avramiou,** which eventually turns into **Ioanni Theotoki.** The **KTEL (green) bus terminal's** long driveway will be on your left as you pass, and the **blue bus terminal's** station is in the square. The **Old Town** can be reached by walking along the waterfront toward the Old Port. If you follow the waterfront with the water on your left past the Old Port square, circling the Old Town, you will see the **palace** on your left and a long park known as the **"Spianada,"** the town's social center, straight in front of you. Two streets encircle the Spianada: **Eleftherias** (which becomes **Kapodistriou**) is farther inland; **Polytechniou** curves around the outside.

Tourist Office: Tourist Information (☎26610 12 177) is on Pl. San Rocco in a green kiosk. Friendly, English-speaking staff help with any questions. Open daily 8am-10pm.

Banks: Banks with **24hr. ATMs** line the larger streets and the waterfront by the ports. **National Bank,** Alexandras 30 (☎26610 47 728), is on the corner of Alexandras and Rizopaston Voulefton across from the post office. Open M-Th 8am-2:30pm, F 8:30am-1:30pm.

Work Opportunities: The Pink Palace (p. 543) hires hotel and club staff and DJs. Mail a letter of introduction, resume, and photo in advance. Min. 2 month commitment.

Bookstore: Xenoglosso, Markora 45 (☎26610 23 923). From the police station, walking away from San Rocco, turn left onto Markora. The wonderful collection includes classic novels, books about Greece, and language materials. Limited selection in English. Open M, W, Sa 8am-2pm, Tu, Th-F 8:30am-2pm and 5-8:30pm.

Laundromat: "New Port" Laundry, Sp. Mouriki 2 (☎26610 38 457), on the road perpendicular to the waterfront, opposite port customs, washes and dries for €8 per load. Open M-F 8:30am-3pm and 5:30-9pm, Sa 5:30-8:30pm.

Police: ☎26610 39 294. Heading toward the New Port, turn right off I. Theotoki along Pl. San Rocco on to the short street that intersects Markora. Open 24hr. In an **emergency,** dial ☎100. The **tourist police** (☎26610 30 265) are located on the 4th fl. of the police building. Open daily 7am-2pm.

Hospital: Corfu General Hospital (☎26610 88 200 or 26610 45 811), on I. Andreadi. The tourist office or tourist police can help find an English-speaking doctor. For an **ambulance,** call ☎166.

Internet Access: Netoikos Cafe, Kaloheretou 12-14 (☎26610 47 479), behind Ag. Spiridon church. €3 per hr. Open M-Sa 10am-midnight, Su 6-midnight. **Eden** (☎26610 35 284), in Saroco by the info kiosk, has 10 terminals. €3 per hr. Open 8am-midnight.

Post Office: ☎26610 25 544. On the corner of Alexandras and R. Voulefton. **Poste Restante** and **currency exchange** available. Open M-F 7:30am-8pm. **Postal Code:** 49100.

🔒 ACCOMMODATIONS

There's no getting around the fact that Corfu Town is expensive. Relatively cheap accommodations do exist, though, especially in low season. Travelers looking for bargains may have some luck with the **Association of Owners of Private Rooms and Apartments in Corfu,** Iak. Polila 24, which has a complete list of rooms in Corfu and the phone numbers of the landlords who lease them. (☎26610 26 133. Open M-F 9am-3pm and 5-8pm.) If you are traveling in high season, call several weeks in advance to ensure availability. Otherwise, towns and campgrounds just outside the city can be worthwhile alternatives. Prices in general, however, are flexible and depend on the duration of your stay, the time of year, and the vacancy of the hotel or domatia. Since competition is fierce, don't hesitate to ask for a lower fee.

Hotel Konstantinoupolis, K. Zavitsianou 1 (☎26610 48 716), at the Old Port, is a beautiful building that has been greeting guests since 1878 with its traditional long Venetian shutters. Airy rooms, some with balconies that yield amazing views, have TV, A/C, and a perfect location in the middle of the large square at Spilia. Call in advance for rooms in high season. Breakfast €7. Laundry services available. Reception 24hr. Singles €50-70; doubles €70-98; triples €79-117. ❹

Hotel Hermes, G. Markora 14 (☎26610 39 268), around the bend from the police station, by the noisy public market. Complete with an old-fashioned push-button phone operator in the reception area, this hotel has an undeniably retro style. Spacious, clean rooms include mini-fridges and fans. Breakfast €5. Reception 24hr. Singles €30, with bath €35; doubles €38/50; triples €45. MC/V. ❸

Hotel Astron, Donzelot 15 (☎26610 39 505), past Spilia with the water on your left. The wooden furniture and marble steps may feel anachronistic, but large rooms have modern amenities, like TV, A/C, and baths; some have balconies. Breakfast €5. Prices inflate to the listed high by Aug. 6. Singles and doubles €30-80; triples €50-90. ❹

Hotel Europa, P. Gitsiali 10 (☎26610 39 304). Europa rents simple, small rooms with decent views, though the location is not particularly convenient or well-lit. Breakfast €6. Reception 24hr. Singles €20, with bath €35; doubles €35-45; triples €50-60. ❷

☐ FOOD

The main restaurant areas are by the **Spianada** and the **Old Port.** Lots of similar tavernas are scattered throughout the Old Town's maze of small alleyways. While in Corfu, you can experiment with the many local specialties. Homemade wines and beers are available all over the island: light white *kakotrygis*, richer white *moscato*, dry *petrokorintho* red, and dark *skopelitiko*. Bottles of light yellow *tsitsibira* (ginger beer) are another of Corfu's specialties. A daily **open-air market** sells inexpensive produce on Dessila, off G. Theotoki and below the new fortress. (Open daily 6am-2pm.) **Supermarkets** are located on I. Theotoki, in Pl. San Rocco, and beyond the bus station on Alexandras. (Open M-F 8am-9pm, Sa 8am-8pm.)

To Paradosiakon, Odos Solomou 20 (☎26610 37 578), at the corner of Ag. Sofias. Look for the pink walls. Highly recommended by locals, this small restaurant, whose name means "tradition," makes amazing, freshly cooked food. The chef cooks whatever she buys in the market each day, giving the classic meals a sense of spontaneity. Entrees €4-8.50. Open daily March-Nov. 10am-midnight. ❷

Restaurant Antranik/Pizza Pete, Arseniou 21 (☎26610 22 301), a 2min. walk past Hotel Astron with the water on your left. In addition to the large entrees (3-person pizza; €9.20), this waterfront taverna also makes 20 types of homemade ice cream (€5-7). Open daily spring-summer 9am-midnight. AmEx/MC/V. ❷

Aegli, Kapodistriou 23 (☎26610 31 949), is the oldest restaurant in town, and the years of experience show in the excellent service and somewhat fancier ambiance. Tables either sit on the side of the restaurant in a snug walkway, or look out onto the beautiful Spianada. *Kleftiko* (lamb in a clay dish with tomatoes, onions, potatoes, and melted feta; €12.50) is a Corfiot favorite. Open 10am-midnight. AmEx/MC/V. ❸

Best Top Restaurant, Filellinon 33 (☎26610 24 010). From the plateia at the Spilia end of Donzelot, walk up the stairs to the left; it's in the 2nd little plateia. At the end of Filellinon's tourist- and gift shop-clogged alleyway, Best Top is an oasis where you can watch the masses pass you by. A friendly staff serves Corfiot specialties like *sofrito* (beef slow cooked in white sauce; €6.50). Open daily 9:30am-midnight. AmEx/MC/V. ❷

Cafe En Plo, Pili Ag. Nikolaou (☎26610 81 813), juts into the water with tables literally on the rocks and has a magnificent view of the Old Fortress. From the Spianada, walk under the palace's arch; En Plo is down on the water to your left. While sipping a cup of coffee (€2.80), it's easy to imagine the Turks attempting to scale the massive walls. The freshly netted seafood mix (shrimp, calamari, mussels, and octopus; €24) easily feeds 4-5. Salads €5-7.50. Open daily 9:30am-2:30am. ❷

◉ 🏛 SIGHTS AND MUSEUMS

After invading Vandals and Goths destroyed ancient Corfu (Paleopolis) in the AD 5th and 6th centuries, residents built a more defensible city between the twin peaks of the Old Fortress. Wary of Ottoman raids, the Venetians strengthened the existing structure, constructed the New Fortress, and built thick walls around the growing city. A series of underground tunnels, now closed, connected the Old Fortress to the new one and all parts of Corfu Town. They later provided refuge for Corfiots after the first WWII air raids in 1940.

■ **MON REPOS ESTATE.** In a grandiose effort to please his Corfiot wife, Sir Frederic Adams, the second British High Commissioner of the Ionian Islands, mandated the construction of one of the most elegant and expansive estates in Greece. Only two years after they moved in, however, the Adamses relocated to Madras, India, and so the grounds changed hands many times until they became the summer home of Greece's ex-royal family in 1864. Today, a walk through the estate gives a glimpse of Corfu's gorgeous terrain (including 2000 trees Adams received as a house-warming gift from the British Empire) and passes by excavation sites. Look for the intriguing **Museum of Paleopolis,** which exhibits an eclectic collection of period rooms from the palace, along with archaeological finds from excavations around Corfu. Each display, including the particularly memorable ancient version of a cosmetics kit and a collection of 510 silver Corinthian and Corycian coins, is labeled with full explanations in English and Greek. Those tired of perusing ancient artifacts will still be able to take it all in at the amazingly well-done multimedia exhibit that gives a thorough summary of local history. *(☎26610 41 369. To reach the palace, head up the path to the right just inside the main gate. Estate open daily 8am-7pm. Free. Museum open Tu-Su 8:30am-3pm. €3, EU students €2.)* From the palace, with the water on your left, follow the forested path overlooking the sea to the tiny, pebble-filled **Kardaki beach.** Legend claims that anyone who drinks from its spring will remain on the island forever. To the right of the palace as you face the museum entrance, a path leads to two Doric temples: the last remains of the **Temple of Hera** (the Heraion), and the more impressive **Kardaki Temple,** thought to have been dedicated to either Poseidon, Apollo, or Asclepius. *(Take the #2 bus toward Mouse Island and tell the driver you want to be dropped off at Mon Repos; 10min., €0.60.)*

■ **PALACE OF SAINT MICHAEL AND SAINT GEORGE.** Built by Adams's predecessor, British Lord High Commissioner Sir Thomas Maitland, this palace, which presides over the Spianada, combines Neoclassical and mythology-based sculpture with Asian artifacts. First intended to house the High Commissioner, the Ionian parliament, and the ceremonies of the orders of St. Michael and George, and later used by the ex-royal family as a ceremonial palace, the building was renovated to hold the EU summit meeting in 1994. Once inside, a glance around reveals the intricate ceilings and the impressive "throne room." The palace also contains the **Museum of Asian Art,** which displays over 11,000 artifacts from five formerly private collections. This well-organized collection, with such treasures as Samurai weapons and a set of six-fold screens, includes objects from Afghanistan, Cambodia, China, India, Japan, Nepal, Pakistan, and Tibet. *(☎26610 30 443. Open Tu-Su 8:30am-3pm. €3, students and seniors €2, EU students free.)* The **Municipal Modern Art Gallery (Dimotiko Pinakothiki),** behind the palace and through the garden, has a small display of Corfiot paintings and various rotating exhibits. *(☎26610 48 690. Open Tu-F 9am-5pm, but hours vary with special exhibits. €1.50, students and seniors €1.)*

ARCHAEOLOGICAL MUSEUM. Ancient coins, bronze laurel leaves, and detailed statuettes will likely catch any visitor's attention, but the hands-down highlight of this large collection is the **Gorgon Pediment** (590-580 BC) from Corfu's Doric Temple of Artemis. The oldest surviving pediment in Greece, it shows Medusa with her offspring, Pegasus and Chrysaor. According to mythology, the creatures were born at the moment when Perseus cut off their mother's snake-covered head, though in the pediment she appears full of life. The entire room displays finds from the temple. *(Armeni Vraila 1, down the steps leading to the Spianada, past Hotel Corfu Palace on the right. ☎ 26610 30 680. Open Tu-Su 8:30am-3pm. €3, students and seniors €2, children and EU students free. Combined ticket for the Old Fortress, Byzantine Museum, Archaeological Museum, and Museum of Asian Art €8; students and seniors €4; available at any of the sights.)*

OLD FORTRESS (PALEO FROURIO). Linked to the Spianada by a 60m iron bridge that goes over the AD 10th-century moat, the Old Fortress is a symbol of Corfu's history. The Byzantines, Venetians, and British all fortified the two hilltops, and ruins from each period remain. Most visitors find themselves drawn to the red **bell tower** near the summit and the **Church of Saint George,** which unfortunately is often closed to the public. Amazing panoramic views of the city and the sea (and gallons of sweat) await the determined who climb to the top of the tower. In the summer, Greek rock stars perform on the vast plateau next to the church (ask at the tourist information kiosk for concert schedule). Explanations in English are sparse, so you may consider buying a guidebook (€4-6) from the museum. *(Just east of the Spianada. ☎ 26610 48 311. Open daily 8am-7pm. €4, students and seniors €2, EU students free.)*

NEW FORTRESS. The result of the Venetians' second attempt to protect their city, the 350-year-old walls of the New Fortress were once considered the archetype of military architecture. Currently, the massive edifice hosts a small art gallery (which is almost always closed), a playground, and the occasional stray dog. Despite its somewhat paltry offerings, the fortress's location above the docks yields panoramic views of the town. Concerts and theatrical events take place here during the summer. *(Look for signs as you walk along Velissariou from the Old Port. It is at the top of Solomou. ☎ 26610 45 000. Open daily 9am-9pm. €2, EU students free.)*

BYZANTINE MUSEUM. This impressive collection of religious artifacts is housed in the small, late 15th-century **Church of the Most Holy Virgin Antivouniotissa,** which still operates as a church on the December 26 and August 23 feasts of the Virgin. Gold communion cups, 15th- through 19th-century priestly vestments, and iron-covered gospel books are some of the highlights of the permanent exhibit in the room next to the church. The collection of **Cretan School** icons is also worth seeing, if only to observe the painted "wallpaper" (a red floral pattern that adorns much of the church) and wood ceiling carvings. The museum's 90 icons are merely a gilded background for the famed 16th-century icon of Mary Magdalene calling Jesus "Rabouni" ("my teacher"), as described in the Gospel of John. The many different styles and influences in the collection are attributed to the influx of Cretan artists who stopped in Corfu on their way to Venice after the 1646 fall of Rethymno. *(Past the Old Port with the waterfront on the left; there are signs on Arseniou. ☎ 26610 38 313. Open Tu-Su 8:30am-3pm. €2, students and seniors €1, EU students free. Modest dress required.)*

CHURCH OF AGIOS SPIRIDON. Housing the embalmed body of the island's patron saint, Ag. Spiridon, this church is an important Orthodox pilgrimage point. The biblical scenes on the 18th-century Baroque ceiling and the Renaissance-style icons draw tourists as well. Inside, a silver casket holds the remains of the 3rd-century saint, whose spirit is believed to wander the streets performing good deeds for the island's people. Rumor has it that if the priest opens the gold cover of Spiridon's casket during your visit, you can still catch a glimpse of his blackened face. *(Take Ag. Spiridon off the Spianada; it's on the left. Open daily 6am-9pm. Modest dress required.)*

KANONI AND MOUSE ISLAND. Praised in traditional songs about Corfu, Mouse Island (*Pontikonisi*) is located near the beautiful bay at Kanoni. Take the #2 bus or a taxi (€10-12) to Kanoni and enjoy the jaw-dropping view at the now-famous Cafe Kanoni, serving since 1864. *(Coffee €1.50. Snacks €3.50-6.50. Open in summer daily 8am-5pm.)* Then walk down to the water, where the tiny Vlacherna Monastery of the Virgin Mary juts into the water. A small water taxi can then take you to Mouse Island (10am-9pm, €2.50). There, the only building you will find among the rich flora is the 13th-century Byzantine Church of the Pantocrator, with its single cell.

OTHER MUSEUMS. Located in the house where he spent the last 20 years of his life, the **Solomos Museum** pays tribute to the beloved national poet, Dionysios Solomos. The first to use Demotic Greek in poetry, Solomos was part of the vibrant artistic community that once made the Old City its headquarters. His *Hymn to Freedom* provided the lyrics of Greece's national anthem; beyond myriad photographs and photocopies, the museum holds pieces of the tree that apparently inspired the poet. *(Look for the sign in an alleyway on Arseniou just west of the Byzantine Museum, toward the New Port. ☎ 26610 30 674. Open M-F 9:30am-1:30pm. €1, students free.)* If you can't get enough of the coins in archaeological museums, feed your love for money even more at the **Museum of Paper Currency** in the Ionian Bank Building, down N. Theotoki from the Spianada. As well as examples of all Greek currency ever circulated, the museum is the proud owner of the first bank note printed in Greece. The collection makes it seem as if today's euros are just another step after Alexander the Great's drachmas. *(☎ 26610 41 552. Open M-F 10am-2pm. Free.)*

🎵 🎭 ENTERTAINMENT AND NIGHTLIFE

The **Phoenix cinema,** G. Theotoki 42 (☎ 26610 28 310), is two blocks from Saroco after Dessila on the left and plays movies in English regularly. Look for placards on G. Theotoki (tickets €7). The **municipal theater** (☎ 26610 33 598), between Dessila and Mantzarou one block from G. Theotoki, has occasional drama, dance, and music performances, publicized on bulletin boards all over town. **Carnival** season, beginning in February or March (depending on the date of Orthodox Easter), is largely secular in Corfu. Celebrating generally means dining, drinking, and dancing; most restaurants stay open all night long. The most entertaining traditions include "the Gossip," on the final Thursday of Carnival. In something like a street theater performance, women call out the latest gossip from windows across alleys in the center of the Old Town. Though this age-old custom is not practiced with the same fervor as in the past, some juicy secrets are still spilled. On the last Sunday, the festival culminates with the burning of King Carnival, when the effigy "King" is tried and sentenced to death by fire for his hand in all the year's misfortunes. Corfu's animated **Easter** celebrations are reflected in the ornate Palm Sunday procession of the embalmed body of Ag. Spiridon, Corfu's conspicuous saint. On Holy Saturday (the day before Easter), for good luck, Corfiots throw pots full of water out of their windows at 11am; kids can often be seen walking the streets, happily waiting to be drenched. In August, Corfu is once again filled with festivities, this time celebrating the **Barcarola** festival.

 STARING CONTEST. Greek men are notorious for casting intense, longing gazes at women in clubs and cafes. The penetrating glares can intimidate those unfamiliar with the culture, but they are usually a harmless, if annoyingly ubiquitous, part of the bar scene. In Greek slang, the men who cast these predatory looks are known as *kamaki*, the Greek word for "harpoon." Unless a woman is looking to be hooked, she should feel free to swim away.

Less than 2km west of the New Port, the so-called **Disco Strip** is the undisputed center of nightlife in Corfu Town in July and August. Crowds of locals and tourists intermingle in the plethora of bars and cafes, each of which offers its own take on the ideal evening out. Most clubs here close down for low season, and, when they reopen, frequently change names and/or ownership; it may be a good idea to ask the locals about the status of various clubs before heading out. **Crystal,** at the end of the strip (open midnight-7am), and **Prime,** in the center of the strip (open 10pm-5am), may be your best bets for an international dance-off, as both Corfiots and mostly European tourists come for the relatively cheap alcohol, plentiful happy hours, and loud music. Popular **Envy,** where Corfiots go to lose the foreign masses, blasts Greek music. (Open 11pm-4am.) **Ekarti** wins as Corfu's bona fide hot spot. The club for Greeks who know how to party and are willing to shell out plenty of euros for it, Ekarti often has no cover but doesn't serve drinks for under €6. If you're going to try to snag a table for the night, be ready to part with up to €130 for a single bottle of whisky, as is common among the rich and famous who come here to see and be seen. (Open 10pm-4:30am.) The best way to get to the strip, located on Eth. Antistasios, is by taxi (€4-7, more after midnight). Once there, beer is generally €3-5.50, and mixed drinks are €5-9.

Since these clubs are only open in high season, earlier in the summer you can take a taxi (€7-9) to **Gouvia's** small club scene. **Whispers Bar** fills with groups of friends, talking and listening to the music that ranges from the latest club hits to 60s classics. In Corfu Town itself, the elegant little cafes that line the Spianda, usually lively until about 1am, are open year-round. On the palace side of the park, sip one of 10 sinfully rich frappés (€4.50) at **Cafe au Chokolat,** Eleftherias 36. As you try desperately to decide if you want your chocolate cold or hot and with or without whipped cream, you can take a break from the mental anguish by reading the facts about chocolate also printed on the menu. (☎26610 80 019. Open 9am-1am.)

⚡ DAYTRIP FROM CORFU TOWN

🏛ACHILLION PALACE

In Gastouri. Take bus #10 from a spot on Methodiou, 200m west of Pl. San Rocco (20min.; M-Sa 6 per day 7:20am-8pm, Su 4 per day 9am-8pm; €0.90). ☎26610 56 210. Open daily 8am-7pm. €6; groups €3; EU students, holders of ISIC card, and children free.

From housing an estranged empress to providing the filming location for the 1981 James Bond flick *For Your Eyes Only,* the Achillion Palace has continually intrigued visitors with its exquisite architecture, ornate designs, and flourishing gardens. Built in 1889, the magnificent property first belonged to the Austrian Empress Elizabeth, whose turbulent familial affairs brought her to this secluded estate. Having developed a penchant for Classical literature, she christened her palace after the nearly invincible hero Achilles. The empress spent her summers here until she was assassinated by an Italian anarchist in 1898. The palace then changed hands a number of times—first sold to German Kaiser Wilhelm II, it served as a military hospital for French troops during WWI and then became a Nazi headquarters in WWII. Entrepreneurs jumped on the bandwagon as well, making it the home of the first Greek casino. Today the palace itself has become a museum whose ornate rooms and beautiful grounds will make any visitor wish he or she was born with blue blood. A stroll through the rooms will take you past preserved personal items belonging to both the empress and the Kaiser. The most impressive piece of art, a sculpture of Achilles dying, stands on the veranda.

IONIAN ISLANDS

WESTERN CORFU

A beach lover's paradise, western Corfu's wide expanses of golden sand, hidden crystal coves, majestic cliffs, and rock formations serve as a backdrop for the glimmering cerulean sea. While it sees its share of tour buses, the area doesn't suffer from the same degree of over-development that mars the east and south, making its towns and more remote beaches a continual delight.

■ PELEKAS Πέλεκας ☎26610

Removed from the mass tourism of the beach resorts, the village of Pelekas sits at the top of a hill that towers over the island, allowing visitors to see breathtaking landscapes and famously beautiful sunsets. Its relaxed mentality, friendly people, and proximity to Corfu's nicest beaches make this town an essential stop on the island. A 5min. walk uphill from the center of the village takes you to the natural "balcony" known as **"Kaiser's throne";** according to locals, Wilhelm II would spend hours on end in silence on this hilltop, staring at the beauty that spread out below him. Indeed, sunsets from this spot match the best in the world, and a visit at any point during the day will let you admire all of Corfu's glory at once.

Staying in Pelekas is overwhelmingly peaceful—the village is not tourist-drowned (although it certainly deserves the attention), and its people extend genuine Greek hospitality to visitors. Rooms to let are plentiful and well priced, but call ahead in high season to secure a spot. ■**Pension Tellis and Brigitte ❷,** down the hill from the bus stop on the left side of the street, has the friendliest hosts in town, who do their best to make each visitor feel at home. The comfy rooms fill the little yellow house covered with bougainvillea and gigantic sunflowers. Balconies have superb views of the surrounding countryside. (☎26610 94 326. Singles €18; doubles €25-30.) **Jimmy's Pension ❸,** right under Jimmy's restaurant, has fantastic rooms with A/C, TV, fridges, large baths, and tall ceilings that make the already large rooms seem even more spacious. (☎26610 94 284. Reception in restaurant 8am-midnight. Singles €30, in low season €20; doubles €40/30; triples €50/40. AmEx/MC/V.) On the road to the beach, next to the fork for Glyfada, **Pension Paradise ❷** rents rooms with mountain views, big baths, TV, fridges, and fully equipped kitchens. (☎26610 94 530. Doubles €30; triples €40. Open 9am-10pm.) Pelekas has a disproportionately large number of restaurants and tavernas that, combined with the bird's eye view from most of them, can offer both dinner and a spectacular view. On top of a 300-year-old olive orchard is Pelakas's gastronomical all-star, the ■ **Taverna Pink Panther ❷,** which serves Greek and Italian food. Take a left at the fork above the bus station, and continue for 300m downhill. Each member of the owner's family takes part in the delicious enterprise, making and serving creamy cake (€2 per slice), large pizzas (from €7), and plentiful drinks. (☎26610 94 361. Open 8am-3am.) As you walk up the main hill toward Glyfada, **Jimmy's ❷** serves Greek specialties and many vegetarian options, including the traditional *tsigareli* (seasonal green vegetables in spicy tomato sauce). Wooden floors and furniture lend a comfortable feel to the simple but excellent food. (☎26610 94 284. Entrees €5-8. Open 8am-midnight.) At the top of the winding road that leads to the Kaiser's old lookout is **Sunset Restaurant ❸,** where the more costly food may be worth the majestic view. (☎26610 94 230. Entrees €7-12. Open 9am-1am. MC/V.)

Take **bus #11** from Saroco in Corfu Town (20min., 7 per day 7am-8:30pm, €1). A free shuttle bus (8 per day 10am-10pm) goes between town, the main sandy **beach,** and the nearby beach of Glyfada. The same bus will also take you to the more isolated beach of **Myrtiotissa** (p. 542). From the drop-off point, it's a 20min. walk to the water. Signs with bus times are posted all over town.

GLYFADA Γλυφάδα ☎26610

Glyfada attracts more tourists than Pelekas, 5km down the coast, but its seemingly endless shore accommodates the throngs admirably. Cliffs bracket both of Glyfada's shallow **beaches**, where crashing waves make swimming a bit unpredictable. Those not sunbathing can partake in many activities—the beaches have parasailing (singles €34; doubles €50), water-skiing (€47 per 30min.), and jet-skiing (€80 per hr. or €200 per day), and rent motorboats, kayaks, inner tubes, and paddle boats. Though this is the ultimate laid-back vacation spot, relatively expensive accommodations and a lack of anything but sand might persuade you to stay in nearby Pelekas and take daily excursions here. In July and August, tan-centric mornings turn into dance-and-drink-fueled afternoons at **Aloha Bar** (open until 9pm), on the beach, which attracts youth from all over Corfu. Green KTEL **buses** leave from Corfu Town (30min., 4 per day 9am-4pm, €1.70), and a free bus that leaves from the parking lot by the beach connects Pelekas to Glyfada (10min., 8 per day 10am-10pm). Budget accommodations are scarce, but it's easy to make the trip from Pelekas or Corfu Town. North of Glyfada, accessible via a dirt path off the main Pelekas road, lies isolated **Myrtiotissa beach**, extolled by author and Corfu resident Lawrence Durrell as the most beautiful in the world. A section of Myrtiotissa is an unofficial nude beach—unless local monks complain to the police, who reluctantly bring offending nudists to court. A short walk up the road is the monastery, **Moni Myrtidion**, which takes its name from an icon of the Virgin found in myrtle bushes over 700 years ago. (Open 7am-7pm. Modest dress required.)

PALEOKASTRITSA Παλαιοκαστρίτσα ☎26610

Paleokastritsa **beach** rests among six small coves and sea caves, and locals claim its waters are Corfu's coldest and most beautiful. From the sapphire sea to the bright green hills, just the colors are a sight in themselves. As you look out into the sea from the main beach, a large rock that looks like a boat juts out. Legend tells that this was Odysseus's ship, which passed through the area on his famed journey, turned to stone by Poseidon's wrath. Poseidon must have since calmed down, though, as the beach today bustles with vendors selling their goods, the expected tourist attractions, and a bizarre number of travelers with their dogs. Green KTEL **buses** arrive from Corfu Town (45min., 6 per day 9am-6pm, €2). Hiring or renting a motorboat (30min., €10), paddle boat (€11 per hr.), or kayak (singles €4 per hr.; doubles €7) will enable you to reach the caves where, according to legend, Phoenician princess Nausicaä found the shipwrecked Odysseus washed ashore. You can also hop on a taxi boat from the main beach (☎69799 78 619; open 9:30am-6pm) to tour three picturesque caves and travel to incredible off-white beaches, only accessible from the water. Organize pickup time at your leisure. Prices are negotiable, but the standard cave tour (available in English) ranges €8-10 per person. Projecting out from a hill over the sea, bright white **Panagia Theotokos Monastery** (open 7:30am-4pm), founded in 1228, boasts a museum with a collection of Byzantine icons and engraved Bibles. Sunlight reflects off the whitewashed courtyard walls and highlights the colors in the lovely little garden, which offers startlingly beautiful views of the expansive shoreline. Come as early as possible—by mid-morning it's a mess of tour buses.

AGIOS GORDIOS Άγιος Γόρδιος ☎26610

Fourteen kilometers west of Corfu Town, Agios Gordios is highlighted by impressive rock formations and a lovely, surprisingly wide **beach**. The main road, running perpendicular to the sand, has a short stretch of touristy restaurants, mini-marts, and souvenir shops. But in reality, most visitors to Agios Gordios couldn't tell you where those shops are; the majority never make it beyond the premises of the town's infamous **Pink Palace Hotel ❷**, a favorite with American and Canadian backpackers in search of instant (and constant) gratification. Regardless of when you arrive, an energetic and remarkably attractive staff member greets you with open arms and a mandatory, eye-opening shot of pink ouzo. From then on, it's up to you how to sin away the day. The Palace's impressive list of amenities makes it a self-contained party resort: there's laundry service (€7.50), Internet access (€1.50 per 35min.), a jacuzzi, basketball and volleyball courts, a nightclub, four-wheel-drive rental (€15 per day), a safari to Mt. Pantokrator (€18 including lunch), clothing-optional cliff-diving (€15), boat daytrips (a.k.a. the "booze cruise"), and various water-sports. Saturday nights bring a weekly dance-and-drink-fest, when some faux-Greek traditions heighten the fun: hundreds of pink toga-wrapped partiers down countless shots of ouzo as Dr. George, the hostel's owner, breaks plates on willing guests' heads in a spirit of revelry that would make Dionysus proud. Nights at the Palace are not for the faint of heart, nor the weak of liver. (☎26610 53 103; www.thepinkpalace.com. Check-out 9am. Dorms, open only in high season, from €20; rooms with A/C, phones, balconies, and baths €25-40. AmEx/MC/V.) To get to the Palace from Corfu Town, take the green bus to Agios Gordios, which leaves from the New Port and has an Ag. Gordios sign. (45min.; M-Sa 5 per day 8:15am-8pm, Su 3 per day 9:30am-3:30pm; €1.50). Dr. George sends staff to meet incoming ferries at the port, and buses arranged by the Palace run to and from Athens, bypassing Patras. The bus runs every other day, so call for the exact schedule. (€46. Breakfast, dinner, and pickup/drop-off at the Corfu Town ferry included.)

EASTERN CORFU

The eastern coast of Corfu is the most developed and least aesthetically pleasing part of the island. The first 20km north of Corfu Town are thoroughly Anglicized by throngs of rowdy expats, and the beaches are thin strips that edge a busy, clamorous coastal road; try to avoid them unless you're looking for sweaty crowds and overpriced junk. Everything—beach, restaurants, hotels, and night-life—is consolidated into one strip. It's slightly cheaper than beautiful Corfu Town, but close enough to enable frequent trips, so it would be easy to make this area your base for exploring the island if you could stand the neon lights, plas-ticy shops, and third-rate restaurants that stretch as far as the eye can see. **Gou-via** and **Dassia,** the first two resorts north of Corfu Town, thrive off package tours. A bit farther north, visitors to the small but notorious town of **Ipsos** have unlimited access to a myriad of souvenir stands, fast-food joints, and C-class hotels that line the flat stretch of road from across the mountain. Guests guzzle the day away at tacky bars like the depressingly named "Alcoholics Anony-mous," only to collapse a few hours later onto the yellow sand like beached whales. The scene is almost identical at night, as clubs offer gimmicks like free shots and foam parties to anyone willing to drop a few euros. **Pirgi,** a quieter extension of Ipsos, has much of the same €2-per-pint atmosphere. Your best bet may be to settle down at a nearby campground like **Karda Beach Camping ❶,** between Dassia and Ipsos on the main road. The site's proximity to the bus sta-tion makes Corfu Town and the rest of the island easily accessible. (☎26610 93 595; www.kardacamp.gr. Playground, mini-mart, showers, pool. Sites €3.50; €6 per person; €5 per tent, 4-5 person tent €24; apartment-style bungalows €39. Electricity €4.) **KTEL green buses** serve Ipsos and Pirgi (30min.; M-F 9 per day 7am-8pm, Sa 5 per day 9am-4pm, Su 9:30am; €1.20). **Blue buses** head to Dassia via Gouvia (every 30min. 7-9am and 7-10:30pm, €1). Buy tickets onboard.

NORTHERN CORFU

Past Pirgi, the road winds below steep cliffs. **Mount Pantokrator,** a bare rock jutting out of the forested hills, towers 1km above, while dramatic vistas of dark, wooded

Albania appear across the straits. Roman emperors Tiberius and Nero both vacationed here, though tourism has erased most traces of the ancient world on the northern coast. Like the eastern coast, this area is not Corfu's most attractive, but the mountain road and a couple of lovely small beaches make it worth a short visit.

A mere 15min. drive from bustling Sidari, the wide, sandy beach of **Agios Stefanos** is set into a long curving gulf of high sandstone cliffs. Less developed than the island's resorts, there are only two or three tavernas on the beach, though watersports are still available (single canoe €8.20, double €11.40; parasailing €31). The trip there is a treat in itself: the coastal road curves inland past fern-filled hillsides of figs, olives, and cypresses, and through a picturesque mountain village. Though this area is better visited as a daytrip, the few who decide to stay will find expensive hotels and domatia around €35-40. **Buses** run from Corfu Town (1½hr.; M-F 4 per day 5:15am-4pm, Sa 3 per day 5:30am-2pm; €3) to Kassiopi and Sidari (M-F 4 per day 9:30am-4pm, Sa-Su 6 per day 9:30am-4pm; €1). There is **no bank or ATM** in town, so bring enough cash for your stay.

The sheer slopes of northeastern Corfu cradle several fine **beaches,** including **Barbati,** 10km north of Ipsos, nearby **Nissaki,** and the twin beaches **Kalami** and **Kouloura.** Kalami, with its spacious flat-stoned beach, is a welcome respite from the masses that pack the eastern coast. Less known for its clear water than its status as home to author Lawrence Durrell, the area attracts visitors who come to see his house, still "set like a dice on a rock" in the southern end of town. Durrell's former abode is now the pleasant **Taverna White House ❷,** which serves typical Greek fare like stuffed vine leaves (€6) and overlooks the sea. (Entrees €5.50-11.50.) Super-secluded Kouloura, a 10min. walk along the road from Kalami, is a small beach composed of mixed sand, eucalyptus leaves, and stones, with nary an umbrella or paddle boat in sight. **Taverna Kouloura ❷,** right on the shore, has vegetarian options, fish cooked less than 1hr. after they are caught, and a nice view of the marina. (Entrees €4-8. Fish dishes €11-28.) It can be expensive to stay in the area overnight, and there are no accommodations in Kouloura itself.

Take the **green KTEL bus** from Corfu Town to Kassiopi (1hr.; M-Sa 5 per day 5:45am-4pm, Su 9:30am; €2.50) which also stops at most beaches along the northeastern coast; ask the driver to be let off at less popular destinations. Kouloura and Kalami are a brief walk from the main road north of Gimari village. Head down from the bus stop on the main road; soon you'll see a yellow sign on the right marking the shortcut path to Kalami. If you're going to Kouloura, continue down the road until you reach a fork with signs for Kouloura and Kalami; turn right down this road. Blue "To the Beach" signs on the left mark the path down to Kouloura, while signs on the right side of the road point you toward Kalami.

Sidari, popular with tourists, is home to the famous **Canal D'Amour,** a small strip of water between towering rocks that have been shaped into beautiful monuments by the wind and waves. As the name implies, the small beach would be a lovers' haven—if it weren't jam-packed with slightly nauseating tourist traps.

Mount Pantokrator offers breathtaking views of all of Corfu. To get to the top, start at **Spartillas,** a village 7km north of and inland from Pirgi along the bus route. Follow the road used each summer by villagers on their way to the annual festival at Pantokrator Monastery. There is no footpath, but hikers can embark on a nice 4-5hr. walk to the top by taking the same dirt road as the cars. The windy road leads you through small clusters of houses and green orchards; if you look toward the west in the early evening, you may see one of the famous Corfiot sunsets that paint the entire sky a dazzling gold. **Cafe Pantokrator ❶,** which serves small snacks and drinks, is perched on the top of the mountain, at the entrance to the church. (Coffee €1.50. Egg salad sandwich €4.50. Open 9:15am-9pm.)

LEFKADA Λευκάδα

Thucydides reported that Lefkada was part of the mainland until 427 BC when the inhabitants dug a canal and made their home an island. A bridge now connects Lefkada to the mainland, just 50m away, which has made it easier for the tourism industry to seep in. But despite the excessive souvenir shops, miles of white-sand beaches and stunning mountainous terrain remain; with a little effort, you can skirt the patches of tacky tourism and find the island's unspoiled secrets.

LEFKADA TOWN   ☎ 26450

Lefkada Town, facing the mainland, does not, at first glance, introduce visitors to the best the island has to offer. The waterfront and pedestrian streets near the main plateia are the centers of the town's social scene, offering locals and travelers plenty of shops, restaurants, and opportunities to interact with the most conspicuous of tourists. Still, meandering into the tiny alleys off the main street will show you glimpses of Lefkada Town's quiet allure hidden under its bustling surface. Picturesque houses in the old Venetian style are newer than they look, built after extensive damage from earthquakes in 1867 and 1948.

⌐ TRANSPORTATION. From the bus station (☎26450 22 364), past the port and along the water on the left, **buses** cross the canal to Athens (5½hr., 4 per day 9:30am-5pm, €25). Local buses run to: Agios Nikitas (20min.; 6:40am, 2:15pm; €0.90); Nidri (45min., 12 per day 5:30am-7:30pm, €1.10); Vasiliki (1hr., 4 per day, €2.50). Pick up a recent schedule at the station for additional routes and return times; service is reduced on Sundays and expanded in high season. **Ferries** leaving from Nidri and Vasiliki link Lefkada with Ithaka and Kephalonia. **Taxis** (☎26450 21 001) line up by the start of Str. Mela and by the bus station. **Eurocar** (☎26450 23 581), on Panagou, two blocks to the right of Hotel Nirikos, rents **mopeds** (€8 per day). There are many rental shops along the road, so feel free to bargain.

▣◪ ORIENTATION AND PRACTICAL INFORMATION. Legend has it that the Venetians designed the town in the shape of a fish bone. The main road, **Stratigou Ioannou Mela** (a.k.a **Dörpfeld**) runs from the right end of the waterfront, facing inland, through town. Str. Mela and the winding streets branching off from it are pedestrian- and bike-only until they hit the central **plateia**, packed with cafes and the occasional traveling music act. A beltway, which becomes the waterfront road to the left of the start of Str. Mela as you face inland, envelops the entire downtown area and leads out to Vasiliki. This road is **8th Merarhias** on maps, but on street signs it is D. Golemi, I. Polytechniou, and Ag. Sikelianou for some stretches.

There is no tourist office, but try the travel agencies on Str. Mela for info about ferries, tours, or sights. A **National Bank** (open M-Th 8am-2:30pm, F 8am-2pm) with a **24hr. ATM** and several **pharmacies** sit on Str. Mela. The **tourist police** can be found on 8th Merarhias. Facing the bus station, walk left and follow the road as it leads away from the water; the **tourist police** are in a small kiosk in front of the **police** station on your left. (☎26450 29 370. General info and help with accommodations. Open 8am-2pm.) For the **OTE**, turn right off Str. Mela onto Skiardesi, just before the National Bank; turn left when it dead-ends at I. Marinou and walk 100m farther. (Open M-F 7:30am-1:30pm.) **Internet C@fe Lefkada,** past the police station on 8th Merarhias on the third side road on the left, has **Internet access,** as its name suggests. (☎26450 21 507. €2.40 per hr. Coffee €1.50. Open M-Sa 8am-2am, Su 10am-2am.) Past the bus station with the water on your left, look for **Cafezinho,** Golemi

14, on your right which also has Internet access. (☎26450 22 965. €3 per hr. Coffee under €2.) The **post office** is on Str. Mela about 150m past the National Bank on the left facing inland. (☎26450 24 225. Open M-F 7:30am-2pm.) **Postal Code:** 31100.

⬛ **ACCOMMODATIONS.** Most hotel rooms in Lefkada Town cost upwards of €40 in high season, so budget travelers should consider staying elsewhere. Travel agencies suggest **Ligia**, a domatia-packed village 4km outside of town. (Frequent buses to and from Nidri and Vasiliki pass through Ligia; 10min.) If you do stay in Lefkada Town, there are reasonably priced domatia a few blocks from the harbor, to the right of Str. Mela facing inland. Walk along the road and have your pick of the signs sticking out from between the numerous bars and cafes. One relatively affordable option is **Hotel Nikiros ❸**, at the beginning of Str. Mela at the waterfront. All rooms come with baths, TV, and A/C; request a room with a balcony overlooking the water for the same price. Nikiros houses a delightful cafe and restaurant. (☎26450 24 132. Breakfast included. Singles €30; doubles €40. AmEx/MC/V.) **Hotel Santa Maura ❹**, two blocks from the water on Str. Mela, has clean rooms in a 19th-century building; all come with baths, A/C, TV, and balconies. (☎26450 21 308. Reservations recommended. Singles €30-50; doubles €40-60.) Directly across the street is **Pirofani Pension ❹**. Despite its stuffy lobby, the rooms upstairs are spacious with matching furniture and TV, A/C, fridges, private baths, balconies, and plentiful sunlight. (☎26450 25 844. Singles €35-67; doubles €40-67.)

⬛⬛ **FOOD AND NIGHTLIFE.** Dining options in Lefkada Town, especially along Str. Mela, are pricey and tourist-oriented; you'll have to work a little to find authenticity. Walking up Str. Mela, you'll see the clock of Ag. Nikolaos church on your left and a yellow sign on your right that leads to **Lighthouse Tavern ❷**. This small restaurant is known for its peaceful, flower-filled garden (complete with chirping pet birds) and budget-friendly prices. Enjoy moussaka (€6) under the old-fashioned hanging lanterns outside. (☎26450 25 117. Entrees €5-12. Open daily 5pm-2am.) One of the oldest local favorites is the family-owned **Taverna Regantos ❷**, 75m down Dimarmou Verrioti, the first right as you approach the plateia from the waterfront. As you dine on well-priced seafood, ask for a translation of the quotes and song lyrics painted on the walls. (☎26450 22 855. Salads €2-3. Octopus in red sauce €6. Fish from €20 per kg. Open daily 7am-2am.) Sea lovers can have a truly marine experience at **Alkiona ❸**, 100m to the left of the bus station facing inland, where they can eat fish while watching boats meander around the harbor. (☎26450 22 458. Salads €2.50-4. Calamari €10. Entrees €6-13. Open daily noon-4pm and 7pm-1am. AmEx/V.) Reward yourself for making it through Str. Mela's tourist traps at **To Petrano ❶**, just before the plateia. Crepes (€1.50-6) can be topped with a wide variety of confections and ice cream (€1.10), and slushies (€1.50) are good for beating the heat. (☎26450 22 642. Open daily 9am-3am.)

As the sun sets, the party gets started at the small cafe-clubs located to the right of Str. Mela (facing inland). At **Cafe Excess** (☎26450 24 704) and **Coconut Groove**, Ag. Sikelianou 4, stylish rooms swell with sweaty locals dancing to pounding rock tunes. (Cafe Excess open daily 9am-1:30pm. Coconut Groove open daily Sept.-July 6pm-late; Aug. 24hr.) Nightlife elitists find themselves returning to **Capital**, the two-story venue that makes the scene at any other club in town look like a middle-school mixer. A swimming pool and blasting pop hits make for (in)famous all-night parties. Walk with the water on your right past the large white museum building and then go on past two schools; it's on the left, about 1km from town. Taxis cost roughly €4. (☎26450 25 138. Beer €3. Mixed drinks €6-7. Cover €5, only in Aug. Open daily mid-July to mid-Aug.; mid-Aug. to mid-July F-Sa.)

🔲🔲 **SIGHTS AND BEACHES.** The **Archaeological Museum** is located 1km down the waterfront road; make a left as you exit Str. Mela and follow the road with the water on your right for 1km; it's the big white building on the right. This wonderful museum houses a collection of artifacts from ancient Lefkas, a prominent city from the 7th century BC, as well as finds from ancient graves at Nidri. Panels thoroughly explain the objects in English and give interesting information on Lefkas's history and culture. The museum also documents the work of 19th-century archaeologist Wilhelm Dorpfeld, who was convinced that Lefkada, not Ithaka, was Odysseus's mythic home. Focal points include 6th-century BC terracotta figurines of dancing nymphs and a sarcophagus with its original skeleton and burial goods still inside. (☎26450 21 635. Open Tu-Su 8:30am-3pm. Free.) In late August, Lefkada hosts the annual **Folklore Festival,** bringing dance troupes from around the world to perform in the streets. (Afternoon performances. Free.)

While Lefkada Town has no sandy beaches, the northwestern coast has kilometers of white pebbles and clear water. Catch a bus to the best stretch of beaches along the island's west coast, starting at **Agios Nikitas** (3 per day, €0.90) and continuing to serene **Faneromenis Monastery,** which treats visitors to stunning views. (☎26450 21 105. Open daily 7am-2pm and 5-9pm. Free. Modest dress required.)

VASILIKI Βασιλική ☎26450

Vasiliki's position between mountains creates distinct wind patterns that make it one of the world's premier windsurfing towns. The long beach gives a sweeping view of multicolored sails; boats run to pebbled coves nearby. Avoid the garishly touristed main street and harbor and you'll find untouched, world-class beaches.

🔲🔲 **ORIENTATION AND PRACTICAL INFORMATION.** Almost everything in Vasiliki lies either along the waterfront or on the main road running perpendicular to the harbor. To reach the road from the ferry docks, walk 5min. with the water on your left; it will be before the road curves to the left. The main bakery at the end of the main road's commercial stretch on the right doubles as the town's bus stop. Four **buses** per day (7:15am-8:45pm) run to and from Lefkada Town (1hr., €3) and Nidri (30min., €2). A **ferry** leaves at least once daily for Fiskardo (1hr., €6). A 2min. walk up the main road from the bus station leads to the incredibly helpful ◼**Samba Tours,** which provides **ferry** and **bus information,** boat excursions, faxes, car rental, plane tickets, photocopying, safety deposit boxes, **currency exchange,** accommodations advice, and **Internet access.** They also sell local olive oil and eggs. (☎26450 31 555. Internet €4 per hr. Open daily 9am-11pm.) **GM Rentals,** located on the main road, offers mopeds (€10 per day) and cars (€25 per day)—renting either one is a good idea if you want to avoid overly touristed beach towns. There are plenty of rental places in town, so feel free to bargain. (☎26450 31 650. Open daily 8:30am-11pm.) There are no banks in Vasiliki, only **ATMs. Emporiki Bank** has one on the left of the waterfront as you face inland, next to the elementary school. A self-service **laundromat,** open 24hr., is available at the right end of the waterfront, facing inland. (€4 per wash.) The 24hr. **police station** is inland around the left side of Hotel Vasiliki Bay. (☎26450 31 218. Main office open daily 8am-2pm.) For medical **emergencies,** contact the **health center** (☎26450 31 065); on the main road, go straight through the intersection with the bakery/bus stop. To reach the **post office,** walk toward the port from the bus station. It is after the crossroads, on the left side of the main road. (Open M-F 7:30am-2pm.) **Postal Code:** 31082.

🔲 **ACCOMMODATIONS AND CAMPING.** Rooms for rent are plentiful along the waterfront, the main road past the bakery, and the side streets branching off them.

With a little work you should be able to find **domatia** for €15 per person or less in low season, and for as low as €25 in high season. The friendly brothers who own the mini-mart opposite the ferry dock, to the right side of the waterfront when facing inland, let spacious rooms with private baths and balconies at **Hotel Dimitrius ❷**. (☎26450 31 221. Singles €20-45; doubles €30-45.) To find **Hotel Vasiliki Bay ❸**, walk past the main road along the harbor and take the first right. The hotel is another 200m on the left. Rustic green furniture, large bathrooms, fridges, balconies, TV, and A/C make these rooms a great deal. (☎26450 31 077. Singles €25; doubles €30; triples €40.) **Vasiliki Beach Camping ❶**, popular among the windsurfing crowd, is a clean, affordable campsite only 80m from the beach. The bar, laundry, showers, nearby supermarket, and waterfront location will make travelers glad they traded in A/C for a tent. (☎26450 31 308. €5.50-7 per person; €5-5.50 per small tent, €5.50-6.50 per large tent; €3.50-5 per car.) ₊

▮▮ FOOD AND NIGHTLIFE. Nearly all the restaurants in Vasiliki are on a short stretch of the waterfront and are indistinguishable in both quality and price. If you can sift through the ordinary, though, you can find a quality, well-prepared, and still inexpensive meal. **Miramare ❷**, toward the far right side of the waterfront facing inland, is on its own pier, both literally and figuratively, as it combines excellent quality and hefty portions with low prices. (Entrees €5.50-8.50. MC/V.) **Evi's Pirate Place ❸**, on the main road from the bus station, is a local favorite. Evi, owner of the intimate stone restaurant, prepares all the dishes herself. (☎26450 31 811. Salads €4-5. Entrees €6-17. Open 6pm-late.) Check out a Greek take on Chinese food at **Jasmine Garden ❷**, facing inland, at the far right corner of the waterfront. Szechuan beef (€7) and *satay* shrimp (€11) are the house specialties, but various vegetable dishes (€4-5) are available. (Entrees €5-15. MC/V.)

Nightlife options in Vasiliki are slim pickings, but **Zeus's Bar**, on the waterfront, has a slew of shots and mixed drinks to soothe the sting of a sunburn or a thunderbolt. Don't question the god's determination: the trance, techno, rock, and pop play all night until the two full dance floors are empty. (☎26450 31 560. Drinks €6-7. Open daily 10am-"when people leave.") **Abraxa's Tunnel Bar** plays classic rock in a cozy space. (Beer €2. Mixed drinks €4.50. Happy hour 8:30-10:30pm.) **Remezzo Beach Bar**, on the beach all the way to the left of the waterfront (facing inland), is the site of the most popular spot among the younger crowd. Remezzo lets you relax during the day in chairs on the harbor's pebble beaches, but when the sun goes down, the beats of American and Greek pop start bumping and the venue turns into a full-fledged club. (Open May-Sept. Beer €4-5. Mixed drinks €6-7.)

▨ SIGHTS. **Boat tours** to several of the island's beaches leave from Vasiliki. During high season, Samba Tours leads weekly trips to Lefkada's best beach, breathtaking **◪Porto Katsiki** (Port of the Goat), at the base of towering white cliffs (40-50min., round-trip leaves 11am and returns 5pm, €8). Porto Katsiki is also accessible by car or moped: drive to the end of the main road, turn left, and keep an eye out for signs. The drive takes about 1hr., and then you have to walk the rest of the way on a difficult path for about 30min. The boat ride to Porto Katsiki also passes a **lighthouse** built on the site of the **Temple of Lefkas Apollo**, on the southernmost tip of the island. The ancient poet **Sappho**, rejected by her beloved Phaon, is said to have leapt to her death from these 70m-high cliffs. Boat excursions will take you to the best views of Sappho's jumping point. **Trekking Hellas**, on the main road toward the bus station, offers outdoor activities that show Vasiliki's wilder side. (☎26450 31 130; www.vassiliki.com.gr. Guided walks around deserted villages €18-28. Scuba diving €35-190. Tours all morning. Office open daily 8-10pm.)

ITHAKA Ιθάκη

Traverse Odysseus's legendary home to see the pebbled beaches, rocky hillsides, and terraced olive groves that drew him back here through countless obstacles. Perhaps the most beautiful of the Ionian Islands, Ithaka's close-knit, genuinely Greek flavor is rare amid its heavily-touristed neighbors. Villages, where the ambling pace of life creates a far more relaxing and quiet atmosphere than that found on nearby Kephalonia or Lefkada, surround Ithaka's many natural harbors. Hidden on both sides of the island, empty beaches wait to be discovered.

VATHY Βαθύ ☎ 26740

Ithaka's lovely capital wraps around a circular bay, where fishing boats and luxurious yachts bob, and precipitous green hillsides that roll down to the water. At dusk, the dying sun deepens the tint of Vathy's traditional red-shingled roofs and pastel-painted houses. The old-fashioned street lamps and calm evening air evoke nostalgic memories and bring out the romantic in any visitor.

▐▓ TRANSPORTATION AND PRACTICAL INFORMATION. Facing inland, Vathy's **ferry docks** are on the far right of the waterfront, about a 4min. walk along the water to the right of the town plateia. **Ferries** depart from Frikes, on the northern tip of Ithaka, to Vasiliki, Lefkada, via Kephalonia (2½hr., 10am, €6). Departures from Piso Aetos go to Sami, Kephalonia (45min., 4 per day, €2) or from Vathy to Sami (1hr., 7am, €5.10). A taxi ride to Piso Aetos from Sami costs €10. Ferries also go to mainland Patras in the Peloponnese (4hr., 7am, €13.30). Schedules vary seasonally and ferries run considerably more frequently in July and August; check with the staff at **Delas Tours** in the main plateia. (☎ 26740 32 104. Open daily 6-7am, 9am-1pm, and 5-9:30pm; low season 9am-1pm and 5-9:30pm.) Or consult **Polyctor Tours,** along the far side of the plateia as you approach from the port police. (☎ 26740 33 120. Open daily 9am-1:30pm and 5:30-9pm.) **Taxis** (☎ 26740 33 030) tend to be pricey; they line up by the water, in front of the plateia. Be sure to call ahead for a taxi, as there are not many on the island. Ithaka is small enough to explore in a day by car—to rent one, try **AGS Rent a Car** on the waterfront two blocks to the right of the plateia. (☎ 26740 32 702. €30-35 including insurance. Open daily 8:30am-9pm.) **Rent a Scooter,** on a side street off the waterfront directly across from the port police and to the right before the plateia, rents from €10 per day. (☎ 26740 32 840. Open daily 8:30am-1pm and 5-9pm.)

The **National Bank** is in the far right corner of the plateia, with Polyctor Tours on your left; it has a **24hr. ATM** and **currency exchange.** (☎ 26740 32 720. Open M-Th 8am-2:30pm, F 8am-2pm.) **Alpha Bank,** a few doors left of Net, on the plateia, offers the same services. (☎ 26740 33 690. Open M-Th 8am-2:30pm, F 8am-2pm.) For **laundry, Polifimos** is behind the National Bank, in the far right corner of the plateia. Walk past the bank on the right, take the first left, and it will be set back in the first building on your right. (☎ 26740 32 032. Wash and dry €4 per kg. Open M-Sa 8am-1pm and 6-9pm.) To reach the 24hr. **police station** (☎ 26740 32 205, 100 in emergencies) from the plateia, turn right on the first street after Drakouli, and walk straight uphill for three blocks. It will be on the right side. There is a **pharmacy** 20m to the right of the post office. (☎ 26740 33 105. Open daily 8:30am-2pm.) To get to the **health center** (☎ 26740 32 222), turn right after Drakouli and walk uphill about 150m past the police station. The **OTE** is on the waterfront, just before Hotel Mentor when coming from the plateia with the water on your left. (☎ 26740 32 299. Open M-F 7:30am-2:30pm, depend-

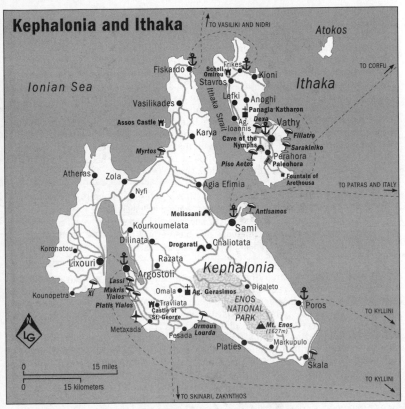

Kephalonia and Ithaka

ing on the season.) **Internet access** is available at **Net,** on the left side of the plateia facing inland, which has a full bar (mixed drinks €4) as well as two floors of Internet access and touch-screen gaming. (☎26740 33 450. €4 per hr. Open daily 8am-2:30pm and 6pm-late.) **Nirito Cafe** has coffee (€2) and baklava (€2.50) as well as limited Internet access. (☎26740 32 437. €4 per hr. Open daily 7am-2am.) The **post office** is in the plateia near Delas Tours. (☎26740 32 386. Open M-Th 8am-2:30pm, F 8am-2pm.) **Postal Code:** 28300.

ACCOMMODATIONS. Cheap **domatia** are definitely the way to go over tempting but pricey hotel rooms. ▓**Sophia's ❸,** located in a classic blue-and-white stucco house about 300m from the central plateia, offers some of the lowest prices in town. Bear left at the National Bank, walk straight past Niko's Taverna, and go two blocks uphill; Delas Tours will give travelers a ride. Each room comes with a spacious bathroom, kitchen, satellite TV, and A/C, which makes up for the spartan furnishings. (☎26740 32 104. Rooms €25. Reservations recommended.) A clean and convenient option is **Aktaion Domatia ❸,** across from the ferry dock on the far right side of the waterfront (facing inland), with a pleasant view of the bay. Immaculate rooms include baths, TV, A/C, and minifridges. Many vehicles going to Vathy pass by here, so light sleepers should ask for a room on the inside. (☎26740 32 387. Singles, offered only in low season, €25;

doubles €30-60. Negotiate for discounts in low season.) **Ms. Martha ❸** has old-fashioned rooms with private baths, kitchenettes, fans, and access to a white marble balcony with a great harbor view. To find her, bear left in front of the National Bank, past Niko's Taverna, turn right at the T-shaped intersection, walk one more block, and turn left; the rooms are a few houses down on the left, marked by a small sign. Make sure to bargain, as prices are negotiable depending on season and length of stay. (☎26740 32 352. Singles €30-60; doubles €40-70.) Facing inland, **Hotel Mentor ❹** is on the far left of the waterfront with a large sign. The biggest hotel on the island, Mentor has basic but spacious rooms with baths, balconies, A/C, and TV; some have harbor views. If the hotel is out of your price range, ask about renting one of its studios (€45-50) or apartments (€70-80), whose A/C, TV, bath, and kitchen will make it a good deal for larger parties. The apartments are closer to the plateia than the hotel. (☎26740 32 433; www.hotelmentor.gr. Breakfast included. Singles €50-75; doubles €72-98.)

▶TIP◀ GONE, BUT NOT FOR LONG. Greek hotel and hostel owners often leave their reception desks unattended while they linger at a nearby cafe or run a quick errand. Don't be deterred by unanswered knocks or vacant offices—managers usually return soon enough and often expect prospective clients to dial their mobile numbers, which they've posted on business cards or on the door.

◻ **FOOD.** Of the seemingly endless tavernas and seafood restaurants lining the waterfront, locals recommend **Kantouni ❸** for the best quality and fastest service. The taverna's special lobster pasta is a staggering €120-150, but you can get an equally tasty meal for a fraction of the price. (☎26740 32 918. Pork with wine €7. Mixed vegetable plate €5. MC/V.) Carnivores rejoice at **Niko's Taverna ❷**, behind the National Bank, where the menu is organized by how the meat is cooked—grilled, roasted, minced, and so on. Specialties include moussaka (€6) and calamari (€5.50), and decent salads (€3-4.50) are available for vegetarians. (☎26740 32 039. Open May-Oct. 7pm-2am.) Behind the post office, you'll find a respite from the touristy harbor at **Taverna To Trexantiri ❷**, where home-cooked dishes and low prices make up for the fluorescent ambience. (☎26740 33 066. Salads €3-4. Entrees €5-7. Open 6pm-late.) Across the street, to the right of Trexantiri, the blue-and-white patio of **Sirene's ❸** is enveloped by a canopy of pink flowers. The restaurant offers a distinctive Ithakan omelette (€6) and basic Greek fare with home-grown vegetables. (☎26740 33 001. Entrees €7-10. Open 7pm-late. MC/V.) For a snack, stop by **Drakouli ❶**, a mansion-turned-cafe on the left end of the waterfront facing inland. Inside a turquoise door are a palm-lined garden with a lake, casually displayed antiques, and wood-paneled floors. These touches of class are as sweet as the ice cream (€1.50) or the signature sundae (€7) combining several flavors. (☎26740 33 435. Coffee €2-3. Open 9am-midnight.)

◧ **SIGHTS.** Though small, Ithaka has so much historical tradition that each little village has something worth seeing. In Vathy, most everything is located near the central plateia. Turn right after Dragoumi cafe and take the first left to find the **Vathy Archaeological Museum,** two blocks down on the right. The tiny collection displays finds from ongoing excavations at the **Sanctuary of Apollo at Aetos**—a site containing the ruins of an ancient city dating back to 700 BC—as well as ceramics and artifacts from the Dark Age. Animal-shaped ritual vases from the 7th or 6th century BC and ivory and amber jewelry from the Geometric period are highlights. (☎26470 32 200. Open Tu-Su 8:30am-3pm. Free.) Turn right onto the footpath near Alpha Bank to find the **Folklore and Nautical Museum.** The peach-colored museum houses a large collection of nautical equipment and memorabilia as well as artifacts from Ithaka's colonial period. Art and literature buffs will appreciate early 19th-century illustrations of Homer's characters on the second floor. (☎26740 33 398. Open Tu-Sa 10am-2pm and 5-9pm. €1.)

☞ ♫! BEACHES AND THE OUTDOORS. Ithaka's beaches are slightly out of the way, but their beauty justifies the effort to reach them. Because most tourists are disinclined to hike the winding, hilly roads (or pay for a pricey taxi), you may find yourself pleasantly alone. Jaw-dropping **■Filiatro** and **Sarakiniko,** 3.5km and 2.5km away from Vathy, respectively, have trees that reach the clear, glowing waters to make for a shimmering combination of shade and sunshine. To get there, walk with the water to your left and, after Hotel Mentor, turn right and keep heading toward the mountain to the left of town as you face inland; take the steep uphill road. Eventually the road to Filiatro will turn left off the main road—it's a 50min. walk, but the views alone are well worth it. There is a small cafe at Filiatro, but its selection is limited, so you may want to bring your own lunch. The closest beach to the plateia is family-oriented **Dexa,** with a long, pebbled shore and plenty of shady olive trees. To get there from Vathy, follow the main road out of town (with the water on your right) up and over the hill with the gas station; the walk will take about 30min. To spend a languid afternoon on the shores of **Gidaki,** a deserted island, you'll need to take a boat (round-trip €7-8), which runs twice a day during high season. The island's sole **bus,** which doubles as a school bus, runs north from Vathy to **Frikes** (30-40min., €2) and exceptionally beautiful **■Kioni** (1hr., €2), a small village whose crystal blue harbors and white pebble beaches make it a favorite of locals and tourists. In high season, the bus generally runs twice a day: once at 5:30am and again at 2pm, both returning immediately. Around 3km south of Kioni, little **Stavros** sits high in the mountains, with delightfully cheesy papier-mache models of Odysseus's journey in the town square. The **Archaeological Museum** houses a collection of excavated items from Pilicata Hill, another archaeological site on Ithaka. Keep an eye out for signs; it's 700m past the town's church off a side street on the right-hand side. (Open Tu-Su 8am-2pm. Small donation expected.) Near the village of **Agios Ioannis,** on the island's western side, are several stunning pebble beaches with views of Kephalonia alongside some of the island's ritziest real estate. A taxi from the plateia costs €18.

⚑ DAYTRIPS FROM VATHY. Trying to get to most of the sights on this small island without a taxi or car may make you feel like Odysseus on his beleaguered journey home. If you are planning on seeing many sights, the cheapest option is to rent a motorbike or car, or hire a taxi by the hour (€30 per 1hr., but bargain).

The **Monastery of Panagia Katharon,** dedicated to the Virgin Kathariotissa (patroness of the island), is more than 600m up on Ithaka's highest mountain, **■Mount Neritos;** take a moped or taxi (round-trip €25) toward Anoghi and follow the signs. This monastery, open from sunrise to sunset, has operated as a church since the 1500s and holds an icon of the Virgin Mary said to be a miracle-worker painted by St. Luke. Women must cover their legs in the sanctuary, and all visitors must observe the monks' rule to close the front door in order to keep wandering goats off the premises. Bring a camera—on a clear day, your snapshots may match the common postcard images depicting the view from this mountain.

In nearby Anoghi, the island's former capital, the modest church of **Agia Panagia,** with delicately-worn frescoes, has occupied the town s.quare for over 300 years.

Outside is a bell tower and a relic of a tank used to fight the Germans in WWII. The church is usually locked, so get the key from the adjacent cafe on the left.

Two kilometers outside of Vathy is the **Cave of the Nymphs**, where water nymphs (*naiads*) were worshipped and, according to legend, where Odysseus hid the treasure the Phoenicians gave him. Archaeologists have been excavating the cave in recent years and, consequently, it is sometimes closed to visitors. Check with taxi drivers and tour operators before going. If it is closed, you can still walk around the site and view the two separate entrances (one for the gods and one for mere mortals) and perhaps chat with a few archaeologists. To get to the cave, walk around the harbor with the water on your right on the road out of town leading to Piso Aetos and Stavros, then follow the signs along the road winding up the mountain. The hike itself provides impressive views of Vathy, and the entrance is up a flight of steps to the right, just before the paved road ends.

For a great view and a literal taste of modern Greek culture, make your way to **Perahora**, a small village on the frighteningly steep mountainside 4km above Vathy; a **wine festival** invites visitors here at the end of July each year. The real treasure, though, is the ruins of **Paleohora**, the island's capital until it was abandoned in the early 16th century. To find them, follow the signs in Perahora to the community center until you reach a footpath that leads through olive groves. Here lie intact architectural ruins as well as abandoned Byzantine **churches** with the remains of frescoes clinging to the inner walls. In the village, you can marvel at the intricately-designed icon screen of the church of the Dormition of the Virgin. The road leading to Perahora is on the far right of the waterfront as you face inland (opposite the road to Stavros)—follow the signs uphill. A taxi from Vathy costs €7.

In Stavros is a site that locals call *"Scholi Omirou"* ("Homer's School"), where Odysseus's Palace is said to have stood. Until very recently, the location, and even the existence, of this palace had been little more than a rumor. In the last decade, however, after a resurgence of interest in the area, archaeologists have found Mycenaean ruins, intact architectural structures, Hellenistic towers, and even an untouched Roman grave. On the hike up, notice the mountainside *melanithros*, or natural springs. From Stavros, go past the Archaeological Museum on the main road, which turns into a dirt road, and follow it to the end. The ruins are 150m along a footpath up the hill. (Free. Taxi from Vathy €20.)

KEPHALONIA Κεφαλονιά

Massive mountains, subterranean lakes and rivers, caves, dense forests, and more than 250km of sand-and-pebble coastline make Kephalonia a nature-lover's paradise. Though it is the largest of the Ionians, Kephalonia lacks convenient buses. Appreciating its beauty and avoiding its many tourist traps thus requires a car or a moped. With your own transportation, you'll uncover villages perched on lush hillsides and untouched, never-ending beaches that blend into brilliant sunsets.

ARGOSTOLI Αργοστόλι ☎ 26710

The capital and by far the largest town on Kephalonia or Ithaka, Argostoli is a lively city packed with yellow and orange buildings that dot the hills. Other parts of the island may be more picturesque, but Argostoli offers urban convenience and access to the rest of Kephalonia. Though there's no shortage of hotels, restaurants, or shops, the main plateia is the only place to go for the limited nightlife.

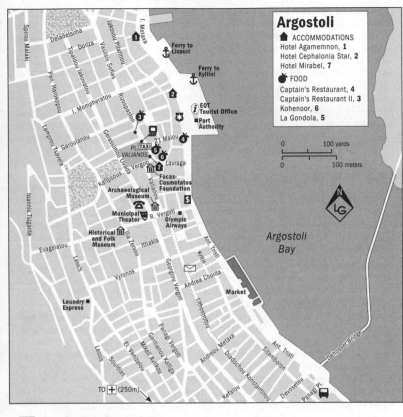

Argostoli

🏠 ACCOMMODATIONS
Hotel Agamemnon, **1**
Hotel Cephalonia Star, **2**
Hotel Mirabel, **7**

🍴 FOOD
Captain's Restaurant, **4**
Captain's Restaurant II, **3**
Kohenoor, **6**
La Gondola, **5**

Argostoli
Bay

🚏 TRANSPORTATION

Flights: Olympic Airways, R. Vergoti 1 (☎26710 28 808), has 2 flights per day to Athens (€75) during high season. They also offer 3 flights per week to: **Corfu** (€25); **Preveza** (€30); **Thessaloniki** (€95); **Zakynthos** (€29). Open M-F 8am-3:30pm.

Ferries: Kephalonia has multiple ports for different destinations. Buses connect Argostoli to other ports, including **Sami** (p. 559), where ferries leave for **Corfu, Ithaka,** and **Patras,** in addition to **Italy** in July-Aug. Prices and times are seasonal; inquire at a travel agency. From Argostoli boats go to **Kyllini** on the Peloponnese (2 per day, 30min., €7.30) and **Lixouri, Kephalonia** (20min., 1 per hr. until 10:30pm, €1.40). From Poros, on the southeastern coast, ferries leave for **Kyllini** (2 per day, €6.50). Ferries head to the tiny port of **Ag. Nikolaos** (2 per day, €4) on the northern end of Zakynthos from Pesada, a similarly small and inconvenient port on the southern coast of Kephalonia. Buses do not go from Pesada to Argostoli, so you'll have to take a taxi (€16-20); also, buses in Zakynthos do not regularly go to Ag. Nikolaos. Multiple ferry companies operate out of Argostoli, so check with the tourist office for updated times and prices.

Buses: ☎ 26710 22 281. On the southern end of the waterfront, in a light pink building all the way to the left as you face inland. Brochures with schedules, prices, and return times available. Open daily 7am-8pm. Buses head to: **Agios Gerasimos/Omala** (30min.; 10am, 12:30, 2pm; €1); **Fiskardo** (1½hr.; 10am, 2pm; €4); **Poros** (1½hr., 4 per day 10:30am-2pm, €3.50); **Sami** (40min., 4 per day, €3); **Skala** (10am, 2pm; €3). For **Travliata,** take either the Skala or Poros buses (€1). Buses meet the ferry and continue to **Athens** (4 per day, €26). Buses to Argostoli meet the ferry arriving in **Sami** (3-4 per day, €3). Local service reduced Sa-Su.

Taxis: ☎ 26710 28 505 or 26710 22 700. Plenty line up in the plateia. Available 24hr.

Rentals: There are many rentals along the waterfront. **Sunbird,** Antoni Tristi 139 (☎ 26710 23 723), near the Port Authority, rents cars (from €30) and mopeds (from €10). Open daily 8:30am-2pm and 5-9pm.

■ ⑦ ORIENTATION AND PRACTICAL INFORMATION

The town's cafe-packed and hotel-lined main plateia is two blocks from the water. Walk from the water on **21 Maiou,** across from the Port Authority and GNTO/EOT. To the left of the plateia, facing inland, **Lithostrotou** is a pedestrian area with high-rent stores like Diesel and Benetton and dozens of leather, postcard, and jewelry shops. Many museums and galleries are between the plateia and Lithostrotou.

Tourist Office: ☎ 26710 22 248. Beside the Port Authority near the ferry docks. Helpful staff provides free **maps,** information and brochures about sights and beaches, and some assistance with accommodations and restaurants. Information in English, French, German, Greek, and Italian. Open daily 7am-2:30pm.

Bank: National Bank, between Hotel Olga and Hotel Tourist along the harbor, offers **currency exchange** and **24hr. ATM.** Open M-Th 8am-2:30pm, F 8am-2pm. Other banks and ATMs line the waterfront.

Laundromat: Laundry Express, Lassis 46b. Walk inland on Vyronos for 9 blocks, turning left onto Lassis. The laundromat is 2 blocks farther on your right. Self-service. Wash and dry €5.40 per load. If the owners are not there, buy tokens from the mini-mart across the street. Open daily 9am-2:30pm and 5-10pm.

Police: ☎ 26710 22 200. On I. Metaxa across from the tourist office. Open 24hr.

Tourist Police: ☎ 26710 22 815. In the police station. Open daily 7am-10pm.

Telephones: OTE (☎ 26710 28 599). On Gerassimou Livada, to the left of the Archaeological Museum. Open M-Th 7:30am-1:30pm, F 7:30am-1pm.

Internet Access: B.B.'s Club (☎ 26710 25 469), in the bottom right corner of the plateia (facing inland). "B.B.'s" both stands for "Bad Boys" and for the full Bar and Billiards. €2.50 per hr., €1 min. Open 9am-2am.

Post Office: ☎ 26710 23 173. 2 blocks up from the water on Lithostrotou, at the intersection of Kerkyras. Open M-F 7:30am-2pm. **Postal Code:** 28100.

⌂ ACCOMMODATIONS

Rooms in bustling Argostoli are in high demand for travelers waiting to board ferries and small-town Greeks looking for bigger-city partying. In high season, private rooms are often the cheapest option, though many are relatively far from the center of town. Bargain, but don't expect to find a room for much less than €35. All other times during the year, however, the prices of domatia and hotels are fairly similar. If you plan to stay in a hotel, call ahead. Otherwise, renting a car or moped allows you to stay in the small-town **domatia** and still have access to the beach. The tourist office maintains a listing of available domatia.

🗾 **Hotel Agamemnon, I.** Metaxa 36 (☎69720 90 844), about 5 blocks north of the police station along the waterfront, above Pizza Mella. The entrance is on the side. Agamemnon offers rooms on the harbor for almost half the price of other hotels in town. Egyptian and ancient Greek decorations line the hallways that lead to immaculate, quiet rooms with A/C, baths, and balconies. Singles €15-30; doubles €25-50. ❷

🗾 **Hotel Cephalonia Star, I.** Metaxa 60 (☎/fax 26710 23 180), farther along on the waterfront; the door just says "Hotel C Star." 42 elegant, colorful, and comfortable rooms are conveniently near the water and central plateia, making them worth the price. Amenities include A/C, TV, phone, balconies, fridges, and small baths. Breakfast included. Singles €30-40; doubles €40-50; triples €50-60. ❹

Hotel Mirabel, Central Square 281 (☎26710 25 381), in the left corner of the main square, facing inland, has small but fully equipped rooms with A/C, TV, and ample closet space. The breakfast area and garden are pleasant. Book early. Breakfast included. Singles start at €30; doubles €40; triples €60. Prices rise in the summer. ❹

🍴 FOOD

Food may be cheaper on the waterfront, but try to avoid the generic restaurants that line Ant. Tristi; selection and quality are better in the plateia. Those visiting on Saturday mornings can check out the well-organized **farmers' market** for fresh fruits and vegetables; the fruit shops, bakeries, and supermarkets that line the water between the bus station and port are less ephemeral. **Polatos,** Ant. Tristi 32, across from Alpha Bank, has a large selection of fresh fruits at the lowest prices. (Open daily 7am-10pm.) 🗾**Captain's Restaurant** ❸ has two large spaces: one on the waterfront (I. Metaxa and 21 Maiou), and one to the right of the plateia, facing inland (Rizospaston 3). Live Greek music plays while you munch on fresh bread rolls with delicious chive cream; when it's time for the main course, friendly waiters bring out large, tasty portions from either the regular or vegetarian menu. (Salads €2.50-8. Most entrees €5-9.) **La Gondola** ❷ has ample but often packed seating on 21 Maiou. They serve Greek dishes, but people come for divine Italian dishes like *risotto d'oro* (€8.60), which comes with pumpkin and shrimp. (Pizza €7-9. Pasta €4.20-9. Greek entrees €6-9. Wine €8.50-25. Open 4:30pm-1am. MC/V.) **Kohenoor** ❸, at the intersection of Str. Metaxa and Lavraga, one block from the plateia, is marked by sign reading simply "Indian Restaurant"—more than enough to identify it among Argostoli's limited options. Inside you'll

PARTY CULTURE

Geographically and historically set apart from the rest of Greece, Ionian Islands pride themselves on their distinctiveness, pointing to the landscape, rural villages, and Venetian influences. This pride culminates in the "Cultural Summers" that occur throughout the region, mainly in August. The festivals are as much about celebrating a collective identity as they are about attracting visitors, and they range from tame to wild and religious to hedonistic.

In quaint Lefkada Town, during the annual **Folklore Festival,** dance troupes from all over the world put on shows every afternoon on the main pedestrian street, Str. Mela, and in a nearby theater. Afterward, the town turns into a giant party, teeming with performers and travelers reinvigorated by the afternoon's shows. With hotels typically booked to the max, it's a good idea to make reservations early.

The festivals on Kephalonia— in Sami and its neighboring villages—center on religious celebrations. On August 15, Sami commemorates the Virgin Mary and St. Erasmus, with performances by Greek singers and bands. The Cultural Summer there lasts from the end of July through mid-August, with nightly song and dance performances, and occasional joyous parades. For more information, consult the local tourist office.

find tasty curries at relatively reasonable prices. (Chicken *tikka* €9. *Rogan josh* €9. Appetizers €4-5. Open daily 6:30pm-midnight. MC/V.)

👁 SIGHTS

Argostoli's **Archaaeological Museum** is housed in a beautiful building a few blocks south of the plateia, across from the Municipal Theater on R. Vergoti. Pottery and jewelry from excavations around the island and Melissani Lake are displayed with explanations in Greek and English. Vintage photographs of an 1899 excavation at Sami are on display, as are some of the 3rd-century BC tombstones found there—complete with remarkably well-preserved names of the dead. Make sure to stop by the **mosaic** from the temple of Poseidon from the 2nd century BC. (☎26710 28 300. Open Tu-Su 8:30am-3pm. €3, seniors and students €2, children and EU students free.) The **Historical and Folk Museum,** two blocks from the Archaeological Museum, on the road to the left of the theater, contains an exhaustive display of 19th-century objects. Of particular interest are the 20th-century photos of Argostoli, including shots of damage from the devastating 1953 earthquake, and religious items and tiles that survived the quake. (☎26710 28 835. Open M-Sa 9am-2pm. €3, students €1.50, children under 12 free.) The **Focas-Cosmetatos Foundation,** one block left of the plateia facing inland, has a large collection of 18th- and 19th-century furniture, coins, and paintings, as well as photos from the period of the 1953 disaster. The Foundation is building a botanical garden to showcase and preserve the plants of the Ionian Islands and the Mediterranean basin. (☎26710 26 595. Open M-Sa 9:30am-12:45pm and 7-9:45pm. €3, children under 14 free.)

🔳 DAYTRIPS FROM ARGOSTOLI

Renting a moped or car allows you to roam between sights and beaches, unrestrained by inconvenient bus schedules. You can also get to ⚑**Myrtos beach** (p. 562) on the western coast, considered one of Europe's best.

CASTLE OF ST. GEORGE. The Venetian castle is 9km southeast of Argostoli, overlooking the village of Travliata. From its 18th-century battlements, you can admire the panorama that once inspired Lord Byron or imagine running through the underground tunnels that once connected the castle to Argostoli and were used as a getaway system through WWII. *(By moped, head toward Skala and bear left when the road splits, or take either the Poros or Skala buses (10min., €1). Open M-Sa 8am-8pm. Free.)*

LIXOURI. In the center of the western peninsula, Lixouri is a large and vibrant town, yet less touristed than the capital. If you wish to spend the day here, you can rent a **moped** at several places in town and explore the charming villages in the area. You can also take one of the local **buses,** including the one that runs twice a day to **Xi** (15min., returns immediately; 9:15am, 2:45pm; €1), a red sand beach surrounded by cliffs. And the town itself, with its small cafes and bakeries, is a wonderful place to settle and unwind. For a change of scenery, a small beach is at the far left of the waterfront, facing inland; it's a 5min. walk along a lovely tree-lined promenade. *(Boat from Argostoli 30min., every 30min., €1.10. Buy tickets onboard.)*

SOUTHERN COAST BEACHES. A few beaches and noteworthy towns dot the area south of Argostoli. Closer to the capital city than white-sanded **Ormous Lourda, Makris Yialos** and **Platis Yialos** share breathtaking shorelines below an enormous cliff. You can sit above the sands and listen to the crashing waves or join the tanning population on the lounge chairs below. *(Take the Lassi bus; 5min., 10 per day 9am-6:30pm, €1. You can also walk from the central plateia. Facing inland, take the road to the left side of the plateia and follow the signs. The beaches are about 3km away.)*

EAST OF ARGOSTOLI. The **Monastery of Agios Gerasimos** was built around the underground cove where Ag. Gerasimos spent his last days on earth. Today, a small ladder toward the back of the church allows guests access to that cove. When a large enough crowd forms at the monastery, the monks open the silver casket which holds his preserved body. On the night of August 15, nearby **Omala** hosts a festival and vigil in the saint's church; for two days, Omala's residents honor him by drinking their fill of wine. On the saint's name-days (Aug. 16 and Oct. 20), **Marcupulo**, another nearby village, throws its own wild party to celebrate Ag. Gerasimos. *(Ask at the tourist office for info on the festival. Buses run from Argostoli to Ag. Gerasimos/Omala at 10am, 12:30, 2pm; €1.)* **Skala** is yet another village with a never-ending beach; this one is pebble and sand. The small town offers bathers crystal-clear water 37km from Argostoli and history buffs the remains of a 2nd-century Roman villa. Almost all of its structure is gone, but the mosaic floors are remarkably well-preserved. *(Look for the signs as you walk down the road from the bus stop toward the water. Open daily 10am-2pm. If it's closed, a view is still available from the sides. Free.)* The ruins of an ancient temple are 2km in the other direction. *(Walk with the water on your right side and follow the signs.)* There's no shortage of dining choices along the beach, but the **Sun Rise Restaurant ❷**, all the way to the left (facing inland), serves fresh, inexpensive seafood. Tasty fish entrees start at €5, and thrifty couples can share special platters for two (red snapper, prawns, and sardines; €8).

SAMI Σάμη ☎ 26740

As you stroll through Sami, stunning views in all directions make it difficult to decide which is more lovely: the tempestuous blue waves crashing on the long, white-sand beach or the lush, village-dotted hills cradling the town. Sami's main advantages are its central location as a small port and its proximity to the natural wonders of Melissani Lake, Drogarati cave, and Antisamos beach, whose beauty makes it a good place to spend the afternoon and night before catching a ferry. In the late 1990s, Nicolas Cage starred as an Italian military officer occupying Kephalonia during WWII in *Captain Corelli's Mandolin*. The picturesque Venetian buildings seen in the film, however, were actually created by skilled set-makers; in reality, the 1953 earthquake wiped out most of Sami, leaving unremarkable modern architecture in its wake.

⌫ TRANSPORTATION. From Sami, **ferries** sail to Patras (2½hr.; 8:30am, 5pm; €14) and Vathy, Ithaka (1hr., 11:30pm, €6). In July and August, international ferries go to Brindisi, Italy (daily, €35). **Buses** leave the station on the left end of the waterfront, facing inland, for Argostoli (45min., 4 per day, €3) and Fiskardo (1hr.; 10:15am, 2pm; €2). Buy tickets onboard. There are no buses on Sundays. Expensive **taxis** (☎ 26740 22 308) line up on the waterfront facing the plateia.

⬛🔢 ORIENTATION AND PRACTICAL INFORMATION. Poseidonos, the waterfront street lined with cafes, intersects the main plateia. White sandy beaches lie both to the left and right of the town center. Ferries land on either side of the town plateia. From the bus station, facing the water, turn left to reach the plateia. You may be able to see the top of the blue-and-white Hotel Kyma, which sits on I. Metaxa, Sami's main road; this road runs parallel to the water one block inland.

The plateia lies between the road and the waterfront. If you follow it with the water on your right, it leads to Argostoli. The staff at **Blue Sea Travel**, next to the bus station, sells ferry tickets and offers general information. (☎26740 23 007; www.samistar.com. Open daily 8am-11pm.) Sami has several **banks; Emporiki Trapeza**, on the waterfront to the right of the plateia as you face inland, has **currency exchange** and a **24hr ATM**. (Open M-Th 8am-2:30pm, F 8am-2pm.) The 24hr. **police** station, I. Metaxa 14 (☎26740 22 100), is located on the main road toward Argostoli, near the post office, three blocks from the plateia. **Pharmacies** are on the main road to Argostoli. If you take a right onto the road from the plateia facing inland, and one will be on your left at I. Metaxa 37. (☎26740 22 266. Open daily 7:30am-2pm and 3-10:30pm.) The **OTE** is one block past the post office. (Open M-F 7:30am-10pm.) For **Internet access**, try **Internet Break**, under Hotel Kastro along the waterfront. (☎26740 23 770. €5 per hr. Open M-Sa 9am-3pm and 5-9:30pm, Su 5-9:30pm.) The **post office** is on the road to Argostoli, two blocks off the right corner of the plateia at the fork in the road. (Open M-F 7:30am-2pm.) **Postal Code:** 28080.

⌂ ACCOMMODATIONS AND CAMPING. Because Sami is a convenient base for travel within Kephalonia, there can be a high demand for rooms, which get relatively expensive in the summer. The street leading to the nearby village of **Karavomilos**, toward Melissani Lake, is lined with **domatia**. The rooms above **Riviera Restaurant ❷** along the harbor, a block from the bus station, have kitchens, baths, A/C, and wooden furniture for a low price. The rooms are accessible by a white marble staircase to the side of the restaurant. (Singles €30.) If you are dying to stay in town, the **Hotel Kyma ❷**, in the middle of the plateia, has decent if sparsely furnished rooms with shared baths, fans, and balconies. Quieter rooms are in the back. (☎26740 22 064. Singles €20-30; doubles €40-60; triples €59-78.) **Hotel Melissania ❸**, two blocks inland from the Port Authority, on the far left of the waterfront, has 15 rooms with balconies, fridges, TV, and private baths. Ask for a top-floor room for a private roof-top patio. (☎26740 22 464. Breakfast €7. Singles €25-37; doubles €30-58; triples €45-70.) **Karavomilos Beach Camping ❶**, a 15min. walk from town with the water on your right, is in a huge field. The site is clean, with hot showers, electricity, laundry, Internet access, and a mini-mart. (☎26740 22 480; www.camping-karavomilos.gr. Office open 8:30am-noon and 4:30-7:30pm. €5-6.50 per person; €3.50-4 per small tent, €4.50-5.50 per large tent. Electricity €3.50.)

◫◧ FOOD AND NIGHTLIFE. Taka Taka Mam ❶ serves standard Greek fare by the ocean at a great bargain. Some of its plates run up to €8, but travelers can keep it cheap with gyros (€1.80) and souvlaki (€1.50). **Mermaid Restaurant ❷**, Taka's waterfront neighbor, is less tacky than other harborside options and has many vegetarian options (Salads €3-4. Grilled peppers €4.50.) **Pizza Tereza ❷**, toward the far right end of the waterfront cafes (facing inland), provides a little taste of Italy in very big portions. (Sizable pizzas €6.90-8.)

At night, young locals drive around the main square blasting Greek pop; at the few bars along the harbor, they can drink all night long. **Calypso Bar**, next to the bank along the harbor, pays homage to a very different group of islands with chilled-out reggae. (Beer €2.50. Mixed drinks €6. Open daily 7:30pm-4am.)

◉◖ SIGHTS AND BEACHES. Sami's two popular caves are a short drive from town. Stalactite- and stalagmite-filled **Melissani**, 2km from Sami, is part of the huge, underground Lake Karavomilos. Its deep blue waters run up to 15m deep and come from as far as Argostoli. Finding it is simple, though the walk will take 30-45min.; go along the beach with the water to your right until you come to a small ocean-fed "lake" with a waterwheel on the far side. Turn left after the restaurant by the lake, walk inland to the road about 30m, and turn right; you'll see signs down this street. The boat tour of the cave lasts 10-15min., and the knowledgeable boatmen explain the history and pose for photos. Because the cave has an open roof measuring 50m by 30m, you'll want to go when the sun is high in the sky. (☎26740 22 997. Open daily 9am-late afternoon. €5 entrance. Tipping the boatman €1-3 is encouraged.) **Drogarati,** 5km from Sami, is a large cavern full of spectacular stalactites and stalagmites over 150 million years old. To find it, head inland on the road to Argostoli and follow the signs (1-1½hr.) or take the bus to Argostoli and ask to be let off at Drogarati; you'll likely be dropped off at the fork, 1.5km from the caves. (☎26740 22 950. Open until dark. €3.) **Agia Efimia,** 10km north of Sami, is a pretty harbor town, popular with the yachting crowd, that definitely deserves a visit. Buses (15min., 2 per day, €3) run from Sami to Agia Efimia. Ask the Fiskardo bus to let you off there (15min., €3). Isolated and alluring ▓**Antisamos** beach is a must if you get to this side of Kephalonia. The long, white pebble beach is enclosed by rolling green hills, home to the island's colorful butterflies and many wandering goats. You can take a taxi to Antisamos (€7) or you can hike there (1¼hr.) by following the waterfront left from the plateia as you face inland; take the road next to the Port Authority. Since the hike is uphill, fairly long, and challenging, bring plenty of water and wear good shoes.

FISKARDO   Φισκάρδο   ☎26740

The road north ends at must-see Fiskardo, one of the few Kephalonian villages to escape the 1953 earthquake. That stroke of luck has left it a rare example of the island's 18th- and 19th-century architecture. The crescent-shaped waterfront is tinged with the pastel hues of the modest buildings surrounding it. At night a romantic aura pervades the town, which twinkles with the dim lights of boats resting in the water. A splendid walk through the woods or swim from the rocks takes you to the forested bit of land across the harbor, home to a lighthouse and a ruined 15th-century Venetian fortress. The town's charm is accented by the sweet perfume of its ubiquitous flowers. Fiskardo's white pebble beach is only 500m from town, on the road to Argostoli, in a quiet cove with flat rocks for sunbathing.

▐▘▟ TRANSPORTATION AND PRACTICAL INFORMATION. Ferries go to Nidri, Lefkada (2hr., 1-5 per day, €6) and Vasiliki (1hr., €6). In July and August, the same boats also run to Ithaka (€3). **Buses** for Argostoli leave from the parking lot next to the church, uphill from the town. Two buses per day run to and from Argostoli (1½hr.; 6:30am, 4:30pm; €4) and Sami (1½hr.; 6:30am, 4:30pm; €3). **Nautilus Travel Agency,** at the right end of the waterfront, answers transportation and lodgings questions and provides **Internet access** (€6 per hr.) and **currency exchange.** (☎26740 41 440. Open daily 9am-10pm.) In high season, you can rent motorboats from **Regina,** past Nicholas Taverna and by the ferry docks, starting at €50 per day. (☎69389 84 647. Open daily 8:30am-6pm.)

▐▘▐▘ ACCOMMODATIONS AND FOOD. Rooms are not cheap in Fiskardo, even in the scattered **domatia.** Early in summer, simple doubles start at €40. For the best view in the village, stay at ▓**Tavern Inn ❸,** whose rooms have baths, fans and, most importantly, balconies. Hanging over the rocks and crashing waves, guests can look toward the famed lighthouse and nearby Ithaka. To find the Inn, walk with the water on your left for 100m out of the town center. (Singles €35; doubles €55.) The well-maintained rooms at **Anatoli ❸,** next to Elli's Restaurant and Cafe on the right side of the harbor, have A/C, TV, and common kitchens. (☎26740 41

204. Singles €40; doubles €60.) Some cheap rooms are just outside of town. Ask at **Tassia Restaurant ❷**, on the waterfront, which offers apartments for four with two rooms, baths, and kitchens 2.5km out of town. (☎26740 41 205. €58.)

Although the town is full of excellent restaurants, most are tourist havens with hefty price tags to match, especially along the harbor. An exception is the pink-and-blue **Lagoudera ❷**, just off the waterfront next to the post office. Though it lacks a waterfront view, the food is delicious and the mood set by lanterns and flowers isn't bad either. (Entrees €5-8.) At **Nicholas Taverna ❸**, located 200m to the right of the port (facing inland), waiters and a playground occupy kids so couples can enjoy a romantic dinner by the water. Gregarious Nicholas attests to his family-run taverna's status as a dining institution by tacking up newspaper and magazine clippings about, well, himself. On Fridays, he teaches patrons to dance. (☎26740 41 307. Salads €3.50-5. Fish €45-50 per kg. Entrees €8-13. MC/V.) Wasting your money and your appetite on pre-packaged ice cream is pointless when you can try the local-recommended frozen treats at **Dodoni ❷**, next to Nautilus Tours. (Ice cream €1.50. Other desserts €3-4.50.)

🏛🏖 **SIGHTS AND BEACHES.** Venturing away from the waterfront proves quite rewarding. To reach the old-fashioned lighthouse, walk all the way around the waterfront with the sea on your right to Nicholas Taverna. A short and shaded path picks up where the road ends, and is marked with yellow circles all the way. Ruins of an old fortress are nearby. If you need to cool off and aren't in the mood for a trek, a smaller, though heavily trafficked, pebble beach offers first-rate views of neighboring Ithaka. With the water on your left, head along the waterfront road for about 10min.; the beach is on your left just past the Roman graves on your right. Off the road from Argostoli and Sami to Fiskardo is one of Europe's most breathtaking beaches, **◼Myrtos.** The snowy white pebbles and clear, blue water are stunning enough, but the beach's location, pressed against the cliffs, makes it divine. Buses from Fiskardo to Sami and Argostoli stop at the turn-off to Myrtos, 4km from the gasp-inducing beauty of the beach. Ten kilometers up the road from the Myrtos turn-off is the equally incredible Venetian **Castle of Assos,** on a steep, wooded peninsula connected to the island by a narrow isthmus. Completed in the early part of the 17th century, much of the castle is well preserved. Fiskardo buses stop at the Assos turn-off; it's a 4km walk to the small, peaceful village, also worth a visit, and another few kilometers to the castle.

ZAKYNTHOS Ζάκυνθος

The varied landscapes of Zakynthos (or Zante) are filled with an exceptionally subtle palette of colors—white cliffs rise from aquamarine water, sun-bleached wheat fields wave in the shadow of evergreens, and magenta flowers frame the twisting streets. Known as the greenest of the Ionian Islands, Zakynthos shelters thousands of plant and flower species, some of them found nowhere else. A large population of endangered loggerhead sea turtles also takes refuge off its shores. Still, in Zakynthos Town and on its neighboring beaches, you'll encounter more sweaty tourists and sleazy street vendors than natural wonders; only in the countryside can you appreciate Zakynthos's true beauty, from its famous beaches in the east to the caves in the north. Those who do venture away from the shops selling oversized, plush sea turtles will quickly come to understand why the Venetians called Zakynthos the "Flower of the East."

ZAKYNTHOS TOWN ☎ 26950

Arcaded streets and delicate Old World buildings welcome visitors to Zakynthos Town. After an earthquake destroyed the city in 1953, locals recreated the Venetian architecture in areas such as Pl. Solomou, creating a romantic, nostalgic air. Though buzzing crowds of tourists and street vendors may make things hectic earlier in the day, walking through the streets or by the waterfront is a true pleasure at sunset. With many tour companies clamoring for clients, Zakynthos Town is a convenient base for daytrips to see the island. If the call of the wild burns in your veins, seek the serene beauty of the more remote beaches.

▶ TRANSPORTATION

Flights: The **airport** (☎ 26950 28 322) is 6km south of town. Flights to: **Athens** (45min., 1-2 per day, €74); **Corfu** (3 per week, €46); **Kephalonia** (3 per week, €28); **Thessaloniki** (3 per week, €96). The **Olympic Airways** office, Al. Roma 16 (☎ 26950 28 611), is 2 blocks past Il Primo and 3 blocks inland along the pedestrian shopping street. Open M-F 8am-2:30pm.

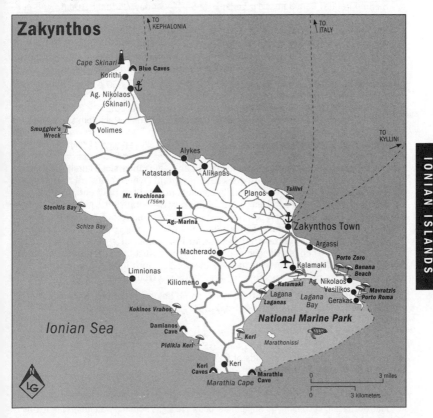

Zakynthos

IONIAN ISLANDS

Ferries: Ferries for **Kyllini** in the Peloponnese (1½hr., 5-7 per day 5:30am-8pm, €6) depart from the southern dock, on the left side of the waterfront as you face inland. Tickets for Kyllini ferries can be bought at **Praktoreio Ploion** (☎26278 22 083), next to Hertz on Lomvardou past the police station with the water on your right. Open daily 8:30am-8:30pm. **Agios Nikolaos (Skinari),** about 40km north of Zakynthos Town, has ferries to **Pesada, Kephalonia** (1½hr., 1-2 per day, €4). Be warned that both Pesada and Ag. Nikolaos are very small; Kephalonian buses do not go to Pesada, which lacks accommodations, and Zakynthian buses do not run to Ag. Nikolaos. You'll need to take a taxi (€40), and be prepared to wait 30min. for it. Due to such difficulties, you might save time and money by flying from the airport near Argostoli directly to Zakynthos Town. Returning to Kyllini and heading to Kephalonia by ferry is another alternative. For more information, call the **port police** (☎26950 28 117 or 26950 28 118).

Buses: Filita 42 (☎26950 22 255), behind the Praktoreio Ploion. From Pl. Solomou, walk 6 blocks south (with the water on your left) and 1 block inland. Schedules change monthly; check the info window. To **Athens** (6hr., 5 per day 5am-7pm, €19 including ferry) via **Patras** (3hr., €6 including ferry) and **Thessaloniki** (10hr., Su-Th 7:30am, €36.20 including ferry). **Local buses** run to: **Alykes** (M-F 4 per day 6:50am-4:45pm, Sa-Su 4 per day 7:40am-4:30pm; €1.20); **Argassi** (M-F 8 per day 6:45am-7:30pm, Sa-Su 4 per day 9am-3pm; €1); **Lagana** (M-Sa 13 per day 7:15am-8:10pm, Su 8 per day 7:15am-8pm; €1); **Kalamaki** (M-Sa 11 per day 7:15am-8:10pm, Su 8 per day 7:15am-8pm; €1); **Tsilivi** (M-Sa 10 per day 6:40am-8:10pm, Su 5 per day 7am-3:30pm; €1); **Vasilikos** (M-F 3 per day 6:45am-2:30pm, Sa-Su 10am, 3pm; €1.20).

Taxis: ☎26950 48 400. On side streets off the waterfront. Available 24hr., but those seeking rides in the early morning should make arrangements the day before.

Rentals: Hertz, Lomvardou 38 (☎26950 45 706). Cars from €60 per day, but can be bargained to €35-40; includes unlimited mileage, insurance, and tax. Open daily 8am-2pm and 5:30-9pm. **EuroSky Rentals,** A. Makri 6 (☎26950 26 278), 2 blocks inland on A. Makri, by Pl. Solomou. Mopeds €15 per day. Open daily 9am-2pm and 6-9pm.

✴ 🛈 ORIENTATION AND PRACTICAL INFORMATION

The waterfront runs between **Plateia Solomou** and **Agios Dionysios church.** Each end has a dock: Kyllini ferries usually dock at the left end (when facing inland), by Ag. Dionysios; all other boats (such as daily cruises) dock at the right end, by Pl. Solomou. The waterfront street, **Lomvardou,** is lined with restaurants, gift shops, ferry agencies, and car and moped rentals. The next street inland is **Filita,** with the bus station and fast-food stands; Filita becomes **Klavdianou** toward Pl. Solomou. Behind it are **Foskolou, Alexandrou Roma,** and **Tertseti,** all of which either change names or end between **Martinegou** and Ag. Dionysios. Just inland from Pl. Solomou is **Plateia Agiou Markou,** a major gathering spot for both locals and tourists. Al. Roma becomes a pedestrian shopping area between **Tzoulati** and Pl. Ag. Markou.

Banks: National Bank (☎26950 26 808), on Pl. Solomou, **exchanges currency** and has a **24hr. ATM.** Open daily M-F 8am-2:30pm. Other ATMs sit along Lomvardou and around Pl. Solomou.

Police: ☎26950 24 480, emergency 100. At the intersection of Lomvardou and Fra. Tzoulati. Open 24hr. The **tourist police** (☎26950 24 482) are in the same building. Enter through the door to the side of Fra. Tzoulati, take a right, and they are at the end of the hallway. Open daily 7:30am-2:30pm.

Hospital: ☎26950 42 514 or 26950 42 515. Uphill and 600m inland from the city center. Walk down Lomvardou to Ag. Eleftheriou. Follow this road inland to Kokkini, where the road goes right, becoming Ag. Spiridona. Follow the signs from the waterfront. Open 24hr.

Internet Access: Connect Internet, 18 Ag. Dionysios (☎ 26950 44 622). €4 per hr.; €2 min. Take a right on Voltera, the road before the park facing the church of Ag. Dionysios, and then take a left; the cafe will be on the right. Open daily 10am-2pm and 4-11pm.

Post Office: ☎ 26950 42 418. On Tertseti, the 4th street inland from the waterfront, near Xenou. **Exchanges currency.** Open M-F 7:30am-3:30pm. **Postal Code:** 29100.

⌐▪ ACCOMMODATIONS AND FOOD

Rooms in Zakynthos Town fill up in July and August, though they tend to be expensive year-round. Large waterfront hotels charge around €90 for a double in high season; reasonably priced hotels with lower-quality service seem to overflow in the blocks to the very right of the waterfront, facing inland, after the port. One option is to stay in Argassi, 3km away, where domatia and hotels crowd the main street. If you do want to stay in town, put on your poker face and bargain. **Athina Marouda Rooms for Rent ❶,** on Tzoulati and Koutouzi, is three blocks inland from the police. The central location, common kitchen, and simple rooms with sparse furnishings and a shared bath are good enough to keep people strapped for cash nicely satisfied. (☎ 26950 45 194. Singles €10-15; doubles €20-35.) **Hotel Diana ❹,** in Pl. St. Markou, adjacent to the Catholic church, offers location and luxury for predictably higher prices. Elegant rooms have A/C, baths, and TV. (☎ 26950 28 547; www.dianahotels.gr. Breakfast included. Singles €35-80; doubles €50-80. MC/V.) **Hotel Yria ❸,** Kapodistrou 4, two blocks past Pl. Ag. Markou to the far right of the waterfront facing inland, rents plush, carpeted rooms with A/C, TV, phones, sizable baths, and small balconies. Look for a building with vines and flowers wrapping its walls. (☎ 26950 44 682; www.zakynthos-net.gr/yria. Singles €30-40; doubles €40-50; triples €50-60.) The unassuming and slightly cramped lobby at **Hotel Aegli ❸,** on Lomvardou, two blocks south from Pl. Solomou with the water on your left, leads to bright, colorful rooms with TV, balconies, A/C, and admirably large private baths. (Singles €30-40; doubles €45-55; triples €45-55.)

Restaurants with menus that resemble full-length novels line the waterfront and Pl. Ag. Markou. On Al. Roma, every other store is either a cafe or a candy shop. The **Veropoulos Supermarket,** on Lomvardou, 50m to the right of the police station, facing inland, sells a wide variety of fruit, vegetables, cereal, and snacks. In the sweltering summer, swing by for the freezing-cold A/C even if you're not hungry. (Open M-F 8am-9pm, Sa 8am-7pm.) **Village Inn ❸,** Lomvardou 20, is the best option on the waterfront, with tables facing the water. Musicians fill the beautiful garden area with Greek melodies. (☎ 26950 26 991. Lamb in lemon sauce €8.50. Moussaka €5. Open daily 9am-midnight.) In Pl. Ag. Markou, the appropriately named **Venetsiana ❷** exudes an Italian air, with a much classier ambience than its sister restaurant in Argassi. Beef *stamnas* (€7), the house specialty, is as delightful as the live music played in August. The takeout paradise **Molos ❷,** 26 Lomvardou, displays its diverse and delicious dishes in a convenient location near the pick-up points for many boat tours. (☎ 26950 23 939. *Pastitsio* €5. Club sandwich plate €5. Open 10am-12am.) **Il Primo ❷,** Lomvardou 18, is next to Village Inn. Filling portions of Italian cuisine will satisfy both the appetite and the budget. (☎ 26950 45 919. Pasta €4-7. Vegetarian dishes €4-6. Pizza €4-7. V.) Even the tourist traffic and higher prices at **House of Latas (To Spiti to Lata) ❹,** 2km above the city (follow the signs to Bohalis), near the Venetian castle, can't detract from its spectacular view. Have a beer (€2.50) at sunset if you don't want to break the bank. (☎ 26950 41 585. Salads €4-8. Grilled entrees from €7. Open daily 6pm-late. MC/V.)

🔍 SIGHTS

The intricate, glittering designs throughout the **Church of Agios Dionysios,** named in honor of the island's patron saint, make its colorful frescoes pale in comparison. In a room enclosed by silver walls, a silver chest holds some of the saint's relics. At night, only the iconostasis is lit up, making it visible from the street. (Open 7am-1pm and 5-10pm. Modest dress required.) Directly behind is the ◪**Ecclesiastical Museum,** which features beautifully sculpted crosses, Ag. Dionysios's vestments, and his handwritten documents. Engraved Bibles from the 13th through 17th centuries were salvaged from repeated pirate attacks on the Monastery of Strofades, where the saint lived. Letters written in Latin between late 16th-century religious leaders are remarkably well-preserved, and magnificent paintings line the stairs to the second floor. (☎26950 44 126. Open daily 9am-1pm and 5-9pm. €2, under 18 free.) In Pl. Solomou, the **Byzantine Museum** houses two floors of icons from the Ionian School, a distinctive local hybrid of Byzantine and Renaissance art styles. Two 17th-century iconostases on the first floor are extravagantly detailed, and a 16th-century iconostasis from St. Andreas's monastery fills the walls of its entire second floor room. When you reach the Renaissance-style room with the magnificent *Virgin and Child with Angels* from the Church of Panagia Phaneromeni (late 18th century), make sure to look up at the equally majestic paintings on the museum's ceiling. Many of these artifacts were rescued by locals who risked their lives to pluck them from the dusty rubble of area churches after the 1953 earthquake, as documented in poignant photos. (☎26950 42 714. Open Tu-Su 8am-2:30pm. €3, seniors and students €2, EU students free.) Perhaps most fascinating is the **Museum of Dionysios Solomos,** in Pl. Ag. Markou. Solomos, born in Zakynthos and buried inside the museum, is Greece's national poet; the first verses of his "Hymn to Liberty" became the Greek National Anthem. The exhibit includes everything from the dust from Solomos's first grave, to inkpots used by the poet, to handwritten manuscripts of his most famous poetry. It also highlights the lives of other famous Greeks, such as the piano of composer Paul Karren. There is little explanation provided, but tours in English and Greek can be arranged with the museum staff for a small donation. (Open daily 9am-2pm. Info booklet €3. €3, seniors and students €2, under 12 free.)

A hearty walk (or nice drive) gets you to **Stranis Hill,** 3km above town, which has a ruined Venetian castle. Solomos's home also stands atop of this hill, where the famous "Free Besieged" was written. Take Tertseti, which becomes N. Koluva, to the edge of town, or head inland from Pl. Ag. Markou, take a right onto Therianou, a left onto Filikon, and follow the signs uphill to Bohalis. Turn left at the junction and go 500m farther. The views of Zakynthos are particularly dazzling at night.

🔳 DAYTRIPS FROM ZAKYNTHOS TOWN

You can see all of Zakynthos, including the otherwise-inaccessible **western cliffs,** by boat. Shop around for a cruise on Lomvardou. The tours that highlight most of the island's sites usually run €18-25. Most tours leave in the morning, usually around 9am, return around 5:30 or 6pm, and prefer reservations be made the day before. Don't buy from hawkers around gift shops—while the ticket prices are usually about the same as the agencies', they do not offer refunds and give little explanation after they take your money. For reliable ser-

! Sunbathers should note that they share Zakynthos's beaches with a resident population of **endangered sea turtles;** a simple stroll through the sand could potentially destroy hundreds of turtle eggs. Zakynthos is gradually making efforts to protect the turtles and their nests, encouraging waterfront properties to certain precautions and indicating which beaches have nests. Gerakas, Kalamaki, and Laganas have turtle populations; ask at tour companies which other beaches are also turtle territory.

vice, try **Caretta Tours,** off Lomvardou. (☎26950 25 032. Open daily 9am-2:30pm and 5:30-9:30pm.) Cruises go to many of the island's most spectacular sights, including the **Blue Caves** on the northeastern shore past Ag. Nikolaos. The azure sea reflects off the ceilings of the stalactite-filled caverns, creating a blue glow throughout. For a more intimate experience, skip the huge ships and take a small fishing boat from Ag. Nikolaos. If you go swimming by the caves, watch out for the jellyfish. Southwest of the Blue Caves is the ◪**Smuggler's Wreck,** a large boat skeleton which has made the beach one of the most photographed in the world. Most cruises stop for 30min.-1hr. on the beach. To avoid noontime crowds, try to go in the mid-afternoon. Other cruises from Zakynthos Town may visit **Marathonissi,** also called Turtle Island because of its proximity to loggerhead turtle nesting grounds and its turtle-like shape. Inquire at the tourist police or one of the agencies in town. Renting a **moped** will let you explore with far less hassle—there are rental agencies at many beaches (€10-15). If you decide to go solo, buy a road map (€1-5) and ask directions; the island is developing rapidly, and new roads may not appear on old maps.

The bustling beach town of **Argassi** is 4km south of Zakynthos Town. Buses run to the village daily (20min.; M-F 8 per day 6:45am-7:30pm, Sa-Su 4 per day 9am-3pm; €1), but it's an easy 30-40min. walk on the main road out of town with the water on your left. Argassi is Zakynthos Town gone wrong, with many of the same conveniences and twice the tourist to local ratio. Like a cheesy cruise ship, the garish bars host nightly parties with themes like Toga Night; one spot, **Avalon,** is a re-creation of a medieval castle. Moped and car rental agencies, many restaurants, and a children's go-kart race track are just a few of Argassi's amenities.

FROM THE ROAD

GO WITH THE FLOW

Of all the strangely worded and creatively translated phrases I have encountered in the Greek islands, the worst is "ferry schedule," a term which leads one to believe that a regular pattern of departures and arrivals exists, and that ferry companies run accordingly. Neither assumption, however, is entirely valid. The "schedules" change constantly, and even if a boat is listed to depart or arrive, it's possible that nothing will materialize.

As an American trained to swear by my daily planner, the Greek people's lack of frustration with the ferries' unpredictably was even more mysterious than the "schedule" itself. While being stranded drove me crazy, Greeks reacted to my frustration with confusion: "Go tomorrow, go the next day, why rush?"

Maybe this nonchalance about scheduling (or lack thereof) stems from acclimatization; the locals expect ferries not to run on time and are surprised when they do. Or perhaps it simply reflects more relaxed cultural values.

Though the ferry system's forced deviances took some getting used to, the frustration at being "stuck" on an island soon become opportunistic relief. When a planned two-day whirlwind suddenly became a luxurious five-day stay, it was easy to go beyond the standard beach-and-acropolis routine, and delve into the local culture.

—Laurie Schnidman

Wide, sandy **Tsilivi beach,** 6km up Zakynthos Town's waterfront road with the water on your right, is not the place to go if you're fleeing the tourist masses. Lined with chairs, the beach is crowded with sun-seeking foreigners and people playing adventure sports. Tsilivi is nearly as close as Argassi, but the mountainous terrain and the higher number of oblivious tour bus drivers make reaching Tsilivi on foot more challenging. Local buses run daily from Zakynthos Town (20min.; M-Sa 10 per day 6:40am-8:10pm, Su 5 per day 7am-2:30pm; €1). Follow the signs down the main road from the bus stop leading to the beach.

> **SANDY BED? YES PLEASE.** If you want to spend days exploring Zakynthos's many beaches without being tied to a particular town, grab your sleeping bag and head to **Zante Camping ❶,** 1.5km past Planos on Ampula beach, which is one of the island's only beach campsites. Its quiet location, amid beautiful flora and sands devoid of tourist footprints, makes it a wonderful place to get acquainted with the island while its numerous amenities, including a cafeteria, mini-mart, pool, and car rental, ensure that you'll be staying in comfort. To get there, catch the Tsilivi bus from Zakynthos Town. (☎26950 61 710. €5, children free; €2 per tent, €3 per car. Electricity free.)

For those dying to escape the crowds, nearly untouched beaches carpet the peninsula that stretches out 18km from Zakynthos Town. Farthest south, 2km past Vasilikos, are the serene sands and crystal-clear water of **Porto Roma.** A few minutes north, though, **Mavratzis** ensures that the hedonistic carousal is never too far away. Its adventure sports and party resort draw a young, international crowd. **Porto Zoro** and **Banana Beach** can't be beat for quiet afternoons of sipping pina coladas and lounging under the sun. Buses leave Zakynthos Town for Vasilikos (M-F 4 per day 6:45am-2:30pm, Sa-Su 10am, 3pm; €1.20). For a unique experience, rent a bicycle in Zakynthos Town and take an early morning ride to Porto Roma (or catch the early bus and store your bike with the luggage). Then spend the day heading back to town, stopping at each beach along the way, perhaps even spending the night in one of the many rooms to let by the beaches. Travelers should note that some spots on the western coast of the peninsula are protected areas that must be vacated in the evenings, when sea turtles come ashore to nest.

The soft, white-sand beaches that fringe Alykes, 20km from Zakynthos Town, are popular with families but are often less crowded than their southern counterparts. In the true spirit of Greek hospitality, many hotels and pool clubs offer free lounge chairs and umbrellas. Buses run from Zakynthos Town (M-F 4 per day 6:50am-4:45pm, Sa-Su 4 per day 9am-6:30pm; €1.20).

AGIOS NIKOLAOS (SKINARI) Άγιος Νικόλαος ☎26950

At the extreme northern tip of Zakynthos, a breathtaking drive away from the bustle of tourist-centric beach towns, is tiny Agios Nikolaos, a village about the length of a city block, and the port of Cape Skinari. (Confusingly, Agios Nikalaos is itself sometimes referred to as Skinari.) Ferries to Pesada, Kephalonia depart from here. Bus service is nonexistent, so incoming ferry passengers need to arrange their own transportation to Zakynthos Town, which might require a taxi (€40), as Skinari has no rental agencies. Above La Grotta restaurant, in the middle of the village and to the right of the port, facing inland, is **Hotel La Grotta ❷,** the only hotel in town. Spacious rooms come with A/C, small balconies, and showers. Since most travelers only make Agios Nikolaos a daytrip, proprietors are often willing to bargin. (☎26950 31 224. Singles €20-30; doubles €40-50. MC/V.) **Domatia** with similar amenities can be found on the road 200m before and after the town. Farther down the street, **La Storia Restaurant ❷** serves traditional Greek cuisine on the beach. You might want to go for the seafood (€6-18), as there are only four other main courses available. (☎26950 31 635. MC/V.) Those who prefer more variety can try **La Grotta Restaurant ❷**, which offers a cornucopia of salads (€3-6), from the typical Greek salad to the "La Grotta Special." The barbecue burger (€6) is surprisingly zesty. (☎26950 31 224.) You can buy tickets on the waterfront for a fishing boat tour of the **Blue Caves** (45min., starting 9-9:30am, €8) and the ◼**Smuggler's Wreck** (2hr., starting 11-11:30am, €15), accessible only by water (p. 566). These tours are smaller and considerably shorter than those from Zakynthos Town, so if you end up in Agios Nikolaos, take advantage of this convenience; during high season, boats leave every 5-15min. from the dock. For more information, contact **Actipis Cruises** (☎26950 31 224). You can also rent canoes on the beach.

CRETE Κρήτη

Crete awes with its sheer geographic variety. Palm tree forests collide with precipitous mountains; sheltered coves lie alongside stepped vineyards; and windmill-strewn plains are only minutes from dramatic gorges. Yet the region's diversity is as cultural as it is environmental. Isolating mountain ranges have preserved rural lifestyles that seem completely removed from the cities and tourist towns along the coast. Because it is so far south, the island has been influenced by the Egyptians and Phoenicians along with the Turks, Venetians, and Germans who overran the rest of Greece. Its architecture is thus a unique fusion of Eastern, African, Mediterranean, and European styles.

SUGGESTED ITINERARIES: CRETE

FIVE DAYS Explore western Crete, basing your trip in bustling **Hania** (p. 571). Hike the **Samaria Gorge** (p. 579), the longest in Europe, before sunning yourself on **Plakias's** (p. 588) expansive beach. See what remains of the Minoans at under-visited **Phaistos** (p. 602).

TWO WEEKS After seeing Hania's (p. 571) Venetian arsenal, climbing past the wild goats of the Samaria Gorge (p. 579),

and ascending to the ancient palaces of Phaistos (p. 602), quench your thirst with water from **Zaros's** (p. 599) famous spring. Spend 1 day in **Iraklion** (p. 590), then rent a car and circle the quiet, mountain-ringed villages of the **Lasithi Plateau** (p. 613). Continue your eastward journey to **Sitia** (p. 617), from which you can take daytrips to the palm-tree forest of **Vai** (p. 620) and the ironically life-filled **Valley of Death** (p. 621).

The seeds of civilization were planted in Crete, with records of life on the island dating back to 6000 BC and ruins that predate Hellenic culture attesting to the advancement of Minoan society. Disasters—earthquakes, a tidal wave from an enormous volcanic eruption on Santorini, and Mycenaean invasions—plagued 3rd millenium BC Minoan society until one final cataclysm wiped the civilization out entirely. The Dorians occupied the island in the 8th century BC, followed 1000 years later by Romans. Next Crete fell under rickety Byzantine rule, before Arabs conquered the island in AD 827. The Byzantines eventually regained control but lost it again to Frankish crusaders in 1204. When sold to the Venetian Empire, Crete became a commercial hub. Trade led to the development of a middle class, dominated by Venetian nobles and local merchants. In 1646 the island fell to the Turks, who ruled until the Cretans won independence in 1898, 70 years after most of Greece. After the Balkan Wars, Crete joined the Greek state. A strong guerilla resistance combated the German occupation here during WWII, leaving the islanders with a justifiable sense of pride about their revolutionary nature.

Though Crete is divided into four prefectures—Hania, Rethymno, Iraklion, and Lasithi—the territorial divisions do little to convey its unified feel. According to a Greek saying, a Cretan's first loyalty is to his island, his second to his country. Crete's sense of identity, however, also expresses itself in an overwhelming hospitality, as its people eagerly strive to show visitors why their island is so exceptional. Yet Crete's spirit is almost impossible to capture or define, as its most tangible qualities—the relaxed pace of life, rebellious streak, and seemingly infinite diversity—are only minute samples of the island's rich offerings.

✈ **GETTING THERE.** **Olympic Airways** (☎21096 66 666) and **Aegean/Cronus Airlines** (☎21099 88 300) run frequent, cheap, and fast domestic flights from Athens to **Iraklion, Hania,** and **Sitia.** Consult the **Transportation** section of your destination for more information on flights. Many travelers take the 10hr. **ferry** from Piraeus to Crete, landing in Iraklion, Hania, Sitia, or occasionally Rethymno or Agios Nikolaos. Boats run frequently during the summer, but often irregularly. All prices listed are for deck-class accommodations; bring a sleeping bag to snooze on the deck.

HANIA PREFECTURE

Gorgeous beaches, steep, rocky gorges, and pine-covered hills dot the western tip of Crete. Tourists flock to these natural wonders in droves, so it's impressive that Hania has managed to maintain some semblance of its distinct character. By day, the region's small villages and pristine beaches call nature lovers to brush up against untapped wilderness and local hospitality. By night, the capital city welcomes party animals seeking hedonistic pleasure, but also beckons the weary traveler to come sip coffee at a cafe alongside the majestic Venetian harbor.

HANIA Χάνια   ☎28210

The island's second largest city, Hania takes on its avalanche of summer tourists with a refined ease typical of this port town's urban sophistication. The gritty outer streets give way to pedestrian boulevards of stylish shops and cafes down by the Old Venetian Harbor. Visitors meander through maze-like cobblestone roads, listening to folk music from streetside cafes or waiting for the setting sun to silhouette the lighthouse and nearby Ottoman domes. A day in Hania is easily spent people-watching from cafes, window-shopping, or absorbing the aura of the Old Town by casting maps aside and blazing your own route.

▉ TRANSPORTATION

Flights: Olympic Airways, Tzanakaki 88 (☎28210 537 60), across from the municipal gardens. Tickets sold daily 8:15am-3:30pm. Flights to **Athens** (4-5 per day, €55-90) and **Thessaloniki** (1½hr., 3 per week, €115).

Ferries: ANEK Office, Pl. Market 2 (☎28210 27 500). From Hania's port town, **Souda,** ferries go to **Piraeus** (9½hr.; 9, 11:30pm; €24). Open daily 7:30am-9pm. Catch the bus to Souda in front of the municipal market where El. Venizelou meets Giannari (25min., every 20min. 6am-10:40pm, €1).

Buses: The **central bus station** (☎28210 93 052) fills the block of Kidonias, Zymvrakakidon, Smyrnis, and Kelaidi. To: **Elafonisi** (2½hr., daily, €8); **Hora Sfakion** (2hr., 3-4 per day, €6); **Iraklion** (2½hr., 20 per day 5:30am-10pm, €11); **Kastelli** (1hr., 14 per day 6:30am-10pm, €4.20); **Paleohora** (2hr., 4 per day, €6); **Platanias** (20min., every 30min. 6:30am-11:30pm, €1.40); **Rethymno** (1hr., 20 per day 5:30am-9pm, €6); **Samaria Gorge** (1hr., 4 per day, €6); **Sougia** (2hr., 1-2 per day, €10).

Taxis: ☎28210 98 700. In Pl. Machis Tis Kritis and on Pl. 1866's eastern side. 24hr.

Car and Moped Rental: Agencies are on Halidon. Mopeds €18-25 per day; cars €25-50. Most rentals only allow for 100km; driving more may cost €0.06-0.20 per km.

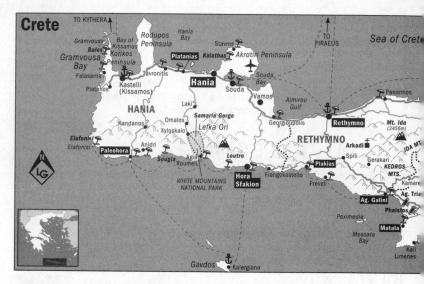

◼◼ ORIENTATION AND PRACTICAL INFORMATION

To get to the city center from the bus station, turn right onto **Kidonias**, walk one block, then turn left onto **Zymvrakakidon**, which runs along one side of a long park called "**Plateia 1866**." At the far end of Pl. 1866, the road becomes **Halidon** and leads to the **Old Venetian Harbor**, full of outdoor restaurants, pensions, and narrow alleyways. **Skalidi** intersects Zymvrakakidon where it becomes Halidon; to the right, Skalidi becomes **Chatzimichali** and then **Giannari**. One hundred meters far-

> ◼ **CAR COUNTRY.** Though bus service between major hubs in Crete like Hania, Iraklion, and Rethymno is surprisingly prompt, frequent, and cheap, it will only get you as far as the next trampled tourist destination. To really mine the island's gems, consider renting your own wheels.

ther, Giannari splits into **Tzanakaki** and **Eleftheriou Venizelou.** If you're arriving by ferry, you'll dock in the nearby port of **Souda.** Take the bus from the dock, which stops on Zymvrakakidon by Pl. 1866 (15min., €1). Hania's business district is across from the **Municipal Market** near the fork in Giannari. Sunbathers should head west of the harbor along the waterfront to find a well-populated long, thin stretch of sand at **Nea Hora.** The top of **Promahonas Hill**, on Baladinou just off of Halidon, yields an overview of Hania.

Tourist Office: Kidonias 29 (☎ 28210 36 155; www.chania.gr), in the city hall. Provides free **maps** of the city and information on buses, museums, monasteries, **Samaria Gorge** hikes, and boats on the southern coast. Open M-F 9am-8pm, Sa 9am-2pm.

Bank: National Bank (☎28210 38 934), on the corner of El. Venizelou and Tzanakaki. Open M-Th 8am-2:30pm, F 8am-2pm. **24hr. ATM.**

Luggage Storage: At the bus station. €1.50 per bag for 24hr. Open daily 6am-9pm.

Bookstores: Several pricey bookstores line Halidon. **Newsstand,** Skalidi 8 (☎28210 95 888), sells guidebooks, newspapers, and a large selection of Dutch, English, French,

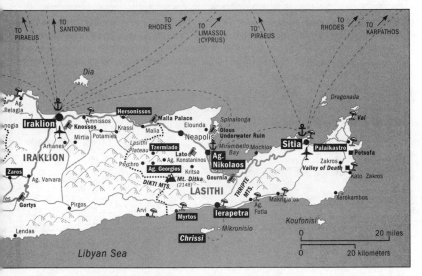

German, and Italian magazines. Open daily 8am-11:30pm. The American owner of **To Pazari,** Daskalogianni 46, buys and sells used books in English, French, and German. Open M, W 8:30am-2pm, Tu, Th-F 8:30am-1:30pm and 6-9pm, Sa 8:30am-3pm.

Public Toilets: In Pl. 1866 near the bus stop and at the corner of El. Venizelou and A. Papandreou near the Municipal Market.

Police: (☎28210 25 811), 250m down Apokronou, which becomes Irakliou, on the left. Open daily 8am-2pm. The **tourist police** (☎28210 25 931) is in the tourist office. Another location is next to the mosque in the Old Harbor. Open daily 10am-2pm.

Hospital: ☎28210 22 000. Located in Mournies, 6km south of Hania. Open 24hr.

Telephones: OTE, Tzanakaki 5 (☎121). Open M, W 7:30am-2pm, Tu, Th-F 7:30am-1pm.

Internet Access: The Park Internet Corner (☎28210 93 478), on Baladinou, just off Halidon, burns CDs and uploads digital photos. Internet €3 per hr. Coffee €1.80-2.80. Open daily 10am-midnight. **K@f Odon** (☎28210 23 130), Isodion 10 at Karaolli Dimitrou in the Old Harbor. Internet €3 per hr. Open 9am-1am.

Post Office: Tzanakaki 3 (☎28210 28 445). **Western Union** available. Open M-F 7:30am-8pm. **Postal Code:** 73100.

ACCOMMODATIONS AND CAMPING

Inexpensive rooms are hard to come by, especially since a number of hotels and hostels have recently renovated their rooms and raised rates accordingly. The New Town pensions have dazzling views of the harbor but are near noisy night spots. Small hotels sprout from the beaches to the west, but expect to pay dearly for rooms by the brown sands of Nea Kydonia and Agia Marina. Reasonable prices, though, can still be found in the Old Town. The tourist agencies around Pl. 1866 can help you find a room.

■ **Hotel Neli,** Isodion 21-23 (☎28210 55 533; www.nelistudios.com). You'll feel like a Venetian *doge* standing on your own wrought-iron balcony overlooking narrow cobblestone streets at this classy pension in the Old Harbor. Spacious and elegant rooms, with

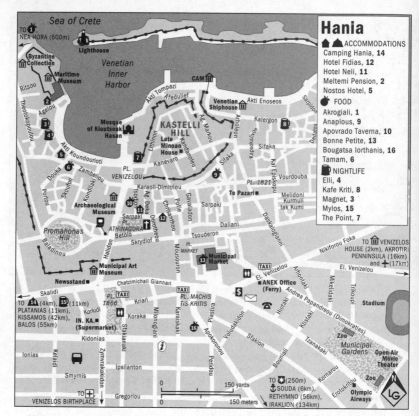

Hania

▲ ACCOMMODATIONS
Camping Hania, 14
Hotel Fidias, 12
Hotel Neli, 11
Meltemi Pension, 2
Nostos Hotel, 5

🍴 FOOD
Akrogiali, 1
Anaplous, 9
Apovrado Taverna, 10
Bonne Petite, 13
Bougatsa Iorthanis, 16
Tamam, 6

🍸 NIGHTLIFE
Elli, 4
Kafe Kriti, 8
Magnet, 3
Mylos, 15
The Point, 7

kitchenettes, fridges, baths, TV, and A/C, sit only blocks away from the center of the city at Pl. El. Venizelou. Singles €28; doubles €35-45; triples €40-50; quads €50-60. ❸

Hotel Fidias, Sarpaki 6 (☎28210 52 494). Walking toward the harbor on Halidon, turn right onto Athinagora. Half a block past the cathedral on the right, Athinagora becomes Sarpaki, and the pension is on your right. Stelios, owner and master host, provides bright, simple rooms with balconies along with invaluable travel tips and nuggets of general wisdom. Free luggage storage. Laundry €7 for wash and dry. Reception 7am-10pm. Singles €12; doubles €15-25; triples €25-35. ❷

Nostos Hotel, Zambeliou 42-46 (☎28210 94 743). Unique rooms, in a classic Venetian mansion on Zambeliou in the Old City, defy standardization with dual-level suites, harbor views, and fireplaces. All rooms have private baths, kitchens, A/C, and TV. Breakfast included. Singles €35-45; doubles €65-80; triples €75-90. AmEx/MC/V. ❹

Meltemi Pension, Agelou 2 (☎28210 92 802), on the western side of the harbor, by the Maritime Museum. High ceilings and clear views only add to the open feel of these large rooms. Meltemi Cafe downstairs serves frappés (€2.20), breakfast (€4-6), and mixed drinks (€4.50). Doubles €20-30; triples €30-40. ❸

Camping Hania, Ag. Apostoli (☎28210 31 138). Walking, take Skalidi west out of town and continue as it becomes Kisamou. 4km down the road, take a right at the sign. Alternatively take the bus to Kallimaki (15min., every 15min., €1) from Pl. 1866 and get off once you see the signs. Sequestered within walls between a number of hotels and apartments, this site has laundry (€4.50), a pool, a restaurant, and a mini-mart. Proximity to the beach (450m) is another plus. €5 per person, €4.50 per large tent, €3.50 per small tent; tent rental €8. ❶

🍴 FOOD

You can build a fantasy meal from the exotic snacks at the open-air **Municipal Market** in cleverly named Pl. Market. The smells of cheeses (€7-8.30 per wheel), meats (€4-9.50 per kg), fish (€2-10 per kg), spices, and baked goods waft from the shops into visitors' nostrils. (Open daily 8am-2:30pm, Tu, Th-F 8am-2:30pm and 6-9pm.) Inside, **Restaurant Bonne Petite** ❸ provides freshly cooked seafood for the salivating masses. (Most fish dishes €6-8. Open daily 10am-4pm.) For other cheap options, try the well-stocked and convenient **IN.KA. Supermarket** (☎28210 90 558), in Pl. 1866, on the right coming from Halidon. (Open M-F 8am-9pm, Sa 8am-6pm.)

🍽 **Anaplous** (☎28210 41 320), on the right on Sifaka when headed away from the harbor. This romantic open-air bistro is located in pink stone ruins with soft, low light; flower vines serve as the ceiling. Brothers Angelos and Nikos claim to offer the only *pilino* (pork and lamb cooked 6-7hr. in fresh clay; €25) in Greece. Breaking the clay for this dish may also bust your wallet, but it serves 3. Anaplous moves to a Venetian house across the street during winter. Complimentary *raki,* berries, and nuts in honey for dessert. Open daily 7:30pm-12:30am. AmEx/MC/V. ❷

Tamam, Zambeliou 49 (☎28210 96 080). Served in an former Turkish bath complex, the stellar food here has long been a secret among locals. The wine list (wines €6-28) is longer than the menu. Many vegetarian alternatives. Pork with cheese in white sauce €7. Complimentary *raki* and honey cake. Open daily 1pm-12:30am. ❷

Bougatsa Iorthanis, Apokronou 24 (☎28210 88 855). This local favorite serves 1 dish and 1 dish only: *bougatsa* (€2.10), a scrumptious goat cheese pastry available with or without sugar. Open daily 6am-2pm. ❶

Akrogiali, Akti Papanikoli 19 (☎28210 73 110), on the waterfront in Nea Hora, a 12min. walk westward along the water past the Maritime Museum. This beachfront restaurant caters to hordes of hungry Greeks. House specialties include calamari (€8) and swordfish fillet (€9). Open M-Sa 6pm-1am, Su 11am-1am. ❸

Apovrado Taverna (☎28210 58 151), at Sarpaki and Isodion. Candle-lit tables spill out onto the Athinagora, under fuchsia bougainvilleas and the shadow of Mitropolis Church. In this quietly sophisticated setting, you can sample Anna's rabbit onion stew (€8) or aubergine with cheese and tomato (€5.50). Open daily 10am-midnight. ❷

🔵 SIGHTS

VENETIAN INNER HARBOR. The **Venetian lighthouse** marks the entrance to Hania's stunning architectural relic, the Venetian Inner Harbor. The inlet has retained its original breakwater and Venetian arsenal, and the Egyptians restored the lighthouse during their occupation of Crete in the late 1830s. On the western side of the main harbor, the **Maritime Museum** describes the tumultuous 6000 years of Crete's naval and merchant history in maps and models. The second floor houses a large exhibition on Crete's remarkable expulsion of the Nazis in 1941. (☎28210 91 875. Open daily Apr.-Oct. 9am-4pm; Nov.-Mar. 9am-2pm. €2, students €1.) The newly renovated **Venetian Shiphouse,** at the end of the harbor where Arholeon meets Akti Enoseos, hosts Hania's annual **International Art Festival,** a large exhibition each July of hundreds of contemporary artists from around the world, along with other exhibits throughout the year. *(Hours and prices vary by exhibi-*

CRETE

tion, most open daily 10am-10pm. Most free. For information on the International Art Festival, contact the Omma Center of Contemporary Art, ☎28210 42 100; www.omma.gr.) Turning left on the waterfront from Arholeon you will come to **CAM,** an art museum featuring rotating exhibits on photography and painting in a modern, air-conditioned building. *(☎28210 27 184. Open daily 10am-2pm and 7-10pm. Free.)* At the corner of Kandanoleu and Kanevaro, just north of Kanevaro on **Kastelli Hill,** lie reminders of Hania's Bronze Age prosperity, including the **Late Minoan House** (1450 BC) and other fenced-off and unmarked monuments.

MUNICIPAL GARDENS. Flee the traffic-filled streets in favor of the floral shade of the Municipal Gardens (Dimotikos Kypos), to the left as you walk down Tzanakaki from the city center. Once the property of a *muezzin* (Islamic prayer caller), the garden is now home to an open-air **movie theater** that screens international films *(☎28210 41 427; €7; shows 8:45, 10:45pm)* and two tiny zoos that boast an amusing combination of goats and peacocks. UNICEF sets up an annual **International Fair** in the gardens—consult the tourist office for details.

ARCHAEOLOGICAL MUSEUM. The Archaeological Museum, on Halidon about 40m past the cathedral, features a broad collection of Cretan artifacts, from early Minoan to Hellenistic times. First a Venetian monastery, then the mosque of Yusuf Pasha, the building's high-ceilinged halls are lined with clay shards, gold jewelry, and Roman floor mosaics similar to those found at Pompeii. A modern room to the right of the entrance displays a bronze cup with a rare inscription in Linear A, the Minoans' mysterious, undeciphered script. The ancient coin collection includes gold tokens once placed in the mouths of the dead to pay Charon to ferry souls to the Underworld. *(☎28210 90 334. Open Tu-Su 8:30am-3pm. €2, students €1, EU students free.)* You can buy a ticket at the Archaeological Museum that admits you to the **Byzantine Collection,** on Theotokopoulou, which charts the history of Hania from early Christian times to Ottoman rule in wall paintings, mosaics, coins, and icons inside a church-like building. *(☎28210 96 046. Open Tu-Su 8:30am-3pm. €2, students and seniors €1, EU students free; joint ticket €3.)*

OTHER MUSEUMS. Those eager to learn more about Eleftherios Venizelos, the most important figure in modern Greek history can visit **Venizelos House,** the prime minister's former residence-turned-museum. Just follow the predictably named El. Venizelou heading west until you get to (you guessed it) Pl. Venizelou. For a more scenic walk, follow the coastline west from the Old Harbor until it meets with El. Venizelou. *(Pl. Venizelou, in Halepa, 2km outside the Old Harbor. ☎28210 56 008. Open M-F 11:30am-1:30pm and 7-9pm, Sa-Su 7-9pm. Free.)* Near the intersection with Skalidi, the **Municipal Art Gallery,** Halidon 98-102, shows rotating exhibits of modern art, which usually last one to three months, in a sleek, three-story building. *(☎28210 92 294. Open M-F 10am-1pm and 7-10pm, Sa 10am-1pm. €2; students €1; seniors, artists with ID, military personnel, and children under 17 free. Su free.)*

☒ NIGHTLIFE

Hania offers several entertainment options. For traditional music and local company, head to **Kafe Kriti,** Kalergon 2, on the eastern side of the harbor. Live music plays nightly at 8:30pm; ask the owner, an instructor of traditional dance, to teach you some moves. *(☎28210 58 661. Beer €3. Bottle of raki €5. Open daily 6pm-3am.)* Pounding hard rock and an image of St. Mark's lion liven up the vaulted stone walls of **Magnet,** a waterfront club with a serious strobe light. (☎28210 93 400; www.magnet-club.com. Beer €3-4. Mixed drinks €5.50-6. Open daily 10am-dawn.) Next door, **Elli** cranks 1970s American rock up loud enough to be heard over Magnet's thumping bass. (☎28210 72 130. Beer €3-4. Mixed drinks €6.) **The Point,** Sourmeli 2, also on the Old Harbor, is an oasis for those maxed out on techno and *bouzouki.* The eclectic music, from 1960s hits to hip-hop, and balconies with harbor views draw both locals and tourists. (☎28210 57 556; www.pointchania.com. Mixed drinks €6. Open 9pm-late. AmEx/MC/V.) **Mylos,** a dance club for beach-party devotees, is a €10 taxi away in Platanias (p. 577).

🡢 DAYTRIPS FROM HANIA

PLATANIAS Πλατανιάς
Patanias is 30min. from Hania by bus (every 30min., €1.40). To get back to Hania, either take a cab (€11) or party until the 6:30am bus arrives the next morning.

Platanias's long, pretty beaches seem to have 1000 tourists for every local. The area's fame sprang from a large rock island just offshore, better known as **Kracken,** the sea monster whom Perseus turned to stone with the aid of Medusa's severed head. At present-day Platanias's most famous phenomenon, swanky rock club **Mylos,** the hard, pumping beats have the opposite effect, driving enormous numbers of partiers to bump and gyrate. White canvas sheets decorate the ceiling of the converted bread mill, massive amplifiers hang from braided rope, and the DJ spins tunes from a crow's nest above the dance floor. The massive, oval-shaped bar and neon-blue fishtanks draw nightly crowds of suave Europeans from midnight until morning. Take the last bus from Hania, get off at the bus stop at Platanias Center, and continue walking away from Hania. After about 450m, a huge sign will alert you to the right-hand turn-off that leads past a large parking lot to Mylos and the **beach.** (☎28210 60 449. Wine €6. Beer €7. Mixed drinks €8. M-Th, Su cover €8, F-Sa €10; includes 1 drink. Open daily June-Sept. midnight-8am.)

AKROTIRI PENINSULA
The Akrotiri Peninsula is best navigated by car, which will allow you to visit all of the sites in 1 day. You will need 2 days using the bus due to erratic schedules.

Just northeast of Hania is the sparsely populated peninsula of Akrotiri, home to herds of goats, rows of olive trees, several monasteries, and sheltered coves. Since WWII, it's also been inhabited by American soldiers who live in the US military base there and coexist, sometimes uneasily, with Hania's natives. At **Kalathas,** a small white sand beach 11km from Hania, sunbeds with umbrellas

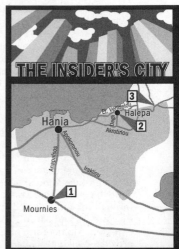

VENIZELOS'S HANIA

Eleftherios Venizelos's name is plastered throughout Greece, from microscopic hilltop villages to bustling seaside cities. To really understand this former prime minister, however, you'll have to come to his hometown.

1 In Mournies, 5km south of Hania's Old Harbor, you can visit the former politician's **childhood home** and see his cradle. Go to the town hall and ask for the keys. (Open M-F 8am-2pm. Free.)

2 The **house** Venizelos lived in as an adult is in Halepa, 2km west of the Old Harbor. A variety of memorabilia, including two bloody shirts from assassination attempts, is displayed here. (☎28210 56 008. Open M-F 11:30am-1:30pm and 7-9pm, Sa-Su 7-9pm. Free.)

3 In a courtyard atop a hill, **Venizelos's grave** overlooks the city of Hania and the sea beyond. Drive west on Akrotirou and follow signs to the park. (Open 24hr. Free.)

go for €5 per day. Enjoy the soothing Mediterranean sun from the shore, or swim out to the little island facing the beach for a view of the mountains. Kalathas lies on the route of the bus to **Stavros**, another glorious beach with a handful of cafes, a calm, sheltered cove, a winding stream, and a mining hill you may recognize from the movie Zorba the Greek. Take the bus (1hr., 6 per day 6:45am-8pm, €1.50) and get off at the end of the line in front of **Cristiana's Restaurant ❷** (☎28210 39 152), one of the few restaurants in town, set under a large wooden roof on stone floors, with a view of the water. (Greek salad €3.50. Shrimp with bacon €17. Open daily 7:30am-11pm.) On the sand, rent an umbrella and deck chair (€5 per day) or take a walk down to the rockier, more private, end of the beach for cost-free sunbathing. Get refreshments under a grape arbor 100m inland at **Zorba's Original Tavern ❶**. (☎28210 39 402. Souvlaki €5. Open daily 8:30am-midnight.) Just past the Hania airport, 16.5km from the city, is the monastery of **Agia Triada** (☎28210 63 310), which was built in 1606 near ruins of a Minoan temple and has produced traditional olive oil since 1632. Take the bus to Agia Triada (30min., 2-3 per day, €2) and enjoy a peaceful walk through the grounds and small **museum,** with its collection of mostly 19th-century pieces and three 17th-century Byzantine paintings. You can bottle the experience in the form of the famous olive oil (€6 per L). Visit early to beat the crowds. (Open M-Sa 9am-7pm, Su 10am-7pm. €1.50. Modest dress required.) Monastery buffs who just can't get enough may want to follow the road up into the hills (complete with wild goats and narcissus flowers) 4km to **Gouverneto**, a similar but smaller monastery, which receives fewer visitors than Agia Triada. (☎28210 63 319. Open daily 7am-2pm and 4-8pm. Free.) From the monastery, the stone path leading down toward the sea passes several small Venetian ruins and **Bear Cave** (600m, about 15min.). Legend tells that a monk drinking from the cave's fountains was attacked by a bear. Before any harm was done, though, the animal was turned into stone by a miracle, saving the monk and preserving the outline of the beast in the distinctive shape of the cave's stalagmite patterns.

BALOS

You can only reach Balos by car or boat. Most cars can handle the harrowing drive, but a 4x4 will make it far more pleasant. To get there, take Skalidi west out of Hania toward Kissamos. You will hit Kissamos after about 40km of beautiful countryside. Go through the town for another 2km and look for a sign for a phone on the side of the road. Make a right at the phone (you will also see signs for Kaliviani), and make an immediate left by the sign for the Balos Hotel. After about 1km, you will pass through a tiny town. Just outside of it, make a right at the small sign for Balos. After 5km on this road, you will pass a white chapel; the parking lot lies another 3km beyond the church. When you finally arrive at the parking lot, take the small marked path and hike 30min. to the lagoon.

Nestled away on the northwestern tip of Crete, Balos's heavenly ✎**blue lagoon** is Crete's uncontested best beach, where sand, sea, and sky melt into one. Almost entirely enclosed by bright-white sand, the lagoon's ankle-deep, warm water drifts seamlessly into the deeper, brilliant blue water closer to shore. For those willing to see the jade-colored lagoon brimming with other bathers, **boat cruises** leave from Kissamos port, 3km outside of town along the main road heading away from Hania (May-Oct. departs daily 10:15am, returns 5:30pm; round-trip €20). Buy tickets at Kissamos port from companies such as **Gramvousa-Balos Daily Cruises** (☎28220 24 344). Before arriving at Balos, the boat stops at nearby **Gramvousa,** an island with a Venetian fortress on its summit. The steep walk up to the fortress yields a breathtaking view of the sheer cliffs of Crete and the water below.

SAMARIA GORGE Φαράγγι της Σαμαριάς

The most popular excursion on Crete is the spectacular 5-6hr. hike down the longest gorge in Europe, the ⬛Samaria Gorge, a formidable 16km pass through the White Mountains National Park. (Open May-Oct. 15 6am-6pm. €5, children under 15 and student groups free. Hang on to your ticket, as you have to give it back as you exit.) Sculpted over 14 million years by rainwater, the gorge retains its allure despite mobs of international visitors. The rocky trail can trip you up, but if you take a look around you'll see epiphytes (plants that don't need soil to grow) peeking out from sheer rock walls, wild flowers bordering the path, elusive *agrimi* (wild goats) clambering around one of their last natural homes, and endangered gryphon vultures and golden eagles soaring overhead. People have settled here for centuries, as the gorge's namesake, the 1379 church of **Saint Maria of Egypt,** attests.

If you want to spend the night in Omalos, **Gigilos Hotel ❷,** on the main road, is a good place to rest up before the hike. (☎28210 67 181. Singles €15-20; doubles €20-25; triples €30-35.) Though it's possible to reach the gorge from any number of major tourist towns, **Hania** is the closest and allows for the most flexibility. **Buses** from Hania go to Omalos and Xyloskalo, the town at the trailhead (1½hr., 4 per day, €5.50). Early buses (6:15, 7:30, 8:30am) can get you to Xyloskalo in time for a dayhike. From Rethymno, take the 7am bus through Hania to Omalos (€11). Earlier risers can take the 5:30am bus from Iraklion through Rethymno and Hania to Omalos (€16). For gorge information, call the **Hania Forest Service** (☎28210 97 317) or consult the Hania, Rethymno, or Iraklion tourist offices.

The base town of Xyloskalo boasts no more than the ticket booth, a cafeteria, a shop, and toilets—the last of their kind that you'll see for hours. From the trailhead you begin a long descent, following a noisy but nearly dry river with turquoise waterfalls, passing between stunningly steep cliff walls as high as 600m and as narrow as 3.5m. Much of the hike is shaded by clumps of pines and by the walls of the gorge itself. For the first 6km, the trail continues the steady, seemingly neverending descent into the gorge. After 1km more, hikers reach the former village of Samaria, inhabited from prehistoric times until the creation of the national park here in 1962. The trail continues past Samaria on flatter ground and a rocky riverbed through the narrowest part of the gorge. You'll end up in the small beach town of Agia Roumeli on the southern coast; from there, experienced hikers can embark on a 10hr. trail to **Hora Sfakion** (p. 580) along one of the more outstanding coastlines in Greece, or take a path from Xyloskalo that ascends **Mount Gigilos** to the west. If you're only interested in the gorge's final, dramatic tail, you can start at Agia Roumeli; the path begins behind Hotel Livikon at the rear of the village. Known as "Samaria the Lazy Way," this 2hr. climb to the north takes you to the gorge's narrowest pass: the **Iron Gates.**

If you go early, the lack of heat or crowds combined with the soft morning light lends the park a surreal, lunar feel. Whichever route you choose, it's always smart to bring water, trail snacks, and supportive shoes with good treads. One small water bottle will suffice; potable water sources line the trail. There are enforced rules concerning littering, so take all trash out with you. The gorge is dry and dusty in summer and worn stones on the path are very slippery. The altitude can also make the top of the gorge cold and rainy. If you get tired, look for **donkey taxis** that wait to pick up weary travelers at sporadic rest stations. Be sure to bring enough **cash** to get to the gorge and home again; there are no banks on either end.

The town of **Agia Roumeli,** at the end of the gorge, caters primarily to tired, hungry hikers. Though it has little more than restaurants, grocery stores, souvenirs, and lodgings, the peaceful beach is a well-deserved reward for a hard day's hike. It's a relief to reach the town, but the inflated prices are less than comforting. **Hotel Agia Roumeli ❸** is a good place to crash, with easy sea access along with A/C, fridges, and balconies. (☎28250 91 241. Doubles €40; triples €45.) **Kri-Kri ❸,** on the left on the street from the gorge, has reasonably priced but somewhat cramped rooms with A/C, fridges, and small balconies. (☎28250 91 089. Doubles and triples €30-40. AmEx/MC/V.) **Ferries** (☎28250 91 251) run from Agia Roumeli to Hora Sfakion (1¼hr., 3-4 per day, €5.40) via Loutro (45min.) and to Paleohora (1½hr.: daily Apr.-Oct.; Nov.-Mar. 3 per week: €7.20) via Sougia (45min., €3.20). Call in advance for ferry times. The last **bus** (to Hania or Rethymno €5.50; to Iraklion €9) from Hora Sfakion leaves at 7:30pm, after the last ferry has come in (6pm).

HORA SFAKION Χώρα Σφακίων ☎28250

The tiny port town of Hora Sfakion, often called simply "Sfakion," lacks the intimacy of Plakias to the east or Paleohora to the west but serves as the southern coast's transportation hub. Its quiet streets and tavernas are a common resting spot after the Samaria Gorge hike, and the location makes it a convenient base for daytrips to the area's smaller gorges and lovely beaches.

Hotel owners in Hora Sfakion are aware that their town is a convenient rest stop for those who have hiked the gorge, and they charge accordingly. Following the right fork of the harbor road uphill past the bakery leads to **Stavris ❷,** where the friendly owner offers clean rooms with private baths and balconies with the best view in town of the western coastline. Some rooms have A/C for €4 extra per night. (☎28250 91 220. Singles €20; doubles €22-25; triples €25-27.) The air-conditioned rooms with balconies at **Hotel Samaria ❷,** one of the first buildings on the harbor road, let you cool down without spending a fortune. (☎28250 91 261. Doubles €25, with breakfast €27. AmEx/MC/V.) Grotto-like **Hotel Xenia ❷,** on the harbor road at the far end away from the ferry landing, has pleasant, spacious rooms with refrigerators and phones. (☎28250 91 490. Check-out noon. Singles €28; doubles €33; triples from €38.)

The town consists of one main harborfront road, which opens off a plateia 50m uphill from the ferry dock. Four **buses** (☎28210 91 288) per day go to Hania (2hr., last bus 7:15pm, €6), dropping off passengers bound for Iraklion (3hr., €11.50) and Rethymno (2hr., €6) at Vrises. Buses leave Vrises for Rethymno and Iraklion every hour. Don't worry if your ferry is late—the buses wait for the boats to arrive. **Ferries** from Hora Sfakion go to Agia Roumeli (1¼hr., 3-4 per day, €5). From April to October, most routes stop in Loutro. To get to Loutro in the winter, go by foot or fishing boat. Schedules can change, so you may want to check with the ticket office (☎28250 91 221). **Boats** also run three days a week to Gavdos, a sparsely populated island that is the southernmost point in Europe (1½hr., F-Su 10:30am, €10.20). Daily **fishing boats** to Sweetwater beach leave at 10am and return at 5:30pm (€3 one-way). **Taxis** (☎28250 91 269) pick up at the ferry dock. In the plateia you'll find **Sfakia Tours,** where you can **rent cars.** (☎28250 91 272. Cars €35 per day. Open daily 8am-10pm.) The **police station** lies in Komitades, 4km away (☎28250 91 205). Next to Sfakia Tours is the **post office.** (☎28250 91 244. Open M-F 7:30am-2pm.) **Postal Code:** 73011.

PALEOHORA Παλαιοχώρα ☎28230

Paleohora, 77km south of Hania, is a peninsular retreat flanked by a rocky harbor, smooth beaches, and splendid mountains. Small enough to do without street names, Paleohora welcomes beachgoers, monastery-lovers, hikers, and archaeologists with friendly smiles and warm meals.

E TRANSPORTATION. The bus station (☎ 28230 41 914) is on El. Venizelou on the edge of town. **Buses** go to Hania (2hr., 3-5 per day, €6) and Samaria (1½hr., 6:15am, €5.50). **Ferries** leave the port for Agia Roumeli (2hr., 2 per day, €7.20) via Sougia (1hr., €4.40). Ferries then go from Agia Roumeli to Hora Skafion (1hr., 4 per day, €5) via Loutro (30min.). One boat per day departs Paleohora for Elafonisi at 10am and returns at 4pm (1hr., €4.50). A boat goes to Gavdos three times per week (3½hr.; Tu 8:30am, returns 2:30pm; €10.20.) For a taxi, contact the **Paleohora Taxi Office.** (☎28230 41 128. Open daily 8am-11:30pm.) You can rent a **car** (about €25-45), **moped** (€10-20), or **bicycle** (€3-10) at any of Paleohora's travel agencies.

■ ⁊ ORIENTATION AND PRACTICAL INFORMATION. The town's restaurants and bars cluster around the main thoroughfare, **Eleftheriou Venizelou,** which runs down the center of the peninsula from north to south. Heading north on El. Venizelou takes you to Hania; going south puts you at the ruins of an old castle. El. Venizelou crosses **Kentekaki,** which leads west to the beach and east to the harbor. Most accommodations are located on the side streets off El. Venizelou. For information about boats and tickets, visit the friendly people at **Notos Rentals,** to the left as you walk up El. Venizelou from the bus station. (☎28230 42 110. Open daily 8am-2pm and 5-11pm.) **Syia Travel,** a right on Kentekaki past the pharmacy, is a general tourist office that is helpful for ferry information and tickets, as well as for basic information about the region. (☎28230 41 198. Open daily 9am-1:30pm and 6-9:30pm.) **National Bank,** with its **24hr. ATM,** is three blocks up El. Venizelou on your right. (☎28230 41 430. Open M-Th 8am-2:30pm, F 8am-2pm.) The **port police** (☎28230 41 214) are four blocks farther down the main street on the right. Turning left toward the harbor at the OTE leads to the **police station** (☎28230 41 111), one block down on your left. The port is one block past the police. The multi-talented staff at Notos Rentals also does **laundry, exchange currency,** and offers **Internet access.** (Wash and dry €8. Internet €1 per 30min. Open daily 8am-2pm and 5-11pm.) There is a **pharmacy** on El. Venizelou, diagonally across from the OTE. (☎28230 41 498. Open M-Sa 8:30am-2pm and 5:30-10:30pm.) Taking a right toward the beach behind the OTE will get you to the **public health center.** (☎28230 41 211. Open M-F 9am-2pm.) The **OTE** is a block beyond the National Bank. (☎28230 41 212. Open M-F 7:30am-3pm.) To find the **post office,** turn right on Kentekaki toward the beach, then turn right again on the beach road and walk 100m. (☎28230 41 206. Open M-F 7:30am-2pm.) **Postal Code:** 73001.

⁊ ACCOMMODATIONS AND CAMPING. Small hotels line the road closest to the harbor, while cheaper rooms can be found in the Old Town past the harbor on the far side of Kentekaki. At ▨**Dream Rooms ❷,** a white building in the middle of the harbor road, your deepest wishes will actually come true if you've been hoping for fans, private baths, and a common fridge. Rooms with balconies facing the front of the building overlook the charming harbor and the surrounding mountains; back balconies trade more space for less view. (☎28230 41 112. Singles €20; doubles €25; triples €30.) **Villa Anna ❹** is a good choice for groups or families. Large apartments with private baths, a lush garden, and a playground are a great alternative to Paleohora's homogenous hotels. Facing the castle ruins on the main street, turn right before the tourist office, take the second right, and walk toward the beach; the Villa is on the right after two streets. (☎28230 46 428. 1-bedroom apartment for 2-3 people €40-50; 2-bedroom for 4-5 €60.) **Camping Paleohora ❶** is a 15min. walk to the east of town. The campsite has its own **restaurant** and a beautiful beach. Walk away from town on El. Venizelou, turn right just after the bus station, take the second left

CRETE

on the last paved road before the beach, and follow the signs 1km to the site. (☎28230 41 120. Open Apr.-Oct. €3-3.50 per person, €2.10 per child, under 5 free, €2-2.50 per tent, €2.10 per car; €2 tent rental.)

🖸🖻 FOOD AND ENTERTAINMENT. At sunset the main street closes to vehicles and restaurants set up rows of tables, converting the street into one long dining area. Off the main street, the ▧**Third Eye Vegetarian Restaurant ❶** is one of the few remaining bastions of Paleohora's counterculture days. The proprietors have a repertoire of over 50 Asian, Greek, and European dishes, all created from organic ingredients grown on their family farm; each night, they prepare 20 dishes and 14 salads for diners. This unique, ecologically run restaurant even offers complimentary table water, a rarity on Crete. To get there, take Kentekaki in the direction of the beach and look for the signs directing you left. (☎28230 41 234. Entrees under €5. Open daily Apr.-Oct. 8:30am-3pm and 6-11pm.) To reach **Niki's Pizzeria ❷**, walk toward the beach past Syia Travel and take the second left; the garden seating area is on the right. Niki's tasty pizzas (€4-6) are cooked in an outdoor, igloo-shaped brick oven. (☎28230 41 532. Open daily 11am-2pm and 6pm-1am.)

The local **cinema** shows American films in the evenings, often at 10pm (€5). **Club Paleohora,** across from Camping Paleohora, is the town's popular disco. Follow the directions to the campsite or take the minibus (every 20-40min. 11pm-4am, free) that transports clients from Skala bar in front of the port to the disco. (☎28230 41 225. Beer €3. Mixed drinks €4. Cover F-Sa €5; includes 1 drink. Open May-July 14 and Oct. F-Sa 11pm-5am; July 15-Sept. daily 11pm-5am.)

🞫 DAYTRIPS FROM PALEOHORA. Elafonisi is a beach across from a small uninhabited island at the southwestern corner of Crete. Visitors start on the mainland side of the beach and wade across the shallow 100m inlet that divides the mainland from the lovely island. Though crowded with tourists in the summer, walking away from the mainland along the island brings you to increasingly umbrella-free, pristine beaches of fine-grained sand and translucent waters speckled with small islands. Back on the mainland side are restrooms and a **taverna ❶** with upright logs for seats. (Sandwiches €2.50-3. Burgers €2.50. Donuts €1.50. Beer €2. Open daily 8am-10pm.) A 300m walk up the dry, dusty road will get you a table overlooking the beach at **Panorama ❷.** (☎28220 61 548. Chicken with lemon €4.50. Swordfish €5. Open daily Apr.-Oct. 8am-11pm.) Panorama also has **rooms ❸,** if you miss your boat back (doubles €30-40). Those tired of prostrating themselves before the sun can pay homage of another sort at the cliffside monastery **Chrysoskalitissa,** built from and supported by the cliffs and operated by an order of nuns. Walk 6km up the road from Elafonisi to get there. The cream-colored monastery will appear on your left when you come to a small church on the left side of the road; continue walking along the main road into the village and take a sharp left toward the monastery at the sign. (Open daily sunrise-sunset. Free. Modest dress required.) To reach Elafonisi, take the ferry from Paleohora along the southern coast (1¼hr.; leaves 10am, returns 4pm; €5) or the bus from Hania (2½hr.; leaves 8:30, 9:30am, returns 2, 4pm; €8).

Escape the crowds of Paleohora's beach at nearby **Anidri beach,** accessible by car or foot. Hikers should take the road out of town past Camping Paleohora and continue 5min. until the road forks. The low road to the right (the easy way) takes you on a lingering but prominent street along the coast to the beach (45min.). The high road to the left (the exciting way) will take you through the mountains and up to the sweet village of Anidri itself. For the latter route, hike up the high road into the mountains to the village cafe (1hr.). Take a right just before the cafe (locals can show you where) and onto a road with a sign pointing to a church, the gorge, and the beach. Follow this road to its end and make another right. You'll reach a stone road with a sign pointing back to the cafe; turn left and go down to the dry riverbed. Follow the occasional sign and stone marker through the small gorge to the beach (40min. from town). The beautiful path is fairly difficult and your only company will be roaming goats; wear sturdy shoes and bring water and snacks. The beaches at the bottom, especially the one farthest to your left, are smooth, unblemished strips of pale, if somewhat rocky, sand surrounded by high cliffs. Some bathers choose not to weigh themselves down with bathing suits. Most visitors leave by taking the coastal road, which returns you to the right branch of the fork near Camping Paleohora.

RETHYMNO PREFECTURE

Western Crete has struggled for years to maintain its identity amid surging tourism. Rethymno has met success where its neighbor Iraklion has largely failed, as each town in the area has managed to maintain a sense of individuality. Modest seaside towns fill only short sections of the shore with tavernas, leaving long stretches to the birds, waves, and hikers. The melding of Ottoman, Venetian, and Greek architecture complements the blue waters of the southwestern coast and the rich, dark mountains and deep canyons of the interior.

RETHYMNO   Ρέθυμνο   ☎28310

Rethymno has a reputation for bizarre power struggles. According to myth, Zeus was born to Rhea in the cave of Idaion Andron outside this regional capital. The titan Cronus, antsy about his infant son's approaching dominion, came up with the obvious solution of eating him. Luckily for Greek religion, Rhea tricked Cronus into swallowing a stone instead, and baby Zeus grew up to be king of the gods. Warlike humans followed Cronus's quest for power, though they decided to sack and rebuild cities—visible in Rethymno's skyline of minarets and ruined Venetian fortresses—instead of eating babies. Potent raki, Crete's answer to ouzo, may cloud the minds of travelers seeking to understand the cycles of history that have passed through this city, but it will certainly help them understand Cretan living.

▐ TRANSPORTATION

For **flights,** go to **Olympic Airways,** Koumoundorou 5, opposite the public gardens. (☎28310 22 257. Open M-Sa 8am-3:45pm.) If you want to leave by **ferry,** buy tickets to Piraeus (daily 8pm, €20) at any travel office. **Buses** run from the **Rethymno-Hania station** (☎28310 29 644), overlooking the water off I. Gavriil, and go to: Agia Galini (1hr., 3-5 per day, €5); Arkadi Monastery (1hr., 3-4 per day, €2.10); Hania (1hr., 20 per day 7am-10:30pm, €6); Iraklion (1½hr., 21 per day 6:30am-10:15pm, €6.50); Plakias (45min., 4 per day, €3.50). **Taxis** (☎28310 22 316) congregate at Pl. Martiron 4, Pl. Iroon, and the Public Gardens, and are available 24hr.

▟ ▛ ORIENTATION AND PRACTICAL INFORMATION

Plateia Martiron, between the **Old City** to the north and the **New City** to the south, is a 15min. walk from anywhere you want to go. To get to the plateia from the bus station, climb the stairs at the back of the station's parking lot onto **Igoumenou Gavriil** and go left; Pl. Martiron is to your left just after the **public gardens.** The **waterfront** lies at the north end of the Old City, with a maze of ancient streets filling the space between the main thoroughfare of I. Gavriil and the .water. The Venetian **Fortezza** overlooks the waterfront, and a beach meets the city's edge.

Rethymno

🏠🏔 ACCOMMODATIONS
Elizabeth Camping, **15**
Hotel Leo, **7**
Olga's Pension, **9**
Park Hotel, **13**
Youth Hostel, **12**

🍎 FOOD
Akri, **10**
Katerina's, **1**
Ovelisterio, **11**
Taverna Garden Ftochiko, **8**
Taverna Kyria Maria, **2**

🍸 NIGHTLIFE
Dimman Bar, **3**
Karma Cafe, **4**
Rock Cafe Club, **6**

Tourist Office: (☎ 28310 29 148; www.rethymnon.gr). By the waterfront on El. Venizelou. Pick up free town **maps,** bus and ferry schedules, and info on rooms, restaurants, and Rethymno prefecture. Open M-F 8:30am-2pm.

Bank: Numerous banks with **24hr. ATMs** line Koundouriotou to the east of the public gardens. The **National Bank** (☎ 28310 55 228), on Koundouriotou next to the town hall, has excellent exchange rates. Also in the Old City on Tsouderon. Open M-Th 8am-2:30pm, F 8am-2pm.

Bookstore: Spontidaki Toula, Souliou 43 (☎ 28310 54 307), buys and sells new and used books. Open daily 9am-11pm. **Newsstand,** in Pl. Iroön (☎ 28310 25 110), carries a wide selection of English books, travel guides, and foreign magazines and newspapers. Open daily 9am-midnight.

Laundromat: Tombazi 45 (☎ 28310 56 196). Wash and dry €9. Open M, W 8am-2:15pm and 6-8:30pm, Tu, Th-F 8am-2:15pm and 5-9pm, Sa 8am-3pm.

Public Toilets: On the corner of the public gardens closest to Pl. Martiron.

Police: ☎ 100. In Pl. Iroön Polytechniou. Open 24hr.

Tourist Police: El. Venizelou 5 (☎ 28310 28 156), next to the tourist information office. Open daily 8am- 2:30pm.

Pharmacy: Over 35 pharmacies dot the city, each marked by a green cross and a sign reading "φαρμακείο." Each pharmacy's door lists which is open all night that evening.

CRETE

Hospital: Trandalidou 18 (☎28310 87 100). From I. Gavriil at the bus station, take a right on Kriari and turn left onto Trandalidou. Open 24hr.

Telephones: OTE, Koundouriotou 23 (☎28310 59 500). Open M, W 7:30am-2:30pm, Tu, Th-F 7:30am-8pm, Sa 8am-2:30pm.

Internet Access: Game Net Cafe, Koundouriotou 8, in Pl. Martiron. This cafe has the best rates in town at €2.50 per hr., €1.50 after midnight. **Cafe Galero** (☎28310 54 345), at the Rimondi Fountain, has Internet access for €3 per hr. Open daily 6am-3am.

Post Office: Main branch, Moatsou 19 (☎28310 22 303). From the OTE, walk down G. Hatzidaki into the New City. **Western Union** available M-F 7:30am-8pm. Open M-F 7:30am-8pm. **Postal Code:** 74100.

ACCOMMODATIONS AND CAMPING

Picturesque streets near the fortress and the Venetian port are lined with ideally located but expensive hotels and domatia. A few, however, offer both low prices and an location in the Old City.

▧ Youth Hostel, Tombazi 41-43 (☎28310 22 848; www.yhrethymno.com). From the bus station, walk down I. Gavriil and take the first left at Pl. Martiron through the Porta Megali; Tombazi is the 2nd right. The gardens and outdoor bar (beer and wine; €1.50-1.70) buzz with backpackers. Outdoor beds available in the summer. Breakfast €2-4. Solar-powered hot showers during daylight. Sheets €1. Internet €3 per hr. Reception 8am-noon and 5-9pm. Check-out 10:30am. Dorms €7.50. ❶

▧ Olga's Pension, Souliou 57 (☎28310 53 206), off Antistasis. You'll feel like part of the family with owners George, Stella, and Yiannis. Enjoy Stella's delicious cooking either downstairs or in the roof-top garden. All rooms have ceiling fans, TV, and fridges; some have private baths or balconies. Breakfast and lunch €5. Singles €25; doubles €30. ❷

Hotel Leo, Vafe 2 (☎28310 26 197), just off of Souliou. Romantically decorated with wood floors, high windows, antique lamps, and white stucco, the rooms in Leo's 650-year-old building also boast private baths and a quiet atmosphere. Singles €30; doubles €35; triples €40; quads €45. ❷

Elizabeth Camping (☎28310 28 694), 3km east of town on the old road to Iraklion. Take the hotel bus from the Rethymno station and ask the driver to stop at the campsite (every 30min. 7:30am-9:30pm, €0.75). Pitch your tent under a bamboo cover at this warm, family-owned campground, and take advantage of your proximity to the wide beach. Campers gather at Th barbecues (€5-8) and at Save the Sea Turtles slide shows every F (free). Taverna open 8:30am-10pm. Laundry €4, with soap €4.50. Parking €2.50-3. Safe available. Open mid-Apr. to Oct. €5-6.50 per person, €3-5 per tent, €4-5 per caravan. Tent rental €6-7. 10% discount for stays of 7 days or more. ❶

Park Hotel, I. Gavriil 37 (☎28310 29 958). A good option for those who want to be near the bus station and prefer the New City over the Old. Rooms have private baths, TV, A/C, and phones, and overlook I. Gavriil. Singles €30; doubles €35; triples €45. ❷

FOOD

An **open-air market** on El. Venizelou by the New Town marina opens Thursdays at 7am and closes around 2:30pm, though the selection has dwindled by 10am. If you have a hankering for bruised fruit or need to save a few euros, though, come at the end for the best deals as the vendors try to shed their remaining products. For affordable nighttime eats, tourists and locals head to **Plateia Titou Petichaki.**

Taverna Kyria Maria, Moskovitou 20 (☎28310 29 078), to the right down the small alley behind the Rimondi fountain, is under a vine-draped grape arbor filled with hanging bird cages. From the initially charming entrance to the complimentary desert of raki and honey-drizzled cheese pie, Kyria Maria is one of the best bets in town. Octopus in wine sauce (€8) is their specialty. Open daily mid-Mar. to Oct. 11am-11pm. MC/V. ❷

Taverna Garden Ftochiko, Souliou 37 (☎28310 28 136). Ftochiko's spacious seating under aromatherapeutic lemon trees defies the crowds and cramped quarters of Souliou. Gyros plate €7. Complimentary apple pie. Open daily noon-midnight. MC/V. ❸

Ovelisterio (☎28310 55 249), on the corner of Arkadiou and Varda Kallergi. Look for the round wooden entrance and a sign that says "O Nikos." Enjoy delicious, inexpensive gyros pitas (€1.50) or gyros plates (€5) with locals in this tiny hole in the wall on the big shopping street of Arkadiou. Open 10am-midnight. ❶

Katerina's, Melissinou 34 (☎28310 57 024). Flavored raki and bright blue, yellow, and pink seating beneath the Fortezz accent the fixed menus. Moussaka, Greek salad, *tzatziki,* wine, and coffee for 2, €13.50. Open daily noon-11pm. ❷

Akri, Kornarou 27 (☎28310 50 719). The interior's electric orange glow is surprisingly calming, and the cafe, in a quiet alleyway, is a nice change from the bustling shopping district outside. Pastitsio €5.50. Open daily 11am-11pm. ❷

🅖 SIGHTS

The sprawling 🅜**Venetian Fortezza,** a fortress built in 1580, is the high point of the city (both literally and figuratively) and provides magnificent views of the coast and surrounding towns. Exploring the series of caves, churches, and crumbling facades that comprise the ruins can entertain visitors for half an hour or half a day; many choose to bring a picnic and dine overlooking the water. (☎28310 28 101. Open Tu-Su 9am-8pm, last entry at 7:15pm. €3, under 16 €2.50, under 12 and students with ID free.) Rethymno's **Archaeological Museum** occupies a former Ottoman prison adjacent to the fortress. In a single, large room, the collection contains an eclectic mix of knives, coins, lamps, sarcophagi, and statues from Minoan and Classical times. (☎28310 54 668. Open Tu-Su 8:30am-3pm. €3, students and seniors €2, EU students and children under 12 free.) The **L. Kanakakis Municipal Gallery of Contemporary Art,** Himaras 5, at the corner of Salaminos, displays 19th- and 20th-century Greek art, and hosts temporary exhibits in twin galleries across from each other in the Old City. (☎28310 52 530; www.rca.gr. Open Tu-F 9am-1pm and 7-10pm, Sa-Su 11am-3pm. €3, students €1.50, under 12 free.) The **Historical and Folklore Museum,** Vernardou 28-30, showcases artifacts of Cretan social history. (☎28310 23 398. Open M-Sa 9:30am-2:30pm. €3, students €1.50.) Tattooed with graffiti, Rethymno's Ottoman monuments are in a state of forlorn disarray. Struggling for space in the modern city's streets are the **Neratzes Minaret** on Antistasios; **Nerdjes Mosque,** a former Franciscan church located a block away on Fragkiskou 1 and called "St. Francis" on many maps; the **Kara Pasha Mosque** on Arkadiou near Pl. Iroön; and the **Valides Minaret,** which presides over the gate called **"Porta Megali"** at Pl. Martiron (if you're having trouble finding it, look up). On the corner of Pl. Martiron, the **public gardens** are a much-needed oasis of shade in the scorching Greek sun. Tall, exotic trees line shady paths toward the central fountain, while a diverse menagerie borders the walkways. Deer, gazelle, donkeys, water fowl, and ostriches occupy pens under the trees, and a massive flock of pigeons puts on its own exhibition over at the central fountain.

Rethymno's **Wine Festival,** which takes place at the end of July, is a crowded all-you-can-drink celebration, with a local dance troupe performance each evening. The city's **Renaissance Festival,** featuring theater (tickets €20), concerts, and exhibitions, is held in the fortress in July and August. Rethymno's February **Carnival** is

CRETE

the largest celebration in all of Crete. Attractions include a parade, a masked ball, and a treasure hunt. Call the tourist office for information.

NIGHTLIFE

The bar scene in Rethymno centers on **Ioulias Petichaki, Nearchou,** and **Plateia Plasteira** near the western end of the harbor. A handful of chic clubs cater predominantly to locals looking to meet friends for drinks; dancing is minimal. **⧉Rock Cafe Club,** I. Petichaki 6 (☎69445 08 299), is one of the few popular dancing locations. The patrons are unpretentious, the DJs are savvy, and drinks issue from not one, but three fully stocked bars. (Beer €4. Mixed drinks €7. Open M-Th, Su 11pm-4am, F-Sa 11pm-morning.) **Dimman Bar,** upstairs at Arkadiou 220, has a small interior covered in a collage of outdated currency and images of classic movie stars. Diman's highlight is its wraparound balcony, which serves as a perfect vantage point for watching dressed-up and decked-out Greeks scamper from club to club. (Open daily 10pm-3am.) **Karma Cafe,** Plastira 2 (☎28310 57 564), is popular mostly with twenty-something Greeks. In the heart of tight-black-pants territory, this cover-free nightclub stands out with its tastefully swanky Asian-themed interior.

DAYTRIP FROM RETHYMNO

⧉ARKADI MONASTERY Μονή Αρκαδή
Take the bus from Rethymno (1hr., 3-4 per day, €2.10; return trips 30min. later). Site open daily 9am-7pm. €2. Modest dress required.

The site of one of the most famous battles in the War of Independence, Arkadi Monastery became a symbol to accompany the rallying motto "Freedom or Death." Greeks refer to the event that took place here as the Holocaust of 1866. In November of that year, Greeks and Turks fought a two-day standoff at the monastery, where Greek villagers had gathered to seek refuge from over 2000 Turkish soldiers. When Greek defenses gave way, the monks and guerrilla fighters holding out in the monastery set off their own ammunition supply, sacrificing themselves to kill hundreds of Turks. Today a bust commemorates the sole survivor, a young girl who lived to tell the tale. A few monks maintain what is left of the monastery: the frame of the church and the outer complex, a roofless chamber where the ammunition was set off, and a small museum containing 200-year-old Bibles and a portion of the church's original decoration, including Byzantine paintings and Orthodox vestments. Despite its devastated state, Arkadi is a stunning

PHYLLO: BEHIND THE DOUGH

Paper-thin phyllo dough has likely become part of the daily diet of anyone traveling in Greece; the ubiquitous tiropita, spanikopita, and baklava all share this flaky common denominator.

If you're wondering how the dough gets thin enough to see through, visit Katerina and her husband at Rethymno's unassuming **Filo Factory.** The simple two-room building produces fresh phyllo by the pound every day, and the owners are more than happy to welcome onlookers.

In the back room, Katerina's husband begins by mixing the ingredients and kneading the dough, using a pin roller to stretch and flatten it to its delicate consistency. He then leaves the dough in sheets the size of small rugs to dry in the front room, stacked in piles separated by wax paper. After allowing the dough to sit for a while, Katerina folds, wraps, and bakes it into flaky phyllo pastries like *kandaifi*, dripping with honey and powdered sugar.

Whether you actually eat the fresh baklava (€5) or just watch it being made, Katerina and her Filo Factory will leave you astounded at the time, care, and affection that go into making this multi-purpose Greek staple.

*The **Filo Factory,** Vernarou 30, is next to the History and Folklore Museum. ☎28310 29 488. Open daily 8am-8pm.*

example of 15th-century Cretan architecture. A stroll through the rose-lined gardens and dilapidated rooms gives a sense both of what once was and of what remains. The small room across from the parking lot houses the skulls of the freedom fighters.

PLAKIAS Πλακιάς ☎ 28320

Though it has increasingly sacrificed its seclusion to tourists, Plakias remains wonderfully underdeveloped and inexpensive compared to most Cretan beach towns. Towering mountains and steep gorges shelter the palm trees, olive groves, and stunning hiking terrain that engulf the town. Though most people stay on the main street that runs along the sandy beach, the enchanting interior is filled with palm fronds and the sound of chirping cicadas.

▐▀ ▌ TRANSPORTATION AND PRACTICAL INFORMATION. You'll be able to find anything you need on either the beach road or the paths that head inland from it. Facing the water at the bus stop, the main road goes left toward the umbrella beach and west toward the pier. **Buses** drop off and pick up at the beach, and run to Preveli (30min., daily, €1.50) and Rethymno (50min., 4 per day, €3.50). **Taxis** pick up next to the bus stop. (☎ 28320 31 610. Available 7am-11pm.) Find **rental cars** (€29-40) and **mopeds** (€10-20) at **Monza Travel**, on the beach road to the left of the bus stop if you're facing the beach. (☎ 28320 31 433. Open daily 9am-9pm.) **Bikes** are available to rent at **Asklepias**, 50m down the road that meets the beach at the Argo taverna. (☎ 28320 31 645. €5-14 per day. Open 9:30am-2pm and 6-9pm.) A **24hr. ATM** is on the side of Old Alianthos Taverna; another is next to the town hall, one block past the bridge coming from the bus stop. The **laundromat** is around the bend past the pier. (☎ 28320 31 471. Wash €5, dry €5. Open daily 9am-noon and 5-7:30pm.) The **police** (☎ 28320 22 027) are 20km away in Spili. Behind Monza Travel is a **pharmacy**. (☎ 28320 31 666. Open M-Sa 9:15am-1pm and 5:15-8:30pm.) The **hospital** (☎ 28310 27 814) is in Rethymno. A **doctor's office** is next to the pharmacy. (☎ 28320 31 770, 24hr. assistance ☎ 69734 34 934. Open M-Sa 9:30am-1pm and 5-8:30pm.) **Internet access** is available at **Plakias Youth Hostel**. (€4.50 per hr.; open daily 8am-8pm) and at **Forum**, across the street from the bus stop (☎ 28320 32 084; €4 per hr.; open daily 10am-late). The **post office**, next to the doctor's office, has **Western Union**. (☎ 28320 31 212. Open M-F 7:30am-2pm.) **Postal Code:** 74060.

▐ ACCOMMODATIONS AND CAMPING. Facing the beach at the bus stop, turn left and walk 50m and then turn left again at Monza Travel; go left at the end of the road and follow the signs to reach the **◪Plakias Youth Hostel ❶**, the self-proclaimed southernmost hostel in Europe. Set in an olive grove, this happening place goes all-out with hot showers, good music, friendly people, and cheap alcohol (beer €1.05; 0.75L wine €1.50), making it an oasis that backpackers enthusiastically endorse. (☎ 28320 32 118; www.yhplakias.com. Internet access €0.75 per 10min. Reception 9am-noon and 5-8pm. Open Mar.-Nov. Dorms €7.50.) At the far right end of town if you're facing the beach, **On The Rocks ❸** provides amazing views of the smaller, rock-guarded beach and surrounding cliffs. Warm, hospitable owners offer rooms with fridges, kettles, private baths, and A/C. Rooms on the lower-floor have small, private balconies with laundry lines, and those on the upper-floor share a single, spacious balcony. Downstairs is a lovely restaurant. (☎ 28320 32 115; www.cretaspirit.com. Singles €29; doubles €33; triples €38.) At **Pension Kyriakos ❷**, at the turn of the road behind Monza Travel, rooms are equipped with fridges and private baths. Air flows freely between the open doors of the communal front balcony and private back balconies, cooling the rooms with

The **laundromat** (wash and dry €10) is behind the post office at the bus stop. (Open 10am-4pm.) Free **public toilets** sit across the street from the post office, on the way to the beach. The **police, pharmacy,** and **hospital** are in Mires, 17km to the northeast. In an **emergency,** call ☎28920 51 111 for the Mires police, ☎166 for first aid, and ☎28920 51 219 for the medical center. **Internet access** is available at the **Kafaneio Coffee Shop,** on the right side of the road about 100m past the bus stop. (☎28920 45 460. €4 per hr. Coffee €2-5. Ice cream €4. Open daily 8am-2am.) The nearest **post office** is in Mires, but you can buy stamps from any *periptero* and use the ubiquitous yellow drop boxes to mail letters. **Postal Code:** 70200.

⌐ ACCOMMODATIONS AND CAMPING. Though it may be tempting as hotels in town can be pricey, sleeping on the beach or in the caves is illegal, and the law is heavily enforced. Instead, you can find reasonable prices in a quieter setting once you get off the main street. Last along the row of flashy pensions lining the road to Red Beach, **Xenos Dias Hotel ❷** distinguishes itself with its subdued, sophisticated hospitality. Spacious, quiet rooms all have private baths, fridges, and balconies that overlook the sea or the ancient Minoan ruins and vineyards in the backyard. Apartments are also available with kitchens and dining tables. (☎28920 45 116. A/C and breakfast each €5 extra. Singles €15-20; doubles €20-30; triples €25-35; apartments €35-50.) If you're driving, you may want to consider staying at **Dimitri's Villa ❷,** an oasis about 250m off the main road with plenty of room for parking, a precious commodity in cramped Matala. On foot, walk 200m toward Phaistos, turn right before the mini-mart, and follow the blue signs. Dimitri's rooms have baths, balconies, fridges, TV, safes, and phones. (☎28920 45 002. Breakfast included. Singles €20-25; doubles €25-30; triples €30-40.) The owner at **Pension Matala View ❷,** 20m down the road to Red Beach, offers simple rooms with private baths, balconies, and a common kitchen. (☎28920 45 114; www.cretehouses.com. A/C €5. Singles €15-20; doubles €20-30; triples €22-32.) **Matala Camping ❶** has the best location in town, behind the beach at the end of the road in a wooded grove. (☎28920 42 720. Showers available. Quiet hours after midnight. Reception 24hr. €4.10 per person, €3.20 per tent, €2.50 per car.)

◖◗ FOOD AND NIGHTLIFE. Only a few restaurants in town are budget-friendly. Despite sometimes-brusque service, **Waves Restaurant ❷,** on the western end of the beach, stuns with panoramic views of Matala and serves standard fare at reasonable prices. (☎28920 45 361. Greek salad €3. Grilled octopus €8. Open daily 9am-late.) For good souvlaki (€2.50) and gyros (€2), head to **Notos ❶,** between the waterfront and the covered market. (☎28920 45 533. Open daily 11am-midnight.) Evening activities tend to be low-key. Cluttered with candles and commanding a view of the main plateia, **Kantari** is a popular place to catch world music. (☎28920 45 404. Open daily 9am-late. Beer €2. Mixed drinks €4.50.) Groups of 20-somethings convene at **Zafiria Cafe,** on the main road next to the bookshop. (☎28920 45 496. Open daily 8am-late. Cretan wine €1-3.)

◙◪ SIGHTS AND BEACHES. Matala attracts visitors with three tiers of spectacular **caves** to the right of the main beach. As you sit in the damp interior, reflect on the caves' previous occupants—Roman corpses, Nazis searching for British submarines, and songwriter Joni Mitchell. Matala is blessed with some of Crete's best **beaches,** many of which are spawning grounds for endangered **sea turtles.** Environmentalists run a kiosk at the bus stop, where they provide info on the turtles and their habitat; if you want to support the cause, pick up a purple ⬛Save the Turtles t-shirt (€12). The main beach is a beautiful rounded cove with pebbly yellow sand and aquamarine water. The phrase "today is life, tomorrow never comes," painted in block letters on its eastern side, captures Matala's former spirit. A 35min. hike, tough enough to necessitate hiking boots, past the pension-lined street and over a steep trail, will bring you to a magnificent strip of sand known as **Red beach**. Once you reach a fence, follow it to the right, and go through the goat herd gate to the shore. Cliffs surround this isolated and amazingly picturesque beach with nude bathers. Five kilometers from Matala stretches long, pebbly **Kommos**, dotted with enclaves of nude bathers and free from development save one taverna. Archaeologists are currently excavating a Minoan site there. Take the Matala-Iraklion **bus**, ask to be let off at Kommos (€1.10), and walk 500m down to the beach. Neither beach is shaded, leading to speculation that Red beach may take its name from the lobster skin-tone of unprepared visitors and not its clay-colored sand.

■ PHAISTOS Φαιστός

Buses from Phaistos go to: Agia Galini (25min., 7 per day, €1.70); Iraklion (1½hr., 4 per day, €5); Matala (20min., 5 per day, €1.50); Mires (10min., 4 per day, €1). ☎ 28920 42 315. Open 8am-7pm. €4; students and EU seniors €2; classics students, under 18, and EU students free; combined ticket with Agia Triada €6.

Seated royally on a plateau with magnificent views of the mountains, the ruins of Phaistos are one of the finest reminders of the grandeur of Minoan palaces, though the site has undergone less interpretive renovation than its more famous counterpart, Knossos (p. 596), and attracts fewer tourists. If you arrive during the first two hours that the site is open, though, you can avoid the crowds that do come by. The ruins span epochs of Greek history; archaeologists have identified structures at Phaistos from the Neolithic to the Hellenic periods. Four palaces have been discovered on the site. The first, built around 1900 BC, was destroyed by the earthquake that hit Crete around 1700 BC. The second structure was leveled by the mysterious **cataclysm** (p. 54) in 1450 BC; traces of two even older palaces were detected by an excavation in 1952. Since then, minor reconstructive work has been done on the walls, chambers, and cisterns. Built according to the standard Minoan blueprint, the complex included a great central court surrounded by royal quarters, servant quarters, storerooms, and chambers for state occasions.

There are no signs or labels in the palace complex, but you can pick up a free map at the entrance or buy a more comprehensive guidebook (€3.50) at the gift shop. Visitors enter Phaistos and immediately see the **West Courtyard** and **theater area** at the lower level on their right. Next to the theater area, the intact **grand staircase** leads to the foot of the regal **propylaea** on the left. The staircase, the largest of its kind on Crete, showcases the Minoans' advancement, as its steps were built in a slightly convex form to shed rainwater. The propylaea, consisting of a landing, portico, central column, and well, served as the ceremonial entrance to the palace. Its resemblance to the propylaea of the Acropolis in Athens demonstrates the influence of Minoan architecture on that of Classical Greece. Walk through the propylaea and take the next left to reach the **main hall,** containing a central fenced-off **storeroom** that housed the massive *pithoi.*

On the perimeter of the central court, columns and boxes mark the place where sentries used to stand guard. The covered **royal apartments,** with a queen's **magaron** and a beautiful lustral basin (covered purifying pool), sit past the entrance gate. Just beyond, in the **peristyle hall,** the remains of some of the Minoans' signature cigar-shaped columns can be seen lining the walls. In the opposite direction, northeast of the central court, are the halls of the palace **workshops** along with the seven-compartmented room where the renowned **Phaistos disc**, now in the Archaeological Museum in Iraklion (p. 594), was discovered.

AGIA TRIADA Άγια Τριάδα

Follow the signs from the main road near Phaistos; the side road dead-ends 3km later at the parking lot. ☎ 28920 91 564. Open daily 10am-4:30pm. €3, ticket with Phaistos €6.

The ruins near the medieval town of Agia Triada draw fewer tourists than Phaistos, but still provide an enticing window into Greek history. The oldest sections of the site date from the second millennium BC, while the newest part is a church from the AD 14th century. Some archaeologists believe that the structures at Agia Triada were a seasonal residence for the kings at Phaistos, but others argue that Minoans moved there after Phaistos began to decline in prestige.

The ruins sit on the side of a hill in a roughly backwards L-shape; visitors enter from the corner of the L. Straight ahead from the entrance, the long open space with eight evenly spaced stone blocks is the **agora,** and is surrounded by the residents' living quarters. Looking to the left from the entrance, the **Mycenaean megaron** features an advanced waste-water disposal system in the form of troughs running between the rooms. Before the megaron, the paved **road to Phaistos** was the connection between the two ancient settlements. Walking past the megaron brings you to a "Minoan house," the room with benches and slabs of gypsum stone on the walls. At the top of the hill beyond the road to Phaistos sits the small church of **Agios Giorgios.** The only complete building on the site, the church displays impressive examples of Christian frescoes.

AGIA GALINI Άγα Γαλήνη ☎28320

The narrow streets in tiny Agia Galini wind down the hillside, leading fishermen to their boats and tourists to the small, chair-lined beach. Only 50km from Rethymno, the intimate community welcomes visitors to explore its covered market and gaze at the sea from dramatic cliffs or the bustling harbor.

🖅🛈 TRANSPORTATION AND PRACTICAL INFORMATION. The town's main street runs downhill from the bus station to the harbor and contains all practical necessities. Off the main drag, more winding streets are so steep that they are often composed of steps rather than pavement; most have restaurants and accommodations. Turn left from the harbor to reach the long beach, where numerous oceanside tavernas cater to dehydrated sunbathers. **Ferries** run to Preveli (daily 10am, round-trip €22). **Buses** go to: Iraklion (2hr., 6-10 per day, €5.50); Matala (1hr., 4-5 per day, €2.40); Phaistos (30min., 6-9 per day, €1.70); Rethymno (1hr., 3-5 per day, €4.40). Opposite the bus stop, **Monza Travel** provides tourist info, rents mopeds (€15-25) and cars (€28-35), and calls **taxis.** (☎28320 91 004. Open daily 9am-9pm.) The street is full of **24hr. ATMs** and places that **exchange currency.** Coming from the bus stop, the **Laundry Center** is on your right (☎28320 91 336. Wash and dry €7.) Continuing downhill, you'll pass the **police station** on the right (☎28320 91 210; open 24hr.) and a **pharmacy** on the left (☎28320 91 168; open M-Sa 9:30am-2pm and 5-8pm). There is **no doctor** in town, so health needs are addressed at the **Spili health center** (☎28320 91 111), in the same building as the police, or at the **hospital** in Rethymno (☎28310 27 814). **Internet access** is available at **Christos Cafe-Bar,** near the harbor on the street ending at a small fountain. (☎28320 91 144. €4 per hr. Beer €3. Open 9am-late.) The **post office** is on the left a block past the bus stop toward the harbor. (☎28320 91 393. Open M-F 7:30am-2pm.) **Postal Code:** 74056.

🏠 ACCOMMODATIONS AND CAMPING. Some pensions are reasonably priced and close to the beach. **🏕Camping Agia Galini No Problem ❶,** however, makes indoor accommodations seem overrated. This spectacular campsite has a pool, a mini-mart, a kitchen, and a taverna (see below). To get to the campgrounds, walk along the beach and take a left on the dirt path past the footbridges; follow for 150m and the entrance to the campsite will be on your right. (☎28320 91 386. Reception open at 8:30am. €6 per person, €4 per tent, €3 per car.) Matriarch Marika presides over the unassuming **Pela Rooms ❷** with a firm but kind hand. Clean and airy rooms with kitchenettes, private baths, and balconies are tucked in a prime location along the quiet side street behind the bus station. (☎28320 91 143. A/C €2. Singles €20; doubles €25-30.) Beach lovers should check out the bright rooms with wooden ceilings and gorgeous views at **Stochos ❸**, only 10m from the sand. (☎28320 91 433. Doubles and triples €35. AmEx/MC/V.) With a nice view of the harbor, **Akteon Hotel ❷** has well-priced rooms with A/C. Walk along the harbor and turn up the street opposite a small fountain; make the first right and the hotel is at the top of the stairs. (☎28320 91 208. Singles €20; doubles €25-30; triples €30-40.)

◖◗ **FOOD AND NIGHTLIFE.** Owner Bobby takes pride in offering patrons traditional meals made from local natural products at **Taverna Knossos ❸** (www.cretanatural.com), including rabbit *stifado* in wine (€8) and Cretan pies with honey (€2.50). Directly across from the fountain in the harbor, it is up one flight of stairs to the left. To the left after the post office and around the corner, **Medusa Taverna ❷** serves diners next to a clever brick and plaster outline of Crete on the wall. (☎28320 91 487. Crepes €4-5. Gyros €2. Fresh fruit drinks €2. Open May-Oct. 11am-1am. MC/V.) The No Problem campsite's **taverna ❷** serves farm-fresh food cooked over the embers of a traditional wood stove. (Greek salad €3.20. Pizzas €5-6. Fish from €5.) The small **bakery ❶**, on the main road next to the bus stop, has traditional Cretan sweets for under €1.50. (Open daily 8am-9pm.)

At night, people gather at mellow waterfront bars or head to retro **Jukebox,** just off the harbor across from the fountain. The bar here extends from indoors to the street outside. (☎69372 31 381; www.jukeboxclub.gr. Beer €2-5. Mixed drinks €2-6. Open daily 10pm-7am.)

HERSONISSOS Χερσόνησος   ☎28970

With numerous bars, discos, and nightclubs around its harbor, Hersonissos (hehr-SON-i-sos) becomes a playground for Dutch, Irish, and German teenagers every summer. Minigolf, go-karts, and waterslides clutter the beachfront, and lounging sunbathers become energetic club-hoppers who overrun the town. Authentic Cretan culture is preserved only in a well-polished open-air museum.

▐ TRANSPORTATION

There is no bus station, just a kiosk at the western perimeter of town. Tickets can be purchased on the **buses,** which go to: Agios Nikolaos (1hr., 17-20 per day 7:10am-10:10pm, €3); Ierapetra (2hr., 8 per day 7:10am-8:10pm, €7.50); Iraklion (45min., 4 per hr. 6:20am-11:20pm, €2.50); Malia (20min., 4 per hr. 7:10am-10:40pm, €1.20); Sitia (2½hr., 6 per day 7:10am-7:10pm, €10). A 24hr. **taxi** stand (☎28970 23 723) is by the bus stop on El. Venizelou. Countless **rental agencies** line El. Venizelou. **Autotravel,** El. Venizelou 20 (☎28970 22 761), rents **cars.** (€30-40 per day, full insurance and tax included; reduced for multiple days.) **Motorbike rentals** can be found on nearly every street (€10-20 per day).

◩ ▟ ORIENTATION AND PRACTICAL INFORMATION

Hersonissos is 26km east of Iraklion. The main road, **Eleftheriou Venizelou,** has the town's offices, markets, and discos. Perpendicular streets lead to either the beach or the hills. Turning right beyond the bus stop on your way toward Iraklion puts you on **Dimokratias,** a less-congested stretch of supermarkets and travel agencies.

Budget Travel: Serapis Travel, El. Venizelou 141 (☎28970 24 610). Open 10am-11pm. **Zakros Tours,** Dimokratias 12 (☎28970 22 776), rents cars, sells boat and plane tickets, **exchanges currency,** finds rooms, and has **maps.** Open 9am-10:30pm.

Banks: Several on El. Venizelou **exchange currency** and have **24hr. ATMs.** A **National Bank** is at El. Venizelou 106 (☎28970 22 377). Open M-Th 8am-2:30pm, F 8am-2pm.

Laundromat: Laundrysalon, Minos 15 (☎28970 24 908). Turn toward the beach from El. Venizelou by the Q Club. Wash €5.50, dry €3. Open daily 9:30am-11pm.

Police: Minos 8 (☎28970 22 100 or 28970 22 222). Has a detailed map of town on its wall. The **tourist police** are in the same building (☎28970 21 000). Walk toward the beach 2 blocks after the bus stop.

Medical Services: Cretan Medicare, El. Venizelou 19 (☎28970 25 141, 28970 25 142, or 28970 25 143), 500m from the bus station on the way to Iraklion. Open 24hr.

Telephones: OTE, Eleftherias 11 (☎28970 22 299). Go in the direction of the mountains just before Jackpot Internet Cafe and look for the sign. Open M-F 7:30am-2:30pm.

Internet Access: Cafe Hersonissos, Papadogiri 10 (☎28970 25 292). Turn facing the beach from El. Venizelou near the church. €3.20 per hr. Ice cream €3.50. Open daily 10am-2am. **Jackpot Internet Cafe,** El. Venizelou 30 (☎28970 22 911), 250m toward Malia past the bus stop. €2.50 per hr. Open daily 9am-late.

Post Office: ☎28970 22 022. Open M-F 7:30am-2pm. **Western Union** available. **Postal Code:** 70014.

⌐ ACCOMMODATIONS AND CAMPING

Hotels line El. Venizelou and rent rooms for €20-55. Tour companies book most of the rooms in town for the height of tourist season, so reserve in advance if you're visiting in late July or August. Walking from the bus kiosk on the main road away from Iraklion, turn toward the beach two streets past RnB Bar, and you'll arrive at **Selena Pension ❷,** Em. Maragaki 13. Small, bright rooms have private baths and spacious balconies. (☎28970 25 180. Check-out noon. Doubles €30-45.) **Hotel Despina ❷,** Vitsentzou Kornarou 10, is slightly more upscale, with a relaxed, comfy lounge and bar. Its small rooms include private baths and balconies; some have fridges. (☎28970 22 966. Check-out noon. Singles €20; doubles €25; triples €30-35.) To get to **Camping Caravan ❶,** by the port of Hersonissos, walk 1km from the fork in the road along the beach at the eastern side of town toward Agios Nikolaos. The campsite is past the Star beach water park. (☎28970 24 718. Restaurant, bar, and hot water. €6 per person, €3 per car; 2-person bungalow €20-35.)

◗ FOOD

On the Hersonissos waterfront, "traditional Greek food" is often code for pre-packaged facsimiles whose pictures grace menus with the plasticky sheen of tourism. Sandwich and fast-food places line the main road by the beach; the outskirts of town contain far calmer eateries. **Passage to India ❷,** on Petrakis, just off the beach road, marked by signs, complements its delicious Indian dishes with boudoir-like drapery. It has several options for vegetarians. (☎28970 23 776. Chicken *tikka masala* €7.60. Open daily 6pm-midnight.) At **Ristorante Vesuvios ❷,** just off El. Venizelou across from the Q Club, an international clientele dines to multilingual background music under a vine-covered trellis that evokes an Italian villa. (☎28970 21 474. Pizza €7-10. Pasta €7-12. Open daily 6pm-2am.) **Elli Taverna ❶,** Sanoudaki 2, is just after Cretan Medicare, on your right when heading toward Iraklion. There's no menu, but patrons can peek under pot lids and choose from a rotating selection of dishes, all cooked by the owner in homemade olive oil. Simple and authentic, Elli is a welcome escape from the overwhelmingly generic fare. (☎28970 24 758. Most entrees €7. Vegetarian entrees €6. Open noon-midnight.)

◉ SIGHTS

The **Lychnostatis Open-Air Museum** provides the only alternative to Hersonissos's bright beaches and water slides. The outdoor museum recreates a traditional life-sized Cretan village with a windmill, small chapel, and pleasant-smelling herb shop. On Wednesday, visitors can stomp on grapes and sample wine at the museum's Grape Fest (€14). Walk down El. Venizelou toward Malia, then follow the beach road to the left at the fork in the eastern end of town. The entrance on the left is past the water park and Camping Caravan. (☎28970 23 660; www.lychnostatis.gr. Open Apr.-Oct. 9:30am-2pm. €4.50, students €3, children 4-12 €2; prices reduced for groups. Tours in English every hr. 9:30am-1:30pm.)

> 🏁**TIP**   **OUTSMARTING THE HERD.** To truly take advantage of Hersonissos's sparkling blue-flag beaches, avoid the midday crowds and enjoy an early morning swim or pre-dinner dip. The masses will be busy either preparing for or recovering from the evening's debauchery, leaving you to enjoy your cleverly timed solitude with the best the area has to offer.

◉ NIGHTLIFE

Hersonissos's nighttime hubs typically open at dusk and close at dawn, but you'll be lonely at most of them before midnight. You can't stray a block without encountering yet another bar or disco; they generally charge no cover and sell beer for €4 and mixed drinks for around €6. Many clubs also have "happy hour all night long," which means that with the purchase of one severely overpriced drink, you get your second free. Find **Amnesia Club,** at the western end of town, by taking a right off El. Venizelou onto Ag. Paraskimis when walking toward Iraklion. With fancy laser-light displays, it's one of the hottest clubs in town. The best dancers strut their stuff on elevated platforms, while the masses below grind to the tunes spun by one of the rotating DJs. (☎28970 25 490; www.amnesiaclub.gr. Opens 10pm.) A diverse crowd shimmies to international rave music at **Camelot Dancing Club,** across from Amnesia. Fake torches above the dance floor and real candles at the twin bars contribute to the club's medieval theme. (☎28970 22 734. Open M-Th, Su 10:30pm-4:30am, F-Sa 10:30pm-6am.) **Status,** Ag. Paraskevis 47, with impressively chic decor including a spiral staircase and illuminated, stepped floors, is consistently crowded. (www.status-club.gr. Open 9pm-late.)

LASITHI PREFECTURE

The Lasithi Prefecture doesn't make a great first impression. The heavily touristed towns on the western side seem to be British outposts incongruously placed on the coast, where all local culture is lost in a flurry of summertime hedonism and over-ripe sunburns. The road east from Iraklion, however, eventually passes over these jam-packed, overpriced resort towns and transports you to the quiet, scenic inland region. The smaller villages that line the eastern edge, sustained not by tourism but by thriving local agriculture, are spread out between olive groves and stretches of unblemished coastline. Lasithi has an abundance of stunning and uncommon natural sights—the palm tree forest at Vai, the Valley of Death near Kato Zakros, and the desert island of Chrissi off the coast of Ierapetra will make you forget even the tackiest of resort towns.

AGIOS NIKOLAOS Άγιος Νικόλαος ☎28410

On a small peninsula on Crete's northeastern edge, Agios Nikolaos is a nouveau resort town where vacationers, mostly from northern Europe, huff and puff their way up steep, boutique-lined streets, then stop in at posh harborside cafes to catch their breath. The hills lend magnificent views of the central lake and the sea, and many hotels and restaurants occupy prime overlooks. Catering to beach-obsessed tourists, one-stop holiday-makers, and hikers on their way to more obscure destinations, Agios Nikolaos is lively, glamorous, and definitely not cheap.

⌸ TRANSPORTATION

Flights: Olympic Airways, Plastira 18 (☎28410 22 033), overlooking the lake. Open M-F 8am-3:30pm. The closest **airports** are in Iraklion and Sitia.

Buses: ☎28410 22 234. Just off Epimendiou. To: **Ierapetra** (1hr., 10 per day 5:30am-9pm, €3); **Iraklion** (1½hr., 22 per day 5:30am-10:30pm, €5.30) via **Malia** and **Hersonissos**; **Kritsa** (15min., 10 per day 6am-8:30pm, €1.20); **Sitia** (1½hr., 7 per day 6:15am-8pm, €6). Buses to **Elounda** (20min., 15 per day 6am-8pm, €1) and **Plaka** (40min., 7 per day 6am-7pm, €2) leave from across from the tourist office.

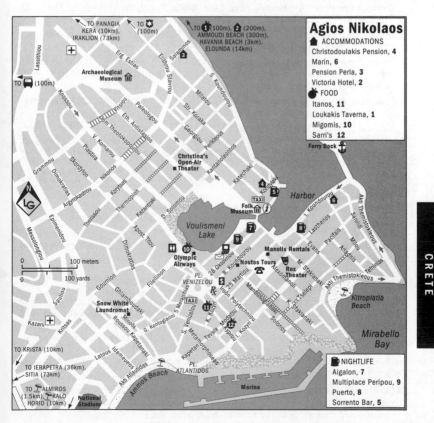

Agios Nikolaos

🏠 ACCOMMODATIONS
Christodoulakis Pension, **4**
Marin, **6**
Pension Perla, **3**
Victoria Hotel, **2**
🍴 FOOD
Itanos, **11**
Loukakis Taverna, **1**
Migomis, **10**
Sarri's **12**
⚓ Ferry Dock

🎶 NIGHTLIFE
Aigalon, **7**
Multiplace Peripou, **9**
Puerto, **8**
Sorrento Bar, **5**

CRETE

Ferries: Go to: **Karpathos** (7hr., 2 per week, €20.10); **Kassos** (6hr., 3 per week, €17); **Piraeus** (12hr., 3 per week, €31) via **Milos** (7hr., €20.40); **Rhodes** (12hr., 2 per week, €26); **Sitia** (1hr., 2 per week, €7.20); **Spinalonga** (2 per day, €15). **Nostos Tours,** R. Koundourou 30 (☎28410 22 819), sells tickets. Open 8am-9pm.

Taxis: ☎28410 24 000. Wait at Pl. Venizelou and the bridge by the tourist office. 24hr.

Rentals: A number of agencies are on I. Koundourou. Most rent **cars** for about €35-40 per day, including insurance. **Manolis** (☎28410 24 940), down the hill from the OTE on 25 Martiou, rents **mopeds** (€15 per day, including insurance) and **bicycles** (€8).

✈ 🛈 ORIENTATION AND PRACTICAL INFORMATION

Agios Nikolaos is easy to get around—it's on a small peninsula with beaches on three sides and most services, hotels, restaurants, and discos in the center. The one exception to the navigational simplicity is that **R. Koundourou, I. Koundourou,** and **S. Koundourou** are three different streets.

Tourist Office: S. Koundourou 21A (☎28410 22 357; www.aghiosnikolaos.gr), across the bridge at the harbor. Helps with accommodations, **exchanges currency,** and has transportation schedules and **maps.** Open daily Apr.-Nov. 8am-9:30pm.

Banks: Several on 28 Oktovriou have **24hr. ATMs.** The **National Bank** (☎28410 23 725) on R. Koundourou **exchanges currency.** Open M-Th 8am-2:30pm, F 8am-2pm.

Laundromat: Snow White Laundromat, Fillelinon 21 (☎28410 25 674). Wash, dry, and soap €3 per kg. Open M-Sa 8:30am-9pm.

Police: Stavrou 25 (☎28410 91 418 or 28410 91 417). Walk up E. Stavrou off Paleologou from the harbor; it's on the left. Open 24hr. The **tourist police** (☎28410 91 408) are in the same building. Open 8am-2pm.

Pharmacy: Doctor Theodore Furakis (☎28410 24 011; www.furakis.gr), Pl. Venizelou 23. Open M, W-F 8am-2pm and 5:30-9pm.

Medical Services: The **hospital** (☎28410 66 000) is on Paleologou, at the northern end of town. From the lake, walk up Paleologou, 1 block past the Archaeological Museum. For **emergencies,** go to **Cretan Medicare,** Kazani 7 (☎28410 27 551 or 28410 27 552). Open 24hr.

Telephones: OTE, ☎28410 95 314. On the corner of 25 Martiou and K. Sfakianaki. Open M-F 7:30am-1pm.

Internet Access: 💻 **Multiplace Peripou,** 28 Oktovriou 25 (☎28410 24 876). €4 per hr. (p. 610). **Du Lac Cafe** (☎28410 22 711), by the post office on 28 Oktovriou. €4 per hr., €6 per 2hr. Coffee €2. Beer €3.40. Open daily 9am-2am.

Post Office: 28 Oktovriou 9 (☎28410 22 062). Open M-F 7:30am-2pm. **Western Union** available. **Postal Code:** 72100.

🏠 ACCOMMODATIONS

Many larger hotels in Agios Nikolaos fill up months in advance. **Pensions** rent clean, cheap rooms, but they are in great demand, so reservations are recommended. The tourist office has a bulletin board that lists many of the city's pensions and their prices. Cheaper accommodations cluster inland near the Archaeological Museum and off I. Koundourou. For all rooms, prices are generally reduced 20-40% in low season.

💻 **Christodoulakis Pension,** Stratigou Koraka 7 (☎28410 22 525). From the tourist office, turn away from the water and turn right onto the street behind the taxi stand. Walk up the hill and turn left onto Stratigou Koraka. The pension, the 2nd building after you turn the corner, is unmarked; look for the profusion of plants. The kind, upbeat owners offer bright rooms with harbor views, and the sea breeze keeps everything cool. Also has a common kitchen with fridge, common baths, and a large balcony for sunbathing and socializing. Singles €20; doubles €20-25; triples €30-40. ❷

Marin, I. Koundourou 6 (☎28410 23 830), on the waterfront past the ramp to the ferry landing. Hidden in a garden courtyard away from crowded waterfront cafes, Marin's homey rooms in a great location come with private baths, TV, balconies, A/C, and ceiling fans. Open Mar.-Nov. Singles and doubles €35; triples €40. ❸

Victoria Hotel (☎28410 22 731), about 1km from the harbor on S. Koundourou, near Ammoudi beach. The white stucco hotel has a comfy, 2-fl. lounge area and basic rooms with baths, phones, ceiling fans, and small balconies. Prices vary by view, floor, and season. Singles €20-28; doubles €30-37; triples €36-45. ❷

Pension Perla, Salaminos 4 (☎28410 23 379). Walk away from the harbor on S. Koundourou and turn onto Salaminos. Near S. Koundourou's scenic waterfront, the pension has a TV lounge and rooms that include private baths and a waterfront view. Singles €14-15; doubles €15-17; triples €20. ❷

❑ FOOD

While Agios Nikolaos's waterfront suffers from a super-chic strain of the tourist-restaurant virus, there are **supermarkets** throughout the city, and you can find tasty and semi-cheap food if you look hard enough. **Loukakis Taverna ❷,** S. Koundourou 24, is a 10min. walk past the tourist office. The oldest taverna in Agios Nikolaos, its authentic, satisfying, cheap meals are like water in the desert of €6 Greek salads. (☎28410 28 022. *Stifado* €6.20. Stuffed green peppers €3.20. Open daily 9am-midnight.) **Migomis ❸,** Plastira 24, epitomizes a "special occasion" restaurant. The tasty but pricey food (entrees €8.50-21) is served in the classiest of classy settings—live piano plays every night, and the dining room has a tremendous panorama of the city. (☎28410 24 353. Appetizers €6-11.50. Open daily noon-midnight.) **Itanos ❷,** on Kyprou just off Pl. Venizelou, is tourist-friendly without being touristy. Homemade wine is served straight out of the barrel to tables in the

> 𝕽𝕯 **THE REAL DEAL.** Though Agios Nikolaos has plenty of convenient eateries, the "priceless" sea views come with a hefty bill. Don't be surprised to find that the very same Greek salad you enjoyed in Plakias for €3.50 costs twice as much here. Consider hitting 1 of the many markets lining S. Koundourou and 28 Oktovriou and whipping something up yourself.

outdoor seating area. (☎28410 25 340. Stuffed eggplant €5. Greek salad €3.50. Open daily 10am-11pm.) The vine-covered outdoor enclave at **Sarri's ❷,** Kyprou 15, is a quiet retreat from the nearby city center. To get there, start from the harbor bridge, walk up 28 Oktovriou, and turn left onto Kyprou at Pl. Venizelou; it's one block up. Portions are modest, but the food is flavorful, with all-encompassing lunch specials (€5.50-6.50) that include soup, *tzatziki*, souvlaki, potatoes, and a glass of wine. (☎28410 28 059. Open 8:30am-3pm and 6pm-midnight.)

◉ ❑ SIGHTS AND BEACHES

Interspersed between hilly Agios Nikolaos's colorful pedestrian streets lined with boutiques are goat-inhabited archaeological sites, a handful of the seemingly required museums, and beautiful, super-clean beaches.

C R E T E

MARKET. The kaleidoscopic weekly market sells a variety of inexpensive clothes and cracked cutlery, along with sundry items like paintings, knock-off Prada bags, and underwear. At the top of the street, displays of watermelons, tomatoes, fresh cheeses, and Cretan honey jockey for space. *(On Eth. Antistasis. Open W 7am-1pm.)*

MUSEUMS. Head away from the harbor on Paleologou to reach the **Archaeological Museum,** whose collection includes Minoan clay sarcophagi, a well-documented ancient coin collection, and art from the under-represented 7th-century BC Daedalic period. The last room contains two of the collection's all-stars: an athlete's skull, adorned with both a gold-leaf wreath and a coin to pay the toll to the afterlife, and a bowl of knuckle bones used by the ancients to divine the future or amuse themselves. *(☎28410 24 943. Open Tu-Su 8:30am-3pm. €3; seniors €2; students, classicists, and under 18 free.)* The **Folk Museum,** next to the tourist office, displays tapestries, icons, and objects from daily life on Crete in the 16th-19th centuries BC. *(☎28410 25 093. Open M-F, Su 10am-4pm. €3, under 12 €1.50.)* On the road from Agios Nikolaos, 1km before Kritsa, Crete's Byzantine treasure, the tiny **Panagia Kera** church, honors the Assumption of the Virgin in several narrative cycles. A crumbling patchwork of smoky 14th-century paintings adorns the central nave, while the wings display muted 15th-century frescoes. *(Open daily 8:30am-3pm. €3.)*

BEACHES. All of Agios Nikolaos's beaches are rated ▨**blue flag beaches** by the EU, which means they're the cleanest of the clean. Constant sunshine and lack of rain make them perfect tanning spots. Three of the more mediocre beaches are a quick walk from the main harbor, but the farther you venture, the better they get. Some choose to sunbathe on the concrete piers that jut out from S. Koundourou, while others head to **Ammos** by the National Stadium, **Kitroplatia** between Akti Panagou, and the marina (**Ammoudi**) farther up S. Koundourou away from town. Those with more lofty aspirations can catch the hourly bus to Ierapetra or Sitia and get off at **Almiros** (1½km east of Agios Nikolaos). With the rusting hulk of an old fishing boat adding a picturesque flair to the translucent waters and an island outcropping flying the Greek flag, Almiros is arguably the area's best beach. Just up the hill lies an EU-protected **wildlife reserve.** A river runs through the reserve and gushes water into the sea at Almiros; the hot springs mix with the cold jet for a spa-quality, refreshing swim. Sandy **Kalo Horio,** 10km farther, is equally spectacular and less crowded. Tell the bus driver to let you off at the **Kavos Taverna.** Another beautiful but somewhat touristy spot is **Havania,** at the Havania stop on the Elounda bus.

🎵 🍷 ENTERTAINMENT AND NIGHTLIFE

Upbeat crowds gather at the fashionable clubs around the harbor on I. Koundourou and S. Koundourou. Both Greek and American movies play at **Christina's open-air theater** on Eth. Antistasis; from October to April, films are also shown indoors at the **Rex** theater on Lasthenos (€6). Every other year (in 2006 and 2008), the last week in June or the first in July brings **Nautical Week.** Greek seamen race in the waters around Agios Nikolaos during the day, and music and dancing fill the late nights. Call the tourist office for details. The **Feast of All Saints,** on one of the last weekends of June, gives both tourists and locals the coveted chance to visit the forbidden **Island of All Saints.** Due to its archaeological and ecological value, visitors are normally banned from the uninhabited island, and the endangered Kri-Kri goats are granted free rein.

▨ **Multiplace Peripou,** 28 Oktovriou 25 (☎28410 24 876). A 1-stop entertainment spot with a cafe, Internet access (€4 per hr.), and book and music store. Live music (Greek traditional to jazz) Oct.-May Sa. Open daily 9:30am-2am.

Sorrento Bar (☎28410 24 310), at S. Koundourou on the harbor waterfront, may as well answer to Queen Elizabeth. The cozy, lively bar is decorated with British soccer club insignias and plays a Britpop and retro mix. The wig-wearing bartenders often break out into crazy renditions of pop songs. Beer €2.50. Mixed drinks €5. Open daily noon-4am.

Aigalon (☎28410 22 535), by the bridge, serves wine (€5) and other drinks under an oak ceiling. The balcony's peaceful views of the bridge, lake, and harbor contrast with the interior's techno-dance groove. Beer €3-5. Mixed drinks €5. Open daily 9am-late.

Puerto, at the corner of I. Koundourou and Evans, caters to sophisticated local hipsters who sip fruity drinks in the low-slung harbor seats or on plush stools in the music-driven interior. Frappés €2.80. Beer €4-5. Mixed drinks €6-7. Open daily 9am-4am.

▶ DAYTRIPS FROM AGIOS NIKOLAOS

SPINALONGA Σπιναλόγκα

There are 2 ways to get to Spinalonga. Nostos Tours, in Agios Nikolaos, offers guided boat rides and walking tours of the island (€15). Several other companies offer boat excursions there but don't run tours on the island itself. Most boats make 20min. swim stops, so you may want to bring your bathing suit. You can get there at a slightly cheaper cost, though you won't have a guide, if you catch a bus to Elounda (€1.10) and take a ferry from there to Spinalonga (Apr.-Oct., every 30min. 9:30am-4:30pm, €8). The site itself is €2, EU students and children under 12 free.

The most touted—and most disconcerting—excursion in eastern Crete is the trip to Spinalonga Island. This island-wide museum's seeming simplicity hardly hints at the area's long and bizarre history. In 1204, after purchasing the entire island of Crete, the Venetians destroyed fortresses in Barba Rossa and Agios Nikolaos before spending 75 years building a third, almost impregnable fortress on Spinalonga. When Crete gained independence in 1898, residents were determined to rid the island of all outsiders, including the Turks who had overtaken Spinalonga in 1715. They did this by establishing a leper colony there, which simultaneously frightened away the Turks and sequestered the infected, who had previously inhabited mountain caves. On October 22, 1903, the first lepers arrived at their new home. Though the island was certainly not luxurious, it was a drastic improvement for the lepers, who had previously been locked away from all society in a life of solitude. On Spinalonga the residents were able to form communities, open tavernas, have weddings, and even welcome guests. In 1957, following the development of an effective treatment for leprosy, the colony closed, and the residents were taken to Athens and cured. The last leper colony in Europe, Spinalonga was reopened in 1970, leaving 13 years to ensure a safe absence of the bacteria. Today the island is a ghost town of crumbling stone facades and hanging door frames, a disintegrating and subtly eerie remnant of the area's madcap history.

When you arrive, you will enter as the lepers did, in a grim, dark procession through **Dante's Gate** and an iron-barred tunnel. Just after the gate, the stone steps to the right lead up to the battlements of the old fortress and a spectacular view of the turquoise Mediterranean. Following the main road leads to the brightly colored stacks of reconstructed Venetian and Turkish houses that line the agora. At the end of the street is the **Church of Agios Pandelemonis,** founded by the Venetians in 1709 and dedicated to the Roman doctor Pandelemon, the Greek Orthodox saint of the sick. Stairs lead from the church to the **laundry,** where water was collected into tubs, heated over fires, and used to rinse bandages. The **hospital,** halfway up the hill, is identifiable by its eight-window facade. The lofty location theoretically allowed the wind to carry away the odor of rotting flesh. Beyond the laundry, steps lead to the sea; to their right are the modern concrete **apartment buildings** where the lepers lived. The original arched entrance to the **fortress** is at the bottom of the steps. In front is the **disinfecting room,** where everything from bedsheets to clothing to coins was sterilized. Continuing on the path around the rest of the island, you will find the small orange-roofed **Church of Agios Giorgios.** Built in 1661 by the Venetians, this is where the lepers took communion. Past this church, at the top of the ramp leading back to Dante's Gate, is the cemetery and its 44 graves, left unmarked so they could be reused.

MALIA Μάλια
Follow the road from Agios Nikolaos toward the town of Malia and turn right toward the sea when you see signs for the palace. ☎ *28970 31 597. Open Tu-Su 8:30am-3pm. €4, students and seniors €2, EU students and classicists free.*

Malia's majestic ruins remind visitors that the town was one of the three great cities of Minoan Crete. Although its **palace** lacks the labyrinthine plan of Knossos and Phaistos, it was a long-time center of Minoan power. First built in 1900 BC, the palace was destroyed around 1650 BC, rebuilt on a larger scale, and then destroyed again by the mysterious cataclysm that decimated all Minoan civilization around 1450 BC. The **Hall of Columns,** located on the northern side of the large central courtyard, with its six columns supporting the roof, has remained impressive over the millennia. The **loggia,** a raised chamber on the western side, was used for state ceremonies; west of it are the palace's living quarters and archives. Northwest of the loggia and main site is the **Hypostyle Crypt,** which was possibly a social center for Malia's most-educated citizens. Signs marking the site help visitors locate each structure. Though it is less touristed than Knossos, most of the palace is open to visitors. The admission fee also includes entrance to a small gallery with a three-dimensional reconstruction of the site and photographs of its excavation.

OLOUS Ολούς
The ancient city of Olous competed with Gournia and Malia as a center of trade in Minoan days. Now the city is completely **underwater,** submerged near the causeway connecting modern Elounda with the Kolokytha peninsula. In Elounda, you can walk 1km along the shore to the causeway and see outlines of buildings in the shoals. More adventurous travelers can put on their snorkeling mask and swim out from either side of the causeway to see more buildings in the deeper waters.

ANCIENT LATO Λατω
Take the bus to Kritsa and follow the signs 4km out of town. ☎ *28410 24 943. Open June-Nov. 8 daily 8:30am-3pm. €3.*

The ancient Dorian city of Lato, home to **Nearchos,** an admiral of Alexander the Great, towers above the Mirabello Bay in a saddle between two peaks. In the late first millennium BC the city struck alliances with Pergamon, Rhodes, and Teos; while its residents fought bitterly with neighboring Olous over shared borders. The city established a port, **Kamara,** which became so successful by the 2nd century BC that the residents abandoned Lato and moved there; the new settlement became modern Agios Nikolaos. Around the corner from the entrance, visitors can see the well-preserved ruins of ancient stone residences, complete with stone cisterns. The **agora** sat in the middle of the saddle, near a central ring of stones by a deep pit. With the bay to your right, face uphill to see the steep steps leading up to the ruins of the **Prytaneion,** the central administrative building. The remains of a two-room **temple** made of large stone blocks, with an altar at the back, are on the opposite side of the hill. Downhill from the temple lies the **theatrical area.**

GOURNIA Γουρνιά
Take either the Ierapetra bus or the Sitia bus and ask to be let off at Gournia, 30min. from Agios Nikolaos. ☎ *28420 93 028. Open Tu-Su 8:30am-3pm. €2, students free.*

Though the town's ancient name is unknown, the beautifully preserved ruins at Gournia provide an excellent example of an average Minoan town from the early second millennium BC. Visitors can see the layout of the entire town and its buildings, complete with stone-paved streets and an administrative center. Though the upper-level living quarters of the houses have not survived, the workshop and storage levels on the ground floor are still intact. Houses in traditional Cretan villages were built using this same format until only a few decades ago. From the entrance to the site, walk along the narrow, stone-paved street along the bottom of the hill and follow it around the edge of the site to the **courtyard**, where the Cretan sport of bull-leaping took place. Turn right to see the L-shaped steps of the **theatrical area**, and the slab of stone to their left, commonly thought to be a sacrificial stone. Going up the steps takes you into the **palace**, which, like the one at Knossos, was an administrative center of government as well as a royal residence.

LASITHI PLATEAU Οροπέδιο Λασίθιου

The inland route to Agios Nikolaos evades the jagged northern coastline to traverse the Lasithi Plateau, ringed by steep, crumbling mountains. This flat, fertile plain, where you might very well encounter fields overflowing with magnificent opium-red poppies, is home to 12 whitewashed villages full of exhausted donkeys and field-tilling farmers. The residents of the region once harnessed the plain's persistent breezes with thousands of wind-powered water pumps; black and white pictures of their windmill-strewn fields adorn the walls of travel agencies across the northern coast. Electric pumps have taken over in recent decades, leaving the carpet of defunct mills in a state of romantic rusting decay. Much of modern life has taken to the coastal road and bypassed Lasithi, preserving a rural hospitality and tranquility that seem utterly isolated from the urbanity just beyond the sequestering cliffs. All the basics can be found in Tzermiado ("Dzermiado" on many signs), the capital of Lasithi and the only large village in the plain.

⌗ TRANSPORTATION. It's best to visit Lasithi with a **rental car** or **moped.** Those who use the infrequent and irregular bus service may find themselves stranded for hours in one town or limited to the few towns within walking distance. If you're coming from **Iraklion,** take the coastal road 8km past Gournes and then turn right on the road to **Kastelli** (not the one on the western coast). After about 6km, the road forks right to Kastelli; stay left, heading toward **Potamies.** On the way, you'll pass the giant plane tree in the center of the town, whose trunk can be hugged by no fewer than 12 men. Signs to the Plateau guide you along the main road which winds around mountain ridges, cuts through the ruins of the stone windmills of the Seli Ambelou pass, and finally descends into the Lasithi Plateau. If you're coming from **Malia,** you have two options. To reach the more manageable road, head west along the coastal road and turn left about 3km outside of town at the turn-off for Mochos; this road takes you onto one that passes through Krassi and heads toward signs for the plateau. Your second option from Malia is to take 25 Martiou out of town and follow the signs. This road is faster than the Mochos route, but it is often empty and involves even more hairpin turns. **Buses** go from the plateau to Iraklion (2hr.; M, W, F-Sa 3:30pm; €5.25), but the schedule changes frequently. The bus makes its way around the whole Plateau, so you can stop at any of the towns.

⌗ ORIENTATION AND PRACTICAL INFORMATION. The bus stops at the center of **Tzermiado's** main plateia in front of the Kronio Restaurant. Continuing from Tzermiado 3km around the plateau brings you to **Agios Konstantinos** and then **Agios Giorgios,** 1km farther along the way. The town of **Psychro** is across the plains, 6km from Agios Giorgios. The **Agricultural Bank** in Tzermiado **exchanges currency** and has a **24hr. ATM.** (☎28440 22 390. Open M-Th 8am-2:30pm, F 8am-2pm.) The

Plateau's **tourist police** are in Agios Nikolaos, but the regular **police station** is in Tzermiado, on the second floor a few doors down from Kronio. (☎28440 22 208. Open 24hr.) The **pharmacy** is 100m from the bus stop along the road to Agios Nikolaos past the post office. (☎28440 22 310. Open M-F 8:30am-2pm and 6-9:30pm, Sa 9am-2pm and 6-9pm, Su 10:30am-2pm and 6-8pm.) The **OTE** is past the police station. (☎28440 22 299. Open M-F 7:30am-3:10pm.) The **post office** is next door to Kronio. (☎28440 22 248. Open M-F 7:30am-2pm.) **Postal Code:** 72052.

▐▏◨ ACCOMMODATIONS AND FOOD. In **Tzermiado**, you'll find **Hotel Kourites ❸** by following the road with the pharmacy and post office past the gas station. You can also check in at the hotel's other building and taverna farther along the road. The roomy bedrooms come with baths and balconies. (☎28440 22 194. Breakfast included. Singles €25; doubles €40; triples €55.) In **Agios Giorgios,** there are several good choices. ▨**Hotel Maria ❷,** 500m off the main road, marked by frequent signs, puts a hip spin on traditional style, with newly remodeled, sparklingly clean rooms, immaculate bathrooms, and an outdoor dining area draped in ivy. If you're lucky, the owner, Giorgos, may give you cherries fresh off his tree. (☎28440 31 209. Breakfast included. €19 per person.) **Dias Hotel ❶,** on the main road, has a few rooms with private sinks and common bathrooms at amazing prices. The rooms are decorated with the friendly owner's handmade crafts. (☎28440 31 207. Breakfast €3. Singles €10; doubles €15; triples €25.) In **Magoulas,** just a few kilometers from Dikteon Cave, **Hotel Dionysos ❷** has large, modern rooms with baths, sun-drenched interiors, and breathtaking views of the plateau. (☎28440 31 672. Doubles €25; triples €30.)

Most restaurants in Lasithi Plateau are linked to hotels. An exception to the rule is the family-owned **Kronio Restaurant ❷,** the oldest taverna in Lasithi, at the center of **Tzermiado.** In addition to the hospitable atmosphere and flavorful food, the corner by Kronio gives a fabulously unfettered view of bustling tourists buying embroidery and locals haggling to settle bills. (☎28440 22 375. Greek salad €3.50. Moussaka €5. *Stifado* €6. Open daily Apr.-Oct. 8am-10pm.) The **Kri Kri Taverna ❶** has a limited selection of tourist fare amid amusingly incongruous ivy-covered walls and a homey fireplace. (☎28440 22 170. Moussaka €5. Omelette €3. Lamb €6. Open daily 9am-11pm.) The **Dikti Taverna ❶,** on the main road in **Agios Konstantinos,** decorated with traditional tapestries and baskets, serves moussaka (€5) and Greek coffee. (☎28440 31 255. Open daily Apr.-Nov. 7am-7pm.) In **Agios Giorgios,** the only restaurants are attached to hotels, though *kafeneios* abound. The owner of **Taverna Stavros ❶,** a rest stop on the way to Dikteon in **Psychro,** offers a complimentary post-meal *raki* to fortify you for the climb up the cave. (☎28440 31 453. *Tzatziki* €1.50. Feta €1.50. Moussaka €6. Open daily 7am-1am.)

◙ SIGHTS. The **folklore museum** in **Agios Giorgios,** in a restored 19th-century hut, displays old tools, looms, costumes, and photographs, providing a well-rounded overview of the local culture. Next door is the **Eleftherios Venizelos Museum,** a hall dedicated to the former prime minister, who was born in Hania. (Open daily Apr.-Oct. 10am-4pm. Admission to both museums €2.50, groups €1.50 per person.)

Psychro serves as a starting point for exploring ▨**Dikteon Cave,** 1km up the hill. In the early 20th century, archaeologists found hundreds of Minoan artifacts crammed into the cave's ribbed stalactites; many are now exhibited at Iraklion's Archaeological Museum. Sir Arthur Evans, who also spearheaded the dig at Knossos, excavated this spot and, in a blast of misguided enthusiasm, blew apart the entrance. To get there, follow signs from Ag. Giorgios. The uphill walk is grueling, but it should only take about 30min., and local members of the donkey drivers will probably offer to taxi you up (€10) as you climb. Inside, the massive cave has multiple levels and irregular hanging rock formations. (Open daily 9am-4:30pm. €4. Parking €2.) The more modest but also more storied **Kronion Cave,** perched above the plateau, lacks Dikteon's crowds. Signs outside of Tzermiado will direct you to the 1km route to the grotto, which was the home of Zeus's parents, Cronus and Rhea. A stone staircase up the side of the mountain leads to the entrance. Stay on the people path (as opposed to the goat paths), and don't forget a flashlight to view the dripping swirls of stone where Greece's famed mythological history began.

The drive to Lasithi is dotted with small, incandescent, white monasteries wedged into the cliffs; watch the sides of the road for signs. Just before the Seli Ambelou pass lies the **Monastery of the Panagia Kera.** Currently under restoration, it has a small church and a magnificent view. (Open 8am-8pm. Donations requested.) Continuing along the road, you will also see a turn-off for the **Vivandi Monastery,** which has impressive ruins.

IERAPETRA Ιεράπετρα   ☎28420

Ierapetra (yer-AH-peh-tra) is one of the few vacation towns on Crete that still welcomes more Greeks than foreigners. It's touted as Europe's southernmost city, but this title is difficult to confirm—after a few days in the labyrinthine streets, you won't know which way is south anyway. Many visitors to Ierapetra use it as a base for venturing out to Chrissi Island, 15km offshore. Arabs, Venetians, and Turks once made this a busy, worldly city, but today a laid-back pace and friendly locals preserve a small-town atmosphere.

⊟ TRANSPORTATION. The bus station, Lasthenous 41 (☎28420 28 237), sends **buses** to Iraklion (2½hr., 10 per day, €8) via Agios Nikolaos (1hr., €3), Myrtos (20min., 6 per day 6:30am-8:15pm, €1.50), and Sitia (1½hr., 6 per day 6:15am-8:15pm, €4.60). **Radio Taxis** (☎28420 26 600) wait in Pl. Plastira, Pl. Venizelou, and Pl. Kanoupaki 24hr. **Driver's Club,** behind Ierapetra Express, arranges **car rentals.** (☎28420 25 583. Cars €30. Open daily 8:30am-2pm and 4-9:30pm.)

◪◪ ORIENTATION AND PRACTICAL INFORMATION. Although not a large city, Ierapetra can be difficult to navigate because of its long, maze-like streets. It has four main plateias, connected by three roads that run north-south. With your back to the bus station, **Plateia Plastira** will be on your right. Walking straight for a block on **Lasthenous** leads you to **Plateia Venizelou.** At this plateia, Lasthenous becomes pedestrian-only **Koundouriotou.** Next is the central square: spacious, triangular **Plateia Eleftherias.** Keep walking in the same direction for about 100m to reach the final plateia, **Plateia Kanoupaki.** Beyond it is the **Old Town,** where the stone streets are crooked and the houses are nestled cozily together.

Tourist information and **maps** are available at the **town hall** in Pl. Kanoupaki (☎28420 90 027). The travel agency **Ierapetra Express,** Eleftherias 25, offers **currency exchange** and **Western Union.** (☎28420 28 673. Open M-F 8am-2pm and 5-9pm, Sa 8am-2pm.) The **National Bank,** next to Ierapetra Express, **exchanges currency** and has a **24hr. ATM.** (☎28420 28 374 Open M-Th 8am-3:15pm, F 8am-2:45pm.) The **police station,** between Pl. Eleftherias and Pl. Kanoupaki, is in the big yellow building on the waterfront. (☎28420 90 160. Open 24hr.) The **tourist police** are also in that building. (☎28420 90 176. Open 24hr.) One of the city's many **pharmacies** is in Pl. Eleftherias. (☎28420 22 236. Open M, W 8am-2pm, Tu, Th-F 8am-2pm and 6-9pm.) The **hospital** is north of the bus station, left off Lasthenous at Kalimerake 6. (☎28420 90 222, 28420 90 223, or 28420 90 224. Open 24hr.) There is an **OTE** at Koraka 25. (☎28420 22 799. Open M-F 7:30am-2:30pm.) For **Internet access** and a break from the ever-present *bouzouki* soundtrack, head to hip, sophisticated ▓**Odeion,** Lasthenous 18. (☎28420 27 429. €2.50 per hr. Wine €4. Open 10am-late, kitchen opens 8:30pm.) The **post office** is on V. Kornarou, on the western side of the Old Town. (☎28420 24 915. Open M-F 7:30am-2pm.) **Postal Code:** 72200.

⌂ ACCOMMODATIONS AND CAMPING. Ierapetra makes most of its beds for upscale tourists, who want only the best after a day of sunbathing on Chrissi Island. Bargain-hunters looking for a slightly different (e.g. cheaper) scene avoid the waterfront and knock on doors offering domatia in the streets surrounding the bus station. After making a sharp right out of the bus station, you'll see signs leading to several moderately priced pensions, including the sparkling **Cretan Villa ❸**, Lakerda 16. The 206-year-old building's white stone and stucco-walled rooms, which all have clean baths and satellite TV, hide a central garden. The owner, a University of Missouri alum, speaks fluent English. (☎28420 28 522; www.cretanvilla.com. A/C €6 per night. Singles €28-34; doubles €35-40; triples €40-42.) Good deals also nestle in the streets of the Old Town. Walk down Kyrva past the taxis to the waterfront and make a right onto Ioanidou after passing the port police. To the right is **Hotel Coral ❸**, Ioanidou 18. Its bright rooms have bathtubs, fridges, A/C, TV, and free luggage storage. (☎28420 22 846. Doubles €30; triples €40.) Camping at sites like **Koutsounari ❶**, 7km from Ierapetra on the coastal road to Sitia near the restaurant, bar, and beach, is unquestionably the cheapest option. Take the bus to Sitia via Makri Gialo (20min., 6 per day, €1) and ask to be let off at the campgrounds. (☎28420 61 213. €5 per person, €3.50 per tent, €2.70 per car.)

◻ FOOD. Most of Ierapetra's waterfront restaurants are identically priced, so make your choice based on which food looks most appealing. Piled with enough pastries to make even an ascetic start salivating, **Veterano ❶**, a cafe and dessert bar on the corner of Pl. Eleftherias, boasts a superior view of the palm-edged main plateia. Contemplating a second piece of *kalitsounia* (€0.50), an Ierapetrian sweet cheese tart, seems inevitable while sitting at the inviting spot, sipping a cappuccino and joining the locals in watching a soccer game on TV. (☎28420 23 175. Open daily 7:30am-midnight.) Many of the restaurants lining the waterfront specialize in local seafood. The lively, multilingual staff at **Castello ❷**, 200m past Tunes World Cafe, grills fish (€7-9) and meat (€5) out in the open. The owner's mother prepares the appetizers fresh every day. (☎28420 24 424. Mussels *saganaki* €6. Open daily 10:30am-1am. AmEx/MC/V.) **Helvetia ❸**, 300m past the fortress overlooking the marina, taps into local atmosphere, as laughs and local gossip float through clusters of diners. (☎09728 39 206. Greek salad €3. Cuttlefish fritter €5. Open daily 7:30am-12:30am.)

◙ SIGHTS. Although Ierapetra's beaches receive the highest scores for cleanliness, their gravelly texture makes for a harrowing sunbathing experience. Unfortunately Ierapetra's historical sights aren't that fabulous either. In the Old Town at Tzami Sq., just off Nik. Vassarmidi, a 19th-century **mosque** and a decaying **Ottoman fountain** are covered with Greek graffiti. The 13th-century restored **Venetian fortress** at the southern end of the old harbor, reputedly built by Genoese pirates, provides a nice view of the town and sea, though it is rather modest compared to some of the other fortresses on Crete. (Open Tu-Su 8:30am-3pm. Free.) The **Kyrvia Festival**, held each summer in July and August, features music, dance, and theater performances at local schools; call the town hall (☎28420 90 027) for information. Ierapetra's **Archaeological Museum**, at Pl. Kanoupaki across from the taxi stand, has Minoan artifacts from the southern coast, red figure vases, and a worthwhile collection of Greek and Roman statues, all with helpful explanations in English. The sarcophagi in the second room, adorned by hunting scenes, are particularly well-preserved examples of Minoan painting. The town's pride and joy, a near-mint condition **Persephone statue** from the AD 2nd century, sits prominently in the third room. (☎28420 28 721. Open Tu-Sa 8:30am-3pm. €2, EU students free.)

⚡ DAYTRIP FROM IERAPETRA: CHRISSI ISLAND. Ierapetra's star attraction is uninhabited Chrissi Island, 15km offshore. Water-starved trees and shrubs grow on sand dunes in the interior, while the higher ground to the left of the ferry landing is dotted with multicolored volcanic rocks. Chrissi is home to several endangered species, and visitors are asked to treat the local fauna and flora with care. Most people, however, come to Chrissi for its **beaches.** Two long arcs of sand, one on the sea side by the ferry landing and the other facing Crete, draw two boatloads of sunbathers daily. The dockside **taverna ❶** serves a tasty tomato and feta bread (€2), and offers the only significant **shade** on the island. (☎69455 94 759. Sandwiches €3. Beer €2.50. Soda €2. Open daily June-Oct. 9am-2am.) **Ferries** leave Ierapetra daily May-Oct. at 10:30am and 12:30pm and return at 5 and 6pm (€20 roundtrip). Tickets are sold onboard and at a number of waterfront agencies.

MYRTOS Μύρτος ☎28420

Perched on the coast 14km west of Ierapetra, the small village of Myrtos draws smaller crowds than its neighbor does, giving travelers a peaceful respite from urban life. Myrtos's size makes it easy to navigate; facing the bus stop, walk down the road with the mountains behind you. The intersection with the main street before the waterfront, 300m from the bus stop, is the center of town. Follow the sign to the small but fascinating ⚑**museum** for lessons in archaeology, rural lifestyles, and Myrtos's history. The gracious attendant offers **tours** (20min., free with admission) that also give information about the local Minoan site. (☎28420 51 065. Open June-Oct. M-F 9am-1pm. €1.50, children under 12 free.) Sunbathers can access the **beach** from staircases by the waterfront. Numerous "rooms to let" signs occupy walls and street corners. **Cretan House ❸,** next to the museum, has tidy rooms with private baths and a common kitchen off the vine-covered porch. (☎28420 26 435. Singles €30-35; doubles and triples €30-40; quads €50.) Walk 20m past the bus stop toward town to reach **Despina Rent Rooms ❷** on your left. The rooms' common balcony, private baths, and fridges pleasantly supplement the convenient location. (☎28420 51 343. Doubles €20; triples €25.) The **supermarket** and **bakery** in town fulfill basic food needs, but the authentic tavernas sit along the waterfront. **Restaurant Votsalo ❷** shades its patrons at bamboo-roofed outdoor tables overlooking the beach. (☎28420 51 457. Yogurt with fruit and honey €3. Open daily 8am-midnight.) The streetside tables at **Myrtos Taverna ❷,** next to the Myrtos Hotel, gives visitors a chance to watch as the town goes about its day. (☎28420 51 227. Omelettes €3.50-4. Open daily 7am-midnight.) **Buses** run to Ierapetra (20min., 6 per day 7am-8:30pm, €1.40). Myrtos has a single **taxi** (☎69448 36 576). To get to **Prima Tours,** walk past Myrtos Taverna away from town and turn right. There you'll find **car rentals** (€30 per day), **currency exchange, Internet access** (€2 for the first 30min., €1.50 every 30min. after), and helpful advice. (Open daily 8:30am-12:30pm and 6-9pm.) Myrtos also has a **police station** (☎28420 51 204) and **medical assistance** (☎28420 51 222). Other services are in Ierapetra.

SITIA Σητεία ☎28430

A winding drive on coastal mountain roads from Agios Nikolaos leads to the port town of Sitia. The tourism industry has found its way here, but the town maintains a spunk all its own that goes beyond the gaudiness of souvenir stands and gift shops. Travelers blend with locals at the seaside tavernas and fishing supplies mix with beach blankets at the local stores. Sitia makes an excellent base for exploring Crete's eastern coast, and is the most convenient port for departures to Rhodes.

⌐ TRANSPORTATION

Flights: The **airport** (☎28430 24 666) connects Sitia to **Athens** (1hr.; 3 per week, in winter 2 per week; €70). Buy tickets at **Olympic Airways,** 4 Septemvriou 4 (☎28430 22 270), off Karamanli toward the tourist office. Open M-F 8am-3:30pm.

Ferries: Dikta Travel, Kornarou 150 (☎28430 25 080). Turn right off of Kapetan Sifi from Pl. Polytechniou. Open M-F 8am-8pm, Sa-Su 8am-3pm. 5 ferries per week go to **Milos** (10hr., €22) and **Piraeus** (15hr., €31) via **Agios Nikolaos** (1¼hr., €7.20). 3 per week go to **Karpathos** (4½hr., €18.30), **Kassos** (2½hr., €11), and **Rhodes** (10hr., €25). 1 per week goes to **Santorini** (6½hr., €21).

Buses: ☎28430 22 272. Out of town off Papandreou, inland from the tourist office. To: **Ierapetra** (1½hr., 3-6 per day, €4.40); **Iraklion** (3¼hr., 8 per day, €10) via **Agios Nikolaos** (1½hr., €5.50); **Kato Zakros** (1¼hr., 2-3 per day, €4); **Vai** (1hr., 3-5 per day, €2.50) via **Palaikastro** (25min., €2).

Taxis: ☎28430 22 700. In Pl. Polytechniou. Available 24hr.

Car Rentals: Porto-Belis Travel, Karamanli 34 (☎28430 22 370; www.portobelis-crete.gr), along the waterfront, rents cars (€30-45, including insurance). Open daily July-Sept. 9am-9pm; Apr.-June, Oct. 9am-3pm and 5-8:30pm.

◖◗ ORIENTATION AND PRACTICAL INFORMATION

Plateia Iroön Polytechniou, the main square, is on the waterfront. With the bus station on your left and the Archaeological Museum on your right, head down the street, following the signs for "port." Turn right onto Papandreou to reach the tourist office on the water. Turn left at the tourist office to reach Pl. Polytechniou.

Tourist Office: ☎28430 28 300. In the small white building on the waterfront. Has **maps, currency exchange,** and info on accommodations. Open June-Oct. M-F 9:30am-2:30pm and 5:30-9pm, Sa 10am-2:30pm.

Banks: National Bank (☎28430 22 250), in Pl. Polytechniou, has a **24hr. ATM.** Open M-Th 8am-2:30pm, F 8am-2pm.

Police: Therissou 31 (☎28430 22 266). Follow Kapetan Sifi 2 blocks to Mysonos; go left and continue until it becomes Therissou. Also serves as **tourist police.** Open 24hr.

Medical Services: Hospital ☎28430 24 311. Past the police off Therissou. Open 24hr.

Telephones: OTE, Kapetan Sifi 22 (☎28430 28 099). From Pl. Polytechniou, go inland past the National Bank for 3 blocks. Open M-F 7am-2pm.

Internet Access: EnterNet, El. Venizelou 95 (☎28430 22 949). €2.50 per hr. Open daily 8am-midnight.

Post Office: Dimokritou 10 (☎28430 22 283). Walk inland on El. Venizelou and go left on Dimokritou; it will be on your right. Offers **currency exchange** and **Western Union.** Open M-F 7:30am-2pm. **Postal Code:** 72300.

⌐ ACCOMMODATIONS

Many of the hotels and pensions crowd behind the waterfront on Kornarou and Kondilaki. Call ahead for reservations in August.

▨ **Rooms to Let Apostolis,** Kazantzakis 27 (☎28430 22 993). From Pl. Polytechniou, head inland on Kapetan Sifi and turn right onto Fountalidou, then go left onto Kazantzakis after 2 blocks. Bright granite stairs lead to spacious rooms with private baths, A/C, and fans. Friendly owners, a basic common kitchen area, and a balconied dining area complete the welcoming atmosphere. Doubles €30-35; triples €40-45. ❸

Hotel Arhontiko, Kondilaki 16 (☎28430 28 172). From Kapetan Sifi, take a right on Kondilaki and walk 3 blocks. Sparkling common bathrooms, wood floors, and private sinks complement the simple rooms. Singles €22; doubles €28; triples €34. ❷

Venus Rooms to Let, Kondilaki 60 (☎28430 24 307). Go uphill on Kapetan Sifi from the main plateia and take the 1st right after the OTE. Has 6 rooms with high ceilings and comfortable balconies in a flower-lined home. Watch your head on the stairs up to the 3rd fl. Doubles €20-25, with bath €25-30; triples €28/33. ❷

Hotel Apollon, Kapetan Sifi 28 (☎28430 22 733), about 3 blocks back from the main plateia. Clean, modern rooms have TV, baths, and A/C. Lobby area has a breakfast cafe-lounge. Breakfast €5. Singles €25-35; doubles €35-45; triples €38-47. ❸

◖ FOOD

On the waterfront, identical outdoor cafes under awnings serve a hodgepodge of Greek dishes, pizza, and meat. To get a more local experience, you'll have to give up the waterfront view and head to the tavernas on the inland streets.

Il Forno (☎28430 23 270), on El. Venizelou past Pl. Polytechniou toward the fortress. Diners can fill crepes (€2-5) with whatever strikes their fancy, and eat them in the pleasant harborside seating area. Delivery available. Pizza €7. Open daily 7pm-1am. ❷

Cretan House, Karamanli 10 (☎28430 25 133). Turn right off the main plateia as you face the water and continue past the tourist office. The intriguing array of Cretan appetizers spices up the traditional menu at this waterfront taverna. Entrees €5-8. Complimentary ouzo or *raki* after the meal. Open daily 10am-midnight. MC/V. ❷

Taverna Mixos, V. Kornarou 117 (☎28430 22 416), 1 block up from Pl. Polytechniou, serves varied souvlaki, including swordfish-mushroom (€8.50) and calamari (€5). Coffee-sipping, card-playing Cretan youths linger at its chic seaside tables. Live Greek music Oct.-Apr. F-Sa around 10pm. ❷

Taverna Kali Kardia, Fountalidou 22 (☎28430 22 249). Walk up Kapetan Sifi and turn left onto Fountalidou. Decent food with a local flavor in a laid-back environment. Ask for the *escargots* (€4.50) and a lesson on how to eat them. Complimentary fruit for dessert. Souvlaki €5. Open daily 8am-midnight. ❷

◙ SIGHTS

A modest **fortress** presides over the town from a high hill, offering a decent panorama to those who choose to make the short trek. (Open Tu-Su 8:30am-2:30pm. Free.) It hosts Sitia's **Kornareia Festival,** which runs through July and August, with open-air theater (€10-15) and free concerts of Greek music and dancing. The tourist office has details. The **Archaeological Museum,** opposite the bus station, contains treasures from the many excavation sites around Sitia, which were once prominent Minoan sanctuaries and villas. It also shows items from the palace complex at Kato Zakros. The Minoan Palaikastro *kouros* at the entrance is a small ivory and gold masterpiece. (☎28430 23 917. Open Tu-Su 8:30am-3pm. €2, students and seniors €1, children and EU students free.) Sitia's **Folk Art Museum** exhibits traditional 19th-century items from carvings to coins. Walk up Kapetan Sifi from the main plateia; the museum is on the right. (☎28430 22 861. Open M-Sa 10am-1pm. €2.) The long, pebbly **beach** extends

3km past the tourist office. Close to town, a busy roadway edges the beach, but the road turns inland farther down, leaving an empty expanse of sand.

🔊 NIGHTLIFE

At **Pulse's** outdoor club, past Pl. Polytechniou on El. Venizelou in the direction of the fortress, the party starts before midnight and ends late. (☎69741 94 416. Beer €3. Mixed drinks €7.) Two blocks farther, **Morfes** flaunts its tech-savvy skills with sophisticated blue lighting inside and a big-screen television outside. (Mixed drinks €6. Open daily 9pm-late.) Along the beach, 500m past the tourist office, **Oasis** (☎28430 29 056) is a two-floor nightclub with palm-tree decor and spacious outdoor seating. (Beer €3. Mixed drinks €6-7.)

🏃 DAYTRIP FROM SITIA

VAI Βαι

Buses from Sitia to Vai (40min., 3 per day, €2.50) via Palaikastro (€2) stop in the parking lot in front of the beach. Bathrooms (free) and showers (€0.50) are available in the parking lot. Chairs on the beach €3.50. Parking €3, motorbikes €1.50.

Not long ago, travelers headed to Vai to get off the beaten path. Today several buses roll into this outpost daily, depositing tourists at the smooth, sandy **beach**, eager to swim and rest under the shady fronds of Europe's only indigenous **palm tree forest.** Legend tells that the forest sprouted from date seeds that littering Egyptian soldiers dropped on their way to war in the 2nd century BC. In the 1960s and 70s, Vai became a haven for British bands like Cream and Led Zeppelin, who would camp out, smoke out, and rock out under the palms. Nowadays, both camping and smoking are prohibited, while rocking out is merely frowned upon. The palm trees have been mostly fenced off except for a small patch in the area immediately next to the beach. The sand is less crowded over the hill; those in search of a still more secluded beach experience should go left along the cliff. Although camping is forbidden in the park, many unroll their sleeping bags in this cove to the south of the palm beach. If sandy pajamas and the possibility of arrest don't appeal to you, though, you can rent a room in quiet **Palaikastro** (see below), 8km back toward Sitia. Although there is one more **restaurant** and a **snack bar** ❶ (small sandwiches €2.20) in Vai, you're better off packing a picnic or eating in one of the nearby towns. A **watersports center** rents jet-skis (€30 per 15min. for 1 person, €35 per 15min. for 2), and the **Vai Scuba Diving Club** organizes dives at noon and 3pm (☎28430 71 543; €50 per session).

PALAIKASTRO Παλαίκαστρο ☎28430

At a crossroads between major tourist attractions, Palaikastro is a good base for exploring local beaches and archaeological sites. The town's slow pace makes a pleasant contrast to a day's excitement at the sights of eastern Crete.

🚍 TRANSPORTATION AND PRACTICAL INFORMATION. Buses leave from the main plateia for Kato Zakros (30min., 1-2 per day, €2.50), Sitia (30min., 3-4 per day, €2), and Vai (15min., 3 per day, €1). You can buy tickets at a cafe in the plateia. For **taxis**, call ☎28430 61 380. **Hermes Rent a Car**, in the plateia opposite the church, rents cars for €35-57 per day. (☎28430 61 101. Open daily 9am-9pm.) The helpful **tourist information office**, 100m down the road to Sitia on your right, has an

CRETE

ATM, currency exchange, accommodations and restaurant info, and **maps** of the town, region, and local trails. (☎28430 61 546; www.palaikastro.com. Open M-F 9:30am-1:30pm and 3-9:30pm, Sa-Su 9:30am-1pm and 6-9pm.) The **police station,** across from Hellas restaurant, in the main plateia, is one flight upstairs in a building marked by Greek flags. (☎28430 61 222. Open 24hr.) The **pharmacy** is across the street from the tourist office. (☎28430 61 410. Open M-F 8am-2pm and 5:30-9pm, Sa 8am-2pm.) A **doctor** (☎28430 61 2143) visits the village three times per week, seeing patients in the medical building behind the tourist office. **Internet access** is available at the **Art and Light,** past the church on the road to Zakros, with the maroon and white striped awning. (☎28430 61 305. €4 per hr.) Or you can go to **Argo Bookstore,** across from the church, which also has used English-language books for €3. (☎28430 29 640. €4.50 per hr. Open M-Sa 9am-2pm and 5-10:30pm.)

ⓕⓒ ACCOMMODATIONS AND FOOD. You can find clean rooms, a common fridge, and plenty of hospitality in the home of **Yiannis Perakis ❷.** From the bus, go past the church and follow the road to Angathia, 200m to Pegasos Taverna. Take the small gravel road to the left immediately before Pegasos to the house on the left. (☎28430 61 310. Singles €12; doubles €25; triples €30.) On the same path, **Pegasos Rooms ❷,** above Pegasos Taverna, has balconies, fridges, A/C and private baths. (☎28430 61 479. Doubles €30; triples €35-40; 5-person rooms €50.)

For the basics, visit one of the village's **mini-marts** in the center of town, and the **bakery,** 20m down the road to Vai. **Restaurant Mythos ❷,** in the plateia, is well-loved by locals. (Moussaka and *stifado* €4-6. Stuffed grape leaves €3. Open daily noon-3pm and 6pm-midnight.) **Hotel Hellas ❶** serves delicious souvlaki (€5.50) and has a lovely view of the plateia. (☎28430 61 455. Fried cheese €2.50. Open daily 9am-11pm.) At **Vaios ❶,** a popular family restaurant 300m past Pegasos in Angathia, each meal is a feast. (☎28430 61 403. Entrees €2.50-5. Open daily Apr.-Nov. 7pm-midnight.)

◙ⓖ SIGHTS AND BEACHES. Archaeological sites and sequestered beaches abound near Palaikastro; to reach a few of the closer sights, follow the signs along the road east to the tiny village of **Agathias.** Past Agathias, the road forks; a small, well-marked dirt path to the right leads to the ruins of a Minoan city at **Roussolakos.** The main road continues to the left and goes to **Hiona,** the area's most famous sand strip after Vai. **Karoumes** is another nearby beach; take the bus to Kato Zakros and ask the driver to let you off at **Chochlakes.** From this village, follow signs through the valley to the beach.

ⓕ DAYTRIP FROM PALAIKASTRO. Surrounded by cliffs, streams, and geysers, and carpeted in brilliant wildflowers, the 6½km hike through the ▨**Valley of Death** leads from the quiet village of **Zakros** to the beach enclave **Kato Zakros.** The ravine, also known as "Death's Gorge," got its morbid name from the beehive of surrounding caves in which the Minoans buried their dead. The landscape, however, is vibrant enough to compensate for the area's macabre past. A fast-flowing stream, bounded by sprouting plant life, winds its way between sheer cliffs. The wildlife includes the usual herds of fearless wild goats, along with a charming selection of snakes and scorpions. Although it's impossible to wander too far astray in any gorge, the path here is occasionally hard to follow, as it is only sporadically marked by red arrows. Bring plenty of water and snacks, and wear good hiking shoes and long pants to protect against brambles and bugs. Keep an eye out for *phaskomilo*, a sweet-smelling tea plant with small, fuzzy leaves, and onion plants, whose purple flowers are virtually inescapable in the gorge. The small village of Zakros is a convenient starting point for the hike; take the **bus** from Sitia (1hr., 3 per day, €3), which drops off at the bus stop in the main plateia.

At the end of the gorge, turn left on the dirt path and look for the sign leading to the coast and the **Minoan Palace** of Zakros. Destroyed in 1450 BC by the mysterious cataclysm, the royal rubble, still undergoing excavation, extends up a hill. The stone outlines of chambers and courtyards hint at ancient Crete's opulence. Royalty once bathed in pools near the bottom of the hill, now home to many **turtles.** The palace is also thought to have been a center of the Minoan navy. (☎28430 93 207. Open daily 8am-7pm. €3. Students free.)

Continue along the path away from the palace to the town of **Kato Zakros.** Its waterfront is largely free from clutter, and its beach is pleasant, if pebbly. **Nikos Platanias ❷,** under shady pine trees, has friendly, multilingual waiters who serve fresh fish and vegetables from the owner's farm. (☎28430 26 887. Entrees €4-6. Open daily Apr.-Nov. 8:30am-midnight. MC/V.) If you're staying the night, try **George's Villa ❷,** up the road past the palace and gorge trail, which has bright, flower-laced rooms with private baths, fridges, and shady balconies overlooking the hazy sea. If George isn't around, inquire at his taverna. (☎28430 26 883. Singles €20; doubles €30; triples €35.) **Buses** from Kato Zakros go to Sitia (1¾hr., 3 per day, €4) and Zakros (15min., 3 per day, €0.10).

APPENDIX

CLIMATE

The climate varies significantly between regions of Greece, despite the country's relatively small size. Southern islands like Crete and Santorini can be exceedingly hot and dry, while the lush Ionians are cooler and receive more rainfall. High-altitude areas (especially in the north) are cooler, and snow remains on some mountain tops through summer. For the most part, **summer** is sunny, hot, and generally dry. In **winter,** temperatures vacillate around 50°F, and snow occasionally falls as far south as Athens. The rainy season is October to March.

Avg. Temp. (hi/lo)	JANUARY		APRIL		JULY		OCTOBER	
Precipitation	°F	in.	°F	in.	°F	in.	°F	in.
Athens	55/44	1.9	66/52	0.9	89/73	0.2	73/60	2.1
Thessaloniki	48/34	1.6	65/46	1.4	88/66	0.9	70/52	1.8
Larisa	49/33	1.4	66/45	1.2	90/65	0.8	70/51	2.3
Naxos	57/50	3.5	65/56	0.7	79/73	0.1	70/64	1.8

To convert from degrees Fahrenheit to degrees Celsius, subtract 32 and multiply by 5/9. To convert from Celsius to Fahrenheit, multiply by 9/5 and add 32.

°CELSIUS	-5	0	5	10	15	20	25	30	35	40
°FAHRENHEIT	23	32	41	50	59	68	77	86	95	104

METRIC CONVERSIONS

1 inch (in.) = 2.54cm	1 centimeter (cm) = 0.39 in.
1 foot (ft.) = 0.30m	1 meter (m) = 3.28 ft.
1 mile (mi.) = 1.61km	1 kilometer (km) = 0.62 mi.
1 ounce (oz.) = 28.35g	1 gram (g) = 0.035 oz.
1 pound (lb.) = 0.454kg	1 kilogram (kg) = 2.202 lb.
1 fluid ounce (fl. oz.) = 29.57ml	1 milliliter (ml) = 0.034 fl. oz.
1 gallon (gal.) = 3.785L	1 liter (L) = 0.264 gal.
1 square mile (sq. mi.) = 2.59 sq. km	1 square kilometer (sq. km) = 0.386 sq. mi.

TELEPHONE CODES

See **Keeping in Touch** (p. 39) for full information and advice about telephone calls in Greece, including international access.

COUNTRY	CODE	COUNTRY	CODE	COUNTRY	CODE
Australia	61	Greece	30	South Africa	27
Canada	1	Ireland	353	Spain	34
Cyprus	357	Italy	39	Turkey	90
France	33	Japan	81	UK	44
Germany	49	New Zealand	64	US	1

GLOSSARY OF USEFUL TERMS

acropolis fortified high place atop a city

amphora two-handled vessel for oil or wine storage

apse nook beyond the altar of a church

architrave lintel/lowest part of the entablature resting on columns

atrium Roman house's open interior courtyard

basilica church with a saint's relic (especially holy)

bouzouki pear-shaped stringed instrument

capital top of a column

catamaran double-hulled boat; usually high-speed and used for island transport

cella inner sanctum of an ancient temple or Byzantine church

Corinthian column ornate column with engraved acanthus leaves and volutes

cornice top of the entablature of a temple

Cyclopean walls massive, irregularly-cut Minoan and Mycenaean stone walls, so called because only a Cyclops could lift such stones

domatia rooms to rent in private homes; rooms to let

Doric column austere columns with wide fluted shafts, cushion tops (or capitals), and no bases

entablature upper parts of a temple facade, atop columns

exedra curved recess in Classical/Byzantine architecture

exonarthex outer vestibule in a Byzantine church

Faneromeni term used in Orthodox symbolism to refer to the revealed Virgin Mary

forum Roman public square or marketplace

frieze decorated middle part of a temple exterior (in particular, the entablature); see *metopes* and *triglyph*

heroon shrine to a demigod

iconostasis screen that displays Byzantine icons

Ionic column slender column topped with twin scrolling spirals (volutes)

Katharevusa snooty, "pure" Greek literary language, taken from ancient Greek

katholikon monastery's main church or chapel

koini "common" Greek used before the Byzantine era

kore female statue

kouros male nude statue

KTEL inter-city bus service

malaka common obscenity connoting masturbation

megaron large hall in a house or palace

meltemi unusually strong north wind in the Cyclades and Dodecanese

metopes painted or sculpted square block in a Doric frieze that contains scenes with figures; *metopes* are separated by *triglyphs*

naos holy innermost part of a temple or church

narthex vestibule on the west side of a Byzantine church

nave central area of a church

New Democracy conservative Greek political party

nomos Greek province

odeon semi-circular theater

OTE the Greek national telephone company

palaestra Classical gymnasium

Panagia the Virgin Mary

panigiri local festival, often religious

pediment triangular sculpture-decorated space in an ancient temple's facade

peristyle colonnade around a building

plateia town square

portico colonnade or peristyle

pronaos outer column-lined temple porch

propylaion sanctuary entrance

prytaneion public dining room and symbolic heart of a city-state

stele stone slab that marks a tomb or holds an inscription

stoa public building fronted by rows of columns in ancient marketplaces

tholos earth-covered, beehive-shaped Mycenaean tomb

triglyph part of a Doric frieze comprised of 3 vertical grooves that alternate with *metopes*

trireme ancient ship with 3 sets of oars

ANCIENT GODS

GREEK GOD	ROMAN NAME	JOB DESCRIPTION
Zeus	Jupiter	King of gods; in charge of the sky and weather; quick to punish with a thunderbolt.
Hera	Juno	Queen of Olympus; Zeus's sister and wife; goddess of marriage and women.
Ares	Mars	God of war and the spirit of battle; often seen with his sidekick Eris (strife).
Hephæstus	Vulcan	Fire god; patron of blacksmiths and all craftsmen; Aphrodite's homely husband.
Demeter	Ceres	Harvest and fertility goddess; created seasons.
Aphrodite	Venus	Goddess of love, beauty, seduction, and sex; mom and boss of Eros (Cupid).
Athena	Minerva	Goddess of wisdom, craft, and war; Athens's protectress; born from Zeus's head.
Hades	Pluto	God of the underworld; rules over the dead and precious metals. Greedy for both.
Poseidon	Neptune	God of the water: controlled seas, rivers, earthquakes, and floods; Zeus's brother.
Apollo	Apollo	God of light, music, song, poetry, healing, and prophecy; Artemis's twin.
Artemis	Diana	Virgin goddess of the hunt, the moon, wild animals, the woods, and childbirth.
Dionysus	Bacchus	God of wine, fertility, and revelry.
Hermes	Mercury	Messenger god; known for trickery and persuasion; patron god of ■ travelers.

GREEK ALPHABET

The Greek alphabet has 24 letters. In the chart below, the left column gives the name of each letter in Greek, the middle column shows lower case and capital letters, and the right column shows the pronunciation. Greek words often have an accent mark called a *tonos* (τόνος). The *tonos* appears over the vowels of multi-syllabic words and tells you where the stress lies. The stress can change the meaning of the word, so the tonos is essential for understanding and communication.

LETTER	SYMBOL	PRONUNCIATION	LETTER	SYMBOL	PRONUNCIATION
alpha	α A	*a* as in father	nu	ν N	*n* as in net
beta	β B	*v* as in velvet	xi	ξ Ξ	*x* as in mix
gamma	γ Γ	*y* as in yo or *g* as in go	omicron	o O	*o* as in row
delta	δ Δ	*th* as in there	pi	π Π	*p* as in peace
epsilon	ε E	*e* as in jet	rho	ρ P	*r* as in roll
zeta	ζ Z	*z* as in zebra	sigma	σ ς Σ	*s* as in sense
eta	η H	*ee* as in queen	tau	τ T	*t* as in tent
theta	θ Θ	*th* as in health	upsilon	υ Y	*ee* as in green
iota	ι I	*ee* as in tree	phi	φ Φ	*f* as in fog
kappa	κ K	*k* as in cat	chi	χ X	*h* as in horse or *ch* as in Bach
lambda	λ Λ	*l* as in land	psi	ψ Ψ	*ps* as in oops
mu	μ M	*m* as in moose	omega	ω Ω	*o* as in Let's Go

Greek has a few sounds that are not intuitive for English speakers. For example **gh** marks a muted "g" sound produced from the back of your throat. **Dth** denotes a hard "th" as in thee as opposed to a soft "th" as in three. Delta is most often pronounced with a hard "th." An asterisk (*) marks a syllable that can be pronounced either with a diphthong, to rhyme with "pow"—or without, to rhyme with "flow."

Below is a list of challenging double consonants and vowels that do not follow the above letter pronunciations.

SYMBOL	PRONUNCIATION	SYMBOL	PRONUNCIATION
μπ	*b* as in baby	τζ	*j* as jockey
ντ	*d* as in dune	ει	*ee* as in beet
γγ	*ng* as in English	οι	*ee* as in beet
γκ	*g* as in god	υι	*ee* as in beet
αυ	*ahf/ahv* as in coffin/improv	ευ	*ef/ev* as in effort/ever
αι	*eh* as in element	ου	*oo* as in soon

USEFUL WORDS AND PHRASES

BASICS

Yes.	Ναι.	NEH.
No.	Οχι.	OH-hee.
Okay.	Εντάξει.	en-DAH-xee.
Please/You're welcome.	Παρακαλώ.	pah-rah-kah-LO.
Thank you (very much).	Ευχαριστώ (πολύ).	ef-kah-ree-STO (po-LEE).
Sorry/Pardon me.	Συγνόμη.	sigh-NO-mee.
Do you speak English?	Μιλάτε αγγλικά;	mee-LAH-teh eng-lee-KAH?
Help!	Βοήτηεια!	vo-EE-tee-ah!
How much does it cost?	Πόσο κάνει;	PO-so KAH-nee?
I am ill.	Είμαι άρρωστος.	EE-meh AH-rose-tose.
I don't understand.	Δεν καταλαβαίνω.	DTHEN kah-tah-lah-VEH-no.
I don't speak Greek.	Δεν μιλαώ ελληνικά.	DTHEN mee-LOW* el-lee-nee-KAH.
It does (not) matter.	(Δεν) Πειράζει.	(DTHEN) peer-AH-zee.
Leave me alone!	Ασεμε!	AH-seh-meh!
Maybe, I'm thinking about it.	Το σκέπτομαι.	tow SKEP-to-meh.
Where? Who? When?	Πού; Πιός; Πότε;	POO? PIOS? POH-teh?
Where is...?	Πού είναι...;	poo EE-neh...?
Why?	Γιατί;	yah-TEE?

FEELINGS

I love you.	Σ'αγαπώ.	sah-gah-POW.
I miss you.	Μου λείπεις.	moo LEE-pees.
I want you.	Σε θέλω.	seh THEH-lo.
friend (male/female)	φίλος/φίλη	FEE-los/FEE-lee
happy	χαρούμενος	ha-ROO-meh-nos
single, free	ελεύθερος	eh-LEF-the-ros
upset, sad, disappointed	επικρέμενος	eh-pee-KREH-meh-nos

GREETINGS

Good morning/Good day.	Καλημέρα.	kah-lee-MEH-rah.
Good evening.	Καλησπέρα.	kah-lee-SPEH-rah.
Good night.	Καληνύχτα.	kah-lee-NEE-ktah.
Hello/Goodbye. (polite plural)	Γεια σας.	YAH-sahs.
Hello/Goodbye. (familiar)	Γεια σου.	YAH-soo.
Mr./Sir	Κύριος	KEE-ree-os

GREETINGS, CONT'D

Ms./Madam	Κυρία	kee-REE-ah
My name is...	Με λένε...	meh LEH-neh...
What is your name?	Πώς σε λένε;	po seh-LEH-neh?

TRANSPORTATION

How much will the trip cost?	Πόσο θα κάνει ο δρόμος;	PO-so THA KAH-nee O DRO-mose?
I am going to...	Πηγαίνω σε...	pee-YEH-no seh...
I am lost.	Χάθηκα.	HA-thee-ka.
I need a ticket.	Χρειάζομαι εισιτήριο.	kree-AH-zo-meh ee-see-TEE-ree-o.
Start the meter!	Αρχίστε το μετρητή!	ar-HEE-steh TO me-tree-TEE!
When do we leave?	Τι ώρα φεύγουμε;	tee O-rah FEV-goo-meh?
Where are you going?	Πού πας;	POO PAHS?
airplane	αεροπλάνο	ah-eh-ro-PLAH-no
bus	λεωφορείο	leh-o-fo-REE-o
car	αυτοκίνητο	af-to-KEE-nee-to
ferry	πλοίο	PLEE-o
here, there	εδώ, εκεί	eh-DTHO, eh-KEE
international	εξωτερικός	ex-oh-teh-ree-KOS
island capital/main town	χώρα	HO-rah
left	αριστερά	ah-rees-teh-RAH
long-distance	υπεραστικός	ee-peh-ras-tee-KOS
passport	διαβατηρίο	dthya-vah-TEE-rio
port	λιμάνι	lee-MAH-nee
right	δεξιά	dthe-XYAH
stop (as a noun)	στάση	STAH-see
suitcase	βαλίτσα	vah-LEE-tsah
taxi	ταξί	tah-XEE
ticket	εισιτήριο	ee-see-TEE-ree-o
train	τραίνο	TREH-no

TIME

Monday	Δευτέρα	dtheh-FTEH-ra
Tuesday	Τρίτη	TREE-tee
Wednesday	Τέταρτη	TEH-tar-tee
Thursday	Πέμπτη	PEM-ptee
Friday	Παρασκευί	pah-rah-skeh-VEE
Saturday	Σάββατο	SAH-vah-to
Sunday	Κυριακή	kee-ree-ah-KEE
morning	πρωί	pro-EE
afternoon	απόγευμα	ah-PO-yev-mah
evening	βράδυ	VRAH-dthee
weekend	Σαββατοκύριακο	sah-vah-to-KEE-rya-ko
yesterday	χτες	KTAYS
today	σήμερα	SEE-mer-a
tomorrow	αύριο	AV-ree-o

APPENDIX

TIME, CONT'D

daily	καθημερινός	kah-thee-meh-ree-NOS
now	τώρα	TO-rah
What time is it?	Τί ώρα είναι;	TEE O-rah EE-neh?
year	χρόνος, έτος	HRO-nos, EH-tos

SIGNS

bank	τράπεζα	TRAH-peh-zah
church	εκκλησία	eh-klee-SEE-ah
doctor	γιατρός	yah-TROSE
hospital	νοσοκομείο	no-so-ko-MEE-o
hotel	ξενοδοχείο	xhe-no-dtho-HEE-o
market	αγορά	ah-go-RAH
museum	μουσείο	moo-SEE-o
open, closed	ανοικτό, κλειστό	ah-nee-KTO, klee-STO
pharmacy	φαρμακείο	fahr-mah-KEE-o
police	αστυνομία	as-tee-no-MEE-a
post office	ταχυδρομείο	ta-hee-dthro-MEE-o
room	δωμάτιο	dtho-MAH-tee-o
toilet	τουαλέτα, λουτρό	twa-LE-ta, loo-TRO

COMMERCE

Can I see a room?	Μπορώ να δω ένα δωμάτιο;	bo-RO NAH DTHO E-nah dtho-MAH-tee-o?
Do you have...?	Μηπώς έχετε...;	mee-POSE EK-he-teh...?
I need...	χρειάζομαι...	kree-AH-zo-meh...
I want...	θέλω...	THEH-lo...
I will buy this one.	Θα αγοράζω αυτό.	THAH ah-go-RAH-zo ahf-TO.
I would like...	Θα ήθελα...	THAH EE-the-lah...
cheap	φτηνό	ftee-NO
expensive	ακριβό	ah-kree-VO
good	καλό	kah-LO

FOOD

raki (anise-flavored liqueur)	ρακή	rah-KEE
baklava (nut and honey pastry)	μπακλαβά	bah-klah-VAH
bread	ψωμί	pso-MEE
butter	βούτυρο	VOO-tee-ro
cafe	καφενείο	kah-feh-NEE-o
casual restaurant	ταβέρνα	ta-VEHR-na
Cheers!	Γεια μας!	YAH MAHS!
cheese	τυρί	ti-REE
chicken	κοτόπουλο	ko-TO-poo-lo
cigarette	τσιγάρο	tsee-GAH-ro
coffee with a little milk and sugar	καφές μέτριος	kah-FES MET-ree-os
cucumber	αγγούρι	ahng-OU-ree
custard and honey pastry	γαλατομπούρικο	ghah-lah-to-BOO-ree-ko

FOOD, CONT'D

dairy shop	γαλακτοπωλείο	gah-lahk-to-po-LEE-o
egg	αβγό	ahv-GAH
egg-lemon soup or sauce	αβγολέμονο	ahv-go-LEH-meh-no
fish	ψάρι	PSAH-ree
grape leaves stuffed with rice and/or meat (large/small)	δολμάδες/δολμαδάκια	dthol-MAH-dthes/dthol-mah-DTHAH-kya
Greek meatballs	κεφτές	kef-TES
gyro (meat sandwich wrapped in pita)	γυρό	yee-RO
hard yellow cheese	κασέρι	kah-SEH-ree
ice cream	παγωτό	pah-yo-TOE
lamb	αρνάκι	ar-NA-kee
meat-and-onion stew	στιφάδο	stee-FAH-do
mezedes (assorted appetizers)	μεζέδες/μεζεδάκια	meh-ZEH-dthes/meh-zeh-DTHAH-kya
milk	γάλα	GAH-lah
moussaka (lasagna-like dish with eggplant and meat)	μουσακά	moo-sah-KAH
nuts	καρύδια	kah-REE-dthya
ouzo (strong Greek liqueur)	ούζο	OO-zo
pastry-cheese pie	τυρόπιτα	tee-RO-pee-tah
restaurant	εστιατόριο	es-tee-ah-TO-ree-o
salt	αλάτι	ah-LA-tee
sharp white wine	ρετσίνα	reh-TSEE-nah
souvlaki (meat on a skewer)	σουβλάκι	soo-VLAH-kee
sugar	ζάχαρη	ZAH-hah-ree
sweets	γλύκα	GLEE-kah
water	νερό	ne-RO
Does this have meat?	Έχει κρέα αυτό εδώ;	EK-hee KRAY-a auf-TO e-DTHO?
I am allergic to...	Είμαι αλλεργικός σε...	EE-may ah-lehr-gee-KOS SEH...
The bill, please.	Ο λογαριασμός, παρακαλώ.	OH lo-gah-ree-yah-SMOS, pah-rah-kah-LOW.

NUMBERS

zero	μηδέν	mee-DTHEN
one	ένα	EH-nah
two	δύο	DTHEE-o
three	τρία	TREE-ah
four	τέσσερα	TES-eh-rah
five	πέντε	PEN-dtheh
six	έξι	EH-xee
seven	επτά	ep-TAH
eight	οκτώ	okh-TO
nine	εννιά	en-YAH
ten	δέκα	DTHEH-kah

APPENDIX

NUMBERS, CONT'D		
eleven	ένδεκα	EN-dheh-kah
twelve	δώδεκα	DTHO-dheh-kah
thirteen	δεκα–τρία	dthe-kah-TREE-ah
fourteen	δεκα–τέσσερα	dthe-kah-TES-ser-ah
fifteen	δεκα–πέντε	dthe-kah-PEN-dheh
sixteen	δεκα–έξι	dthe-kah-EH-xee
seventeen	δεκα–επτά	dthe-kah-ep-TAH
eighteen	δεκα–οκτώ	dthe-kah-okh-TO
nineteen	δεκα–εννιά	dthe-kah-en-YAH
twenty	είκοσι	EE-ko-see
thirty	τριάντα	tree-AHN-dah
forty	σαράντα	sa-RAHN-dah
fifty	πενήντα	peh-NEEN-dah
sixty	εξήντα	eh-XEEN-dah
seventy	εβδομήντα	ev-dho-MEEN-dah
eighty	ογδόντα	og-DHON-dah
ninety	ενήντα	eh-NEEN-dah
hundred	εκατό	eh-kah-TO
thousand(s)	χιλιά(δες)	hil-YAH(-dthes)
million	εκατομμύριο	eh-kah-to-MEE-ree-o

ON THE HORIZON

CYPRUS

Cyprus, 480km away from the nearest Greek island, is currently embroiled in a cross-country tension. After enduring a long succession of conquerors, a chunk of Cyprus now exists independently, but the island is caught between its own independent status, its northern Turkish territory, and allegiance to Greece. Although visiting Cyprus can be expensive, more and more tourists seem convinced that the trip is worthwhile. **The Republic of Cyprus** (Southern Cyprus) is accessible from Greece by ferry or plane—**Olympic Airways** (Cyprus ☎24 627 950; US 800 223 1226; www.olympic-airways.gr), **Cyprus Airways** (Cyprus ☎22 443 054; US 212 714 2190; www.cyprusair.com.cy), and many other major airlines run routes to the island. Tourists with valid passports from the Australia, Canada, Ireland, the UK , and the US do not need a **visa** to enter Southern Cyprus for stays of up to 90 days. For information on longer stays contact your country's embassy. Trips to Northern Cyprus can be logistically difficult because of the political situation.

TURKEY

The Turkish Aegean coast is full of laid-back beach towns, beautiful mosques, and ancient Greek ruins. Daytrips to Turkey are cheap and easy from several Greek islands, including Samos (p. 490), Chios (p. 500), and Kos (p. 470). For a daytrip, catch a ferry to the Aegean coast from a nearby island. Not every daytrip is accessible by direct ferry, however; if your destination is Çanakkale, Eceabat, İzmir, Ephesus (Efes), or Selçuk, you'll need to head to Bodrum, Çeşme, or Kuşadası and catch a bus to your destination. For travelers headed to İstanbul or the Aegean overland, go through Alexandroupoli. American travelers need a visa and a passport to enter Turkey; **visas,** which are generally valid for three months, can be purchased upon entry into Turkey or at a Turkish Consulate in the US.

INDEX

MAP INDEX

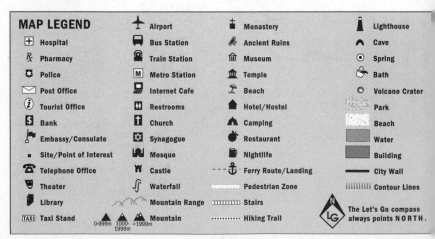

MAP LEGEND

✈	Airport
■	Monastery
🛆	Lighthouse
✚	Hospital
🚌	Bus Station
Ancient Ruins	
∧	Cave
℞	Pharmacy
🚂	Train Station
🏛	Museum
⊙	Spring
✪	Police
Ⓜ	Metro Station
🏛	Temple
Bath
✉	Post Office
🖥	Internet Cafe
Beach
○	Volcano Crater
ⓘ	Tourist Office
Restrooms
Hotel/Hostel
Park
$	Bank
†	Church
Camping
Beach
Embassy/Consulate		Synagogue	Restaurant	Water
Site/Point of Interest	Mosque	Nightlife	Building
☎ Telephone Office	Castle	⚓ Ferry Route/Landing	City Wall
Theater	Waterfall	Pedestrian Zone	Contour Lines
Library	Mountain Range	Stairs
TAXI Taxi Stand	Mountain	Hiking Trail	The Let's Go compass always points NORTH.

0-999m   1000-1999m   >1999m